COLLINS

ITALIAN ★ ENGLISH
ENGLISH ★ ITALIAN
DICTIONARY

CATHERINE E. LOVE

BERKLEY BOOKS, NEW YORK

General Editor
R. H. Thomas

The text of this dictionary has been
adapted from the Collins Gem
Italian-English, English-Italian
Dictionary prepared for Collins
Publishers by Lexus
1982

First published in this edition 1982

Contributors
Paolo L. Rossi with Davina M. Chaplin,
Fernando Villa, Ennio Bilucaglia

This Berkley book contains the complete
text of the original edition.
It has been completely reset in a typeface
designed for easy reading and was printed
from new film.

COLLINS ITALIAN/ENGLISH · ENGLISH/ITALIAN
DICTIONARY

A Berkley Book / published by arrangement with
Collins Publishers

PRINTING HISTORY
Collins Gem edition published 1982
Berkley edition / August 1982

ISBN: 0-425-10271-8

A BERKLEY BOOK ® TM 757,375
Berkley Books are published by The Berkley Publishing Group,
200 Madison Avenue, New York, New York 10016.
The name "BERKLEY" and the "B" logo
are trademarks belonging to Berkley Publishing Corporation.

PRINTED IN THE UNITED STATES OF AMERICA

10   9   8   7

INTRODUCTION

The user whose aim is to read and understand Italian will find in this dictionary a comprehensive and up-to-date wordlist including numerous phrases in current use. He will also find listed alphabetically the main irregular forms with a cross-reference to the basic form where a translation is given, as well as some of the most common abbreviations, acronyms and geographical names.

The user who wishes to communicate and to express himself in Italian will find clear and detailed treatment of all the basic words, with numerous indications pointing to the appropriate translation, and helping him to use it correctly.

INTRODUZIONE

Questo dizionario offre a chi deve leggere e comprendere l'inglese una nomenclatura dettagliata e aggiornata, con vocaboli e locuzioni idiomatiche parlate e scritte della lingua inglese contemporanea. Vi figurano anche, in ordine alfabetico, le principali forme irregolari, con un rimando alla forma di base dove si trova la traduzione, così come i più comuni nomi di luogo, le sigle e le abbreviazioni.

A loro volta, quanti hanno la necessità di esprimersi in inglese trovano in questo dizionario una trattazione chiara ed essenziale di tutti i vocaboli di base, con numerose indicazioni per una esatta traduzione e un uso corretto ed appropriato.

abbreviations	iv	abbreviazioni
phonetic symbols	vii	simboli fonetici
Italian pronunciation	viii	la pronunzia dell'italiano
ITALIAN-ENGLISH	1	ITALIANO-INGLESE
ENGLISH-ITALIAN	199	INGLESE-ITALIANO
verb tables	402	verbi
numbers	406	i numeri
time	407	l'ora

Abbreviations

Abbreviazioni

adjective	**a**	aggettivo
abbreviation	**abbr**	abbreviazione
adverb	**ad**	avverbio
administration	**ADMIN**	amministrazione
flying, air travel	**AER**	aeronautica, viaggi aerei
adjective	**ag**	aggettivo
agriculture	**AGR**	agricoltura
administration	**AMM**	amministrazione
anatomy	**ANAT**	anatomia
architecture	**ARCHIT**	architettura
astronomy, astrology	**ASTR**	astronomia, astrologia
the motor car and motoring	**AUT**	l'automobile
adverb	**av**	avverbio
flying, air travel	**AVIAT**	aeronautica, viaggi aerei
biology	**BIOL**	biologia
botany	**BOT**	botania
British English	**Brit**	inglese di Gran Bretagna
consonant	**C**	consonante
conjunction	**cj**	congiunzione
colloquial usage (! particularly offensive)	**col(!)**	familiare (! da evitare)
commerce, finance, banking	**COMM**	commercio, finanza, banca
conjunction	**cong**	congiunzione
compound element: noun used as adjective and which cannot follow the noun it qualifies	**cpd**	sostantivo usato come aggettivo, non può essere usato né come attributo, né dopo il sostantivo qualificato
cookery	**CULIN, CUC**	cucina
before	**dav**	davanti a
determiner: article, demonstrative etc	**det**	determinativo: articolo, aggettivo dimostrativo o indefinito etc
law	**DIR**	diritto
economics	**ECON**	economia
building	**EDIL**	edilizia
electricity, electronics	**ELEC, ELETTR**	elettricità, elettronica
exclamation	**excl, escl**	esclamazione

feminine	**f**	femminile
colloquial usage (! particularly offensive)	**fam(!)**	familiare (! da evitare)
railways	**FERR**	ferrovia
figurative use	**fig**	figurato
physiology	**FISIOL**	fisiologia
photography	**FOT**	fotografia
(phrasal verb) where the particle cannot be separated from main verb	**fus**	(verbo inglese) la cui particella è inseparabile dal verbo
in most or all senses; generally	**gen**	nella maggior parte dei sensi; generalmente
geography, geology	**GEO**	geografia, geologia
geometry	**GEOM**	geometria
computers	**INFORM**	informatica
schooling, schools and universities	**INS**	insegnamento, sistema scolastico e universitario
invariable	**inv**	invariabile
irregular	**irg**	irregolare
grammar, linguistics	**LING**	grammatica, linguistica
masculine	**m**	maschile
mathematics	**MAT(H)**	matematica
medical term, medicine	**MED**	termine medico, medicina
the weather, meteorology	**METEOR**	il tempo, meteorologia
either masculine or feminine depending on sex	**m/f**	maschile o femminile, secondo il sesso
military matters	**MIL**	esercito, lingua militare
music	**MUS**	musica
noun	**n**	sostantivo
sailing, navigation	**NAUT**	nautica
numeral adjective or noun	**num**	numerale (aggettivo, sostantivo)
oneself	**o.s.**	
derogatory, pejorative	**pej, peg**	peggiorativo
photography	**PHOT**	fotografia
physiology	**PHYSIOL**	fisiologia
plural	**pl**	plurale
politics	**POL**	politica
past participle	**pp**	participio passato
preposition	**prep**	preposizione
psychology, psychiatry	**PSYCH, PSIC**	psicologia, psichiatria

past tense	pt	tempo del passato
uncountable noun : not used in the plural	q	sostantivo che non si usa al plurale
	qc	qualcosa
	qd	qualcuno
religions, church service	REL	religione, liturgia
noun	s	sostantivo
somebody	sb	
schooling, schools and universities	SCOL	insegnamento, sistema scolastico e universitario
singular	sg	singolare
(grammatical) subject	sog	soggetto (grammaticale)
something	sth	
subjunctive	sub	congiuntivo
(grammatical) subject	subj	soggetto (grammaticale)
technical term, technology	TECH, TECN	termine tecnico, tecnologia
telecommunications	TEL	telecomunicazioni
typography, printing	TIP	tipografia
television	TV	televisione
typography, printing	TYP	tipografia
American English	US	inglese degli Stati Uniti
vowel	V	vocale
verb	vb	verbo
verb or phrasal verb used intransitively	vi	verbo o gruppo verbale con funzione intransitiva
reflexive verb	vr	verbo riflessivo
verb or phrasal verb used transitively	vt	verbo o gruppo verbale con funzione transitiva
zoology	ZOOL	zoologia
registered trademark	®	marca depositata
introduces a cultural equivalent	≈	introduce un'equivalenza culturale
auxiliary verb 'essere' in compound tenses	2	verbo ausiliare 'essere' nei tempi composti

TRASCRIZIONE FONETICA

PHONETIC TRANSCRIPTION

CONSONANTS CONSONANTI

VOWELS VOCALI

NB. The pairing of some vowel sounds only indicates approximate equivalence/La messa in equivalenza di certi suoni indica solo una rassomiglianza approssimativa.

NB. **p, b, t, d, k, g** are not aspirated in Italian/sono seguiti da un'aspirazione in inglese.

		heel bead i: i	*vino idea*
		hit pity ı	
		e	*stella edera*
puppy	p	*padre*	*set tent* ɛ *epoca*
baby	b	*bambino*	eccetto
tent	t	*tutto*	*apple bat* æ a *mamma*
daddy	d	*dado*	*amore*
cork kiss chord	k	*cane che*	*after car calm* ɑ:
gag guess	g	*gola ghiro*	*fun cousin* ʌ
so rice kiss	s	*sano*	*over above* ə
cousin buzz	z	*svago esame*	*urn fern work* ə:
sheep sugar	ʃ	*scena*	*wash pot* ɔ *rosa occhio*
pleasure beige	ʒ		*born cork* ɔ: *ponte*
church	tʃ	*pece lanciare*	*ognuno*
judge general	dʒ	*giro gioco*	*full soot* u *utile zucca*
farm raffle	f	*aʃa faro*	*boon lewd* u:
very rev	v	*vero bravo*	
thin maths	θ		
that other	ð		
little ball	l	*letto ala*	
	ʎ	*gli*	

DIPHTHONGS DITTONGHI

rat brat	r	*rete arco*
mummy comb	m	*ramo madre*
no ran	n	*no fumante*
	ɲ	*gnomo*
singing bank	ŋ	
hat reheat	h	
yet	j	*buio piacere*
wall bewail	w	*uomo guaio*
loch	x	

ıə	*beer tier*
ɛə	*tear fair there*
eı	*date plaice day*
aı	*life buy cry*
au	*owl foul now*
əu	*low no*
ɔı	*boil boy oily*
uə	*poor tour*

MISCELLANEOUS

VARIE

* per l'inglese: la 'r' finale viene pronunciata se seguita da una vocale.

' precedes the stressed syllable/precede la sillaba accentata.

ITALIAN PRONUNCIATION

Vowels

Where the vowel **e** or the vowel **o** appears in a stressed syllable it can be either open [ɛ], [ɔ] or closed [e], [o]. As the open or closed pronunciation of these vowels is subject to regional variation, the distinction is of little importance to the user of this dictionary. Phonetic transcription for headwords containing these vowels will therefore only appear where other pronunciation difficulties are present.

Consonants

c before 'e' or 'i' is pronounced *tch*.

ch is pronounced like the 'k' in 'kit'.

g before 'e' or 'i' is pronounced like the 'j' in 'jet'.

gl before 'e' or 'i' is normally pronounced like the 'lli' in 'million', and in a few cases only like the 'gl' in 'glove'.

gn is pronounced like the 'ny' in 'canyon'.

sc before 'e' or 'i' is pronounced *sh*.

z is pronounced like the 'ts' in 'stetson', or like the 'd's' in 'bird's-eye'.

Headwords containing the above consonants and consonantal groups have been given full phonetic transcription in this dictionary.

NB. All double written consonants in Italian are fully sounded: eg. the *tt* in 'tutto' is pronounced as in 'hat *t*rick'.

ITALIANO - INGLESE
ITALIAN - ENGLISH

A

a *prep* (*a + il* = **al,** *a + lo* = **allo,** *a + l'* = **all',** *a + la* = **alla,** *a + i* = **ai,** *a + gli* = **agli,** *a + le* = **alle**) (*stato in luogo, tempo*) at; in; (*moto a luogo, complemento di termine*) to; (*mezzo*) with, by; **essere ~ Roma/alla posta/~ casa** to be in Rome/at the post office/at home; **~ 18 anni** at 18 (years of age); **~ mezzanotte/Natale** at midnight/ Christmas; **alle 3 at 3** (o'clock); **~ maggio** in May; **~ piedi/cavallo** on foot/horseback; **una barca ~ motore** a motorboat; **alla milanese** the Milanese way, in the Milanese fashion; **~ 500 lire il chilo** 500 lire a *o* per kilo; **viaggiare ~ 100 chilometri l'ora** to travel at 100 kilometres an *o* per hour; **~ 10 chilometri da Firenze** 10 kilometres from Florence; **~ domani!** see you tomorrow!; **~ uno ~ uno** one by one.

a'bate *sm* abbot.

abbacchi'ato, a [abbak'kjato] *ag* downhearted, in low spirits.

abbagli'ante [abbaʎ'ʎante] *ag* dazzling; **~i** *smpl* (*AUT*): **accendere gli ~i** to put one's headlights on full beam.

abbagli'are [abbaʎ'ʎare] *vt* to dazzle; (*illudere*) to delude; **ab'baglio** *sm* blunder; **prendere un abbaglio** to blunder, make a blunder.

abbai'are *vi* to bark.

abba'ino *sm* dormer window; (*soffitta*) attic room.

abban'donare *vt* to leave, abandon, desert; (*trascurare*) to neglect; (*rinunciare a*) to abandon, give up; **~rsi** *vr* to let o.s. go; **~rsi a** (*ricordi, vizio*) to give o.s. up to; **abban'dono** *sm* abandoning; neglecting; (*stato*) abandonment; neglect; (*SPORT*) withdrawal; (*fig*) abandon.

abbas'sare *vt* to lower; (*radio*) to turn down; **~rsi** *vr* (*chinarsi*) to stoop; (*livello, sole*) to go down; (*fig: umiliarsi*) to demean o.s.; **~ i fari** (*AUT*) to dip one's lights.

ab'basso *escl*: **~ il re!** down with the king!

abbas'tanza [abbas'tantsa] *av* (*a sufficienza*) enough; (*alquanto*) quite, rather, fairly; **un vino ~ dolce** quite a sweet wine, a fairly sweet wine; **averne ~ di qd/qc** to have had enough of sb/sth.

ab'battere *vt* (*muro, casa*) to pull down; (*ostacolo*) to knock down; (*albero*) to fell; (*sog: vento*) to bring down; (*bestie da macello*) to slaughter; (*cane, cavallo*) to destroy, put down; (*selvaggina, aereo*) to shoot down; (*fig: sog: malattia*) to leave prostrate; **~rsi** *vr* (*avvilirsi*) to lose heart.

abba'zia [abbat'tsia] *sf* abbey.

abbece'dario [abbetʃe'darjo] *sm* primer.

abbel'lire *vt* to make beautiful; (*ornare*) to embellish.

abbeve'rare *vt* to water; **abbevera'toio** *sm* drinking trough.

'abbi, 'abbia, abbi'amo, 'abbiano, abbi'ate *forme del vb* **avere**.

abbicci [abbit'tʃi] *sm inv* alphabet; (*sillabario*) primer; (*fig*) rudiments *pl*.

abbi'ente *ag* well-to-do, well-off.

abbi'etto, a *ag* = **abietto**.

abbiglia'mento [abbiʎʎa'mento] *sm* dress *q*; (*indumenti*) clothes *pl*; (*industria*) clothing industry.

abbigli'are [abbiʎ'ʎare] *vt* to dress up.

abbi'nare *vt* to combine, put together.

abbindo'lare *vt* (*fig*) to cheat, trick.

abbocca'mento *sm* talks *pl*, meeting.

abboc'care *vt* (*tubi, canali*) to connect, join up // *vi* (*pesce*) to bite; (*fig*) to swallow the bait; (*tubi*) to join.

abbona'mento *sm* subscription; (*alle ferrovie etc*) season ticket; **fare l'~** to take out a subscription (*o* season ticket).

abbo'nare *vt* = **abbuonare**; **~rsi** *vr*: **~rsi a un giornale** to take out a subscription to a newspaper; **~rsi al teatro/alle ferrovie** to take out a season ticket for the theatre/the train; **abbo-'nato, a** *sm/f* subscriber; season-ticket holder.

abbon'dante *ag* abundant, plentiful; (*giacca*) roomy.

abbon'danza [abbon'dantsa] *sf* abundance.

abbon'dare *vi* to abound, be plentiful; **~ in** *o* **di** to be full of, abound in.

abbor'dabile *ag* (*persona*) approachable; (*prezzo*) reasonable.

abbor'dare *vt* (*nave*) to board; (*persona*) to approach; (*argomento*) to tackle; **~ una curva** to take a bend.

abbotto'nare *vt* to button up, do up.

abboz'zare [abbot'tsare] *vt* to sketch, outline; (*SCULTURA*) to rough-hew; **~ un sorriso** to give a ghost of a smile; **ab-'bozzo** *sm* sketch, outline; (*DIR*) draft.

abbracci'are [abbrat'tʃare] *vt* to embrace; (*persona*) to hug, embrace; (*professione*) to take up; (*contenere*) to include; **~rsi** *vr* to hug *o* embrace (one another); **~rsi a qd/qc** to cling to sb/sth; **ab'braccio** *sm* hug, embrace.

abbrevi'are *vt* to shorten; (*parola*) to abbreviate, shorten; **abbreviazi'one** *sf* abbreviation.

abbron'zante [abbron'dzante] *ag* tanning, sun *cpd.*

abbron'zare [abbron'dzare] *vt* (*pelle*) to tan; (*metalli*) to bronze; **~rsi** *vr* to tan, get a tan; **abbronza'tura** *sf* tan, suntan.

abbrusto'lire *vt* (*pane*) to toast; (*caffè*) to roast.

abbui'are *vi* (*annottare*) to grow dark; **~rsi** *vr* to grow dark; (*vista*) to grow dim; (*fig*) to grow sad.

abbuo'nare *vt* (*perdonare*) to forgive.

abbu'ono *sm* (*COMM*) allowance, discount; (*SPORT*) handicap.

abdi'care *vi* to abdicate; **~ a** to give up, renounce; **abdicazi'one** *sf* abdication.

aberrazi'one [aberrat'tsjone] *sf* aberration.

a'bete *sm* fir (tree); **~ rosso** spruce.

abi'etto, a *ag* despicable, abject.

'abile *ag* (*idoneo*) suitable, fit; (*capace*) able; (*astuto*) clever; (*accorto*) skilful; (*MIL*): **~ alla leva** fit for military service; **abilità** *sf inv* ability; cleverness; skill.

abili'tato, a *ag* qualified; **abilitazi'one** *sf* qualification.

a'bisso *sm* abyss, gulf.

abi'tante *sm/f* inhabitant.

abi'tare *vt* to live in, dwell in // *vi*: **~ in campagna/a Roma** to live in the country/in Rome; **abi'tato, a** *ag* inhabited; lived in // *sm* built-up area; **abitazi'one** *sf* residence; house.

'abito *sm* dress *q*; (*da uomo*) suit; (*da donna*) dress; (*abitudine, disposizione, REL*) habit; **~i** *smpl* clothes; **in ~ da sera** in evening dress.

abitu'ale *ag* usual, habitual.

abitu'are *vt*: **~ qd a** to get sb used *o* accustomed to; **~rsi a** to get used to, accustom *o.s.* to.

abitudi'nario, a *ag* of fixed habits; **~i** *smpl* regular customers.

abi'tudine *sf* habit; **d'~** usually; **per ~** from *o* out of habit.

abiu'rare *vt* to renounce.

abnegazi'one [abnegat'tsjone] *sf* (self-)abnegation, self-denial.

abo'lire *vt* to abolish; (*DIR*) to repeal; **abolizi'one** *sf* abolition; repeal.

abomi'nevole *ag* abominable.

abo'rigeno [abo'ridʒeno] *sm* aborigine.

abor'rire *vt* to abhor, detest.

abor'tire *vi* (*MED: accidentalmente*) to miscarry, have a miscarriage; (: *deliberatamente*) to have an abortion; (*fig*) to miscarry, fail; **a'borto** *sm* miscarriage; abortion; (*fig*) freak.

abrasi'one *sf* abrasion; **abra'sivo, a** *ag, sm* abrasive.

abro'gare *vt* to repeal, abrogate.

A'bruzzo *sm*: **l'~, gli ~i** the Abruzzi.

'abside *sf* apse.

abu'sare *vi*: **~ di** to abuse, misuse; (*alcool*) to take to excess; (*approfittare, violare*) to take advantage of; **~ dei cibi** to eat to excess; **a'buso** *sm* abuse, misuse; excessive use.

a.C. (*abbr di avanti Cristo*) B.C.

'acca *sf* letter H.

acca'demia *sf* (*società*) learned society; (*scuola: d'arte, militare*) academy; **acca-'demico, a, ci, che** *ag* academic // *sm* academician.

acca'dere *vb impers* (2) to happen, occur; **acca'duto** *sm* event; **raccontare l'accaduto** to describe what has happened.

accalappi'are *vt* to catch; (*fig*) to trick, dupe.

accal'care *vt* to crowd, throng.

accal'darsi *vr* to grow hot.

accalo'rarsi *vr* (*fig*) to get excited.

accampa'mento *sm* camp.

accam'pare *vt* to encamp; (*fig*) to put forward, advance; **~rsi** *vr* to camp.

accani'mento *sm* fury; (*tenacia*) tenacity, perseverance.

acca'nirsi *vr* (*infierire*) to rage; (*ostinarsi*): **~ in** to persist in; **acca'nito, a** *ag* (*odio, gelosia*) fierce, bitter; (*lavoratore*) assiduous, dogged; (*fumatore*) inveterate.

ac'canto *av* near, nearby; **~ a** *prep* near, beside, close to.

accanto'nare *vt* (*problema*) to shelve; (*somma*) to set aside.

accaparra'mento *sm* (*COMM*) cornering, buying up.

accapar'rare *vt* to corner, buy up; (*versare una caparra*) to pay a deposit on; **~rsi qc** (*fig: simpatia, voti*) to secure sth (for *o.s.*).

accapigli'arsi [akkapiʎ'ʎarsi] *vr* to come to blows; (*fig*) to quarrel.

accappa'toio *sm* bathrobe.

accappo'nare *vi*: **mi si accappona la pelle per il freddo** the cold is giving me goosepimples *o* gooseflesh.

accarez'zare [akkaret'tsare] *vt* to caress, stroke, fondle; (*fig*) to toy with.

acca'sarsi *vr* to set up house; to get married.

accasci'arsi [akkaʃ'ʃarsi] *vr* to collapse; (*fig*) to lose heart.

accatto'naggio [akkatto'naddʒo] *sm* begging.

accat'tone, a *sm/f* beggar.

accaval'lare *vt* (*gambe*) to cross; **~rsi** *vr* (*sovrapporsi*) to overlap; (*addensarsi*) to gather.

acce'care [attʃe'kare] *vt* to blind // *vi* (2) to go blind.

ac'cedere [at'tʃedere] *vi* (2): **~ a** to enter; (*richiesta*) to grant, accede to.

accele'rare [attʃele'rare] *vt* to speed up // *vi* (*AUT*) to accelerate; **~ il passo** to quicken one's pace; **accele'rato, a** *ag* quick, rapid; accelerated // *sm* (*FERR*) slow train; **accele'ratore** *sm* (*AUT*) accelerator; **accelerazi'one** *sf* acceleration.

ac'cendere [at'tʃendere] *vt* (*fuoco, sigaretta*) to light; (*luce, televisione*) to put *o* switch *o* turn on; (*AUT: motore*) to switch on; (*COMM: conto*) to open; (*fig: suscitare*) to inflame, stir up; **~rsi** *vr* (*luce*) to come *o* go on; (*legna*) to catch fire, ignite; **accen-**

'dino sm, **accendi'sigaro** sm (cigarette) lighter.

accen'nare [attʃen'nare] vt to indicate, point out; (disegno) to sketch; (MUS) to pick out the notes of; to hum // vi: ~ **a** to beckon to; (col capo) to nod to; (fig: alludere a) to hint at; (: parlare brevemente di) to touch on; (: far vista di) to look as if; (: far atto di) to make as if.

ac'cenno [at'tʃenno] sm (cenno) sign; nod; (allusione) hint.

accensi'one [attʃen'sjone] sf (vedi accendere) lighting; switching on; opening; (AUT) ignition.

accen'tare [attʃen'tare] vt (parlando) to stress; (scrivendo) to accent.

ac'cento [at'tʃento] sm accent; (FONETICA, fig) stress; (inflessione) tone (of voice).

accen'trare [attʃen'trare] vt to centralize.

accentu'are [attʃentu'are] vt to stress, emphasize; ~**rsi** vr to become more noticeable.

accerchi'are [attʃer'kjare] vt to surround, encircle.

accerta'mento [attʃerta'mento] sm check; assessment.

accer'tare [attʃer'tare] vt to ascertain; (verificare) to check; (reddito) to assess.

ac'ceso, a [at'tʃeso] pp di accendere // ag lit; on; open; (colore) bright.

acces'sibile [attʃes'sibile] ag (luogo) accessible; (persona) approachable; (prezzo) reasonable; (idea): ~ **a qd** within the reach of sb.

ac'cesso [at'tʃesso] sm access; (MED) attack, fit; (impulso violento) fit, outburst.

acces'sorio, a [attʃes'sorjo] ag secondary, of secondary importance; ~**i** smpl accessories.

ac'cetta [at'tʃetta] sf hatchet.

accet'tabile [attʃet'tabile] ag acceptable.

accet'tare [attʃet'tare] vt to accept; ~ **di fare qc** to agree to do sth; **accettazi'one** sf acceptance; (locale di servizio pubblico) reception.

ac'cetto, \a [at'tʃetto] ag agreeable; (persona) liked.

accezi'one [attʃet'tsjone] sf meaning.

acchiap'pare [akkjap'pare] vt to catch.

acci'acco, chi [at'tʃakko] sm ailment.

acciaie'ria [attʃaje'ria] sf steelworks sg.

acci'aio [at'tʃajo] sm steel.

acciden'tale [attʃiden'tale] ag accidental.

acciden'tato, a [attʃiden'tato] ag (terreno etc) uneven.

acci'dente [attʃi'dɛnte] sm (caso imprevisto) accident; (disgrazia) mishap; (MED) stroke; ~**i!** (fam: per rabbia) damn (it)!; (: per meraviglia) good heavens!

ac'cidia [at'tʃidja] sf (REL) sloth.

accigli'ato, a [attʃiʎ'ʎato] ag frowning.

ac'cingersi [at'tʃindʒersi] vr: ~ **a fare** to be about to do.

acciuf'fare [attʃuf'fare] vt to seize, catch.

acci'uga, ghe [at'tʃuga] sf anchovy.

accla'mare vt (applaudire) to applaud;

(eleggere) to acclaim; **acclamazi'one** sf applause; acclamation.

acclima'tare vt to acclimatize; ~**rsi** vr to become acclimatized.

ac'cludere vt to enclose; **ac'cluso, a** pp di **accludere** // ag enclosed.

accocco'larsi vr to crouch.

accogli'ente [akkoʎ'ʎɛnte] ag welcoming, friendly; **accogli'enza** sf reception; welcome.

ac'cogliere [ak'kɔʎʎere] vt (ricevere) to receive; (dare il benvenuto) to welcome; (approvare) to agree to, accept; (contenere) to hold, accommodate.

accol'lato, a ag (vestito) high-necked.

accoltel'lare vt to knife, stab.

ac'colto, a pp di **accogliere**.

accoman'dita sf (DIR) limited partnership.

accomoda'mento sm agreement, settlement.

accomo'dante ag accommodating.

accomo'dare vt (aggiustare) to repair, mend; (riordinare) to tidy; (conciliare) to settle; ~**rsi** vr to make o.s. comfortable o at home; (adattarsi) to make do; ~**rsi a sedere/in casa** to sit down/come in.

accompagna'mento [akkompaɲ-ɲa'mento] sm (MUS) accompaniment.

accompa'gnare [akkompaɲ'nare] vt to accompany, come o go with; (MUS) to accompany; (unire) to couple.

accomu'nare vt to pool, share; (avvicinare) to unite.

acconcia'tura [akkontʃa'tura] sf hairstyle.

ac'concio, a, ci, ce [ak'kontʃo] ag suitable.

accondi'scendere [akkondiʃ'ʃendere] vi: ~ **a** to agree o consent to; **accondi-'sceso, a** pp di **accondiscendere**.

acconsen'tire vi: ~ **(a)** to agree o consent (to).

acconten'tare vt to satisfy; ~**rsi di** to be satisfied with, content o.s. with.

ac'conto sm part payment; **pagare una somma in** ~ to pay a sum of money as a deposit.

accoppia'mento sm coupling, pairing off; mating.

accoppi'are vt to couple, pair off; (BIOL) to mate; ~**rsi** vr to pair off; to mate.

accorci'are [akkor'tʃare] vt to shorten; ~**rsi** vr to become shorter.

accor'dare vt to reconcile; (colori) to match; (MUS) to tune; (LING): ~ **qc con qc** to make sth agree with sth; (DIR) to grant; ~**rsi** vr to agree, come to an agreement; (colori) to match.

ac'cordo sm agreement; (armonia) harmony; (MUS) chord; **essere d'**~ to agree; **andare d'**~ to get on well together; **d'**~**!** all right!, agreed!

ac'corgersi [ak'kordʒersi] vr: ~ **di** to notice; (fig) to realize; **accorgi'mento** sm shrewdness q; (espediente) trick, device.

ac'correre *vi* (*2*) to run up.

ac'corto, a *pp di* accorgersi // *ag* shrewd; stare ~ to be on one's guard.

accos'tare *vt* (*avvicinare*): ~ qc a to bring sth near to, put sth near to; (*avvicinarsi a*) to approach; (*socchiudere: imposte*) to half-close; (: *porta*) to leave ajar // *vi* (*NAUT*) to come alongside; ~rsi a to draw near, approach; (*fig*) to support.

accovacci'arsi [akkovat'tʃarsi] *vr* to crouch.

accoz'zaglia [akkot'tsaʎʎa] *sf* jumble, hotchpotch; (*peg: di persone*) mob.

accredi'tare *vt* (*notizia*) to confirm the truth of; (*COMM*) to credit; (*diplomato*) to accredit; ~rsi *vr* (*fig*) to gain credit.

ac'crescere [ak'kreʃere] *vt* to increase; ~rsi *vr* to increase, grow; accresci-'mento *sm* increase, growth; accre-sci'uto, a *pp di* accrescere.

accucci'arsi [akkut'tʃarsi] *vr* (*cane*) to lie down.

accu'dire *vt* (*anche: vi:* ~ a) to attend to.

accumu'lare *vt* to accumulate; accumu-la'tore *sm* (*ELETTR*) accumulator; accumulazi'one *sf* accumulation.

accura'tezza [akkura'tettsa] *sf* care; accuracy.

accu'rato, a *ag* (*diligente*) careful; (*preciso*) accurate.

ac'cusa *sf* accusation; (*DIR*) charge.

accu'sare *vt:* ~ qd di qc to accuse sb of sth; (*DIR*) to charge sb with sth; ~ ricevuta di (*COMM*) to acknowledge receipt of.

accu'sato, a *sm/f* accused; defendant.

accusa'tore, 'trice *sm/f* accuser // *sm* (*DIR*) prosecutor.

a'cerbo, a [a'tʃerbo] *ag* bitter; (*frutta*) sour, unripe.

'acero [a'tʃero] *sm* maple.

a'cerrimo, a [a'tʃerrimo] *ag* very fierce.

a'ceto [a'tʃeto] *sm* vinegar.

A.C.I. *sm* (*abbr di Automobile Club d'Italia*) ≈ A.A.

acidità [atʃidi'ta] *sf* acidity; sourness.

'acido, a ['atʃido] *ag* (*sapore*) acid, sour; (*CHIM*) acid // *sm* (*CHIM*) acid.

'acino ['atʃino] *sm* berry; ~ d'uva grape.

'acne *sf* acne.

'acqua *sf* water; (*pioggia*) rain; ~e *sfpl* waters; fare ~ (*NAUT*) to leak, take in water; ~ corrente running water; ~ dolce fresh water; ~ minerale mineral water; ~ potabile drinking water; ~ salata salt water; ~ tonica tonic water.

acqua'forte, *pl* acque'forti *sf* etching.

a'cquaio *sm* sink.

acqua'ragia [akkwa'radʒa] *sf* turpentine.

a'cquario *sm* aquarium; (*dello zodiaco*): A~ Aquarius.

acqua'santa *sf* holy water.

acqua'vite *sf* brandy.

acquaz'zone [akkwat'tsone] *sm* cloudburst, heavy shower.

acque'dotto *sm* aqueduct; waterworks *pl*, water system.

acque'rello *sm* watercolour.

acque'rugiola [akkwe'rudʒola] *sf* drizzle.

acquie'tare *vt* to appease; (*dolore*) to ease; ~rsi *vr* to calm down.

acqui'rente *sm/f* purchaser, buyer.

acqui'sire *vt* to acquire.

acquis'tare *vt* to purchase, buy; (*fig*) to gain; a'cquisto *sm* purchase; fare acquisti to go shopping.

acqui'trino *sm* bog, marsh.

acquo'lina *sf:* far venire l'~ in bocca a qd to make sb's mouth water.

a'cquoso, a *ag* watery.

'acre *ag* acrid, pungent; (*fig*) harsh, biting.

a'crobata, i, e *sm/f* acrobat.

acro'batica *sf* acrobatics *sg*.

acro'bazia [akrobat'tsia] *sf* acrobatic feat.

acu'ire *vt* to sharpen.

a'culeo *sm* (*ZOOL*) sting; (*BOT*) prickle.

a'cume *sm* acumen, perspicacity.

a'custica *sf* (*scienza*) acoustics *sg*; (*di una sala*) acoustics *pl*.

a'cuto, a *ag* (*appuntito*) sharp, pointed; (*suono, voce*) shrill, piercing; (*MAT, LING, MED*) acute; (*MUS*) high-pitched; (*fig: dolore, desiderio*) intense; (: *perspicace*) acute, keen.

ad *prep* (*dav V*) = a.

adagi'are [ada'dʒare] *vt* to lay *o* set down carefully; ~rsi *vr* to lie down, stretch out.

a'dagio [a'dadʒo] *av* slowly // *sm* (*MUS*) adagio; (*proverbio*) adage, saying.

adatta'mento *sm* adaptation.

adat'tare *vt* to adapt; (*applicare*) to fit; ~rsi (a) (*ambiente, tempi*) to adapt (to).

a'datto, a *ag:* ~ (a) suitable (for), right (for).

addebi'tare *vt:* ~ qc a qd to debit sb with sth; (*fig: incolpare*) to blame sb for sth.

adden'sare *vt* to thicken; ~rsi *vr* to thicken; (*folla, nuvole*) to gather.

adden'tare *vt* to bite into.

adden'trarsi *vr:* ~ in to penetrate, go into.

ad'dentro *av* inside, within; (*fig*) deeply; essere molto ~ in qc to be well-versed in sth.

addestra'mento *sm* training.

addes'trare *vt* ~rsi *vr* to train; ~rsi in qc to practise sth.

ad'detto, a *ag:* ~ a assigned to; (*occupato in un lavoro*) employed in, attached to // *sm* employee; (*funzionario*) attaché; ~ commerciale/stampa commercial/ press attaché.

addì *av* (*AMM*): ~ 3 luglio 1978 on the 3rd of July 1978.

addi'etro *av* (*indietro*) behind; (*nel passato, prima*) before, ago.

ad'dio *sm, escl* goodbye, farewell.

addirit'tura *av* (*veramente*) really, absolutely; (*perfino*) even; (*direttamente*) directly, right away.

ad'dirsi *vr:* ~ a to suit, be suitable for.

addi'tare *vt* to point out; (*fig*) to expose.

addi'tivo *sm* additive.

addizio'nare [addittsjo'nare] *vt* (*MAT*) to add (up); **addizl'one** *sf* addition.

addob'bare *vt* to decorate; **ad'dobbo** *sm* decoration.

addol'cire [addol'tʃire] *vt* (*caffè etc*) to sweeten; (*acqua, fig: carattere*) to soften; ~**rsi** *vr* (*fig*) to mellow, soften.

addolo'rare *vt* to pain, grieve; ~**rsi (per)** to be distressed (by).

ad'dome *sm* abdomen.

addomesti'care *vt* to tame.

addormen'tare *vt* to put to sleep; ~**rsi** *vr* to fall asleep.

addos'sare *vt* (*appoggiare*): ~ **qc a qc** to lean sth against sth; (*fig*): ~ **qc a qd** to saddle sb with sth; ~ **la colpa a qd** to lay the blame on sb; ~**rsi qc** (*responsabilità etc*) to shoulder.

ad'dosso *av* (*sulla persona*) on; **mettersi** ~ **il cappotto** to put one's coat on; ~ **a** *prep* (*sopra*) on; (*molto vicino*) right next to.

ad'durre *vt* (*DIR*) to produce; (*citare*) to cite.

adegu'are *vt*: ~ **qc a qc** to adjust *o* relate sth to; ~**rsi** *vr* to adapt; **adegu'ato, a** *ag* adequate; (*conveniente*) suitable; (*equo*) fair.

a'dempiere, adem'pire *vt* to fulfil, carry out.

ade'rente *ag* adhesive; (*vestito*) close-fitting // *sm/f* follower; **ade'renza** *sf* adhesion; **aderenze** *sfpl* (*fig*) connections, contacts.

ade'rire *vi* (*stare attaccato*) to adhere, stick; ~ **a** to adhere to, stick to; (*fig: società, partito*) to join; (*: opinione*) to support; (*richiesta*) to agree to; **adesl'one** *sf* adhesion; (*fig*) agreement, acceptance; **ade'sivo, a** *ag, sm* adhesive.

a'desso *av* (*ora*) now; (*or ora, poco fa*) just now; (*tra poco*) any moment now.

adia'cente [adja'tʃɛnte] *ag* adjacent.

adi'bire *vt* (*usare*): ~ **qc a** to turn sth into.

adi'rarsi *vr*: ~ (**con** *o* **contro qd per qc**) to get angry (with sb over sth).

a'dire *vt* (*tribunale*) to resort to; ~ **le vie legali** to take legal proceedings.

'adito *sm* entrance; access.

adocchi'are [adok'kjare] *vt* (*scorgere*) to catch sight of; (*occhieggiare*) to eye.

adole'scente [adoleʃ'ʃɛnte] *ag, sm/f* adolescent; **adole'scenza** *sf* adolescence.

adom'brare *vt* (*fig*) to veil, conceal; ~**rsi** *vr* (*cavallo*) to shy; (*persona*) to grow suspicious; (*: aversene a male*) to be offended.

adope'rare *vt* to use; ~**rsi** *vr* to strive; ~**rsi per qd/qc** to do one's best for sb/sth.

ado'rare *vt* to adore; (*REL*) to adore, worship; **adorazi'one** *sf* adoration; worship.

ador'nare *vt* to adorn.

adot'tare *vt* to adopt; (*decisione, provvedimenti*) to pass; **adot'tivo, a** *ag* (*genitori*) adoptive; (*figlio, patria*) adopted; **adozl'one** *sf* adoption.

adri'atico, a, ci, che *ag* Adriatic // *sm*: **l'A~, il mare A~** the Adriatic, the Adriatic Sea.

adu'lare *vt* to adulate, flatter.

adulte'rare *vt* to adulterate.

adul'terio *sm* adultery; **a'dultero, a** *ag* adulterous // *sm/f* adulterer/adulteress.

a'dulto, a *ag* adult; (*fig*) mature // *sm* adult, grown-up.

adu'nanza [adu'nantsa] *sf* assembly, meeting.

adu'nare *vt*, ~**rsi** *vr* to assemble, gather; **adu'nata** *sf* (*MIL*) parade, muster.

a'dunco, a, chi, che *ag* hooked.

a'ereo, a *ag* air *cpd*; (*radice*) aerial // *sm* aerial; (*abbr di* **aeroplano**) plane; **aerodi'namico, a, ci, che** *ag* aerodynamic; (*affusolato*) streamlined // *sf* aerodynamics *sg*; **aero'nautica** *sf* (*scienza*) aeronautics *sg*; **aeronautica militare** air force; **aero'plano** *sm* aeroplane; **aero'porto** *sm* airport; **aero-'sol** *sm inv* aerosol; **aerospazi'ale** *ag* aerospace.

'afa *sf* sultriness.

af'fabile *ag* affable.

affaccen'darsi [affattʃen'darsi] *vr*: ~ **intorno a qc** to busy o.s. with sth; **affaccen'dato, a** *ag* busy.

affacci'arsi [affat'tʃarsi] *vr*: ~ (**a**) to appear (at).

affa'mare *vt* to starve; **affa'mato, a** *ag* starving; (*fig*): **affamato (di)** eager (for).

affan'nare *vt* to leave breathless; (*fig*) to worry; ~**rsi** *vr*: ~**rsi per qd/qc** to worry about sb/sth; **af'fanno** *sm* breathlessness; (*fig*) anxiety, worry; **affan'noso, a** *ag* (*respiro*) difficult; (*fig*) troubled, anxious.

af'fare *sm* (*cosa, faccenda*) matter, affair; (*COMM*) piece of business, (*business*) deal; (*DIR*) case; (*fam: cosa*) thing; ~**i** *smpl* (*COMM*) business *sg*; **ministro degli A~i esteri** Foreign Secretary; **affa'rista, i** *sm* profiteer, unscrupulous businessman.

affasci'nare [affaʃʃi'nare] *vt* to bewitch; (*fig*) to charm, fascinate.

affati'care *vt* to tire; ~**rsi** *vr* (*durar fatica*) to tire o.s. out.

af'fatto *av* completely; **non ...** ~ not ... at all.

affer'mare *vi* (*dire di sì*) to say yes // *vt* (*dichiarare*) to maintain, affirm; ~**rsi** *vr* to assert o.s., make one's name known; **affermazi'one** *sf* affirmation, assertion; (*successo*) achievement.

affer'rare *vt* to seize, grasp; (*fig: idea*) to grasp; ~**rsi** *vr*: ~**rsi a** to cling to.

affet'tare *vt* (*tagliare a fette*) to slice; (*ostentare*) to affect; **affet'tato, a** *ag* sliced; affected // *sm* sliced cold meat; **affettazi'one** *sf* affectation.

affet'tivo, a *ag* emotional, affective.

af'fetto *sm* affection; **affettu'oso, a** *ag* affectionate.

affezio'narsi [affettsjo'narsi] *vr*: ~ a to grow fond of.

affezi'one [affet'tsjone] *sf* (*affetto*) affection; (*MED*) ailment, disorder.

affian'care *vt* to place side by side; (*MIL*) to flank; (*fig*) to support; ~ **qc a qc** to place sth next to o beside sth; ~**rsi a qd** to stand beside sb.

affia'tarsi *vr* to get on well together.

affibbi'are *vt* to buckle, do up; (*fig: dare*) to give.

affida'mento *sm* (*fiducia*) confidence, trust; (*garanzia*) assurance; **fare** ~ **su qd** to rely on sb.

affi'dare *vt*: ~ **qc a qd** to entrust sb with sth; ~**rsi** *vr*: ~**rsi a** to place one's trust in.

affievo'lirsi *vr* to grow weak.

af'figgere [af'fiddʒere] *vt* to stick up, post up.

affi'lare *vt* to sharpen.

affili'are *vt* to affiliate; ~**rsi** *vr*: ~**rsi a** to become affiliated to.

affi'nare *vt* to sharpen.

affinché [affin'ke] *cong* in order that, so that.

af'fine *ag* similar; **affinità** *sf inv* affinity.

affio'rare *vi* to emerge.

affissi'one *sf* bill-posting.

af'fisso, a *pp di* **affiggere** // *sm* bill, poster; (*LING*) affix.

affit'tare *vt* (*dare in affitto*) to let, rent (out); (*prendere in affitto*) to rent; **af'fitto** *sm* rent; (*contratto*) lease.

af'fliggere [af'fliddʒere] *vt* to torment; ~**rsi** *vr* to grieve; **af'flitto, a** *pp di* **affliggere**; **afflizi'one** *sf* distress, torment.

afflosci'arsi [affloʃ'ʃarsi] *vr* to go limp; (*frutta*) to go soft.

afflu'ente *sm* tributary; **afflu'enza** *sf* flow; (*di persone*) crowd.

afflu'ire *vi* (2) to flow; (*fig: merci, persone*) to pour in; **af'flusso** *sm* influx.

affo'gare *vt, vi* to drown; ~**rsi** *vr* to drown; (*deliberatamente*) to drown o.s.

affol'lare *vt*, ~**rsi** *vr* to crowd; **affol-'lato, a** *ag* crowded.

affon'dare *vt* to sink.

affran'care *vt* to free, liberate; (*AMM*) to redeem; (*lettera*) to stamp; (*automaticamente*) to frank; ~**rsi** *vr* to free o.s.; **affranca'tura** *sf* (*di francobollo*) stamping; franking; (*tassa di spedizione*) postage.

af'franto, a *ag* (*esausto*) worn out; (*abbattuto*) overcome.

af'fresco, schi *sm* fresco.

affret'tare *vt* to quicken, speed up; ~**rsi** *vr* to hurry; ~**rsi a fare qc** to hurry o hasten to do sth.

affron'tare *vt* (*pericolo etc*) to face; (*assalire: nemico*) to confront; ~**rsi** *vr* (*reciproco*) to come to blows.

af'fronto *sm* affront, insult.

affumi'care *vt* to fill with smoke; to blacken with smoke; (*alimenti*) to smoke.

affuso'lato, a *ag* tapering.

a'foso, a *ag* sultry, close.

'Africa *sf*: l'~ Africa; **afri'cano, a** *ag, sm/f* African.

afrodi'siaco, a, ci, che *ag, sm* aphrodisiac.

a'genda [a'dʒenda] *sf* diary.

a'gente [a'dʒente] *sm* agent; ~ **di cambio** stockbroker; ~ **di polizia** police officer; ~ **di vendita** sales agent; **agen-'zia** *sf* agency; (*succursale*) branch; **agenzia immobiliare** estate agent's (office); **agenzia pubblicitaria/viaggi** advertising/travel agency.

agevo'lare [adʒevo'lare] *vt* to facilitate, make easy.

a'gevole [a'dʒevole] *ag* easy; (*strada*) smooth.

agganci'are [aggan'tʃare] *vt* to hook up; (*FERR*) to couple.

ag'geggio [ad'dʒeddʒo] *sm* gadget, contraption.

agget'tivo [addʒet'tivo] *sm* adjective.

agghiacci'are [aggjat'tʃare] *vt* to freeze; (*fig*) to make one's blood run cold; ~**rsi** *vr* to freeze.

aggior'nare [addʒor'nare] *vt* (*opera, manuale*) to bring up-to-date; (*seduta etc*) to postpone; ~**rsi** *vr* to bring (o keep) o.s. up-to-date.

aggi'rare [addʒi'rare] *vt* to go round; (*fig: ingannare*) to trick; ~**rsi** *vr* to wander about; **il prezzo s'aggira sul milione** the price is around the million mark.

aggiudi'care [addʒudi'kare] *vt* to award; (*all'asta*) to knock down; ~**rsi qc** to win sth.

ag'giungere [ad'dʒundʒere] *vt* to add; **aggi'unto, a** *pp di* **aggiungere** // *ag* assistant *cpd* // *sm* assistant // *sf* addition; **sindaco aggiunto** deputy mayor.

aggius'tare [addʒus'tare] *vt* (*accomodare*) to mend, repair; (*riassettare*) to adjust; (*fig: lite*) to settle; ~**rsi** *vr* (*arrangiarsi*) to make do; (*con senso reciproco*) to come to an agreement.

agglome'rato *sm* (*di rocce*) conglomerate; (*di legno*) chipboard; ~ **urbano** built-up area.

aggrap'parsi *vr*: ~ **a** to cling to.

aggra'vare *vt* (*aumentare*) to increase; (*appesantire: anche fig*) to weigh down, make heavy; (*fig: pena*) to make worse; ~**rsi** *vr* (*fig*) to worsen, become worse.

aggrazi'ato, a [aggrat'tsjato] *ag* graceful.

aggre'dire *vt* to attack, assault.

aggre'gare *vt*: ~ **qd a qc** to admit sb to sth; ~**rsi** *vr* to join; ~**rsi a** to join, become a member of; **aggre'gato, a** *ag* associated // *sm* aggregate; **aggregato di case** block of houses.

aggressi'one *sf* aggression; (*atto*) attack, assault.

aggres'sivo, a *ag* aggressive.

aggres'sore *sm* aggressor, attacker.

aggrot'tare *vt*: ~ **le sopracciglia** to frown.

aggrovigli'are [aggroviʎ'ʎare] *vt* to

tangle; ~rsi vr (fig) to become complicated.

aggru'marsi vr to clot.

agguan'tare vt to catch, seize.

aggu'ato sm trap; (imboscata) ambush; tendere un ~ a qd to set a trap for sb.

agi'ato, a [a'dʒato] ag (vita) easy; (persona) well-off, well-to-do.

'agile ['adʒile] ag agile, nimble; agilità sf agility, nimbleness.

'agio ['adʒo] sm ease, comfort; ~i smpl comforts; mettersi a proprio ~ to make o.s. at home o comfortable.

a'gire [a'dʒire] vi to act; (esercitare un'azione) to take effect; (TECN) to work, function; ~ su (influire su) to affect; ~ contro qd (DIR) to take action against sb.

agi'tare [adʒi'tare] vt (bottiglia) to shake; (mano, fazzoletto) to wave; (fig: turbare) to disturb; (: incitare) to stir (up); (: dibattere) to discuss; ~rsi vr (mare) to be rough; (malato, dormitore) to toss and turn; (bambino) to fidget; (emozionarsi) to get upset; (POL) to agitate; agi'tato, a ag rough; restless; fidgety; upset, perturbed; agitazi'one sf agitation; (POL) unrest, agitation; mettere in agitazione qd to upset o distress sb.

'agli ['aʎʎi] prep + det vedi a.

'aglio ['aʎʎo] sm garlic.

a'gnello [aɲ'ɲɛllo] sm lamb.

'ago, pl aghi sm needle.

ago'nia sf agony.

ago'nistico, a, ci, che ag athletic; (fig) competitive.

agoniz'zare [agonid'dzare] vi to be dying.

agopun'tura sf acupuncture.

a'gosto sm August.

a'grario, a ag agrarian, agricultural; (riforma) land cpd // sm landowner // sf agriculture.

a'gricolo, a ag agricultural, farm cpd; agricol'tore sm farmer; agricol'tura sf agriculture, farming.

agri'foglio [agri'fɔʎʎo] sm holly.

agrimen'sore sm land surveyor.

'agro, a ag sour, sharp.

a'grume sm (spesso al pl: pianta) citrus; (: frutto) citrus fruit.

aguz'zare [agut'tsare] vt to sharpen; ~ gli orecchi to prick up one's ears.

a'guzzo, a [a'guttso] ag sharp.

'ai prep + det vedi a.

'aia sf threshing-floor.

'Aia sf: l'~ the Hague.

ai'rone sm heron.

aiu'ola sf flower bed.

aiu'tante sm/f assistant // sm (MIL) adjutant; (NAUT) master-at-arms; ~ di campo aide-de-camp.

aiu'tare vt to help.

ai'uto sm help, assistance, aid; (aiutante) assistant; venire in ~ di qd to come to sb's aid; ~ chirurgo assistant surgeon.

aiz'zare [ait'tsare] vt to incite; ~ i cani contro qd to set the dogs on sb.

al prep + det vedi a.

'ala, pl 'ali sf wing; fare ~ to fall back, make way; ~ destra/sinistra (SPORT) right/left wing.

ala'bastro sm alabaster.

'alacre ag quick, brisk.

a'lano sm Great Dane.

a'lare ag wing cpd; ~i smpl firedogs.

'alba sf dawn.

Alba'nia sf: l'~ Albania.

'albatro sm albatross.

albeggi'are [albed'dʒare] (2) vi, vb impers to dawn.

albera'tura sf (NAUT) masts pl.

alberga'tore, 'trice sm/f hotelier, hotel-keeper.

alberghi'ero, a [alber'gjero] ag hotel cpd.

al'bergo, ghi sm hotel.

'albero sm tree; (NAUT) mast; (TECN) shaft; ~ di Natale Christmas tree; ~ maestro mainmast; ~ di trasmissione transmission shaft.

albi'cocca, che sf apricot; albi'cocco, chi sm apricot tree.

'albo sm (registro) register, roll; (AMM) notice board.

'album sm album; ~ da disegno sketch book.

al'bume sm albumen.

albu'mina sf albumin.

'alce ['altʃe] sm elk.

al'chimia [al'kimja] sf alchemy; alchi'mista, i sm alchemist.

al'colico, a, ci, che ag alcoholic // sm alcoholic drink.

alcoliz'zato, a [alkolid'dzato] sm/f alcoholic.

'alcool sm alcohol; alco'olico etc vedi alcolico etc.

al'cova sf alcove.

al'cuno, a det (dav sm: alcun +C, V, alcuno + s impura, gn, pn, ps, x, z; dav sf: alcuna +C, alcun' +V) (nessuno): non ... ~ no, not any; ~i(e) det pl, pronome pl some, a few; non c'è ~a fretta there's no hurry, there isn't any hurry; senza alcun riguardo without any consideration.

a'letta sf (TECN) fin; tab.

alfa'beto sm alphabet.

alfi'ere sm standard-bearer; (MIL) ensign; (SCACCHI) bishop.

al'fine av finally, in the end.

'alga, ghe sf seaweed q, alga.

'algebra ['aldʒebra] sf algebra.

Alge'ria [aldʒe'ria] sf: l'~ Algeria.

ali'ante sm (AER) glider.

'alibi sm inv alibi.

alie'nare vt (DIR) to alienate, transfer; (rendere ostile) to alienate; ~rsi qd to alienate sb; alie'nato, a ag alienated; transferred; (fuor di senno) insane // sm lunatic, insane person; alienazi'one sf alienation; transfer; insanity.

ali'eno, a ag (avverso): ~ (da) opposed (to), averse (to).

alimen'tare vt to feed; (TECN) to feed; to supply; (fig) to sustain // ag food cpd;

alimentazi'one *sf* feeding; supplying; sustaining; (*gli alimenti*) diet.

ali'mento *sm* food; ~i *smpl* food *sg*; (*DIR*) alimony.

a'liquota *sf* share; (*d'imposta*) rate.

alis'cafo *sm* hydrofoil.

'alito *sm* breath.

all. (*abbr di* allegato) encl.

'alla *prep + det vedi* **a.**

allacci'are [allat'tʃare] *vt* (*scarpe*) to tie, lace (up); (*cintura*) to do up, fasten; (*due località*) to link; (*luce, gas*) to connect; (*amicizia*) to form.

allaga'mento *sm* flooding *q*; flood.

allar'gare *vt* to widen; (*vestito*) to let out; (*aprire*) to open; (*fig: dilatare*) to extend.

allar'mare *vt* to alarm.

al'larme *sm* alarm; ~ **aereo** air-raid warning.

allat'tare *vt* to feed.

'alle *prep + det vedi* **a.**

alle'anza [alle'antsa] *sf* alliance.

alle'arsi *vr* to form an alliance; **alle'ato, a** *ag* allied // *sm/f* ally.

alle'gare *vt* (*accludere*) to enclose; (*DIR: citare*) to cite, adduce; (*denti*) to set on edge; **alle'gato, a** *ag* enclosed // *sm* enclosure; **in allegato** enclosed.

allegge'rire [alleddʒe'rire] *vt* to lighten, make lighter; (*fig: sofferenza*) to alleviate, lessen; (*: lavoro, tasse*) to reduce; ~**rsi** *vr* to put on lighter clothes.

allego'ria *sf* allegory.

alle'gria *sf* gaiety, cheerfulness.

al'legro, a *ag* cheerful, merry; (*un po' brillo*) merry, tipsy; (*vivace: colore*) bright // *sm* (*MUS*) allegro.

allena'mento *sm* training.

alle'nare *vt*, ~**rsi** *vr* to train; **allena'tore** *sm* (*SPORT*) trainer, coach.

allen'tare *vt* to slacken; (*disciplina*) to relax; ~**rsi** *vr* to become slack; (*ingranaggio*) to work loose.

aller'gia, 'gie [aller'dʒia] *sf* allergy; **al'lergico, a, ci, che** *ag* allergic.

alles'tire *vt* (*cena*) to prepare; (*esercito, nave*) to equip, fit out; (*spettacolo*) to stage.

allet'tare *vt* to lure, entice.

alleva'mento *sm* breeding, rearing; (*luogo*) stock farm.

alle'vare *vt* (*animale*) to breed, rear; (*bambino*) to bring up.

allevi'are *vt* to alleviate.

alli'bire *vi* (2) to be astounded.

allie'tare *vt* to cheer up, gladden.

alli'evo *sm* pupil; (*apprendista*) apprentice; (*MIL*) cadet.

alliga'tore *sm* alligator.

alline'are *vt* (*persone, cose*) to line up; (*TIP*) to align; (*fig: economia, salari*) to adjust, align; ~**rsi** *vr* to line up; (*fig: a idee*): ~**rsi a** to come into line with.

'allo *prep + det vedi* **a.**

al'locco, a, chi, che *sm* tawny owl // *sm/f* dolt.

allocuzi'one [allokut'tsjone] *sf* address, solemn speech.

al'lodola *sf* (sky)lark.

alloggi'are [allod'dʒare] *vt* to put up, give accommodation to; (*MIL*) to quarter; to billet // *vi* to live; (*MIL*) to be quartered; to be billeted; **al'loggio** *sm* lodging, accommodation; (*appartamento*) flat; (*MIL*) quarters *pl*; billet.

allontana'mento *sm* removal; dismissal.

allonta'nare *vt* to send away, send off; (*impiegato*) to dismiss; (*pericolo*) to avert, remove; (*estraniare*) to alienate; ~**rsi** *vr*: ~**rsi (da)** to go away (from); (*estraniarsi*) to become estranged (from).

al'lora *av* (*in quel momento*) then // *cong* (*in questo caso*) well then; (*dunque*) well then, so; **la gente d'~** people then *o* in those days; **da ~ in poi** from then on.

al'loro *sm* laurel.

'alluce ['allutʃe] *sm* big toe.

allucinazi'one [allutʃinat'tsjone] *sf* hallucination.

al'ludere *vi*: ~ **a** to allude to, hint at.

allu'minio *sm* aluminium.

allun'gare *vt* to lengthen; (*distendere*) to prolong, extend; (*diluire*) to water down; ~**rsi** *vr* to lengthen; (*ragazzo*) to stretch, grow taller; (*sdraiarsi*) to lie down, stretch out.

allusi'one *sf* hint, allusion.

alluvi'one *sf* flood.

alma'nacco, chi *sm* almanac.

al'meno *av* at least // *cong* if only; ~ **piovesse!** if only it would rain!

a'lone *sm* halo.

'Alpi *sfpl*: **le** ~ the Alps.

alpi'nismo *sm* mountaineering, climbing; **alpi'nista, i, e** *sm/f* mountaineer, climber.

al'pino, a *ag* Alpine; mountain *cpd*.

al'quanto *av* rather, a little; ~**, a** *det a* certain amount of, some // *pronome a* certain amount, some; ~**i(e)** *det pl*, *pronome pl* several, quite a few.

alt *escl* halt!, stop!

alta'lena *sf* (*a funi*) swing; (*in bilico, anche fig*) seesaw.

al'tare *sm* altar.

alte'rare *vt* to alter, change; (*cibo*) to adulterate; (*registro*) to falsify; (*persona*) to irritate; ~**rsi** *vr* to alter; (*cibo*) to go bad; (*persona*) to lose one's temper; **alterazi'one** *sf* alteration, change; adulteration; falsification; annoyance.

al'terco, chi *sm* altercation, wrangle.

alter'nare *vt*, ~**rsi** *vr* to alternate; **alterna'tivo, a** *ag* alternating // *sf* (*avvicendamento*) alternation; (*scelta*) alternative; **alterna'tore** *sm* alternator.

al'terno, a *ag* alternate; **a giorni** ~**i** on alternate days, every other day.

al'tezza [al'tettsa] *sf* height; width; breadth; depth; pitch; (*GEO*) latitude; (*titolo*) highness; (*fig: nobiltà*) greatness; **essere all'**~ **di** to be on a level with; (*fig*) to be up to *o* equal to; **altez'zoso, a** *ag* haughty.

alti'tudine *sf* altitude.

'alto, a *ag* high; (*persona*) tall; (*tessuto*)

wide, broad; (sonno, acque) deep; (suono) high(-pitched); (GEO) upper; (: settentrionale) northern // sm top (part) // av high; (parlare) aloud, loudly; **il palazzo è ~ 20 metri** the building is 20 metres high; **il tessuto è ~ 70 cm** the material is 70 cm wide; **ad ~a voce** aloud; **a notte ~a** in the dead of night; **in ~** up, upwards; at the top; **dall'~** in o **al basso** up and down; **degli ~i e bassi** (fig) ups and downs; **~a fedeltà** high fidelity, hi-fi; **~a moda** haute couture.

alto'forno sm blast furnace.

altopar'lante sm loudspeaker.

altret'tanto, a ag, pronome as much; (pl) as many // av equally; **tanti auguri! — grazie, ~** all the best! — thank you, the same to you.

'altri pronome inv (qualcuno) somebody; (: in espressioni negative) anybody; (un'altra persona) another (person).

altri'menti av otherwise.

'altro, a det other; **un ~ libro** (supplementare) another book, one more book; (diverso) another book, a different book; **un ~** another (one); **l'~** the other (one); **gli ~i** (la gente) others, other people; **desidera ~?** do you want anything else?; **aiutarsi l'un l'~** to help one another; **l'uno e l'~** both (of them); **l'~ giorno** the other day; **l'~ ieri** the day before yesterday; **domani l'~** the day after tomorrow; **quest'~ mese** next month; **da un giorno all'~** from day to day; (qualsiasi giorno) any day now; **d'~a parte** on the other hand; **tra l'~** among other things; **ci mancherebbe ~!** that's all we need!; **non faccio ~ che studiare** I do nothing but study; **sei contento? — ~ che!/tutt'~!** are you pleased? — and how!/on the contrary!; **noi/voi ~i** us/you (lot).

al'tronde av: **d'~** on the other hand.

al'trove av elsewhere, somewhere else.

al'trui ag inv other people's // sm other people's belongings pl.

altru'ista, i, e ag altruistic.

al'tura sf (rialto) height, high ground; (alto mare) open sea; **pesca d'~** deep-sea fishing.

a'lunno, a sm/f pupil.

alve'are sm hive.

al'zare [al'tsare] vt to raise, lift; (issare) to hoist; (costruire) to build, erect; **~rsi** vr to rise; (dal letto) to get up; (crescere) to grow tall (o taller); **~ le spalle** to shrug one's shoulders; **~ le carte** to cut the cards; **~rsi in piedi** to stand up, get to one's feet; **al'zata** sf lifting, raising; **un'alzata di spalle** a shrug.

a'mabile ag lovable; (vino) sweet.

a'maca, che sf hammock.

amalga'mare vt, **~rsi** vr to amalgamate.

a'mante ag: **~ di** (musica etc) fond of // sm/f lover/mistress.

a'mare vt to love; (amico, musica, sport) to like.

ama'rena sf sour black cherry.

ama'rezza [ama'rettsa] sf bitterness.

a'maro, a ag bitter // sm bitterness; (liquore) bitters pl.

ambasce'ria [ambaʃʃe'ria] sf embassy.

am'bascia, sce [am'baʃʃa] sf (MED) difficulty in breathing; (fig) anguish.

ambasci'ata [ambaʃ'ʃata] sf embassy; (messaggio) message; **ambascia'tore, 'trice** sm/f ambassador/ambassadress.

ambe'due ag inv: **~ i ragazzi** both boys // pronome inv both.

ambien'tare vt to acclimatize; (romanzo, film) to set; **~rsi** vr to get used to one's surroundings.

ambi'ente sm environment; (fig: insieme di persone) milieu; (stanza) room.

ambiguità sf inv ambiguity.

am'biguo, a ag ambiguous; (persona) shady.

am'bire vt (anche: vi: **~ a**) to aspire to.

'ambito sm sphere, field.

ambizi'one [ambit'tsjone] sf ambition; **ambizi'oso, a** ag ambitious.

'ambra sf amber; **~ grigia** ambergris.

ambu'lante ag travelling, itinerant.

ambu'lanza [ambu'lantsa] sf ambulance.

ambula'torio sm (studio medico) surgery.

amenità sf inv pleasantness q; (facezia) pleasantry.

a'meno, a ag pleasant; (strano) funny, strange; (spiritoso) amusing.

A'merica sf: **l'~** America; **l'~ latina** Latin America; **ameri'cano, a** ag, sm/f American.

ame'tista sf amethyst.

a'mica sf vedi **amico.**

ami'chevole [ami'kevole] ag friendly.

ami'cizia [ami'tʃittsja] sf friendship; **~e** sfpl (amici) friends.

a'mico, a, ci, che sm/f friend; (amante) boyfriend/girlfriend; **~ del cuore** o **intimo** bosom friend.

'amido sm starch.

ammac'care vt (pentola) to dent; (persona) to bruise; **~rsi** vr to bruise; **ammacca'tura** sf dent; bruise.

ammaes'trare vt (animale) to train; (persona) to teach.

ammai'nare vt to lower, haul down.

amma'larsi vr to fall ill; **amma'lato, a** ag ill, sick // sm/f sick person; (paziente) patient.

ammali'are vt (fig) to enchant, charm; **ammalia'tore, 'trice** sm/f enchanter/enchantress.

am'manco, chi sm (ECON) deficit.

ammanet'tare vt to handcuff.

ammas'sare vt (ammucchiare) to amass; (raccogliere) to gather together; **~rsi** vr to pile up; to gather; **am'masso** sm mass; (mucchio) pile, heap; (ECON) stockpile.

ammat'tire vi (2) to go mad.

ammaz'zare [ammat'tsare] vt to kill; **~rsi** vr (uccidersi) to kill o.s.; (rimanere ucciso) to be killed; **~rsi di lavoro** to work o.s. to death.

am'menda sf amends pl; (DIR, SPORT) fine; **fare ~ di qc** to make amends for sth.

am'messo, a pp di **ammettere** // cong: **~ che** supposing that.

am'mettere vt to admit; (riconoscere: fatto) to acknowledge, admit; (permettere) to allow, accept; (supporre) to suppose; **ammettiamo che ...** let us suppose that ... .

ammic'care vi: **~ (a)** to wink (at).

amminis'trare vt to run, manage; (REL, DIR) to administer; **amministra'tivo, a** ag administrative; **amministra'tore** sm administrator; (direttore di azienda) manager; (consigliere di società) director; **amministratore delegato** managing director; **amministrazi'one** sf management; administration.

ammiragli'ato [ammiraʎ'ʎato] sm admiralty.

ammi'raglio [ammi'raʎʎo] sm admiral.

ammi'rare vt to admire; **ammira'tore, 'trice** sm/f admirer; **ammirazi'one** sf admiration.

ammis'sibile ag admissible, acceptable.

ammissi'one sf admission; (approvazione) acknowledgement.

ammobili'are vt to furnish.

am'modo, a 'modo av properly // ag inv respectable, nice.

ammol'lare vt (panni etc) to soak.

ammo'niaca sf ammonia.

ammoni'mento sm warning; admonishment.

ammo'nire vt (avvertire) to warn; (rimproverare) to admonish; (DIR) to caution.

ammon'tare vi (2): **~ a** to amount to // sm (total) amount.

ammonticchi'are [ammontik'kjare] vt to pile up, heap up.

ammorbi'dire vt to soften.

ammortiz'zare [ammortid'dzare] vt (ECON) to pay off, amortize; (: spese d'impianto) to write off; (AUT, TECN) to absorb, deaden; **ammortizza'tore** sm (AUT, TECN) shock-absorber.

ammucchi'are [ammuk'kjare] vt, **~rsi** vr to pile up, accumulate.

ammuf'fire vi (2) to go mouldy.

ammutina'mento sm mutiny.

ammuti'narsi vr to mutiny.

ammuto'lire vi to be struck dumb.

amne'sia sf amnesia.

amnis'tia sf amnesty.

'amo sm (PESCA) hook; (fig) bait.

a'more sm love; (~i) love affairs; **il tuo bambino è un ~** your baby's a darling; **fare l'~ o all'~** to make love; **per ~ o per forza** by hook or by crook; **amor proprio** self-esteem, pride; **amo'revole** ag loving, affectionate.

a'morfo, a ag amorphous; (fig: persona) lifeless.

amo'roso, a ag (affettuoso) loving, affectionate; (d'amore: sguardo) amorous; (: poesia, relazione) love cpd.

ampi'ezza [am'pjettsa] sf width, breadth; spaciousness; (fig: importanza) scale, size.

'ampio, a ag wide, broad; (spazioso) spacious; (abbondante: vestito) loose; (: gonna) full; (: spiegazione) ample, full.

am'plesso sm (eufemismo) embrace.

ampli'are vt (ingrandire) to enlarge; (allargare) to widen.

amplifi'care vt to amplify; (magnificare) to extol; **amplifica'tore** sm (TECN, MUS) amplifier.

am'polla sf (vasetto) cruet.

ampol'loso, a ag bombastic, pompous.

ampu'tare vt (MED) to amputate; **amputazi'one** sf amputation.

anabbagli'ante [anabbaʎ'ʎante] ag (AUT) dipped; **~i** smpl dipped headlights.

a'nagrafe sf (registro) register of births, marriages and deaths; (ufficio) registry office.

analfa'beta, i, e ag, sm/f illiterate.

a'nalisi sf inv analysis; (MED: esame) test; **~ grammaticale** parsing; **ana'lista, i, e** sm/f analyst; (PSIC) (psycho)analyst.

analiz'zare [analid'dzare] vt to analyse; (MED) to test.

analo'gia, 'gie [analo'dʒia] sf analogy.

a'nalogo, a, ghi, ghe ag analogous.

'ananas sm inv pineapple.

anar'chia [anar'kia] sf anarchy; **a'narchico, a, ci, che** ag anarchic(al) // sm/f anarchist.

ana'tema, i sm anathema.

anato'mia sf anatomy; **ana'tomico, a, ci, che** ag anatomical; (sedile) contoured.

'anatra sf duck.

'anca, che sf (ANAT) hip; (ZOOL) haunch.

'anche ['anke] av also; (perfino) even; **vengo anch'io!** I'm coming too!; **~ se** even if.

an'cora av still; (di nuovo) again; (di più) some more; (: in frasi negative) any more; (persino): **~ più forte** even stronger; **non ~ not yet; ~ un po'** a little more; (di tempo) a little longer.

'ancora sf anchor; **gettare/levare l'~** to cast/weigh anchor; **anco'raggio** sm anchorage; **anco'rare** vt, **ancorarsi** vr to anchor.

anda'mento sm progress, movement; course; state.

an'dante ag (corrente) current; (di poco pregio) cheap, second-rate // sm (MUS) andante.

an'dare sm (l'andatura) walk, gait; **a lungo ~** in the long run // vi (2) to go; (essere adatto): **~ a** to suit; (moneta) to be legal tender; (piacere): **il suo comportamento non mi va** I don't like the way he behaves; **ti va di andare al cinema?** do you feel like going to the cinema?; **andarsene** to go away; **questa camicia va lavata** this shirt needs a wash o should be washed; **~ a cavallo** to ride; **~ in macchina/aereo** to go by car/plane; **~ a male** to go bad; **come va? — bene, grazie!** how are you? — fine, thanks!; **ne va della nostra vita** our lives are at stake; **an'data** *sf* going; (*viaggio*) outward journey; **biglietto di sola andata/di andata e ritorno** single/return ticket; **anda'tura** *sf* (*modo di andare*) walk, gait; (*SPORT*) pace; (*NAUT*) tack.

an'dazzo [an'dattso] *sm* (*peg*) current (bad) practice.

andirivi'eni *sm inv* coming and going.

'andito *sm* corridor, passage.

an'drone *sm* entrance-hall.

a'neddoto *sm* anecdote.

ane'lare *vi*: ~ **a** (*fig*) to long for, yearn for.

a'nelito *sm* (*fig*): ~ **di** longing *o* yearning for.

a'nello *sm* ring; (*di catena*) link.

ane'mia *sf* anaemia; **a'nemico, a, ci, che** *ag* anaemic.

a'nemone *sm* anemone.

aneste'sia *sf* anaesthesia; **anes'tetico, a, ci, che** *ag, sm* anaesthetic.

an'fibio, a *ag* amphibious.

anfite'atro *sm* amphitheatre.

an'fratto *sm* ravine.

an'gelico, a, ci, che [an'dʒeliko] *ag* angelic(al).

'angelo ['andʒelo] *sm* angel; ~ **custode** guardian angel.

anghe'ria [ange'ria] *sf* vexation.

an'gina [an'dʒina] *sf* angina.

angli'cano, a *ag* Anglican.

angli'cismo [angli'tʃizmo] *sm* anglicism.

anglo'sassone *ag* Anglo-Saxon.

ango'lare *ag* angular.

'angolo *sm* corner; (*MAT*) angle.

an'goscia, sce [an'gɔʃʃa] *sf* deep anxiety, anguish *q*; **angosci'oso, a** *ag* (*d'angoscia*) anguished; (*che dà angoscia*) distressing, painful.

angu'illa *sf* eel.

an'guria *sf* watermelon.

an'gustia *sf* (*ansia*) anguish, distress; (*povertà*) poverty, want.

angusti'are *vt* to distress; ~**rsi** *vr*: ~**rsi (per)** to worry (about).

an'gusto, a *ag* (*stretto*) narrow; (*fig*) mean, petty.

'anice ['anitʃe] *sm* (*CUC*) aniseed; (*BOT*) anise.

'anima *sf* soul; (*fig: persona*) person, soul; (: *abitante*) inhabitant.

ani'male *sm, ag* animal.

ani'mare *vt* to give life to, liven up; (*incoraggiare*) to encourage; ~**rsi** *vr* to become animated, come to life; **ani'mato, a** *ag* animate; (*vivace*) lively, animated; (: *strada*) busy; **anima'tore, 'trice** *sm/f* guiding spirit; (*CINEMA*) animator; (*di festa*) life and soul; **animazi'one** *sf* liveliness; (*di strada*) bustle; (*CINEMA*) animation.

'animo *sm* (*mente*) mind; (*cuore*) heart; (*coraggio*) courage; (*disposizione*) character, disposition; (*inclinazione*) inclination; (*proposito*) intention; **avere in ~ di fare qc** to intend *o* have a mind to do sth; **fare qc di buon/mal ~** to do sth

willingly/unwillingly; **perdersi d'**~ to lose heart; **animosità** *sf* animosity; **ani'moso, a** *ag* hostile; (*coraggioso*) spirited, bold.

'anitra *sf* = **anatra**.

anna'cquare *vt* to water down, dilute.

annaffi'are *vt* to water; **annaffia'tolo** *sm* watering can.

an'nali *smpl* annals.

an'nata *sf* year; (*importo annuo*) annual amount.

annebbi'are *vt* (*fig*) to cloud; ~**rsi** *vr* (*tempo*) to become foggy, become misty; (*vista*) to become dim.

annega'mento *sm* drowning.

anne'gare *vt, vi* (2) to drown; ~**rsi** *vr* (*accidentalmente*) to drown; (*deliberatamente*) to drown o.s.

anne'rire *vt* to blacken // *vi* (2) to become black.

an'nessi *smpl* (*edifici*) outbuildings; ~ **e connessi** appurtenances.

annessi'one *sf* (*POL*) annexation.

an'nesso, a *pp di* **annettere.**

an'nettere *vt* (*POL*) to annex; (*accludere*) to attach.

annichi'lare, annichi'lire [anniki'lare, anniki'lire] *vt* to annihilate.

anni'darsi *vr* to nest.

annienta'mento *sm* annihilation, destruction.

annien'tare *vt* to annihilate, destroy.

anniver'sario, a *ag*: **giorno** ~ anniversary // *sm* anniversary.

'anno *sm* year; ~**i fa** years ago.

anno'dare *vt* to knot, tie; (*fig: rapporto*) to form.

annoi'are *vt* to bore; (*seccare*) to annoy; ~**rsi** *vr* to be bored; to be annoyed.

anno'tare *vt* (*registrare*) to note, note down; (*commentare*) to annotate; **annotazi'one** *sf* note; annotation.

annove'rare *vt* to number.

annu'ale *ag* annual.

annu'ario *sm* yearbook.

annu'ire *vi* to nod; (*acconsentire*) to agree.

annulla'mento *sm* annihilation, destruction; cancellation; annulment; quashing.

annul'lare *vt* to annihilate, destroy; (*contratto, francobollo*) to cancel; (*matrimonio*) to annul; (*sentenza*) to quash; (*risultati*) to declare void.

annunci'are [annun'tʃare] *vt* to announce; (*dar segni rivelatori*) to herald; **annuncia'tore, 'trice** *sm/f* (*RADIO, TV*) announcer; **l'Annunciazi'one** *sf* the Annunciation.

an'nuncio [an'nuntʃo] *sm* announcement; (*fig*) sign; ~ **pubblicitario** advertisement; ~**i economici** classified advertisements, small ads.

'annuo, a *ag* annual, yearly.

annu'sare *vt* to sniff, smell; (*fig*) to smell, suspect.

anoma'lia *sf* anomaly.

a'nomalo, a *ag* anomalous.

a'nonimo, a *ag* anonymous // *sm* (*autore*) anonymous writer (*o painter etc*).

anor'male *ag* abnormal // *sm/f* subnormal person; (*eufemismo*) homosexual; **anormalità** *sf inv* abnormality.

'ansa *sf* (*manico*) handle; (*di fiume*) bend, loop.

'ansia, ansietà *sf* anxiety.

ansi'mare *vi* to pant.

ansi'oso, a *ag* anxious.

antago'nismo *sm* antagonism; **antago-'nista, i, e** *sm/f* antagonist.

an'tartico, a, ci, che *ag* Antarctic // *sm*: **l'A~** the Antarctic.

antece'dente [antetʃe'dɛnte] *ag* preceding, previous.

ante'fatto *sm* previous events *pl*; previous history.

antegu'erra *sm* pre-war period.

ante'nato *sm* ancestor, forefather.

an'tenna *sf* (*RADIO, TV*) aerial; (*ZOOL*) antenna, feeler; (*NAUT*) yard.

ante'prima *sf* preview.

anteri'ore *ag* (*ruota, zampa*) front; (*fatti*) previous, preceding.

antia'ereo, a *ag* anti-aircraft.

antibi'otico, a, ci, che *ag, sm* antibiotic.

anti'camera *sf* anteroom; **fare ~** to wait (for an audience).

antichità [antiki'ta] *sf inv* antiquity; (*oggetto*) antique.

antici'clone [antitʃi'klone] *sm* anticyclone.

antici'pare [antitʃi'pare] *vt* (*consegna, visita*) to bring forward, anticipate; (*somma di denaro*) to pay in advance; (*notizia*) to disclose // *vi* to be ahead of time; **anticipazi'one** *sf* anticipation; (*di notizia*) advance information; (*somma di denaro*) advance; **an'ticipo** *sm* anticipation; (*di denaro*) advance; **in anticipo** early, in advance.

an'tico, a, chi, che *ag* (*quadro, mobili*) antique; (*dell'antichità*) ancient.

anticoncezio'nale [antikontʃettsjo'nale] *sm* contraceptive.

an'tidoto *sm* antidote.

An'tille *sfpl*: **le ~** the West Indies.

an'tilope *sf* antelope.

anti'pasto *sm* hors d'œuvre.

antipa'tia *sf* antipathy, dislike; **anti-'patico, a, ci, che** *ag* unpleasant, disagreeable.

an'tipodi *smpl*: **gli ~** the antipodes.

antiquari'ato *sm* antique trade.

anti'quario *sm* antique dealer.

anti'quato, a *ag* antiquated, old-fashioned.

anti'settico, a, ci, che *ag, sm* antiseptic.

an'titesi *sf* antithesis.

antolo'gia, 'gie [antolo'dʒia] *sf* anthology.

'antro *sm* cavern; (*fig*) hole.

antro'pofago, gi *sm* cannibal.

antropolo'gia [antropolo'dʒia] *sf* anthropology.

anu'lare *ag* ring *cpd* // *sm* ring finger.

'anzi ['antsi] *av* (*invece*) on the contrary; (*o meglio*) or rather, or better still; (*di più*) indeed; **~ che** = **anziché**.

anzianità [antsjani'ta] *sf* old age; (*AMM*) seniority.

anzi'ano, a [an'tsjano] *ag* old; (*AMM*) senior // *sm/f* old person; senior member.

anziché [antsi'ke] *cong* rather than.

anzi'tutto [antsi'tutto] *av* first of all.

apa'tia *sf* apathy, indifference; **a'patico, a, ci, che** *ag* apathetic, indifferent.

'ape *sf* bee.

aperi'tivo *sm* aperitif.

a'perto, a *pp di* **aprire** // *ag* open; **all'~** in the open (air).

aper'tura *sf* opening; (*ampiezza*) width, spread; (*POL*) approach; (*FOT*) aperture; **~ alare** wing span; **~ mentale** open-mindedness.

'apice ['apitʃe] *sm* apex; (*fig*) height.

apicol'tore *sm* beekeeper.

a'polide *ag* stateless.

apoples'sia *sf* (*MED*) apoplexy.

a'postolo *sm* apostle.

a'postrofo *sm* apostrophe.

appa'gare *vt* to satisfy; **~rsi** *vr*: **~rsi di** to be satisfied with.

appai'are *vt* to couple, pair.

ap'palto *sm* (*COMM*) contract; **dare/prendere in ~ un lavoro** to let out/undertake a job on contract.

appan'nare *vt* (*vetro*) to mist; (*metallo*) to tarnish; (*vista*) to dim; **~rsi** *vr* to mist over; to tarnish; to grow dim.

appa'rato *sm* (*messinscena*) display; (*ANAT, TECN*) apparatus; **~ scenico** (*TEATRO*) props *pl*.

apparecchi'are [apparek'kjare] *vt* to prepare; (*tavola*) to set // *vi* to set the table.

appa'recchio [appa'rekkjo] *sm* piece of apparatus, device; (*aeroplano*) aircraft *inv*; **~ televisivo/telefonico** television set/telephone.

appa'rente *ag* apparent; **appa'renza** *sf* appearance; **in o all'apparenza** apparently, to all appearances.

appa'rire *vi* (2) to appear; (*sembrare*) to seem, appear; **appari'scente** *ag* (*colore*) garish, gaudy; (*bellezza*) striking; **appari-zi'one** *sf* apparition.

apparta'mento *sm* flat, apartment (*US*).

appar'tarsi *vr* to withdraw; **appar'tato, a** *ag* secluded.

appar'tenere *vi*: **~ a** to belong to.

appassio'nare *vt* to thrill; (*commuovere*) to move; **~rsi a qc** to take a great interest in sth; to be deeply moved by sth; **appassio'nato, a** *ag* passionate; **appassionato per la musica** passionately fond of music.

appas'sire *vi* (2) to wither.

appel'lare *vi* (*DIR*) to appeal; **~rsi** *vr* (*ricorrere*): **~rsi a** to appeal to; (*DIR*): **~rsi contro** to appeal against; **ap'pello** *sm* roll-call; (*implorazione, DIR*) appeal;

fare appello a to appeal to.
ap'pena av (a stento) hardly, scarcely; (solamente, da poco) just // cong as soon as; ~ furono arrivati ... as soon as they had arrived ...; ~ ... che o quando no sooner ... than.
ap'pendere vt to hang (up).
appen'dice [appen'ditʃe] sf appendix.
appendi'cite [appendi'tʃite] sf appendicitis.
Appen'nini smpl: gli ~ the Apennines.
appesan'tire vt to make heavy; ~rsi vr to grow stout.
ap'peso, a pp di appendere.
appe'tito sm appetite; appeti'toso, a ag appetising; (fig) attractive, desirable.
appia'nare vt to level; (fig) to smooth away, iron out.
appiat'tire vt to flatten; ~rsi vr to become flatter; (farsi piatto) to flatten o.s.; ~rsi al suolo to lie flat on the ground.
appicci'care [appittʃi'kare] vt to stick; (fig): ~ qc a qd to palm sth off on sb; ~rsi vr to stick; (fig: persona) to cling.
appigli'arsi [appiʎ'ʎarsi] vr: ~ a (afferrarsi) to take hold of; (fig) to cling to; ap'piglio sm hold; (fig) pretext.
appiso'larsi vr to doze off.
applau'dire vt, vi to applaud; ap'plauso sm applause.
appli'care vt to apply; (regolamento) to enforce; ~rsi vr to apply o.s.; applicazi'one sf application; enforcement.
appoggi'are [appod'dʒare] vt (mettere contro): ~ qc a qc to lean o rest sth against sth; (fig: sostenere) to support; ~rsi vr: ~rsi a to lean against; (fig) to rely upon; ap'poggio sm support.
ap'porre vt to affix.
appor'tare vt to bring.
ap'posito, a ag appropriate.
ap'posta av on purpose, deliberately.
appos'tare vt to lie in wait for; ~rsi vr to lie in wait.
ap'prendere vt (imparare) to learn; (comprendere) to grasp.
appren'dista, i, e sm/f apprentice.
apprensi'one sf apprehension; appren'sivo, a ag apprehensive.
ap'presso av (accanto, vicino) close by, near; (dietro) behind; (dopo, più tardi) after, later; ~ a prep (vicino a) near, close to.
appres'tare vt to prepare, get ready; ~rsi vr: ~rsi a fare qc to prepare o get ready to do sth.
apprez'zabile [appret'tsabile] ag noteworthy, significant.
apprezza'mento [apprettsa'mento] sm appreciation; (giudizio) opinion.
apprez'zare [appret'tsare] vt to appreciate.
ap'proccio [ap'prottʃo] sm approach.
appro'dare vi (NAUT) to land; (fig): non ~ a nulla to come to nothing; ap'prodo sm landing; (luogo) landing-place.

approfit'tare vi: ~ di to make the most of, profit by.
approfon'dire vt to deepen; (fig) to study in depth.
appropri'ato, a ag appropriate.
approssi'marsi vr: ~ a to approach.
approssima'tivo, a ag approximate, rough; (impreciso) inexact, imprecise.
appro'vare vt (condotta, azione) to approve of; (candidato) to pass; (progetto di legge) to approve; approvazi'one sf approval.
approvvigiona'mento [approvvidʒona-'mento] sm supplying; stocking up; ~i smpl (MIL) supplies.
approvvigio'nare [approvvidʒo'nare] vt to supply; ~rsi vr to lay in provisions, stock up; ~ qd di qc to supply sb with sth.
appunta'mento sm appointment; (amoroso) date; darsi ~ to arrange to meet (one another).
appun'tare vt (rendere aguzzo) to sharpen; (fissare) to pin, fix; (annotare) to note down.
ap'punto sm note; (rimprovero) reproach // av (proprio) exactly, just; per l'~!, ~! exactly!
appu'rare vt to check, verify.
apribot'tiglie [apribot'tiʎʎe] sm inv bottleopener.
a'prile sm April.
a'prire vt to open; (via, cadavere) to open up; (gas, luce, acqua) to turn on // vi to open; ~rsi vr to open; ~rsi a qd to confide in sb, open one's heart to sb.
apris'catole sm inv tin opener.
a'quario sm = acquario.
'aquila sf (ZOOL) eagle; (fig) genius.
aqui'lone sm (giocattolo) kite; (vento) North wind.
A'rabia 'Saudita sf: l'~ Saudi Arabia.
'arabo, a ag, sm/f Arab // sm Arabic.
a'rachide [a'rakide] sf peanut.
ara'gosta sf crayfish; lobster.
a'raldica sf heraldry.
a'raldo sm herald.
a'rancia, ce [a'rantʃa] sf orange; aranci'ata sf orangeade; a'rancio sm (BOT) orange tree; (colore) orange // ag inv (colore) orange.
a'rare vt to plough.
a'ratro sm plough.
a'razzo [a'rattso] sm tapestry.
arbi'traggio [arbi'raddʒo] sm (SPORT) refereeing; umpiring; (DIR) arbitration.
arbi'trare vt (SPORT) to referee; to umpire; (DIR) to arbitrate.
arbi'trario, a ag arbitrary.
ar'bitrio sm will; (abuso, sopruso) arbitrary act.
'arbitro sm arbiter, judge; (DIR) arbitrator; (SPORT) referee; (: TENNIS, CRICKET) umpire.
ar'busto sm shrub.
'arca, che sf (sarcofago) sarcophagus; l'~ di Noè Noah's ark.

ar'caico, a, ci, che ag archaic.
ar'cangelo [ar'kandʒelo] sm archangel.
ar'cano, a ag arcane, mysterious.
ar'cata sf (ARCHIT, ANAT) arch; (ordine di archi) arcade.
archeolo'gia [arkeolo'dʒia] sf archaeology; arche'ologo, a, gi, ghe sm/f archaeologist.
ar'chetto [ar'ketto] sm (MUS) bow.
archi'tetto [arki'tetto] sm architect; architet'tura sf architecture.
ar'chivio [ar'kivjo] sm archives pl.
arci'ere [ar'tʃɛre] sm archer.
ar'cigno, a [ar'tʃiɲɲo] ag grim, severe.
arci'pelago, ghi [artʃi'pɛlago] sm archipelago.
arci'vescovo [artʃi'veskovo] sm archbishop.
'arco sm (arma, MUS) bow; (ARCHIT) arch; (MAT) arc.
arcoba'leno sm rainbow.
arcu'ato, a ag curved, bent; dalle gambe ~e bow-legged.
ar'dente ag burning; (fig) burning, ardent.
'ardere vt, vi (2) to burn.
ar'desia sf slate.
ar'dire vi to dare; ar'dito, a ag brave, daring, bold; (sfacciato) bold.
ar'dore sm blazing heat; (fig) ardour, fervour.
'arduo, a ag arduous, difficult.
'area sf area; (EDIL) land, ground.
a'rena sf arena; (sabbia) sand.
are'narsi vr to run aground.
areo'plano sm = aeroplano.
'argano sm winch.
argente'ria [ardʒente'ria] sf silverware, silver.
argenti'ere [ardʒen'tjɛre] sm silversmith.
Argen'tina [ardʒen'tina] sf: l'~ Argentina.
ar'gento [ar'dʒɛnto] sm silver; ~ vivo quicksilver.
ar'gilla [ar'dʒilla] sf clay.
'argine ['ardʒine] sm embankment, bank; (diga) dyke.
argomen'tare vi to argue.
argo'mento sm argument; (motivo) motive; (materia, tema) subject.
argu'ire vt to deduce.
ar'guto, a ag sharp, quick-witted; (spiritoso) witty; ar'guzia sf wit; (battuta) witty remark.
'aria sf air; (espressione, aspetto) air, look; (MUS: melodia) tune; (: di opera) aria; mandare all'~ qc to ruin o upset sth; all'~ aperta in the open (air).
'arido, a ag arid.
arieggi'are [arjed'dʒare] vt (cambiare aria) to air; (imitare) to imitate.
ari'ete sm ram; (MIL) battering ram; (dello zodiaco): A~ Aries.
a'ringa, ghe sf herring inv.
'arista sf (CUC) chine of pork.
aristo'cratico, a, ci, che ag aristocratic.
aristocra'zia [aristokrat'tsia] sf aristocracy.

arit'metica sf arithmetic.
arlec'chino [arlek'kino] sm harlequin.
'arma, i sf weapon, arm; (parte dell'esercito) arm; chiamare alle ~i to call up; sotto le ~i in the army (o forces); alle ~i! to arms!; ~ da fuoco firearm.
ar'madio sm cupboard; (per abiti) wardrobe.
armamen'tario sm equipment, instruments pl.
arma'mento sm (MIL) armament; (: materiale) arms pl, weapons pl; (NAUT) fitting out; manning.
ar'mare vt to arm; (arma da fuoco) to cock; (NAUT: nave) to rig, fit out; to man; (EDIL: volta, galleria) to prop up, shore up; ~rsi vr to arm o.s.; (MIL) to take up arms; ar'mata sf (MIL) army; (NAUT) fleet; arma'tore sm shipowner; arma'tura sf (struttura di sostegno) framework; (impalcatura) scaffolding; (STORIA) armour q, suit of armour.
armis'tizio [armis'tittsjo] sm armistice.
armo'nia sf harmony; ar'monico, a, ci, che ag harmonic; (fig) harmonious; armoni'oso, a ag harmonious.
armoniz'zare [armonid'dzare] vt to harmonize; (colori, abiti) to match // vi to be in harmony; to match.
ar'nese sm tool, implement; (oggetto indeterminato) thing, contraption; male in ~ (malvestito) badly dressed; (di salute malferma) in poor health; (di condizioni economiche) down-at-heel.
'arnia sf hive.
a'roma, i sm aroma; fragrance; ~i smpl herbs and spices; aro'matico, a, ci, che ag aromatic; (cibo) spicy.
'arpa sf (MUS) harp.
ar'peggio [ar'peddʒo] sm (MUS) arpeggio.
ar'pia sf (anche fig) harpy.
arpi'one sm (gancio) hook; (cardine) hinge; (PESCA) harpoon.
arrabat'tarsi vr to do all one can, strive.
arrabbi'are vi (2) (cane) to be affected with rabies; ~rsi vr (essere preso dall'ira) to get angry, fly into a rage; arrabbi'ato, a ag rabid, with rabies; furious, angry.
arrampi'carsi vr to climb (up).
arran'giare [arran'dʒare] vt to arrange; ~rsi vr to manage, do the best one can.
arre'care vt to bring; (causare) to cause.
arreda'mento sm (studio) interior design; (mobili etc) furnishings pl.
arre'dare vt to furnish; ar'redo sm fittings pl, furnishings pl.
ar'rendersi vr to surrender.
arres'tare vt (fermare) to stop, halt; (catturare) to arrest; ~rsi vr (fermarsi) to stop; ar'resto sm (cessazione) stopping; (fermata) stop; (cattura, MED) arrest; subire un arresto to come to a stop o standstill; mettere agli arresti to place under arrest.
arre'trare vt, vi (2) to withdraw; arre'trato, a ag (lavoro) behind schedule;

(*paese, bambino*) backward; (*numero di giornale*) back *cpd*.

arric'chire [arrik'kire] *vt* to enrich; ~**rsi** *vr* to become rich.

arricci'are [arrit'tʃare] *vt* to curl; ~ **il naso** to turn up one's nose.

ar'ringa, ghe *sf* harangue; (*DIR*) address by counsel.

arrischi'are [arris'kjare] *vt* to risk; ~**rsi** *vr* to venture, dare; **arrischi'ato, a** *ag* risky; (*temerario*) reckless, rash.

arri'vare *vi* (2) to arrive; (*accadere*) to happen, occur; ~ **a** (*livello, grado etc*) to reach; **lui arriva a Roma alle 7** he gets to *o* arrives at Rome at 7; **non ci arrivo** I can't reach it; (*fig: non capisco*) I can't understand it.

arrive'derci [arrive'dertʃi] *escl* goodbye!

arrive'derla *escl* (*forma di cortesia*) goodbye!

arri'vista, i, e *sm/f* go-getter.

ar'rivo *sm* arrival; (*SPORT*) finish, finishing-line.

arro'gante *ag* arrogant.

arro'lare *vb* = **arruolare.**

arros'sire *vi* (*per vergogna, timidità*) to blush, flush; (*per gioia, rabbia*) to flush.

arros'tire *vt* to roast; (*pane*) to toast; (*ai ferri*) to grill.

ar'rosto *sm, ag inv* roast.

arro'tare *vt* to sharpen; (*investire con un veicolo*) to run over.

arroto'lare *vt* to roll up.

arroton'dare *vt* (*forma, oggetto*) to round; (*stipendio*) to add to; (*somma*) to round off.

arruf'fare *vt* to ruffle; (*fili*) to tangle; (*fig: questione*) to confuse.

arruggi'nire [arruddʒi'nire] *vt* to rust; ~**rsi** *vr* to rust; (*fig*) to become rusty.

arruola'mento *sm* (*MIL*) enlistment.

arruo'lare (*MIL*) *vt* to enlist; ~**rsi** *vr* to enlist, join up.

arse'nale *sm* (*MIL*) arsenal; (*cantiere navale*) dockyard.

ar'senico *sm* arsenic.

'arso, a *pp di* **ardere** // *ag* (*bruciato*) burnt; (*arido*) dry; **ar'sura** *sf* (*calore opprimente*) burning heat; (*siccità*) drought.

'arte *sf* art; (*abilità*) skill.

ar'tefice [ar'tefitʃe] *sm/f* craftsman/woman; (*autore*) author.

ar'teria *sf* artery.

'artico, a, ci, che *ag* Arctic.

artico'lare *ag* (*ANAT*) of the joints, articular // *vt* to articulate; (*suddividere*) to divide, split up.

ar'ticolo *sm* article; ~ **di fondo** (*STAMPA*) leader, leading article.

'Artide *sf*: **l'~** the Arctic.

artifici'ale [artifi'tʃale] *ag* artificial.

arti'ficio [arti'fitʃo] *sm* (*espediente*) trick, artifice; (*ricerca di effetto*) artificiality; **artifi'cioso, a** *ag* cunning; (*non spontaneo*) affected.

artigia'nato [artidʒa'nato] *sm* craftsmanship; craftsmen *pl*.

artigi'ano,   a [arti'dʒano]   *sm/f* craftsman/woman.

artiglie'ria [artiʎʎe'ria] *sf* artillery.

ar'tiglio [ar'tiʎʎo] *sm* claw; (*di rapaci*) talon.

ar'tista, i, e *sm/f* artist; **ar'tistico, a, ci, che** *ag* artistic.

'arto *sm* (*ANAT*) limb.

ar'trite *sf* (*MED*) arthritis.

ar'zillo, a [ar'dzillo] *ag* lively, sprightly.

a'scella [aʃ'ʃella] *sf* (*ANAT*) armpit.

ascen'dente [aʃʃen'dɛnte] *sm* ancestor; (*fig*) ascendancy.

ascensi'one [aʃʃen'sjone] *sf* (*ALPINISMO*) ascent; (*REL*): **l'A~** the Ascension.

ascen'sore [aʃʃen'sore] *sm* lift.

a'scesa [aʃ'ʃesa] *sf* ascent; (*al trono*) accession.

a'scesso [aʃ'ʃɛsso] *sm* (*MED*) abscess.

a'sceta, i [aʃ'ʃɛta] *sm* ascetic.

'ascia, pl 'asce [ˈaʃʃa] *sf* axe.

asciugaca'pelli [aʃʃugaka'pelli] *sm* hair-drier.

asciuga'mano [aʃʃuga'mano] *sm* towel.

asciu'gare [aʃʃu'gare] *vt* to dry; ~**rsi** *vr* to dry o.s.; (*diventare asciutto*) to dry.

asci'utto, a [aʃ'ʃutto] *ag* dry; (*fig: magro*) lean; (: *burbero*) curt; **restare a bocca ~a** (*fig*) to be disappointed; **restare all'~** (*fig*) to be left penniless.

ascol'tare *vt* to listen to; **ascolta'tore, 'trice** *sm/f* listener; **as'colto** *sm*: **essere** *o* **stare in ascolto** to be listening; **dare** *o* **prestare ascolto (a)** to pay attention (to).

as'falto *sm* asphalt.

asfis'sia *sf* asphyxia, asphyxiation.

'Asia *sf*: **l'A~** Asia; **asi'atico, a, ci, che** *ag, sm/f* Asiatic, Asian.

a'silo *sm* refuge, sanctuary; ~ **(d'infanzia)** nursery(-school); ~ **politico** political asylum.

'asino *sm* donkey, ass.

'asma *sf* asthma.

'asola *sf* buttonhole.

as'parago, gi *sm* asparagus *q*.

asperità *sf inv* roughness *q*; (*fig*) harshness *q*.

aspet'tare *vt* to wait for; (*anche COMM*) to await; (*aspettarsi*) to expect // *vi* to wait; ~**rsi** *vr* to expect; ~ **un bambino** to be expecting (a baby); **questo non me l'aspettavo** I wasn't expecting this; **aspetta'tiva** *sf* wait; expectation; **inferiore all'aspettativa** worse than expected.

as'petto *sm* (*apparenza*) aspect, appearance, look; (*punto di vista*) point of view.

aspi'rante *ag* (*attore etc*) aspiring // *sm/f* candidate, applicant.

aspira'polvere *sm inv* vacuum cleaner.

aspi'rare *vt* (*respirare*) to breathe in, inhale; (*sog: apparecchi*) to suck (up) // *vi*: ~ **a** to aspire to; **aspira'tore** *sm* extractor fan.

aspi'rina *sf* aspirin.

aspor'tare vt (anche MED) to remove, take away.

as'prezza [as'prettsa] sf sourness, tartness; pungency; harshness; roughness; rugged nature.

'aspro, a ag (sapore) sour, tart; (odore) acrid, pungent; (voce, clima, fig) harsh; (superficie) rough; (paesaggio) rugged.

assaggi'are [assad'dʒare] vt to taste; **as'saggio** sm tasting; (piccola quantità) taste; (campione) sample.

as'sai av (abbastanza) enough; (molto) a lot, much // ag inv (quantità) a lot of, much; (numero) a lot of, many; **~ contento** very pleased.

assa'lire vt to attack, assail.

as'salto sm attack, assault.

assassi'nare vt to murder; to assassinate; (fig) to ruin; **assas'sinio** sm murder; assassination; **assas'sino, a** ag murderous // sm/f murderer; assassin.

'asse sm (TECN) axle; (MAT) axis // sf board; ~ **f da stiro** ironing board.

assedi'are vt to besiege; **as'sedio** sm siege.

asse'gnare [assenjnare] vt to assign, allot.

as'segno [as'sennjo] sm allowance; (anche: **~ bancario**) cheque; **contro ~** cash on delivery; **~ circolare** bank draft; **~ sbarrato** crossed cheque; **~ a vuoto** dud cheque; **~i familiari** family allowance sg.

assem'blea sf assembly.

assen'nato, a ag sensible.

as'senso sm assent, consent.

as'sente ag absent; (fig) faraway, vacant; **as'senza** sf absence.

asses'sore sm (POL) councillor.

assesta'mento sm (sistemazione) arrangement; (EDIL) settlement.

asses'tare vt (mettere in ordine) to put in order, arrange; **~rsi** vr to settle in; **~ un colpo a qd** to deal sb a blow.

asse'tato, a ag thirsty, parched.

as'setto sm order, arrangement; (NAUT, AER) trim.

assicu'rare vt (accertare) to ensure; (infondere certezza) to assure; (fermare, legare) to make fast, secure; (fare un contratto di assicurazione) to insure; **~rsi** vr (accertarsi): **~rsi (di)** to make sure (of); (contro il furto etc): **~rsi (contro)** to insure o.s. (against); **assicurazi'one** sf assurance; insurance.

assidera'mento sm exposure.

as'siduo, a ag (costante) assiduous; (regolare) regular.

assi'eme av (insieme) together; **~ a** prep (together) with.

assil'lare vt to pester, torment.

as'sillo sm (fig) worrying thought.

assimi'lare vt to assimilate.

as'sise sfpl (DIR) assizes; **Corte f d'A~** Court of Assizes.

assis'tente sm/f assistant; **~ sociale** social worker.

assis'tenza [assis'tɛntsa] sf assistance,

help; treatment; (presenza) presence; **~ sociale** welfare services pl.

as'sistere vt (aiutare) to assist, help; (curare) to treat // vi: **~ (a qc)** (essere presente) to be present (at sth), to attend (sth).

'asso sm ace; **piantare qd in ~** to leave sb in the lurch.

associ'are [asso't∫are] vt to associate; (rendere partecipe): **~ qd a** (affari) to take sb into partnership in; (partito) to make sb a member of; **~rsi** vr to enter into partnership; **~rsi a** to become a member of, join; (dolori, gioie) to share in.

associazi'one [assot∫at'tsjone] sf association; (COMM) association, society.

assogget'tare [assoddʒet'tare] vt to subject, subjugate.

asso'lato, a ag sunny.

assol'dare vt to recruit.

as'solto, a pp di **assolvere.**

assoluta'mente av absolutely.

asso'luto, a ag absolute.

assoluzi'one [assolut'tsjone] sf (DIR) acquittal; (REL) absolution.

as'solvere vt (DIR) to acquit; (REL) to absolve; (adempiere) to carry out, perform.

assomigli'are [assomiʎ'ʎare] vi: **~ a** to resemble, look like.

asso'pirsi vr to doze off.

assor'bente ag absorbent // sm: **~ igienico** sanitary towel.

assor'bire vt to absorb; (fig: far proprio) to assimilate.

assor'dare vt to deafen.

assorti'mento sm assortment.

assor'tito, a ag assorted; matched, matching.

as'sorto, a ag absorbed, engrossed.

assottigli'are [assottiʎ'ʎare] vt to make thin, to thin; (aguzzare: anche fig) to sharpen; (ridurre) to reduce; **~rsi** vr to grow thin; (fig: ridursi) to be reduced.

assue'fare vt to accustom; **~rsi a** to get used to, accustom o.s. to.

as'sumere vt (impiegato) to take on, engage; (responsabilità) to assume, take upon o.s.; (contegno, espressione) to assume, put on; **as'sunto, a** pp di **assumere** // sm (tesi) proposition.

assurdità sf inv absurdity; **dire delle ~** to talk nonsense.

as'surdo, a ag absurd.

'asta sf pole; (modo di vendita) auction.

as'temio, a ag abstemious.

aste'nersi vr: **~ (da)** to abstain (from), refrain (from); (POL) to abstain (from); **astensi'one** sf abstention.

aste'risco, schi sm asterisk.

asti'nenza [asti'nɛntsa] sf abstinence.

'astio sm rancour, resentment.

as'tratto, a ag abstract.

'astro sm star.

'astro... prefisso: **astrolo'gia** [astrolo'dʒia] sf astrology; **as'trologo, a, ghi, ghe** sm/f astrologer; **astro'nauta, i, e** sm/f astronaut; **astro'nave** sf space ship; **astrono'mia** sf astronomy; **astro- 'nomico, a, ci, che** ag astronomic(al); **as- 'tronomo** sm astronomer.

as'tuccio [as'tuttʃo] sm case, box, holder.

as'tuto, a ag astute, cunning, shrewd; **as- 'tuzia** sf astuteness, shrewdness; (azione) trick.

ate'ismo sm atheism.

A'tene sf Athens.

'ateo, a ag, sm/f atheist.

at'lante sm atlas.

at'lantico, a, ci, che ag Atlantic // sm: **l'A~, l'Oceano A~** the Atlantic, the Atlantic Ocean.

at'leta, i, e sm/f athlete; **at'letica** sf athletics sg.

atmos'fera sf atmosphere; **atmos'ferico, a, ci, che** ag atmospheric.

a'tomico, a, ci, che ag atomic; (nucleare) atomic, atom cpd, nuclear.

'atomo sm atom.

'atrio sm entrance-hall, lobby.

a'troce [a'trotʃe] ag (che provoca orrore) dreadful; (terribile) atrocious; **atrocità** sf inv atrocity.

attacca'mento sm (fig) attachment, affection.

attacca'panni sm hook, peg; (mobile) hall stand.

attac'care vt (unire) to attach; (far aderire) to stick (on); (appendere) to hang (up); (assalire: anche fig) to attack; (iniziare) to begin, start; (fig: contagiare) to pass on // vi to stick, adhere; ~**rsi** vr to stick, adhere; (trasmettersi per contagio) to be contagious; (afferrarsi): ~**rsi (a)** to cling (to); (fig: affezionarsi): ~**rsi (a)** to become attached (to); ~ **discorso** to start a conversation; **at'tacco, chi** sm (punto di unione) junction; (azione offensiva: anche fig) attack; (MED) attack, fit.

atteggia'mento sm [atteddʒa'mento] attitude.

atteggi'arsi [atted'dʒarsi] vr: ~ **a** to pose as.

at'tendere vt to wait for, await // vi: ~ **a** to attend to.

atte'nersi vr: ~ **a** to keep o stick to.

atten'tare vi: ~ **a** to make an attempt on; **atten'tato** sm attack; **attentato alla vita di qd** attempt on sb's life.

at'tento, a ag attentive; (accurato) careful, thorough; **stare ~ a qc** to pay attention to sth // escl be careful!

attenu'ante sf (DIR) extenuating circumstance.

attenu'are vt , to attenuate; (dolore, rumore) to lessen, deaden; (pena, tasse) to alleviate; ~**rsi** vr to ease, abate.

attenzi'one [atten'tsjone] sf attention // escl watch out!, be careful!

atter'raggio [atter'raddʒo] sm landing.

atter'rare vt to bring down // vi to land.

atter'rire vt to terrify; ~**rsi** vr to be terrified.

at'teso, a pp di **attendere** // sf waiting; (tempo trascorso aspettando) wait.

attes'tato sm certificate.

'attico, ci sm attic.

at'tiguo, a ag adjacent, adjoining.

attil'lato, a ag (vestito) close-fitting, tight; (persona) dressed up.

'attimo sm moment; **in un ~** in a moment.

atti'nente ag: ~ **a** relating to, concerning.

atti'rare vt to attract.

atti'tudine sf (disposizione) aptitude; (atteggiamento) attitude.

atti'vare vt to activate; (far funzionare) to set going, start.

attività sf inv activity; (COMM) assets pl.

at'tivo, a ag active; (COMM) profit-making, credit cpd // sm (COMM) assets pl.

attiz'zare [attit'tsare] vt (fuoco) to poke; (fig) to stir up.

'atto sm act; (azione, gesto) action, act, deed; (DIR: documento) deed, document; ~**i** smpl (di congressi etc) proceedings; **mettere in ~** to put into action.

at'tonito, a ag dumbfounded, astonished.

attorcigli'are [attortʃiʎ'ʎare] vt, ~**rsi** vr to twist.

at'tore, 'trice sm/f actor/actress.

at'torno av, ~ **a** prep round, around, about.

attra'ente ag attractive.

at'trarre vt to attract; **attrat'tiva** sf (fig: fascino) attraction, charm; **at'tratto, a** pp di **attrarre**.

attraver'sare vt to cross; (città, bosco, fig: periodo) to go through; (sog: fiume) to run through.

attra'verso prep through; (da una parte all'altra) across.

attrazi'one [attrat'tsjone] sf attraction.

attrez'zare [attret'tsare] vt to equip; (NAUT) to rig; **attrezza'tura** sf equipment q; rigging; **at'trezzo** sm tool, instrument; (SPORT) piece of equipment.

attribu'ire vt: ~ **qc a qd** (assegnare) to give o award sth to sb; (quadro etc) to attribute sth to sb; **attri'buto** sm attribute.

at'trice [at'tritʃe] sf vedi **attore**.

attu'ale ag (presente) present; (di attualità) topical; (che è in atto) actual; **attualità** sf inv topicality; (avvenimento) current event; **essere di attualità** to be topical; to be fashionable.

attu'are vt to carry out; ~**rsi** vr to be realized.

attu'tire vt to deaden, reduce; ~**rsi** vr to die down.

au'dace [au'datʃe] ag audacious, daring, bold; (provocante) provocative; (sfacciato) impudent, bold; **au'dacia** sf audacity, daring; boldness; provocativeness; impudence.

audiovi'sivo, a ag audiovisual.

audi'torio sm auditorium.

audizi'one [audit'tsjone] sf hearing; (MUS) audition.

augu'rare vt to wish; ~**rsi qc** to hope for sth.

au'gurio *sm* (*presagio*) omen; (*voto di benessere etc*) (good) wish; **fare gli ~i a qd** to give sb one's best wishes; **tanti ~i!** all the best!

'aula *sf* (*scolastica*) classroom; (*universitaria*) lecture-theatre; (*di edificio pubblico*) hall.

aumen'tare *vt, vi* (2) to increase; **au'mento** *sm* increase.

au'reola *sf* halo.

au'rora *sf* dawn.

ausili'are *ag, sm, sm/f* auxiliary.

aus'picio [aus'pitʃo] *sm* omen; (*protezione*) patronage; **sotto gli ~i di** under the auspices of.

austerità *sf inv* austerity.

aus'tero, a *ag* austere.

Aus'tralia *sf:* **l'A~** Australia; **australi'ano, a** *ag, sm/f* Australian.

'Austria *sf:* **l'A~** Austria; **aus'triaco, a, ci, che** *ag, sm/f* Austrian.

autenti'care *vt* to authenticate.

au'tentico, a, ci, che *ag* (*quadro, firma*) authentic, genuine; (*fatto*) true, genuine.

au'tista, i *sm* driver.

'auto *sf inv* car.

autobiogra'fia *sf* autobiography.

'autobus *sm inv* bus.

auto'carro *sm* lorry.

au'tografo, a *ag, sm* autograph.

auto'linea *sf* bus route.

au'toma, i *sm* automaton.

auto'matico, a, ci, che *ag* automatic // *sm* (*bottone*) snap fastener; (*fucile*) automatic.

auto'mezzo [auto'mɛddzo] *sm* motor vehicle.

auto'mobile *sf* (motor) car.

autono'mia *sf* autonomy; (*di volo*) range.

au'tonomo, a *ag* autonomous.

autop'sia *sf* post-mortem (examination), autopsy.

auto'radio *sf inv* (*apparecchio*) car radio; (*autoveicolo*) radio car.

au'tore, 'trice *sm/f* author; **l'~ del furto** the person who committed the robbery.

auto'revole *ag* authoritative; (*persona*) influential.

autori'messa *sf* garage.

autorità *sf inv* authority.

autoriz'zare [autorid'dzare] *vt* (*permettere*) to authorize; (*giustificare*) to allow, sanction; **autorizzazi'one** *sf* authorization.

autoscu'ola *sf* driving school.

autos'top *sm* hitchhiking; **autostop'pista, i, e** *sm/f* hitchhiker.

autos'trada *sf* motorway.

auto'treno *sm* articulated lorry.

autove'icolo *sm* motor vehicle.

au'tunno *sm* autumn.

avam'braccio, *pl(f)* **cia** [avam'brattʃo] *sm* forearm.

avangu'ardia *sf* vanguard.

a'vanti *av* (*stato in luogo*) in front; (*moto: andare, venire*) forward; (*tempo: prima*) before // *escl* (*entrate*) come (*o* go) in!; (MIL) forward!; (*suvvia*) come on! // *ag inv* (*precedente*) before; **il giorno ~** the day before; (*che si trova davanti*) front *cpd* // *sm inv* (SPORT) forward; **~ e indietro** backwards and forwards; **andare ~** to go forward; (*precedere*) to go ahead; (*continuare*) to go on; (*orologio*) to be fast; **essere ~ negli studi** to be well advanced with one's studies.

avanza'mento [avantsa'mento] *sm* progress; promotion.

avan'zare [avan'tsare] *vt* (*spostare in avanti*) to move forward, advance; (*domanda*) to put forward; (*superare*) to surpass; (*vincere*) to beat; (*promuovere*) to promote; (*essere creditore*): **~ qc da qd** to be owed sth by sb // *vi* (2) (*andare avanti*) to move forward, advance; (*fig: progredire*) to make progress; (*essere d'avanzo*) to be left, remain; **~rsi** *vr* to move forward, advance; **avan'zata** *sf* (MIL) advance; **a'vanzo** *sm* (*residuo*) remains *pl*, leftovers *pl*; (MAT) remainder; (COMM) surplus; **averne d'avanzo di qc** to have more than enough of sth.

ava'ria *sf* (*guasto*) damage; (: *meccanico*) breakdown.

ava'rizia [ava'rittsja] *sf* avarice.

a'varo, a *ag* avaricious, miserly // *sm* miser.

a'vena *sf* oats *pl*.

a'vere *sm* (COMM) credit; **~i** *smpl* (*ricchezza*) wealth *sg*, possessions // *vt, vb* *ausiliare* to have; *vedi* **freddo, fame** *etc*; **~ da mangiare/bere** to have something to eat/drink; **~ da** *o* **a fare qc** to have to do sth; **~ (a) che fare** *o* **vedere con qd/qc** to have to do with sb/sth; **ho 28 anni** I am 28 (years old); **avercela con qd** to have something against sb.

avia'tore, 'trice *sm/f* aviator, pilot.

aviazi'one [avjat'tsjone] *sf* aviation; (MIL) air force.

avidità *sf* eagerness; greed.

'avido, a *ag* eager; (*peg*) greedy.

'avi *smpl* ancestors, forefathers.

avo'cado *sm* avocado.

a'vorio *sm* ivory.

Avv. *abbr* di **avvocato**.

avvalla'mento *sm* sinking *q*; (*effetto*) depression.

avvalo'rare *vt* to confirm.

avvantaggi'are [avvantad'dʒare] *vt* to favour; **~rsi** *vr* (*trarre vantaggio*): **~rsi di** to take advantage of; (*prevalere*): **~rsi negli affari/sui concorrenti** to get ahead in business/of one's competitors.

avvelena'mento *sm* poisoning.

avvele'nare *vt* to poison.

avve'nente *ag* attractive, charming.

avveni'mento *sm* event.

avve'nire *vi, vb impers* (2) to happen, occur // *sm* future.

avven'tarsi *vr:* **~ su** *o* **contro qd/qc** to hurl o.s. *o* rush at sb/sth.

avven'tato, a *ag* rash, reckless.

av'vento *sm* advent, coming; (*REL*): **l'A~** Advent.

avven'tura *sf* adventure; (*amorosa*) affair.

avventu'rarsi *vr* to venture.

avventuri'ero, a *sm/f* adventurer/adventuress.

avventu'roso, a *ag* adventurous.

avve'rarsi *vr* to come true.

av'verbio *sm* adverb.

avver'sare *vt* to oppose.

avver'sario, a *ag* opposing // *sm* opponent, adversary.

avversi'one *sf* aversion.

avversità *sf inv* adversity, misfortune.

av'verso, a *ag* (*contrario*) contrary; (*sfavorevole*) unfavourable.

avver'tenza [avver'tentsa] *sf* (*ammonimento*) warning; (*cautela*) care; (*premessa*) foreword; **~e** *sfpl* (*istruzioni per l'uso*) instructions.

avverti'mento *sm* warning.

avver'tire *vt* (*avvisare*) to warn; (*rendere consapevole*) to inform, notify; (*percepire*) to feel.

av'vezzo, a [av'vettso] *ag*: ~ **a** used to.

avvia'mento *sm* (*atto*) starting; (*effetto*) start; (*AUT*) starting; (*: dispositivo*) starter; (*COMM*) goodwill.

avvi'are *vt* (*mettere sul cammino*) to direct; (*impresa*) to begin, start; (*motore*) to start; **~rsi** *vr* to set off, set out.

avvicina'mento [avvitʃina'mento] *sm* approach.

avvici'nare [avvitʃi'nare] *vt* to bring near; (*trattare con: persona*) to approach; **~rsi** *vr*: **~rsi a qd/qc**) to approach (sb/sth), draw near to (sb/sth).

avvili'mento *sm* humiliation; disgrace; discouragement.

avvi'lire *vt* (*umiliare*) to humiliate; (*degradare*) to disgrace; (*scoraggiare*) to dishearten, discourage; **~rsi** *vr* (*abbattersi*) to lose heart.

avvinaz'zato, a [avvinat'tsato] *ag* drunk.

av'vincere [av'vintʃere] *vt* to charm, enthral.

avvinghi'are [avvin'gjare] *vt* to clasp; **~rsi** *vr*: **~rsi a** to cling to.

avvi'sare *vt* (*far sapere*) to inform; (*mettere in guardia*) to warn; **av'viso** *sm* warning; (*annuncio*) announcement; (*: affisso*) notice; (*inserzione pubblicitaria*) advertisement; **a mio avviso** in my opinion.

avvi'tare *vt* to screw down (*o* in).

avviz'zire [avvit'tsire] *vi* (*2*) to wither.

avvo'cato, 'essa *sm/f* (*DIR*) barrister; (*fig*) defender, advocate.

av'volgere [av'voldʒere] *vt* to roll up; (*avviluppare*) to wrap up; **~rsi** *vr* (*avvilupparsi*) to wrap o.s. up; **avvol'gibile** *sm* roller blind.

avvol'toio *sm* vulture.

azi'enda [ad'dzjenda] *sf* business, firm, concern; **~ agricola** farm.

azi'one [at'tsjone] *sf* action; (*COMM*) share; **azio'nista, i, e** *sm/f* (*COMM*) shareholder.

azzan'nare [attsan'nare] *vt* to sink one's teeth into.

azzar'darsi [addzar'darsi] *vr* to dare; **azzar'dato, a** *ag* (*impresa*) risky; (*risposta*) rash.

az'zardo [ad'dzardo] *sm* risk.

azzuf'farsi [attsuf'farsi] *vr* to come to blows.

az'zurro, a [ad'dzurro] *ag* blue // *sm* (*colore*) blue; **gli ~i** (*SPORT*) the Italian national team.

B

bab'beo *sm* simpleton.

'babbo *sm* (*fam*) dad, daddy; **B~ natale** Father Christmas.

bab'buccia, ce [bab'buttʃa] *sf* slipper; (*per neonati*) bootee.

ba'bordo *sm* (*NAUT*) port side.

ba'cato, a *ag* worm-eaten, rotten.

'bacca, che *sf* berry.

baccalà *sm* dried salted cod.

bac'cano *sm* din, clamour.

bac'cello [bat'tʃello] *sm* pod.

bac'chetta [bak'ketta] *sf* (*verga*) stick, rod; (*di direttore d'orchestra*) baton; (*di tamburo*) drumstick; **~ magica** magic wand.

baci'are [ba'tʃare] *vt* to kiss; **~rsi** *vr* to kiss (one another).

baci'nella [batʃi'nella] *sf* basin.

ba'cino [ba'tʃino] *sm* basin; (*MINERALOGIA*) field, bed; (*ANAT*) pelvis; (*NAUT*) dock.

'bacio ['batʃo] *sm* kiss.

'baco, chi *sm* worm; **~ da seta** silkworm.

ba'dare *vi* (*fare attenzione*) to take care, be careful; (*occuparsi di*): **~ a** to look after, take care of; (*dar ascolto*): **~ a** to pay attention to; **bada ai fatti tuoi!** mind your own business!

ba'dia *sf* abbey.

ba'dile *sm* shovel.

'baffi *smpl* moustache *sg*; (*di animale*) whiskers; **ridere sotto i ~** to laugh up one's sleeve; **leccarsi i ~** to lick one's lips.

bagagli'aio [bagaʎ'ʎajo] *sm* luggage-van; (*AUT*) boot.

ba'gagli [ba'gaʎʎi] *smpl* luggage *sg*.

bagat'tella *sf* trifle, trifling matter.

bagli'ore [baʎ'ʎore] *sm* flash, dazzling light; **un ~ di speranza** a sudden ray of hope.

ba'gnante [baɲ'ɲante] *sm/f* bather.

ba'gnare [baɲ'ɲare] *vt* to wet; (*inzuppare*) to soak; (*innaffiare*) to water; (*sog: fiume*) to flow through; (*: mare*) to wash, bathe; **~rsi** *vr* (*al mare*) to go swimming *o* bathing; (*in vasca*) to have a bath.

ba'gnino [baɲ'ɲino] *sm* lifeguard.

'bagno ['baɲɲo] *sm* bath; (*locale*) bathroom; **~i** *smpl* (*stabilimento*) baths; **fare il ~** to have a bath; (*nel mare*) to go swimming *o* bathing; **fare il ~ a qd** to give sb a bath.

'**baia** *sf* bay.

baio'netta *sf* bayonet.

balaus'trata *sf* balustrade.

balbet'tare *vi* to stutter, stammer; (*bimbo*) to babble // *vt* to stammer out.

balbuzi'ente [balbut'tsjɛnte] *ag* stuttering, stammering.

bal'cone *sm* balcony.

baldac'chino [baldak'kino] *sm* canopy.

bal'danza [bal'dantsa] *sf* self-confidence, boldness.

'**baldo, a** *ag* bold, daring.

bal'doria *sf* merrymaking *q*; noisy party.

ba'lena *sf* whale.

bale'nare (2) *vb impers*: **balena** there's lightning // *vi* to flash; **mi balenò un'idea** an idea flashed through my mind; **ba'leno** *sm* flash of lightning; **in un baleno** in a flash.

ba'lestra *sf* crossbow.

'**balia** *sf* wet-nurse.

ba'lia *sf*: **in ~ di** at the mercy of; **cadere in ~ di qd** to fall into sb's hands.

'**balla** *sf* (*di merci*) bale; (*fandonia*) (tall) story.

bal'lare *vt, vi* to dance; **bal'lata** *sf* ballad.

balle'rina *sf* dancer; ballet dancer; (*scarpa*) ballet shoe.

balle'rino *sm* dancer; ballet dancer.

bal'letto *sm* ballet.

'**ballo** *sm* dance; (*azione*) dancing *q*; **essere in ~** (*fig: persona*) to be involved; (*: cosa*) to be at stake.

ballot'taggio [ballot'taddʒo] *sm* (POL) second ballot.

balne'are *ag* seaside *cpd*; (*stagione*) bathing.

ba'locco, chi *sm* toy.

ba'lordo, a *ag* stupid, senseless; (*stordito*) stupefied, dopey.

'**balsamo** *sm* (*aroma*) balsam; (*lenimento, fig*) balm.

'**Baltico** *sm*: **il (mar) ~** the Baltic (Sea).

balu'ardo *sm* bulwark.

'**balza** ['baltsa] *sf* (*dirupo*) crag; (*di stoffa*) frill.

bal'zare [bal'tsare] *vi* to bounce; (*lanciarsi*) to jump, leap; '**balzo** *sm* bounce; jump, leap; (*del terreno*) crag.

bam'bagia [bam'badʒa] *sf* (*ovatta*) cotton wool; (*cascame*) cotton waste.

bam'bina *ag, sf vedi* **bambino**.

bambi'naia *sf* nanny, nurse(maid).

bam'bino, a *ag* child *cpd*; (*non sviluppato*) immature // *sm/f* child.

bam'boccio [bam'bɔttʃo] *sm* plump child; (*pupazzo*) rag doll.

'**bambola** *sf* doll.

bambù *sm* bamboo.

ba'nale *ag* banal, commonplace; **banalità** *sf inv* banality.

ba'nana *sf* banana; **ba'nano** *sm* banana tree.

'**banca, che** *sf* bank.

banca'rella *sf* stall.

ban'cario, a *ag* banking, bank *cpd* // *sm* bank clerk.

banca'rotta *sf* bankruptcy; **fare ~** to go bankrupt.

ban'chetto [ban'ketto] *sm* banquet.

banchi'ere [ban'kjɛre] *sm* banker.

ban'china [ban'kina] *sf* (*di porto*) quay; (*per pedoni, ciclisti*) path; (*di stazione*) platform; **~ spartitraffico** (AUT) central reservation; **~e non transitabili** (AUT) soft verges.

'**banco, chi** *sm* bench; (*di negozio*) counter; (*di mercato*) stall; (*di officina*) (work-)bench; (GEO, *banca*) bank; **~ degli imputati** dock; **~ di prova** (*fig*) testing ground; **~ dei testimoni** witness box.

banco'nota *sf* banknote.

'**banda** *sf* band; (*di stoffa*) band, stripe; (*lato, parte*) side.

banderu'ola *sf* pennant; (METEOR) weathercock, weathervane.

bandi'era *sf* flag, banner.

ban'dire *vt* to proclaim; (*esiliare*) to exile; (*fig*) to dispense with.

ban'dito *sm* outlaw, bandit.

bandi'tore *sm* (*di aste*) auctioneer.

'**bando** *sm* proclamation; (*esilio*) exile, banishment.

bar *sm inv* bar.

'**bara** *sf* bier.

ba'racca, che *sf* shed, hut; (*peg*) hovel; **mandare avanti la ~** to keep things going; **far ~** to make merry.

bara'onda *sf* hubbub, bustle.

ba'rare *vi* to cheat.

'**baratro** *sm* abyss.

barat'tare *vt*: **~ qc con** to barter sth for, swap sth for; **ba'ratto** *sm* barter.

ba'rattolo *sm* (*di latta*) tin; (*di vetro*) jar; (*di coccio*) pot.

'**barba** *sf* beard; **farsi la ~** to shave; **farla in ~ a qd** (*fig*) to do sth to sb's face; **che ~!** what a bore!

barbabi'etola *sf* beetroot; **~ da zucchero** sugar beet.

bar'barico, a, ci, che *ag* barbarian; barbaric.

bar'barie *sf* barbarity.

'**barbaro, a** *ag* barbarous; **~i** *smpl* barbarians.

barbi'ere *sm* barber.

bar'bone *sm* (*cane*) poodle; (*vagabondo*) tramp.

bar'buto, a *ag* bearded.

'**barca, che** *sf* boat; **~ a remi** rowing boat; **barcai'olo** *sm* boatman; (*noleggiatore*) boat hirer.

barcol'lare *vi* to stagger.

bar'cone *sm* (*per ponti di barche*) pontoon.

ba'rella *sf* (*lettiga*) stretcher.

ba'rile *sm* barrel, cask.

ba'rista, i, e *sm/f* barman/maid; bar owner.

ba'ritono *sm* baritone.

bar'lume *sm* glimmer, gleam.

ba'rocco, a, chi, che *ag, sm* baroque.

ba'rometro *sm* barometer.

ba'rone *sm* baron; **baro'nessa** *sf* baroness.

'barra *sf* bar; (*NAUT*) helm; (*linea grafica*) line, stroke.

barri'care *vt* to barricade; **barri'cata** *sf* barricade.

barri'era *sf* barrier; (*GEO*) reef.

ba'ruffa *sf* scuffle.

barzel'letta [bardzel'letta] *sf* joke, funny story.

ba'sare *vt* to base, found; **~rsi** *vr*: **~rsi su** (*sog: fatti, prove*) to be based *o* founded on; (: *persona*) to base one's arguments on.

'basco, schi *sm* (*copricapo*) beret.

'base *sf* base; (*fig: fondamento*) basis; (*POL*) rank and file; **di ~** basic; **in ~ a** on the basis of, according to; **a ~ di caffè** coffee-based.

ba'setta *sf* sideburn.

ba'silica, che *sf* basilica.

ba'silico *sm* basil.

'basso, a *ag* low; (*di statura*) short; (*meridionale*) southern // *sm* bottom, lower part; (*MUS*) bass; **la ~a Italia** southern Italy.

basso'fondo, pl bassifondi (*GEO*) shallows *pl*; **bassifondi** *smpl* (*fig*) dregs.

bassorili'evo *sm* bas-relief.

'basta *escl* (that's) enough!, that will do!

bas'tardo, a *ag* (*animale, pianta*) hybrid, crossbreed; (*persona*) illegitimate, bastard (*peg*) // *sm/f* illegitimate child, bastard (*peg*).

bas'tare *vi, vb impers* (2) to be enough, be sufficient; **~ a qd** to be enough for sb; **basta chiedere a un vigile** you have only to *o* need only ask a policeman.

basti'mento *sm* ship, vessel.

basto'nare *vt* to beat, thrash.

bas'tone *sm* stick; **~ da passeggio** walking stick.

bat'taglia [bat'taʎʎa] *sf* battle; fight.

bat'taglio [bat'taʎʎo] *sm* (*di campana*) clapper; (*di porta*) knocker.

battagli'one [battaʎ'ʎone] *sm* battalion.

bat'tello *sm* boat.

bat'tente *sm* (*imposta: di porta*) wing, flap; (: *di finestra*) shutter; (*batacchio: di porta*) knocker; (: *di orologio*) hammer.

'battere *vt* to beat; (*grano*) to thresh; (*percorrere*) to scour // *vi* (*bussare*) to knock; (*urtare*): **~ contro** to hit *o* strike against; (*pioggia, sole*) to beat down; (*cuore*) to beat; (*TENNIS*) to serve; **~rsi** *vr* to fight; **~ le mani** to clap; **~ i piedi** to stamp one's feet; **~ le ore** to strike the hours; **~ su un argomento** to hammer home an argument; **~ a macchina** to type; **~ bandiera italiana** to fly the Italian flag; **~ in testa** (*AUT*) to knock; **in un batter d'occhio** in the twinkling of an eye.

bat'teri *smpl* bacteria.

batte'ria *sf* battery; (*MUS*) drums *pl*.

bat'tesimo *sm* baptism; christening.

battez'zare [batted'dzare] *vt* to baptize; to christen.

batticu'ore *sm* palpitations *pl*; **avere il ~** to be frightened to death.

batti'mano *sm* applause.

batti'panni *sm inv* carpet-beater.

battis'tero *sm* baptistry.

battis'trada *sm inv* (*di pneumatico*) tread; (*di gara*) pacemaker.

'battito *sm* beat, throb; **~ cardiaco** heartbeat; **~ della pioggia/ dell'orologio** beating of the rain/ticking of the clock.

bat'tuta *sf* blow; (*di macchina da scrivere*) stroke; (*MUS*) bar; beat; (*TEATRO*) cue; (*di caccia*) beating; (*POLIZIA*) combing, scouring; (*TENNIS*) service.

ba'ule *sm* trunk; (*AUT*) boot.

'bava *sf* dribble; (*di cane etc*) slaver, slobber; (*di vento*) breath.

bava'glino [bavaʎ'ʎino] *sm* bib.

ba'vaglio [ba'vaʎʎo] *sm* gag.

'bavero *sm* collar.

ba'zar [bad'dzar] *sm inv* bazaar.

baz'zecola [bad'dzekola] *sf* trifle.

bazzi'care [battsi'kare] *vt* to frequent // *vi*: **~ in/con** to frequent.

beati'tudine *sf* bliss.

be'ato, a *ag* blessed; (*fig*) happy; **~ te!** lucky you!

bec'caccia, ce [bek'kattʃa] *sf* woodcock.

bec'care *vt* to peck; (*fig: raffreddore*) to pick up, catch; **~rsi** *vr* (*fig*) to squabble.

beccheggi'are [bekked'dʒare] *vi* to pitch.

bec'chino [bek'kino] *sm* gravedigger.

'becco, chi *sm* beak, bill; (*di caffettiera etc*) spout; lip.

Be'fana *sf* old woman who, according to legend, brings children their presents at the Epiphany; (*Epifania*) Epiphany; (*donna brutta*): **b~** hag, witch.

'beffa *sf* practical joke; **bef'fardo, a** *ag* scornful, mocking; **bef'fare** *vt* (*anche*: **beffarsi di**) to make a fool of, mock.

'bega, ghe *sf* quarrel.

'begli ['bɛʎʎi] **'bei, bel** *ag* vedi **bello**.

be'iare *vi* to bleat.

'belga, gi, ghe *ag, sm/f* Belgian.

'Belgio ['bɛldʒo] *sm*: **il ~** Belgium.

bel'lezza [bel'lettsa] *sf* beauty.

belli'coso, a *ag* warlike.

bellige'rante [bellidʒe'rante] *ag* belligerent.

'bello, a *ag* (*dav sm* **bel** +*C*, **bell'** +*V*, **bello** + *s impura, gn, pn, ps, x, z, pl* **bei** +*C*, **begli** + *s impura etc o V*) beautiful, fine, lovely; (*uomo*) handsome // *sm* (*bellezza*) beauty; (*tempo*) fine weather // *sf* (*SPORT*) decider // *av*: **fa ~** the weather is fine, it's fine; **una ~a cifra** a considerable sum of money; **un bel niente** absolutely nothing; **è una truffa ~a e buona!** it's a real fraud!; **è bell'e finito** it's already finished; **sul più ~** at the crucial point; **belle arti** fine arts.

'belva *sf* wild animal.

belve'dere *sm inv* panoramic viewpoint.

benché [ben'ke] *cong* although.

'benda *sf* bandage; (*per gli occhi*) blindfold; **ben'dare** *vt* to bandage; to blindfold.

'bene *av* well; (*completamente, affatto*): **è**

ben difficile it's very difficult // *ag inv*: **gente** ~ well-to-do people // *sm* good; **~i smpl** (*averi*) property *sg*, estate *sg*; **io sto ~/poco** ~ I'm well/not very well; **va** ~ all right; **volere un** ~ **dell'anima a qd** to love sb very much; **un uomo per** ~ a respectable man; **fare** ~ to do the right thing; **fare** ~ **a** (*salute*) to be good for; **fare del** ~ **a qd** to do sb a good turn; **~i di consumo** consumer goods.

bene'detto, a *pp di* **benedire** // *ag* blessed, holy.

bene'dire *vt* to bless; to consecrate; **benedizi'one** *sf* blessing.

benedu'cato, a *ag* well-mannered.

benefat'tore, 'trice *sm/f* benefactor/benefactress.

benefi'care *vt* to help, benefit.

benefi'cenza [benefi'tʃɛntsa] *sf* charity.

bene'ficio [bene'fitʃo] *sm* benefit.

be'nefico, a, ci, che *ag* beneficial; charitable.

bene'merito, a *ag* meritorious.

be'nessere *sm* well-being.

benes'tante *ag* well-to-do.

benes'tare *sm* consent, approval.

benevo'lenza [benevo'lɛntsa] *sf* benevolence.

be'nevolo, a *ag* benevolent.

be'nigno, a [be'ɲiɲɲo] *ag* kind, kindly; (*critica etc*) favourable; (*MED*) benign.

benin'teso *av* of course.

bensì *cong* but (rather).

benve'nuto, a *ag, sm* welcome; **dare il** ~ **a qd** to welcome sb.

ben'zina [ben'dzina] *sf* petrol; **fare** ~ to get petrol; **benzi'naio** *sm* petrol pump attendant.

'bere *vt* to drink; (*assorbire*) to soak up.

ber'lina *sf* (*AUT*) saloon (car).

Ber'lino *sf* Berlin.

ber'noccolo *sm* bump; (*inclinazione*) bent, flair.

ber'retto *sm* cap.

bersagli'are [bersaʎ'ʎare] *vt* to shoot at; (*colpire ripetutamente, fig*) to bombard; **bersagliato dalla sfortuna** dogged by ill fortune.

ber'saglio [ber'saʎʎo] *sm* target.

bes'temmia *sf* blasphemy; oath, curse, swearword.

bestemmi'are *vi* to blaspheme; to curse, swear // *vt* to blaspheme; to curse, swear at.

'bestia *sf* animal; ~ **da soma** beast of burden; **besti'ale** *ag* bestial; brutal; **besti'ame** *sm* livestock; (*bovino*) cattle *pl*.

'bettola *sf* (*peg*) dive.

be'tulla *sf* birch.

be'vanda *sf* drink, beverage.

bevi'tore, 'trice *sm/f* drinker.

be'vuto, a *pp di* **bere** // *sf* drink.

bi'ada *sf* fodder.

bianche'ria [bjanke'ria] *sf* linen; ~ **intima** underwear; ~ **da donna** ladies' underwear, lingerie.

bi'anco, a, chi, che *ag* white; (*non*

scritto) blank // *sm* white; blank, blank space; (*intonaco*) whitewash // *sm/f* white, white man/woman; **in** ~ (*foglio, assegno*) blank; **mangiare in** ~ to follow a bland diet; **pesce in** ~ boiled fish; ~ **dell'uovo** egg-white.

biasi'mare *vt* to disapprove of, censure; **bi'asimo** *sm* disapproval, censure.

'bibbia *sf* bible.

bibe'ron *sm inv* feeding bottle.

'bibita *sf* (soft) drink.

biblio'teca, che *sf* library; (*mobile*) bookcase; **bibliote'cario, a** *sm/f* librarian.

bicarbo'nato *sm*: ~ **(di sodio)** bicarbonate (of soda).

bicchi'ere [bik'kjɛre] *sm* glass.

bici'cletta [bitʃi'kletta] *sf* bicycle.

bidé *sm inv* bidet.

bi'dello, a *sm/f* (*INS*) janitor.

bi'done *sm* drum, can; (*anche:* ~ **dell'immondizia**) (dust)bin; (*fam: truffa*) swindle.

bien'nale *ag* biennial.

bi'etola *sf* beet.

bifor'carsi *vr* to fork; **biforcazi'one** *sf* fork.

biga'mia *sf* bigamy.

bighello'nare [bigello'nare] *vi* to loaf (about).

bigiotte'ria [bidʒotte'ria] *sf* costume jewellery; (*negozio*) jeweller's (*selling only costume jewellery*).

bigli'ardo [biʎ'ʎardo] *sm* = **biliardo**.

bigliette'ria [biʎʎette'ria] *sf* (*di stazione*) ticket office; booking office; (*di teatro*) box office.

bigli'etto [biʎ'ʎetto] *sm* (*per viaggi, spettacoli etc*) ticket; (*cartoncino*) card; (*anche:* ~ **di banca**) (bank)note; ~ **d'auguri/da visita** greetings/visiting card.

bigo'dino *sm* roller, curler.

bi'gotto, a *ag* over-pious // *sm/f* church fiend.

bi'lancia, ce *sf* (*pesa*) scales *pl*; (*: di precisione*) balance; (*dello zodiaco*): **B~** Libra; ~ **commerciale/dei pagamenti** balance of trade/payments; **bilanci'are** *vt* (*pesare*) to weigh; (*: fig*) to weigh up; (*pareggiare*) to balance.

bi'lancio [bi'lantʃo] *sm* (*COMM*) balance(-sheet); (*statale*) budget; **fare il** ~ **di** (*fig*) to assess; ~ **consuntivo** (final) balance; ~ **preventivo** budget.

'bile *sf* bile; (*fig*) rage, anger.

bili'ardo *sm* billiards *sg*; billiard table.

'bilico, chi *sm* unstable equilibrium; **in** ~ in the balance; **tenere qd in** ~ to keep sb in suspense.

bi'lingue *ag* bilingual.

bili'one *sm* (*mille milioni*) thousand million; (*milione di milioni*) billion.

'bimbo, a *sm/f* little boy/girl.

bimen'sile *ag* fortnightly.

bimes'trale *ag* two-monthly, bimonthly.

bi'nario *sm* (railway) track *o* line;

(*piattaforma*) platform; ~ **morto** dead-end track.
bi'nocolo *sm* binoculars *pl.*
bio... *prefisso*: **bio'chimica** [bio'kimika] *sf* biochemistry; **biodegra'dabile** *ag* biodegradable; **biogra'fia** *sf* biography; **biolo'gia** *sf* biology; **bio'logico, a, ci, che** *ag* biological.
bi'ondo, a *ag* blond, fair.
bir'bante *sm* rogue, rascal.
biri'chino, a [biri'kino] *ag* mischievous // *sm/f* scamp, little rascal.
bi'rillo *sm* skittle; ~**i** *smpl* (*gioco*) skittles *sg.*
'birra *sf* beer; **a tutta** ~ (*fig*) at top speed; **birre'ria** *sf* ≈ bierkeller.
bis *escl, sm inv* encore.
bisbigli'are [bisbiʎ'ʎare] *vt, vi* to whisper; **bis'biglio** *sm* whisper; (*notizia*) rumour; **bisbi'glio** *sm* whispering.
'bisca, sche *sf* gambling-house.
'biscia, sce ['biʃʃa] *sf* snake; ~ **d'acqua** grass snake.
bis'cotto *sm* biscuit.
bises'tile *ag*: **anno** ~ leap year.
bis'lungo, a, ghi, ghe *ag* oblong.
bis'nonno, a *sm/f* great-grandfather/grandmother.
biso'gnare [bizoɲ'ɲare] *vb impers*: **bisogna che tu parta/lo faccia** you'll have to go/do it; **bisogna parlargli** we'll (*o* I'll) have to talk to him // *vi* (*esser utile*) to be necessary; **mi bisognano quei fogli** I need those sheets of paper.
bi'sogno [bi'zoɲɲo] *sm* need; ~**i** *smpl*: **fare i propri** ~**i** to relieve o.s.; **avere** ~ **di qc/di fare qc** to need sth/to do sth; **al** ~, **in caso di** ~ if need be; **biso'gnoso, a** *ag* needy, poor; **bisognoso di** in need of, needing.
bis'tecca, che *sf* steak, beefsteak.
bisticci'are [bistit'tʃare] *vi*, ~**rsi** *vr* to quarrel, bicker; **bis'ticcio** *sm* quarrel, squabble; (*gioco di parole*) pun.
'bisturi *sm* scalpel.
bi'sunto, a *ag* very greasy.
'bitter *sm inv* bitters *pl.*
bi'vacco, chi *sm* bivouac.
'bivio *sm* fork; (*fig*) dilemma.
'bizza ['biddza] *sf* tantrum; **fare le** ~**e** (*bambino*) to be naughty.
biz'zarro, a [bid'dzarro] *ag* bizarre, strange.
biz'zeffe [bid'dzɛffe]: **a** ~ *av* in plenty, galore.
blan'dire *vt* to soothe; to flatter.
'blando, a *ag* mild, gentle.
bla'sone *sm* coat of arms.
blate'rare *vi* to chatter, blether.
'blatta *sf* cockroach.
blin'dato, a *ag* armoured.
bloc'care *vt* to block; (*isolare*) to isolate, cut off; (*porto*) to blockade; (*prezzi, beni*) to freeze; (*meccanismo*) to jam.
'blocco, chi *sm* block; (*MIL*) blockade; (*dei fitti*) restriction; (*quadernetto*) pad; (*fig: unione*) coalition; (*il bloccare*) blocking;

isolating, cutting-off; blockading; freezing; jamming; **in** ~ (*nell'insieme*) as a whole; (*COMM*) in bulk.
blu *ag inv, sm* dark blue.
'blusa *sf* (*camiciotto*) smock; (*camicetta*) blouse.
'boa *sm inv* (*ZOOL*) boa constrictor; (*sciarpa*) feather boa // *sf* buoy.
bo'ato *sm* rumble, roar.
bo'bina *sf* reel, spool; (*di pellicola*) spool; (*di film*) reel; (*ELETTR*) coil.
'bocca, che *sf* mouth; **in** ~ **al lupo!** good luck!
boc'caccia, ce [bok'kattʃa] *sf* (*smorfia*) grimace.
boc'cale *sm* jug; ~ **da birra** tankard.
boc'cetta [bot'tʃetta] *sf* small bottle.
boccheggi'are [bokked'dʒare] *vi* to gasp.
boc'chino [bok'kino] *sm* (*di sigaretta, sigaro: cannella*) cigarette-holder; cigar-holder; (*di pipa, strumenti musicali*) mouthpiece; ~ **con filtro** filter tip.
'boccia, ce ['bottʃa] *sf* bottle; (*da vino*) decanter, carafe; (*palla*) bowl; **gioco di** ~**ce** bowls *sg.*
bocci'are [bot'tʃare] *vt* (*respingere*) to reject; (*: INS*) to fail; (*nel gioco delle bocce*) to hit; **boccia'tura** *sf* failure.
bocci'olo [bot'tʃɔlo] *sm* bud.
boc'cone *sm* mouthful, morsel.
boc'coni *av* face downwards.
'boia *sm inv* executioner; hangman.
boi'ata *sf* botch.
boicot'tare *vt* to boycott.
Bo'livia *sf*: **la** ~ Bolivia.
'bolla *sf* bubble; (*MED*) blister; ~ **papale** papal bull.
bol'lare *vt* to stamp; (*fig*) to brand.
bol'lente *ag* boiling; boiling hot.
bol'letta *sf* bill; (*ricevuta*) receipt; **essere in** ~ to be hard up.
bollet'tino *sm* bulletin; (*COMM*) note; ~ **di spedizione** consignment note.
bol'lire *vt, vi* to boil; **bol'lito** *sm* (*CUC*) boiled meat; **bolli'tura** *sf* boiling.
'bollo *sm* stamp.
bol'lore *sm* boiling (point); (*caldo intenso*) torrid heat; ~**i di gioventù** youthful enthusiasm *sg.*
'bomba *sf* bomb; **tornare a** ~ (*fig*) to get back to the point; ~ **atomica** atom bomb.
bombarda'mento *sm* bombardment; bombing.
bombar'dare *vt* to bombard; (*da aereo*) to bomb.
bombardi'ere *sm* bomber.
bom'betta *sf* bowler (hat).
'bombola *sf* cylinder.
bo'naccia, ce [bo'nattʃa] *sf* dead calm.
bo'nario, a *ag* good-natured, kind.
bo'nifica, che *sf* reclamation; reclaimed land.
bo'nifico, ci *sm* (*COMM: abbuono*) discount; (*: versamento*) credit transfer.
bontà *sf* goodness; (*cortesia*) kindness; **aver la** ~ **di fare qc** to be good *o* kind enough to do sth.

borbot'tare *vi* to mumble; (*stomaco*) to rumble.

'borchia ['borkja] *sf* stud.

borda'tura *sf* (*SARTORIA*) border, trim.

'bordo *sm* (*NAUT*) ship's side; (*orlo*) edge; (*striscia di guarnizione*) border, trim; **prendere a ~** to take on board; **a ~ della macchina** inside the car.

bor'dura *sf* border.

bor'gata *sf* hamlet.

bor'ghese [bor'geze] *ag* (*spesso peg*) middle-class; bourgeois; **abito ~** civilian dress; **borghe'sia** *sf* middle classes *pl*; bourgeoisie.

'borgo, ghi *sm* (*paesino*) village; (*quartiere*) district.

'boria *sf* self-conceit, arrogance; **bori'oso, a** *ag* arrogant.

boro'talco *sm* talcum powder.

bor'raccia, ce [bor'rattʃa] *sf* canteen, water-bottle.

'borsa *sf* bag; (*anche:* **~ da signora**) handbag; (*ECON*): **la B~** (*valori*) the Stock Exchange; **~ nera** black market; **~ della spesa** shopping bag; **~ di studio** grant; **borsai'olo** *sm* pickpocket; **borsel'lino** *sm* purse; **bor'setta** *sf* handbag; **bor'sista, i, e** *sm/f* (*ECON*) speculator; (*INS*) grant-holder.

bos'caglia [bos'kaʎʎa] *sf* woodlands *pl*.

boscai'olo *sm* woodcutter; forester.

'bosco, schi *sm* wood; **bos'coso, a** *ag* wooded.

'bossolo *sm* cartridge-case.

bo'tanico, a, ci, che *ag* botanical // *sm* botanist // *sf* botany.

'botola *sf* trap door.

'botta *sf* blow; (*rumore*) bang.

'botte *sf* barrel, cask.

bot'tega, ghe [bot'teɡa] *sf* shop; (*officina*) workshop; **botte'gaio, a** *sm/f* shopkeeper; **botte'ghino** *sm* ticket office; (*del lotto*) public lottery office.

bot'tiglia [bot'tiʎʎa] *sf* bottle; **bottiglie'ria** *sf* wine shop.

bot'tino *sm* (*di guerra*) booty; (*di rapina, furto*) loot.

'botto *sm* bang; crash; **di ~** suddenly.

bot'tone *sm* button; (*BOT*) bud; **botton d'oro** buttercup.

bo'vino, a *ag* bovine; **~i** *smpl* cattle.

boxe [bɔks] *sf* boxing.

'bozza ['bɔttsa] *sf* draft; sketch; (*TIP*) proof; **boz'zetto** *sm* sketch.

'bozzolo ['bɔttsolo] *sm* cocoon.

brac'care *vt* to hunt.

brac'cetto [brat'tʃetto] *sm*: **a ~** arm in arm.

bracci'ale [brat'tʃale] *sm* bracelet; (*distintivo*) armband; **braccia'letto** *sm* bracelet, bangle.

bracci'ante [brat'tʃante] *sm* (*AGR*) day labourer.

bracci'ata [brat'tʃata] *sf* armful; (*nel nuoto*) stroke.

'braccio ['brattʃo] *sm* (*pl(f)* **braccia**: *ANAT*) arm; (*pl(m)* **bracci**: *di gru, fiume*) arm; (*: di edificio*) wing; **~ di mare** sound; **~ di terra** promontory; **bracci'olo** *sm* (*appoggio*) arm.

'bracco, chi *sm* hound.

bracconi'ere *sm* poacher.

'brace ['bratʃe] *sf* embers *pl*; **braci'ere** *sm* brazier.

braci'ola [bra'tʃɔla] *sf* (*CUC*) chop.

'branca, che *sf* branch.

'branchia ['brankja] *sf* (*ZOOL*) gill.

'branco, chi *sm* (*di cani, lupi*) pack; (*di uccelli, pecore*) flock; (*mandria*) herd; (*peg: di persone*) gang, pack.

branco'lare *vi* to grope, feel one's way.

'branda *sf* camp bed.

bran'dello *sm* scrap, shred; **a ~i** in tatters, in rags.

bran'dire *vt* to brandish.

'brano *sm* piece; (*di libro*) passage.

bra'sare *vt* to braise.

Bra'sile *sm*: **il ~** Brazil; **brasili'ano, a** *ag, sm/f* Brazilian.

'bravo, a *ag* (*abile*) clever, capable, skilful; (*buono*) good, honest; (*: bambino*) good; (*coraggioso*) brave; **~! **well done!; (*al teatro*) bravo!

bra'vura *sf* cleverness, skill.

'breccia, ce ['brettʃa] *sf* breach.

bre'tella *sf* (*AUT*) link; **~e** *sfpl* braces.

'breve *ag* brief, short; **in ~** in short.

brevet'tare *vt* to patent.

bre'vetto *sm* patent; **~ di pilotaggio** pilot's licence.

brevità *sf* brevity.

'brezza ['breddza] *sf* breeze.

'bricco, chi *sm* jug, pot; **~ del caffè** coffeepot.

bric'cone, a *sm/f* rogue, rascal.

'briciola ['britʃola] *sf* crumb.

'briciolo ['britʃolo] *sm* bit.

'briga, ghe *sf* (*fastidio*) trouble, bother; **pigliarsi la ~ di fare qc** to take the trouble to do sth.

brigadi'ere *sm* (*dei carabinieri etc*) ≈ sergeant.

bri'gante *sm* bandit.

bri'gare *vi* to scheme.

bri'gata *sf* (*MIL*) brigade; (*gruppo*) group, party.

'briglia ['briʎʎa] *sf* rein; **a ~ sciolta** at full gallop; (*fig*) at full speed.

bril'lante *ag* bright; brilliant; (*che luccica*) shining // *sm* diamond.

bril'lare *vi* to shine; (*mina*) to blow up.

'brillo, a *ag* merry, tipsy.

'brina *sf* hoarfrost.

brin'dare *vi*: **~ a qd/qc** to drink to *o* toast sb/sth.

'brindisi *sm inv* toast.

'brio *sm* liveliness, go; **bri'oso, a** *ag* lively.

bri'tannico, a, ci, che *ag* British.

bri'vido *sm* shiver; (*di ribrezzo*) shudder; (*fig*) thrill.

brizzo'lato, a [brittso'lato] *ag* (*persona*) going grey; (*barba, capelli*) greying.

'brocca, che *sf* jug.

broc'cato *sm* brocade.

'broccolo sm broccoli sg.

'brodo sm broth; (per cucinare) stock; ~ **ristretto** consommé.

'brogli ['brɔʎʎi] smpl (DIR) malpractices.

brogli'accio [broʎ'ʎattʃo] sm scribbling pad.

bron'chite [bron'kite] sf (MED) bronchitis.

'broncio ['brontʃo] sm sulky expression; **fare il** ~ to sulk.

bronto'lare vi to grumble; (stomaco) to rumble.

'bronzo ['brondzo] sm bronze.

bru'care vt to browse on, nibble at.

brucia'pelo [brutʃa'pelo]: **a** ~ av point-blank.

bruci'are [bru'tʃare] vt to burn; (scottare) to scald // vi (2) to burn; **brucia'tore** sm burner; **brucia'tura** sf burning q; burn; (scottatura) scald; **bruci'ore** sm burning o smarting sensation.

'bruco, chi sm caterpillar; grub.

brughi'era [bru'gjɛra] sf heath, moor.

bruli'care vi to swarm.

'brullo, a ag bare, bleak.

'bruma sf mist.

'bruno, a ag brown, dark; (persona) dark(-haired).

'brusco, a, schi, sche ag (sapore) sharp; (modi, persona) brusque, abrupt; (movimento) abrupt, sudden.

bru'sio sm buzz, buzzing.

bru'tale ag brutal; **brutalità** sf inv brutality.

'bruto, a ag brute cpd; brutal // sm brute.

brut'tezza [brut'tettsa] sf ugliness.

'brutto, a ag ugly; (cattivo) bad; (malattia, strada, affare) nasty, bad; ~ **tempo** bad weather; **brut'tura** sf (cosa brutta) ugly thing; (sudiciume) filth; (azione meschina) mean action.

Bru'xelles [bry'sɛl] sf Brussels.

'buca, che sf hole; (avvallamento) hollow; ~ **delle lettere** letterbox.

buca'neve sm inv snowdrop.

bu'care vt (forare) to make a hole (o holes) in; (pungere) to pierce; (biglietto) to punch; ~ **una gomma** to have a puncture.

bu'cato sm (operazione) washing; (panni) wash, washing.

'buccia, ce ['buttʃa] sf skin, peel; (corteccia) bark.

bucherel'lare [bukerel'lare] vt to riddle with holes.

'buco, chi sm hole.

bu'dello sm intestine; (fig: tubo) tube; ~ **a** sfpl bowels, guts.

bu'dino sm pudding.

'bue sm ox; (anche: **carne di** ~) beef.

'bufalo sm buffalo.

bu'fera sf storm; ~ **di vento** gale.

'buffo, a ag funny; (TEATRO) comic.

buf'fone sm buffoon.

bu'gia, 'gie [bu'dʒia] sf lie; (candeliere) candleholder; **bugi'ardo, a** ag lying, deceitful // sm/f liar.

bugi'gattolo [budʒi'gattolo] sm poky little room.

'buio, a ag dark // sm dark, darkness; **fa** ~ **pesto** it's pitch-dark.

'bulbo sm (BOT) bulb; ~ **oculare** eyeball.

Bulga'ria sf: **la** ~ Bulgaria.

bul'lone sm bolt.

buongus'taio, a sm/f gourmet.

buon'gusto sm good taste.

bu'ono, a ag (dav sm **buon** + C o V, **buono** + s impura, gn, pn, ps, x, z; dav sf **buon'** +V) good; (benevolo): ~ **(con)** good (to), kind (to); (adatto): ~ **a/da** fit for/to // sm good; (COMM) voucher, coupon; **alla buona** ag simple // av in a simple way, without any fuss; **buona fortuna** good luck; **buona notte** good night; **buona sera** good evening; **buon compleanno** happy birthday; **buon divertimento** have a nice time; **buon giorno** good morning (o afternoon); **a buon mercato** cheap; **di buon'ora** early; ~ **di cassa** cash voucher; ~ **fruttifero** bond bearing interest; ~ **a nulla** good-for-nothing; ~ **del tesoro** Treasury bill; **buon riposo** sleep well; **buon senso** common sense; **buon viaggio** bon voyage, have a good trip.

buontem'pone, a sm/f jovial person.

burat'tino sm puppet.

'burbero, a ag surly, gruff.

'burla sf prank, trick; **bur'lare** vt: **burlare qc/qd, burlarsi di qc/qd** to make fun of sth/sb.

bu'rocrate sm bureaucrat; **buro'cratico, a, ci, che** ag bureaucratic; **burocra'zia** sf bureaucracy.

bur'rasca, sche sf storm; **burras'coso, a** ag stormy.

'burro sm butter.

bur'rone sm ravine.

bus'care vt anche: ~**rsi**: (raffreddore) to get, catch; **buscarle** (fam) to get a hiding.

bus'sare vi to knock.

'bussola sf compass; **perdere la** ~ (fig) to lose one's bearings.

'busta sf (da lettera) envelope; (astuccio) case; **in** ~ **aperta** in an unsealed envelope; ~ **paga** pay packet.

busta'rella sf bribe, backhander.

'busto sm bust; (indumento) corset, girdle.

but'tare vt to throw; (anche: ~ **via**) to throw away; ~ **giù** (scritto) to scribble down, dash off; (cibo) to gulp down; (edificio) to pull down, demolish; (pasta, verdura) to put into boiling water; ~**rsi dalla finestra** to jump o throw o.s. out of the window.

C

ca'bina sf (di nave) cabin; (da spiaggia) beach hut; (di autocarro, treno) cab; (di aereo) cockpit; (di ascensore) cage; ~ **telefonica** call box, (tele)phone box o booth.

ca'cao sm cocoa.

'caccia ['kattʃa] sf hunting; (con fucile)

shooting; (*inseguimento*) chase; (*cacciagione*) game; ~ **grossa** big-game hunting; ~ **all'uomo** manhunt // *sm inv* (*aereo*) fighter; (*nave*) destroyer.

cacciabombardi'ere [kattʃabombar-'djere] *sm* fighter-bomber.

cacciagi'one [kattʃa'dʒone] *sf* game.

cacci'are [kat'tʃare] *vt* to hunt; (*mandar via*) to chase away; (*ficcare*) to shove, stick // *vi* to hunt; ~**rsi** *vr* (*mettersi*): ~**rsi tra la folla** to plunge into the crowd; **dove s'è cacciata la mia borsa?** where has my bag got to?; ~ **fuori qc** to whip *o* pull sth out; ~ **un urlo** to let out a yell; **caccia'tore** *sm* hunter; **cacciatore di frodo** poacher.

caccia'vite [kattʃa'vite] *sm inv* screwdriver.

'cactus *sm inv* cactus.

ca'davere *sm* (dead) body, corpse.

ca'dente *ag* falling; (*casa*) tumbledown; (*persona*) decrepit.

ca'denza [ka'dɛntsa] *sf* cadence; (*andamento ritmico*) rhythm; (*MUS*) cadenza.

ca'dere *vi* (2) to fall; (*denti, capelli*) to fall out; (*tetto*) to fall in; **questa gonna cade bene** this skirt hangs well; **lasciar cadere** (*anche fig*) to drop; ~ **dal sonno** to be falling asleep on one's feet; ~ **ammalato** to fall ill.

ca'detto *sm* cadet.

ca'duta *sf* fall; ~ **di temperatura** drop in temperature.

caffè *sm inv* coffee; (*locale*) café; ~ **macchiato** coffee with a dash of milk; ~ **macinato** ground coffee.

caffel'latte *sm inv* white coffee.

caffetti'era *sf* coffeepot.

cagio'nare [kadʒo'nare] *vt* to cause, be the cause of.

cagio'nevole [kadʒo'nevole] *ag* delicate, weak.

cagli'are [kaʎ'ʎare] *vi* (2) to curdle.

'cagna ['kaɲɲa] *sf* (*ZOOL, peg*) bitch.

ca'gnesco, a, schi, sche [kaɲ'ɲesko] *ag* (*fig*): **guardare qd in** ~ to scowl at sb.

cala'brone *sm* hornet.

cala'maio *sm* inkpot; inkwell.

cala'maro *sm* squid.

cala'mita *sf* magnet.

calamità *sf inv* calamity, disaster.

ca'lare *vt* (*far discendere*) to lower; (*MAGLIA*) to decrease // *vi* (2) (*discendere*) to go (*o* come) down; (*tramontare*) to set, go down; ~ **di peso** to lose weight.

'calca *sf* throng, press.

cal'cagno [kal'kaɲɲo] *sm* heel.

cal'care *sm* limestone // *vt* (*premere coi piedi*) to tread, press down; (*premere con forza*) to press down; (*mettere in rilievo*) to stress.

'calce ['kaltʃe] *sm*: **in** ~ at the foot of the page // *sf* lime; ~ **viva** quicklime.

calces'truzzo [kaltʃes'truttso] *sm* concrete.

calci'are [kal'tʃare] *vt, vi* to kick; **calcia'tore** *sm* footballer.

cal'cina [kal'tʃina] *sf* (lime) mortar.

'calcio ['kaltʃo] *sm* (*pedata*) kick; (*sport*) football, soccer; (*di pistola, fucile*) butt; (*CHIM*) calcium; ~ **di punizione** (*SPORT*) free kick.

'calco, chi *sm* (*ARTE*) casting, moulding; cast, mould.

calco'lare *vt* to calculate, work out, reckon; (*ponderare*) to weigh (up); **calcola'tore, 'trice** *ag* calculating // *sm* calculator; (*fig*) calculating person // *sf* calculator; **calcolatore elettronico** computer.

'calcolo *sm* (*anche MAT*) calculation; (*infinitesimale etc*) calculus; (*MED*) stone; **fare i propri** ~**i** (*fig*) to weigh the pros and cons; **per** ~ out of self-interest.

cal'daia *sf* boiler.

caldeggi'are [kalded'dʒare] *vt* to support warmly, favour.

'caldo, a *ag* warm; (*molto caldo*) hot; (*fig: appassionato*) keen; hearty // *sm* heat; **ho** ~ I'm warm; I'm hot; **fa** ~ it's warm; it's hot.

calen'dario *sm* calendar.

'calibro *sm* (*di arma*) calibre, bore; (*TECN*) callipers *pl*; (*fig*) calibre; **i grossi** ~**i** (*anche fig*) the big guns.

'calice ['kalitʃe] *sm* goblet; (*REL*) chalice.

ca'ligine [ka'lidʒine] *sf* fog; (*mista con fumo*) smog.

'callo *sm* callus; (*ai piedi*) corn; **fare il** ~ **a qc** to get used to sth.

'calma *sf* calm.

cal'mante *sm* sedative, tranquillizer.

cal'mare *vt* to calm; (*lenire*) to soothe; ~**rsi** *vr* to grow calm, calm down; (*vento*) to abate; (*dolore*) to ease.

calmi'ere *sm* controlled price.

'calmo, a *ag* calm, quiet.

'calo *sm* (*COMM: di prezzi*) fall; (: *di volume*) shrinkage; (: *di peso*) loss.

ca'lore *sm* warmth; heat; **essere in** ~ (*ZOOL*) to be on heat.

calo'ria *sf* calorie.

calo'roso, a *ag* warm.

calpes'tare *vt* to tread on, trample on; **'è vietato** ~ **l'erba'** 'keep off the grass'.

ca'lunnia *sf* slander; (*scritta*) libel.

cal'vario *sm* (*fig*) affliction, cross.

cal'vizie [kal'vittsje] *sf* baldness.

'calvo, a *ag* bald.

'calza ['kaltsa] *sf* (*da donna*) stocking; (*da uomo*) sock.

cal'zare [kal'tsare] *vt* (*scarpe, guanti: mettersi*) to put on; (: *portare*) to wear // *vi* (2) to fit; **calza'tura** *sf* footwear.

calzet'tone [kaltset'tone] *sm* heavy knee-length sock.

cal'zino [kal'tsino] *sm* sock.

calzo'laio [kaltso'lajo] *sm* shoemaker; (*che ripara scarpe*) cobbler; **calzole'ria** *sf* (*negozio*) shoe shop.

calzon'cini [kaltson'tʃini] *smpl* shorts.

cal'zone [kal'tsone] *sm* trouser leg; (*CUC*)

savoury turnover made with pizza dough; ~i smpl trousers.

camale'onte sm chameleon.

cambi'ale sf bill (of exchange); (pagherò cambiario) promissory note.

cambia'mento sm change.

cambi'are vt to change; (modificare) to alter, change; (barattare) to exchange // vi (2) to change, alter; **~rsi** vr (variare abito) to change; **~ casa** to move (house); **~ idea** to change one's mind; **~ aspetto** to change (in appearance); **~ treno** to change trains.

'cambio sm change; (modifica) alteration, change; (scambio, COMM) exchange; (corso dei cambi) rate (of exchange); (TECN, AUT) gears pl; **in ~ di** in exchange for; **dare il ~ a qd** to take over from sb.

'camera sf room; (anche: **~ da letto**) bedroom; (COMM, TECN) chamber; (POL) chamber, house; (FOT) camera; **~ ardente** mortuary chapel; **~ d'aria** inner tube; (di pallone) bladder; **C~ dei Deputati** Chamber of Deputies, **~** House of Commons; **~ a gas** gas chamber; **~ a un letto/a due letti/matrimoniale** single/twin-bedded/double room; **~ oscura** (FOT) dark room.

came'rata, i, e sm/f companion, mate // sf dormitory; **camera'tismo** sm comradeship.

cameri'era sf (domestica) maid; (che serve a tavola) waitress; (che fa le camere) chambermaid.

cameri'ere sm (man)servant; (di ristorante) waiter.

came'rino sm (TEATRO) dressing room.

'camice ['kamitʃe] sm (REL) alb; (per medici etc) white coat.

cami'cetta [kami'tʃetta] sf blouse.

ca'micia, cie [ka'mitʃa] sf (da uomo) shirt; (da donna) blouse; **~ di forza** straitjacket; **camici'otto** sm smock; workman's top.

ca'mino sm chimney; (focolare) fireplace, hearth.

'camion sm inv lorry; **camion'cino** sm van.

cam'mello sm (ZOOL) camel; (tessuto) camel hair.

cam'meo sm cameo.

cammi'nare vi to walk; (funzionare) to work, go.

cam'mino sm walk; (sentiero) path; (itinerario, direzione, tragitto) way; **mettersi in ~** to set o start off; **cammin facendo** on the way.

camo'milla sf camomile; (infuso) camomile tea.

ca'morra sf camorra; racket.

ca'moscio [ka'moʃʃo] sm chamois.

cam'pagna [kam'paɲɲa] sf country, countryside; (POL, COMM, MIL) campaign; **in ~** in the country; **fare una ~** to campaign; **campa'gnolo, a** ag country cpd // sf (AUT) land rover.

cam'pale ag field cpd; (fig): **una giornata ~** a hard day.

cam'pana sf bell; (anche: **~ di vetro**) bell jar; **campa'nella** sf small bell; (di tenda) curtain ring; (di porta) (ring-shaped) knocker; **campa'nello** sm (all'uscio, da tavola) bell.

campa'nile sm bell tower, belfry; **campani'lismo** sm parochialism.

cam'pare vi (2) to live; (tirare avanti) to get by, manage; **~ alla giornata** to live from day to day.

cam'pato, a ag: **~ in aria** unsound, unfounded.

campeggi'are [kamped'dʒare] vi to camp; (risaltare) to stand out; **cam'peggio** sm camping; (terreno) camp site; **fare (del) campeggio** to go camping.

cam'pestre ag country cpd, rural.

campio'nario, a ag: **fiera ~a** a trade fair // sm collection of samples.

campio'nato sm championship.

campi'one, 'essa sm/f (SPORT) champion // sm (COMM) sample.

'campo sm field; (MIL) field; (: accampamento) camp; (spazio delimitato: sportivo etc) ground; field; (di quadro) background; **i ~i** (campagna) the countryside; **~ da aviazione** airfield; **~ di concentramento** concentration camp; **~ di golf** golf course; **~ da tennis** tennis court; **~ visivo** field of vision.

campo'santo, pl **campisanti** sm cemetery.

camuf'fare vt to disguise.

'Canada sm: **il ~** Canada; **cana'dese** ag, sm/f Canadian.

ca'naglia [ka'naʎʎa] sf rabble, mob; (persona) scoundrel, rogue.

ca'nale sm (anche fig) channel; (artificiale) canal.

'canapa sf hemp.

cana'rino sm canary.

cancel'lare [kantʃel'lare] vt (con la gomma) to rub out, erase; (con la penna) to strike out; (annullare) to annul, cancel; (disdire) to cancel.

cancelle'ria [kantʃelle'ria] sf chancery; (quanto necessario per scrivere) stationery.

cancelli'ere [kantʃel'ljere] sm chancellor; (di tribunale) clerk of the court.

can'cello [kan'tʃello] sm gate.

can'crena sf gangrene.

'cancro sm (MED) cancer; (dello zodiaco): **C~** Cancer.

can'dela sf candle; **~ (di accensione)** (AUT) sparking plug.

cande'labro sm candelabra.

candeli'ere sm candlestick.

candi'dato, a sm/f candidate; (aspirante a una carica) applicant.

'candido, a ag white as snow; (puro) pure; (sincero) sincere, candid.

can'dito, a ag candied.

can'dore sm brilliant white; purity; sincerity, candour.

cane sm dog; (di pistola, fucile) cock; **fa un freddo ~** it's bitterly cold; **non c'era un ~** there wasn't a soul; **quell'attore è un**

~ he's a rotten actor; ~ **da guardia** guard dog; ~ **lupo** alsatian.

ca'nestro sm basket.

cangi'ante [kan'dʒante] ag iridescent; **seta** ~ shot silk.

can'guro sm kangaroo.

ca'nile sm kennel; (di allevamento) kennels pl; ~ **municipale** dog pound.

ca'nino, a ag, sm canine.

'canna sf (pianta) reed; (: indica, da zucchero) cane; (bastone) stick, cane; (di fucile) barrel; (di organo) pipe; ~ **fumaria** chimney flue; ~ **da pesca** (fishing) rod; ~ **da zucchero** sugar cane.

can'nella sf (CUC) cinnamon.

can'nibale sm cannibal.

cannocchi'ale [kannok'kjale] sm telescope.

can'none sm (MIL) gun; (: STORIA) cannon; (tubo) pipe, tube; (piega) box pleat; (fig) ace.

can'nuccia, ce [kan'nuttʃa] sf (drinking) straw.

ca'noa sf canoe.

'canone sm canon, criterion; (mensile, annuo) rent; fee; **ca'nonico, ci** sm (REL) canon.

canoniz'zare [kanonid'dzare] vt to canonize.

ca'noro, a ag (uccello) singing, song cpd.

canot'taggio [kanot'taddʒo] sm rowing.

canotti'era sf vest.

ca'notto sm small boat, dinghy; canoe.

cano'vaccio [kano'vattʃo] sm (tela) canvas; (strofinaccio) duster; (trama) plot.

can'tante sm/f singer.

can'tare vt, vi to sing; **cantau'tore, 'trice** sm/f singer-composer.

canterel'lare vt to hum, sing to oneself.

canti'ere sm (EDIL) (building) site; (anche: ~ **navale**) shipyard.

canti'lena sf (filastrocca) lullaby; (fig) sing-song voice.

can'tina sf (locale) cellar; (bottega) wine shop.

'canto sm song; (arte) singing; (REL) chant; (chanting; (poesia) poem, lyric; (parte di una poesia) canto; (angolo di due muri) corner; (parte, lato) side; **d'altro** ~ on the other hand.

can'tone sm (in Svizzera) canton.

can'tuccio [kan'tuttʃo] sm corner, nook.

ca'nuto, a ag white, whitehaired.

canzo'nare [kantso'nare] vt to tease.

can'zone [kan'tsone] sf song; (POESIA) canzone; **canzoni'ere** sm (MUS) songbook; (LETTERATURA) collection of poems.

'caos sm inv chaos; **ca'otico, a, ci, che** ag chaotic.

C.A.P. abbr vedi **codice**.

ca'pace [ka'patʃe] ag able, capable; (ampio, vasto) large, capacious; **sei** ~ **di farlo?** can you o are you able to do it?; **capacità** sf inv ability; (DIR, di recipiente) capacity; **capaci'tarsi** vr: **capacitarsi di** to make out, understand.

ca'panna sf hut.

capan'none sm (AGR) barn; (fabbricato industriale) (factory) shed.

ca'parbio, a ag stubborn.

ca'parra sf deposit, down payment.

ca'pello sm hair; ~**i** smpl (capigliatura) hair sg; **capel'luto, a** ag having thick hair.

capez'zale [kapet'tsale] sm bolster; (fig) bedside.

ca'pezzolo [ka'pettsolo] sm nipple.

capi'enza [ka'pjentsa] sf capacity.

capiglia'tura [kapiʎʎa'tura] sf hair.

ca'pire vt to understand.

capi'tale ag (mortale) capital; (fondamentale) main, chief // sf (città) capital // sm (ECON) capital; **capita'lismo** sm capitalism; **capita'lista, i, e** ag, sm/f capitalist.

capi'tano sm captain.

capi'tare (2) vi (giungere casualmente) to happen to go, find o.s.; (accadere) to happen; (presentarsi: cosa) to turn up, present itself // vb impers to happen.

capi'tello sm (ARCHIT) capital.

capito'lare vi to capitulate.

ca'pitolo sm chapter.

capi'tombolo sm headlong fall, tumble.

'capo sm head; (persona) head, leader; (: in ufficio) head, boss; (: in tribù) chief; (di oggetti) head; top; end; (GEO) cape; **andare a** ~ to start a new paragraph; **da** ~ over again; ~ **di bestiame** head inv of cattle; ~ **di vestiario** item of clothing.

'capo... prefisso: **Capo'danno** sm New Year; **capo'fitto: a capofitto** av headfirst, headlong; **capo'giro** sm dizziness q; **capola'voro, i** sm masterpiece; **capo'linea, pl capi'linea** sm terminus; **capolu'ogo, pl ghi** o **capi-lu'oghi** sm chief town, administrative centre; **capo'mastro, pl i** o **capi'mastri** sm master builder.

capo'rale sm (MIL) lance corporal.

'capo... prefisso: **capo'saldo, pl capi'saldi** sm stronghold; (fig: fondamento) basis, cornerstone; **capostazi'one, pl capostazi'oni** sm station master; **capo-'treno, pl capi'treno** o **capo'treni** sm guard.

capo'volgere [kapo'voldʒere] vt to overturn; (fig) to reverse; ~**rsi** vr to overturn; (barca) to capsize; (fig) to be reversed.

capo'volto, a pp di **capovolgere**.

'cappa sf (mantello) cape, cloak; (del camino) hood.

cap'pella sf (REL) chapel; **cappel'lano** sm chaplain.

cap'pello sm hat.

'cappero sm caper.

cap'pone sm capon.

cap'potto sm (over)coat.

cappuc'cino [kapput'tʃino] sm (frate) Capuchin monk; (bevanda) frothy white coffee.

cap'puccio [kap'puttʃo] sm (copricapo) hood; (della biro) cap.

'capra sf (she-)goat; **ca'pretto** sm kid.

ca'priccio [ka'prittʃo] sm caprice, whim; (bizza) tantrum; **fare i ~i** to be very naughty; **capricci'oso, a** ag capricious, whimsical; naughty.

Capri'corno sm Capricorn.

capri'ola sf somersault.

capri'olo sm roe deer.

'capro sm billy-goat; **~ espiatorio** (fig) scapegoat.

'capsula sf capsule; (di proiettile) primer; cap.

cap'tare vt (RADIO, TV) to pick up; (cattivarsi) to gain, win.

carabini'ere sm carabiniere.

ca'raffa sf carafe.

cara'mella sf sweet.

ca'rattere sm character; (caratteristica) characteristic, trait; **avere un buon ~** to be good-natured; **caratte'ristico, a, ci, che** ag characteristic // sf characteristic, trait, peculiarity; **caratteriz'zare** vt to characterize, distinguish.

car'bone sm coal.

carbu'rante sm (motor) fuel.

carbura'tore sm carburettor.

car'cassa sf carcass.

carce'rato, a [kartʃe'rato] sm/f prisoner.

'carcere ['kartʃere] sm prison; (pena) imprisonment.

carci'ofo [kar'tʃɔfo] sm artichoke.

car'diaco, a, ci, che ag cardiac, heart cpd.

cardi'nale ag, sm cardinal.

'cardine sm hinge.

'cardo sm thistle.

ca'rena sf (NAUT) bottom, hull.

ca'renza [ka'rɛntsa] sf lack, scarcity; (vitaminica) deficiency.

cares'tia sf famine; (penuria) scarcity, dearth.

ca'rezza [ka'rettsa] sf caress; **carez'zare** vt to caress, stroke, fondle.

'carica sf vedi **carico**.

cari'care vt to load; (aggravare: anche fig) to weigh down; (orologio) to wind up; (batteria, MIL) to charge.

carica'tura sf caricature.

'carico, a, chi, che ag (che porta un peso): **~ di** loaded o laden with; (fucile) loaded; (orologio) wound up; (batteria) charged; (colore) deep; (caffè, tè) strong // sm (il caricare) loading; (ciò che si carica, ELETTR) load; (fig: peso) burden, weight // sf (mansione ufficiale) office, position; (MIL, TECN, ELETTR) charge; (fig: energia) drive; **persona a ~** dependent; **essere a ~ di qd** (spese etc) to be charged to sb.

'carie sf (dentaria) decay.

ca'rino, a ag lovely, pretty, nice; (simpatico) nice.

carità sf charity; **per ~!** (escl di rifiuto) good heavens, no!

carnagi'one [karna'dʒone] sf complexion.

car'nale ag (amore) carnal; (fratello) blood cpd.

'carne sf flesh; (bovina, ovina etc) meat; **~ di manzo/maiale/pecora** beef/pork/mutton; **~ tritata** mince, minced meat.

car'nefice [kar'nefitʃe] sm executioner; hangman.

carne'vale sm carnival.

car'nivoro, a ag carnivorous.

car'noso, a ag fleshy.

'caro, a ag (amato) dear; (costoso) dear, expensive.

ca'rogna [ka'roɲɲa] sf carrion; (fig: fam) swine.

caro'sello sm merry-go-round.

ca'rota sf carrot.

caro'vana sf caravan.

caro'vita sm high cost of living.

carpenti'ere sm carpenter.

car'pire vt: **~ qc a qd** (segreto etc) to get sth out of sb.

car'poni av on all fours.

car'rabile ag suitable for vehicles.

car'raio, a ag: **passo ~** vehicle entrance.

carreggi'ata [karred'dʒata] sf carriageway.

car'rello sm trolley; (AER) undercarriage; (CINEMA) dolly; (di macchina da scrivere) carriage.

car'retto sm cart.

carri'era sf career; **fare ~** to get on; **a gran ~** at full speed.

carri'ola sf wheelbarrow.

'carro sm cart, wagon; **~ armato** tank.

car'rozza [kar'rɔttsa] sf carriage.

carrozze'ria [karrottse'ria] sf body, coachwork; (officina) coachbuilder's workshop.

carroz'zina [karrot'tsina] sf pram.

'carta sf paper; (al ristorante) menu; (GEO) map; plan; (documento, da gioco) card; (costituzione) charter; **~e sfpl** (documenti) papers, documents; **~ assorbente** blotting paper; **~ di credito** credit card; **~ (geografica)** map; **~ d'identità** identity card; **~ igienica** toilet paper; **~ da lettere** writing paper; **~ da parati** wallpaper; **~ verde** (AUT) green card; **~ vetrata** sandpaper.

cartacar'bone, pl **cartecar'bone** sf carbon paper.

car'taccia, ce [kar'tattʃa] sf waste paper.

cartamo'neta sf paper money.

carta'pecora sf parchment.

carta'pesta sf papier-mâché.

car'teggio [kar'tedd'zo] sm correspondence.

car'tella sf (scheda) card; (custodia: di cartone) folder; (: di uomo d'affari etc) briefcase; (: di scolaro) schoolbag, satchel.

car'tello sm sign; (pubblicitario) poster; (stradale) sign, signpost; (ECON) cartel; (in dimostrazioni) placard; **cartel'lone** sm (pubblicitario) advertising poster; (della tombola) scoring frame; (TEATRO) playbill; **tenere il cartellone** (spettacolo) to have a long run.

carti'era sf paper mill.
carti'lagine [karti'ladʒine] sf cartilage.
car'toccio [kar'tɔttʃo] sm paper bag.
cartole'ria sf stationer's (shop).
carto'lina sf postcard.
car'tone sm cardboard; (ARTE) cartoon; ~i animati smpl (CINEMA) cartoons.
car'tuccia, ce [kar'tuttʃa] sf cartridge.
'casa sf house; (specialmente la propria casa) home; (COMM) firm, house; **essere a** ~ to be at home; **vado a** ~ **mia/tua** I'm going home/to your house; ~ **di cura** nursing home; ~ **dello studente** student hostel; ~**e popolari** ≈ council houses (o flats).
ca'sacca, che sf military coat; (di fantino) blouse.
casalingo, a, ghi, ghe ag household, domestic; (fatto a casa) home-made; (semplice) homely; (amante della casa) home-loving // sf housewife; ~**ghi** smpl household articles; **cucina** ~**a** plain home cooking.
cas'care vi to fall; **cas'cata** sf fall; (d'acqua) cascade, waterfall.
'casco, schi sm helmet; (del parrucchiere) hair-drier.
ca'sella sf pigeon-hole; ~ **postale (C.P.)** post office box (P.O. box).
ca'sello sm (di autostrada) toll-house.
ca'serma sf barracks pl.
ca'sino sm (confusione) row, racket; (casa di prostituzione) brothel.
casinò sm inv casino.
'caso sm chance; (fatto, vicenda) event, incident; (possibilità) possibility; (MED, LING) case; **a** ~ at random; **per** ~ by chance, by accident; **in ogni** ~, **in tutti i** ~**i** in any case, at any rate; **al** ~ should the opportunity arise; **nel** ~ **che** in case; ~ **mai** if by chance; ~ **limite** borderline case.
'cassa sf case, crate, box; (bara) coffin; (mobile) chest; (involucro: di orologio etc) case; (macchina) cash register; (luogo di pagamento) cash desk; (fondo) fund; (istituto bancario) bank; ~ **mutua** o **malattia** health insurance scheme; ~ **toracica** (ANAT) chest; ~ **di risparmio** savings bank.
cassa'forte, pl casseforti sf safe.
cassa'panca, pl cassapanche o **cassepanche** sf settle.
casseru'ola, casse'rola sf saucepan.
cas'setta sf box; (per registratore) cassette; (CINEMA, TEATRO) box-office takings pl; ~ **di sicurezza** strongbox; ~ **delle lettere** letterbox.
cas'setto sm drawer; **casset'tone** sm chest of drawers.
cassi'ere, a sm/f cashier; (di banca) teller.
'casta sf caste.
cas'tagna [kas'taɲɲa] sf chestnut.
cas'tagno [kas'taɲɲo] sm chestnut (tree).
cas'tello sm castle; (TECN) scaffolding.
casti'gare vt to punish; **cas'tigo, ghi** sm punishment.

castità sf chastity.
'casto, a ag chaste, pure.
cas'toro sm beaver.
cas'trare vt to castrate; to geld; to doctor.
casu'ale ag chance cpd.
cata'comba sf catacomb.
ca'talogo, ghi sm catalogue.
catarifran'gente [catarifran'dʒɛnte] sm (AUT) reflector.
ca'tarro sm catarrh.
ca'tasta sf stack, pile.
ca'tasto sm land register; land registry office.
ca'tastrofe sf catastrophe, disaster.
cate'chismo [kate'kizmo] sm catechism.
catego'ria sf category; **cate'gorico, a, ci, che** ag categorical.
ca'tena sf chain; ~ **di montaggio** assembly line; ~**e da neve** (AUT) snow chains; **cate'naccio** sm bolt.
cate'ratta sf cataract; (chiusa) sluice-gate.
cati'nella sf: **piovere a** ~**e** to pour, rain cats and dogs.
ca'tino sm basin.
ca'trame sm tar.
'cattedra sf teacher's desk; (di università) chair.
catte'drale sf cathedral.
catti'veria sf malice, spite; naughtiness; (atto) spiteful act; (parole) malicious o spiteful remark.
cattività sf captivity.
cat'tivo, a ag bad; (malvagio) bad, wicked; (turbolento: bambino) bad, naughty; (: mare) rough; (odore, sapore) nasty, bad.
cattoli'cesimo [kattoli'tʃezimo] sm Catholicism.
cat'tolico, a, ci, che ag, sm/f (Roman) Catholic.
cat'tura sf capture.
cattu'rare vt to capture.
cauc'ciù [kaut'tʃu] sm rubber.
'causa sf cause; (DIR) lawsuit, case, action; **fare** o **muovere** ~ **a qd** to take legal action against sb.
cau'sare vt to cause.
'caustico, a, ci, che ag caustic.
cau'tela sf caution, prudence.
caute'lare vt to protect.
'cauto, a ag cautious, prudent.
cauzi'one [kaut'tsjone] sf security; (DIR) bail.
cav. abbr di **cavaliere.**
'cava sf quarry; (di carbone) open-cast mine.
caval'care vt (cavallo) to ride; (muro) to sit astride; (sog: ponte) to span; **caval'cata** sf ride; (gruppo di persone) riding party.
cavalca'via sm inv flyover.
cavalci'oni [kaval'tʃoni]: **a** ~ **di** prep astride.
cavali'ere sm rider; (feudale, titolo) knight; (soldato) cavalryman; (che accompagna una donna) escort; (: al ballo) partner; **cavalle'resco, a, schi, sche** ag

chivalrous; **cavalle'ria** *sf* chivalry; (*milizia a cavallo*) cavalry.

cavalle'rizzo, a [kavalle'rittso] *sm/f* horseman/woman.

caval'letta *sf* grasshopper.

caval'letto *sm* (*FOT*) tripod; (*da pittore*) easel.

ca'vallo *sm* horse; (*SCACCHI*) knight; (*AUT: anche:* ~ **vapore**) horsepower; (*dei pantaloni*) crotch; **a** ~ on horseback; **a** ~ **di** astride, straddling; ~ **di corsa** racehorse.

ca'vare *vt* (*togliere*) to draw out, extract, take out; (: *giacca, scarpe*) to take off; (: *fame, sete, voglia*) to satisfy; **cavarsela** to get away with it; to manage, get on all right.

cava'tappi *sm inv* corkscrew.

ca'verna *sf* cave.

ca'vezza [ka'vettsa] *sf* halter.

'cavia *sf* guinea pig.

cavi'ale *sm* caviar.

ca'viglia [ka'viʎʎa] *sf* ankle.

cavil'lare *vi* to quibble.

cavità *sf inv* cavity.

'cavo, a *ag* hollow // *sm* (*ANAT*) cavity; (*grossa corda*) rope, cable; (*ELETTR, TEL*) cable.

cavolfi'ore *sm* cauliflower.

'cavolo *sm* cabbage; ~ **di Bruxelles** Brussels sprout.

cazzu'ola [kat'tswɔla] *sf* trowel.

c/c *abbr di* **conto corrente.**

ce [tʃe] *pron, av vedi* **ci.**

cecità [tʃetʃi'ta] *sf* blindness.

Cecoslo'vacchia [tʃekoslo'vakkja] *sf:* **la** ~ Czechoslovakia; **cecoslo'vacco, a, chi, che** *ag, sm/f* Czechoslovakian.

'cedere ['tʃedere] *vt* (*concedere: posto*) to give up; (*DIR*) to transfer, make over // *vi* (*cadere*) to give way, subside; ~ **(a)** to surrender (to), yield (to), give in (to); **ce'devole** *ag* (*terreno*) soft; (*fig*) yielding.

'cedola ['tʃedola] *sf* (*COMM*) coupon; voucher.

'cedro ['tʃedro] *sm* cedar; (*albero da frutto*) lime tree.

C.E.E. *abbr f vedi* **comunità.**

cef'fone [tʃef'fone] *sm* slap, smack.

ce'larsi [tʃe'larsi] *vr* to hide.

cele'brare [tʃele'brare] *vt* to celebrate; **celebrazi'one** *sf* celebration.

'celebre ['tʃelebre] *ag* famous, celebrated; **celebrità** *sf inv* fame; (*persona*) celebrity.

'celere ['tʃelere] *ag* fast, swift; (*corso*) crash *cpd.*

ce'leste [tʃe'leste] *ag* celestial; heavenly; (*colore*) sky-blue.

celi'bato [tʃeli'bato] *sm* bachelorhood; (*REL*) celibacy.

'celibe ['tʃelibe] *ag* single, unmarried // *sm* bachelor.

'cella ['tʃella] *sf* cell.

'cellula ['tʃellula] *sf* (*BIOL, ELETTR, POL*) cell.

cemen'tare [tʃemen'tare] *vt* (*anche fig*) to cement.

ce'mento [tʃe'mento] *sm* cement; ~ **armato** reinforced concrete.

'cena ['tʃena] *sf* dinner; (*leggera*) supper.

ce'nare [tʃe'nare] *vi* to dine, have dinner.

'cencio ['tʃentʃo] *sm* piece of cloth, rag; (*da spolverare*) duster.

'cenere ['tʃenere] *sf* ash.

'cenno ['tʃenno] *sm* (*segno*) sign, signal; (*gesto*) gesture; (*col capo*) nod; (*con la mano*) wave; (*allusione*) hint, mention; (*spiegazione sommaria*) short account; **far** ~ **di sì/no** to nod (one's head)/shake one's head.

censi'mento [tʃensi'mento] *sm* census.

cen'sore [tʃen'sore] *sm* censor.

cen'sura [tʃen'sura] *sf* censorship; censor's office; (*fig*) censure; **censu'rare** *vt* to censor; to censure.

cente'nario, a [tʃente'narjo] *ag* (*che ha cento anni*) hundred-year-old; (*che ricorre ogni cento anni*) centennial, centenary *cpd* // *sm/f* centenarian // *sm* centenary.

cen'tesimo, a [tʃen'tezimo] *ag, sm* hundredth.

cen'tigrado, a [tʃen'tigrado] *ag* centigrade; **20 gradi** ~**i** 20 degrees centigrade.

cen'timetro [tʃen'timetro] *sm* centimetre.

centi'naio, a *pl(f)* **aia** [tʃenti'najo] *sm:* **un** ~ **(di)** a hundred; about a hundred.

'cento ['tʃento] *num* a hundred, one hundred.

cen'trale [tʃen'trale] *ag* central // *sf:* ~ **telefonica** (telephone) exchange; ~ **elettrica** electric power station; **centra'lino** *sm* (telephone) exchange; (*di albergo etc*) switchboard; **centrali'nista** *sm/f* operator; **centraliz'zare** *vt* to centralize.

cen'trare [tʃen'trare] *vt* to hit the centre of; (*TECN*) to centre.

cen'trifuga [tʃen'trifuga] *sf* spin-drier.

'centro ['tʃentro] *sm* centre.

'ceppo ['tʃeppo] *sm* (*di albero*) stump; (*pezzo di legno*) log.

'cera ['tʃera] *sf* wax; (*aspetto*) appearance, look.

ce'ramica, che [tʃe'ramika] *sf* ceramic; (*ARTE*) ceramics *sg.*

'cerca ['tʃerka] *sf:* **in** *o* **alla** ~ **di** in search of.

cer'care [tʃer'kare] *vt* to look for, search for // *vi:* ~ **di fare qc** to try to do sth.

'cerchia ['tʃerkja] *sf* circle.

'cerchio ['tʃerkjo] *sm* circle; (*giocattolo, di botte*) hoop.

cere'ale [tʃere'ale] *sm* cereal.

cere'brale [tʃere'brale] *ag* cerebral.

ceri'monia [tʃeri'mɔnja] *sf* ceremony; **cerimoni'ale** *sm* etiquette, ceremonial; **cerimoni'oso, a** *ag* formal, ceremonious.

ce'rino [tʃe'rino] *sm* wax match.

'cernia ['tʃernja] *sf* (*ZOOL*) stone bass.

cerni'era [tʃer'njera] *sf* hinge; ~ **lampo** zip (fastener).

cer'nita ['tʃernita] *sf* selection.

'cero ['tʃero] *sm* (church) candle.

ce'rotto [tʃe'rɔtto] *sm* sticking plaster.

cer'tezza [tʃer'tettsa] *sf* certainty.

certifi'care [tʃertifi'kare] *vt* to certify.

certifi'cato *sm* certificate; ~ **medico/di nascita** medical/birth certificate.

'certo, a ['tʃerto] *ag* certain; (*sicuro*) ~ **(di/che)** certain *o* sure (of/that) // *det* certain // *av* certainly, of course; ~**i** *pronome pl* some; **un** ~ **non so che** an indefinable something; **di una** ~**a età** past one's prime, not so young; **sì** ~ yes indeed; **no** ~ certainly not; **di** ~ certainly.

cer'tuni [tʃer'tuni] *pronome pl* some (people).

cer'vello, *pl* **i** (*anche*: *pl(f)* **a** *o* **e**) [tʃer'vɛllo] *sm* brain.

'cervo, a ['tʃervo] *sm/f* stag/hind // *sm* deer; ~ **volante** stag beetle.

cesel'lare [tʃezel'lare] *vt* to chisel; (*fig*) to polish, finish with care.

ce'sello [tʃe'zɛllo] *sm* chisel.

ce'soie [tʃe'zoje] *sfpl* shears.

'cespite ['tʃɛspite] *sm* source of income.

ces'puglio [tʃes'puʎʎo] *sm* bush.

ces'sare [tʃes'sare] *vi* (2), *vt* to stop, cease; ~ **di fare qc** to stop doing sth; **cessate il fuoco** *sm* ceasefire.

'cesso ['tʃɛsso] *sm* (*fam*) bog.

'cesta ['tʃesta] *sf* (large) basket.

ces'tino [tʃes'tino] *sm* basket; (*per la carta straccia*) wastepaper basket.

'cesto ['tʃesto] *sm* basket.

'ceto ['tʃɛto] *sm* (social) class.

cetrio'lino [tʃetrio'lino] *sm* gherkin.

cetri'olo [tʃetri'ɔlo] *sm* cucumber.

cfr. (*abbr di confronta*) cf.

che [ke] *pronome* (*relativo*: *persona*: *soggetto*) who; (: *oggetto*) whom; (: *cosa*) which, that; **l'uomo** ~ **io vedo** the man (whom) I see; **il libro** ~ **è sul tavolo** the book which *o* that is on the table; **il giorno** ~ ... the day (that) ...; **la sera** ~ **ti ho visto** the evening I saw you; (*interrogativo*, *esclamativo*) what; ~ **(cosa) fai?** what are you doing?; **a** ~ **(cosa) pensi?** what are you thinking about?; **non sa** ~ **fare** he doesn't know what to do // *det* what; (*di numero limitato*) which; ~ **vestito ti vuoi mettere?** what (*o* which) dress do you want to put on?; ~ **tipo di film hai visto?** what sort of film did you see?; ~ **bel vestito!** what a lovely dress!; ~ **buono!** how delicious! // *cong* that; **so** ~ **tu c'eri** I know (that) you were there; **voglio** ~ **tu studi** I want you to study; (*affinché*) **vieni qua,** ~ **ti veda** come here, so that I can see you; (*temporale*) **arrivai** ~ **eri già partito** you had already left when I arrived; **sono anni** ~ **non lo vedo** I haven't seen him in years; (*in frasi imperative*): ~ **venga pure** let him come by all means; **non** ~ **sia stupido** not that he's stupid; *vedi* **non, più, meno** etc.

cheru'bino [keru'bino] *sm* cherub.

cheti'chella [keti'kɛlla]: **alla** ~ *av* stealthily, unobtrusively.

'cheto, a ['keto] *ag* quiet, silent.

chi [ki] *pronome* (*interrogativo*: *soggetto*) who; (: *oggetto*): **di** ~ **è questo libro?** whose book is this?; **con** ~ **parli?** to whom are you talking?, who are you talking to?; (*relativo*: *colui/colei che*) he/she who; (: *complemento*): **dillo a** ~ **vuoi** tell it to whoever you like; ~ **dice una cosa** ~ **un'altra** some say one thing some another.

chiacchie'rare [kjakkje'rare] *vi* to chat; (*discorrere futilmente*) to chatter; (*far pettegolezzi*) to gossip; **chi'acchiere** *sfpl* chatter *q*; gossip *q*; **fare due** *o* **quattro chiacchiere** to have a chat; **chiacchie'rone, a** *ag* talkative, chatty; gossipy.

chia'mare [kja'mare] *vt* to call; (*rivolgersi a qd*) to call (in), send for; ~**rsi** *vr* (*aver nome*) to be called; **mi chiamo Paolo** my name is Paolo, I'm called Paolo; ~ **alle armi** to call up; ~ **in giudizio** to summon; **chia'mata** *sf* call; (*MIL*) call-up; **chiamata interurbana** (*TEL*) trunk call.

chia'rezza [kja'rettsa] *sf* clearness; clarity.

chiarifi'care [kjarifi'kare] *vt* (*anche fig*) to clarify.

chia'rire [kja'rire] *vt* to make clear; (*fig*: *spiegare*) to clear up, explain; ~**rsi** *vr* to become clear.

chi'aro, a ['kjaro] *ag* clear; (*luminoso*) clear, bright; (*colore*) pale, light.

chiaroveg'gente [kjaroved'dʒente] *sm/f* clairvoyant.

chi'asso ['kjasso] *sm* uproar, row; **chias'soso, a** *ag* noisy, rowdy.

chi'ave ['kjave] *sf* key // *ag inv* key *cpd*; ~ **inglese** monkey wrench; **chiavis'tello** *sm* bolt.

chi'azza ['kjattsa] *sf* stain; splash.

chic [ʃik] *ag inv* chic, elegant.

'chicco, chi ['kikko] *sm* (*di cereale, riso*) grain; (*di caffè*) bean; ~ **d'uva** grape.

chi'edere ['kjedere] *vt* (*per sapere*) to ask; (*per avere*) to ask for // *vi*: ~ **di qd** to ask after sb; (*chiamare*: *al telefono*) to ask for *o* want sb; ~ **qc a qd** to ask sb sth; to ask sb for sth.

chi'erico, ci ['kjɛriko] *sm* cleric; altar boy.

chi'esa ['kjɛza] *sf* church.

chi'esto, a *pp di* **chiedere.**

'chiglia ['kiʎʎa] *sf* keel.

'chilo ['kilo] *sm* (*abbr di* **chilogrammo**) kilo; **chilo'grammo** *sm* kilogram(me); **chi'lometro** *sm* kilometre.

'chimico, a, ci, che ['kimiko] *ag* chemical // *sm/f* chemist // *sf* chemistry.

'china ['kina] *sf* (*pendio*) slope, descent; (*inchiostro di*) ~ Indian ink.

chi'nare [ki'nare] *vt* to lower, bend; ~**rsi** *vr* to stoop, bend.

chincaglie'ria [kinkaʎʎe'ria] *sf* fancy-goods shop; ~**e** *sfpl* fancy goods, knick-knacks.

chi'nino [ki'nino] *sm* quinine.

chi'occia, ce ['kjɔttʃa] *sf* brooding hen.

chi'occiola ['kjɔttʃola] *sf* snail.

chi'odo ['kjɔdo] *sm* nail; (*fig*) obsession.

chi'oma ['kjɔma] sf (capelli) head of hair; (di albero) foliage.

chi'osco, schi ['kjɔsko] sm kiosk.

chi'ostro ['kjɔstro] sm cloister.

chirur'gia [kirur'dʒia] sf surgery; **chi'rurgo, ghi** o **gi** sm surgeon.

chissà [kis'sa] av who knows, I wonder.

chi'tarra [ki'tarra] sf guitar; **chitar'rista, i, e** sm/f guitarist, guitar player.

chi'udere ['kjudere] vt to close, shut; (luce, acqua) to put off, turn off; (definitivamente: fabbrica) to close down, shut down; (strada) to close; (recingere) to enclose; (porre termine) to end // vi to close, shut; to close down, shut down; to end; **~rsi** vr to shut, close; (ritirarsi: anche fig) to shut o.s. away; (ferita) to close up.

chi'unque [ki'unkwe] pronome (relativo) whoever; (indefinito) anyone, anybody.

chi'uso, a ['kjuso] pp di **chiudere** // sf (di corso d'acqua) sluice, lock; (recinto) enclosure; (di discorso etc) conclusion, ending; **chiu'sura** sf closing; shutting; closing o shutting down; enclosing; putting o turning off; ending; (dispositivo) catch; fastening; fastener.

ci [tʃi] (dav lo, la, li, le, ne diventa **ce**) pronome (personale) us; (: complemento di termine) (to) us; (: riflessivo) ourselves; (: reciproco) one another; (dimostrativo: di ciò, su ciò, in ciò etc) about (o on o of) it; **non so cosa far~** I don't know what to do about it; **che c'entro io?** what have I got to do with it? // av (qui) here; (lì) there; **esser~** vedi **essere**.

C.ia (abbr di **compagnia**) Co.

cia'batta [tʃa'batta] sf mule, slipper.

ci'alda ['tʃalda] sf (CUC) wafer.

ciam'bella [tʃam'bella] sf (CUC) ring-shaped cake; (salvagente) rubber ring.

ci'ao ['tʃao] escl (all'arrivo) hello!; (alla partenza) cheerio!, bye!

ciarla'tano [tʃarla'tano] sm charlatan.

cias'cuno, a [tʃas'kuno] (dav sm: ciascun +C, V, ciascuno +s impura, gn, pn, ps, x, z; dav sf: ciascuna +C, ciascun' +V) det, pronome each.

'cibo ['tʃibo] sm food.

ci'cala [tʃi'kala] sf cicada.

cica'trice [tʃika'tritʃe] sf scar; **cicatriz'zarsi** vr to form a scar, heal (up).

'cicca ['tʃikka] sf cigarette end.

'ciccia ['tʃittʃa] sf (fam: carne) meat; (: grasso umano) fat, flesh.

cice'rone [tʃitʃe'rone] sm guide.

cicla'mino [tʃikla'mino] sm cyclamen.

ci'clismo [tʃi'klizmo] sm cycling; **ci'clista, i, e** sm/f cyclist.

'ciclo ['tʃiklo] sm cycle; (di malattia) course.

ciclomo'tore [tʃiklomo'tore] sm moped.

ci'clone [tʃi'klone] sm cyclone.

ciclos'tile [tʃiklos'tile] sm cyclostyle.

ci'cogna [tʃi'koɲɲa] sf stork.

ci'coria [tʃi'kɔrja] sf chicory.

ci'eco, a, chi, che ['tʃɛko] ag blind // sm/f blind man/woman.

ci'elo ['tʃɛlo] sm sky; (REL) heaven.

'cifra ['tʃifra] sf (numero) figure; numeral; (somma di denaro) sum, figure; (monogramma) monogram, initials pl; (codice) code, cipher; **ci'frare** vt to embroider with a monogram; to code.

'ciglio ['tʃiʎʎo] sm (margine) edge, verge; (pl(f) **ciglia**: delle palpebre) eye(lash); eye(lid); (sopracciglio) eyebrow.

'cigno ['tʃiɲɲo] sm swan.

cigo'lare [tʃigo'lare] vi to squeak, creak.

'Cile ['tʃile] sm: il ~ Chile.

cilecca [tʃi'lekka] sf: far ~ to fail.

cili'egia, gie o **ge** [tʃi'ljedʒa] sf cherry; **cili'egio** sm cherry tree.

cilin'drata [tʃilin'drata] sf (AUT) (cubic) capacity; **una macchina di grossa** ~ a big-engined car.

ci'lindro [tʃi'lindro] sm cylinder; (cappello) top hat.

'cima ['tʃima] sf (sommità) top; (di monte) top, summit; (estremità) end; **da** ~ **a fondo** from top to bottom; (fig) from beginning to end.

cimen'tare [tʃimen'tare] vt to put to the test.

'cimice ['tʃimitʃe] sf (ZOOL) bug; (puntina) drawing pin.

cimini'era [tʃimi'njɛra] sf chimney; (di nave) funnel.

cimi'tero [tʃimi'tɛro] sm cemetery.

ci'murro [tʃi'murro] sm (di cani) distemper.

'Cina ['tʃina] sf: la ~ China.

'cinema ['tʃinema] sm inv cinema; **cinematogra'fare** vt to film; **cine'presa** sf cine-camera.

ci'nese [tʃi'nese] ag, sm/f, sm Chinese inv.

ci'netico, a, ci, che [tʃi'nɛtiko] ag kinetic.

'cingere ['tʃindʒere] vt (attorniare) to surround, encircle; ~ **la vita con una cintura** to put a belt round one's waist.

'cinghia ['tʃingja] sf strap; (cintura, TECN) belt.

cinghi'ale [tʃin'gjale] sm wild boar.

cinguet'tare [tʃingwet'tare] vi to twitter.

'cinico, a, ci, che ['tʃiniko] ag cynical // sm/f cynic.

cin'quanta [tʃin'kwanta] num fifty; **cinquan'tesimo, a** num fiftieth.

cinquan'tina [tʃinkwan'tina] sf (serie): **una** ~ **(di)** about fifty; (età): **essere sulla** ~ to be about fifty.

'cinque ['tʃinkwe] num five; **avere** ~ **anni** to be five (years old); **il** ~ **dicembre 1982** the fifth of December 1982; **alle** ~ **(ora)** at five (o'clock).

cinque'cento [tʃinkwe'tʃento] num five hundred // sm: **il C**~ the sixteenth century.

'cinto, a ['tʃinto] pp di **cingere**.

cin'tura [tʃin'tura] sf belt; ~ **di salvataggio** lifebelt; ~ **di sicurezza** (AUT, AER) safety belt.

ciò [tʃɔ] pronome this; that; ~ **che** what; ~ **nondimeno** in spite of this (o that).

ci'occa, che ['tʃɔkka] *sf* (*di capelli*) lock.

ciocco'lata [tʃokko'lata] *sf* chocolate; (*bevanda*) (hot) chocolate; **cioccola'tino** *sm* chocolate; **ciocco'lato** *sm* chocolate.

cioè [tʃo'ɛ] *av* that is (to say).

ciondo'lare [tʃondo'lare] *vi* to dangle; (*fig*) to loaf (about); **ci'ondolo** *sm* pendant.

ci'otola ['tʃɔtola] *sf* bowl.

ci'ottolo ['tʃɔttolo] *sm* pebble; (*di strada*) cobble(stone).

ci'polla [tʃi'polla] *sf* onion; (*di tulipano etc*) bulb.

ci'presso [tʃi'prɛsso] *sm* cypress (tree).

'cipria ['tʃiprja] *sf* (face) powder.

cipri'ota, i, e [tʃipri'ɔta] *ag*, *sm/f* Cypriot.

'Cipro ['tʃipro] *sm* Cyprus.

'circa ['tʃirka] *av* about, roughly // *prep* about, concerning; **a mezzogiorno** ~ about midday.

'circo, chi ['tʃirko] *sm* circus.

circo'lare [tʃirko'lare] *vi* to circulate; (*AUT*) to drive (along), move (along) // *ag* circular // *sf* (*AMM*) circular; (*di autobus*) circle (line); **circolazi'one** *sf* circulation; (*AUT*): **la circolazione** (the) traffic.

'circolo ['tʃirkolo] *sm* circle.

circon'dare [tʃirkon'dare] *vt* to surround.

circonfe'renza [tʃirkonfe'rɛntsa] *sf* circumference.

circonvalazi'one [tʃirkonvallat'tsjone] *sf* ring road; (*per evitare una città*) by-pass.

circos'critto, a [tʃirkos'kritto] *pp di* **circoscrivere**

circos'crivere [tʃirkos'krivere] *vt* to circumscribe; (*fig*) to limit, restrict; **circoscrizi'one** *sf* (*AMM*) district, area; **circoscrizione elettorale** constituency.

circos'petto, a [tʃirkos'petto] *ag* circumspect, cautious.

circos'tante [tʃirkos'tante] *ag* surrounding, neighbouring.

circos'tanza [tʃirkos'tantsa] *sf* circumstance; (*occasione*) occasion.

cir'cuito [tʃir'kuito] *sm* circuit.

'ciste ['tʃiste] *sf* = **cisti.**

cis'terna [tʃis'tɛrna] *sf* tank, cistern.

'cisti ['tʃisti] *sf* cyst.

C.I.T. [tʃit] *abbr f di Compagnia Italiana Turismo.*

ci'tare [tʃi'tare] *vt* (*DIR*) to summon; (*autore*) to quote; (*a esempio, modello*) to cite; **citazi'one** *sf* summons *sg*; quotation; (*di persona*) mention.

ci'tofono [tʃi'tɔfono] *sm* entry phone; (*in uffici*) intercom.

città [tʃit'ta] *sf inv* town; (*importante*) city; ~ **universitaria** university campus.

cittadi'nanza [tʃittadi'nantsa] *sf* citizens *pl*, inhabitants *pl* of a town (o city); (*DIR*) citizenship.

citta'dino, a [tʃitta'dino] *ag* town *cpd*; city *cpd* // *sm/f* (*di uno Stato*) citizen; (*abitante di città*) towndweller.

ci'uco, a, chi, che ['tʃuko] *sm/f* ass, donkey.

ci'uffo ['tʃuffo] *sm* tuft.

ci'vetta [tʃi'vetta] *sf* (*ZOOL*) owl; (*fig: donna*) coquette, flirt.

'civico, a, ci, che ['tʃiviko] *ag* civic; (*museo*) municipal, town *cpd*; **city cpd.**

ci'vile [tʃi'vile] *ag* civil; (*non militare*) civilian; (*nazione*) civilized // *sm* civilian.

civiliz'zare [tʃivilid'dzare] *vt* to civilize; **civilizzazi'one** *sf* civilization.

civiltà [tʃivil'ta] *sf* civilization; (*cortesia*) civility.

ci'vismo [tʃi'vizmo] *sm* public spirit.

'clacson *sm inv* (*AUT*) horn.

cla'more *sm* (*frastuono*) din, uproar, clamour; (*fig*) outcry; **clamo'roso, a** *ag* noisy; (*fig*) sensational.

clandes'tino, a *ag* clandestine; (*POL*) underground, clandestine // *sm/f* stowaway.

clari'netto *sm* clarinet.

'classe *sf* class; **di** ~ (*fig*) with class; of excellent quality.

classi'cismo [klassi'tʃizmo] *sm* classicism.

'classico, a, ci, che *ag* classical; (*tradizionale: moda*) classic(al) // *sm* classic; classical author.

clas'sifica *sf* classification; (*SPORT*) placings *pl*.

classifi'care *vt* to classify; (*candidato, concorrente*) to grade; (*compito*) to mark; ~**rsi** *vr* to be placed; **classificazi'one** *sf* classification; grading; marking.

'clausola *sf* (*DIR*) clause.

'clava *sf* club.

clavi'cembalo [klavi'tʃembalo] *sm* harpsichord.

cla'vicola *sf* (*ANAT*) collar bone.

cle'mente *ag* merciful; (*clima*) mild; **cle'menza** *sf* mercy, clemency; mildness.

cleri'cale *ag* clerical.

'clero *sm* clergy.

cli'ente *sm/f* customer, client; **clien'tela** *sf* customers *pl*, clientèle.

'clima, i *sm* climate; **cli'matico, a, ci, che** *ag* climatic; **climatizzazi'one** *sf* (*TECN*) air conditioning.

'clinico, a, ci, che *ag* clinical // *sm* (*medico*) clinician // *sf* (*scienza*) clinical medicine; (*casa di cura*) clinic, nursing home; (*ospedale*) clinic.

clo'aca, che *sf* sewer.

cloro'filla *sf* chlorophyll.

cloro'formio *sm* chloroform.

club *sm inv* club.

coabi'tare *vi* to live together, live under the same roof.

coagu'lare *vt* to coagulate // *vi* (2), ~**rsi** *vr* to coagulate; (*latte*) to curdle.

coalizi'one [koalit'tsjone] *sf* coalition.

co'atto, a *ag* (*DIR*) compulsory, forced.

'cobra *sm inv* cobra.

coca'ina *sf* cocaine.

cocci'nella [kottʃi'nɛlla] *sf* ladybird.

'coccio ['kɔttʃo] *sm* earthenware; (*vaso*) earthenware pot; ~**i** *smpl* fragments (of pottery).

cocci'uto, a [kot'tʃuto] *ag* stubborn, pigheaded.

'cocco, chi *sm* (*pianta*) coconut palm; (*frutto*): **noce di ~** coconut // *sm/f* (*fam*) darling.

cocco'drillo *sm* crocodile.

cocco'lare *vt* to cuddle, fondle.

co'cente [ko'tʃente] *ag* (*anche fig*) burning.

co'comero *sm* watermelon.

co'cuzzolo [ko'kuttsolo] *sm* top; (*di capo, cappello*) crown.

'coda *sf* tail; (*fila di persone, auto*) queue; (*di abiti*) train; (*dell'occhio*) corner; **mettersi in ~** to queue (up); to join the queue; **~ di cavallo** (*acconciatura*) ponytail.

co'dardo, a *ag* cowardly // *sm/f* coward.

'codice ['koditʃe] *sm* code; **~ di avviamento postale (C.A.P.)** postal code; **~ della strada** highway code.

codifi'care *vt* (*DIR*) to codify; (*cifrare*) to code.

coe'rente *ag* coherent; **coe'renza** *sf* coherence.

coesi'one *sf* cohesion.

coe'sistere *vi* (2) to coexist.

coe'taneo, a *ag, sm/f* contemporary.

'cofano *sm* (*AUT*) bonnet; (*forziere*) chest.

'cogli ['koʎʎi] *prep* + *det vedi* **con.**

'cogliere ['koʎʎere] *vt* (*fiore, frutto*) to pick, gather; (*sorprendere*) to catch, surprise; (*bersaglio*) to hit; (*fig: momento opportuno etc*) to grasp, seize, take; (: *capire*) to grasp; **~ qd in flagrante** *o* **in fallo** to catch sb red-handed.

co'gnato, a [koɲ'ɲato] *sm/f* brother-/sister-in-law.

cognizi'one [koɲɲit'tsjone] *sf* knowledge.

co'gnome [koɲ'ɲome] *sm* surname.

'coi *prep* + *det vedi* **con.**

coinci'denza [kointʃi'dɛntsa] *sf* coincidence; (*FERR, AER, di autobus*) connection.

coin'volgere [koin'vɔldʒere] *vt*: **~ in** to involve in.

col *prep* + *det vedi* **con.**

cola'brodo *sm inv* strainer.

cola'pasta *sm inv* colander.

co'lare *vt* (*liquido*) to strain; (*pasta*) to drain; (*oro fuso*) to pour // *vi* (*sudore*) to drip; (*botte*) to leak; (*cera*) to melt; **~ a picco** *vt, vi* (*nave*) to sink.

co'lata *sf* (*di lava*) flow; (*FONDERIA*) casting.

colazi'one [kolat'tsjone] *sf* (*anche:* **prima ~**) breakfast; (*anche:* **seconda ~**) lunch; **fare ~** to have breakfast (*o* lunch).

co'lei *pronome vedi* **colui.**

co'lera *sm* (*MED*) cholera.

'colica *sf* (*MED*) colic.

'colla *sf* glue; (*di farina*) paste.

collabo'rare *vi* to collaborate; **~ a** to collaborate on; (*giornale*) to contribute to; **collabora'tore, 'trice** *sm/f* collaborator; contributor; **collaborazi'one** *sf* collaboration; contribution.

col'lana *sf* necklace; (*collezione*) collection, series.

col'lant [kɔ'lã] *sm inv* tights *pl.*

col'lare *sm* collar.

col'lasso *sm* (*MED*) collapse.

collau'dare *vt* to test, try out; **col'laudo** *sm* testing *q*; test.

'colle *sm* hill.

col'lega, ghi, ghe *sm/f* colleague.

collega'mento *sm* connection; (*MIL*) liaison.

colle'gare *vt* to connect, join, link; **~rsi** *vr* (*RADIO, TV*) to link up; **~rsi con** (*TEL*) to get through to.

col'legio [kol'lɛdʒo] *sm* college; (*convitto*) boarding school; **~ elettorale** (*POL*) constituency.

'collera *sf* anger.

col'lerico, a, ci, che *ag* quick-tempered, irascible.

col'letta *sf* collection.

collettività *sf* community.

collet'tivo, a *ag* collective; (*interesse*) general, everybody's; (*biglietto, visita etc*) group *cpd* // *sm* (*POL*) (political) group.

col'letto *sm* collar.

collezio'nare [kollettsjo'nare] *vt* to collect.

collezi'one [kollet'tsjone] *sf* collection.

colli'mare *vi* to correspond, coincide.

col'lina *sf* hill.

col'lirio *sm* eyewash.

collisi'one *sf* collision.

'collo *sm* neck; (*di abito*) neck, collar; (*pacco*) parcel; **~ del piede** instep.

colloca'mento *sm* (*impiego*) employment; (*disposizione*) placing, arrangement.

collo'care *vt* (*libri, mobili*) to place; (*persona: trovare un lavoro per*) to find a job for, place; (*COMM: merce*) to find a market for; **~rsi** *vr* to take one's place; to find a job.

col'loquio *sm* conversation, talk; (*ufficiale*) interview, talk; (*INS*) preliminary oral exam.

col'mare *vt*: **~ di** (*anche fig*) to fill with; (*dare in abbondanza*) to load *o* overwhelm with; **'colmo, a** *ag*: **colmo (di)** full (of) // *sm* summit, top; (*fig*) height; **al colmo della disperazione** in the depths of despair; **è il colmo!** it's the last straw!

co'lombo, a *sm/f* dove; pigeon.

co'lonia *sf* colony; (*per bambini*) holiday camp; **acqua di ~** (eau de) cologne; **coloni'ale** *ag* colonial // *sm/f* colonist, settler.

coloniz'zare [kolonid'dzare] *vt* to colonize.

co'lonna *sf* column; **~ vertebrale** spine, spinal column.

colon'nello *sm* colonel.

co'lono *sm* (*coltivatore*) tenant farmer.

colo'rante *sm* colouring.

colo'rare *vt* to colour; (*disegno*) to colour in.

co'lore *sm* colour; **a ~i** in colour, colour

cpd; **farne di tutti i** ~**i** to get up to all sorts of mischief.

colo'rito, a *ag* coloured; (*viso*) rosy, pink; (*linguaggio*) colourful // *sm* (*tinta*) colour; (*carnagione*) complexion.

co'loro *pronome pl vedi* **colui.**

colos'sale *ag* colossal, enormous.

co'losso *sm* colossus.

'colpa *sf* fault; (*biasimo*) blame; (*colpevolezza*) guilt; (*azione colpevole*) offence; (*peccato*) sin; **di chi è la** ~**?** whose fault is it?; **per** ~ **di** through, owing to; **col'pevole** *ag* guilty.

col'pire *vt* to hit, strike; (*fig*) to strike; **rimanere colpito da qc** to be amazed *o* struck by sth.

'colpo *sm* (*urto*) knock; (: *affettivo*) blow, shock; (: *aggressivo*) blow; (*di pistola*) shot; (*SPORT*) stroke; shot; blow; (*MED*) stroke; **di** ~ suddenly; **fare** ~ to make a strong impression; ~ **di grazia** coup de grâce; ~ **di sole** sunstroke; ~ **di Stato** coup d'état; ~ **di telefono** phone call; ~ **di testa** (sudden) impulse *o* whim; ~ **di vento** gust (of wind).

coltel'lata *sf* stab.

col'tello *sm* knife; ~ **a serramanico** clasp knife.

colti'vare *vt* to cultivate; (*verdura*) to grow, cultivate; (*MINERALOGIA*) to work; **coltiva'tore** *sm* farmer; **coltivazi'one** *sf* cultivation; growing; working.

'colto, a *pp di* **cogliere** // *ag* (*istruito*) cultured, educated.

'coltre *sf* blanket.

col'tura *sf* (*di terra*) cultivation; (*di verdura*) growing; cultivation.

co'lui, co'lei, *pl* **co'loro** *pronome* the one; ~ **che parla** the one *o* the man *o* the person who is speaking; **colei che amo** the one *o* the woman *o* the person (whom) I love.

'coma *sm inv* coma.

comanda'mento *sm* (*REL*) commandment.

coman'dante *sm* (*MIL*) commander, commandant; (*di reggimento*) commanding officer; (*NAUT, AER*) captain.

coman'dare *vt* to command; (*imporre*) to order, command; (*meccanismo*) to control; **co'mando** *sm* (*ingiunzione*) order, command; (*autorità*) command; (*TECN*) control.

combaci'are [kombat'tʃare] *vi* to meet; (*fig: coincidere*) to coincide, correspond.

combat'tente *ag* fighting // *sm* combatant; **ex**~~ ex-serviceman.

com'battere *vt* to fight; (*fig*) to combat, fight against // *vi* to fight; **combatti'mento** *sm* fight; fighting *q*; (*di pugilato*) match.

combi'nare *vt* to combine; (*organizzare*) to arrange; (*fam: fare*) to make, cause; ~**rsi** *vr* to combine; (*mettersi d'accordo*) to come to an agreement; **combinazi'one** *sf* combination; (*caso fortuito*) coincidence; (*biancheria*) combinations *pl*; (*tuta: da aviatore*) flying suit; (: *da operaio*) boiler

suit; **per combinazione** by chance.

combus'tibile *ag* combustible // *sm* fuel.

combusti'one *sf* combustion.

com'butta *sf* (*peg*) gang; **in** ~ in league.

'come *av* like; (*in qualità di*) as; (*interrogativo, esclamativo*) how; (*che cosa, prego*): ~**?** pardon?, sorry? // *cong* as; (*che, in quale modo*) how; (*appena che, quando*) as soon as; ~ **stai?** how are you?; ~ **sei cresciuto!** how you've grown!; ~ **se** as if, as though; *vedi* **così, tanto.**

co'meta *sf* comet.

'comico, a, ci, che *ag* (*TEATRO*) comic; (*buffo*) comical // *sm* (*attore*) comedian, comic actor; (*comicità*) comic spirit, comedy.

co'mignolo [ko'miɲɲolo] *sm* chimney top.

cominci'are [komin'tʃare] *vt, vi* to begin, start; ~ **a fare/col fare** to begin to do/by doing.

comi'tato *sm* committee.

comi'tiva *sf* party, group.

co'mizio [ko'mittsjo] *sm* (*POL*) meeting, assembly.

com'mando *sm inv* commando (squad).

com'media *sf* comedy; (*opera teatrale*) play; (: *che fa ridere*) comedy; (*fig*) playacting *q*; **commedi'ante** *sm/f* (*peg*) third-rate actor/actress; (: *fig*) sham.

commemo'rare *vt* to commemorate; **commemorazi'one** *sf* commemoration.

commen'tare *vt* to comment on; (*testo*) to annotate; (*RADIO, TV*) to give a commentary on; **commenta'tore, 'trice** *sm/f* commentator; **com'mento** *sm* comment; (*a un testo*) commentary, notes *pl*; (*RADIO, TV*) commentary.

commerci'ale [kommer'tʃale] *ag* commercial, trading; (*peg*) commercial.

commerci'ante [kommer'tʃante] *sm/f* trader, dealer; (*bottegaio*) shopkeeper.

commerci'are [kommer'tʃare] *vi*: ~ **in** to deal *o* trade in.

com'mercio [kom'mertʃo] *sm* trade, commerce; **essere in** ~ (*prodotto*) to be on the market *o* on sale; **essere nel** ~ (*persona*) to be in business; ~ **all'ingrosso/al minuto** wholesale/retail trade.

com'messo, a *pp di* **commettere** // *sm/f* shop assistant // *sm* (*impiegato subalterno*) clerk // *sf* (*COMM*) order; ~ **viaggiatore** commercial traveller.

commes'tibile *ag* edible.

com'mettere *vt* to commit.

commi'nare *vt* (*DIR*) to threaten; to inflict.

commise'rare *vt* to sympathize with, commiserate with.

commissari'ato *sm* (*AMM*) commissionership; (: *sede*) commissioner's office; (: *di polizia*) police station.

commis'sario *sm* commissioner; (*di pubblica sicurezza*) ≈ police superintendent; (*SPORT*) steward; (*membro di commissione*) member of a committee *o* board.

commissio'nario *sm* (*COMM*) selling agent.

commissi'one *sf* (*incarico*) message; errand; (*comitato, percentuale*) commission; (*COMM: ordinazione*) order; ~**i** *sfpl* (*acquisti*) shopping *sg*.

commit'tente *sm/f* (*COMM*) purchaser, buyer.

com'mosso, a *pp di* **commuovere.**

commo'vente *ag* moving.

commozi'one [kommot'tsjone] *sf* emotion, deep feeling; ~ **cerebrale** concussion.

commu'overe *vt* to move, affect; ~**rsi** *vr* to be moved.

commu'tare *vt* (*pena*) to commute; (*ELETTR*) to change *o* switch over.

comò *sm inv* chest of drawers.

como'dino *sm* bedside table.

comodità *sf inv* comfort; convenience.

'comodo, a *ag* comfortable; (*facile*) easy; (*conveniente*) convenient; (*utile*) useful, handy; (*persona*) easy-going // *sm* comfort; convenience; **con** ~ at one's convenience *o* leisure; **fare il proprio** ~ to do as one pleases; **far** ~ to be useful *o* handy.

compae'sano, a *sm/f* fellow-countryman; person from the same town.

com'pagine [kom'padʒine] *sf* (*squadra*) team.

compa'gnia [kompaɲ'ɲia] *sf* company; (*gruppo*) gathering.

com'pagno, a [kom'paɲɲo] *sm/f* (*di classe, gioco*) companion; (*POL*) comrade; (*COMM: socio*) partner; ~ **di squadra** team mate.

compa'rare *vt* to compare.

compara'tivo, a *ag, sm* comparative.

comparazi'one [komparat'tsjone] *sf* comparison.

compa'rire *vi* (2) to appear; (*spiccare: persona*) to stand out; **com'parso, a** *pp di* **comparire** // *sf* appearance; (*TEATRO*) walk-on; (*CINEMA*) extra.

compartecipazi'one [kompartetʃipat-'tsjone] *sf* sharing; (*quota*) share; ~ **agli utili** profit-sharing.

comparti'mento *sm* (*suddivisione*) division, compartment; (*FERR*) compartment; (*AMM*) department.

compassi'one *sf* compassion, pity; **avere** ~ **di qd** to feel sorry for sb, to pity sb; **compassio'nevole** *ag* compassionate.

com'passo *sm* (pair of) compasses *pl*; callipers *pl*.

compa'tibile *ag* (*scusabile*) excusable; (*conciliabile*) compatible.

compati'mento *sm* compassion; indulgence.

compa'tire *vt* (*aver compassione di*) to sympathize with, feel sorry for; (*scusare*) to make allowances for.

compatri'ota, i, e *sm/f* compatriot.

com'patto, a *ag* compact; (*roccia*) solid; (*folla*) dense; (*fig: partito*) united, close-knit.

compendi'are *vt* to summarize.

com'pendio *sm* summary; (*libro*) compendium.

compene'trare *vt* to permeate.

compen'sare *vt* (*equilibrare*) to compensate for, make up for; ~ **qd di** (*rimunerare*) to pay *o* remunerate sb for; (*risarcire*) to pay compensation to sb for; (*fig: fatiche, dolori*) to reward sb for; **com-'penso** *sm* compensation; payment, remuneration; reward; **in compenso** in compensation; (*in cambio*) in return.

'compera *etc* = **compra** *etc*.

compe'tente *ag* competent; (*mancia*) apt, suitable; **compe'tenza** *sf* competence; **competenze** *sfpl* (*onorari*) fees.

com'petere *vi* to compete, vie; (*DIR: spettare*): ~ **a** to lie within the competence of; **competi'tore, 'trice** *sm/f* competitor; **competizi'one** *sf* competition.

compia'cente [kompja'tʃente] *ag* courteous, obliging; **compia'cenza** *sf* courtesy.

compia'cere [kompja'tʃere] *vi*: ~ **a** to gratify, please // *vt* to humour; ~**rsi** *vr* (*provare soddisfazione*): ~**rsi di** *o* **per qc** to be delighted at sth; (*rallegrarsi*): ~**rsi con qd** to congratulate sb; (*degnarsi*): ~**rsi di fare** to be so good as to do; **compiaci'uto, a** *pp di* **compiacere.**

compi'angere [kom'pjandʒere] *vt* to sympathize with, feel sorry for; **com-pi'anto, a** *pp di* **compiangere.**

'compiere *vt* (*concludere*) to finish, end, complete; (*adempiere*) to carry out, fulfil; ~**rsi** *vr* (*avverarsi*) to be fulfilled, come true; ~ **gli anni** to have one's birthday.

compi'lare *vt* to compile.

com'pire *vb* = **compiere.**

compi'tare *vt* to spell out.

'compito *sm* (*incarico*) task, duty; (*dovere*) duty; (*INS*) exercise; (*: a casa*) homework.

com'pito, a *ag* well-mannered, polite.

comple'anno *sm* birthday.

complemen'tare *ag* complementary; (*INS: materia*) subsidiary.

comple'mento *sm* complement; (*MIL*) reserve (troops); ~ **oggetto** (*LING*) direct object.

complessità *sf* complexity.

comples'sivo, a *ag* (*globale*) comprehensive, overall; (*totale: cifra*) total.

com'plesso, a *ag* complex // *sm* (*PSIC, EDIL*) complex; (*MUS: corale*) ensemble; (*: orchestrina*) band; (*: di musica pop*) group; **in** *o* **nel** ~ on the whole.

comple'tare *vt* to complete.

com'pleto, a *ag* complete; (*teatro, autobus*) full // *sm* suit; **al** ~ full; (*tutti presenti*) all present.

compli'care *vt* to complicate; ~**rsi** *vr* to become complicated; **complicazi'one** *sf* complication.

'complice ['komplitʃe] *sm/f* accomplice.

complimen'tarsi *vr*: ~ **con** to congratulate.

compli'mento *sm* compliment; ~**i** *smpl*

(*cortesia eccessiva*) ceremony *sg*; (*ossequi*) regards, compliments; ~**il** congratulations!; **senza** ~**il** don't stand on ceremony!; make yourself at home!; help yourself!

complot'tare *vi* to plot, conspire.

com'plotto *sm* plot, conspiracy.

compo'nente *sm/f* member // *sm o f* component (part).

componi'mento *sm* (*DIR*) settlement; (*INS*) composition; (*poetico, teatrale*) work.

com'porre *vt* (*musica, testo*) to compose; (*formare*) to make up, form; (*motore*) to make up, put together; (*mettere in ordine*) to arrange; (*DIR: lite*) to settle; (*TIP*) to set.

comporta'mento *sm* behaviour.

compor'tare *vt* (*implicare*) to involve; (*consentire*) to permit, allow (of); ~**rsi** *vr* (*condursi*) to behave.

composi'tore, 'trice *sm/f* composer; (*TIP*) compositor, typesetter.

composizi'one [kompozit'tsjone] *sf* composition; (*DIR*) settlement.

com'posta *sf vedi* **composto**.

compos'tezza [kompos'tettsa] *sf* composure; decorum.

com'posto, a *pp di* **comporre** // *ag* (*persona*) composed, self-possessed; (: *decoroso*) dignified; (*formato da più elementi*) compound *cpd* // *sm* compound // *sf* (*CUC*) stewed fruit *q*; (*AGR*) compost.

'compra *sf* purchase.

com'prare *vt* to buy; **compra'tore, 'trice** *sm/f* buyer, purchaser.

com'prendere *vt* (*contenere*) to comprise, consist of; (*capire*) to understand.

comprensi'one *sf* understanding.

compren'sivo, a *ag* (*prezzo*): ~ **di** inclusive of; (*indulgente*) understanding.

com'preso, a *pp di* **comprendere** // *ag* (*incluso*) included.

com'pressa *sf vedi* **compresso**.

compressi'one *sf* compression; (*pressione*) pressure.

com'presso, a *pp di* **comprimere** // *ag* pressed; compressed; repressed // *sf* (*MED: garza*) compress; (: *pastiglia*) tablet.

com'primere *vt* (*premere*) to press; (*FISICA*) to compress; (*fig*) to repress.

compro'messo, a *pp di* **compromettere** // *sm* compromise.

compro'mettere *vt* to compromise.

compro'vare *vt* to confirm.

com'punto, a *ag* contrite; **compunzi'one** *sf* compunction.

compu'tare *vt* to calculate; (*addebitare*): ~ **qc a qd** to debit sb with sth; **computiste'ria** *sf* accounting, book-keeping; **'computo** *sm* calculation.

comu'nale *ag* municipal; town *cpd*, ≈ borough *cpd*.

comu'nanza [komu'nantsa] *sf* community.

co'mune *ag* common; (*consueto*) common, everyday; (*di livello medio*) average; (*ordinario*) ordinary // *sm* (*AMM*) commune, ≈ town council; (: *sede*) town

hail // *sf* (*di persone*) commune; **fuori del** ~ out of the ordinary; **mettere in** ~ to share.

comuni'care *vt* (*notizia*) to pass on, convey; (*malattia*) to pass on; (*ansia etc*) to communicate; (*trasmettere: calore etc*) to transmit, communicate; (*REL*) to administer communion to // *vi* to communicate; ~**rsi** *vr* (*propagarsi*): ~**rsi a** to spread to; (*REL*) to receive communion; **comunica-'tivo, a** *ag* (*sentimento*) infectious; (*persona*) communicative.

comuni'cato *sm* communiqué.

comunicazi'one [komunikat'tsjone] *sf* communication; (*TEL*): ~ (**telefonica**) (telephone) call; **dare la** ~ **a qd** to put sb through; **ottenere la** ~ to get through.

comuni'one *sf* communion.

comu'nismo *sm* communism; **comu-'nista, i, e** *ag, sm/f* communist.

comunità *sf inv* community; **C**~ **Economica Europea (C.E.E.)** European Economic Community (EEC).

co'munque *cong* however, no matter how // *av* (*in ogni modo*) in any case; (*tuttavia*) however, nevertheless.

con *prep* (*nei seguenti casi* **con** *può fondersi con l'articolo definito:* **con** + **il** = **col**, **con** + **gli** = **cogli**, **con** + **i** = **coi**) with; **partire col treno** to leave by train; ~ **mio grande stupore** to my great astonishment; ~ **tutto ciò** for all that.

co'nato *sm*: ~ **di vomito** retching.

'conca, che *sf* (*GEO*) valley.

'concavo, a *ag* concave.

con'cedere [kon't∫edere] *vt* (*accordare*) to grant; (*ammettere*) to admit, concede; ~**rsi qc** to treat o.s. to sth, to allow o.s. sth.

concentra'mento [kont∫entra'mento] *sm* concentration.

concen'trare [kont∫en'trare] *vt*, ~**rsi** *vr* to concentrate; **concentrazi'one** *sf* concentration.

concepi'mento [kont∫epi'mento] *sm* conception.

conce'pire [kont∫e'pire] *vt* (*bambino*) to conceive; (*progetto, idea*) to conceive (of); (*metodo, piano*) to devise; (*affetto, speranze*) to entertain.

con'cernere [kon't∫ernere] *vt* to concern.

concer'tare [kont∫er'tare] *vt* (*MUS*) to harmonize; (*ordire*) to devise, plan; ~**rsi** *vr* to agree.

con'certo [kon't∫erto] *sm* (*MUS*) concert; (: *componimento*) concerto.

concessio'nario [kont∫essjo'narjo] *sm* (*COMM*) agent, dealer.

concessi'one [kont∫es'sjone] *sf* concession.

con'cesso, a [kon't∫esso] *pp di* **concedere**.

con'cetto [kon't∫etto] *sm* (*pensiero, idea*) concept; (*opinione*) opinion.

concezi'one [kont∫et'tsjone] *sf* conception.

con'chiglia [kon'kiʎʎa] *sf* shell.

'concia ['kɔnt∫a] *sf* (*di pelle*) tanning; (*di*

tabacco) curing; (*sostanza*) tannin.

conci'are [kon'tʃare] *vt* (*pelle*) to tan; (*tabacco*) to cure; (*fig: ridurre in cattivo stato*) to beat up; ~**rsi** *vr* (*sporcarsi*) to get in a mess; (*vestirsi male*) to dress badly.

concili'abolo [kontʃi'ljabolo] *sm* clandestine meeting.

concili'are [kontʃi'ljare] *vt* to reconcile; (*contravvenzione*) to pay on the spot; (*favorire: sonno*) to be conducive to, induce; (*procurare: simpatia*) to gain; ~**rsi qc** to gain *o* win sth (for o.s.); ~**rsi qd** to win sb over; ~**rsi con** to be reconciled with; **conciliazi'one** *sf* reconciliation; (*DIR*) settlement.

con'cilio [kon'tʃiljo] *sm* (*REL*) council.

con'cime [kon'tʃime] *sm* manure; (*chimico*) fertilizer.

con'ciso, a [kon'tʃizo] *ag* concise, succinct.

conci'tato, a [kontʃi'tato] *ag* excited, emotional.

concitta'dino, a [kontʃitta'dino] *sm/f* fellow citizen.

con'clave *sm* conclave.

con'cludere *vt* to conclude; (*portare a compimento*) to conclude, finish, bring to an end; (*operare positivamente*) to achieve // *vi* (*essere convincente*) to be conclusive; ~**rsi** *vr* to come to an end, close; **conclusi'one** *sf* conclusion; (*risultato*) result; **conclu'sivo, a** *ag* conclusive; (*finale*) final; **con'cluso, a** *pp di* **concludere**.

concor'danza [konkor'dantsa] *sf* (*anche* *LING*) agreement.

concor'dare *vt* (*tregua*) to agree on; (*LING*) to make agree // *vi* to agree; **concor'dato** *sm* agreement; (*DIR*) composition; (*REL*) concordat.

con'corde *ag* (*d'accordo*) in agreement; (*simultaneo*) simultaneous.

con'cordia *sf* harmony, concord.

concor'rente *ag* competing; (*MAT*) concurrent // *sm/f* competitor; (*INS*) candidate; **concor'renza** *sf* competition.

con'correre *vi:* ~ (**in**) (*MAT*) to converge *o* meet (in); ~ (**a**) (*competere*) to compete (for); (: *INS: a una cattedra*) to apply (for); (*partecipare: a un'impresa*) to take part (in), contribute (to); **con'corso, a** *pp di* **concorrere** // *sm* competition; (*INS*) competitive examination.

con'creto, a *ag* concrete.

concussi'one *sf* (*DIR*) extortion.

con'danna *sf* sentence; conviction; condemnation.

condan'nare *vt* (*DIR*): ~ **a** to sentence to; ~ **per** to convict of; (*disapprovare*) to condemn; **condan'nato, a** *sm/f* convict.

conden'sare *vt*, ~**rsi** *vr* to condense; **condensazi'one** *sf* condensation.

condi'mento *sm* seasoning; dressing.

con'dire *vt* to season; (*insalata*) to dress.

condiscen'dente [kondiʃʃen'dɛnte] *ag* compliant; indulgent, easy-going.

condi'scendere [kondiʃ'ʃɛndere] *vi:* ~ **a**

to agree to; **condi'sceso, a** *pp di* **condiscendere**.

condi'videre *vt* to share; **condi'viso, a** *pp di* **condividere**.

condizio'nale [kondittsjo'nale] *ag* conditional // *sm* (*LING*) conditional // *sf* (*DIR*) suspended sentence.

condizio'nare [kondittsjo'nare] *vt* to condition; (*determinare*) to determine.

condizi'one [kondit'tsjone] *sf* condition; ~**i** *sfpl* (*di pagamento etc*) terms, conditions; **a** ~ **che** on condition that, provided that.

condogli'anze [kondoʎ'ʎantse] *sfpl* condolences.

condo'minio *sm* joint ownership; (*edificio*) jointly-owned building.

condo'nare *vt* (*DIR*) to remit; **con'dono** *sm* remission.

con'dotta *sf vedi* **condotto**.

con'dotto, a *pp di* **condurre** // *ag:* **medico** ~ local authority doctor (*in country district*) // *sm* (*canale, tubo*) pipe, conduit; (*ANAT*) duct // *sf* (*modo di comportarsi*) conduct, behaviour; (*di un affare etc*) handling; (*di acqua*) piping; (*incarico sanitario*) country medical practice controlled by a local authority.

condu'cente [kondu'tʃɛnte] *sm* driver.

con'durre *vt* to conduct; (*azienda*) to manage; (*accompagnare: bambino*) to take; (*automobile*) to drive; (*trasportare: acqua, gas*) to convey, conduct; (*fig*) to lead // *vi* to lead; **condursi** *vr* to behave, conduct o.s.; ~ **una vita felice** to lead a happy life.

condut'tore *sm* (*conducente*) driver; (*FERR*) guard; (*ELETTR, FISICA*) conductor.

con'farsi *vr:* ~ **a** to suit, agree with.

confederazi'one [konfederat'tsjone] *sf* confederation.

confe'renza [konfe'rɛntsa] *sf* (*discorso*) lecture; (*riunione*) conference; **conferenzi'ere, a** *sm/f* lecturer.

confe'rire *vt:* ~ **qc a qd** to give sth to sb, bestow sth on sb // *vi* to confer.

con'ferma *sf* confirmation.

confer'mare *vt* to confirm.

confes'sare *vt*, ~**rsi** *vr* to confess; **confessio'nale** *ag, sm* confessional; **confessi'one** *sf* confession; (*setta religiosa*) denomination; **confes'sore** *sm* confessor.

con'fetto *sm* sugared almond; (*MED*) pill.

confezio'nare [konfettsjo'nare] *vt* (*vestito*) to make (up); (*merci, pacchi*) to package.

confezi'one [konfet'tsjone] *sf* tailoring; dressmaking; packaging; ~**i** *sfpl* garments, clothes; ~ **regalo** gift pack.

confic'care *vt:* ~ **qc in** to hammer *o* drive sth into; ~**rsi** *vr* to stick.

confi'dare *vi:* ~ **in** to confide in, rely on // *vt* to confide; ~**rsi con qd** to confide in sb; **confi'dente** *sm/f* (*persona amica*) confidant/confidante; (*spia*) informer; **confi'denza** *sf* (*familiarità*) intimacy, familiarity; (*fiducia*) trust, confidence; (*rivelazione*) confidence; **confidenzi'ale** *ag* familiar, friendly; (*notizia*) confidential.

configu'rarsi *vr*: ~ a to assume the shape *o* form of; **configurazi'one** *sf* configuration. .

confi'nare *vi*: ~ **con** to border on // *vt* (*POL*) to intern; (*fig*) to confine; ~**rsi** *vr* (*isolarsi*): ~**rsi in** to shut o.s. up in; (*fig: limitarsi*): ~**rsi a** to confine o.s. to.

con'fine *sm* boundary; (*di paese*) border, frontier.

con'fino *sm* internment.

confis'care *vt* to confiscate.

conflagrazi'one [konflagrat'tsjone] *sf* conflagration.

con'flitto *sm* conflict.

conflu'enza [konflu'entsa] *sf* (*di fiumi*) confluence; (*di strade*) junction.

conflu'ire *vi* (*fiumi*) to flow into each other, meet; (*strade*) to meet.

con'fondere *vt* to mix up, confuse; (*imbarazzare*) to embarrass; ~**rsi** *vr* (*mescolarsi*) to mingle; (*turbarsi*) to be confused; (*sbagliare*) to get mixed up.

confor'mare *vt* (*adeguare*): ~ a to adapt *o* conform to // *vr*: ~**rsi (a)** to conform (to).

conforme'mente *av* accordingly; ~ **a** in accordance with.

confor'mista, i, e *sm/f* conformist.

confor'tare *vt* to comfort, console; **confor'tevole** *ag* (*consolante*) comforting; (*comodo*) comfortable; **con'forto** *sm* comfort, consolation; comfort.

confron'tare *vt* to compare.

con'fronto *sm* comparison; **in** *o* **a** ~ **di** in comparison with, compared to; **nei miei** (*o* **tuoi** *etc*) ~**i** towards me (*o* you *etc*).

confusi'one *sf* confusion; (*imbarazzo*) embarrassment.

con'fuso, a *pp di* **confondere** // *ag* (*vedi confondere*) confused; embarrassed.

confu'tare *vt* to refute.

conge'dare [kondʒe'dare] *vt* to dismiss; (*MIL*) to demob; ~**rsi** *vr* to take one's leave; **con'gedo** *sm* (*anche MIL*) leave; **prendere congedo da qd** to take one's leave of sb; **congedo assoluto** (*MIL*) discharge.

conge'gnare [kondʒeɲ'ɲare] *vt* to construct, put together; **con'gegno** *sm* device, mechanism.

conge'lare [kondʒe'lare] *vt* to freeze; **congela'tore** *sm* freezer.

con'genito, a [kon'dʒɛnito] *ag* congenital.

congestio'nare [kondʒestjo'nare] *vt* to congest.

congesti'one [kondʒes'tjone] *sf* congestion.

conget'tura [kondʒet'tura] *sf* conjecture, supposition.

con'giungere [kon'dʒundʒere] *vt* to join (together); (*porre in comunicazione*) to connect, link (up); ~**rsi** *vr* to join (together); to connect, link (up).

congiunti'vite [kondʒunti'vite] *sf* conjunctivitis.

congiun'tivo [kondʒun'tivo] *sm* (*LING*) subjunctive.

congi'unto, a [kon'dʒunto] *pp di* **congiungere** // *ag* (*unito*) joined; (: *da parentela*) related.

congiun'tura [kondʒun'tura] *sf* (*giuntura*) junction, join; (*ANAT*) joint; (*circostanza*) juncture; (*ECON*) economic situation.

congiunzi'one [kondʒun'tsjone] *sf* (*LING*) conjunction.

congi'ura [kon'dʒura] *sf* conspiracy; **congiu'rare** *vi* to conspire.

conglome'rato *sm* (*GEO*) conglomerate; (*fig*) conglomeration; (*EDIL*) concrete.

congratu'larsi *vr*: ~ **con qd per qc** to congratulate sb on sth.

congratulazi'oni [kongratulat'tsjoni] *sfpl* congratulations.

congrega, ghe *sf* band, bunch.

congregazi'one [kongregat'tsjone] *sf* congregation.

con'gresso *sm* congress.

conguagli'are [kongwaʎ'ʎare] *vt* to balance; **congu'aglio** *sm* balancing, adjusting; (*somma di denaro*) balance.

coni'are *vt* to mint, coin; (*fig*) to coin.

'conico, a, ci, che *ag* conical.

co'nifera *sf* conifer.

co'niglio [ko'niʎʎo] *sm* rabbit.

coniu'gare *vt* (*LING*) to conjugate; ~**rsi** *vr* to get married; **coniugazi'one** *sf* (*LING*) conjugation.

'coniuge ['kɔnjudʒe] *sm/f* spouse.

connazio'nale [konnattsjo'nale] *sm/f* fellow-countryman/woman.

connessi'one *sf* connection.

con'nesso, a *pp di* **connettere**.

con'nettere *vt* to connect, join // *vi* (*fig*) to think straight.

conni'vente *ag* conniving.

conno'tati *smpl* distinguishing marks.

'cono *sm* cone; ~ **gelato** ice-cream cone.

cono'scente [konoʃ'ʃente] *sm/f* acquaintance.

cono'scenza [konoʃ'ʃentsa] *sf* (*il sapere*) knowledge *q*; (*persona*) acquaintance; (*facoltà sensoriale*) consciousness *q*; **perdere** ~ to lose consciousness.

co'noscere [ko'noʃʃere] *vt* to know; **ci siamo conosciuti a Firenze** we (first) met in Florence; **conosci'tore, 'trice** *sm/f* connoisseur; **conosci'uto, a** *pp di* **conoscere** // *ag* well-known.

con'quista *sf* conquest.

conquis'tare *vt* to conquer; (*fig*) to gain, win.

consa'crare *vt* (*REL*) to consecrate; (: *sacerdote*) to ordain; (*dedicare*) to dedicate; (*fig: uso etc*) to sanction; ~**rsi a** to dedicate o.s. to.

consangu'ineo, a *sm/f* blood relation.

consa'pevole *ag*: ~ **di** aware *o* conscious of; **consapevo'lezza** *sf* awareness, consciousness.

'conscio, a, sci, sce ['kɔnʃo] *ag*: ~ **di** aware *o* conscious of.

consecu'tivo, a *ag* consecutive;

(*successivo: giorno*) following, next.

con'segna [kon'seɲɲa] *sf* delivery; (*merce consegnata*) consignment; (*custodia*) trust, custody; (*MIL: ordine*) orders *pl*; (: *punizione*) confinement to barracks; (*DIR: di malfattore*) handing over; **alla ~ on delivery; dare qc in ~ a qd** to entrust sth to sb.

conse'gnare [konseɲ'ɲare] *vt* to deliver; (*affidare*) to entrust, hand over; (*MIL*) to confine to barracks.

consegu'ente *ag* consequent.

consegu'enza [konse'gwɛntsa] *sf* consequence; **per *o* di ~** consequently.

consegu'ire *vt* to achieve // *vi* (2) to follow, result.

con'senso *sm* consent; (*fra due o più persone*) agreement.

consen'tire *vi*: **~ a** to consent *o* agree to // *vt* to allow, permit.

con'serva *sf* (*CUC*) preserve; **~ di frutta** jam; **~ di pomodoro** tomato purée.

conser'vare *vt* (*CUC*) to preserve; (*custodire*) to keep; (: *dalla distruzione etc*) to preserve, conserve; **~rsi** *vr* to keep; **~rsi sano** to keep healthy.

conserva'tore, 'trice *sm/f* (*POL*) conservative.

conservazi'one [konservat'tsjone] *sf* preservation.

conside'rare *vt* to consider; (*reputare*) to consider, regard; **~ molto qd** to think highly of sb; **considerazi'one** *sf* consideration; regard, esteem; **conside- 'revole** *ag* considerable.

consigli'are [konsiʎ'ʎare] *vt* (*persona*) to advise; (*metodo, azione*) to recommend, advise, suggest; **~rsi con qd** to ask sb for advice; **consigli'ere, a** *sm/f* adviser // *sm:* **consigliere d'amministrazione** board member; **consigliere comunale** town councillor; **con'siglio** *sm* (*suggerimento*) advice *q*, piece of advice; (*assemblea*) council; **consiglio d'amministrazione** board; **il Consiglio dei Ministri** (*POL*) ≈ the Cabinet.

consis'tente *ag* thick; solid; (*fig*) sound, valid; **consis'tenza** *sf* consistency, thickness; solidity; validity.

con'sistere *vi*: **~ in** to consist of; **consis- 'tito, a** *pp di* **consistere.**

conso'iare *ag* consular // *vt* (*confortare*) to console, comfort; (*rallegrare*) to cheer up; **~rsi** *vr* to be comforted; to cheer up.

conso'lato *sm* consulate.

consolazi'one [konsolat'tsjone] *sf* consolation *q*, comfort *q*.

'console *sm* consul.

consoli'dare *vt* to strengthen, reinforce; (*MIL, terreno*) to consolidate; **~rsi** *vr* to consolidate.

conso'nante *sf* consonant.

conso'nanza [konso'nantsa] *sf* consonance.

con'sorte *sm/f* consort.

con'sorzio [kon'sɔrtsjo] *sm* consortium.

con'stare (2) *vi*: **~ di** to consist of // *vb impers:* **mi consta che** it has come to my

knowledge that, it appears that.

consta'tare *vt* to establish, verify; (*notare*) to notice, observe.

consu'eto, a *ag* habitual, usual; **consue- 'tudine** *sf* habit, custom; (*usanza*) custom.

consu'lente *sm/f* consultant; **consu- 'lenza** *sf* consultancy.

consul'tare *vt* to consult; **~rsi con qd** to seek the advice of sb; **consultazi'one** *sf* consultation; **consultazioni** *sfpl* (*POL*) talks.

consu'mare *vt* (*logorare: abiti, scarpe*) to wear out; (*usare*) to consume, use up; (*mangiare, bere*) to consume; (*DIR*) to consummate; **~rsi** *vr* to wear out; to be used up; (*anche fig*) to be consumed; (*combustibile*) to burn out; **consuma'tore** *sm* consumer; **consumazi'one** *sf* consumption; (*bibita*) drink; (*spuntino*) snack; (*DIR*) consummation; **con'sumo** *sm* consumption; wear; use.

consun'tivo *sm* (*ECON*) final balance.

con'sunto, a *ag* worn-out; (*viso*) wasted.

con'tabile *ag* accounts *cpd*, accounting // *sm/f* accountant; **contabilità** *sf* (*attività, tecnica*) accounting, accountancy; (*insieme dei libri etc*) books *pl*, accounts *pl*; (*ufficio*) accounts department.

conta'dino, a *sm/f* countryman/woman; farm worker; (*peg*) peasant.

contagi'are [konta'dʒare] *vt* to infect.

con'tagio [kon'tadʒo] *sm* infection; (*per contatto diretto*) contagion; **contagi'oso, a** *ag* infectious; contagious.

contami'nare *vt* to contaminate; **contaminazi'one** *sf* contamination.

con'tante *sm* cash; **pagare in ~i** to pay cash.

con'tare *vt* to count; (*considerare*) to consider // *vi* to count, be of importance; **~ su qd** to count *o* rely on sb; **~ di fare qc** to intend to do sth; **conta'tore** *sm* meter.

contat'tare *vt* to contact.

con'tatto *sm* contact.

'conte *sm* count.

conteggi'are [konted'dʒare] *vt* to charge, put on the bill; **con'teggio** *sm* calculation; **conteggio alla rovescia** countdown.

con'tegno [kon'teɲɲo] *sm* (*comportamen- to*) behaviour; (*atteggiamento*) attitude; **conte'gnoso, a** *ag* reserved, dignified.

contem'plare *vt* to contemplate, gaze at; (*DIR*) to make provision for.

contempo'raneo, a *ag, sm/f* contemporary.

conten'dente *sm/f* opponent, adversary.

con'tendere *vi* (*competere*) to compete; (*litigare*) to quarrel // *vt* to contest.

conte'nere *vt* to contain; **conteni'tore** *sm* container.

conten'tare *vt* to please, satisfy; **~rsi di** to be satisfied with, content o.s. with.

conten'tezza [konten'tettsa] *sf* contentment.

con'tento, a *ag* pleased, glad; **~ di** pleased with.

conte'nuto sm contents pl; (argomento) content.

con'teso, a pp di **contendere** // sf dispute, argument.

con'tessa sf countess.

contes'tare vt (DIR) to notify; (fig) to dispute.

con'testo sm context.

con'tiguo, a ag: ~ (a) adjacent (to).

continen'tale ag, sm/f continental.

conti'nente ag continent // sm (GEO) continent; (: terra ferma) mainland; **conti'nenza** sf continence.

contin'gente [kontin'dʒɛnte] sm (COMM) quota; (MIL) contingent; **contin'genza** sf circumstance.

continu'are vt to continue (with), go on with // vi to continue, go on; ~ **a fare qc** to go on o continue doing sth; **continua-zi'one** sf continuation.

continuità sf continuity.

con'tinuo, a ag (numerazione) continuous; (pioggia) continual, constant; (ELETTR): **corrente** ~**a** direct current; **di** ~ continually.

'conto sm (calcolo) calculation; (COMM, ECON) account; (di ristorante, albergo) bill; (fig: stima) consideration, esteem; **fare i** ~**i con qd** to settle one's account with sb; **fare** ~ **su qd/qc** to count o rely on sb; **rendere** ~ **a qd di qc** to be accountable to sb for sth; **tener** ~ **di qd/qc** to take sb/sth into account; **per** ~ **di** on behalf of; **per** ~ **mio** as far as I'm concerned; **a** ~ **corrente** current account; **a** ~**i fatti, in fin dei** ~**i** all things considered.

con'torcere [kon'tortʃere] vt to twist; (panni) to wring (out); ~**rsi** vr to twist, writhe.

contor'nare vt to surround.

con'torno sm (linea) outline, contour; (ornamento) border; (CUC) vegetables pl.

contorsi'one sf contortion.

con'torto, a pp di **contorcere**.

contrabbandi'ere, a sm/f smuggler.

contrab'bando sm smuggling, contraband; **merce di** ~ contraband, smuggled goods pl.

contraccambi'are vt (favore etc) to return; **contrac'cambio** sm return; **in contraccambio di** in return o exchange for.

contrac'colpo sm rebound; (di arma da fuoco) recoil; (fig) repercussion.

contrad'detto, a pp di **contraddire**.

contrad'dire vt to contradict; **contraddit'torio, a** ag contradictory // sm debate; **contraddizi'one** sf contradiction.

contraf'fare vt (persona) to mimic; (alterare: voce) to disguise; (firma) to forge, counterfeit; **contraf'fatto, a** pp di **contraffare** // ag counterfeit; **contraffazi'one** sf mimicking q; disguising q; forging q; (cosa contraffatta) forgery.

con'tralto sm (MUS) contralto.

contrap'peso sm counterbalance, counterweight.

contrap'porre vt (opporre) to oppose, set against; **contrap'posto, a** pp di **contrapporre**.

contraria'mente av: ~ **a** contrary to.

contrari'are vt (contrastare) to thwart, oppose; (irritare) to annoy, bother; ~**rsi** vr to get annoyed.

contrarietà sf adversity; (fig) aversion.

con'trario, a ag opposite; (sfavorevole) unfavourable // sm opposite; ~ **a** contrary to; **al** ~ on the contrary.

con'trarre vt, **contrarsi** vr to contract.

contrasse'gnare [kontrasseɲ'nare] vt to mark; **contras'segno** sm mark; (distintivo) distinguishing mark.

contras'tante ag contrasting.

contras'tare vt (avversare) to oppose; (impedire) to bar; (negare: diritto) to contest, dispute // vi: ~ (**con**) (essere in disaccordo) to contrast (with); (lottare) to struggle (with); **con'trasto** sm contrast; (conflitto) conflict; (litigio) dispute.

contrat'tacco sm counterattack.

contrat'tare vt, vi to negotiate.

contrat'tempo sm hitch.

con'tratto, a pp di **contrarre** // sm contract; **contrattu'ale** ag contractual.

contravve'leno sm antidote.

contravve'nire vi: ~ **a** (legge) to contravene; (obbligo) to fail to meet; **contravvenzi'one** sf contravention; (ammenda) fine.

contrazi'one [kontrat'tsjone] sf contraction; (di prezzi etc) reduction.

contribu'ente sm/f taxpayer; ratepayer.

contribu'ire vi to contribute; **contri'buto** sm contribution; (tassa) tax.

con'trito, a ag contrite, penitent.

'contro prep against; ~ **di me/lui** against me/him; ~ **pagamento** (COMM) on payment // prefisso: **contro'battere** vt (fig: a parole) to answer back; (: confutare) to refute; **controfi'gura** sf (CINEMA) double; **controfir'mare** vt to countersign.

control'lare vt (accertare) to check; (sorvegliare) to watch, control; (tenere nel proprio potere, fig: dominare) to control; **con'trollo** sm check; watch; control; **controllo delle nascite** birth control; **control'lore** sm (FERR, AUTOBUS) (ticket) inspector.

controprodu'cente [kontroprodu'tʃɛnte] ag producing the opposite effect.

contro'senso sm (contraddizione) contradiction in terms; (assurdità) nonsense.

controspio'naggio [kontrospio'naddʒo] sm counterespionage.

contro'versia sf controversy.

contro'verso, a ag controversial.

contro'voglia [kontro'vɔʎʎa] av unwillingly.

contu'macia [kontu'matʃa] sf (DIR) default.

contur'bare vt to disturb, upset.

contusi'one sf (MED) bruise.
convale'scente [konvaleʃˈʃɛnte] ag, sm/f convalescent; **convale'scenza** sf convalescence.
convali'dare vt to confirm.
con'vegno [konˈveɲɲo] sm (incontro) meeting; (congresso) convention, congress; (luogo) meeting place.
conve'nevoli smpl civilities.
conveni'ente ag suitable; (pratico) convenient, handy; (vantaggioso) profitable, advantageous; (prezzo) cheap; **conveni'enza** sf suitability; convenience; advantage; **le convenienze** sfpl social conventions.
conve'nire vi (2: riunirsi) to gather, assemble; (concordare) to agree; (essere opportuno, addirsi) to be suitable; (tornare utile) to be worthwhile // vb impers (2): **conviene fare questo** it is advisable to do this; **conviene andarsene** we should go; **ne convengo I** agree.
con'vento sm (di frati) monastery; (di suore) convent.
convenzio'nale [konventsjoˈnale] ag conventional.
convenzi'one [konvenˈtsjone] sf (DIR) agreement; (nella società) convention; **le ~ i** sfpl convention sg, social conventions.
conver'gente [konverˈdʒente] ag convergent.
con'vergere [konˈverdʒere] vi (2) to converge.
conver'sare vi to converse.
conversazi'one [konversatˈtsjone] sf conversation.
conversi'one sf conversion.
con'verso, a pp di **convergere**.
conver'tire vt (trasformare) to change; (POL, REL) to convert; **~rsi** vr: **~rsi (in)** to change (to); **~rsi (a)** to be converted (to); **conver'tito, a** sm/f convert.
con'vesso, a ag convex.
con'vincere [konˈvintʃere] vt to convince; **~ qd di qc** to convince sb of sth; **~ qd a fare qc** to persuade sb to do sth; **con'vinto, a** pp di **convincere**; **convinzi'one** sf conviction, firm belief.
convis'suto, a pp di **convivere**.
con'vitto sm (INS) boarding school; **convit'tore, 'trice** sm/f boarder.
con'vivere vi to live together.
convo'care vt to call, convene; (DIR) to summon; **convocazi'one** sf meeting; summons sg.
convogli'are [konvoʎˈʎare] vt to convey; (dirigere) to direct, send; **con'voglio** sm (di veicoli) convoy; (FERR) train; **convoglio funebre** funeral procession.
convul'sione sf convulsion.
con'vulso, a ag (pianto) violent, convulsive; (attività) feverish.
coope'rare vi: **~ (a)** to cooperate (in); **coope'rativa** sf cooperative; **coopera-zi'one** sf cooperation.
coordi'nare vt to coordinate; **coordi-'nate** sfpl (MAT, GEO) coordinates; **coordinazi'one** sf coordination.

co'perchio [koˈperkjo] sm cover; (di pentola) lid.
co'perta sf cover; (di lana) blanket; (da viaggio) rug; (NAUT) deck.
coper'tina sf (STAMPA) cover, jacket.
co'perto, a pp di **coprire** // ag covered; (cielo) overcast // sm place setting; (posto a tavola) place; (al ristorante) cover charge; **~ di** covered in o with.
coper'tone sm (telo impermeabile) tarpaulin; (AUT) rubber tyre.
coper'tura sf (anche ECON, MIL) cover; (di edificio) roofing.
'copia sf copy; (stesura) draught, copy; **brutta/bella ~** rough/final draft.
copi'are vt to copy; **copia'trice** sf copier, copying machine.
copi'one sm (CINEMA, TEATRO) script.
'coppa sf (bicchiere) goblet; (per frutta, gelato) dish; (trofeo) cup, trophy; **~ dell'olio** oil sump.
'coppia sf couple.
coprifu'oco, chi sm curfew.
copri'letto sm bedspread.
co'prire vt to cover; (occupare: carica, posto) to hold; **~rsi** vr (cielo) to cloud over; (vestirsi) to wrap up, cover up; (ECON) to cover o.s.; **~rsi di** (fiori, muffa) to become covered in.
co'raggio [koˈraddʒo] sm courage, bravery; **coraggi'oso, a** ag courageous, brave.
co'rale ag choral; (approvazione) unanimous.
co'rallo sm coral.
co'rano sm (REL) Koran.
co'razza [koˈrattsa] sf armour; (di animali) carapace, shell; (MIL) armour(-plating); **coraz'zata** sf battleship.
corbelle'ria sf stupid action; howler; **~e** sfpl nonsense q.
'corda sf cord; (fune) rope; (spago, MUS) string; **tenere sulla ~ qd** to keep sb on tenterhooks; **tagliare la ~** to slip away, sneak off; **~e vocali** vocal cords.
cordi'ale ag cordial, warm // sm (bevanda) cordial.
cor'doglio [korˈdɔʎʎo] sm grief; (lutto) mourning.
cor'done sm cord, string; (linea: di polizia) cordon; **~ ombelicale** umbilical chord.
coreogra'fia sf choreography.
core'ografo, a sm/f choreographer.
cori'andoli smpl confetti sg.
cori'care vt to put to bed; **~rsi** vr to go to bed.
'corna sfpl vedi **corno**.
cor'nacchia [korˈnakkja] sf crow.
corna'musa sf bagpipes pl.
'cornea sf (ANAT) cornea.
cor'netta sf (MUS) cornet; (TEL) receiver.
cor'netto sm (CUC) croissant; **~ acustico** ear trumpet.
cor'nice [korˈnitʃe] sf frame.
'corno sm (ZOOL: pl(f) **~a**, MUS) horn; **fare le ~a a qd** to be unfaithful to sb; **cor'nuto, a** ag (con corna) horned; (faml:

marito) cuckolded // *sm* (*fam!*) cuckold; (: *insulto*) bastard (!).

'**coro** *sm* chorus; (*REL*) choir.

co'**rona** *sf* crown; (*di fiori*) wreath; ~ **del rosario** rosary, rosary beads *pl*; coro-'**nare** *vt* to crown.

'**corpo** *sm* body; (*cadavere*) (dead) body; (*militare, diplomatico*) corps *inv*; (*di opere*) corpus; **prendere** ~ to take shape; **a** ~ **a** ~ hand-to-hand; ~ **di ballo** corps de ballet; ~ **di guardia** guardroom; ~ **insegnante** teaching staff.

corpo'**rale** *ag* bodily; (*punizione*) corporal.

corpora'**tura** *sf* build, physique.

corporazi'**one** [korporat'tsjone] *sf* corporation.

cor'**poreo, a** *ag* bodily, physical.

corpu'**lento, a** *ag* stout.

corre'**dare** *vt*: ~ **di** to provide *o* furnish with; cor'**redo** *sm* equipment; (*di sposa*) trousseau.

cor'**reggere** [kor'rɛddʒere] *vt* to correct; (*compiti*) to correct, mark.

cor'**rente** *ag* (*fiume*) flowing; (*acqua del rubinetto*) running; (*moneta, prezzo*) current; (*comune*) everyday // *sm*: **essere al** ~ to be well-informed // *sf* (*movimento di liquido*) current, stream; (*spiffero*) draught; (*ELETTR, METEOR*) current; (*fig*) trend, tendency.

'**correre** *vi* (2) to run; (*precipitarsi*) to rush; (*partecipare a una gara*) to race, run; (*fig: diffondersi*) to go round // *vt* (*SPORT: gara*) to compete in; (*rischio*) to run; (*pericolo*) to face; ~ **dietro a qd** to run after sb.

cor'**retto, a** *pp di* **correggere** // *ag* (*comportamento*) correct, proper.

correzi'**one** [korret'tsjone] *sf* correction; marking; ~ **di bozze** proofreading.

corri'**doio** *sm* corridor.

corri'**dore** *sm* (*SPORT*) runner; (: *su veicolo*) racer.

corri'**era** *sf* coach, bus.

corri'**ere** *sm* (*diplomatico, di guerra*) courier; (*posta*) mail, post; (*COMM*) carrier.

corri'**gendo, a** [korri'dʒɛndo] *sm/f* (*DIR*) young offender.

corrispon'**dente** *ag* corresponding // *sm/f* correspondent.

corrispon'**denza** [korrispon'dɛntsa] *sf* correspondence.

corris'**pondere** *vi* to correspond; (*stanze*) to communicate; (*fig: contraccambiare*): ~ **a** to return; corris'**posto, a** *pp di* **corrispondere**.

corrobo'**rare** *vt* to strengthen, fortify; (*fig*) to corroborate, bear out.

cor'**rodere** *vt*, ~**rsi** *vr* to corrode.

cor'**rompere** *vt* to corrupt; (*comprare*) to bribe.

corrosi'**one** *sf* corrosion.

corro'**sivo, a** *ag* corrosive.

cor'**roso, a** *pp di* **corrodere.**

cor'**rotto, a** *pp di* **corrompere** // *ag* corrupt.

corrucci'**arsi** [korrut'tʃarsi] *vr* to grow angry *o* vexed.

corru'**gare** *vt* to wrinkle; ~ **la fronte** to knit one's brows.

corruzi'**one** [korrut'tsjone] *sf* corruption; bribery.

'**corsa** *sf* running *q*; (*gara*) race; (*di autobus, taxi*) journey, trip; **fare una** ~ to run, dash; (*SPORT*) to run a race.

cor'**sia** *sf* (*AUT, SPORT*) lane; (*di ospedale*) ward.

cor'**sivo** *sm* cursive (writing); (*TIP*) italics *pl*.

'**corso, a** *pp di* **correre** // *sm* course; (*strada cittadina*) main street; (*di unità monetaria*) circulation; (*di titoli, valori*) rate, price; **dar libero** ~ **a** to give free expression to; **in** ~ in progress, under way; (*annata*) current; ~ **serale** evening class.

'**corte** *sf* (court)yard; (*DIR, regale*) court; **fare la** ~ **a qd** to court sb; ~ **marziale** court-martial.

cor'**teccia, ce** [kòr'tettʃa] *sf* bark.

corteggi'**are** [korted'dʒare] *vt* to court.

cor'**teo** *sm* procession.

cor'**tese** *ag* courteous; corte'**sia** *sf* courtesy.

cortigi'**ano, a** [korti'dʒano] *sm/f* courtier // *sf* courtesan.

cor'**tile** *sm* (court)yard.

cor'**tina** *sf* curtain; (*anche fig*) screen.

'**corto, a** *ag* short; **essere a** ~ **di qc** to be short of sth; ~ **circuito** short-circuit.

'**corvo** *sm* raven.

'**cosa** *sf* thing; (*faccenda*) affair, matter, business *q*; (**che**) ~? what?; **a** ~ **pensi?** what are you thinking about?; **a** ~ **e fatte** when it's all over.

'**coscia, sce** ['kɔʃʃa] *sf* thigh.

cosci'**ente** [koʃ'ʃɛnte] *ag* conscious; ~ **di** conscious *o* aware of; **cosci'enza** *sf* conscience; (*consapevolezza*) consciousness; **coscienzi'oso, a** *ag* conscientious.

cosci'**otto** [koʃ'ʃɔtto] *sm* (*CUC*) leg.

cos'**critto** *sm* (*MIL*) conscript.

coscrizi'**one** [koskrit'tsjone] *sf* conscription.

così *av* so; (*in questo modo*) like this, like that; ~ **lontano** so far away; **un ragazzo** ~ **intelligente** such an intelligent boy // *ag inv* (*tale*): **non ho mai visto un film** ~ I've never seen such a film // *cong* (*perciò*) so, therefore; ~ ... **come as ... as**; **non è** ~ **bravo come te** he's not as good as you; **come stai?** — ~ ~ how are you? — so-so; **non ho detto** ~ I didn't say that; **e** ~ **via** and so on; **per** ~ **dire** so to speak.

così**detto, a** *ag* so-called.

cos'**metico, a, ci, che** *ag, sm* cosmetic.

'**cosmo** *sm* cosmos.

cosmo'**nauta, i, e** *sm/f* cosmonaut.

cosmopo'**lita, i, e** *ag* cosmopolitan.

cos'**pargere** [kos'pardʒere] *vt*: ~ **di** to sprinkle with; **cos'parso, a** *pp di* **cospargere.**

cos'**petto** *sm*: **al** ~ **di** in front of; in the presence of.

cos'picuo, a *ag* conspicuous, remarkable; (*grande*) considerable, large.

cospi'rare *vi* to conspire; **cospira'tore, 'trice** *sm/f* conspirator; **cospirazi'one** *sf* conspiracy.

'costa *sf* (*tra terra e mare*) coast(line); (*litorale*) shore; (*pendio*) slope; (ANAT) rib.

costà *av* there.

cos'tante *ag* constant; (*persona*) steadfast // *sf* constant.

cos'tare *vi* (2), *vt* to cost; ~ caro to be expensive, cost a lot.

costeggi'are [kosted'dʒare] *vt* to be close to; to run alongside.

cos'tei *pronome vedi* costui.

costellazi'one [kostellat'tsjone] *sf* constellation.

costernazi'one [kosternat'tsjone] *sf* dismay, consternation.

costi'ero, a *ag* coastal, coast *cpd* // *sf* stretch of coast.

costitu'ire *vt* (*comitato, gruppo*) to set up, form; (*collezione*) to put together, build up; (*sog: elementi, parti: comporre*) to make up, constitute; (*rappresentare*) to constitute; (DIR) to appoint; ~rsi alla polizia to give o.s. up to the police.

costituzio'nale [kostituttsjo'nale] *ag* constitutional.

costituzi'one [kostitut'tsjone] *sf* setting up; building up; constitution.

'costo *sm* cost; a ogni o qualunque ~, a tutti i ~i at all costs.

'costola *sf* (ANAT) rib; (*di libro, pettine*) spine.

costo'letta *sf* (CUC) cutlet.

cos'toro *pronome vedi* costui.

cos'toso, a *ag* expensive, costly.

cos'tretto, a *pp di* costringere.

cos'tringere [kos'trindʒere] *vt*: ~ qd a fare qc to force sb to do sth; costrizi'one *sf* coercion.

costru'ire *vt* to construct, build; costruzi'one *sf* construction, building.

cos'tui, cos'tei, *pl* cos'toro *pronome* (*soggetto*) he/she; *pl* they; (*complemento*) him/her; *pl* them.

cos'tume *sm* (*uso*) custom; (*foggia di vestire, indumento*) costume; ~i *smpl* morals, morality *sg*; il buon ~ public morality; ~ da bagno bathing o swimming costume, swimsuit; (*da uomo*) bathing o swimming trunks *pl*.

co'tenna *sf* hide; (*di maiale*) pigskin; (*del lardo*) rind.

co'togna [ko'toɲɲa] *sf* quince.

co'tone *sm* cotton; ~ idrofilo cotton wool.

'cotta *sf* (REL) surplice; (*fam: innamoramento*) crush.

'cottimo *sm* piecework; lavorare a ~ to do piecework.

'cotto, a *pp di* cuocere // *ag* cooked; (*fam: innamorato*) head-over-heels in love.

cot'tura *sf* cooking; (*in forno*) baking; (*in umido*) stewing.

co'vare *vt* to hatch; (*fig: malattia*) to be

sickening for; (*: odio, rancore*) to nurse // *vi* (*fuoco, fig*) to smoulder.

'covo *sm* den.

co'vone *sm* sheaf.

'cozza ['kɔttsa] *sf* mussel.

coz'zare [kot'tsare] *vi*: ~ contro to bang into, collide with; 'cozzo *sm* collision.

C.P. *abbr vedi* casella.

'crampo *sm* cramp.

'cranio *sm* skull.

cra'tere *sm* crater.

cra'vatta *sf* tie.

cre'anza [kre'antsa] *sf* manners *pl*.

cre'are *vt* to create; cre'ato *sm* creation; crea'tore, 'trice *ag* creative // *sm* creator; crea'tura *sf* creature; (*bimbo*) baby, infant; creazi'one *sf* creation; (*fondazione*) foundation, establishment.

cre'dente *sm/f* (REL) believer.

cre'denza [kre'dɛntsa] *sf* belief; (*credito*) credit; (*armadio*) sideboard.

credenzi'ali [kreden'tsjali] *sfpl* credentials.

'credere *vt* to believe // *vi*: ~ in, ~ a to believe in; ~ qd onesto to believe sb (to be) honest; ~ che to believe o think that; ~rsi furbo to think one is clever; cre'dibile *ag* credible, believable.

'credito *sm* (*anche* COMM) credit; (*reputazione*) esteem, repute; comprare a ~ to buy on credit.

'credo *sm inv* credo.

'credulo, a *ag* credulous.

'crema *sf* cream; (*con uova, zucchero etc*) custard.

cre'mare *vt* to cremate; cremazi'one *sf* cremation.

Crem'lino *sm*: il ~ the Kremlin.

'crepa *sf* crack.

cre'paccio [kre'pattʃo] *sm* large crack, fissure; (*di ghiacciaio*) crevasse.

crepacu'ore *sm* broken heart.

cre'pare *vi* (2) (*fam: morire*) to snuff it, kick the bucket; (*spaccarsi*) to crack; ~ dalle risa to split one's sides laughing; ~ dall'invidia to be green with envy.

crepi'tare *vi* (*fuoco*) to crackle; (*pioggia*) to patter.

cre'puscolo *sm* twilight, dusk.

cre'scendo [kreʃ'ʃendo] *sm* (MUS) crescendo.

'crescere ['kreʃʃere] *vi* (2) to grow; 'crescita *sf* growth; cresci'uto, a *pp di* crescere.

'cresima *sf* (REL) confirmation; cresi'mare *vt* to confirm.

'crespo, a *ag* (*capelli*) frizzy; (*vestito*) wrinkled // *sm* crêpe.

'cresta *sf* crest; (*di polli, uccelli*) crest, comb.

'creta *sf* chalk; clay.

'Creta *sf* Crete.

cre'tino, a *sm/f* idiot, fool.

'cric *sm inv* (TECN) jack.

'cricca, che *sf* clique.

'cricco, chi *sm* = cric.

crimi'nale *ag, sm/f* criminal.

'**crimine** *sm* (*DIR*) crime.

'**crine** *sm* horsehair; **crini'era** *sf* mane.

'**cripta** *sf* crypt.

crisan'temo *sm* chrysanthemum.

'**crisi** *sf inv* crisis; (*MED*) attack, fit; ~ **di nervi** attack *o* fit of nerves.

cristalliz'zare [kristalid'dʒare] *vi* (2), ~**rsi** *vr* to crystallize; (*fig*) to become fossilized.

cris'tallo *sm* crystal.

cristia'nesimo *sm* Christianity.

cristianità *sf* Christianity; (*i cristiani*) Christendom.

cristi'ano, a *ag, sm/f* Christian.

'**Cristo** *sm* Christ.

cri'terio *sm* criterion; (*buon senso*) (*common*) sense.

'**critica, che** *sf vedi* **critico**.

criti'care *vt* to criticize.

'**critico, a, ci, che** *ag* critical // *sm* critic // *sf* criticism; **la ~a** (*attività*) criticism; (*persone*) the critics *pl*.

cri'vello *sm* riddle.

'**croce** ['krotʃe] *sf* cross; **in** ~ (*di traverso*) crosswise; (*fig*) on tenterhooks; **la C~ Rossa** the Red Cross.

croce'figgere [krotʃe'fiddʒere] *etc* = **crocifiggere** *etc.*

croce'via [krotʃe'via] *sm inv* crossroads *sg*.

croci'ata [kro'tʃata] *sf* crusade.

cro'cicchio [kro'tʃikkjo] *sm* crossroads *sg*.

croci'era [kro'tʃera] *sf* (*viaggio*) cruise; (*ARCHIT*) transept.

croci'figgere [krotʃi'fiddʒere] *vt* to crucify; **crocifissi'one** *sf* crucifixion; **croci'fisso, a** *pp di* **crocifiggere**.

crogi'olo, crogiu'olo [kro'dʒɔlo] *sm* crucible; (*fig*) melting pot.

crol'lare *vi* (2) to collapse; '**crollo** *sm* collapse; (*di prezzi*) slump, sudden fall.

cro'mato, a *ag* chromium-plated.

'**cromo** *sm* chrome, chromium.

cromo'soma, i *sm* chromosome.

'**cronaca, che** *sf* chronicle; (*STAMPA*) news *sg*; (: *rubrica*) column; (*TV, RADIO*) commentary; **fatto** *o* **episodio di** ~ news item; ~ **nera** crime news *sg*; crime column.

'**cronico, a, ci, che** *ag* chronic.

cro'nista, i *sm* (*STAMPA*) reporter, columnist.

cronolo'gia [kronolo'dʒia] *sf* chronology.

'**crosta** *sf* crust.

cros'tacei [kros'tatʃei] *smpl* shellfish.

'**cruccio** ['kruttʃo] *sm* worry, torment.

cruci'verba *sm inv* crossword (puzzle).

cru'dele *ag* cruel; **crudeltà** *sf* cruelty.

'**crudo, a** *ag* (*non cotto*) raw; (*aspro*) harsh, severe.

cru'miro *sm* (*peg*) blackleg, scab.

'**crusca** *sf* bran.

crus'cotto *sm* (*AUT*) dashboard.

'**Cuba** *sf*: **la** ~ Cuba.

'**cubico, a, ci, che** *ag* cubic.

'**cubo, a** *ag* cubic // *sm* cube; **elevare al** ~ (*MAT*) to cube.

cuc'cagna [kuk'kaɲɲa] *sf*: **paese della** ~ land of plenty; **albero della** ~ greasy pole (*fig*).

cuc'cetta [kut'tʃetta] *sf* (*FERR*) couchette; (*NAUT*) berth.

cucchiai'ata [kukja'jata] *sf* spoonful.

cucchia'ino [kukkja'ino] *sm* teaspoon; coffee spoon.

cucchi'aio [kuk'kjajo] *sm* spoon.

'**cuccia, ce** ['kuttʃa] *sf* dog's bed; **a** ~**!** down!

'**cucciolo** ['kuttʃolo] *sm* puppy.

cu'cina [ku'tʃina] *sf* (*locale*) kitchen; (*arte culinaria*) cooking, cookery; (*le vivande*) food, cooking; (*apparecchio*) cooker; **fare da** ~ to cook; ~ **componibile** fitted kitchen; **cuci'nare** *vt* to cook.

cu'cire [ku'tʃire] *vt* to sew, stitch; **cuci-'tura** *sf* sewing, stitching; (*costura*) seam.

cucù *sm inv*, **cu'culo** *sm* cuckoo.

'**cuffia** *sf* bonnet, cap; (*da bagno*) (bathing) cap; (*per ascoltare*) headphones *pl*, headset.

cu'gino, a [ku'dzino] *sm/f* cousin.

'**cui** *pronome* (*nei complementi indiretti*): **la persona a** ~ **accennava** the person you were referring to *o* to whom you referred; **il libro di** ~ **parlavo** the book I was talking about *o* about which I was talking; **il quartiere in** ~ **abito** the district where I live; (*inserito tra l'articolo e il sostantivo*) whose; **il** ~ **nome** whose name; **la** ~ **madre** whose mother.

culi'naria *sf* cookery.

'**culla** *sf* (*anche fig*) cradle.

cul'lare *vt* to rock.

culmi'nare *vi* to culminate.

'**culmine** *sm* top, summit.

'**culo** *sm* (*fam!*) arse (*!*), bum.

'**culto** *sm* (*religione*) religion; (*adorazione*) worship, adoration; (*venerazione: anche fig*) cult.

cul'tura *sf* culture; education, learning; **cultu'rale** *ag* cultural.

cumu'lare *vt* to accumulate, amass; **cumula'tivo, a** *ag* cumulative; (*prezzo*) inclusive; (*biglietto*) group *cpd*.

'**cumulo** *sm* (*mucchio*) pile, heap; (*METEOR*) cumulus.

'**cuneo** *sm* wedge.

cu'ocere ['kwɔtʃere] *vt* (*alimenti*) to cook; (*mattoni etc*) to fire // *vi* (2) to cook; **cu'oco, a, chi, che** *sm/f* cook; **primo cuoco** chef.

cu'oio *sm* leather; ~ **capelluto** scalp.

cu'ore *sm* heart; ~**i** *smpl* (*CARTE*) hearts; **avere buon** ~ to be kind-hearted; **di** (**buon**) ~ willingly.

cupi'digia [kupi'didʒa] *sf* greed, covetousness.

'**cupo, a** *ag* dark; (*fig*) gloomy, dismal.

'**cupola** *sf* dome; cupola.

'**cura** *sf* care; (*MED: trattamento*) (course of) treatment; **aver** ~ **di** (*occuparsi di*) to look after; **a** ~ **di** (*libro*) edited by.

cu'rare *vt* (*malato, malattia*) to treat; (: *guarire*) to cure; (*aver cura di*) to take care of; (*testo*) to edit; ~**rsi** *vr* to take care of o.s.; (*MED*) to follow a course of treatment; ~**rsi di** to pay attention to.

cu'rato *sm* parish priest; (*protestante*) vicar.

cura'tore, 'trice *sm/f* (*DIR*) trustee; (*di antologia etc*) editor.

'curia *sf* (*REL*): la ~ romana the Roman curia.

curiosità *sf inv* curiosity; (*cosa rara*) curio, curiosity.

curi'oso, a *ag* (*che vuol sapere*) curious, inquiring; (*ficcanaso*) curious, inquisitive; (*bizzarro*) strange, curious.

'curva *sf* curve; (*stradale*) bend, curve.

cur'vare *vt* to bend // *vi* (*veicolo*) to take a bend; (*strada*) to bend, curve; ~**rsi** *vr* to bend; (*legno*) to warp.

'curvo, a *ag* curved; (*piegato*) bent.

cusci'netto [kuʃʃi'netto] *sm* pad; (*TECN*) bearing // *ag inv*: **stato** ~ buffer state; ~ a **sfere** ball bearing.

cu'scino [kuʃ'ʃino] *sm* cushion; (*guanciale*) pillow.

'cuspide *sf* (*ARCHIT*) spire.

cus'tode *sm/f* keeper, custodian.

cus'todia *sf* care; (*DIR*) custody; (*astuccio*) case, holder.

custo'dire *vt* (*conservare*) to keep; (*assistere*) to look after, take care of; (*fare la guardia*) to guard.

'cute *sf* (*ANAT*) skin.

cu'ticola *sf* cuticle.

C.V. (*abbr di* cavallo vapore) h.p.

D

da *prep* (*da* + *il* = dal, *da* + *lo* = dallo, *da* + *l'* = dall', *da* + *la* = dalla, *da* + *i* = dai, *da* + *gli* = dagli, *da* + *le* = dalle) (*agente*) by; (*provenienza*) from; (*causale*) with; (*moto a luogo: riferito a persone*): vado ~ Pietro/dal giornalaio I'm going to Pietro's (house)/to the newsagent's; (*stato in luogo: riferito a persone*): sono ~ Pietro I'm at Pietro's (house); (*moto per luogo*) through; (*fuori da*) out of, from; (*tempo*): vivo qui ~ un anno I have been living here for a year; è dalle 3 che ti aspetto I've been waiting for you since 3 (o'clock); comportarsi ~ bambino to behave like a child; ~ bambino piangevo molto I cried a lot as a o when I was a child; una ragazza dai capelli biondi a girl with blonde hair; un vestito ~ 100,000 lire a 100,000 lire dress; ~ ... a from ... to; ~ oggi in poi from today onwards; l'ho fatto ~ me I did it myself; macchina ~ corsa racing car.

dab'bene *ag inv* honest, decent.

dac'capo, da 'capo *av* (*di nuovo*) (once) again; (*dal principio*) all over again, from the beginning.

dacché [dak'ke] *cong* since.

'dado *sm* (*da gioco*) dice *o* die (*pl* dice); (*CUC*) stock cube; ~**i** *smpl* (*game of*) dice.

daf'fare, da 'fare *sm* work, toil.

'dagli ['daʎʎi], 'dai *prep* + *det vedi* da.

'daino *sm* (*fallow*) deer *inv*; (*pelle*) buckskin.

dal, dall', 'dalla, 'dalle, 'dallo *prep* + *det vedi* da.

'dama *sf* lady; (*nei balli*) partner; (*gioco*) draughts *sg*.

damigi'ana [dami'dʒana] *sf* demijohn.

da'naro *sm* = denaro.

da'nese *ag* Danish // *sm/f* Dane // *sm* (*LING*) Danish.

Dani'marca *sf*: la ~ Denmark.

dan'nare *vt* (*REL*) to damn; far ~ qd to drive sb mad; dannazi'one *sf* damnation.

danneggi'are [danned'dʒare] *vt* to damage; (*rovinare*) to spoil; (*nuocere*) to harm.

'danno *sm* damage; (*a persona*) harm, injury; ~**i** *smpl* (*DIR*) damages; dan'noso, a *ag*: dannoso (a) harmful (to), bad (for).

Da'nubio *sm*: il ~ the Danube.

'danza ['dantsa] *sf*: la ~ dancing; una ~ a dance.

dan'zare [dan'tsare] *vt*, *vi* to dance.

dapper'tutto *av* everywhere.

dap'poco *ag inv* inept, worthless.

dap'presso *av* (*vicino*) near, close at hand; (*da vicino*) closely.

dap'prima *av* at first.

'dardo *sm* dart.

'dare *sm* (*COMM*) debit // *vt* to give; (*produrre: frutti, suono*) to produce // *vi* (*guardare*): ~ su to look (out) onto; ~**rsi** *vr*: ~**rsi a** to dedicate o.s. to; ~**rsi al commercio** to go into business; ~**rsi al bere** to take to drink; ~**rsi a correre** to start to run; ~ per certo qc to consider sth certain; ~ per morto qd to give sb up for dead.

'darsena *sf* dock; dockyard.

'data *sf* date.

da'tare *vt* to date // *vi*: ~ da to date from.

'dato, a *ag* given // *sm* datum; ~**i** *smpl* data *pl*; ~ che given that.

'dattero *sm* date.

dattilogra'fare *vt* to type; dattilogra'fia *sf* typing; datti'lografo, a *sm/f* typist.

da'vanti *av* in front; (*dirimpetto*) opposite // *ag inv* front // *sm* front; ~ a *prep* in front of; facing, opposite; (*in presenza di*) before, in front of.

davan'zale [davan'tsale] *sm* windowsill.

da'vanzo, d'a'vanzo [da'vantso] *av* more than enough.

dav'vero *av* really, indeed.

'dazio ['dattsjo] *sm* (*somma*) duty; (*luogo*) customs *pl*.

d. C. (*abbr di* dopo Cristo) A.D.

'dea *sf* goddess.

'debito, a *ag* due, proper // *sm* debt; (*COMM: dare*) debit; a tempo ~ at the right time; debi'tore, 'trice *sm/f* debtor.

'debole *ag* weak, feeble; (*suono*) faint; (*luce*) dim; debo'lezza *sf* weakness.

debut'tare *vi* to make one's début; de'butto *sm* début.

deca'dente *ag* decadent, in decline; deca-

'denza *sf* decline; (*DIR*) loss, forfeiture.

decaffei'nare *vt* to decaffeinate.

de'cano *sm* (*REL*) dean.

decapi'tare *vt* to decapitate, behead.

decappot'tabile *ag, sf* convertible.

dece'duto, a [detʃe'duto] *ag* deceased.

de'cenne [de'tʃɛnne] *ag* ten-year-old; (*predicativo*) ten years old; **de'cennio** *sm* decade.

de'cente [de'tʃɛnte] *ag* decent, respectable, proper; (*accettabile*) satisfactory, decent; **de'cenza** *sf* decency, propriety.

de'cesso [de'tʃɛsso] *sm* death; **atto di ~** death certificate.

de'cidere [de'tʃidere] *vt*: **~ qc** to decide on sth; (*questione, lite*) to settle sth; **~ di fare/che** to decide to do/that; **~ di qc** (*sog: cosa*) to determine sth; **~rsi (a fare)** to decide (to do), make up one's mind (to do).

deci'frare [detʃi'frare] *vt* to decode; (*fig*) to decipher, make out.

deci'male [detʃi'male] *ag* decimal.

deci'mare [detʃi'mare] *vt* to decimate.

'decimo, a ['detʃimo] *num* tenth.

de'cina [de'tʃina] *sf* ten; (*circa dieci*): **una ~ (di)** about ten.

decisi'one [detʃi'zjone] *sf* decision; **prendere una ~** to make a decision.

de'ciso, a [de'tʃizo] *pp di* **decidere**.

declas'sare *vt* to downgrade; to lower in status.

decli'nare *vi* to go down; (*fig: diminuire*) to decline; (*tramontare*) to set, go down // *vt* to decline; **declinazi'one** *sf* (*LING*) declension; **de'clino** *sm* decline.

de'clivio *sm* (downward) slope.

decol'lare *vi* (*AER*) to take off; **de'collo** *sm* take-off.

decolo'rare *vt* to bleach.

decom'porre *vt*, **decomporsi** *vr* to decompose; **decomposizi'one** *sf* decomposition; **decom'posto, a** *pp di* **decomporre**.

deconge'lare [dekondʒe'lare] *vt* to defrost.

deco'rare *vt* to decorate; **decora'tore, 'trice** *sm/f* (interior) decorator; **decorazi'one** *sf* decoration.

de'coro *sm* decorum; **deco'roso, a** *ag* decorous, dignified.

de'correre *vi* (2) to pass, elapse; (*avere effetto*) to run, have effect; **de'corso, a** *pp di* **decorrere** // *sm* passing; (*evoluzione: anche MED*) course.

de'crepito, a *ag* decrepit.

de'crescere [de'kreʃʃere] *vi* (2) (*diminuire*) to decrease, diminish; (*acque*) to subside, go down; (*prezzi*) to go down; **decresci'uto, a** *pp di* **decrescere**.

de'creto *sm* decree.

'dedalo *sm* maze, labyrinth.

'dedica, che *sf* dedication.

dedi'care *vt* to dedicate.

'dedito, a *ag*: **~ a** (*studio etc*) dedicated *o* devoted to; (*vizio*) addicted to.

de'dotto, a *pp di* **dedurre**.

de'durre *vt* (*concludere*) to deduce; (*defalcare*) to deduct; **deduzi'one** *sf* deduction.

defal'care *vt* to deduct.

defe'rente *ag* respectful, deferential.

defe'rire *vt* (*DIR*) to refer.

defezi'one [defet'tsjone] *sf* defection, desertion.

defici'ente [defi'tʃɛnte] *ag* (*mancante*) insufficient; (*minorato*) mentally deficient; (*stupido*) idiotic // *sm/f* mental defective; idiot; **defici'enza** *sf* shortage; (*lacuna*) gap; (*MED*) mental deficiency.

'deficit ['dɛfitʃit] *sm inv* (*ECON*) deficit.

defi'nire *vt* to define; (*risolvere*) to settle; **defini'tivo, a** *ag* definitive, final; **definizi'one** *sf* definition; settlement.

deflazi'one [deflat'tsjone] *sf* (*ECON*) deflation.

de'flusso *sm* (della marea) ebb.

defor'mare *vt* (*alterare*) to put out of shape; (*corpo*) to deform; (*pensiero, fatto*) to distort; **~rsi** *vr* to lose its shape.

de'forme *ag* deformed; disfigured; **deformità** *sf inv* deformity.

defrau'dare *vt*: **~ qd di qc** to defraud sb of sth, cheat sb out of sth.

de'funto, a *ag* late *cpd* // *sm/f* deceased.

degene'rare [dedʒene'rare] *vi* to degenerate; **de'genere** *ag* degenerate.

de'gente [de'dʒɛnte] *ag* bedridden.

'degli ['deʎʎi] *prep + det vedi* **di**.

de'gnarsi [deɲ'narsi] *vr*: **~ di fare** to deign *o* condescend to do.

'degno, a *ag* dignified; **~ di** worthy of; **~ di lode** praiseworthy.

degra'dare *vt* (*MIL*) to demote; (*privare della dignità*) to degrade; **~rsi** *vr* to demean o.s.

degus'tare *vt* to sample, taste; **degusta-zi'one** *sf* sampling, tasting.

'dei, del *prep + det vedi* **di**.

dela'tore, 'trice *sm/f* police informer.

'delega, ghe *sf* (*procura*) proxy.

dele'gare *vt* to delegate; **dele'gato** *sm* delegate; **delegazi'one** *sf* delegation.

del'fino *sm* dolphin.

delibe'rare *vt, vi* to deliberate.

delica'tezza [delika'tettsa] *sf* (*anche CUC*) delicacy; frailty; thoughtfulness; tactfulness.

deli'cato, a *ag* delicate; (*salute*) delicate, frail; (*fig: gentile*) thoughtful, considerate; (*: pieno di tatto*) tactful.

delimi'tare *vt* to circumscribe, define.

deline'are *vt* to outline; **~rsi** *vr* to be outlined; (*fig*) to emerge.

delin'quente *sm/f* criminal, delinquent; **delin'quenza** *sf* criminality, delinquency; **delinquenza minorile** juvenile delinquency.

deli'rare *vi* to be delirious, rave; (*fig*) to rave.

de'lirio *sm* delirium; (*ragionamento insensato*) raving; (*fig*) frenzy.

de'litto sm crime; **delittu'oso, a** ag criminal.

de'lizia [de'littsja] sf delight; **delizi'oso, a** ag delightful; (cibi) delicious.

dell', 'della, 'delle, 'dello prep + det vedi **di.**

'delta sm inv delta.

delta'plano sm hang-glider; **volo col** ~ hang gliding.

de'ludere vt to disappoint; **delusi'one** sf disappointment; **de'luso, a** pp di **deludere.**

dema'gogo, ghi sm demagogue.

de'manio sm state property.

de'mente ag (MED) demented, mentally deranged; **de'menza** sf dementia; (stupidità) foolishness.

demo'cratico, a, ci, che ag democratic.

democra'zia [demokrat'tsia] sf democracy.

democristi'ano, a ag, sm/f Christian Democrat.

demo'lire vt to demolish; **demolizi'one** sf demolition.

'demone sm demon.

de'monio sm demon, devil; **il D**~ the Devil.

demoraliz'zare [demoralid'dzare] vt to demoralize.

de'naro sm money.

deni'grare vt to denigrate, run down.

denomi'nare vt to name; ~**rsi** vr to be named o called; **denomina'tore** sm (MAT) denominator; **denominazi'one** sf name; denomination.

deno'tare vt to denote, indicate.

densità sf inv density.

'denso, a ag thick, dense.

den'tale ag dental.

den'tario, a ag dental.

'dente sm tooth; (di forchetta) prong; (GEO: cima) jagged peak; **al** ~ (CUC: pasta) cooked so as to be firm when eaten; ~**i dei giudizio** wisdom teeth; **denti'era** sf (set of) false teeth pl.

denti'fricio [denti'fritʃo] sm toothpaste.

den'tista, i, e sm/f dentist.

'dentro av in, inside; (fig: nell'intimo) inwardly, in one's mind // prep in, inside; (entro) within; ~ **a,** ~ **in** in, inside; within; **qui/là** ~ in here/there; ~ **di sé** (pensare, brontolare) to oneself; **di** ~ from inside.

de'nuncia, ce o **cie** [de'nuntʃa], **de-'nunzia** [de'nuntsja] sf denunciation; accusation; declaration; ~ **del reddito** (income) tax return.

denunci'are [denun'tʃare], **denunzi'are** [denun'tsjare] vt to denounce; (accusare) to accuse; (dichiarare) to declare.

denutrizi'one [denutrit'tsjone] sf malnutrition.

deodo'rante sm deodorant.

depe'rire vi to waste away.

depila'torio sm depilatory.

deplo'rare vt to deplore; to lament; **deplo'revole** ag deplorable.

de'porre vt (depositare) to put down; (rimuovere: da una carica) to remove; (: re) to depose; (DIR) to testify.

depor'tare vt to deport.

deposi'tare vt (GEO, ECON) to deposit; (lasciare) to leave; (merci) to store.

de'posito sm deposit; (luogo) warehouse; depot; (: MIL) depot; ~ **bagagli** left-luggage office.

deposizi'one [depozit'tsjone] sf deposition; (da una carica) removal.

de'posto, a pp di **deporre.**

depra'vare vt to corrupt, deprave.

depre'care vt to deprecate, disapprove of.

depre'dare vt to rob, plunder.

depressi'one sf depression.

de'presso, a pp di **deprimere** // ag depressed.

deprez'zare [depret'tsare] vt (ECON) to depreciate.

de'primere vt to depress.

depu'rare vt to purify.

depu'tare vt to delegate; ~ **qd a** to send sb (as a representative) to; **depu'tato, a** o **'essa** sm/f (POL) deputy, ≈ Member of Parliament; **deputazi'one** sf deputation; (POL) position of deputy, ≈ parliamentary seat.

deraglia'mento [deraʎʎa'mento] sm derailment.

deragli'are [deraʎ'ʎare] vi to be derailed; **far** ~ to derail.

dere'litto, a ag derelict.

dere'tano sm bottom, buttocks pl.

de'ridere vt to mock, deride; **derisi'one** sf derision, mockery; **de'riso, a** pp di **deridere.**

de'riva sf (NAUT, AER) drift; **andare alla** ~ (anche fig) to drift.

deri'vare vi (2): ~ **da** to derive from // vt to derive; (corso d'acqua) to divert; **derivazi'one** sf derivation; diversion.

dero'gare vi: ~ **a** to go against, depart from; (legge) to repeal in part.

der'rate sfpl commodities; ~ **alimentari** foodstuffs.

deru'bare vt to rob.

des'critto, a pp di **descrivere.**

des'crivere vt to describe; **descrizi'one** sf description.

de'serto, a ag deserted // sm (GEO) desert; **isola** ~**a** desert island.

deside'rare vt to want, wish for; (sessualmente) to desire; ~ **fare/che qd faccia** to want o wish to do/sb to do; **desidera fare una passeggiata?** would you like to go for a walk?

desi'derio sm wish; (forte, carnale) desire.

deside'roso, a ag: ~ **di** longing o eager for.

desi'gnare [desiɲ'ɲare] vt to designate, appoint; (data) to fix.

desi'nare vi to dine, have dinner // sm dinner.

de'sistere vi: ~ **da** to give up, desist from; **desis'tito, a** pp di **desistere.**

deso'lare vt (affliggere) to distress, grieve.

deso'lato, a ag (paesaggio) desolate; (persona: spiacente) sorry; **desolazi'one** sf desolation.

'despota, i sm despot.

des'tare vt to wake (up); (fig) to awaken, arouse; ~**rsi** vr to wake (up).

desti'nare vt to destine; (assegnare) to appoint, assign; (indirizzare) to address; ~ **qc a qd** to intend to give sth to sb, intend sb to have sth.

destinazi'one [destinat'tsjone] sf destination; (uso) purpose.

des'tino sm destiny, fate.

destitu'ire vt to dismiss, remove.

'desto, a ag (wide) awake.

'destra sf vedi **destro**.

destreggi'arsi [destred'dʒarsi] vr to manoeuvre.

des'trezza [des'trettsa] sf skill, dexterity.

'destro, a ag right, right-hand; (abile) skilful, adroit // sf (mano) right hand; (parte) right (side); (POL): la ~ the Right; **a** ~**a** on the right.

dete'nere vt (incarico, primato) to hold; (un bene) to be in possession of; (in prigione) to detain, hold; **dete'nuto, a** sm/f prisoner; **detenzi'one** sf holding; possession; detention.

deter'gente [deter'dʒente] sm detergent.

deterio'rare vt to damage; ~**rsi** vr to deteriorate.

determi'nare vt to determine; ~**rsi a fare qc** to make up one's mind to do sth; **determinazi'one** sf determination; (decisione) decision.

deter'sivo sm detergent.

detes'tare vt to detest, hate.

deto'nare vi to detonate.

de'trarre vt: ~ (da) to deduct (from), take away (from); **de'tratto, a** pp di **detrarre**.

detri'mento sm detriment, harm; **a** ~ **di** to the detriment of.

de'trito sm (GEO) detritus.

dettagli'ante [dettaʎ'ʎante] sm/f (COMM) retailer.

dettagli'are [dettaʎ'ʎare] vt to detail, give full details of.

det'taglio [det'taʎʎo] sm detail; (COMM): il ~ retail; **al** ~ (COMM) retail; separately.

det'tare vt to dictate; **det'tato** sm dictation; **detta'tura** sf dictation.

'detto, a pp di **dire** // ag (soprannominato) called, known as; (già nominato) above-mentioned // sm saying; ~ **fatto** no sooner said than done.

detur'pare vt to disfigure; (moralmente) to sully.

devas'tare vt to devastate; (fig) to ravage; **devastazi'one** sf devastation; ravages pl.

devi'are vi to swerve, veer off // vt to divert; **deviazi'one** sf (anche AUT) diversion.

devo'luto, a pp di **devolvere**.

devoluzi'one [devolut'tsjone] sf (DIR) devolution, transfer.

de'volvere vt (DIR) to transfer, devolve.

de'voto, a ag (REL) devout, pious; (affezionato) devoted.

devozi'one [devot'tsjone] sf devoutness; (anche REL) devotion.

di prep (di + il = **del**, di + lo = **dello**, di + l' = **dell'**, di + la = **della**, di + i = **dei**, di + gli = **degli**, di + le = **delle**) of; (causa) with; for; of; (mezzo) with; (provenienza) from // det: **del pane** (some) bread; **dei libri** (some) books; **la sorella** ~ **mio padre** my father's sister; **un sacchetto** ~ **plastica/orologio d'oro** a plastic bag/gold watch; **tremare** ~ **paura** to tremble with fear; **un bambino** ~ **tre anni** a child of three, a three-year-old child; ~ **primavera/giugno** in spring/June; ~ **mattina/sera** in the morning/evening; ~ **notte** by night; at night; in the night; ~ **domenica** on Sundays; ~ ... **in** from ... to; vedi **più**, **meno** etc.

dia'bete sm diabetes sg.

dia'bolico, a, ci, che ag diabolical.

di'acono sm (REL) deacon.

dia'dema, i sm diadem; (di donna) tiara.

dia'framma, i sm (divisione) screen; (ANAT, FOT) diaphragm.

di'agnosi [di'aɲɲozi] sf diagnosis sg; **diagnosti'care** vt to diagnose.

diago'nale ag, sf diagonal.

dia'gramma, i sm diagram.

dia'letto sm dialect.

di'alogo, ghi sm dialogue.

dia'mante sm diamond.

di'ametro sm diameter.

di'amine escl: **che** ~ ... ? what on earth ... ?

diaposi'tiva sf transparency, slide.

di'ario sm diary.

diar'rea sf diarrhoea.

di'avolo sm devil.

di'battere vt to debate, discuss; ~**rsi** vr to struggle; **di'battito** sm debate, discussion.

di'cembre [di'tʃembre] sm December.

dicas'tero sm ministry.

dichia'rare [dikja'rare] vt to declare; **dichiarazi'one** sf declaration.

dician'nove [ditʃan'nɔve] num nineteen.

dicias'sette [ditʃas'sɛtte] num seventeen.

dici'otto [di'tʃɔtto] num eighteen.

dici'tura [ditʃi'tura] sf words pl, wording.

di'dattico, a, ci, che ag didactic.

di'eci ['djɛtʃi] num ten; **die'cina** sf = **decina**.

'diesel ['dizal] sm inv diesel engine.

di'eta sf diet; **essere a** ~ to be on a diet.

di'etro av behind // prep behind; (tempo: dopo) after // sm back, rear; **le zampe di** ~ the back legs, the hind legs; ~ **richiesta** on demand; (scritta) on application.

di'fendere vt to defend; **difen'sivo, a** ag defensive // sf: **stare sulla difensiva**

(*anche fig*) to be on the defensive; **difen-'sore, a** *sm/f* defender; **avvocato difensore** counsel for the defence; **di'feso, a** *pp di* **difendere** // *sf* defence.

difet'tare *vi* to be defective; ~ **di** to be lacking in, lack; **difet'tivo, a** *ag* defective.

di'fetto *sm* (*mancanza*): ~ **di** lack of; shortage of; (*di fabbricazione*) fault, flaw, defect; (*morale*) fault, failing, defect; (*fisico*) defect; **far** ~ to be lacking; **in** ~ at fault; in the wrong; **difet'toso, a** *ag* defective, faulty.

diffa'mare *vt* to defame, slander; to libel.

diffe'rente *ag* different.

diffe'renza [diffe'rɛntsa] *sf* difference; **a** ~ **di** unlike.

differenzi'ale [differen'tsjale] *ag, sm* differential.

differenzi'are [differen'tsjare] *vt* to differentiate; ~**rsi da** to differentiate o.s. from; to differ from.

diffe'rire *vt* to postpone, defer // *vi* to be different.

dif'ficile [dif'fitʃile] *ag* difficult; (*persona*) hard to please, difficult (to please); (*poco probabile*): **è** ~ **che sia libero** it is unlikely that he'll be free // *sm* difficult part, difficulty; **difficoltà** *sf inv* difficulty.

dif'fida *sf* (*DIR*) warning, notice.

diffi'dare *vi*: ~ **di** to be suspicious *o* distrustful of // *vt* (*DIR*) to warn; **diffi-'dente** *ag* suspicious, distrustful; **diffi-'denza** *sf* suspicion, distrust.

dif'fondere *vt* (*calore*) to diffuse; (*notizie*) to spread, circulate; ~**rsi** *vr* to spread; **diffusi'one** *sf* diffusion; spread; (*anche di giornale*) circulation; (*FISICA*) scattering; **dif'fuso, a** *pp di* **diffondere**.

difi'lato *av* (*direttamente*) straight, directly; (*subito*) straight away.

difte'rite *sf* (*MED*) diphtheria.

'diga, ghe *sf* dam; (*argine litoraneo*) dyke.

dige'rire [didʒe'rire] *vt* to digest; **diges-ti'one** *sf* digestion; **diges'tivo, a** *ag* digestive // *sm* (*after-dinner*) liqueur.

digi'tale [didʒi'tale] *ag* digital; (*delle dita*) finger *cpd*, digital // *sf* (*BOT*) foxglove.

digiu'nare [didʒu'nare] *vi* to starve o.s.; (*REL*) to fast; **digi'uno, a** *ag*: **essere digiuno** not to have eaten // *sm* fast; **a digiuno** on an empty stomach.

dignità [diɲɲi'ta] *sf inv* dignity; **digni-'tario** *sm* dignitary; **digni'toso, a** *ag* dignified.

digressi'one *sf* digression.

digri'gnare [digriɲ'ɲare] *vt*: ~ **i denti** to grind one's teeth.

dila'gare *vi* to flood; (*fig*) to spread.

dilapi'dare *vt* to squander, waste.

dila'tare *vt* to dilate; (*gas*) to cause to expand; (*passaggio, cavità*) to open (up); ~**rsi** *vr* to dilate; (*FISICA*) to expand.

dilazio'nare [dilattsjo'nare] *vt* to delay, defer; **dilazi'one** *sf* delay; (*COMM: di pagamento etc*) extension; (*rinvio*) postponement.

dileggi'are [dileddʒare] *vt* to mock, deride.

dilegu'are *vi*, ~**rsi** *vr* to vanish, disappear.

di'lemma, i *sm* dilemma.

dilet'tante *sm/f* dilettante; (*anche SPORT*) amateur.

dilet'tare *vt* to give pleasure to, delight; ~**rsi** *vr*: ~**rsi di** to take pleasure in, enjoy.

di'letto, a *ag* dear, beloved // *sm* pleasure, delight.

dili'gente [dili'dʒente] *ag* (*scrupoloso*) diligent; (*accurato*) careful, accurate; **dili-'genza** *sf* diligence; care; (*carrozza*) stagecoach.

dilu'ire *vt* to dilute.

dilun'garsi *vr* (*fig*): ~ **su** to talk at length on *o* about.

diluvi'are *vb impers* to pour (down).

di'luvio *sm* downpour; (*inondazione, fig*) flood.

dima'grire *vi* (2) to get thinner, lose weight.

dime'nare *vt* to wave, shake; ~**rsi** *vr* to toss and turn; (*fig*) to struggle; ~ **la coda** (*sog: cane*) to wag its tail.

dimensi'one *sf* dimension; (*grandezza*) size.

dimenti'canza [dimenti'kantsa] *sf* forgetfulness; (*errore*) oversight, slip; **per** ~ inadvertently.

dimenti'care *vt* to forget; ~**rsi di qc** to forget sth.

di'messo, a *pp di* **dimettere** // *ag* (*voce*) subdued; (*uomo, abito*) modest, humble.

dimesti'chezza [dimesti'kettsa] *sf* familiarity.

di'mettere *vt*: ~ **qd da** to dismiss sb from; (*dall'ospedale*) to discharge sb from; ~**rsi (da)** to resign (from).

dimez'zare [dimed'dzare] *vt* to halve.

diminu'ire *vt* to reduce, diminish // *vi* (2) to decrease, diminish, go down; **diminu-zi'one** *sf* decreasing, diminishing.

dimissi'oni *sfpl* resignation *sg*; **dare** *o* **presentare le** ~ to resign, hand in one's resignation.

di'mora *sf* residence.

dimo'rare *vi* to reside.

dimos'trare *vt* to demonstrate, show; (*provare*) to prove, demonstrate; ~**rsi** *vr*: ~**rsi molto abile** to show o.s. *o* prove to be very clever; **dimostra'tivo, a** *ag* (*anche LING*) demonstrative; **dimostra-zi'one** *sf* demonstration; proof.

di'namico, a, ci, che *ag* dynamic // *sf* dynamics *sg*.

dina'mismo *sm* dynamism.

dina'mite *sf* dynamite.

'dinamo *sf inv* dynamo.

di'nanzi [di'nantsi]: ~ **a** *prep* in front of.

dinas'tia *sf* dynasty.

dini'ego, ghi *sm* refusal; denial.

din'torno *av* round, (round) about; ~**i** *smpl* outskirts; **nei** ~**i di** in the vicinity *o* neighbourhood of.

'dio, pl 'dei *sm* god; **D**~ God; **gli dei** the gods.

di'ocesi [di'ɔtʃezi] sf diocese.

dipa'nare vt (lana) to wind into a ball; (fig) to disentangle, sort out.

diparti'mento sm department.

dipen'dente ag dependent // sm/f employee; **dipen'denza** sf dependence; **essere alle dipendenze di qd** to be employed by sb o in sb's employ.

di'pendere vi (2): ~ **da** to depend on; (finanziariamente) to be dependent on; (derivare) to come from, be due to; **di'peso**, a pp di **dipendere**.

di'pingere [di'pindʒere] vt to paint; ~**rsi** vr to make up, put on makeup; **di'pinto, a** pp di **dipingere** // sm painting.

di'ploma, i sm diploma.

diplo'matico, a, ci, che ag diplomatic // sm diplomat.

diploma'zia [diplomat'tsia] sf diplomacy.

di'porto sm: **imbarcazione** f **da** ~ pleasure craft.

dira'dare vt to thin (out); (visite) to reduce, make less frequent; ~**rsi** vr to disperse; (nebbia) to clear (up).

dira'mare vt to issue, send out // vi, ~**rsi** vr to branch.

'dire vt to say; (segreto, fatto) to tell; ~ **qc a qd** to tell sb sth; ~ **a qd di fare qc** to tell sb to do sth; ~ **di sì/no** to say yes/no; **si dice che** ... they say that ...; **si direbbe che** ... it looks (o sounds) as though ... ; **dica, signora?** (in un negozio) yes, Madam, can I help you?

diret'tissimo sm (FERR) fast (through) train.

di'retto, a pp di **dirigere** // ag direct // sm (FERR) through train.

diret'tore, 'trice sm/f (d'impresa) director; manager/ess; (di scuola elementare) headmaster/mistress; ~ **d'orchestra** conductor.

direzi'one [diret'tsjone] sf board of directors; management; (senso di movimento) direction; **in** ~ **di** in the direction of, towards.

diri'gente [diri'dʒɛnte] sm/f executive; (POL) leader.

di'rigere [di'ridʒere] vt to direct; (impresa) to run, manage; (MUS) to conduct; ~**rsi** vr: ~**rsi verso** o a to make o head for.

diri'gibile [diri'dʒibile] sm dirigible.

dirim'petto av opposite; ~ **a** prep opposite, facing.

di'ritto, a ag straight; (onesto) straight, upright; (destro) right // av straight, directly; **andare** ~ to go straight on // sm right side; (prerogativa) right; (leggi, scienza): **il** ~ **law**; ~**i** smpl (tasse) duty sg; **stare** ~ to stand upright.

dirit'tura sf (SPORT) straight; (fig) rectitude.

diroc'cato, a ag tumbledown, in ruins.

dirot'tare vt (nave, aereo) to change the course of; (aereo: sotto minaccia) to hijack; (traffico) to divert // vi (nave, aereo) to change course; **dirotta'tore, 'trice** sm/f hijacker.

di'rotto, a ag (pioggia) torrential; (pianto) unrestrained; **piovere a** ~ to pour, rain cats and dogs; **piangere a** ~ to cry one's heart out.

di'rupo sm crag, precipice.

disabi'tato, a ag uninhabited.

disabitu'arsi vr: ~ **a** to get out of the habit of.

disac'cordo sm disagreement.

disadat'tato, a ag (PSIC) maladjusted.

disa'datto, a ag: ~ **(a o per)** unsuited (to).

disa'dorno, a ag plain, unadorned.

disagi'ato, a [diza'dʒato] ag poor, needy; (vita) hard.

di'sagio [di'zadʒo] sm discomfort; (disturbo) inconvenience; (fig: imbarazzo) embarrassment; ~**i** smpl hardship sg, poverty sg; **essere a** ~ to be ill at ease.

disappro'vare vt to disapprove of; **disapprovazi'one** sf disapproval.

disap'punto sm disappointment.

disar'mare vt, vi to disarm; **di'sarmo** sm (MIL) disarmament.

di'sastro sm disaster; **disas'troso, a** ag disastrous.

disat'tento, a ag inattentive.

disa'vanzo [diza'vantso] sm (ECON) deficit.

disavve'duto, a ag careless, thoughtless.

disavven'tura sf misadventure, mishap.

dis'brigo, ghi sm (prompt) clearing up o settlement.

dis'capito sm disadvantage, detriment; **a** ~ **di qd** to sb's cost.

discen'dente [diʃʃen'dɛnte] ag descending // sm/f descendant.

di'scendere [diʃʃendere] vt to go (o come) down // vi (2) to go (o come) down; (strada) to go down; (smontare) to get off; ~ **da** (famiglia) to be descended from; **dalla macchina/dal treno** to get out of the car/out of o off the train; ~ **da cavallo** to dismount, get off one's horse.

di'scepolo, a [diʃʃepolo] sm/f disciple.

di'scernere [diʃʃernere] vt to discern, make out; **discerni'mento** sm judgment, discernment.

di'sceso, a [diʃʃeso] pp di **discendere** // sf descent; (pendio) slope; **in** ~**a** (strada) downhill.

disci'ogliere [diʃʃɔʎʎere] vt, ~**rsi** vr to dissolve; (fondere) to melt; **disci'olto, a** pp di **disciogliere**.

disci'plina [diʃʃi'plina] sf discipline; **discipli'nare** ag disciplinary // vt to discipline.

'disco, schi sm disc; (SPORT) discus; (fonografico) record, disc; ~ **orario** (AUT) parking disc; ~ **volante** flying saucer.

discol'pare vt to clear of blame.

disco'noscere [disko'noʃʃere] vt to refuse to acknowledge; (figlio) to disown; **disconosci'uto, a** pp di **disconoscere**.

dis'corde ag conflicting, clashing; **dis'cordia** sf discord; (dissidio) disagreement, clash.

dis'correre vi: ~ (**di**) to talk (about).
dis'corso, a pp di **discorrere** // sm speech; (conversazione) conversation, talk.
dis'costo, a ag faraway, distant // av far away; ~ **da** prep far from.
disco'teca, che sf (raccolta) record library; (luogo di ballo) discothèque.
discredi'tare vt to discredit.
discre'panza [diskre'pantsa] sf disagreement.
dis'creto, a ag discreet; (abbastanza buono) reasonable, fair; **discrezi'one** sf discretion; (giudizio) judgment, discernment; **a discrezione di** at the discretion of.
discriminazi'one [diskriminat'tsjone] sf discrimination.
discussi'one sf discussion; (litigio) argument.
dis'cusso, a pp di **discutere**.
dis'cutere vt to discuss, debate; (contestare) to question, dispute // vi to talk; (contrastare) to argue; ~ **di** to discuss.
disde'gnare [disde ɲ'nare] vt to scorn; **dis'degno** sm scorn, disdain.
dis'detto, a pp di **disdire** // sf retraction; cancellation; (sfortuna) bad luck.
dis'dire vt (ritrattare) to retract, take back; (annullare) to cancel.
dise'gnare [diseɲ'nare] vt to draw; (progettare) to design; (fig) to outline; **disegna'tore, 'trice** sm/f designer.
di'segno [di'seɲno] sm drawing; design; outline.
diser'tare vt, vi to desert; **diser'tore** sm (MIL) deserter; **diserzi'one** sf (MIL) desertion.
dis'fare vt to undo; (valigie) to unpack; (lavoro, paese) to destroy; (neve) to melt; ~**rsi** vr to melt; ~ **il letto** to strip the bed; ~**rsi in lacrime** to dissolve into tears; ~**rsi di qd** (liberarsi) to get rid of sb; **dis'fatto, a** pp di **disfare** // sf (sconfitta) rout.
disfunzi'one [disfun'tsjone] sf (MED) disorder.
disge'lare [dizdʒe'lare] vt, vi, ~**rsi** vr to thaw; **dis'gelo** sm thaw.
dis'grazia [diz'grattsja] sf (sventura) misfortune; (incidente) accident, mishap; **disgrazi'ato, a** ag unfortunate // sm/f wretch.
disgre'gare vt, ~**rsi** vr to break up.
disgu'ido sm: ~ **postale** error in postal delivery.
disgus'tare vt to disgust; ~**rsi** vr: ~**rsi di** to be disgusted by.
dis'gusto sm disgust; **disgus'toso, a** ag disgusting.
disidra'tare vt to dehydrate.
disil'ludere vt to disillusion, disenchant; **disillusi'one** sf disillusion, disenchantment.
disimpa'rare vt to forget.
disimpe'gnare [dizimpeɲ'nare] vt (oggetto dato in pegno) to redeem, get out of pawn; (liberare) to release, free;

(sbrigare: ufficio) to carry out; ~**rsi** vr to free o.s.; (cavarsela) to manage.
disinfet'tante ag, sm disinfectant.
disinfet'tare vt to disinfect; **disinfezi'one** sf disinfection.
disingan'nare vt to disabuse, disillusion.
disinte'grare vt, vi (2) to disintegrate.
disinteres'sarsi vr: ~ **di** to take no interest in.
disinte'resse sm indifference; (generosità) unselfishness.
disin'volto, a ag casual, free and easy; **disinvol'tura** sf casualness, ease.
dislo'care vt to station, position.
dismi'sura sf excess; **a** ~ to excess, excessively.
disobbe'dire etc = **disubbidire** etc.
disoccu'pato, a ag unemployed // sm/f unemployed person; **disoccupazi'one** sf unemployment.
disonestà sf dishonesty.
diso'nesto, a ag dishonest.
disono'rare vt to dishonour, bring disgrace upon.
diso'nore sm dishonour, disgrace.
di'sopra av (con contatto) on top; (senza contatto) above; (al piano superiore) upstairs // ag inv (superiore) upper; **la gente** ~ the people upstairs; **il piano** ~ the floor above // sm.inv top, upper part.
disordi'nare vt to mess up, disarrange; (fig) to upset, confuse; (MIL) to throw into disorder // vi: ~ **nel bere** etc to take drink etc to excess; **disordi'nato, a** ag untidy; (privo di misura) irregular, wild.
di'sordine sm (confusione) disorder, confusion; (sregolatezza) debauchery.
disorien'tare vt to disorientate; ~**rsi** vr (fig) to get confused, lose one's bearings.
di'sotto av below, underneath; (in fondo) at the bottom; (al piano inferiore) downstairs // ag inv (inferiore) lower; bottom cpd; **la gente** ~ the people downstairs; **il piano** ~ the floor below // sm inv (parte inferiore) lower part; bottom.
dis'paccio [dis'pattʃo] sm dispatch.
dispa'rato, a ag disparate.
'dispari ag inv odd, uneven.
disparità sf inv disparity.
dis'parte: in ~ av (da lato) aside, apart; **tenersi o starsene in** ~ to keep to o.s., hold aloof.
dispendi'oso, a ag expensive.
dis'pensa sf pantry, larder; (mobile) sideboard; (DIR) exemption; (REL) dispensation; (fascicolo) number, issue.
dispen'sare vt (elemosine, favori) to distribute; (esonerare) to exempt.
dispe'rare vi: ~ (**di**) to despair (of); ~**rsi** vr to despair; **dispe'rato, a** ag desperate; **disperazi'one** sf desperation.
dis'perdere vt (disseminare) to disperse; (MIL) to scatter, rout; (fig: consumare) to waste, squander; ~**rsi** vr to disperse; to scatter; **dispersi'one** sf dispersion, dispersal; (FISICA, CHIM) dispersion; **dis'perso, a** pp di **disperdere** // sm missing soldier.

dis'petto sm spite q, spitefulness q; **fare un ~ a** qd to play a (nasty) trick on sb; **a ~ di** in spite of; **dispet'toso, a** ag spiteful.

dispia'cere [dispja'tʃere] sm (rammarico) regret, sorrow; (dolore) grief; **~i** smpl troubles, worries // vi: **~ a** to displease // vb impers: **mi dispiace (che)** I am sorry (that); **se non le dispiace, me ne vado adesso** if you don't mind, I'll go now; **displaci'uto, a** pp di **dispiacere.**

dispo'nibile ag available.

dis'porre vt (sistemare) to arrange; (preparare) to prepare; (DIR) to order; (persuadere): **~ qd a** to incline o dispose sb towards // vi (decidere) to decide; (usufruire): **~ di** to use, have at one's disposal; (essere dotato): **~ di** to have; **disporsi** vr (ordinarsi) to place o.s., arrange o.s.; **disporsi a fare** to get ready to do; **disposizi'one** sf arrangement, layout; (stato d'animo) mood; (tendenza) bent, inclination; (comando) order; (DIR) provision, regulation; **a disposizione di** qd at sb's disposal; **dis'posto, a** pp di **disporre.**

dis'potico, a, ci, che ag despotic.

disprez'zare [dispret'tsare] vt to despise.

dis'prezzo [dis'prettso] sm contempt.

'disputa sf dispute, quarrel.

dispu'tare vt (contendere) to dispute, contest; (SPORT: partita) to play; (: gareggiare) to take part in // vi to quarrel; **~ di** to discuss; **~rsi** qc to fight for sth.

dissangua'mento sm loss of blood.

disse'care vt to dissect.

dissec'care vt, **~rsi** vr to dry up.

dissemi'nare vt to scatter; (fig: notizie) to spread.

dis'senso sm dissent; (disapprovazione) disapproval.

dissente'ria sf dysentery.

dissen'tire vi: **~ (da)** to disagree (with).

dissertazi'one [dissertat'tsjone] sf dissertation.

disser'vizio [disser'vittsjo] sm inefficiency.

disses'tare vt (ECON) to ruin; **dis'sesto** sm (financial) ruin.

disse'tante ag refreshing.

disse'tare vt to quench the thirst of.

dissezi'one [disset'tsjone] sf dissection.

dissi'dente ag, sm/f dissident.

dis'sidio sm disagreement.

dis'simile ag different, dissimilar.

dissimu'lare vt (fingere) to dissemble; (nascondere) to conceal.

dissi'pare vt (dissipare; (scialacquare) to squander, waste; **dissipa'tezza** sf dissipation; **dissipazi'one** sf squandering.

dissoci'are [disso'tʃare] vt to dissociate.

dis'solto, a pp di **dissolvere.**

disso'lubile ag soluble.

disso'luto, a pp di **dissolvere** // ag dissolute, licentious.

dis'solvere vt to dissolve; (neve) to melt;

(fumo) to disperse; **~rsi** vr to dissolve; to melt; to disperse.

disso'nante ag discordant.

dissu'adere vt: **~ qd da** to dissuade sb from; **dissu'aso, a** pp di **dissuadere.**

distac'care vt to detach, separate; (SPORT) to leave behind; **~rsi** vr to be detached; (fig) to stand out; **~rsi da** (fig: allontanarsi) to grow away from.

dis'tacco, chi sm (separazione) separation; (fig: indifferenza) detachment; (SPORT): **è arrivato con un ~ di 10 minuti dai primi** he came in 10 minutes behind the leaders.

dis'tante av far away // ag distant, far away.

dis'tanza [dis'tantsa] sf distance.

distanzi'are [distan'tsjare] vt to space out, place at intervals; (SPORT) to outdistance; (fig: superare) to outstrip, surpass.

dis'tare vi: **distiamo pochi chilometri da Roma** we are only a few kilometres (away) from Rome.

dis'tendere vt (coperta) to spread out; (gambe) to stretch (out); (mettere a giacere) to lay; (rilassare: muscoli, nervi) to relax; **~rsi** vr (rilassarsi) to relax; (sdraiarsi) to lie down; **distensi'one** sf stretching; relaxation; (POL) détente.

dis'teso, a pp di **distendere** // sf expanse, stretch.

distil'lare vt to distil.

distille'ria sf distillery.

dis'tinguere vt to distinguish.

dis'tinta sf (nota) note; (elenco) list.

distin'tivo, a ag distinctive; distinguishing // sm badge.

dis'tinto, a pp di **distinguere** // ag (dignitoso ed elegante) distinguished; **"~i saluti"** "Yours faithfully".

distinzi'one [distin'tsjone] sf distinction.

dis'togliere [dis'tɔʎʎere] vt: **~ da** to take away from; (fig) to dissuade from; **dis'tolto, a** pp di **distogliere.**

distorsi'one sf (MED) sprain; (alterazione) distortion.

dis'trarre vt to distract; (divertire) to entertain, amuse; **distrarsi** vr (svagarsi) to amuse o enjoy o.s.; **dis'tratto, a** pp di **distrarre** // ag absent-minded; (disattento) inattentive; **distrazi'one** sf absent-mindedness; inattention; (svago) distraction, entertainment.

dis'tretto sm district.

distribu'ire vt to distribute; (CARTE) to deal (out); (consegnare: posta) to deliver; **distribu'tore** sm (di benzina) petrol pump; (AUT, ELETTR) distributor; (automatico) vending o slot machine; **distribuzi'one** sf distribution; delivery.

distri'care vt to disentangle, unravel.

dis'truggere [dis'truddʒere] vt to destroy; **distrut'tivo, a** ag destructive; **dis'trutto, a** pp di **distruggere**; **distruzi'one** sf destruction.

distur'bare vt to disturb, trouble; (sonno,

lezioni) to disturb, interrupt; **~rsi** *vr* to put o.s. out.

dis'turbo *sm* trouble, bother, inconvenience; (*indisposizione*) (slight) disorder, ailment; **~i** *smpl* (*RADIO, TV*) static *sg*.

disubbidi'ente *ag* disobedient; **disubbidi'enza** *sf* disobedience.

disubbi'dire *vi*: **~ (a qd)** to disobey (sb).

disugu'ale *ag* unequal; (*diverso*) different; (*irregolare*) uneven.

disu'mano, a *ag* inhuman.

disu'nire *vt* to divide, disunite.

di'suso *sm* disuse; **andare** *o* **cadere in ~** to fall into disuse.

'dita *fpl di* **dito**.

di'tale *sm* thimble.

'dito, *pl(f)* **'dita** *sm* finger; (*misura*) finger, finger's breadth; **~ (del piede)** toe.

'ditta *sf* firm, business.

ditta'tore *sm* dictator.

ditta'tura *sf* dictatorship.

dit'tongo, ghi *sm* diphthong.

di'urno, a *ag* day *cpd*, daytime *cpd* // *sm* (*anche*: **albergo ~**) public toilets with washing and shaving facilities etc.

'diva *sf vedi* **divo**.

diva'gare *vi* to digress; **divagazi'one** *sf* digression.

divam'pare *vi* (2) to flare up, blaze up.

di'vano *sm* sofa; divan.

divari'care *vt* to open wide.

di'vario *sm* difference.

dive'nire *vi* (2) = **diventare**; **dive'nuto, a** *pp di* **divenire**.

diven'tare *vi* (2) to become; **~ famoso/professore** to become famous/a teacher.

di'verbio *sm* altercation.

diver'gente [diver'dʒɛnte] *ag* divergent.

di'vergere [di'vɛrdʒere] *vi* to diverge.

diversifi'care *vt* to diversify, vary; to differentiate.

diversi'one *sf* diversion.

diversità *sf inv* difference, diversity; (*varietà*) variety.

diver'sivo *sm* diversion, distraction.

di'verso, a *ag* (*differente*): **~ (da)** different (from); **~i, e** *det pl* several, various; (*COMM*) sundry // *pronome pl* several (people); many (people).

diver'tente *ag* amusing.

diverti'mento *sm* amusement, pleasure; (*passatempo*) pastime, recreation.

diver'tire *vt* to amuse, entertain; **~rsi** *vr* to amuse *o* enjoy o.s.

divi'dendo *sm* dividend.

di'videre *vt* (*anche MAT*) to divide; (*distribuire, ripartire*) to divide (up), split (up).

divi'eto *sm* prohibition; **"~ di sosta"** (*AUT*) "no parking".

divinco'larsi *vr* to wriggle, writhe.

divinità *sf inv* divinity.

di'vino, a *ag* divine.

di'visa *sf* (*MIL etc*) uniform; (*COMM*) foreign currency.

divisi'one *sf* division.

di'viso, a *pp di* **dividere**.

'divo, a *sm/f* star.

divo'rare *vt* to devour.

divorzi'are [divor'tsjare] *vi*: **~ (da qd)** to divorce (sb).

di'vorzio [di'vɔrtsjo] *sm* divorce.

divul'gare *vt* to divulge, disclose; (*rendere comprensibile*) to popularize; **~rsi** *vr* to spread.

dizio'nario [ditsjo'narjo] *sm* dictionary.

dizi'one [dit'tsjone] *sf* diction; pronunciation.

do *sm* (*MUS*) C; (*: solfeggiando la scala*) do(h).

'doccia, ce ['dottʃa] *sf* shower; (*condotto*) pipe.

do'cente [do'tʃɛnte] *ag* teaching // *sm/f* teacher; (*di università*) lecturer; **do'cenza** *sf* university teaching *o* lecturing.

'docile ['dɔtʃile] *ag* docile.

documen'tare *vt* to document; **~rsi** *vr*: **~rsi (su)** to gather information *o* material (about).

documen'tario, a *ag, sm* documentary.

documentazi'one [dokumenta'tsjone] *sf* documentation.

docu'mento *sm* document; **~i** *smpl* (*d'identità etc*) papers.

'dodici ['doditʃi] *num* twelve.

do'gana *sf* (*ufficio*) customs *pl*; (*tassa*) (customs) duty; **passare la ~** to go through customs; **doga'nale** *ag* customs *cpd*; **dogani'ere** *sm* customs officer.

'doglie ['dɔʎʎe] *sfpl* (*MED*) labour *sg*, labour pains.

'dogma, i *sm* dogma.

'dolce ['doltʃe] *ag* sweet; (*colore*) soft; (*fig: mite: clima*) mild; (*non ripido: pendio*) gentle // *sm* (*sapore dolce*) sweetness, sweet taste; (*CUC: portata*) sweet, dessert; (*: torta*) cake; **dol'cezza** *sf* sweetness; softness; mildness; gentleness; **dolci'umi** *smpl* sweets.

do'lente *ag* sorrowful, sad.

do'lere *vi* (2) to be sore, hurt, ache; **~rsi** *vr* to complain; (*essere spiacente*): **~rsi di** to be sorry for; **mi duole la testa** my head aches, I've got a headache.

'dollaro *sm* dollar.

'dolo *sm* (*DIR*) malice.

Dolo'miti *sfpl*: **le ~** the Dolomites.

do'lore *sm* (*fisico*) pain; (*morale*) sorrow, grief; **dolo'roso, a** *ag* painful; sorrowful, sad.

do'loso, a *ag* (*DIR*) malicious.

do'manda *sf* (*interrogazione*) question; (*richiesta*) demand; (*: cortese*) request; (*DIR: richiesta scritta*) application; (*ECON*): **la ~** demand; **fare una ~ a qd** to ask sb a question.

doman'dare *vt* (*per avere*) to ask for; (*per sapere*) to ask; (*esigere*) to demand; **~rsi** *vr* to wonder; to ask o.s.; **~ qc a qd** to ask sb for sth; to ask sb sth.

do'mani *av* tomorrow // *sm*: **il ~** (*il futuro*) the future; (*il giorno successivo*) the next day; ~ **l'altro** the day after tomorrow.

do'**mare** vt to tame.

domat'**tina** av tomorrow morning.

do'**menica, che** sf Sunday; **di** o **la** ~ on Sundays; **domeni'cale** ag Sunday cpd.

do'**mestica, che** sf vedi **domestico**.

domesti'**chezza** [domesti'kettsa] sf = **dimestichezza**.

do'**mestico, a, ci, che** ag domestic // sm/f servant, domestic.

domi'**cilio** [domi'tʃiljo] sm (DIR) domicile, place of residence.

domi'**nare** vt to dominate; (fig: sentimenti) to control, master // vi to be in the dominant position; ~**rsi** vr (controllarsi) to control o.s.; ~ **su** (fig) to surpass, outclass; **dominazi'one** sf domination.

do'**minio** sm dominion; (fig: campo) field, domain.

do'**nare** vt to give, present; (per beneficenza etc) to donate // vi (fig): ~ **a** to suit, become; **dona'tore, 'trice** sm/f donor; **donatore di sangue** blood donor; **donazi'one** sf donation.

dondo'**lare** (cullare) to rock; ~**rsi** vr to swing, sway; '**dondolo** sm: **sedia/cavallo a dondolo** rocking chair/horse.

'**donna** sf woman; ~ **di casa** housewife; home-loving woman; ~ **di servizio** maid.

donnai'**olo** sm ladykiller.

don'**nesco, a, schi, sche** ag women's, woman's.

'**donnola** sf weasel.

'**dono** sm gift.

'**dopo** av (tempo) afterwards; (luogo) after, next // prep after // cong (temporale): ~ **aver studiato** after having studied; ~ **mangiato va a dormire** after having eaten o after a meal he goes for a sleep // ag inv: **il giorno** ~ the following day; **un anno** ~ a year later; ~ **di me/lui** after me/him.

dopodo'**mani** av the day after tomorrow.

dopogu'**erra** sm postwar years pl.

dopo'**pranzo** [dopo'prandzo] av after lunch (o dinner).

doposcì [dopoʃ'ʃi] sm inv après-ski outfit.

doposcu'**ola** sm inv sort of school club offering extra tuition and recreational facilities.

dopo'**tutto** av after all.

doppi'**aggio** [dop'pjaddʒo] sm (CINEMA) dubbing.

doppi'**are** vt (NAUT) to round; (SPORT) to lap; (CINEMA) to dub.

'**doppio, a** ag double; (fig: falso) double-dealing, deceitful // sm (quantità): **il** ~ **(di)** twice as much (o many), double the amount (o number) of; (SPORT) doubles pl // av double.

doppi'**one** sm duplicate (copy).

doppio'**petto** sm double-breasted jacket.

do'**rare** vt to gild; (CUC) to brown; **dora-'tura** sf gilding.

dormicchi'**are** [dormik'kjare] vi to doze.

dormigli'**one, a** [dormiʎ'ʎone] sm/f sleepyhead.

dor'**mire** vt, vi to sleep; **dor'mita** sf (good) sleep.

dormi'**torio** sm dormitory.

dormi'**veglia** [dormi'veʎʎa] sm drowsiness.

'**dorso** sm back; (di montagna) ridge, crest; (di libro) spine; **a** ~ **di cavallo** on horseback.

do'**sare** vt to measure out; (MED) to dose.

'**dose** sf quantity, amount; (MED) dose.

'**dosso** sm (dorso) back; **levarsi di** ~ **i vestiti** to take one's clothes off.

do'**tare** vt: ~ **di** to provide o supply with; (fig) to endow with; **dotazi'one** sf (insieme di beni) endowment; (di macchine etc) equipment.

'**dote** sf (di sposa) dowry; (assegnata a un ente) endowment; (fig) gift, talent.

Dott. (abbr di **dottore**) Dr.

'**dotto, a** ag (colto) learned // sm (sapiente) scholar; (ANAT) duct.

dotto'**rato** sm degree; (di ricerca) doctorate, doctor's degree.

dot'**tore, essa** sm/f doctor.

dot'**trina** sf doctrine.

Dott.ssa (abbr di **dottoressa**) Dr.

'**dove** av where; (in cui) where, in which; (dovunque) wherever; **di** ~ **sei?** where are you from?; **da** ~ **abito vedo tutta la città** I can see the whole city from where I stay; **per** ~ **si passa?** which way should we go?

do'**vere** sm (obbligo) duty // vt (essere debitore): ~ **qc (a qd)** to owe (sb) sth // vi (seguito dall'infinito: obbligo) to have to; **lui deve farlo** he has to do it, he must do it; **è dovuto partire** he had to leave; **ha dovuto pagare** he had to pay; (: intenzione): **devo partire domani** I'm (due) to leave tomorrow; (: probabilità) **dev'essere tardi** it must be late.

dove'**roso, a** ag (right and) proper.

do'**vunque** av (in qualunque luogo) wherever; (dappertutto) everywhere; ~ **io vada** wherever I go.

do'**vuto, a** ag (causato): ~ **a** due to.

doz'**zina** [dod'dzina] sf dozen; **una** ~ **di uova** a dozen eggs.

dozzi'**nale** [doddzi'nale] ag cheap, second-rate.

dra'**gare** vt to dredge.

'**drago, ghi** sm dragon.

'**dramma, i** sm drama; **dram'matico, a, ci, che** ag dramatic; **drammatiz'zare** vt to dramatize; **dramma'turgo, ghi** sm playwright, dramatist.

drappeggi'**are** [draped'dʒare] vt o drape.

drap'**pello** sm (MIL) squad; (gruppo) band, group.

dre'**naggio** [dre'naddʒo] sm drainage.

dre'**nare** vt to drain.

'**dritto, a** ag, av = **diritto**.

driz'**zare** [drit'tsare] vt (far tornare diritto) to straighten; (volgere: sguardo, occhi) to turn, direct; (*innalzare: antenna, muro*) to erect; ~**rsi** *vr* to stand up; ~ **le orecchie** to prick up one's ears.

'droga, ghe *sf* (*sostanza aromatica*) spice; (*stupefacente*) drug; **dro'gare** *vt* to season, spice; to drug, dope; **drogarsi** *vr* to take drugs; **dro'gato, a** *sm/f* drug addict.

droghe'ria [droge'ria] *sf* grocer's shop.

drome'dario *sm* dromedary.

'dubbio, a *ag* (*incerto*) doubtful, dubious; (*ambiguo*) dubious // *sm* (*incertezza*) doubt; **avere il** ~ **che** to be afraid that, suspect that; **mettere in** ~ **qc** to question sth; **dubbi'oso, a** *ag* doubtful, dubious.

dubi'tare *vi*: ~ **di** to doubt; (*risultato*) to be doubtful of; **dubita'tivo, a** *ag* doubtful, dubious.

'duca, chi *sm* duke.

du'chessa [du'kessa] *sf* duchess.

'due *num* two.

due'cento [due'tʃɛnto] *num* two hundred // *sm*: **il D**~ the thirteenth century.

du'ello *sm* duel.

due'pezzi [due'pɛttsi] *sm* (*costume da bagno*) two-piece swimsuit; (*abito femminile*) two-piece suit *o* costume.

du'etto *sm* duet.

'duna *sf* dune.

'dunque *cong* (*perciò*) so, therefore; (*riprendendo il discorso*) well (then).

du'omo *sm* cathedral.

dupli'cato *sm* duplicate.

'duplice ['duplitʃe] *ag* double, twofold; **in** ~ in duplicate.

du'rante *prep* during.

du'rare *vi* to last; (*perseverare*): ~ **in qc/a fare qc** to persist *o* persevere in sth/in doing sth; ~ **fatica a** to have difficulty in; **du'rata** *sf* length (of time); duration; **dura'turo, a** *ag*, **du'revole** *ag* lasting.

du'rezza [du'rettsa] *sf* hardness; stubbornness; harshness; toughness.

'duro, a *ag* (*pietra, lavoro, materasso, problema*) hard; (*persona: ostinato*) stubborn, obstinate; (: *severo*) harsh, hard; (*voce*) harsh; (*carne*) tough // *sm* (*persona*) tough guy; ~ **d'orecchi** hard of hearing; ~ **di testa** (*fig: fam*) slow-witted.

du'rone *sm* hard skin.

E

e, *dav* V *spesso* **ed** *cong* and.

E. (*abbr di* **est**) E.

è *forma del vb* **essere.**

'ebano *sm* ebony.

eb'bene *cong* well (then).

eb'brezza [eb'brettsa] *sf* intoxication.

'ebbro, a *ag* drunk; ~ **di** (*gioia etc*) beside o.s. *o* wild with.

'ebete *ag* stupid, idiotic.

eboliizi'one [ebollit'tsjone] *sf* boiling; **punto di** ~ boiling point.

e'braico, a, ci, che *ag* Hebrew, Hebraic // *sm* (*LING*) Hebrew.

e'breo, a *ag* Jewish // *sm/f* Jew/Jewess.

ecc *av* (*abbr di* **eccetera**) etc.

ecce'denza [ettʃe'dɛntsa] *sf* excess, surplus.

ec'cedere [et'tʃɛdere] *vt* to exceed // *vi* to go too far; ~ **nel bere/mangiare** to indulge in drink/food to excess.

eccel'lente [ettʃel'lɛnte] *ag* excellent; **eccel'lenza** *sf* excellence; (*titolo*) Excellency.

ec'cellere [et'tʃellere] *vi* to excel; ~ **su tutti** to surpass everyone; **ec'celso, a** *pp di* **eccellere.**

ec'centrico, a, ci, che [et'tʃɛntriko] *ag* eccentric; (*quartiere*) outlying.

ecces'sivo, a [ettʃes'sivo] *ag* excessive.

ec'cesso [et'tʃɛsso] *sm* excess; **all'**~ (*gentile, generoso*) to excess, excessively; **dare in** ~**i** to fly into a rage.

ec'cetera [et'tʃɛtera] *av* et cetera, and so on.

ec'cetto [et'tʃɛtto] *prep* except, with the exception of; ~ **che** *cong* except, other than; ~ **che (non)** unless.

eccettu'are [ettʃettu'are] *vt* to except.

eccezio'nale [ettʃetsjo'nale] *ag* exceptional.

eccezi'one [ettʃet'tsjone] *sf* exception; (*DIR*) objection; **a** ~ **di** with the exception of, except for; **d'**~ exceptional.

ecci'tare [ettʃi'tare] *vt* (*curiosità, interesse*) to excite, arouse; (*folla*) to incite; ~**rsi** *vr* to get excited; **eccita- zi'one** *sf* excitement.

ecclesi'astico, a, ci, che *ag* ecclesiastical, church *cpd*; clerical // *sm* ecclesiastic.

'ecco *av* (*per dimostrare*): ~ **il treno!** here's *o* here comes the train!; (*dav pronome*): ~**mi!** here I am!; ~**ne uno!** here's one (of them)!; (*dav pp*): ~ **fatto!** there, that's it done!

echeggi'are [eked'dʒare] *vi* to echo.

e'clissi *sf* eclipse.

'eco, *pl*(*m*) **'echi** *sm o f* echo.

ecolo'gia [ekolo'dʒia] *sf* ecology.

econo'mia *sf* economy; (*scienza*) economics *sg*; (*risparmio: azione*) saving; ~**e** *sfpl* (*denari risparmiati*) savings; **fare** ~**e** to save; **eco'nomico, a, ci, che** *ag* (*ECON*) economic; (*poco costoso*) economical; **econo'mista, i** *sm* economist; **economiz'zare** *vi* to save; **e'conomo, a** *ag* thrifty // *sm/f* (*INS*) bursar.

ed *cong vedi* **e.**

'edera *sf* ivy.

e'dicola *sf* newspaper kiosk.

edifi'care *vt* to build; (*fig: teoria, azienda*) to establish; (*indurre al bene*) to edify.

edi'ficio [edi'fitʃo] *sm* building; (*fig*) structure.

e'dile *ag* building *cpd*; **edi'lizio, a** *ag* building *cpd* // *sf* building, building trade.

edi'tore, 'trice *ag* publishing *cpd* // *sm/f* publisher; (*curatore*) editor; **edito'ria** *sf* publishing; **editori'ale** *ag* publishing *cpd* // *sm* editorial, leader.

edizi'one [edit'tsjone] *sf* edition; (*tiratura*) printing; (*di manifestazioni, feste etc*) production.

edu'care *vt* to educate; (*abituare*): ~ **(a)** to train (for); **edu'cato, a** *ag* polite, well-mannered; **educazi'one** *sf* education; (*comportamento*) (good) manners *pl*; **educazione fisica** (*INS*) physical training *o* education.

effemi'nato, a *ag* effeminate.

efferve'scente [efferveʃ'ʃɛnte] *ag* effervescent.

effet'tivo, a *ag* (*reale*) real, actual; (*operaio, professore*) permanent; (*MIL*) regular // *sm* (*MIL*) strength; (*di patrimonio etc*) sum total.

ef'fetto *sm* effect; (*fig: impressione*) impression; **cercare l'~** to look for attention; **in ~i** in fact, actually; **effettu'are** *vt* to effect, carry out.

effi'cace [effi'katʃe] *ag* effective.

effici'ente [effi'tʃɛnte] *ag* efficient; **effici'enza** *sf* efficiency; **in piena efficienza** (*persona*) fit; (*macchina*) in perfect working order.

ef'figie [ef'fidʒe] *sf inv* effigy.

ef'fimero, a *ag* ephemeral.

effusi'one *sf* effusion.

E'geo [e'dʒɛo] *sm*: **l'~, il mare ~** the Aegean (Sea).

E'gitto [e'dʒitto] *sm*: **l'~** Egypt.

'egli ['eʎʎi] *pronome* he; ~ **stesso** he himself.

ego'ismo *sm* selfishness, egoism; **ego'ista, i, e** *ag* selfish, egoistic // *sm/f* egoist.

egr. *abbr di* **egregio**.

e'gregio, a, gi, gie [e'grɛdʒo] *ag* distinguished; (*nelle lettere*): **E~ Signore** Dear Sir.

eguagli'anza [egwaʎ'ʎantsa] *etc vedi* **uguaglianza** *etc*.

elabo'rare *vt* (*progetto*) to work out, elaborate; (*dati*) to process; (*digerire*) to digest; **elaborazi'one** *sf* elaboration; digestion; **elaborazione dei dati** data processing.

e'lastico, a, ci, che *ag* elastic // *sm* (*gommino*) rubber band; (*per il cucito*) elastic *q*.

ele'fante *sm* elephant.

ele'gante *ag* elegant; **ele'ganza** *sf* elegance.

e'leggere [e'lɛddʒere] *vt* to elect.

elemen'tare *ag* elementary; ~**i** *sfpl* primary school.

ele'mento *sm* element; (*parte componente*) element, component, part; ~**i** *smpl* (*della scienza etc*) elements, rudiments.

ele'mosina *sf* charity, alms *pl*.

elen'care *vt* to list.

e'lenco, chi *sm* list; ~ **telefonico** telephone directory.

e'letto, a *pp di* **eleggere** // *sm/f* (*nominato*) elected member; **eletto'rale** *ag* electoral, election *cpd*; **eletto'rato** *sm*

electorate; **elet'tore, 'trice** *sm/f* voter, elector.

elet'trauto *sm inv* workshop for car electrical repairs; (*tecnico*) car electrician.

elettri'cista, i [elettri'tʃista] *sm* electrician.

elettri'cità [elettritʃi'ta] *sf* electricity.

e'lettrico, a, ci, che *ag* electric(al).

elettrifi'care *vt* to electrify.

elettriz'zare [elettrid'dzare] *vt* to electrify.

e'lettro... *prefisso*: **elettrocardio-'gramma, i** *sm* electrocardiogram; **e'lettrodo** *sm* electrode; **elettrodo-'mestico, a, ci, che** *ag*: **apparecchi elettrodomestici** domestic (electrical) appliances; **elettroma'gnetico, a, ci, che** *ag* electromagnetic; **elet'trone** *sm* electron; **elet'tronico, a, ci, che** *ag* electronic // *sf* electronics *sg*; **elettro-'treno** *sm* electric train.

ele'vare *vt* to raise; (*edificio*) to erect; (*multa*) to impose; **elevazi'one** *sf* elevation; (*l'elevare*) raising.

elezi'one [elet'tsjone] *sf* election; ~**i** *sfpl* (*POL*) election(s).

'elica, che *sf* propeller.

eli'cottero *sm* helicopter.

elimi'nare *vt* to eliminate; **elimina'toria** *sf* eliminating round.

'elio *sm* helium.

'ella *pronome* she; (*forma di cortesia*) you; ~ **stessa** she herself; you yourself.

el'metto *sm* helmet.

e'logio [e'lɔdʒo] *sm* (*discorso, scritto*) eulogy; (*lode*) praise (*di solito q*).

elo'quente *ag* eloquent; **elo'quenza** *sf* eloquence.

e'ludere *vt* to evade; **elu'sivo, a** *ag* evasive.

ema'nare *vt* to send out, give out; (*fig: leggi, decreti*) to issue // *vi* (2): ~ **da** to come from.

emanci'pare [emantʃi'pare] *vt* to emancipate; ~**rsi** *vr* (*fig*) to become liberated *o* emancipated; **emancipa-zi'one** *sf* emancipation.

em'blema, i *sm* emblem.

embri'one *sm* embryo.

emenda'mento *sm* amendment.

emen'dare *vt* to amend.

emer'genza [emer'dʒɛntsa] *sf* emergency; **in caso di** ~ in an emergency.

e'mergere [e'mɛrdʒere] *vi* to emerge; (*sommergibile*) to surface; (*fig: distinguersi*) to stand out; **e'merso, a** *pp di* **emergere**.

e'messo, a *pp di* **emettere**.

e'mettere *vt* (*suono, luce*) to give out, emit; (*onde radio*) to send out; (*assegno, francobollo*) to issue; (*fig: giudizio*) to express, voice.

emi'crania *sf* migraine.

emi'grante *ag, sm/f* emigrant.

emi'grare *vi* to emigrate; **emigrazi'one** *sf* emigration.

emi'nente *ag* eminent, distinguished; **emi'nenza** *sf* eminence.

emis'fero *sm* hemisphere; ∼ **boreale/australe** northern/southern hemisphere.

emissi'one *sf* emission; sending out; issue; (RADIO) broadcast.

emit'tente *ag* (*banca*) issuing; (RADIO) broadcasting, transmitting // *sf* (RADIO) transmitter.

emorra'gia, 'gie [emorra'dʒia] *sf* haemorrhage.

emo'tivo, a *ag* emotional.

emozio'nante [emottsjo'nante] *ag* exciting, thrilling.

emozio'nare [emottsjo'nare] *vt* (*eccitare*) to excite; (*commuovere*) to move; (*turbare*) to upset; ∼**rsi** *vr* to be excited; to be moved; to be upset.

emozi'one [emot'tsjone] *sf* emotion; (*agitazione*) excitement.

'empio, a *ag* (*sacrilego*) impious; (*spietato*) cruel, pitiless; (*malvagio*) wicked, evil.

em'pire *vt* to fill (up).

em'porio *sm* market, commercial centre; (*grande magazzino*) department store.

emu'lare *vt* to emulate.

emulsi'one *sf* emulsion.

en'ciclica, che [en'tʃiklika] *sf* (REL) encyclical.

enciclope'dia [entʃiklope'dia] *sf* encyclopaedia.

endove'noso, a *ag* (MED) intravenous.

ener'gia, 'gie [ener'dʒia] *sf* (FISICA) energy; (*fig*) energy, strength, vigour; **e'nergico, a, ci, che** *ag* energetic, vigorous; (*efficace*) powerful, strong.

'enfasi *sf* emphasis; (*peg*) bombast, pomposity; **en'fatico, a, ci, che** *ag* pompous.

e'nigma, i *sm* enigma; **enig'matico, a, ci, che** *ag* enigmatic.

E.N.I.T. *abbr di Ente Nazionale Italiano per il Turismo.*

en'nesimo, a *ag* (MAT, *fig*) nth; **per l'∼a volta** for the umpteenth time.

e'norme *ag* enormous, huge; **enormità** *sf inv* enormity, huge size; (*assurdità*) absurdity; **non dire** ∼! don't talk nonsense!

'ente *sm* (*istituzione*) body, board, corporation; (FILOSOFIA) being.

en'trambi, e *pronome pl* both (of them) // *ag pl:* ∼ **i ragazzi** both boys, both of the boys.

en'trare *vi* (2) to enter, go (*o* come) in; ∼ **in** (*luogo*) to enter, go (*o* come) into; (*trovar posto, poter stare*) to fit into; (*essere ammesso a: club etc*) to join, become a member of; ∼ **in automobile** to get into the car; **questo non c'entra** (*fig*) that's got nothing to do with it; **en'trata** *sf* entrance, entry; **entrate** *sfpl* (COMM) receipts, takings; (ECON) income *sg*.

'entro *prep* (*temporale*) within.

entusias'mare *vt* to excite, fill with enthusiasm; ∼**rsi (per qc/qd)** to become enthusiastic (about sth/sb); **entusi'asmo**

sm enthusiasm; **entusi'asta, i, e** *ag* enthusiastic // *sm/f* enthusiast; **entu-si'astico, a, ci, che** *ag* enthusiastic.

enume'rare *vt* to enumerate, list.

enunci'are [enun'tʃare] *vt* (*teoria*) to enunciate, set out.

'epico, a, ci, che *ag* epic.

epide'mia *sf* epidemic.

Epifa'nia *sf* Epiphany.

epiles'sia *sf* epilepsy.

e'pilogo, ghi *sm* conclusion.

epi'sodio *sm* episode.

e'pistola *sf* epistle.

e'piteto *sm* epithet.

'epoca, che *sf* (*periodo storico*) age, era; (*tempo*) time; (GEO) age.

ep'pure *cong* and yet, nevertheless.

epu'rare *vt* (POL) to purge; (: *persona*) to expel, remove.

equa'tore *sm* equator.

equazi'one [ekwat'tsjone] *sf* (MAT) equation.

e'questre *ag* equestrian.

equi'latero, a *ag* equilateral.

equili'brare *vt* to balance; **equi'librio** *sm* balance; (*bilancia*) equilibrium.

e'quino, a *ag* horse *cpd*, equine.

equi'nozio [ekwi'nɔttsjo] *sm* equinox.

equipaggi'are [ekwipad'dʒare] *vt* (*di persone*) to man; (*di mezzi*) to equip; **equi-'paggio** *sm* crew.

equipa'rare *vt* to make equal.

equità *sf* equity, fairness.

equitazi'one [ekwitat'tsjone] *sf* (horse-)riding.

equiva'lente *ag, sm* equivalent; **equiva-'lenza** *sf* equivalence.

equivo'care *vi* to misunderstand; **e'quivoco, a, ci, che** *ag* equivocal, ambiguous; (*sospetto*) dubious // *sm* misunderstanding; **a scanso di equivoci** to avoid any misunderstanding; **giocare sull'equivoco** to equivocate.

'equo, a *ag* fair, just.

'era *sf* era.

'erba *sf* grass; (*aromatica, medicinale*) herb; **in** ∼ (*fig*) budding; **er'baccia, ce** *sf* weed; **er'boso, a** *ag* grassy.

e'rede *sm/f* heir; **eredità** *sf* (DIR) inheritance; (BIOL) heredity; **lasciare qc in eredità a qd** to leave *o* bequeath sth to sb; **eredi'tare** *vt* to inherit; **eredi'tario, a** *ag* hereditary.

ere'mita, i *sm* hermit.

ere'sia *sf* heresy; **e'retico, a, ci, che** *ag* heretical // *sm/f* heretic.

e'retto, a *pp di* **erigere** // *ag* erect, upright; **erezi'one** *sf* (FISIOL) erection.

er'gastolo *sm* (DIR: *pena*) life imprisonment; (: *luogo di pena*) prison.

'erica *sf* heather.

e'rigere [e'ridʒere] *vt* to erect, raise; (*fig:* *fondare*) to found.

ermel'lino *sm* ermine.

er'metico, a, ci, che *ag* hermetic.

'ernia *sf* (MED) hernia.

e'roe *sm* hero.

ero'gare *vt* (*somme*) to distribute; (: *per beneficenza*) to donate; (*gas, servizi*) to supply.

e'roico, a, ci, che *ag* heroic.

ero'ina *sf* heroine; (*droga*) heroin.

ero'ismo *sm* heroism.

erosi'one *sf* erosion.

e'rotico, a, ci, che *ag* erotic.

'erpice ['erpitʃe] *sm* (*AGR*) harrow.

er'rare *vi* (*vagare*) to wander, roam; (*sbagliare*) to be mistaken; **er'roneo, a** *ag* erroneous, wrong; **er'rore** *sm* error, mistake; (*morale*) error; **per errore** by mistake.

'erta *sf* steep slope; **stare all'~** to be on the alert.

eru'dito, a *ag* learned, erudite.

erut'tare *vi* to belch // *vt* (*sog: vulcano*) to throw out.

eruzi'one [erut'tsjone] *sf* eruption.

esacer'bare [ezatʃer'bare] *vt* to exacerbate.

esage'rare [ezadʒe'rare] *vt* to exaggerate // *vi* to exaggerate; (*eccedere*) to go too far; **esagerazi'one** *sf* exaggeration.

e'sagono *sm* hexagon.

esal'tare *vt* to exalt; (*entusiasmare*) to excite, stir; **esal'tato** *sm* fanatic.

e'same *sm* examination; (*INS*) exam, examination; **dare un ~** to sit an exam; **~ del sangue** blood test.

esami'nare *vt* to examine.

e'sanime *ag* lifeless.

esaspe'rare *vt* to exasperate; to exacerbate; **~rsi** *vr* to become annoyed *o* exasperated; **esasperazi'one** *sf* exasperation.

esat'tezza [ezat'tettsa] *sf* exactitude, accuracy, precision.

e'satto, a *pp* di **esigere** // *ag* (*calcolo, ora*) correct, right, exact; (*preciso*) accurate, precise; (*puntuale*) punctual.

esat'tore *sm* (*di imposte etc*) collector.

esau'dire *vt* to grant, fulfil.

esauri'ente *ag* exhaustive.

esauri'mento *sm* exhaustion; **~ nervoso** nervous breakdown.

esau'rire *vt* (*stancare*) to exhaust, wear out; (*provviste, miniera*) to exhaust; **~rsi** *vr* to exhaust o.s., wear o.s. out; (*provviste*) to run out; **esau'rito, a** *ag* exhausted; (*merci*) sold out; (*libri*) out of print; **e'sausto, a** *ag* exhausted.

'esca, *pl* **esche** *sf* bait; (*sostanza infiammabile*) tinder.

escande'scenza [eskandeʃ'ʃentsa] *sf*: **dare in ~e** to lose one's temper, fly into a rage.

'esce, 'esci ['eʃe,'eʃi] *forme del vb* **uscire**.

escla'mare *vi* to exclaim, cry out; **esclamazi'one** *sf* exclamation.

es'cludere *vt* to exclude; **esclusi'one** *sf* exclusion.

esclu'sivo, a *ag* exclusive // *sf* (*DIR*) exclusive *o* sole rights *pl*.

es'cluso, a *pp* di **escludere**.

'esco, 'escono *forme del vb* **uscire**.

'escono *forma del vb* **uscire**.

escre'menti *smpl* excrement *sg*, faeces.

escursi'one *sf* (*gita*) excursion, trip; (: *a piedi*) hike, walk; (*METEOR*) range.

ese'crare *vt* to loathe, abhor.

esecu'tivo, a *ag, sm* executive.

esecu'tore, 'trice *sm/f* (*MUS*) performer; (*DIR*) executor.

esecuzi'one [ezekut'tsjone] *sf* execution, carrying out; (*MUS*) performance; **~ capitale** execution.

esegu'ire *vt* to carry out, execute; (*MUS*) to perform, execute.

e'sempio *sm* example; **per ~** for example, for instance; **esem'plare** *ag* exemplary // *sm* example; (*copia*) copy; **esemplifi'care** *vt* to exemplify.

esen'tare *vt*: **~qd/qc da** to exempt sb/sth from.

e'sente *ag*: **~ da** (*dispensato da*) exempt from; (*privo di*) free from; **esenzi'one** *sf* exemption.

e'sequie *sfpl* funeral rites; funeral service *sg*.

eser'cente [ezer'tʃente] *sm/f* trader, dealer; shopkeeper.

eserci'tare [ezertʃi'tare] *vt* (*professione*) to practise; (*allenare: corpo, mente*) to exercise, train; (*diritto*) to exercise; (*influenza, pressione*) to exert; **~rsi** *vr* to practise; **~rsi alla lotta** to practise fighting; **esercitazi'one** *sf* (*scolastica, militare*) exercise.

e'sercito [e'zertʃito] *sm* army.

eser'cizio [ezer'tʃittsjo] *sm* practise; exercising; (*fisico, di matematica*) exercise; (*ECON*) financial year; (*azienda*) business, concern; **in ~** (*medico etc*) practising.

esi'bire *vt* to exhibit, display; (*documenti*) to produce, present; **~rsi** *vr* (*attore*) to perform; (*fig*) to show off; **esibizi'one** *sf* exhibition; (*di documento*) presentation; (*spettacolo*) show, performance.

esi'gente [ezi'dʒente] *ag* demanding; **esi-'genza** *sf* demand, requirement.

e'sigere [e'zidʒere] *vt* (*pretendere*) to demand; (*richiedere*) to demand, require; (*imposte*) to collect.

e'siguo, a *ag* small, slight.

'esile *ag* slender, slim; (*suono*) faint.

esili'are *vt* to exile; **e'silio** *sm* exile.

e'simere *vt*: **~ qd/qc da** to exempt sb/sth from.

esis'tenza [ezis'tentsa] *sf* existence.

e'sistere *vi* (2) to exist.

esis'tito, a *pp* di **esistere**.

esi'tare *vi* to hesitate; **esitazi'one** *sf* hesitation.

'esito *sm* result, outcome.

'esodo *sm* exodus.

esone'rare *vt*: **~ qd da** to exempt sb from.

esorbi'tante *ag* exorbitant, excessive.

esorciz'zare [ezortʃid'dʒare] *vt* to exorcize.

e'sordio *sm* début.

esor'tare vt: ~ qd a fare to urge sb to do.

e'sotico, a, ci, che ag exotic.

es'pandere vt to expand; (confini) to extend; (influenza) to extend, spread; ~rsi vr to expand; espansi'one sf expansion; espan'sivo, a ag expansive, communicative.

espatri'are vi (2) to leave one's country. espedi'ente sm expedient.

es'pellere vt to expel.

esperi'enza [espe'rjɛntsa] sf experience; (SCIENZA: prova) experiment; parlare per ~ to speak from experience.

esperi'mento sm experiment.

es'perto, a ag, sm expert.

espi'are vt to atone for.

espi'rare vt, vi to breathe out.

espli'care vt (attività) to carry out, perform.

es'plicito, a [es'plitʃito] ag explicit.

es'plodere vi (anche fig) to explode; (fucile) to go off // vt to fire.

esplo'rare vt to explore; esplora'tore, 'trice sm/f explorer; (anche: giovane esploratore) (boy) scout/(girl) guide // sm (NAUT) scout (ship); esplorazi'one sf exploration.

esplosi'one sf explosion; esplo'sivo, a ag, sm explosive; es'ploso, a pp di esplodere.

espo'nente sm/f (rappresentante) representative.

es'porre vt (merci) to display; (quadro) to exhibit, show; (fatti, idee) to explain, set out; (porre in pericolo, FOT) to expose.

espor'tare vt to export; esporta'tore, 'trice ag exporting // sm exporter; esportazi'one sf exportation; export.

esposizi'one [espozit'tsjone] sf displaying; exhibiting; setting out; (anche FOT) exposure; (mostra) exhibition; (narrazione) explanation, exposition.

es'posto, a pp di esporre // ag: ~ a nord facing north // sm (AMM) statement, account; (: petizione) petition.

espressi'one sf expression.

espres'sivo, a ag expressive.

es'presso, a pp di esprimere // ag express // sm (lettera) express letter; (anche: treno ~) express train; (anche: caffè ~) espresso.

es'primere vt to express; ~rsi vr to express o.s.

espulsi'one sf expulsion; es'pulso, a pp di espellere.

'essa pronome f, 'esse pronome fpl vedi esso.

es'senza [es'sɛntsa] sf essence; essenzi'ale ag essential; l'essenziale the main o most important thing.

'essere sm being; ~ umano human being // vi, vb con attributo (2) to be // vb ausiliare (2) to have (o qualche volta be); è giovane/professore he is young/a teacher; è l'una it's one o'clock; sono le otto it's eight o'clock; esserci: c'è/ci sono there is/there are; che c'è? what's wrong?; ci siamo! here we are!; (fig) this

is it!; (: siamo alle solite) here we go again!; ~ di (appartenenza) to belong to; (origine) to be from; è di mio fratello it belongs to my brother, it's my brother's.

'esso, a pronome it; (fam: riferito a persona: soggetto) he/she; (: complemento) him/her; ~i, e pronome pl they; (complemento) them.

est sm east.

'estasi sf ecstasy.

es'tate sf summer.

es'tatico, a, ci, che ag ecstatic.

es'tendere vt to extend; ~rsi vr (diffondersi) to spread; (territorio, confini) to extend; estensi'one sf extension; (di superficie) expanse; (MUS) range.

esteri'ore ag outward, external.

es'terno, a ag (porta, muro) outer, outside; (scala) outside; (alunno, impressione) external // sm outside, exterior // sm/f (allievo) day pupil; per uso ~ for external use only.

'estero, a ag foreign // sm: all'~ abroad.

es'teso, a pp di estendere // ag extensive, large; scrivere per ~ to write in full.

es'tetico, a, ci, che ag aesthetic // sf aesthetics sg; este'tista sf beautician.

'estimo sm (valuation); (disciplina) surveying.

es'tinguere vt to extinguish, put out; (debito) to pay off; ~rsi vr to go out; (famiglia, animali) to become extinct; es'tinto, a pp di estinguere; estin'tore sm (fire) extinguisher; estinzi'one sf putting out; (di famiglia, animali) extinction.

es'tivo, a ag summer cpd.

es'torcere [es'tortʃere] vt: ~ qc (a qd) to extort sth (from sb); estorsi'one sf extortion; es'torto, a pp di estorcere.

estradizi'one [estradit'tsjone] sf extradition.

es'traneo, a ag foreign; (discorso) extraneous, unrelated // sm/f stranger; rimanere ~ a qc to take no part in sth.

es'trarre vt to extract, pull out; (minerali) to mine; (sorteggiare) to draw; es'tratto, a pp di estrarre // sm extract; (di documento) abstract; estratto conto statement of account; estrazi'one sf extraction; mining; drawing q; draw.

estre'mista, i, e sm/f extremist.

estremità sf inv extremity, end // sfpl (ANAT) extremities.

es'tremo, a ag, sm extreme; l'~ Oriente the Far East.

'estro sm (capriccio) whim, fancy; (ispirazione creativa) inspiration; es'troso, a ag whimsical, capricious; inspired.

estro'verso, a ag, sm extrovert.

estu'ario sm estuary.

esube'rante ag exuberant.

'esule sm/f exile.

età sf inv age; all'~ di 8 anni at the age of 8, at 8 years of age; raggiungere la maggiore ~ to come of age; essere in ~ minore to be under age.

'etere sm ether; e'tereo, a ag ethereal.

eternità *sf* eternity.

e'terno, a *ag* eternal.

etero'geneo, a [etero'dʒɛneo] *ag* heterogeneous.

'etica *sf vedi* **etico.**

eti'chetta [eti'ketta] *sf* label; (*cerimoniale*) etiquette.

'etico, a, ci, che *ag* ethical // *sf* ethics *sg.*

etimolo'gia, **'gie** [etimolo'dʒia] *sf* etymology.

Eti'opia *sf:* **l'**~ Ethiopia.

'Etna *sm:* **l'**~ Etna.

'etnico, a, ci, che *ag* ethnic.

e'trusco, a, schi, sche *ag, sm/f* Etruscan.

'ettaro *sm* hectare (= *10,000 m²).*

'etto *sm abbr di* **ettogrammo.**

etto'grammo *sm* hectogram(me) (= *100 grams).*

Eucaris'tia *sf:* **l'**~ the Eucharist.

eufe'mismo *sm* euphemism.

Eu'ropa *sf:* **l'**~ Europe; **euro'peo, a** *ag, sm/f* European.

eutana'sia *sf* euthanasia.

evacu'are *vt* to evacuate; **evacuazi'one** *sf* evacuation.

e'vadere *vi* (2) (*fuggire*): ~ **da** to escape from // *vt* (*sbrigare*) to deal with, dispatch; (*tasse*) to evade.

evan'gelico, a, ci, che [evan'dʒɛliko] *ag* evangelical; **evange'lista, i** *sm* evangelist; **evan'gelo** *sm* = **vangelo.**

evapo'rare *vi* to evaporate; **evapora-zi'one** *sf* evaporation.

evasi'one *sf* escape; ~ **fiscale** tax evasion.

eva'sivo, a *ag* evasive.

e'vaso, a *pp di* **evadere** // *sm* escapee.

e'vento *sm* event.

eventu'ale *ag* possible.

evi'dente *ag* evident, obvious; **evi'denza** *sf* obviousness; **mettere in evidenza** to point out, highlight.

evi'tare *vt* to avoid; ~ **di fare** to avoid doing; ~ **qc a qd** to spare sb sth.

'evo *sm* age, epoch.

evo'care *vt* to evoke.

evo'luto, a *pp di* **evolvere.**

evoluzi'one [evolut'tsjone] *sf* evolution.

e'volversi *vr* to evolve.

ev'viva *escl* hurrah!; ~ **il re!** long live the king!, hurrah for the king!

ex *prefisso* ex-.

'extra *prep* outside, outwith // *ag inv* first-rate; top-quality // *sm inv* extra; **extraconiu'gale** *ag* extramarital.

F

fa *forma del vb* **fare** // *sm inv* (*MUS*) F; (: *solfeggiando la scala*) fa // *av:* **10 anni** ~ 10 years ago.

'fabbrica *sf* factory; **fabbri'cante** *sm* manufacturer, maker; **fabbri'care** *vt* to build; (*produrre*) to manufacture, make; (*fig*) to fabricate, invent.

'fabbro *sm* (black)smith.

fac'cenda [fat'tʃɛnda] *sf* matter, affair; (*cosa da fare*) task, chore.

fac'chino [fak'kino] *sm* porter.

'faccia, ce ['fattʃa] *sf* face; (*di moneta, disco etc*) side; ~ **a** ~ face to face.

facci'ata [fat'tʃata] *sf* façade; (*di pagina*) side.

'faccio ['fattʃo] *forma del vb* **fare.**

fa'ceto, a [fa'tʃeto] *ag* witty, humorous.

'facile ['fatʃile] *ag* easy; (*affabile*) easy-going; (*disposto*): ~ **a** inclined to, prone to; (*probabile*): **è** ~ **che piova** it's likely to rain; **facilità** *sf* easiness; (*disposizione, dono*) aptitude; **facili'tare** *vt* to make easier.

facino'roso, a [fatʃino'roso] *ag* violent.

facoltà *sf inv* faculty; (*potere*) power.

facolta'tivo, a *ag* optional; (*fermata d'autobus*) request *cpd.*

'faggio ['faddʒo] *sm* beech.

fagi'ano [fa'dʒano] *sm* pheasant.

fagio'lino [fadʒo'lino] *sm* French bean.

fagi'olo [fa'dʒolo] *sm* bean.

fa'gotto *sm* bundle; (*MUS*) bassoon; **far** ~ (*fig*) to pack up and go.

'fai *forma del vb* **fare.**

'falce ['faltʃe] *sf* scythe; **fal'cetto** *sm* sickle; **falci'are** *vt* to cut; (*fig*) to mow down.

'falco, chi *sm* hawk.

fal'cone *sm* falcon.

'falda *sf* layer, stratum; (*di cappello*) brim; (*di monte*) lower slope; (*di tetto*) pitch; **nevica a larghe** ~**e** the snow is falling in large flakes; **abito a** ~**e** tails *pl.*

fale'gname [falɛɲ'ɲame] *sm* joiner.

fal'lace [fal'latʃe] *ag* misleading, deceptive.

falli'mento *sm* failure; bankruptcy.

fal'lire *vi* (2: *non riuscire*): ~ (**in**) to fail (in); (*DIR*) to go bankrupt // *vt* (*bersaglio, preda*) to miss; **fal'lito, a** *ag* unsuccessful; bankrupt // *sm* bankrupt.

'fallo *sm* error, mistake; (*imperfezione*) defect, flaw; (*SPORT*) foul; fault; **senza** ~ without fail.

falò *sm inv* bonfire.

fal'sare *vt* to distort, misrepresent; **fal-'sario** *sm* forger; counterfeiter; **falsifi-'care** *vt* to forge; (*monete*) to forge, counterfeit.

'falso, a *ag* false; (*errato*) wrong, incorrect; (*falsificato*) forged; fake // *sm* forgery; **giurare il** ~ to commit perjury.

'fama *sf* fame; (*reputazione*) reputation, name.

'fame *sf* hunger; **aver** ~ to be hungry; **fa-'melico, a, ci, che** *ag* ravenous.

fa'miglia [fa'miʎʎa] *sf* family.

famili'are *ag* (*della famiglia*) family *cpd*; (*ben noto*) familiar; (*tono*) friendly, informal; (*LING*) informal, colloquial // *sm* relative, relation; **familiarità** *sf* familiarity; informality.

fa'moso, a *ag* famous, well-known.

fa'nale *sm* (*AUT*) light, lamp; (*NAUT*) beacon; ~ **di coda** (*AUT*) tail-light.

fa'natico, a, ci, che *ag* fanatical; (*del teatro, calcio etc*): ~ **di** *o* **per** mad *o* wild about // *sm/f* fanatic; (*tifoso*) fan.

fanciul'lezza [fantʃulˈlettsa] *sf* childhood.

fanci'ullo, a [fanˈtʃullo] *sm/f* child.

fan'donia *sf* tall story; ~**e** *sfpl* nonsense *sg*.

fan'fara *sf* brass band; (*musica*) fanfare.

'fango, ghi *sm* mud; **fan'goso, a** *ag* muddy.

'fanno *forma del vb* fare.

fannul'lone, a *sm/f* idler, loafer.

fantasci'enza [fantaʃˈʃentsa] *sf* science fiction.

fanta'sia *sf* fantasy, imagination; (*capriccio*) whim, caprice // *ag inv:* **vestito** ~ patterned dress.

fan'tasma, i *sm* ghost, phantom; (*immagine*) fantasy.

fantasteche'ria [fantastikeˈria] *sf* daydream.

fan'tastico, a, ci, che *ag* fantastic; (*potenza, ingegno*) imaginative.

'fante *sm* infantryman; (*CARTE*) jack, knave; **fante'ria** *sf* infantry.

fan'toccio [fanˈtɔttʃo] *sm* puppet.

far'dello *sm* bundle; (*fig*) burden.

'fare *vt* to make; (*operare, agire*) to do; (*TEATRO*) to act; ~ **l'avvocato/il medico** to be a lawyer/doctor; ~ **del tennis** to play tennis; ~ **il morto/l'ignorante** to act dead/the fool; **non fa niente** it doesn't matter; **2 più 2 fa 4** 2 and 2 are *o* make 4; **non ce la faccio più** I can't go on any longer; **farla a qd** to get the better of sb; **farla finita con qc** to have done with sth // *vi* (*essere adatto*) to be suitable; (*stare per*): **fece per parlare quando ...** he was about to speak when ...; ~ **in modo di** to act in such a way that; **faccia pure!** go ahead!; ~ **da** (*fare le funzioni di*) to act as // *vb impers:* vedi **bello, freddo** *etc*; ~ **piangere/ridere qd** to make sb cry/laugh; ~ **venire qd** to have sb come; **fammi vedere** let me see; ~**rsi** *vr* (*diventare*) to become; ~**rsi la macchina** to get a car for o.s.; ~**rsi avanti** to come forward; ~**rsi notare** to get o.s. noticed.

far'falla *sf* butterfly.

fa'rina *sf* flour.

fa'ringe [faˈrindʒe] *sf* (*ANAT*) pharynx.

farma'ceutico, a, ci, che [farmaˈtʃeutiko] *ag* pharmaceutical.

farma'cia, 'cie [farmaˈtʃia] *sf* pharmacy; (*locale*) chemist's (shop), pharmacy; **farma'cista, i, e** *sm/f* chemist, pharmacist.

'farmaco, ci *o* **chi** *sm* drug, medicine.

'faro *sm* (*NAUT*) lighthouse; (*AER*) beacon; (*AUT*) headlight, headlamp.

'farsa *sf* farce.

'fascia, sce [ˈfaʃʃa] *sf* band, strip; (*MED*) bandage; (*di carta*) wrapper; (*di sindaco, ufficiale*) sash; (*parte di territorio*) strip, belt.

fasci'are [faʃˈʃare] *vt* to bandage.

fa'scicolo [faʃˈʃikolo] *sm* (*di documenti*) file, dossier; (*di rivista*) issue, number; (*opuscolo*) booklet, pamphlet.

'fascino [ˈfaʃʃino] *sm* charm, fascination.

'fascio [ˈfaʃʃo] *sm* bundle, sheaf; (*di fiori*) bunch.

fa'scismo [faʃˈʃizmo] *sm* fascism.

'fase *sf* phase.

fas'tidio *sm* (*molestia*) annoyance, bother, trouble; (*scomodo*) inconvenience; **dare** ~ **a qd** to bother *o* annoy sb; **sento** ~ **allo stomaco** my stomach's upset; **fastidi'oso, a** *ag* annoying, tiresome; (*schifiltoso*) fastidious.

'fasto *sm* pomp, splendour.

'fata *sf* fairy.

fa'tale *ag* fatal; (*inevitabile*) inevitable; (*fig*) irresistible; **fatalità** *sf* inevitability; (*avversità*) misfortune; (*fato*) fate, destiny.

fa'tica, che *sf* hard work, toil; (*sforzo*) effort; (*di metalli*) fatigue; **a** ~ with difficulty; **fati'care** *vi* to toil; **faticare a fare qc** to have difficulty doing sth; **fati'coso, a** *ag* tiring, exhausting; hard, difficult.

'fato *sm* fate, destiny.

'fatto, a *pp di* fare // *ag:* **un uomo** ~ a grown man; ~ **a mano/in casa** hand-/home-made // *sm* fact; (*azione*) deed; (*di romanzo, film*) action, story; (*affare, caso*) event; **cogliere qd sul** ~ to catch sb red-handed; **il** ~ **sta** *o* **è che** the fact remains *o* is that; **in** ~ **di** as for, as far as ... is concerned.

fat'tore *sm* (*AGR*) farm manager; (*elemento costitutivo*) factor.

fatto'ria *sf* farm; farmhouse.

fatto'rino *sm* errand-boy; office-boy.

fat'tura *sf* (*di abito, scarpa*) cut, design; (*lavorazione*) workmanship; (*COMM*) invoice; (*malia*) spell.

fattu'rare *vt* (*COMM*) to invoice; (*vino*) to adulterate.

'fatuo, a *ag* vain, fatuous.

'fauna *sf* fauna.

fau'tore *sm* advocate, supporter.

fa'vella *sf* speech.

fa'villa *sf* spark.

'favola *sf* (*fiaba*) fairy tale; (*d'intento morale*) fable; (*fandonia*) yarn; **favo'loso, a** *ag* fabulous.

fa'vore *sm* favour; **per** ~ please; **favo'revole** *ag* favourable.

favo'rire *vt* to favour; (*il commercio, l'industria, le arti*) to promote, encourage; **vuole** ~? won't you help yourself?; **favorisca in salotto** please come into the sitting room; **favo'rito, a** *ag, sm/f* favourite.

fazi'one [fatˈtsjone] *sf* faction.

fazzo'letto [fattsoˈletto] *sm* handkerchief; (*per la testa*) (head)scarf.

feb'braio *sm* February.

'febbre *sf* fever; **aver la** ~ to have a high temperature; ~ **da fieno** hay fever; **feb'brile** *ag* (*anche fig*) feverish.

'feccia, ce [ˈfettʃa] *sf* dregs *pl*.

'fecola *sf* potato flour.

fecon'dare vt to fertilize.
fe'condo, a ag fertile.
'fede sf (credenza) belief, faith; (REL) faith; (fiducia) faith, trust; (fedeltà) loyalty; (anello) wedding ring; (attestato) certificate; **aver ~ in qd** to have faith in sb; **fe'dele** ag: **fedele (a)** faithful (to) // sm/f follower; **i fedeli** (REL) the faithful; **fedeltà** sf faithfulness; (coniugale, RADIO) fidelity.
'federa sf pillowslip, pillowcase.
fede'rale ag federal.
federazi'one [federat'tsjone] sf federation.
'fegato sm liver; (fig) guts pl, nerve.
'felce ['feltʃe] sf fern.
fe'lice [fe'litʃe] ag happy; (fortunato) lucky; **felicità** sf happiness.
felici'tarsi [felitʃi'tarsi] vr (congratularsi): **~ con qd per qc** to congratulate sb on sth.
fe'lino, a ag feline.
'feltro sm felt; (cappello) felt hat.
'femmina sf (ZOOL, TECN) female; (figlia) girl, daughter; (spesso peg) woman; **femmi'nile** ag feminine; (sesso) female; (lavoro) woman's // sm (LING) feminine; **femmi'nismo** sm feminism.
'fendere vt to split, cleave; (attraversare) to force one's way through.
fe'nomeno sm phenomenon.
'feretro sm coffin.
feri'ale ag working cpd, work cpd, week cpd; **giorno ~** weekday.
'ferie sfpl holidays.
fe'rire vt to injure; (deliberatamente: MIL etc) to wound; (colpire) to hurt; **fe'rita** sf injury; wound.
'ferma sf (MIL) (period of) service; (CACCIA): **cane da ~** pointer.
fer'maglio [fer'maʎʎo] sm clasp; (gioiello) brooch.
fer'mare vt to stop, halt; (POLIZIA) to detain, hold; (bottone etc) to fasten, fix // vi to stop; **~rsi** vr to stop, halt; **~ l'attenzione su qc/qd** to focus one's attention on sth.
fer'mata sf stop; **~ dell'autobus** bus stop.
fer'mento sm (anche fig) ferment; (lievito) yeast.
fer'mezza [fer'mettsa] sf (fig) firmness, steadfastness.
'fermo, a ag still, motionless; (veicolo) stationary; (orologio) not working; (saldo: anche fig) firm; (fissato: occhi) fixed // escl stop!; keep still! // sm (chiusura) catch, lock; (DIR) detention.
fe'roce [fe'rotʃe] ag (bestia) wild, fierce, ferocious; (persona) cruel, fierce; (fame, dolore) raging; **fe'rocia, cie** sf ferocity.
ferra'gosto sm (festa) feast of the Assumption; (periodo) August holidays pl.
ferra'menta sfpl ironmongery sg, hardware sg; **negozio di ~** ironmonger's, hardware shop.
fer'rare vt (cavallo) to shoe.

'ferreo, a ag iron.
'ferro sm iron; **una bistecca ai ~i** a grilled steak; **~ battuto** wrought iron; **~ di cavallo** horseshoe; **~ da stiro** iron.
ferro'via sf railway; **le ~e** the railways; **ferrovi'ario, a** ag railway cpd; **ferro-vi'ere** sm railwayman.
'fertile ag fertile; **fertiliz'zante** sm fertilizer.
fer'vente ag fervent, ardent.
fer'vore sm fervour, ardour; (punto culminante) height.
'fesso, a pp di **fendere** // ag (fam: sciocco) crazy, cracked.
fes'sura sf crack, split; (per gettone, moneta) slot.
'festa sf (religiosa) feast; (pubblica) holiday; (compleanno) birthday; (onomastico) name day; (cerimonia) celebration, party; **far ~ a qd** to have a holiday; to live it up; **far ~ a qd** to give sb a warm welcome.
festeggi'are [fested'dʒare] vt to celebrate; (amici, sposi) to give a warm welcome to.
fes'tino sm party; (con balli) ball.
fes'tivo, a ag Sunday cpd; holiday cpd; **giorno ~** holiday.
fes'toso, a ag merry, joyful.
fe'ticcio [fe'tittʃo] sm fetish.
'feto sm foetus.
'fetta sf slice.
feu'dale ag feudal.
FF.SS. abbr di Ferrovie dello Stato.
fi'aba sf fairy tale.
fi'acca sf weariness; (svogliatezza) listlessness.
fiac'care vt to weaken.
fi'acco, a, chi, che ag (stanco) tired, weary; (svogliato) listless; (debole) weak; (mercato) slack.
fi'accola sf torch.
fi'ala sf phial.
fi'amma sf flame; (NAUT) pennant.
fiammeggi'are [fjammed'dʒare] vi to blaze.
fiam'mifero sm match.
fiam'mingo, a, ghi, ghe ag Flemish // sm/f Fleming // sm (LING) Flemish; (ZOOL) flamingo; **i F~ghi** the Flemish.
fiancheggi'are [fjanked'dʒare] vt to border; (fig) to support, back (up); (MIL) to flank.
fi'anco, chi sm side; (MIL) flank; **di ~** sideways, from the side; **a ~ a ~** side by side.
fi'asco, schi sm flask; (fig) fiasco; **fare ~** to be a fiasco.
fi'ato sm breath; (SPORT) stamina; **avere il ~ grosso** to be out of breath; **prendere ~** to catch one's breath.
'fibbia sf buckle.
'fibra sf fibre; (fig) constitution.
fic'care vt to push, thrust, drive.
'fico, chi sm (pianta) fig tree; (frutto) fig; **~ d'India** prickly pear; **~ secco** dried fig.

fidanza'mento [fidantsa'mento] *sm* engagement.

fidan'zarsi [fidan'tsarsi] *vr* to get engaged; **fidan'zato, a** *sm/f* fiancé/fiancée.

fi'darsi *vr*: ~ **di** to trust; **fi'dato, a** *ag* reliable, trustworthy.

'fido *sm* (*seguace*) loyal follower; (*COMM*) credit.

fi'ducia [fi'dutʃa] *sf* confidence, trust; **incarico di** ~ position of trust, responsible position; **persona di** ~ reliable person.

fi'ele *sm* (*MED*) bile; (*fig*) bitterness.

fie'nile *sm* barn; hayloft.

fi'eno *sm* hay.

fi'era *sf* fair.

fie'rezza [fje'rettsa] *sf* pride.

fi'ero, a *ag* proud; (*crudele*) fierce, cruel; (*audace*) bold.

'fifa *sf* (*fam*): **aver** ~ to have the jitters.

'figlia ['fiʎʎa] *sf* daughter.

figli'astro, a [fiʎ'ʎastro] *sm/f* stepson/daughter.

'figlio ['fiʎʎo] *sm* son; (*senza distinzione di sesso*) child; ~ **di papà** spoilt, wealthy young man; **figli'occio, a, ci, ce** *sm/f* godchild, godson/daughter.

fi'gura *sf* figure; (*forma, aspetto esterno*) form, shape; (*illustrazione*) picture, illustration; **far** ~ to look smart; **fare una brutta** ~ to make a bad impression.

figu'rare *vt* (*plasmare*) to model; (*simboleggiare*) to symbolize, stand for // *vi* to appear; ~**rsi** *qc* to imagine sth; **figurati!** imagine that!; **ti do noia? - ma figurati!** am I disturbing you? - not at all!

figura'tivo, a *ag* figurative.

'fila *sf* row, line; (*coda*) queue; (*serie*) series, string; **di** ~ in succession; **fare la** ~ to queue; **in** ~ **indiana** in single file.

fila'mento *sm* filament.

filantro'pia *sf* philanthropy.

fi'lare *vt* to spin; (*NAUT*) to pay out // *vi* (*baco, ragno*) to spin; (*liquido*) to trickle out; (*discorso*) to hang together; (*fam: amoreggiare*) to go steady; (*4: muoversi a forte velocità*) to go at full speed; (*: andarsene lestamente*) to make o.s. scarce; ~ **diritto** (*fig*) to toe the line.

filar'monico, a, ci, che *ag* philharmonic.

filas'trocca, che *sf* nursery rhyme.

filate'lia *sf* philately, stamp collecting.

fi'lato, a *ag* spun // *sm* yarn; **3 giorni** ~**i** 3 days running *o* on end; **fila'tura** *sf* spinning; (*luogo*) spinning mill.

fi'letto *sm* braid, trimming; (*di vite*) thread; (*di carne*) fillet.

fili'ale *ag* filial // *sf* (*di impresa*) branch.

fili'grana *sf* (*in oreficeria*) filigree; (*su carta*) watermark.

film *sm inv* film; **fil'mare** *vt* to film.

'filo *sm* (*anche fig*) thread; (*filato*) yarn; (*metallico*) wire; **per** ~ **e per segno** in detail; ~ **d'erba** blade of grass; ~ **di perle** string of pearls; ~ **spinato** barbed

wire; **con un** ~ **di voce** in a whisper.

'filobus *sm inv* trolley bus.

fi'lone *sm* (*di minerali*) seam, vein; (*pane*) Vienna loaf; (*fig*) trend.

filoso'fia *sf* philosophy; **fi'losofo, a** *sm/f* philosopher.

fil'trare *vt, vi* (2) to filter.

'filtro *sm* filter.

'filza ['filtsa] *sf* (*anche fig*) string.

fin *av, prep* = **fino**.

fi'nale *ag* final // *sm* (*di opera*) end, ending; (*: MUS*) finale // *sf* (*SPORT*) final; **finalità** *sf* (*scopo*) aim, purpose; **final'mente** *av* finally, at last.

fi'nanza [fi'nantsa] *sf* finance; ~**e** *sfpl* (*di individuo, Stato*) finances; **finanzi'ario, a** *ag* financial; **finanzi'ere** *sm* financier; (*guardia di finanza: doganale*) customs officer; (*: tributaria*) inland revenue official.

finché [fin'ke] *cong* (*per tutto il tempo che*) as long as; (*fino al momento in cui*) until; **aspetta** ~ **io (non) sia ritornato** wait until I get back.

'fine *ag* (*lamina, carta*) thin; (*capelli, polvere*) fine; (*vista, udito*) keen, sharp; (*persona: raffinata*) refined, distinguished; (*osservazione*) subtle // *sf end* // *sm* aim, purpose; (*esito*) result, outcome; **secondo** ~ ulterior motive; **in** *o* **alla** ~ in the end, finally; ~ **settimana** *sm o f inv* weekend.

fi'nestra *sf* window; **fines'trino** *sm* (*di treno, auto*) window.

'fingere ['findʒere] *vt* to feign; (*supporre*) to imagine, suppose; ~**rsi** *vr*: ~**rsi ubriaco/pazzo** to pretend to be drunk/mad; ~ **di fare** to pretend to do.

fini'menti *smpl* (*di cavallo etc*) harness *sg*.

fini'mondo *sm* pandemonium.

fi'nire *vt* to finish // *vi* (2) to finish, end; ~ **di fare** (*compiere*) to finish doing; (*smettere*) to stop doing; ~ **ricco** to end up *o* finish up rich; **fini'tura** *sf* finish.

Fin'landia *sf*: **la** ~ Finland.

'fino, a *ag* (*capelli, seta*) fine; (*oro*) pure; (*fig: acuto*) shrewd // *av* (*spesso troncato in* **fin**: *pure, anche*) even // *prep* (*spesso troncato in* **fin**: *tempo*): **fin quando?** till when?; (*: luogo*): **fin qui** as far as here; ~ **a** (*tempo*) until, till; (*luogo*) as far as, (up) to; **fin da domani** from tomorrow onwards; **fin da ieri** since yesterday; **fin dalla nascita** from *o* since birth.

fi'nocchio [fi'nɔkkjo] *sm* fennel; (*fam: pederasta*) queer.

fi'nora *av* up till now.

'finto, a *pp di* **fingere** // *sf* pretence, sham; (*SPORT*) feint; **far** ~**a (di fare)** to pretend (to do).

finzi'one [fin'tsjone] *sf* pretence, sham.

fi'occo, chi *sm* (*di nastro*) bow; (*di stoffa, lana*) flock; (*di neve*) flake; (*NAUT*) jib; **coi** ~**chi** (*fig*) first-rate; ~**chi d'avena** oatflakes.

fi'ocina ['fjɔtʃina] *sf* harpoon.

fi'oco, a, chi, che *ag* faint, dim.

fi'onda *sf* catapult.

fio'raio, a *sm/f* florist.

fio'rami *smpl*: **a** ~ flowered, with a floral pattern.

fi'ordo *sm* fjord.

fi'ore *sm* flower; ~**i** *smpl* (*CARTE*) clubs; **a fior d'acqua/di pelle** on the surface of the water/skin.

fioren'tino, a *ag* Florentine.

fio'retto *sm* (*SCHERMA*) foil.

fio'rire *vi* (*2*) (*rosa*) to flower; (*albero*) to blossom; (*fig*) to flourish; (*ammuffire*) to become mouldy.

Fi'renze [fi'rɛntse] *sf* Florence.

'firma *sf* signature; (*reputazione*) name.

firma'mento *sm* firmament.

fir'mare *vt* to sign.

fisar'monica *sf* accordion.

fis'cale *ag* fiscal, tax *cpd*.

fischi'are [fis'kjare] *vi* to whistle // *vt* to whistle; (*attore*) to boo, hiss.

'fischio ['fiskjo] *sm* whistle.

'fisco *sm* tax authorities *pl*, ≈ Inland Revenue.

'fisico, a, ci, che *ag* physical // *sm/f* physicist // *sm* physique // *sf* physics *sg*.

fisiolo'gia [fizjolo'dʒia] *sf* physiology.

fisiono'mia *sf* face, physiognomy.

fisiotera'pia *sf* physiotherapy.

fis'sare *vt* to fix, fasten; (*guardare intensamente*) to stare at; (*data, condizioni*) to fix, establish, set; (*prenotare*) to book; ~**rsi su** (*sog: sguardo, attenzione*) to focus on; (*fig: idea*) to become obsessed with; **fissazi'one** *sf* (*PSIC*) fixation.

'fisso, a *ag* fixed; (*stipendio, impiego*) regular; (*occhi*) staring.

'fitta *sf vedi* **fitto.**

fit'tizio, a *ag* fictitious, imaginary.

'fitto, a *ag* thick, dense // *sm* depths *pl*, middle; (*affitto, pigione*) rent // *sf* sharp pain; **a capo** ~ head first.

fiu'mana *sf* swollen river; (*fig*) stream, flood.

fi'ume *sm* river.

fiu'tare *vt* to smell, sniff; (*sog: animale*) to scent; (*fig: inganno*) to get wind of, smell; **fi'uto** *sm* (*sense of smell*) (*fig*) nose.

fla'gelio [fla'dʒɛllo] *sm* scourge.

fla'grante *ag* flagrant; **cogliere qd in** ~ to catch sb red-handed.

fla'nella *sf* flannel.

flash [flaʃ] *sm inv* (*FOT*) flash; (*giornalistico*) newsflash.

'flauto *sm* flute.

'flebile *ag* faint, feeble.

'flemma *sf* (*calma*) coolness, phlegm; (*MED*) phlegm.

fles'sibile *ag* pliable; (*fig: che si adatta*) flexible.

'flesso, a *pp di* **flettere.**

flessu'oso, a *ag* supple, lithe.

'flettere *vt* to bend.

F.lli (*abbr di* **fratelli**) Bros.

'flora *sf* flora.

'florido, a *ag* flourishing; (*fig*) glowing with health.

'floscio, a, sci, sce ['flɔʃʃo] *ag* floppy, soft; (*muscoli*) flabby.

'flotta *sf* fleet.

'fluido, a *ag, sm* fluid.

flu'ire *vi* (*2*) to flow.

fluore'scente [fluoreʃ'ʃɛnte] *ag* fluorescent.

fluo'oro *sm* fluorine.

fluo'ruro *sm* fluoride.

'flusso *sm* flow; (*del mare*) flood tide; (*FISICA, MED*) flux; ~ **e riflusso** ebb and flow.

fluttu'are *vi* to rise and fall; (*ECON*) to fluctuate; (*fig*) to waver.

fluvi'ale *ag* river *cpd*, fluvial.

'foca, che *sf* (*ZOOL*) seal.

fo'caccia, ce [fo'kattʃa] *sf* kind of pizza; (*dolce*) bun.

'foce ['fotʃe] *sf* (*GEO*) mouth.

foco'laio *sm* (*MED*) centre of infection; (*fig*) hotbed.

foco'lare *sm* hearth, fireside; (*TECN*) furnace.

'fodera *sf* lining; (*di libro, poltrona*) cover; **fode'rare** *vt* to line; to cover.

'fodero *sm* sheath.

'foga *sf* enthusiasm, ardour.

'foggia, ge ['fɔddʒa] *sf* (*maniera*) style; (*aspetto*) form, shape; (*moda*) fashion, style.

'foglia ['fɔʎʎa] *sf* leaf; ~ **d'argento/d'oro** silver/gold leaf; **fogli'ame** *sm* foliage, leaves *pl*.

'foglio ['fɔʎʎo] *sm* (*di carta*) sheet (of paper); (*di metallo*) sheet; (*documento*) document; (*banconota*) (bank)note; ~ **rosa** (*AUT*) provisional licence; ~ **volante** pamphlet.

'fogna ['foɲɲa] *sf* drain, sewer; **fogna'tura** *sf* drainage, sewerage.

folgo'rare *vt* (*sog: fulmine*) to strike down; (: *alta tensione*) to electrocute.

'folla *sf* crowd, throng.

'folle *ag* mad, insane; (*TECN*) idle; **in** ~ (*AUT*) in neutral.

fol'lia *sf* folly, foolishness; foolish act; (*pazzia*) madness, lunacy.

'folto, a *ag* thick.

fomen'tare *vt* to stir up, foment.

fonda'mento *sm* foundation; ~**a** *sfpl* (*EDIL*) foundations.

fon'dare *vt* to found; (*edificio*) to lay the foundations for; (*fig: dar base*): ~ **qc su** to base sth on; **fondazi'one** *sf* founding; (*ente morale*) foundation; **fondazi'oni** *sfpl* (*EDIL*) foundations.

'fondere *vt* (*neve*) to melt; (*metallo*) to fuse, melt; (*fig: colori*) to merge, blend // *vi* to melt; ~**rsi** *vr* to melt; (*fig: partiti, correnti*) to unite, merge; **fonde'ria** *sf* foundry.

'fondo, a *ag* deep // *sm* (*di recipiente, pozzo*) bottom; (*di stanza*) back; (*quantità di liquido che resta, deposito*) dregs *pl*; (*sfondo*) background; (*unità immobiliare*) property, estate; (*somma di denaro*) fund; (*SPORT*) long-distance race; ~**i** *smpl* (*denaro*) funds; **in** ~ **a** at the bottom of; at the back of; **andare a** ~ (*nave*) to sink;

conoscere a ~ to know inside out; **in** ~ (fig) after all, all things considered; **andare fino in** ~ **a** (fig) to examine thoroughly; **a** ~ **perduto** (COMM) without security; **~i di caffè** coffee grounds; **~i di magazzino** old o unsold stock sg.

fo'netica sf phonetics sg.

fon'tana sf fountain.

'fonte sf spring, source; (fig) source.

fo'raggio [fo'raddʒo] sm fodder, forage.

fo'rare vt to pierce, make a hole in; (biglietto) to punch; ~ **una gomma** to burst a tyre.

'forbici ['fɔrbitʃi] sfpl scissors.

forbi'cina [forbi'tʃina] sf earwig.

'forca, che sf (AGR) fork, pitchfork; (patibolo) gallows sg.

for'cella [for'tʃɛlla] sf fork; (di monte) pass.

for'chetta [for'ketta] sf fork.

for'cina [for'tʃina] sf hairpin.

'forcipe ['fɔrtʃipe] sm forceps pl.

fo'resta sf forest.

foresti'ero, a ag foreign // sm/f foreigner.

'forfora sf dandruff.

'forgia, ge ['fɔrdʒa] sf forge; forgi'are vt to forge.

'forma sf form; (aspetto esteriore) form, shape; (DIR: procedura) procedure; (per calzature) last; (stampo da cucina) mould; ~**e** sfpl (del corpo) figure, shape; **le** ~**e** (convenzioni) appearances; **essere in** ~ to be in good shape.

formag'gino [formad'dʒino] sm processed cheese.

for'maggio [for'maddʒo] sm cheese.

for'male ag formal; formalità sf inv formality.

for'mare vt to form, shape, make; (fig: carattere) to form, mould; ~**rsi** vr to form, take shape; for'mato sm format, size; formazi'one sf formation; (fig: educazione) training.

for'mica, che sf ant; formi'caio sm anthill.

formico'lare vi (2: gamba, braccio) to tingle; (brulicare: anche fig): ~ **di** to be swarming with; **mi formicola la gamba** I've got pins and needles in my leg, my leg's tingling; formico'lio sm pins and needles pl; swarming.

formi'dabile ag powerful, formidable; (straordinario) remarkable.

'formula sf formula.

formu'lare vt to formulate; to express.

for'nace [for'natʃe] sf (per laterizi etc) kiln; (per metalli) furnace.

for'naio sm baker.

for'nello sm (elettrico, a gas) ring; (di pipa) bowl.

for'nire vt: ~ qd di qc, ~ qc a qd to provide o supply sb with sth, to supply sth to sb.

'forno sm (di cucina) oven; (panetteria) bakery; (TECN: per calce etc) kiln; (: per metalli) furnace.

'foro sm (buco) hole; (STORIA) forum; (tribunale) (law) court.

'forse av perhaps, maybe; (circa) about; **essere in** ~ to be in doubt.

forsen'nato, a ag mad, insane.

'forte ag strong; (suono) loud; (spesa) considerable, great; (passione, dolore) great, deep // av strongly; (velocemente) fast; (a voce alta) loud(ly) // sm (edificio) fort; (specialità) forte, strong point; **essere** ~ **in qc** to be good at sth.

for'tezza [for'tettsa] sf (morale) strength; (luogo fortificato) fortress.

fortifi'care vt to fortify, strengthen.

for'tuito, a ag fortuitous.

for'tuna sf (destino) fortune, luck; (buona sorte) success, fortune; (eredità, averi) fortune; **per** ~ luckily, fortunately; **di** ~ makeshift, improvised; **atterraggio di** ~ emergency landing; fortu'nato, a ag lucky, fortunate; (impresa) successful.

forvi'are vt, vi = fuorviare.

'forza ['fɔrtsa] sf strength; (potere) power; (FISICA) force; ~ **e** sfpl (fisiche) strength sg; (MIL) forces // escl come on!; **per** ~ against one's will; (naturalmente) of course; **a viva** ~ by force; **a** ~ **di** by dint of; ~ **maggiore** circumstances beyond one's control; **la** ~ **pubblica** the police pl.

for'zare [for'tsare] vt to force; ~ **qd a fare** to force sb to do; for'zato, a ag forced // sm (DIR) prisoner sentenced to hard labour.

fos'chia [fos'kia] sf mist, haze.

'fosco, a, schi, sche ag dark, gloomy.

fos'fato sm phosphate.

'fosforo sm phosphorous.

'fossa sf pit; (di cimitero) grave; ~ **biologica** septic tank.

fos'sato sm ditch; (di fortezza) moat.

fos'setta sf dimple.

'fossile ag, sm fossil.

'fosso sm ditch; (MIL) trench.

'foto sf (abbr di fotografia) photo // pref: foto'copia sf photocopy; fotocopi'are vt to photocopy; fotogra'fare vt to photograph; fotogra'fia sf (procedimento) photography; (immagine) photograph; fo'tografo, a sm/f photographer; foto-ro'manzo sm romantic picture story.

fra prep = tra.

fracas'sare vt to shatter, smash; ~**rsi** vr to shatter, smash; (veicolo) to crash; fra-'casso sm smash; crash; (baccano) din, racket.

'fradicio, a, ci, ce ['fraditʃo] ag (guasto) rotten; (molto bagnato) soaking (wet); **ubriaco** ~ blind drunk.

'fragile ['fradʒile] ag fragile; (fig: salute) delicate.

'fragola sf strawberry.

frago'roso, a ag crashing, roaring.

fra'grante ag fragrant.

frain'tendere vt to misunderstand; frain'teso, a pp di fraintendere.

fram'mento sm fragment.

'**frana** *sf* landslide; **fra'nare** *vi* (*2*) to slip, slide down.

fran'cese [fran'tʃeze] *ag* French // *sm/f* Frenchman/woman // *sm* (*LING*) French; **i F~i** the French.

fran'chezza [fran'kettsa] *sf* frankness, openness.

'**Francia** ['frantʃa] *sf*: **la ~** France.

'**franco, a, chi, che** *ag* (*COMM*) free; (*sincero*) frank, open, sincere // *sm* (*moneta*) franc; **farla ~a** (*fig*) to get off scot-free; **~ di dogana** duty-free; **~ a domicilio** delivered free of charge; **prezzo ~ fabbrica** ex-works price; **~ tiratore** sniper.

franco'bollo *sm* (postage) stamp.

fran'gente [fran'dʒɛnte] *sm* breaker.

'**frangia, ge** ['frandʒa] *sf* fringe; (*fig: abbellimento*) frill, embellishment.

frantu'mare *vt*, **~rsi** *vr* to break into pieces, shatter; **fran'tumi** *smpl* pieces, bits; (*schegge*) splinters.

'**frasca, sche** *sf* (leafy) branch.

'**frase** *sf* (*LING*) sentence; (*locuzione, espressione, MUS*) phrase; **~ fatta** set phrase.

'**frassino** *sm* ash (tree).

frastu'ono *sm* hubbub, din.

'**frate** *sm* friar, monk.

fratel'lanza [fratel'lantsa] *sf* brotherhood; (*associazione*) fraternity.

fra'tello *sm* brother; **~i** *smpl* brothers; (*nel senso di fratelli e sorelle*) brothers and sisters.

fra'terno, a *ag* fraternal, brotherly.

frat'tanto *av* in the meantime, meanwhile.

frat'tempo *sm*: **nel ~** in the meantime, meanwhile.

frat'tura *sf* fracture.

fraudo'lento, a *ag* fraudulent.

frazi'one [frat'tsjone] *sf* fraction; (*borgata*): **~ di comune** hamlet.

'**freccia, ce** ['frettʃa] *sf* arrow; **~ di direzione** (*AUT*) indicator.

fred'dare *vt* to shoot dead.

fred'dezza [fred'dettsa] *sf* coldness.

'**freddo, a** *ag, sm* cold; **fa ~** it's cold; **aver ~** to be cold; **a ~** (*fig*) deliberately; **freddo'loso, a** *ag* sensitive to the cold.

fred'dura *sf* pun.

fre'gare *vt* to rub; (*fam: truffare*) to take in, cheat; (: *rubare*) to swipe, pinch; **fregarsene** (*fam!*): **chi se ne frega?** who gives a damn (about it)?

fre'gata *sf* rub; (*fam*) swindle; (*NAUT*) frigate.

'**fregio** ['fredʒo] *sm* (*ARCHIT*) frieze; (*ornamento*) decoration.

'**fremere** *vi*: **~ di** to tremble *o* quiver with; '**fremito** *sm* tremor, quiver.

fre'nare *vt* (*veicolo*) to slow down; (*cavallo*) to rein in; (*lacrime*) to restrain, hold back // *vi* to brake; **~rsi** *vr* (*fig*) to restrain o.s., control o.s.; **fre'nata** *sf*: **fare una frenata** to brake.

frene'sia *sf* frenzy; mania; **fre'netico, a, ci, che** *ag* frenzied.

'**freno** *sm* brake; (*morso*) bit; (*fig*) check; **~ a disco** disc brake; **~ a mano** handbrake.

frequen'tare *vt* (*luoghi*) to frequent; (*persone*) to see (often).

fre'quente *ag* frequent; **di ~** frequently; **fre'quenza** *sf* frequency; (*assiduità*) attendance.

fres'chezza [fres'kettsa] *sf* freshness.

'**fresco, a, schi, sche** *ag* fresh; (*temperatura*) cool; (*notizia*) recent, fresh // *sm*: **godere il ~** to enjoy the cool air; **stare ~** (*fig*) to be in for it; **mettere al ~** to put in a cool place.

'**fretta** *sf* hurry, haste; **in ~** in a hurry; **in ~ e furia** in a mad rush; **aver ~** to be in a hurry; **fretto'loso, a** *ag* hurried, rushed.

fri'abile *ag* (*terreno*) friable; (*pasta*) crumbly.

'**friggere** ['friddʒere] *vt* to fry // *vi* (*olio etc*) to sizzle.

'**frigido, a** ['fridʒido] *ag* (*MED*) frigid.

'**frigo** *sm* fridge.

frigo'rifero, a *ag* refrigerating // *sm* refrigerator.

frin'guello *sm* chaffinch.

frit'tata *sf* omelette; **fare una ~** (*fig*) to make a mess of things.

frit'tella *sf* (*CUC*) pancake; (: *ripiena*) fritter.

'**fritto, a** *pp di* **friggere** // *ag* fried // *sm* fried food; **~ misto** mixed fry.

'**frivolo, a** *ag* frivolous.

frizi'one [frit'tsjone] *sf* friction; (*di pelle*) rub, rub-down; (*AUT*) clutch.

friz'zante [frid'dzante] *ag* (*acqua*) fizzy, sparkling; (*vento, fig*) biting.

'**frizzo** ['friddzo] *sm* witticism.

fro'dare *vt* to defraud, cheat.

'**frode** *sf* fraud; **~ fiscale** tax evasion.

'**frollo, a** *ag* (*carne*) tender; (: *di selvaggina*) high; (*fig: persona*) soft; **pasta ~a** short(crust) pastry.

'**fronda** *sf* (leafy) branch; (*di partito politico*) internal opposition; **~e** *sfpl* foliage *sg*.

fron'tale *ag* frontal; (*scontro*) head-on.

'**fronte** *sf* (*ANAT*) forehead; (*di edificio*) front, façade // *sm* (*MIL, POL, METEOR*) front; **a ~, di ~** facing, opposite; **di ~ a** (*posizione*) opposite, facing, in front of; (*paragone di*) compared with.

fronteggi'are [fronted'dʒare] *vt* (*avversari, difficoltà*) to face, stand up to; (*sog: edificio*) to face.

fronti'era *sf* border, frontier.

fronzolo ['frondzolo] *sm* frill.

'**frottola** *sf* fib; **~e** *sfpl* nonsense *sg*.

fru'gale *ag* frugal.

fru'gare *vi* to rummage // *vt* to search.

frul'lare *vt* (*CUC*) to whisk // *vi* (*uccelli*) to flutter; **frulla'tore** *sm* electric mixer; **frul'lino** *sm* whisk.

fru'mento *sm* wheat.

fru'scio [fruʃ'ʃio] *sm* rustle; rustling; (*di acque*) murmur.

'frusta *sf* whip; (*CUC*) whisk.

frus'tare *vt* to whip.

frus'tino *sm* riding crop.

frus'trare *vt* to frustrate; **frustrazi'one** *sf* frustration.

'frutta *sf* fruit; (*portata*) dessert; ~ **candita/secca** candied/dried fruit.

frut'teto *sm* orchard.

frutti'vendolo, a *sm/f* greengrocer.

'frutto *sm* fruit; (*fig: risultato*) result(s); (*ECON: interesse*) interest; (: *reddito*) income; ~**i di mare** seafood *sg*.

FS *abbr di* Ferrovie dello Stato.

fu *forma del vb* **essere** // *ag inv:* **il** ~ **Paolo Bianchi** the late Paolo Bianchi.

fuci'lare [futʃi'lare] *vt* to shoot; **fuci'lata** *sf* rifle shot.

fu'cile [fu'tʃile] *sm* rifle, gun; (*da caccia*) shotgun, gun.

fu'cina [fu'tʃina] *sf* forge.

'fuga *sf* flight; (*di gas, liquidi*) leak; (*MUS*) fugue; **prendere la** ~ to take flight, flee.

fu'gace [fu'gatʃe] *ag* fleeting, transient.

fug'gevole [fud'dʒevole] *ag* fleeting.

fuggi'asco, a, schi, sche [fud'dʒasko] *ag, sm/f* fugitive.

fuggi'fuggi [fuddʒi'fuddʒi] *sm* scramble, stampede.

fug'gire [fud'dʒire] *vi* (2) to flee, run away; (*fig: passar veloce*) to fly // *vt* to avoid; **fuggi'tivo, a** *sm/f* fugitive, runaway.

'fulcro *sm* fulcrum.

ful'gore *sm* brilliance, splendour.

fu'liggine [fu'liddʒine] *sf* soot.

fulmi'nare *vt* to strike down; (*sog: alta tensione*) to electrocute.

'fulmine *sm* thunderbolt; lightning *q*.

fumai'olo *sm* (*di nave*) funnel; (*di fabbrica*) chimney-stack.

fu'mare *vi* to smoke; (*emettere vapore*) to steam // *vt* to smoke; **fu'mata** *sf* puff of smoke; (*segnale*) smoke signal; (*di tabacco*) smoke; **fare una fumata** to have a smoke; **fuma'tore, 'trice** *sm/f* smoker.

fu'metto *sm* comic strip; ~**i** *smpl* comics.

'fumo *sm* smoke; (*vapore*) steam; (*il fumare tabacco*) smoking; ~**i** *smpl* fumes; **vendere** ~ to deceive, cheat; **fu'moso, a** *ag* smoky.

fu'nambolo, a *sm/f* tightrope walker.

'fune *sf* rope, cord; (*più grossa*) cable.

'funebre *ag* (*rito*) funeral; (*aspetto*) gloomy, funereal.

fune'rale *sm* funeral.

'fungere ['fundʒere] *vi:* ~ **da** to act as.

'fungo, ghi *sm* fungus; (*commestibile*) mushroom; ~ **velenoso** toadstool.

funico'lare *sf* funicular railway.

funi'via *sf* cable railway.

funzio'nare [funtsjo'nare] *vi* to work, function; (*fungere*): ~ **da** to act as.

funzio'nario [funtsjo'narjo] *sm* official.

funzi'one [fun'tsjone] *sf* function; (*carica*) post, position; (*REL*) service; **entrare in**

~ to take up one's post; to take up office.

fu'oco, chi *sm* fire; (*fornello*) ring; (*FOT, FISICA*) focus; **dare** ~ **a qc** to set fire to sth; **far** ~ (*sparare*) to fire; ~ **d'artificio** firework.

fuorché [fwor'ke] *cong, prep* except.

fu'ori *av* outside; (*all'aperto*) outdoors, outside; (*fuori di casa, SPORT*) out; (*esclamativo*) get out! // *prep:* ~ **(di)** out of, outside // *sm* outside; **lasciar** ~ **qc/qd** to leave sth/sb out; **far** ~ **qd** (*fam*) to kill sb, do sb in; **essere** ~ **di sé** to be beside o.s.; ~ **luogo** (*inopportuno*) out of place, uncalled for; ~ **mano** out of the way, remote; ~ **pericolo** out of danger; ~ **uso** old-fashioned; obsolete.

fu'ori... *prefisso:* **fuori'bordo** *sm* speedboat (with outboard motor); outboard motor; **fuori'classe** *sm/f inv* (undisputed) champion; **fuorigi'oco** *sm* offside; **fuori'legge** *sm/f inv* outlaw; **fuori'serie** *ag inv* (*auto etc*) custom-built; **fuoru'scito, a, fuoriu'scito, a** *sm/f* exile; **fuorvi'are** *vt* to mislead, put on the wrong track; (*fig*) to lead astray // *vi* to go astray.

'furbo, a *ag* cunning, sly; (*astuto*) shrewd.

fu'rente *ag:* ~ (**contro**) furious (with).

fur'fante *sm* rascal, scoundrel.

fur'gone *sm* van.

'furia *sf* (*ira*) fury, rage; (*fig: impeto*) fury, violence; (*fretta*) rush; **a** ~ **di** by dint of; **montare in** ~ to fly into a rage; **furi'bondo, a** *ag* furious.

furi'oso, a *ag* furious; (*mare, vento*) raging.

fu'rore *sm* fury; (*esaltazione*) frenzy; **far** ~ to be all the rage.

fur'tivo, a *ag* furtive; (*merce*) stolen.

'furto *sm* theft; ~ **con scasso** burglary.

'fusa *sfpl:* **fare le** ~ to purr.

fu'sibile *sm* (*ELETTR*) fuse.

fusi'one *sf* (*di metalli*) fusion, melting; (*colata*) casting; (*COMM*) merger; (*fig*) merging.

'fuso, a *pp di* **fondere** // *sm* (*FILATURA*) spindle; ~ **orario** time zone.

fus'tagno [fus'taɲɲo] *sm* corduroy.

'fusto *sm* stem; (*ANAT, di albero*) trunk; (*recipiente: in metallo*) drum, can; (: *in legno*) barrel, cask.

'futile *ag* vain, futile; **futilità** *sf inv* futility.

fu'turo, a *ag, sm* future.

G

gab'bare *vt* to take in, dupe; ~**rsi** *vr:* ~**rsi di qd** to make fun of sb.

'gabbia *sf* cage; (*DIR*) dock; (*da imballaggio*) crate; ~ **dell'ascensore** lift shaft; ~ **toracica** (*ANAT*) rib cage.

gabbi'ano *sm* (sea)gull.

gabi'netto *sm* (*MED etc*) consulting room; (*POL*) cabinet; (*di decenza*) toilet, lavatory; (*INS: di fisica etc*) laboratory.

gagli'ardo, a [gaʎ'ʎardo] *ag* strong, vigorous.

gai'ezza [ga'jettsa] *sf* gaiety, cheerfulness.

'gaio, a *ag* gay, cheerful.

'gala *sf* (*sfarzo*) pomp; (*festa*) ala.

ga'lante *ag* gallant, courteous; (*avventura, poesia*) amorous; **galante'ria** *sf* gallantry.

galantu'omo, *pl* **galantu'omini** *sm* gentleman.

ga'lassia *sf* galaxy.

gala'teo *sm* (good) manners *pl.*

gale'otto *sm* (*rematore*) galley slave; (*carcerato*) convict.

ga'lera *sf* prison.

'galla *sf* (*BOT*) gall; **a** ~ afloat.

galleggi'ante [galled'dʒante] *ag* floating // *sm* (*natante*) barge; (*di pescatore, lenza, TECN*) float.

galleggi'are [galled'dʒare] *vi* to float.

galle'ria *sf* (*traforo*) tunnel; (*ARCHIT, d'arte*) gallery; (*TEATRO*) circle; (*strada coperta con negozi*) arcade; ~ **del vento** *o* **aerodinamica** (*AER*) wind tunnel.

'Galles *sm*: **il** ~ Wales.

gal'lina *sf* hen.

'gallo *sm* cock.

gal'lone *sm* piece of braid; (*MIL*) stripe; (*misura inglese e americana*) gallon.

galop'pare *vi* to gallop.

ga'loppo *sm* gallop; **al** *o* **di** ~ at a gallop.

galvaniz'zare [galvanid'dzare] *vt* to galvanize.

'gamba *sf* leg; (*asta: di lettera*) stem; **in** ~ (*in buona salute*) well; (*bravo*) bright, smart; **prendere qc sotto** ~ (*fig*) to treat sth too lightly.

gambe'retto *sm* prawn; shrimp.

'gambero *sm* (*di acqua dolce*) crayfish; (*di mare*) lobster.

'gambo *sm* stem; (*di pianta*) stalk, stem; (*TECN*) shank.

'gamma *sf* (*MUS*) scale; (*di colori, fig*) range, gamut.

ga'nascia, sce [ga'naʃʃa] *sf* jaw; ~ **sce del freno** (*AUT*) brake shoes.

'gancio ['gantʃo] *sm* hook.

'ganghero ['gangero] *sm* (*arpione di ferro*) hinge; (*gancetto*) hook; **uscire dai** ~**i** (*fig*) to fly into a temper.

'gara *sf* competition; (*SPORT*) competition; contest; match; (*: corsa*) race; **fare a** ~ to compete, vie.

garan'tire *vt* to guarantee; (*dare per certo*) to assure.

garan'zia [garan'tsia] *sf* guarantee; (*pegno*) security.

gar'bato, a *ag* courteous, polite.

'garbo *sm* (*buone maniere*) politeness, courtesy; (*di vestito etc*) grace, style.

gareggi'are [gared'dʒare] *vi* to compete.

garga'rismo *sm* gargle; **fare i** ~**i** to gargle.

ga'rofano *sm* carnation; **chiodo di** ~ clove.

'garza ['gardza] *sf* (*per bende*) gauze.

gar'zone [gar'dzone] *sm* boy; ~ **di stalla** stableboy.

gas *sm inv* gas; **a tutto** ~ at full speed; **dare** ~ (*AUT*) to accelerate; ~ **lacrimogeno** tear gas.

ga'solio *sm* diesel oil.

ga's(s)are *vt* to aerate, carbonate; (*asfissiare*) to gas.

gas'soso, a *ag* gaseous; gassy // *sf* lemonade.

'gastrico, a, ci, che *ag* gastric.

gastrono'mia *sf* gastronomy.

gat'tino *sm* kitten.

'gatto, a *sm/f* cat, tomcat/she-cat; ~ **selvatico** wildcat.

gatto'pardo *sm*: ~ **africano** serval; ~ **americano** ocelot.

gat'tuccio [gat'tuttʃo] *sm* dogfish.

gau'dente *sm/f* pleasure-seeker.

ga'vetta *sf* (*MIL*) mess tin.

'gazza ['gaddza] *sf* magpie.

gaz'zella [gad'dzɛlla] *sf* gazelle.

gaz'zetta [gad'dzetta] *sf* news sheet; **G**~ **Ufficiale** *official publication containing details of new laws.*

gaz'zoso, a [gad'dzoso] *ag* = **gassoso.**

ge'lare [dʒe'lare] *vt, vi, vb impers* to freeze; **ge'iata** *sf* frost.

gelate'ria [dʒelate'ria] *sf* ice-cream shop.

gela'tina [dʒela'tina] *sf* gelatine; ~ **esplosiva** dynamite; ~ **di frutta** fruit jelly.

ge'lato, a [dʒe'lato] *ag* frozen // *sm* ice cream.

'gelido, a ['dʒɛlido] *ag* icy, ice-cold.

'gelo ['dʒɛlo] *sm* (*temperatura*) intense cold; (*brina*) frost; (*fig*) chill; **ge'lone** *sm* chilblain.

gelo'sia [dʒelo'sia] *sf* (*stato d'animo*) jealousy; (*persiana*) shutter.

ge'loso, a [dʒe'loso] *ag* jealous.

'gelso ['dʒɛlso] *sm* mulberry (tree).

gelso'mino [dʒelso'mino] *sm* jasmine.

ge'mello, a [dʒe'mɛllo] *ag, sm/f* twin; ~**i** *smpl* (*di camicia*) cufflinks; (*dello zodiaco*): **G**~**i** Gemini *sg.*

'gemere ['dʒɛmere] *vi* to moan, groan; (*cigolare*) to creak; (*gocciolare*) to drip, ooze; **'gemito** *sm* moan, groan.

'gemma ['dʒɛmma] *sf* (*BOT*) bud; (*pietra preziosa*) gem.

gene'rale [dʒene'rale] *ag, sm* general; **in** ~ (*per sommi capi*) in general terms; (*di solito*) usually, in general; **a** ~ **richiesta** by popular request; **generalità** *sfpl* (*dati d'identità*) particulars; **generaliz'zare** *vt, vi* to generalize.

gene'rare [dʒene'rare] *vt* (*dar vita*) to give birth to; (*produrre*) to produce; (*causare*) to arouse; (*TECN*) to produce, generate; **genera'tore** *sm* (*TECN*) generator; **generazi'one** *sf* generation.

'genere ['dʒenere] *sm* kind, type, sort; (*BIOL*) genus; (*merce*) article, product; (*LING*) gender; (*ARTE, LETTERATURA*) genre; **in** ~ generally, as a rule; **il** ~ **umano** mankind; ~**i alimentari** foodstuffs.

ge'nerico, a, ci, che [dʒe'nɛriko] *ag* generic; (*persona: non specializzata*) general, non-specialized.

'genero ['dʒɛnero] *sm* son-in-law.

generosità [dʒenerosi'ta] *sf* generosity.

gene'roso, a [dʒene'roso] ag generous.

'genesi ['dʒɛnesi] sf genesis.

ge'netico, a, ci, che [dʒe'nɛtiko] ag genetic // sf genetics sg.

gen'giva [dʒen'dʒiva] sf (ANAT) gum.

geni'ale [dʒe'njale] ag (persona) of genius; (idea) ingenious, brilliant.

'genio ['dʒɛnjo] sm genius; (attitudine, talento) talent, flair, genius; andare a ~ a qd to be to sb's liking, appeal to sb.

geni'tale [dʒeni'tale] ag genital; ~i smpl genitals.

geni'tore [dʒeni'tore] sm parent, father o mother; ~i smpl parents.

gen'naio [dʒen'najo] sm January.

'Genova ['dʒɛnova] sf Genoa.

gen'taglia [dʒen'taʎʎa] sf (peg) rabble.

'gente ['dʒɛnte] sf people pl.

gen'tile [dʒen'tile] ag (persona, atto) kind; (: garbato) courteous, polite; (nelle lettere): G ~ Signore Dear Sir; (: sulla busta): G ~ Signor Fernando Villa Mr Fernando Villa; genti'lezza sf kindness; courtesy, politeness; per gentilezza (per favore) please.

genuflessi'one [dʒenufles'sjone] sf genuflection.

genu'ino, a [dʒenu'ino] ag genuine.

geogra'fia [dʒeogra'fia] sf geography; geo'grafico, a, ci, che ag geographical.

geolo'gia [dʒeolo'dʒia] sf geology; geo'logico, a, ci, che ag geological.

ge'ometra, i, e [dʒe'ɔmetra] sm/f (professionista) surveyor.

geome'tria [dʒeome'tria] sf geometry; geo'metrico, a, ci, che ag geometric(al).

ge'ranio [dʒe'ranjo] sm geranium.

gerar'chia [dʒerar'kia] sf hierarchy.

ge'rente [dʒe'rɛnte] sm/f manager/manageress.

'gergo, ghi ['dʒɛrgo] sm jargon; slang.

geria'tria [dʒerja'tria] sf geriatrics sg.

Ger'mania [dʒer'manja] sf: la ~ Germany.

'germe ['dʒɛrme] sm germ.

germogli'are [dʒermoʎ'ʎare] vi to sprout; to germinate; ger'moglio sm shoot; bud.

gero'glifico, ci [dʒero'glifiko] sm hieroglyphic.

'gesso ['dʒɛsso] sm chalk; (SCULTURA, MED, EDIL) plaster; (minerale) gypsum.

gestazi'one [dʒestat'tsjone] sf gestation.

gestico'lare [dʒestiko'lare] vi to gesticulate.

gesti'one [dʒes'tjone] sf management.

ges'tire [dʒes'tire] vt to run, manage.

'gesto ['dʒɛsto] sm gesture.

ges'tore [dʒes'tore] sm manager.

Gesù [dʒe'zu] sm Jesus.

gesu'ita, i [dʒezu'ita] sm Jesuit.

get'tare [dʒet'tare] vt to throw; (anche: ~ via) to throw away o out; (SCULTURA) to cast; (EDIL) to lay; (emettere) to spout, gush; ~rsi in (sog: fiume) to flow into; ~ uno sguardo su to take a quick look at;

get'tata sf (di cemento, metalli) cast; (diga) jetty.

'getto ['dʒɛtto] sm (di gas, liquido, AER) jet; (BOT) shoot; a ~ continuo uninterruptedly; di ~ (fig) straight off, in one go.

get'tone [dʒet'tone] sm token; (per giochi) counter; (: roulette etc) chip; ~ telefonico telephone token.

'ghetto ['getto] sm ghetto.

ghiacci'aio [gjat'tʃajo] sm glacier.

ghiacci'are [gjat'tʃare] vt to freeze; (fig): ~ qd to make sb's blood run cold // vi to freeze, ice over.

ghi'accio ['gjattʃo] sm ice.

ghiacci'olo [gjat'tʃɔlo] sm icicle; (tipo di gelato) ice(d) lolly.

ghi'aia ['gjaja] sf gravel.

ghi'anda ['gjanda] sf (BOT) acorn.

ghi'andola ['gjandola] sf gland.

ghigliot'tina [giʎʎot'tina] sf guillotine.

ghi'gnare [gin'nare] vi to sneer.

ghi'otto, a ['gjotto] ag greedy; (cibo) delicious, appetizing; ghiot'tone, a sm/f glutton.

ghiri'bizzo [giri'biddzo] sm whim.

ghiri'goro [giri'gɔro] sm scribble, squiggle.

ghir'landa [gir'landa] sf garland, wreath.

'ghiro ['giro] sm dormouse.

'ghisa ['giza] sf cast iron.

già [dʒa] av already; (ex, in precedenza) formerly // escl of course!, yes indeed!

gi'acca, che ['dʒakka] sf jacket; ~ a vento windcheater.

giacché [dʒak'ke] cong since, as.

giac'chetta [dʒak'ketta] sf (light) jacket.

gia'cenza [dʒa'tʃɛntsa] sf: merce in ~ goods in stock; capitale in ~ uninvested capital; ~e di magazzino unsold stock.

gia'cere [dʒa'tʃere] vi (2) to lie; giaci-'mento sm deposit.

gia'cinto [dʒa'tʃinto] sm hyacinth.

gi'ada ['dʒada] sf jade.

giaggi'olo [dʒad'dʒɔlo] sm iris.

giagu'aro [dʒa'gwaro] sm jaguar.

gi'allo ['dʒallo] ag yellow; (carnagione) sallow // sm yellow; (anche: romanzo ~) detective novel; (anche: film ~) detective film; ~ dell'uovo yolk.

giam'mai [dʒam'mai] av never.

Giap'pone [dʒap'pone] sm Japan; giappo-'nese ag, sm/f, sm Japanese.

gi'ara ['dʒara] sf jar.

giardi'naggio [dʒardi'naddʒo] sm gardening.

giardini'ere, a [dʒardi'njɛre] sm/f gardener // sf (misto di sottaceti) mixed pickles pl; (automobile) estate car.

giar'dino [dʒar'dino] sm garden; ~ d'infanzia nursery school; ~ pubblico public gardens pl, (public) park.

giarretti'era [dʒarret'tjɛra] sf garter.

giavel'lotto [dʒavel'lɔtto] sm javelin.

gi'gante, 'essa [dʒi'gante] sm/f giant // ag giant, gigantic; gigan'tesco, a, schi, sche ag gigantic.

'giglio ['dʒiʎʎo] *sm* lily.

gilè [dʒi'lε] *sm inv* waistcoat.

gin [dʒin] *sm* gin.

ginecolo'gia [dʒinekolo'dʒia] *sf* gynaecology.

gi'nepro [dʒi'nepro] *sm* juniper.

gi'nestra [dʒi'nεstra] *sf* (BOT) broom.

Gi'nevra [dʒi'nevra] *sf* Geneva.

gingil'larsi [dʒindʒil'larsi] *vr* to fritter away one's time.

gin'gillo [dʒin'dʒillo] *sm* plaything.

gin'nasio [dʒin'nazjo] *sm the* 4th and 5th year of secondary school in Italy.

gin'nasta, i, e [dʒin'nasta] *sm/f* gymnast; **gin'nastica** *sf* gymnastics *sg*; keep-fit exercises.

gi'nocchio [dʒi'nɔkkjo], *pl(m)* **gi'nocchi** *o pl(f)* **gi'nocchia** *sm* knee; **stare in ~** to kneel, be on one's knees; **ginocchi'oni** *av* on one's knees.

gio'care [dʒo'kare] *vt* to play; (*scommettere*) to stake, wager, bet; (*ingannare*) to take in // *vi* to play; (*a roulette etc*) to gamble; (*fig*) to play a part, be important; (TECN: *meccanismo*) to be loose; **~ a** (*gioco, sport*) to play; (*cavalli*) to bet on; **gioca'tore, 'trice** *sm/f* player; gambler.

gio'cattolo [dʒo'kattolo] *sm* toy.

gio'chetto [dʒo'ketto] *sm:* **è un ~** it's child's play.

gi'oco, chi ['dʒɔko] *sm* game; (*divertimento*, TECN) play; (*al casinò*) gambling; (CARTE) hand; (*insieme di pezzi etc necessari per un gioco*) set; **per ~** for fun; **fare il doppio ~ con qd** to double-cross sb; **~ d'azzardo** game of chance; **~ della palla** football; **~ degli scacchi** chess set; **i giochi olimpici** the Olympic games.

gio'coso, a [dʒo'koso] *ag* playful, jesting.

gio'gaia [dʒo'gaja] *sf* (GEO) range of mountains.

gi'ogo, ghi ['dʒɔgo] *sm* yoke.

gi'oia ['dʒɔja] *sf* joy, delight; (*pietra preziosa*) jewel, precious stone.

gioielle'ria [dʒojelle'ria] *sf* jeweller's craft; jeweller's (shop).

gioielli'ere, a [dʒojel'ljεre] *sm/f* jeweller.

gioi'ello [dʒo'jεllo] *sm* jewel, piece of jewellery; **~i** *smpl* jewellery *sg*.

gioi'oso, a [dʒo'joso] *ag* joyful.

Gior'dania [dʒor'danja] *sf:* **la ~** Jordan.

giorna'laio, a [dʒorna'lajo] *sm/f* newsagent; news-vendor.

gior'nale [dʒor'nale] *sm* (*news*)paper; (*diario*) journal, diary; (COMM) journal; **~ di bordo** log; **~ radio** radio news *sg*.

giornali'ero, a [dʒorna'ljεro] *ag* daily; (*che varia: umore*) changeable // *sm/f* day labourer.

giorna'lismo [dʒorna'lizmo] *sm* journalism.

giorna'lista, i, e [dʒorna'lista] *sm/f* journalist.

gior'nata [dʒor'nata] *sf* day; **~ lavorativa** working day.

gi'orno ['dʒorno] *sm* day; (*opposto alla notte*) day, daytime; (*luce del ~*) daylight; **al ~** per day; **di ~** by day; **al ~ d'oggi** nowadays.

gi'ostra ['dʒɔstra] *sf* merry-go-round; (*torneo storico*) joust.

gi'ovane ['dʒovane] *ag* young; (*giovanile*) youthful // *sm/f* youth/girl, young man/woman; **i ~i** young people; **giova'nile** *ag* youthful; **giova'notto** *sm* young man.

gio'vare [dʒo'vare] *vi:* **~ a** (*essere utile*) to be useful to; (*far bene*) to be good for // *vb impers* (*essere bene, utile*) to be useful; **~rsi di qc** to take advantage of sth.

giovedì [dʒove'di] *sm* Thursday; **di o il ~** on Thursdays.

gioventù [dʒoven'tu] *sf* youth; (*i giovani*) young people *pl*, youth.

giovi'ale [dʒo'vjale] *ag* jovial, jolly.

giovi'nezza [dʒovi'nettsa] *sf* youth.

gira'dischi [dʒira'diski] *sm inv* record player.

gl'raffa [dʒi'raffa] *sf* giraffe.

giran'dola [dʒi'randola] *sf* (*fuoco d'artificio*) Catherine wheel; (*giocattolo*) toy windmill; (*banderuola*) weather vane, weather cock.

gi'rare [dʒi'rare] *vt* (*far ruotare*) to turn; (*percorrere, visitare*) to go round; (CINEMA) to shoot; to make; (COMM) to endorse // *vi* to turn; (*più veloce*) to spin; (*andare in giro*) to wander, go around; **~rsi** *vr* to turn; **attorno a** to go round; to revolve round; **far ~ la testa a qd** to make sb dizzy; (*fig*) to turn sb's head.

girar'rosto [dʒirar'rɔsto] *sm* (CUC) spit.

gira'sole [dʒira'sole] *sm* sunflower.

gi'rata [dʒi'rata] *sf* (*passeggiata*) stroll; (*con veicolo*) drive; (COMM) endorsement.

gira'volta [dʒira'vɔlta] *sf* twirl, turn; (*curva*) sharp bend; (*fig*) about-turn.

gi'revole [dʒi'revole] *ag* revolving, turning.

gi'rino [dʒi'rino] *sm* tadpole.

'giro ['dʒiro] *sm* (*cerchio*) circle; (*di manovella*) turn; (*viaggio*) tour, excursion; (*passeggiata*) stroll, walk; (*in macchina*) drive; (*in bicicletta*) ride; (SPORT: *della pista*) lap; (*di denaro*) circulation; (CARTE) hand; (TECN) revolution; **prendere in ~ qd** (*fig*) to pull sb's leg; **fare un ~** to go for a walk (o a drive o a ride); **andare in ~** to go about, walk around; **a stretto ~ di posta** by return of post; **nel ~ di un mese** in a month's time; **~ d'affari** (COMM) turnover; **~ di parole** circumlocution; **~ di prova** (AUT) test drive; **giro'collo** *sm:* **a girocollo** crewneck *cpd*; **gi'rone** *sm* (SPORT) series of games; **girone di andata/ritorno** (CALCIO) first/second half of the season.

gironzo'lare [dʒirondzo'lare] *vi* to stroll about.

girova'gare [dʒirova'gare] *vi* to wander about.

'gita ['dʒita] *sf* excursion, trip.

gi'tano, a [dʒi'tano] *sm/f* gipsy.

giù [dʒu] av down; (*dabbasso*) downstairs; **in ~** downwards, down; **~ di lì** (*pressappoco*) thereabouts; **bambini dai 6 anni in ~** children aged 6 and under; **~ per: cadere ~ per le scale** to fall down the stairs; **portare i capelli ~ per le spalle** to have shoulder-length hair; **essere ~** (*fig: di salute*) to be run down; (: *di spirito*) to be depressed.

giub'botto [dʒub'bɔtto] *sm* jerkin.

giubi'lare [dʒubi'lare] *vi* to rejoice // *vt* to pension off.

gi'ubilo ['dʒubilo] *sm* rejoicing.

giudi'care [dʒudi'kare] *vt* to judge; **~ qd/qc bello** to consider sb/sth (to be) beautiful.

gi'udice ['dʒuditʃe] *sm* judge; **~ conciliatore** justice of the peace.

giu'dizio [dʒu'dittsjo] *sm* judgment; (*opinione*) opinion; (*DIR*) judgment, sentence; (: *processo*) trial; (: *verdetto*) verdict; **aver ~** to be wise *o* prudent; **giudizi'oso, a** *ag* prudent, judicious.

gi'ugno ['dʒunno] *sm* June.

giul'lare [dʒul'lare] *sm* jester.

giu'menta [dʒu'menta] *sf* mare.

gi'unco, chi ['dʒunko] *sm* rush.

gi'ungere ['dʒundʒere] *vi* (2) to arrive // *vt* (*mani etc*) to join; **~ a** to arrive at, reach.

gi'ungla [dʒungla] *sf* jungle.

gi'unto, a ['dʒunto] *pp di* **giungere** // *sm* addition; (*organo esecutivo, amministrativo*) council, board; **per ~a** into the bargain, in addition; **~a militare** military junta; **giun'tura** *sf* joint.

giuo'care [dʒwo'kare] *vt, vi* = **giocare**; **giu'oco** *sm* = **gioco**.

giura'mento [dʒura'mento] *sm* oath; **~ falso** perjury.

giu'rare [dʒu'rare] *vt* to swear // *vi* to swear, take an oath; **giu'rato, a** *ag*: **nemico giurato** sworn enemy // *sm/f* juror, juryman/woman.

giu'ria [dʒu'ria] *sf* jury.

giu'ridico, a, ci, ci [dʒu'ridiko] *ag* legal.

giurisdizi'one [dʒurizdit'tsjone] *sf* jurisdiction.

giurispru'denza [dʒurispru'dentsa] *sf* jurisprudence.

giustifi'care [dʒustifi'kare] *vt* to justify; **giustificazi'one** *sf* justification; (*INS*) (note of) excuse.

gius'tizia [dʒus'tittsja] *sf* justice; **giustizi'are** *vt* to execute, put to death; **giustizi'ere** *sm* executioner.

gi'usto, a ['dʒusto] *ag* (*equo*) fair, just; (*vero*) true, correct; (*adatto*) right, suitable; (*preciso*) exact, correct // *av* (*esattamente*) exactly, precisely; (*per l'appunto, appena*) just; **arrivare ~** to arrive just in time; **ho ~ bisogno di te** you're just the person I need.

giaci'ale [gla'tʃale] *ag* glacial.

'glandola *sf* = **ghiandola.**

gli [ʎi] *det mpl* (*dav V, s impura, gn, pn, ps, x, z*) the // *pronome* (*a lui*) to him; (*a esso*) to

it; (*in coppia con lo, la, li, le, ne: a lui, a lei, a loro etc*): **gliele do** I'm giving them to him (*o her o* them).

glice'rina [glitʃe'rina] *sf* glycerine.

gli'ela [ʎ'Aela] *etc vedi* **gli.**

glo'bale *ag* overall.

'globo *sm* globe.

'globulo *sm* globule; (*ANAT*) corpuscle.

'gloria *sf* glory; **glorifi'care** *vt* to exalt, glorify; **glori'oso, a** *ag* glorious.

glos'sario *sm* glossary.

glu'cosio *sm* glucose.

'gnocchi ['ɲɔkki] *smpl* (*CUC*) small dumplings made of semolina pasta or potato.

'gnomo ['ɲɔmo] *sm* gnome.

'gobba *sf* (*ANAT*) hump; (*protuberanza*) bump.

'gobbo, a *ag* hunchbacked; (*ricurvo*) round-shouldered // *sm/f* hunchback.

'goccia, ce ['gottʃa] *sf* drop; **goccio'lare** *vi* (2), *vt* to drip; **goccio'lio** *sm* dripping.

go'dere *vi* (*compiacersi*): **~ (di)** to be delighted (at), rejoice (at); (*trarre vantaggio*): **~ di** to enjoy, benefit from // *vt* to enjoy; **~rsi la vita** to enjoy life; **~sela** to have a good time, enjoy o.s.; **godi'mento** *sm* enjoyment.

'goffo, a *ag* clumsy, awkward.

'gola *sf* (*ANAT*) throat; (*golosità*) gluttony, greed; (*di camino*) flue; (*di monte*) gorge; **fare ~** (*anche fig*) to tempt.

golf *sm inv* (*SPORT*) golf; (*maglia*) cardigan.

'golfo *sm* gulf.

go'loso, a *ag* greedy.

'gomito *sm* elbow; (*di strada etc*) sharp bend.

go'mitolo *sm* ball.

'gomma *sf* rubber; (*colla*) gum; (*per cancellare*) rubber, eraser; (*di veicolo*) tyre; **~ a terra** flat tyre; **gommapi'uma** *sf* (*®*) foam rubber.

'gondola *sf* gondola; **gondoli'ere** *sm* gondolier.

gonfa'lone *sm* banner.

gonfi'are *vt* (*pallone*) to blow up, inflate; (*dilatare, ingrossare*) to swell; (*fig: persona*) to flatter; (: *notizia*) to exaggerate; **~rsi** *vr* to swell; (*fiume*) to rise; **'gonfio, a** *ag* swollen; (*stomaco*) bloated; **gonfi'ore** *sm* swelling.

gongo'lare *vi* to look pleased with o.s.; **~ di gioia** to be overjoyed.

'gonna *sf* skirt.

'gonzo ['gondzo] *sm* simpleton, fool.

gorgheggi'are [gorged'dʒare] *vi* to warble; to trill.

'gorgo, ghi *sm* whirlpool.

gorgogli'are [gorgoʎ'Aare] *vi* to gurgle.

go'rilla *sm inv* gorilla.

'gotico, a, ci, che *ag, sm* Gothic.

'gotta *sf* gout.

gover'nante *sm/f* ruler // *sf* (*di bambini*) governess; (*donna di servizio*) housekeeper.

gover'nare *vt* (*Stato*) to govern, rule; (*azienda*) to manage, run; (*pilotare, guidare*) to steer; (*bestiame*) to tend, look after; **governa'tivo, a** *ag* government *cpd*, state *cpd*; **governa'tore** *sm* governor.

go'verno *sm* government; management, running; steering; tending; ~ **della casa** housekeeping.

gozzo'viglia [gottso'vi ʎa] *sf* carousing.

gracchi'are [grak'kjare] *vi* to caw.

graci'dare [gratʃi'dare] *vi* to croak.

'gracile ['gratʃile] *ag* frail, delicate.

gra'dasso *sm* boaster.

gradazi'one [gradat'tsjone] *sf* (*sfumatura*) gradation; ~ **alcolica** alcoholic content, strength.

gra'devole *ag* pleasant, agreeable.

gradi'mento *sm* pleasure, satisfaction.

gradi'nata *sf* flight of steps; (*in teatro, stadio*) tiers *pl*.

gra'dino *sm* step; (*ALPINISMO*) foothold.

gra'dire *vt* (*accettare con piacere*) to accept; (*desiderare*) to wish, like; **gra'dito, a** *ag* pleasing; welcome.

'grado *sm* (*MAT, FISICA etc*) degree; (*stadio*) degree, level; (*MIL, sociale*) rank; **essere in ~ di fare** to be in a position to do.

gradu'ale *ag* gradual.

gradu'are *vt* to grade; **gradu'ato, a** *ag* (*esercizi*) graded; (*scala, termometro*) graduated // *sm* (*MIL*) non-commissioned officer; **graduazi'one** *sf* graduation.

'graffa *sf* (*gancio*) clip; (*segno grafico*) brace.

graffi'are *vt* to scratch.

'graffio *sm* scratch.

gra'fia *sf* spelling; (*scrittura*) handwriting.

'grafico, a, ci, che *ag* graphic // *sm* graph; (*persona*) graphic designer // *sf* graphic arts *pl*.

gra'migna [gra'miɲɲa] *sf* weed; couch grass.

gram'matica, che *sf* grammar; **grammati'cale** *ag* grammatical; **gram-'matico, a, ci, che** *ag* = **grammaticale**.

'grammo *sm* gram(me).

gram'mofono *sm* gramophone.

gran *ag vedi* **grande**.

'grana *sf* (*granello, di minerali, corpi spezzati*) grain; (*fam: seccatura*) trouble; (: *soldi*) cash // *sm inv* Parmesan (cheese).

gra'naio *sm* granary, barn.

gra'nata *sf* (*scopa*) broom; (*frutto*) pomegranate; (*pietra preziosa*) garnet; (*proiettile*) grenade.

Gran Bre'tagna [gran bre'taɲɲa] *sf*: **la ~** Great Britain.

'granchio ['grankjo] *sm* crab; (*fig*) blunder.

grandango'lare *sm* wide-angle lens *sg*.

'grande, *qualche volta* **gran** *+C,* **grand'** *+V ag* (*grosso, largo, vasto*) big, large; (*alto*) tall; (*lungo*) long; (*in sensi astratti*) great // *sm/f* (*persona adulta*) adult, grown-up; (*chi ha ingegno e potenza*) great man/woman; **fare le cose in ~** to do things in style; **una gran bella donna** a very beautiful woman; **non è una gran cosa** *o* **un gran che** it's nothing special; **non ne so gran che** I don't know very much about it.

grandeggi'are [granded'dʒare] *vi* (*emergere per grandezza*): ~ **su** to tower over; (*darsi arie*) to put on airs.

gran'dezza [gran'dettsa] *sf* (*dimensione*) size; magnitude; (*fig*) greatness; **in ~ naturale** lifesize.

grandi'nare *vb impers* to hail.

'grandine *sf* hail.

grandi'oso, a *ag* grand, grandiose.

gran'duca, chi *sm* grand duke.

gra'nello *sm* (*di cereali, uva*) seed; (*di frutta*) pip; (*di sabbia etc*) grain.

gra'nita *sf* kind of water ice.

gra'nito *sm* granite.

'grano *sm* (*in quasi tutti i sensi*) grain; (*frumento*) wheat; (*di rosario, collana*) bead; ~ **di pepe** peppercorn.

gran'turco *sm* maize.

'granulo *sm* granule; (*MED*) pellet.

'grappa *sf* (*alcool*) rough, strong brandy; (*EDIL*) cramp (iron).

'grappolo *sm* bunch, cluster.

'grasso, a *ag* fat; (*cibo*) fatty; (*pelle*) greasy; (*terreno*) rich; (*fig: guadagno, annata*) plentiful; (: *volgare*) coarse, lewd // *sm* (*di persona, animale*) fat; (*sostanza che unge*) grease; **gras'soccio, a, ci, ce** *ag* plump.

'grata *sf* grating.

gra'ticcio [gra'tittʃo] *sm* trellis; (*stuoia*) mat.

gra'ticola *sf* grill.

gra'tifica, che *sf* bonus.

'gratis *av* free, for nothing.

grati'tudine *sf* gratitude.

'grato, a *ag* grateful; (*gradito*) pleasant, agreeable.

gratta'capo *sm* worry, headache.

grattaci'elo [gratta'tʃɛlo] *sm* skyscraper.

grat'tare *vt* (*pelle*) to scratch; (*raschiare*) to scrape; (*pane, formaggio, carote*) to grate; (*fam: rubare*) to pinch // *vi* (*stridere*) to grate; (*AUT*) to grind; ~**rsi** *vr* to scratch o.s.

grat'tugia, gie [grat'tudʒa] *sf* grater; **grattugi'are** *vt* to grate.

gra'tuito, a *ag* free; (*fig*) gratuitous.

gra'vame *sm* tax; (*fig*) burden, weight.

gra'vare *vt* to burden // *vi* (2): ~ **su** to weigh on.

'grave *ag* heavy; (*fig: danno, pericolo, peccato etc*) grave, serious; (: *responsabilità*) heavy, grave; (: *contegno*) grave, solemn; (*voce, suono*) deep, low-pitched; (*LING*): **accento ~** grave accent; **un malato ~** a person who is seriously ill.

gravi'danza [gravi'dantsa] *sf* pregnancy.

'gravido, a *ag* pregnant.

gravità *sf* seriousness; (*anche FISICA*) gravity.

gra'voso, a *ag* heavy, onerous.

'grazia ['grattsja] *sf* grace; (*favore*) favour; (*DIR*) pardon; **grazi'are** *vt* (*DIR*) to pardon.

'grazie ['grattsje] *escl* thank you!; ~

mille! o **tante!** o **infinite!** thank you very much!; ~ **a thanks to.**

grazi'oso, a [grat'tsjoso] ag charming, delightful; (gentile) gracious.

'Grecia ['grɛtʃa] sf: **la** ~ Greece; **'greco, a, ci, che** ag, sm/f Greek.

gre'gario sm (CICLISMO) supporting rider.

'gregge, pl(f) **i** ['greddʒe] sm flock.

'greggio, a, gi, ge ['greddʒo] ag raw, crude, rough; (fig) unrefined // sm (anche: **petrolio** ~) crude (oil).

grembi'ule sm apron; (sopravveste) overall.

'grembo sm lap; (ventre della madre) womb.

gre'mire vt to pack, cram; ~**rsi** vr: ~**rsi (di)** to become packed o crowded (with); **gre'mito, a** ag packed, crowded.

'gretto, a ag mean, stingy; (fig) narrow-minded.

'greve ag heavy.

'grezzo, a ['greddzo] ag = **greggio.**

gri'dare vi (per chiamare) to shout, cry (out); (strillare) to scream, yell // vt to shout (out), yell (out).

'grido, pl(m) **i** o pl(f) **a** sm shout, cry; scream, yell; (di animale) cry; **di** ~ famous.

'grigio, a, gi, gie ['gridʒo] ag grey.

'griglia ['griʎʎa] sf (per arrostire) grill; (ELETTR) grid; **alla** ~ (CUC) grilled.

gril'letto sm trigger.

'grillo sm (ZOOL) cricket; (fig) whim.

grimal'dello sm picklock.

'grinta sf grim expression; (SPORT) fighting spirit.

'grinza ['grintsa] sf crease, wrinkle; (ruga) wrinkle.

grip'pare vi (TECN) to seize.

gris'sino sm bread-stick.

'gronda sf eaves pl.

gron'daia sf gutter.

gron'dare vi (di) to pour; (essere bagnato): ~ **di** to be soaking o dripping with // vt to drip with.

'groppa sf (di animale) back, rump; (fam: dell'uomo) back, shoulders pl.

'groppo sm tangle; **avere un** ~ **alla gola** (fig) to have a lump in one's throat.

'grossa sf (unità di misura) gross.

gros'sezza [gros'settsa] sf size; thickness.

gros'sista, i, e sm/f (COMM) wholesaler.

'grosso, a ag big, large; (di spessore) thick; (grossolano: anche fig) coarse; (grave, insopportabile) serious, great; (tempo, mare) rough // sm: **il** ~ **di** the bulk of; **farla** ~**a** to do something very stupid; **dirle** ~**e** to tell tall stories; **sbagliarsi di** ~ to be completely wrong.

grosso'lano, a ag rough, coarse; (fig) coarse, crude.

grosso'modo av roughly.

'grotta sf cave; grotto.

grot'tesco, a, schi, sche ag grotesque.

grovi'era sm o f gruyère (cheese).

gro'viglio [gro'viʎʎo] sm tangle; (fig) muddle.

gru sf inv crane.

'gruccia, ce ['gruttʃa] sf (per camminare) crutch; (per abiti) coat-hanger.

gru'gnire [gruɲ'ɲire] vi to grunt; **gru'gnito** sm grunt.

'grugno, ['gruɲɲo] sm snout.

'grullo, a ag silly, stupid.

'grumo sm (di sangue) clot; (di farina etc) lump.

'gruppo sm group; ~ **sanguigno** blood group.

guada'gnare [gwadaɲ'ɲare] vt (ottenere) to gain; (soldi, stipendio) to earn; (vincere) to win; (raggiungere) to reach.

gua'dagno [gwa'daɲɲo] sm earnings pl; (COMM) profit; (vantaggio, utile) advantage, gain; ~ **lordo/netto** gross/net earnings pl.

gu'ado sm ford; **passare a** ~ to ford.

gu'ai escl: ~ **a te** (o lui etc)! woe betide you (o him etc)!

gua'ina sf (fodero) sheath; (indumento per donna) girdle.

gu'aio sm trouble, mishap; (inconveniente) trouble, snag.

gua'ire vi to whine, yelp.

gu'ancia, ce ['gwantʃa] sf cheek.

guanci'ale [gwan'tʃale] sm pillow.

gu'anto sm glove.

gu'arda... prefisso: ~**'boschi** sm inv forester; ~**'caccia** sm inv gamekeeper; ~**'coste** sm inv coastguard; (nave) coastguard patrol vessel; ~**'linee** sm inv (SPORT) linesman.

guar'dare vt (con lo sguardo: osservare) to look at; (film, televisione) to watch; (custodire) to look after, take care of // vi to look; (badare): ~ **a** to pay attention to; (luoghi: esser orientato): ~ **a** to face; ~**rsi** vr to look at o.s.; ~**rsi da** (astenersi) to refrain from; (stare in guardia) to beware of; ~**rsi da fare** to take care not to do; ~ **a vista qd** to keep a close watch on sb.

guarda'roba sm inv wardrobe; (locale) cloakroom; **guardarobi'ere, a** sm/f cloakroom attendant.

gu'ardia sf guard; (vigilanza, custodia) watch, guard; **fare la** ~ **a qc/qd** to guard sth/sb; **stare in** ~ (fig) to be on one's guard; ~ **di finanza** (corpo) customs pl; (persona) customs officer.

guardi'ano, a sm/f (di carcere) warder; (di villa etc) caretaker; (di museo) custodian; ~ **notturno** night watchman.

guar'dingo, a, ghi, ghe ag wary, cautious.

guardi'ola sf porter's lodge; (MIL) look-out tower.

guarigi'one [gwari'dʒone] sf recovery.

gua'rire vt (persona, malattia) to cure; (ferita) to heal // vi (2) to recover, be cured; to heal (up).

guarnigi'one [gwarni'dʒone] sf garrison.

guar'nire vt (ornare) to decorate, ornament; (: abiti) to trim; (CUC) to garnish; (MIL) to garrison; **guarnizi'one** sf decoration; trimming; garnish; (TECN) gasket.

guasta'feste sm/f inv spoilsport.

guas'tare vt to spoil, ruin; (meccanismo) to break; ~**rsi** vr (cibo) to go bad; (meccanismo) to break down; (tempo) to change for the worse; (fig) to be spoiled, be ruined; (: amici) to quarrel, fall out.

gu'asto, a ag (non funzionante) broken; (: telefono) out of order; (andato a male) bad, rotten; (: dente) decayed, bad; (fig: corrotto) depraved // sm breakdown, failure; (danno) damage; (fig) something rotten.

gu'azza ['gwattsa] sf heavy dew.

guazza'buglio [gwattsa'buʎʎo] sm muddle.

gu'azzo ['gwattso] sm puddle, pool; (PITTURA) gouache.

gu'ercio, a, ci, ce ['gwertʃo] ag cross-eyed.

gu'erra sf war; (tecnica: atomica, chimica etc) warfare; **fare la ~ (a)** to wage war (against); ~ **mondiale** world war; **guerreggi'are** vi to wage war; **guer-'resco, a, schi, sche** ag (di guerra) war cpd; (incline alla guerra) warlike; **guerri'ero, a** ag warlike // sm warrior; **guerrigli'ero** sm guerrilla.

'gufo sm owl.

gu'ida sf guide; (comando, direzione) guidance, direction; (AUT) driving; (: sterzo) steering; (tappeto, di tenda, cassetto) runner; ~ **a destra/sinistra** (AUT) right-/left-hand drive.

gui'dare vt to guide; (condurre a capo) to lead; (auto) to drive; (aereo, nave) to pilot; **sai ~?** can you drive?; **guida'tore** sm (conducente) driver.

guin'zaglio [gwin'tsaʎʎo] sm leash, lead.

gu'isa sf: **a ~ di** like, in the manner of.

guiz'zare [gwit'tsare] vi to dart; to flash; to flicker; to leap.

'guscio ['guʃʃo] sm shell.

gus'tare vt (cibi) to taste; (: assaporare con piacere) to enjoy, savour; (fig) to enjoy, appreciate // vi (2) to please; **non mi gusta affatto** I don't like it at all.

'gusto sm taste; (sapore) flavour; (godimento) enjoyment; **al ~ di fragola** strawberry-flavoured; **mangiare di ~** to eat heartily; **prenderci ~: ci ha preso** ~ he's acquired a taste for it, he's got to like it; **gus'toso, a** ag tasty; (fig) agreeable.

guttu'rale ag guttural.

H

ha, 'hai [a, ai] forme del vb **avere**.

'handicap ['handikap] sm inv handicap.

'hanno ['anno] forma del vb **avere**.

'hascisc ['haʃiʃ] sm hashish.

ho [ɔ] forma del vb **avere**.

'hobby ['hɔbi] sm inv hobby.

'hockey ['hɔki] sm hockey; ~ **su ghiaccio** ice hockey.

I

i det mpl the.

i'ato sm hiatus.

ibernazi'one [ibernat'tsjone] sf hibernation.

'ibrido, a ag, sm hybrid.

i'cona sf icon.

Id'dio sm God.

i'dea sf idea; (opinione) opinion, view; (ideale) ideal; ~ **fissa** obsession; **neanche** o **neppure per ~!** not on your life!, certainly not!

ide'ale ag, sm ideal; **idea'lismo** sm idealism; **idea'lista, i, e** sm/f idealist; **idealiz'zare** vt to idealize.

ide'are vt (immaginare) to think up, conceive; (progettare) to plan.

i'dentico, a, ci, che ag identical.

identifi'care vt to identify; **identifica-zi'one** sf identification.

identità sf inv identity.

ideolo'gia, 'gie [ideolo'dʒia] sf ideology.

i'dillico, a, ci, che ag idyllic.

idi'oma, i sm idiom, language; **idio-'matico, a, ci, che** ag idiomatic.

idiosincra'sia sf idiosyncrasy.

idi'ota, i, e ag idiotic // sm/f idiot.

idio'tismo sm idiom, idiomatic phrase.

idola'trare vt to worship; (fig) to idolize.

'idolo sm idol.

idoneità sf suitability.

i'doneo, a ag: ~ **a** a suitable for, fit for; (MIL) fit for; (qualificato) qualified for.

i'drante sm hydrant.

i'draulico, a, ci, che ag hydraulic // sm plumber // sf hydraulics sg.

idroe'lettrico, a, ci, che ag hydroelectric.

idro'filo, a ag: vedi **cotone**.

idrofo'bia sf rabies sg.

i'drogeno [i'drɔdʒeno] sm hydrogen.

idros'calo sm seaplane base.

idrovo'lante sm seaplane.

i'ena sf hyena.

i'eri av yesterday; ~ **l'altro** the day before yesterday; ~ **sera** yesterday evening.

igi'ene [i'dʒene] sf hygiene; ~ **pubblica** public health; **igi'enico, a, ci, che** ag hygienic; (salubre) healthy.

i'gnaro, a [iɲ'naro] ag: ~ **di** unaware of, ignorant of.

i'gnobile [iɲ'nɔbile] ag despicable, vile.

igno'minia [iɲɲo'minja] sf ignominy.

igno'rante [iɲɲo'rante] ag ignorant; **igno-'ranza** sf ignorance.

igno'rare [iɲɲo'rare] vt (non sapere, conoscere) to be ignorant o unaware of, not to know; (fingere di non vedere, sentire) to ignore.

i'gnoto, a [iɲ'nɔto] ag unknown.

il det m the.

'ilare ag cheerful; **ilarità** sf hilarity, mirth.

illangui'dire vi (2) to grow weak o feeble.

il'lecito, a [il'lɛtʃito] *ag* illicit.
ille'gale *ag* illegal.
illeg'gibile [illed'dʒibile] *ag* illegible.
illegittimità [illedʒittimi'ta] *sf* illegitimacy.
ille'gittimo, a [ille'dʒittimo] *ag* illegitimate.
il'leso, a *ag* unhurt, unharmed.
illette'rato, a *ag* illiterate.
illimi'tato, a *ag* boundless; unlimited.
il'logico, a, ci, che [il'lɔdʒiko] *ag* illogical.
il'ludere *vt* to deceive, delude; ~**rsi** *vr* to deceive o.s., delude o.s.
illumi'nare *vt* to light up; (*con riflettori*) to illuminate, floodlight; (*fig*) to enlighten; ~**rsi** *vr* to light up; **illuminazi'one** *sf* lighting; illumination, floodlighting; (*fig*) flash of inspiration.
illusi'one *sf* illusion; **farsi delle** ~**i** to delude o.s.
illusio'nismo *sm* conjuring.
il'luso, a *pp di* **illudere.**
illus'trare *vt* to illustrate; **illustra'tivo, a** *ag* illustrative; **illustrazi'one** *sf* illustration.
il'lustre *ag* eminent, renowned.
imbacuc'care *vt*, ~**rsi** *vr* to wrap up.
imbal'laggio [imbal'laddʒo] *sm* packing q.
imbal'lare *vt* to pack; (*AUT*) to race; ~**rsi** *vr* (*AUT*) to race.
imbalsa'mare *vt* to embalm.
imbaraz'zare [imbarat'tsare] *vt* (*ostacolare*) to hamper; (*confondere*) to puzzle, perplex; (*mettere in imbarazzo*) to embarrass.
imba'razzo [imba'rattso] *sm* (*ostacolo*) hindrance, obstacle; (*perplessità*) bewilderment, puzzlement; (*disagio*) embarrassment; ~ **di stomaco** indigestion.
imbarca'dero *sm* landing stage.
imbar'care *vt* (*passeggeri*) to embark; (*merci*) to load; ~**rsi** *vr* to board; ~ **acqua** (*NAUT*) to ship water.
imbarcazi'one [imbarkat'tsjone] *sf* (small) boat, (small) craft *inv*; ~ **di salvataggio** lifeboat.
im'barco, chi *sm* embarkation; loading; boarding; (*banchina*) landing stage.
imbas'tire *vt* (*cucire*) to tack; (*fig: abbozzare*) to sketch, outline.
im'battersi *vr*: ~ **in** (*incontrare*) to bump *o* run into; (*avere la sorte*) to meet with.
imbat'tibile *ag* unbeatable, invincible.
imbavagli'are [imbavaʎ'ʎare] *vt* to gag.
imbec'cata *sf* (*TEATRO*) prompt.
imbe'cille [imbe'tʃille] *ag* idiotic // *sm/f* idiot; (*MED*) imbecile.
imbel'lire *vt* to adorn, embellish.
im'berbe *ag* beardless.
im'bevere *vt* to soak; ~**rsi** *vr*: ~**rsi di** to soak up, absorb.
imbian'care *vt* to whiten; (*muro*) to whitewash // *vi* (2) to become *o* turn white.

imbian'chino [imbjan'kino] *sm* (house) painter, painter and decorator.
imboc'care *vt* (*bambino*) to feed; (*fig: imbeccare*): ~ **qd** to prompt sb, put the words into sb's mouth; (*entrare: strada*) to enter, turn into; (*tromba*) to put to one's mouth // *vi*: ~ **in** (*sog: strada*) to lead into; (: *fiume*) to flow into.
imbocca'tura *sf* (*apertura*) opening; mouth; (*ingresso*) entrance; (*MUS*) mouthpiece.
im'bocco, chi *sm* entrance.
imbos'care *vt* to hide; ~**rsi** *vr* (*MIL*) to evade military service.
imbos'cata *sf* ambush.
imbottigli'are [imbottiʎ'ʎare] *vt* to bottle; (*NAUT*) to blockade; (*MIL*) to hem in; ~**rsi** *vr* to be stuck in a traffic jam.
imbot'tire *vt* to stuff; (*giacca*) to pad; **imbot'tita** *sf* quilt; **imbotti'tura** *sf* stuffing; padding.
imbrat'tare *vt* to dirty, smear, daub.
imbrigli'are [imbriʎ'ʎare] *vt* to bridle.
imbroc'care *vt* (*fig*) to guess correctly.
imbrogli'are [imbroʎ'ʎare] *vt* to mix up; (*CARTE*) to shuffle; (*fig: raggirare*) to deceive, cheat; (: *confondere*) to confuse, mix up; ~**rsi** *vr* to get tangled; (*fig*) to become confused; **im'broglio** *sm* (*groviglio*) tangle; (*situazione confusa*) mess; (*truffa*) swindle, trick; **imbrogli'one, a** *sm/f* cheat, swindler.
imbronci'are [imbron'tʃare] *vi* (2) (*anche:* ~**rsi**) to sulk.
imbru'nire *vi, vb impers* (2) to grow dark; **sull'**~ at dusk.
imbrut'tire *vt* to make ugly // *vi* (2) to become ugly.
imbu'care *vt* to post.
imbur'rare *vt* to butter.
im'buto *sm* funnel.
imi'tare *vt* to imitate; (*riprodurre*) to copy; (*assomigliare*) to look like; **imitazi'one** *sf* imitation.
immaco'lato, a *ag* spotless; immaculate.
immagazzi'nare [immagaddzi'nare] *vt* to store.
immagi'nare [immadʒi'nare] *vt* to imagine; (*supporre*) to suppose; (*inventare*) to invent; **s'immagini** don't mention it!, not at all!; **immagi'nario, a** *ag* imaginary; **immaginazi'one** *sf* imagination; (*cosa immaginata*) fancy.
im'magine [im'madʒine] *sf* image; (*rappresentazione grafica, mentale*) picture.
imman'cabile *ag* certain; unfailing.
immangi'abile [imman'dʒabile] *ag* inedible.
immatrico'lare *vt* to register; ~**rsi** *vr* (*INS*) to matriculate, enrol; **immatricolazi'one** *sf* registration; matriculation, enrolment.
imma'turo, a *ag* (*frutto*) unripe; (*persona*) immature; (*prematuro*) premature.
immedesi'marsi *vr*: ~ **in** to identify with.
immedi'ato, a *ag* immediate.
im'memore *ag*: ~ **di** forgetful of.

im'menso, a *ag* immense.
im'mergere [im'mɛrdʒere] *vt* to immerse, plunge; **~rsi** *vr* to plunge; (*sommergibile*) to dive, submerge; (*dedicarsi a*): **~rsi in** to immerse o.s. in.
immeri'tato, a *ag* undeserved.
immeri'tevole *ag* undeserving, unworthy.
immersi'one *sf* immersion; (*di sommergibile*) submersion, dive; (*di palombaro*) dive.
im'merso, a *pp di* **immergere**.
immi'grante *ag, sm/f* immigrant.
immi'grare *vi* (2) to immigrate; **immi'grato, a** *sm/f* immigrant; **immigrazi'one** *sf* immigration.
immi'nente *ag* imminent.
immischi'are [immis'kjare] *vt*: **~ qd in** to involve sb in; **~rsi in** to interfere o meddle in.
im'mobile *ag* motionless, still; (**beni**) **~i** *smpl* real estate *sg*; **immobili'are** *ag* (*DIR*) property *cpd*; **immobilità** *sf* stillness; immobility; **immobiliz'zare** *vt* to immobilize; (*ECON*) to lock up.
immode'rato, a *ag* excessive.
immo'desto, a *ag* immodest.
immo'lare *vt* to sacrifice, immolate.
immon'dizia [immon'dittsja] *sf* dirt, filth; (*spesso al pl: spazzatura, rifiuti*) rubbish *q*, refuse *q*.
im'mondo, a *ag* filthy, foul.
immo'rale *ag* immoral.
immorta'lare *vt* to immortalize.
immor'tale *ag* immortal.
im'mune *ag* (*esente*) exempt; (*MED, DIR*) immune; **immunità** *sf* immunity; **immunità parlamentare** parliamentary privilege; **immuniz'zare** *vt* (*MED*) to immunize.
immu'tabile *ag* immutable; unchanging.
impacchet'tare [impakket'tare] *vt* to pack up.
impacci'are [impat'tʃare] *vt* to hinder, hamper; **impacci'ato, a** *ag* awkward, clumsy; (*imbarazzato*) embarrassed; **im'paccio** *sm* obstacle; (*imbarazzo*) embarrassment; (*situazione imbarazzante*) awkward situation.
im'pacco, chi *sm* (*MED*) compress.
impadro'nirsi *vr*: **~ di** to seize, take possession of; (*fig: apprendere a fondo*) to master.
impa'gabile *ag* priceless.
impagli'are [impaʎ'ʎare] *vt* to stuff (with straw).
impa'lato, a *ag* (*fig*) stiff as a poker.
impalca'tura *sf* scaffolding; (*anche fig*) framework.
impalli'dire *vi* (2) to turn pale; (*fig*) to fade.
impa'nare *vt* (*CUC*) to dip in breadcrumbs.
impanta'narsi *vr* to sink (in the mud); (*fig*) to get bogged down.
impappi'narsi *vr* to stammer, falter.
impa'rare *vt* to learn.

impareggi'abile [impared'dʒabile] *ag* incomparable.
imparen'tarsi *vr*: **~ con** to marry into.
'impari *ag inv* (*disuguale*) unequal; (*dispari*) odd.
impar'tire *vt* to bestow, give.
imparzi'ale [impar'tsjale] *ag* impartial, unbiased.
impas'sibile *ag* impassive.
impas'tare *vt* (*pasta*) to knead; (*colori*) to mix.
im'pasto *sm* (*anche fig*) mixture; (*di pane*) dough.
im'patto *sm* impact.
impau'rire *vt* to scare, frighten // *vi* (2) (*anche*: **~rsi**) to become scared o frightened.
impazi'ente [impat'tsjɛnte] *ag* impatient; **impazi'enza** *sf* impatience.
impaz'zire [impat'tsire] *vi* (2) to go mad; **~ per qd/qc** to be crazy about sb/sth.
impec'cabile *ag* impeccable, flawless.
impedi'mento *sm* obstacle, hindrance.
impe'dire *vt* (*vietare*): **~ a qd di fare** to prevent sb from doing; (*ostruire*) to obstruct; (*impacciare*) to hamper, hinder.
impe'gnare [impeɲ'ɲare] *vt* (*dare in pegno*) to pawn; (*onore etc*) to pledge; (*prenotare*) to book, reserve; (*obbligare*) to oblige; (*occupare*) to keep busy; (*MIL: nemico*) to engage; **~rsi** *vr* (*vincolarsi*): **~rsi a fare** to undertake to do; (*mettersi risolutamente*): **~rsi in qc** to devote o.s. to sth; **impegna'tivo, a** *ag* binding; (*lavoro*) demanding, exacting; **impe'gnato, a** *ag* (*occupato*) busy; (*fig: romanzo, autore*) committed, engagé.
im'pegno [im'peɲɲo] *sm* (*obbligo*) obligation; (*promessa*) promise, pledge; (*zelo*) diligence, zeal; (*compito, d'autore*) commitment.
impel'lente *ag* pressing, urgent.
impene'trabile *ag* impenetrable.
impen'narsi *vr* (*cavallo*) to rear up; (*AER*) to nose up; (*fig*) to bridle.
impen'sato, a *ag* unforeseen, unexpected.
impensie'rire *vt*, **~rsi** *vr* to worry.
impe'rare *vi* (*anche fig*) to reign, rule.
impera'tivo, a *ag, sm* imperative.
impera'tore, 'trice *sm/f* emperor/empress.
impercet'tibile [impertʃet'tibile] *ag* imperceptible.
imperdo'nabile *ag* unforgivable, unpardonable.
imper'fetto, a *ag* imperfect // *sm* (*LING*) imperfect (tense); **imperfezi'one** *sf* imperfection.
imperi'ale *ag* imperial.
imperi'oso, a *ag* (*persona*) imperious; (*motivo, esigenza*) urgent, pressing.
impe'rizia [impe'rittsja] *sf* lack of experience.
imperma'lirsi *vr* to take offence.
imperme'abile *ag* waterproof // *sm* raincoat.

im'pero sm empire; (forza, autorità) rule, control.

imperscru'tabile ag inscrutable.

imperso'nale ag impersonal.

imperso'nare vt to personify; (TEATRO) to play, act (the part of).

imperter'rito, a ag fearless, undaunted; impassive.

imperti'nente ag impertinent; **imperti-'nenza** sf impertinence.

impertur'babile ag imperturbable.

imperver'sare vi to rage.

'impeto sm (moto, forza) force, impetus; (assalto) onslaught; (fig: impulso) impulse; (: slancio) transport; **con ~** energetically; vehemently.

impet'tito, a ag stiff, erect.

impetu'oso, a ag (vento) strong, raging; (persona) impetuous.

impian'tare vt (motore) to install; (azienda, discussione) to establish, start.

impi'anto sm (installazione) installation; (apparecchiature) plant; (sistema) system; **~ elettrico** wiring; **~ sportivo** sports complex.

impias'trare vt to smear, dirty.

impi'astro sm poultice.

impic'care vt to hang; **~rsi** vr to hang o.s.

impicci'are [impit'tʃare] vt to hinder, hamper; **~rsi** vr to meddle, interfere; **im-'piccio** sm (ostacolo) hindrance; (seccatura) trouble, bother; (affare imbrogliato) mess.

impie'gare vt (usare) to use, employ; (assumere) to employ, take on; (spendere: denaro, tempo) to spend; (investire) to invest; **~rsi** vr to get a job, obtain employment; **impie'gato, a** sm/f employee.

impi'ego, ghi sm (uso) use; (occupazione: impiego) (posto) (regular) job, post; (ECON) investment.

impieto'sire vt to move to pity; **~rsi** vr to be moved to pity.

impigli'are [impiʎ'ʎare] vt to catch, entangle; **~rsi** vr to get caught up o entangled.

impi'grire vt to make lazy // vi (2) (anche: **~rsi**) to grow lazy.

impiom'bare vt (pacco) to seal (with lead); (dente) to fill.

impli'care vt to imply; (coinvolgere) to involve; **~rsi** vr to become involved; **implicazi'one** sf implication.

im'plicito, a [im'plitʃito] ag implicit.

implo'rare vt to implore.

impoltro'nire vt to make lazy // vi (2) (anche: **~rsi**) to grow lazy.

impolve'rare vt to cover with dust; **~rsi** vr to get dusty.

impo'nente ag imposing, impressive.

impo'nibile ag taxable // sm taxable income.

impopo'lare ag unpopular; **impopolarità** sf unpopularity.

im'porre vt to impose; (costringere) to force, make; (far valere) to impose, enforce; **imporsi** vr (persona) to assert o.s.; (cosa: rendersi necessario) to become necessary; **~ a qd di fare** to force sb to do, make sb do.

impor'tante ag important; **impor'tanza** sf importance; **dare importanza a qc** to attach importance to sth.

impor'tare vt (introdurre dall'estero) to import // vi (2) to matter, be important // vb impers (2) (essere necessario) to be necessary; (interessare) to matter; **non importa!** it doesn't matter!; **non me ne importa!** I don't care!; **importazi'one** sf importation; (merci importate) imports pl.

im'porto sm (total) amount.

importu'nare vt to bother.

impor'tuno, a ag irksome, annoying.

imposizi'one [impozit'tsjone] sf imposition; order, command; (onere, imposta) tax.

imposses'sarsi vr: **~ di** to seize, take possession of.

impos'sibile ag impossible; **im-possibilità** sf impossibility; **essere nell'impossibilità di fare qc** to be unable to do sth.

im'posta sf (di finestra) shutter; (tassa) tax; **~ sul reddito** income tax; **~ sul valore aggiunto (I.V.A.)** value added tax (VAT).

impos'tare vt (imbucare) to post; (preparare) to plan, set out; (avviare) to begin, start off; (voce) to pitch.

im'posto, a pp di **imporre**.

impos'tore, a sm/f impostor.

impo'tente ag weak, powerless; (anche MED) impotent; **impo'tenza** sf weakness, powerlessness; impotence.

impove'rire vt to impoverish // vi (2) (anche: **~rsi**) to become poor.

imprati'cabile ag (strada) impassable; (campo da gioco) unplayable.

imprati'chire [imprati'kire] vt to train; **~rsi in qc** to practise sth.

impre'ciso, a [impre'tʃizo] ag imprecise, vague.

impre'gnare [impreɲ'pare] vt: **~ (di)** (imbevere) to soak o impregnate (with); (riempire: anche fig) to fill (with).

imprendi'tore sm entrepreneur; (appaltatore) contractor; **piccolo ~** small businessman.

im'presa sf (iniziativa) enterprise; (azione) exploit; (azienda) firm, concern.

impre'sario sm (TEATRO) manager, impresario; **~ di pompe funebri** funeral director.

imprescin'dibile [impreʃʃin'dibile] ag not to be ignored.

impressio'nante ag impressive; upsetting.

impressio'nare vt to impress; (turbare) to upset; (FOT) to expose; **~rsi** vr to be easily upset.

impressi'one sf impression; (fig: sensazione) sensation, feeling; (stampa) printing; **fare ~** to impress; (turbare) to frighten, upset; **fare buona/cattiva ~ a** to make a good/bad impression on.

im'presso, a pp di **imprimere.**

impreve'dibile ag unforeseeable; (persona) unpredictable.

imprevi'dente ag lacking in foresight.

impre'visto, a ag unexpected, unforeseen // sm unforeseen event; **salvo ~i** unless anything unexpected happens.

imprigiona'mento [impridʒona'mento] sm imprisonment.

imprigio'nare [impridʒo'nare] vt to imprison.

im'primere vt (anche fig) to impress, stamp; (stampare) to print; (comunicare: movimento) to transmit, give.

impro'babile ag improbable, unlikely.

im'pronta sf imprint, impression, sign; (di piede, mano) print; (fig) mark, stamp; **~ digitale** fingerprint.

impro'perio sm insult; **~i** smpl abuse sg.

im'proprio, a ag improper.

improvvisa'mente av suddenly; unexpectedly.

improvvi'sare vt to improvise; **~rsi** vr: **~rsi cuoco** to (decide to) act as cook; **improvvi'sata** sf (pleasant) surprise.

improv'viso, a ag (imprevisto) unexpected; (subitaneo) sudden; **all'~** unexpectedly; suddenly.

impru'dente ag unwise, rash.

impu'dente ag impudent; **impu'denza** sf impudence.

impu'dico, a, chi, che ag immodest.

impu'gnare [impuɲ'ɲare] vt to grasp, grip; (DIR) to contest; **impugna'tura** sf grip, grasp; (manico) handle; (: di spada) hilt.

impul'sivo, a ag impulsive.

im'pulso sm impulse.

impu'nito, a ag unpunished.

impun'tarsi vr to stop dead, refuse to budge; (fig) to be obstinate.

impurità sf inv impurity.

im'puro, a ag impure.

impu'tare vt (ascrivere): **~ qc a** to attribute sth to; (DIR: accusare): **~ qd di** to charge sb with, accuse sb of; **impu'tato, a** sm/f (DIR) accused, defendant; **imputazi'one** sf (DIR) charge.

imputri'dire vi (2) to rot.

in prep (in + il = **nel**, in + lo = **nello**, in + l' = **nell'**, in + la = **nella**, in + i = **nei**, in + gli = **negli**, in + le = **nelle**) in; (moto a luogo) to; (: dentro) into; (mezzo): ~ **autobus/treno** by bus/train; (composizione): ~ **marmo** made of marble, marble cpd; **essere ~ casa** to be at home; **andare ~ Austria** to go to Austria; **Maria Bianchi ~ Rossi** Maria Rossi née Bianchi; **siamo ~ quattro** there are four of us.

i'nabile ag: ~ **a** incapable of; (fisicamente, MIL) unfit for; **inabilità** sf incapacity.

inabi'tabile ag uninhabitable.

inacces'sibile [inattʃes'sibile] ag inaccessible; (persona) unapproachable.

inaccet'tabile [inattʃet'tabile] ag unacceptable.

ina'datto, a ag: ~ **(a)** unsuitable o unfit (for).

inadegu'ato, a ag inadequate.

inadempi'ente sm/f defaulter.

inaffer'rabile ag elusive; (concetto, senso) difficult to grasp.

ina'lare vt to inhale; **inala'tore** sm inhaler.

inal'bere vt (NAUT) to hoist, raise; **~rsi** vr (impennarsi) to rear up; (fig) to flare up, fly off the handle.

inalte'rabile ag unchangeable; (colore) fast, permanent; (affetto) constant.

inalte'rato, a ag unchanged.

inami'dare vt to starch; **inamidato, a** ag starched.

inammis'sibile ag inadmissible.

inani'mato, a ag inanimate; (senza vita: corpo) lifeless.

inappa'gabile ag insatiable.

inappel'labile ag (DIR) final, not open to appeal.

inappun'tabile ag irreproachable, flawless.

inar'care vt (schiena) to arch; (sopracciglia) to raise; **~rsi** vr to arch.

inari'dire vt to make arid, dry up // vi (2) (anche: **~rsi**) to dry up, become arid.

inaspet'tato, a ag unexpected.

inas'prire vt to embitter; to exacerbate; **~rsi** vr to grow bitter.

inattac'cabile ag (MIL) unassailable; (fig: fama)~ unimpeachable; ~ **dalle tarme** moth-proof.

inatten'dibile ag unreliable.

inat'teso, a ag unexpected.

inat'tivo, a ag inactive, idle; (CHIM) inactive.

inattu'abile ag impracticable.

inau'dito, a ag unheard of.

inaugu'rale ag inaugural.

inaugu'rare vt to inaugurate, open; (monumento) to unveil; **inaugurazi'one** sf inauguration; unveiling.

inavve'duto, a ag careless, inadvertent.

inavver'tenza [inavver'tɛntsa] sf carelessness, inadvertence.

incagli'are [inkaʎ'ʎare] vi (2) (NAUT: anche: **~rsi**) to run aground // vt (intralciare) to hamper, hinder; **in'caglio** sm (NAUT) running aground; (ostacolo) obstacle, hindrance.

incalco'labile ag incalculable.

incal'lito, a ag calloused; (fig) hardened, inveterate; (: insensibile) hard.

incal'zare [inkal'tsare] vt to follow o pursue closely; (fig) to press // vi (urgere) to be pressing; (essere imminente) to be imminent.

incame'rare vt (DIR) to expropriate.

incammi'nare vt (fig: avviare) to start up; **~rsi** vr to set off.

incande'scente [inkandeʃ'ʃente] ag incandescent, white-hot.

incan'tare vt to enchant, bewitch; **~rsi**

vr (*rimanere intontito*) to be spellbound; to be in a daze; (*meccanismo: bloccarsi*) to jam; **incanta'tore, 'trice** *ag* enchanting, bewitching // *sm/f* enchanter/enchantress; **incan'tesimo** *sm* spell, charm; **incan'tevole** *ag* charming, enchanting.

in'canto *sm* spell, charm, enchantment; (*asta*) auction; **come per ~** as if by magic; **mettere all'~** to put up for auction.

incanu'tire *vi* (2) to go white.

inca'pace [inka'patʃe] *ag* incapable; **incapacità** *sf* inability; (*DIR*) incapacity.

incapo'nirsi *vr* to be stubborn, be determined.

incap'pare *vi* (2): **~ in qc/qd** (*anche fig*) to run into sth/sb.

incapricci'arsi [inkaprit'tʃarsi] *vr:* **~ di** to take a fancy to *o* for.

incapsu'lare *vt* (*dente*) to crown.

incarce'rare [inkartʃe'rare] *vt* to imprison.

incari'care *vt:* **~ qd di fare** to give sb the responsibility of doing; **~rsi di** to take care *o* charge of; **incari'cato, a** *ag:* **incaricato (di)** in charge (of), responsible (for) // *sm/f* delegate, representative; **incaricato d'affari** (*POL*) chargé d'affaires.

in'carico, chi *sm* task, job.

incar'nare *vt* to embody; **~rsi** *vr* to be embodied; (*REL*) to become incarnate; **incarnazi'one** *sf* incarnation.

incarta'mento *sm* dossier, file.

incar'tare *vt* to wrap (in paper).

incas'sare *vt* (*merce*) to pack (in cases); (*gemma: incastonare*) to set; (*ECON: riscuotere*) to collect; (*PUGILATO: colpi*) to take, stand up to; **in'casso** *sm* cashing, encashment; (*introito*) takings *pl.*

incasto'nare *vt* to set; **incastona'tura** *sf* setting.

incas'trare *vt* to fit in, insert; **~rsi** *vr* to stick; **in'castro** *sm* slot, groove.

incate'nare *vt* to chain up; (*fig*) to tie.

incatra'mare *vt* to tar.

in'cauto, a *ag* imprudent, rash.

inca'vare *vt* to hollow out; **inca'vato, a** *ag* hollow; (*occhi*) sunken; **incava'tura** *sf* hollow; **in'cavo** *sm* hollow; (*solco*) groove.

incendi'are [intʃen'djare] *vt* to set fire to; **~rsi** *vr* to catch fire, burst into flames.

incendi'ario, a [intʃen'djarjo] *ag* incendiary // *sm/f* arsonist.

in'cendio [in'tʃendjo] *sm* fire.

incene'rire [intʃene'rire] *vt* to burn to ashes, incinerate; (*cadavere*) to cremate; **~rsi** *vr* to be burnt to ashes.

in'censo [in'tʃenso] *sm* incense.

incensu'rato, a [intʃensu'rato] *ag* (*DIR*): **essere ~** to have a clean record.

incen'tivo [intʃen'tivo] *sm* incentive.

incep'pare [intʃep'pare] *vt* to obstruct, hamper; **~rsi** *vr* to jam.

ince'rata [intʃe'rata] *sf* (*tela*) tarpaulin; (*impermeabile*) oilskins *pl.*

incer'tezza [intʃer'tettsa] *sf* uncertainty.

in'certo, a [in'tʃerto] *ag* uncertain; (*irresoluto*) undecided, hesitating // *sm* uncertainty.

inces'sante [intʃes'sante] *ag* incessant.

in'cesto [in'tʃesto] *sm* incest.

in'cetta [in'tʃetta] *sf* buying up; **fare ~ di qc** to buy up sth.

inchi'esta [in'kjesta] *sf* investigation, inquiry.

inchi'nare [inki'nare] *vt* to bow; **~rsi** *vr* to bend down; (*per riverenza*) to bow; (: *donna*) to curtsy; **in'chino** *sm* bow; curtsy.

inchio'dare [inkjo'dare] *vt* to nail; (*chiudere con chiodi*) to nail down (*o* up).

inchi'ostro [in'kjɔstro] *sm* ink; **~ simpatico** invisible ink.

inciam'pare [intʃam'pare] *vi* to trip, stumble.

inci'ampo [in'tʃampo] *sm* obstacle; **essere d'~ a qd** (*fig*) to be in sb's way.

inciden'tale [intʃiden'tale] *ag* incidental.

inci'dente [intʃi'dɛnte] *sm* accident; **~ d'auto** car accident.

inci'denza [intʃi'dɛntsa] *sf* incidence.

in'cidere [in'tʃidere] *vi:* **~ su** to bear upon, affect // *vt* (*tagliare incavando*) to cut into; (*ARTE*) to engrave; to etch; (*canzone*) to record.

in'cinta [in'tʃinta] *ag f* pregnant.

incipi'ente [intʃi'pjɛnte] *ag* incipient.

incipri'are [intʃi'prjare] *vt* to powder.

in'circa [in'tʃirka] *av:* **all'~** more or less, very nearly.

incisi'one [intʃi'zjone] *sf* cut; (*disegno*) engraving; etching; (*registrazione*) recording; (*MED*) incision.

inci'sivo, a [intʃi'zivo] *ag* incisive.

in'ciso [in'tʃizo] *sm:* **per ~** incidentally, by the way.

inci'tare [intʃi'tare] *vt* to incite.

inci'vile [intʃi'vile] *ag* uncivilized; (*villano*) impolite.

incivi'lire [intʃivi'lire] *vt* to civilize.

incl. (*abbr di incluso*) encl.

incli'nare *vt* to tilt // *vi* (*fig*): **~ a qc/a fare** to incline towards sth/doing; to tend towards sth/to do; **inclinato, a** *ag* (*anche fig*) inclined; **inclinazi'one** *sf* slope; (*fig*) inclination, tendency; **in'cline** *ag:* **incline a** inclined to.

in'cludere *vt* to include; (*accludere*) to enclose; **inclusi'one** *sf* inclusion; **inclu'sivo, a** *ag:* **inclusivo di** inclusive of; **in'cluso, a** *pp di* **includere** // *ag* included; enclosed.

incoe'rente *ag* incoherent; (*contraddittorio*) inconsistent; **incoe'renza** *sf* incoherence; inconsistency.

in'cognito, a [in'kɔɲnito] *ag* unknown // *sm:* **in ~** incognito // *sf* (*MAT, fig*) unknown quantity.

incol'lare *vt* to glue, gum; (*unire con colla*) to stick together.

incolon'nare *vt* to draw up in columns.

inco'lore *ag* colourless.

incol'pare *vt:* **~ qd di** to charge sb with.

in'colto, a *ag* (*terreno*) uncultivated;

(trascurato: capelli) neglected; (persona) uneducated.

in'colume ag safe and sound, unhurt.

in'combere vi (sovrastare minacciando): ~ su to threaten, hang over; (spettare): ~ a to rest o be incumbent upon.

incominci'are [inkomin'tʃare] vi (2), vt to begin, start.

in'comodo, a ag uncomfortable; (inopportuno) inconvenient // sm inconvenience, bother.

incompa'rabile ag incomparable.

incompa'tibile ag (non ammissibile: negligenza) intolerable; (inconciliabile) incompatible.

incompe'tente ag incompetent; incompe'tenza sf incompetence.

incompi'uto, a ag unfinished, incomplete.

incom'pleto, a ag incomplete.

incompren'sibile ag incomprehensible.

incomprensi'one sf incomprehension.

incom'preso, a ag not understood; misunderstood.

inconce'pibile [inkontʃe'pibile] ag inconceivable.

inconcili'abile [inkontʃi'ljabile] ag irreconcilable.

inconclu'dente ag inconclusive; (persona) ineffectual.

incondizio'nato, a [inkondittsjo'nato] ag unconditional.

inconfu'tabile ag irrefutable.

incongru'ente ag inconsistent.

in'congruo, a ag incongruous.

inconsa'pevole ag: ~ di unaware of, ignorant of.

in'conscio, a, sci, sce [in'konʃo] ag unconscious // sm (PSIC): l'~ the unconscious.

inconsis'tente ag insubstantial; unfounded.

inconso'labile ag inconsolable.

inconsu'eto, a ag unusual.

incon'sulto, a ag rash.

inconti'nenza [inkonti'nɛntsa] sf incontinence.

incon'trare vt to meet; (difficoltà) to meet with; ~rsi vr to meet.

incontras'tabile ag incontrovertible, indisputable.

in'contro av: ~ a (verso) towards // sm meeting; (SPORT) match; meeting; ~ di calcio football match.

inconveni'ente sm drawback, snag.

incoraggia'mento [inkoraddʒa'mento] sm encouragement.

incoraggi'are [inkorad'dʒare] vt to encourage.

incornici'are [inkorni'tʃare] vt to frame.

incoro'nare vt to crown; incoronazi'one sf coronation.

incorpo'rare vt to incorporate; (fig: annettere) to annex.

incorreg'gibile [inkorred'dʒibile] ag incorrigible.

in'correre vi (2): ~ in to meet with, run into.

incorrut'tibile ag incorruptible.

incosci'ente [inkoʃ'ʃɛnte] ag (inconscio) unconscious; (irresponsabile) reckless, thoughtless; incosci'enza sf unconsciousness; recklessness, thoughtlessness.

incre'dibile ag incredible, unbelievable.

in'credulo, a ag incredulous, disbelieving.

incremen'tare vt to increase; (dar sviluppo a) to promote.

incre'mento sm (sviluppo) development; (aumento numerico) increase, growth.

incres'parsi vr (acqua) to ripple; (capelli) to go frizzy; (pelle, tessuto) to wrinkle.

incrimi'nare vt (DIR) to charge.

incri'nare vt, ~rsi vr to crack; incrina'tura sf crack.

incroci'are [inkro'tʃare] vt to cross; (incontrare) to meet // vi (NAUT, AER) to cruise; ~rsi vr (strade) to cross, intersect; (persone, veicoli) to pass each other; ~ le braccia/le gambe to fold one's arms/cross one's legs; incrocia'tore sm cruiser.

in'crocio [in'krotʃo] sm (anche FERR) crossing; (di strade) crossroads.

incros'tare vt to encrust.

incuba'trice [inkuba'tritʃe] sf incubator.

incubazi'one [inkubat'tsjone] sf incubation.

'incubo sm nightmare.

in'cudine sf anvil.

incul'care vt: ~ qc in to inculcate sth into, instill sth into.

incune'are vt to wedge.

incu'rabile ag incurable.

incu'rante ag: ~ (di) heedless (of), careless (of).

incurio'sire vt to make curious; ~rsi vr to become curious.

incursi'one sf raid.

incur'vare vt, ~rsi vr to bend, curve.

in'cusso, a pp di incutere.

incusto'dito, a ag unguarded, unattended.

in'cutere vt to arouse; ~ timore/rispetto a qd to strike fear into sb/command sb's respect.

'indaco sm indigo.

indaffa'rato, a ag busy.

inda'gare vt to investigate.

in'dagine [in'dadʒine] sf investigation, inquiry; (ricerca) research, study.

indebi'tare vt to get into debt; ~rsi vr to run o get into debt.

in'debito, a ag undue; undeserved.

indebo'lire vt, vi (2) (anche: ~rsi) to weaken.

inde'cente [inde'tʃɛnte] ag indecent; inde'cenza sf indecency.

indeci'frabile [indetʃi'frabile] ag indecipherable.

indecisi'one [indetʃi'zjone] sf indecisiveness; indecision.

inde'ciso, a [inde'tʃizo] ag indecisive; (irrisoluto) undecided.

inde'fesso, a ag untiring, indefatigable.

indefi'nibile ag indefinable.

indefi'nito, a *ag* (*anche* LING) indefinite; (*impreciso, non determinato*) undefined.

in'degno, a [in'deɲɲo] *ag* unworthy.

inde'lebile *ag* indelible.

indelica'tezza [indelika'tettsa] *sf* tactlessness.

indemoni'ato, a *ag* possessed (by the devil).

in'denne *ag* unhurt, uninjured; **indennità** *sf inv* (*rimborso: di spese*) allowance; (: *di perdita*) compensation, indemnity; **indennità di contingenza** cost-of-living allowance; **indennità di trasferta** travel expenses *pl*.

indenniz'zare [indennid'dzare] *vt* to compensate; **inden'nizzo** *sm* (*somma*) compensation, indemnity.

indero'gabile *ag* binding.

indeside'rabile *ag* undesirable.

indetermi'nato, a *ag* indefinite, indeterminate.

'India *sf*: l'~ India; **indi'ano, a** *ag* Indian // *sm/f* (*d'India*) Indian; (*d'America*) Red Indian.

indiavo'lato, a *ag* possessed (by the devil); (*vivace, violento*) wild.

indi'care *vt* (*mostrare*) to show, indicate; (: *col dito*) to point to, point out; (*consigliare*) to suggest, recommend; **indica'tivo, a** *ag* indicative // *sm* (LING) indicative (mood); **indica'tore** *sm* (*elenco*) guide; directory; (TECN) gauge; indicator; **indicazi'one** *sf* indication; (*notizia*) information *q*; **indicazioni per l'uso** instructions for use.

'indice ['inditʃe] *sm* (ANAT: *dito*) index finger, forefinger; (*lancetta*) needle, pointer; (*fig: indizio*) sign; (TECN, MAT, *nei libri*) index.

indi'cibile [indi'tʃibile] *ag* inexpressible.

indietreggi'are [indietred'dʒare] *vi* to draw back, retreat.

indi'etro *av* back; (*guardare*) behind, back; (*andare, cadere: anche:* **all'~**) backwards; **rimanere ~** (*col lavoro*) to be left behind; **essere ~** (*col lavoro*) to be behind; (*orologio*) to be slow; **rimandare qc ~** to send sth back.

indiffe'rente *ag* indifferent; **indiffe'renza** *sf* indifference.

in'digeno, a [in'didʒeno] *ag* indigenous, native // *sm/f* native.

indi'gente [indi'dʒɛnte] *ag* poverty-stricken, destitute; **indi'genza** *sf* extreme poverty.

indigesti'one [indidʒes'tjone] *sf* indigestion.

indi'gesto, a [indi'dʒɛsto] *ag* indigestible.

indi'gnare [indiɲ'ɲare] *vt* to fill with indignation; **~rsi** *vr* to be (*o* get) indignant; **indignazi'one** *sf* indignation.

indimenti'cabile *ag* unforgettable.

indipen'dente *ag* independent; **indipen'denza** *sf* independence.

indi'retto, a *ag* indirect.

indiriz'zare [indirit'tsare] *vt* (*dirigere*) to direct; (*mandare*) to send; (*lettera*) to address; **~ la parola a qd** to address sb.

indi'rizzo [indi'rittso] *sm* address; (*direzione*) direction; (*avvio*) trend, course.

indisci'plina [indiʃʃi'plina] *sf* indiscipline.

indis'creto, a *ag* indiscreet; **indiscrezi'one** *sf* indiscretion.

indis'cusso, a *ag* unquestioned.

indispen'sabile *ag* indispensable, essential.

indispet'tire *vt* to irritate, annoy // *vi* (2) (*anche:* **~rsi**) to get irritated *o* annoyed.

indis'posto, a *pp di* **indisporre** // *ag* indisposed, unwell.

indisso'lubile *ag* indissoluble.

indis'tinto, a *ag* indistinct.

indistrut'tibile *ag* indestructible.

in'divia *sf* endive.

individu'ale *ag* individual; **individualità** *sf* individuality.

individu'are *vt* (*dar forma distinta a*) to characterize; (*determinare*) to locate; (*riconoscere*) to single out.

indi'viduo *sm* individual.

indi'viso, a *ag* undivided.

indizi'are [indit'tsjare] *vt*: **~ qd di qc** to cast suspicion on sb for sth; **indizi'ato, a** *ag* suspected // *sm/f* suspect.

in'dizio [in'dittsjo] *sm* (*segno*) sign, indication; (POLIZIA) clue; (DIR) piece of evidence.

'indole *sf* nature, character.

indo'lente *ag* indolent; **indo'lenza** *sf* indolence.

indolen'zito, a [indolen'tsito] *ag* stiff, aching; (*intorpidito*) numb.

indo'lore *ag* painless.

indo'mani *sm*: l'~ the next day, the following day.

Indo'nesia *sf*: l'~ Indonesia.

indos'sare *vt* (*mettere indosso*) to put on; (*avere indosso*) to have on; **indossa'tore, 'trice** *sm/f* model.

in'dotto, a *pp di* **indurre.**

indottri'nare *vt* to indoctrinate.

indovi'nare *vt* (*scoprire*) to guess; (*immaginare*) to imagine, guess; (*il futuro*) to foretell; **indovi'nato, a** *ag* successful; (*scelta*) inspired; **indovi'nello** *sm* riddle; **indo'vino** *a*, *sm/f* fortuneteller.

indubbia'mente *av* undoubtedly.

in'dubbio, a *ag* certain, undoubted.

indugi'are [indu'dʒare] *vi* to take one's time, delay; **~rsi** *vr* (*soffermarsi*) to linger.

in'dugio [in'dudʒo] *sm* (*ritardo*) delay; **senza ~** without delay.

indul'gente [indul'dʒɛnte] *ag* indulgent; (*giudice*) lenient; **indul'genza** *sf* indulgence; leniency.

in'dulgere [in'duldʒere] *vi*: **~ a** (*accondiscendere*) to comply with; (*abbandonarsi*) to indulge in; **in'dulto, a** *pp di* **indulgere** // *sm* (DIR) pardon.

indu'mento *sm* article of clothing, garment; **~i** *smpl* clothes.

indu'rire *vt* to harden // *vi* (2) (*anche:* **~rsi**) to harden, become hard.

in'durre vt to induce, persuade, lead; ~ qd in errore to mislead sb.

in'dustria sf industry; **industri'ale** ag industrial // sm industrialist.

industrializ'zare [industrialid'dzare] vt to industrialize; **industrializzazi'one** sf industrialization.

industri'arsi vr to do one's best, try hard.

industri'oso, a ag industrious, hard-working.

induzi'one [indut'tsjone] sf induction.

inebe'tito, a ag dazed, stunned.

inebri'are vt (anche fig) to intoxicate; ~rsi vr to become intoxicated.

inecce'pibile [inettʃe'pibile] ag unexceptionable.

i'nedia sf starvation.

i'nedito, a ag unpublished.

ineffi'cace [ineffi'katʃe] ag ineffective.

ineffici'ente [ineffi'tʃɛnte] ag inefficient.

inegu'ale ag unequal; (irregolare) uneven.

ine'rente ag: ~ a concerning, regarding.

i'nerme ag unarmed; defenceless.

inerpi'carsi vr: ~ (su) to clamber (up).

i'nerte ag inert; (inattivo) indolent, sluggish; **i'nerzia** sf inertia; indolence, sluggishness.

ine'satto, a ag (impreciso) inexact; (erroneo) incorrect; (AMM: non riscosso) uncollected.

inesau'ribile ag inexhaustible.

inesis'tente ag non-existent.

ineso'rabile ag inexorable, relentless.

inesperi'enza [inespe'rjɛntsa] sf inexperience.

ines'perto, a ag inexperienced.

inespli'cabile ag inexplicable.

inesti'mabile ag inestimable.

i'netto, a ag (incapace) inept; (che non ha attitudine): ~ (a) unsuited (to).

inevi'tabile ag inevitable.

i'nezia [i'nɛttsja] sf trifle, thing of no importance.

infagot'tare vt to bundle up, wrap up; ~rsi vr to wrap up.

infal'libile ag infallible.

infa'mare vt to defame; **infama'torio, a** ag defamatory.

in'fame ag infamous; (fig: cosa, compito) awful, dreadful; **in'famia** sf infamy.

infan'tile ag child cpd; childlike; (adulto, azione) childish; **letteratura** ~ children's books pl.

in'fanzia [in'fantsja] sf childhood; (bambini) children pl; **prima** ~ babyhood, infancy.

infari'nare vt to cover with (o sprinkle with o dip in) flour; ~ **di zucchero** to sprinkle with sugar; **infarina'tura** sf (fig) smattering.

in'farto sm (MED): ~ **(cardiaco)** coronary.

infasti'dire vt to annoy, irritate; ~rsi vr to get annoyed o irritated.

infati'cabile ag tireless, untiring.

in'fatti cong as a matter of fact, in fact, actually.

infatu'arsi vr: ~ di o per to become infatuated with, fall for; **infatuazi'one** sf infatuation.

in'fausto, a ag unpropitious, unfavourable.

infe'condo, a ag infertile.

infe'dele ag unfaithful; **infedeltà** sf infidelity.

infe'lice [infe'litʃe] ag unhappy; (sfortunato) unlucky, unfortunate; (inopportuno) inopportune, ill-timed; (mal riuscito: lavoro) bad, poor; **infelicità** sf unhappiness.

inferi'ore ag lower; (per intelligenza, qualità) inferior // sm/f inferior; ~ **a** (numero, quantità) less o smaller than; (meno buono) inferior to; ~ **alla media** below average; **inferiorità** sf inferiority.

inferme'ria sf sick bay.

infermi'ere, a sm/f nurse.

infermità sf inv illness; infirmity.

in'fermo, a ag (ammalato) ill; (debole) infirm; ~ **di mente** mentally ill.

infer'nale ag infernal; (proposito, complotto) diabolical.

in'ferno sm hell.

inferri'ata sf grating.

infervo'rare vt to arouse enthusiasm in; ~rsi vr to get excited, get carried away.

infes'tare vt to infest.

infet'tare vt to infect; ~rsi vr to become infected; **infet'tivo, a** ag infectious; **in'fetto, a** ag infected; (acque) polluted, contaminated; **infezi'one** sf infection.

inflac'chire [infjak'kire] vt to weaken // vi (2) (anche: ~rsi) to grow weak.

infiam'mabile ag inflammable.

infiam'mare vt to set alight; (fig, MED) to inflame; ~rsi vr to catch fire; (MED) to become inflamed; (fig): ~rsi di to be fired with; **infiammazi'one** sf (MED) inflammation.

infias'care vt to bottle.

in'fido, a ag unreliable, treacherous.

in'figgere [in'fiddʒere] vt: ~ **qc in** to thrust o drive sth into; ~rsi in to penetrate, sink deeply into.

infi'lare vt (ago) to thread; (mettere: chiave) to insert; (: anello, vestito) to slip o put on; ~rsi vr: ~ in/per to slip into/through; ~ **l'uscio** to slip in; to slip out.

infil'trarsi vr to penetrate, seep through; (MIL) to infiltrate; **infiltrazi'one** sf infiltration.

infil'zare [infil'tsare] vt (infilare) to string together; (trafiggere) to pierce.

'infimo, a ag lowest.

in'fine av finally; (insomma) in short.

infinità sf infinity; (in quantità): **un'~ di** an infinite number of.

infi'nito, a ag infinite; (LING) infinitive // sm infinity; (LING) infinitive; **all'~** (senza fine) endlessly.

infinocchi'are [infinok'kjare] vt (fam) to hoodwink.

infischi'arsi [infis'kjarsi] *vr*: ~ **di** not to care about.

in'fisso, a *pp di* **infiggere** // *sm* fixture; (*di porta, finestra*) frame.

infit'tire *vt, vi* (2) (*anche:* ~**rsi**) to thicken.

inflazi'one [inflat'tsjone] *sf* inflation.

infles'sibile *ag* inflexible; (*ferreo*) unyielding.

inflessi'one *sf* inflexion.

in'fliggere [in'flidd3ere] *vt* to inflict; **in-'flitto, a** *pp di* **infliggere**.

influ'ente *ag* influential; **influ'enza** *sf* influence; (*MED*) influenza, flu.

influ'ire *vi*: ~ **su** to influence.

in'flusso *sm* influence.

infol'tire *vt, vi* (2) to thicken.

infon'dato, a *ag* unfounded, groundless.

in'fondere *vt*: ~ **qc in qd** to instill sth in sb.

infor'care *vt* to fork (up); (*bicicletta, cavallo*) to get on; (*occhiali*) to put on.

infor'mare *vt* to inform, tell; ~**rsi** *vr*: ~**rsi (di)** to inquire (about); **infor-'matica** *sf* computer science; **informa-'tivo, a** *ag* informative; **informa'tore** *sm* informer; **informazi'one** *sf* piece of information; **informazioni** *sfpl* information *sg*.

in'forme *ag* shapeless.

infor'tunio *sm* accident; ~ **sul lavoro** industrial accident, accident at work.

infos'sarsi *vr* (*avvallarsi*) to sink; (*incavarsi*) to become hollow; **infos'sato, a** *ag* hollow; (*occhi*) deep-set; (: *per malattia*) sunken.

in'frangere [in'frand3ere] *vt* to smash; (*fig: patti*) to break; ~**rsi** *vr* to smash, break; **infran'gibile** *ag* unbreakable; **in-'franto, a** *pp di* **infrangere** // *ag* broken.

infra'rosso, a *ag, sm* infrared.

infrastrut'tura *sf* infrastructure.

infrazi'one [infrat'tsjone] *sf*: ~ **a** breaking of, violation of.

infredda'tura *sf* slight cold.

infreddo'lito, a *ag* cold, chilled.

infre'quente *ag* infrequent, rare.

infruttu'oso, a *ag* fruitless.

infu'ori *av* out; **all'**~ outwards; **all'**~ **di** (*eccetto*) except, with the exception of.

infuri'are *vi* to rage; ~**rsi** *vr* to fly into a rage.

infusi'one *sf* infusion.

in'fuso, a *pp di* **infondere** // *sm* infusion; ~ **di camomilla** camomile tea.

Ing. *abbr di* **ingegnere**.

ingabbi'are *vt* to cage; **ingabbia'tura** *sf* (*EDIL*) supporting frame.

ingaggi'are [ingad'd3are] *vt* (*assumere con compenso*) to take on, hire; (*SPORT*) to sign on; (*MIL*) to engage; **in'gaggio** *sm* hiring; signing on.

ingan'nare *vt* to deceive; (*coniuge*) to be unfaithful to; (*fisco*) to cheat; (*eludere*) to dodge, elude; (*fig: tempo*) to while away // *vi* (*apparenza*) to be deceptive; ~**rsi** *vr* to

be mistaken, be wrong; **ingan'nevole** *ag* deceptive.

in'ganno *sm* deceit, deception; (*azione*) trick; (*menzogna, frode*) cheat, swindle; (*illusione*) illusion.

ingarbugli'are [ingarbuʎ'ʎare] *vt* to tangle; (*fig*) to confuse, muddle; ~**rsi** *vr* to become confused o muddled.

inge'gnarsi [ind3eɲ'ɲarsi] *vr* to do one's best, try hard; ~ **per vivere** to live by one's wits.

inge'gnere [ind3eɲ'ɲere] *sm* engineer; ~ **civile/navale** civil/naval engineer; **ingegne'ria** *sf* engineering.

in'gegno [in'd3eɲɲo] *sm* (*intelligenza*) intelligence, brains *pl*; (*capacità creativa*) ingenuity; (*disposizione*) talent; **inge-'gnoso, a** *ag* ingenious, clever.

ingelo'sire [ind3elo'zire] *vt* to make jealous // *vi* (2) (*anche:* ~**rsi**) to become jealous.

in'gente [in'd3ente] *ag* huge, enormous.

ingenuità [ind3enui'ta] *sf* ingenuousness.

in'genuo, a [in'd3enuo] *ag* ingenuous, naïve.

inge'rirsi [ind3e'rirsi] *vr* to interfere, meddle.

inges'sare [ind3es'sare] *vt* (*MED*) to put in plaster; **ingessa'tura** *sf* plaster.

Inghil'terra [ingil'tɛrra] *sf*: **l'**~ England.

inghiot'tire [ingjot'tire] *vt* to swallow.

ingial'lire [ind3al'lire] *vi* (2) to go yellow.

ingigan'tire [ind3igan'tire] *vt* to enlarge, magnify // *vi* (2) to become gigantic o enormous.

inginocchi'arsi [ind3inok'kjarsi] *vr* to kneel (down).

ingiù [in'd3u] *av* down, downwards.

ingi'uria [in'd3urja] *sf* insult; (*fig: danno*) damage; **ingiuri'are** *vt* to insult, abuse; **ingiuri'oso, a** *ag* insulting, abusive.

ingius'tizia [ind3us'tittsja] *sf* injustice.

ingi'usto, a [in'd3usto] *ag* unjust, unfair.

in'glese *ag* English // *sm/f* Englishman/woman // *sm* (*LING*) English; **gli l**~**i** the English; **andarsene** o **filare all'**~ to take French leave.

ingoi'are *vt* to gulp (down); (*fig*) to swallow (up).

ingol'fare *vt*, ~**rsi** *vr* (*motore*) to flood.

ingom'brare *vt* (*strada*) to block; (*stanza*) to clutter up; **in'gombro** *sm* obstacle; (*di macchina*): **lunghezza/larghezza/al-tezza d'ingombro** maximum length/width/height.

in'gordo, a *ag*: ~ **di** greedy for; (*fig*) greedy o eager for.

ingor'garsi *vr* to be blocked up, be choked up.

in'gorgo, ghi *sm* blockage, obstruction; ~ **di traffico** traffic jam.

ingoz'zare [ingot'tsare] *vt* (*inghiottire*) to gulp down, gobble; (*costringere a mangiare: animali*) to fatten.

ingra'naggio [ingra'nadd3o] *sm* gear; (*fig*) mechanism; ~**i** *smpl* gears, gearing *sg*.

ingra'nare *vi* to mesh, engage // *vt* to

engage; ~ **la marcia** to get into gear.
ingrandi'mento *sm* enlargement; extension.
ingran'dire *vt* (*anche* FOT) to enlarge; (*estendere*) to extend; (OTTICA, *fig*) to magnify // *vi* (2) (*anche*: ~**rsi**) to become larger *o* bigger; (*aumentare*) to grow, increase; (*espandersi*) to expand.
ingras'sare *vt* to make fat; (*animali*) to fatten; (AGR: *terreno*) to manure; (*lubrificare*) to oil, lubricate // *vi* (2) (*anche*: ~**rsi**) to get fat, put on weight; **in'grasso** *sm* (*di animali*) fattening; (*di terreno*) manuring *q*; manure.
ingrati'tudine *sf* ingratitude.
in'grato, a *ag* ungrateful; (*lavoro*) thankless, unrewarding.
ingrazi'are [ingrat'tsjare] *vt*: ~**rsi qd** to ingratiate o.s. with sb.
ingredi'ente *sm* ingredient.
in'gresso *sm* (*porta*) entrance; (*atrio*) hall; (*l'entrare*) entrance, entry; (*facoltà di entrare*) admission; **"~ libero"** "admission free".
ingros'sare *vt* to increase; (*folla, livello*) to swell // *vi* (2) (*anche*: ~**rsi**) to increase; to swell.
in'grosso *av*: **all'**~ (COMM) wholesale; (*all'incirca*) roughly, about.
ingual'cibile [ingwal'tʃibile] *ag* crease-resistant.
ingua'ribile *ag* incurable.
'inguine *sm* (ANAT) groin.
ini'bire *vt* to forbid, prohibit; (PSIC) to inhibit; **inibizi'one** *sf* prohibition; inhibition.
iniet'tare *vt* to inject; ~**rsi di sangue** (*occhi*) to become bloodshot; **iniezi'one** *sf* injection.
inimi'carsi *vr*: ~ **con qd** to fall out with sb.
inimi'cizia [inimi'tʃittsja] *sf* animosity.
ininter'rotto, a *ag* unbroken; uninterrupted.
iniquità *sf inv* iniquity; (*atto*) wicked action.
i'niquo, a *ag* iniquitous.
inizi'ale [init'tsjale] *ag, sf* initial.
inizi'are [init'tsjare] *vi* (2), *vt* to begin, start; ~ **qd a** to initiate sb into; (*pittura etc*) to introduce sb to.
inizia'tiva [inittsja'tiva] *sf* initiative; ~ **privata** private enterprise.
i'nizio [i'nittsjo] *sm* beginning; **all'**~ at the beginning, at the start; **dare** ~ **a qc** to start sth, get sth going.
innaffi'are *etc* = **annaffiare** *etc*.
innal'zare [innal'tsare] *vt* (*sollevare, alzare*) to raise; (*rizzare*) to erect; ~**rsi** *vr* to rise.
innamo'rare *vt* to enchant, charm; ~**rsi** *vr*: ~**rsi (di qd)** to fall in love (with sb); **innamo'rato, a** *ag* (*che nutre amore*): **innamorato (di)** in love (with); (*appassionato*): **innamorato di** very fond of.
in'nanzi [in'nantsi] *av* (*stato in luogo*) in front, ahead; (*moto a luogo*) forward, on;

(*tempo: prima*) before // prep (*prima*) before; ~ **a** in front of; **d'ora** ~ from now on.
in'nato, a *ag* innate.
innatu'rale *ag* unnatural.
inne'gabile *ag* undeniable.
innervo'sire *vt*: ~ **qd** to get on sb's nerves; ~**rsi** *vr* to get irritated *o* upset.
innes'care *vt* to prime; **in'nesco, schi** *sm* primer.
innes'tare *vt* (BOT, MED) to graft; (TECN) to engage; (*inserire: presa*) to insert; **in'nesto** *sm* graft; grafting *q*; (TECN) clutch; (ELETTR) connection.
'inno *sm* hymn; ~ **nazionale** national anthem.
inno'cente [inno'tʃɛnte] *ag* innocent; **inno'cenza** *sf* innocence.
in'nocuo, a *ag* innocuous, harmless.
inno'vare *vt* to change, make innovations in; **innovazi'one** *sf* innovation.
innume'revole *ag* innumerable.
inocu'lare *vt* (MED) to inoculate.
ino'doro, a *ag* odourless.
inol'trare *vt* (AMM) to pass on, forward; ~**rsi** *vr* (*addentrarsi*) to advance, go forward.
i'noltre *av* besides, moreover.
inon'dare *vt* to flood; **inondazi'one** *sf* flooding *q*; flood.
inope'roso, a *ag* inactive, idle.
inoppor'tuno, a *ag* untimely, ill-timed; inappropriate; (*momento*) inopportune.
inor'ganico, a, ci, che *ag* inorganic.
inorgo'glire [inorgoʎ'ʎire] *vt* to make proud // *vi* (2) (*anche*: ~**rsi**) to become proud; ~**rsi di qc** to pride o.s. on sth.
inorri'dire *vt* to horrify // *vi* (2) to be horrified.
inospi'tale *ag* inhospitable.
inosser'vato, a *ag* (*non notato*) unobserved; (*non rispettato*) not observed, not kept.
inossi'dabile *ag* stainless.
inqua'drare *vt* (*foto, immagine*) to frame; (*fig*) to situate, set.
inquie'tare *vt* (*turbare*) to disturb, worry; ~**rsi** *vr* to worry, become anxious; (*impazientirsi*) to get upset.
inqui'eto, a *ag* restless; (*preoccupato*) worried, anxious; **inquie'tudine** *sf* anxiety, worry.
inqui'lino, a *sm/f* tenant.
inquina'mento *sm* pollution.
inqui'nare *vt* to pollute.
inqui'sire *vt, vi* to investigate; **inquisi'tore, 'trice** *ag* (*sguardo*) inquiring; (DIR) investigating; **inquisizi'one** *sf* (STORIA) inquisition.
insa'lata *sf* salad; **insalati'era** *sf* salad bowl.
insa'lubre *ag* unhealthy.
insa'nabile *ag* incurable; unhealable.
insangui'nare *vt* to stain with blood.
in'sania *sf* insanity.
insa'puta *sf*: **all'**~ **di qd** without sb knowing.

insazi'abile [insat'tsjabile] *ag* insatiable.
insce'nare [inʃe'nare] *vt* (*TEATRO*) to stage, put on; (*fig*) to stage.
in'segna [in'seɲɲa] *sf* sign; (*emblema*) sign, emblem; (*bandiera*) flag, banner; ~e *sfpl* (*decorazioni*) insignia *pl*.
insegna'mento [inseɲɲa'mento] *sm* teaching.
inse'gnante [insen'ɲante] *ag* teaching // *sm/f* teacher.
inse'gnare [insen'ɲare] *vt, vi* to teach; ~ a qd qc to teach sb sth; ~ qd a fare qc to teach sb (how) to do sth.
insegui'mento *sm* pursuit, chase.
insegui're *vt* to pursue, chase; **insegui-'tore, 'trice** *sm/f* pursuer.
inselvati'chire [inselvati'kire] *vi* (2) (*anche*: ~rsi) to grow wild.
insena'tura *sf* inlet, creek.
insen'sato, a *ag* senseless, stupid.
insen'sibile *ag* (*nervo*) insensible; (*movimento*) imperceptible; (*persona*) indifferent.
insepa'rabile *ag* inseparable.
inse'rire *vt* to insert; (*ELETTR*) to connect; ~rsi *vr* (*fig*): ~rsi in to become part of; **in'serto** *sm* (*pubblicazione*) insert.
inservi'ente *sm/f* attendant.
inserzi'one [inser'tsjone] *sf* insertion; (*avviso*) advertisement; **fare un'~** (**sui giornale**) to put an advertisement in the paper.
insetti'cida, i [insetti'tʃida] *sm* insecticide.
in'setto *sm* insect.
in'sidia *sf* snare, trap; (*pericolo*) hidden danger; **insidi'are** *vt, vi*: **insidiare a** to lay a trap for; **insidi'oso, a** *ag* insidious.
insi'eme *av* together // *prep*: ~ a o con together with // *sm* whole; (*MAT, servizio, assortimento*) set; (*MODA*) ensemble, outfit; **tutti** ~ all together; **tutto** ~ all together; (*in una volta*) at one go; **nell'~** on the whole; **d'~** (*veduta etc*) overall.
insignifi'cante [insiɲɲifi'kante] *ag* insignificant.
insi'gnire [insiɲ'ɲire] *vt* to decorate.
insin'cero, a [insin'tʃero] *ag* insincere.
insinda'cabile *ag* unquestionable.
insinu'are *vt* (*introdurre*): ~ qc in to slip o slide sth into; (*fig*) to insinuate, imply; ~rsi *vr*: ~rsi in to seep into; (*fig*) to creep into; to worm one's way into; **insinuazi'one** *sf* (*fig*) insinuation.
in'sipido, a *ag* insipid.
insis'tente *ag* insistent; persistent; **insis-'tenza** *sf* insistence; persistence.
in'sistere *vi*: ~ su qc to insist on sth; ~ in qc/a fare (*perseverare*) to persist in sth/in doing; **insis'tito, a** *pp di* **insistere**.
insoddis'fatto, a *ag* dissatisfied.
insoffe'rente *ag* intolerant.
insolazi'one [insolat'tsjone] *sf* insolation; (*MED*) sunstroke.
inso'lente *ag* insolent; **insolen'tire** *vi* (2) to grow insolent // *vt* to insult, be rude to; **inso'lenza** *sf* insolence.

in'solito, a *ag* unusual, out of the ordinary.
inso'lubile *ag* insoluble.
inso'luto, a *ag* (*non risolto*) unsolved; (*non pagato*) unpaid, outstanding.
insol'vibile *ag* insolvent.
in'somma *av* (*in breve, in conclusione*) in short; (*dunque*) well // *escl* for heaven's sake!
in'sonne *ag* sleepless; **in'sonnia** *sf* insomnia, sleeplessness.
insonno'lito, a *ag* sleepy, drowsy.
insoppor'tabile *ag* unbearable.
in'sorgere [in'sordʒere] *vi* (2) (*ribellarsi*) to rise up, rebel; (*apparire*) to come up, arise.
in'sorto, a *pp di* **insorgere** // *sm/f* rebel, insurgent.
insospet'tire *vt* to make suspicious // *vi* (2) (*anche*: ~rsi) to become suspicious.
inspi'rare *vt* to breathe in, inhale.
in'stabile *ag* (*carico, indole*) unstable; (*tempo*) unsettled; (*equilibrio*) unsteady.
instal'lare *vt* to install; ~rsi *vr* (*sistemarsi*): ~rsi in to settle in; **installa-zi'one** *sf* installation.
instan'cabile *ag* untiring, indefatigable.
instau'rare *vt* to introduce, institute; ~rsi *vr* to start, begin.
instra'dare *vt* to direct.
insubordinazi'one [insubordinat'tsjone] *sf* insubordination.
insuc'cesso [insut'tʃesso] *sm* failure, flop.
insudici'are [insudi'tʃare] *vt* to dirty; ~rsi *vr* to get dirty.
insuffici'ente [insuffi'tʃente] *ag* insufficient; (*compito, allievo*) inadequate; **insuffici'enza** *sf* insufficiency; inadequacy; (*INS*) fail.
insu'lare *ag* insular.
insu'lina *sf* insulin.
in'sulso, a *ag* (*sciocco*) inane, silly; (*persona*) dull, insipid.
insul'tare *vt* to insult, affront.
in'sulto *sm* insult, affront.
insurrezi'one [insurret'tsjone] *sf* revolt, insurrection.
insussis'tente *ag* non-existent.
intac'care *vt* (*fare tacche*) to cut into; (*corrodere*) to corrode; (*fig: cominciare ad usare: risparmi*) to break into; (: *ledere*) to damage.
intagli'are [intaʎ'ʎare] *vt* to carve; **in-'taglio** *sm* carving.
intan'gibile [intan'dʒibile] *ag* untouchable; inviolable.
in'tanto *av* (*nel frattempo*) meanwhile, in the meantime; (*per cominciare*) just to begin with; ~ che *cong* while.
intarsi'are *vt* to inlay; **in'tarsio** *sm* inlaying q, marquetry q; inlay.
inta'sare *vt* to choke (up), block (up); (*AUT*) to obstruct, block; ~rsi *vr* to become choked o blocked.
intas'care *vt* to pocket.
in'tatto, a *ag* intact; (*puro*) unsullied.
intavo'lare *vt* to start, enter into.

inte'grale *ag* complete; (*MAT*): **calcolo ~** integral calculus.

inte'grante *ag*: **parte ~** integral part.

inte'grare *vt* to complete; (*MAT*) to integrate; **~rsi** *vr* (*persona*) to integrate; **integrazi'one** *sf* integration.

integrità *sf* integrity.

'integro, a *ag* (*intatto, intero*) complete, whole; (*retto*) upright.

intelaia'tura *sf* frame; (*fig*) structure, framework.

intel'letto *sm* intellect; **intellettu'ale**, *sm/f* intellectual.

intelli'gente [intelli'dʒɛnte] *ag* intelligent; **intelli'genza** *sf* intelligence; **intelli'gibile** *ag* intelligible.

intem'perie *sfpl* bad weather *sg*.

intempes'tivo, a *ag* untimely.

inten'dente *sm* principal administrator; **inten'denza** *sf*: **intendenza di finanza** finance office; **intendenza generale** (*MIL*) supplies office.

in'tendere *vt* (*avere intenzione*): ~ **fare qc** to intend *o* mean to do sth; (*comprendere*) to understand; (*udire*) to hear; (*significare*) to mean; **~rsi** *vr* (*conoscere*): **~rsi di** to know a lot about, be a connoisseur of; (*accordarsi*) to get on (well); **intendersela con qd** (*avere una relazione amorosa*) to have an affair with sb; **intendi'mento** *sm* (*intelligenza*) understanding; (*proposito*) intention; **intendi'tore, 'trice** *sm/f* connoisseur, expert.

intene'rire *vt* (*fig*) to move (to pity); **~rsi** *vr* (*fig*) to be moved.

intensifi'care *vt*, **~rsi** *vr* to intensify.

intensità *sf* intensity.

inten'sivo, a *ag* intensive.

in'tenso, a *ag* intense.

in'tento, a *ag* (*teso, assorto*): ~ **(a)** intent (on), absorbed (in) // *sm* aim, purpose.

intenzio'nale [intentsjo'nale] *ag* intentional.

intenzi'one [inten'tsjone] *sf* intention; (*DIR*) intent; **avere ~ di fare qc** to intend *o* do sth, have the intention of doing sth.

interca'lare *sm* pet phrase, stock phrase // *vt* to insert.

inter'cedere [inter'tʃedere] *vi* to intercede; **intercessi'one** *sf* intercession.

intercet'tare [intertʃet'tare] *vt* to intercept; (*telefono*) to tap.

inter'correre *vi* (2) (*esserci*) to exist; (*passare: tempo*) to elapse.

inter'detto, a *pp di* **interdire** // *ag* forbidden, prohibited; (*sconcertato*) dumbfounded // *sm* (*REL*) interdict.

inter'dire *vt* to forbid, prohibit, ban; (*REL*) to interdict; (*DIR*) to deprive of civil rights; **interdizi'one** *sf* prohibition, ban.

interessa'mento *sm* interest.

interes'sante *ag* interesting; **essere in stato ~** to be expecting (a baby).

interes'sare *vt* to interest; (*concernere*) to concern, be of interest to; (*far intervenire*): ~ **qd a** to draw sb's attention

to // *vi*: ~ **a** to interest, matter to; **~rsi** *vr* (*mostrare interesse*): **~rsi a** to take an interest in, be interested in; (*occuparsi*): **~rsi di** to take care of.

inte'resse *sm* (*anche COMM*) interest.

interfe'renza [interfe'rɛntsa] *sf* interference.

interfe'rire *vi* to interfere.

interiezi'one [interjet'tsjone] *sf* exclamation, interjection.

interi'ora *sfpl* entrails.

interi'ore *ag* interior, inner, inside, internal; (*fig*) inner.

inter'ludio *sm* (*MUS*) interlude.

intermedi'ario, a *ag*, *sm/f* intermediary.

inter'medio, a *ag* intermediate.

inter'mezzo [inter'mɛddzo] *sm* (*intervallo*) interval; (*breve spettacolo*) intermezzo.

intermi'nabile *ag* interminable, endless.

inter'nare *vt* (*arrestare*) to intern; (*MED*) to commit (to a mental institution).

internazio'nale [internattsjo'nale] *ag* international.

in'terno, a *ag* (*di dentro*) internal, interior, inner; (: *mare*) inland; (*nazionale*) domestic, home *cpd*, internal; (*allievo*) boarding // *sm* inside, interior; (*di paese*) interior; (*fodera*) lining; (*di appartamento*) flat (number); (*TEL*) extension // *sm/f* (*INS*) boarder; **~i** *smpl* (*CINEMA*) interior shots; **all'~** inside; **ministro dell'I~** Minister of the Interior, ≈ Home Secretary; ~ **destro/sinistro** (*CALCIO*) inside right/left.

in'tero, a *ag* (*integro, intatto*) whole, entire; (*completo, totale*) complete; (*numero*) whole; (*non ridotto: biglietto*) full.

interpel'lare *vt* to consult.

inter'porre *vt* to interpose; **interporsi** *vr* to intervene; **inter'posto, a** *pp di* **interporre**.

interpre'tare *vt* to interpret; **interpretazi'one** *sf* interpretation; **in'terprete** *sm* interpreter; (*TEATRO*) actor, performer; (*MUS*) performer.

interro'gare *vt* to question; (*INS*) to test; **interroga'tivo, a** *ag* (*occhi, sguardo*) questioning, inquiring; (*LING*) interrogative // *sm* question; (*fig*) mystery; **interroga'torio, a** *ag* interrogatory, questioning // *sm* (*DIR*) questioning *q*; **interrogazi'one** *sf* questioning *q*; (*INS*) oral test.

inter'rompere *vt* to interrupt; (*studi, trattative*) to break off, interrupt; **~rsi** *vr* to break off, stop; **inter'rotto, a** *pp di* **interrompere**.

interrut'tore *sm* switch.

interruzi'one [interrut'tsjone] *sf* interruption; break.

interse'care *vt*, **~rsi** *vr* to intersect.

inter'stizio [inter'stittsjo] *sm* interstice, crack.

interur'bano, a *ag* inter-city; (*TEL*: *chiamata*) trunk *cpd*, long-distance; (: *telefono*) long-distance // *sf* trunk call, long-distance call.

inter'vallo *sm* interval; (*spazio*) space, gap.

interve'nire *vi* (2) (*partecipare*): ~ **a** to be present at, attend; (*intromettersi: anche POL*) to intervene; (*MED: operare*) to operate; **inter'vento** *sm* presence, attendance; (*inframmettenza*) intervention; (*MED*) operation.

inter'vista *sf* interview; **intervis'tare** *vt* to interview.

in'teso, a *pp di* **intendere** // *ag* agreed // *sf* (*fra amici, paesi*) understanding; (*accordo*) agreement, understanding; (*SPORT*) teamwork; **non darsi per ~ di qc** to take no notice of sth.

intes'tare *vt* to head; (*casa*): ~ **qc a** to put *o* register sth in the name of; **~rsi** *vr* (*ostinarsi*): **~rsi a fare** to take it into one's head to do; **intestazi'one** *sf* heading; (*su carta da lettere*) letterhead; (*registrazione*) registration.

intes'tino, a *ag* (*lotte*) internal, civil // *sm* (*ANAT*) intestine.

inti'mare *vt* to order, command; **intimazi'one** *sf* order, command.

intimidazi'one [intimidat'tsjone] *sf* intimidation.

intimi'dire *vt* to intimidate // *vi* (2) (*anche:* **~rsi**) to grow shy.

intimità *sf* intimacy; privacy; (*familiarità*) familiarity.

'intimo, a *ag* intimate; (*affetti, vita*) private; (*fig: profondo*) inmost // *sm* (*persona*) intimate *o* close friend; (*dell'animo*) bottom, depths *pl*.

intimo'rire *vt* to frighten; **~rsi** *vr* to become frightened.

in'tingolo *sm* sauce; (*pietanza*) stew.

intiriz'zire [intirid'dzire] *vt* to numb // *vi* (2) (*anche:* **~rsi**) to go numb.

intito'lare *vt* to give a title to; (*dedicare*) to dedicate.

intolle'rabile *ag* intolerable.

intolle'rante *ag* intolerant.

intona'care *vt* to plaster.

in'tonaco, ci *o* **chi** *sm* plaster.

into'nare *vt* (*canto*) to start to sing; (*strumenti*) to tune; (*armonizzare*) to match; **~rsi** *vr* to be in tune; to match; **intonazi'one** *sf* intonation.

inton'tire *vt* to stun, daze // *vi* (2) to be stunned *o* dazed.

in'toppo *sm* stumbling block, obstacle.

in'torno *av* around; ~ **a** *prep* (*attorno a*) around; (*riguardo, circa*) about.

intorpi'dire *vt* to numb; (*fig*) to make sluggish // *vi* (2) (*anche:* **~rsi**) to grow numb; (*fig*) to become sluggish.

intossi'care *vt* to poison; **intossica-zi'one** *sf* poisoning.

intralci'are [intral'tʃare] *vt* to hamper, hold up.

intransi'gente [intransi'dʒente] *ag* intransigent, uncompromising.

intransi'tivo, a *ag, sm* intransitive.

intrapren'dente *ag* enterprising, go-ahead.

intra'prendere *vt* to undertake.

intrat'tabile *ag* intractable.

intratte'nere *vt* to entertain; to engage in conversation; **~rsi** *vr* to linger; **~rsi su qc** to dwell on sth.

intrave'dere *vt* to catch a glimpse of; (*fig*) to foresee.

intrecci'are [intret'tʃare] *vt* (*capelli*) to plait, braid; (*intessere: anche fig*) to weave, interweave, intertwine; **~rsi** *vr* to intertwine, become interwoven; ~ **le mani** to clasp one's hands; **in'treccio** *sm* (*fig: trama*) plot, story.

in'trepido, a *ag* fearless, dauntless.

intri'gare *vi* to manoeuvre, scheme; **~rsi** *vr* to interfere, meddle; **in'trigo, ghi** *sm* plot, intrigue.

in'trinseco, a, ci, che *ag* intrinsic; (*amico*) close, intimate.

in'triso, a *ag*: ~ (**di**) soaked (in).

intro'durre *vt* to introduce; (*chiave etc*): ~ **qc in** to insert sth into; (*persone: far entrare*) to show in; **introdursi** *vr* (*moda, tecniche*) to be introduced; **introdursi in** (*persona: penetrare*) to enter; (*: entrare furtivamente*) to steal *o* slip into; **introdu-zi'one** *sf* introduction.

in'troito *sm* income, revenue.

intro'mettersi *vr* to interfere, meddle; (*interporsi*) to intervene.

intro'verso, a *ag* introverted // *sm* introvert.

in'truglio [in'truʎʎo] *sm* concoction.

intrusi'one *sf* intrusion; interference.

in'truso, a *sm/f* intruder.

intu'ire *vt* to perceive by intuition; (*rendersi conto*) to realise; **in'tuito** *sm* intuition; (*perspicacia*) perspicacity; **intui-zi'one** *sf* intuition.

inu'mano, a *ag* inhuman.

inumi'dire *vt* to dampen, moisten; **~rsi** *vr* to become damp *o* wet.

i'nutile *ag* useless; (*superfluo*) pointless, unnecessary; **inutilità** *sf* uselessness; pointlessness.

inva'dente *ag* (*fig*) interfering, nosey.

in'vadere *vt* to invade; (*affollare*) to swarm into, overrun; (*sog: acque*) to flood; **invadi'trice** *ag vedi* **invasore**.

invalidità *sf* infirmity; disability; (*DIR*) invalidity.

in'valido, a *ag* (*infermo*) infirm, invalid; (*al lavoro*) disabled; (*DIR*) invalid // *sm/f* invalid; disabled person.

in'vano *av* in vain.

invari'abile *ag* invariable.

invasi'one *sf* invasion.

in'vaso, a *pp di* **invadere**.

inva'sore, invadi'trice [invadi'tritʃe] *ag* invading // *sm* invader.

invecchi'are [invek'kjare] *vi* (2) (*persona*) to grow old; (*vino, popolazione*) to age; (*moda*) to become dated // *vt* to age; (*far apparire più vecchio*) to make look older.

in'vece [in'vetʃe] *av* instead; (*al contrario*) on the contrary; ~ **di** *prep* instead of.

inve'ire *vi*: ~ **contro** to rail against.

inven'tare *vt* to invent; (*pericoli, pettegolezzi*) to make up, invent.

inven'tario *sm* inventory; (*COMM*) stocktaking *q*.

inven'tivo, a *ag* inventive // *sf* inventiveness.

inven'tore *sm* inventor.

invenzi'one [inven'tsjone] *sf* invention; (*bugia*) lie, story.

inver'nale *ag* winter *cpd*; (*simile all'inverno*) wintry.

in'verno *sm* winter.

invero'simile *ag* unlikely.

inversi'one *sf* inversion; reversal; ~ **di marcia** (*AUT*) reversing; **"divieto d'~"** "no U-turns".

in'verso, a *ag* reverse; opposite; (*MAT*) inverse // (*in senso* contrary, opposite; **in senso** ~ in the opposite direction; **nell'ordine** ~ in the reverse order.

inverte'brato, a *ag, sm* invertebrate.

inver'tire *vt* to invert, reverse; ~ **la marcia** to reverse; **inver'tito, a** *sm/f* homosexual.

investi'gare *vt, vi* to investigate; **inves'tigatore** *sm* investigator, detective; **investigazi'one** *sf* investigation, inquiry.

investi'mento *sm* (*ECON*) investment; (*scontro, urto*) crash, collision; (*incidente stradale*) road accident.

inves'tire *vt* (*denaro*) to invest; (*sog: veicolo: pedone*) to knock down; (: *altro veicolo*) to crash into; (*sog: nave*) to collide with; (*apostrofare*) to assail; (*incaricare*): ~ **qd di** to invest sb with; **investi'tura** *sf* investiture.

invete'rato, a *ag* inveterate.

invet'tiva *sf* invective.

invi'are *vt* to send; **invi'ato, a** *sm/f* envoy; (*STAMPA*) correspondent.

in'vidia *sf* envy; **invidi'are** *vt* to envy; **invidi'oso, a** *ag* envious.

invigo'rire *vt* to strengthen, invigorate // *vi* (2) (*anche:* ~**rsi**) to gain strength.

invin'cibile [invin'tʃibile] *ag* invincible.

in'vio, 'vii *sm* sending; (*insieme di merci*) consignment.

invio'labile *ag* inviolable.

invipe'rito, a *ag* furious.

invi'sibile *ag* invisible.

invi'tare *vt* to invite; ~ **qd a fare** to invite sb to do; (*sog: cosa*) to tempt sb to do; **invi'tato, a** *sm/f* guest; **in'vito** *sm* invitation.

invo'care *vt* (*chiedere: aiuto, pace*) to cry out for; (*appellarsi: la legge, Dio*) to appeal to, invoke.

invogli'are [invoʎ'ʎare] *vt*: ~ **qd a fare** to tempt sb to do, induce sb to do; ~**rsi di** to take a fancy to.

involon'tario, a *ag* (*errore*) unintentional; (*gesto*) involuntary.

invol'tino *sm* (*CUC*) roulade.

in'volto *sm* (*pacco*) parcel; (*fagotto*) bundle.

in'volucro *sm* cover, wrapping.

invo'luto, a *ag* involved, intricate.

invulne'rabile *ag* invulnerable.

inzacche'rare [intsakke'rare] *vt* to spatter with mud.

inzup'pare [intsup'pare] *vt* to soak; ~**rsi** *vr* to get soaked.

'io *pronome* I // *sm inv*: **l'~** the ego, the self; ~ **stesso(a)** I myself.

i'odio *sm* iodine.

i'ogurt *sm inv* = **yoghurt.**

i'one *sm* ion.

l'onio *sm*: **lo** ~ the Ionian (Sea).

ipermer'cato *sm* hypermarket.

ipertensi'one *sf* high blood pressure, hypertension.

ip'nosi *sf* hypnosis; **ip'notico, a, ci, che** *ag* hypnotic; **ipno'tismo** *sm* hypnotism; **ipnotiz'zare** *vt* to hypnotize.

ipocri'sia *sf* hypocrisy.

i'pocrita, i, e *ag* hypocritical // *sm/f* hypocrite.

ipo'teca, che *sf* mortgage; **ipote'care** *vt* to mortgage.

i'potesi *sf inv* hypothesis; **ipo'tetico, a, ci, che** *ag* hypothetical.

'ippico, a, ci, che *ag* horse *cpd* // *sf* horseracing.

ippocas'tano *sm* horse chestnut.

ip'podromo *sm* racecourse.

ippo'potamo *sm* hippopotamus.

'ira *sf* anger, wrath.

l'ran *sm*: **l'~** Iran.

l'raq *sm*: **l'~** Iraq.

'iride *sf* (*arcobaleno*) rainbow; (*ANAT, BOT*) iris.

Ir'landa *sf*: **l'~** Ireland; **irlan'dese** *ag* Irish // *sm/f* Irishman/woman; **gli Irlandesi** the Irish.

iro'nia *sf* irony; **i'ronico, a, ci, che** *ag* ironic(al).

irradi'are *vt* to radiate; (*sog: raggi di luce: illuminare*) to shine on, irradiate // *vi* (2) (*diffondersi: anche:* ~**rsi**) to radiate; **irradiazi'one** *sf* radiation; irradiation.

irragio'nevole [irradʒo'nevole] *ag* irrational; unreasonable.

irrazio'nale [irrattsjo'nale] *ag* irrational.

irre'ale *ag* unreal.

irrecu'sabile *ag* (*offerta*) not to be refused; (*prova*) irrefutable.

irrefu'tabile *ag* irrefutable.

irrego'lare *ag* irregular; (*terreno*) uneven; **irregolarità** *sf inv* irregularity; unevenness.

irremo'vibile *ag* (*fig*) unshakeable, unyielding.

irrepa'rabile *ag* irreparable; (*fig*) unavoidable.

irrepe'ribile *ag* nowhere to be found.

irrequi'eto, a *ag* restless.

irresis'tibile *ag* irresistible.

irreso'luto, a *ag* irresolute.

irrespon'sabile *ag* irresponsible.

irrevo'cabile *ag* irrevocable.

irridu'cibile [irridu'tʃibile] *ag* irreducible; (*fig*) indomitable.

irri'gare *vt* (*annaffiare*) to irrigate; (*sog:*

fiume etc) to flow through; **irrigazi'one** *sf* irrigation.

irrigi'dire [irridʒi'dire] *vt*, ~**rsi** *vr* to stiffen.

irri'sorio, a *ag* derisory.

irri'tabile *ag* irritable.

irri'tare *vt* (*mettere di malumore*) to irritate, annoy; (MED) to irritate; ~**rsi** *vr* (*stizzirsi*) to become irritated *o* annoyed; **irritazi'one** *sf* irritation; annoyance.

ir'rompere *vi*: ~ **in** to burst into.

irro'rare *vt* to sprinkle; (AGR) to spray.

irru'ente *ag* (*fig*) impetuous, violent.

irruzi'one [irrut'tsjone] *sf* irruption *q*; **fare** ~ **in** to burst into.

'irto, a *ag* bristly; ~ **di** bristling with.

is'critto, a *pp di* **iscrivere** // *sm/f* member; **per** *o* **in** ~ in writing.

is'crivere *vt* to register, enter; (*persona*) to register, enrol; ~**rsi** *vr*: ~**rsi (a)** (*club, partito*) to join; (*università*) to register *o* enrol (at); (*esame, concorso*) to register *o* enter (for); **iscrizi'one** *sf* (*epigrafe etc*) inscription; (*a scuola, società*) enrolment, registration; (*registrazione*) registration.

Is'landa *sf*: **l'**~ Iceland.

'isola *sf* island; ~ **pedonale** (AUT) traffic island.

isola'mento *sm* isolation; (TECN) insulation.

iso'lano, a *ag* island *cpd* // *sm/f* islander.

iso'lante *ag* insulating // *sm* insulator.

iso'lare *vt* to isolate; (TECN) to insulate; (*acusticamente*) to soundproof; **iso'lato, a** *ag* isolated; insulated // *sm* (EDIL) block.

ispetto'rato *sm* inspectorate.

ispet'tore *sm* inspector.

ispezio'nare [ispettsjo'nare] *vt* to inspect.

ispezi'one [ispet'tsjone] *sf* inspection.

'ispido, a *ag* bristly, shaggy.

ispi'rare *vt* to inspire; ~**rsi** *vr*: ~**rsi a** to draw one's inspiration from; **ispirazi'one** *sf* inspiration.

Isra'ele *sm*: **l'**~ Israel; **israeli'ano, a** *ag, sm/f* Israeli.

is'sare *vt* to hoist.

istan'taneo, a *ag* instantaneous // *sf* (FOT) snapshot.

is'tante *sm* instant, moment; **all'**~, **sull'**~ instantly, immediately.

is'tanza [is'tantsa] *sf* petition, request.

is'terico, a, ci, che *ag* hysterical.

iste'rismo *sm* hysteria.

isti'gare *vt* to incite, instigate; **istiga-zi'one** *sf* instigation.

istin'tivo, a *ag* instinctive.

is'tinto *sm* instinct.

istitu'ire *vt* (*fondare*) to institute, found; (*porre*: *confronto*) to establish; (*intraprendere: inchiesta*) to set up.

isti'tuto *sm* institute; (*ente*, DIR) institution; ~ **di bellezza** beauty salon.

istituzi'one [istitut'tsjone] *sf* institution.

'istmo *sm* (GEO) isthmus.

'istrice ['istritʃe] *sm* porcupine.

istri'one *sm* (*peg*) ham actor.

istru'ire *vt* (*insegnare*) to teach;

(*ammaestrare*) to train; (*informare*) to instruct, inform; (DIR) to prepare; **istrut-'tivo, a** *ag* instructive; **istrut'tore, 'trice** *sm/f* instructor // *ag*: **giudice istruttore** examining magistrate; **istrut'toria** *sf* (DIR) (preliminary) investigation and hearing; **istruzi'one** *sf* education; training; (*direttiva*) instruction; (DIR) = **istruttoria**; **istruzioni** *sfpl* (*norme per l'uso*) instructions, directions.

I'talia *sf*: **l'**~ Italy.

itali'ano, a *ag* Italian // *sm/f* Italian // *sm* (LING) Italian; **gli I**~**i** the Italians.

itine'rario *sm* itinerary.

itte'rizia [itte'rittsja] *sf* (MED) jaundice.

'ittico, a, ci, che *ag* fish *cpd*; fishing *cpd*.

Iugos'lavia *sf* = **Jugoslavia**.

iugos'lavo, a *ag, sm/f* = **jugoslavo, a**.

i'uta *sf* jute.

I.V.A. ['iva] *abbr f vedi* **imposta**.

J

jazz [dʒaz] *sm* jazz.

jeans [dʒinz] *smpl* jeans.

Jugos'lavia [jugoz'lavja] *sf*: **la** ~ Yugoslavia; **jugos'lavo, a** *ag, sm/f* Yugoslav(ian).

'juta ['juta] *sf* = **iuta**.

L

l' *det vedi* **la, lo.**

la *det f* (*dav V* **l'**) the // *pronome* (*dav V* **l'**) (*oggetto: persona*) her; (: *cosa*) it; (: *forma di cortesia*) you // *sm inv* (MUS) A; (: *solfeggiando la scala*) la.

là *av* there; **di** ~ (*da quel luogo*) from there; (*in quel luogo*) in there; (*dall'altra parte*) over there; **di** ~ **di** beyond; **per di** ~ that way; **andare in** ~ (*procedere*) to go on, proceed; **più in** ~ further on; (*tempo*) later on; *vedi* **quello**.

'labbro *sm* (*pl(f)*: **labbra**: *solo nel senso* ANAT) lip.

labi'rinto *sm* labyrinth, maze.

labora'torio *sm* (*di ricerca*) laboratory; (*di arti, mestieri*) workshop; ~ **linguistico** language laboratory.

labori'oso, a *ag* (*faticoso*) laborious; (*attivo*) hard-working.

labu'rista, i, e *ag* Labour *cpd* // *sm/f* Labour Party member.

'lacca, che *sf* lacquer.

'laccio ['lattʃo] *sm* noose; (*lazo*) lasso; (*di scarpa*) lace; (*fig*) snare.

lace'rare [latʃe'rare] *vt* to tear to shreds, lacerate; ~**rsi** *vr* to tear; **'lacero, a** *ag* (*logoro*) torn, tattered.

la'conico, a, ci, che *ag* laconic, brief.

'lacrima *sf* tear; (*goccia*) drop; **in** ~**e** in tears; **lacri'mare** *vi* to weep, shed tears; **lacri'mogeno, a** *ag*: *vedi* **gas**; **lacri'moso, a** *ag* tearful; (*commovente*) pitiful, pathetic.

la'cuna *sf* (*fig*) gap.

'ladro *sm* thief; **ladro'cinio** *sm* theft, larceny.

laggiù [lad'dʒu] *av* down there; (*di là*) over there.

la'gnarsi [laɲ'ɲarsi] *vr:* ~ **(di)** to complain (about).

'lago, ghi *sm* lake.

'lagrima *etc* = **lacrima** *etc.*

la'guna *sf* lagoon.

'laico, a, ci, che *ag* (*apostolato*) lay; (*vita*) secular; (*scuola*) non-denominational // *sm/f* layman/ woman // *sm* lay brother.

'lama *sf* blade // *sm inv* (ZOOL) llama; (REL) lama.

lambic'care *vt* to distil; ~**rsi il cervello** to rack one's brains.

lam'bire *vt* to lick; to lap.

la'mella *sf* (*di metallo etc*) thin sheet, thin strip; (*di fungo*) gill.

lamen'tare *vt* to lament; ~**rsi** *vr* (*emettere lamenti*) to moan, groan; (*rammaricarsi*): ~**rsi (di)** to complain (about); **lamen'tela** *sf* complaining *q*; **lamen'tevole** *ag* (*voce*) complaining, plaintive; (*destino*) pitiful; **la'mento** *sm* moan, groan; wail; **lamen'toso, a** *ag* plaintive.

la'metta *sf* razor blade.

lami'era *sf* sheet metal.

'lamina *sf* (*lastra sottile*) thin sheet (*o* layer *o* plate); ~ **d'oro** gold leaf; gold foil; **lami'nare** *vt* to laminate; **lami'nato, a** *ag* laminated; (*tessuto*) lamé // *sm* laminate; lamé.

'lampada *sf* lamp; ~ **da saldatore** blowlamp; ~ **da tavolo** table lamp.

lampa'dario *sm* chandelier.

lampa'dina *sf* light bulb; ~ **tascabile** pocket torch.

lam'pante *ag* (*fig: evidente*) crystal clear, evident.

lampi'one *sm* street light *o* lamp.

'lampo *sm* (METEOR) flash of lightning; (*di luce, fig*) flash; ~**i** *smpl* lightning *q* // *ag inv:* **cerniera** ~ zip (fastener); **guerra** ~ blitzkrieg.

lam'pone *sm* raspberry.

'lana *sf* wool; ~ **d'acciaio** steel wool; **pura** ~ **vergine** pure new wool; ~ **di vetro** glass wool.

lan'cetta [lan'tʃetta] *sf* (*indice*) pointer, needle; (*di orologio*) hand.

'lancia ['lantʃa] *sf* (*arma*) lance; (: *picca*) spear; (*imbarcazione*) launch.

lanciafi'amme [lantʃa'fjamme] *sm inv* flamethrower.

lanci'are [lan'tʃare] *vt* to throw, hurl, fling; (SPORT) to throw; (*far partire: automobile*) to get up to full speed; (*bombe*) to drop; (*razzo, prodotto, moda*) to launch; ~**rsi** *vr:* ~**rsi contro/su** to throw *o* hurl *o* fling o.s. against/on; ~**rsi in** (*fig*) to embark on.

lanci'nante [lantʃi'nante] *ag* (*dolore*) shooting, throbbing; (*grido*) piercing.

'lancio ['lantʃo] *sm* throwing *q*; throw; dropping *q*; drop; launching *q*; launch; ~ **del peso** putting the shot.

'landa *sf* (GEO) moor.

'languido, a *ag* (*fiacco*) languid, weak; (*tenero, malinconico*) languishing.

langu'ire *vi* to languish; (*conversazione*) to flag.

langu'ore *sm* weakness, languor.

lani'ero, a *ag* wool *cpd*, woollen.

lani'ficio [lani'fitʃo] *sm* woollen mill.

la'noso, a *ag* woolly.

lan'terna *sf* lantern; (*faro*) lighthouse.

la'nugine [la'nudʒine] *sf* down.

lapi'dare *vt* to stone.

lapi'dario, a *ag* (*fig*) terse.

'lapide *sf* (*di sepolcro*) tombstone; (*commemorativa*) plaque.

'lapis *sm inv* pencil.

'lapsus *sm inv* slip.

'lardo *sm* bacon fat, lard.

larghegi'are [larged'dʒare] *vi:* ~ **di** *o* **in** to be generous *o* liberal with.

lar'ghezza [lar'gettsa] *sf* width; breadth; looseness; generosity; ~ **di vedute** broad-mindedness.

'largo, a, ghi, ghe *ag* wide; broad; (*maniche*) wide; (*abito: troppo ampio*) loose; (*fig*) generous // *sm* width; breadth; (*mare aperto*): **il** ~ the open sea; ~ **due metri** two metres wide; ~ **di spalle** broad-shouldered; ~ **di vedute** broad-minded; **su** ~ **scala** on a large scale; **al** ~ (NAUT) offshore; **farsi** ~ **tra la folla** to push one's way through the crowd.

'larice ['laritʃe] *sm* (BOT) larch.

la'ringe [la'rindʒe] *sf* larynx; **larin'gite** *sf* laryngitis.

'larva *sf* larva; (*fig*) shadow.

la'sagne [la'zaɲɲe] *sfpl* lasagna *sg*.

lasci'are [laʃ'ʃare] *vt* to leave; (*abbandonare*) to leave, abandon, give up; (*cessare di tenere*) to let go of // *vb ausiliare:* ~ **fare qd** to let sb do // *vi:* ~ **di fare** (*smettere*) to stop doing; ~**rsi andare/truffare** to let o.s. go/be cheated; ~ **andare** *o* **correre** *o* **perdere** to let things go their own way; ~ **stare qc/qd** to leave sth/sb alone.

'lascito ['laʃito] *sm* (DIR) legacy.

la'scivo, a [laʃ'ʃivo] *ag* lascivious.

'laser ['lazer] *ag, sm inv:* **(raggio)** ~ laser (beam).

lassa'tivo, a *ag, sm* laxative.

'lasso *sm:* ~ **di tempo** interval, lapse of time.

lassù *av* up there.

'lastra *sf* (*di pietra*) slab; (*di metallo, FOT*) plate; (*di ghiaccio, vetro*) sheet; (*radiografica*) X-ray (plate).

lastri'care *vt* to pave; **lastri'cato,** *sm,* **'lastrico, ci** *o* **chi** *sm* pavement.

la'tente *ag* latent.

late'rale *ag* lateral, side *cpd* // *sm* (CALCIO) half-back.

late'rizi [late'rittsi] *smpl* bricks; tiles.

lati'fondo *sm* large estate.
la'tino, a *ag, sm* Latin; **~ ameri'cano a** *ag* Latin-American.
lati'tante *sm/f* fugitive (from justice).
lati'tudine *sf* latitude.
'lato, a *ag* (*fig*) wide, broad // *sm* side; (*fig*) aspect, point of view; **in senso ~** broadly speaking.
la'trare *vi* to bark.
la'trina *sf* latrine.
latro'cinio [latro'tʃinjo] *sm* = **ladrocinio**.
'latta *sf* tin; (*recipiente*) tin, can.
lat'taio, a *sm/f* milkman/ dairywoman.
lat'tante *ag* unweaned.
'latte *sm* milk; **~ detergente** cleansing milk *o* lotion; **~ secco** *o* **in polvere** dried *o* powdered milk; **~ scremato** skimmed milk; **'latteo, a** *ag* milky; (*dieta, prodotto*) milk *cpd*; **latte'ria** *sf* dairy; **latti'cini** *smpl* dairy products.
lat'tina *sf* (*di birra etc*) can.
lat'tuga *sf* lettuce.
'laurea *sf* degree; **laure'ando, a** *sm/f* final-year student; **laure'are** *vt* to confer a degree on; **laurearsi** *vr* to graduate; **laure'ato, a** *sm, ag/f* graduate.
'lauro *sm* laurel.
'lava *sf* lava.
la'vabile *ag* washable.
la'vabo *sm* washbasin.
la'vaggio [la'vaddʒo] *sm* washing *q*; **~ del cervello** brainwashing *q*.
la'vagna [la'vaɲɲa] *sf* (*GEO*) slate; (*di scuola*) blackboard.
'lavanda *sf* (*anche MED*) wash; (*BOT*) lavender; **lavan'daia** *sf* washerwoman; **lavande'ria** *sf* laundry; **lavanderia automatica** launderette; **lavan'dino** *sm* sink.
lavapi'atti *sm/f* dishwasher.
la'vare *vt* to wash; **~rsi** *vr* to wash, have a wash; **~ a secco** to dry-clean; **~rsi le mani/i denti** to wash one's hands/clean one's teeth.
lava'secco *sm o f inv* drycleaner's.
lavasto'viglie [lavasto'viʎʎe] *sm o f inv* (*macchina*) dishwasher.
lava'toio *sm* (public) washhouse.
lava'trice [lava'tritʃe] *sf* washing machine.
lava'tura *sf* washing *q*; **~ di piatti** dishwater.
lavo'rante *sm* workman.
lavo'rare *vi* to work; (*fig: bar, studio etc*) to do good business // *vt* to work; (*fig: persuadere*) to work on; **~ a** to work on; **~ a maglia** to knit; **~ la terra** to till the land; **lavora'tivo, a** *ag* working; **lavora-'tore, 'trice** *sm/f* worker // *ag* working; **lavorazi'one** *sf* manufacture; (*di materie prime*) processing; (*produzione*) production; **lavo'rio** *sm* intense activity.
la'voro *sm* work; (*occupazione*) job, work *q*; (*opera*) piece of work, job; (*ECON*) labour; **~i forzati** hard labour *sg*;

ministro dei L~i pubblici Minister of Works.
le *det fpl* the // *pronome* (*oggetto*) them; (: *a lei, a essa*) to her; (: *forma di cortesia*) to you.
le'ale *ag* loyal; (*sincero*) sincere; (*onesto*) fair; **lealtà** *sf* loyalty; sincerity; fairness.
'lebbra *sf* leprosy.
'lecca 'lecca *sm inv* lollipop.
leccapi'edi *sm/f inv* (*peg*) toady, bootlicker.
lec'care *vt* to lick; (*sog: gatto: latte etc*) to lick *o* lap up; (*fig*) to flatter; **~rsi i baffi** *o* **le labbra** to lick one's lips; **lec'cata** *sf* lick.
'leccio ['lettʃo] *sm* holm oak, ilex.
leccor'nia *sf* titbit, delicacy.
'lecito, a ['lɛtʃito] *ag* permitted, allowed.
'ledere *vt* to damage, injure; **~ gli interessi di qd** to be prejudicial to sb's interests.
'lega, ghe *sf* league; (*di metalli*) alloy.
le'gaccio [le'gattʃo] *sm* string, lace.
le'gale *ag* legal // *sm* lawyer; **legalità** *sf* legality, lawfulness; **legaliz'zare** *vt* to authenticate; (*regolarizzare*) to legalize.
le'game *sm* (*corda, fig: affettivo*) tie, bond; (*nesso logico*) link, connection.
lega'mento *sm* (*ANAT*) ligament.
le'gare *vt* (*prigioniero, capelli, cane*) to tie (up); (*libro*) to bind; (*CHIM*) to alloy; (*fig: collegare*) to bind, join // *vi* (*far lega*) to unite; (*fig*) to get on well.
lega'tario, a *sm/f* (*DIR*) legatee.
le'gato *sm* (*REL*) legate; (*DIR*) legacy, bequest.
lega'tura *sf* tying *q*; binding *q*; (*di libro*) binding; (*MUS*) ligature.
legazi'one [legat'tsjone] *sf* legation.
'legge ['leddʒe] *sf* law.
leg'genda [led'dʒɛnda] *sf* (*narrazione*) legend; (*di carta geografica etc*) key, legend; (*di disegno*) caption, legend; **leg-gen'dario, a** *ag* legendary.
'leggere ['leddʒere] *vt, vi* to read.
legge'rezza [leddʒe'rettsa] *sf* lightness; thoughtlessness; fickleness.
leg'gero, a [led'dʒɛro] *ag* light; (*agile, snello*) nimble, agile, light; (*tè, caffè*) weak; (*fig: non grave, piccolo*) slight; (: *spensierato*) thoughtless; (: *incostante*) fickle; free and easy; **alla ~a** thoughtlessly.
leggi'adro, a [led'dʒadro] *ag* pretty, lovely; (*movimenti*) graceful.
leg'gibile [led'dʒibile] *ag* legible; (*libro*) readable, worth reading.
leggi'ero, a [led'dʒɛro] *ag* = **leggero.**
leg'gio, 'gii [led'dʒio] *sm* lectern; (*MUS*) music stand.
legio'nario [ledʒo'narjo] *sm* (*romano*) legionary; (*volontario*) legionnaire.
legi'one [le'dʒone] *sf* legion; **~ straniera** foreign legion.
legisla'tivo, a [ledʒizla'tivo] *ag* legislative.
legisla'tore [ledʒizla'tore] *sm* legislator.

legisla'tura [ledʒizla'tura] *sf* legislature.
legislazi'one [ledʒizlat'tsjone] *sf* legislation.
legittimità [ledʒittimi'ta] *sf* legitimacy.
le'gittimo, a [le'dʒittimo] *ag* legitimate; *(fig: giustificato, lecito)* justified, legitimate; **~a difesa** *(DIR)* self-defence.
legna ['leɲɲa] *sf* firewood; **le'gname** *sm* wood, timber.
legno ['leɲɲo] *sm* wood; *(pezzo di —)* piece of wood; **di ~** wooden; **~ compensato** plywood; **le'gnoso, a** *ag* wooden; woody; *(carne)* tough.
le'gumi *smpl* *(BOT)* pulses.
'lei *pronome (soggetto)* she; *(oggetto: per dare rilievo, con preposizione)* her; *(forma di cortesia: anche:* **L~**) you // *sm:* **dare del ~ a qd** to address sb as 'lei'; **~ stessa** she herself; you yourself.
'lembo *sm (di abito, strada)* edge; *(striscia sottile: di terra)* strip.
lemma, i *sm* headword.
'lemme 'lemme *av* (very) very slowly.
'lena *sf (fig)* energy, stamina.
le'nire *vt* to soothe.
'lente *sf* *(OTTICA)* lens *sg*; **~ d'ingrandimento** magnifying glass; **~i a contatto** *o* **corneali** contact lenses.
len'tezza [len'tettsa] *sf* slowness.
len'ticchia [len'tikkja] *sf (BOT)* lentil.
len'tiggine [len'tiddʒine] *sf* freckle.
'lento, a *ag* slow; *(molle: fune)* slack; *(non stretto: vite, abito)* loose.
lenza ['lɛntsa] *sf* fishing-line.
lenzu'olo [len'tswɔlo] *sm* sheet; **~a** *sfpl* pair of sheets.
le'one *sm* lion; *(dello zodiaco):* **L~** Leo.
leo'pardo *sm* leopard.
'lepido, a *ag* witty.
lepo'rino, a *ag:* **labbro ~** harelip.
'lepre *sf* hare.
'lercio, a, ci, cie ['lertʃo] *ag* filthy.
'lesbica, che *sf* lesbian.
lesi'nare *vt* to be stingy with // *vi:* **~ (su)** to skimp (on), be stingy with).
lesi'one *sf (MED)* lesion; *(DIR)* injury, damage; *(EDIL)* crack.
le'sivo, a *ag:* **~ (di)** damaging (to), detrimental (to).
'leso, a *pp di* **ledere** // *ag (offeso)* injured.
les'sare *vt (CUC)* to boil.
'lessico, ci *sm* vocabulary; lexicon.
'lesso, a *ag* boiled // *sm* boiled meat.
'lesto, a *ag* quick; *(agile)* nimble; *(cosa: sbrigativa)* hasty, hurried; **~ di mano** *(per rubare)* light-fingered; *(per picchiare)* free with one's fists.
le'tale *ag* lethal; fatal.
leta'maio *sm* dunghill.
le'tame *sm* manure, dung.
le'targo, ghi *sm* lethargy; *(ZOOL)* hibernation.
le'tizia [le'tittsja] *sf* joy, happiness.
'lettera *sf* letter; **~e** *sfpl (letteratura)* literature *sg*; *(studi umanistici)* arts (subjects); **alla ~** literally; **in ~e** in words, in full; **lette'rale** *ag* literal.

lette'rario, a *ag* literary.
lette'rato, a *ag* well-read, scholarly.
lettera'tura *sf* literature.
let'tiga, ghe *sf (portantina)* litter; *(barella)* stretcher.
'letto, a *pp di* **leggere** // *sm* bed; **~ a castello** bunk beds *pl*; **~ a una piazza/a due piazze** *o* **matrimoniale** single/double bed.
let'tore, 'trice *sm/f* reader; *(INS)* (foreign language) assistant.
let'tura *sf* reading.
leuce'mia [leutʃe'mia] *sf* leukaemia.
'leva *sf* lever; *(MIL)* conscription; **far ~ su qd** to work on sb; **~ del cambio** *(AUT)* gear lever.
le'vante *sm* east; *(vento)* East wind; **il L~** the Levant.
le'vare *vt (occhi, braccio)* to raise; *(sollevare, togliere: tassa, divieto)* to lift; *(indumenti)* to take off, remove; *(rimuovere)* to take away; *(: dal di sopra)* to take off; *(: dal di dentro)* to take out; **~rsi** *vr* to get up; *(sole)* to rise; **le'vata** *sf* rising; *(di posta)* collection.
leva'toio, a *ag:* **ponte ~** drawbridge.
leva'tura *sf* intelligence, mental capacity.
levi'gare *vt* to smooth; *(con carta vetrata)* to sand.
levri'ero *sm* greyhound.
lezi'one [let'tsjone] *sf* lesson; *(all'università, sgridata)* lecture; **fare ~** to teach; to lecture.
lezi'oso, a [let'tsjoso] *ag* affected; simpering.
'lezzo ['leddzo] *sm* stench, stink.
li *pronome pl (oggetto)* them.
lì *av* there; **di** *o* **da ~** from there; **per di ~** that way; **di ~ a pochi giorni** a few days later; **~ per ~** there and then; at first; **essere ~ (~) per fare** to be on the point of doing, be about to do; **~ dentro** in there; **~ sotto** under there; **~ sopra** on there; up there; *vedi* quello.
Li'bano *sm:* **il ~** the Lebanon.
'libbra *sf (peso)* pound.
li'beccio [li'bettʃo] *sm* south-west wind.
li'bello *sm* libel.
li'bellula *sf* dragonfly.
libe'rale *ag, sm/f* liberal.
liberaliz'zare [liberalid'dzare] *vt* to liberalize.
libe'rare *vt* to free, liberate; *(prigioniero: sog: autorità, TECN)* to release; *(sottrarre a danni)* to rescue; **libera'tore, 'trice** *ag* liberating // *sm/f* liberator; **liberazi'one** *sf* liberation, freeing; release; rescuing.
'libero, a *ag* free; *(strada)* clear; *(non occupato: posto etc)* vacant; not taken; empty; not engaged; **~ di fare qc** free to do sth; **~ da** free from; **~ arbitrio** free will; **~ professionista** professional man; **~ scambio** free trade; **libertà** *sf inv* freedom; *(tempo disponibile)* free time // *sfpl (licenza)* liberties; **in libertà provvisoria/vigilata** on bail/probation; **libertà di riunione** right to hold meetings.

liber'tino, a *ag* libertine.
'Libia *sf*: **la ~** Libya; **'libico, a, ci, che** *ag, sm/f* Libyan.
li'bidine *sf* lust; **libidi'noso, a** *ag* lustful, libidinous.
li'bido *sf* libido.
li'braio *sm* bookseller.
li'brarsi *vr* to hover.
li'brario, a *ag* book *cpd.*
libre'ria *sf* (*bottega*) bookshop; (*stanza*) library; (*mobile*) bookcase.
li'bretto *sm* booklet; (*taccuino*) notebook; (*MUS*) libretto; **~ degli assegni** cheque book; **~ di risparmio** (savings) bank-book, passbook; **~ universitario** student's report book.
'libro *sm* book; **~ di cassa** cash book; **~ paga** payroll.
li'cenza [li'tʃɛntsa] *sf* (*permesso*) permission, leave; (*di pesca, caccia, circolazione*) permit, licence; (*MIL*) leave; (*INS*) leaving certificate, diploma; (*libertà*) liberty; licence; licentiousness; **andare in ~** (*MIL*) to go on leave.
licenzia'mento [litʃentsja'mento] *sm* dismissal; **indennità di ~** redundancy payment.
licenzi'are [litʃen'tsjare] *vt* (*impiegato*) to dismiss; (*INS*) to award a certificate to; **~rsi** *vr* (*impiegato*) to resign, hand in one's notice; (*INS*) to obtain one's school-leaving certificate.
licenzi'oso, a [litʃen'tsjoso] *ag* licentious.
li'ceo [li'tʃɛo] *sm* (*INS*) secondary school (*for 14- to 19-year-olds*).
li'chene [li'kene] *sm* (*BOT*) lichen.
licitazi'one [litʃitat'tsjone] *sf* (*offerta*) bid.
'lido *sm* beach, shore.
li'eto, a *ag* happy, glad; **"molto ~"** (*nelle presentazioni*) "pleased to meet you".
li'eve *ag* light; (*di poco conto*) slight; (*sommesso: voce*) faint, soft.
lievi'tare *vi* (2) (*anche fig*) to rise // *vt* to leaven.
li'evito *sm* yeast; **~ di birra** brewer's yeast.
'ligio, a, gi, gie ['lidʒo] *ag* faithful, loyal.
'lilla, lillà *sm inv* lilac.
'lima *sf* file.
limacci'oso, a [limat'tʃoso] *ag* slimy; muddy.
li'mare *vt* to file (down); (*fig*) to polish.
'limbo *sm* (*REL*) limbo.
li'metta *sf* nail file.
limi'tare *sm* (*anche fig*) threshold // *vt* to limit, restrict; (*circoscrivere*) to bound, surround; **limita'tivo, a** *ag* limiting, restricting; **limi'tato, a** *ag* limited, restricted; **limitazi'one** *sf* limitation, restriction.
'limite *sm* limit; (*confine*) border, boundary; **~ di velocità** speed limit.
li'mitrofo, a *ag* neighbouring.
limo'nata *sf* lemonade; lemon squash.
li'mone *sm* (*pianta*) lemon tree; (*frutto*) lemon.
'limpido, a *ag* clear; (*acqua*) limpid, clear.

'lince ['lintʃe] *sf* lynx.
linci'are *vt* to lynch.
'lindo, a *ag* tidy, spick and span; (*biancheria*) clean.
'linea *sf* line; (*di mezzi pubblici di trasporto: itinerario*) route; (: *servizio*) service; **a grandi ~e** in outline; **mantenere la ~** to look after one's figure; **di ~: aereo di ~** airliner; **nave di ~** liner; **~ di partenza/d'arrivo** (*SPORT*) starting/finishing line; **~ di tiro** line of fire.
linea'menti *smpl* features; (*fig*) outlines.
line'are *ag* linear; (*fig*) coherent, logical.
line'etta *sf* (*trattino*) dash; (*d'unione*) hyphen.
lin'gotto *sm* ingot, bar.
'lingua *sf* (*ANAT, CUC*) tongue; (*idioma*) language; **mostrare la ~** to stick out one's tongue; **di ~ italiana** Italian-speaking; **~ madre** mother tongue; **una ~ di terra** a spit of land; **linguacci'uto, a** *ag* gossipy.
lingu'aggio [lin'gwaddʒo] *sm* language.
lingu'etta *sf* (*di strumento*) reed; (*di scarpa, TECN*) tongue; (*di busta*) flap.
lingu'ista, i, e *sm/f* linguist; **lingu'istico, a, ci, che** *ag* linguistic // *sf* linguistics *sg.*
lini'mento *sm* liniment.
'lino *sm* (*pianta*) flax; (*tessuto*) linen.
li'noleum *sm inv* linoleum, lino.
lio'corno *sm* unicorn.
lique'fare *vt* (*render liquido*) to liquefy; (*fondere*) to melt; **~rsi** *vr* to liquefy; to melt.
liqui'dare *vt* (*società, beni; persona: uccidere*) to liquidate; (*persona: sbarazzarsene*) to get rid of; (*conto, problema*) to settle; (*COMM: merce*) to sell off, clear; **liquidazi'one** *sf* liquidation; settlement; clearance sale.
liquidità *sf* liquidity.
'liquido, a *ag, sm* liquid; **~ per freni** brake fluid.
liqui'rizia [likwi'rittsja] *sf* (*BOT*) liquorice.
li'quore *sm* liqueur.
'lira *sf* (*unità monetaria*) lira; (*MUS*) lyre; **~ sterlina** pound sterling.
'lirico, a, ci, che *ag* lyric(al); (*MUS*) lyric // *sf* (*poesia*) lyric poetry; (*componimento poetico*) lyric; (*MUS*) opera; **cantante/teatro ~** opera singer/house.
Lis'bona *sf* Lisbon.
'lisca, sche *sf* (*di pesce*) fishbone.
lisci'are [liʃ'ʃare] *vt* to smooth; (*accarezzare*) to stroke; (*fig*) to flatter.
'liscio, a, sci, sce ['liʃʃo] *ag* smooth; (*capelli*) straight; (*mobile*) plain; (*bevanda alcolica*) neat; (*fig*) straightforward, simple // *av*: **andare ~** to go smoothly; **passarla ~a** to get away with it.
'liso, a *ag* worn out, threadbare.
'lista *sf* (*striscia*) strip; (*elenco*) list; **~ elettorale** electoral roll; **~ delle vivande** menu; **lis'tare** *vt* to edge, border.
lis'tino *sm* list; **~ dei cambi** (foreign) exchange rate; **~ dei prezzi** price list.

lita'nia *sf* litany.

'lite *sf* quarrel, argument; (*DIR*) lawsuit.

liti'gare *vi* to quarrel; (*DIR*) to litigate.

li'tigio [li'tidʒo] *sm* quarrel; **litigi'oso, a** *ag* quarrelsome; (*DIR*) litigious.

litogra'fia *sf* (*sistema*) lithography; (*stampa*) lithograph.

lito'rale *ag* coastal, coast *cpd* // *sm* coast.

'litro *sm* litre.

litur'gia, 'gie [litur'dʒia] *sf* liturgy.

li'uto *sm* lute.

li'vella *sf* level; ~ **a bolla d'aria** spirit level.

livel'lare *vt* to level, make level; ~**rsi** *vr* to become level; (*fig*) to level out, balance out.

li'vello *sm* level; (*fig*) level, standard; **ad alto** ~ (*fig*) high-level; ~ **del mare** sea level.

'livido, a *ag* livid; (*per percosse*) bruised, black and blue; (*cielo*) leaden // *sm* bruise.

li'vore *sm* malice, spite.

Li'vorno *sf* Livorno, Leghorn.

li'vrea *sf* livery.

'lizza ['littsa] *sf* lists *pl*; **scendere in** ~ (*anche fig*) to enter the lists.

lo *det m* (*dav s impura, gn, pn, ps, x, z*; *dav V I'*) the // *pronome* (*dav V I'*) (*oggetto: persona*) him; (*: cosa*) it; ~ **sapevo** I knew it; ~ **so** I know; **sii buono, anche se lui non** ~ **è** be good, even if he isn't.

'lobo *sm* lobe; ~ **dell'orecchio** ear lobe.

lo'cale *ag* local // *sm* room; (*luogo pubblico*) premises *pl*; ~ **notturno** nightclub; **località** *sf inv* locality; **localiz-'zare** *vt* (*circoscrivere*) to confine, localize; (*accertare*) to locate, place.

lo'canda *sf* inn; **locandi'ere, a** *sm/f* innkeeper.

loca'tario, a *sm/f* tenant.

loca'tore, 'trice *sm/f* landlord/lady.

locazi'one [lokat'tsjone] *sf* (*da parte del locatario*) renting *q*; (*da parte del proprietario*) renting out *q*, letting *q*; (*effetto*) rent(al).

locomo'tiva *sf* locomotive.

locomo'tore *sm* electric locomotive.

locomozi'one [lokomot'tsjone] *sf* locomotion; **mezzi di** ~ vehicles, means of transport.

lo'custa *sf* locust.

locuzi'one [lokut'tsjone] *sf* phrase, expression.

lo'dare *vt* to praise.

'lode *sf* praise; (*INS*): **laurearsi con la** ~ ≈ to graduate with a first-class honours degree; **lo'devole** *ag* praiseworthy.

loga'ritmo *sm* logarithm.

'loggia, ge ['lɔddʒa] *sf* (*ARCHIT*) loggia; (*circolo massonico*) lodge; **loggi'one** *sm* (*di teatro*): **il loggione** the Gods *sg*.

'logico, a, ci, che ['lɔdʒiko] *ag* logical // *sf* logic.

logo'rare *vt* to wear out; (*sciupare*) to waste; ~**rsi** *vr* to wear out; (*fig*) to wear o.s. out.

logo'rio *sm* wear and tear; (*fig*) strain.

'logoro, a *ag* (*stoffa*) worn out, threadbare; (*persona*) worn out.

lom'baggine [lom'baddʒine] *sf* lumbago.

Lombar'dia *sf*: **la** ~ Lombardy.

lom'bata *sf* (*taglio di carne*) loin.

'lombo *sm* (*ANAT*) loin.

lom'brico, chi *sm* earthworm.

'Londra *sf* London.

longevità [londʒevi'ta] *sf* longevity.

lon'gevo, a [lon'dʒevo] *ag* long-lived.

longi'tudine [londʒi'tudine] *sf* longitude.

lonta'nanza [lonta'nantsa] *sf* distance; absence.

lon'tano, a *ag* (*distante*) distant, faraway; (*assente*) absent; (*vago: sospetto*) slight, remote; (*tempo: remoto*) far-off, distant; (*parente*) distant, remote // *av* far; **è** ~**a la casa?** is it far to the house?, is the house far from here?; **è** ~ **un chilometro** it's a mile away *o* a mile from here; **più** ~ farther; **da** *o* **di** ~ from a distance; ~ **da** a long way from; **alla** ~**a** slightly, vaguely.

'lontra *sf* otter.

lo'quace [lo'kwatʃe] *ag* talkative, loquacious; (*fig: gesto etc*) eloquent.

'lordo, a *ag* dirty, filthy; (*peso, stipendio*) gross; **lor'dura** *sf* filth.

'loro *pronome pl* (*oggetto, con preposizione*) them; (*complemento di termine*) to them; (*soggetto*) they; (*forma di cortesia: anche*: L~) you; to you; **il(la)** ~, **i(le)** ~ *det* their; (*forma di cortesia: anche*: L~) your // *pronome* theirs; (*forma di cortesia: anche*: L~) yours; ~ **stessi(e)** they themselves; you yourselves.

'losco, a, schi, sche *ag* (*fig*) shady, suspicious.

'loto *sm* lotus.

'lotta *sf* struggle, fight; (*SPORT*) wrestling; **lot'tare** *vi* to fight, struggle; to wrestle; **lotta'tore** *sm* wrestler.

lotte'ria *sf* lottery; (*di gara ippica*) sweepstake.

'lotto *sm* (*gioco*) (state) lottery; (*parte*) lot; (*EDIL*) site.

lozi'one [lot'tsjone] *sf* lotion.

'lubrico, a, ci, che *ag* lewd, lascivious.

lubrifi'cante *sm* lubricant.

lubrifi'care *vt* to lubricate.

luc'chetto [luk'ketto] *sm* padlock.

lucci'care [luttʃi'kare] *vi* to sparkle, glitter, twinkle.

'luccio ['luttʃo] *sm* (*ZOOL*) pike.

'lucciola ['luttʃola] *sf* (*ZOOL*) firefly; glowworm.

'luce ['lutʃe] *sf* light; (*finestra*) window; **alla** ~ **di** by the light of; **fare** ~ **su qc** (*fig*) to shed *o* throw light on sth; ~ **del sole/della luna** sun/moonlight; **lu'cente** *ag* shining.

lu'cerna [lu'tʃerna] *sf* oil-lamp.

lucer'nario [lutʃer'narjo] *sm* skylight.

lu'certola [lu'tʃertola] *sf* lizard.

luci'dare [lutʃi'dare] *vt* to polish; (*ricalcare*) to trace.

lucidità [lutʃidi'ta] *sf* lucidity.

'lucido, a ag shining, bright; (lucidato) polished; (fig) lucid // sm shine, lustre; (per scarpe etc) polish; (disegno) tracing.

lu'cignolo [lu'tʃiɲɲolo] sm wick.

lu'crare vt to earn, make.

'lucro sm profit, gain; **lu'croso, a** ag lucrative, profitable.

lu'dibrio sm mockery q; (oggetto di scherno) laughing-stock.

'luglio ['luʎʎo] sm July.

'lugubre ag gloomy.

'lui pronome (soggetto) he; (oggetto: per dare rilievo, con preposizione) him; ~ **stesso** he himself.

lu'maca, che sf slug; (chiocciola) snail.

'lume sm light; (lampada) lamp; (fig): **chiedere ~i a qd** to ask sb for advice.

lumi'naria sf (per feste) illuminations pl.

lumi'noso, a ag (che emette luce) luminous; (cielo, colore, stanza) bright; (sorgente) of light, light cpd; (fig) obvious, clear; **idea ~a** bright idea.

'luna sf moon; ~ **nuova/piena** new/full moon; ~ **di miele** honeymoon.

'luna park sm inv amusement park, funfair.

lu'nare ag lunar, moon cpd.

lu'nario sm almanac.

lu'natico, a, ci, che ag whimsical, temperamental.

lunedì sm inv Monday; **di o il ~** on Mondays.

lun'gaggine [lun'gaddʒine] sf slowness; ~i **della burocrazia** red tape.

lun'ghezza [lun'gettsa] sf length; ~ **d'onda** (FISICA) wavelength.

'lungo, a, ghi, ghe ag long; (lento: persona) slow; (diluito: caffè, brodo) weak, watery, thin // sm length ,/ prep along; ~ **3 metri** 3 metres long; **a ~** for a long time; **a ~ andare** in the long run; **di gran ~a** (molto) by far; **andare in ~** o **per le lunghe** to drag on; **saperla ~a** to know what's what; **in ~ e in largo** far and wide, all over; ~ **il corso dei secoli** throughout the centuries.

lungo'mare sm promenade.

lu'notto sm (AUT) rear o back window.

lu'ogo, ghi sm place; (posto: di incidente etc) scene, site; (punto, passo di libro) passage; **in ~ di** instead of; **in primo ~** in the first place; **aver ~** to take place; **dar ~ a** to give rise to; ~ **comune** commonplace; ~ **geometrico** locus.

luogote'nente sm (MIL) lieutenant.

lu'para sf sawn-off shotgun.

'lupo, a sm/f wolf.

'luppolo sm (BOT) hop.

'lurido, a ag filthy.

lu'singa, ghe sf (spesso al pl) flattery q.

lusin'gare vt to flatter; ~rsi vr (sperare) to deceive o.s.; **lusinghi'ero, a** ag flattering, gratifying.

lus'sare vt (MED) to dislocate.

Lussem'burgo sm: il ~ Luxembourg.

'lusso sm luxury; **di ~** luxury cpd; **lus-su'oso, a** ag luxurious.

lussureggi'are [lussured'dʒare] vi to be luxuriant.

lus'suria sf lust.

lus'trare vt to polish, shine.

lustras'carpe sm/f inv shoeshine.

lus'trino sm sequin.

'lustro, a ag shiny; (pelliccia) glossy // sm shine, gloss; (fig) prestige, glory; (quinquennio) five-year period.

'lutto sm mourning; **essere in/portare il ~** to be in/wear mourning; **luttu'oso, a** ag mournful, sad.

M

ma cong but; ~ **insomma!** for goodness sake!; ~ **no!** of course not!

'macabro, a ag gruesome, macabre.

macché [mak'ke] escl not at all!, certainly not!

macche'roni [makke'roni] smpl macaroni sg.

'macchia ['makkja] sf stain, spot; (chiazza di diverso colore) spot; splash, patch; (tipo di boscaglia) scrub; **macchi'are** vt (sporcare) to stain, mark; **macchiarsi** vr (persona) to get o.s. dirty; (stoffa) to stain; to get stained o marked.

'macchina ['makkina] sf machine; (elettrica, a vapore) engine; (automobile) car; (fig: meccanismo) machinery; **andare in ~** (AUT) to go by car; (STAMPA) to go to press; ~ **da cucire** sewing machine; ~ **fotografica** camera; ~ **da scrivere** typewriter; ~ **a vapore** steam engine.

macchi'nare [makki'nare] vt to plot.

macchi'nario [makki'narjo] sm machinery.

macchi'netta [makki'netta] sf (fam: caffettiera) percolator; (: accendino) lighter.

macchi'nista [makki'nista] sm (di treno) engine-driver; (di nave) engineer; (TEATRO, TV) stagehand.

macchi'noso, a [makki'noso] ag complex, complicated.

mace'donia [matʃe'dɔnja] sf fruit salad.

macel'laio [matʃel'lajo] sm butcher.

macel'lare [matʃel'lare] vt to slaughter, butcher; **macelle'ria** sf butcher's (shop); **ma'cello** sm (mattatoio) slaughterhouse, abattoir; (fig) slaughter, massacre; (: disastro) shambles sg.

mace'rare [matʃe'rare] vt to macerate; (fig) to mortify; ~rsi vr to waste away; (fig): ~rsi in to be consumed with.

ma'cerie [ma'tʃerje] sfpl rubble sg, debris sg.

ma'cigno [ma'tʃiɲɲo] sm (masso) rock, boulder.

maci'lento, a [matʃi'lɛnto] ag emaciated.

ma'cina [ma'tʃina] sf (pietra) millstone; (macchina) grinder; **macinacaffè** sm inv coffee grinder; **macina'pepe** sm inv peppermill.

maci'nare [matʃi'nare] vt to grind; maci-'nato sm meal, flour; (carne) mince, minced meat.

maci'nino [matʃi'nino] sm coffee grinder; peppermill.

'madido, a ag: ~ (di) wet o moist (with).

Ma'donna sf (REL) Our Lady.

mador'nale ag enormous, huge.

'madre sf mother; (matrice di bolletta) counterfoil // ag inv mother cpd; ragazza ~ unmarried mother; scena ~ (TEATRO) principal scene.

madre'lingua sf mother tongue, native language.

madre'perla sf mother-of-pearl.

madri'gale sm madrigal.

ma'drina sf godmother.

maestà sf inv majesty; maes'toso, a ag majestic.

ma'estra sf vedi maestro.

maes'trale sm north-west wind, mistral.

maes'tranze [maes'trantse] sfpl workforce sg.

maes'tria sf mastery, skill.

ma'estro, a sm/f (INS: anche: ~ elementare) primary teacher; (persona molto preparata) expert // sm (artigiano, fig: guida) master; (MUS) maestro // ag (principale) main; (di grande abilità) masterly, skilful; ~ di cerimonie master of ceremonies; ~a giardiniera nursery teacher.

'mafia sf Mafia; mafi'oso sm member of the Mafia.

'maga sf sorceress.

ma'gagna [ma'gaɲɲa] sf defect, flaw, blemish.

ma'gari escl (esprime desiderio): ~ fosse vero! if only it were true!; ti piacerebbe andare in Scozia? — ~! would you like to go to Scotland? — and how! // av (anche) even; (forse) perhaps.

magaz'zino [magad'dzino] sm warehouse; (grande emporio) department store.

'maggio ['maddʒo] sm May.

maggio'rana [maddʒo'rana] sf (BOT) (sweet) marjoram.

maggio'ranza [maddʒo'rantsa] sf majority.

maggio'rare [maddʒo'rare] vt to increase, raise.

maggior'domo [maddʒor'dɔmo] sm butler.

maggi'ore [mad'dʒore] ag (comparativo: più grande) bigger, larger; taller; greater; (: più vecchio: sorella, fratello) older, elder; (: di grado superiore) senior; (: più importante, MIL, MUS) major; (superlativo) biggest, largest; tallest; greatest; oldest, eldest // sm/f (di grado) superior; (di età) elder; (MIL) major; (: AER) squadron leader; la maggior parte the majority; maggio'renne ag of age // sm/f person who has come of age; maggio'rente sm notable; maggior'mente av much more; (con senso superlativo) most.

ma'gia [ma'dʒia] sf magic; 'magico, a, ci, che ag magic; (fig) fascinating, charming, magical.

'magio ['madʒo] sm (REL): i re Magi the Magi, the Three Wise Men.

magis'tero [madʒis'tero] sm (INS) teaching; (fig: maestria) skill; magis'trale ag primary teachers', primary teaching cpd; skilful.

magis'trato [madʒis'trato] sm magistrate; magistra'tura sf magistrature; (magistrati): la magistratura the Bench.

'maglia ['maʎʎa] sf stitch; (lavoro ai ferri) knitting q; (tessuto, SPORT) jersey; (maglione) jersey, sweater; (di catena) link; (di rete) mesh; avviare/diminuire le ~e to cast on/cast off; ~ diritta/rovescia plain/purl; magli'eria sf knitwear; (negozio) knitwear shop; magli'etta sf (canottiera) vest; (tipo camicia) T-shirt; magli'ficio sm knitwear factory.

'maglio ['maʎʎo] sm mallet; (macchina) power hammer.

ma'gnanimo, a [maɲ'ɲanimo] ag magnanimous.

ma'gnesia [maɲ'ɲezja] sf (CHIM) magnesia.

ma'gnesio [maɲ'ɲezjo] sm (CHIM) magnesium.

ma'gnete [maɲ'ɲete] sm magnet; ma-'gnetico, a, ci, che ag magnetic; magne-'tismo sm magnetism.

magne'tofono [maɲɲe'tɔfono] sm tape recorder.

magnifi'cenza [maɲɲifi'tʃentsa] sf magnificence, splendour.

ma'gnifico, a, ci, che [maɲ'ɲifiko] ag magnificent, splendid; (ospite) generous.

ma'gnolia [maɲ'ɲɔlja] sf magnolia.

'mago, ghi av (stregone) magician, wizard; (illusionista) magician.

ma'grezza [ma'grettsa] sf thinness.

'magro, a ag (very) thin, skinny; (carne) lean; (formaggio) low-fat; (fig: scarso, misero) meagre, poor; (: meschino: scusa) poor, lame; mangiare di ~ not to eat meat.

'mai av (nessuna volta) never; (talvolta) ever; non ... ~ never; ~ più never again; come ~? why (o how) on earth?; chi/dove/quando ~? whoever/wher-ever/whenever?

mai'ale sm (ZOOL) pig; (carne) pork.

maio'nese sf mayonnaise.

'mais sm inv maize.

mai'uscolo, a ag (lettera) capital; (fig) enormous, huge // sf capital letter.

mal av, sm vedi male.

malac'corto, a ag rash, careless.

mala'copia sf rough copy.

malafede sf bad faith.

mala'mente av badly; dangerously.

malan'dato, a ag (persona: di salute) in poor health; (: di condizioni finanziarie) badly off; (trascurato) shabby.

ma'lanimo sm ill will, malevolence; di ~ unwillingly.

ma'lanno *sm* (*disgrazia*) misfortune; (*malattia*) ailment.

mala'pena *sf*: a ~ hardly, scarcely.

ma'laria *sf* (MED) malaria.

mala'sorte *sf* bad luck.

mala'ticcio, a [mala'tittʃo] *ag* sickly.

ma'lato, a *ag* ill, sick; (*gamba*) bad; (*pianta*) diseased // *sm/f* sick person; (*in ospedale*) patient; **malat'tia** *sf* (*infettiva etc*) illness, disease; (*cattiva salute*) illness, sickness.

malau'gurio *sm* bad o ill omen.

mala'vita *sf* underworld.

mala'voglia [mala'voʎʎa] *sf* reluctance, unwillingness; **di** ~ unwillingly, reluctantly.

mal'concio, a, ci, ce [mal'kontʃo] *ag* in a sorry state.

malcon'tento *sm* discontent.

malcos'tume *sm* immorality.

mal'destro, a *ag* (*inabile*) inexpert, inexperienced; (*goffo*) awkward.

maldi'cente [maldi'tʃente] *ag* slanderous.

maldis'posto, a *ag*: ~ (**verso**) ill-disposed (towards).

'male *av* badly // *sm* (*ciò che è ingiusto, disonesto*) evil; (*danno, svantaggio*) harm; (*sventura*) misfortune; (*dolore fisico, morale*) pain, ache; **di** ~ **in peggio** from bad to worse; **sentirsi** ~ to feel ill; **far** ~ (*dolere*) to hurt; **far** ~ **alla salute** to be bad for one's health; **far del** ~ **a qd** to hurt o harm sb; **restare** o **rimanere** ~ to be sorry; to be disappointed; to be hurt; **andare a** ~ to go bad; **come va?** — **non c'è** ~ how are you? — not bad; **mal di mare** seasickness; **avere mal di gola/testa** to have a sore throat/a headache.

male'detto, a *pp di* **maledire** // *ag* cursed, damned; (*fig: fastidioso*) damned, wretched.

male'dire *vt* to curse; **maledizi'one** *sf* curse; **maledizione!** damn it!

maledu'cato, a *ag* rude, ill-mannered.

male'ficio [male'fitʃo] *sm* witchcraft.

ma'lefico, a, ci, che *ag* (*aria, cibo*) harmful, bad; (*influsso, azione*) evil.

ma'lessere *sm* indisposition, slight illness; (*fig*) uneasiness.

ma'levolo, a *ag* malevolent.

malfa'mato, a *ag* notorious.

mal'fatto, a *ag* (*persona*) deformed; (*cosa*) badly made.

malfat'tore, 'trice *sm/f* wrongdoer.

mal'fermo, a *ag* unsteady, shaky; (*salute*) poor, delicate.

malformazi'one [malformat'tsjone] *sf* malformation.

malgo'verno *sm* maladministration.

mal'grado *prep* in spite of, despite // *cong* although; **mio** (o **tuo** *etc*) ~ against my (o your *etc*) will.

ma'lia *sf* spell; (*fig: fascino*) charm.

mali'gnare [maliɲ'ɲare] *vi*: ~ **su** to malign, speak ill of.

ma'ligno, a [ma'liɲɲo] *ag* (*malvagio*)

malicious, malignant; (MED) malignant.

malinco'nia *sf* melancholy, gloom; **malin'conico, a, ci, che** *ag* melancholy.

malincu'ore: **a** ~ *av* reluctantly, unwillingly.

malintenzio'nato, a [malintentsjo'nato] *ag* ill-intentioned.

malin'teso, a *ag* misunderstood; (*riguardo, senso del dovere*) mistaken, wrong // *sm* misunderstanding.

ma'lizia [ma'littsja] *sf* (*malignità*) malice; (*furbizia*) cunning; (*espediente*) trick; **malizi'oso, a** *ag* malicious; cunning; (*vivace, birichino*) mischievous.

malle'abile *ag* malleable.

malme'nare *vt* to beat up; (*fig*) to ill-treat.

mal'messo, a *ag* (*persona*) shabby, badly-dressed; (*casa*) badly-furnished.

malnu'trito, a *ag* undernourished; **malnutrizi'one** *sf* malnutrition.

ma'locchio [ma'lɔkkjo] *sm* evil eye.

ma'lora *sf* ruin; **andare in** ~ to go to the dogs; **va in** ~! go to hell!

ma'lore *sm* feeling of faintness; feeling of discomfort.

mal'sano, a *ag* unhealthy.

malsi'curo, a *ag* unsafe; (*fig*) uncertain; (: *testimonianza*) unreliable.

'malta *sf* (EDIL) mortar.

mal'tempo *sm* bad weather.

'malto *sm* malt.

maltrat'tare *vt* to ill-treat.

malu'more *sm* bad mood; (*irritabilità*) bad temper; (*discordia*) ill feeling; **di** ~ in a bad mood.

mal'vagio, a, gi, gie [mal'vadʒo] *ag* wicked, evil.

malversazi'one [malversat'tsjone] *sf* (DIR) embezzlement.

mal'visto, a *ag*: ~ (**da**) disliked (by), unpopular (with).

malvi'vente *sm* criminal.

malvolenti'eri *av* unwillingly, reluctantly.

malvo'lere *vt*: **farsi** ~ **da qd** to make o.s. unpopular with sb // *sm* (*avversione*) ill will; (*scarsa volontà*) unwillingness.

'mamma *sf* mummy, mum; ~ **mia!** my goodness!

mam'mario, a *ag* (ANAT) mammary.

mam'mella *sf* (ANAT) breast; (*di vacca, capra etc*) udder.

mam'mifero *sm* mammal.

'mammola *sf* (BOT) violet.

ma'nata *sf* (*colpo*) slap; (*quantità*) handful.

'manca *sf vedi* **manco**.

man'canza [man'kantsa] *sf* lack; (*carenza*) shortage, scarcity; (*fallo*) fault; (*imperfezione*) failing, shortcoming; **per** ~ **di tempo** through lack of time; **in** ~ **di meglio** for lack of anything better.

man'care *vi* (2: *essere insufficiente*) to be lacking; (: *venir meno*) to fail; (: *non esserci*) to be missing, not to be there; (: *essere lontano*): ~ (**da**) to be away (from) // *vt* to miss; ~ **di** to lack; ~ **a**

(*promessa*) to fail to keep; **tu mi manchi** I miss you; **mancò poco che morisse** he very nearly died; **mancano ancora 10 sterline** we're still £10 short; **manca un quarto alle 6** it's a quarter to 6; **man'cato, a** *ag* (*tentativo*) unsuccessful; (*artista*) failed.

'mancia, ce ['mantʃa] *sf* tip; ~ **competente** reward.

manci'ata [man'tʃata] *sf* handful.

man'cino, a [man'tʃino] *ag* (*braccio*) left; (*persona*) left-handed; (*fig*) underhand.

'manco, a, chi, che *ag* left // *sf* left hand // *av* (*nemmeno*) not even.

man'dare *vt* to send; (*far funzionare: macchina*) to drive; (*emettere*) to send out; (: *grido*) to give, utter, let out; ~ **a chiamare qd** to send for sb; ~ **giù** to send down; (*anche fig*) to swallow; ~ **via** to send away; (*licenziare*) to fire.

manda'rino *sm* mandarin (orange), tangerine; (*cinese*) mandarin.

man'data *sf* (*spedizione*) sending; (*quantità*) lot, batch; (*di chiave*) turn.

manda'tario *sm* (*DIR*) representative, agent.

man'dato *sm* (*incarico*) commission; (*DIR: provvedimento*) warrant; (*di deputato etc*) mandate; (*ordine di pagamento*) postal *o* money order; ~ **d'arresto** warrant for arrest.

man'dibola *sf* mandible, jaw.

'mandorla *sf* almond; **'mandorlo** *sm* almond tree.

'mandria *sf* herd.

maneggi'are [maned'dʒare] *vt* (*creta*) to mould, work, fashion; (*arnesi, utensili*) to handle; (: *adoperare*) to use; (*fig: persone*) to handle, deal with; **ma'neggio** *sm* moulding; handling; use; (*intrigo*) plot, scheme; (*per cavalli*) riding school.

ma'nesco, a, schi, sche *ag* free with one's fists.

ma'netta *sf* hand lever; ~e *sfpl* handcuffs.

manga'nello *sm* club.

manga'nese *sm* manganese.

'mangano *sm* mangle.

mange'reccio, a, ci, ce [mandʒe'rettʃo] *ag* edible.

mange'ria [mandʒe'ria] *sf* extortion.

mangia'dischi [mandʒa'diski] *sm inv* record player.

mangi'are [man'dʒare] *vt* to eat; (*intaccare*) to eat into *o* away; (*CARTE, SCACCHI etc*) to take //. *vi* to eat // *sm* eating; (*cibo*) food; (*cucina*) cooking; ~**rsi le parole** to mumble; **mangia'toia** *sf* feeding-trough.

man'gime [man'dʒime] *sm* fodder.

'mango, ghi *sm* mango.

ma'nia *sf* (*PSIC*) mania; (*fig*) obsession, craze; **ma'niaco, a, ci, che** *ag* suffering from a mania; **maniaco (di)** obsessed (by), crazy (about).

'manica *sf* sleeve; (*fig: gruppo*) gang, bunch; (*GEO*): **la M~** the (English) Channel; **essere di ~ larga/stretta** to

be easy-going/strict; ~ **a vento** (*AER*) wind sock.

mani'chino [mani'kino] *sm* (*di sarto, vetrina*) dummy.

'manico, ci *sm* handle; (*MUS*) neck.

mani'comio *sm* mental hospital; (*fig*) madhouse.

mani'cotto *sm* muff; (*TECN*) coupling; sleeve.

mani'cure *sf inv* manicurist.

mani'era *sf* way, manner; (*stile*) style, manner; ~e *sfpl* manners; **in ~ che** so that; **in ~ da** so as to; **in tutte le ~e** at all costs.

manie'rato, a *ag* affected.

manifat'tura *sf* (*lavorazione*) manufacture; (*stabilimento*) factory.

manifes'tare *vt* to show, display; (*esprimere*) to express; (*rivelare*) to reveal, disclose // *vi* to demonstrate; ~**rsi** *vr* to show o.s.; ~**rsi amico** to prove o.s. (to be) a friend; **manifestazi'one** *sf* show, display; expression; (*sintomo*) sign, symptom; (*dimostrazione pubblica*) demonstration; (*cerimonia*) event.

mani'festo, a *ag* obvious, evident // *sm* poster, bill; (*scritto ideologico*) manifesto.

ma'niglia [ma'niʎʎa] *sf* handle; (*sostegno: negli autobus etc*) strap.

manipo'lare *vt* to manipulate; (*alterare: vino*) to adulterate; **manipolazi'one** *sf* manipulation; adulteration.

manis'calco, chi *sm* farrier.

'manna *sf* (*REL*) manna.

man'naia *sf* (*del boia*) (executioner's) axe; (*per carni*) cleaver.

man'naro: lupo ~ *sm* werewolf.

'mano, i *sf* hand; (*strato: di vernice etc*) coat; **di prima ~** (*notizia*) first-hand; **di seconda ~** second-hand; **man ~** little by little, gradually; **man ~ che** as; **darsi** *o* **stringersi la ~** to shake hands; **mettere le ~i avanti** (*fig*) to safeguard o.s.; **a ~** by hand; ~**i in alto!** hands up!

mano'dopera *sf* labour.

ma'nometro *sm* gauge, manometer.

mano'mettere *vt* (*alterare*) to tamper with; (*frugare, aprire*) to break open illegally; (*ledere: diritti*) to violate, infringe; **mano'messo, a** *pp di* **manomettere**.

ma'nopola *sf* (*dell'armatura*) gauntlet; (*guanto*) mitt; (*di impugnatura*) hand-grip; (*pomello*) knob.

manos'critto, a *ag* handwritten // *sm* manuscript.

mano'vale *sm* labourer.

mano'vella *sf* handle; (*TECN*) crank; **albero a ~** crankshaft.

ma'novra *sf* manoeuvre; (*FERR*) shunting; **mano'vrare** *vt* to manoeuvre; (*congegno*) to operate // *vi* to manoeuvre.

manro'vescio [manro'veʃʃo] *sm* slap (*with back of hand*).

man'sarda *sf* attic.

mansi'one *sf* task, duty, job.

mansu'eto, a *ag* gentle, docile.

man'tello *sm* cloak; (*fig: di neve etc*)

blanket, mantle; (*TECN: involucro*) casing, shell; (*ZOOL*) coat.

mante'nere *vt* to maintain; (*adempiere: promesse*) to keep, abide by; (*provvedere a*) to support, maintain; ~**rsi** *vr*: ~**rsi calmo/ giovane** to stay calm/young; **manteni'mento** *sm* maintenance.

'**mantice** ['mantitʃe] *sm* bellows *pl*; (*di carrozza, automobile*) hood.

'**manto** *sm* cloak; ~ **stradale** road surface.

manu'ale *ag* manual // *sm* (*testo*) manual, handbook.

ma'nubrio *sm* handle; (*di bicicletta etc*) handlebars *pl*; (*SPORT*) dumbbell.

manu'fatto, a *ag* manufactured.

manutenzi'one [manuten'tsjone] *sf* maintenance, upkeep; (*d'impianti*) maintenance, servicing.

'**manzo** ['mandzo] *sm* (*ZOOL*) steer; (*carne*) beef.

'**mappa** *sf* (*GEO*) map; **mappa'mondo** *sm* map of the world; (*globo girevole*) globe.

ma'rasma, i *sm* (*fig*) decay, decline.

mara'tona *sf* marathon.

'**marca, che** *sf* mark; (*bollo*) stamp; (*COMM: di prodotti*) brand; (*contrassegno, scontrino*) ticket, check; ~ **da bollo** official stamp; ~ **di fabbrica** trademark.

mar'care *vt* (*munire di contrassegno*) to mark; (*a fuoco*) to brand; (*SPORT: gol*) to score; (*: avversario*) to mark; ~ **visita** (*MIL*) to report sick.

mar'chese, a [mar'keze] *sm/f* marquis *o* marquess/marchioness.

marchi'are [mar'kjare] *vt* to brand; '**marchio** *sm* (*di bestiame, COMM, fig*) brand; **marchio di fabbrica** trademark; **marchio depositato** registered trademark.

'**marcia, ce** ['martʃa] *sf* (*anche MUS, MIL*) march; (*funzionamento*) running; (*il camminare*) walking; (*AUT*) gear; **mettere in** ~ to start; **mettersi in** ~ to get moving; **far** ~ **indietro** (*AUT*) to reverse; (*fig*) to back-pedal.

marciapi'ede [martʃa'pjɛde] *sm* (*di strada*) pavement; (*FERR*) platform.

màrci'are [mar'tʃare] *vi* to march; (*andare: treno, macchina*) to go; (*funzionare*) to run, work.

'**marcio, a, ci, ce** ['martʃo] *ag* (*frutta, legno*) rotten, bad; (*MED*) festering; (*fig*) corrupt, rotten.

mar'cire [mar'tʃire] *vi* (*2*) (*andare a male*) to go bad, rot; (*suppurare*) to fester; (*fig*) to rot, waste away.

'**marco, chi** *sm* (*unità monetaria*) mark.

'**mare** *sm* sea; **in** ~ at sea; **andare al** ~ (*in vacanza etc*) to go to the seaside; **il** ~ **del Nord** the North Sea.

ma'rea *sf* tide; **alta/bassa** ~ high/low tide.

mareggi'ata [mared'dʒata] *sf* heavy sea.

ma'remma *sf* (*GEO*) maremma, swampy coastal area.

mare'moto *sm* seaquake.

maresci'allo [mareʃ'ʃallo] *sm* (*MIL*) marshal; (*: sottufficiale*) warrant officer.

marga'rina *sf* margarine.

marghe'rita [marge'rita] *sf* (ox-eye) daisy, marguerite; **margheri'tina** *sf* daisy.

margi'nale [mardʒi'nale] *ag* marginal.

'**margine** ['mardʒine] *sm* margin; (*di bosco, via*) edge, border.

ma'rina *sf* navy; (*costa*) coast; ~ **militare/mercantile** navy/merchant navy.

mari'naio *sm* sailor.

mari'nare *vt* (*CUC*) to marinate; ~ **la scuola** to play truant; **mari'nata** *sf* marinade.

ma'rino, a *ag* maritime, sea *cpd*.

mario'netta *sf* puppet.

mari'tale *ag* marital.

mari'tare *vt* to marry; ~**rsi** *vr*: ~**rsi a** *o* **con qd** to marry sb, get married to sb.

ma'rito *sm* husband.

ma'rittimo, a *ag* maritime, sea *cpd*.

mar'maglia [mar'maʎʎa] *sf* mob, riff-raff.

marmel'lata *sf* jam; (*di agrumi*) marmalade.

mar'mitta *sf* (*recipiente*) pot; (*AUT*) silencer.

'**marmo** *sm* marble.

mar'mocchio [mar'mɔkkjo] *sm* (*fam*) tot, kid.

mar'motta *sf* (*ZOOL*) marmot.

Ma'rocco *sm*: **il** ~ Morocco.

'**marra** *sf* hoe.

mar'rone *ag inv* brown // *sm* (*BOT*) chestnut.

mar'sina *sf* tails *pl*, tail coat.

martedì *sm inv* Tuesday; **di** *o* **il** ~ on Tuesdays; ~ **grasso** Shrove Tuesday.

martel'lare *vt* to hammer // *vi* to hammer; (*pulsare*) to throb.

mar'tello *sm* hammer; (*di uscio*) knocker.

marti'netto *sm* (*TECN*) jack.

'**martire** *sm/f* martyr; **mar'tirio** *sm* martyrdom; (*fig*) agony, torture.

'**martora** *sf* marten.

martori'are *vt* to torment, torture.

marza'pane [martsa'pane] *sm* marzipan.

marzi'ale [mar'tsjale] *ag* martial.

'**marzo** ['martso] *sm* March.

mascal'zone [maskal'tsone] *sm* rascal, scoundrel.

ma'scella [maʃ'ʃella] *sf* (*ANAT*) jaw.

'**maschera** ['maskera] *sf* mask; (*travestimento*) disguise; (*: per un ballo etc*) fancy dress; (*TEATRO, CINEMA*) usher/usherette; (*personaggio del teatro*) stock character; **maschera'mento** *sm* disguise; (*MIL*) camouflage; **masche'rare** *vt* to mask; (*travestire*) to disguise; to dress up; (*fig: celare*) to hide, conceal; (*MIL*) to camouflage; ~**rsi da** to disguise o.s. as; to dress up as; (*fig*) to masquerade as.

mas'chile [mas'kile] *ag* masculine; (*sesso, popolazione*) male; (*abiti*) men's; (*per ragazzi: scuola*) boys'.

'**maschio, a** ['maskjo] *ag* (*BIOL*) male;

(*virile*) manly // *sm* male; (*ragazzo*) boy; (*figlio*) son.

masco'lino, a *ag* masculine.

mas'cotte *sf inv* mascot.

'massa *sf* mass; (*di errori etc*): **una ~ di** heaps of, masses of; (*di gente*) mass, multitude; (*ELETTR*) earth; **in ~** (*COMM*) in bulk; (*tutti insieme*) en masse; **adunata in ~** mass meeting; **la ~ dei popolo** the masses *pl*.

massa'crare *vt* to massacre, slaughter; **mas'sacro** *sm* massacre, slaughter; (*fig*) mess, disaster.

massaggi'are [massad'dʒare] *vt* to massage; **mas'saggio** *sm* massage.

mas'saia *sf* housewife.

masse'ria *sf* large farm.

masse'rizie [masse'rittsje] *sfpl* (household) furnishings.

mas'siccio, a, ci, ce [mas'sittʃo] *ag* (*oro, legno*) solid; (*palazzo*) massive; (*corporatura*) stout // *sm* (*GEO*) massif.

'massima *sf vedi* **massimo.**

massi'male *sm* maximum.

'massimo, a *ag, sm* maximum // *sf* (*sentenza, regola*) maxim; (*METEOR*) maximum temperature; **al ~** at (the) most; **in linea di ~**a generally speaking.

'masso *sm* rock, boulder.

mas'sone *sm* freemason; **massone'ria** *sf* freemasonry.

masti'care *vt* to chew.

'mastice ['mastitʃe] *sm* mastic; (*per vetri*) putty.

mas'tino *sm* mastiff.

masturbazi'one [masturbat'tsjone] *sf* masturbation.

ma'tassa *sf* skein; **trovare il bandolo della ~** (*fig*) to get to the bottom of a complicated matter.

mate'matico, a, ci, che *ag* mathematical // *sm/f* mathematician // *sf* mathematics *sg*.

mate'rasso *sm* mattress; **~ a molle** spring o interior-sprung mattress.

ma'teria *sf* (*FISICA*) matter; (*TECN, COMM*) material, matter *q*; (*disciplina*) subject; (*argomento*) subject matter, material; **~e prime** raw materials; **materi'ale** *ag* material; (*fig: grossolano*) rough, rude // *sm* material; (*insieme di strumenti etc*) equipment *q*, materials *pl*; **materia'lista, i, e** *ag* materialistic.

maternità *sf* motherhood, maternity; (*clinica*) maternity hospital.

ma'terno, a *ag* (*amore, cura etc*) maternal, motherly; (*nonno*) maternal; (*lingua, terra*) mother *cpd*.

ma'tita *sf* pencil.

ma'trice [ma'tritʃe] *sf* matrix; (*COMM*) counterfoil.

ma'tricola *sf* (*registro*) register; (*numero*) registration number; (*nell'università*) freshman, fresher.

ma'trigna [ma'triɲɲa] *sf* stepmother.

matrimoni'ale *ag* matrimonial, marriage *cpd*.

matri'monio *sm* marriage, matrimony;

(*durata*) marriage, married life; (*cerimonia*) wedding.

ma'trona *sf* (*fig*) matronly woman.

mat'tina *sf* morning; **matti'nata** *sf* morning; (*spettacolo*) matinée, afternoon performance; **mattini'ero, a** *ag*: **essere mattiniero** to be an early riser; **mat'tino** *sm* morning.

'matto, a *ag* mad, crazy; (*fig: falso*) false, imitation; (: *opaco*) matt, dull // *sm/f* madman/woman; **avere una voglia ~a di qc** to be dying for sth.

mat'tone *sm* brick.

matto'nella *sf* tile.

matu'rare *vi* (2) (*anche*: **~rsi**) (*frutta, grano*) to ripen; (*ascesso*) to come to a head; (*fig: persona, idea, ECON*) to mature // *vt* to ripen; to (make) mature.

maturità *sf* maturity; (*di frutta*) ripeness, maturity; (*INS*) school-leaving examination, ≈ GCE A-levels.

ma'turo, a *ag* mature; (*frutto*) ripe, mature.

mauso'leo *sm* mausoleum.

'mazza ['mattsa] *sf* (*bastone*) club; (*martello*) sledge-hammer; (*SPORT: da golf*) club; (: *da baseball, cricket*) bat.

'mazzo ['mattso] *sm* (*di fiori, chiavi etc*) bunch; (*di carte da gioco*) pack.

me *pronome* me; **~ stesso/a** myself; **sei bravo quanto ~** you are as clever as I (am) o as me.

M.E.C. [mek] *sm* (*abbr di* **Mercato Comune Europeo**) EEC.

mec'canico, a, ci, che *ag* mechanical // *sm* mechanic // *sf* mechanics *sg*; (*attività tecnologica*) mechanical engineering; (*meccanismo*) mechanism.

mecca'nismo *sm* mechanism.

me'daglia [me'daʎʎa] *sf* medal; **medagli'one** *sm* (*ARCHIT*) medallion; (*gioiello*) locket.

me'desimo, a *ag* same; (*in persona*): **io ~** I myself.

'media *sf vedi* **medio.**

medi'ano, a *ag* median; (*valore*) mean // *sm* (*CALCIO*) half-back.

medi'ante *prep* by means of.

medi'are *vt* (*fare da mediatore*) to act as mediator in; (*MAT*) to average.

media'tore, 'trice *sm/f* mediator; (*COMM*) middle man, agent.

mediazi'one [medjat'tsjone] *sf* mediation.

medica'mento *sm* medicine, drug.

medi'care *vt* to treat; (*ferita*) to dress; **medicazi'one** *sf* treatment, medication; dressing.

medi'cina [medi'tʃina] *sf* medicine; **~ legale** forensic medicine; **medici'nale** *ag* medicinal // *sm* drug, medicine.

'medico, a, ci, che *ag* medical // *sm* doctor; **~ generico** general practitioner, G.P.

medie'vale *ag* medieval.

'medio, a *ag* average; (*punto, ceto*) middle; (*altezza, statura*) medium // *sm* (*dito*) middle finger // *sf* average; (*MAT*) mean;

(*INS: voto*) end-of-term average.
medi'ocre *ag* mediocre, poor.
medioe'vale *ag* = **medievale**.
medio'evo *sm* Middle Ages *pl*.
medi'tare *vt* to ponder over, meditate on; (*progettare*) to plan, think out // *vi* to meditate; **meditazi'one** *sf* meditation.
mediter'raneo, a *ag* Mediterranean; **il (mare) M~** the Mediterranean (Sea).
me'dusa *sf* (*ZOOL*) jellyfish.
me'gafono *sm* megaphone.
'meglio ['mɛʎʎo] *av, ag inv* better; (*con senso superlativo*) best // *sm* (*la cosa migliore*): **il ~** the best (thing); **alla ~** as best one can; **andar di bene in ~** to get better and better; **fare del proprio ~** to do one's best; **per il ~** for the best; **aver la ~ su qd** to get the better of sb.
'mela *sf* apple; **~ cotogna** quince.
mela'grana *sf* pomegranate.
melan'zana [melan'dzana] *sf* aubergine.
me'lassa *sf* molasses *sg*, treacle.
me'lenso, a *ag* dull, stupid.
mel'lifluo, a *ag* (*peg*) sugary, honeyed.
'melma *sf* mud, mire.
'melo *sm* apple tree.
melo'dia *sf* melody; **me'lodico, a, ci, che** *ag* melodic; **melodi'oso, a** *ag* melodious.
melo'dramma, i *sm* melodrama.
me'lone *sm* (musk)melon.
'membra *sfpl* vedi **membro**.
mem'brana *sf* membrane.
'membro *sm* member; (*pl(f)* **~a**: *arto*) limb.
memo'rabile *ag* memorable.
memo'randum *sm inv* memorandum.
me'moria *sf* memory; **~e** *sfpl* (*opera autobiografica*) memoirs; **a ~** (*imparare, sapere*) by heart; **a ~ d'uomo** within living memory; **memori'ale** *sm* (*raccolta di memorie*) memoirs *pl*; (*DIR*) memorial.
mena'dito: a ~ *av* perfectly, thoroughly; **sapere qc a ~** to have sth at one's fingertips.
me'nare *vt* to lead; (*picchiare*) to hit, beat; (*dare: colpi*) to deal; **~ la coda** (*cane*) to wag its tail.
mendi'cante *sm/f* beggar.
mendi'care *vt* to beg for // *vi* to beg.
'meno *av* less; (*in frasi comparative*): **~ freddo che** not as cold as, less cold than; (*: seguito da nome, pronome*): **~ alto di** not as tall as, less tall than; **~ denaro di** less money than, not as much money as; (*in frasi superlative*): **il(la) ~ bravo(a)** the least clever; (*di temperatura*) below (zero), minus; (*MAT*) minus, less; (*l'ora*): **sono le 8 ~ un quarto** it's a quarter to eight // *ag inv* (*tempo, denaro*) less; (*errori, persone*) fewer // *prep* except (for) // *sm inv* (*la parte minore*): **il ~** the least; (*MAT*) minus; **i ~** (*la minoranza*) the minority; **a ~ che** *cong* unless; **fare a ~ di qc** (*privarsene*) to do without sth; (*rinunciarvi*) to give sth up; **fare a ~ di fumare** to give up smoking; **non potevo fare a ~ di ridere** I couldn't help laughing; **mille lire in ~**

a thousand lire less; **~ male** so much the better; thank goodness.
meno'mare *vt* (*danneggiare*) to maim, disable; (*diminuire: meriti*) to diminish, lessen.
meno'pausa *sf* menopause.
'mensa *sf* (*locale*) canteen; (*: MIL*) mess; (*: nelle università*) refectory.
men'sile *ag* monthly // *sm* (*periodico*) monthly (magazine); (*stipendio*) monthly salary.
'mensola *sf* bracket; (*ripiano*) shelf; (*ARCHIT*) corbel.
'menta *sf* mint; (*anche: ~ peperita*) peppermint.
men'tale *ag* mental; **mentalità** *sf inv* mentality.
'mente *sf* mind; **imparare/sapere qc a ~** to learn/know sth by heart; **avere in ~ qc** to have sth in mind; **passare di ~ a qd** to slip sb's mind.
men'tire *vi* to lie.
'mento *sm* chin.
'mentre *cong* (*temporale*) while; (*avversativo*) whereas.
menzio'nare [mentsjo'nare] *vt* to mention.
menzi'one [men'tsjone] *sf* mention; **fare ~ di** to mention.
men'zogna [men'tsɔɲa] *sf* lie.
mera'viglia [mera'viʎʎa] *sf* amazement, wonder; (*persona, cosa*) marvel, wonder; **a ~** perfectly, wonderfully; **meravigli'are** *vt* to amaze, astonish; **meravigliarsi (di)** to marvel (at); (*stupirsi*) to be amazed (at), be astonished (at); **meravigli'oso, a** *ag* wonderful, marvellous.
mer'cante *sm* merchant; **~ di cavalli** horse dealer; **mercanteggi'are** *vt* (*onore, voto*) to sell // *vi* to bargain, haggle; **mercan'tile** *ag* commercial, mercantile, merchant *cpd* // *sm* (*nave*) merchantman; **mercan'zia** *sf* merchandise, goods *pl*.
mer'cato *sm* market; **~ dei cambi** exchange market; **M~ Comune (Europeo)** (European) Common Market; **~ nero** black market.
'merce ['mɛrtʃe] *sf* goods *pl*, merchandise; **~ deperibile** perishable goods *pl*.
mercé [mer'tʃe] *sf* mercy.
merce'nario, a [mertʃe'narjo] *ag, sm* mercenary.
merce'ria [mertʃe'ria] *sf* (*bottega, articoli*) haberdashery.
mercoledì *sm inv* Wednesday; **di** *o* **il ~** on Wednesdays; **~ delle Ceneri** Ash Wednesday.
mer'curio *sm* mercury.
'merda *sf* (*fam!*) shit (!).
me'renda *sf* afternoon snack.
meridi'ano, a *ag* meridian; midday *cpd*, noonday // *sm* meridian // *sf* (*orologio*) sundial.
meridio'nale *ag* southern // *sm/f* southerner.
meridi'one *sm* south.
me'ringa, ghe *sf* (*CUC*) meringue.
meri'tare *vt* to deserve, merit.

meri'tevole ag worthy.

'merito sm merit; (valore) worth; **in ~ a** as regards, with regard to; **dare ~ a qd di** to give sb credit for; **meri'torio, a** ag praiseworthy.

mer'letto sm lace.

'merlo sm (ZOOL) blackbird; (ARCHIT) battlement.

mer'luzzo [mer'luttso] sm (ZOOL) cod.

mes'chino, a [mes'kino] ag wretched; (scarso) scanty, poor; (persona: gretta) mean; (: limitata) narrow-minded, petty.

'mescita ['meʃʃita] sf public house.

mesco'lanza [mesko'lantsa] sf mixture.

mesco'lare vt to mix; (colori) to blend; (mettere in disordine) to mix up, muddle up; (carte) to shuffle; **~rsi** vr to mix; to blend; to get mixed up; (fig): **~rsi in** to get mixed up in, meddle in.

'mese sm month.

'messa sf (REL) mass; (il mettere): **~ in moto** starting; **~ in piega** set; **~ a punto** (TECN) adjustment; (AUT) tuning; (fig) clarification; **~ in scena** vedi **messinscena**.

messag'gero [messad'dʒero] sm messenger.

mes'saggio [mes'saddʒo] sm message.

mes'sale sm (REL) missal.

'messe sf harvest.

Mes'sia sm inv (REL): **il ~** the Messiah.

'Messico sm: **il ~** Mexico.

messin'scena [messin'ʃɛna] sf (TEATRO) production.

'messo, a pp di **mettere** // sm messenger.

mesti'ere sm (professione) job; (: manuale) trade; (: artigianale) craft; (fig: abilità nel lavoro) skill, technique; **essere del ~** to know the tricks of the trade.

'mesto, a ag sad, melancholy.

'mestola sf (CUC) ladle; (EDIL) trowel.

'mestolo sm (CUC) ladle.

mestruazi'one [mestruat'tsjone] sf menstruation.

'meta sf destination; (fig) aim, goal.

metà sf inv half; (punto di mezzo) middle; **dividere qc a o per ~** to divide sth in half, halve sth; **fare a ~** (di qc con qd) to go halves (with sb in sth); **a ~ prezzo** at half price; **a ~ strada** halfway.

metabo'lismo sm metabolism.

meta'fisica sf metaphysics sg.

me'tafora sf metaphor.

me'tallico, a, ci, che ag (di metallo) metal cpd; (splendore etc) metallic.

me'tallo sm metal; **metallur'gia** sf metallurgy.

meta'morfosi sf metamorphosis.

me'tano sm methane.

me'teora sf meteor.

meteo'rite sm meteorite.

meteorolo'gia [meteorolo'dʒia] sf meteorology; **meteoro'logico, a, ci, che** ag meteorological, weather cpd.

me'ticcio, a, ci, ce [me'tittʃo] sm/f half-caste, half-breed.

metico'loso, a ag meticulous.

me'todico, a, ci, che ag methodical.

'metodo sm method; (manuale) tutor, manual.

'metrico, a, ci, che ag metric; (POESIA) metrical // sf metrics sg.

'metro sm metre; (nastro) tape measure; (asta) (metre) rule.

me'tropoli sf metropolis.

metropoli'tano, a ag metropolitan // sm (city) policeman // sf underground, subway.

'mettere vt to put; (abito) to put on; (: portare) to wear; (installare: telefono) to put in; (fig: provocare): **~ fame/allegria a qd** to make sb hungry/happy; (supporre): **mettiamo che ...** let's suppose o say that ... ; **~rsi** vr (disporsi: faccenda) to turn out; **~rsi a sedere** to sit down; **~rsi a letto** to get into bed; (per malattia) to take to one's bed; **~rsi il cappello** to put on one's hat; **~rsi a** (cominciare) to begin to, start to; **~rsi al lavoro** to set to work; **~rci** **~rci molta cura/molto tempo** to take a lot of care/a lot of time; **ci ho messo 3 ore per venire** it's taken me 3 hours to get here; **~ a tacere qd/qc** to keep sb/sth quiet; **~ su casa** to set up house; **~ su un negozio** to start a shop; **~ via** to put away.

mez'zadro [med'dzadro] sm (AGR) sharecropper.

mezza'luna [meddza'luna] sf half-moon; (dell'islamismo) crescent; (coltello) (semicircular) chopping knife.

mezza'nino [meddza'nino] sm mezzanine (floor).

mez'zano, a [med'dzano] ag (medio) average, medium // sm/f (intermediario) go-between; (ruffiano) pimp.

mezza'notte [meddza'nɔtte] sf midnight.

'mezzo, a ['mɛddzo] ag half; **un ~ litro/panino** half a litre/roll // av half-; **~ morto** half-dead // sm (metà) half; (parte centrale: di strada etc) middle; (per raggiungere un fine) means sg; (veicolo) vehicle; (nell'indicare l'ora): **le nove e ~** half past nine; **mezzogiorno e ~** half past twelve; **~i** smpl (possibilità economiche) means; **di ~a età** middle-aged; **di ~** middle, in the middle; **andarci di ~** (patir danno) to suffer; **levarsi o togliersi di ~** to get out of the way; **in ~ a** in the middle of; **per o a ~ di** by means of; **~i di comunicazione di massa** mass media pl; **~i pubblici** public transport sg; **~i di trasporto** means of transport.

mezzogi'orno [meddzo'dʒorno] sm midday, noon; (GEO) south; **a ~** at 12 (o'clock) o midday o noon; **il ~ d'Italia** southern Italy.

mez'z'ora, mez'zora [med'dzora] sf half-hour, half an hour.

mi pronome (dav lo, la, li, le, ne diventa **me**) (oggetto) me; (complemento di termine) to me; (riflessivo) myself // sm (MUS) E; (: solfeggiando la scala) mi.

'mia vedi **mio.**

miago'lare *vi* to miaow, mew.
'**mica** *sf* (*CHIM*) mica // *av* (*fam*): **non ...**
~ **not ... at all; non sono** ~ **stanco** I'm
not a bit tired; ~ **male** not bad.
'**miccia, ce** ['mittʃa] *sf* fuse.
micidi'ale [mitʃi'djale] *ag* fatal;
(*dannosissimo*) deadly.
'**microbo** *sm* microbe.
mi'crofono *sm* microphone.
micros'copico, a, ci, che *ag*
microscopic.
micros'copio *sm* microscope.
mi'dollo, *pl*(*f*) ~**a** *sm* (*ANAT*) marrow.
'**mie, mi'ei** *vedi* **mio.**
mi'ele *sm* honey.
mi'etere *vt* (*AGR*) to reap, harvest; (*fig:
vite*) to take, claim.
migli'aio [miʎ'ʎajo], *pl*(*f*) ~**a** *sm*
thousand; **un** ~ (**di**) about a thousand; a
~**a** by the thousand, in thousands.
'**miglio** ['miʎʎo] *sm* (*BOT*) millet; (*pl*(*f*)
~**a:** *unità di misura*) mile; ~ **marino** *o*
nautico nautical mile.
miglio'rare [miʎʎo'rare] *vt, vi* to
improve.
migli'ore [miʎ'ʎore] *ag* (*comparativo*)
better; (*superlativo*) best // *sm:* **il** ~ the
best (thing) // *sm/f.* **il(la)** ~ the best
(person); **il miglior vino di questa
regione** the best wine in this area.
'**mignolo** ['miɲɲolo] *sm* (*ANAT*) little
finger, pinkie; (: *dito del piede*) little toe.
mi'grare *vi* to migrate; **migrazi'one** *sf*
migration.
'**mila** *pl di* **mille.**
Mi'lano *sf* Milan.
miliar'dario, a *sm/f* millionaire.
mili'ardo *sm* milliard, thousand million.
mili'are *ag:* **pietra** ~ milestone.
mili'one *sm* million; **un** ~ **di lire** a
million lire.
mili'tante *ag, sm/f* militant.
mili'tare *vi* (*MIL*) to be a soldier, serve;
(*fig: in un partito*) to be a militant // *ag*
military // *sm* serviceman; ~ **a favore di**
(*sog: argomenti etc*) to militate in favour
of; **fare il** ~ to do one's military service.
'**milite** *sm* soldier.
mi'lizia [mi'littsja] *sf* (*corpo armato*)
militia.
millanta'tore, 'trice *sm/f* boaster.
'**mille** *num* (*pl* **mila**) a *o* one thousand;
dieci mila ten thousand.
mille'foglie [mille'fɔʎʎe] *sm inv* (*CUC*)
cream *o* vanilla slice.
mil'lennio *sm* millennium.
millepi'edi *sm inv* centipede.
mil'lesimo, a *ag, sm* thousandth.
milli'grammo *sm* milligram(me). .
mil'limetro *sm* millimetre.
'**milza** ['miltsa] *sf* (*ANAT*) spleen.
mimetiz'zare [mimetid'dzare] *vt* to
camouflage; ~**rsi** *vr* to camouflage o.s.
'**mimica** *sf* (*arte*) mime.
'**mimo** *sm* (*attore, componimento*) mime.
mi'mosa *sf* mimosa.
'**mina** *sf* (*esplosiva*) mine; (*di matita*) lead.

mi'naccia, ce [mi'nattʃa] *sf* threat;
minacci'are *vt* to threaten; **minacci'oso, a** *ag* threatening.
mi'nare *vt* (*MIL*) to mine; (*fig*) to
undermine.
mina'tore *sm* miner.
mina'torio, a *ag* threatening.
mine'rale *ag, sm* mineral; **mineralo'gia**
sf mineralogy.
mine'rario, a *ag* (*delle miniere*) mining;
(*dei minerali*) ore *cpd.*
mi'nestra *sf* soup; ~ **in brodo** noodle
soup; **mines'trone** *sm* thick vegetable
and pasta soup.
mingher'lino, a [minger'lino] *ag* thin,
slender.
minia'tura *sf* miniature.
mini'era *sf* mine.
'**minimo, a** *ag* minimum, least, slightest;
(*piccolissimo*) very small, slight; (*il più
basso*) lowest, minimum // *sm* minimum;
al ~ at least; **girare al** ~ (*AUT*) to idle.
minis'tero *sm* (*POL, REL*) ministry;
(*governo*) government; ~ **delle Finanze**
Ministry of Finance, ≈ Treasury.
mi'nistro *sm* (*POL, REL*) minister; ~ **delle
Finanze** Minister of Finance, ≈
Chancellor of the Exchequer.
mino'ranza [mino'rantsa] *sf* minority.
mino'rato, a *ag* handicapped // *sm/f*
physically (*o* mentally) handicapped
person.
mi'nore *ag* (*comparativo*) less; (*più
piccolo*) smaller; (*numero*) lower;
(*inferiore*) lower, inferior; (*meno
importante*) minor; (*più giovane*) younger;
(*superlativo*) least; smallest; lowest;
youngest // *sm/f* (*minorenne*) minor,
person under age.
mino'renne *ag* under age // *sm/f* minor,
person under age.
mi'nuscolo, a *ag* (*scrittura, carattere*)
small; (*piccolissimo*) tiny // *sf* small letter.
mi'nuta *sf* rough copy, draft.
mi'nuto, a *ag* tiny, minute; (*pioggia*) fine;
(*corporatura*) delicate, fine; (*lavoro*)
detailed // *sm* (*unità di misura*) minute; **al**
~ (*COMM*) retail.
'**mio, 'mia, mi'ei, 'mie** *det:* **il** ~, **la mia**
etc my // *pronome:* **il** ~, **la mia** *etc* mine;
i miei my family; **un** ~ **amico** a friend
of mine.
'miope *ag* short-sighted.
'**mira** *sf* (*anche fig*) aim; (*bersaglio*) target;
(*congegno di mira*) sight; **prendere la** ~
to take aim; **prendere di** ~ **qd** (*fig*) to
pick on sb.
mi'rabile *ag* admirable, wonderful.
mi'racolo *sm* miracle; **miraco'loso, a** *ag*
miraculous.
mi'raggio [mi'raddʒo] *sm* mirage.
mi'rare *vi:* ~ **a** to aim at.
mi'rino *sm* (*TECN*) sight; (*FOT*) viewer,
viewfinder.
mir'tillo *sm* bilberry, whortleberry.
'**mirto** *sm* myrtle.
mi'santropo, a *sm/f* misanthropist.

mi'scela [miʃ'ʃela] *sf* mixture; (*di caffè*) blend.

miscel'lanea [miʃʃel'lanea] *sf* miscellany.

'mischia ['miskja] *sf* scuffle.

mischi'are [mis'kjare] *vt*, **~rsi** *vr* to mix, blend.

mis'cuglio [mis'kuʎʎo] *sm* mixture, hotchpotch, jumble.

mise'rabile *ag* (*infelice*) miserable, wretched; (*povero*) poverty-stricken; (*di scarso valore*) miserable.

mi'seria *sf* extreme poverty; (*infelicità*) misery; **~e** *sfpl* (*del mondo etc*) misfortunes, troubles; **porca ~!** (*fam*), **~ ladra!** (*fam*) blast!, damn!

miseri'cordia *sf* mercy, pity.

'misero, a *ag* miserable, wretched; (*povero*) poverty-stricken; (*insufficiente*) miserable.

mis'fatto *sm* misdeed, crime.

mi'sogino [mi'zɔdʒino] *sm* misogynist.

'missile *sm* missile.

missio'nario, a *ag, sm/f* missionary.

missi'one *sf* mission.

misteri'oso, a *ag* mysterious.

mis'tero *sm* mystery.

'mistico, a, ci, che *ag* mystic(al) // *sm* mystic.

mistifi'care *vt* to fool, bamboozle.

'misto, a *ag* mixed; (*scuola*) mixed, coeducational // *sm* mixture.

mis'tura *sf* mixture.

mi'sura *sf* measure; (*misurazione, dimensione*) measurement; (*taglia*) size; (*provvedimento*) measure, step; (*moderazione*) moderation; (*MUS*) time; (: *divisione*) bar; (*fig: limite*) bounds *pl*, limit; **a ~ che** as; **su ~** made to measure.

misu'rare *vt* (*ambiente, stoffa*) to measure; (*terreno*) to survey; (*abito*) to try on; (*pesare*) to weigh; (*fig: parole etc*) to weigh up; (: *spese, cibo*) to limit; **~rsi** *vr*: **~rsi con qd** to have a confrontation with sb; to compete with sb; **misu'rato, a** *ag* (*ponderato*) measured; (*prudente*) cautious; (*moderato*) moderate; **misurazi'one** *sf* measuring; (*di terreni*) surveying.

'mite *ag* mild; (*prezzo*) moderate, reasonable.

miti'gare *vt* to mitigate, lessen; (*lenire*) to soothe, relieve; **~rsi** *vr* (*odio*) to subside; (*tempo*) to become milder.

'mito *sm* myth; **mitolo'gia, 'gie** *sf* mythology.

'mitra *sf* (*REL*) mitre // *sm inv* (*arma*) submachine gun.

mitraglia'trice [mitraʎʎa'tritʃe] *sf* machine gun.

mit'tente *sm/f* sender.

'mobile *ag* mobile; (*parte di macchina*) moving; (*DIR: bene*) movable, personal // *sm* (*arredamento*) piece of furniture; **~i** *smpl* furniture *sg*.

mo'bilia *sf* furniture.

mobili'are *ag* (*DIR*) personal, movable.

mo'bilio *sm* = **mobilia.**

mobilità *sf* mobility.

mobili'tare *vt* to mobilize; **mobilitazi'one** *sf* mobilization.

mocas'sino *sm* moccasin.

'moccolo *sm* (*di candela*) candle-end; (*fam: bestemmia*) oath; (: *moccio*) snot; **reggere il ~** to play gooseberry.

'moda *sf* fashion; **alla ~**, **di ~** fashionable, in fashion.

modalità *sf inv* formality.

mo'della *sf* model.

model'lare *vt* (*creta*) to model, shape; **~rsi** *vr*: **~rsi su** to model o.s. on.

mo'dello *sm* model; (*stampo*) mould // *ag inv* model *cpd*; **~ di carta** (*SARTORIA*) (paper) pattern.

mode'rare *vt* to moderate; **~rsi** *vr* to restrain o.s.; **mode'rato, a** *ag* moderate.

modera'tore, 'trice *sm/f* moderator.

moderazi'one [moderat'tsjone] *sf* moderation.

mo'derno, a *ag* modern.

mo'destia *sf* modesty.

mo'desto, a *ag* modest.

'modico, a, ci, che *ag* reasonable, moderate.

mo'difica, che *sf* modification.

modifi'care *vt* to modify, alter; **~rsi** *vr* to alter, change.

'modo *sm* way, manner; (*mezzo*) means, way; (*occasione*) opportunity; (*LING*) mood; (*MUS*) mode; **~i** *smpl* manners; **a suo ~, a ~ suo** in his own way; **ad o in ogni ~** anyway; **di o in ~ che** so that; **in ~ da** so as to; **in tutti i ~i** at all costs; (*comunque sia*) anyway; (*in ogni caso*) in any case; **in qualche ~** somehow or other; **~ di dire** turn of phrase; **per ~ di dire** so to speak.

modu'lare *vt* to modulate; **modulazi'one** *sf* modulation; **modulazione di frequenza** frequency modulation.

'modulo *sm* form; (*lunare, di comando*) module.

'mogano *sm* mahogany.

'mogio, a, gi, gie ['mɔdʒo] *ag* down in the dumps, dejected.

'moglie ['moʎʎe] *sf* wife.

mo'ine *sfpl* cajolery *sg*; (*leziosità*) affectation *sg*.

'mola *sf* millstone; (*utensile abrasivo*) grindstone.

mo'lare *vt* to grind // *ag* (*pietra*) mill *cpd* // *sm* (*dente*) molar.

'mole *sf* mass; (*dimensioni*) size; (*edificio grandioso*) massive structure.

mo'lecola *sf* molecule.

moles'tare *vt* to bother, annoy; **mo'lestia** *sf* annoyance, bother; **recar molestia a qd** to bother sb; **mo'lesto, a** *ag* annoying.

'molla *sf* spring; **~e** *sfpl* tongs.

mol'lare *vt* to release, let go; (*NAUT*) to ease; (*fig: ceffone*) to give // *vi* (*cedere*) to give in.

'molle *ag* soft; (*peg*) flabby, limp; (: *fig*) weak, feeble; (*bagnato*) wet.

mol'letta *sf* (*per capelli*) hairgrip; (*per*

panni stesi) clothes peg; ~e *sfpl* (*per zucchero*) tongs.

mol'lezza [mol'lettsa] *sf* softness; flabbiness, limpness; weakness, feebleness; ~e *sfpl*: **vivere nelle ~e** to live in the lap of luxury.

'mollica, che *sf* crumb, soft part; ~**che** *sfpl* (*briciole*) crumbs.

mol'lusco, schi *sm* mollusc.

'molo *sm* mole, breakwater; jetty.

mol'teplice [mol'teplitʃe] *ag* (*formato di più elementi*) complex; (*numeroso*) numerous; (: *interessi, attività*) many, manifold; **molteplicità** *sf* multiplicity.

moltipli'care *vt* to multiply; ~**rsi** *vr* to multiply; to increase in number; **moltiplica'tore** *sm* multiplier; **moltiplicazi'one** *sf* multiplication.

molti'tudine *sf* multitude; **una ~ di** a vast number *o* a multitude of.

'molto, a *det* much, a lot of; (*con sostantivi al plurale*): ~**i(e)** many, a lot of; (*lungo: tempo*) long // *av* a lot; (*in frasi negative*) much; (*intensivo*) very // *pronome* much, a lot; ~**i(e)** *pronome pl* many, a lot; ~ **meglio** much *o* a lot better; ~ **buono** very good; **per ~ (tempo)** for a long time.

momen'taneo, a *ag* momentary, fleeting.

mo'mento *sm* moment; **capitare nel ~ buono** to come at the right time; **da un ~ all'altro** at any moment; (*all'improvviso*) suddenly; **al ~ di fare** just as I was (*o* you were *o* he was *etc*) doing; **per il ~** for the time being; **dal ~ che** ever since; (*dato che*) since.

'monaca, che *sf* nun.

'monaco, ci *sm* monk.

'Monaco *sf* Monaco, ~ **(di Baviera)** Munich.

mo'narca, chi *sm* monarch; **monar'chia** *sf* monarchy.

monas'tero *sm* (*di monaci*) monastery; (*di monache*) convent; **mo'nastico, a, ci, che** *ag* monastic.

'monco, a, chi, che *ag* maimed; (*fig*) incomplete; ~ **d'un braccio** one-armed.

mon'dana *sf* prostitute.

mon'dano, a *ag* (*anche fig*) worldly; (*dell'alta società*) society *cpd*; fashionable.

mon'dare *vt* (*frutta, patate*) to peel; (*piselli*) to shell; (*pulire*) to clean.

mondi'ale *ag* (*campionato, popolazione*) world *cpd*; (*influenza*) world-wide.

'mondo *sm* world; (*grande quantità*): **un ~ di** lots of, a host of; **il gran** *o* **bel ~** high society.

mo'nello, a *sm/f* street urchin; (*ragazzo vivace*) scamp, imp.

mo'neta *sf* coin; (*ECON: valuta*) currency; (*denaro spicciolo*) (small) change; ~ **estera** foreign currency; ~ **legale** legal tender; **mone'tario, a** *ag* monetary.

mongo'loide *ag, sm/f* (*med*) mongol.

'monito *sm* warning.

'monitor *sm inv* (*TECN, TV*) monitor.

mo'nocolo *sm* (*lente*) monocle, eyeglass.

monoco'lore *ag* (*POL*) one-party.

mono'gramma, i *sm* monogram.

mo'nologo, ghi *sm* monologue.

mono'piano *sm* monoplane.

mono'polio *sm* monopoly; **monopoliz-'zare** *vt* to monopolize.

mono'sillabo, a *ag* monosyllabic // *sm* monosyllable.

monoto'nia *sf* monotony.

mo'notono, a *ag* monotonous.

monsi'gnore [monsiɲ'ɲore] *sm* (*REL: titolo*) Your (*o* His) Grace.

mon'sone *sm* monsoon.

monta'carichi [monta'kariki] *sm inv* hoist, goods lift.

mon'taggio [mon'taddʒo] *sm* (*TECN*) assembly; (*CINEMA*) editing.

mon'tagna [mon'taɲɲa] *sf* mountain; (*zona montuosa*): **la ~** the mountains *pl*; ~**e russe** roller coaster *sg*, big dipper *sg*; **monta'gnoso, a** *ag* mountainous.

monta'naro, a *ag* mountain *cpd* // *sm/f* mountain dweller.

mon'tano, a *ag* mountain *cpd*; alpine.

mon'tare *vt* to go (*o* come) up; (*apparecchiatura*) to set up, assemble; (*CUC*) to whip; (*ZOOL*) to cover; (*incastonare*) to mount, set; (*CINEMA*) to edit // *vi* (2) to go (*o* come) up; (*a cavallo*): ~ **bene/male** to ride well/badly; (*aumentare di livello, volume*) to rise; ~**rsi** *vr* to become big-headed; ~ **qc** to exaggerate sth; ~ **qd** *o* **la testa a qd** to turn sb's head; ~ **in bicicletta/treno** to get on a bicycle/train; ~ **a cavallo** to get on *o* mount a horse.

monta'tura *sf* assembling *q*; (*di occhiali*) frames *pl*; (*di gioiello*) mounting, setting; (*fig*): ~ **pubblicitaria** publicity stunt.

'monte *sm* mountain; **a ~** upstream; **mandare a ~ qc** to upset sth, cause sth to fail; **il M~ Bianco** Mont Blanc; ~ **dei pegni** pawnshop.

mon'tone *sm* (*ZOOL*) ram.

montu'oso, a *ag* mountainous.

monu'mento *sm* monument.

'mora *sf* (*del rovo*) blackberry; (*del gelso*) mulberry; (*DIR*) delay; (: *somma*) arrears *pl*.

mo'rale *ag* moral // *sf* (*scienza*) ethics *sg*, moral philosophy; (*complesso di norme*) moral standards *pl*, morality; (*condotta*) morals *pl*; (*insegnamento morale*) moral // *sm* morale; **moralità** *sf* morality; (*condotta*) morals *pl*.

'morbido, a *ag* soft; (*pelle*) soft, smooth.

mor'billo *sm* (*MED*) measles *sg*.

'morbo *sm* disease.

mor'boso, a *ag* (*fig*) morbid.

'morchia ['mɔrkja] *sf* (*residuo grasso*) dregs *pl*; oily deposit.

mor'dace [mor'datʃe] *ag* biting, cutting.

mor'dente *sm* (*fig*) push, drive.

'mordere *vt* to bite; (*addentare*) to bite into; (*corrodere*) to eat into.

mor'fina *sf* morphine.

mori'bondo, a *ag* dying, moribund.

morige'rato, a [moridʒe'rato] *ag* of good morals.

mo'rire *vi* (2) to die; (*abitudine, civiltà*) to die out; ~ **di fame** to die of hunger; (*fig*) to be starving; ~ **di noia** to be bored to death; **fa un caldo da** ~ it's terribly hot.

mormo'rare *vi* to murmur; (*brontolare*) to grumble; **mormo'rio** *sm* murmuring; grumbling.

'moro, a *ag* dark(-haired); dark(-complexioned); **i M~i** *smpl* (*STORIA*) the Moors.

mo'roso, a *ag* in arrears // *sm/f* (*fam: innamorato*) sweetheart.

'morsa *sf* vice.

morsi'care *vt* to nibble (at), gnaw (at); (*sog: insetto*) to bite.

'morso, a *pp di* **mordere** // *sm* bite; (*di insetto*) sting; (*parte della briglia*) bit; **~i della fame** pangs of hunger.

mor'taio *sm* mortar.

mor'tale *ag, sm* mortal; **mortalità** *sf* mortality, death rate.

'morte *sf* death.

mortifi'care *vt* to mortify.

'morto, a *pp di* **morire** // *ag* dead // *sm/f* dead man/woman; **i ~i** the dead; **fare il** ~ (*nell'acqua*) to float on one's back.

mor'torio *sm* (*anche fig*) funeral.

mo'saico, ci *sm* mosaic.

'mosca, sche *sf* fly; ~ **cieca** blind-man's-buff.

'Mosca *sf* Moscow.

mos'cato *sm* muscatel (wine).

mosce'rino [moʃʃe'rino] *sm* midge, gnat.

mos'chea [mos'kɛa] *sf* mosque.

mos'chetto [mos'ketto] *sm* musket.

'moscio, a, sci, sce ['mɔʃʃo] *ag* (*fig*) lifeless.

mos'cone *sm* (*ZOOL*) bluebottle; (*barca*) pedalo; (: *a remi*) kind of pedalo with oars.

'mossa *sf* movement; (*nel gioco*) move.

'mosso, a *pp di* **muovere** // *ag* (*mare*) rough; (*capelli*) wavy; (*FOT*) blurred; (*ritmo, prosa*) animated.

mos'tarda *sf* mustard.

'mostra *sf* exhibition, show; (*ostentazione*) show; **in** ~ on show; **far** ~ **di** (*fingere*) to pretend; **far** ~ **di sé** to show off.

mos'trare *vt* to show // *vi*: ~ **di fare** to pretend to do; **~rsi** *vr* to appear.

'mostro *sm* monster; **mostru'oso, a** *ag* monstrous.

mo'tel *sm inv* motel.

moti'vare *vt* (*causare*) to cause; (*giustificare*) to justify, account for; **motivazi'one** *sf* justification; motive; (*PSIC*) motivation.

mo'tivo *sm* (*causa*) reason, cause; (*movente*) motive; (*letterario*) (central) theme; (*disegno*) motif, design, pattern; (*MUS*) motif; **per quale** ~? why?, for what reason?

'moto *sm* (*anche FISICA*) motion; (*movimento, gesto*) movement; (*esercizio fisico*) exercise; (*sommossa*) rising, revolt; (*commozione*) feeling, impulse // *sf inv* (*motocicletta*) motor-bike; **mettere in** ~

to set in motion; (*AUT*) to start up.

motoci'cletta [mototʃi'kletta] *sf* motorcycle; **motoci'clismo** *sm* motorcycling, motorcycle racing; **motoci'clista, i, e** *sm/f* motorcyclist.

mo'tore, 'trice *ag* motor; (*TECN*) driving // ~ *sm* engine, motor; **a** ~ motor *cpd*, power-driven; ~ **a combustione interna/a reazione** internal combustion/jet engine; **moto'rino** *sm* moped; **motorino di avviamento** (*AUT*) starter; **motoriz'zato, a** *ag* (*truppe*) motorized; (*persona*) having a car *o* transport.

motos'cafo *sm* motorboat.

mot'teggio [mot'teddʒo] *sm* banter.

'motto *sm* (*battuta scherzosa*) witty remark; (*frase emblematica*) motto, maxim.

mo'vente *sm* motive.

movimen'tare *vt* to liven up.

movi'mento *sm* movement; (*fig*) activity, hustle and bustle; (*MUS*) tempo, movement.

mozi'one [mot'tsjone] *sf* (*POL*) motion.

moz'zare [mot'tsare] *vt* to cut off; (*coda*) to dock; ~ **il fiato** *o* **il respiro a qd** (*fig*) to take sb's breath away.

mozza'rella [mottsa'rɛlla] *sf* mozzarella (*a moist Neapolitan curd cheese*).

mozzi'cone [mottsi'kone] *sm* stub, butt, end; (*anche*: ~ **di sigaretta**) cigarette end.

'mozzo *sm* ['mɔddzo] (*MECCANICA*) hub; ['mottso] (*NAUT*) ship's boy; ~ **di stalla** stable boy.

'mucca, che *sf* cow.

'mucchio ['mukkjo] *sm* pile, heap; (*fig*): **un** ~ **di** lots of, heaps of.

'muco, chi *sm* mucus.

mu'cosa *sf* mucous membrane.

'muffa *sf* mould, mildew.

mug'gire [mud'dʒire] *vi* (*vacca*) to low, moo; (*toro*) to bellow; (*fig*) to roar; **mug-'gito** *sm* low, moo; bellow; roar.

mu'ghetto [mu'getto] *sm* lily of the valley.

mu'gnaio, a [muɲ'najo] *sm/f* miller.

mugo'lare *vi* (*cane*) to whimper, whine; (*fig: persona*) to moan.

muli'nare *vi* to whirl, spin (round and round).

muli'nello *sm* (*moto vorticoso*) eddy, whirl; (*per aria*) ventilating fan; (*di canna da pesca*) reel; (*NAUT*) windlass.

mu'lino *sm* mill; ~ **a vento** windmill.

'mulo *sm* mule.

'multa *sf* fine; **mul'tare** *vt* to fine.

multico'lore *ag* multicoloured.

'multiplo, a *ag, sm* multiple.

'mummia *sf* mummy.

'mungere ['mundʒere] *vt* (*anche fig*) to milk.

munici'pale [munitʃi'pale] *ag* municipal; town *cpd*.

muni'cipio [muni'tʃipjo] *sm* town council, corporation; (*edificio*) town hall.

mu'nire vt: ~ qc/qd di to equip sth/sb with.

munizi'oni [munit'tsjoni] sfpl (MIL) ammunition sg.

'munto, a pp di **mungere**.

mu'overe vt to move; (ruota, macchina) to drive; (sollevare: questione, obiezione) to raise, bring up; (: accusa) to make, bring forward; ~rsi vr to move; **muoviti!** hurry up!, get a move on!

'mura sfpl vedi **muro**.

mu'raglia [mu'raʎʎa] sf (high) wall.

mu'rale ag wall cpd; mural.

mu'rare vt (persona, porta) to wall up.

mura'tore sm mason; bricklayer.

'muro sm wall; ~**a** sfpl (cinta cittadina) walls; **a ~ wall** cpd; (armadio etc) built-in; ~ **del suono** sound barrier.

'muschio ['muskjo] sm (ZOOL) musk; (BOT) moss.

musco'lare ag muscular, muscle cpd.

'muscolo sm (ANAT) muscle.

mu'seo sm museum.

museru'ola sf muzzle.

'musica sf music; **scrivere una ~** to write a piece of music; ~ **da ballo/camera** dance/chamber music; **musi'cale** ag musical; **musi'cista, i, e** sm/f musician.

'muso sm muzzle; (di auto, aereo) nose; **tenere il ~** to sulk; **mu'sone, a** sm/f sulky person.

'mussola sf muslin.

'muta sf (ZOOL) moulting; (: di serpenti) sloughing; (cambio) change; (di sentinella) relief; (per immersioni subacquee) diving suit; (gruppo di cani) pack.

muta'mento sm change.

mu'tande sfpl (da uomo) (under)pants; **mutan'dine** sfpl (da donna, bambino) pants; **mutandine di plastica** plastic pants.

mu'tare vt, vi (2) to change, alter; **mutazi'one** sf change, alteration; (BIOL) mutation; **mu'tevole** ag changeable.

muti'lare vt to mutilate, maim; (fig) to mutilate, deface; **muti'lato, a** sm/f disabled person (through loss of limbs); **mutilazi'one** sf mutilation.

mu'tismo sm (MED) mutism; (atteggiamento) (stubborn) silence.

'muto, a ag (MED) dumb; (emozione, dolore, CINEMA) silent; (LING) silent, mute; (carta geografica) blank; ~ **per lo stupore** etc speechless with amazement etc.

'mutua sf (anche: **cassa ~**) health insurance scheme.

mutu'are vt (fig) to borrow.

mutu'ato, a sm/f member of a health insurance scheme.

'mutuo, a ag (reciproco) mutual // sm (ECON) (long-term) loan.

N

N. (abbr di nord) N.

'nacchere ['nakkere] sfpl castanets.

'nafta sf naphtha; (per motori diesel) diesel oil.

'naia sf (ZOOL) cobra; (MIL) slang term for national service.

'nailon sm nylon.

'nanna sf (linguaggio infantile): **andare a ~** to go bye-byes.

'nano, a ag, sm/f dwarf.

napole'tano, a ag, sm/f Neapolitan.

'Napoli sf Naples.

'nappa sf tassel.

nar'ciso [nar'tʃizo] sm narcissus.

nar'cosi sf narcosis.

nar'cotico, ci sm narcotic.

na'rice [na'ritʃe] sf nostril.

nar'rare vt to tell the story of, recount; **narra'tivo, a** ag narrative // sf (branca letteraria) fiction; **narra'tore, 'trice** sm/f narrator; **narrazi'one** sf narration; (racconto) story, tale.

na'sale ag nasal.

'nascere ['naʃʃere] vi (2) (bambino) to be born; (pianta) to come o spring up; (fiume) to rise, have its source; (sole) to rise; (dente) to come through; (fig: derivare, conseguire): ~ **da** to arise from, be born out of; **è nata nel 1952** she was born in 1952; **'nascita** sf birth.

nas'condere vt to hide, conceal; ~rsi vr to hide; **nascon'diglio** sm hiding place; **nascon'dino** sm (gioco) hide-and-seek; **nas'costo, a** pp di **nascondere** // ag hidden; **di nascosto** secretly.

na'sello sm (ZOOL) hake.

'naso sm nose.

'nastro sm ribbon; (magnetico, isolante, SPORT) tape; ~ **adesivo** adhesive tape; ~ **dattilografico** typewriter ribbon; ~ **trasportatore** conveyor belt.

nas'turzio [nas'turtsjo] sm nasturtium.

na'tale ag of one's birth // sm (REL): **N~** Christmas; (giorno della nascita) birthday; **natalità** sf birth rate; **nata'lizio, a** ag (del Natale) Christmas cpd; (di nascita) of one's birth.

na'tante ag floating // sm craft inv, boat.

'natica, che sf (ANAT) buttock.

na'tio, a, 'tii, 'tie ag native.

Nativi'tà sf (REL) Nativity.

na'tivo, a ag, sm/f native.

'nato, a pp di **nascere** // ag: **un attore ~** a born actor; ~**a Pieri** née Pieri.

na'tura sf nature; **pagare in ~** to pay in kind; ~ **morta** still life.

natu'rale ag natural; **natura'lezza** sf naturalness; **natura'lista, i, e** sm/f naturalist.

naturaliz'zare [naturalid'dzare] vt to naturalize.

natural'mente av naturally; (certamente, sì) of course.

naufra'gare vi (nave) to be wrecked;

(*persona*) to be shipwrecked; (*fig*) to fall through; **nau'fragio** *sm* shipwreck; (*fig*) ruin, failure; **'naufrago, ghi** *sm* castaway, shipwreck victim.

'nausea *sf* nausea; **nausea'bondo, a** *ag* nauseating, sickening; **nause'are** *vt* to nauseate, make (feel) sick.

'nautico, a, ci, che *ag* nautical // *sf* (art of) navigation.

na'vale *ag* naval.

na'vata *sf* (*anche:* ~ **centrale**) nave; (*anche:* ~ **laterale**) aisle.

'nave *sf* ship, vessel; ~ **cisterna** tanker; ~ **da guerra** warship; ~ **spaziale** spaceship.

na'vetta *sf* shuttle; (*servizio di collegamento*) shuttle (service).

navi'cella [navi'tʃella] *sf* (*di aerostato*) gondola.

navi'gabile *ag* navigable.

navi'gare *vi* to sail; **navigazi'one** *sf* navigation.

na'viglio [na'viʎʎo] *sm* fleet, ships *pl*; (*canale artificiale*) canal; ~ **da pesca** fishing fleet.

nazio'nale [nattsjo'nale] *ag* national // *sf* (*SPORT*) national team; **naziona'lismo** *sm* nationalism; **nazionalità** *sf inv* nationality; **nazionaliz'zare** *vt* to nationalize.

nazi'one [nat'tsjone] *sf* nation.

ne *pronome* of him/her/it/them; about him/her/it/them; ~ **riconosco la voce** I recognize his (*o* her) voice; **non parliamone più!** let's not talk about him (*o* her *o* it *o* them) any more!; (*con valore partitivo*): **hai dei libri?** — **sì,** ~ **ho** have you any books? — yes, I have (some); **hai del pane?** — **no, non** ~ **ho** have you any bread? — no, I don't have any; **quanti anni hai?** — **ho 17** how old are you? — I'm 17 // *av* (*moto da luogo*) from there.

né *cong*: ~ ... ~ neither ... nor; ~ **l'uno** ~ **l'altro lo vuole** neither of them wants it; **non parla** ~ **l'italiano** ~ **il tedesco** he speaks neither Italian nor German, he doesn't speak either Italian or German; **non piove** ~ **nevica** it isn't raining or snowing.

ne'anche [ne'anke] *av, cong* not even; **non ... ~** not even; ~ **se volesse potrebbe venire** he couldn't come even if he wanted to; **non l'ho visto** — ~ **io** I didn't see him — neither did I *o* I didn't either; ~ **per idea** *o* **sogno!** not on your life!

'nebbia *sf* fog; (*foschia*) mist; **nebbi'oso, a** *ag* foggy; misty.

necessaria'mente [netʃessarja'mente] *av* necessarily.

neces'sario, a [netʃes'sarjo] *ag* necessary.

necessità [netʃessi'ta] *sf inv* necessity; (*povertà*) need, poverty; **necessi'tare** *vt* to require // *vi* (*2*) (*aver bisogno*): **necessitare di** to need // *vb impers* to be necessary.

necro'logio [nekro'lɔdʒo] *sm* obituary notice; (*registro*) register of deaths.

necrosco'pia *sf* postmortem (examination).

ne'fando, a *ag* infamous, wicked.

ne'fasto, a *ag* inauspicious, ill-omened.

ne'gare *vt* to deny; (*rifiutare*) to deny, refuse; ~ **di aver fatto/che** to deny having done/that; **nega'tivo, a** *ag, sf* negative; **negazi'one** *sf* denial; (*contrario*) negation; (*LING*) negative.

neghit'toso, a [negit'toso] *ag* slothful.

ne'gletto, a [ne'ʎʎetto] *ag* (*trascurato*) neglected.

'negli ['neʎʎi] *prep* + *det vedi* **in**.

negli'gente [negli'dʒɛnte] *ag* negligent, careless; **negli'genza** *sf* negligence, carelessness.

negozi'ante [negot'tsjante] *sm/f* trader, dealer; (*bottegaio*) shopkeeper.

negozi'are [negot'tsjare] *vt* to negotiate // *vi*: ~ **in** to trade *o* deal in; **negozi'ato** *sm* negotiation.

ne'gozio [ne'gɔttsjo] *sm* (*locale*) shop; (*affare*) (piece of) business *q*.

'negro, a *ag, sm/f* Negro.

'nei, nel, nell', 'nella, 'nelle, 'nello *prep* + *det vedi* **in**.

'nembo *sm* (*METEOR*) nimbus.

ne'mico, a, ci, che *ag* hostile; (*MIL*) enemy *cpd* // *sm/f* enemy; **essere** ~ **di** to be strongly averse *o* opposed to.

nem'meno *av, cong* = **neanche**.

'nenia *sf* dirge; (*motivo monotono*) monotonous tune.

'neo *sm* mole; (*fig*) (slight) flaw.

'neo... ** *prefisso* neo...; **neo'litico, a, ci, che *ag* neolithic.

'neon *sm* (*CHIM*) neon.

neo'nato, a *ag* newborn // *sm/f* newborn baby.

neozelan'dese [neoddzelan'dese] *ag* New Zealand *cpd* // *sm/f* New Zealander.

nep'pure *av, cong* = **neanche**.

'nerbo *sm* lash; (*fig*) strength, backbone; **nerbo'ruto, a** *ag* muscular; robust.

ne'retto *sm* (*TIP*) bold type.

'nero, a *ag* black; (*scuro*) dark // *sm* black.

nerva'tura *sf* (*ANAT*) nervous system; (*BOT*) venation; (*ARCHIT, TECN*) rib.

'nervo *sm* (*ANAT*) nerve; (*BOT*) vein; **avere i** ~**i** to be on edge; **dare sui** ~**i a qd** to get on sb's nerves; **ner'voso, a** *ag* nervous; (*irritabile*) irritable // *sm* (*fam*): **far venire il nervoso a qd** to get on sb's nerves.

'nespola *sf* (*BOT*) medlar; (*fig*) blow, punch; **'nespolo** *sm* medlar tree.

'nesso *sm* connection, link.

nes'suno, a *det* (*dav sm* **nessun** + *C, V,* **nessuno** + *s impura, gn, pn, ps, x, z; dav sf* **nessuna** + *C,* **nessun'** + *V*) (*non uno*) no, *espressione negativa* + any; (*qualche*) any // *pronome* (*non uno*) no one, nobody, *espressione negativa* + any(one); (: *cosa*) none, *espressione negativa* + any; (*qualcuno*) anyone, anybody; (*qualcosa*) anything; **non c'è nessun libro** there isn't any book, there is no book; **hai** ~ **a**

obiezione? do you have any objections?; ~ **è venuto, non è venuto** ~ nobody came; **nessun altro** no one else, nobody else; **nessun'altra cosa** nothing else; **in nessun luogo** nowhere.

net'tare vt to clean // sm ['nɛttare] nectar.

net'tezza [net'tettsa] sf cleanness, cleanliness; ~ **urbana** cleansing department.

'netto, a ag (pulito) clean; (chiaro) clear, clear-cut; (deciso) definite; (ECON) net.

nettur'bino sm dustman.

neurolo'gia [neurolo'dʒia] sf neurology.

neu'rosi sf = **nevrosi**.

neu'trale ag neutral; **neutralità** sf neutrality; **neutraliz'zare** vt to neutralize.

'neutro, a ag neutral; (LING) neuter // sm (LING) neuter.

ne'vaio sm snowfield.

'neve sf snow; **nevi'care** vb impers to snow; **nevi'cata** sf snowfall.

ne'vischio [ne'viskjo] sm sleet.

ne'voso, a ag snowy; snow-covered.

nevral'gia [nevral'dʒia] sf neuralgia.

ne'vrosi sf neurosis.

'nibbio sm (ZOOL) kite.

'nicchia ['nikkja] sf niche.

nicchi'are [nik'kjare] vi to shilly-shally, hesitate.

'nichel ['nikel] sm nickel.

nico'tina sf nicotine.

'nido sm nest; **a** ~ **d'ape** (tessuto etc) honeycomb cpd.

ni'ente pronome (nessuna cosa) nothing; (qualcosa) anything; **non ...** ~ nothing, espressione negativa + anything // sm nothing // av (in nessuna misura): **non è** ~ **buono** it's not good at all; **una cosa da** ~ a trivial thing; ~ **affatto** not at all, not in the least; **nient'altro** nothing else; **nient'altro che** nothing but; just, only; ~ **di** ~ absolutely nothing; **per** ~ (invano, gratuitamente) for nothing; **non ... per** ~ not ... at all.

nientedi'meno, niente'meno av actually, even // escl really!, I say!

'nimbo sm halo.

'ninfa sf nymph.

nin'fea sf water lily.

ninna-'nanna sf lullaby.

'ninnolo sm (balocco) plaything; (gingillo) knick-knack.

ni'pote sm/f (di zii) nephew/niece; (di nonni) grandson/daughter, grandchild.

'nitido, a ag clear; (specchio) bright.

ni'trato sm nitrate.

'nitrico, a, ci, che ag nitric.

ni'trire vi to neigh.

ni'trito sm (di cavallo) neighing q; neigh; (CHIM) nitrite.

nitroglice'rina [nitroglitʃe'rina] sf nitroglycerine.

'niveo, a ag snow-white.

no av (risposta) no; **vieni o** ~? are you coming or not?; **perché** ~? why not?

'nobile ag noble // sm/f noble, nobleman/woman; **nobili'are** ag noble; **nobiltà** sf nobility; (di azione etc) nobleness.

'nocca, che sf (ANAT) knuckle.

nocci'ola [not'tʃɔla] sf hazelnut.

'nocciolo ['nɔttʃolo] sm (di frutto) stone; (fig) heart, core; [not'tʃolo] (albero) hazel.

'noce ['notʃe] sm (albero) walnut tree // sf (frutto) walnut; ~ **moscata** nutmeg.

no'civo, a [no'tʃivo] ag harmful, noxious.

'nodo sm (di cravatta, legname, NAUT) knot; (AUT, FERR) junction; (MED, ASTR, BOT) node; (fig: legame) bond, tie; (: punto centrale) heart, crux; **avere un** ~ **alla gola** to have a lump in one's throat; **no'doso, a** ag (tronco) gnarled.

'noi pronome (soggetto) we; (oggetto: per dare rilievo, con preposizione) us; ~ **stessi(e)** we ourselves; (oggetto) ourselves.

'noia sf boredom; (disturbo, impaccio) bother q, trouble q; **avere qd/qc a** ~ not to like sb/sth; **mi è venuto a** ~ I'm tired of it; **dare** ~ **a** to annoy; **avere delle** ~**e con qd** to have trouble with sb.

noi'altri pronome we.

noi'oso, a ag boring; annoying, troublesome.

noleggi'are [noled'dʒare] vt (prendere a noleggio) to hire; (dare a noleggio) to hire out; (aereo, nave) to charter; **no'leggio** sm hire; charter.

'nolo sm hire; charter; (per trasporto merci) freight; **prendere/dare a** ~ **qc** to hire/hire out sth.

'nomade ag nomadic // sm/f nomad.

'nome sm name; (LING) noun; **in/a** ~ **di** in the name of; **di o per** ~ (chiamato) called, named; **conoscere qd di** ~ to know sb by name; ~ **d'arte** stage name; ~ **depositato** trade name; ~ **di famiglia** surname.

no'mea sf notoriety.

no'mignolo [no'miɲɲolo] sm nickname.

'nomina sf appointment.

nomi'nale ag nominal; (LING) noun cpd.

nomi'nare vt to name; (eleggere) to appoint; (citare) to mention.

nomina'tivo, a ag (LING) nominative; (ECON) registered // sm (LING: anche: **caso** ~) nominative (case); (AMM) name.

non av not // prefisso non-; vedi **affatto**, **appena** etc.

nonché [non'ke] cong (tanto più, tanto meno) let alone; (e inoltre) as well as.

noncu'rante ag: ~ (**di**) careless (of), indifferent (to); **noncu'ranza** sf carelessness, indifference.

nondi'meno cong (tuttavia) however; (nonostante) nevertheless.

'nonno, a sm/f grandfather/ mother; (in senso più familiare) grandma/grandpa; ~**i** smpl grandparents.

non'nulla sm inv: **un** ~ nothing, a trifle.

'nono, a ag, sm ninth.

nonos'tante prep in spite of,

notwithstanding // *cong* although, even though.

nontiscordardimé *sm inv* (*BOT*) forget-me-not.

nord *sm* North // *ag inv* north; northern; **nor'dest** *sm* North-East; **'nordico, a, ci, che** *ag* nordic, northern European; **nor'dovest** *sm* North-West.

'norma *sf* (*criterio*) norm; (*regola*) regulation, rule; (*avvertenza*) instruction; **a ~ di legge** according to law, as laid down by law.

nor'male *ag* normal; (*che dà una norma: lettera*) standard *cpd*; **normalità** *sf* normality; **normaliz'zare** *vt* to normalize, bring back to normal.

normal'mente *av* normally.

norve'gese [norve'dʒese] *ag, sm/f, sm* Norwegian.

Nor'vegia [nor'vedʒa] *sf*: **la ~** Norway.

nostal'gia [nostal'dʒia] *sf* (*di casa, paese*) homesickness; (*del passato*) nostalgia; **nos'talgico, a, ci, che** *ag* homesick; nostalgic.

nos'trano, a *ag* local; national; home-produced.

'nostro, a *det*: **il(la) ~(a)** *etc* our // *pronome*: **il(la) ~(a)** *etc* ours; **i ~i** (*soldati etc*) our own people.

'nota *sf* (*segno*) mark; (*comunicazione scritta, MUS*) note; (*fattura*) bill; (*elenco*) list; **degno di ~** noteworthy, worthy of note; **~e caratteristiche** distinguishing marks *o* features.

no'tabile *ag* notable; (*persona*) important // *sm* prominent citizen.

no'taio *sm* notary.

no'tare *vt* (*segnare: errori*) to mark; (*registrare*) to note (down), write down; (*rilevare, osservare*) to note, notice; **farsi ~** to get o.s. noticed.

notazi'one [notat'tsjone] *sf* marking; annotation; (*MUS*) notation.

no'tevole *ag* (*talento*) notable, remarkable; (*peso*) considerable.

no'tifica, che *sf* notification.

notifi'care *vt* (*DIR*): **~ qc a qd** to notify sb of sth, give sb notice of sth; **notifica-zi'one** *sf* notification.

no'tizia [no'tittsja] *sf* (*piece of*) news *sg*; (*informazione*) piece of information; **~e** *sfpl* news *sg*; information *sg*; **notizi'ario** *sm* (*RADIO, TV, STAMPA*) news *sg*.

'noto, a *ag* (well-)known.

notorietà *sf* fame; notoriety.

no'torio, a *ag* well-known; (*peg*) notorious.

not'tambulo *sm* night-bird.

not'tata *sf* night; **far ~** to sit up all night.

'notte *sf* night; **di ~** at night; (*durante la notte*) in the night, during the night; **peggio che andar di ~** worse than ever; **~ bianca** sleepless night; **notte'tempo** *av* at night; during the night.

not'turno, a *ag* nocturnal; (*servizio, guardiano*) night *cpd*.

no'vanta *num* ninety; **novan'tesimo, a** *num* ninetieth; **novan'tina** *sf*: **una novantina (di)** about ninety.

'nove *num* nine.

nove'cento [nove'tʃento] *num* nine hundred // *sm*: **il N~** the twentieth century.

no'vella *sf* (*LETTERATURA*) short story.

novel'lino, a *ag* (*pivello*) green, inexperienced.

no'vello, a *ag* (*piante, patate*) new; (*animale*) young; (*sposo*) newly-married.

no'vembre *sm* November.

novi'lunio *sm* (*ASTR*) new moon.

novità *sf inv* novelty; (*innovazione*) innovation; (*cosa originale, insolita*) something new; (*notizia*) (piece of) news *sg*; **le ~ della moda** the latest fashions.

novizi'ato [novit'tsjato] *sm* (*REL*) novitiate; (*tirocinio*) apprenticeship.

no'vizio, a [no'vittsjo] *sm/f* (*REL*) novice; (*tirocinante*) beginner, apprentice.

nozi'one [not'tsjone] *sf* notion, idea; **~i** *sfpl* basic knowledge *sg*, rudiments.

'nozze ['nɔttse] *sfpl* wedding *sg*, marriage *sg*; **~ d'argento/d'oro** silver/golden wedding *sg*.

ns. *abbr commerciale di* nostro.

'nube *sf* cloud; **nubi'fragio** *sm* cloudburst.

'nubile *ag* (*donna*) unmarried, single.

'nuca *sf* nape of the neck.

nucle'are *ag* nuclear.

'nucleo *sm* nucleus; (*gruppo*) team, unit, group; (*MIL*) squad.

nu'dista, i, e *sm/f* nudist.

nudità *sf inv* nudity, nakedness; (*di paesaggio*) bareness // *sfpl* (*parti nude del corpo*) nakedness *sg*.

'nudo, a *ag* (*persona*) bare, naked, nude; (*membra*) bare, naked; (*montagna*) bare // *sm* (*ARTE*) nude.

'nulla *pronome, av* = niente // *sm*: **il ~** nothing.

nulla'osta *sm inv* authorization.

nullità *sf inv* nullity; (*persona*) nonentity.

'nullo, a *ag* useless, worthless; (*DIR*) null (and void); (*SPORT*): **incontro ~** draw.

nume'rale *ag, sm* numeral.

nume'rare *vt* to number; **numerazi'one** *sf* numbering; (*araba, decimale*) notation.

nu'merico, a, ci, che *ag* numerical.

'numero *sm* number; (*romano, arabo*) numeral; (*di spettacolo*) act, turn; **~ civico** house number; **nume'roso, a** *ag* numerous, many; (*con sostantivo sg: adunanza etc*) large.

'nunzio ['nuntsjo] *sm* (*REL*) nuncio.

nu'ocere ['nwɔtʃere] *vi*: **~ a** to harm, damage; **nuoci'uto, a** *pp di* nuocere.

nu'ora *sf* daughter-in-law.

nuo'tare *vi* to swim; (*galleggiare: oggetti*) to float; **nuota'tore, 'trice** *sm/f* swimmer; **nu'oto** *sm* swimming; **nuoto sul dorso** backstroke.

nu'ova *sf vedi* nuovo.

nuova'mente *av* again.

nu'ovo, a *ag* new // *sf* (*notizia*) (piece of) news *sg*; **di ~** again; **~ fiammante** *o* **di zecca** brand-new; **la N~a Zelanda** New Zealand.

nutri'ente ag nutritious, nourishing.

nutri'mento sm food, nourishment.

nu'trire vt to feed; (fig: sentimenti) to harbour, nurse; **nutri'tivo, a** ag nutritional; (alimento) nutritious; **nutri-zi'one** sf nutrition.

'nuvola sf cloud; **'nuvolo, a** ag, **nuvo-'loso, a** ag cloudy.

nuzi'ale [nut'tsjale] ag nuptial; wedding cpd.

O

o cong (dav V spesso **od**) or; ~ ... ~ either ... or; ~ **l'uno** ~ **l'altro** either (of them).

O. (abbr di ovest) W.

'oasi sf inv oasis.

obbedi'ente etc vedi **ubbidiente** etc.

obbli'gare vt (costringere): ~ **qd a fare** to force o oblige sb to do; (DIR) to bind; ~**rsi** vr: ~**rsi a fare** to undertake to do; **obbli'gato, a** ag (costretto, grato) obliged; **obbliga'torio, a** ag compulsory, obligatory; **obbligazi'one** sf obligation; (COMM) bond, debenture; **'obbligo, ghi** sm obligation; (dovere) duty; **avere l'obbligo di fare, essere nell'obbligo di fare** to be obliged to do.

ob'brobrio sm disgrace.

obesità sf obesity.

o'beso, a ag obese.

obiet'tare vt to object; ~ **su qc** to object to sth, raise objections concerning sth.

obiettività sf objectivity.

obiet'tivo, a ag objective; (imparziale) unbiased, impartial // sm (OTTICA, FOT) lens sg, objective; (MIL, fig) objective.

obiet'tore sm objector; ~ **di coscienza** conscientious objector.

obiezi'one [objet'tsjone] sf objection.

obi'torio sm morgue, mortuary.

o'bliquo, a ag oblique; (inclinato) slanting; (fig) devious, underhand; **sguardo** ~ sidelong glance.

oblite'rare vt to obliterate.

oblò sm inv porthole.

o'blungo, a, ghi, ghe ag oblong.

'oboe sm (MUS) oboe.

obsole'scenza [obsoleʃ'ʃɛntsa] sf (ECON) obsolescence.

'oca, pl 'oche sf goose.

occasi'one sf (caso favorevole) opportunity; (causa, motivo, circostanza) occasion; (COMM) bargain; **d'**~ (a buon prezzo) bargain cpd; (usato) secondhand.

occhi'aia [ok'kjaja] sf eye socket; ~**e** sfpl shadows (under the eyes).

occhi'ali [ok'kjali] smpl glasses, spectacles; ~ **da sole** sunglasses.

occhi'ata [ok'kjata] sf look, glance; **dare un'**~ a to have a look at.

occhieggi'are [okkjed'dʒare] vt to eye, ogle // vi (apparire qua e là) to peep (out).

occhi'ello [ok'kjɛllo] sm buttonhole; (asola) eyelet.

'occhio ['ɔkkjo] sm eye; ~**!** careful!, watch out!; **a** ~ **nudo** with the naked eye; **a**

quattr'~**i** privately, tête-à-tête; **dare all'**~ o **nell'**~ **a qd** to catch sb's eye; **fare l'**~ **a qc** to get used to sth; **tenere d'**~ **qd** to keep an eye on sb; **vedere di buon/mal** ~ **qc** to look favourably/unfavourably on sth.

occhio'lino [okkjo'lino] sm: **fare l'**~ **a qd** to wink at sb.

occiden'tale [ottʃiden'tale] ag western // sm/f Westerner.

occi'dente [ottʃi'dɛnte] sm west; (POL): **l'O**~ the West.

oc'cipite [ot'tʃipite] sm back of the head, occiput.

oc'cludere vt to block; **occlusi'one** sf blockage, obstruction; **oc'cluso, a** pp di **occludere**.

occor'rente ag necessary // sm all that is necessary.

occor'renza [okkor'rɛntsa] sf necessity, need; **all'**~ in case of need.

oc'correre (2) vi to be needed, be required // vb impers: **occorre farlo** it must be done; **occorre che tu parta** you must leave, you'll have to leave; **oc'corso, a** pp di **occorrere**.

occul'tare vt to hide, conceal.

oc'culto, a ag hidden, concealed; (scienze, forze) occult.

occu'pare vt to occupy; (manodopera) to employ; (ingombrare) to occupy, take up; ~**rsi** vr to occupy o.s., keep o.s. busy; (impiegarsi) to get a job; ~**rsi di** (interessarsi) to take an interest in; (prendersi cura di) to look after, take care of; **occu'pato, a** ag (MIL, POL) occupied; (persona: affaccendato) busy; (posto, sedia) taken; (toilette, TEL) engaged; **occu-pa'tore, 'trice** sm/f occupier; **occupa-zi'one** sf occupation; (impiego, lavoro) job; (ECON) employment.

o'ceano [o'tʃeano] sm ocean.

'ocra sf ochre.

ocu'lare ag ocular, eye cpd.

ocu'lato, a ag (attento) cautious, prudent; (accorto) shrewd.

ocu'lista, i, e sm/f eye specialist, oculist.

'ode sf ode.

odi'are vt to hate, detest.

odi'erno, a ag today's, of today; (attuale) present.

'odio sm hatred; **avere in** ~ **qc/qd** to hate o detest sth/sb; **odi'oso, a** ag hateful, odious.

odo'rare vt (annusare) to smell; (profumare) to perfume, scent // vi: ~ (di) to smell (of); **odo'rato** sm sense of smell.

o'dore sm smell; **gli** ~**i** smpl (CUC) (aromatic) herbs; **odo'roso, a** ag sweet-smelling.

of'fendere vt to offend; (violare) to break, violate; (insultare) to insult; (ferire) to injure; ~**rsi** vr (con senso reciproco) to insult one another; (risentirsi): ~**rsi (di)** to take offence (at), be offended (by); **offen'sivo, a** ag, sf offensive; **offen'sore,**

offendi'trice *sm/f* offender; (*MIL*) aggressor.

offe'rente *sm* (*in aste*): **al maggior ~** to the highest bidder.

of'ferto, a *pp di* **offrire** // *sf* offer; (*donazione, anche REL*) offering; (*in gara d'appalto*) tender; (*in aste*) bid; (*ECON*) supply.

of'feso, a *pp di* **offendere** // *ag* offended // *sm/f* offended party // *sf* insult, affront; (*MIL*) attack; (*DIR*) offence.

offi'cina [offi'tʃina] *sf* workshop.

of'frire *vt* to offer; **~rsi** *vr* (*proporsi*) to offer (o.s.), volunteer; (*occasione*) to present itself; (*esporsi*): **~rsi a** to expose o.s. to; **ti offro da bere** I'll buy you a drink.

offus'care *vt* to obscure, darken; (*fig: intelletto*) to dim, cloud; (: *fama*) to obscure, overshadow; **~rsi** *vr* to grow dark; to cloud, grow dim; to be obscured.

of'talmico, a, ci, che *ag* ophthalmic.

oggettività [oddʒettivi'ta] *sf* objectivity.

ogget'tivo, a [oddʒet'tivo] *ag* objective.

og'getto [od'dʒetto] *sm* object; (*materia, argomento*) subject (matter).

'oggi ['ɔddʒi] *av, sm* today; **~ a otto** a week today; **oggi'orno** *av* nowadays.

o'giva [o'dʒiva] *sf* (*ARCHIT*) diagonal rib; (*MIL*) warhead; **arco a ~** lancet arch.

'ogni ['oɲɲi] *det* every, each; (*tutti*) all; **~ uomo è mortale** all men are mortal; (*con valore distributivo*) every; **viene ~ due giorni** he comes every two days; **~ cosa** everything; **in ~ luogo** everywhere; **~ tanto** every so often; **~ volta che** every time that.

Ognis'santi [oɲɲis'santi] *sm* All Saints' Day.

o'gnuno [oɲ'ɲuno] *pronome* everyone, everybody.

'ohi *escl* oh!; (*esprimente dolore*) ow!

ohimè *escl* oh dear!

O'landa *sf*: **l'~** Holland; **olan'dese** *ag* Dutch // *sm* (*LING*) Dutch // *sm/f* Dutchman/woman; **gli Olandesi** the Dutch.

oleo'dotto *sm* oil pipeline.

ole'oso, a *ag* oily; (*che contiene olio*) oil-yielding.

ol'fatto *sm* sense of smell.

oli'are *vt* to oil; **olia'tore** *sm* oil-can, oiler.

oli'era *sf* oil cruet.

olim'piadi *sfpl* Olympic games; **o'limpico, a, ci, che** *ag* Olympic.

'olio *sm* oil; **sott'~** (*CUC*) in oil; **~ d'oliva** olive oil; **~ di fegato di merluzzo** cod liver oil.

o'liva *sf* olive; **oli'vastro, a** *ag* olive(-coloured); (*carnagione*) sallow; **oli'veto** *sm* olive grove; **o'livo** *sm* olive tree.

'olmo *sm* elm.

oltraggi'are [oltrad'dʒare] *vt* to outrage; to offend gravely.

ol'traggio [ol'traddʒo] *sm* outrage; offence, insult; **~ alla magistratura** contempt of court; **oltraggi'oso, a** *ag* offensive.

ol'tralpe *av* beyond the Alps.

ol'tranza [ol'trantsa] *sf*: **a ~** to the last, to the bitter end.

'oltre *av* (*più in là*) further; (*di più: aspettare*) longer, more // *prep* (*di là da*) beyond, over, on the other side of; (*più di*) more than, over; (*in aggiunta a*) besides; (*eccetto*): **~ a** except, apart from; **oltre-'mare** *av* overseas; **oltrepas'sare** *vt* to go beyond, exceed.

o'maggio [o'maddʒo] *sm* (*dono*) gift; (*segno di rispetto*) homage, tribute; **~i** *smpl* (*complimenti*) respects; **rendere ~ a** to pay homage o tribute to; **copia in ~** (*STAMPA*) complimentary copy.

ombeli'cale *ag* umbilical.

ombe'lico, chi *sm* navel.

'ombra *sf* (*zona non assolata, fantasma*) shade; (*sagoma scura*) shadow; **sedere all'~** to sit in the shade.

ombreggi'are [ombred'dʒare] *vt* to shade.

om'brello *sm* umbrella; **ombrel'lone** *sm* beach umbrella.

om'bretto *sm* eyeshadow.

om'broso, a *ag* shady, shaded; (*cavallo*) nervous, skittish; (*persona*) touchy, easily offended.

ome'lia *sf* (*REL*) homily, sermon.

meopa'tia *sf* homoeopathy.

omertà *sf* conspiracy of silence.

o'messo, a *pp di* **omettere**.

o'mettere *vt* to omit, leave out; **~ di fare** to omit o fail to do.

omi'cida, i, e [omi'tʃida] *ag* homicidal, murderous // *sm/f* murderer/eress.

omi'cidio [omi'tʃidjo] *sm* murder; **~ colposo** culpable homicide.

omissi'one *sf* omission.

omogeneiz'zato [omodʒeneid'dzato] *sm* baby food.

omo'geneo, a [omo'dʒɛneo] *ag* homogeneous.

omolo'gare *vt* to approve, recognize; to ratify.

o'monimo, a *sm/f* namesake // *sm* (*LING*) homonym.

omosessu'ale *ag, sm/f* homosexual.

'oncia, ce ['ontʃa] *sf* ounce.

'onda *sf* wave; **mettere o mandare in ~** (*RADIO, TV*) to broadcast; **~e corte/medie/lunghe** short/medium/long wave; **on'data** *sf* wave, billow; (*fig*) wave, surge; **a ondate** in waves; **ondata di caldo** heatwave.

'onde *cong* (*affinché: con il congiuntivo*) so that, in order that; (: *con l'infinito*) so as to, in order to.

ondeggi'are [onded'dʒare] *vi* (*acqua*) to ripple; (*muoversi sulle onde: barca*) to rock, roll; (*fig: muoversi come le onde, barcollare*) to sway; (: *essere incerto*) to waver.

ondula'torio, a *ag* undulating; (*FISICA*) undulatory, wave *cpd*.

ondulazi'one [ondulat'tsjone] *sf* undulation; (*acconciatura*) wave; **permanente** permanent wave, perm.

'onere *sm* burden; **~i fiscali** taxes; **one-'roso, a** *ag* (*fig*) heavy, onerous.

onestà *sf* honesty.

o'nesto, a *ag* (*probo, retto*) honest; (*giusto*) fair; (*casto*) chaste, virtuous.

'onice ['ɔnitʃe] *sf* onyx.

onnipo'tente *ag* omnipotent.

onnisci'ente [onniʃ'ʃɛnte] *ag* omniscient.

onniveg'gente [onnived'dʒɛnte] *ag* all-seeing.

ono'mastico, ci *sm* name-day.

ono'ranze [ono'rantse] *sfpl* honours.

ono'rare *vt* to honour; (*far onore a*) to do credit to; **~rsi** *vr*: **~rsi di** to feel honoured at, be proud of.

ono'rario, a *ag* honorary // *sm* fee.

o'nore *sm* honour; **in ~ di** in honour of; **fare gli ~i di casa** to play host (*o* hostess); **fare ~ a** to honour; (*pranzo*) to do justice to; (*famiglia*) to be a credit to; **farsi ~** to distinguish o.s.; **ono'revole** *ag* honourable // *sm* (POL) Member of Parliament; **onorifi'cenza** *sf* honour; decoration; **ono'rifico, a, ci, che** *ag* honorary.

'onta *sf* shame, disgrace.

'O.N.U. ['ɔnu] *sf* (*abbr di Organizzazione delle Nazioni Unite*) UN, UNO.

o'paco, a, chi, che *ag* (*vetro*) opaque; (*metallo*) dull, matt.

o'pale *sm o f* opal.

'opera *sf* work; (*azione rilevante*) action, deed, work; (MUS) work; opus; (: *melodramma*) opera; (: *teatro*) opera house; (*ente*) institution, organization; **~ d'arte** work of art; **~e pubbliche** public works.

ope'raio, a *ag* working-class; workers' // *sm/f* worker; **classe ~a** working class.

ope'rare *vt* to carry out, make; (MED) to operate on // *vi* to operate, work; (*rimedio*) to act, work; (MED) to operate: **~rsi** *vr* to occur, take place; **opera'tivo, a** *ag* operative, operating; **opera'tore, 'trice** *sm/f* operator; (MED) surgeon; (TV, CINEMA) cameraman; **operatore economico** agent, broker; **opera'torio, a** *ag* (MED) operating; **operazi'one** *sf* operation.

ope'retta *sf* (MUS) operetta, light opera.

ope'roso, a *ag* busy, active, hard-working.

opi'ficio [opi'fitʃo] *sm* factory, works *pl*.

opini'one *sf* opinion.

'oppio *sm* opium.

oppo'nente *ag* opposing // *sm/f* opponent.

op'porre *vt* to oppose; **opporsi** *vr*: **opporsi (a qc)** to oppose (sth); to object (to sth); **~ resistenza/un rifiuto** to offer resistance/refuse.

opportu'nista, i, e *sm/f* opportunist.

opportunità *sf inv* opportunity; (*convenienza*) opportuneness, timeliness.

oppor'tuno, a *ag* timely, opportune.

opposi'tore *sm* opposer, opponent.

opposizi'one [oppozit'tsjone] *sf* opposition; (DIR) objection.

op'posto, a *pp di* **opporre** // *ag* opposite;

(*opinioni*) conflicting // *sm* opposite, contrary; **all'~** on the contrary.

oppressi'one *sf* oppression.

oppres'sivo, a *ag* oppressive.

op'presso, a *pp di* **opprimere**.

oppres'sore *sm* oppressor.

op'primere *vt* (*premere, gravare*) to weigh down; (*estenuare*: *sog*: *caldo*) to suffocate, oppress; (*tiranneggiare*: *popolo*) to oppress.

oppu'gnare [oppuɲ'ɲare] *vt* (*fig*) to refute.

op'pure *cong* or (else).

op'tare *vi*: **~ per** to opt for.

opu'lento, a *ag* (*ricco*) rich, wealthy; (: *arredamento etc*) opulent.

o'puscolo *sm* booklet, pamphlet.

opzi'one [op'tsjone] *sf* option.

'ora *sf* (*60 minuti*) hour; (*momento*) time; **che ~ è?, che ~e sono?** what time is it?; **non veder l'~ di fare** to long to do, look forward to doing; **alla buon'~!** at last!; **~ legale (estiva)** summer time; **~ locale** local time; **~ di punta** (AUT) rush hour // *av* (*adesso*) now; (*poco fa*): **è uscito proprio ~** he's just gone out; (*tra poco*) presently, in a minute; (*correlativo*): **~ ... ~ ...** now ... now; **d'~ in avanti** from now on; **or ~** just now, a moment ago.

o'racolo *sm* oracle.

'orafo *sm* goldsmith.

o'rale *ag, sm* oral.

ora'mai *av* = **ormai**.

o'rario, a *ag* hourly; (*velocità*) per hour // *sm* timetable, schedule; (*di ufficio, visite etc*) hours *pl*, time(s *pl*).

ora'tore, 'trice *sm/f* speaker; orator.

ora'torio, a *ag* oratorical // *sm* (REL) oratory; (MUS) oratorio // *sf* (*arte*) oratory.

or'bene *cong* so, well (then).

'orbita *sf* (ASTR, FISICA) orbit; (ANAT) (eye-)socket.

or'chestra [or'kɛstra] *sf* orchestra; **orches'trale** *ag* orchestral // *sm/f* orchestra player; **orches'trare** *vt* to orchestrate; (*fig*) to mount, stage-manage.

orchi'dea [orki'dɛa] *sf* orchid.

'orcio ['ortʃo] *sm* jar.

'orco, chi *sm* ogre.

'orda *sf* horde.

or'digno [or'diɲɲo] *sm* (*esplosivo*) explosive device.

ordi'nale *ag* ordinal.

ordina'mento *sm* order, arrangement; (*regolamento*) regulations *pl*, rules *pl*; **~ scolastico/giuridico** education/legal system.

ordi'nanza [ordi'nantsa] *sf* (DIR, MIL) order; (*persona*: MIL) orderly, batman; **d'~** (MIL) regulation *cpd*.

ordi'nare *vt* (*mettere in ordine*) to arrange, organize; (COMM) to order; (*prescrivere*: *medicina*) to prescribe; (*comandare*): **~ a qd di fare qc** to order *o* command sb to do sth; (REL) to ordain.

ordi'nario, a *ag* (*comune*) ordinary;

everyday; standard; (*grossolano*) coarse, common // *sm* ordinary; (*INS: di università*) full professor.

ordina'tivo, a *ag* regulating, regulative.

ordi'nato, a *ag* tidy, orderly.

ordinazi'one [ordinat'tsjone] *sf* (*COMM*) order; (*REL*) ordination.

'ordine *sm* order; (*carattere*): **d'~ pratico** of a practical nature; **all'~** (*COMM: assegno*) to order; **di prim'~** first-class; **fino a nuovo ~** until further notice; **mettere in ~** to put in order, tidy (up); **~ del giorno** (*di seduta*) agenda; (*MIL*) order of the day; **l'~ pubblico** law and order; **~i (sacri)** (*REL*) Holy orders.

or'dire *vt* (*fig*) to plot, scheme; **or'dito** (*fig*) plot.

orec'chino [orek'kino] *sm* earring.

o'recchio [o'rekkjo], *pl*(*f*) **o'recchie** *sm* (*ANAT*) ear.

orecchi'oni [orek'kjoni] *smpl* (*MED*) mumps *sg*.

o'refice [o'refitʃe] *sm* goldsmith; jeweller; **orefice'ria** *sf* (*arte*) goldsmith's art; (*negozio*) jeweller's (shop).

'orfano, a *ag* orphan(ed) // *sm/f* orphan; **~ di padre/madre** fatherless/motherless; **orfano'trofio** *sm* orphanage.

orga'netto *sm* barrel organ; (*armonica a bocca*) mouth organ; (*fisarmonica*) accordion.

or'ganico, a, ci, che *ag* organic // *sm* personnel, staff.

organi'gramma, i *sm* organization chart.

orga'nismo *sm* (*BIOL*) organism; (*corpo umano*) body; (*AMM*) body, organism.

orga'nista, i, e *sm/f* organist.

organiz'zare [organid'dzare] *vt* to organize; **~rsi** *vr* to get organized; **organizza'tore, 'trice** *ag* organizing // *sm/f* organizer; **organizzazi'one** *sf* organization.

'organo *sm* organ; (*di congegno*) part; (*portavoce*) spokesman, mouthpiece.

or'gasmo *sm* (*FISIOL*) orgasm; (*fig*) agitation, anxiety.

'orgia, ge ['ordʒa] *sf* orgy.

or'goglio [or'gɔʎʎo] *sm* pride; **orgogli'oso, a** *ag* proud.

orien'tale *ag* oriental; eastern; east.

orienta'mento *sm* positioning; orientation; direction; **senso di ~** sense of direction; **~ professionale** careers guidance.

orien'tare *vt* (*situare*) to position; (*fig*) to direct, orientate; **~rsi** *vr* to find one's bearings; (*fig: tendere*) to tend, lean; (: *indirizzarsi*): **~rsi verso** to take up, go in for.

ori'ente *sm* east; **l'O~** the East, the Orient.

o'rigano *sm* oregano.

origi'nale [oridʒi'nale] *ag* original; (*bizzarro*) eccentric // *sm* original; **originalità** *sf* originality; eccentricity.

origi'nare [oridʒi'nare] *vt* to bring about,

produce // *vi* (2): **~ da** to arise o spring from.

origi'nario, a [oridʒi'narjo] *ag* original; **essere ~ di** to be a native of; (*provenire da*) to originate from; to be native to.

o'rigine [o'ridʒine] *sf* origin; **all'~** originally; **d'~ inglese** of English origin; **dare ~ a** to give rise to.

origli'are [oriʎ'ʎare] *vi*: **~ (a)** to eavesdrop (on).

o'rina *sf* urine; **ori'nale** *sm* chamberpot.

ori'nare *vi* to urinate // *vt* to pass; **orina'toio** *sm* (*public*) urinal.

ori'undo, a *ag*: **~ (di)** native (of).

orizzon'tale [oriddzon'tale] *ag* horizontal.

oriz'zonte [orid'dzonte] *sm* horizon.

or'lare *vt* to hem; **orla'tura** *sf* hemming *q*; hem.

'orlo *sm* edge, border; (*di recipiente*) rim, brim; (*di vestito etc*) hem.

'orma *sf* (*di persona*) footprint; (*di animale*) track; (*impronta, traccia*) mark, trace.

or'mai *av* by now, by this time; (*adesso*) now; (*quasi*) almost, nearly.

ormeggi'are [ormed'dʒare] *vt* (*NAUT*) to moor; **or'meggio** *sm* (*atto*) mooring *q*; (*luogo*) moorings *pl*.

or'mone *sm* hormone.

ornamen'tale *ag* ornamental, decorative.

orna'mento *sm* ornament, decoration.

or'nare *vt* to adorn, decorate; **or'nato, a** *ag* ornate.

ornitolo'gia [ornitolo'dʒia] *sf* ornithology.

'oro *sm* gold; **d'~, in ~** gold *cpd*; **d'~** (*fig*) golden.

orologe'ria [orolodʒe'ria] *sf* watchmaking *q*; watchmaker's (shop); clockmaker's (shop); **bomba a ~** time bomb.

orologi'aio [orolo'dʒajo] *sm* watchmaker; clockmaker.

oro'logio [oro'lɔdʒo] *sm* clock; (*da tasca, da polso*) watch; **~ da polso** wristwatch; **~ a sveglia** alarm clock.

o'roscopo *sm* horoscope.

or'rendo, a *ag* (*spaventoso*) horrible, awful; (*bruttissimo*) hideous.

or'ribile *ag* horrible.

'orrido, a *ag* fearful, horrid.

orripi'lante *ag* hair-raising, horrifying.

or'rore *sm* horror; **avere in ~** qd/qc to loathe o detest sb/sth.

orsacchi'otto [orsak'kjɔtto] *sm* teddy bear.

'orso *sm* bear; **~ bruno/bianco** brown/polar bear.

or'taggio [or'taddʒo] *sm* vegetable.

or'tica, che *sf* (*stinging*) nettle.

orti'caria *sf* nettle rash.

orticol'tura *sf* horticulture.

'orto *sm* vegetable garden, kitchen garden; **~ industriale** market garden.

orto'dosso, a *ag* orthodox.

ortogra'fia *sf* spelling.

orto'lano, a *sm/f* (*venditore*) greengrocer.

ortope'dia *sf* orthopaedics *sg*; **orto-**

'pedico, a, ci, che *ag* orthopaedic // *sm* orthopaedic specialist.

orzai'olo [ordza'jɔlo] *sm* (MED) stye.

or'zata [or'dzata] *sf* barley water.

'orzo ['ordzo] *sm* barley.

o'sare *vt, vi* to dare; ~ **fare** to dare (to) do.

oscenità [oʃʃeni'ta] *sf inv* obscenity.

o'sceno, a [oʃ'ʃeno] *ag* obscene; (*ripugnante*) ghastly.

oscil'lare [oʃʃil'lare] *vi* (*pendolo*) to swing; (*dondolare: al vento etc*) to rock; (*variare*) to fluctuate; (*TECN*) to oscillate; (*fig*): ~ **fra** to waver *o* hesitate between; **oscillazi'one** *sf* oscillation; (*di prezzi, temperatura*) fluctuation.

oscura'mento *sm* darkening; obscuring; (*in tempo di guerra*) blackout.

oscu'rare *vt* to darken, obscure; (*fig*) to obscure; ~**rsi** *vr* to grow dark.

os'curo, a *ag* dark; (*fig*) obscure; humble, lowly // *sm*: **all'**~ in the dark; **tenere qd all'**~ **di qc** to keep sb in the dark about sth.

ospe'dale *sm* hospital.

ospi'tale *ag* hospitable; **ospitalità** *sf* hospitality.

ospi'tare *vt* to give hospitality to; (*sog: albergo*) to accommodate.

'ospite *sm/f* (*persona che ospita*) host/hostess; (*persona ospitata*) guest.

os'pizio [os'pittsjo] *sm* (*per vecchi etc*) home.

'ossa *sfpl vedi* **osso**.

ossa'tura *sf* (ANAT) skeletal structure, frame; (TECN, fig) framework.

'osseo, a *ag* bony; (*tessuto etc*) bone *cpd*.

osse'quente *ag* respectful, deferential; ~ **alla legge** law-abiding.

os'sequio *sm* deference, respect; ~**i** *smpl* (*saluto*) respects, regards; **ossequi'oso, a** *ag* obsequious.

osser'vanza [osser'vantsa] *sf* observance.

osser'vare *vt* to observe, watch; (*esaminare*) to examine; (*notare, rilevare*) to notice, observe; (DIR: *la legge*) to observe, respect; (*mantenere: silenzio*) to keep, observe; **far** ~ **qc a qd** to point sth out to sb; **osserva'tore, 'trice** *ag* observant, perceptive // *sm/f* observer; **osserva'torio** *sm* (ASTR) observatory; (MIL) observation post; **osservazi'one** *sf* observation; (*di legge etc*) observation; (*considerazione critica*) observation, remark; (*rimprovero*) reproof; **in osservazione** under observation.

ossessio'nare *vt* to obsess, haunt; (*tormentare*) to torment, harass.

ossessi'one *sf* obsession.

os'sesso, a *ag* (*spiritato*) possessed.

os'sia *cong* that is, to be precise.

ossi'dare *vt*, ~**rsi** *vr* to oxidize.

'ossido *sm* oxide; ~ **di carbonio** carbon monoxide.

ossige'nare [ossidʒe'nare] *vt* to oxygenate; (*decolorare*) to bleach.

os'sigeno *sm* oxygen.

'osso *sm* (*pl(f)* **ossa** *nel senso* ANAT) bone; **d'**~ (*bottone etc*) of bone, bone *cpd*.

osso'buco, *pl* **ossi'buchi** *sm* (CUC) marrowbone; (: *piatto*) stew made with knuckle of veal in tomato sauce.

os'suto, a *ag* bony.

ostaco'lare *vt* to block, obstruct.

os'tacolo *sm* obstacle; (EQUITAZIONE) hurdle, jump.

os'taggio [os'taddʒo] *sm* hostage.

'oste, os'tessa *sm/f* innkeeper.

osteggi'are [osted'dʒare] *vt* to oppose, be opposed to.

os'tello *sm*: ~ **della gioventù** youth hostel.

osten'sorio *sm* (REL) monstrance.

osten'tare *vt* to make a show of, flaunt; **ostentazi'one** *sf* ostentation, show.

oste'ria *sf* inn.

os'tessa *sf vedi* **oste**.

os'tetrico, a, ci, che *ag* obstetric // *sm* obstetrician // *sf* midwife.

'ostia *sf* (REL) host; (*per medicinali*) wafer.

'ostico, a, ci, che *ag* (*fig*) harsh; hard, difficult; unpleasant.

os'tile *ag* hostile; **ostilità** *sf inv* hostility // *sfpl* (MIL) hostilities.

osti'narsi *vr* to insist, dig one's heels in; ~ **a fare** to persist (obstinately) in doing; **osti'nato, a** *ag* (*caparbio*) obstinate; (*tenace*) persistent, determined; **ostinazi'one** *sf* obstinacy; persistence.

ostra'cismo [ostra'tʃizmo] *sm* ostracism.

'ostrica, che *sf* oyster.

ostru'ire *vt* to obstruct, block; **ostruzi'one** *sf* obstruction, blockage.

'otre *sm* (*recipiente*) goatskin.

ottago'nale *ag* octagonal.

ot'tagono *sm* octagon.

ot'tanta *num* eighty; **ottan'tesimo, a** *num* eightieth; **ottan'tina** *sf*: **una ottantina (di)** about eighty.

ot'tavo, a *num* eighth // *sf* octave.

ottempe'rare *vi*: ~ **a** to comply with, obey.

ottene'brare *vt* to darken; (*fig*) to cloud.

otte'nere *vt* to obtain, get; (*risultato*) to achieve, obtain.

'ottico, a, ci, che *ag* (*della vista: nervo*) optic; (*dell'ottica*) optical // *sm* optician // *sf* (*scienza*) optics *sg*; (FOT: *lenti, prismi etc*) optics *pl*.

ottima'mente *av* excellently, very well.

otti'mismo *sm* optimism; **otti'mista, i, e** *sm/f* optimist.

'ottimo, a *ag* excellent, very good.

'otto *num* eight.

ot'tobre *sm* October.

otto'cento [otto'tʃento] *num* eight hundred // *sm*: **l'O**~ the nineteenth century.

ot'tone *sm* brass; **gli** ~**i** (MUS) the brass.

ottuage'nario, a [ottuadʒe'narjo] *ag*, *sm/f* octogenarian.

ot'tundere *vt* (*fig*) to dull.

ottu'rare *vt* to close (up); (*dente*) to fill; **ottura'tore** *sm* (FOT) shutter; (*nelle armi* breechblock; **otturazi'one** sf closing (up); (dentaria) filling.

ot'tuso, a pp di **ottundere** // ag (smussato) blunt, dull; (MAT, fig) obtuse; (suono) dull.

o'vaia sf, **o'vaio** sm (ANAT) ovary.

o'vale ag, sm oval.

o'vatta sf cotton wool; (per imbottire) padding, wadding.

ovazi'one [ovat'tsjone] sf ovation.

'ovest sm west.

o'vile sm pen, enclosure.

o'vino, a ag sheep cpd, ovine.

ovulazi'one [ovulat'tsjone] sf ovulation.

'ovulo sm (FISIOL) ovum.

ov'vero cong (ossia) that is, to be precise; (oppure) or (else).

ovvi'are vi: ~ **a** to obviate.

'ovvio, a ag obvious.

ozi'are [ot'tsjare] vi to laze, idle.

'ozio ['ottsjo] sm idleness; (tempo libero) leisure; **ore d'~** leisure time; **stare in ~** to be idle; **ozi'oso, a** ag idle.

o'zono [o'dzono] sm ozone.

P

pa'cato, a ag quiet, calm.

pac'chetto [pak'ketto] sm packet.

'pacco, chi sm parcel; (involto) bundle.

'pace ['patʃe] sf peace; **darsi ~** to resign o.s.

pacifi'care [patʃifi'kare] vt (riconciliare) to reconcile, make peace between; (mettere in pace) to pacify.

pa'cifico, a, ci, che [pa'tʃifiko] ag (persona) peaceable; (vita) peaceful; (fig: indiscusso) indisputable; (: ovvio) obvious, clear // sm: **il P~, l'Oceano P~** the Pacific (Ocean).

paci'fista, i, e [patʃi'fista] sm/f pacifist.

pa'della sf frying pan; (per infermi) bedpan.

padigli'one [padiʎ'ʎone] sm pavilion; (AUT) roof.

'Padova sf Padua.

'padre sm father; **~i** smpl (antenati) forefathers; **pa'drino** sm godfather.

padro'nanza [padro'nantsa] sf command, mastery.

pa'drone, a sm/f master/mistress; (proprietario) owner; (datore di lavoro) employer; **essere ~ di sé** to be in control of o.s.; **~ di casa** master/mistress of the house; (per gli inquilini) landlord/lady; **padroneggi'are** vt to rule, command; (fig: sentimenti) to master, control; (: materia) to master, know thoroughly.

pae'saggio [pae'zaddʒo] sm landscape.

pae'sano, a ag country cpd // sm/f villager; countryman.

pa'ese sm country; land; region; village; **i P~i Bassi** the Netherlands.

paf'futo, a ag chubby, plump.

'paga, ghe sf pay, wages pl.

paga'mento sm payment.

pa'gano, a ag, sm/f pagan.

pa'gare vt to pay; (acquisto, fig: colpa) to pay for; (contraccambiare) to repay, pay back // vi to pay; **quanto l'hai pagato?** how much did you pay for it?; **~ un assegno a qd** (sog: banca) to cash sb a cheque.

pa'gella [pa'dʒɛlla] sf (INS) report card.

'paggio ['paddʒo] sm page(boy).

paggi'erò [page'rɔ] sm inv acknowledgement of a debt, IOU.

'pagina ['padʒina] sf page.

'paglia ['paʎʎa] sf straw.

pagliac'cetto [paʎʎat'tʃetto] sm (per bambini) rompers pl.

pagli'accio [paʎ'ʎattʃo] sm clown.

pagli'etta [paʎ'ʎetta] sf (cappello per uomo) (straw) boater; (per tegami etc) steel wool.

pagli'uzza [paʎ'ʎuttsa] sf (blade of) straw; (d'oro etc) tiny particle, speck.

pa'gnotta [paɲ'ɲɔtta] sf round loaf.

pa'goda sf pagoda.

'paio, pl(f) 'paia sm pair; **un ~ di** (alcuni) a couple of.

pai'olo, paiu'olo sm (copper) pot.

'pala sf shovel; (di remo, ventilatore, elica) blade; (di ruota) paddle.

pa'lato sm palate.

pa'lazzo [pa'lattso] sm (reggia) palace; (edificio) building; **~ di giustizia** courthouse; **~ dello sport** sports stadium.

pal'chetto [pal'ketto] sm shelf.

'palco, chi sm (TEATRO) box; (tavolato) platform, stand; (ripiano) layer.

palco'scenico, ci [palkoʃ'ʃeniko] sm (TEATRO) stage.

pale'sare vt to reveal, disclose; **~rsi** vr to reveal o show o.s.

pa'lese ag clear, evident.

Pales'tina sf: la ~ Palestine.

pa'lestra sf gymnasium; (esercizio atletico) exercise, training; (fig) training ground, school.

pa'letta sf spade; (per il focolare) shovel; (del capostazione) signalling disc.

pa'letto sm stake, peg; (spranga) bolt.

'palio sm (gara): **il P~** horserace run at Siena; **mettere qc in ~** to offer sth as a prize.

paliz'zata [palit'tsata] sf palisade.

'palla sf ball; (pallottola) bullet; **~ canestro** sm basketball; **~ nuoto** sm water polo; **~ volo** sm volleyball.

palleggi'are [palled'dʒare] vi (CALCIO) to practise with the ball; (TENNIS) to knock up.

pallia'tivo sm palliative; (fig) stopgap measure.

'pallido, a ag pale.

pal'lina sf (bilia) marble.

pallon'cino [pallon'tʃino] sm balloon; (lampioncino) chinese lantern.

pal'lone sm (palla) ball; (CALCIO) football; (aerostato) balloon; **gioco del ~** football.

pal'lore sm pallor, paleness.

pal'lottola *sf* pellet; (*proiettile*) bullet.

'palma *sf* (ANAT) = palmo; (BOT, *simbolo*) palm; ~ da datteri date palm.

'palmo *sm* (ANAT) palm; restare con un ~ di naso to be badly disappointed.

'palo *sm* (*legno appuntito*) stake; (*sostegno*) pole; fare da o il ~ (*fig*) to act as lookout.

palom'baro *sm* diver.

pa'lombo *sm* (*pesce*) dogfish.

pal'pare *vt* to feel, finger.

'palpebra *sf* eyelid.

palpi'tare *vi* (*cuore, polso*) to beat; (: *più forte*) to pound, throb; (*fremere*) to quiver; palpitazi'one *sf* palpitation; 'palpito *sm* (*del cuore*) beat; (*fig: d'amore etc*) throb.

paltò *sm inv* overcoat.

pa'lude *sf* marsh, swamp; palu'doso, a *ag* marshy, swampy.

pa'lustre *ag* marsh *cpd*, swamp *cpd*.

'pampino *sm* vine leaf.

pana'cea [pana'tʃea] *sf* panacea.

'panca, che *sf* bench.

pan'cetta [pan'tʃetta] *sf* (CUC) bacon.

pan'chetto [pan'ketto] *sm* stool; footstool.

pan'china [pan'kina] *sf* garden seat; (*di giardino pubblico*) (park) bench.

'pancia, ce ['pantʃa] *sf* belly, stomach; mettere *o* fare ~ to be getting a paunch; avere mal di ~ to have stomach ache *o* a sore stomach.

panci'otto [pan'tʃɔtto] *sm* waistcoat.

pan'cone *sm* workbench.

'pancreas *sm* pancreas.

'panda *sm inv* panda.

pande'monio *sm* pandemonium.

'pane *sm* bread; (*pagnotta*) loaf (of bread); (*forma*) un ~ di burro/cera *etc* a pat of butter/bar of wax *etc*; ~ integrale wholemeal bread; ~ tostato toast.

panette'ria *sf* (*forno*) bakery; (*negozio*) baker's (shop), bakery.

panetti'ere, a *sm/f* baker.

panet'tone *sm* a kind of spiced brioche with sultanas, eaten at Christmas.

pangrat'tato *sm* breadcrumbs *pl*.

'panico, a, ci, che *ag, sm* panic.

pani'ere *sm* basket.

pani'ficio [pani'fitʃo] *sm* (*forno*) bakery; (*negozio*) baker's (shop), bakery.

pa'nino *sm* roll; ~ imbottito filled roll; sandwich.

'panna *sf* (CUC) cream; (TECN) breakdown; essere in ~ to have broken down; ~ montata whipped cream.

pan'nello *sm* panel.

'panno *sm* cloth; ~i *smpl* (*abiti*) clothes.

pan'nocchia [pan'nɔkkja] *sf* (*di mais etc*) ear.

panno'lino *sm* (*per bambini*) nappy.

pano'rama, i *sm* panorama; pano'ramico, a, ci, che *ag* panoramic.

panta'loni *smpl* trousers *pl*, pair of trousers.

pan'tano *sm* bog.

pan'tera *sf* panther.

pan'tofola *sf* slipper.

panto'mima *sf* pantomime.

pan'zana [pan'tsana] *sf* fib, tall story.

pao'nazzo, a [pao'nattso] *ag* purple.

'papa, i *sm* pope.

papà *sm inv* dad(dy).

pa'pale *ag* papal.

pa'pato *sm* papacy.

pa'pavero *sm* poppy.

'papero, a *sm/f* (ZOOL) gosling // *sf* (*fig*) slip of the tongue, blunder.

pa'piro *sm* papyrus.

'pappa *sf* baby's cereal.

pappa'gallo *sm* parrot; (*fig: uomo*) Romeo, wolf.

pappa'gorgia, ge [pappa'gɔrdʒa] *sf* double chin.

'para *sf*: suole di ~ crepe soles.

pa'rabola *sf* (MAT) parabola; (REL) parable.

para'brezza [para'breddza] *sm inv* (AUT) windscreen.

paraca'dute *sm inv* parachute; paracadu'tista, i, e *sm/f* parachutist.

para'carro *sm* kerbstone.

para'diso *sm* paradise.

parados'sale *ag* paradoxical.

para'dosso *sm* paradox.

para'fango, ghi *sm* mudguard.

paraf'fina *sf* paraffin, paraffin wax.

parafra'sare *vt* to paraphrase.

para'fulmine *sm* lightning conductor.

pa'raggi [pa'raddʒi] *smpl*: nei ~ in the vicinity, in the neighbourhood.

parago'nare *vt*: ~ con/a to compare with/to.

para'gone *sm* comparison; (*esempio analogo*) analogy, parallel; reggere al ~ to stand comparison.

pa'ragrafo *sm* paragraph.

pa'ralisi *sf* paralysis; para'litico, a, ci, che *ag, sm/f* paralytic.

paraliz'zare [paralid'dzare] *vt* to paralyze.

paral'lelo, a *ag* parallel // *sm* (GEO) parallel; (*comparazione*): fare un ~ tra to draw a parallel between // *sf* parallel (line); ~e *sfpl* (*attrezzo ginnico*) parallel bars.

para'lume *sm* lampshade.

pa'rametro *sm* parameter.

para'noia *sf* paranoia; para'noico, a, ci, che *ag, sm/f* paranoiac.

para'occhi [para'ɔkki] *smpl* blinkers.

para'petto *sm* parapet.

para'piglia [para'piʎʎa] *sm* commotion, uproar.

pa'rare *vt* (*addobbare*) to adorn, deck; (*proteggere*) to shield, protect; (*scansare: colpo*) to parry; (CALCIO) to save // *vi*: dove vuole andare a ~? what are you driving at?; ~rsi *vr* (*presentarsi*) to appear, present o.s.

para'sole *sm inv* parasol, sunshade.

paras'sita, i *sm* parasite.

pa'rata *sf* (SPORT) save; (MIL) review, parade.

para'tia *sf* (*di nave*) bulkhead.

para'urti sm inv (AUT) bumper.

para'vento sm folding screen.

par'cella [par'tʃɛlla] sf account, fee (of lawyer etc).

parcheggi'are [parked'dʒare] vt to park; **par'cheggio** sm parking q; (luogo) car park.

par'chimetro [par'kimetro] sm parking meter.

'parco, chi sm park; (spazio per deposito) depot; (complesso di veicoli) fleet.

'parco, a, chi, che ag: ~ (in) (sobrio) moderate (in); (avaro) sparing (with).

pa'recchio, a [pa'rekkjo] det quite a lot of; (tempo) quite a lot of, ~i(e) det pl quite a lot of, several // pronome quite a lot, quite a bit; (tempo) quite a while, a long time; ~i(e) pronome pl quite a lot, several // av (con ag) quite, rather; (con vb) quite a lot, quite a bit.

pareggi'are [pared'dʒare] vt to make equal; (terreno) to level, make level; (bilancio, conti) to balance // vi (SPORT) to draw; **pa'reggio** sm (ECON) balance; (SPORT) draw.

paren'tado sm relatives pl, relations pl.

pa'rente sm/f relative, relation.

paren'tela sf (vincolo di sangue, fig) relationship; (insieme dei parenti) relations pl, relatives pl.

pa'rentesi sf (segno grafico) bracket, parenthesis; (frase incisa) parenthesis; (digressione) parenthesis, digression.

pa'rere sm (opinione) opinion; (consiglio) advice, opinion; **a mio** ~ in my opinion // (2) vi to seem, appear // vb impers: pare che it seems o appears that, they say that; **mi pare che** it seems to me that; **fai come ti pare** do as you like; **che ti pare del mio libro?** what do you think of my book?

pa'rete sf wall.

'pari ag inv (uguale) equal, same; (in giochi) equal; drawn, tied; (fig: adeguato): ~ a equal to; (MAT) even // sm (POL: di Gran Bretagna) peer // sm/f peer, equal; **alla** ~ on the same level; **ragazza alla** ~ au pair girl; **mettersi alla** ~ **con** to place o.s. on the same level as; **mettersi in** ~ **con** to catch up with; **andare di** ~ **passo con qd** to keep pace with sb.

Pa'rigi [pa'ridʒi] sf Paris.

pa'riglia [pa'riʎʎa] sf pair; **rendere la** ~ to give tit for tat.

parità sf parity, equality; (SPORT) draw, tie.

parlamen'tare ag parliamentary // sm/f member of parliament // vi to negotiate, parley.

parla'mento sm parliament.

parlan'tina sf (fam) talkativeness; **avere una buona** ~ to have the gift of the gab.

par'lare vi to speak, talk; (confidare cose segrete) to talk // vt to speak; ~ **(a qd) di** to speak o talk (to sb) about; **parla'tore, 'trice** sm/f speaker; **parla'torio** sm (di carcere etc) visiting room; (REL) parlour.

parmigi'ano [parmi'dʒano] sm (grana) Parmesan (cheese).

paro'dia sf parody.

pa'rola sf word; (facoltà) speech; ~e sfpl (chiacchiere) talk sg; **chiedere la** ~ to ask permission to speak; ~ **d'onore** word of honour; ~ **d'ordine** (MIL) password; ~e **incrociate** crossword (puzzle) sg; **paro'laccia, ce** sf bad word, swearword.

par'rocchia [par'rɔkkja] sf parish; parish church.

'parroco, ci sm parish priest.

par'rucca, che sf wig.

parrucchi'ere, a [parruk'kjɛre] sm/f hairdresser // sm barber.

parsi'monia sf frugality, thrift.

'parso, a pp di **parere**.

'parte sf part; (lato) side; (quota spettante a ciascuno) share; (direzione) direction; (POL) party; faction; (DIR) party; **a** ~ ag separate // av separately; **scherzi a** ~ joking aside; **a** ~ **ciò** apart from that; **da** ~ (in disparte) to one side, aside; **d'altra** ~ on the other hand; **da** ~ **di** (per conto di) on behalf of; **da** ~ **mia** as far as I'm concerned, as for me; **da** ~ **a** ~ right through; **da ogni** ~ on all sides, everywhere; (moto da luogo) from all sides; **prendere** ~ **a qc** to take part in sth; **mettere qd a** ~ **di qc** to inform sb of sth.

parteci'pare [partetʃi'pare] vi: ~ **a** to take part in, participate in; (utili etc) to share in; (spese etc) to contribute to; (dolore, successo di qd) to share (in); **partecipazi'one** sf participation; sharing; (ECON) interest; **partecipazione agli utili** profit-sharing; **par'tecipe** ag participating; **essere partecipe di** to take part in, participate in; to share (in); (consapevole) to be aware of.

parteggi'are [parted'dʒare] vi: ~ **per** to side with, be on the side of.

par'tenza [par'tɛntsa] sf departure; (SPORT) start; **essere in** ~ to be about to leave, be leaving.

parti'cella [parti'tʃɛlla] sf particle.

parti'cipio [parti'tʃipjo] sm participle.

partico'lare ag (specifico) particular; (proprio) personal, private; (speciale) special, particular; (caratteristico) distinctive, characteristic; (fuori dal comune) peculiar // sm detail, particular; **in** ~ in particular, particularly; **particolareggi'are** vt to give full details of, detail; **particolarità** sf inv particularity; detail; characteristic, feature.

partigi'ano, a [parti'dʒano] ag partisan // sm (fautore) supporter, champion; (MIL) partisan.

par'tire vi (2) to go, leave; (allontanarsi) to go o (drive etc) away o off; (petardo, colpo) to go off; (fig: avere inizio, SPORT) to start; **sono partita da Roma alle 7** I left Rome at 7; **il volo parte da Ciampino** the flight leaves from Ciampino; **a** ~ **da** from.

par'tita sf (COMM) lot, consignment; (ECON: registrazione) entry, item; (CARTE, SPORT:

gioco) game; (: *competizione*) match, game; ~ **di caccia** hunting party.

par'tito *sm* (*POL*) party; (*decisione*) decision, resolution; (*persona da maritare*) match.

'parto *sm* (*MED*) delivery, (child)birth; labour; **parto'rire** *vt* to give birth to; (*fig*) to produce.

parzi'ale [par'tsjale] *ag* (*limitato*) partial; (*non obiettivo*) biased, partial.

'pascere ['paʃʃere] *vi* to graze // *vt* (*brucare*) to graze on; (*far pascolare*) to graze, pasture; (*nutrire*: *persone, animali*) to feed, nourish; **pasci'uto, a** *pp di* **pascere**.

pasco'lare *vt, vi* to graze.

'pascolo *sm* pasture.

'Pasqua *sf* Easter; **pas'quale** *ag* Easter *cpd*.

pas'sabile *ag* fairly good, passable.

pas'saggio [pas'saddʒo] *sm* passing *q*, passage; (*traversata*) crossing *q*, passage; (*luogo, prezzo della traversata, brano di libro etc*) passage; (*su veicolo altrui*) lift; (*SPORT*) pass; (*di* ~ *persona*) passing through; ~ **pedonale/a livello** pedestrian/level crossing.

pas'sante *sm/f* passer-by // *sm* loop.

passa'porto *sm* passport.

pas'sare *vi* (2) (*andare*) to go; (*veicolo, pedone*) to pass (by), go by; (*fare una breve sosta: postino etc*) to come, call; (: *amico: per fare una visita*) to call o drop in; (*sole, aria, luce*) to get through; (*trascorrere: giorni, tempo*) to pass, go by; (*fig: proposta di legge*) to be passed; (: *dolore*) to pass, go away; (: *essere trasferito*): ~ **di ... in** to pass from ... to; (*CARTE*) to pass // *vt* (*attraversare*) to cross; (*trasmettere: messaggio*): ~ **qc a qd** to pass sth on to sb; (*dare*): ~ **qc a qd** to pass sth to sb, give sb sth; (*trascorrere: tempo*) to spend; (*superare: esame*) to pass; (*triturare: verdura*) to strain; (*approvare*) to pass, approve; (*oltrepassare, sorpassare: anche fig*) to go beyond, pass; (*fig: subire*) to go through; ~ **per** (*anche fig*) to go through; ~ **per stupido/un genio** to be taken for a fool/a genius; ~ **sopra** (*anche fig*) to pass over; ~ **attraverso** (*anche fig*) to go through; ~ **alla storia** to pass into history; ~ **a un esame** to go up (to the next class) after an exam; ~ **inosservato** to go unnoticed; ~ **di moda** to go out of fashion; **le passo il Signor X** (*al telefono*) here is Mr X; I'm putting you through to Mr X; **lasciar** ~ **qd/qc** to let sb/sth through; **passarsela: come te la passi?** how are you getting on o along?

pas'sata *sf*: **dare una** ~ **di vernice a qc** to give sth a coat of paint; **dare una** ~ **al giornale** to have a look at the paper, skim through the paper.

passa'tempo *sm* pastime, hobby.

pas'sato, a *ag* past; (*sfiorito*) faded // *sm* past; (*LING*) past (tense); ~ **prossimo** (*LING*) present perfect; ~ **remoto** (*LING*)

past historic; ~ **di verdura** (*CUC*) vegetable purée.

passaver'dura *sm inv* vegetable mill.

passeg'gero, a [passed'dʒero] *ag* passing // *sm/f* passenger.

passeggi'are [passed'dʒare] *vi* to go for a walk; (*in veicolo*) to go for a drive; **passeggi'ata** *sf* walk; drive; (*luogo*) promenade; **fare una passeggiata** to go for a walk (o drive); **passeg'gino** *sm* pushchair; **pas'seggio** *sm* walk, stroll; (*luogo*) promenade.

passe'rella *sf* footbridge; (*di nave, aereo*) gangway; (*pedana*) catwalk.

'passero *sm* sparrow.

pas'sibile *ag*: ~ **di** liable to.

passi'one *sf* passion.

pas'sivo, a *ag* passive // *sm* (*LING*) passive; (*ECON*) debit; (: *complesso dei debiti*) liabilities *pl*.

'passo *sm* step; (*andatura*) pace; (*rumore*) (foot)step; (*orma*) footprint; (*passaggio, fig: brano*) passage; (*valico*) pass; **a** ~ **d'uomo** at walking pace; ~ **(a)** ~ step by step; **fare due o quattro** ~**i** to go for a walk o a stroll; **'~ carraio'** 'vehicle entrance — keep clear'.

'pasta *sf* (*CUC*) dough; (: *impasto per dolce*) pastry; (: *anche*: ~ **alimentare**) pasta; (*massa molle di materia*) paste; (*fig: indole*) nature; ~**e** *sfpl* (*pasticcini*) pastries; ~ **di legno** wood pulp.

pastasci'utta [pastaʃ'ʃutta] *sf* pasta.

pas'tella *sf* batter.

pas'tello *sm* pastel.

pas'tetta *sf* (*CUC*) = **pastella**.

pas'ticca, che *sf* = **pastiglia**.

pasticce'ria [pastittʃe'ria] *sf* (*pasticcini*) pastries *pl*, cakes *pl*; (*negozio*) cake shop; (*arte*) confectionery.

pasticci'are [pastit'tʃare] *vt* to mess up, make a mess of // *vi* to make a mess.

pasticci'ere, a [pastit'tʃere] *sm/f* pastrycook; confectioner.

pas'ticcio [pas'tittʃo] *sm* (*CUC*) pie; (*lavoro disordinato, imbroglio*) mess; **trovarsi nei** ~**i** to get into trouble.

pasti'ficio [pasti'fitʃo] *sm* pasta factory.

pas'tiglia [pas'tiʎʎa] *sf* pastille, lozenge.

pas'tina *sf* small pasta shapes used in soup.

pasti'naca, che *sf* parsnip.

'pasto *sm* meal.

pasto'rale *ag* pastoral.

pas'tore *sm* shepherd; (*REL*) pastor, minister; (*anche: cane* ~) shepherd dog.

pastoriz'zare [pastorid'dzare] *vt* to pasteurize.

pas'toso, a *ag* doughy; pasty; (*fig: voce, colore*) mellow, soft.

pas'trano *sm* greatcoat.

pas'tura *sf* pasture.

pa'tata *sf* potato; ~**e fritte** chips, French fried potatoes; **pata'tine** *sfpl* (*potato*) crisps.

pata'trac *sm* (*crollo: anche fig*) crash.

pa'tella *sf* (*ZOOL*) limpet.

pa'tema, i *sm* anxiety, worry.

pa'tente sf licence; (anche: ~ **di guida**) driving licence.

paternità sf paternity, fatherhood.

pa'terno, a ag (affetto, consigli) fatherly; (casa, autorità) paternal.

pa'tetico, a, ci, che ag pathetic; (commovente) moving, touching.

'pathos ['patos] sm pathos.

pa'tibolo sm gallows sg, scaffold.

patina sf (su rame etc) patina; (sulla lingua) fur, coating.

pa'tire vt, vi to suffer.

pa'tito, a sm/f enthusiast, fan, lover.

patolo'gia [patolo'dʒia] sf pathology; **pato'logico, a, ci, che** ag pathological.

'patria sf homeland.

patri'arca, chi sm patriarch.

pa'trigno [pa'triɲɲo] sm stepfather.

patri'monio sm estate, property; (fig) heritage.

patri'ota, i, e sm/f patriot; **patri'ottico, a, ci, che** ag patriotic; **patriot'tismo** sm patriotism.

patroci'nare [patrotʃi'nare] vt (DIR: difendere) to defend; (sostenere) to sponsor, support; **patro'cinio** sm defence; support, sponsorship.

patro'nato sm patronage; (istituzione benefica) charitable institution o society.

pa'trono sm (REL) patron saint; (socio di patronato) patron; (DIR) counsel.

'patta sf flap; (dei pantaloni) fly.

patteggi'are [patted'dʒare] vt, vi to negotiate.

patti'naggio [patti'naddʒo] sm skating.

patti'nare vi to skate; **pattina'tore, 'trice** sm/f skater; **'pattino** sm skate; (di slitta) runner; (AER) skid; (TECN) sliding block; **pattini (da ghiaccio)** (ice) skates; **pattini a rotelle** roller skates; **[pat'tino]** (barca) kind of pedalo with oars.

'patto sm (accordo) pact, agreement; (condizione) term, condition; **a ~ che** on condition that.

pat'tuglia [pat'tuʎʎa] sf (MIL) patrol.

pattu'ire vt to reach an agreement on.

pattumi'era sf (dust)bin.

pa'ura sf fear; **aver ~ di/di fare/che** to be frightened o afraid of/of doing/that; **far ~ a** to frighten; **per ~ di/che** for fear of/that; **pau'roso, a** ag (che fa paura) frightening; (che ha paura) fearful, timorous.

'pausa sf (sosta) break; (nel parlare, MUS) pause.

pavi'mento sm floor.

pa'vone sm peacock; **pavoneggi'arsi** vr to strut about, show off.

pazien'tare [pattsjen'tare] vi to be patient.

pazi'ente [pat'tsjɛnte] ag, sm/f patient; **pazi'enza** sf patience.

paz'zesco, a, schi, sche [pat'tsesko] ag mad, crazy.

paz'zia [pat'tsia] sf (MED) madness, insanity; (azione) folly; (di azione, decisione) madness, folly.

'pazzo, a ['pattso] ag (MED) mad, insane; (strano) wild, mad // sm/f madman/woman; ~ **di** (gioia etc) mad o crazy with; ~ **per qc/qd** mad o crazy about sth/sb.

'pecca, che sf defect, flaw, fault.

peccami'noso, a ag sinful.

pec'care vi to sin; (fig) to err.

pec'cato sm sin; **è un ~ che** it's a pity that; **che ~!** what a shame o pity!

pecca'tore, 'trice sm/f sinner.

'pece ['petʃe] sf pitch.

'pecora sf sheep; **peco'raio** sm shepherd; **peco'rino** sm sheep's milk cheese.

peculi'are ag: ~ **di** peculiar to.

pecuni'ario, a ag financial, money cpd.

pe'daggio [pe'daddʒo] sm toll.

pedago'gia [pedago'dʒia] sf pedagogy, educational methods pl.

peda'lare vi to pedal; (andare in bicicletta) to cycle.

pe'dale sm pedal.

pe'dana sf (SPORT: nel salto) springboard; (: nella scherma) piste; (tappetino) rug.

pe'dante ag pedantic // sm/f pedant.

pe'data sf (impronta) footprint; (colpo) kick.

pede'rasta, i sm pederast; homosexual.

pe'destre ag prosaic, pedestrian.

pedi'atra, i, e sm/f paediatrician; **pedia'tria** sf paediatrics sg.

pedi'cure sm/f inv chiropodist.

pe'dina sf (della dama) draughtsman; (fig) pawn.

pedi'nare vt to shadow, tail.

pedo'nale ag pedestrian.

pe'done, a sm/f pedestrian // sm (SCACCHI) pawn.

'peggio ['peddʒo] av, ag inv worse // sm o f: **il o la ~** the worst; **alla ~** at worst, if the worst comes to the worst; **peggiora-'mento** sm worsening; **peggio'rare** vt to make worse, worsen // vi to grow worse, worsen; **peggiora'tivo, a** ag pejorative; **peggi'ore** ag (comparativo) worse; (superlativo) worst // sm/f: **il(la) peggiore** the worst (person).

'pegno ['peɲɲo] sm (DIR) security, pledge; (nei giochi di società) forfeit; (fig) pledge, token; **dare in ~ qc** to pawn sth.

pe'lame sm (di animale) coat, fur.

pe'lare vt (spennare) to pluck; (spellare) to skin; (sbucciare) to peel; (fig) to make pay through the nose; ~**rsi** vr to go bald.

pel'lame sm skins pl, hides pl.

'pelle sf skin; (di animale) skin, hide; (cuoio) leather; **avere la ~ d'oca** to have goose pimples o goose flesh.

pellegri'naggio [pellegri'naddʒo] sm pilgrimage.

pelle'grino, a sm/f pilgrim.

pelle'rossa, pelli'rossa, pl pelli'rosse sm/f Red Indian.

pellette'ria sf leather goods pl; leather goods shop.

pelli'cano sm pelican.

pellicce'ria [pellittʃe'ria] sf (negozio)

furrier's (shop); (*quantità di pellicce*) furs *pl*.

pel'liccia, ce [pel'littʃa] *sf* (*mantello di animale*) coat, fur; (*indumento*) fur coat.

pel'licola *sf* (*membrana sottile*) film, layer; (*FOT, CINEMA*) film.

'pelo *sm* hair; (*pelame*) coat, hair; (*pelliccia*) fur; (*di tappeto*) pile; (*di liquido*) surface; **per un ~**: **per un ~ non ho perduto il treno** I very nearly missed the train; **c'è mancato un ~ che affogasse** he escaped drowning by the skin of his teeth; **pe'loso, a** *ag* hairy.

'peltro *sm* pewter.

pe'luria *sf* down.

'pena *sf* (*DIR*) sentence; (*punizione*) punishment; (*sofferenza*) sadness *q*, sorrow; (*fatica*) trouble *q*, effort; (*difficoltà*) difficulty; **far ~** to be pitiful; **mi fai ~** I feel sorry for you; **prendersi** *o* **darsi la ~ di fare** to go to the trouble of doing; **~ di morte** death sentence; **~ pecuniaria** fine; **pe'nale** *ag* penal; **penalità** *sf inv* penalty; **penaliz'zare** *vt* (*SPORT*) to penalize.

pe'nare *vi* (*patire*) to suffer; (*faticare*) to struggle.

pen'dente *ag* hanging; leaning // *sm* (*ciondolo*) pendant; (*orecchino*) drop earring; **pen'denza** *sf* slope, slant; (*grado d'inclinazione*) gradient; (*ECON*) outstanding account.

'pendere *vi* (*essere appeso*) **~ da** to hang from; (*essere inclinato*) to lean; (*fig: incombere*) **~ su** to hang over.

pen'dio, 'dii *sm* slope, slant; (*luogo in pendenza*) slope.

'pendola *sf* pendulum clock.

pendo'lare *ag* pendulum *cpd*, pendular // *sm/f* commuter.

'pendolo *sm* (*peso*) pendulum; (*anche*: **orologio a ~**) pendulum clock.

'pene *sm* penis.

pene'trante *ag* piercing, penetrating.

pene'trare *vi* to come *o* get in // *vt* to penetrate; **~ in** to enter; (*sog: proiettile*) to penetrate; (: *acqua, aria*) to go *o* come into.

penicil'lina [penitʃil'lina] *sf* penicillin.

pe'nisola *sf* peninsula.

peni'tente *ag, sm/f* penitent; **peni'tenza** *sf* penitence; (*punizione*) penance.

penitenzi'ario [peniten'tsjarjo] *sm* prison.

'penna *sf* (*di uccello*) feather; (*per scrivere*) pen; **~ a feltro/ stilografica/a sfera** felt-tip/ fountain/ballpoint pen.

pennel'lare *vi* to paint.

pen'nello *sm* brush; (*per dipingere*) (paint)brush; **a ~** (*perfettamente*) to perfection, perfectly; **~ per la barba** shaving brush.

pen'nino *sm* nib.

pen'none *sm* (*NAUT*) yard; (*stendardo*) banner, standard.

pe'nombra *sf* half-light, dim light.

pe'noso, a *ag* painful, distressing; (*faticoso*) tiring, laborious.

pen'sare *vi* to think // *vt* to think; (*inventare, escogitare*) to think out; **~ a** to think of; (*amico, vacanze*) to think of *o* about; (*problema*) to think about; **~ di fare qc** to think of doing sth.

pensi'ero *sm* thought; (*modo di pensare, dottrina*) thinking *q*; (*preoccupazione*) worry, care, trouble; **stare in ~ per qd** to be worried about sb; **pensie'roso, a** *ag* thoughtful.

'pensile *ag* hanging.

pensio'nante *sm/f* (*presso una famiglia*) lodger; (*di albergo*) guest.

pensio'nato, a *sm/f* pensioner.

pensi'one *sf* (*al prestatore di lavoro*) pension; (*vitto e alloggio*) board and lodging; (*albergo*) boarding house; **andare in ~** to retire.

pen'soso, a *ag* thoughtful, pensive, lost in thought.

pen'tagono *sm* pentagon.

Pente'coste *sf* Pentecost, Whit Sunday.

penti'mento *sm* repentance, contrition.

pen'tirsi *vr*: **~ di** to repent of; (*rammaricarsi*) to regret, be sorry for.

'pentola *sf* pot; **~ a pressione** pressure cooker.

pe'nultimo, a *ag* last but one, penultimate.

pe'nuria *sf* shortage.

penzo'lare [pendzo'lare] *vi* to dangle, hang loosely; **penzo'loni** *av* dangling, hanging down; **stare penzoloni** to dangle, hang down.

'pepe *sm* pepper; **~ macinato/in grani** ground/whole pepper.

pepe'rone *sm* pepper, capsicum; (*piccante*) chili.

pe'pita *sf* nugget.

per *prep* for; (*moto attraverso luogo*) through; (*mezzo, modo*) by; (*causa*) because of, owing to // *cong*: **~ fare** (so as) to do, in order to do; **~ aver fatto** for having done; **partire ~ l'Inghilterra** to leave for England; **sedere ~ terra** to sit on the ground; **~ lettera/ferrovia** by letter/rail; **assentarsi ~ malattia** to be off because of *o* through *o* owing to illness; **uno ~ uno** one by one; **~ persona** per person; **moltiplicare/dividere 9 ~ 3** to multiply/divide 9 by 3; **~ cento** per cent; **~ poco che sia** however little it may be, little though it may be.

'pera *sf* pear.

pe'raltro *av* moreover, what's more.

per'bene *ag inv* respectable, decent // *av* (*con cura*) properly, well.

percentu'ale [pertʃentu'ale] *sf* percentage.

perce'pire [pertʃe'pire] *vt* (*sentire*) to perceive; (*ricevere*) to receive; **percet'tibile** *ag* perceptible; **percezi'one** *sf* perception.

perché [per'ke] *av* why // *cong* (*causale*) because; (*finale*) in order that, so that; (*consecutivo*): **è troppo forte ~ si possa batterlo** he's too strong to be beaten.

perciò [per'tʃɔ] *cong* so, for this (*o* that) reason.

per'correre *vt* (*luogo*) to go all over; (: *paese*) to travel up and down, go all over; (*distanza*) to cover.

per'corso, a *pp di* **percorrere** // *sm* (*tragitto*) journey; (*tratto*) route.

per'cosso, a *pp di* **percuotere** // *sf* blow.

percu'otere *vt* to hit, strike.

percussi'one *sf* percussion; **strumenti a** ~ (*MUS*) percussion instruments.

'perdere *vt* to lose; (*lasciarsi sfuggire*) to miss; (*sprecare: tempo, denaro*) to waste; (*mandare in rovina: persona*) to ruin // *vi* to lose; (*serbatoio etc*) to leak; ~**rsi** *vr* (*smarrirsi*) to get lost; (*svanire*) to disappear, vanish; **saper** ~ to be a good loser; **lascia** ~**!** forget it!, never mind!

perdigi'orno [perdi'dʒorno] *sm/f inv* idler, waster.

'perdita *sf* loss; (*spreco*) waste; (*fuoriuscita*) leak; **in** ~ (*COMM*) at a loss; **a** ~ **d'occhio** as far as the eye can see.

perdi'tempo *sm* waste of time // *sm/f inv* waster, idler.

perdo'nare *vt* to pardon, forgive; (*scusare*) to excuse, pardon.

per'dono *sm* forgiveness; (*DIR*) pardon.

perdu'rare *vi* to go on, last; (*perseverare*) to persist.

perduta'mente *av* desperately, passionately.

per'duto, a *pp di* **perdere**.

peregri'nare *vi* to wander, roam.

pe'renne *ag* eternal, perpetual, perennial; (*BOT*) perennial.

peren'torio, a *ag* peremptory; (*decisivo*) final.

per'fetto, a *ag* perfect // *sm* (*LING*) perfect (tense).

perfezio'nare [perfettsjo'nare] *vt* to improve, perfect; ~**rsi** *vr* to improve; (*INS*) to specialize.

perfezi'one [perfet'tsjone] *sf* perfection.

'perfido, a *ag* perfidious, treacherous.

per'fino *av* even.

perfo'rare *vt* to perforate; to punch a hole (*o* holes) in; (*banda, schede*) to punch; (*trivellare*) to drill; **perfora'tore, 'trice** *sm/f* punch-card operator // *sm* (*utensile*) punch; **perforatore di schede** card punch // *sf* (*TECN*) boring *o* drilling machine; (*INFORM*) card punch; **perforazi'one** *sf* perforation; punching; drilling; (*INFORM*) punch; (*MED*) perforation.

perga'mena *sf* parchment.

'pergamo *sm* pulpit.

perico'lante *ag* precarious.

pe'ricolo *sm* danger; **mettere in** ~ **to** endanger, put in danger; **perico'loso, a** *ag* dangerous.

perife'ria *sf* periphery; (*di città*) outskirts *pl*.

pe'rifrasi *sf* circumlocution.

pe'rimetro *sm* perimeter.

peri'odico, a, ci, che *ag* periodic(al);

(*MAT*) recurring // *sm* periodical.

pe'riodo *sm* period.

peripe'zie [peripet'tsie] *sfpl* ups and downs, vicissitudes.

pe'rire *vi* (2) to perish, die.

peris'copio *sm* periscope.

pe'rito, a *ag* expert, skilled // *sm/f* expert; (*agronomo, navale*) surveyor; **un** ~ **chimico** a qualified chemist.

pe'rizia [pe'rittsja] *sf* (*abilità*) ability; (*consulenza*) expert opinion; expert's report; (*valutazione*) survey, appraisal.

'perla *sf* pearl; **per'lina** *sf* bead.

perlus'trare *vt* to patrol.

perma'loso, a *ag* touchy.

perma'nente *ag* permanent // *sf* permanent wave, perm; **perma'nenza** *sf* permanence; (*soggiorno*) stay.

perma'nere *vi* (2) to remain.

perme'are *vt* to permeate.

per'messo, a *pp di* **permettere** // *sm* (*autorizzazione*) permission, leave; (*dato a militare, impiegato*) leave; (*licenza*) licence, permit; (*MIL: foglio*) pass; ~**?, è** ~**?** (*posso entrare?*) may I come in?; (*posso passare?*) excuse me; ~ **di lavoro/pesca** work/fishing permit.

per'mettere *vt* to allow, permit; ~ **a qd di fare/qc** to allow sb to do/sth.

permutazi'one [permutat'tsjone] *sf* (*baratto*) exchange, barter; (*MAT*) permutation.

per'nice [per'nitʃe] *sf* partridge.

pernici'oso, a [perni'tʃoso] *ag* pernicious.

'perno *sm* pivot.

pernot'tare *vi* to spend the night, stay overnight.

'pero *sm* pear tree.

però *cong* (*ma*) but; (*tuttavia*) however, nevertheless.

pero'rare *vt* to defend, support.

perpendico'lare *ag, sf* perpendicular.

perpen'dicolo *sm* plumbline; **a** ~ perpendicularly.

perpe'trare *vt* to perpetrate.

perpetu'are *vt* to perpetuate.

per'petuo, a *ag* perpetual.

per'plesso, a *ag* perplexed; uncertain, undecided.

perqui'sire *vt* to search; **perquisizi'one** *sf* (police) search.

persecu'tore *sm* persecutor.

persecuzi'one [persekut'tsjone] *sf* persecution.

persegu'ire *vt* to pursue.

persegui'tare *vt* to persecute.

perseve'rante *ag* persevering; **perseve-'ranza** *sf* perseverance.

perseve'rare *vi* to persevere.

'Persia *sf*: **la** ~ Persia.

persi'ano, a *ag, sm/f* Persian // *sf* shutter; ~ **a avvolgibile** Venetian blind.

'persico, a, ci, che *ag* (*GEO*) Persian; **il golfo P**~ the Persian Gulf.

per'sino *av* = **perfino**.

persis'tente *ag* persistent.

per'sistere *vi* to persist; ~ **a fare** to

persist in doing; **persis'tito, a** *pp di* **persistere**.

'perso, a *pp di* **perdere**.

per'sona *sf* person; *(qualcuno)*: **una ~** someone, somebody, *espressione interrogativa* + anyone *o* anybody; **~e** *sfpl* people; **non c'è ~ che ...** there's nobody who ..., there isn't anybody who ... .

perso'naggio [perso'naddʒo] *sm* (*persona ragguardevole*) personality, figure; *(tipo)* character, individual; *(LETTERATURA)* character.

perso'nale *ag* personal // *sm* staff; personnel.

personalità *sf inv* personality.

personifi'care *vt* to personify; to embody.

perspi'cace [perspi'katʃe] *ag* shrewd, discerning.

persu'adere *vt* to persuade; **~ qd di qc/a fare** to persuade sb of sth/to do; **persuasi'one** *sf* persuasion; **persua'sivo, a** *ag* persuasive; **persu'aso, a** *pp di* **persuadere**.

per'tanto *cong (quindi)* so, therefore.

'pertica, che *sf* pole.

perti'nace [perti'natʃe] *ag* determined; persistent.

perti'nente *ag*: **~ (a)** relevant (to), pertinent (to).

per'tosse *sf* whooping cough.

per'tugio [per'tudʒo] *sm* hole, opening.

pertur'bare *vt* to disrupt; *(persona)* to disturb, perturb; **perturbazi'one** *sf* disruption; perturbation; **perturbazione atmosferica** atmospheric disturbance.

per'vadere *vt* to pervade; **per'vaso, a** *pp di* **pervadere**.

perve'nire *vi (2)*: **~ a** to reach, arrive at, come to; *(venire in possesso)*: **gli pervenne una fortuna** he inherited a fortune; **far ~ qc a** to have sth sent to; **perve'nuto, a** *pp di* **pervenire**.

perversi'one *sf* perversion.

per'verso, a *ag* depraved; perverse.

perver'tire *vt* to pervert.

p. es. *(abbr di per esempio)* e.g.

'pesa *sf* weighing *q*; weighbridge.

pe'sante *ag* heavy; *(fig: noioso)* dull, boring.

pe'sare *vt* to weigh // *vi (avere un peso)* to weigh; *(essere pesante)* to be heavy; *(fig)* to carry weight; **~ su** *(fig)* to lie heavy on; to influence; to hang over; **mi pesa sgridarlo** I find it hard to scold him.

'pesca *sf (pl: pesche: frutto)* peach; *(il pescare)* fishing; **andare a ~** to go fishing; **~ con la lenza** angling.

pes'care *vt* to fish for; *(annegato)* to fish out; *(fig: trovare)* to get hold of, find.

pesca'tore *sm* fisherman; angler.

'pesce ['peʃe] *sm* fish *gen inv*; **P~i** *(dello zodiaco)* Pisces; **~ d'aprile!** April Fool!; **~ spada** swordfish; **pesce'cane** *sm* shark.

pesche'reccio [peske'rettʃo] *sm* fishing boat.

pesche'ria [peske'ria] *sf* fishmonger's (shop).

peschi'era [pes'kjɛra] *sf* fishpond.

pesci'vendolo, a [peʃʃi'vɛndolo] *sm/f* fishmonger.

'pesco, schi *sm* peach tree.

pes'coso, a *ag* abounding in fish.

'peso *sm* weight; *(SPORT)* shot; **rubare sul ~** to give short weight; **~ lordo/netto** gross/net weight; **~ piuma/mosca/ gallo/medio/massimo** *(PUGILATO)* feather/fly/bantam/middle/heavyweight.

pessi'mismo *sm* pessimism; **pessi'mista, i, e** *ag* pessimistic // *sm/f* pessimist.

'pessimo, a *ag* very bad, awful.

pes'tare *vt* to tread on, trample on; *(sale, pepe)* to grind; *(uva, aglio)* to crush; **~ il muso a qd** to smash sb's face in.

'peste *sf* plague; *(persona)* nuisance, pest.

pes'tello *sm* pestle.

pesti'lenza [pesti'lentsa] *sf* pestilence; *(fetore)* stench.

'pesto, a *ag (alimentari)* ground; crushed // *sm (CUC)* sauce made with basil, garlic, cheese and oil; **c'è buio ~** it's pitch-dark; **occhio ~** black eye.

'petalo *sm (BOT)* petal.

pe'tardo *sm* banger, firecracker.

petizi'one [petit'tsjone] *sf* petition.

'peto *sm (fam!)* fart (!).

petrol'chimica [petrol'kimika] *sf* petrochemical industry.

petroli'era *sf (nave)* oil tanker.

petro'lifero, a *ag* oil-bearing; oil *cpd*.

pe'trolio *sm* oil, petroleum; *(per lampada, fornello)* paraffin.

pettego'lare *vi* to gossip.

pettego'lezzo [petteɡo'leddzo] *sm* gossip *q*; **fare ~i** to gossip.

pet'tegolo, a *ag* gossipy // *sm/f* gossip.

petti'nare *vt* to comb (the hair of); **~rsi** *vr* to comb one's hair; **pettina'tura** *sf* combing *q*; *(acconciatura)* hairstyle.

'pettine *sm* comb; *(ZOOL)* scallop.

petti'rosso *sm* robin.

'petto *sm* chest; *(seno)* breast, bust; *(CUC: di carne bovina)* brisket; *(: di pollo etc)* breast; **a doppio ~** *(abito)* double-breasted; **petto'ruto, a** *ag* broad-chested; full-breasted; *(fig)* haughty, puffed up with pride.

petu'lante *ag* insolent.

'pezza ['pettsa] *sf* piece of cloth; *(toppa)* patch; *(cencio)* rag, cloth.

pez'zato, a [pet'tsato] *ag* piebald.

pez'zente [pet'tsɛnte] *sm/f* beggar.

'pezzo ['pettso] *sm (gen)* piece; *(brandello, frammento)* piece, bit; *(di macchina, arnese etc)* part; *(STAMPA)* article; *(di tempo)*: **aspettare un ~** to wait quite a while *o* some time; **in *o* a ~i** in pieces; **andare in ~i** to break into pieces; **un bel ~ d'uomo** a fine figure of a man; **abito a due ~i** two-piece suit; **~ di cronaca** *(STAMPA)* report; **~ grosso** *(fig)* bigwig; **~ di ricambio** spare part.

pia'cente [pja'tʃɛnte] ag attractive, pleasant.

pia'cere [pja'tʃere] vi (2) to please; una ragazza che piace a likeable girl; an attractive girl; ~ a: mi piace I like it; quei ragazzi non mi piacciono I don't like those boys; gli piacerebbe andare al cinema // sm pleasure; (favore) favour; '~!' (nelle presentazioni) 'pleased to meet you!'; con ~ certainly, with pleasure; per ~! please; fare un ~ a qd to do sb a favour; pia'cevole ag pleasant, agreeable; piaci'uto, a pp di piacere.

pi'aga, ghe sf (lesione) sore; (ferita: anche fig) wound; (fig: flagello) scourge, curse; (: persona) pest, nuisance.

piagnis'teo [pjaɲɲis'tɛo] sm whining, whimpering.

piagnuco'lare [pjaɲɲuko'lare] vi to whimper.

pi'alla sf (arnese) plane; pial'lare vt to plane.

pi'ana sf stretch of level ground; (più esteso) plain.

pianeggi'ante [pjaned'dʒante] ag flat, level.

piane'rottolo sm landing.

pi'aneta sm (ASTR) planet.

pi'angere ['pjandʒere] vi to cry, weep; (occhi) to water // vt to cry, weep; (lamentare) to bewail, lament; (: morto) to mourn (for).

pianifi'care vt to plan; pianificazi'one sf planning.

pia'nista, i, e sm/f pianist.

pi'ano, a ag (piatto) flat, level; (MAT) plane; (facile) straightforward, simple; (chiaro) clear, plain // av (adagio) slowly; (a bassa voce) softly; (con cautela) slowly, carefully // sm (MAT) plane; (GEO) plain; (livello) level, plane; (di edificio) floor; (programma) plan; (MUS) piano; pian ~ very slowly; (poco a poco) little by little; in primo/secondo ~ in the foreground/background; di primo ~ (fig) prominent, high-ranking; ~ stradale roadway.

piano'forte sm piano, pianoforte.

pi'anta sf (BOT) plant; (ANAT: anche: ~ del piede) sole (of the foot); (grafico) plan; (topografica) map; in ~ stabile on the permanent staff; piantagi'one sf plantation; pian'tare vt to plant; (conficcare) to drive o hammer in; (tenda) to put up, pitch; (fig: lasciare) to leave, desert; ~rsi davanti a qd to plant o.s. in front of sb; piantala! (fam) cut it out!

pianter'reno sm ground floor.

pi'anto, a pp di piangere // sm tears pl, crying.

pian'tone sm (vigilante) sentry, guard; (soldato) orderly; (AUT) steering column.

pia'nura sf plain.

pi'astra sf plate; (di pietra) slab.

pias'trella sf tile.

pias'trina sf (MIL) identity disc.

piatta'forma sf (anche fig) platform.

pi'atto, a ag flat; (fig: scialbo) dull // sm (recipiente, vivanda) dish; (portata) course; (parte piana) flat (part); ~i smpl (MUS) cymbals; ~ fondo soup dish; ~ forte main course; ~ del giradischi turntable.

pi'azza ['pjattsa] sf square; (COMM) market; far ~ pulita to make a clean sweep; piazza'forte, pl piazze'forti sf (MIL) stronghold; piaz'zale sm (large) square.

piaz'zare [pjat'tsare] vt to place; (COMM) to market, sell; ~rsi vr (SPORT) to be placed.

piaz'zista, i [pjat'tsista] sm (COMM) commercial traveller.

piaz'zola [pjat'tsola] sf (AUT) lay-by.

'picca, che sf pike; ~che sfpl (CARTE) spades.

pic'cante ag hot, pungent; (fig) racy; biting.

pic'carsi vr: ~ di fare to pride o.s. on one's ability to do; ~ per qc to take offence at sth.

pic'chetto [pik'ketto] sm (MIL, di scioperanti) picket.

picchi'are [pik'kjare] vt (percuotere) to thrash, beat; (colpire) to strike, hit // vi (bussare) to knock; (: con forza) to bang; (colpire) to hit, strike; picchi'ata sf knock; bang; blow; (percosse) beating, thrashing; (AER) dive.

picchiet'tare [pikkjet'tare] vt (punteggiare) to spot, dot; (colpire) to tap.

'picchio ['pikkjo] sm woodpecker.

pic'cino, a [pit'tʃino] ag tiny, very small.

piccio'naia [pittʃo'naja] sf pigeon-loft; (TEATRO): la ~ the Gods sg.

picci'one [pit'tʃone] sm pigeon.

'picco, chi sm peak; a ~ vertically.

'piccolo, a ag small; (oggetto, mano, di età: bambino) small, little (dav sostantivo); (di breve durata: viaggio) short; (fig) mean, petty // sm/f child, little one; ~i smpl (di animale) young pl; in ~ in miniature.

pic'cone sm pick(-axe).

pic'cozza [pik'kɔttsa] sf ice-axe.

pic'nic sm inv picnic.

pi'docchio [pi'dɔkkjo] sm louse.

pi'ede sm foot; (di mobile) leg; in ~i standing; a ~i on foot; a ~i nudi barefoot; su due ~i (fig) at once; prendere ~ (fig) to gain ground, catch on; sul ~ di guerra (MIL) ready for action; ~ di porco crowbar.

piedis'tallo, piedes'tallo sm pedestal.

pi'ega, ghe sf (piegatura, GEO) fold; (di gonna) pleat; (di pantaloni) crease; (grinza) wrinkle, crease; (fig: andamento) turn.

pie'gare vt to fold; (braccia, gambe, testa) to bend // vi to bend; ~rsi vr to bend; (fig): ~rsi (a) to yield (to), submit (to); piega'tura sf folding q; bending q; fold; bend; pieghet'tare vt to pleat; pie'ghevole ag pliable, flexible; (porta) folding; (fig) yielding, docile.

Pie'monte sm: il ~ Piedmont.

pi'ena sf vedi pieno.

pi'eno, a ag full; (muro, mattone) solid //

sm (colmo) height, peak; (carico) full load // sf (di fiume) flood, spate; (gran folla) crowd, throng; ~ di (full of); in ~ a notte in the middle of the night; fare il ~ (di benzina) to fill up (with petrol).

pietà sf pity; (REL) piety; senza ~ pitiless, merciless; avere ~ di (compassione) to pity, feel sorry for; (misericordia) to have pity o mercy on.

pie'tanza [pje'tantsa] sf dish; (main) course.

pie'toso, a ag (compassionevole) pitying, compassionate; (che desta pietà) pitiful.

pi'etra sf stone; ~ preziosa precious stone, gem; pie'traia sf (terreno) stony ground; pie'trame sm stones pl; pietrifi-'care vt to petrify; (fig) to transfix, paralyze.

'piffero sm (MUS) fife.

pigi'ama [pi'dʒama] sm pyjamas pl.

'pigia 'pigia ['pidʒa'pidʒa] sm crowd, press.

pigi'are [pi'dʒare] vt to press; pigia'trice sf (macchina) wine press.

pigi'one [pi'dʒone] sf rent; dare/prendere a ~ to let o rent out/rent.

pigli'are [piʎ'ʎare] vt to take, grab; (afferrare) to catch.

'piglio ['piʎʎo] sm look, expression.

pig'mento sm pigment.

pig'meo, a sm/f pygmy.

'pigna ['piɲɲa] sf pine cone.

pi'gnolo, a [piɲ'ɲolo] ag pernickety.

pigo'lare vi to cheep, chirp.

pi'grizia [pi'grittsja] sf laziness.

'pigro, a ag lazy; (fig: ottuso) slow, dull.

'pila sf (catasta, di ponte) pile; (ELETTR) battery; (vasca) basin.

pi'lastro sm pillar.

'pillola sf pill; prendere la ~ to be on the pill.

pi'lone sm (di ponte) pier; (di linea elettrica) pylon.

pi'lota, i, e sm/f pilot; (AUT) driver // ag inv pilot cpd; ~ automatico automatic pilot; pilo'tare vt to pilot; to drive.

piluc'care vt (acini d'uva) to pick off, pluck (one at a time); (biscotto) to nibble at.

pi'mento sm pimento, allspice.

pinaco'teca, che sf art gallery.

pi'neta sf pinewood.

ping-'pong [piŋ'pɔŋ] sm table tennis.

'pingue ag fat, corpulent; pingu'edine sf corpulence.

pingu'ino sm (ZOOL) penguin.

'pinna sf fin; (di pinguino, spatola di gomma) flipper.

pin'nacolo sm pinnacle.

'pino sm pine (tree); pi'nolo sm pine kernel.

'pinza ['pintsa] sf pliers pl; (MED) forceps pl; (ZOOL) pincer.

pin'zette [pin'tsette] sfpl tweezers.

'pio, a, 'pii, 'pie ag pious; (opere, istituzione) charitable, charity cpd.

pi'oggia, ge ['pjɔddʒa] sf rain.

pi'olo sm peg; (di scala) rung.

piom'bare vi to fall heavily; (gettarsi con impeto): ~ su to fall upon, assail // vt (dente) to fill; quel vestito piomba bene that dress hangs well; piomba'tura sf (di dente) filling.

piom'bino sm (sigillo) (lead) seal; (del filo a piombo) plummet; (PESCA) sinker.

pi'ombo sm (CHIM) lead; (sigillo) (lead) seal; (proiettile) (lead) shot; a ~ (cadere) straight down.

pioni'ere, a sm/f pioneer.

pi'oppo sm poplar.

pi'overe (2) vb impers to rain // vi (fig: scendere dall'alto) to rain down; (: affluire in gran numero): ~ in to pour into; pioviggi'nare vb impers to drizzle; pio-'voso, a ag rainy.

pi'ovra sf octopus.

'pipa sf pipe.

pipi sf (fam): fare ~ to have a wee (wee).

pipis'trello sm (ZOOL) bat.

pi'ramide sf pyramid.

pi'rata, i sm pirate; ~ della strada hit-and-run driver.

Pire'nei smpl: i ~ the Pyrenees.

'pirico, a, ci, che ag: polvere ~a gunpowder.

pi'rite sf pyrite.

piro'etta sf pirouette.

pi'rofilo, a ag heat-resistant.

pi'roga, ghe sf dug-out canoe.

pi'romane sm/f pyromaniac; arsonist.

pi'roscafo sm steamer, steamship.

pisci'are [piʃ'ʃare] vi (fam!) to piss (!), pee (!).

pi'scina [piʃ'ʃina] sf (swimming) pool; (stabilimento) (swimming) baths pl.

pi'sello sm pea.

piso'lino sm nap.

'pista sf (traccia) track, trail; (di stadio) track; (di pattinaggio) rink; (da sci) run; (AER) runway; (di circo) ring; ~ da ballo dance floor.

pis'tacchio [pis'takkjo] sm pistachio (tree); pistachio (nut).

pis'tillo sm (BOT) pistil.

pis'tola sf pistol, gun; ~ a spruzzo spray gun.

pis'tone sm piston.

pi'tocco, chi sm skinflint, miser.

pi'tone sm python.

pit'tore, 'trice sm/f painter; pitto'resco, a, schi, sche ag picturesque; pit'torico, a, ci, che ag of painting, pictorial.

pit'tura sf painting; pittu'rare vt to paint.

più av more; (in frasi comparative) more, aggettivo corto + ...er; (in frasi superlative) most, aggettivo corto + ...est; (negativo): non ... ~ no more, espressione negativa + any more; no longer; (di temperatura) above zero; (MAT) plus // prep plus, besides // ag inv more; (parecchi) several // sm inv (la parte maggiore): il ~ the most; (MAT) plus (sign); i ~ the majority; ~ che/di more than; ~ grande che bigger than; ~ **di 10 persone/te** more than 10 people/you; **il ~ intelligente/grande** the most intelligent/biggest; **di ~** more; (*inoltre*) what's more, moreover; **3 ore/litri di ~ che** 3 hours/litres more than; **3 chili in ~** 3 kilos more, 3 extra kilos; **a ~ non posso** as much as possible; **al ~ presto** as soon as possible; **al ~ tardi** at the latest; **~ o meno** more or less; **né ~ né meno** no more, no less.

piucchepper'fetto [pjukkepper'fetto] *sm* (*LING*) pluperfect, past perfect.

pi'uma *sf* feather; **~e** *sfpl* down *sg*; (*piumaggio*) plumage *sg*, feathers; **piu'maggio** *sm* plumage, feathers *pl*; **piu'mino** *sm* (*eider*)down; (*coperta*) eiderdown; (*per cipria*) powder puff; (*per spolverare*) feather duster.

piut'tosto *av* rather; **~ che** (*anziché*) rather than.

pi'vello, a *sm/f* greenhorn.

'pizza ['pittsa] *sf* pizza; **pizze'ria** *sf* place where pizzas are made, sold or eaten.

pizzi'cagnolo, a [pittsi'kaɲnolo] *sm/f* specialist grocer.

pizzi'care [pittsi'kare] *vt* (*stringere*) to nip, pinch; (*pungere*) to sting; to bite; (*MUS*) to pluck // *vi* (*prudere*) to itch, be itchy; (*sentir bruciare*) to sting, tingle; (*cibo*) to be hot o spicy.

pizziche'ria [pittsike'ria] *sf* delicatessen (shop).

'pizzico, chi ['pittsiko] *sm* (*pizzicotto*) pinch, nip; (*piccola quantità*) pinch, dash; (*d'insetto*) sting; bite.

pizzi'cotto [pittsi'kɔtto] *sm* pinch, nip.

'pizzo ['pittso] *sm* (*merletto*) lace; (*barbetta*) goatee beard.

pla'care *vt* to placate, soothe; **~rsi** *vr* to calm down.

'placca, che *sf* plate; (*con iscrizione*) plaque; (*d'eczema etc*) patch; **plac'care** *vt* to plate; **placcato in oro/argento** gold-/silver-plated.

pla'centa [pla'tʃɛnta] *sf* placenta.

'placido, a ['platʃido] *ag* placid, calm.

plagi'are [pla'dʒare] *vt* (*copiare*) to plagiarize; **'plagio** *sm* plagiarism.

pla'nare *vi* (*AER*) to glide.

'plancia, ce ['plantʃa] *sf* (*NAUT*) bridge.

'plancton *sm* plankton.

plane'tario, a *ag* planetary // *sm* (*locale*) planetarium.

'plasma *sm* plasma.

plas'mare *vt* to mould, shape.

'plastico, a, ci, che *ag* plastic // *sm* (*rappresentazione*) relief model; (*esplosivo*): **bomba al ~** plastic bomb // *sf* (*arte*) plastic arts *pl*; (*MED*) plastic surgery; (*sostanza*) plastic.

plasti'lina *sf* [®] plasticine [®].

'platano *sm* plane tree.

pla'tea *sf* (*TEATRO*) stalls *pl*.

'platino *sm* platinum.

pla'tonico, a, ci, che *ag* platonic.

plau'sibile *ag* plausible.

'plauso *sm* (*fig*) approval.

ple'baglia [ple'baʎʎa] *sf* (*peg*) rabble, mob.

'plebe *sf* common people; **ple'beo, a** *ag* plebeian; (*volgare*) coarse, common; **plebi'scito** *sm* plebiscite.

ple'nario, a *ag* plenary.

pleni'lunio *sm* full moon.

'plettro *sm* plectrum.

pleu'rite *sf* pleurisy.

'plico, chi *sm* bundle; (*pacco*) parcel; **in ~ a parte** (*COMM*) under separate cover.

plo'tone *sm* (*MIL*) platoon; **~ d'esecuzione** firing squad.

'plumbeo, a *ag* leaden.

plu'rale *ag, sm* plural; **pluralità** *sf* plurality; (*di voti etc*) majority.

plusva'lore *sm* (*ECON*) surplus.

pluvi'ale *ag* rain *cpd*, pluvial.

pneu'matico, a, ci, che *ag* inflatable; pneumatic // *sm* (*AUT*) tyre.

po' *av, sm vedi* **poco.**

'poco, a, chi, che *ag* (*quantità*) little, negazione + (*very*) much; (*numero*) few, negazione + (*very*) many // *av* little, espressione negativa + much; (*con ag*) espressione negativa + very // *pronome* (*very*) little; **~chi(che)** *pronome pl* few // *sm*: **il ~ che guadagna ...** what little he earns ...; **un po'** a little, a bit; **sono un po' stanco** I'm a bit tired; **un po' di soldi/pane** a little money/bread; **~ prima/dopo** shortly before/afterwards; **~ fa** a short time ago; **a ~ a ~** little by little; **fra ~ o un po'** in a little while.

po'dere *sm* (*AGR*) farm.

pode'roso, a *ag* powerful.

podestà *sm inv* (*nel fascismo*) podestà, mayor.

'podio *sm* dais, platform; (*MUS*) podium.

po'dismo *sm* (*SPORT*) track events *pl*.

po'ema, i *sm* poem.

poe'sia *sf* (*arte*) poetry; (*componimento*) poem.

po'eta, 'essa *sm/f* poet/poetess; **poe'tare** *vi* to write poetry; **po'etico, a, ci, che** *ag* poetic(al).

poggi'are [pod'dʒare] *vt* to lean, rest; (*posare*) to lay, place; **poggia'testa** *sm inv* (*AUT*) headrest.

'poggio ['pɔddʒo] *sm* hillock, knoll.

poi *av* then; (*avversativo*) but; (*alla fine*) finally, at last; **e ~** and (then).

poiché [poi'ke] *cong* since, as.

'poker *sm* poker.

po'lacco, a, chi, che *ag* Polish // *sm/f* Pole.

po'lare *ag* polar.

'polca, che *sf* polka.

po'lemico, a, ci, che *ag* polemic(al), controversial // *sf* controversy.

po'lenta *sf* (*CUC*) sort of thick porridge made with maize flour.

'poli... *prefisso*: poli'clinico, ci *sm* polyclinic; **poliga'mia** *sf* polygamy; **po'ligono** *sm* polygon.

'polio(mie'lite) *sf* polio(myelitis).

'polipo *sm* polyp.

polisti'rolo sm polystyrene.
poli'tecnico, ci sm postgraduate technical college.
politiciz'zare [politiʃid'dzare] vt to politicize.
po'litico, a, ci, che ag political // sm/f politician // sf politics sg; (linea di condotta) policy.
poli'zia [polit'tsia] sf police; ~ **giudiziaria** ≈ Criminal Investigation Department, C.I.D.; ~ **stradale** traffic police; **polizi'esco, a schi, sche** ag police cpd; (film, romanzo) detective cpd; **poli-zi'otto** sm policeman; **cane poliziotto** police dog; **donna poliziotto** policewoman.
'polizza ['polittsa] sf (COMM) bill; ~ **di assicurazione** insurance policy; ~ **di carico** bill of lading.
pol'laio sm henhouse.
pollai'olo, a sm/f poulterer.
pol'lame sm poultry.
pol'lastro sm (ZOOL) cockerel.
'pollice ['pollitʃe] sm thumb.
'polline sm pollen.
'pollo sm chicken.
pol'mone sm lung; **polmo'nite** sf pneumonia.
'polo sm (GEO, FISICA) pole; (gioco) polo.
Po'lonia sf: **la** ~ Poland.
'polpa sf flesh, pulp; (carne) lean meat.
pol'paccio [pol'pattʃo] sm (ANAT) calf.
pol'petta sf (CUC) meatball; **polpet'tone** sm (CUC) meatloaf.
'polpo sm octopus.
pol'poso, a ag fleshy.
pol'sino sm cuff.
'polso sm (ANAT) wrist; (pulsazione) pulse; (fig: forza) drive, vigour.
pol'tiglia [pol'tiʎʎa] sf (composto) mash, mush; (fango) mire.
pol'trire vi to laze about.
pol'trona sf armchair; (TEATRO: posto) seat in the front stalls.
pol'trone ag lazy, slothful.
'polvere sf dust; (anche: ~ **da sparo**) (gun)powder; (sostanza ridotta minutissima) powder, dust; **latte in** ~ dried or powdered milk; **caffè in** ~ instant coffee; **sapone in** ~ soap powder; ~ **di carbone** coal dust; **polveri'era** sf powder magazine; **polveriz'zare** vt to pulverize; (nebulizzare) to atomize; (fig) to crush, pulverize; to smash; **polve'rone** sm thick cloud of dust; **polve'roso, a** ag dusty.
po'mata sf ointment, cream.
po'mello sm knob.
pomeridi'ano, a ag afternoon cpd; **nelle ore** ~ **e** in the afternoon.
pome'riggio [pome'riddʒo] sm afternoon.
'pomice ['pomitʃe] sf pumice.
'pomo sm (mela) apple; (ornamentale) knob; (di sella) pommel; ~ **d'Adamo** (ANAT) Adam's apple.
pomo'doro sm tomato.
'pompa sf pump; (sfarzo) pomp (and ceremony); ~ **e funebri** funeral parlour

sg, undertaker's sg; **pom'pare** vt to pump; (trarre) to pump out; (gonfiare d'aria) to pump up.
pom'pelmo sm grapefruit.
pompi'ere sm fireman.
pom'poso, a ag pompous.
ponde'rare vt to ponder over, consider carefully.
ponde'roso, a ag (anche fig) weighty.
po'nente sm west.
'ponte sm bridge; (di nave) deck; (: anche: ~ **di comando**) bridge; (impalcatura) scaffold; **fare il** ~ (fig) to take the extra day off (between 2 public holidays); **governo/soluzione** ~ interim government/solution; ~ **aereo** airlift; ~ **sospeso** suspension bridge; ~ **di volo** flight deck.
pon'tefice [pon'tefitʃe] sm (REL) pontiff.
pontifi'care vi (anche fig) to pontificate; **pontifi'cato** sm pontificate; **ponti'ficio, a, ci, cie** ag papal.
popo'lano, a ag popular, of the people.
popo'lare ag popular; (quartiere, clientela) working-class // vt (rendere abitato) to populate; (abitare) to inhabit; (riempire di gente) to fill with people; ~ **rsi** vr to fill with people, get crowded; **popolarità** sf popularity; **popolazi'one** sf population.
'popolo sm people; **popo'loso, a** ag densely populated.
po'pone sm melon.
'poppa sf (di nave) stern; (mammella) breast.
pop'pare vt to suck.
poppa'toio sm (feeding) bottle.
porcel'lana [portʃel'lana] sf porcelain, china; piece of china.
porcel'lino, a [portʃel'lino] sm/f piglet.
porche'ria [porke'ria] sf filth, muck; (fig) obscenity; (: azione disonesta) dirty trick; (cosa mal fatta) rubbish.
por'cile [por'tʃile] sm pigsty.
por'cino, a [por'tʃino] ag of pigs, pork cpd // sm (fungo) type of edible mushroom.
'porco, ci sm pig; (carne) pork.
porcos'pino sm porcupine.
'porgere ['pordʒere] vt to hand, give; (tendere) to hold out.
pornogra'fia sf pornography; **porno-'grafico, a, ci, che** ag pornographic.
'poro sm pore; **po'roso, a** ag porous.
'porpora sf purple; **di** ~ purple.
'porre vt (mettere) to put; (collocare) to place; (posare) to lay (down), put (down); (fig: supporre): **poniamo che ...** let's suppose that ...; **porsi** vr (mettersi): **porsi a sedere/in cammino** to sit down/set off; ~ **una domanda a qd** to ask sb a question, put a question to sb; ~ **mente a qc** to turn one's mind to sth.
'porro sm (BOT) leek; (MED) wart.
'porta sf door; (SPORT) goal; ~ **e** sfpl (di città) gates; ~ **principale** main door; front door; **a** ~ **e chiuse** (DIR) in camera.
'porta... prefisso: portaba'gagli sm inv (facchino) porter; (AUT, FERR) luggage

rack; **portabandi'era** *sm inv* standard bearer; **porta'cenere** *sm inv* ashtray; **portachi'avi** *sm inv* keyring; **porta-'cipria** *sm inv* powder compact; **por-ta'erei** *sf inv* (*nave*) aircraft carrier // *sm inv* (*aereo*) aircraft transporter; **porta-fi'nestra**, *pl* **portefi'nestre** *sf* French window; **porta'foglio** *sm* (*busta*) wallet; (*borsa*) briefcase; (*POL, BORSA*) portfolio; **portafor'tuna** *sm inv* lucky charm; mascot; **portagi'oie** *sm inv*, **porta-gioi'elli** *sm inv* jewellery box.

por'tale *sm* portal.

porta'lettere *sm/f inv* postman/woman.

porta'mento *sm* carriage, bearing; (*fig*) behaviour, conduct.

portamo'nete *sm inv* purse.

por'tante *ag* (*muro etc*) supporting, load-bearing.

portan'tina *sf* sedan chair; (*per ammalati*) stretcher.

por'tare *vt* (*sostenere, sorreggere: peso, bambino, pacco*) to carry; (*indossare: abito, occhiali*) to wear; (: *capelli lunghi*) to have; (*avere: nome, titolo*) to have, bear; (*recare*): ~ **qc a qd** to take (*o* bring) sth to sb; (*fig: sentimenti*) to bear; ~**rsi** *vr* (*trasferirsi*) to go; (*agire*) to behave, act; ~ **i bambini a spasso** to take the children for a walk; ~ **fortuna** to bring good luck.

portasiga'rette *sm inv* cigarette case.

portas'pilli *sm inv* pincushion.

por'tata *sf* (*vivanda*) course; (*AUT*) carrying (*o* loading) capacity; (*di arma*) range; (*volume d'acqua*) (rate of) flow; (*fig: limite*) scope, capability; (: *importanza*) impact, import; **alla ~ di qd** at sb's level, within sb's capabilities; **a/fuori ~ (di)** within/out of reach (of); **a ~ di mano** within (arm's) reach.

por'tatile *ag* portable.

por'tato, a *ag* (*incline*): ~ **a fare** inclined *o* apt to do.

porta'tore, 'trice *sm/f* (*anche* *COMM*) bearer; (*MED*) carrier.

portau'ovo *sm inv* eggcup.

porta'voce [porta'votʃe] *sm/f inv* spokesman/woman // *sm inv* loudhailer.

por'tento *sm* wonder, marvel.

'portico, ci *sm* portico.

porti'era *sf* door.

porti'ere *sm* (*portinaio*) doorman, commissionaire; (*nel calcio*) goalkeeper.

porti'naio, a *sm/f* porter, doorkeeper.

portine'ria *sf* porter's lodge.

'porto, a *pp di* **porgere** // *sm* (*NAUT*) harbour, port; (*spesa di trasporto*) carriage // *sm inv* port (wine); ~ **abusivo d'armi** unlawful carrying of arms.

Porto'gallo *sm*: **il ~** Portugal; **porto-'ghese** *ag, sm/f, sm* Portuguese.

por'tone *sm* main entrance, main door.

portu'ale *ag* harbour *cpd*, port *cpd* // *sm* dock worker.

porzi'one [por'tsjone] *sf* portion, share; (*di cibo*) portion, helping.

'posa *sf* laying *q*; settling *q*; (*riposo*) rest,

peace; (*FOT*) exposure; (*atteggiamento, di modello*) pose.

po'sare *vt* to put (down), lay (down) // *vi* (*fig: fondarsi*): ~ **su** to be based on; (: *atteggiarsi*) to pose; (*liquidi*) to settle; ~**rsi** *vr* (*ape, aereo*) to land.

po'sata *sf* piece of cutlery; ~**e** *sfpl* cutlery *sg*.

po'sato, a *ag* serious.

pos'critto *sm* postscript.

posi'tivo, a *ag* positive; (*persona: pratica*) down-to-earth, practical; **di ~** (*certo*) for sure.

posizi'one [pozit'tsjone] *sf* position; **prendere ~** (*fig*) to take a stand; **luci di ~** (*AUT*) sidelights.

posolo'gia, 'gie [pozolo'dʒia] *sf* dosage, directions *pl* for use.

pos'porre *vt* to place after; (*differire*) to postpone, defer; **pos'posto, a** *pp di* **posporre**.

posse'dere *vt* to own, possess; (*qualità, virtù*) to have, possess; (*conoscere a fondo: lingua etc*) to have a thorough knowledge of; (*sog: ira etc*) to possess; **possedi-'mento** *sm* possession.

posses'sivo, a *ag* possessive.

pos'sesso *sm* ownership *q*; possession.

posses'sore *sm* owner.

pos'sibile *ag* possible // *sm*: **fare tutto il ~** to do everything possible; **nei limiti del ~** as far as possible; **al più tardi ~** as late as possible; **possibilità** *sf inv* possibility // (*mezzi*) means; **aver la possibilità di fare** to be in a position to do; to have the opportunity to do.

possi'dente *sm/f* landowner.

'posta *sf* (*servizio*) post, postal service; (*corrispondenza*) post, mail; (*ufficio postale*) post office; (*nei giochi d'azzardo*) stake; ~**e** *sfpl* (*amministrazione*) post office; ~ **aerea** airmail; **ministro delle P~e e Telecomunicazioni** Postmaster General; **posta'giro** *sm* postal giro; **pos'tale** *ag* postal, post office *cpd*.

post'bellico, a, ci, che *ag* postwar.

posteggi'are [posted'dʒare] *vt, vi* to park; **pos'teggio** *sm* car park; **posteggio per auto pubbliche** taxi rank.

postelegra'fonico, a, ci, che *ag* postal, telegraphic and telephonic.

posteri'ore *ag* (*dietro*) back; (*dopo*) later // *sm* (*fam*) behind.

posterità *sf* posterity.

pos'ticcio, a, ci, ce [pos'tittʃo] *ag* false // *sm* hairpiece.

postici'pare [postitʃi'pare] *vt* to defer, postpone.

pos'tilla *sf* marginal note.

pos'tino *sm* postman.

'posto, a *pp di* **porre** // *sm* (*sito, posizione*) place; (*impiego*) job; (*spazio libero*) room, space; (*di parcheggio*) space; (*sedile: al teatro, in treno etc*) seat; (*MIL*) post; **a ~** (*in ordine*) in place, tidy; (*fig*) settled; (: *persona*) reliable; **mettere a ~ qd** (*dargli un lavoro*) to fix sb up with a job; **al ~ di**

in place of; **sul** ~ on the spot; ~ **di blocco** roadblock.

pos'tribolo *sm* brothel.

'postumo, a *ag* posthumous; (*tardivo*) belated; ~**i** *smpl* (*conseguenze*) after-effects, consequences.

po'tabile *ag* drinkable; **acqua** ~ drinking water.

po'tare *vt* to prune.

po'tassio *sm* potassium.

po'tente *ag* (*nazione*) strong, powerful; (*veleno*) potent, strong; **po'tenza** *sf* power; (*forza*) strength.

potenzi'ale [poten'tsjale] *ag, sm* potential.

po'tere *vb + infinito* can; (*sog: persona*) can, to be able to; (*autorizzazione*) can, may; (*possibilità, ipotesi*) may // *vb impers*: **può darsi** perhaps; **può darsi che** perhaps, it may be that // *sm* power; **avresti potuto dirmelo!** you could *o* might have told me!; **non ne posso più** I'm exhausted; I can't take any more; ~ **d'acquisto** purchasing power.

potestà *sf* (*potere*) power; (*DIR*) authority.

'povero, a *ag* poor; (*disadorno*) plain, bare // *sm/f* poor man/woman; **i** ~**i** the poor; ~ **di** lacking in, having little; **povertà** *sf* poverty.

pozi'one [pot'tsjone] *sf* potion.

'pozza ['pottsa] *sf* pool.

poz'zanghera [pot'tsangera] *sf* puddle.

'pozzo ['pottso] *sm* well; (*cava: di carbone*) pit; (*di miniera*) shaft; ~ **petrolifero** oil well.

pran'zare [pran'dzare] *vi* to dine, have dinner; to lunch, have lunch.

'pranzo ['prandzo] *sm* dinner; (*a mezzogiorno*) lunch.

'prassi *sf* usual procedure.

'pratica, che *sf* practice; (*esperienza*) experience; (*conoscenza*) knowledge, familiarity; (*tirocinio*) training, practice; (*AMM: affare*) matter, case; (: *incartamento*) file, dossier; ~**che** *sfpl* dealings, negotiations; **in** ~ (*praticamente*) in practice; **mettere in** ~ to put into practice.

prati'cabile *ag* (*progetto*) practicable, feasible; (*luogo*) passable, practicable.

prati'cante *sm/f* apprentice, trainee; (*REL*) (regular) churchgoer.

prati'care *vt* to practise; (*attuare*) to put into practice; (*frequentare: persona*) to associate *o* mix with; (: *luogo*) to frequent; (*eseguire*) to carry out, perform; (: *apertura, buco*) to make.

'pratico, a, ci, che *ag* practical; ~ **di** (*esperto*) experienced *o* skilled in; (*familiare*) familiar with.

'prato *sm* meadow; (*di giardino*) lawn.

preavvi'sare *vt* to forewarn; to inform in advance; **preav'viso** *sm* notice; **telefonata con preavviso telefonico** personal *o* person to person call.

pre'cario, a *ag* precarious.

precauzi'one [prekaut'tsjone] *sf* caution, care; (*misura*) precaution.

prece'dente [pretʃe'dɛnte] *ag* previous //

sm precedent; **il discorso/film** ~ the previous *o* preceding speech/film; **prece-'denza** *sf* priority, precedence; (*AUT*) right of way.

pre'cedere [pre'tʃedere] *vt* to precede; (*camminare, guidare innanzi*) to be ahead of.

pre'cetto [pre'tʃetto] *sm* precept; (*MIL*) call-up notice.

precet'tore [pretʃet'tore] *sm* (private) tutor.

precipi'tare [pretʃipi'tare] *vi* (2) (*cadere: anche fig*) to fall headlong, plunge (down) // *vt* (*gettare dall'alto in basso*) to hurl, fling; (*fig: affrettare*) to rush; ~**rsi** *vr* (*gettarsi*) to hurl *o* fling o.s.; (*affrettarsi*) to rush; **precipitazi'one** *sf* (*METEOR*) precipitation; (*fig*) haste; **precipi'toso, a** *ag* (*caduta, fuga*) headlong; (*fig: avventato*) rash, reckless; (: *affrettato*) hasty, rushed.

preci'pizio [pretʃi'pittsjo] *sm* precipice; **a** ~ (*fig: correre*) headlong.

pre'cipuo, a [pre'tʃipuo] *ag* principal, main.

preci'sare [pretʃi'zare] *vt* to state, specify; (*spiegare*) to explain (in detail).

precisi'one [pretʃiz'jone] *sf* precision; accuracy.

pre'ciso, a [pre'tʃizo] *ag* (*esatto*) precise; (*accurato*) accurate, precise; (*uguale*): **2 vestiti** ~**i** 2 dresses exactly the same; **sono le 9** ~**e** it's exactly 9 o'clock.

pre'cludere *vt* to block, obstruct; **pre-'cluso, a** *pp di* **precludere**.

pre'coce [pre'kɔtʃe] *ag* early; (*bambino*) precocious; (*vecchiaia*) premature.

precon'cetto, a [prekon'tʃetto] *ag* preconceived.

precur'sore *sm* forerunner, precursor.

'preda *sf* (*bottino*) booty; (*animale, fig*) prey; **essere** ~ **di** to fall prey to; **essere in** ~ **a** to be prey to; **preda'tore** *sm* predator.

predeces'sore, a [predetʃes'sore] *sm/f* predecessor.

pre'della *sf* platform, dais; altar-step.

predesti'nare *vt* to predestine.

pre'detto, a *pp di* **predire**.

'predica, che *sf* sermon; (*fig*) lecture, talking-to.

predi'care *vt, vi* to preach.

predi'cato *sm* (*LING*) predicate.

predi'letto, a *pp di* **prediligere** // *ag, sm/f* favourite.

predilezi'one [predilet'tsjone] *sf* fondness, partiality; **avere una** ~ **per qc/qd** to be partial to sth/fond of sb.

predi'ligere [predi'lidʒere] *vt* to prefer, have a preference for.

pre'dire *vt* to foretell, predict.

predis'porre *vt* to get ready, prepare; ~ **qd a qc** to predispose sb to sth; **predis-'posto, a** *pp di* **predisporre**.

predizi'one [predit'tsjone] *sf* prediction.

predomi'nare *vi* to predominate; (*prevalere*) to prevail; **predo'minio** *sm* predominance; supremacy.

prefabbri'cato, a ag (EDIL) prefabricated.

prefazi'one [prefat'tsjone] sf preface, foreword.

prefe'renza [prefe'rɛntsa] sf preference; **preferenzi'ale** ag preferential.

prefe'rire vt to prefer, like better; **~ il caffè al tè** to prefer coffee to tea, like coffee better than tea.

pre'fetto sm prefect; **prefet'tura** sf prefecture.

pre'figgere [pre'fiddʒere] vt to fix o arrange in advance; **~rsi uno scopo** to set o.s. a goal.

pre'fisso, a pp di **prefiggere** // sm (LING) prefix; (TEL) dialling code.

pre'gare vi to pray // vt (REL) to pray to; (implorare) to beg; (chiedere): **~ qd di fare** to ask sb to do; **farsi ~** to need coaxing o persuading.

pre'gevole [pre'dʒevole] ag valuable.

preghi'era [pre'gjɛra] sf (REL) prayer; (domanda) request.

pregi'arsi [pre'dʒarsi] vr: **mi pregio di farle sapere che ...** I am pleased o honoured to inform you that ... .

'pregio ['prɛdʒo] sm (stima) esteem, regard; (qualità) (good) quality, merit; (valore) value, worth.

pregiudi'care [predʒudi'kare] vt to prejudice, harm, be detrimental to; **pregiudi'cato, a** sm/f (DIR) previous offender.

pregiu'dizio [predʒu'dittsjo] sm (idea errata) prejudice; (danno) harm q.

'pregno, a ['prɛɲɲo] ag (gravido) pregnant; (saturo): **~ di** full of, saturated with.

'prego escl (a chi ringrazia) don't mention it!; (invitando qd ad accomodarsi) please sit down!; (invitando qd ad andare prima) after you!

pregus'tare vt to look forward to.

preis'torico, a, ci, che ag prehistoric.

pre'lato sm prelate.

prele'vare vt (denaro) to withdraw; (campione) to take; (sog: polizia) to take, capture.

preli'evo sm (MED): **fare un ~ (di)** to take a sample (of).

prelimi'nare ag preliminary; **~i** smpl preliminary talks; preliminaries.

pre'ludio sm prelude.

pre-ma'man [prema'mã] sm inv maternity dress.

prema'turo, a ag premature.

premeditazi'one [premeditat'tsjone] sf (DIR) premeditation; **con ~** ag premeditated // av with intent.

'premere vt to press // vi: **~ su** to press down on; (fig) to put pressure on; **~ a** (fig: importare) to matter to.

pre'messo, a pp di **premettere** // sf introductory statement, introduction.

pre'mettere vt to put before; (dire prima) to start by saying, state first.

premi'are vt to give a prize to; to reward.

premi'nente ag pre-eminent.

'premio sm prize, award; (ricompensa) reward; (COMM) premium; (AMM: indennità) bonus.

premu'nirsi vr: **~ di** to provide o.s. with; **~ contro** to protect o.s. from, guard o.s. against.

pre'mura sf (fretta) haste, hurry; (riguardo) attention, care; **premu'roso, a** ag thoughtful, considerate.

prena'tale ag antenatal.

'prendere vt to take; (andare a prendere) to get, fetch; (ottenere) to get; (guadagnare) to get, earn; (catturare: ladro, pesce) to catch; (collaboratore, dipendente) to take on; (passeggero) to pick up; (chiedere: somma, prezzo) to charge, ask; (trattare: persona) to handle // vi (colla, cemento) to set; (pianta) to take; (fuoco: nel camino) to catch; (: incendio) to start; (voltare): **~ a destra** to turn to the right; **~rsi** vr (azzuffarsi): **~rsi a pugni** to come to blows; **~ a fare qc** to start doing sth; **~ qd/qc per** (scambiare) to take sb/sth for; **~ le armi** to take up arms; **~ fuoco** to catch fire; **~ parte a** to take part in; **~rsi cura di qd/qc** to look after sb/sth; **prendersela** (adirarsi) to get annoyed; (preoccuparsi) to get upset, worry.

preno'tare vt to book, reserve; **prenotazi'one** sf booking, reservation.

preoccu'pare vt to worry; to preoccupy; **~rsi** vr: **~rsi di qd/qc** to worry about sb/sth; **~rsi per qd** to be anxious for sb; **preoccupazi'one** sf worry, anxiety.

prepa'rare vt to prepare; (esame, concorso) to prepare for; **~rsi** vr: **~rsi (a qc/a fare)** to get ready o prepare (o.s.) (for sth/to do); **prepara'tivi** smpl preparations; **prepa'rato** sm (prodotto) preparation; **prepara'torio, a** ag preparatory; **preparazi'one** sf preparation.

pre'porre vt to place before; (fig) to prefer.

preposizi'one [prepozit'tsjone] sf (LING) preposition.

pre'posto, a pp di **preporre**.

prepo'tente ag domineering, arrogant; (bisogno, desiderio) overwhelming, pressing // sm/f bully; **prepo'tenza** sf arrogance; arrogant behaviour.

pre'puzio [pre'puttsjo] sm (ANAT) foreskin.

preroga'tiva sf prerogative.

'presa sf taking q; catching q; (di città) capture; (indurimento: di cemento) setting; (appiglio, SPORT) hold; (ELETTR): **~ (di corrente)** socket; (: al muro) point; (piccola quantità: di sale etc) pinch; (CARTE) trick; **far ~** to catch, hold; (cemento) to set; (pianta) to take root; **~ d'acqua** water supply point; tap; **~ d'aria** air inlet; **~ di terra** (ELETTR) earth; **essere alle ~e con qc** (fig) to be struggling with sth.

pre'sagio [pre'zadʒo] sm omen.

presa'gire [preza'dʒire] *vt* to foresee.
'presbite *ag* long-sighted.
presbiteri'ano, a *ag, sm/f* Presbyterian.
presbi'terio *sm* presbytery.
pre'scindere [preʃ'ʃindere] *vi:* ~ **da** to leave out of consideration; **a** ~ **da** apart from.
pres'critto, a *pp di* **prescrivere**.
pres'crivere *vt* to prescribe; **prescri- zi'one** *sf* (*MED, DIR*) prescription; (*norma*) rule, regulation.
presen'tare *vt* to present; (*far conoscere*): ~ **qd (a)** to introduce sb (to); (*AMM: inoltrare*) to submit; ~**rsi** *vr* (*in comune etc*) to report, come; (*in giudizio*) to appear; (*farsi conoscere*) to introduce o.s.; (*occasione*) to arise; ~**rsi candidato** (*POL*) to stand as a candidate; ~**rsi bene/male** to look good/bad; **presentazi'one** *sf* presentation; introduction.
pre'sente *ag* present; (*questo*) this // **sm** present; **i** ~**i** those present; **aver** ~ **qc/qd** to remember sth/sb.
presenti'mento *sm* premonition.
pre'senza [pre'zentsa] *sf* presence; (*aspetto esteriore*) appearance; ~ **di spirito** presence of mind.
pre'sepio, **pre'sepe** *sm* crib.
preser'vare *vt* to protect; to save; **preserva'tivo** *sm* sheath, condom.
'preside *sm/f* (*INS*) headmaster/mistress; (*di facoltà universitaria*) dean.
presi'dente *sm* (*POL*) president; (*di assemblea, COMM*) chairman; **presiden- 'tessa** *sf* president; president's wife; chairwoman; **presi'denza** *sf* presidency; office of president; chairmanship; **presidenzi'ale** *ag* presidential.
presidi'are *vt* to garrison; **pre'sidio** *sm* garrison.
presi'edere *vt* to preside over // *vi:* ~ **a** to direct, be in charge of.
'preso, a *pp di* **prendere**.
'pressa *sf* crowd, throng; (*TECN*) press.
pressap'poco *av* about, roughly.
pres'sare *vt* to press.
pressi'one *sf* pressure; **far** ~ **su qd** to put pressure on sb; ~ **sanguigna** blood pressure.
'presso *av* (*vicino*) nearby, close at hand // *prep* (*vicino a*) near; (*accanto a*) beside, next to; (*in casa di*): ~ **qd** at sb's home; (*nelle lettere*) care of (*abbr* c/o); **lavora** ~ **di noi** he works for *o* with us.
pressuriz'zare [pressurid'dzare] *vt* to pressurize.
presta'nome *sm/f inv* (*peg*) figurehead.
pres'tante *ag* good-looking.
pres'tare *vt* to lend; ~**rsi** *vr* (*adoperarsi*): ~**rsi per qd/a fare** to help sb/to do; (*essere adatto*): ~**rsi a** to lend itself to, be suitable for; ~ **aiuto** to lend a hand; ~ **orecchio** to listen; **prestazi'oni** *sfpl* (*di macchina, atleta*) performance *sg*; (*di persona: servizi*) services.
prestigia'tore, **'trice** [prestidʒa'tore] *sm/f* conjurer.

pres'tigio [pres'tidʒo] *sm* (*potere*) prestige; (*illusione*): **gioco di** ~ conjuring trick.
'prestito *sm* lending *q*; loan; **dar in** *o* **a** ~ to lend; **prendere in** ~ to borrow.
'presto *av* (*tra poco*) soon; (*in fretta*) quickly; (*di buon'ora*) early; **a** ~ see you soon; **fare** ~ **a fare qc** to hurry up and do sth; (*non costare fatica*) to have no trouble doing sth; **si fa** ~ **a criticare** it's easy to criticize.
pre'sumere *vt* to presume, assume // *vi:* ~ **di** to overrate; **pre'sunto,** a *pp di* **presumere**.
presuntu'oso, a *ag* presumptuous.
presunzi'one [prezun'tsjone] *sf* presumption.
presup'porre *vt* to suppose; to presuppose.
'prete *sm* priest.
preten'dente *sm/f* pretender // *sm* (*corteggiatore*) suitor.
pre'tendere *vt* (*esigere*) to demand, require; (*sostenere*): ~ **che** to claim that // *vi* (*presumere*) to think, presume; **pretende di aver sempre ragione** he thinks he's always right; ~ **a** to lay claim to; **pretensi'one** *sf* claim; pretentiousness; **pretenzi'oso,** a *ag* pretentious.
pre'teso, a *pp di* **pretendere** // *sf* (*esigenza*) claim, demand; (*presunzione, sfarzo*) pretentiousness; **senza** ~**e** unpretentious.
pre'testo *sm* pretext, excuse.
pre'tore *sm* magistrate.
preva'lente *ag* prevailing; **preva'lenza** *sf* predominance.
preva'lere *vi* to prevail; **pre'valso,** a *pp di* **prevalere**.
preve'dere *vt* (*indovinare*) to foresee; (*presagire*) to foretell; (*considerare*) to make provision for.
preve'nire *vt* (*anticipare*) to forestall; to anticipate; (*evitare*) to avoid, prevent; (*avvertire*): ~ **qd (di)** to warn sb (of); to inform sb (of).
preventi'vare *vt* (*COMM*) to estimate.
preven'tivo, a *ag* preventive // *sm* (*COMM*) estimate.
prevenzi'one [preven'tsjone] *sf* prevention; (*preconcetto*) prejudice.
previ'dente *ag* showing foresight; prudent; **previ'denza** *sf* foresight; **istituto di previdenza** provident institution; **previdenza sociale** social security.
previsi'one *sf* forecast, prediction; ~**i meteorologiche** *o* **del tempo** weather forecast *sg*.
pre'visto, a *pp di* **prevedere** // *ag* foreseen, expected; **più/meno del** ~ more/less than expected.
prezi'oso, a [pret'tsjoso] *ag* precious; invaluable // *sm* jewel; valuable.
prez'zemolo [pret'tsemolo] *sm* parsley.
'prezzo ['prettso] *sm* price; ~

prigione [pri'dʒone] sf prison; **prigio'nia**
sf imprisonment; **prigioni'ero, a** ag
captive // sm/f prisoner.

'prima sf vedi **primo** // av before; (in
anticipo) in advance, beforehand; (per
l'addietro) at one time, formerly; (più
presto) sooner, earlier; (in primo luogo)
first // cong: ~ **di fare/che parta** before
doing/he leaves; ~ **di** prep before; ~ **o**
poi sooner or later.

pri'mario, a ag primary; (principale)
chief, leading, primary.

pri'mate sm (REL) primate.

pri'mato sm supremacy; (SPORT) record.

prima'vera sf spring; **primave'rile** ag
spring cpd.

primeggi'are [primed'dʒare] vi to excel,
be one of the best.

primi'tivo, a ag primitive; original.

pri'mizie [pri'mittsje] sfpl early produce
sg.

'primo, a ag first; (fig) initial; basic; prime
// sf (TEATRO) first night; (CINEMA)
première; (AUT) first (gear); **le ~e ore**
del mattino the early hours of the
morning; **ai ~i di maggio** at the
beginning of May; **viaggiare in ~a** to
travel first-class; **in ~ luogo** first of all, in
the first place; **di prim'ordine** o **~a**
qualità first-class, first-rate; **in un ~**
tempo at first; **~a donna** leading lady;
(di opera lirica) prima donna.

primo'genito, a [primo'dʒenito] ag, sm/f
firstborn.

primordi'ale ag primordial.

'primula sf primrose.

princi'pale [printʃi'pale] ag main,
principal // sm manager, boss.

princi'pato [printʃi'pato] sm principality.

'principe ['printʃipe] sm prince; **~**
ereditario crown prince; **princi'pessa** sf
princess.

principi'ante [printʃi'pjante] sm/f
beginner.

principi'are [printʃi'pjare] vt, vi to start,
begin.

prin'cipio [prin'tʃipjo] sm (inizio)
beginning, start; (origine) origin, cause;
(concetto, norma) principle; **al** o **in ~** at
first; **per ~** on principle.

pri'ore sm (REL) prior.

priorità sf priority.

'prisma, i sm prism.

pri'vare vt: ~ **qd di** to deprive sb of;
~rsi di to go o do without.

priva'tiva sf (ECON) monopoly.

pri'vato, a ag private // sm/f private
citizen; **in ~** in private.

privazi'one [privat'tsjone] sf privation,
hardship.

privilegi'are [privile'dʒare] vt to grant a
privilege to.

privi'legio [privi'ledʒo] sm privilege.

'privo, a ag: ~ **di** without, lacking.

pro prep for, on behalf of // sm inv (utilità)
advantage, benefit; **a che ~?** what's the

use?; **il ~ e il contro** the pros and cons.

pro'babile ag probable, likely; **pro-**
babilità sf inv probability.

pro'bante ag convincing.

probità sf integrity, probity.

pro'blema, i sm problem.

pro'boscide [pro'boʃʃide] sf (di elefante)
trunk.

procacci'are [prokat'tʃare] vt to get,
obtain.

pro'cedere [pro'tʃedere] vi to proceed;
(comportarsi) to behave; (iniziare): ~ **a** to
start; ~ **contro** (DIR) to start legal
proceedings against; **procedi'mento** sm
(modo di condurre) procedure; (di
avvenimenti) course; (comportamento)
behaviour; (TECN) process; **proce'dura** sf
(DIR) procedure.

proces'sare [protʃes'sare] vt (DIR) to try.

processi'one [protʃes'sjone] sf
procession.

pro'cesso [pro'tʃesso] sm (DIR) trial;
proceedings pl; (metodo) process.

pro'cinto [pro'tʃinto] sm: **in ~ di fare**
about to do, on the point of doing.

pro'clama, i sm proclamation.

procla'mare vt to proclaim;
proclamazi'one sf proclamation,
declaration.

procrastinazi'one [prokrastinat'tsjone]
sf procrastination.

procre'are vt to procreate.

pro'cura sf (DIR) proxy; power of
attorney; (ufficio) attorney's office.

procu'rare vt: ~ **qc a qd** (provvedere) to
get o obtain sth for sb; (causare: noie etc)
to bring o give sb sth.

procura'tore, 'trice sm/f (DIR) ≈
solicitor; (: chi ha la procura) attorney;
proxy; ~ **generale** (in corte d'appello)
public prosecutor; (in corte di cassazione)
Attorney General; ~ **della Repubblica**
(in corte d'assise, tribunale) public
prosecutor.

prodi'gare vt to be lavish with; **~rsi per**
qd to do all one can for sb.

pro'digio [pro'didʒo] sm marvel, wonder;
(persona) prodigy; **prodigi'oso, a** ag
prodigious; phenomenal.

'prodigo, a, ghi, ghe ag lavish,
extravagant.

pro'dotto, a pp di **produrre** // sm
product; **~i agricoli** farm produce sg.

pro'durre vt to produce; **prodursi** vr
(attore) to perform, appear; **produttività**
sf productivity; **produt'tivo, a** ag
productive; **produt'tore, 'trice** sm/f
producer; **produzi'one** sf production;
(rendimento) output.

pro'emio sm introduction, preface.

Prof. (abbr di professore) Prof.

profa'nare vt to desecrate.

pro'fano, a ag (mondano) secular;
profane; (sacrilego) profane.

profe'rire vt to utter.

profes'sare vt to profess; (medicina etc)
to practise.

professio'nale ag professional.

professi'one *sf* profession; **professio-'nista, i, e** *sm/f* professional.

profes'sore, 'essa *sm/f* (*INS*) teacher; (: *di università*) lecturer; (: *titolare di cattedra*) professor.

pro'feta, i *sm* prophet; **profetiz'zare** *vt* to prophesy; **profe'zia** *sf* prophecy.

pro'ficuo, a *ag* useful, profitable.

profi'lare *vt* to outline; (*ornare: vestito*) to edge; (*aereo*) to streamline; **~rsi** *vr* to stand out, be silhouetted; to loom up.

pro'filo *sm* profile; (*contorno*) contour, line; (*breve descrizione*) sketch, outline; **di ~ in** profile.

profit'tare *vi*: **~ in** to make progress in; **~ di** (*trarre profitto*) to profit by; (*approfittare*) to take advantage of.

pro'fitto *sm* advantage, profit, benefit; (*fig: progresso*) progress; (*COMM*) profit.

pro'fondere *vt* (*lodi*) to lavish; (*denaro*) to squander; **~rsi in** to be profuse in.

profondità *sf inv* depth.

pro'fondo, a *ag* deep; (*rancore, meditazione*) profound // *sm* depth(s *pl*), bottom; **~ 8 metri** 8 metres deep.

'profugo, a, ghi, ghe *sm/f* refugee.

profu'mare *vt* to perfume // *vi* (2) to be fragrant; **~rsi** *vr* to put on perfume *o* scent.

profume'ria *sf* perfumery; (*negozio*) perfume shop; **~e** *sfpl* perfumes.

pro'fumo *sm* (*prodotto*) perfume, scent; (*fragranza*) scent, fragrance.

profusi'one *sf* profusion; **a ~** in plenty.

pro'fuso, a *pp di* **profondere**.

proget'tare [prodʒet'tare] *vt* to plan; (*TECN: edificio*) to plan, design; **pro'getto** *sm* plan; (*idea*) plan, project; **progetto di legge** bill.

pro'gramma, i *sm* programme; (*TV, RADIO*) programmes *pl*; (*INS*) syllabus, curriculum; (*INFORM*) program; **program-'mare** *vt* (*TV, RADIO*) to put on; (*INFORM*) to program; (*ECON*) to plan; **programma-'tore, 'trice** *sm/f* (*INFORM*) computer programmer; (*ECON*) planner; **program-mazi'one** *sf* programming; planning.

progre'dire *vi* to progress, make progress.

progressi'one *sf* progression.

progres'sivo, a *ag* progressive.

pro'gresso *sm* progress *q*; **fare ~i** to make progress.

proi'bire *vt* to forbid, prohibit; **proibi-'tivo, a** *ag* prohibitive; **proibizi'one** *sf* prohibition.

proiet'tare *vt* (*gettare*) to throw out (*o* off *o* up); (*CINEMA*) to project; (: *presentare*) to show, screen; (*luce, ombra*) to throw, cast, project; **proi'ettile** *sm* projectile, bullet (*o* shell *etc*); **proiet'tore** *sm* (*CINEMA*) projector; (*AUT*) headlamp; (*MIL*) searchlight; **proiezi'one** *sf* (*CINEMA*) projection; showing.

'prole *sf* children *pl*, offspring.

proletari'ato *sm* proletariat.

prole'tario, a *ag, sm* proletarian.

prolife'rare *vi* (*fig*) to proliferate.

pro'lifico, a, ci, che *ag* prolific.

pro'lisso, a *ag* verbose.

'prologo, ghi *sm* prologue.

pro'lunga, ghe *sf* (*di cavo elettrico etc*) extension.

prolun'gare *vt* (*discorso, attesa*) to prolong; (*linea, termine*) to extend.

prome'moria *sm inv* memorandum.

pro'messa *sf* promise.

pro'messo, a *pp di* **promettere**.

pro'mettere *vt* to promise // *vi* to be *o* look promising; **~ a qd di fare** to promise sb that one will do.

promi'nente *ag* prominent; **promi-'nenza** *sf* prominence.

promiscuità *sf* promiscuousness.

promon'torio *sm* promontory, headland.

pro'mosso, a *pp di* **promuovere**.

promo'tore *sm* promoter, organizer.

promozi'one [promot'tsjone] *sf* promotion.

promul'gare *vt* to promulgate.

promu'overe *vt* to promote.

proni'pote *sm/f* (*di nonni*) great-grandchild, great-grandson/grand-daughter; (*di zii*) great-nephew/niece.

pro'nome *sm* (*LING*) pronoun.

pronosti'care *vt* to foretell, predict; to presage.

pron'tezza [pron'tettsa] *sf* readiness; quickness, promptness.

'pronto, a *ag* ready; (*rapido*) fast, quick, prompt; **~!** (*TEL*) hello!; **~ all'ira** quick-tempered; **~ soccorso** first aid.

prontu'ario *sm* manual, handbook.

pro'nuncia [pro'nuntʃa] *etc* = **pronunzia** *etc*.

pro'nunzia [pro'nuntsja] *sf* pronunciation; **pronunzi'are** *vt* (*parola, sentenza*) to pronounce; (*dire*) to utter; (*discorso*) to deliver; **pronunziarsi** *vr* to declare one's opinion; **pronunzi'ato, a** *ag* (*spiccato*) pronounced, marked; (*sporgente*) prominent.

propa'ganda *sf* propaganda.

propa'gare *vt* (*fig*) to spread; (*BIOL*) to propagate; **~rsi** *vr* to spread; to propagate; (*FISICA*) to be propagated.

pro'pendere *vi*: **~ per** to favour, lean towards; **propensi'one** *sf* inclination, propensity; **pro'penso, a** *pp di* **propendere**.

propi'nare *vt* to administer.

pro'pizio, a [pro'pittsjo] *ag* favourable.

pro'porre *vt* (*suggerire*): **~ qc (a qd)/di fare** to suggest sth (to sb)/doing, propose to do; (*candidato*) to put forward; (*legge, brindisi*) to propose; **proporsi di fare** to propose *o* intend to do; **proporsi una meta** to set o.s. a goal.

proporzio'nale [proportsjo'nale] *ag* proportional.

proporzio'nare [proportsjo'nare] *vt*: **~ qc a** to proportion *o* adjust sth to.

proporzi'one [propor'tsjone] *sf* proportion; **in ~ a** in proportion to.

pro'posito *sm* (*intenzione*) intention, aim;

(*argomento*) subject, matter; **a ~ di** regarding, with regard to; **di ~** (*apposta*) deliberately, on purpose; **a ~ by** the way; **capitare a ~** (*cosa, persona*) to turn up at the right time.

proposizi'one [propozit'tsjone] *sf* (*LING*) clause; (: *periodo*) sentence.

pro'posto, a *pp di* **proporre** // *sf* suggestion; proposal.

proprietà *sf inv* (*diritto*) ownership; (*ciò che si possiede*) property *gen* q, estate; (*caratteristica*) property; (*correttezza*) correctness; **proprie'tario**, a *sm/f* owner; (*di albergo etc*) proprietor, owner; (*per l'inquilino*) landlord/lady.

'proprio, a *ag* (*possessivo*) own; (: *impersonale*) one's; (*esatto*) exact, correct, proper; (*senso, significato*) literal; (*LING: nome*) proper; (*particolare*): **~ di** characteristic of, peculiar to // *av* (*precisamente*) just, exactly, precisely; (*davvero*) really; (*affatto*): **non ... ~** not ... at all.

propulsi'one *sf* propulsion.

'prora *sf* (*NAUT*) bow(s *pl*), prow.

'proroga, **ghe** *sf* extension; postponement; **proro'gare** *vt* to extend; (*differire*) to postpone, defer.

pro'rompere *vi* to burst out; **pro'rotto**, a *pp di* **prorompere**.

'prosa *sf* prose; **pro'saico**, a, **ci**, **che** *ag* (*fig*) prosaic, mundane.

pro'sciogliere [prof'ʃɔʎʎere] *vt* to release; (*DIR*) to acquit; **prosci'olto**, a *pp di* **prosciogliere**.

prosciu'gare [proʃʃu'gare] *vt* (*terreni*) to drain, reclaim; **~rsi** *vr* to dry up.

prosci'utto [proʃ'ʃutto] *sm* ham.

pros'critto, a *pp di* **proscrivere** // *sm* exile.

pros'crivere *vt* to exile, banish.

prosecuzi'one [prosekut'tsjone] *sf* continuation.

prosegui'mento *sm* continuation; **buon ~!** all the best!; (*a chi viaggia*) enjoy the rest of your journey!

prosegu'ire *vt* to carry on with, continue // *vi* to carry on, go on.

prospe'rare *vi* to thrive; **prosperità** *sf* prosperity; **'prospero**, a *ag* (*fiorente*) flourishing, thriving, prosperous; (*favorevole*) favourable; **prospe'roso**, a *ag* (*robusto*) hale and hearty; (: *ragazza*) buxom.

prospet'tare *vt* (*esporre*) to point out, show; **~rsi** *vr* to look, appear.

prospet'tiva *sf* (*ARTE*) perspective; (*veduta*) view; (*fig: previsione*) prospect.

pros'petto *sm* (*veduta*) view, prospect; (*facciata*) façade, front; (*tabella*) table.

prospici'ente [prospi'tʃɛnte] *ag*: **~ qc** facing *o* overlooking sth.

prossimità *sf* nearness, proximity; **in ~ di** near (to), close to.

'prossimo, a *ag* (*vicino*): **~ a** near (to), close to; (*che viene subito dopo*) next; (*parente*) close // *sm* neighbour, fellow man.

prosti'tuta *sf* prostitute; **prostituzi'one** *sf* prostitution.

pros'trare *vt* (*fig*) to exhaust, wear out; **~rsi** *vr* (*fig*) to humble o.s.

protago'nista, **i**, **e** *sm/f* protagonist.

pro'teggere [pro'tɛddʒere] *vt* to protect.

prote'ina *sf* protein.

pro'tendere *vt* to stretch out; **pro'teso**, a *pp di* **protendere**.

pro'testa *sf* protest; (*dichiarazione*) protestation, profession.

protes'tante *ag*, *sm/f* Protestant.

protes'tare *vt*, *vi* to protest; **~rsi** *vr*: **~rsi innocente** *etc* to protest one's innocence *o* that one is innocent *etc*.

protet'tivo, a *ag* protective.

pro'tetto, a *pp di* **proteggere**.

protet'torato *sm* protectorate.

protet'tore, **'trice** *sm/f* protector; (*sostenitore*) patron.

protezi'one [protet'tsjone] *sf* protection; (*patrocinio*) patronage.

protocol'lare *vt* to register // *ag* formal; of protocol.

proto'collo *sm* protocol; (*registro*) register of documents.

pro'totipo *sm* prototype.

pro'trarre *vt* (*prolungare*) to prolong; (*differire*) to put off; **pro'tratto**, a *pp di* **protrarre**.

protube'ranza [protube'rantsa] *sf* protuberance, bulge.

'prova *sf* (*esperimento, cimento*) test, trial; (*tentativo*) attempt, try; (*MAT, testimonianza, documento etc*) proof; (*DIR*) evidence q, proof; (*INS*) exam, test; (*TEATRO*) rehearsal; (*di abito*) fitting; **a ~ di** (*in testimonianza di*) as proof of; **a ~ di fuoco** fireproof; **mettere in ~** (*vestito*) to try on; **mettere alla ~** to put to the test; **viaggio** *o* **corsa di ~** test *o* trial run; **~ generale** (*TEATRO*) dress rehearsal.

pro'vare *vt* (*sperimentare*) to test; (*tentare*) to try, attempt; (*assaggiare*) to try, taste; (*sperimentare in sé*) to experience; (*sentire*) to feel; (*cimentare*) to put to the test; (*dimostrare*) to prove; (*abito*) to try on // *vi* to try; **~rsi** *vr*: **~rsi (a fare)** to try *o* attempt (to do); **~ a fare** to try *o* attempt to do.

proveni'enza [prove'njɛntsa] *sf* origin, source.

prove'nire *vi* (2): **~ da** to come from.

pro'venti *smpl* revenue *sg*.

prove'nuto, a *pp di* **provenire**.

pro'verbio *sm* proverb.

pro'vetta *sf* test tube.

pro'vetto, a *ag* skilled, experienced.

pro'vincia, **ce** *o* **cie** [pro'vintʃa] *sf* province; **provinci'ale** *ag* provincial.

pro'vino *sm* (*CINEMA*) screen test; (*campione*) specimen.

provo'cante *ag* (*attraente*) provocative.

provo'care *vt* (*causare*) to cause, bring about; (*eccitare: riso, pietà*) to arouse; (*irritare, sfidare*) to provoke; **provoca-**

'torio, a ag provocative; **provocazi'one** sf provocation.

provve'dere vi (disporre): ~ **(a)** to provide (for); (prendere un provvedimento) to take steps, act // vt to provide, supply; ~**rsi** vr: ~**rsi di** to provide o.s. with; **provvedi'mento** sm measure; (di previdenza) precaution.

provvi'denza [provvi'dɛntsa] sf: **la** ~ providence; **provvidenzi'ale** ag providential.

provvigi'one [provvi'dʒone] sf (COMM) commission.

provvi'sorio, a ag temporary; (DIR) provisional.

prov'vista sf provision, supply.

'prua sf (NAUT) = **prora**.

pru'dente ag cautious, careful, prudent; (assennato) sensible, wise; **pru'denza** sf prudence; (cautela) caution, care.

'prudere vi to itch, be itchy.

'prugna ['prуɲɲa] sf plum; ~ **secca** prune; **'prugno** sm plum tree.

prurigi'noso, a [pruridʒi'noso] ag itchy.

pru'rito sm itchiness q; itch.

P.S. (abbr di postscriptum) P.S.; abbr di Pubblica Sicurezza.

pseu'donimo sm pseudonym.

psica'nalisi sf psychoanalysis; **psicana-'lista, i, e** sm/f psychoanalyst; **psicana-liz'zare** vt to psychoanalyse.

'psiche ['psike] sf (PSIC) psyche.

psichi'atra, i, e [psi'kjatra] sm/f psychiatrist; **psichia'tria** sf psychiatry.

psicolo'gia [psikolo'dʒia] sf psychology; **psico'logico, a, ci, che** ag psychological; **psi'cologo, a, gi, ghe** sm/f psychologist.

psico'patico, a, ci, che ag psychopathic // sm/f psychopath.

P.T. (abbr di Posta e Telegrafi) P.O.

pubbli'care vt to publish.

pubblicazi'one [pubblikat'tsjone] sf publication; ~**i** (**matrimoniali**) sfpl (marriage) banns.

pubbli'cista, i, e [pubbli'tʃista] sm/f (STAMPA) occasional contributor.

pubblicità [pubblitʃi'ta] sf (diffusione) publicity; (attività) advertising; (annunci nei giornali) advertisements pl; **pubblici-'tario, a** ag advertising cpd; (trovata, film) publicity cpd.

'pubblico, a, ci, che ag public; (statale: scuola etc) state cpd // sm public; (spettatori) audience; **in** ~ in public; ~ **funzionario** civil servant; **P~ Ministero** Public Prosecutor's Office; **la P~a Sicurezza** the Police.

'pube sm (ANAT) pubis.

pubertà sf puberty.

'pudico, a, ci, che ag modest.

pu'dore sm modesty.

puericul'tura sf paediatric nursing; infant care.

pue'rile ag childish.

pugi'lato [pudʒi'lato] sm boxing.

'pugile ['pudʒile] sm boxer.

pugna'lare [puɲɲa'lare] vt to stab.

pu'gnale [puɲ'ɲale] sm dagger.

'pugno ['puɲɲo] sm fist; (colpo) punch; (quantità) fistful.

'pulce ['pultʃe] sf flea.

pul'cino [pul'tʃino] sm chick.

pu'ledro, a sm/f colt/filly.

pu'leggia, ge [pu'leddʒa] sf pulley.

pu'lire vt to clean; (lucidare) to polish; **pu-'lito, a** ag (anche fig) clean; (ordinato) neat, tidy // sf quick clean; **puli'tura** sf cleaning; **puli'zia** sf cleaning; cleanness; **fare le pulizie** to do the cleaning, do the housework.

'pullman sm inv coach.

pul'lover sm inv pullover, jumper.

pullu'lare vi to swarm, teem.

pul'mino sm minibus.

'pulpito sm pulpit.

pul'sante sm (push-)button.

pul'sare vi to pulsate, beat; **pulsazi'one** sf beat.

pul'viscolo sm fine dust.

'puma sm inv puma.

pun'gente [pun'dʒɛnte] ag prickly; stinging; (anche fig) biting.

'pungere ['pundʒere] vt to prick; (sog: insetto, ortica) to sting; (: freddo) to bite; (fig) to wound, offend.

pungigli'one [pundʒiʎ'ʎone] sm sting.

pungo'lare vt to goad.

pu'nire vt to punish; **puni'tivo, a** ag punitive; **punizi'one** sf punishment.

'punta sf point; (parte terminale) tip, end; (di monte) peak; (di costa) promontory; (minima parte) touch, trace; **in** ~ **di piedi** on tip-toe; **ore di** ~ peak hours; **uomo di** ~ front-rank o leading man.

pun'tare vt (piedi a terra, gomiti sul tavolo) to plant; (dirigere: pistola) to point; (scommettere) to bet // vi (mirare): ~ **a** to aim at; (avviarsi): ~ **su** to head o make for; (fig: contare): ~ **su** to count o rely on.

pun'tata sf (gita) short trip; (scommessa) bet; (parte di opera) instalment; **romanzo a ~e** serial.

punteggi'are [punted'dʒare] vt to dot; (forare) to make holes in; (LING) to punctuate; **punteggia'tura** sf (LING) punctuation.

pun'teggio [pun'teddʒo] sm score.

puntel'lare vt to support.

pun'tello sm prop, support.

pun'tiglio [pun'tiʎʎo] sm obstinacy, stubbornness.

pun'tina sf: ~ **da disegno** drawing pin.

pun'tino sm dot; **fare qc a** ~ to do sth properly.

'punto, a pp di **pungere** // sm (segno, macchiolina) spot; (LING) full stop; (MAT, momento, di punteggio, fig: argomento) point; (posto) spot; (a scuola) mark; (nel cucire, nella maglia, MED) stitch // av: **non** ... ~ not ... at all; **due** ~**i** sm (LING) colon; **sul** ~ **di fare** (just) about to do; **fare il** ~ (NAUT) to take a bearing; (fig): **fare il** ~ **su qc** to define sth; **alle 6 in** ~ at 6 o'clock sharp o on the dot; **essere a buon**

~ to have reached a satisfactory stage; **mettere a** ~ **to** adjust; (*motore*) to tune; (*cannocchiale*) to focus; (*fig*) to settle; **di** ~ **in bianco** point-blank; ~ **cardinale** point of the compass, cardinal point; ~ **debole** weak point; ~ **esclamativo/ interrogativo** exclamation/question mark; ~ **di riferimento** landmark; (*fig*) point of reference; ~ **di vendita** retail outlet; ~ **e virgola** semicolon; ~ **di vista** (*fig*) point of view; **~i di sospensione** suspension points.

puntu'ale *ag* punctual; precise, exact; **puntualità** *sf* punctuality; precision, exactness.

pun'tura *sf* (*di ago*) prick; (*di insetto*) sting, bite; (*MED*) puncture; (: *iniezione*) injection; (*dolore*) sharp pain.

punzecchi'are [puntsek'kjare] *vt* to prick; (*fig*) to tease.

pun'zone [pun'tsone] *sm* (*per metalli*) stamp, die.

'pupa *sf* doll.

pu'pazzo [pu'pattso] *sm* puppet.

pu'pillo, a *sm/f* (*DIR*) ward; (*prediletto*) favourite, pet // *sf* (*ANAT*) pupil.

purché [pur'ke] *cong* provided that, on condition that.

'pure *cong* (*tuttavia*) and yet, nevertheless; (*anche se*) even if // *av* (*anche*) too, also; **pur di** (*al fine di*) just to; **faccia** ~! go ahead!, please do!

purè *sm*, **pu'rea** *sf* (*CUC*) purée; (*di patate*) mashed potatoes.

pu'rezza [pu'rettsa] *sf* purity.

'purga, ghe *sf* (*MED*) purging q; purge; (*POL*) purge.

pur'gante *sm* (*MED*) purgative, purge.

pur'gare *vt* (*MED, POL*) to purge; (*pulire*) to clean.

purga'torio *sm* purgatory.

purifi'care *vt* to purify; (*metallo*) to refine.

puri'tano, a *ag, sm/f* Puritan.

'puro, a *ag* pure; (*acqua*) clear, limpid; (*vino*) undiluted; **puro'sangue** *sm/f inv* thoroughbred.

pur'troppo *av* unfortunately.

pus *sm* pus.

pusil'lanime *ag* fainthearted.

'pustola *sf* pimple.

puti'ferio *sm* rumpus, row.

putre'fare *vi* (2) to putrefy, rot; **putre- 'fatto, a** *pp di* **putrefare**.

'putrido, a *ag* putrid, rotten.

put'tana *sf* (*fam!*) whore (!).

'puzza ['puttsa] *sf* = **puzzo**.

puz'zare [put'tsare] *vi* to stink.

'puzzo ['puttso] *sm* stink, foul smell.

'puzzola ['puttsola] *sf* polecat.

puzzo'lente [puttso'lɛnte] *ag* stinking.

Q

qua *av* here; **in** ~ (*verso questa parte*) this way; **da un anno in** ~ for a year now; **per di** ~ (*passare*) this way; **al di** ~ **di**

(*fiume, strada*) on this side of; *vedi* **questo**.

qua'derno *sm* notebook; (*per scuola*) exercise book.

qua'drangolo *sm* quadrangle.

qua'drante *sm* quadrant; (*di orologio*) face.

qua'drare *vi* (*bilancio*) to balance, tally; (*descrizione*) to correspond; (*fig*): ~ **a** to please, be to one's liking // *vt* (*MAT*) to square; **non mi quadra** I don't like it; **qua'drato, a** *ag* square; (*fig: equilibrato*) level-headed, sensible // *sm* (*MAT*) square; (*PUGILATO*) ring; **5 al quadrato** 5 squared.

qua'dretto *sm*: **a ~i** (*tessuto*) checked.

quadri'foglio [kwadri'fɔʎʎo] *sm* four-leaf clover.

'quadro *sm* (*pittura*) painting, picture; (*quadrato*) square; (*tabella*) table, chart; (*TECN*) board, panel; (*TEATRO*) scene; (*fig: scena, spettacolo*) sight; (: *descrizione*) outline, description; **~i** *smpl* (*POL*) party organizers; (*MIL*) cadres; (*CARTE*) diamonds.

qua'drupede *sm* quadruped.

quadrupli'care *vt* to quadruple.

'quadruplo, a *ag, sm* quadruple.

quaggiù [kwad'dʒu] *av* down here.

'quaglia ['kwaʎʎa] *sf* quail.

'qualche ['kwalke] *det* some; (*alcuni*) a few; (*in espressioni interrogative*) any; (*uno*): **c'è** ~ **medico?** is there a doctor?; **ho comprato** ~ **libro** I've bought some *o* a few books; **hai** ~ **sigaretta?** have you any cigarettes?; **una persona di** ~ **rilievo** a person of some importance; ~ **cosa** = **qualcosa**; **in** ~ **modo** somehow; ~ **volta** sometimes; **qualche'duno** *pronome* = **qualcuno**.

qual'cosa *pronome* something; (*in espressioni interrogative*) anything; **qual- cos'altro** something else; anything else; ~ **di nuovo** something new; anything new.

qual'cuno *pronome* (*persona*) someone, somebody; (: *in espressioni interrogative*) anyone, anybody; (*alcuni*) some; ~ **è favorevole a noi** some are on our side; **qualcun altro** someone *o* somebody else; anyone *o* anybody else.

'quale (*spesso troncato in* **qual**) *det* what; (*discriminativo*) which; (*come*) as // *pronome* (*interrogativo*) what; which; (*relativo*): **il(la)** ~ (*persona: soggetto*) who; (: *oggetto, con preposizione*) whom; (*cosa*) which; (*possessivo*): **la signora della** ~ **ammiriamo la bellezza** the lady whose beauty we admire // *av* (*in qualità di*) as; ~ **disgrazia!** what a misfortune!

qua'lifica, che *sf* qualification; (*titolo*) title.

qualifi'care *vt* to qualify; (*definire*): ~ **qd/qc come** to describe sb/sth as; **~rsi** *vr* (*anche SPORT*) to qualify; **qualifica- 'tivo, a** *ag* qualifying; **qualificazi'one** *sf* qualification.

qualità *sf inv* quality; **in** ~ **di** in one's capacity as.

qua'lora *cong* in case, if.

qual'siasi, qua'lunque *det inv* any; (*quale che sia*) whatever; (*discriminativo*) whichever; (*posposto: mediocre*) poor, indifferent; ordinary; ~ **cosa accada** whatever happens; **a** ~ **costo** at any cost, whatever the cost; **l'uomo** ~ **the man in the street;** ~ **persona** anyone, anybody.

'quando *cong, av* when; ~ **sarò ricco** when I'm rich; **da** ~ (*dacché*) since; (*interrogativo*): **da** ~ **sei qui?** how long have you been here?; **quand'anche** even if.

quantità *sf inv* quantity; (*gran numero*): **una** ~ **di** a great deal of; a lot of; **in grande** ~ in large quantities.

'quanto, a *det* (*interrogativo: quantità*) how much; (: *numero*) how many; (*esclamativo*) what a lot of, how much (*o* many); (*relativo*) as much ... as; as many ... as; **ho** ~ **denaro mi occorre** I have as much money as I need // *pronome* (*interrogativo*) how much; how many; (: *tempo*) how long; (*relativo*) as much as; as many as; ~**i(e)** *pronome pl* (*persone*) all those who // *av* (*interrogativo: con ag, av*) how; (: *con vb*) how much; (*esclamativo: con ag, av*) how; (: *con vb*) how much, what a lot; (*con valore relativo*) as much as; **studierò** ~ **posso** I'll study as much as *o* all I can; ~**i ne abbiamo oggi?** what is the date today?; ~**i anni hai?** how old are you?; ~ **costa?, quant'è?** how much does it cost?, how much is it?; **in** ~ *av* (*in qualità di*) as; (*poiché*) since, as; **per** ~ **sia brava, fa degli errori** however good she may be, she makes mistakes; **per** ~ **io sappia** as far as I know; ~ **a** as regards, as for; ~ **prima** as soon as possible; ~ **tempo?** how long?, how much time?; ~ **più ... tanto meno** the more ... the less; ~ **più ... tanto più** the more ... the more.

quan'tunque *cong* although, though.

qua'ranta *num* forty.

quaran'tena *sf* quarantine.

quaran'tesimo, a *num* fortieth.

quaran'tina *sf*: **una** ~ (**di**) about forty.

qua'resima *sf*: **la** ~ Lent.

'quarta *sf vedi* **quarto**.

quar'tetto *sm* quartet(te).

quarti'ere *sm* district, area; (*MIL*) quarters *pl*; ~ **generale** headquarters *pl*, HQ.

'quarto, a *ag* fourth // *sm* fourth; (*quarta parte*) quarter // *sf* (*AUT*) fourth (gear); ~ **d'ora** quarter of an hour; **le 6 e un** ~ **a** quarter past six.

'quarzo ['kwartso] *sm* quartz.

'quasi *av* almost, nearly // *cong* (*anche*: ~ **che**) as if; (**non**) ... ~ **mai** hardly ever; ~ ~ **me ne andrei** I've half a mind to leave.

quassù *av* up here.

'quatto, a *ag* crouched, squatting; (*silenzioso*) silent; ~ ~ very quietly; stealthily.

quat'tordici [kwat'torditʃi] *num* fourteen.

quat'trini *smpl* money *sg*, cash *sg*.

'quattro *num* four; **in** ~ **e quatt'otto** in less than no time; (*aprire*) **quattro'cento** *num* four hundred // *sm*: **il Quattrocento** the fifteenth century; **quattro'mila** *num* four thousand.

'quello, a *det* (*dav sm* **quel** + *C,* **quell'** + *V,* **quello** + *s impura, gn, pn, ps, x, z; pl* **quei** + *C,* **quegli** + *V o s impura, gn, pn, ps, x, z; dav sf* **quella** + *C,* **quell'** + *V; pl* **quelle**) that; those *pl* // *pronome* that (one); those (ones) *pl*; (*ciò*) that; ~**(a) che** the one who; ~**i(e) che** those who; **ho fatto** ~ **che potevo** I did what I could; ~**(a) ... lì** *o* **là** *det* that; **quell'uomo lì** that man; ~**(a) lì** *o* **là** *pronome* that one.

'quercia, ce ['kwertʃa] *sf* oak (tree); (*legno*) oak.

que'rela *sf* (*DIR*) (legal) action; **quere'lare** *vt* to bring an action against.

que'sito *sm* question, query; problem.

questio'nare *vi*: ~ **di/su qc** to argue about/over sth.

questio'nario *sm* questionnaire.

questi'one *sf* problem, question; (*affare*) matter; issue; (*litigio*) quarrel; **in** ~ in question; **fuor di** ~ out of the question; **è** ~ **di tempo** it's a matter *o* question of time.

'questo, a *det* this; these *pl* // *pronome* this (one); these (ones) *pl*; (*ciò*) this; ~**(a) ... qui** *o* **qua** *det* this; ~ **ragazzo qui** this boy; ~**(a) qui** *o* **qua** *pronome* this one; **lo prendo** ~ **cappotto, tu prendi quello** I'll take this coat, you take that one; **preferisce** ~ **i o quelli?** do you prefer these (ones) or those (ones)?; **vengono Paolo e Folco:** ~ **da Roma, quello da Palermo** Paolo and Folco are coming: the latter from Rome, the former from Palermo; **quest'oggi** today.

ques'tore *sm* ≈ chief constable.

'questua *sf* collection (of alms).

ques'tura *sf* police headquarters *pl*.

qui *av* here; **da** *o* **di** ~ **from here; di** ~ **in avanti** from now on; **di** ~ **a poco/una settimana** in a little while/a week's time; ~ **dentro/sopra/vicino** in/up/near here; *vedi* **questo**.

quie'tanza [kwje'tantsa] *sf* receipt.

quie'tare *vt* to calm, soothe.

qui'ete *sf* quiet, quietness; calmness; stillness; peace.

qui'eto, a *ag* quiet; (*calmo*) calm, still; (*tranquillo*) quiet, calm; (*pacifico*) peaceful; (: *persona*) peaceable.

'quindi *av* then // *cong* therefore, so.

'quindici ['kwinditʃi] *num* fifteen.

quindi'cina [kwindi'tʃina] *sf* (*serie*): **una** ~ (**di**) about fifteen; **fra una** ~ **di giorni** in a fortnight.

quin'quennio *sm* period of five years.

quin'tale *sm* quintal (*100 kg*).

'quinte *sfpl* (*TEATRO*) wings.

quin'tetto *sm* quintet(te).

'quinto, a *num* fifth.

'quorum *sm* quorum.

'quota *sf* (*ripartizione*) quota, share; (*rata*) instalment; (*AER*) height, altitude; (*IPPICA*) odds *pl*; **prendere/perdere** ~ (AER) to gain/lose height *o* altitude.

quo'tare *vt* (BORSA) to quote; **quotazi'one** *sf* quotation.

quotidi'ano, **a** *ag* daily; *(banale)* everyday // *sm (giornale)* daily (paper).

quozi'ente [kwot'tsjɛnte] *sm* (MAT) quotient; ~ **d'intelligenza** intelligence quotient, IQ.

R

ra'barbaro *sm* rhubarb.

'rabbia *sf (ira)* anger, rage; *(accanimento, furia)* fury; (MED: *idrofobia*) rabies *sg*.

rab'bino *sm* rabbi.

rabbi'oso, **a** *ag* angry, furious; *(facile all'ira)* quick-tempered; *(forze, acqua etc)* furious, raging; (MED) rabid, mad.

rabbo'nire *vt*, ~**rsi** *vr* to calm down.

rabbrivi'dire *vi* (2) to shudder, shiver.

rabbui'arsi *vr* to grow dark.

raccapez'zare [rakkapet'tsare] *vt (denaro)* to scrape together; *(senso)* to make out, understand; ~**rsi** *vr*: **non** ~**rsi** to be at a loss.

raccapricci'ante [rakkaprit'tʃante] *ag* horrifying.

raccatta'palle *sm inv* (SPORT) ballboy.

raccat'tare *vt* to pick up.

rac'chetta [rak'ketta] *sf (per tennis)* racket; *(per ping-pong)* bat; ~ **da neve** snowshoe; ~ **da sci** ski stick.

racchi'udere [rak'kjudere] *vt* to contain; **racchi'uso**, **a** *pp di* **racchiudere**.

rac'cogliere [rak'kɔʎʎere] *vt* to collect; *(raccattare)* to pick up; *(frutti, fiori)* to pick, pluck; (AGR) to harvest; *(approvazione, voti)* to win; *(profughi)* to take in; ~**rsi** *vr* to gather; *(fig)* to gather one's thoughts; to meditate; **raccogli'mento** *sm* meditation; **raccogli'tore**, **'trice** *sm/f* collector // *sm (cartella)* folder, binder; **raccoglitore a fogli mobili** loose-leaf binder.

rac'colto, **a** *pp di* **raccogliere** // *ag (rannicchiato)* curled up; *(pensoso)* thoughtful; *(assorto)* absorbed, engrossed // *sm* (AGR) crop, harvest // *sf* collecting *q*; collection; (AGR) harvesting *q*, gathering *q*; harvest, crop; *(adunata)* gathering.

raccoman'dare *vt* to recommend; *(affidare)* to entrust; *(lettera)* to register; ~**rsi a qd** to commend o.s. to sb; **mi raccomando!** don't forget!; **raccoman-'data** *sf (anche:* **lettera raccomandata**) registered letter; **raccomandazi'one** *sf* recommendation.

raccomo'dare *vt (rassettare)* to put in order; *(riparare)* to repair, mend.

raccon'tare *vt*: ~ **a qd** *(dire)* to tell (sb); *(narrare)* to relate to (sb), tell (sb) about; **rac'conto** *sm* telling *q*, relating *q*; *(fatto raccontato)* story, tale.

raccorci'are [rakkor'tʃare] *vt* to shorten.

raccor'dare *vt* to link up, join; **rac'cordo** *sm* (TECN: *giunzione*) connection, joint;

(AUT: di autostrada) slip road; **raccordo anulare** (AUT) ring road.

ra'chitico, **a**, **ci**, **che** [ra'kitiko] *ag* suffering from rickets; *(fig)* scraggy, scrawny.

rachi'tismo [raki'tizmo] *sm* (MED) rickets *sg*.

racimo'lare [ratʃimo'lare] *vt (fig)* to scrape together, glean.

'rada *sf (natural)* harbour.

'radar *sm* radar.

raddol'cire [raddol'tʃire] *vt* to sweeten; *(fig: lenire)* to ease, soothe; (: *voce, colori*) to soften; ~**rsi** *vr (tempo)* to grow milder.

raddoppi'are *vt* to double; *(accrescere: anche fig)* to redouble, increase // *vi* to double.

raddriz'zare [raddrit'tsare] *vt* to straighten; *(fig: correggere)* to put straight, correct.

'radere *vt (barba)* to shave off; *(mento)* to shave; *(fig: rasentare)* to graze; to skim; ~**rsi** *vr* to shave (o.s.); ~ **al suolo** to raze to the ground.

radi'ale *ag* radial.

radi'are *vt* to strike off.

radia'tore *sm* radiator.

radiazi'one [radjat'tsjone] *sf* (FISICA) radiation; *(cancellazione)* striking off.

radi'cale *ag* radical // *sm* (LING) root.

ra'dicchio [ra'dikkjo] *sm* chicory.

ra'dice [ra'ditʃe] *sf* root.

'radio *sf inv* radio // *sm* (CHIM) radium; **radioattività** *sf* radioactivity; **radioat-'tivo**, **a** *ag* radioactive; **radiodiffusi'one** *sf* (radio) broadcasting; **radiogra'fia** *sf* radiography; *(foto)* X-ray photograph; **radiogra'fare** *vt* to X-ray; **radi'ologo**, **a**, **gi**, **ghe** *sm/f* radiologist.

radi'oso, **a** *ag* radiant.

radiostazi'one [radjostat'tsjone] *sf* radio station.

'rado, **a** *ag (capelli)* sparse, thin; *(visite)* infrequent; **di** ~ rarely.

radu'nare *vt*, ~**rsi** *vr* to gather, assemble.

ra'dura *sf* clearing.

'rafano *sm* radish.

raffazzo'nare [raffattso'nare] *vt* to patch up.

raf'fermo, **a** *ag* stale.

'raffica, **che** *sf* (METEOR) gust (of wind); *(di colpi: scarica)* burst of gunfire.

raffigu'rare *vt* to represent.

raffi'nare *vt* to refine; **raffina'tezza** *sf* refinement; **raffi'nato**, **a** *ag* refined; **raffine'ria** *sf* refinery.

raffor'zare [raffor'tsare] *vt* to reinforce.

raffredda'mento *sm* cooling.

raffred'dare *vt* to cool; *(fig)* to dampen, have a cooling effect on; ~**rsi** *vr* to grow cool *o* cold; *(prendere raffreddore)* to catch a cold; *(fig)* to cool (off).

raffred'dore *sm* (MED) cold.

raf'fronto *sm* comparison.

'rafia *sf (fibra)* raffia.

ra'gazzo, **a** [ra'gattso] *sm/f* boy/girl; *(fam:*

fidanzato) boyfriend/girlfriend.

raggi'ante [rad'dʒante] *ag* radiant, shining.

'raggio ['raddʒo] *sm* (*di sole etc*) ray; (*MAT, distanza*) radius; (*di ruota etc*) spoke; ~ **d'azione** range; ~**i X** X-rays.

raggi'rare [raddʒi'rare] *vt* to take in, trick; **rag'giro** *sm* trick.

raggi'ungere [rad'dʒundʒere] *vt* to reach; (*persona: riprendere*) to catch up (with); (*bersaglio*) to hit; (*fig: meta*) to achieve; **raggi'unto, a** *pp di* **raggiungere**.

raggomito'larsi *vr* to curl up.

raggranel'lare *vt* to scrape together.

raggrin'zare [raggrin'tsare] *vt, vi* (2) (*anche*: ~**rsi**) to wrinkle.

raggrup'pare *vt* to group (together).

ragguagli'are [raggwaʎ'ʎare] *vt* (*paragonare*) to compare; (*informare*) to inform; **raggu'aglio** *sm* comparison; piece of information.

ragguar'devole *ag* (*degno di riguardo*) distinguished, notable; (*notevole: somma*) considerable.

'ragia ['radʒa] *sf* resin; **acqua** ~ turpentine.

ragiona'mento [radʒona'mento] *sm* reasoning *q*; arguing *q*; argument.

ragio'nare [radʒo'nare] *vi* (*usare la ragione*) to reason; (*discorrere*): ~ **(di)** to argue (about).

ragi'one [ra'dʒone] *sf* reason; (*dimostrazione, prova*) argument, reason; (*diritto*) right; **aver** ~ to be right; **aver** ~ **di qd** to get the better of sb; **in** ~ **di** at the rate of; to the amount of; according to; **a o con** ~ rightly, justly; **perdere la** ~ to become insane; (*fig*) to take leave of one's senses; **a ragion veduta** after due consideration.

ragione'ria [radʒone'ria] *sf* accountancy; accounts department.

ragio'nevole [radʒo'nevole] *ag* reasonable.

ragioni'ere, a [radʒo'njere] *sm/f* accountant.

ragli'are [raʎ'ʎare] *vi* to bray.

ragna'tela [raɲɲa'tela] *sf* cobweb, spider's web.

'ragno ['raɲɲo] *sm* spider.

ragù *sm inv* (*CUC*) meat sauce; stew.

RAI-TV [raiti'vu] *abbr f di Radio televisione italiana.*

rallegra'menti *smpl* congratulations.

ralle'grare *vt* to cheer up; ~**rsi** *vr* to cheer up; (*provare allegrezza*) to rejoice; ~**rsi con qd** to congratulate sb.

rallenta'mento *sm* slowing down; lessening, slackening.

rallen'tare *vt* to slow down; (*fig*) to lessen, slacken // *vi* to slow down; ~**rsi** *vr* (*fig*) to lessen, slacken (off).

raman'zina [raman'dzina] *sf* lecture, telling-off.

'rame *sm* (*CHIM*) copper.

ramificazi'one [ramifikat'tsjone] *sf* ramification.

rammari'carsi *vr*: ~ **(di)** (*rincrescersi*) to be sorry (about), regret; (*lamentarsi*) to complain (about); **ram'marico, chi** *sm* regret.

rammen'dare *vt* to mend; (*calza*) to darn; **ram'mendo** *sm* mending *q*; darning *q*; mend; darn.

rammen'tare *vt* to remember, recall; (*richiamare alla memoria*): ~ **qc a qd** to remind sb of sth; ~**rsi** *vr*: ~**rsi (di qc)** to remember (sth).

rammol'lire *vt* to soften // *vi* (2) (*anche*: ~**rsi**) to go soft.

'ramo *sm* branch.

ramo'scello [ramoʃ'ʃello] *sm* twig.

'rampa *sf* flight (of stairs); ~ **di lancio** launching pad.

rampi'cante *ag* (*BOT*) climbing.

ram'pino *sm* (*gancio*) hook; (*NAUT*) grapnel; (*fig*) pretext, excuse.

ram'pone *sm* harpoon; (*ALPINISMO*) crampon.

'rana *sf* frog.

'rancido, a ['rantʃido] *ag* rancid.

ran'core *sm* rancour, resentment.

ran'dagio, a, gi, gie o ge [ran'dadʒo] *ag* (*gatto, cane*) stray.

ran'dello *sm* club, cudgel.

'rango, ghi *sm* (*condizione sociale, MIL: riga*) rank.

rannicchi'arsi [rannik'kjarsi] *vr* to crouch, huddle.

rannuvo'larsi *vr* to cloud over, become overcast.

ra'nocchio [ra'nɔkkjo] *sm* (edible) frog.

'rantolo *sm* wheeze; (*di agonizzanti*) death rattle.

'rapa *sf* (*BOT*) turnip.

ra'pace [ra'patʃe] *ag* (*animale*) predatory; (*fig*) rapacious, grasping // *sm* bird of prey.

ra'pare *vt* (*capelli*) to crop, cut very short.

'rapida *sf vedi* **rapido.**

rapidità *sf* speed.

'rapido, a *ag* fast; (*esame, occhiata*) quick, rapid // *sm* (*FERR*) express (train) // *sf* (*di fiume*) rapid.

rapi'mento *sm* kidnapping; (*fig*) rapture.

ra'pina *sf* robbery; (*bottino*) loot; ~ **a mano armata** armed robbery; **rapi'nare** *vt* to rob; **rapina'tore, 'trice** *sm/f* robber.

ra'pire *vt* (*cose*) to steal; (*persone*) to kidnap; (*fig*) to enrapture, delight; **rapi'tore, 'trice** *sm/f* kidnapper.

rappez'zare [rappet'tsare] *vt* to patch.

rappor'tare *vt* (*riferire*) to report; (*confrontare*) to compare; (*riprodurre*) to reproduce.

rap'porto *sm* (*resoconto*) report; (*legame*) relationship; (*MAT, TECN*) ratio; ~**i** *smpl* (*fra persone, paesi*) relations; ~**i sessuali** sexual intercourse *sg*.

rap'prendersi *vr* to coagulate, clot; (*latte*) to curdle.

rappre'saglia [rappre'saʎʎa] *sf* reprisal, retaliation.

rappresen'tante *sm/f* representative;

rappresen'tanza sf delegation, deputation; (COMM: ufficio, sede) agency.

rappresen'tare vt to represent; (TEATRO) to perform; **rappresenta'tivo, a** ag representative; **rappresentazi'one** sf representation; performing q; (spettacolo) performance.

rap'preso, a pp di **rapprendere**.

rapso'dia sf rhapsody.

rare'fare vt, ~**rsi** vr to rarefy; **rare-'fatto, a** pp di **rarefare**.

rarità sf inv rarity.

'raro, a ag rare.

ra'sare vt (barba etc) to shave off; (siepi, erba) to trim, cut; ~**rsi** vr to shave (o.s.).

raschi'are [ras'kjare] vt to scrape; (macchia, fango) to scrape off // vi to clear one's throat.

rasen'tare vt (andar rasente) to keep close to; (sfiorare) to skim along (o over); (fig) to border on.

ra'sente prep: ~ (a) close to, very near.

'raso, a pp di **radere** // ag (barba) shaved; (capelli) cropped; (con misure di capacità) level; (pieno: bicchiere) full to the brim // sm (tessuto) satin; ~ **terra** close to the ground; **un cucchiaio** ~ a level spoonful.

ra'soio sm razor; ~ **elettrico** electric shaver o razor.

ras'segna [ras'senna] sf (MIL) inspection, review; (esame) inspection; (resoconto) review, survey; (pubblicazione letteraria etc) review; (mostra) exhibition, show; **passare in** ~ (MIL) to inspect, review.

rasse'gnare [rassen'nare] vt to resign, relinquish; ~**rsi** vr (accettare) to resign o.s.; **rassegnazi'one** sf resignation.

rasse'renarsi vr (tempo) to clear up.

rasset'tare vt to tidy, put in order; (aggiustare) to repair, mend.

rassicu'rare vt to reassure.

rasso'dare vt to harden, stiffen; (fig) to strengthen, consolidate.

rassomigli'anza [rassomiʎ'ʎantsa] sf resemblance.

rassomigli'are [rassomiʎ'ʎare] vi: ~ **a** to resemble, look like.

rastrel'lare vt to rake; (fig: perlustrare) to comb.

rastrelli'era sf rack; (per piatti) dishrack.

ras'trello sm rake.

'rata sf (quota) instalment; **pagare a** ~**e** to pay by instalments o on hire purchase; **rate'are, rateiz'zare** vt to divide into instalments.

ratifi'care vt (DIR) to ratify.

'ratto sm (DIR) abduction; (ZOOL) rat.

rattop'pare vt to patch; **rat'toppo** sm patching q; patch.

rattrap'pire vt to make stiff; ~**rsi** vr to be stiff.

rattris'tare vt to sadden; ~**rsi** vr to become sad.

'rauco, a, chi, che ag hoarse.

rava'nello sm radish.

ravi'oli smpl ravioli sg.

ravve'dersi vr to mend one's ways.

ravvici'nare [ravvitʃi'nare] vt (avvicinare): ~ **qc a** to bring sth nearer to; (: due tubi) to bring closer together; (riconciliare) to reconcile, bring together.

ravvi'sare vt to recognize.

ravvi'vare vt to revive; (fig) to brighten up, enliven; ~**rsi** vr to revive; to brighten up.

razio'cinio [ratsjo'tʃinjo] sm reasoning q; reason; (buon senso) common sense.

razio'nale [rattsjo'nale] ag rational.

razio'nare [rattsjo'nare] vt to ration.

razi'one [rat'tsjone] sf ration; (porzione) portion, share.

'razza ['rattsa] sf race; (ZOOL) breed; (discendenza, stirpe) stock, race; (sorta) sort, kind.

raz'zia [rat'tsia] sf raid, foray.

razzi'ale [rat'tsjale] ag racial.

raz'zismo [rat'tsizmo] sm racism, racialism.

raz'zista, i, e [rat'tsista] ag, sm/f racist, racialist.

'razzo ['raddzo] sm rocket.

razzo'lare [rattso'lare] vi (galline) to scratch about.

re sm inv (sovrano) king; (MUS) D; (: solfeggiando la scala) re.

rea'gire [rea'dʒire] vi to react.

re'ale ag real; (di, da re) royal // sm: **il** ~ reality; **rea'lismo** sm realism; **rea'lista, i, e** sm/f realist; (POL) royalist.

realiz'zare [realid'dzare] vt (progetto etc) to realize, carry out; (sogno, desiderio) to realize, fulfil; (scopo) to achieve; (COMM: titoli etc) to realize; (CALCIO etc) to score; ~**rsi** vr to be realized; **realizzazi'one** sf realization; fulfilment; achievement; **realizzazione scenica** stage production.

real'mente av really, actually.

realtà sf inv reality.

re'ato sm offence.

reat'tore sm (FISICA) reactor; (AER: aereo) jet; (: motore) jet engine.

reazio'nario, a [reattsjo'narjo] ag (POL) reactionary.

reazi'one [reat'tsjone] sf reaction.

'rebbio sm prong.

recapi'tare vt to deliver.

re'capito sm (indirizzo) address; (consegna) delivery.

re'care vt (portare) to bring; (avere su di sé) to carry, bear; (cagionare) to cause, bring; ~**rsi** vr to go.

re'cedere [re'tʃedere] vi to withdraw.

recensi'one [retʃen'sjone] sf review; **recen'sire** vt to review; **recen'sore, a** sm/f reviewer.

re'cente [re'tʃente] ag recent; **di** ~ recently.

recessi'one [retʃes'sjone] sf (ECON) recession.

re'cidere [re'tʃidere] vt to cut off, chop off.

reci'divo, a [retʃi'divo] sm/f (DIR) second (o habitual) offender, recidivist.

re'cinto [re'tʃinto] sm enclosure; (ciò che

recinge) fence; surrounding wall.
recipi'ente [retʃi'pjɛnte] *sm* container.
re'ciproco, a, ci, che [re'tʃiproko] *ag* reciprocal.
re'ciso, a [re'tʃizo] *pp di* **recidere.**
'recita ['rɛtʃita] *sf* performance.
'recital ['rɛtʃital] *sm inv* recital.
reci'tare [retʃi'tare] *vt* (*poesia, lezione*) to recite; (*dramma*) to perform; (*ruolo*) to play *o* act (the part of); **recitazi'one** *sf* recitation; (*di attore*) acting.
recla'mare *vi* to complain // *vt* (*richiedere*) to demand, claim; (*necessitare*) to need, require.
ré'clame [re'klam] *sf inv* advertising *q*; advert(isement).
re'clamo *sm* complaint.
reclusi'one *sf* (*DIR*) imprisonment.
re'cluso, a *sm/f* prisoner.
'recluta *sf* recruit; **recluta'mento** *sm* recruitment; **reclu'tare** *vt* to recruit.
re'condito, a *ag* secluded; (*fig*) secret, hidden.
recriminazi'one [rekriminat'tsjone] *sf* recrimination.
recrude'scenza [rekrudeʃ'ʃɛntsa] *sf* fresh outbreak.
redargu'ire *vt* to rebuke.
re'datto, a *pp di* **redigere; redat'tore, 'trice** *sm/f* (*giornalista*) writer; sub-editor; (*di casa editrice*) editor; **redazi'one** *sf* writing; editing; (*sede*) editorial office(s); (*personale*) editorial staff; (*versione*) version.
reddi'tizio, a [reddi'tittsjo] *ag* profitable.
'reddito *sm* income; (*dello Stato*) revenue; (*di un capitale*) yield.
re'dento, a *pp di* **redimere.**
redenzi'one [reden'tsjone] *sf* redemption.
re'digere [re'didʒere] *vt* to write; (*contratto*) to draw up.
re'dimere *vt* to deliver; (*REL*) to redeem.
'redini *sfpl* reins.
redi'vivo, a *ag* returned to life, reborn.
'reduce ['rɛdutʃe] *ag*: ~ **da** returning from, back from // *sm/f* survivor.
'refe *sm* thread.
refe'rendum *sm inv* referendum.
refe'renza [refe'rɛntsa] *sf* reference.
re'ferto *sm* medical report.
refet'torio *sm* refectory.
refrat'tario, a *ag* refractory; (*fig*): **essere** ~ **alla matematica** to have no aptitude for mathematics.
refrige'rare [refridʒe'rare] *vt* to refrigerate; (*rinfrescare*) to cool, refresh; **refrigerazi'one** *sf* refrigeration.
rega'lare *vt* to give (as a present), make a present of.
re'gale *ag* regal.
re'galo *sm* gift, present.
re'gata *sf* regatta.
reg'gente [red'dʒɛnte] *sm/f* regent; **reg-'genza** *sf* regency.
'reggere ['rɛddʒere] *vt* (*tenere*) to hold; (*sostenere*) to support, bear, hold up; (*portare*) to carry, bear; (*resistere*) to

withstand; (*dirigere: impresa*) to manage, run; (*governare*) to rule, govern; (*LING*) to take, be followed by // *vi* (*resistere*): ~ **a** to stand up to, hold out against; (*sopportare*): ~ **a** to stand; (*durare*) to last; ~**rsi** *vr* (*stare ritto*) to stand; (*fig: dominarsi*) to control o.s.; ~**rsi sulle gambe** *o* **in piedi** to stand up.
'reggia, ge ['rɛddʒa] *sf* royal palace.
reggi'calze [reddʒi'kaltse] *sm inv* suspender belt.
reggi'mento [reddʒi'mento] *sm* (*MIL*) regiment.
reggi'petto [reddʒi'pɛtto] *sm*, **reggi-'seno** [reddʒi'seno] *sm* bra.
re'gia, 'gie [re'dʒia] *sf* (*TV, CINEMA etc*) direction.
re'gime [re'dʒime] *sm* (*POL*) regime; (*DIR: aureo, patrimoniale etc*) system; (*MED*) diet; (*TECN*) (engine) speed; **essere a** ~ to be on a diet.
re'gina [re'dʒina] *sf* queen.
'regio, a, gi, gie ['rɛdʒo] *ag* royal.
regio'nale [redʒo'nale] *ag* regional.
regi'one [re'dʒone] *sf* region; (*territorio*) region, district, area.
re'gista, i, e [re'dʒista] *sm/f* (*TV, CINEMA etc*) director.
regis'trare [redʒis'trare] *vt* (*AMM*) to register; (*COMM*) to enter; (*notare*) to note, take note of; (*canzone, conversazione, sog: strumento di misura*) to record; (*mettere a punto*) to adjust, regulate; **registra'tore** *sm* (*strumento di misura*) recorder, register; (*magnetofono*) tape recorder; (*classificatore*) folder; **registratore di cassa** cash register; **registrazi'one** *sf* recording; (*AMM*) registration; (*COMM*) entry.
re'gistro [re'dʒistro] *sm* (*libro*) register; ledger; logbook; (*DIR*) registry; (*MUS, TECN*) register.
re'gnare [reɲ'ɲare] *vi* to reign, rule; (*fig*) to reign.
'regno ['reɲɲo] *sm* kingdom; (*periodo*) reign; (*fig*) realm; **il** ~ **animale/vegetale** the animal/ vegetable kingdom; **il R**~ **Unito** the United Kingdom.
'regola *sf* rule; **a** ~ **d'arte** duly; perfectly; **in** ~ in order.
regola'mento *sm* (*complesso di norme*) regulations *pl*; (*di debito*) settlement; ~ **di conti** (*fig*) settling of scores.
rego'lare *ag* regular; (*in regola: domanda*) in order, lawful // *vt* to regulate, control; (*apparecchio*) to adjust, regulate; (*questione, conto, debito*) to settle; ~**rsi** *vr* (*moderarsi*): ~**rsi nel bere/nello spendere** to control one's drinking/spending; (*comportarsi*) to behave, act; **regolarità** *sf inv* regularity.
'regolo *sm* ruler; ~ **calcolatore** slide rule.
reinte'grare *vt* to restore; (*in una carica*) to reinstate.
relatività *sf* relativity.
rela'tivo, a *ag* relative.

relazi'one [relat'tsjone] *sf* (*fra cose, persone*) relation(ship); (*resoconto*) report, account; ~**i** *sfpl* (*conoscenze*) connections.

rele'gare *vt* to banish; (*fig*) to relegate.

religi'one [reli'dʒone] *sf* religion; (*rispetto*) veneration, reverence; **religi'oso, a** *ag* religious // *sm/f* monk/nun.

re'liquia *sf* relic.

re'litto *sm* wreck; (*fig*) down-and-out.

re'mare *vi* to row.

remini'scenze [reminiʃ'ʃentse] *sfpl* reminiscences.

remissi'one *sf* remission; (*deferenza*) submissiveness, compliance.

remis'sivo, a *ag* submissive, compliant.

'remo *sm* oar.

re'moto, a *ag* remote.

'rendere *vt* (*ridare*) to return, give back; (: *saluto etc*) to return; (*produrre*) to yield, bring in; (*esprimere, tradurre*) to render; (*far diventare*): ~ **qc possibile** to make sth possible; ~ **la vista a qd** to restore sb's sight; ~ **grazie a qd** to thank sb; ~**rsi utile** to make o.s. useful; ~**rsi conto di qc** to realize sth.

rendi'conto *sm* (*rapporto*) report, account; (*COMM*) statement of account.

rendi'mento *sm* (*reddito*) yield; (*di manodopera, TECN*) efficiency; (*capacità di produrre*) output; (*di studenti*) performance.

'rendita *sf* (*di individuo*) private *o* unearned income; (*COMM*) revenue; ~ **annua** annuity.

'rene *sm* kidney.

'reni *sfpl* back *sg*.

reni'tente *ag* reluctant, unwilling; ~ **ai consigli di qd** unwilling to follow sb's advice; **essere** ~ **alla leva** (*MIL*) to fail to report for military service.

'renna *sf* reindeer *inv.*

'Reno *sm:* **il** ~ the Rhine.

'reo, a *sm/f* (*DIR*) offender.

re'parto *sm* department, section; (*MIL*) detachment.

repel'lente *ag* repulsive.

repen'taglio [repen'taʎʎo] *sm:* **mettere a** ~ to jeopardize, risk.

repen'tino, a *ag* sudden, unexpected.

repe'ribile *ag* to be found, available.

re'perto *sm* (*ARCHEOLOGIA*) find; (*MED*) report.

reper'torio *sm* (*TEATRO*) repertory; (*elenco*) index, (alphabetical) list.

'replica, che *sf* repetition; reply, answer; (*obiezione*) objection; (*TEATRO, CINEMA*) repeat performance; (*copia*) replica.

repli'care *vt* (*ripetere*) to repeat; (*rispondere*) to answer, reply.

repressi'one *sf* repression.

re'presso, a *pp di* **reprimere.**

re'primere *vt* to suppress, repress.

re'pubblica, che *sf* republic; **repubbli'cano, a** *ag, sm/f* republican.

repu'tare *vt* to consider, judge.

reputazi'one [reputat'tsjone] *sf* reputation.

'requie *sf* rest.

requi'sire *vt* to requisition.

requi'sito *sm* requirement.

requisizi'one [rekwizit'tsjone] *sf* requisition.

'resa *sf* (*l'arrendersi*) surrender; (*restituzione, rendimento*) return; ~ **dei conti** rendering of accounts; (*fig*) day of reckoning.

resi'dente *ag* resident; **resi'denza** *sf* residence; **residenzi'ale** *ag* residential.

re'siduo, a *ag* residual, remaining // *sm* remainder; (*CHIM*) residue.

'resina *sf* resin.

resis'tente (*che resiste*): ~ **a** resistant to; (*forte*) strong; (*duraturo*) long-lasting, durable; ~ **al caldo** heat-resistant; **resis'tenza** *sf* resistance; (*di persona*) endurance, resistance.

re'sistere *vi* to resist; ~ **a** (*assalto, tentazioni*) to resist; (*dolore, sog: pianta*) to withstand; (*non patir danno*) to be resistant to; **resis'tito, a** *pp di* **resistere.**

'reso, a *pp di* **rendere.**

reso'conto *sm* report, account.

respin'gente [respin'dʒente] *sm* (*FERR*) buffer.

res'pingere [res'pindʒere] *vt* to drive back, repel; (*rifiutare*) to reject; (*INS: bocciare*) to fail; **res'pinto, a** *pp di* **respingere.**

respi'rare *vi* to breathe; (*fig*) to get one's breath; to breathe again // *vt* to breathe (in), inhale; **respira'tore** *sm* respirator; **respira'torio, a** *ag* respiratory; **respirazi'one** *sf* breathing; **respirazione artificiale** artificial respiration; **res'piro** *sm* breathing *q*; (*singolo atto*) breath; (*fig*) respite, rest; **mandare un respiro di sollievo** to give a sigh of relief.

respon'sabile *ag* responsible // *sm/f* person responsible; (*capo*) person in charge; ~ **di** responsible for; (*DIR*) liable for; **responsabilità** *sf inv* responsibility; (*legale*) liability.

res'ponso *sm* answer.

'ressa *sf* crowd, throng.

res'tare *vi* (2) (*rimanere*) to remain, stay; (*diventare*): ~ **orfano/cieco** to become *o* be left an orphan/become blind; (*trovarsi*): ~ **sorpreso** to be surprised; (*avanzare*) to be left, remain; ~ **d'accordo** to agree; **non resta più niente** there's nothing left; **restano pochi giorni** there are only a few days left.

restau'rare *vt* to restore; **restaurazi'one** *sf* (*POL*) restoration; **res'tauro** *sm* (*di edifici etc*) restoration.

res'tio, a, 'tii, 'tie *ag* restive; (*persona*): ~ **a** reluctant to.

restitu'ire *vt* to return, give back; (*energie, forze*) to restore.

'resto *sm* remainder, rest; (*denaro*) change; (*MAT*) remainder; ~**i** *smpl* leftovers; (*di città, mortali*) remains; **del** ~ moreover, besides.

res'tringere [res'trindʒere] *vt* to reduce; (*vestito*) to take in; (*stoffa*) to shrink; (*fig*) to restrict, limit; **~rsi** vr (strada) to narrow; (stoffa) to shrink; (persone) to draw closer together; **restrizi'one** sf restriction.

'rete sf net; (fig) trap, snare; (di recinzione) wire netting; (AUT, FERR, di spionaggio etc) network; **segnare una ~** (CALCIO) to score a goal.

reti'cente [reti'tʃɛnte] ag reticent.

retico'lato sm grid; (rete metallica) wire netting.

'retina sf (ANAT) retina.

re'torico, a, ci, che ag rhetorical // sf rhetoric.

retribu'ire vt to pay; (premiare) to reward; **retribuzi'one** sf payment; reward.

re'trivo, a ag (fig) reactionary.

'retro sm inv back // av (dietro): **vedi ~** see over(leaf).

retro'cedere [retro'tʃɛdere] vi (2) to withdraw // vt (CALCIO) to relegate; (MIL) to degrade.

retroda'tare vt (AMM) to backdate.

re'trogrado, a ag (fig) reactionary, backward-looking.

retrogu'ardia sf (MIL) rearguard.

retro'marcia [retro'martʃa] sf (AUT) reverse; (: dispositivo) reverse gear.

retrospet'tivo, a ag retrospective.

retrovi'sore sm (AUT) driving mirror.

'retta sf (MAT) straight line; (di convitto) charge for bed and board; (fig: ascolto): **dar ~ a** to listen to, pay attention to.

rettango'lare ag rectangular.

ret'tangolo, a ag right-angled // sm rectangle.

ret'tifica, che sf rectification, correction.

rettifi'care vt (curva) to straighten; (fig) to rectify, correct.

'rettile sm reptile.

retti'lineo, a ag rectilinear; (fig: condotta) upright, honest.

retti'tudine sf rectitude, uprightness.

'retto, a pp di **reggere** // ag straight; (MAT): **angolo ~** right angle; (onesto) honest, upright; (giusto, esatto) correct, proper, right.

ret'tore sm (REL) rector; (di università) ≈ chancellor.

reuma'tismo sm rheumatism.

reve'rendo, a ag: **il ~ padre Belli** the Reverend Father Belli.

rever'sibile ag reversible.

revisio'nare vt (componimento) to revise; (conti) to audit; (TECN) to overhaul, service; (DIR: processo) to review.

revisi'one sf revision; auditing q; audit; servicing q; overhaul; review.

revi'sore sm: **~ di conti/bozze** auditor/proofreader.

'revoca sf revocation.

revo'care vt to revoke.

re'volver sm inv revolver.

riabili'tare vt to rehabilitate; (fig) to restore to favour; **riabilitazi'one** sf rehabilitation.

rial'zare [rial'tsare] vt to raise, lift; (alzare di più) to heighten, raise; (aumentare: prezzi) to increase, raise // vi (2) (prezzi) to rise, increase; **ri'alzo** sm (di prezzi) increase, rise; (sporgenza) rise.

ria'prire vt, **~rsi** vr to reopen, open again.

ri'armo sm (MIL) rearmament.

rias'setto sm (di stanza etc) rearrangement; (ordinamento) reorganization.

rias'sumere vt (riprendere) to resume; (impiegare di nuovo) to re-employ; (sintetizzare) to summarize; **rias'sunto, a** pp di **riassumere** // sm summary.

ria'vere vt to have again; (avere indietro) to get back; (riacquistare) to recover; **~rsi** vr to recover.

riba'dire vt (fig) to confirm.

ri'balta sf flap; (TEATRO: proscenio) front of the stage; (: apparecchio d'illuminazione) footlights pl; (fig) limelight.

ribal'tabile ag (sedile) tip-up.

ribal'tare vt, vi (2) (anche: **~rsi**) to turn over, tip over.

ribas'sare vt to lower, bring down // vi (2) to come down, fall; **ri'basso** sm reduction, fall.

ri'battere vt to return, hit back; (confutare) to refute // vi to retort; **~ su qc** (fig) to harp on about sth.

ribel'larsi vr: **~ (a)** to rebel (against); **ri'belle** ag (soldati) rebel; (ragazzo) rebellious // sm/f rebel; **ribelli'one** sf rebellion.

'ribes sm inv currant; redcurrant; **~ nero** blackcurrant.

ribol'lire vi (fermentare) to ferment; (fare bolle) to bubble, boil; (fig) to seethe.

ri'brezzo [ri'breddzo] sm disgust, loathing; **far ~ a** to disgust.

ribut'tante ag disgusting, revolting.

rica'dere vi (2) to fall again; (scendere a terra, fig: nel peccato etc) to fall back; (vestiti, capelli etc) to hang (down); (riversarsi: fatiche, colpe): **~ su** to fall on; **rica'duta** sf (MED) relapse.

rical'care vt (disegni) to trace; (fig) to follow faithfully.

rica'mare vt to embroider.

ricambi'are vt to change again; (contraccambiare) to repay, return; **ri'cambio** sm exchange, return; (FISIOL) metabolism; **ricambi** smpl, **pezzi di ricambio** spare parts.

ri'camo sm embroidery.

ricapito'lare vt to recapitulate, sum up.

ricat'tare vt to blackmail; **ricatta'tore, 'trice** sm/f blackmailer; **ri'catto** sm blackmail.

rica'vare vt (estrarre) to draw out, extract; (ottenere) to obtain, gain; **ri'cavo** sm proceeds pl.

ric'chezza [rik'kettsa] sf wealth; (fig) richness; **~e** sfpl (beni) wealth sg, riches.

'riccio, a ['rittʃo] ag curly // sm (zool) hedgehog; (: anche: **~ di mare**) sea urchin; **'ricciolo** *sm* curl; **ricci'uto, a** *ag* curly.

'ricco, a, chi, che *ag* rich; *(persona, paese)* rich, wealthy // *sm/f* rich man/woman; **i ~chi** the rich; **~ di** full of; rich in.

ri'cerca, che [ri'tʃerka] *sf* search; *(indagine)* investigation, inquiry; *(studio)*: **la ~** research; **una ~** piece of research.

ricer'care [ritʃer'kare] *vt (cercare con cura)* to look for, search for; *(indagare)* to investigate; *(tentare di scoprire: verità etc)* to try to find; **ricer'cato, a** *ag (apprezzato)* much sought-after; *(affettato)* studied, affected // *sm (POLIZIA)* wanted man.

ri'cetta [ri'tʃetta] *sf (MED)* prescription; *(CUC)* recipe.

ricettazi'one [ritʃettat'tsjone] *sf (DIR)* receiving (stolen goods).

ri'cevere [ri'tʃevere] *vt* to receive; *(stipendio, lettera)* to get, receive; *(accogliere: ospite)* to welcome; *(vedere: cliente, rappresentante etc)* to see // *vi* to receive visitors; to see clients *etc*; **ricevi-'mento** *sm* receiving *q*; *(accoglienza)* welcome, reception; *(trattenimento)* reception; **ricevi'tore** *sm (TECN)* receiver; **ricevitore delle imposte** tax collector; **rice'vuta** *sf* receipt; **ricezi'one** *sf (RADIO, TV)* reception.

richia'mare [rikja'mare] *vt (chiamare indietro, ritelefonare)* to call back; *(ambasciatore, truppe)* to recall; *(rimproverare)* to reprimand; *(attirare)* to attract, draw; *(riportare)* to cite; **~rsi a** *(riferirsi a)* to refer to; **~ qc alla mente** to recall sth; **richi'amo** *sm* call; *(MIL, di ambasciatore)* recall; *(attrazione)* attraction, call, appeal.

richi'edere [ri'kjedere] *vt* to ask again for; *(chiedere indietro)*: **~ qc** to ask for sth back; *(chiedere: per sapere)* to ask; *(: per avere)* to ask for; *(AMM: documenti)* to apply for; *(esigere)* to need, require; **ri-chi'esto, a** *pp di* **richiedere** // *sf (domanda)* request; *(AMM)* application, request; *(esigenza)* demand, request; **a richiesta** on request.

'ricino ['ritʃino] *sm*: **olio di ~** castor oil.

ricognizi'one [rikoɲɲit'tsjone] *sf (MIL)* reconnaissance; *(DIR)* recognition, acknowledgement.

ricominci'are [rikomin'tʃare] *vt, vi* to start again, begin again.

ricom'pensa *sf* reward.

ricompen'sare *vt* to reward.

riconcili'are [rikontʃi'ljare] *vt* to reconcile; **~rsi** *vr* to be reconciled; **riconciliazi'one** *sf* reconciliation.

ricono'scente [rikonoʃ'ʃɛnte] *ag* grateful; **ricono'scenza** *sf* gratitude.

rico'noscere [riko'noʃʃere] *vt* to recognize; *(DIR: figlio, debito)* to acknowledge; *(ammettere: errore)* to admit, acknowledge; *(MIL)* to reconnoitre; **riconosci'mento** *sm* recognition; acknowledgement; *(identificazione)*

identification; **riconosci'uto, a** *pp di* **riconoscere**.

rico'prire *vt* to re-cover; *(coprire)* to cover; *(occupare: carica)* to hold.

ricor'dare *vt* to remember, recall; *(richiamare alla memoria)*: **~ qc a qd** to remind sb of sth; **~rsi** *vr*: **~rsi (di)** to remember; **~rsi di qc/di aver fatto** to remember sth/having done.

ri'cordo *sm* memory; *(regalo)* keepsake, souvenir; *(di viaggio)* souvenir; **~i** *smpl (memorie)* memoirs.

ricor'rente *ag* recurrent, recurring; **ricor'renza** *sf* recurrence; *(festività)* anniversary.

ri'correre *vi (2) (ripetersi)* to recur; **~ a** *(rivolgersi)* to turn to; *(: DIR)* to appeal to; *(servirsi di)* to have recourse to; **ri'corso, a** *pp di* **ricorrere** // *sm* recurrence; *(DIR)* appeal; **far ricorso a = ricorrere a**.

ricostitu'ire *vt* to re-establish, reconstitute; *(MED)* to restore.

ricostru'ire *vt (casa)* to rebuild; *(fatti)* to reconstruct; **ricostruzi'one** *sf* rebuilding *q*; reconstruction.

ri'cotta *sf* soft white unsalted cheese made from sheep's milk.

ricove'rare *vt* to give shelter to; **~ qd in ospedale** to admit sb to hospital.

ri'covero *sm* shelter, refuge; admission (to hospital); *(per vecchi, indigenti)* home.

ricre'are *vt* to recreate; *(rinvigorire)* to restore; *(fig: distrarre)* to amuse.

ricreazi'one [rikreat'tsjone] *sf* recreation, entertainment; *(INS)* break.

ri'credersi *vr* to change one's mind.

ricupe'rare *vt (rientrare in possesso di)* to recover, get back; *(tempo perduto)* to make up for; *(NAUT)* to salvage; *(: naufraghi)* to rescue; *(delinquente)* to rehabilitate.

ricu'sare *vt* to refuse.

ridacchi'are [ridak'kjare] *vi* to snigger.

ri'dare *vt* to return, give back.

'ridere *vi* to laugh; *(deridere, beffare)*: **~ di** to laugh at, make fun of.

ri'detto, a *pp di* **ridire**.

ri'dicolo, a *ag* ridiculous, absurd.

ridimensio'nare *vt* to reorganize; *(fig)* to see in the right perspective.

ri'dire *vt* to repeat; *(criticare)* to find fault with; to object to; **trova sempre qualcosa da ~** he always manages to find fault.

ridon'dante *ag* redundant.

ri'dotto, a *pp di* **ridurre**.

ri'durre *vt (anche CHIM, MAT)* to reduce; *(prezzo, spese)* to cut, reduce; *(accorciare: vestito)* to shorten; *(: opera letteraria)* to abridge; *(: RADIO, TV)* to adapt; **ridursi** *vr (diminuirsi)* to be reduced, shrink; **ridursi a** to be reduced to; **ridursi pelle e ossa** to be reduced to skin and bone; **ridu-zi'one** *sf* reduction; abridgement; adaptation.

riempi'mento *sm* filling.

riem'pire *vt* to fill (up); *(modulo)* to fill in *o* out; **~rsi** *vr* to fill (up); *(mangiare* *troppo*) to stuff o.s.; ~ **qc di** to fill sth (up) with; **riempi'tivo, a** *ag* filling // *sm* (*anche fig*) filler.

rien'tranza [rien'trantsa] *sf* recess; indentation.

rien'trare *vi* (2) (*entrare di nuovo*) to go (*o* come) back in; (*tornare*) to return; (*fare una rientranza*) to go in, curve inwards; to be indented; (*riguardare*): ~ **in** to be included among, form part of; **ri'entro** *sm* (*ritorno*) return; (*anche* ASTR) re-entry.

riepilo'gare *vt* to summarize // *vi* to recapitulate.

ri'fare *vt* to do again; (*riparare*) to repair; (*imitare*) to imitate, copy; ~**rsi** *vr* (*ristabilirsi: malato*) to recover; (*: tempo*) to clear up; (*ricominciare*) to start again; (*vendicarsi*) to get even; (*risarcirsi*): ~**rsi di** to make up for; ~ **il letto** to make the bed; ~**rsi una vita** to make a new life for o.s.; **ri'fatto, a** *pp di* **rifare**.

riferi'mento *sm* reference; **in** *o* **con** ~ **a** with reference to.

rife'rire *vt* (*riportare*) to report; (*ascrivere*): ~ **qc a** to attribute sth to // *vi* to make a report; ~**rsi** *vr*: ~**rsi a** to refer to.

rifi'nire *vt* to finish off, put the finishing touches to; **rifini'tura** *sf* finish; finishing touches *pl*.

rifiu'tare *vt* to refuse; ~ **di fare** to refuse to do; **rifi'uto** *sm* refusal; **rifiuti** *smpl* (*spazzatura*) rubbish *sg*, refuse *sg*.

riflessi'one *sf* (FISICA, *meditazione*) reflection; (*il pensare*) thought, reflection; (*osservazione*) remark.

rifles'sivo, a *ag* (*persona*) thoughtful, reflective; (LING) reflexive.

ri'flesso *pp di* **riflettere** // *sm* (*di luce, rispecchiamento*) reflection; (FISIOL) reflex; **di** *o* **per** ~ indirectly.

ri'flettere *vt* to reflect // *vi* to think; ~**rsi** *vr* to be reflected; ~ **su** to think about.

riflet'tore *sm* reflector; (*proiettore*) floodlight; searchlight.

ri'flusso *sm* flowing back; (*della marea*) ebb.

ri'fondere *vt* (*rimborsare*) to refund, repay.

ri'forma *sf* reform; (MIL) declaration of unfitness for service; discharge (*on health grounds*); **la R** ~ (REL) the Reformation.

rifor'mare *vt* to re-form; (*cambiare, innovare*) to reform; (MIL: *recluta*) to declare unfit for service; (*: soldato*) to invalid out, discharge; **riforma'torio** *sm* (DIR) approved school.

riforni'mento *sm* supplying, providing; restocking; ~**i** *smpl* supplies, provisions.

rifor'nire *vt* (*provvedere*): ~ **di** to supply *o* provide with; (*fornire di nuovo: casa etc*) to restock.

ri'frangere [ri'frandʒere] *vt* to refract; **ri'fratto, a** *pp di* **rifrangere**; **rifrazi'one** *sf* refraction.

rifug'gire [rifud'dʒire] *vi* (2) to escape again; (*fig*): ~ **da** to shun.

rifugi'arsi [rifu'dʒarsi] *vr* to take refuge; **rifugi'ato, a** *sm/f* refugee.

ri'fugio [ri'fudʒo] *sm* refuge, shelter; ~ **antiaereo** air-raid shelter.

'riga, ghe *sf* line; (*striscia*) stripe; (*di persone, cose*) line, row; (*regolo*) ruler; (*scriminatura*) parting; **mettersi in** ~ to line up; **a** ~**ghe** (*foglio*) lined; (*vestito*) striped.

ri'gagnolo [ri'gaɲɲolo] *sm* rivulet.

ri'gare *vt* (*foglio*) to rule // *vi*: ~ **diritto** (*fig*) to toe the line.

rigatti'ere *sm* junk dealer.

riget'tare [ridʒet'tare] *vt* (*gettare indietro*) to throw back; (*fig: respingere*) to reject; (*vomitare*) to bring *o* throw up; **ri'getto** *sm* (*anche* MED) rejection.

rigidità [ridʒidi'ta] *sf* rigidity; stiffness; severity, rigours *pl*; strictness; ~ **cadaverica** rigor mortis.

'rigido, a ['ridʒido] *ag* rigid, stiff; (*membro etc: indurito*) stiff; (METEOR) harsh, severe; (*fig*) strict.

rigi'rare [ridʒi'rare] *vt* to turn; (*ripercorrere*) to go round; (*fig: persona*) to get round; ~**rsi** *vr* to turn round; (*nel letto*) to turn over; ~ **il discorso** to change the subject; **ri'giri** *smpl* (*fig*) tricks.

'rigo, ghi *sm* line; (MUS) staff, stave.

rigogli'oso, a [rigoʎ'ʎoso] *ag* (*anche fig*) exuberant.

ri'gonfio, a *ag* swollen.

ri'gore [ri'gore] (METEOR) harshness, rigours *pl*; (*fig*) severity, strictness; (*anche:* **calcio di** ~) penalty; **di** ~ compulsory; **a rigor di termini** strictly speaking; **rigo'roso, a** *ag* (*severo: persona*) strict, stern; (*: disciplina*) rigorous, strict; (*preciso*) rigorous.

rigover'nare *vt* to wash (up).

riguar'dare *vt* to look at again; (*considerare*) to regard, consider; (*concernere*) to regard, concern; ~**rsi** *vr* (*aver cura di sé*) to look after o.s.; ~**rsi da** to beware of, keep away from.

rigu'ardo *sm* (*attenzione*) care; (*considerazione*) regard, respect; ~ **a** concerning, with regard to; **non aver** ~**i nell'agire/nel parlare** to act/speak freely.

rilasci'are [rilaʃ'ʃare] *vt* (*rimettere in libertà*) to release; (AMM: *documenti*) to issue; **ri'lascio** *sm* release; issue.

rilas'sare *vt* to relax; ~**rsi** *vr* to relax; (*moralità*) to become slack.

rile'gare *vt* (*libro*) to bind; **rilega'tura** *sf* binding.

ri'leggere [ri'leddʒere] *vt* to reread, read again; (*rivedere*) to read over.

ri'lento: a ~ *av* slowly.

rileva'mento *sm* (*topografico, statistico*) survey; (NAUT) bearing.

rile'vante *ag* considerable; important.

rile'vare *vt* (*ricavare*) to find; (*notare*) to notice; (*mettere in evidenza*) to point out; (*venire a conoscere: notizia*) to learn; (*raccogliere: dati*) to gather, collect; (TOPO-

GRAFIA) to survey; (*MIL*) to relieve; (*COMM*) to take over.

rili'evo *sm* (*ARTE*, *GEO*) relief; (*fig: rilevanza*) importance; (*osservazione*) point, remark; (*TOPOGRAFIA*) survey; **dar ~ a** *o* **mettere in ~ qc** (*fig*) to bring sth out, highlight sth.

rilut'tante *ag* reluctant; **rilut'tanza** *sf* reluctance.

'rima *sf* rhyme.

riman'dare *vt* to send again; (*restituire, rinviare*) to send back, return; (*differire*): **~ qc (a)** to postpone sth *o* put sth off (till); (*fare riferimento*): **~ qd a** to refer sb to; **essere rimandato** (*INS*) to have to repeat one's exams; **ri'mando** *sm* (*rinvio*) return; (*dilazione*) postponement; (*riferimento*) cross-reference.

rima'nente *ag* remaining // *sm* rest, remainder; **i ~i** (*persone*) the rest of them, the others; **rima'nenza** *sf* rest, remainder; **rimanenze** *sfpl* (*COMM*) unsold stock *sg*.

rima'nere *vi* (2) (*restare*) to remain, stay; (*avanzare*) to be left, remain; (*restare stupito*) to be amazed; (*restare, mancare*): **rimangono poche settimane a Pasqua** there are only a few weeks left till Easter; **rimane da vedere se** it remains to be seen whether; (*diventare*): **~ vedovo** to be left a widower; (*trovarsi*): **~ confuso/sorpreso** to be confused/surprised.

rimar'chevole [rimar'kevole] *ag* remarkable.

ri'mare *vt, vi* to rhyme.

rimargi'nare [rimardʒi'nare] *vt, vi* (*anche*: **~rsi**) to heal.

ri'masto, a *pp di* **rimanere**.

rima'sugli [rima'suʎʎi] *smpl* leftovers.

rimbal'zare [rimbal'tsare] *vi* to bounce back, rebound; (*proiettile*) to ricochet; **rim'balzo** *sm* rebound; ricochet.

rimbam'bire *vi* (2) to be in one's dotage; (*rincretinire*) to grow foolish.

rimboc'care *vt* (*orlo*) to turn up; (*coperta*) to tuck in; (*maniche, pantaloni*) to turn *o* roll up.

rimbom'bare *vi* to resound.

rimbor'sare *vt* to pay back, repay; **rim'borso** *sm* repayment.

rimedi'are *vi* (2): **~ a** to remedy // *vt* (*fam: procurarsi*) to get *o* scrape together.

ri'medio *sm* (*medicina*) medicine; (*cura, fig*) remedy, cure.

rimesco'lare *vt* to mix well, stir well; (*carte*) to shuffle; **sentirsi ~ il sangue** (*per paura*) to feel one's blood run cold; (*per rabbia*) to feel one's blood boil.

ri'messa *sf* (*locale: per veicoli*) garage; (: *per aerei*) hangar; (*COMM: di merce*) consignment; (: *di denaro*) remittance; (*CALCIO: anche*: **~ in gioco**) throw-in; **vendere a ~** (*COMM*) to sell at a loss.

ri'messo, a *pp di* **rimettere**.

ri'mettere *vt* (*mettere di nuovo*) to put back; (*indossare di nuovo*): **~ qc** to put sth back on, put sth on again; (*restituire*) to

return, give back; (*affidare*) to entrust; (: *decisione*) to refer; (*condonare*) to remit; (*COMM: merci*) to deliver; (: *denaro*) to remit; (*vomitare*) to bring up; (*rimandare*): **~ qc (a)** to postpone sth *o* put sth off (until); **~rsi al bello** (*tempo*) to clear up; **~rsi in salute** to get better, recover one's health.

'rimmel *sm inv* ® mascara.

rimoder'nare *vt* to modernize.

rimon'tare *vt* (*meccanismo*) to reassemble; (*scale*) to go up again; (*SPORT*) to overtake // *vi* (2) to go back up; **~ a** (*risalire a*) to date *o* go back to; **~ a cavallo** to remount.

rimorchi'are [rimor'kjare] *vt* to tow; **rimorchia'tore** *sm* (*NAUT*) tug(boat).

ri'morchio [ri'mɔrkjo] *sm* tow; (*traino*) trailer.

ri'morso *sm* remorse.

rimozi'one [rimot'tsjone] *sf* removal; (*da un impiego*) dismissal; (*PSIC*) repression.

rim'pasto *sm* (*POL*) reshuffle.

rimpatri'are *vi* (2) to return home // *vt* to repatriate; **rim'patrio** *sm* repatriation.

rimpi'angere [rim'pjandʒere] *vt* to regret; (*persona*) to miss; **rimpi'anto, a** *pp di* **rimpiangere** // *sm* regret.

rimpiat'tino *sm* hide-and-seek.

rimpiaz'zare [rimpjat'tsare] *vt* to replace.

rimpicco'lire *vt* to make smaller // *vi* (2) (*anche*: **~rsi**) to become smaller.

rimpin'zare [rimpin'tsare] *vt*: **~ di** to cram *o* stuff with.

rimprove'rare *vt* to rebuke, reprimand; **rim'provero** *sm* rebuke, reprimand.

rimugi'nare [rimudʒi'nare] *vt* (*fig*) to turn over in one's mind.

rimunerazi'one [rimunerat'tsjone] *sf* remuneration; (*premio*) reward.

rimu'overe *vt* to remove; (*destituire*) to dismiss; (*fig: distogliere*) to dissuade.

Rinasci'mento [rinaʃʃi'mento] *sm*: **il ~** the Renaissance.

ri'nascita [ri'naʃʃita] *sf* rebirth, revival.

rincal'zare [rinkal'tsare] *vt* (*sostenere*) to support, prop up; (*lenzuola*) to tuck in; **rin'calzo** *sm* support, prop; (*rinforzo*) reinforcement; (*SPORT*) reserve (player); **rincalzi** *smpl* (*MIL*) reserves.

rinca'rare *vt* to increase the price of // *vi* (2) to go up, become more expensive.

rinca'sare *vi* (2) to go home.

rinchi'udere [rin'kjudere] *vt* to shut (*o* lock) up; **~rsi** *vr*: **~rsi in** to shut o.s. up in; **~rsi in se stesso** to withdraw into o.s.; **rinchi'uso, a** *pp di* **rinchiudere**.

rin'correre *vt* to chase, run after; **rin'corso, a** *pp di* **rincorrere** // *sf* short run.

rin'crescere [rin'kreʃʃere] *vb impers* (2): **mi rincresce che/di non poter fare** I'm sorry that/I can't do, I regret that/being unable to do; **rincresci'mento** *sm* regret; **rincresci'uto, a** *pp di* **rincrescere**.

rincu'lare *vi* (2) to draw back; (*arma*) to recoil.

rinfacci'are [rinfat'tʃare] vt (fig): ~ qc a qd to throw sth in sb's face.

rinfor'zare [rinfor'tsare] vt to reinforce, strengthen // vi (2) (anche: ~rsi) to grow stronger; **rin'forzo** sm reinforcement; (appoggio: anche fig) support; **rinforzi** smpl (MIL) reinforcements.

rinfran'care vt to encourage, reassure.

rinfres'care vt (atmosfera, temperatura) to cool (down); (abito, pareti) to freshen up // vi (2) (tempo) to grow cooler; ~rsi vr (ristorarsi) to refresh o.s.; (lavarsi) to freshen up; **rin'fresco, schi** sm (festa) party; **rinfreschi** smpl refreshments.

rin'fusa sf: **alla** ~ in confusion, higgledy-piggledy.

ringhi'are [rin'gjare] vi to growl, snarl.

ringhi'era [rin'gjεra] sf railing; (delle scale) banister(s pl).

ringiova'nire [rindʒova'nire] vt (sog: vestito, acconciatura etc): ~ qd to make sb look younger; (: vacanze etc) to rejuvenate // vi (2) (anche: ~rsi) to become (o look) younger.

ringrazia'menti [ringrattsja'menti] smpl thanks.

ringrazi'are [ringrat'tsjare] vt to thank; ~ qd di qc to thank sb for sth.

rinne'gare vt (fede) to renounce; (figlio) to disown, repudiate; **rinne'gato, a** sm/f renegade.

rinnova'mento sm renewal.

rinno'vare vt to renew; (ripetere) to repeat, renew; ~rsi vr (fenomeno) to be repeated, recur; **rin'novo** sm renewal; recurrence.

rinoce'ronte [rinotʃe'ronte] sm rhinoceros.

rino'mato, a ag renowned, celebrated.

rinsal'dare vt to strengthen.

rinsa'vire vi (2) to come to one's senses.

rintoc'care vi (campana) to toll; (orologio) to strike.

rintracci'are [rintrat'tʃare] vt to track down.

rintro'nare vi to boom, roar // vt (assordare) to deafen; (stordire) to stun.

rintuz'zare [rintut'tsare] vt (fig: sentimento) to check, repress; (: accusa) to refute.

ri'nuncia [ri'nuntʃa] etc = **rinunzia** etc.

ri'nunzia [ri'nuntsja] sf renunciation.

rinunzi'are [rinun'tsjare] vi: ~ a to give up, renounce.

rinve'nire vt to find, recover; (scoprire) to discover, find out // vi (2) (riprendere i sensi) to come round; (riprendere l'aspetto naturale) to revive.

rinvi'are vt (rimandare indietro) to send back, return; (differire): ~ qc (a) to postpone sth o put sth off (till); to adjourn sth (till); (fare un rimando): ~ qd a to refer sb to.

rinvigo'rire vt to strengthen.

rin'vio, 'vii sm (rimando) return; (differimento) postponement; (: di seduta) adjournment; (in un testo) cross-reference.

ri'one sm district, quarter.

riordi'nare vt (rimettere in ordine) to tidy; (riorganizzare) to reorganize.

riorganiz'zare [riorganid'dzare] vt to reorganize.

ripa'gare vt to repay.

ripa'rare vt (proteggere) to protect, defend; (correggere: male, torto) to make up for; (: errore) to put right; (aggiustare) to repair // vi (mettere rimedio): ~ a to make up for; ~rsi vr (rifugiarsi) to take refuge o shelter; **riparazi'one** sf (di un torto) reparation; (di guasto, scarpe) repairing q; repair; (risarcimento) compensation.

ri'paro sm (protezione) shelter, protection; (rimedio) remedy.

ripar'tire vt (dividere) to divide up; (distribuire) to share out // vi (2) to set off again; to leave again.

ripas'sare vi (2) to come (o go) back // vt (scritto, lezione) to go over (again).

ripen'sare vi to think; (cambiare pensiero) to change one's mind; (tornare col pensiero): ~ a to recall.

ripercu'otere vt (luce) to reflect, throw back; (suono) to throw back; ~rsi vr (luce) to be reflected; (suoni) to reverberate; (fig): ~rsi su to have repercussions on.

ripercussi'one sf reflection; reverberation; ~i sfpl (fig) repercussions.

ri'petere vt to repeat; (ripassare) to go over; **ripetizi'one** sf repetition; (di lezione) revision; **ripetizioni** sfpl (INS) private tutoring o coaching sg.

ripi'ano sm (GEO) terrace; (di mobile) shelf.

'ripido, a ag steep.

ripie'gare vt to refold; (piegare più volte) to fold (up) // vi (MIL) to retreat, fall back; ~rsi vr to bend; **ripi'ego, ghi** sm expedient; **vivere di ripieghi** to live by one's wits.

ripi'eno, a ag full; (CUC) stuffed; (: panino) filled // sm (CUC) stuffing.

ri'porre vt (porre al suo posto) to put back, replace; (mettere via) to put away; (fiducia, speranza): ~ qc in qd to place o put sth in sb.

ripor'tare vt (portare indietro) to bring (o take) back; (riferire) to report; (citare) to quote; (ricevere) to receive, get; (MAT) to carry; (COMM) to carry forward; ~rsi (anche fig) to go back to; (riferirsi a) to refer to; ~ **danni** to suffer damage.

ripo'sare vt (bicchiere, valigia) to put down; (dare sollievo) to rest // vi to rest; ~rsi vr to rest; **ri'poso** sm rest; (MIL); **riposo!** at ease!; **a riposo** (in pensione) retired; **giorno di riposo** day off.

ripos'tiglio [ripos'tiʎʎo] sm lumber-room; hiding-place.

ri'posto, a pp di **riporre**.

ri'prendere vt (prigioniero, fortezza) to recapture; (prendere indietro) to take back; (ricominciare: lavoro) to resume; (andare a prendere) to fetch, come back for; (assumere di nuovo: impiegati) to take on again, re-employ; (*rimproverare*) to tell off; (*restringere: abito*) to take in; (*CINEMA*) to shoot // *vi* to revive; ~**rsi** *vr* to recover; (*correggersi*) to correct o.s.; **ri'preso, a** *pp di* **riprendere** // *sf* recapture; resumption; (*economica, da malattia, emozione*) recovery; (*AUT*) acceleration *q*; (*TEATRO, CINEMA*) rerun; (*CINEMA: presa*) shooting *q*; shot; (*SPORT*) second half; (: *PUGILATO*) round; **a più riprese** on several occasions, several times.

ripristi'nare *vt* to restore.

ripro'durre *vt* to reproduce; **riprodursi** *vr* (*BIOL*) to reproduce; (*riformarsi*) to form again; **riprodut'tivo, a** *ag* reproductive; **riprodu'zione** *sf* reproduction; **riproduzione vietata** all rights reserved.

ripudi'are *vt* to repudiate, disown.

ripu'gnante [ripuɲ'ɲante] *ag* disgusting, repulsive.

ripu'gnare [ripuɲ'ɲare] *vi*: ~ **a qd** to repel *o* disgust sb.

ripu'lire *vt* to clean up; (*sog: ladri*) to clean out; (*perfezionare*) to polish, refine.

ri'quadro *sm* square; (*ARCHIT*) panel.

ri'saia *sf* paddy field.

risa'lire *vi* (2) (*ritornare in su*) to go back up; ~ **a** (*ritornare con la mente*) to go back to; (*datare da*) to date back to, go back to.

risal'tare *vi* (*fig: distinguersi*) to stand out; (*ARCHIT*) to project, jut out; **ri'salto** *sm* prominence; (*sporgenza*) projection; **mettere o porre in risalto qc** to make sth stand out.

risa'nare *vt* (*guarire*) to heal, cure; (*rendere salubre, bonificare*) to reclaim; (*fig: emendare*) to improve.

risa'pere *vt*: ~ **qc** to come to know of sth.

risarci'mento [risartʃi'mento] *sm* compensation.

risar'cire [risar'tʃire] *vt* (*cose*) to pay compensation for; (*persona*): ~ **qd di qc** to compensate sb for sth.

ri'sata *sf* laugh.

riscalda'mento *sm* heating; ~ **centrale** central heating.

riscal'dare *vt* (*scaldare*) to heat; (: *mani, persona*) to warm; (*minestra*) to reheat; ~**rsi** *vr* to warm up.

riscat'tare *vt* (*prigioniero*) to ransom, pay a ransom for; (*DIR*) to redeem; ~**rsi** *vr* (*da disonore*) to redeem o.s.; **ris'catto** *sm* ransom; redemption.

rischia'rare [riskja'rare] *vt* (*illuminare*) to light up; (*colore*) to make lighter; ~**rsi** *vr* (*tempo*) to clear up; (*cielo*) to clear; (*fig: volto*) to brighten up; ~**rsi la voce** to clear one's throat.

rischi'are [ris'kjare] *vt* to risk // *vi*: ~ **di fare qc** to risk *o* run the risk of doing sth.

'rischio ['riskjo] *sm* risk; **rischi'oso, a** *ag* risky, dangerous.

riscia'cquare [riʃʃa'kware] *vt* to rinse.

riscon'trare *vt* (*confrontare: due cose*) to compare; (*esaminare*) to check, verify; (*rilevare*) to find; **ris'contro** *sm* comparison; check, verification; (*AMM*:

lettera di risposta) reply; **mettere a riscontro** to compare.

ris'cosso, a *pp di* **riscuotere** // *sf* (*riconquista*) recovery, reconquest.

riscossi'one *sf* collection.

ris'cuotere *vt* (*anche fig*) to shake, rouse, stir; (*ritirare una somma dovuta*) to collect; (: *stipendio*) to draw, collect; (*fig: successo etc*) to win, earn; ~**rsi** *vr*: ~**rsi (da)** to shake o.s. (out of), rouse o.s. (from).

risenti'mento *sm* resentment.

risen'tire *vt* to hear again; (*provare*) to feel // *vi*: ~ **di** to feel (*o* show) the effects of; ~**rsi** *vr*: ~**rsi per** to take offence at, resent; **risen'tito, a** *ag* resentful.

ri'serbo *sm* reserve.

ri'serva *sf* reserve; (*di caccia, pesca*) preserve; (*restrizione, di indigeni*) reservation; **di** ~ (*provviste etc*) in reserve.

riser'vare *vt* (*tenere in serbo*) to keep, put aside; (*prenotare*) to book, reserve; **riser'vato, a** *ag* (*prenotato, fig: persona*) reserved; (*confidenziale*) confidential; **riserva'tezza** *sf* reserve.

risi'edere *vi*: ~ **a/in** to reside in.

'risma *sf* (*di carta*) ream; (*fig*) kind, sort.

'riso, a *pp di* **ridere** // *sm* (*pl(f)* ~**a**: il ridere*) un ~ a laugh; **il** ~ laughter; (*pianta*) rice.

riso'lino *sm* snigger.

ri'solto, a *pp di* **risolvere**.

risolu'tezza [risolu'tettsa] *sf* determination.

riso'luto, a *ag* determined, resolute.

risolu'zione [risolut'tsjone] *sf* solving *q*; (*MAT*) solution; (*decisione*) resolution.

ri'solvere *vt* (*difficoltà, controversia*) to resolve; (*problema*) to solve; (*decidere*): ~ **di fare** to resolve to do; ~**rsi** *vr* (*decidersi*): ~**rsi a fare** to make up one's mind to do; (*andare a finire*): ~**rsi in** to end up, turn out; ~**rsi in nulla** to come to nothing.

riso'nanza [riso'nantsa] *sf* resonance; **aver vasta** ~ (*fig: fatto etc*) to be known far and wide.

riso'nare *vt, vi* = **risuonare**.

ri'sorgere [ri'sordʒere] *vi* (2) to rise again; **risorgi'mento** *sm* revival; **il Risorgimento** (*STORIA*) the Risorgimento.

ri'sorsa *sf* expedient, resort; ~**e** *sfpl* (*naturali, finanziarie etc*) resources; **persona piena di** ~**e** resourceful person.

ri'sorto, a *pp di* **risorgere**.

ri'sotto *sm* (*CUC*) risotto.

risparmi'are *vt* to save; (*evitare di consumare, non uccidere*) to spare // *vi* to save; ~ **qc a qd** to spare sb sth.

ris'parmio *sm* saving *q*; (*denaro*) savings *pl*.

rispet'tabile *ag* respectable.

rispet'tare *vt* to respect; **farsi** ~ to command respect.

rispet'tivo, a *ag* respective.

ris'petto *sm* respect; ~**i** *smpl* (*saluti*) respects, regards; ~ **a** (*in paragone a*) compared to; (*in relazione a*) as regards, as for; **rispet'toso, a** *ag* respectful.

ris'plendere *vi* to shine.

rispon'dente *ag*: ~ **a** in keeping *o* conformity with; **rispon'denza** *sf* correspondence; harmony; agreement.

ris'pondere *vi* to answer, reply; (*freni*) to respond; ~ **a** (*domanda*) to answer, reply to; (*persona*) to answer; (*invito*) to reply to; (*provocazione, sog: veicolo, apparecchio*) to respond to; (*corrispondere a*) to correspond to; (: *speranze, bisogno*) to answer; ~ **di** to answer for; **ris'posto, a** *pp di* **rispondere** // *sf* answer, reply; **in** *o* **per risposta a** in reply to.

'rissa *sf* brawl.

ristabi'lire *vt* to re-establish, restore; (*persona: sog: riposo etc*) to restore to health; ~**rsi** *vr* to recover.

rista'gnare [ristaɲ'ɲare] *vi* (*acqua*) to become stagnant; (*sangue*) to cease flowing; (*fig: industria*) to stagnate; **ris-'tagno** *sm* stagnation.

ris'tampa *sf* reprinting *q*; reprint.

ristam'pare *vt* to reprint.

risto'rante *sm* restaurant.

risto'rarsi *vr* to have something to eat and drink; (*riposarsi*) to rest, have a rest; **ris'toro** *sm* (*bevanda, cibo*) refreshment; (*sollievo*) relief.

ristret'tezza [ristret'tettsa] *sf* (*strettezza*) narrowness; (*fig: scarsezza*) scarcity, lack; (: *meschinità*) meanness; ~**e** *sfpl* (*povertà*) financial straits.

ris'tretto, a *pp di* **restringere** // *ag* (*racchiuso*) enclosed, hemmed in; (*angusto*) narrow; (*limitato*): ~ **(a)** restricted *o* limited (to); (*riassunto, condensato*) condensed; ~ **di mente** narrow-minded.

risucchi'are [risuk'kjare] *vt* to suck in.

risul'tare *vi* (2) (*conseguire*) to result, ensue; (*dimostrarsi*) to prove (to be), turn out (to be); (*riuscire*) to be, come out; ~ **da** (*provenire*) to result from, be the result of; **risul'tato** *sm* result.

risuo'nare *vi* (*rimbombare*) to resound, reverberate; (: *stanza*) to be resonant.

risurrezi'one [risurret'tsjone] *sf* (REL) resurrection.

risusci'tare [risuʃʃi'tare] *vt* to resuscitate, restore to life; (*fig*) to revive, bring back // *vi* (2) to rise (from the dead).

ris'veglio [riz'veʎʎo] *sm* waking up; (*fig*) revival.

ris'volto *sm* (*di giacca*) lapel; (*di pantaloni*) turn-up; (*di manica*) cuff; (*di tasca*) flap; (*di libro*) inside flap; (*fig*) implication.

ritagli'are [ritaʎ'ʎare] *vt* (*tagliar via*) to cut out; **ri'taglio** *sm* (*di giornale*) cutting, clipping; (*di stoffa etc*) scrap.

ritar'dare *vi* (*persona, treno*) to be late; (*orologio*) to be slow // *vt* (*rallentare*) to slow down; (*impedire*) to delay, hold up; (*differire*) to postpone, delay; **ritarda-'tario, a** *sm/f* latecomer.

ri'tardo *sm* delay; (*di persona aspettata*)

lateness *q*; (*fig: mentale*) backwardness; **in** ~ late.

ri'tegno [ri'teɲɲo] *sm* restraint.

rite'nere *vt* (*trattenere*) to hold back; (: *somma*) to deduct; (*giudicare*) to consider, believe; ~ **qc a memoria** to know sth by heart; **rite'nuta** *sf* (*sul salario*) deduction.

riti'rare *vt* to withdraw; (POL: *richiamare*) to recall; (*andare a prendere: pacco etc*) to collect, pick up; ~**rsi** *vr* to withdraw; (*da un'attività*) to retire; (*stoffa*) to shrink; (*marea*) to recede; **riti'rata** *sf* (MIL) retreat; (*latrina*) lavatory; **ri'tiro** *sm* withdrawal; recall; collection; retirement; shrinking; (*luogo appartato*) retreat.

'ritmico, a, ci, che *ag* rhythmic(al).

'ritmo *sm* rhythm; (*fig*) rate; (: *della vita*) pace, tempo.

'rito *sm* rite; **di** ~ usual, customary.

ritoc'care *vt* (*disegno, fotografia*) to touch up; (*testo*) to alter; **ri'tocco, chi** *sm* touching up *q*; alteration.

ritor'nare *vi* (2) to return, go (*o* come) back; (*ripresentarsi*) to recur; (*ridiventare*): ~ **ricco** to become rich again // *vt* (*restituire*) to return, give back.

ritor'nello *sm* refrain.

ri'torno *sm* return; **essere di** ~ to be back; **far** ~ **di fiamma** (AUT) to backfire.

ri'trarre *vt* (*trarre indietro, via*) to withdraw; (*distogliere: sguardo*) to turn away; (*rappresentare*) to portray, depict; (*ricavare*) to get, obtain.

ritrat'tare *vt* (*disdire*) to retract, take back.

ri'tratto, a *pp di* **ritrarre** // *sm* portrait.

ri'troso, a *ag* (*restio*): ~ **(a)** reluctant (to); (*schivo*) shy; **andare a** ~ to go backwards.

ritro'vare *vt* to find; (*salute*) to regain; (*persona*) to find; to meet again; ~**rsi** *vr* (*essere, capitare*) to find o.s.; (*raccapezzarsi*) to find one's way; (*con senso reciproco*) to meet (again); **ri'trovo** *sm* meeting place; **ritrovo notturno** night club.

'ritto, a *ag* (*in piedi*) standing, on one's feet; (*levato in alto*) erect, raised; (: *capelli*) standing on end; (*posto verticalmente*) upright.

ritu'ale *ag, sm* ritual.

riuni'one *sf* (*adunanza*) meeting; (*riconciliazione*) reunion.

riu'nire *vt* (*ricongiungere*) to join (together); (*riconciliare*) to reunite, bring together (again); ~**rsi** *vr* (*adunarsi*) to meet; (*tornare a stare insieme*) to be reunited.

riu'scire [riuʃ'ʃire] *vi* (2) (*uscire di nuovo*) to go out again, go back out; (*aver esito: fatti, azioni*) to go, turn out; (*aver successo*) to succeed, be successful; (*essere, apparire*) to be, prove; (*raggiungere il fine*) to manage, succeed; ~ **a fare qc** to manage to do *o* succeed in doing *o* be able to do sth; **questo mi riesce nuovo** this is new to me; **riu'scita** *sf* (*esito*) result, outcome; *(buon esito)* success; **cattiva riuscita** failure.

'riva *sf (di fiume)* bank; *(di lago, mare)* shore.

ri'vale *sm/f* rival; **rivalità** *sf* rivalry.

ri'valsa *sf (rivincita)* revenge; *(risarcimento)* compensation.

rivalu'tare *vt (ECON)* to revalue.

rive'dere *vt* to see again; *(ripassare)* to revise; *(verificare)* to check.

rive'lare *vt* to reveal; *(divulgare)* to reveal, disclose; *(dare indizio)* to reveal, show; **~rsi** *vr (manifestarsi)* to be revealed; **~rsi onesto** *etc* to prove to be honest *etc*; **rivela'tore, 'trice** *ag* revealing // *sm (TECN)* detector; *(FOT)* developer; **rivelazi'one** *sf* revelation.

rivendi'care *vt* to claim, demand.

ri'vendita *sf (bottega)* retailer's (shop).

rivendi'tore, 'trice *sm/f* retailer.

riverbe'rare *vt* to reflect; **ri'verbero** *sm (di luce, calore)* reflection; *(di suono)* reverberation.

rive'renza [rive'rɛntsa] *sf* reverence; *(inchino)* bow; curtsey.

rive'rire *vt (rispettare)* to revere; *(salutare)* to pay one's respects to.

river'sare *vt (anche fig)* to pour; **~rsi** *vr (fig: persone)* to pour out.

rivesti'mento *sm (materiale)* covering; coating.

rives'tire *vt (provvedere di abiti)* to dress; *(indossare)* to put on; *(fig: carica)* to hold; *(ricoprire)* to cover; to coat; **~rsi** *vr* to get dressed again; to change (one's clothes); **~ con isolante termico** to lag, insulate.

rivi'era *sf* coast; **la ~ italiana** the Italian Riviera.

ri'vincita [ri'vintʃita] *sf (SPORT)* return match; *(fig)* revenge.

rivis'suto, a *pp di* **rivivere.**

ri'vista *sf* review; *(periodico)* magazine, review; *(TEATRO)* revue; variety show.

ri'vivere *vi (2) (riacquistare forza)* to come alive again; *(tornare in uso)* to be revived // *vt* to relive.

'rivo *sm* stream.

ri'volgere [ri'voldʒere] *vt (attenzione, sguardo)* to turn, direct; *(parole)* to address; *(distogliere)*: **~ da** to turn away from; **~rsi** *vr* to turn round; *(fig: dirigersi per informazioni)*: **~rsi a** to go and see, go and speak to; (: *ufficio)* to enquire at; **rivolgi'mento** *sm* upheaval.

ri'volta *sf* revolt, rebellion.

rivol'tare *vt* to turn over; *(con l'interno all'esterno)* to turn inside out; *(provocare disgusto: stomaco)* to upset, turn; (: *fig)* to revolt; to outrage; **~rsi** *vr (ribellarsi)*: **~rsi (a)** to rebel (against).

rivol'tella *sf* revolver.

ri'volto, a *pp di* **rivolgere.**

rivoluzio'nare [rivoluttsjo'nare] *vt* to revolutionize.

rivoluzio'nario, a [rivoluttsjo'narjo] *ag, sm/f* revolutionary.

rivoluzi'one [rivolut'tsjone] *sf* revolution.

riz'zare [rit'tsare] *vt* to raise, erect; **~rsi**

vr to stand up; *(capelli)* to stand on end.

'roba *sf* stuff, things *pl*; *(possessi, beni)* belongings *pl*, things *pl*, possessions *pl*; **~ da mangiare** things *pl* to eat, food; **~ da matti** sheer madness *o* lunacy.

'robot *sm inv* robot.

ro'busto, a *ag* robust, sturdy; *(solido: catena)* strong.

'rocca, che *sf* fortress.

rocca'forte *sf* stronghold.

roc'chetto [rok'ketto] *sm* reel, spool.

'roccia, ce [ˈrɔttʃa] *sf* rock.

ro'daggio [ro'daddʒo] *sm* running in; **in ~** running in.

ro'dare *vt (AUT, TECN)* to run in.

'rodere *vt* to gnaw (at); *(distruggere poco a poco)* to eat into.

'Rodi *sf* Rhodes.

rodi'tore *sm (ZOOL)* rodent.

rodo'dendro *sm* rhododendron.

'rogna [ˈrɔɲa] *sf (MED)* scabies *sg*; *(fig)* bother, nuisance.

ro'gnone [roɲˈɲone] *sm (CUC)* kidney.

'rogo, ghi *sm (per cadaveri)* (funeral) pyre; *(supplizio)*: **il ~** the stake.

rol'lio *sm* roll(ing).

'Roma *sf* Rome.

Roma'nia *sf*: **la ~** Romania.

ro'manico, a, ci, che *ag* Romanesque.

ro'mano, a *ag, sm/f* Roman.

romanti'cismo [romanti'tʃizmo] *sm* romanticism.

ro'mantico, a, ci, che *ag* romantic.

ro'manza [ro'mandza] *sf (MUS, LETTERATURA)* romance.

roman'zesco, a, schi, sche [roman-'dzesko] *ag (cavalleresco)* romance *cpd*; *(del romanzo)* of the novel; *(fig)* storybook *cpd*.

romanzi'ere [roman'dzjere] *sm* novelist.

ro'manzo, a [ro'mandzo] *ag (LING)* romance *cpd* // *sm (medievale)* romance; *(moderno)* novel; **~ d'appendice** serial (story).

rom'bare *vi* to rumble, thunder, roar.

'rombo *sm* rumble, thunder, roar; *(MAT)* rhombus; *(ZOOL)* turbot, brill.

ro'meno, a *ag, sm/f, sm* = **rumeno, a.**

'rompere *vt* to break; *(conversazione, fidanzamento)* to break off // *vi* to break; **~rsi** *vr* to break; **~ in pianto** to burst into tears; **~rsi un braccio** to break an arm; **rompi'capo** *sm* worry, headache; *(indovinello)* puzzle; *(in enigmistica)* brainteaser; **rompi'collo** *sm* daredevil; **a rompicollo** *av* at breakneck speed; **rompighi'accio** *sm (NAUT)* icebreaker; **rompis'catole** *sm/f inv (fam)* pest, pain in the neck.

'ronda *sf (MIL)* rounds *pl*, patrol.

ron'della *sf (TECN)* washer.

'rondine *sf (ZOOL)* swallow.

ron'done *sm (ZOOL)* swift.

ron'zare [ron'dzare] *vi* to buzz, hum.

ron'zino [ron'dzino] *sm (peg: cavallo)* nag.

'rosa *sf* rose // *ag, sm inv* pink; **ro'saio** *sm (pianta)* rosebush, rose tree; *(giardino)* rose garden; **ro'sario** *sm* (REL) rosary; **ro'sato, a** *ag* pink, rosy // *sm* (*vino*) rosé (wine); **ro'seo, a** *ag* (*anche fig*) rosy; **ro'setta** *sf* (*diamante*) rose diamond; (*rondella*) washer.

rosicchi'are [rosik'kjare] *vt* to gnaw (at); (*mangiucchiare*) to nibble (at).

rosma'rino *sm* rosemary.

'roso, a *pp di* **rodere.**

roso'lare *vt* (CUC) to brown.

roso'lia *sf* (MED) German measles *sg*, rubella.

ro'sone *sm* rosette; (*vetrata*) rose window.

'rospo *sm* (ZOOL) toad.

ros'setto *sm* (*per labbra*) lipstick; (*per guance*) rouge.

'rosso, a *ag, sm, sm/f* red; **il mar R~** the Red Sea; **~ d'uovo** egg yolk; **ros'sore** *sm* flush, blush; (*fig*) shame.

rosticce'ria [rostitʃe'ria] *sf* shop selling roast meat and other cooked food.

'rostro *sm* rostrum; (*becco*) beak.

ro'tabile *ag* (*percorribile*): **strada ~** carriageway; (FERR): **materiale m ~** rolling stock.

ro'taia *sf* rut, track; (FERR) rail; **le ~e** (FERR) the rails, the track *sg*.

ro'tare *vt, vi* to rotate; **rotazi'one** *sf* rotation.

rote'are *vt, vi* to whirl; **~ gli occhi** to roll one's eyes.

ro'tella *sf* small wheel; (*di mobile*) castor.

roto'lare *vt, vi* (2) to roll; **~rsi** *vr* to roll (about).

'rotolo *sm* roll; **andare a ~i** (*fig*) to go to rack and ruin.

ro'tondo, a *ag* round // *sf* rotunda.

ro'tore *sm* rotor.

'rotta *sf* (AER, NAUT) course, route; (MIL) rout; **a ~ di collo** at breakneck speed; **essere in ~ con qd** to be on bad terms with sb.

rot'tame *sm* fragment, scrap, broken bit; (*relitto: anche fig*) wreck; **~i di ferro** scrap iron.

'rotto, a *pp di* **rompere** // *ag* broken; (*calzoni*) torn, split; (*persona: pratico, resistente*): **~ a** accustomed *o* inured to; **per il ~ della cuffia** by the skin of one's teeth.

rot'tura *sf* breaking *q*; break; breaking off; (MED) fracture, break.

ro'vente *ag* red-hot.

'rovere *sm* oak.

rovesci'are [roveʃ'ʃare] *vt* (*versare in giù*) to pour; (: *accidentalmente*) to spill; (*capovolgere*) to turn upside down; (*gettare a terra*) to knock down; (: *fig: governo*) to overthrow; (*piegare all'indietro: testa*) to throw back; **~rsi** *vr* to pour down; to spill; (*fig: persone*) to pour (out).

ro'vescio, sci [ro'veʃʃo] *sm* other side, wrong side; (*della mano*) back; (*di moneta*) reverse; (*pioggia*) sudden downpour; (*fig*) setback; (MAGLIA: *anche*: **punto ~**) purl (stitch); (TENNIS) backhand (stroke); **a ~** upside-down; inside-out; **capire qc a ~** to misunderstand sth.

ro'vina *sf* ruin; **~e** *sfpl* ruins; **andare in ~** (*andare a pezzi*) to collapse; (*fig*) to go to rack and ruin.

rovi'nare *vi* (2) to collapse, fall down // *vt* (*far cadere giù: casa*) to demolish; (*danneggiare, fig*) to ruin; **rovi'noso, a** *ag* disastrous; damaging; violent.

rovis'tare *vt* (*casa*) to ransack; (*tasche*) to rummage in (*o* through).

'rovo *sm* (BOT) blackberry bush, bramble bush.

'rozzo, a ['roddzo] *ag* rough, coarse.

'ruba *sf*: **andare a ~** to sell like hot cakes.

ru'bare *vt* to steal; **~ qc a qd** to steal sth from sb.

rubi'netto *sm* tap.

ru'bino *sm* ruby.

ru'brica, che *sf* (STAMPA) column; (*quadernetto*) index book; address book.

'rude *ag* tough, rough.

'ruderi *smpl* ruins.

rudimen'tale *ag* rudimentary, basic.

rudi'menti *smpl* rudiments; basic principles; basic knowledge *sg*.

ruffi'ano *sm* pimp.

'ruga, ghe *sf* wrinkle.

'ruggine ['ruddʒine] *sf* rust.

rug'gire [rud'dʒire] *vi* to roar.

rugi'ada [ru'dʒada] *sf* dew.

ru'goso, a *ag* wrinkled.

rul'lare *vi* (*tamburo, nave*) to roll; (*aereo*) to taxi.

'rullo *sm* (*di tamburi*) roll; (*arnese cilindrico, TIP*) roller; **~ compressore** steam roller; **~ di pellicola** roll of film.

rum *sm* rum.

ru'meno, a *ag, sm/f, sm* Romanian.

rumi'nare *vt* (ZOOL) to ruminate; (*fig*) to ruminate on *o* over, chew over.

ru'more *sm*: **un ~** a noise, a sound; (*fig*) a rumour; **il ~** noise; **rumoreggi'are** *vi* to make a noise; **rumo'roso, a** *ag* noisy.

ru'olo *sm* (*elenco*) roll, register, list; (TEATRO, *fig*) role, part; **di ~** permanent, on the permanent staff.

ru'ota *sf* wheel; **a ~** (*forma*) circular; **~ anteriore/posteriore** front/back wheel; **~ di scorta** spare wheel.

'rupe *sf* cliff.

ru'rale *ag* rural, country *cpd*.

ru'scello [ruʃ'ʃello] *sm* stream.

'ruspa *sf* excavator.

rus'sare *vi* to snore.

'Russia *sf*: **la ~** Russia; **'russo, a** *ag, sm/f, sm* Russian.

'rustico, a, ci, che *ag* rustic; (*fig*) rough, unrefined.

rut'tare *vi* to belch; **'rutto** *sm* belch.

'ruvido, a *ag* rough, coarse.

ruzzo'lare [ruttso'lare] *vi* (2) to tumble down; **ruzzo'loni** *av*: **cadere ruzzoloni** to tumble down; **fare le scale ruzzoloni** to tumble down the stairs.

S

S. *(abbr di* **sud)** S.

sa *forma del vb* **sapere.**

'sabato *sm* Saturday; **di** *o* **il** ~ on Saturdays.

'sabbia *sf* sand; ~**e mobili** quicksand(s); **sabbi'oso,** a *ag* sandy.

sabo'taggio [sabo'taddʒo] *sm* sabotage.

sabo'tare *vt* to sabotage.

'sacca, che *sf* bag; *(bisaccia)* haversack; *(insenatura)* inlet; ~ **da viaggio** travelling bag.

sacca'rina *sf* saccharin(e).

sac'cente [sat'tʃɛnte] *sm/f* know-all.

saccheggi'are [sakked'dʒare] *vt* to sack, plunder; **sac'cheggio** *sm* sack(ing).

sac'chetto [sak'ketto] *sm* (small) bag; (small) sack.

'sacco, chi *sm* bag; *(per carbone etc)* sack; *(ANAT, BIOL)* sac; *(tela)* sacking; *(saccheggio)* sack(ing); *(fig: grande quantità)*: **un** ~ **di** lots of, heaps of; ~ **a pelo** sleeping bag.

sacer'dote [satʃer'dɔte] *sm* priest; **sacer-'dozio** *sm* priesthood.

sacra'mento *sm* sacrament.

sacrifi'care *vt* to sacrifice; ~**rsi** *vr* to sacrifice o.s.; *(privarsi di qc)* to make sacrifices.

sacri'ficio [sakri'fitʃo] *sm* sacrifice.

sacri'legio [sacri'lɛdʒo] *sm* sacrilege.

'sacro, a *ag* sacred.

sacro'santo, a *ag* sacrosanct.

'sadico, a, ci, che *ag* sadistic // *sm/f* sadist.

sa'dismo *sm* sadism.

sa'etta *sf* arrow; *(fulmine: anche fig)* thunderbolt; flash of lightning.

sa'fari *sm inv* safari.

sa'gace [sa'gatʃe] *ag* shrewd, sagacious.

sag'gezza [sad'dʒettsa] *sf* wisdom.

saggi'are [sad'dʒare] *vt* (metalli) to assay; *(fig)* to test.

'saggio, a, gi, ge ['saddʒo] *ag* wise // *sm (persona)* sage; *(operazione sperimentale)* test; (: *dell'oro*) assay; *(fig: prova)* proof; *(campione indicativo)* sample; *(ricerca, esame critico)* essay.

Sagit'tario [sadʒit'tarjo] *sm* Sagittarius.

'sagoma *sf (profilo)* outline, profile; *(forma)* form, shape; *(TECN)* template.

'sagra *sf* festival.

sagres'tano *sm* sacristan; sexton.

sagres'tia *sf* sacristy; *(culto protestante)* vestry.

'sai *forma del vb* **sapere.**

'sala *sf* hall; *(stanza)* room; ~ **d'aspetto** waiting room; ~ **da ballo** ballroom; ~ **operatoria** operating theatre; ~ **da pranzo** dining room; ~ **per concerti** concert hall.

sala'mandra *sf* salamander.

sa'lame *sm* salami *q,* salami sausage.

sala'moia *sf (CUC)* brine.

sa'lare *vt* to salt.

salari'ato, a *sm/f* wage-earner.

sa'lario *sm* pay, wages *pl.*

sa'lato, a *ag (sapore)* salty; *(CUC)* salted, salt *cpd;* *(fig: discorso etc)* biting, sharp; (: *prezzi)* steep, stiff.

sal'dare *vt (congiungere)* to join, bind; *(parti metalliche)* to solder; (: *con saldatura autogena)* to weld; *(conto)* to settle, pay; **salda'tura** *sf* soldering; welding; *(punto saldato)* soldered joint; weld.

sal'dezza [sal'dettsa] *sf* firmness; strength.

'saldo, a *ag (resistente, forte)* strong, firm; *(fermo)* firm, steady, stable; *(fig)* firm, steadfast // *sm (svendita)* sale; *(di conto)* settlement; *(ECON)* balance.

'sale *sm* salt; *(fig)* wit.

'salice ['salitʃe] *sm* willow; ~ **piangente** weeping willow.

sali'ente *ag (fig)* salient, main.

sali'era *sf* salt cellar.

sa'lino, a *ag* saline // *sf* saltworks *sg.*

sa'lire *vi* (2) to go (*o* come) up; *(aereo etc)* to climb, go up; *(passeggero)* to get on; *(sentiero, prezzi, livello)* to go up, rise // *vt (scale, gradini)* to go (*o* come) up; ~ **su** to climb up onto; ~ **sul treno/sull'autobus** to board the train/the bus; ~ **in macchina** to get into the car; **sa'lita** *sf* climb, ascent; *(erta)* hill, slope; **in salita** *ag, av* uphill.

sa'liva *sf* saliva.

'salma *sf* corpse.

'salmo *sm* psalm.

sal'mone *sm* salmon.

sa'lotto *sm* lounge, sitting room; *(mobilio)* lounge suite.

sal'pare *vi* (2) *(NAUT)* to set sail; *(anche:* ~ **l'ancora)** to weigh anchor.

'salsa *sf (CUC)* sauce; ~ **di pomodoro** tomato sauce.

sal'siccia, ce [sal'sittʃa] *sf* pork sausage.

sal'tare *vi* to jump, leap; *(esplodere)* to blow up, explode; (: *valvola)* to blow; *(rompersi)* to snap, burst; *(venir via)* to pop off // *vt* to jump (over), leap (over); *(fig: pranzo, capitolo)* to skip, miss (out); *(CUC)* to sauté; **far** ~ to blow up; to burst open.

saltel'lare *vi* to skip; to hop.

saltim'banco *sm* acrobat.

'salto *sm* jump; *(SPORT)* jumping; **fare un** ~ to jump, leap; **fare un** ~ **da qd** to pop over to sb's (place); ~ **in alto/lungo** high/long jump; ~ **con l'asta** pole vaulting; ~ **mortale** somersault.

saltu'ario, a *ag* occasional, irregular.

sa'lubre *ag* healthy, salubrious.

salume'ria *sf* delicatessen.

sa'lumi *smpl* salted pork meats.

salu'tare *ag* healthy; *(fig)* salutary, beneficial // *vt (per dire buon giorno, fig)* to greet; *(per dire addio)* to say goodbye to; *(MIL)* to salute.

sa'lute *sf* health; ~**!** *(a chi starnutisce)* bless you!; *(nei brindisi)* cheers!; **bere alla** ~ **di qd** to drink (to) sb's health.

sa'luto *sm (gesto)* wave; *(parola)* greeting;

(*MIL*) salute; ~**i** *smpl* greetings; **cari** ~**i** best regards; **vogliate gradire i nostri più distinti** ~**i** Yours faithfully.

'salva *sf* salvo.

salvacon'dotto *sm* (*MIL*) safe-conduct.

salva'gente [salva'dʒɛnte] *sm* (*NAUT*) lifebuoy; (*stradale*) traffic island; ~ **a ciambella;** ~ **a giubbotto** lifejacket.

salvaguar'dare *vt* to safeguard.

sal'vare *vt* to save; (*trarre da un pericolo*) to rescue; (*proteggere*) to protect; ~**rsi** *vr* to save o.s.; to escape; **salva'taggio** *sm* rescue; **salva'tore, 'trice** *sm/f* saviour; **salvazi'one** *sf* (*REL*) salvation.

'salve *escl* (*fam*) hi!

sal'vezza [sal'vettsa] *sf* salvation; (*sicurezza*) safety.

'salvia *sf* (*BOT*) sage.

'salvo, a *ag* safe, unhurt, unharmed; (*fuori pericolo*) safe, out of danger // *prep* (*eccetto*) except; ~ **che** *cong* (*a meno che*) unless; (*eccetto che*) except (that); ~ **imprevisti** barring accidents.

sam'buco *sm* elder (tree).

sa'nare *vt* to heal, cure; (*fig*) to put right.

sana'torio *sm* sanatorium.

san'cire [san'tʃire] *vt* to sanction.

'sandalo *sm* (*BOT*) sandalwood; (*calzatura*) sandal.

'sangue *sm* blood; **farsi cattivo** ~ to fret, get in a state; ~ **freddo** (*fig*) sangfroid, calm; **a** ~ **freddo** in cold blood; **sangu'igno, a** *ag* blood *cpd*; (*colore*) blood-red; **sangui'nare** *vi* to bleed; **sangui'noso, a** *ag* bloody; (*cruento*) bitter, mortal; **sangui'suga** *sf* leech.

sanità *sf* health; (*salubrità*) healthiness; **Ministro della S**~ Minister of Health; ~ **mentale** sanity.

sani'tario, a *ag* health *cpd*; (*condizioni*) sanitary // *sm* (*AMM*) doctor.

'sanno *forma del vb* **sapere**.

'sano, a *ag* healthy; (*denti, costituzione*) healthy, sound; (*integro*) whole, unbroken; (*fig: politica, consigli*) sound; ~ **di mente** sane; **di** ~ **a pianta** completely, entirely; ~ **e salvo** safe and sound.

santifi'care *vt* to sanctify; (*canonizzare*) to canonize; (*venerare*) to honour.

santità *sf* sanctity; holiness; **Sua/Vostra** ~ (*titolo di Papa*) His/Your Holiness.

'santo, a *ag* holy; (*fig*) saintly; (*seguito da nome proprio: dav sm* **san** + *C,* **sant'** + *V,* **santo** + *s impura, gn, pn, ps, x, z; dav sf* **santa** + *C,* **sant'** + *V*) saint // *sm/f* saint; **la S**~**a Sede** the Holy See; **il S**~ **Spirito** the Holy Spirit o Ghost.

santu'ario *sm* sanctuary.

sanzio'nare [santsjo'nare] *vt* to sanction.

sanzi'one [san'tsjone] *sf* sanction; (*penale, civile*) sanction, penalty.

sa'pere *vt* to know; (*essere capace di*): **so nuotare** I know how to swim, I can swim // *vi*: ~ **di** (*aver sapore*) to taste of; (*aver odore*) to smell of; **sa di muffa** it smells of mould, it smells mouldy // *sm* knowledge; **far** ~ **qc a qd** to inform sb about sth, let sb know sth.

sapi'enza [sa'pjɛntsa] *sf* wisdom.

sa'pone *sm* soap; ~ **da bucato** washing soap; **sapo'netta** *sf* cake o bar o tablet of soap.

sa'pore *sm* taste, flavour; **sapo'rito, a** *ag* tasty; (*fig: arguto*) witty; (*: piccante*) racy.

sappi'amo *forma del vb* **sapere**.

saraci'nesca [saratʃi'neska] *sf* (*serranda*) rolling shutter.

sar'casmo *sm* sarcasm *q*; sarcastic remark; **sar'castico, a, ci, che** *ag* sarcastic.

Sar'degna [sar'deɲɲa] *sf*: **la** ~ Sardinia.

sar'dina *sf* sardine.

'sardo, a *ag, sm/f* Sardinian.

sar'donico, a, ci, che *ag* sardonic.

'sarto, a *sm/f* tailor/dressmaker; **sarto'ria** *sf* tailor's (shop); dressmaker's (shop); (*più grande*) fashion house; (*arte*) couture.

'sasso *sm* stone; (*ciottolo*) pebble; (*masso*) rock.

sas'sofono *sm* saxophone.

sas'soso, a *ag* stony; pebbly.

'Satana *sm* Satan; **sa'tanico, a, ci, che** *ag* satanic, fiendish.

sa'tellite *sm, ag* satellite.

'satira *sf* satire; **sa'tirico, a, ci, che** *ag* satiric(al).

satu'rare *vt* to saturate; **saturazi'one** *sf* saturation; **'saturo, a** *ag* saturated; (*fig*): **saturo di** full of.

'sauna *sf* sauna.

Sa'voia *sf*: **la** ~ Savoy.

savoi'ardo, a *ag* of Savoy, Savoyard // *sm* (*biscotto*) sponge finger.

sazi'are [sat'tsjare] *vt* to satisfy, satiate; ~**rsi** *vr* (*riempirsi di cibo*): ~**rsi (di)** to eat one's fill (of); (*fig*): ~**rsi di** to grow tired o weary of.

'sazio, a ['sattsjo] *ag*: ~ (**di**) sated (with), full (of); (*fig: stufo*) fed up (with), sick (of).

sba'dato, a *ag* careless, inattentive.

sbadigli'are [zbadiʎ'ʎare] *vi* to yawn; **sba'diglio** *sm* yawn.

sbagli'are [zbaʎ'ʎare] *vt* to make a mistake in, get wrong // *vi* to make a mistake, be mistaken, be wrong; (*operare in modo non giusto*) to err; ~**rsi** *vr* to make a mistake, be mistaken, be wrong; ~ **la mira/strada** to miss one's aim/take the wrong road; ~ **qd con qd altro** to mistake sb for sb else; **'sbaglio** *sm* mistake, error; (*morale*) error.

sbal'lare *vt* (*merce*) to unpack.

sballot'tare *vt* to toss (about).

sbalor'dire *vt* to stun, amaze // *vi* to be stunned, be amazed; **sbalordi'tivo, a** *ag* amazing; (*prezzo*) incredible, absurd.

sbal'zare [zbal'tsare] *vt* to throw, hurl; (*fig: da una carica*) to remove, dismiss // *vi* (2) (*balzare*) to bounce; (*saltare*) to leap, bound; **'sbalzo** *sm* bounce; leap; (*spostamento improvviso*) jolt, jerk; **a sbalzi** jerkily; (*fig*) in fits and starts.

sban'dare *vi* (*NAUT*) to list; (*AER*) to bank; (*AUT*) to skid; ~**rsi** *vr* (*folla*) to disperse;

(*truppe*) to disband; (*fig: famiglia*) to break up.

sbandie'rare *vt* (*bandiera*) to wave; (*fig*) to parade, show off.

sbaragli'are [zbaraʎ'ʎare] *vt* (MIL) to rout; (*in gare sportive etc*) to beat, defeat.

sba'raglio [zba'raʎʎo] *sm* rout; defeat; **gettarsi allo ~** to risk everything.

sbaraz'zarsi [zbarat'tsarsi] *vr:* **~ di** to get rid of, rid o.s. of.

sbar'care *vt* (*passeggeri*) to disembark; (*merci*) to unload // *vi* (2) to disembark; **~ il lunario** (*fig*) to make ends meet; **'sbarco** *sm* disembarkation; unloading; (MIL) landing.

'sbarra *sf* bar; (*di passaggio a livello*) barrier; (DIR): **presentarsi alla ~** to appear before the court.

sbarra'mento *sm* (*stradale*) roadblock, barricade; (*diga*) dam, barrage; (MIL) barrage.

sbar'rare *vt* (*strada etc*) to block, bar; (*assegno*) to cross; **~ il passo** to bar the way; **~ gli occhi** to open one's eyes wide.

'sbattere *vt* (*porta*) to slam, bang; (*tappeti, ali, CUC*) to beat; (*urtare*) to knock, hit // *vi* (*porta*) to slam, bang; (*agitarsi: ali, vele etc*) to flap; **sbat'tuto, a** *ag* (*viso, aria*) dejected, worn out; (*uovo*) beaten.

sba'vare *vi* to dribble; (*colore*) to smear, smudge.

sbia'dire *vi* (2) (*anche:* **~rsi**), *vt* to fade; **sbia'dito, a** *ag* faded; (*fig*) colourless, dull.

sbian'care *vt* to whiten; (*tessuto*) to bleach // *vi* (2) (*impallidire*) to grow pale o white.

sbi'eco, a, chi, che *ag* (*storto*) squint, askew; **di ~: guardare qd di ~** (*fig*) to look askance at sb; **tagliare una stoffa di ~** to cut a material on the bias.

sbigot'tire *vt* to dismay, stun // *vi* (2) (*anche:* **~rsi**) to be dismayed.

sbilanci'are [zbilan'tʃare] *vt* to throw off balance // *vi* (*perdere l'equilibrio*) to overbalance; (*pendere da una parte*) to be unbalanced; **~rsi** *vr* (*fig*): **non si sbilancia mai** (*nel parlare*) he always weighs his words; (*nello spendere*) he never spends beyond his means.

sbirci'are [zbir'tʃare] *vt* to cast sidelong glances at, eye.

'sbirro *sm* (*peg*) cop.

sbizzar'rirsi [zbiddzar'rirsi] *vr* to indulge one's whims.

sbloc'care *vt* to unblock, free; (*freno*) to release; (*prezzi, affitti*) to decontrol.

sboc'care *vi* (2): **~ in** (*fiume*) to flow into; (*strada*) to lead into; (*persona*) to come (out) into; (*fig: concludersi*) to end (up) in.

sboc'cato, a *ag* (*persona*) foul-mouthed; (*linguaggio*) foul.

sbocci'are [zbot'tʃare] *vi* (2) (*fiore*) to bloom, open (out).

'sbocco, chi *sm* (*apertura*) opening; (*uscita*) way out; (*di fiume*) mouth; (COMM) outlet; (: *mercato*) market.

sbol'lire *vi* (2) (*fig*) to cool down, calm down.

'sbornia *sf* (*fam*): **prendere una ~** to get plastered.

sbor'sare *vt* (*denaro*) to pay out.

sbot'tare *vi* (2) to burst out; **~ a ridere/per la collera** to burst out laughing/explode with anger.

sbotto'nare *vt* to unbutton, undo.

sbracci'ato, a [zbrat'tʃato] *ag* (*camicia*) sleeveless; (*persona*) bare-armed.

sbrai'tare *vi* to yell, bawl.

sbra'nare *vt* to tear to pieces.

sbricio'lare [zbritʃo'lare] *vt*, **~rsi** *vr* to crumble.

sbri'gare *vt* to deal with, get through; (*cliente*) to attend to, deal with; **~rsi** *vr* to hurry (up); **sbri'gativo, a** *ag* (*persona, modo*) quick, expeditious; (*giudizio*) hasty.

sbrindel'lato, a *ag* tattered, in tatters.

sbrodo'lare *vt* to stain, dirty.

'sbronzo, a ['zbrontso] *ag* (*fam*) tight // *sf*: **prendere una ~a** to get tight o plastered.

sbu'care *vi* (2) to come out, emerge; (*apparire improvvisamente*) to pop out (o up).

sbucci'are [zbut'tʃare] *vt* (*arancia, patata*) to peel; (*piselli*) to shell; (*braccio*) to graze.

sbudel'larsi *vr:* **~ dalle risa** to split one's sides laughing.

sbuf'fare *vi* (*persona, cavallo*) to snort; (: *ansimare*) to puff, pant; (*treno*) to puff; **'sbuffo** *sm* snort; puff, pant; (*di aria, fumo, vapore*) puff.

'scabbia *sf* (MED) scabies *sg*.

'scabro, a *ag* rough, harsh.

sca'broso, a *ag* (*fig: delicato*) delicate, awkward; (: *difficile*) difficult.

scacchi'era [skak'kjɛra] *sf* chessboard.

scacci'are [skat'tʃare] *vt* to chase away o out, drive away o out.

'scacco, chi *sm* (*pezzo del gioco*) chessman; (*quadretto di scacchiera*) square; (*fig*) setback, reverse; **~chi** *smpl* (*gioco*) chess *sg*; **a ~chi** (*tessuto*) check(ed); **scacco'matto** *sm* checkmate.

sca'dente *ag* shoddy, of poor quality.

sca'denza [ska'dentsa] *sf* (*di cambiale, contratto*) maturity; (*di passaporto*) expiry date; **a breve/lunga ~** short-/long-term; **lo farò a breve ~** I'll do it in the near future.

sca'dere *vi* (2) (*contratto etc*) to expire; (*debito*) to fall due; (*valore, forze, peso*) to decline, go down.

sca'fandro *sm* (*di palombaro*) diving suit; (*di astronauta*) space-suit.

scaf'fale *sm* shelf; (*mobile*) set of shelves.

'scafo *sm* (NAUT, AER) hull.

scagio'nare [skadʒo'nare] *vt* to exonerate, free from blame.

'scaglia ['skaʎʎa] *sf* (ZOOL) scale; (*scheggia*) chip, flake.

scagli'are [skaʎ'ʎare] *vt* (*lanciare: anche fig*) to hurl, fling; **~rsi** *vr:* **~rsi su o contro** to hurl o fling o.s. at; (*fig*) to rail at.

scaglio'nare [skaʎʎo'nare] *vt* (*pagamenti*) to space out, spread out; (*MIL*) to echelon; **scagli'one** *sm* echelon; (*GEO*) terrace.

'scala *sf* (*a gradini etc*) staircase, stairs *pl*; (*a pioli, di corda*) ladder; (*MUS, GEO, di colori, valori, fig*) scale; **~e** *sfpl* (*scalinata*) stairs; **su vasta ~/~ ridotta** on a large/small scale; **~ a libretto** stepladder; **~ mobile** escalator; (*ECON*) sliding scale; **~ mobile dei salari** index-linked pay scale.

sca'lare *vt* (*ALPINISMO, muro*) to climb, scale; (*debito*) to scale down, reduce; **sca'lata** *sf* scaling *q*, climbing *q*; climb; **scala'tore, 'trice** *sm/f* climber.

scalda'bagno [skalda'baɲɲo] *sm* waterheater.

scal'dare *vt* to heat; **~rsi** *vr* to warm up, heat up; (*al sole*) to warm o.s.; (*fig*) to get excited.

scal'fire *vt* to scratch.

scali'nata *sf* staircase.

sca'lino *sm* (*anche fig*) step; (*di scala a pioli*) rung.

'scalo *sm* (*NAUT*) slipway; (: *porto d'approdo*) port of call; (*AER*) stopover; **fare ~ (a)** (*NAUT*) to call (at), put in (at); (*AER*) to land (at), make a stop (at); **~ merci** (*FERR*) goods yard.

scalop'pina *sf* (*CUC*) escalope.

scal'pello *sm* chisel.

scal'pore *sm* noise, row; **far ~** to make a noise; (*fig*) to cause a sensation *o* a stir.

'scaltro, a *ag* cunning, shrewd.

scal'zare [skal'tsare] *vt* (*albero*) to bare the roots of; (*muro, fig: autorità*) to undermine; (: *escludere: collega*) to oust; **~ i piedi** to take off one's socks and shoes.

'scalzo, a ['skaltso] *ag* barefoot.

scambi'are *vt* to exchange; (*confondere*): **~ qd/qc per** to take *o* mistake sb/sth for; **mi hanno scambiato il cappello** they've given me the wrong hat.

scambi'evole *ag* mutual, reciprocal.

'scambio *sm* exchange; (*FERR*) points *pl*; **~ di persona** case of mistaken identity.

scampa'gnata [skampaɲ'ɲata] *sf* trip to the country.

scampa'nare *vi* to peal.

scam'pare *vt* (*salvare*) to rescue, save; (*evitare: morte, prigione*) to escape // *vi* (2): **~ (a qc)** to survive (sth), escape (sth); **scamparla bella** to have a narrow escape; **'scampo** *sm* escape; **cercare scampo nella fuga** to seek safety in flight.

'scampolo *sm* scrap; (*di tessuto*) remnant.

scanala'tura *sf* (*incavo*) channel, groove.

scandagli'are [skanda'ʎ'ʎare] *vt* (*NAUT*) to sound; (*fig*) to sound out; to probe.

scandaliz'zare [skandalid'dzare] *vt* to shock, scandalize; **~rsi** *vr* to be shocked.

'scandalo *sm* scandal; **scanda'loso, a** *ag* scandalous, shocking.

Scandi'navia *sf*: **la ~** Scandinavia; **scandi'navo, a** *ag, sm/f* Scandinavian.

scan'dire *vt* (*versi*) to scan; (*parole*) to articulate, pronounce distinctly; **~ il tempo** (*MUS*) to beat time.

scan'nare *vt* (*animale*) to butcher, slaughter; (*persona*) to cut *o* slit the throat of.

'scanno *sm* seat, bench.

scansafa'tiche [skansafa'tike] *sm/f inv* idler, loafer.

scan'sare *vt* (*rimuovere*) to move (aside), shift; (*schivare: schiaffo*) to dodge; (*sfuggire*) to avoid; **~rsi** *vr* to move aside.

scan'sia *sf* shelves *pl*; (*per libri*) bookcase.

'scanso *sm*: **a ~ di** in order to avoid, as a precaution against.

scanti'nato *sm* basement.

scanto'nare *vi* to turn the corner; (*svignarsela*) to sneak off.

scapes'trato, a *ag* dissolute.

'scapito *sm* (*perdita*) loss; (*danno*) damage, detriment; **a ~ di** to the detriment of.

'scapola *sf* shoulder blade.

'scapolo *sm* bachelor.

scappa'mento *sm* (*AUT*) exhaust.

scap'pare *vi* (2) (*fuggire*) to escape; (*andare via in fretta*) to rush off; **lasciarsi ~ un'occasione** to let an opportunity go by; **~ di prigione** to escape from prison; **~ di mano** (*oggetto*) to slip out of one's hands; **~ di mente** a qd to slip sb's mind; **mi scappò detto** I let it slip; **scap'pata** *sf* quick visit *o* call; (*scappatella*) escapade; **scappa'tella** *sf* escapade; **scappa'toia** *sf* way out.

scara'beo *sm* beetle.

scarabocchi'are [skarabok'kjare] *vt* to scribble, scrawl; **scara'bocchio** *sm* scribble, scrawl.

scara'faggio [skara'fadd3o] *sm* cockroach.

scaraven'tare *vt* to fling, hurl; (*fig: impiegato*) to shift.

scarce'rare [skartʃe'rare] *vt* to release (from prison).

'scarica, che *sf* (*di arma da fuoco; ELETTR, FISIOL*) discharge; (*di piùarmi*) volley of shots; (*di sassi, pugni*) hail, shower.

scari'care *vt* (*merci, camion etc*) to unload; (*passeggeri*) to set down, put off; (*arma*) to unload; (: *sparare, ELETTR*) to discharge; (*sog: corso d'acqua*) to empty, pour; (*fig: liberare da un peso*) to unburden, relieve; **~rsi** *vr* (*orologio*) to run *o* wind down; (*accumulatore*) to go flat *o* dead; (*fig: rilassarsi*) to unwind; **scarica'tore** *sm* loader; (*di porto*) docker.

'scarico, a, chi, che *ag* unloaded; (*orologio*) run down; (*accumulatore*) dead, flat; (*fig: libero*): **~ di** free from // *sm* (*di merci, materiali*) unloading; (*di immondizie*) dumping, tipping; (: *luogo*) rubbish dump; (*TECN: deflusso*) draining; (: *dispositivo*) drain; (*AUT*) exhaust.

scarlat'tina *sf* scarlet fever.

scar'latto, a *ag* scarlet.

'scarno, a *ag* thin, bony.

'scarpa *sf* shoe; **~e da tennis** tennis shoes.

scar'pata sf escarpment.

scarseggi'are [skarsed'dʒare] vi to be scarce; ~ **di** to be short of, lack.

scar'sezza [skar'settsa] sf scarcity, lack.

'scarso, a ag (insufficiente) insufficient, meagre; (povero: annata) poor, lean; (INS: nota) poor; ~ **di** lacking in; **3 chili** ~**i** just under 3 kilos, barely 3 kilos.

scarta'mento sm (FERR) gauge; ~ **normale/ridotto** standard/ narrow gauge.

scar'tare vt (pacco) to unwrap; (idea) to reject; (MIL) to declare unfit for military service; (carte da gioco) to discard; (CALCIO) to dodge (past) // vi to swerve.

'scarto sm (cosa scartata, anche COMM) reject; (di veicolo) swerve; (differenza) gap, difference.

scassi'nare vt to break, force.

'scasso sm vedi **furto.**

scate'nare vt (fig) to incite, stir up; ~**rsi** vr (fig) to break out; to rage.

'scatola sf box; (di latta) tin, can; **cibi in** ~ tinned o canned foods; ~ **cranica** cranium.

scat'tare vt (fotografia) to take // vi (2) (congegno, molla etc) to be released; (balzare) to spring up; (SPORT) to put on a spurt; (fig: per l'ira) to fly into a rage; ~ **in piedi** to spring to one's feet.

'scatto sm (dispositivo) release; (: di arma da fuoco) trigger mechanism; (rumore) click; (balzo) jump, start; (SPORT) spurt; (fig: di ira etc) fit; (: di stipendio) increment; **di** ~ suddenly.

scatu'rire vi (2) to gush, spring.

scaval'care vt (ostacolo) to pass (o climb) over; (fig) to get ahead of, overtake.

sca'vare vt (terreno) to dig; (legno) to hollow out; (tesoro) to dig up; (città) to excavate.

'scavo sm excavating q; excavation.

'scegliere ['ʃeʎʎere] vt to choose, select.

sce'icco, chi [ʃe'ikko] sm sheik.

scelle'rato, a [ʃelle'rato] ag wicked, evil.

scel'lino [ʃel'lino] sm shilling.

'scelto, a ['ʃelto] pp di **scegliere** // ag (di prima scelta) carefully chosen; select; (di ottima qualità: merce) choice, top quality; (MIL: specializzato) crack cpd, highly skilled // sf choice; selection; **frutta o formaggi a** ~**a** a choice of fruit or cheese.

sce'mare [ʃe'mare] vt to diminish, reduce.

'scemo, a ['ʃemo] ag stupid, silly.

'scempio ['ʃempjo] sm slaughter, massacre; (fig) ruin; **far** ~ **di** (fig) to play havoc with, ruin.

'scena ['ʃena] sf (gen) scene; (palcoscenico) stage; **le** ~**e** (fig: teatro) the stage; **fare una** ~ to make a scene; **andare in** ~ to be staged o put on o performed; **mettere in** ~ to stage.

sce'nario [ʃe'narjo] sm scenery; (di film) scenario.

sce'nata [ʃe'nata] sf row, scene.

'scendere ['ʃendere] vi (2) to go (o come) down; (strada, sole) to go down; (passeggero: fermarsi) to get out, alight;

(fig: temperatura, prezzi) to go o come down, fall, drop // vt (scale, pendio) to go (o come) down; ~ **dal treno** to get off o out of the train; ~ **da cavallo** to dismount, get off one's horse.

'scenico, a, ci, che ['ʃeniko] ag stage cpd, scenic.

scervel'lato, a [ʃervel'lato] ag feather-brained, scatterbrained.

'sceso, a ['ʃeso] pp di **scendere.**

scetti'cismo [ʃetti'tʃizmo] sm scepticism; **'scettico, a, ci, che** ag sceptical.

'scettro ['ʃettro] sm sceptre.

'scheda ['skɛda] sf (index) card; ~ **elettorale** ballot paper; ~ **perforata** punch card; **sche'dare** vt (dati) to file; (libri) to catalogue; (registrare: anche POLIZIA) to put on one's files; **sche'dario** sm file; (mobile) filing cabinet.

'scheggia, ge ['skeddʒa] sf splinter, sliver.

'scheletro ['skɛletro] sm skeleton.

'schema, i ['skɛma] sm (diagramma) diagram, sketch; (progetto, abbozzo) outline, plan.

'scherma ['skɛrma] sf fencing.

scher'maglia [sker'maʎʎa] sf (fig) skirmish.

'schermo ['skermo] sm shield, screen; (CINEMA, TV) screen.

scher'nire [sker'nire] vt to mock, sneer at; **'scherno** sm mockery, derision.

scher'zare [sker'tsare] vi to joke.

'scherzo ['skertso] sm joke; (tiro) trick; (MUS) scherzo; **è uno** ~**!** (una cosa facile) it's child's play!, it's easy!; **per** ~ in jest; for a joke o a laugh; **fare un brutto** ~ **a qd** to play a nasty trick on sb; **scher'zoso, a** ag joking, jesting; (cagnolino etc) playful.

schiaccia'noci [skjattʃa'notʃi] sm inv nutcracker.

schiacci'are [skjat'tʃare] vt (dito) to crush; (noci) to crack; ~ **un pisolino** to have a nap.

schiaffeggi'are [skjaffed'dʒare] vt to slap.

schi'affo ['skjaffo] sm slap.

schiamaz'zare [skjamat'tsare] vi to squawk, cackle.

schian'tare [skjan'tare] vt to break, tear apart; ~**rsi** vr to break (up), shatter; **schi'anto** sm (rumore) crash; tearing sound; (fig: tormento): **provare uno schianto al cuore** to feel a wrench at one's heart; **è uno schianto!** (fam) it's (o he's o she's) terrific!

schia'rire [skja'rire] vt to lighten, make lighter // vi (2) (anche: ~**rsi**) to grow lighter; (tornar sereno) to clear, brighten up; ~**rsi la voce** to clear one's throat.

schiavitù [skjavi'tu] sf slavery.

schi'avo, a ['skjavo] sm/f slave.

schi'ena ['skjɛna] sf (ANAT) back; **schie'nale** sm (di sedia) back.

schi'era ['skjɛra] sf (MIL) rank; (gruppo) group, band.

schiera'mento [skjera'mento] sm lining up, drawing up; (SPORT) formation; line-up.

schie'rare [skje'rare] vt (esercito) to line up, draw up, marshal; ~rsi vr to line up; (fig) to take sides.

schi'etto, a ['skjɛtto] ag (puro) pure; (fig) frank, straightforward; sincere.

'schifo ['skifo] sm disgust; **fare ~** (essere fatto male, dare pessimi risultati) to be awful; **mi fa ~** it makes me sick, it's disgusting; **quel libro è uno ~** that book's rotten; **schi'foso, a** ag disgusting, revolting; (molto scadente) rotten, lousy.

schioc'care [skjɔk'kare] vt (frusta) to crack; (dita) to snap; (lingua) to click; ~ **le labbra** to smack one's lips.

schi'udere ['skjudere] vt, ~rsi vr to open.

schi'uma ['skjuma] sf foam; (di sapone) lather; (fig: feccia) scum; **schiu'mare** vt to skim // vi to foam.

schi'uso, a ['skjuso] pp di **schiudere**.

schi'vare [ski'vare] vt to dodge, avoid.

'schivo, a ['skivo] ag (ritroso) stand-offish, reserved; (timido) shy; ~ **a fare** loath to do, reluctant to do.

schizo'frenico, a, ci, che [skidzo-'freniko] ag schizophrenic.

schiz'zare [skit'tsare] vt (spruzzare) to spurt, squirt; (sporcare) to splash, spatter; (fig: abbozzare) to sketch // vi to spurt, squirt; (saltar fuori) to dart up (o off etc).

schizzi'noso, a [skittsi'noso] ag fussy, finicky.

'schizzo ['skittso] sm (di liquido) spurt, splash, spatter; (abbozzo) sketch.

sci [ʃi] sm (attrezzo) ski; (attività) skiing; ~ **nautico** water-skiing.

'scia, pl 'scie ['ʃia] sf (di imbarcazione) wake; (di profumo) trail.

scià [ʃa] sm inv shah.

sci'abola ['ʃabola] sf sabre.

scia'callo [ʃa'kallo] sm jackal.

sciac'quare [ʃak'kware] vt to rinse.

scia'gura [ʃa'gura] sf disaster, calamity; misfortune; **sciagu'rato, a** ag unfortunate; (malvagio) wicked.

scialac'quare [ʃalak'kware] vt to squander.

scia'lare [ʃa'lare] vi to lead a life of luxury.

sci'albo, a ['ʃalbo] ag pale, dull; (fig) dull, colourless.

sci'alle ['ʃalle] sm shawl.

scia'luppa [ʃa'luppa] sf (anche: ~ di salvataggio) lifeboat.

sci'ame ['ʃame] sm swarm.

scian'cato, a [ʃan'kato] ag lame; (mobile) rickety.

sci'are [ʃi'are] vi to ski.

sci'arpa ['ʃarpa] sf scarf; (fascia) sash.

scia'tore, 'trice [ʃa'tore] sm/f skier.

sci'atto, a ['ʃatto] ag (persona, aspetto) slovenly, unkempt; (lavoro) sloppy, careless.

scien'tifico, a, ci, che [ʃen'tifiko] ag scientific.

sci'enza ['ʃɛntsa] sf science; (sapere) knowledge; ~**e** sfpl (INS) science sg; ~**e**

naturali natural sciences; **scienzi'ato, a** sm/f scientist.

'scimmia ['ʃimmja] sf monkey; **scimmiot'tare** vt to ape, mimic.

scimpanzé [ʃimpan'tse] sm inv chimpanzee.

scimu'nito, a [ʃimu'nito] ag silly, idiotic.

'scindere ['ʃindere] vt, ~rsi vr to split (up).

scin'tilla [ʃin'tilla] sf spark; **scintil'lare** vi to spark; (acqua, occhi) to sparkle.

scioc'chezza [ʃok'kettsa] sf stupidity q; stupid o foolish thing; **dire ~e** to talk nonsense.

sci'occo, a, chi, che ['ʃɔkko] ag stupid, foolish.

sci'ogliere ['ʃɔʎʎere] vt (nodo) to untie; (animale) to untie, release; (fig: persona) to ~ **da** to release from; (neve) to melt; (nell'acqua: zucchero etc) to dissolve; (fig: problema) to resolve; (: muscoli) to loosen up; (fig: porre fine a: contratto) to cancel; (: società, matrimonio) to dissolve; (adempiere: voto etc) to fulfil; ~rsi vr to loosen, come untied; to melt; to dissolve.

sciol'tezza [ʃol'tettsa] sf agility; suppleness; ease.

sci'olto, a ['ʃɔlto] pp di **sciogliere** // ag loose; (agile) agile, nimble; supple; (disinvolto) free and easy; **versi ~i** (POESIA) blank verse.

sciope'rante [ʃope'rante] sm/f striker.

sciope'rare [ʃope'rare] vi to strike, go on strike.

sci'opero ['ʃopero] sm strike; **fare ~** to strike; ~ **bianco** work-to-rule; ~ **selvaggio** wildcat strike; ~ **a singhiozzo** on-off strike.

sci'rocco [ʃi'rɔkko] sm sirocco.

sci'roppo [ʃi'rɔppo] sm syrup.

'scisma, i ['ʃizma] sm (REL) schism.

scissi'one [ʃis'sjone] sf (anche fig) split, division; (FISICA) fission.

'scisso, a ['ʃisso] pp di **scindere**.

sciu'pare [ʃu'pare] vt (abito, libro, appetito) to spoil, ruin; (tempo, denaro) to waste; ~rsi vr to get spoilt o ruined; (rovinarsi la salute) to ruin one's health.

scivo'lare [ʃivo'lare] vi (2) to slide o glide along; (involontariamente) to slip, slide; **'scivolo** sm slide; (TECN) chute.

scle'rosi sf sclerosis.

scoc'care vt (freccia) to shoot // vi (2) (guizzare) to shoot up; (battere: ora) to strike.

scocci'are [skot'tʃare] (fam) vt to bother, annoy; ~rsi vr to be bothered o annoyed.

sco'della sf bowl.

scodinzo'lare [skodintso'lare] vi to wag its tail.

sco'gliera [skoʎ'ʎɛra] sf reef; cliff.

'scoglio ['skoʎʎo] sm (al mare) rock.

scoi'attolo sm squirrel.

sco'lare, a: **età** ~ school age // vt to drain // vi (2) to drip.

scola'resca sf schoolchildren pl, pupils pl.

sco'laro, a sm/f pupil, schoolboy/girl.

sco'lastico, a, ci, che ag school cpd; scholastic.

scol'lare vt (staccare) to unstick; ~rsi vr to come unstuck; scolla'tura sf neckline.

'scolo sm drainage.

scolo'rire vt to fade; to discolour // vi (2) (anche: ~rsi) to fade; to become discoloured; (impallidire) to turn pale.

scol'pire vt to carve, sculpt.

scombi'nare vt to mess up, upset.

scombusso'lare vt to upset.

scom'messo, a pp di scommettere // sf bet, wager.

scom'mettere vt, vi to bet.

scomo'dare vt to trouble, bother; to disturb; ~rsi vr to put o.s. out; ~rsi a fare to go to the bother o trouble of doing.

'scomodo, a ag uncomfortable; (sistemazione, posto) awkward, inconvenient.

scompagi'nare [skompadʒi'nare] vt to upset, disarrange; (TIP) to break up.

scompa'rire vi (2) to disappear, vanish; (fig) to be insignificant; scom'parso, a pp di scomparire // sf disappearance.

scomparti'mento sm (FERR) compartment.

scom'parto sm compartment, division.

scompigli'are [skompiʎ'ʎare] vt (cassetto, capelli) to mess up, disarrange; (fig: piani) to upset; scom'piglio sm mess, confusion.

scom'porre vt (disfare) to break up, take to pieces; (scompigliare) to disarrange, mess up; scomporsi vr (fig) to get upset, lose one's composure; scom'posto, a pp di scomporre // ag (gesto) unseemly; (capelli) ruffled, dishevelled.

sco'munica sf excommunication.

scomuni'care vt to excommunicate.

sconcer'tare [skontʃer'tare] vt to disconcert, bewilder.

'sconcio, a, ci, ce ['skontʃo] ag (osceno) indecent, obscene // sm (cosa riprovevole, mal fatta) disgrace.

sconfes'sare vt to renounce, disavow; to repudiate.

scon'figgere [skon'fiddʒere] vt to defeat, overcome.

sconfi'nare vi to cross the border; (in proprietà privata) to trespass; (fig): ~ da to stray o digress from; sconfi'nato, a ag boundless, unlimited.

scon'fitto, a pp di sconfiggere // sf defeat.

scon'forto sm despondency.

scongiu'rare [skondʒu'rare] vt (implorare) to entreat, beseech, implore; (eludere: pericolo) to ward off, avert; scongi'uro sm entreaty; (esorcismo) exorcism; fare gli scongiuri to touch wood.

scon'nesso, a pp di sconnettere // ag (fig: discorso) incoherent, rambling.

sconosci'uto, a [skonoʃ'ʃuto] ag unknown; new, strange // sm/f stranger; unknown person.

sconquas'sare vt to shatter, smash; (scombussolare) to upset.

sconside'rato, a ag thoughtless, rash.

sconsigli'are [skonsiʎ'ʎare] vt: ~ qc a qd to advise sb against sth; ~ qd da fare qc to advise sb not to do o against doing sth.

sconso'lato, a ag inconsolable; desolate.

scon'tare vt (detrarre) to deduct; (debito) to pay off; (COMM) to discount; (pena) to serve; (colpa, errori) to pay for, suffer for.

scon'tato, a ag (previsto) foreseen, taken for granted; dare per ~ che to take it for granted that.

scon'tento, a ag: ~ (di) discontented o dissatisfied (with) // sm discontent, dissatisfaction.

'sconto sm discount.

scon'trarsi vr (treni etc) to crash, collide; (venire a combattimento, fig) to clash; ~ con to crash into, collide with.

scon'trino sm ticket.

'scontro sm clash, encounter; crash, collision.

scon'troso, a ag sullen, surly; (permaloso) touchy.

sconveni'ente ag unseemly, improper.

scon'volgere [skon'voldʒere] vt to throw into confusion, upset; (turbare) to shake, disturb; upset; scon'volto, a ag pp di sconvolgere.

'scopa sf broom; (CARTE) Italian card game; sco'pare vt to sweep.

sco'perto, a pp di scoprire // ag uncovered; (capo) uncovered, bare; (luogo) open, exposed; (MIL) exposed, without cover; (conto) overdrawn // sf discovery.

'scopo sm aim, purpose; a che ~? what for?

scoppi'are vi (2) (spaccarsi) to burst; (esplodere) to explode; (fig) to break out; ~ in pianto o a piangere to burst out crying; ~ dalle risa o dal ridere to split one's sides laughing; 'scoppio sm explosion; (di tuono, arma etc) crash, bang; (fig: di risa, ira) fit, outburst; (: di guerra) outbreak; a scoppio ritardato delayed-action.

scoppiet'tare vi to crackle.

sco'prire vt to discover; (liberare da ciò che copre) to uncover; (: monumento) to unveil; ~rsi vr to put on lighter clothes; (fig) to give o.s. away.

scoraggi'are [skoradʒ'dʒare] vt to discourage; ~rsi vr to become discouraged, lose heart.

scorcia'toia [skortʃa'toja] sf short cut.

'scorcio ['skortʃo] sm (ARTE) foreshortening; (di secolo, periodo) end, close.

scor'dare vt to forget; ~rsi vr: ~rsi di qc/di fare to forget sth/to do.

'scorgere ['skɔrdʒere] vt to make out, distinguish, see.

'scorno sm ignominy, disgrace.

scorpacci'ata [skorpat'tʃata] sf: fare

una ~ (di) to stuff o.s. (with), eat one's fill (of).

scorpi'one sm scorpion; (dello zodiaco): S~ Scorpio.

scorraz'zare [skorrat'tsare] vi to run about.

'scorrere vt (giornale, lettera) to run o skim through // vi (2) (scivolare) to glide, slide; (colare, fluire) to run, flow; (trascorrere) to pass (by).

scor'retto, a ag incorrect; (sgarbato) impolite; (sconveniente) improper.

scor'revole ag (porta) sliding; (fig: stile) fluent, flowing.

scorri'banda sf (MIL) raid; (escursione) trip, excursion.

'scorso, a pp di **scorrere** // ag last // sf quick look, glance.

scor'soio, a ag: **nodo** ~ noose.

'scorta sf (di personalità, convoglio) escort; (provvista) supply, stock; **scor'tare** vt to escort.

scor'tese ag discourteous, rude; **scorte-'sia** sf lack of courtesy, rudeness.

scorti'care vt to skin.

'scorto, a pp di **scorgere.**

'scorza ['skɔrdza] sf (di albero) bark; (di agrumi) peel, skin; (di pesce, serpente) skin.

sco'sceso, a [skoʃ'ʃeso] ag steep.

'scosso, a pp di **scuotere** // ag (turbato) shaken, upset // sf jerk, jolt, shake; (ELETTR, fig) shock.

scos'tante ag (fig) off-putting, unpleasant.

scos'tare vt to move (away), shift; ~rsi vr to move away.

scostu'mato, a ag immoral, dissolute.

scot'tare vt (ustionare) to burn; (: con liquido bollente) to scald; (sog: offesa) to hurt, offend // vi to burn; (caffè) to be too hot; **scotta'tura** sf burn; scald.

'scotto, a ag overcooked // sm (fig): **pagare lo** ~ (di) to pay the penalty (for).

sco'vare vt to drive out, flush out; (fig) to discover.

'Scozia ['skɔttsia] sf: **la** ~ Scotland; **scoz-'zese** ag Scottish // sm/f Scot.

scredi'tare vt to discredit.

screpo'lare vt, ~**rsi** vr to crack; **screpola'tura** sf cracking q; crack.

screzi'ato, a [skret'tsjato] ag streaked, speckled.

'screzio ['skrɛttsjo] sm disagreement.

scricchio'lare [skrikkjo'lare] vi to creak, squeak.

'scricciolo ['skrittʃolo] sm wren.

'scrigno ['skriɲno] sm casket.

scrimina'tura sf parting.

'scritto, a pp di **scrivere** // ag written // sm writing; (lettera) letter, note // sf inscription; ~**i** smpl (letterari etc) writing sg; per o in ~ in writing.

scrit'toio sm writing desk.

scrit'tore, 'trice sm/f writer.

scrit'tura sf writing; (COMM) entry; (contratto) contract; (REL): **la Sacra S**~ the Scriptures pl; ~**e** sfpl (COMM) accounts, books.

scrittu'rare vt (TEATRO, CINEMA) to sign up, engage; (COMM) to enter.

scriva'nia sf desk.

scri'vente sm/f writer.

'scrivere vt to write; **come lo si scrive?** how is it spelt?, how do you write it?

scroc'cone, a sm/f scrounger.

'scrofa sf (ZOOL) sow.

scrol'lare vt to shake; ~**rsi** vr (anche fig) to give o.s. a shake; ~ **le spalle/il capo** to shrug one's shoulders/shake one's head.

scrosci'are [skroʃ'ʃare] vi (2) (pioggia) to pour down, pelt down; (torrente, fig: applausi) to thunder, roar; **'scroscio** sm pelting; thunder, roar; (di applausi) burst.

scros'tare vt (intonaco) to scrape off, strip; ~**rsi** vr to peel off, flake off.

'scrupolo sm scruple; (meticolosità) care, conscientiousness; **scrupo'loso, a** ag scrupulous; conscientious, thorough.

scru'tare vt to search, scrutinize; (intenzioni, causa) to examine, scrutinize.

scruti'nare vt (voti) to count; **scru'tinio** sm (votazione) ballot; (insieme delle operazioni) poll; (INS) (meeting for) assignment of marks at end of a term or year.

scu'cire [sku'tʃire] vt (orlo etc) to unpick, undo.

scude'ria sf stable.

scu'detto sm (SPORT) (championship) shield; (distintivo) badge.

'scudo sm shield.

scul'tore, 'trice sm/f sculptor.

scul'tura sf sculpture.

scu'ola sf school; ~ **elemen-tare/materna/media** primary/nur-sery/secondary school; ~ **guida** driving school.

scu'otere vt to shake; ~**rsi** vr to jump, be startled; (fig: muoversi) to rouse o.s., stir o.s.; (: commuoversi) to be shaken.

'scure sf axe.

'scuro, a ag dark; (fig: espressione) grim // sm darkness; dark colour; (imposta) (window) shutter; **verde/rosso** etc ~ dark green/red etc.

scur'rile ag scurrilous.

'scusa sf excuse; ~**e** sfpl apology sg, apologies; **chiedere** ~ **a qd (per)** to apologize to sb (for); **chiedo** ~ I'm sorry; (disturbando etc) excuse me.

scu'sare vt to excuse; ~**rsi** vr: ~**rsi (di)** to apologize (for); **(mi) scusi** I'm sorry; (per richiamare l'attenzione) excuse me.

sde'gnare [zdeɲ'ɲare] vt to scorn, despise; ~**rsi** vr (adirarsi) to get angry.

'sdegno ['zdeɲno] sm scorn, disdain; **sde-'gnoso, a** ag scornful, disdainful.

sdolci'nato, a [zdoltʃi'nato] ag mawkish, oversentimental.

sdoppi'are vt (dividere) to divide o split in two.

sdrai'arsi vr to stretch out, lie down.

'sdraio sm: **sedia a** ~ deck chair.

sdruccio'lare [zdruttʃo'lare] vi (2) to slip, slide.

se pronome vedi **si** // cong if; (in frasi

interrogative indirette) if, whether; **non so ~ scrivere o telefonare** I don't know whether *o* if I should write or phone; **~ mai** if, if ever; *(caso mai)* in case; **~ solo** *o* **solamente** if only.

sé *pronome (gen)* oneself; *(esso, essa, lui, lei, loro)* itself; himself; herself; themselves; **~ stesso(a)** *pronome* oneself; itself; himself; herself; **~ stessi(e)** *pronome pl* themselves.

seb'bene *cong* although, though.

sec. *(abbr di secolo)* c.

'secca *sf vedi* **secco.**

sec'care *vt* to dry; *(prosciugare)* to dry up; *(fig: importunare)* to annoy, bother; (: *annoiare)* to bore // *vi (2)* to dry; to dry up; **~rsi** *vr* to dry; to dry up; *(fig)* to grow annoyed; to grow bored; **secca'tura** *sf (fig)* bother *q*, trouble *q*.

'secchia ['sekkja] *sf* bucket, pail.

'secco, a, chi, che *ag* dry; *(fichi, pesce)* dried; *(foglie, ramo)* withered; *(magro: persona)* thin, skinny; *(fig: risposta, modo di fare)* curt, abrupt; (: *colpo)* clean, sharp // *sm (siccità)* drought // *sf (del mare)* shallows *pl*; **restarci ~** *(fig: morire sul colpo)* to drop dead; **mettere in ~** *(barca)* to beach; **rimanere in** *o* **a ~** *(NAUT)* to run aground; *(fig)* to be left in the lurch.

seco'lare *ag* age-old, centuries-old; *(laico, mondano)* secular.

'secolo *sm* century; *(epoca)* age.

se'conda *sf vedi* **secondo.**

secon'dario, a *ag* secondary.

se'condo, a *ag* second // *sm* second; *(di pranzo)* main course // *sf (AUT)* second (gear) // *prep* according to; *(nel modo prescritto)* in accordance with; **~ me** in my opinion, to my mind; **di ~a classe** second-class; **di ~a mano** second-hand; **viaggiare in ~a** to travel second-class; **a ~a di** *prep* according to; in accordance with.

secrezi'one [sekret'tsjone] *sf* secretion.

'sedano *sm* celery.

seda'tivo, a *ag, sm* sedative.

'sede *sf* seat; *(di ditta)* head office; *(di organizzazione)* headquarters *pl*; **in ~ di** *(in occasione di)* during; **~ sociale** registered office.

seden'tario, a *ag* sedentary.

se'dere *vi (2)* to sit, be seated; **~rsi** *vr* to sit down // *sm (deretano)* behind, bottom.

'sedia *sf* chair.

sedi'cente [sedi'tʃɛnte] *ag* self-styled.

'sedici ['seditʃi] *num* sixteen.

se'dile *sm* seat; *(nei giardini)* bench.

sedi'mento *sm* sediment.

sedizi'one [sedit'tsjone] *sf* revolt, rebellion; **sedizi'oso, a** *ag* seditious; rebellious.

se'dotto, a *pp di* **sedurre.**

sedu'cente [sedu'tʃɛnte] *ag* seductive; *(proposta)* very attractive.

se'durre *vt* to seduce.

se'duta *sf* session, sitting; *(riunione)*

meeting; *(di modello)* sitting; **~ stante** *(fig)* immediately.

seduzi'one [sedut'tsjone] *sf* seduction; *(fascino)* charm, appeal.

'sega, ghe *sf* saw.

'segale *sf* rye.

se'gare *vt* to saw; *(recidere)* to saw off; **sega'tura** *sf (residuo)* sawdust.

'seggio ['sɛddʒo] *sm* seat; **~ elettorale** polling station.

'seggiola ['sɛddʒola] *sf* chair; **seggio'lone** *sm (per bambini)* highchair.

seggio'via [seddʒo'via] *sf* chairlift.

seghe'ria [sege'ria] *sf* sawmill.

seg'mento *sm* segment.

segna'lare [seɲɲa'lare] *vt (manovra etc)* to signal; to indicate; *(annunciare)* to announce; to report; *(fig: far conoscere)* to point out; (: *persona)* to single out; **~rsi** *vr (distinguersi)* to distinguish o.s.

se'gnale [seɲ'ɲale] *sm* signal; *(cartello)* sign; **~ d'allarme** alarm signal; *(FERR)* communication chord; **~ orario** time signal; **segna'letica** *sf* signalling, signposting; **segnaletica stradale** roadsigns *pl*.

se'gnare [seɲ'ɲare] *vt* to mark; *(prendere nota)* to note; *(indicare)* to indicate, mark; *(SPORT: goal)* to score; **~rsi** *vr (REL)* to make the sign of the cross, cross o.s.

'segno ['seɲɲo] *sm* sign; *(impronta, contrassegno)* mark; *(limite)* limit, bounds *pl*; *(bersaglio)* target; **fare ~ di sì/no** to nod (one's head)/shake one's head; **fare ~ a qd di fermarsi** to motion (to) sb to stop; **cogliere** *o* **colpire nel ~** *(fig)* to hit the mark.

segre'gare *vt* to segregate, isolate; **segregazi'one** *sf* segregation.

segre'tario, a *sm/f* secretary; **~ comunale** town clerk; **~ di Stato** Secretary of State.

segrete'ria *sf (di ditta, scuola)* (secretary's) office; *(d'organizzazione internazionale)* secretariat; *(POL etc: carica)* office of Secretary.

segre'tezza [segre'tettsa] *sf* secrecy.

se'greto, a *ag* secret // *sm* secret; secrecy *q*; **in ~** in secret, secretly.

segu'ace [se'gwatʃe] *sm/f* follower, disciple.

segu'ente *ag* following, next.

segu'ire *vt* to follow; *(frequentare: corso)* to attend // *vi (2)* to follow; *(continuare: testo)* to continue.

segui'tare *vt* to continue, carry on with // *vi* to continue, carry on.

'seguito *sm (scorta)* suite, retinue; *(discepoli)* followers *pl*; *(favore)* following; *(serie)* sequence, series *sg*; *(continuazione)* continuation; *(conseguenza)* result; **di ~** at a stretch, on end; **in ~** later on; **in ~ a, a ~ di** following; *(a causa di)* as a result of, owing to.

'sei *forma del vb* **essere** // *num* six.

sei'cento [sei'tʃɛnto] *num* six hundred // *sm*: **il S~** the seventeenth century.

selci'ato [sel'tʃato] *sm* pavement.

selezio'nare [selettsjo'nare] vt to select.
selezi'one [selet'tsjone] sf selection.
'sella sf saddle; **sel'lare** vt to saddle.
selvag'gina [selvad'dʒina] sf (animali) game.
sel'vaggio, a, gi, ge [sel'vaddʒo] ag wild; (tribù) savage, uncivilized; (fig) savage, fierce; unsociable // sm/f savage.
sel'vatico, a, ci, che ag wild.
se'maforo sm (AUT) traffic lights pl.
sem'brare (2) vi to seem // vb impers: **sembra che** it seems that; **mi sembra che** it seems to me that; I think (that); ~ **di essere** to seem to be.
'seme sm seed; (sperma) semen; (CARTE) suit.
se'mestre sm half-year; (INS) semester.
'semi... prefisso semi...; **semi'cerchio** sm semicircle; **semifi'nale** sf semifinal; **semi'freddo, a** ag (CUC) chilled // sm ice-cream cake.
'semina sf (AGR) sowing.
semi'nare vt to sow.
semi'nario sm seminar; (REL) seminary.
se'mitico, a, ci, che ag semitic.
sem'mai = se mai; vedi **se**.
'semola sf bran.
semo'lino sm semolina.
'semplice ['semplitʃe] ag simple; (di un solo elemento) single; **semplice'mente** av simply; **semplicità** sf simplicity; **semplifi'care** vt to simplify.
'sempre av always; (ancora) still; **posso ~ tentare** I can always try, anyway, I can try; **per ~** forever; **una volta per ~** once and for all; ~ **che** cong provided (that); ~ **più** more and more; ~ **meno** less and less.
sempre'verde ag, sm o f (BOT) evergreen.
'senape sf (CUC) mustard.
se'nato sm senate; **sena'tore, 'trice** sm/f senator.
se'nile ag senile.
'senno sm judgment, (common) sense.
'seno sm (petto) breast; (ventre materno, fig) womb; (GEO) inlet, creek; (ANAT) sinus; (MAT) sine.
sen'sato, a ag sensible.
sensazio'nale [sensattsjo'nale] ag sensational.
sensazi'one [sensat'tsjone] sf sensation; **fare ~** to cause a sensation, create a stir.
sen'sibile ag sensitive; (ai sensi) perceptible; (rilevante, notevole) appreciable, noticeable; ~ **a** sensitive to; **sensibilità** sf sensitivity.
'senso sm (FISIOL, istinto) sense; (impressione, sensazione) feeling, sensation; (significato) meaning, sense; (direzione) direction; ~ **i smpl** (coscienza) consciousness sg; (sensualità) senses; **ciò non ha ~** that doesn't make sense; **fare ~ a** (ripugnare) to disgust, repel; ~ **comune** common sense; **in ~ orario/antiorario** clockwise/anticlockwise; ~ **unico,** ~ **vietato** (AUT) one-way street.

sensu'ale ag sensual; sensuous; **sensualità** sf sensuality; sensuousness.
sen'tenza [sen'tɛntsa] sf (DIR) sentence; (massima) maxim; **sentenzi'are** vi (DIR) to pass judgment.
senti'ero sm path.
sentimen'tale ag sentimental; (vita, avventura) love cpd.
senti'mento sm feeling.
senti'nella sf sentry.
sen'tire vt (percepire al tatto, fig) to feel; (udire) to hear; (ascoltare) to listen to; (odore) to smell; (avvertire con il gusto, assaggiare) to taste // vi: ~ **di** (avere sapore) to taste of; (avere odore) to smell of; **~rsi bene/male** to feel well/unwell o ill; **~rsi di fare qc** (essere disposto) to feel like doing sth.
sen'tito, a ag (sincero) sincere, warm; **per ~ dire** by hearsay.
'senza ['sɛntsa] prep, cong without; ~ **dir nulla** without saying a word; **fare ~ qc** to do without sth; ~ **di me** without me; ~ **che io lo sapessi** without me o my knowing; **senz'altro** of course, certainly; ~ **dubbio** no doubt; ~ **scrupoli** unscrupulous; ~ **amici** friendless.
sepa'rare vt to separate; (dividere) to divide; (tenere distinto) to distinguish; **~rsi** vr (coniugi) to separate, part; (amici) to part, leave each other; **~rsi da** (coniuge) to separate o part from; (amico, socio) to part company with; (oggetto) to part with; **separazi'one** sf separation.
se'polcro sm sepulchre.
se'polto, a pp di **seppellire**.
seppel'lire vt to bury.
'seppia sf cuttlefish // ag inv sepia.
se'quenza [se'kwentsa] sf sequence.
seques'trare vt (DIR) to impound; (rapire) to kidnap; (costringere in un luogo) to keep, confine; **se'questro** sm (DIR) impoundment; **sequestro di persona** kidnapping; illegal confinement.
'sera sf evening; **di ~** in the evening; **domani ~** tomorrow evening, tomorrow night; **se'rale** ag evening cpd; **se'rata** sf evening; (ricevimento) party.
ser'bare vt to keep; (mettere da parte) to put aside; ~ **rancore/odio verso qd** to bear sb a grudge/hate sb.
serba'toio sm tank; (di apparecchio igienico) cistern; (TECN) reservoir.
'serbo sm: **mettere** (o **tenere** o **avere**) **in ~ qc** to put (o keep) sth aside.
sere'nata sf (MUS) serenade.
serenità sf serenity.
se'reno, a ag (tempo, cielo) clear; (fig) serene, calm.
ser'gente [ser'dʒɛnte] sm (MIL) sergeant.
'serie sf inv (successione) series inv; (gruppo, collezione: di chiavi etc) set; (SPORT) division; league; (COMM): **modello di ~/fuori ~** standard/custom-built model; **in ~** in quick succession; (COMM) mass cpd.
serietà sf seriousness; reliability.
'serio, a ag serious; (impiegato)

responsible, reliable; (*ditta, cliente*) reliable, dependable; **sul** ~ (*davvero*) really, truly; (*seriamente*) seriously, in earnest.

ser'mone *sm* sermon.

serpeggi'are [serped'dʒare] *vi* to wind; (*fig*) to spread.

ser'pente *sm* snake; ~ **a sonagli** rattlesnake.

'serra *sf* greenhouse; hothouse.

ser'randa *sf* roller shutter.

ser'rare *vt* to close, shut; (*a chiave*) to lock; (*stringere*) to tighten; (*premere: nemico*) to close in on; ~ **i pugni/i denti** to clench one's fists/teeth; ~ **le file** to close ranks.

serra'tura *sf* lock.

'serva *sf vedi* **servo.**

ser'vire *vt* to serve; (*clienti: al ristorante*) to wait on; (: *al negozio*) to serve, attend to; (*fig: giovane*) to aid, help // *vi* (*TENNIS*) to serve; (2) (*essere utile*): ~ **a qd** to be of use to sb; ~ **a qc/a fare** (*utensile etc*) to be used for sth/for doing; ~ **(a qd) di** to serve as (for sb); ~**rsi** *vr* (*usare*): ~**rsi di** to use; (*prendere: cibo*): ~**rsi (di)** to help o.s. (to); (*essere cliente abituale*): ~**rsi da** to be a regular customer at, go to.

servitù *sf* servitude; slavery; captivity; (*personale di servizio*) servants *pl*, domestic staff.

servizi'evole [servit'tsjevole] *ag* obliging, willing to help.

ser'vizio [ser'vittsjo] *sm* service; (*compenso: al ristorante*) service (charge); (*STAMPA, TV, RADIO*) report; (*da tè, caffè etc*) set, service; ~**i** *smpl* (*di casa*) kitchen and bathroom; (*ECON*) services; **essere di** ~ to be on duty; **fare** ~ to operate; (*essere aperto*) to be open; (*essere di turno*) to be on duty; ~ **militare** military service; ~**i segreti** secret service *sg*.

'servo *a sm/f* servant.

ses'santa *num* sixty.

sessan'tina *sf*: **una** ~ **(di)** about sixty.

sessi'one *sf* session.

'sesso *sm* sex; **sessu'ale** *ag* sexual, sex *cpd*.

ses'tante *sm* sextant.

'sesto, a *ag, sm* sixth.

'seta *sf* silk.

'sete *sf* thirst; **avere** ~ to be thirsty.

'setola *sf* bristle.

'setta *sf* sect.

set'tanta *num* seventy.

settan'tina *sf*: **una** ~ **(di)** about seventy.

'sette *num* seven.

sette'cento [sette'tʃento] *num* seven hundred // *sm*: **il S**~ the eighteenth century.

set'tembre *sm* September.

settentrio'nale *ag* northern.

settentri'one *sm* north.

'settico, a, ci, che *ag* (*MED*) septic.

setti'mana *sf* week; **settima'nale** *ag, sm* weekly.

'settimo, a *ag, sm* seventh.

set'tore *sm* sector.

severità *sf* severity.

se'vero, a *ag* severe.

se'vizie [se'vittsje] *sfpl* torture *sg*; **sevi-zi'are** *vt* to torture.

sezio'nare [settsjo'nare] *vt* to divide into sections; (*MED*) to dissect.

sezi'one [set'tsjone] *sf* section; (*MED*) dissection.

sfaccen'dato, a [sfattʃen'dato] *ag* idle.

sfacci'ato, a [sfat'tʃato] *ag* (*maleducato*) cheeky, impudent; (*vistoso*) gaudy.

sfa'celo [sfa'tʃelo] *sm* (*fig*) ruin, collapse.

sfal'darsi *vr* to flake (off).

'sfarzo ['sfartso] *sm* pomp, splendour.

sfasci'are [sfaʃ'ʃare] *vt* (*ferita*) to unbandage; (*distruggere: porta*) to smash, shatter; ~**rsi** *vr* (*rompersi*) to smash, shatter; (*fig*) to collapse.

sfa'tare *vt* (*leggenda*) to explode.

sfavil'lare *vi* to spark, send out sparks; (*risplendere*) to sparkle.

sfavo'revole *ag* unfavourable.

'sfera *sf* sphere; **'sferico, a, ci, che** *ag* spherical.

sfer'rare *vt* (*fig: colpo*) to land, deal; (: *attacco*) to launch.

sfer'zare [sfer'tsare] *vt* to whip; (*fig*) to lash out at.

sfiata'toio *sm* blowhole.

sfi'brare *vt* (*indebolire*) to exhaust, enervate.

'sfida *sf* challenge; **sfi'dare** *vt* to challenge; (*fig*) to defy, brave.

sfi'ducia [sfi'dutʃa] *sf* distrust, mistrust.

sfigu'rare *vt* (*persona*) to disfigure; (*quadro, statua*) to deface // *vi* (*far cattiva figura*) to make a bad impression.

sfi'lare *vt* to unthread; (*abito, scarpe*) to slip off // *vi* (*truppe*) to march past; (*atleti*) to parade; ~**rsi** *vr* (*perle etc*) to come unstrung; (*calza*) to run, ladder; **sfi-lata** *sf* march past; parade; **sfilata di moda** fashion show.

'sfinge ['sfindʒe] *sf* sphinx.

sfi'nito, a *ag* exhausted.

sfio'rare *vt* to brush (against); (*argomento*) to touch upon.

sfio'rire *vi* (2) to wither, fade.

sfo'cato, a *ag* (*FOT*) out of focus.

sfoci'are [sfo'tʃare] *vi* (2): ~ **in** to flow into.

sfo'gare *vt* to vent, pour out; ~**rsi** *vr* (*sfogare la propria rabbia*) to give vent to one's anger; (*confidarsi*): ~**rsi (con)** to pour out one's feelings (to); **non sfogarti su di me!** don't take your bad temper out on me!

sfoggi'are [sfod'dʒare] *vt, vi* to show off.

'sfoglia ['sfoʎʎa] *sf* sheet of pasta dough; **pasta** ~ (*CUC*) puff pastry.

sfogli'are [sfoʎ'ʎare] *vt* (*libro*) to leaf through.

'sfogo, ghi *sm* outlet; (*eruzione cutanea*) rash; (*fig*) outburst; **dare** ~ **a** (*fig*) to give vent to.

sfolgo'rare *vi* to blaze.

sfol'lare *vt* to empty, clear // *vi* (2) to disperse; (*in tempo di guerra*): ~ **(da)** to evacuate.

sfon'dare *vt* (*porta*) to break down; (*scarpe*) to wear a hole in; (*cesto, scatola*) to burst, knock the bottom out of; (*MIL*) to break through // *vi* (*riuscire*) to make a name for o.s.

'sfondo *sm* background.

sfor'mato *sm* (*CUC*) type of soufflé.

sfor'nire *vt*: ~ **di** to deprive of.

sfor'tuna *sf* misfortune, ill luck *q*; **sfor-tu'nato, a** *ag* unlucky; (*impresa, film*) unsuccessful.

sfor'zare [sfor'tsare] *vt* to force; ~**rsi** *vr*: ~ **rsi di** *o* **a** *o* **per fare** to try hard to do.

'sforzo ['sfortso] *sm* effort; (*tensione eccessiva, TECN*) strain.

sfrat'tare *vt* to evict; **'sfratto** *sm* eviction.

sfrec'ciare [sfret'tʃare] *vi* (2) to shoot *o* flash past.

sfregi'are [sfre'dʒare] *vt* to slash, gash; (*persona*) to disfigure; (*quadro*) to deface; **'sfregio** *sm* gash; scar; (*fig*) insult.

sfre'nato, a *ag* (*fig*) unrestrained, unbridled.

sfron'tato, a *ag* shameless.

sfrutta'mento *sm* exploitation.

sfrut'tare *vt* (*terreno*) to overwork, exhaust; (*miniera*) to exploit, work; (*fig: operai, occasione, potere*) to exploit.

sfug'gire [sfud'dʒire] *vi* (2) to escape; ~ **a** (*custode*) to escape (from); (*morte*) to escape; ~ **a qd** (*dettaglio, nome*) to escape sb; ~ **di mano a qd** to slip out of sb's hand (*o* hands); **sfug'gita: di sfuggita** *ad* (*rapidamente, in fretta*) in passing.

sfu'mare *vt* (*colori, contorni*) to soften, shade off // *vi* (2) to shade (off), fade; (*svanire*) to vanish, disappear; (*fig: speranze*) to come to nothing; **sfuma'tura** *sf* shading off *q*; (*tonalità*) shade, tone; (*fig*) touch, hint.

sfuri'ata *sf* (*scatto di collera*) fit of anger; (*rimprovero*) sharp rebuke.

sga'bello *sm* stool.

sgabuz'zino [sgabud'dzino] *sm* lumber room.

sgambet'tare *vi* to kick one's legs about; to scurry along.

sgam'betto *sm*: **far lo** ~ **a qd** to trip sb up.

sganasci'arsi [zganaʃ'ʃarsi] *vr*: ~ **dalle risa** to roar with laughter.

sganci'are [zgan'tʃare] *vt* to unhook; (*FERR*) to uncouple; (*bombe: da aereo*) to release, drop; (*fig: fam: soldi*) to fork out.

sganghe'rato, a [zgange'rato] *ag* (*porta*) off its hinges; (*auto*) ramshackle; (*riso*) wild, boisterous.

sgar'bato, a *ag* rude, impolite.

'sgarbo *sm*: **fare uno** ~ **a qd** to be rude to sb.

sgattaio'lare *vi* to sneak away *o* off.

sge'lare [zdʒe'lare] *vi* (2), *vt* to thaw.

'sghembo, a ['zgembo] *ag* (*obliquo*) slanting; (*storto*) crooked.

sghignaz'zare [zgiɲɲat'tsare] *vi* to laugh scornfully.

sgob'bare *vi* (*fam: scolaro*) to swot; (: *operaio*) to slog.

sgoccio'lare [zgottʃo'lare] *vt* (*vuotare*) to drain (to the last drop) // *vi* (*acqua*) to drip; (*recipiente*) to drain.

sgo'larsi *vr* to talk (*o* shout *o* sing) o.s. hoarse.

sgomb(e)'rare *vt* to clear; (*andarsene da: stanza*) to vacate; (*evacuare*) to evacuate.

'sgombro, a *ag*: ~ **(di)** clear (of), free (from) // *sm* (*trasloco*) removal; (*ZOOL*) mackerel.

sgomen'tare *vt* to dismay; ~**rsi** *vr* to be dismayed; **sgo'mento, a** *ag* dismayed // *sm* dismay, consternation.

sgonfi'are *vt* to let down, deflate; ~**rsi** *vr* to go down.

'sgorbio *sm* blot; scribble.

sgor'gare *vi* (2) to gush (out).

sgoz'zare [zgot'tsare] *vt* to cut the throat of.

sgra'devole *ag* unpleasant, disagreeable.

sgra'dito, a *ag* unpleasant, unwelcome.

sgra'nare *vt* (*piselli*) to shell; ~ **gli occhi** to open one's eyes wide.

sgran'chirsi [zgran'kirsi] *vr* to stretch; ~ **le gambe** to stretch one's legs.

sgranocchi'are [zgranok'kjare] *vt* to munch.

'sgravio *sm*: ~ **fiscale** tax relief.

sgrazi'ato, a [zgrat'tsjato] *ag* clumsy, ungainly.

sgreto'lare *vt* to cause to crumble; ~**rsi** *vr* to crumble.

sgri'dare *vt* to scold; **sgri'data** *sf* scolding.

sgual'cire [zgwal'tʃire] *vt* to crumple (up), crease.

sgual'drina *sf* (*peg*) slut.

sgu'ardo *sm* (*occhiata*) look, glance; (*espressione*) look (in one's eye).

sguaz'zare [zgwat'tsare] *vi* (*nell'acqua*) to splash about; (*nella melma*) to wallow; ~ **nella ricchezza** to be rolling in money.

sguinzagli'are [zgwintsaʎ'ʎare] *vt* to let off the leash.

sgusci'are [zguʃ'ʃare] *vt* to shell // *vi* (*uccelli*) to hatch; (*sfuggire di mano*) to slip; (*fig*) to slip *o* slink away.

'shampoo ['ʃampo] *sm inv* shampoo.

shock [ʃɔk] *sm inv* shock.

si *pronome* (*dav lo, la, li, le, ne diventa* **se**) (*riflessivo*) oneself, *m* himself, *f* herself, *soggetto non umano* itself; *pl* themselves; (*reciproco*) one another, each other; (*passivante*): **lo** ~ **ripara facilmente** it is easily repaired; (*possessivo*): **lavarsi le mani** to wash one's hands; (*impersonale*): ~ **vede che è felice** one *o* you can see that he's happy; (*noi*): **tra poco** ~ **parte** we're leaving soon; (*la gente*): ~ **dice che**

they *o* people say that // *sm* (MUS) B; (*: solfeggiando la scala*) ti.

sì *av* yes.

'sia *cong*: ~ ... ~ (*o ... o*): ~ **che lavori,** ~ **che non lavori** whether he works or not; (*tanto ... quanto*): **verranno ~ Luigi** ~ **suo fratello** both Luigi and his brother will be coming.

sia'mese *ag* siamese.

si'amo *forma del vb* **essere.**

Si'beria *sf*: **la ~** Siberia.

sibi'lare *vi* to hiss; (*fischiare*) to whistle; **'sibilo** *sm* hiss; whistle.

si'cario *sm* hired killer.

sicché [sik'ke] *cong* (*perciò*) so (that), therefore; (*e quindi*) (and) so.

siccità [sittʃi'ta] *sf* drought.

sic'come *cong* since, as.

Si'cilia [si'tʃilja] *sf*: **la ~** Sicily; **sicili'ano, a** *ag, sm/f* Sicilian.

sico'moro *sm* sycamore.

sicu'rezza [siku'rettsa] *sf* safety; security; (*fiducia*) confidence; (*certezza*) certainty; **di ~ safety** *cpd*; **la ~ stradale** road safety.

si'curo, a *ag* safe; (*ben difeso*) secure; (*fiducioso*) confident; (*certo*) sure, certain; (*notizia, amico*) reliable; (*esperto*) skilled // *av* (*anche*: **di ~**) certainly; **essere/mettere al ~** to be safe/put in a safe place; **sentirsi ~** to feel safe *o* secure.

siderur'gia [siderur'dʒia] *sf* iron and steel industry.

'sidro *sm* cider.

si'epe *sf* hedge.

si'ero *sm* (MED) serum.

si'esta *sf* siesta, (afternoon) nap.

si'ete *forma del vb* **essere.**

si'filide *sf* syphilis.

si'fone *sm* siphon.

Sig. (*abbr di* **signore**) Mr.

siga'retta *sf* cigarette.

'sigaro *sm* cigar.

Sigg. (*abbr di* **signori**) Messrs.

sigil'lare [sidʒil'lare] *vt* to seal.

si'gillo [si'dʒillo] *sm* seal.

'sigla *sf* initials *pl*; acronym, abbreviation; **~ musicale** signature tune.

si'glare *vt* to initial.

Sig.na *abbr di* **signorina.**

si'gnora [sin'nora] *sf* lady; **la ~ X** Mrs ['mɪsɪz] X; **buon giorno S~/Signore/Signorina** good morning; (*deferente*) good morning Madam/ Sir/Madam; (*quando si conosce il nome*) good morning Mrs/Mr/Miss X; **Gentile S~/Signore/Signorina** (*in una lettera*) Dear Madam/Sir/Madam; **il signor Rossi e ~** Mr Rossi and his wife; **~e e signori** ladies and gentlemen.

si'gnore [sin'nore] *sm* gentleman; (*padrone*) lord, master; (REL): **il S~** the Lord; **il signor X** Mr ['mɪstə*] X; **i ~i**

Bianchi (*coniugi*) Mr and Mrs Bianchi; *vedi anche* **signora.**

signo'rile [sinno'rile] *ag* refined.

signo'rina [sinno'rina] *sf* young lady; **la ~ X** Miss X; *vedi anche* **signora.**

Sig.ra (*abbr di* **signora**) Mrs.

silenzia'tore [silentsja'tore] *sm* silencer.

si'lenzio [si'lentsjo] *sm* silence; **silenzi'oso, a** *ag* silent, quiet.

'sillaba *sf* syllable.

silu'rare *vt* to torpedo; (*fig: privare del comando*) to oust.

si'luro *sm* torpedo.

simboleggi'are [simboled'dʒare] *vt* to symbolize.

sim'bolico, a, ci, che *ag* symbolic(al).

simbo'lismo *sm* symbolism.

'simbolo *sm* symbol.

'simile *ag* (*analogo*) similar; (*di questo tipo*): **un uomo ~** such a man, a man like this; **libri ~i** such books; **~ a** similar to; **i suoi ~i** one's fellow men; one's peers.

simme'tria *sf* symmetry; **sim'metrico, a, ci, che** *ag* symmetrical.

simpa'tia *sf* (*inclinazione*) liking; (*partecipazione ai sentimenti di qd*) sympathy; **avere ~ per qd** to like sb, have a liking for sb; **sim'patico, a, ci, che** *ag* nice, friendly; pleasant; likeable.

simpatiz'zare [simpatid'dzare] *vi*: **~ con** to take a liking to.

sim'posio *sm* symposium.

simu'lare *vt* to sham, simulate; (TECN) to simulate; **simulazi'one** *sf* shamming; simulation.

simul'taneo, a *ag* simultaneous.

sina'goga, ghe *sf* synagogue.

since'rità [sintʃeri'ta] *sf* sincerity.

sin'cero, a [sin'tʃero] *ag* sincere; genuine; heartfelt.

'sincope *sf* syncopation; (MED) blackout.

sincroniz'zare [sinkronid'dzare] *vt* to synchronize.

sinda'cale *ag* (trade-)union *cpd*; **sindaca-'lista, i, e** *sm/f* trade unionist.

sinda'cato *sm* (*di lavoratori*) (trade) union; (AMM, ECON, DIR) syndicate, trust, pool; **~ dei datori di lavoro** employers' association, employers' federation.

'sindaco, ci *sm* mayor.

'sindrome *sf* (MED) syndrome.

sinfo'nia *sf* (MUS) symphony.

singhioz'zare [singjot'tsare] *vi* to sob; to hiccup.

singhi'ozzo [sin'gjottso] *sm* sob; (MED) hiccup; **avere il ~** to have the hiccups; **a ~** (*fig*) by fits and starts.

singo'lare *ag* (*insolito*) remarkable, singular; (LING) singular // *sm* (LING) singular; (TENNIS): **~ maschile/femminile** men's/women's singles.

'singolo, a *ag* single, individual // *sm* (*persona*) individual; (TENNIS) = **singolare.**

si'nistro, a *ag* left, left-hand; (*fig*) sinister // *sm* (*incidente*) accident // *sf* (POL) left (wing); **a ~a** on the left; (*direzione*) to the left.

'**sino** *prep* = **fino**.

si'**nonimo, a** *ag* synonymous // *sm* synonym; **~ di** synonymous with.

sin'**tassi** *sf* syntax.

'**sintesi** *sf* synthesis; (*riassunto*) summary, résumé.

sin'**tetico, a, ci, che** *ag* synthetic.

sintetiz'**zare** [sintetid'dzare] *vt* to synthesize; (*riassumere*) to summarize.

sinto'**matico, a, ci, che** *ag* symptomatic.

'**sintomo** *sm* symptom.

sinu'**oso, a** *ag* (*strada*) winding.

si'**pario** *sm* (TEATRO) curtain.

si'**rena** *sf* (*apparecchio*) siren; (*nella mitologia, fig*) siren, mermaid.

'**Siria** *sf*: **la ~** Syria; **siri'ano, a** *ag, sm/f* Syrian.

si'**ringa, ghe** *sf* syringe.

'**sismico, a, ci, che** *ag* seismic.

sis'**mografo** *sm* seismograph.

sis'**tema, i** *sm* system; method, way; **cambiare ~** to change one's way of life.

siste'**mare** *vt* (*mettere a posto*) to tidy, put in order; (*risolvere: questione*) to sort out, settle; (*procurare un lavoro a*) to find a job for; (*dare un alloggio a*) to settle, find accommodation for; **~rsi** *vr* to settle down; (*trovarsi un lavoro*) to get fixed up with a job; **ti sistemo io!** I'll soon sort you out!

siste'**matico, a, ci, che** *ag* systematic.

sistemazi'**one** [sistemat'tsjone] *sf* arrangement, order; settlement; employment; accommodation.

situ'**are** *vt* to site, situate; **situ'ato, a** *ag*: **situato a/su** situated at/on.

situazi'**one** [situat'tsjone] *sf* situation.

slacci'**are** [zlat'tʃare] *vt* to undo, unfasten.

slanci'**arsi** [zlan'tʃarsi] *vr* to dash, fling o.s.; **slanci'ato, a** *ag* slender; '**slancio** *sm* dash, leap; (*fig*) surge.

sla'**vato, a** *ag* faded, washed out; (*fig: viso, occhi*) pale, colourless.

'**slavo, a** *ag* Slav(onic), Slavic.

sle'**ale** *ag* disloyal; (*concorrenza etc*) unfair.

sle'**gare** *vt* to untie.

'**slitta** *sf* sledge; (*trainata*) sleigh.

slit'**tare** *vi* (2) to slide; (AUT) to skid.

slo'**gare** *vt* (MED) to dislocate.

sloggi'**are** [zlod'dʒare] *vt* (*inquilino*) to turn out; (*nemico*) to drive out, dislodge // *vi* to move out.

smacchi'**are** [zmak'kjare] *vt* to remove stains from.

'**smacco, chi** *sm* humiliating defeat.

smagli'**ante** [zmaʎ'ʎante] *ag* brilliant, dazzling.

smagli'**are** [zmaʎ'ʎare] *vt*, **~rsi** *vr* (*calza*) to ladder.

smalizi'**ato, a** [zmalit'tsjato] *ag* shrewd, cunning.

smal'**tare** *vt* to enamel; (*a vetro*) to glaze; (*unghie*) to varnish.

smal'**tire** *vt* (*merce*) to sell; (: *svendere*) to sell off; (*rifiuti*) to dispose of; (*cibo*) to digest; **~ la sbornia** to sober up.

'**smalto** *sm* (*anche: di denti*) enamel; (*per ceramica*) glaze; **~ per unghie** nail varnish.

'**smania** *sf* agitation, restlessness; (*fig*) longing, desire; **avere la ~ addosso** to have the fidgets; **smani'are** *vi* (*agitarsi*) to be restless *o* agitated; (*fig*): **smaniare di fare** to long *o* yearn to do.

smantel'**lare** *vt* to dismantle.

smarri'**mento** *sm* loss; (*fig*) bewilderment; dismay.

smar'**rire** *vt* to lose; (*non riuscire a trovare*) to mislay; **~rsi** *vr* (*perdersi*) to lose one's way, get lost; (: *oggetto*) to go astray; (*fig: turbarsi*) to be bewildered; (*essere sbigottito*) to be dismayed.

smasche'**rare** [zmaske'rare] *vt* to unmask.

smemo'**rato, a** *ag* forgetful.

smen'**tire** *vt* (*negare*) to deny; (*sbugiardare*) to give the lie to; (*sconfessare*) to retract, take back; **~rsi** *vr* to be inconsistent (in one's behaviour); **smen'tita** *sf* denial; retraction.

sme'**raldo** *sm* emerald.

smerci'**are** [zmer'tʃare] *vt* (COMM) to sell; (: *svendere*) to sell off.

sme'**riglio** [zme'riʎʎo] *sm* emery.

'**smesso, a** *pp di* **smettere**.

'**smettere** *vt* to stop; (*vestiti*) to stop wearing // *vi* to stop, cease; **~ di fare** to stop doing.

'**smilzo, a** ['zmiltso] *ag* thin, lean.

sminu'**ire** *vt* to diminish, lessen; (*fig*) to belittle.

sminuz'**zare** [zminut'tsare] *vt* to break into small pieces; to crumble.

smis'**tare** *vt* (*pacchi etc*) to sort; (FERR) to shunt.

smisu'**rato, a** *ag* boundless, immeasurable; (*grandissimo*) immense, enormous.

smobili'**tare** *vt* to demobilize, demob (*col*).

smo'**dato, a** *ag* immoderate.

smoking ['zmɔukiŋ] *sm inv* dinner jacket.

smon'**tare** *vt* (*mobile, macchina etc*) to take to pieces, dismantle; (*far scendere: da veicolo*) to let off, drop (off); (*fig: scoraggiare*) to dishearten // *vi* (2) (*scendere: da cavallo*) to dismount; (: *da treno*) to get off; (*terminare il lavoro*) to stop (work); **~rsi** *vr* to lose heart; to lose one's enthusiasm.

'**smorfia** *sf* grimace; (*atteggiamento lezioso*) simpering; **fare ~e** to make faces; to simper; **smorfi'oso, a** *ag* simpering.

'**smorto, a** *ag* (*viso*) pale, wan; (*colore*) dull.

smor'**zare** [zmor'tsare] *vt* (*suoni*) to deaden; (*colori*) to tone down; (*luce*) to dim; (*sete*) to quench; (*entusiasmo*) to dampen; **~rsi** *vr* (*attutirsi*) to fade away.

'**smosso, a** *pp di* **smuovere**.

smotta'mento *sm* landslide.

'smunto, a *ag* haggard, pinched.

smu'overe *vt* to move, shift; (*fig: commuovere*) to move; (: *dall'inerzia*) to rouse, stir; ~**rsi** *vr* to move, shift.

smus'sare *vt* (*angolo*) to round off, smooth; (*lama etc*) to blunt; ~**rsi** *vr* to become blunt.

snatu'rato, a *ag* inhuman, heartless.

'snello, a *ag* (*agile*) agile; (*svelto*) slender, slim.

sner'vare *vt* to enervate, wear out; ~**rsi** *vr* to become enervated.

sni'dare *vt* to drive out, flush out.

snob'bare *vt* to snub.

sno'bismo *sm* snobbery.

snoccio'lare [znottʃo'lare] *vt* (*frutta*) to stone; (*fig: orazioni*) to rattle off; (: *verità*) to blab; (: *fam: soldi*) to shell out.

sno'dare *vt* to untie, undo; (*rendere agile, mobile*) to loosen; ~**rsi** *vr* to come loose; (*articolarsi*) to bend; (*strada, fiume*) to wind.

so *forma del vb* **sapere**.

so'ave *ag* sweet, gentle, soft.

sobbal'zare [sobbal'tsare] *vi* to jolt, jerk; (*trasalire*) to jump, start; **sob'balzo** *sm* jerk, jolt; jump, start.

sobbar'carsi *vr*: ~ **a** to take on, undertake.

sob'borgo, ghi *sm* suburb.

sobil'lare *vt* to stir up, incite.

'sobrio, a *ag* temperate; sober.

socchi'udere [sok'kjudere] *vt* (*porta*) to leave ajar; (*occhi*) to half-close; **soc-chi'uso, a** *pp di* **socchiudere**.

soc'correre *vt* to help, assist; **soc'corso, a** *pp di* **soccorrere** // *sm* help, aid, assistance; **soccorsi** *smpl* (*MIL*) reinforcements.

socialdemo'cratico, a, ci, che [sotʃaldemo'kratiko] *sm/f* Social Democrat.

soci'ale [so'tʃale] *ag* social; (*di associazione*) club *cpd*, association *cpd*.

socia'lismo [sotʃa'lizmo] *sm* socialism; **socia'lista, i, e** *ag, sm/f* socialist.

società [sotʃe'ta] *sf inv* society; (*sportiva*) club; (*COMM*) company; ~ **per azioni (S.p.A.)** limited company.

soci'evole [so'tʃevole] *ag* sociable.

'socio [so'tʃo] *sm* (*DIR, COMM*) partner; (*membro di associazione*) member.

'soda *sf* (*CHIM*) soda; (*acqua gassata*) soda (water).

soda'lizio [soda'littsjo] *sm* association, society.

soddis'fare *vt, vi*: ~ **a** to satisfy; (*impegno*) to fulfil; (*debito*) to pay off; (*richiesta*) to meet, comply with; (*offesa*) to make amends for; **soddis'fatto, a** *pp di* **soddisfare** // *ag* satisfied; **soddisfatto di** happy *o* satisfied with; pleased with; **sod-disfazi'one** *sf* satisfaction.

'sodo, a *ag* firm, hard; (*fig*) sound // *av* (*picchiare, lavorare*) hard; **dormire** ~ to sleep soundly.

sofà *sm inv* sofa.

soffe'renza [soffe'rentsa] *sf* suffering.

sof'ferto, a *pp di* **soffrire**.

soffi'are *vt* to blow; (*notizia, segreto*) to whisper // *vi* to blow; ~**rsi il naso** to blow one's nose; ~ **qc/qd a qd** (*fig*) to pinch *o* steal sth/sb from sb; ~ **via qc** to blow sth away.

'soffice ['soffitʃe] *ag* soft.

'soffio *sm* (*di vento*) breath; (*di fumo*) puff; (*MED*) murmur.

sof'fitta *sf* attic.

sof'fitto *sm* ceiling.

soffo'care *vi* (*anche:* ~**rsi**) to suffocate, choke // *vt* to suffocate, choke; (*fig*) to stifle, suppress; **soffocazi'one** *sf* suffocation.

sof'friggere [sof'friddʒere] *vt* to fry lightly.

sof'frire *vt* to suffer, endure; (*sopportare*) to bear, stand // *vi* to suffer; to be in pain; ~ (**di**) **qc** (*MED*) to suffer from sth.

sof'fritto, a *pp di* **soffriggere**.

sofisti'care *vt* (*vino, cibo*) to adulterate // *vi* to split hairs, quibble; **sofisti'cato, a** *ag* sophisticated.

sogget'tivo, a [soddʒet'tivo] *ag* subjective.

sog'getto, a [sod'dʒetto] *ag*: ~ **a** (*sottomesso*) subject to; (*esposto: a variazioni, danni etc*) subject *o* liable to // *sm* subject.

soggezi'one [soddʒet'tsjone] *sf* subjection; (*timidezza*) awe; **avere** ~ **di qd** to stand in awe of sb; to be ill at ease in sb's presence.

sogghi'gnare [soggin'pare] *vi* to sneer.

soggior'nare [soddʒor'nare] *vi* to stay; **soggi'orno** *sm* (*invernale, marino*) stay; (*stanza*) living room.

'soglia ['soʎʎa] *sf* doorstep; (*anche fig*) threshold.

'sogliola ['soʎʎola] *sf* (*ZOOL*) sole.

so'gnare [soŋ'pare] *vt, vi* to dream; ~ **a occhi aperti** to daydream; **sogna'tore, 'trice** *sm/f* dreamer.

'sogno ['soŋpo] *sm* dream.

'soia *sf* (*BOT*) soya.

sol *sm* (*MUS*) G; (: *solfeggiando la scala*) so(h).

so'laio *sm* (*soffitta*) attic.

sola'mente *av* only, just.

so'lare *ag* solar, sun *cpd*.

'solco, chi *sm* (*scavo, fig: ruga*) furrow; (*incavo*) rut, track; (*di disco*) groove; (*scia*) wake.

sol'dato *sm* soldier; ~ **semplice** private.

'soldo *sm* (*fig*): **non avere un** ~ to be penniless; **non vale un** ~ it's not worth a penny; ~**i** *smpl* (*denaro*) money *sg*.

'sole *sm* sun; (*luce*) sun(light); (*tempo assolato*) sun(shine); **prendere il** ~ to sunbathe.

so'lenne *ag* solemn; **solennità** *sf* solemnity; grand occasion.

sol'fato *sm* (*CHIM*) sulphate.

sol'furo *sm* (*CHIM*) sulphur.

soli'dale ag (DIR) joint and several.

solidarietà sf solidarity.

solidifi'care vt, vi (2) (anche: ~rsi) to solidify.

solidità sf solidity.

'solido, a ag solid; (forte, robusto) sturdy, solid; (fig: ditta) sound, solid // sm (MAT) solid.

soli'loquio sm soliloquy.

so'lista, i, e ag solo // sm/f soloist.

solita'mente av usually, as a rule.

soli'tario, a ag (senza compagnia) solitary, lonely; (solo, isolato) solitary, lone; (deserto) lonely // sm (gioiello, gioco) solitaire.

'solito, a ag usual; **essere ~ fare** to be in the habit of doing; **di ~** usually; **più tardi del ~** later than usual; **come al ~** as usual.

soli'tudine sf solitude.

solleci'tare [solletʃi'tare] vt (lavoro) to speed up; (persona) to urge on; (chiedere con insistenza) to press for, request urgently; (stimolare): **~ qd a fare** to urge sb to do; (TECN) to stress; **sollecitazi'one** sf entreaty, request; (fig) incentive; (TECN) stress.

sol'lecito, a [sol'letʃito] ag prompt, quick // sm (lettera) reminder; **solleci'tudine** sf promptness, speed.

solleti'care vt to tickle.

solle'vare vt to lift, raise; (fig: persona: alleggerire): **~ (da)** to relieve (of); (: dar conforto) to comfort, relieve; (: questione) to raise; (: far insorgere) to stir (to revolt); **~rsi** vr to rise; (fig: riprendersi) to recover; (: ribellarsi) to rise up.

solli'evo sm relief; (conforto) comfort.

'solo, a ag alone; (in senso spirituale: isolato) lonely; (unico): **un ~ libro** only one book, a single book; (con ag numerale): **veniamo noi tre ~i** just o only the three of us are coming // av (soltanto) only, just; **non ~ ... ma anche** not only ... but also; **fare qc da ~** to do sth (all) by oneself; **da me ~** single-handed, on my own.

sol'stizio [sol'stittsjo] sm solstice.

sol'tanto av only.

so'lubile ag (sostanza) soluble.

soluzi'one [solut'tsjone] sf solution.

sol'vente ag, sm solvent.

'soma sf load, burden; **bestia da ~** beast of burden.

so'maro sm ass, donkey.

somigli'anza [somiʎ'ʎantsa] sf resemblance.

somigli'are [somiʎ'ʎare] vi (2): **~ a** to be like, resemble; (nell'aspetto fisico) to look like; **~rsi** vr to be (o look) alike.

'somma sf (MAT) sum; (di denaro) sum (of money); (complesso di varie cose) whole amount, sum total.

som'mare vt to add up; (aggiungere) to add; **tutto sommato** all things considered.

som'mario, a ag (racconto, indagine) brief; (giustizia) summary // sm summary.

som'mergere [som'merdʒere] vt to submerge.

sommer'gibile [sommer'dʒibile] sm submarine.

som'merso, a pp di **sommergere**.

som'messo, a ag (voce) soft, subdued.

somminis'trare vt to give, administer.

sommità sf inv top; (di monte) summit, top; (fig) height.

'sommo, a ag highest, topmost; (fig) supreme; (the) greatest // sm (fig) height; **per ~i capi** briefly, covering the main points.

som'mossa sf uprising.

so'naglio [so'naʎʎo] sm bell.

so'nare etc = **suonare** etc.

son'daggio [son'daddʒo] sm sounding; probe; boring, drilling; (indagine) survey; **~ (d'opinioni)** opinion poll.

son'dare vt (NAUT) to sound; (atmosfera, piaga) to probe; (MINERALOGIA) to bore, drill; (fig) to sound out; to probe.

so'netto sm sonnet.

son'nambulo, a sm/f sleepwalker.

sonnecchi'are [sonnek'kjare] vi to doze, nod.

son'nifero sm sleeping drug (o pill).

'sonno sm sleep; **prendere ~** to fall asleep; **aver ~** to be sleepy.

'sono forma del vb **essere**.

so'noro, a ag (ambiente) resonant; (voce) sonorous, ringing; (onde, film) sound cpd.

sontu'oso, a ag sumptuous; lavish.

sopo'rifero, a ag soporific.

soppe'sare vt to weigh in one's hand(s), feel the weight of; (fig) to weigh up.

soppi'atto: di ~ av secretly; furtively.

soppor'tare vt (reggere) to support; (subire: perdita, spese) to bear, sustain; (soffrire: dolore) to bear, endure; (: cosa: freddo) to withstand; (sog: persona: freddo, vino) to take; (tollerare) to put up with, tolerate.

soppressi'one sf suppression; deletion.

sop'presso, a pp di **sopprimere**.

sop'primere vt (carica, privilegi, testimone) to do away with; (pubblicazione) to suppress; (parola, frase) to delete.

'sopra prep (gen) on; (al di sopra di, più in alto di) above; over; (riguardo a) on, about // av on top; (attaccato, scritto) on it; (al di sopra) above; (al piano superiore) upstairs; **donne ~ i 30 anni** women over 30 (years of age); **dormirci ~** (fig) to sleep on it.

so'prabito sm overcoat.

soprac'ciglio [soprat'tʃiʎʎo], pl(f) **soprac'ciglia** sm eyebrow.

sopracco'perta sf (di letto) bedspread; (di libro) jacket.

soprad'detto, a ag aforesaid.

sopraf'fare vt to overcome, overwhelm; **sopraf'fatto, a** pp di **sopraffare**.

sopraf'fino, a ag excellent; (fig) consummate, supreme.

sopraggi'ungere [soprad'dʒundʒere] vi (2) (giungere all'improvviso) to arrive (unexpectedly); (accadere) to occur (unexpectedly).

soprannatu'rale ag supernatural.

sopran'nome sm nickname.

so'prano, a sm/f (persona) soprano // sm (voce) soprano.

soprappensi'ero av lost in thought.

sopras'salto sm: **di ~** with a start; suddenly.

soprasse'dere vi: **~ a** to delay, put off.

soprat'tutto av (anzitutto) above all; (specialmente) especially.

sopravve'nire vi (2) to arrive, appear; (fatto) to occur.

sopravvis'suto, a pp di **sopravvivere.**

soprav'vivere vi (2) to survive; (continuare a vivere): **~ (in)** to live on (in); **~ a** (incidente etc) to survive; (persona) to outlive.

soprinten'dente sm/f supervisor; (statale: di belle arti etc) keeper; **soprinten'denza** sf (ente): **soprintendenza alle Antichità e ai Monumenti** ≈ National Trust.

so'pruso sm abuse of power; **fare un ~ a qd** to treat sb unjustly.

soq'quadro sm: **mettere a ~** to turn upside-down.

sor'betto sm sorbet, water ice.

sor'bire vt to sip; (fig) to put up with.

'sordido, a ag sordid; (fig: gretto) stingy.

sor'dina sf: **in ~** softly; (fig) on the sly.

sordità sf deafness.

'sordo, a ag deaf; (rumore) muffled; (dolore) dull; (lotta) silent, hidden // sm/f deaf person; **sordo'muto, a** ag deaf-and-dumb // sm/f deaf-mute.

so'rella sf sister; **sorel'lastra** sf stepsister.

sor'gente [sor'dʒɛnte] sf (acqua che sgorga) spring; (di fiume, FISICA, fig) source.

'sorgere ['sɔrdʒere] vi (2) to rise; (scaturire) to spring, rise; (fig: difficoltà) to arise.

sormon'tare vt (fig) to overcome, surmount.

sorni'one, a ag sly.

sorpas'sare vt (AUT) to overtake; (fig) to surpass; (: eccedere) to exceed, go beyond; **~ in altezza** to be higher than; (persona) to be taller than.

sor'prendere vt (cogliere: in flagrante etc) to catch; (stupire, prendere a un tratto) to surprise; **~rsi** vr: **~rsi (di)** to be surprised (at); **sor'preso, a** pp di **sorprendere** // sf surprise.

sor'reggere [sor'rɛddʒere] vt to support, hold up; (fig) to sustain; **sor'retto, a** pp di **sorreggere.**

sor'ridere vi to smile; **sor'riso, a** pp di **sorridere** // sf smile.

'sorso sm sip.

'sorta sf sort, kind; **di ~** whatever, of any kind, at all.

'sorte sf (fato) fate, destiny; (evento fortuito) chance; **tirare a ~** to draw lots.

sor'teggio [sor'tedʒo] sm draw.

sorti'legio [sorti'lɛdʒo] sm witchcraft q; (incantesimo) spell; **fare un ~ a qd** to cast a spell on sb.

sor'tire vi (2) (uscire a sorte) to come out, be drawn.

sor'tita sf (MIL) sortie.

'sorto, a pp di **sorgere.**

sorveglï'anza [sorveʎ'ʎantsa] sf watch; supervision; (POLIZIA, MIL) surveillance.

sorveglï'are [sorveʎ'ʎare] vt (bambino, bagagli, prigioniero) to watch, keep an eye on; (malato) to watch over; (territorio, casa) to watch o keep watch over; (lavori) to supervise.

sorvo'lare vt (territorio) to fly over // vi: **~ su** (fig) to skim over.

'sosia sm inv double.

sos'pendere vt (appendere) to hang (up); (interrompere, privare di una carica) to suspend; (rimandare) to defer; **~ un quadro al muro/un lampadario al soffitto** to hang a picture on the wall/a chandelier from the ceiling; **sospensi'one** sf (anche CHIM, AUT) suspension; deferment; **sos'peso, a** pp di **sospendere** // ag (appeso): **sospeso a** hanging on (o from); (fig) anxious; **in sospeso** in abeyance; (conto) outstanding; **tenere in sospeso** (fig) to keep in suspense.

sospet'tare vt to suspect // vi: **~ di** to suspect; (diffidare) to be suspicious of.

sos'petto, a ag suspicious // sm suspicion; **sospet'toso, a** ag suspicious.

sos'pingere [sos'pindʒere] vt to drive, push; **sos'pinto, a** pp di **sospingere.**

sospi'rare vi to sigh // vt to long for, yearn for; **sos'piro** sm sigh.

'sosta sf (fermata) stop, halt; (pausa) pause, break; **senza ~** non-stop, without a break.

sostan'tivo sm noun, substantive.

sos'tanza [sos'tantsa] sf substance; **~e** sfpl (ricchezze) wealth sg, possessions; **in ~** in short, to sum up; **sostanzi'oso, a** ag (cibo) nourishing, substantial.

sos'tare vi (fermarsi) to stop (for a while), stay; (fare una pausa) to take a break.

sos'tegno [sos'teɲɲo] sm support.

soste'nere vt to support; (prendere su di sé) to take on, bear; (resistere) to withstand, stand up to; (affermare): **~ che** to maintain that; **~rsi** vr to hold o.s. up, support o.s.; (fig) to keep up one's strength; **~ gli esami** to sit exams; **soste'nitore, 'trice** sm/f supporter.

sostenta'mento sm maintenance.

soste'nuto, a ag (riservato) reserved, aloof; (stile) elevated; (prezzo) continuing high.

sostitu'ire vt (mettere al posto di): **~ qd/qc a** to substitute sb/sth for; (prendere il posto di: persona) to substitute for; (: cosa) to take the place of.

sosti'tuto, a sm/f substitute.

sostituzi'one [sostitut'tsjone] sf substitution; **in ~ di** as a substitute for, in place of.

sotta'ceti [sotta'tʃeti] smpl pickles.

sot'tana *sf* (*sottoveste*) underskirt; (*gonna*) skirt; (*REL*) soutane, cassock.

sotter'fugio [sotter'fudʒo] *sm* subterfuge.

sotter'raneo, a *ag* underground // *sm* cellar // *sf* (*FERR*) underground.

sotter'rare *vt* to bury.

sottigli'ezza [sottiʎ'ʎettsa] *sf* thinness; slimness; (*fig: acutezza*) subtlety; shrewdness; (~*e sfpl* (*pedanteria*) quibbles.

sot'tile *ag* thin; (*figura, caviglia*) thin, slim, slender; (*fine: polvere, capelli*) fine; (*fig: leggero*) light; (: *vista*) sharp, keen; (: *olfatto*) fine, discriminating; (: *mente*) subtle; shrewd.

sottin'tendere *vt* (*intendere qc non espresso*) to understand; (*implicare*) to imply; **sottin'teso, a** *pp di* **sottintendere** // *sm* allusion; **parlare senza sottintesi** to speak plainly.

'sotto *prep* (*gen*) under; (*più in basso di*) below // *av* underneath, beneath; below; (*al piano inferiore*) downstairs; ~ **il monte** at the foot of the mountain; ~ **la pioggia/il sole** in the rain/sun(shine); ~ **terra** underground; ~ **voce** in a low voice; **chiuso** ~ **vuoto** vacuum packed.

sottoline'are *vt* to underline; (*fig*) to emphasize, stress.

sottoma'rino, a *ag* (*flora*) submarine; (*cavo, navigazione*) underwater // *sm* (*NAUT*) submarine.

sotto'messo, a *pp di* **sottomettere**.

sotto'mettere *vt* to subdue, subjugate; ~**rsi** *vr* to submit.

sottopas'saggio [sottopas'saddʒo] *sm* (*AUT*) underpass; (*pedonale*) subway, underpass.

sotto'porre *vt* (*costringere*) to subject; (*fig: presentare*) to submit; **sottoporsi** *vr* to submit; **sottoporsi a** (*subire*) to undergo; **sotto'posto, a** *pp di* **sottoporre**.

sottos'critto, a *pp di* **sottoscrivere**.

sottos'crivere *vt* to sign // *vi:* ~ **a** to subscribe to; **sottoscrizi'one** *sf* signing; subscription.

sottosegre'tario *sm:* ~ **di Stato** Under-Secretary of State.

sotto'sopra *av* upside-down.

sotto'terra *av* underground.

sotto'titolo *sm* subtitle.

sotto'veste *sf* underskirt.

sotto'voce [sotto'votʃe] *av* in a low voice.

sot'trarre *vt* (*MAT*) to subtract, take away; ~ **qd/qc a** (*togliere*) to remove sb/sth from; (*salvare*) to save *o* rescue sb/sth from; ~ **qc a qd** (*rubare*) to steal sth from sb; **sottrarsi** *vr:* **sottrarsi a** (*sfuggire*) to escape; (*evitare*) to avoid; **sot'tratto, a** *pp di* **sottrarre**; **sottrazi'one** *sf* subtraction; removal.

sovi'etico, a, ci, che *ag* Soviet // *sm/f* Soviet citizen.

sovraccari'care *vt* to overload.

sovrac'carico, a, chi, che *ag:* ~ (**di**) overloaded (with) // *sm* excess load; ~ **di lavoro** extra work.

sovrannatu'rale *ag* = **sopran-naturale**.

so'vrano, a *ag* sovereign; (*fig: sommo*) supreme // *sm/f* sovereign, monarch.

sovras'tare *vi* (2): ~ **a**, *vt* (*vallata, fiume*) to overhang; (*fig*) to hang over, threaten.

sovrinten'dente *sm/f* = **so-printendente**; **sovrinten'denza** *sf* = **soprintendenza**.

sovru'mano, a *ag* superhuman.

sovvenzi'one [sovven'tsjone] *sf* subsidy, grant.

sovver'sivo, a *ag* subversive.

'sozzo, a ['sottso] *ag* filthy, dirty.

S.p.A. *abbr vedi* **società**.

spac'care *vt* to split, break; (*legna*) to chop; ~**rsi** *vr* to split, break; **spacca-'tura** *sf* split.

spacci'are [spat'tʃare] *vt* (*vendere*) to sell (off); (*mettere in circolazione*) to circulate; ~**rsi** *vr:* ~**rsi per** (*farsi credere*) to pass o.s. off as, pretend to be; **spaccia'tore, 'trice** *sm/f* (*di droga*) pusher; (*di denaro falso*) dealer; **'spaccio** *sm* sale; (*bottega*) shop.

'spacco, chi *sm* (*fenditura*) split, crack; (*strappo*) tear; (*di gonna*) slit.

spac'cone *sm/f* boaster, braggart.

'spada *sf* sword.

spae'sato, a *ag* disorientated, lost.

spa'ghetti [spa'getti] *smpl* (*CUC*) spaghetti *sg*.

'Spagna ['spaɲɲa] *sf:* **la** ~ Spain; **spa-'gnolo, a** *ag* Spanish // *sm/f* Spaniard // *sm* (*LING*) Spanish; **gli Spagnoli** the Spanish.

'spago, ghi *sm* string, twine.

spal'ato, a *ag* (*calza, guanto*) odd.

spalan'care *vt,* ~**rsi** *vr* to open wide.

spa'lare *vt* to shovel.

'spalla *sf* shoulder; (*fig: TEATRO*) stooge; ~**e** *sfpl* (*dorso*) back; **spalleggi'are** *vt* to back up, support.

spal'letta *sf* (*parapetto*) parapet.

spalli'era *sf* (*di sedia etc*) back; (*di letto: da capo*) head(board); (: *da piedi*) foot(board); (*GINNASTICA*) wall bars *pl*.

spal'mare *vt* to spread.

'spandere *vt* to spread; (*versare*) to pour (out); ~**rsi** *vr* to spread; ~ **lacrime** to shed tears; **'spanto, a** *pp di* **spandere**.

spa'rare *vt* to fire // *vi* (*far fuoco*) to fire; (*tirare*) to shoot; **spara'tore** *sm* gunman; **spara'toria** *sf* exchange of shots.

sparecchi'are [sparek'kjare] *vt:* ~ (**la tavola**) to clear the table.

spa'reggio [spa'reddʒo] *sm* (*SPORT*) play-off.

'spargere ['spardʒere] *vt* (*gettare all'intorno*) to scatter, strew; (*versare: vino*) to spill; (: *lacrime, sangue*) to shed; (*diffondere*) to spread; (*emanare*) to give off (*o* out); ~**rsi** *vr* to spread; **spargi-'mento** *sm* scattering, strewing; spilling; shedding; **spargimento di sangue** bloodshed.

spa'rire *vi* (2) to disappear, vanish.

spar'lare *vi:* ~ **di** to run down, speak ill of.

'**sparo** *sm* shot.

sparpagli'are [sparpaʎ'ʎare] *vt*, ~**rsi** *vr* to scatter.

'**sparso, a** *pp di* **spargere** // *ag* scattered; *(sciolto)* loose.

spar'tire *vt (eredità, bottino)* to share out; *(avversari)* to separate.

sparti'traffico *sm inv* (AUT) central reservation.

spa'ruto, a *ag (viso etc)* haggard.

sparvi'ero *sm* (ZOOL) sparrowhawk.

spasi'mare *vi* to be in agony; ~ **di fare** *(fig)* to yearn to do; ~ **per qd** to be madly in love with sb.

'**spasimo** *sm* pang; '**spasmo** (MED) spasm; **spas'modico, a, ci, che** *ag (angoscioso)* agonizing; (MED) spasmodic.

spassio'nato, a *ag* dispassionate, impartial.

'**spasso** *sm (divertimento)* amusement, enjoyment; **andare a** ~ to go out for a walk; **essere a** ~ *(fig)* to be out of work; **mandare qd a** ~ to send sb packing.

'**spatola** *sf* spatula.

spau'racchio [spau'rakkjo] *sm* scarecrow.

spau'rire *vt* to frighten, terrify.

spa'valdo, a *ag* arrogant, bold.

spaventa'passeri *sm inv* scarecrow.

spaven'tare *vt* to frighten, scare; ~**rsi** *vr* to be frightened, be scared; to get a fright; **spa'vento** *sm* fear, fright; **far spavento a qd** to give sb a fright; **spaven'toso, a** *ag* frightening, terrible; *(fig: fam)* tremendous, fantastic.

spazien'tire [spattsjen'tire] *vi* (2) *(anche:* ~**rsi)** to lose one's patience.

'**spazio** ['spattsjo] *sm* space; **spazi'oso, a** *ag* spacious.

spazzaca'mino [spattsaka'mino] *sm* chimney sweep.

spaz'zare [spat'tsare] *vt* to sweep; *(foglie etc)* to sweep up; *(cacciare)* to sweep away; **spazza'tura** *sf* sweepings *pl;* *(immondizia)* rubbish; **spaz'zino** *sm* street sweeper.

spazzola [spat'tsola] *sf* brush; ~ **per abiti** clothesbrush; ~ **da capelli** hairbrush; **spazzo'lare** *vt* to brush; **spazzo'lino** *sm* (small) brush; **spazzolino da denti** toothbrush.

specchi'arsi [spek'kjarsi] *vr* to look at o.s. in a mirror; *(riflettersi)* to be mirrored, be reflected; *(fig):* ~ **in qd** to model o.s. on sb.

'**specchio** ['spekkjo] *sm* mirror.

speci'ale [spe'tʃale] *ag* special; **specia'lista, i, e** *sm/f* specialist; **specialità** *sf inv* speciality; *(branca di studio)* special field, speciality; **specializ'zarsi** *vr:* **specializzarsi (in)** to specialize (in); **special'mente** *av* especially, particularly.

'**specie** ['spetʃe] *sf inv* (BIOL, BOT, ZOOL) species *inv;* *(tipo)* kind, sort // *av* especially, particularly; **fare** ~ **a qd** to surprise sb; **la** ~ **umana** mankind.

specifi'care [spetʃifi'kare] *vt* to specify, state.

spe'cifico, a, ci, che [spe'tʃifiko] *ag* specific.

specu'lare *vi* to speculate; ~ **su** (COMM) to speculate in; *(meditare)* to speculate on; *(sfruttare)* to exploit; **speculazi'one** *sf* speculation.

spe'dire *vt* to send; **spedizi'one** *sf* sending; *(collo)* parcel, consignment; *(scientifica etc)* expedition.

'**spegnere** ['speɲɲere] *vt (fuoco, sigaretta)* to put out, extinguish; *(apparecchio elettrico)* to turn o switch off; *(fig: suoni, passioni)* to stifle; *(debito)* to extinguish; ~**rsi** *vr* to go out; to go off; *(morire)* to pass away.

spel'lare *vt (scuoiare)* to skin; *(scorticare)* to graze; ~**rsi** *vr* to peel.

'**spendere** *vt* to spend.

spen'nare *vt* to pluck.

spensie'rato, a *ag* carefree.

'**spento, a** *pp di* **spegnere** // *ag (suono)* muffled; *(colore)* dull; *(civiltà, vulcano)* extinct.

spe'ranza [spe'rantsa] *sf* hope.

spe'rare *vt* to hope for // *vi:* ~ **in** to trust in; ~ **che/di fare** to hope that/to do; **lo spero, spero di sì** I hope so.

sper'duto, a *ag (isolato)* out-of-the-way; *(persona: smarrita, a disagio)* lost.

spergi'uro, a [sper'dʒuro] *sm/f* perjurer // *sm* perjury.

sperimen'tale *ag* experimental.

sperimen'tare *vt* to experiment with, test; *(fig)* to test, put to the test.

'**sperma, i** *sm* (BIOL) sperm.

spe'rone *sm* spur.

sperpe'rare *vt* to squander.

'**spesa** *sf (somma di denaro)* expense; *(costo)* cost; *(acquisto)* purchase; *(fam: acquisto del cibo quotidiano)* shopping; ~**e** *sfpl* expenses; (COMM) costs; charges; **fare la** ~ to do the shopping; **a** ~**e di** *(a carico di)* at the expense of; ~**e generali** overheads; ~**e postali** postage *sg;* ~**e di viaggio** travelling expenses.

'**speso, a** *pp di* **spendere**.

'**spesso, a** *ag (fitto)* thick; *(frequente)* frequent // *av* often; ~**e volte** frequently, often.

spes'sore *sm* thickness.

spet'tabile *ag (abbr:* **Spett.:** *in lettere):* ~ **ditta X** Messrs X and Co.

spet'tacolo *sm (rappresentazione)* performance, show; *(vista, scena)* sight; **dare** ~ **di sé** to make an exhibition o a spectacle of o.s.; **spettaco'loso, a** *ag* spectacular.

spet'tanza [spet'tantsa] *sf (competenza)* concern; **non è di mia** ~ it's no concern of mine.

spet'tare *vi* (2): ~ **a** *(decisione)* to be up to; *(stipendio)* to be due to; **spetta a te decidere** it's up to you to decide.

spetta'tore, 'trice *sm/f* (CINEMA, TEATRO) member of the audience; *(di avvenimento)* onlooker, witness.

spetti'nare *vt*: ~ qd to ruffle sb's hair; ~**rsi** *vr* to get one's hair in a mess.

'spettro *sm* (*fantasma*) spectre; (*FISICA*) spectrum.

'spezie ['spɛttsje] *sfpl* (*CUC*) spices.

spez'zare [spet'tsare] *vt* (*rompere*) to break; (*fig: interrompere*) to break up; ~**rsi** *vr* to break.

spezza'tino [spettsa'tino] *sm* (*CUC*) stew.

spezzet'tare [spettset'tare] *vt* to break up (*o chop*) into small pieces.

'spia *sf* spy; (*confidente della polizia*) informer; (*ELETTR*) indicating light; warning light; (*fessura*) spy hole, peephole; (*fig: sintomo*) sign, indication.

spia'cente [spja'tʃente] *ag* sorry; **essere ~ di qc/di fare qc** to be sorry about sth/for doing sth.

spia'cevole [spja'tʃevole] *ag* unpleasant, disagreeable.

spi'aggia, ge ['spjaddʒa] *sf* beach.

spia'nare *vt* (*terreno*) to level, make level; (*edificio*) to raze to the ground; (*pasta*) to roll out; (*rendere liscio*) to smooth (out).

spi'ano *sm*: **a tutto ~** (*lavorare*) non-stop, without a break; (*spendere*) lavishly.

spian'tato, a *ag* penniless, ruined.

spi'are *vt* to spy on; (*occasione etc*) to watch *o* wait for.

spi'azzo [spj'attso] *sm* open space; (*radura*) clearing.

spic'care *vt* (*staccare*) to detach, cut off; (*foglia, fiore*) to pick, pluck; (*parole*) to pronounce distinctly; (*assegno, mandato di cattura*) to issue // *vi* (*risaltare*) to stand out; ~ **il volo** to fly up; (*fig*) to take flight; ~ **un balzo** to take a leap; **spic'cato, a** *ag* (*marcato*) marked, strong; (*notevole*) remarkable.

'spicchio ['spikkjo] *sm* (*di agrumi*) segment; (*di aglio*) clove; (*parte*) piece, slice.

spicci'arsi [spit'tʃarsi] *vr* to hurry up.

'spicciolo, a ['spittʃolo] *ag*: **moneta ~a, ~i** *smpl* (small) change.

'spicco, chi *sm* prominence; **fare ~** to stand out.

spi'edo *sm* (*CUC*) spit.

spie'gare *vt* (*far capire*) to explain; (*tovaglia*) to unfold; (*vele*) to unfurl; ~**rsi** *vr* to explain o.s., make o.s. clear; **il problema si spiega** one can understand the problem; **avere una spiegazione con qd** to have it out with sb.

spiegaz'zare [spjegat'tsare] *vt* to crease, crumple.

spie'tato, a *ag* ruthless, pitiless.

spiffe'rare *vt* (*fam*) to blurt out, blab // *vi* to whistle.

'spiga, ghe *sf* (*BOT*) ear.

spigli'ato, a [spiʎ'ʎato] *ag* self-possessed, self-confident.

spigo'lare *vt* (*anche fig*) to glean.

'spigolo *sm* corner; (*MAT*) edge.

'spilla *sf* brooch; (*da cravatta, cappello*) pin.

spil'lare *vt* (*vino, fig*) to tap; ~ **denaro/notizie a qd** to tap sb for money/information.

'spillo *sm* pin; (*spilla*) brooch; ~ **di sicurezza** *o* **da balia** safety pin; ~ **di sicurezza** (*MIL*) (safety) pin.

spi'lorcio, a, ci, ce [spi'lortʃo] *ag* mean, stingy.

'spina *sf* (*BOT*) thorn; (*ZOOL*) spine, prickle; (*di pesce*) bone; (*ELETTR*) plug; (*di botte*) bunghole; **birra alla ~** draught beer; ~ **dorsale** (*ANAT*) backbone.

spi'nacio [spi'natʃo] *sm* spinach *q*.

spi'nale *ag* (*ANAT*) spinal.

'spingere ['spindʒere] *vt* to push; (*condurre: anche fig*) to drive; (*stimolare*): ~ **qd a fare** to urge *o* press sb to do; ~**rsi** *vr* (*inoltrarsi*) to push on, carry on; ~**rsi troppo lontano** (*anche fig*) to go too far; **fin dove spinge lo sguardo** as far as the eye can see.

spi'noso, a *ag* thorny, prickly.

'spinto, a *pp di* **spingere** // *sf* (*urto*) push; (*FISICA*) thrust; (*fig: stimolo*) incentive, spur; (*: appoggio*) string-pulling *q*; **dare una ~a a qd** (*fig*) to pull strings for sb.

spio'naggio [spio'naddʒo] *sm* espionage, spying.

spi'overe *vi* (2) (*scorrere*) to flow down; (*ricadere*) to hang down, fall.

'spira *sf* coil.

spi'raglio [spi'raʎʎo] *sm* (*fessura*) chink, narrow opening; (*raggio di luce, fig*) glimmer, gleam; **uno ~ d'aria** a breath of air.

spi'rale *sf* spiral; (*contraccettivo*) coil; **a ~** spiral(-shaped).

spi'rare *vi* (*vento*) to blow; (*2: morire*) to expire, pass away.

spiri'tato, a *ag* possessed; (*fig: persona, espressione*) wild.

spiri'tismo *sm* spiritualism.

'spirito *sm* (*REL, CHIM, disposizione d'animo, di legge etc, fantasma*) spirit; (*pensieri, intelletto*) mind; (*arguzia*) wit; (*umorismo*) humour, wit; **lo S~** **Santo** the Holy Spirit *o* Ghost.

spirito'saggine [spirito'saddʒine] *sf* witticism; (*peg*) wisecrack.

spiri'toso, a *ag* witty.

spiritu'ale *ag* spiritual.

'splendere *vi* to shine.

'splendido, a *ag* splendid; (*splendente*) shining; (*sfarzoso*) magnificent, splendid.

splen'dore *sm* splendour; (*luce intensa*) brilliance, brightness.

spodes'tare *vt* to deprive of power; (*sovrano*) to depose.

'spoglia ['spoʎʎa] *sf vedi* **spoglio**.

spogli'are [spoʎ'ʎare] *vt* (*svestire*) to undress; (*privare, fig: depredare*): ~ **qd di qc** to deprive sb of sth; (*togliere ornamenti: anche fig*): ~ **qd/qc di** to strip sb/sth of; (*fare lo spoglio di*) to go through, peruse; ~**rsi** *vr* to undress, strip; ~**rsi di** (*ricchezze etc*) to deprive o.s. of, give up; (*pregiudizi*) to rid o.s. of; **spoglia'toio** *sm* dressing room; (*di scuola etc*) cloakroom;

(SPORT) changing room; **'spoglio, a** ag (pianta, terreno) bare; (privo): ~ **di** stripped of; lacking in, without // sm going through, perusal // sf (ZOOL) skin, hide; (: di rettile) slough; **spoglie** sfpl (preda) spoils, booty sg.

'spola sf shuttle; (bobina di filo) cop; **fare la ~ (fra)** to go to and fro o shuttle (between).

spol'pare vt to strip the flesh off.

spolve'rare vt (anche CUC) to dust; (con spazzola) to brush; (con battipanni) to beat; (fig) to polish off // vi to dust.

'sponda sf (di fiume) bank; (di mare, lago) shore; (bordo) edge.

spon'taneo, a ag spontaneous; (persona) unaffected, natural.

spopo'lare vt to depopulate // vi (attirare folla) to draw the crowds; ~**rsi** vr to become depopulated.

spo'radico, a, ci, che ag sporadic.

spor'care vt to dirty, make dirty; (fig) to sully, soil; ~**rsi** vr to get dirty.

spor'cizia [spor'tʃittsja] sf (stato) dirtiness; (sudiciume) dirt, filth; (cosa sporca) dirt q, something dirty; (fig: cosa oscena) obscenity.

'sporco, a, chi, che ag dirty, filthy.

spor'genza [spor'dʒentsa] sf projection.

'sporgere ['spordʒere] vt to put out, stretch out // vi (2) (venire in fuori) to stick out; (protendersi) to jut out; ~**rsi** vr to lean out; **querela contro qd** (DIR) to take legal action against sb.

sport sm inv sport.

'sporta sf shopping bag.

spor'tello sm (di treno, auto etc) door; (di banca, ufficio) window, counter.

spor'tivo, a ag (gara, giornale) sports cpd; (persona) sporty; (abito) casual; (spirito, atteggiamento) sporting.

'sporto, a pp di **sporgere**.

'sposa sf bride; (moglie) wife.

sposa'lizio [spoza'littsjo] sm wedding.

spo'sare vt to marry; (fig: idea, fede) to espouse; ~**rsi** vr to get married, marry; ~**rsi con qd** to marry sb, get married to sb.

'sposo sm (bride)groom; (marito) husband; **gli ~i** smpl the newlyweds.

spos'sato, a ag exhausted, weary.

spos'tare vt to move, shift; (cambiare: orario) to change; ~**rsi** vr to move.

'spranga, ghe sf (sbarra) bar; (catenaccio) bolt.

'sprazzo ['sprattso] sm (di sole etc) flash; (fig: di gioia etc) burst.

spre'care vt to waste; ~**rsi** vr (persona) to waste one's energy; **'spreco** sm waste.

spre'gevole [spre'dʒevole] ag contemptible, despicable.

spregiudi'cato, a [spredʒudi'kato] ag unprejudiced, unbiased; (peg) unscrupulous.

'spremere vt to squeeze.

spre'muta sf fresh juice; ~ **d'arancia** fresh orange juice.

sprez'zante [spret'tsante] ag scornful, contemptuous.

sprigio'nare [spridʒo'nare] vt to give off, emit; ~**rsi** vr to emanate; (uscire con impeto) to burst out.

spriz'zare [sprit'tsare] vt, vi (2) to spurt; ~ **gioia/salute** to be bursting with joy/health.

sprofon'dare vi (2) to sink; (casa) to collapse; (suolo) to give way, subside; ~**rsi** vr: ~**rsi in** (poltrona) to sink into; (fig) to become immersed o absorbed in.

spro'nare vt to spur (on).

'sprone sm (sperone, fig) spur.

sproporzio'nato, a [sproportsjo'nato] ag disproportionate, out of all proportion.

sproporzi'one [s_propor'tsjone] sf disproportion.

sproposi'tato, a ag (lettera, discorso) full of mistakes; (fig: costo) excessive, enormous.

spro'posito sm blunder; **a ~** at the wrong time; (rispondere, parlare) irrelevantly.

sprovve'duto, a ag (privo): ~ **di** lacking in, without; (impreparato) unprepared.

sprov'visto, a ag (mancante): ~ **di** lacking in, without; **alla ~a** unawares.

spruz'zare [sprut'tsare] vt (a nebulizzazione) to spray; (aspergere) to sprinkle; (inzaccherare) to splash; **'spruzzo** sm spray; splash.

'spugna ['spuɲɲa] sf (ZOOL) sponge; (tessuto) towelling; **spu'gnoso, a** ag spongy.

'spuma sf (schiuma) foam; (bibita) mineral water.

spu'mante sm sparkling wine.

spu'mare vi to foam.

spumeggi'ante [spumed'dʒante] ag (vino, fig) sparkling.

spu'mone sm (CUC) mousse.

spun'tare vt (coltello) to break the point of; (capelli) to trim // vi (2) (uscire: germogli) to sprout; (: capelli) to begin to grow; (: denti) to come through; (apparire) to appear (suddenly); ~**rsi** vr to become blunt, lose its point; **spuntarla** (fig) to make it, win through.

spun'tino sm snack.

'spunto sm (TEATRO, MUS) cue; (fig) starting point; (di vino) sour taste; **dare lo ~ a** (fig) to give rise to.

spur'gare vt (fogna) to clean, clear; ~**rsi** vr (MED) to expectorate.

spu'tare vt to spit out; (fig) to belch (out) // vi to spit; **'sputo** sm spittle q, spit q.

'squadra sf (strumento) (set) square; (gruppo) team, squad; (di operai) gang, squad; (MIL) squad; (: AER, NAUT) squadron; (SPORT) team; **a o in ~** straight; ~ **doppia** o **a T** T-square.

squa'drare vt to square, make square; (osservare) to look at closely.

squa'driglia [skwa'driʎʎa] sf (AER) flight; (NAUT) squadron.

squa'drone sm squadron.

squagli'arsi [skwaʎ'ʎarsi] vr to melt; (fig) to sneak off.

squa'lifica sf disqualification.
squalifi'care vt to disqualify.
'squallido, a ag wretched, bleak.
squal'lore sm wretchedness, bleakness.
'squalo sm shark.
'squama sf scale; **squa'mare** vt to scale; **squamarsi** vr to flake o peel (off).
squarcia'gola [skwartʃa'gola]: **a ~** av at the top of one's voice.
squar'tare vt to quarter, cut up.
squattri'nato, a ag penniless.
squili'brare vt to unbalance; **squili-'brato, a** ag (PSIC) unbalanced; **squi'li-brio** sm (differenza, sbilancio) imbalance; (PSIC) unbalance.
squil'lante ag shrill, sharp.
squil'lare vi (campanello, telefono) to ring (out); (tromba) to blare; **'squillo** sm ring, ringing q; blare; **ragazza f squillo** inv call girl.
squi'sito, a ag exquisite; (cibo) delicious.
squit'tire vi (uccello) to squawk; (topo) to squeak.
sradi'care vt to uproot; (fig) to eradicate.
sragio'nare [zradʒo'nare] vi to talk nonsense, rave.
srego'lato, a ag (senza ordine: vita) disorderly; (smodato) immoderate; (dissoluto) dissolute.
'stabile ag stable, steady; (tempo: non variabile) settled; (TEATRO: compagnia) resident // sm (edificio) building.
stabili'mento sm establishing q; (edificio) establishment; (fabbrica) plant, factory; **~ carcerario** prison.
stabi'lire vt to establish; (fissare: prezzi, data) to fix; (decidere) to decide; **~rsi** vr (prendere dimora) to settle.
stabilità sf stability.
stabiliz'zare [stabilid'dzare] vt to stabilize; **stabilizza'tore** sm stabilizer.
stac'care vt (levare) to detach, remove; (separare: anche fig) to separate, divide; (strappare) to tear off (o out); (scandire: parole) to pronounce clearly; (SPORT) to leave behind; **~rsi** vr (bottone etc) to come off; (scostarsi): **~rsi (da)** to move away (from); (fig: separarsi): **~rsi da** to leave; **non ~ gli occhi da qd** not to take one's eyes off sb.
'stadio sm (SPORT) stadium; (periodo, fase) phase, stage.
'staffa sf (di sella) stirrup.
staf'fetta sf (messo) dispatch rider; (SPORT) relay race.
stagio'nale [stadʒo'nale] ag seasonal.
stagio'nare [stadʒo'nare] vt (legno) to season; (formaggi, vino) to mature.
stagi'one [sta'dʒone] sf season; **alta/bassa ~** high/low season.
stagli'arsi [staʎ'ʎarsi] vr to stand out, be silhouetted.
sta'gnante [staɲ'ɲante] ag stagnant.
sta'gnare [staɲ'ɲare] vt (vaso, tegame) to tin-plate; (barca, botte) to make watertight; (sangue) to stop // vi to stagnate.

'stagno, a ['staɲɲo] ag watertight; (a tenuta d'aria) airtight // sm (acquitrino) pond; (CHIM) tin.
sta'gnola [staɲ'ɲola] sf tinfoil.
stalag'mite sf stalagmite.
stalat'tite sf stalactite.
'stalla sf (per bovini) cowshed; (per cavalli) stable.
stal'lone sm stallion.
sta'mani, stamat'tina av this morning.
'stampa sf (TIP, FOT: tecnica) printing; (impressione, copia fotografica) print; (insieme di quotidiani, giornalisti etc) press; **~e** sfpl printed matter.
stam'pare vt to print; (pubblicare) to publish; (coniare) to strike, coin; (imprimere: anche fig) to impress.
stampa'tello sm block letters pl.
stam'pella sf crutch.
'stampo sm mould; (fig: indole) type, kind, sort.
sta'nare vt to drive out.
stan'care vt to tire, make tired; (annoiare) to bore; (infastidire) to annoy; **~rsi** vr to get tired, tire o.s. out; **~rsi (di)** to grow weary (of), grow tired (of).
stan'chezza [stan'kettsa] sf tiredness, fatigue.
'stanco, a, chi, che ag tired; **~ di** tired of, fed up with.
standardiz'zare [standardid'dzare] vt to standardize.
'stanga, ghe sm bar; (di carro) shaft.
stan'gata sf (colpo: anche fig) blow; (INS) poor result; (CALCIO) shot.
sta'notte av tonight; (notte passata) last night.
'stante prep owing to, because of; **a sé ~** (appartamento, casa) independent, separate.
stan'tio, a, 'tii, 'tie ag stale; (burro) rancid; (fig) old.
stan'tuffo sm piston.
'stanza ['stantsa] sf room; (POESIA) stanza; **~ da letto** bedroom.
stanzi'are [stan'tsjare] vt to allocate.
stap'pare vt to uncork; to uncap.
'stare vi (2) (restare in un luogo) to stay, remain; (abitare) to stay, live; (essere situato) to be, be situated; (anche: **~ in piedi**) to be, stand; (essere, trovarsi) to be; (dipendere): **se stesse in me** if it were up to me, if it depended on me; (seguito da gerundio): **sta studiando** he's studying; **starci** (esserci spazio): **nel baule non ci sta più niente** there's no more room in the boot; (accettare) to accept; **ci stai?** is that okay with you?; **~ a** (attenersi a) to follow, stick to; (seguito dall'infinito): **stiamo a discutere** we're talking; (toccare a): **sta a te giocare** it's your turn to play; **~ per fare qc** to be about to do sth; **come sta?** how are you?; **io sto bene/male** I'm very well/not very well; **~ a qd** (abiti etc) to fit sb; **queste scarpe mi stanno strette** these shoes are tight for me; **il rosso ti sta bene** red suits you.

starnu'tire *vi* to sneeze; **star'nuto** *sm* sneeze.

sta'sera *av* this evening, tonight.

sta'tale *ag* state *cpd*; government *cpd* // *sm/f* state employee, local authority employee; (*nell'amministrazione*) ≈ civil servant.

sta'tista, i *sm* statesman.

sta'tistico, a, ci, che *ag* statistical // statistics *sg*.

'stato, a *pp di* essere, stare // *sm* (*condizione*) state, condition; (*POL*) state; (*DIR*) status; **essere in ~ d'accusa** (*DIR*) to be committed for trial; **~ d'assedio/d'emergenza** state of siege/emergency; **~ maggiore** (*MIL*) staff; **gli S~i Uniti (d'America)** the United States (of America).

'statua *sf* statue.

statuni'tense *ag* United States *cpd*, of the United States.

sta'tura *sf* (*ANAT*) height, stature; (*fig*) stature.

sta'tuto *sm* (*DIR*) statute; constitution.

sta'volta *av* this time.

stazio'nario, a [stattsjo'narjo] *ag* stationary; (*fig*) unchanged.

stazi'one [stat'tsjone] *sf* station; (*balneare, termale*) resort; **~ degli autobus** bus station; **~ balneare** seaside resort; **~ invernale** winter sports resort; **~ di polizia** police station (*in small town*); **~ di servizio** service *o* petrol *o* filling station; **~ trasmittente** (*RADIO, TV*) transmitting station.

'stecca, che *sf* stick; (*di ombrello*) rib; (*di sigarette*) carton; (*MED*) splint; (*stonatura*): **fare una ~** to sing (*o* play) a wrong note.

stec'cato *sm* fence.

stec'chito, a [stek'kito] *ag* dried up; (*persona*) skinny; **lasciar ~ qd** (*fig*) to leave sb flabbergasted.

'stella *sf* star; **~ alpina** (*BOT*) edelweiss; **~ di mare** (*ZOOL*) starfish.

'stelo *sm* stem; (*asta*) rod; **lampada a ~** standard lamp.

'stemma, i *sm* coat of arms.

stempe'rare *vt* to dilute; to dissolve; melt; (*colori*) to mix.

sten'dardo *sm* standard.

'stendere *vt* (*braccia, gambe*) to stretch (out); (*tovaglia*) to spread (out); (*bucato*) to hang out; (*mettere a giacere*) to lay (down); (*spalmare: colore*) to spread; (*mettere per iscritto*) to draw up; **~rsi** *vr* (*coricarsi*) to stretch out, lie down; (*estendersi*) to extend, stretch.

stenodatti'lografo, a *sm/f* shorthand typist.

stenogra'fare *vt* to take down in shorthand; **stenogra'fia** *sf* shorthand.

sten'tare *vi*: **~ a fare** to find it hard to do, have difficulty doing.

'stento *sm* (*fatica*) difficulty; **~i** *smpl* (*privazioni*) hardship *sg*, privation *sg*; **a ~** *av* with difficulty, barely.

'sterco *sm* dung.

'stereo('fonico, a, ci, che) *ag* stereo(phonic).

stereoti'pato, a *ag* stereotyped.

'sterile *ag* sterile; (*terra*) barren; (*fig*) futile, fruitless; **sterilità** *sf* sterility.

steriliz'zare [sterilid'dzare] *vt* to sterilize; **sterilizzazi'one** *sf* sterilization.

ster'lina *sf* pound (sterling).

stermi'nare *vt* to exterminate, wipe out.

stermi'nato, a *ag* immense; endless.

ster'minio *sm* extermination, destruction.

'sterno *sm* (*ANAT*) breastbone.

ster'zare *vt, vi* (*AUT*) to steer; **'sterzo** *sm* steering; (*volante*) steering wheel.

'steso, a *pp di* stendere.

'stesso, a *ag* same; (*rafforzativo: in persona, proprio*): **il re ~** the king himself *o* in person // *pronome*: **lo(la) ~(a)** the same (one); **i suoi ~i avversari lo ammirano** even his enemies admire him; **fa lo ~ it** doesn't matter; **per me è lo ~** it's all the same to me, it doesn't matter to me; *vedi* **io, tu** etc.

ste'sura *sf* drafting *q*, drawing up *q*; draft.

stetos'copio *sm* stethoscope.

'stigma, i *sm* stigma.

'stigmate *sfpl* (*REL*) stigmata.

sti'lare *vt* to draw up, draft.

'stile *sm* style; **sti'lista, i** *sm* stylist; designer; **stiliz'zato, a** *ag* stylized.

stil'lare *vi* (2) (*trasudare*) to ooze; (*gocciolare*) to drip; **~rsi il cervello** (*fig*) to rack one's brains; **stilli'cidio** *sm* drip, dripping.

stilo'grafica, che *sf* (*anche*: **penna ~**) fountain pen.

'stima *sf* esteem; valuation; assessment, estimate.

sti'mare *vt* (*persona*) to esteem, hold in high regard; (*terreno, casa etc*) to value; (*stabilire in misura approssimativa*) to estimate, assess; (*ritenere*): **~ che** to consider that; **~rsi fortunato** to consider o.s. (to be) lucky.

stimo'lante *ag* stimulating // *sm* (*MED*) stimulant.

stimo'lare *vt* to stimulate; (*incitare*): **~ qd (a fare)** to spur sb on (to do).

'stimolo *sm* (*sollecitazione*) stimulus, spur; (*FISIOL, PSIC*) stimulus; **lo ~ della fame/del rimorso** the pangs of hunger/remorse.

'stinco, chi *sm* shin; shinbone.

'stingere ['stindʒere] *vt, vi* (2) (*anche*: **~rsi**) to fade; **'stinto, a** *pp di* stingere.

sti'pare *vt* to cram, pack; **~rsi** *vr* (*accalcarsi*) to crowd, throng.

sti'pendio *sm* salary.

'stipite *sm* (*di porta, finestra*) jamb.

stipu'lare *vt* (*redigere*) to draw up.

sti'rare *vt* (*abito*) to iron; (*distendere*) to stretch; **~rsi** *vr* (*fam*) to stretch (o.s.); **stira'tura** *sf* ironing.

'stirpe *sf* birth, stock; descendants *pl*.

stiti'chezza [stiti'kettsa] *sf* constipation.

'stitico, a, ci, che *ag* constipated.

'stiva *sf* (*di nave*) hold.

sti'vale *sm* boot.

'stizza ['stittsa] *sf* anger, vexation; **stiz-'zirsi** *vr* to lose one's temper; **stiz'zoso, a** *ag* (*persona*) quick-tempered, irascible; (*risposta*) angry.

stocca'fisso *sm* stockfish, dried cod.

stoc'cata *sf* (*colpo*) stab, thrust; (*fig*) gibe, cutting remark.

'stoffa *sf* material, fabric; (*fig*): **aver la ~ di** to have the makings of.

'stoico, a, ci, che *ag* stoic(al).

'stola *sf* stole.

'stolto, a *ag* stupid, foolish.

'stomaco, chi *sm* stomach; **dare di ~ to** vomit, be sick.

sto'nare *vt* to sing (*o* play) out of tune // *vi* to be out of tune, sing (*o* play) out of tune; (*fig*) to be out of place, jar; (: *colori*) to clash; **stona'tura** *sf* (*suono*) false note.

stop *sm inv* (*TEL*) stop; (*AUT: cartello*) stop sign; (: *fanalino d'arresto*) brake-light.

'stoppa *sf* tow.

'stoppia *sf* (*AGR*) stubble.

stop'pino *sm* wick; (*miccia*) fuse.

'storcere ['stɔrtʃere] *vt* to twist; **~rsi** *vr* to writhe, twist; **~ il naso** (*fig*) to turn up one's nose; **~rsi la caviglia** to twist one's ankle.

stor'dire *vt* (*intontire*) to stun, daze; **~rsi** *vr.* **~rsi col bere** to drown one's sorrows; **stor'dito, a** *ag* stunned; (*sbadato*) scatterbrained, heedless.

'storia *sf* (*scienza, avvenimenti*) history; (*racconto, bugia*) story; (*faccenda, questione*) business *q*; (*pretesto*) excuse, pretext; **~e** *sfpl* (*smancerie*) fuss *sg*; **'storico, a, ci, che** *ag* historic(al) // *sm* historian.

stori'one *sm* (*ZOOL*) sturgeon.

stor'mire *vi* to rustle.

'stormo *sm* (*di uccelli*) flock.

stor'nare *vt* (*COMM*) to transfer.

'storno *sm* starling.

storpi'are *vt* to cripple, maim; (*fig: parole*) to mangle.

'storpio, a *ag* crippled, maimed.

'storto, a *pp di* **storcere** // *ag* (*chiodo*) twisted, bent; (*gamba, quadro*) crooked; (*fig: ragionamento*) false, wrong // *sf* (*distorsione*) sprain, twist; (*recipiente*) retort.

sto'viglie [sto'viʎʎe] *sfpl* dishes *pl*, crockery.

'strabico, a, ci, che *ag* squint-eyed; (*occhi*) squint.

stra'bismo *sm* squinting.

stra'carico, a, chi, che *ag* overloaded.

stracci'are [strat'tʃare] *vt* to tear.

'straccio, a, ci, ce ['strattʃo] *ag* torn // *sm* rag; (*per pulire*) cloth, duster; **carta ~a** waste paper; **stracci'vendolo** *sm* ragman.

stra'cotto, a *ag* overcooked // *sm* (*CUC*) beef stew.

'strada *sf* road; (*di città*) street; (*cammino, via, fig*) way; **farsi ~** (*fig*) to do well for

o.s.; **essere fuori ~** (*fig*) to be on the wrong track; **~ facendo** on the way; **~ senza uscita** dead end; **stra'dale** *ag* road *cpd.*

strafalci'one [strafal'tʃone] *sm* blunder, howler.

stra'fare *vi* to overdo it; **stra'fatto, a** *pp di* **strafare.**

strafot'tente *ag*: **è ~** he doesn't give a damn, he couldn't care less.

'strage ['stradʒe] *sf* massacre, slaughter.

stralu'nare *vt*: **~ gli occhi** to roll one's eyes; **stralu'nato, a** *ag* (*occhi*) rolling; (*persona*) beside o.s., very upset.

stramaz'zare [stramat'tsare] *vi* (2) to fall heavily.

'strambo, a *ag* strange, queer.

strampa'lato, a *ag* odd, eccentric.

stra'nezza [stra'nettsa] *sf* strangeness.

strango'lare *vt* to strangle; **~rsi** *vr* to choke.

strani'ero, a *ag* foreign // *sm/f* foreigner.

'strano, a *ag* strange, odd.

straordi'nario, a *ag* extraordinary; (*treno etc*) special // *sm* (*lavoro*) overtime.

strapaz'zare [strapat'tsare] *vt* to ill-treat; **~rsi** *vr* to tire o.s. out, overdo things; **stra'pazzo** *sm* strain, fatigue; **da strapazzo** (*fig*) third-rate.

strapi'ombo *sm* overhanging rock; **a ~** overhanging.

strapo'tere *sm* excessive power.

strap'pare *vt* to pull out; (*pagina etc*) to tear off, tear out; (*fazzoletto, lenzuolo, foglio*) to tear, rip; (*sradicare*) to pull up; **~ qc a qd** to snatch sth from sb; (*fig*) to wrest sth from sb; **~rsi** *vr* (*lacerarsi*) to rip, tear; (*rompersi*) to break; **'strappo** *sm* pull, tug; tear, rip; **fare uno strappo alla regola** to make an exception to the rule; **strappo muscolare** torn muscle.

strapun'tino *sm* jump *o* foldaway seat.

strari'pare *vi* to overflow.

strasci'care [straʃʃi'kare] *vt* to trail; (*piedi*) to drag; (*parole*) to drawl.

'strascico, chi ['straʃʃiko] *sm* (*di abito*) train; (*conseguenza*) after-effect.

strata'gemma, i [strata'dʒemma] *sm* stratagem.

strate'gia, 'gie [strate'dʒia] *sf* strategy; **stra'tegico, a, ci, che** *ag* strategic.

'strato *sm* layer; (*rivestimento*) coat, coating; (*GEO, fig*) stratum; (*METEOR*) stratus.

stratos'fera *sf* stratosphere.

strava'gante *ag* odd, eccentric; **strava-'ganza** *sf* eccentricity.

stra'vecchio, a [stra'vɛkkjo] *ag* very old.

stra'vizio [stra'vittsjo] *sm* excess.

stra'volgere [stra'vɔldʒere] *vt* (*volto*) to contort; (*fig: animo*) to trouble deeply; (: *verità*) to twist, distort; **stra'volto, a** *pp di* **stravolgere.**

strazi'are [strat'tsjare] *vt* to torture, torment; **'strazio** *sm* torture; (*fam: persona, libro*) bore.

'**strega, ghe** sf witch.
stre'**gare** vt to bewitch.
stre'**gone** sm (mago) wizard; (di tribù) witch doctor.
'**stregua** sf: **alla ~ di** by the same standard as.
stre'**mare** vt to exhaust.
'**stremo** sm very end; **essere allo ~** to be at the end of one's tether.
'**strenna** sf Christmas present.
'**strenuo, a** ag brave, courageous.
strepi'**toso, a** ag clamorous, deafening; (fig: successo) resounding.
'**stretta** sf vedi **stretto**.
stretta'**mente** av tightly; (rigorosamente) strictly.
stret'**tezza** [stret'tettsa] sf narrowness; **~e** sfpl poverty sg, straitened circumstances.
'**stretto, a** pp di **stringere** // ag (non largo) narrow; (: gonna, serrato: nodo) tight; (intimo: parente, amico) close; (rigoroso: osservanza) strict; (preciso: significato) precise, exact // sm (braccio di mare) strait // sf (di mano) grasp; (finanziaria) squeeze; (fig: dolore, turbamento) pang; **a denti ~i** with clenched teeth; **lo ~ necessario** the bare minimum; **essere alle ~e** to have one's back to the wall; stret'**toia** sf bottleneck; (fig) tricky situation.
stri'**ato, a** ag streaked.
stri'**dente** ag strident.
'**stridere** vi (porta) to squeak; (animale) to screech, shriek; (colori) to clash; '**strido, e** pl(f) **strida** sm screech, shriek; stri'**dore** sm screeching, shrieking; '**stridulo, a** ag shrill.
stril'**lare** vt, vi to scream, shriek; '**strillo** sm scream, shriek.
stril'**lone** sm newspaper seller.
strimin'**zito, a** [strimin'tsito] ag (misero) shabby; (molto magro) skinny.
strimpel'**lare** vt (MUS) to strum.
'**stringa, ghe** sf lace.
strin'**gato, a** ag (fig) concise.
'**stringere** ['strindʒere] vt (avvicinare due cose) to press (together), squeeze (together); (tenere stretto) to hold tight, clasp, clutch; (avvitare) to tighten; (abito) to take in; (sog: scarpe) to pinch, be tight for; (fig: concludere: patto) to make; (: accelerare: passo, tempo) to quicken // vi (incalzare) to be pressing; **~rsi** vr (accostarsi) to draw close (to); **~rsi (a)** to draw close (to), press o.s. (to); (restringersi) to squeeze up; **~ la mano a qd** to shake sb's hand; **~ le labbra/gli occhi** to tighten one's lips/screw up one's eyes.
'**striscia, sce** ['striʃʃa] sf (di carta, tessuto etc) strip; (riga) stripe; **~sce (pedonali)** zebra crossing sg.
strisci'**are** [striʃ'ʃare] vt (piedi) to drag; (muro, macchina) to graze // vi to crawl, creep; **~rsi** vr: **~rsi a** (sfregarsi) to rub against; (fig) to grovel before o in front of.
'**striscio** ['striʃʃo] sm graze; (MED) smear; **colpire di ~** to graze.

strito'**lare** vt to grind.
striz'**zare** [strit'tsare] vt (arancia) to squeeze; (panni) to wring (out); **~ l'occhio** to wink.
'**strofe** sf inv, '**strofa** sf strophe.
strofi'**naccio** [strofi'nattʃo] sm duster, cloth.
strofi'**nare** vt to rub.
stron'**care** vt to break off; (fig: ribellione) to suppress, put down; (: film, libro) to tear to pieces.
stropicci'**are** [stropit'tʃare] vt to rub.
stroz'**zare** [strot'tsare] vt (soffocare) to choke, strangle; **~rsi** vr to choke; strozza'**tura** sf (restringimento) narrowing; (di strada etc) bottleneck.
'**struggere** ['struddʒere] vt (sciogliere) to melt; (fig) to consume; **~rsi** vr to melt; (fig): **~rsi di** to be consumed with.
strumen'**tale** ag (MUS) instrumental.
strumentaliz'**zare** [strumentalid'dzare] vt to exploit, use to one's own ends.
stru'**mento** sm (arnese, fig) instrument, tool; (MUS) instrument; **~ a corda/fiato** stringed/wind instrument.
'**strutto** sm lard.
strut'**tura** sf structure; struttu'**rare** vt to structure.
'**struzzo** ['struttso] sm ostrich.
stuc'**care** vt (muro) to plaster; (vetro) to putty; (decorare con stucchi) to stucco.
stuc'**chevole** [stuk'kevole] ag nauseating; (fig) tedious, boring.
'**stucco, chi** sm plaster; (da vetri) putty; (ornamentale) stucco; **rimanere di ~** (fig) to be dumbfounded.
stu'**dente, 'essa** sm/f student; (scolaro) pupil, schoolboy/girl; studen'**tesco, a, schi, sche** ag student cpd; school cpd.
studi'**are** vt to study; **~rsi** vr (sforzarsi): **~rsi di fare** to try o endeavour to do.
'**studio** sm studying; (ricerca, saggio, stanza) study; (di professionista) office; (di artista, CINEMA, TV, RADIO) studio; **~i** smpl (INS) studies.
studi'**oso, a** ag studious, hardworking // sm/f scholar.
'**stufa** sf stove; **~ elettrica** electric fire o heater.
stu'**fare** vt (CUC) to stew; (fig: fam) to bore; stu'**fato** sm (CUC) stew; '**stufo, a** ag (fam): **essere stufo di** to be fed up with, be sick and tired of.
stu'**oia** sf mat.
stupefa'**cente** [stupefa'tʃente] ag stunning, astounding // sm drug, narcotic.
stu'**pendo, a** ag marvellous, wonderful.
stupi'**daggine** [stupi'daddʒine] sf stupid thing (to do o say).
stupidità sf stupidity.
'**stupido, a** ag stupid.
stu'**pire** vt to amaze, stun // vi (2) (anche: **~rsi**) to be amazed, be stunned.
stu'**pore** sm amazement, astonishment.
'**stupro** sm rape.
'**stura** sf: **dare la ~ a** (bottiglia) to uncork; (sentimenti) to give vent to.

stu'rare vt (lavandino) to clear.
stuzzica'denti [stuttsika'dɛnti] sm toothpick.
stuzzi'care [stuttsi'kare] vt (ferita etc) to poke (at), prod (at); (fig) to tease; ~ **i denti** to pick one's teeth.
su prep (su + il = **sul**, su + lo = **sullo**, su + l' = **sull'**, su + la = **sulla**, su + i = **sui**, su + gli = **sugli**, su + le = **sulle**) on; (moto a luogo) on, on to; (intorno a, riguardo a) about, on; (approssimazione: circa) about, around // av up; (sopra) (up) above // escl come on!; **in** ~ av up(wards); **prezzi dalle mille lire in** ~ prices from 1000 lire (upwards); **una ragazza sui 17 anni** a girl of about 17 (years of age); **in 3 casi** ~ **10** in 3 cases out of 10.
'sua vedi suo.
su'bacqueo, a ag underwater // sm skindiver.
sub'buglio [sub'buʎʎo] sm confusion, turmoil.
subcosci'ente [subkoʃ'ʃɛnte] ag, sm subconscious.
'subdolo, a ag underhand, sneaky.
suben'trare vi (2): ~ **a qd in qc** to take over sth from sb.
su'bire vt to suffer, endure.
subis'sare vt (fig): ~ **di** to overwhelm with, load with.
subi'taneo, a ag sudden.
'subito av immediately, at once, straight away.
su'blime ag sublime.
subodo'rare vt (insidia etc) to smell, suspect.
subordi'nato, a ag subordinate; (dipendente): ~ **a** dependent on, subject to // sm/f subordinate.
subur'bano, a ag suburban.
succe'daneo [suttʃe'daneo] sm substitute.
suc'cedere [sut'tʃɛdere] vi (2) (prendere il posto di qd): ~ **a** to succeed; (venire dopo): ~ **a** to follow; (accadere) to happen; ~**rsi** vr to follow each other; ~ **al trono** to succeed to the throne; **successi'one** sf succession; **succes'sivo, a** ag successive; **suc'cesso, a** pp di succedere // sm (esito) outcome; (buona riuscita) success; **succes'sore** sm successor.
succhi'are [suk'kjare] vt to suck (up).
suc'cinto, a [sut'tʃinto] ag (discorso) succinct; (abito) brief.
'succo, chi sm juice; (fig) essence, gist; **suc'coso, a** ag juicy; (fig) pithy; **succu'lento, a** ag succulent.
succur'sale sf branch (office).
sud sm south // ag inv south; (lato) south, southern.
su'dare vi to perspire, sweat; ~ **freddo** to come out in a cold sweat; **su'data** sf sweat; **ho fatto una bella sudata per finirlo in tempo** it was a real sweat to get it finished in time.
sud'detto, a ag above-mentioned.
sud'dito, a sm/f subject.
suddi'videre vt to subdivide; **suddivisi'one** sf subdivision.

su'dest sm south-east.
'sudicio, a, ci, ce ['sudit ʃo] ag dirty, filthy; **sudici'ume** sm dirt, filth.
su'dore sm perspiration, sweat.
su'dovest sm south-west.
'sue vedi suo.
suffici'ente [suffi'tʃɛnte] ag enough, sufficient; (borioso) self-important; (INS) satisfactory; **suffici'enza** sf self-importance; pass mark; **aver sufficienza di qc** to have enough of sth; **a sufficienza** av enough.
suf'fisso sm (LING) suffix.
suf'fragio [suf'fradʒo] sm (voto) vote; ~ **universale** universal suffrage.
suggel'lare [suddʒel'lare] vt (fig) to seal.
suggeri'mento [suddʒeri'mento] sm suggestion; (consiglio) piece of advice, advice q.
sugge'rire [suddʒe'rire] vt (risposta) to tell; (consigliare) to advise; (proporre) to suggest; (TEATRO) to prompt; **suggeri'tore, 'trice** sm/f (TEATRO) prompter.
suggestio'nare [suddʒestjo'nare] vt to influence.
suggesti'one [suddʒes'tjone] sf (PSIC) suggestion; (istigazione) instigation.
sugges'tivo, a [suddʒes'tivo] ag (paesaggio) evocative; (teoria) interesting, attractive.
'sughero ['sugero] sm cork.
'sugli ['suʎʎi] prep + det vedi su.
'sugna ['suɲɲa] sf suet.
'sugo, ghi sm (succo) juice; (di carne) gravy; (condimento) sauce; (fig) gist, essence.
'sui prep + det vedi su.
sui'cida, i, e [sui'tʃida] ag suicidal // sm/f suicide.
suici'darsi [suitʃi'darsi] vr to commit suicide.
sui'cidio [sui'tʃidjo] sm suicide.
su'ino, a ag: **carne ~a** pork // sm pig; **~i** smpl swine pl.
sul, sull', 'sulla, 'sulle, 'sullo prep + det vedi su.
sulta'nina ag f: (uva) ~ sultana.
sul'tano, a sm/f sultan/sultana.
'sunto sm summary.
'suo, 'sua, 'sue, su'oi det: **il ~, la sua** etc (di lui) his; (di lei) her; (di esso) its; (con valore indefinito) one's, his/her; (forma di cortesia: anche: **S**~) your // pronome: **il** ~, **la sua** etc his; hers; yours; **i suoi** (parenti) one's family.
su'ocero, a ['swɔtʃero] sm/f father/mother-in-law; **i ~i** smpl father- and mother-in-law.
su'oi vedi suo.
su'ola sf (di scarpa) sole.
su'olo sm (terreno) ground; (terra) soil.
suo'nare vt (MUS) to play; (campana) to ring; (ore) to strike; (clacson, allarme) to sound // vi to play; (telefono, campana) to ring; (ore) to strike; (clacson, fig: parole) to sound.
su'ono sm sound.

su'ora *sf* (*REL*) sister.
supe'rare *vt* (*oltrepassare: limite*) to exceed, surpass; (*percorrere*) to cover; (*attraversare: fiume*) to cross; (*sorpassare: veicolo*) to overtake; (*fig: essere più bravo di*) to surpass, outdo; (*: difficoltà*) to overcome; (*: esame*) to get through; ~ **qd in altezza/peso** to be taller/heavier than sb; **ha superato la cinquantina** he's over fifty.
su'perbia *sf* pride.
su'perbo, a *ag* proud; (*fig*) magnificent, superb.
superfici'ale [superfi'tʃale] *ag* superficial.
super'ficie, ci [super'fitʃe] *sf* surface.
su'perfluo, a *ag* superfluous.
superi'ore (*piano, arto, classi*) upper; (*più elevato: temperatura, livello*): ~ **(a)** higher (than); (*migliore*): ~ **(a)** superior (to); ~, **a** *sm/f* (*anche REL*) superior; **superiorità** *sf* superiority.
superla'tivo, a *ag, sm* superlative.
supermer'cato *sm* supermarket.
su'perstite *ag* surviving // *sm/f* survivor.
superstizi'one [superstit'tsjone] *sf* superstition; **superstizi'oso, a** *ag* superstitious.
su'pino, a *ag* supine.
suppel'lettile *sf* furnishings *pl*.
suppergiù [supper'dʒu] *av* more or less, roughly.
supple'mento *sm* supplement.
sup'plente *ag* temporary; (*insegnante*) supply *cpd* // *sm/f* temporary member of staff; supply teacher.
'supplica, che *sf* (*preghiera*) plea; (*domanda scritta*) petition, request.
suppli'care *vt* to implore, beseech.
sup'plire *vi*: ~ **a** to make up for, compensate for.
sup'plizio [sup'plittsjo] *sm* torture.
sup'porre *vt* to suppose.
sup'porto *sm* (*sostegno*) support.
supposizi'one [suppozit'tsjone] *sf* supposition.
sup'posta *sf* (*MED*) suppository.
sup'posto, a *pp di* **supporre**.
suppu'rare *vi* to suppurate.
supre'ma'zia [supremat'tsia] *sf* supremacy.
su'premo, a *ag* supreme.
surge'lare [surdʒe'lare] *vt* to (deep-)freeze.
sur'plus *sm inv* (*ECON*) surplus.
surriscal'dare *vt* to overheat.
surro'gato *sm* substitute.
suscet'tibile [suʃʃet'tibile] *ag* (*sensibile*) touchy, sensitive; (*soggetto*): ~ **di miglioramento** that can be improved, open to improvement.
susci'tare [suʃʃi'tare] *vt* to provoke, arouse.
su'sina *sf* plum; **su'sino** *sm* plum (tree).
sussegu'ire *vt* to follow; ~**rsi** *vr* to follow one another.
sussidi'ario, a *ag* subsidiary; auxiliary.

sus'sidio *sm* subsidy.
sussis'tenza [sussis'tɛntsa] *sf* subsistence.
sus'sistere *vi* (2) to exist; to be valid *o* sound.
sussul'tare *vi* to shudder.
sussur'rare *vt, vi* to whisper, murmur; **sus'surro** *sm* whisper, murmur.
su'tura *sf* (*MED*) suture; **sutu'rare** *vt* to stitch up, suture.
sva'gare *vt* (*distrarre*) to distract; (*divertire*) to amuse; ~**rsi** *vr* to amuse o.s.; to enjoy o.s.
'svago, ghi *sm* (*riposo*) relaxation; (*ricreazione*) amusement; (*passatempo*) pastime.
svaligi'are [zvali'dʒare] *vt* to rob, burgle.
svalu'tare *vt* (*ECON*) to devalue; (*fig*) to belittle; **svalutazi'one** *sf* devaluation.
sva'nire *vi* (2) to disappear, vanish.
svan'taggio [zvan'taddʒo] *sm* disadvantage; (*inconveniente*) drawback, disadvantage.
svapo'rare *vi* (2) to evaporate.
svari'ato, a *ag* varied; various.
'svastica *sf* swastika.
sve'dese *ag* Swedish // *sm/f* Swede // (*LING*) Swedish.
'sveglia ['zveʎʎa] *sf* waking up; (*orologio*) alarm (clock); **suonare la ~** (*MIL*) to sound the reveille.
svegli'are [zveʎ'ʎare] *vt* to wake up; (*fig*) to awaken, arouse; ~**rsi** *vr* to wake up; (*fig*) to be revived, reawaken.
'sveglio, a ['zveʎʎo] *ag* awake; (*fig*) alert, quick-witted.
sve'lare *vt* to reveal.
'svelto, a *ag* (*passo*) quick; (*mente*) quick, alert; (*linea*) slim, slender; **alla ~a** *av* quickly.
'svendita *sf* (*COMM*) (clearance) sale.
sveni'mento *sm* fainting fit, faint.
sve'nire *vi* (2) to faint.
sven'tare *vt* to foil, thwart.
sven'tato, a *ag* (*distratto*) scatterbrained; (*imprudente*) rash.
svento'lare *vt, vi* to wave, flutter.
sven'trare *vt* to disembowel.
sven'tura *sf* misfortune; **sventu'rato, a** *ag* unlucky, unfortunate.
sve'nuto, a *pp di* **svenire**.
svergo'gnato, a [zvergoɲ'ɲato] *ag* shameless.
sver'nare *vi* to spend the winter.
sves'tire *vt* to undress; ~**rsi** *vr* to get undressed.
'Svezia ['zvɛttsja] *sf*: **la ~** Sweden.
svez'zare [zvet'tsare] *vt* to wean.
svi'are *vt* to divert; (*fig*) to lead astray; ~**rsi** *vr* to go astray.
svi'gnarsela [zviɲ'ɲarsela] *vr* to slip away, sneak off.
svilup'pare *vt*, ~**rsi** *vr* to develop.
svi'luppo *sm* development.
svinco'lare *vt* to free, release; (*merce*) to clear; **'svincolo** *sm* clearance; (*stradale*) link road.
svi'sare *vt* to distort.

svisce'rare [zviʃʃe'rare] *vt* (*fig: argomento*) to examine in depth; **svisce-'rato, a** *ag* (*amore*) passionate; (*lodi*) obsequious.

'svista *sf* oversight.

svi'tare *vt* to unscrew.

'Svizzera ['zvittsera] *sf:* **la ~** Switzerland.

'svizzero, a ['zvittsero] *ag, sm/f* Swiss.

svogli'ato, a [zvoʎ'ʎato] *ag* listless; (*pigro*) lazy.

svolaz'zare [zvolat'tsare] *vi* to flutter.

'svolgere ['zvɔldʒere] *vt* to unwind; (*srotolare*) to unroll; (*fig: argomento*) to develop; (: *piano, programma*) to carry out; **~rsi** *vr* to unwind; to unroll; (*fig: aver luogo*) to take place; (: *procedere*) to go on; **svolgi'mento** *sm* development; (*andamento*) course.

'svolta *sf* (*atto*) turning *q*; (*curva*) turn, bend; (*fig*) turning-point.

svol'tare *vi* to turn.

'svolto, a *pp di* **svolgere**.

svuo'tare *vt* to empty (out).

T

tabac'caio, a *sm/f* tobacconist.

tabacche'ria [tabakke'ria] *sf* tobacconist's (shop).

ta'bacco, chi *sm* tobacco.

ta'bella *sf* (*tavola*) table; (*elenco*) list.

taber'nacolo *sm* tabernacle.

tabù *ag, sm inv* taboo.

tabula'tore *sm* tabulator.

'tacca, che *sf* notch, nick; **di mezza ~** (*fig*) mediocre.

tac'cagno, a [tak'kaɲɲo] *ag* mean, stingy.

tac'cheggio [tak'keddʒo] *sm* shoplifting.

tac'chino [tak'kino] *sm* turkey.

'taccia, ce ['tattʃa] *sf* bad reputation.

'tacco, chi *sm* heel.

taccu'ino *sm* notebook.

ta'cere [ta'tʃere] *vi* to be silent *o* quiet; (*smettere di parlare*) to fall silent // *vt* to keep to oneself, say nothing about; **far ~ qd** to make sb be quiet; (*fig*) to silence sb.

ta'chimetro [ta'kimetro] *sm* speedometer.

'tacito, a ['tatʃito] *ag* silent; (*sottinteso*) tacit, unspoken.

taci'turno, a [tatʃi'turno] *ag* taciturn.

ta'fano *sm* horsefly.

taffe'ruglio [taffe'ruʎʎo] *sm* brawl, scuffle.

taffettà *sm* taffeta.

'taglia ['taʎʎa] *sf* (*statura*) height; (*misura*) size; (*riscatto*) ransom; (*ricompensa*) reward.

taglia'carte [taʎʎa'karte] *sm inv* paperknife.

tagli'ando [taʎ'ʎando] *sm* coupon.

tagli'are [taʎ'ʎare] *vt* to cut; (*recidere, interrompere*) to cut off; (*intersecare*) to cut across, intersect; (*carne*) to carve; (*vini*) to blend // *vi* to cut; (*prendere una scorciatoia*) to take a short-cut; **~ corto** (*fig*) to cut short.

taglia'telle [taʎʎa'tɛlle] *sfpl* tagliatelle *pl*.

tagli'ente [taʎ'ʎɛnte] *ag* sharp.

'taglio ['taʎʎo] *sm* cutting *q*; cut; (*parte tagliente*) cutting edge; (*di abito*) cut, style; (*di stoffa: lunghezza*) length; (*di vini*) blending; **di ~** on edge, edgeways; **banconote di piccolo/grosso ~** notes of small/large denomination.

tagli'ola [taʎ'ʎola] *sf* trap, snare.

tagliuz'zare [taʎʎut'tsare] *vt* to cut into small pieces.

'talco *sm* talcum powder.

'tale *det* such; (*intensivo*): **un ~/~i ...** such (a)/such ... // *pronome* (*questa, quella persona già menzionata*) the one, the person; (*indefinito*): **un(una) ~** someone; **il ~ giorno alla ~ ora** on such and such a day at such and such a time; **~ quale: il tuo vestito è ~ quale il mio** your dress is just *o* exactly like mine; **quel/quella ~** that person, that man/woman.

ta'lento *sm* talent.

talis'mano *sm* talisman.

tallon'cino [tallon'tʃino] *sm* counterfoil.

tal'lone *sm* heel.

tal'mente *av* so.

ta'lora *av* = **talvolta**.

'talpa *sf* (*ZOOL*) mole.

tal'volta *av* sometimes, at times.

tambu'rello *sm* tambourine.

tambu'rino *sm* drummer.

tam'buro *sm* drum.

Ta'migi [ta'midʒi] *sm:* **il ~** the Thames.

tampo'nare *vt* (*otturare*) to plug; (*urtare: macchina*) to crash *o* ram into.

tam'pone *sm* (*MED*) wad, pad; (*per timbri*) ink-pad; (*respingente*) buffer; **~ assorbente** tampon.

'tana *sf* lair, den.

'tanfo *sm* stench; musty smell.

tan'gente [tan'dʒɛnte] *ag* (*MAT*): **~ a** tangential to // *sf* tangent; (*quota*) share.

tan'gibile [tan'dʒibile] *ag* tangible.

'tango, ghi *sm* tango.

tan'nino *sm* tannin.

tan'tino: un ~ *av* a little, a bit.

'tanto, a *det* (*pane, acqua, soldi*) so much; (*persone, libri*) so many // *pronome* so much (*o* many) // *av* (*con ag, av*) so; (*con vb*) so much, such a lot; (: *così a lungo*) so long; **due volte ~** twice as much; **~ ... quanto: ho ~i libri quanti (ne hanno) loro** I have as many books as they have *o* as them; **conosco ~ Carlo quanto suo padre** I know both Carlo and his father; **è ~ bella quanto buona** she is as beautiful as she is good; **~ più ... più** the more ... the more; **un ~: costa un ~ al metro** it costs so much per metre; **guardare con ~ d'occhi** to gaze wide-eyed at; **~ per cambiare** just for a change; **una volta ~** just once; **~ è inutile** in any case it's useless; **di ~ in ~, ogni ~** every so often.

tapi'oca *sf* tapioca.

'tappa *sf* (*luogo di sosta, fermata*) stop, halt;

(*parte di un percorso*) stage, leg; (*SPORT*) lap; **a ~e** in stages.

tap'pare *vt* to plug, stop up; (*bottiglia*) to cork.

tap'peto *sm* carpet; (*anche:* **tappetino**) rug; (*di tavolo*) cloth; (*SPORT*): **andare al ~** to go down for the count; **mettere sul ~** (*fig*) to bring up for discussion.

tappez'zare [tappet'tsare] *vt* (*con carta*) to paper; (*rivestire*): **~ qc (di)** to cover sth (with); **tappezze'ria** *sf* (*tessuto*) tapestry; (*carta da parato*) wallpaper; (*arte*) upholstery; **far da tappezzeria** (*fig*) to be a wallflower; **tappezzi'ere** *sm* upholsterer.

'tappo *sm* stopper; (*in sughero*) cork.

ta'rantola *sf* tarantula.

tarchi'ato, a [tar'kjato] *ag* stocky, thickset.

tar'dare *vi* to be late // *vt* to delay; **~ a fare** to delay doing.

'tardi *av* late; **più ~** later (on); **al più ~** at the latest; **far ~** to be late; (*restare alzato*) to stay up late.

tar'divo, a *ag* (*primavera*) late; (*rimedio*) belated, tardy; (*fig: bambino*) retarded.

'tardo, a *ag* (*lento, fig: ottuso*) slow; (*tempo: avanzato*) late.

'targa, ghe *sf* plate; (*AUT*) number plate.

ta'riffa *sf* rates *pl*; fares *pl*; tariff; (*prezzo*) rate; fare; (*elenco*) price list; tariff.

'tarlo *sm* woodworm.

'tarma *sf* moth.

ta'rocco, chi *sm* tarot card; **~chi** *smpl* (*gioco*) tarot *sg*.

tartagli'are [tartaʎ'ʎare] *vi* to stutter, stammer.

'tartaro, a *ag, sm* (*in tutti i sensi*) tartar.

tarta'ruga, ghe *sf* tortoise; (*di mare*) turtle; (*materiale*) tortoiseshell.

tar'tina *sf* canapé.

tar'tufo *sm* (*BOT*) truffle.

'tasca, sche *sf* pocket; **tas'cabile** *ag* (*libro*) pocket *cpd*; **tasca'pane** *sm* haversack; **tas'chino** *sm* breast pocket.

'tassa *sf* (*imposta*) tax; (*doganale*) duty; (*per iscrizione: a scuola etc*) fee; **~ di circolazione/di soggiorno** road/tourist tax.

tas'sametro *sm* taximeter.

tas'sare *vt* to tax; to levy a duty on.

tassa'tivo, a *ag* peremptory.

tassazi'one [tassat'tsjone] *sf* taxation.

tas'sello *sm* plug; wedge.

tassì *sm inv* = **taxi**; **tas'sista, i, e** *sm/f* taxi driver.

'tasso *sm* (*di natalità, d'interesse etc*) rate; (*BOT*) yew; (*ZOOL*) badger; **~ di cambio/d'interesse** rate of exchange/interest.

tas'tare *vt* to feel; **~ il terreno** (*fig*) to see how the land lies.

tasti'era *sf* keyboard.

'tasto *sm* key; (*tatto*) touch, feel.

tas'toni *av:* **procedere (a) ~** to grope one's way forward.

'tattico, a, ci, che *ag* tactical // *sf* tactics *pl*.

'tatto *sm* (*senso*) touch; (*fig*) tact; **duro al ~** hard to the touch; **aver ~** to be tactful, have tact.

tatu'aggio [tatu'addʒo] *sm* tattooing; (*disegno*) tattoo.

tatu'are *vt* to tattoo.

'tavola *sf* table; (*asse*) plank, board; (*lastra*) tablet; (*quadro*) panel (painting); (*illustrazione*) plate; **~ calda** snack bar.

tavo'lato *sm* boarding; (*pavimento*) wooden floor.

tavo'letta *sf* tablet, bar.

'tavolo *sm* table.

tavo'lozza [tavo'lottsa] *sf* (*ARTE*) palette.

'taxi *sm inv* taxi.

'tazza ['tattsa] *sf* cup; **~ da caffè/tè** coffee/tea cup.

te *pronome* (*soggetto: in forme comparative, oggetto*) you.

tè *sm inv* tea; (*trattenimento*) tea party.

tea'trale *ag* theatrical.

te'atro *sm* theatre.

'tecnico, a, ci, che *ag* technical // *sm/f* technician // *sf* technique; (*tecnologia*) technology.

tecnolo'gia [teknolo'dʒia] *sf* technology.

te'desco, a, schi, sche *ag, sm/f, sm* German.

'tedio *sm* tedium, boredom.

te'game *sm* (*CUC*) pan.

'tegola *sf* tile.

tei'era *sf* teapot.

'tela *sf* (*tessuto*) cloth; (*per vele, quadri*) canvas; (*dipinto*) canvas, painting; (*TEATRO*) curtain; **~ cerata** oilcloth; (*copertone*) tarpaulin.

te'laio *sm* (*apparecchio*) loom; (*struttura*) frame.

tele'camera *sf* television camera.

telecomunicazi'oni [telekomunikat'tsjoni] *sfpl* telecommunications.

tele'cronaca *sf* television report.

tele'ferica, che *sf* cableway.

telefo'nare *vi* to telephone, ring; to make a phone call // *vt* to telephone; **~ a** to phone up, ring up, call up.

telefo'nata *sf* (*telephone*) call; **~ a carico del destinatario** reverse charge call.

tele'fonico, a, ci, che *ag* (*tele*)phone *cpd*.

telefo'nista, i, e *sm/f* telephonist; (*d'impresa*) switchboard operator.

te'lefono *sm* telephone; **~ a gettoni** ≈ pay phone.

telegior'nale [teledʒor'nale] *sm* television news (programme).

telegra'fare *vt, vi* to telegraph, cable.

telegra'fia *sf* telegraphy; **tele'grafico, a, ci, che** *ag* telegraph *cpd*, telegraphic; **te'legrafo** *sm* telegraph; (*ufficio*) telegraph office.

tele'gramma, i *sm* telegram.

telepa'tia *sf* telepathy.

teles'copio *sm* telescope.

teleselezi'one [teleselet'tsjone] *sf* ≈ subscriber trunk dialling.

telespetta'tore, 'trice sm/f (television) viewer.

televisi'one sf television.

televi'sore sm television set.

'telex sm inv telex.

'tema, i sm theme; (INS) essay, composition.

teme'rario, a ag rash, reckless.

te'mere vt to fear, be afraid of; (essere sensibile a: freddo, calore) to suffer from; (sog: cose) to be easily damaged by // vi to fear; (essere preoccupato): ~ **per** to worry about, fear for; ~ **di/che** to be afraid of/that.

temperama'tite sm inv pencil sharpener.

tempera'mento sm temperament.

tempe'rare vt (aguzzare) to sharpen; (fig) to moderate, control, temper.

tempe'rato, a ag moderate, temperate; (clima) temperate.

tempera'tura sf temperature.

tempe'rino sm penknife.

tem'pesta sf storm; ~ **di sabbia/neve** sand/snowstorm.

tempes'tivo, a ag timely.

tempes'toso, a ag stormy.

'tempia sf (ANAT) temple.

'tempio sm (edificio) temple.

'tempo sm (METEOR) weather; (cronologico) time; (epoca) time, times pl; (di film, gioco: parte) part; (MUS) time; (: battuta) beat; (LING) tense; **un** ~ once; ~ **fa** some time ago; **al** ~ **stesso** o **a un** ~ at the same time; **per** ~ early; **aver fatto il suo** ~ to have had its (o his etc) day; **primo/secondo** ~ (TEATRO) first/second part; (SPORT) first/second half; **in** ~ **utile** in due time o course.

tempo'rale ag temporal // sm (METEOR) (thunder)storm.

tempo'raneo, a ag temporary.

temporeggi'are [tempored'dʒare] vi to play for time, temporize.

tem'prare vt to temper.

te'nace [te'natʃe] ag strong, tough; (fig) tenacious; **te'nacia** sf tenacity.

te'naglie [te'naʎʎe] sfpl pincers pl.

'tenda sf (riparo) awning; (di finestra) curtain; (per campeggio etc) tent.

ten'denza [ten'dɛntsa] sf tendency; (orientamento) trend; **avere** ~ **a qc** to have a bent for sth.

'tendere vt (allungare al massimo) to stretch, draw tight; (porgere: mano) to hold out; (fig: trappola) to lay, set // vi: ~ **a qc/a fare** to tend towards sth/to do; ~ **l'orecchio** to prick up one's ears; **il tempo tende al caldo** the weather is getting hot.

ten'dina sf curtain.

'tendine sm tendon, sinew.

ten'done sm (da circo) tent.

'tenebre sfpl darkness sg; **tene'broso, a** ag dark, gloomy.

te'nente sm lieutenant.

te'nere vt to hold; (conservare, mantenere) to keep; (ritenere, considerare) to consider; (spazio: occupare) to take up, occupy; (seguire: strada) to keep to // vi to hold; (colori) to be fast; (dare importanza): ~ **a** to care about; ~ **a fare** to want to do, be keen to do; ~**rsi** vr (stare in una determinata posizione) to stand; (stimarsi) to consider o.s.; (aggrapparsi): ~**rsi a** to hold on to; (attenersi): ~**rsi a** to stick to; ~ **una conferenza** to give a lecture; ~ **conto di qc** to take sth into consideration; ~ **presente qc** to bear sth in mind.

tene'rezza [tene'rettsa] sf tenderness.

'tenero, a ag tender; (pietra, cera, colore) soft; (fig) tender, loving.

'tenia sf tapeworm.

'tennis sm tennis.

te'nore sm tenor, way; (contenuto) content; (MUS) tenor; ~ **di vita** way of life; (livello) standard of living.

tensi'one sf tension.

ten'tacolo sm (ZOOL) tentacle.

ten'tare vt (indurre) to tempt; (provare): ~ **qc/di fare** to attempt o try sth/to do; **tenta'tivo** sm attempt; **tentazi'one** sf temptation.

tenten'nare vi to shake, be unsteady; (fig) to hesitate, waver // vt: ~ **il capo** to shake one's head.

ten'toni av: **andare (a)** ~ to grope one's way.

'tenue ag (sottile) fine; (colore) soft; (fig) slender, slight.

te'nuta sf (capacità) capacity; (divisa) uniform; (abito) dress; (AGR) estate; **a** ~ **d'aria** airtight; ~ **di strada** roadholding power.

teolo'gia [teolo'dʒia] sf theology; **teo-'logico, a, ci, che** ag theological; **te'ologo, gi** sm theologian.

teo'rema, i sm theorem.

teo'ria sf theory; **te'orico, a, ci, che** ag theoretic(al).

'tepido, a ag = **tiepido.**

te'pore sm warmth.

'teppa sf mob, hooligans pl; **tep'pismo** sm hooliganism; **tep'pista, i** sm hooligan.

tera'pia sf therapy.

tergicris'tallo [terdʒikris'tallo] sm windscreen wiper.

tergiver'sare [terdʒiver'sare] vi to shilly-shally.

'tergo sm: **a** ~ behind; **vedi a** ~ please turn over.

ter'male ag thermal; **stazione** f ~ spa.

'terme sfpl thermal baths.

'termico, a, ci, che ag thermic; (unità) thermal.

termi'nale ag, sm terminal.

termi'nare vt to end; (lavoro) to finish // vi to end.

'termine sm term; (fine, estremità) end; (di territorio) boundary, limit; **contratto a** ~ (COMM) forward contract; **a breve/lungo** ~ short-/long-term; **parlare senza mezzi** ~**i** to talk frankly, not to mince one's words.

terminolo'gia [terminolo'dʒia] sf terminology.

'**termite** sf termite.

ter'**mometro** sm thermometer.

'**termos** sm inv = **thermos.**

termosi'**fone** sm radiator; (**riscaldamento a**) ~ central heating.

ter'**mostato** sm thermostat.

'**terra** sf (gen, ELETTR) earth; (sostanza) soil, earth; (opposto al mare) land q; (regione, paese) land; (argilla) clay; ~**e** sfpl (possedimento) lands, land sg; **a o per** ~ (stato) on the ground (o floor); (moto) to the ground, down; **mettere a** ~ (ELETTR) to earth.

terra'**cotta** sf terracotta; **vasellame m di** ~ earthenware.

terra'**ferma** sf dry land, terra firma; (continente) mainland.

terrapi'**eno** sm embankment, bank.

ter'**razza** [ter'rattsa] sf, **ter'razzo** [ter'rattso] sm terrace.

terre'**moto** sm earthquake.

ter'**reno, a** ag (vita, beni) earthly // sm (suolo, fig) ground; (COMM) land q, plot (of land); site; (SPORT, MIL) field.

ter'**restre** ag (superficie) of the earth, earth's; (di terra: battaglia, animale) land cpd; (REL) earthly, worldly.

ter'**ribile** ag terrible, dreadful.

terrifi'**cante** ag terrifying.

territori'**ale** ag territorial.

terri'**torio** sm territory.

ter'**rore** sm terror; **terro'rismo** sm terrorism; **terro'rista, i, e** sm/f terrorist; **terroriz'zare** vt to terrorize.

'**terso, a** ag clear.

'**terzo, a** ['tɛrtso] ag third // sm (frazione) third; (DIR) third party; ~**i** smpl (altri) others, other people.

'**tesa** sf brim.

'**teschio** ['teskjo] sm skull.

'**tesi** sf thesis.

'**teso, a** pp di **tendere** // ag (tirato) taut, tight; (fig) tense.

teso'**reria** sf treasury.

tesori'**ere** sm treasurer.

te'**soro** sm treasure; **il Ministero del T**~ the Treasury.

'**tessera** sf (documento) card.

'**tessere** vt to weave; '**tessile** ag, sm textile; **tessili** smpl (operai) textile workers; **tessi'tore, 'trice** sm/f weaver; **tessi'tura** sf weaving.

tes'**suto** sm fabric, material; (BIOL) tissue; (fig) web.

'**testa** sf head; (di cose: estremità, parte anteriore) head, front; **di** ~ ag (vettura etc) front; **fare** ~ **a qd** (nemico etc) to face sb; **fare di** ~ **propria** to go one's own way; **in** ~ (SPORT) in the lead; ~ **o croce?** heads or tails?; **avere la** ~ **dura** to be stubborn; ~ **di serie** (TENNIS) seed, seeded player.

testa'**mento** sm (atto) will; (REL): **T**~ Testament.

tes'**tardo, a** ag stubborn, pig-headed.

tes'**tata** sf (parte anteriore) head; (intestazione) heading.

'**teste** sm/f witness.

tes'**ticolo** sm testicle.

testi'**mone** sm/f (DIR) witness.

testimoni'**anza** [testimo'njantsa] sf testimony.

testimoni'**are** vt to testify; (fig) to bear witness to, testify to // vi to give evidence, testify.

'**testo** sm text; **fare** ~ (fig: persona) to be an authority; (: opera) to be the standard work; **testu'ale** ag textual; literal, word for word.

tes'**tuggine** [tes'tuddʒine] sf tortoise; (di mare) turtle.

'**tetano** sm (MED) tetanus.

'**tetro, a** ag gloomy.

'**tetto** sm roof; **tet'toia** sf shed; (di piattaforma etc) roofing.

'**Tevere** sm: **il** ~ the Tiber.

'**thermos** ® ['tɛrmos] sm inv vacuum o Thermos ® flask.

ti pronome (dav lo, la, li, le, ne diventa **te**) (oggetto) you; (complemento di termine) (to) you; (riflessivo) yourself.

ti'**ara** sf (REL) tiara.

'**tibia** sf tibia, shinbone.

tic sm inv tic, (nervous) twitch; (fig) mannerism.

ticchet'**tio** [tikket'tio] sm clicking; (di orologio) ticking; (della pioggia) patter.

'**ticchio** ['tikkjo] sm (ghiribizzo) whim; (tic) tic, (nervous) twitch.

ti'**epido, a** ag lukewarm, tepid.

ti'**fare** vi: ~ **per** to be a fan of; (parteggiare) to side with.

'**tifo** sm (MED) typhus; (fig): **fare il** ~ **per** to be a fan of.

tifoi'**dea** sf typhoid.

ti'**fone** sm typhoon.

ti'**foso, a** sm/f (SPORT etc) fan.

'**tiglio** ['tiʎʎo] sm lime (tree), linden (tree).

'**tigre** sf tiger.

tim'**ballo** sm (strumento) kettle drum; (CUC) timbale.

'**timbro** sm stamp; (MUS) timbre, tone.

'**timido, a** ag shy; timid.

'**timo** sm thyme.

ti'**mone** sm (NAUT) rudder; **timoni'ere** sm helmsman.

ti'**more** sm (paura) fear; (rispetto) awe; **timo'roso, a** ag timid, timorous.

'**timpano** sm (ANAT) eardrum; (MUS): ~**i** smpl kettledrums, timpani.

'**tingere** ['tindʒere] vt to dye.

'**tino** sm vat.

ti'**nozza** [ti'nɔttsa] sf tub.

'**tinta** sf (materia colorante) dye; (colore) colour, shade; **tinta'rella** sf (fam) (sun)tan.

tintin'**nare** vi to tinkle.

'**tinto, a** pp di **tingere.**

tinto'**ria** sf (officina) dyeworks sg; (lavasecco) dry cleaner's (shop).

tin'**tura** sf (operazione) dyeing; (colorante) dye; ~ **di iodio** tincture of iodine.

'**tipico, a, ci, che** ag typical.

'tipo sm type; (genere) kind, type; (fam) chap, fellow.

tipogra'fia sf typography; (procedimento) letterpress (printing); (officina) printing house; **tipo'grafico, a, ci, che** ag typographic(al); letterpress cpd; **ti'pografo** sm typographer.

ti'raggio [ti'radd3o] sm (di camino etc) draught.

tiranneggi'are [tiranned'd3are] vt to tyrannize.

tiran'nia sf tyranny.

ti'ranno, a ag tyrannical // sm tyrant.

ti'rare vt (gen) to pull; (estrarre): ~ qc da to take o pull sth out of; to get sth out of; to extract sth from; (chiudere: tenda etc) to draw, pull; (tracciare, disegnare) to draw, trace; (lanciare: sasso, palla) to throw; (stampare) to print; (pistola, freccia) to fire // vi (pipa, camino) to draw; (vento) to blow; (abito) to be tight; (fare fuoco) to fire; (fare del tiro, CALCIO) to shoot; ~ avanti vi to struggle on // vt to keep going; ~ fuori vt (estrarre) to take out, pull out; ~ giù vt (abbassare) to bring down; ~ su vt to pull up; (capelli) to put up; (fig: bambino) to bring up; ~rsi indietro to move back.

tira'tore sm gunman; **un buon** ~ a good shot; ~ **scelto** marksman.

tira'tura sf (azione) printing; (di libro) (print) run; (di giornale) circulation.

'tirchio, a ['tirkjo] ag mean, stingy.

'tiro sm shooting q, firing q; (colpo, sparo) shot; (di palla: lancio) throwing q; throw; (fig) trick; **cavallo da** ~ draught horse; ~ **a segno** target shooting; (luogo) shooting range.

tiro'cinio [tiro'tʃinjo] sm apprenticeship; (professionale) training.

ti'roide sf thyroid (gland).

Tir'reno sm: **il (mar)** ~ the Tyrrhenian Sea.

ti'sana sf herb tea.

tito'lare ag appointed; (sovrano) titular // sm/f incumbent; (proprietario) owner; (CALCIO) regular player.

'titolo sm title; (di giornale) headline; (diploma) qualification; (COMM) security; (: azione) share; **a che** ~? for what reason?; **a** ~ **di amicizia** out of friendship; **a** ~ **di premio** as a prize; ~ **di credito** share; ~ **di proprietà** title deed.

titu'bante ag hesitant, irresolute.

'tizio, a ['tittsjo] sm/f fellow, chap.

tiz'zone [tit'tsone] sm brand.

toc'cante ag touching.

toc'care vt to touch; (tastare) to feel; (fig: riguardare) to concern; (: commuovere) to touch, move; (: pungere) to hurt, wound; (: far cenno a: argomento) to touch on, mention // vi (2): ~ **a** (accadere) to happen to; (spettare) to be up to; **tocca a te difenderci** it's up to you to defend us; **a chi tocca?** whose turn is it?; **mi toccò pagare** I had to pay.

'tocco, chi sm touch; (ARTE) stroke, touch; **il** ~ (l'una) one o'clock, one p.m.

'toga, ghe sf toga; (di magistrato, professore) gown.

'togliere ['tɔʎʎere] vt (rimuovere) to take away (o off), remove; (riprendere, non concedere più) to take away, remove; (MAT) to take away, subtract; (liberare) to free; ~ **qc a qd** to take sth (away) from sb; **ciò non toglie che** nevertheless, be that as it may; ~**rsi il cappello** to take off one's hat.

to'letta sf toilet; (mobile) dressing table.

tolle'ranza [tolle'rantsa] sf tolerance.

tolle'rare vt to tolerate.

'tolto, a pp di **togliere**.

to'maia sf (di scarpa) upper.

'tomba sf tomb.

tom'bino sm manhole cover.

'tombola sf (gioco) tombola; (ruzzolone) tumble.

tombo'lare vi (2) to tumble.

'tomo sm volume.

'tonaca, che sf (REL) habit.

to'nare vi = **tuonare**.

'tondo, a ag round.

'tonfo sm splash; (rumore sordo) thud.

'tonico, a, ci, che ag, sm tonic.

tonifi'care vt (muscoli, pelle) to tone up; (irrobustire) to invigorate, brace.

tonnel'laggio [tonnel'ladd3o] sm (NAUT) tonnage.

tonnel'lata sf ton.

'tonno sm tuna (fish).

'tono sm (gen) tone; (MUS: di pezzo) key; (di colore) shade, tone.

ton'silla sf tonsil; **tonsil'lite** sf tonsillitis.

ton'sura sf tonsure.

'tonto, a ag dull, stupid.

to'pazio [to'pattsjo] sm topaz.

'topo sm mouse.

topogra'fia sf topography.

'toppa sf (serratura) keyhole; (pezza) patch.

to'race [to'ratʃe] sm chest.

'torba sf peat.

'torbido, a ag (liquido) cloudy; (: fiume) muddy; (fig) dark; troubled; **pescare nel** ~ (fig) to fish in troubled water.

'torcere ['tortʃere] vt to twist; (biancheria) to wring (out); ~**rsi** vr to twist, writhe.

torchi'are [tor'kjare] vt to press; **'torchio** sm (tipo) press; **torchio tipografico/per uva** printing/wine press.

'torcia, ce ['tortʃa] sf torch.

torci'collo [tortʃi'kɔllo] sm stiff neck.

'tordo sm thrush.

To'rino sf Turin.

tor'menta sf snowstorm.

tormen'tare vt to torment; ~**rsi** vr to fret, worry o.s.; **tor'mento** sm torment.

torna'conto sm advantage, benefit.

tor'nado sm tornado.

tor'nante sm hairpin bend.

tor'nare vi (2) to return, go (o come) back; (ridiventare: anche fig) to become (again); (riuscire giusto, esatto: conto) to work out; (risultare) to turn out (to be), prove (to be); ~ **utile** to prove *o* turn out (to be) useful.

torna'sole *sm inv* litmus.

tor'neo *sm* tournament.

'tornio *sm* lathe.

'toro *sm* bull; (*dello zodiaco*): **T**~ Taurus.

tor'pedine *sf* torpedo; **torpedini'era** *sf* torpedo boat.

tor'pore *sm* torpor, drowsiness; (*pigrizia*) torpor, sluggishness.

'torre *sf* tower; (*SCACCHI*) rook, castle.

torrefazi'one [torrefat'tsjone] *sf* roasting.

tor'rente *sm* torrent; **torrenzi'ale** *ag* torrential.

tor'retta *sf* turret.

'torrido, a *ag* torrid.

torri'one *sm* keep.

tor'rone *sm* nougat.

torsi'one *sf* twisting; torsion.

'torso *sm* torso, trunk; (*ARTE*) torso.

'torsolo *sm* (*di cavolo etc*) stump; (*di frutta*) core.

'torta *sf* cake.

torti'era *sf* cake tin.

'torto, a *pp di* **torcere** // *ag* (*ritorto*) twisted; (*storto*) twisted, crooked // *sm* (*ingiustizia*) wrong; (*colpa*) fault; **a** ~ wrongly; **aver** ~ to be wrong.

'tortora *sf* turtle dove.

tortu'oso, a *ag* (*strada*) twisting; (*fig*) tortuous.

tor'tura *sf* torture; **tortu'rare** *vt* to torture.

'torvo, a *ag* menacing, grim.

tosa'erba *sm o f inv* (lawn)mower.

to'sare *vt* (*pecora*) to shear; (*siepe*) to clip, trim.

Tos'cana *sf*: **la** ~ Tuscany.

'tosse *sf* cough; ~ **convulsa** *o* **canina** whooping cough.

'tossico, a, ci, che *ag* toxic.

tossi'comane *sm/f* drug addict.

tos'sire *vi* to cough.

tosta'pane *sm inv* toaster.

tos'tare *vt* to toast; (*caffè*) to roast.

'tosto, a *ag*: **faccia** ~**a** cheek.

to'tale *ag, sm* total; **totalità** *sf*: **la totalità di** all of, the total amount (*o* number) of; **the whole** + *sg*; **totali'tario, a** *ag* totalitarian; **totaliz'zare** *vt* to total; (*SPORT: punti*) to score.

toto'calcio [toto'kaltʃo] *sm* football pools *pl*.

to'vaglia [to'vaʎʎa] *sf* tablecloth; **tova-gli'olo** *sm* napkin.

'tozzo, a ['tɔttso] *ag* squat // *sm*: ~ **di pane** crust of bread.

tra *prep* (*di due persone, cose*) between; (*di più persone, cose*) among(st); (*tempo: entro*) within, in; ~ **5 giorni** in 5 days' time; **litigano** ~ (**di**) **loro** they're fighting amongst themselves; ~ **breve** soon; ~ **sé e sé** (*parlare etc*) to oneself.

traba'llare *vi* to stagger, totter.

trabboc'care *vi* (*2*) to overflow.

trabboc'chetto [trabok'ketto] *sm* (*fig*) trap.

tracan'nare *vt* to gulp down.

'traccia, ce ['trattʃa] *sf* (*segno, striscia*) trail, track; (*orma*) tracks *pl*; (*residuo, testimonianza*) trace, sign; (*abbozzo*) outline.

tracci'are [trat'tʃare] *vt* to trace, mark (out); (*disegnare*) to draw; (*fig: abbozzare*) to outline; **tracci'ato** *sm* (*grafico*) layout, plan.

tra'chea [tra'kɛa] *sf* windpipe, trachea.

tra'colla *sf* shoulder strap; **borsa a** ~ shoulder bag.

tra'collo *sm* (*fig*) collapse, crash.

traco'tante *ag* overbearing, arrogant.

tradi'mento *sm* betrayal; (*DIR, MIL*) treason.

tra'dire *vt* to betray; (*coniuge*) to be unfaithful to; (*doveri: mancare*) to fail in; (*rivelare*) to give away, reveal; **tradi'tore, 'trice** *sm/f* traitor.

tradizio'nale [tradittsjo'nale] *ag* traditional.

tradizi'one [tradit'tsjone] *sf* tradition.

tra'dotto, a *pp di* **tradurre**.

tra'durre *vt* to translate; (*spiegare*) to render, convey; **tradut'tore, 'trice** *sm/f* translator; **traduzi'one** *sf* translation.

tra'ente *sm/f* (*ECON*) drawer.

trafe'lato, a *ag* out of breath.

traffi'cante *sm/f* dealer; (*peg*) trafficker.

traffi'care *vi* (*commerciare*): ~ (**in**) to trade (in), deal (in); (*affaccendarsi*) to busy o.s. // *vt* (*peg*) to traffic in.

'traffico, ci *sm* traffic; (*commercio*) trade, traffic.

tra'figgere [tra'fiddʒere] *vt* to run through, stab; (*fig*) to pierce; **tra'fitto, a** *pp di* **trafiggere**.

trafo'rare *vt* to bore, drill; **tra'foro** *sm* (*azione*) boring, drilling; (*galleria*) tunnel.

tra'gedia [tra'dʒɛdja] *sf* tragedy.

tra'ghetto [tra'getto] *sm* crossing; (*barca*) ferry(boat).

'tragico, a, ci, che ['tradʒiko] *ag* tragic // *sm* (*autore*) tragedian.

tra'gitto [tra'dʒitto] *sm* (*passaggio*) crossing; (*viaggio*) journey.

tragu'ardo *sm* (*SPORT*) finishing line; (*fig*) goal, aim.

traiet'toria *sf* trajectory.

trai'nare *vt* to drag, haul; (*rimorchiare*) to tow; **'traino** *sm* (*carro*) wagon; (*slitta*) sledge; (*carico*) load.

tralasci'are [tralaʃ'ʃare] *vt* (*studi*) to interrupt; (*dettagli*) to leave out, omit.

'tralcio ['traltʃo] *sm* (*BOT*) shoot.

tra'liccio [tra'littʃo] *sm* (*tela*) ticking; (*struttura*) trellis; (*ELETTR*) pylon.

tram *sm inv* tram.

'trama *sf* (*filo*) weft, woof; (*fig: argomento, maneggio*) plot.

traman'dare *vt* to pass on, hand down.

tra'mare *vt* (*fig*) to scheme, plot.

tram'busto *sm* turmoil.

trames'tio *sm* bustle.

tramez'zino [tramed'dzino] *sm* sandwich.

tra'mezzo [tra'mɛddzo] *sm* (*EDIL*) partition.

'tramite *prep* through.

tramon'tare *vi* (2) to set, go down; **tra'monto** *sm* setting; (*del sole*) sunset.

tramor'tire *vi* (2) to faint // *vt* to stun.

trampo'lino *sm* (*per tuffi*) springboard, diving board; (*per lo sci*) ski-jump.

'trampolo *sm* stilt.

tramu'tare *vt* (*trasferire*) to transfer; (*mutare*) to change, transform.

'trancia, ce ['trantʃa] *sf* slice; (*cesoia*) shearing machine.

tra'nello *sm* trap.

trangugi'are [trangu'dʒare] *vt* to gulp down.

'tranne *prep* except (for), but (for).

tranquil'lante *sm* (*MED*) tranquillizer.

tranquillità *sf* calm, stillness; quietness; peace of mind.

tranquilliz'zare [trankwillid'dzare] *vt* to reassure.

tran'quillo, a *ag* calm, quiet; (*bambino, scolaro*) quiet; (*sereno*) with one's mind at rest; **sta' ~** don't worry.

transat'lantico, a, ci, che *ag* transatlantic // *sm* transatlantic liner.

tran'satto, a *pp di* **transigere**.

transazi'one [transat'tsjone] *sf* compromise; (*DIR*) settlement; (*COMM*) transaction, deal.

tran'senna *sf* barrier.

tran'setto *sm* transept.

tran'sigere [tran'sidʒere] *vi* (*DIR*) to reach a settlement; (*venire a patti*) to compromise, come to an agreement.

tran'sistor *sm*, **transis'tore** *sm* transistor.

transi'tabile *ag* passable.

transi'tare *vi* (2) to pass.

transi'tivo, a *ag* transitive.

'transito *sm* transit; **di ~** (*merci*) in transit; (*stazione*) transit *cpd*; **divieto di ~** no thoroughfare.

transi'torio, a *ag* transitory, transient; (*provvisorio*) provisional.

transizi'one [transit'tsjone] *sf* transition.

tran'via *sf* tramway.

'trapano *sm* (*utensile*) drill; (: *MED*) trepan.

trapas'sare *vt* to pierce.

tra'passo *sm* passage.

trape'lare *vi* (2) to leak, drip; (*fig*) to leak out.

tra'pezio [tra'pɛttsjo] *sm* (*MAT*) trapezium; (*attrezzo ginnico*) trapeze.

trapian'tare *vt* to transplant; **trapi'anto** *sm* transplanting; (*MED*) transplant.

'trappola *sf* trap.

tra'punta *sf* quilt.

'trarre *vt* to draw, pull; (*portare*) to take; (*prendere, tirare fuori*) to take (out), draw; (*derivare*) to obtain; **~ origine da qc** to have its origins o originate in sth.

trasa'lire *vi* to start, jump.

trasan'dato, a *ag* shabby.

trasbor'dare *vt* to transfer; (*NAUT*) to tran(s)ship // *vi* to change.

trascenden'tale [traʃʃenden'tale] *ag* transcendental.

trasci'nare [traʃʃi'nare] *vt* to drag; **~rsi** *vr* to drag o.s. along; (*fig*) to drag on.

tras'correre *vt* (*tempo*) to spend, pass; (*libro*) to skim (through) // *vi* (2) to pass; **tras'corso, a** *pp di* **trascorrere**.

tras'critto, a *pp di* **trascrivere**.

tras'crivere *vt* to transcribe; **trascri'zione** *sf* transcription.

trascu'rare *vt* to neglect; (*non considerare*) to disregard; **trascura'tezza** *sf* carelessness, negligence; **trascu'rato, a** *ag* (*casa*) neglected; (*persona*) careless, negligent.

traseco'lato, a *ag* astounded, amazed.

trasferi'mento *sm* transfer; (*trasloco*) removal, move.

trasfe'rire *vt* to transfer; **~rsi** *vr* to move; **tras'ferta** *sf* transfer; (*indennità*) travelling expenses *pl*; (*SPORT*) away game.

trasfigu'rare *vt* to transfigure.

trasfor'mare *vt* to transform, change; **trasforma'tore** *sm* transformer; **trasformazi'one** *sf* transformation.

trasfusi'one *sf* (*MED*) transfusion.

trasgre'dire *vt* to disobey, contravene.

tras'lato, a *ag* metaphorical, figurative.

traslo'care *vt* to move, transfer; **~rsi** *vr* to move; **tras'loco, chi** *sm* removal.

tras'messo, a *pp di* **trasmettere**.

tras'mettere *vt* (*passare*): **~ qc a qd** to pass sth on to sb; (*mandare*) to send; (*TECN, TEL, MED*) to transmit; (*TV, RADIO*) to broadcast; **trasmetti'tore** *sm* transmitter; **trasmissi'one** *sf* (*gen, FISICA, TECN*) transmission; (*passaggio*) transmission, passing on; (*TV, RADIO*) broadcast; **trasmit'tente** *sf* transmitting o broadcasting station.

traso'gnato, a [trasoɲ'ɲato] *ag* dreamy.

traspa'rente *ag* transparent; **traspa'renza** *sf* transparency.

traspa'rire *vi* (2) to show (through).

traspi'rare *vi* (2) to perspire; (*fig*) to come to light, leak out; **traspirazi'one** *sf* perspiration.

traspor'tare *vt* to carry, move; (*merce*) to transport, convey; **lasciarsi ~ (da qc)** to let o.s. be carried away (by sth); **tras'porto** *sm* transport.

trastul'lare *vt* to amuse; **~rsi** *vr* to amuse o.s.

trasu'dare *vi* (2) (*filtrare*) to ooze; (*sudare*) to sweat // *vt* to ooze with.

trasver'sale *ag* transverse, cross(-); running at right angles.

trasvo'lare *vt* to fly over // *vi* (*fig*): **~ su** to barely touch on.

'tratta *sf* (*ECON*) draft; (*di persone*): **la ~ delle bianche** the white slave trade.

tratta'mento *sm* treatment; (*servizio*) service.

trat'tare *vt* (*gen*) to treat; (*commerciare*) to deal in; (*svolgere: argomento*) to discuss, deal with; (*negoziare*) to negotiate // vi: ~ **di** to deal with; ~ **con** (*persona*) to deal with; **si tratta di ...** it's about ...; **tratta'tive** *sfpl* negotiations; **trat'tato** *sm* (*testo*) treatise; (*accordo*) treaty; **trattazi'one** *sf* treatment.

tratteggi'are [tratted'dʒare] *vt* (*disegnare: a tratti*) to sketch, outline; (*: col tratteggio*) to hatch.

tratte'nere *vt* (*far rimanere: persona*) to detain; (*intrattenere: ospiti*) to entertain; (*tenere, frenare, reprimere*) to hold back, keep back; (*astenersi dal consegnare*) to hold, keep; (*detrarre: somma*) to deduct; ~**rsi** *vr* (*astenersi*) to restrain o.s., stop o.s.; (*soffermarsi*) to stay, remain.

tratteni'mento *sm* entertainment; (*festa*) party.

tratte'nuta *sf* deduction.

trat'tino *sm* dash; (*in parole composte*) hyphen.

'tratto, a *pp di* **trarre** // *sm* (*di penna, matita*) stroke; (*parte*) part, piece; (*di strada*) stretch; (*di mare, cielo*) expanse; (*di tempo*) period (of time); (*modo di comportarsi*) ways *pl*, manners *pl*; ~**i** *smpl* (*lineamenti, caratteristiche*) features; **a un** ~, **d'un** ~ suddenly.

trat'tore *sm* tractor.

tratto'ria *sf* restaurant.

'trauma, i *sm* trauma; **trau'matico, a, ci, che** *ag* traumatic.

tra'vaglio [tra'vaʎʎo] *sm* (*angoscia*) pain, suffering; (*MED*) pains *pl*; ~ **di parto** labour pains.

trava'sare *vt* to decant.

trava'tura *sf* beams *pl*.

tra'versa *sf* (*trave*) crosspiece; (*via*) sidestreet; (*FERR*) sleeper; (*CALCIO*) crossbar.

traver'sare *vt* to cross; **traver'sata** *sf* crossing; (*AER*) flight, trip.

traver'sie *sfpl* mishaps, misfortunes.

traver'sina *sf* (*FERR*) sleeper.

tra'verso, a *ag* oblique; **di** ~ *ag* askew // *av* sideways; **andare di** ~ (*cibo*) to go down the wrong way; **guardare di** ~ to look askance at.

travesti'mento *sm* disguise.

traves'tire *vt* to disguise; ~**rsi** *vr* to disguise o.s.; **traves'tito, a** *ag* disguised, in disguise // *sm* (*PSIC*) transvestite.

travi'are *vt* (*fig*) to lead astray.

travi'sare *vt* (*fig*) to distort, misrepresent.

tra'volgere [tra'voldʒere] *vt* to sweep away, carry away; (*fig*) to overwhelm; **tra'volto, a** *pp di* **travolgere**.

trazi'one [trat'tsjone] *sf* traction.

tre *num* three.

trebbi'are *vt* to thresh; **trebbia'trice** *sf* threshing machine.

'treccia, ce ['trettʃa] *sf* plait, braid.

tre'cento [tre'tʃento] *num* three hundred // *sm*: **il T**~ the fourteenth century.

'tredici ['treditʃi] *num* thirteen.

'tregua *sf* truce; (*fig*) respite.

tre'mare *vi* to tremble, shake; ~ **di**

(*freddo etc*) to shiver o tremble with; (*paura*) to shake o tremble with.

tre'mendo, a *ag* terrible, awful.

tremen'tina *sf* turpentine.

tre'mila *num* three thousand.

'tremito *sm* trembling *q*; shaking *q*; shivering *q*.

tremo'lare *vi* to tremble; (*luce*) to flicker; (*foglie*) to quiver.

tre'more *sm* tremor.

'treno *sm* train; ~ **di gomme** set of tyres; ~ **merci** goods train; ~ **viaggiatori** passenger train.

'trenta *num* thirty; **tren'tesimo, a** *ag* thirtieth; **tren'tina** *sf*: **una trentina (di)** thirty or so, about thirty.

'trepido, a *ag* anxious.

treppi'ede *sm* tripod; (*CUC*) trivet.

'tresca, sche *sf* (*fig*) intrigue; (*: relazione amorosa*) affair.

'trespolo *sm* trestle.

tri'angolo *sm* triangle.

tribolazi'one [tribolat'tsjone] *sf* suffering, tribulation.

tribù *sf inv* tribe.

tri'buna *sf* (*podio*) platform; (*in aule etc*) gallery; (*di stadio*) stand.

tribu'nale *sm* court.

tribu'tare *vt* to bestow.

tribu'tario, a *ag* (*imposta*) fiscal, tax *cpd*; (*GEO*): **essere** ~ **di** to be a tributary of.

tri'buto *sm* tax; (*fig*) tribute.

tri'checo, chi [tri'keko] *sm* (*ZOOL*) walrus.

tri'ciclo [tri'tʃiklo] *sm* tricycle.

trico'lore *ag* three-coloured // *sm* tricolour; (*bandiera italiana*) Italian flag.

tri'dente *sm* trident.

tri'foglio [tri'fɔʎʎo] *sm* clover.

'triglia ['triʎʎa] *sf* red mullet.

trigonome'tria *sf* trigonometry.

tril'lare *vi* (*MUS*) to trill.

tri'mestre *sm* period of three months; (*INS*) term; (*COMM*) quarter.

'trina *sf* lace.

trin'cea [trin'tʃea] *sf* trench; **trince'rare** *vt* to entrench.

trinci'are [trin'tʃare] *vt* to cut up.

Trinità *sf* (*REL*) Trinity.

'trio, pl 'trii *sm* trio.

trion'fale *ag* triumphal, triumphant.

trion'fante *ag* triumphant.

trion'fare *vi* to triumph, win; ~ **su** to triumph over, overcome; **tri'onfo** *sm* triumph.

tripli'care *vt* to triple.

'triplice ['triplitʃe] *ag* triple; **in** ~ **copia** in triplicate.

'triplo, a *ag* triple; treble // *sm*: **il** ~ **(di)** three times as much (as); **una somma** ~**a** a sum three times as great, three times as much money.

'tripode *sm* tripod.

'trippa *sf* (*CUC*) tripe.

'triste *ag* sad; (*luogo*) dreary, gloomy; **tris'tezza** *sf* sadness; gloominess.

'tristo, a *ag* (*cattivo*) wicked, evil;

(*meschino*) sorry, poor; **fare una ~a figura** to cut a poor figure.

trita'carne *sm inv* mincer.

tri'tare *vt* to mince.

'trito, a *ag* (*tritato*) minced.

'trittico, ci *sm* (ARTE) triptych.

tri'vella *sf* drill; **trivel'lare** *vt* to drill.

trivi'ale *ag* vulgar, low.

tro'feo *sm* trophy.

'trogolo *sm* (*per maiali*) trough.

'troia *sf* (ZOOL) sow.

'tromba *sf* (MUS) trumpet; (AUT) horn; **~ d'aria** whirlwind; **~ delle scale** stairwell.

trom'bone *sm* trombone.

trom'bosi *sf* thrombosis.

tron'care *vt* to cut off; (*spezzare*) to break off.

'tronco, a, chi, che *ag* cut off; broken off; (LING) truncated; (*fig*) cut short // *sm* (BOT, ANAT) trunk; (*fig: tratto*) section; (: *pezzo: di lancia*) stump.

troneggi'are [troned'dʒare] *vi:* **~ (su)** to tower (over).

'tronfio, a *ag* conceited.

'trono *sm* throne.

tropi'cale *ag* tropical.

'tropico, ci *sm* tropic; **~ci** *smpl* tropics.

'troppo, a *det, pronome* (*quantità*) too much; (*numero*) too many // *av* (*con vb*) too much; (*con ag, av*) too; **di ~**: **qualche tazza di ~** a few cups too many, a few extra cups; **3000 lire di ~** 3000 lire too much.

'trota *sf* trout.

trot'tare *vi* to trot; **trotterel'lare** *vi* to trot along; (*bambino*) to toddle; **'trotto** *sm* trot.

'trottola *sf* spinning top.

tro'vare *vt* to find; (*giudicare*): **trovo che** I find *o* think that; **~rsi** *vr* (*incontrarsi*) to meet; (*essere, stare*) to be; (*arrivare, capitare*) to find o.s.; **andare a ~ qd** to go and see sb; **~ qd colpevole** to find sb guilty; **~rsi bene** to feel well; **tro'vata** *sf* good idea.

truc'care *vt* (*falsare*) to fake; (*attore etc*) to make up; (*travestire*) to disguise; (SPORT) to fix; (AUT) to soup up; **~rsi** *vr* to make up (one's face); **trucca'tore, 'trice** *sm/f* (CINEMA, TEATRO) make-up artist.

'trucco, chi *sm* trick; (*cosmesi*) make-up.

'truce ['trutʃe] *ag* fierce.

truci'dare [trutʃi'dare] *vt* to slaughter.

'truciolo ['trutʃolo] *sm* shaving.

'truffa *sf* fraud, swindle; **truf'fare** *vt* to swindle, cheat.

'truppa *sf* troop.

tu *pronome* you; **dare del ~ a qd** to address sb as 'tu'.

'tua *vedi* **tuo.**

'tuba *sf* (MUS) tuba; (*cappello*) top hat.

tu'bare *vi* to coo.

tuba'tura *sf*, **tubazi'one** [tubat'tsjone] *sf* piping *q*, pipes *pl*.

tuberco'losi *sf* tuberculosis.

tu'betto *sm* tube.

'tubo *sm* tube; pipe; **~ digerente** (ANAT) alimentary canal, digestive tract; **~ di scappamento** (AUT) exhaust pipe.

'tue *vedi* **tuo.**

tuf'fare *vt* to plunge, dip; **~rsi** *vr* to plunge, dive; **'tuffo** *sm* dive; (*breve bagno*) dip.

tu'gurio *sm* hovel.

tuli'pano *sm* tulip.

tumefazi'one [tumefat'tsjone] *sf* (MED) swelling.

'tumido, a *ag* swollen.

tu'more *sm* (MED) tumour.

tu'multo *sm* uproar, commotion; (*sommossa*) riot; (*fig*) turmoil; **tumultu'oso, a** *ag* rowdy, unruly; (*fig*) turbulent, stormy.

'tunica, che *sf* tunic.

Tuni'sia *sf:* **la ~** Tunisia.

'tuo, 'tua, tu'oi, 'tue *det:* **il ~, la tua** *etc* your // *pronome:* **il ~, la tua** *etc* yours.

tuo'nare *vi* to thunder; **tuona** it is thundering, there's some thunder.

tu'ono *sm* thunder.

tu'orlo *sm* yolk.

tu'racciolo [tu'rattʃolo] *sm* cap, top; (*di sughero*) cork.

tu'rare *vt* to stop, plug; (*con sughero*) to cork; **~rsi il naso** to hold one's nose.

turba'mento *sm* disturbance; (*di animo*) anxiety, agitation.

tur'bante *sm* turban.

tur'bare *vt* to disturb, trouble.

tur'bina *sf* turbine.

turbi'nare *vi* to whirl.

'turbine *sm* whirlwind; **~ di polvere/sabbia** dust/sandstorm.

turbo'lento, a *ag* turbulent; (*ragazzo*) boisterous, unruly.

turbo'lenza [turbo'lɛntsa] *sf* turbulence.

turboreat'tore *sm* turbojet engine.

tur'chese [tur'kese] *sf* turquoise.

Tur'chia [tur'kia] *sf:* **la ~** Turkey.

tur'chino, a [tur'kino] *ag* deep blue.

'turco, a, chi, che *ag* Turkish // *sm/f* Turk/Turkish woman // *sm* (LING) Turkish.

tu'rismo *sm* tourism; tourist industry; **tu'rista, i, e** *sm/f* tourist; **tu'ristico, a, ci, che** *ag* tourist *cpd*.

'turno *sm* turn; (*di lavoro*) shift; **di ~** (*soldato, medico, custode*) on duty; **a ~** (*rispondere*) in turn; (*lavorare*) in shifts; **fare a ~ a fare qc** to take turns to do sth; **è il suo ~** it's your (*o his etc*) turn.

'turpe *ag* filthy, vile; **turpi'loquio** *sm* obscene language.

'tuta *sf* overalls *pl*; (SPORT) tracksuit.

tu'tela *sf* (DIR: *di minore*) guardianship; (: *protezione*) protection; (*difesa*) defence; **tute'lare** *vt* to protect, defend.

tu'tore, 'trice *sm/f* (DIR) guardian.

tutta'via *cong* nevertheless, yet.

'tutto, a *det all;* **~ il latte** all the milk, the whole of the milk; **~a la sera** all evening, the whole evening; **~a una bottiglia** a whole bottle; **~i i ragazzi** all the boys; ~ **e le sere** every evening // *pronome* everything, all; ~**i(e)** *pronome pl* all (of them); (*ognuno*) everyone // *av* (*completamente*) completely, quite // *sm* whole; (*l'intero*): **il** ~ all of it, the whole lot; ~**i e due** both *o* each of us (*o* them); ~**i e cinque** all five of us (*o* them); **a** ~ **a velocità** at full *o* top speed; **del** ~ completely; **in** ~ in all; **tutt'altro** on the contrary; (*affatto*) not at all; **tutt'altro che felice** anything but happy; ~ **considerato** all things considered; **a tutt'oggi** so far, up till now; **tutt'al più** at (the) most; (*al più tardi*) at the latest; ~**e le volte che** every time (that).

tutto'fare *ag inv*: **domestica** ~ general maid; **ragazzo** ~ office boy // *sm inv* handyman.

tut'tora *av* still.

U

ubbidi'ente *ag* obedient; **ubbidi'enza** *sf* obedience.

ubbi'dire *vi* to obey; ~ **a** to obey; (*sog: veicolo, macchina*) to respond to.

ubiquità *sf*: **non ho il dono dell'**~ I can't be everywhere at once.

ubria'care *vt*: ~ **qd** to get sb drunk; (*sog: alcool*) to make sb drunk; (*fig*) to make sb's head spin *o* reel; ~**rsi** *vr* to get drunk; ~**rsi di** (*fig*) to become intoxicated with.

ubria'chezza [ubria'kettsa] *sf* drunkenness.

ubri'aco, a, chi, che *ag, sm/f* drunk.

uccelli'era [uttʃel'ljɛra] *sf* aviary.

uc'cello [ut'tʃello] *sm* bird.

uc'cidere [ut'tʃidere] *vt* to kill; ~**rsi** *vr* (*suicidarsi*) to kill o.s.; (*perdere la vita*) to be killed; **uccisi'one** *sf* killing; **uc'ciso, a** *pp di* **uccidere; ucci'sore, uccidi'trice** *sm/f* killer.

u'dibile *ag* audible.

udi'enza [u'djɛntsa] *sf* audience; (*DIR*) hearing, sitting.

u'dire *vt* to hear; **udi'tivo, a** *ag* auditory; **u'dito** *sm* (sense of) hearing; **udi'tore, 'trice** *sm/f* listener; (*INS*) unregistered student (*attending lectures*); **udi'torio** *sm* (*persone*) audience.

uffici'ale [uffi'tʃale] *ag* official // *sm* (*AMM*) official, officer; (*MIL*) officer; ~ **di stato civile** registrar.

uf'ficio [uf'fitʃo] *sm* (*gen*) office; (*dovere*) duty; (*mansione*) task, function, job; (*agenzia*) agency, bureau; (*REL*) service; **d'**~ *ag office cpd*; official // *av* officially; ~ **di collocamento** employment office; ~ **postale** post office.

ufficio'oso, a [uffi'tʃoso] *ag* unofficial.

'ufo: a ~ *av* free, for nothing.

uggi'oso, a [ud'dʒoso] *ag* tiresome; (*tempo*) dull.

uguagli'anza [ugwaʎ'ʎantsa] *sf* equality.

uguagli'are [ugwaʎ'ʎare] *vt* to make equal; (*essere uguale*) to equal, be equal to; (*livellare*) to level; ~**rsi a** *o* **con qd** (*paragonarsi*) to compare o.s. to sb.

ugu'ale *ag* equal; (*identico*) identical, the same; (*uniforme*) level, even; **ugual'mente** *av* equally; (*lo stesso*) all the same.

'ulcera ['ultʃera] *sf* ulcer.

u'liva *etc* = **oliva** *etc*.

ulteri'ore *ag* further.

ulti'mare *vt* to finish, complete.

ulti'matum *sm inv* ultimatum.

'ultimo, a *ag* (*finale*) last; (*estremo*) farthest, utmost; (*recente: notizia, moda*) latest; (*fig: sommo, fondamentale*) ultimate // *sm/f* last (one); **fino all'**~ to the last, until the end; **da** ~, **in** ~ in the end; **abitare all'**~ **piano** to live on the top floor.

ultravio'letto, a *ag* ultraviolet.

ulu'lare *vi* to howl; **ulu'lato** *sm* howling *q*; howl.

umanità *sf* humanity; **umani'tario, a** *ag* humanitarian.

u'mano, a *ag* human; (*comprensivo*) humane.

umbi'lico *sm* = **ombelico**.

umet'tare *vt* to dampen, moisten.

umidità *sf* dampness; humidity.

'umido, a *ag* damp; (*mano, occhi*) moist; (*clima*) humid // *sm* dampness, damp; **carne in** ~ stew.

'umile *ag* humble.

umili'are *vt* to humiliate; ~**rsi** *vr* to humble o.s.; **umiliazi'one** *sf* humiliation.

umiltà *sf* humility, humbleness.

u'more *sm* (*disposizione d'animo*) mood; (*carattere*) temper; **di buon/cattivo** ~ in a good/bad mood.

umo'rismo *sm* humour; **avere il senso dell'**~ to have a sense of humour; **umo'rista, i, e** *sm/f* humorist; **umo'ristico, a, ci, che** *ag* humorous, funny.

un, un', una *vedi* **uno**.

u'nanime *ag* unanimous; **unanimità** *sf* unanimity; **all'unanimità** unanimously.

unci'netto [untʃi'netto] *sm* crochet hook.

un'cino [un'tʃino] *sm* hook.

'undici ['unditʃi] *num* eleven.

'ungere ['undʒere] *vt* to grease, oil; (*REL*) to anoint; (*fig*) to flatter, butter up; ~**rsi** *vr* (*sporcarsi*) to get covered in grease; ~**rsi con la crema** to put on cream.

unghe'rese [unge'rese] *ag, sm/f, sm* Hungarian.

Unghe'ria [unge'ria] *sf*: **l'**~ Hungary.

'unghia ['ungja] *sf* (*ANAT*) nail; (*di animale*) claw; (*di rapace*) talon; (*di cavallo*) hoof; **unghi'ata** *sf* (*graffio*) scratch.

ungu'ento *sm* ointment.

'unico, a, ci, che *ag* (*solo*) only; (*ineguagliabile*) unique; (*singolo: binario*) single.

uni'corno *sm* unicorn.

unifi'care *vt* to unite, unify; (*sistemi*) to standardize; **unificazi'one** *sf* uniting; unification; standardization.

uni'forme *ag* uniform; (*superficie*) even // *sf* (*divisa*) uniform; **uniformità** *sf* uniformity; evenness.

unilate'rale *ag* one-sided; (*DIR*) unilateral.

uni'one *sf* union; (*fig: concordia*) unity, harmony; **l'U~ Sovietica** the Soviet Union.

u'nire *vt* to unite; (*congiungere*) to join, connect; (: *ingredienti, colori*) to combine; (*in matrimonio*) to unite, join together; **~rsi** *vr* to unite; (*in matrimonio*) to be joined together; **~ qc a** to unite sth with; to join *o* connect sth with; to combine sth with; **~rsi a** (*gruppo, società*) to join.

u'nisono *sm*: **all'~** in unison.

unità *sf inv* (*unione, concordia*) unity; (*MAT, MIL, COMM, di misura*) unit; **uni'tario, a** *ag* unitary; **prezzo unitario** price per unit.

u'nito, a *ag* (*paese*) united; (*famiglia*) close; (*tinta*) solid.

univer'sale *ag* universal; general.

università *sf inv* university; **universi- 'tario, a** *ag* university *cpd* // *sm/f* (*studente*) university student; (*insegnante*) academic, university lecturer.

uni'verso *sm* universe.

'uno, a *det, num* (*dav sm* **un** + *C, V, uno* + *s impura, gn, pn, ps, x, z; dav sf* **un'** + *V,* **una** + *C*) *det* a, an + *vocale* // *num* one // *pronome* (*un tale*) someone, somebody; (*con valore impersonale*) one, you // *sf*: **è l'~a** it's one o'clock.

'unto, a *pp di* **ungere** // *ag* greasy, oily // *sm* grease; **untu'oso, a** *ag* greasy, oily.

u'omo, *pl* **u'omini** *sm* man; **da ~** (*abito, scarpe*) men's, for men; **~ d'affari** businessman; for men; **~ di paglia** stooge; **~ rana** frogman.

u'opo *sm*: **all'~** if necessary.

u'ovo, *pl(f)* **u'ova** *sm* egg; **~ affogato** poached egg; **~ bazzotto/sodo** soft/hard-boiled egg; **~ alla coque** boiled egg; **~ di Pasqua** Easter egg; **uova strapazzate** scrambled eggs.

ura'gano *sm* hurricane.

u'ranio *sm* (*CHIM*) uranium.

urba'nesimo *sm* urbanization.

urba'nistica *sf* town planning.

ur'bano, a *ag* urban, city *cpd*, town *cpd*; (*fig*) urbane.

ur'gente [ur'dʒɛnte] *ag* urgent; **ur'genza** *sf* urgency; **in caso d'urgenza** in (case of) an emergency; **d'urgenza** *ag* emergency // *av* urgently, as a matter of urgency.

urgere ['urdʒere] *vi* to be urgent; to be needed urgently.

u'rina *sf* = **orina**.

ur'lare *vi* (*persona*) to scream, yell; (*animale, vento*) to howl // *vt* to scream, yell.

'urlo, *pl(m)* **'urli,** *pl(f)* **'urla** *sm* scream, yell; howl.

'urna *sf* urn; (*elettorale*) ballot-box; **andare alle ~e** to go to the polls.

urrà *escl* hurrah!

U.R.S.S. *abbr f*: **l'~** the USSR.

ur'tare *vt* to bump into, knock against; (*fig: irritare*) to annoy // *vi*: **~ contro** *o* **in** to bump into, knock against, crash into; (*fig: imbattersi*) to come up against; **~rsi**

vr (*reciproco: scontrarsi*) to collide; (: *fig*) to clash; (*irritarsi*) to get annoyed; **'urto** *sm* (*colpo*) knock, bump; (*scontro*) crash, collision; (*fig*) clash.

U.S.A. ['uza] *abbr mpl*: **gli ~** the U.S.A.

u'sanza [u'zantsa] *sf* custom; (*moda*) fashion.

u'sare *vt* to use, employ // *vi* (*servirsi*): **~ di** to use; (: *diritto*) to exercise; (*essere di moda*) to be fashionable; (*essere solito*): **~ fare** to be in the habit of doing, be accustomed to doing; **u'sato, a** *ag* used; (*consumato*) worn; (*di seconda mano*) used, second-hand; **secondo l'usato** as usual; **fuori dell'usato** unusual.

usci'ere [uʃ'ʃɛre] *sm* usher.

'uscio ['uʃʃo] *sm* door.

u'scire [uʃ'ʃire] *vi* (2) (*gen*) to come out; (*partire, andare a passeggio, a uno spettacolo etc*) to go out; (*essere sorteggiato: numero*) to come up; **~ da** (*gen*) to leave; (*posto*) to go (*o* come) out of, leave; (*solco, vasca etc*) to come out of; (*competenza etc*) to be outside; (*infanzia, adolescenza*) to leave behind; (*famiglia nobile etc*) to come from; **~ da** *o* **di casa** to go out; (*fig*) to leave home; **~ in automobile** to go out in the car, go for a drive; **~ di strada** (*AUT*) to go off *o* leave the road.

u'scita [uʃ'ʃita] *sf* (*passaggio, varco*) exit, way out; (*per divertimento*) outing; (*ECON: somma*) expenditure; (*TEATRO*) entrance; (*fig: battuta*) witty remark; **~ di sicurezza** emergency exit.

usi'gnolo [uziɲ'ɲɔlo] *sm* nightingale.

'uso *sm* (*utilizzazione*) use; (*esercizio*) practice; (*abitudine*) custom; **a ~ di** for (the use of); **d'~** (*corrente*) in use; **fuori ~** out of use.

usti'one *sf* burn.

usu'ale *ag* common, everyday.

u'sura *sf* usury; (*logoramento*) wear (and tear); **usu'raio** *sm* usurer.

usur'pare *vt* to usurp.

uten'sile *sm* tool, implement; **~i da cucina** kitchen utensils.

u'tente *sm/f* user.

'utero *sm* uterus.

'utile *ag* useful // *sm* (*vantaggio*) advantage, benefit; (*ECON: profitto*) profit; **utilità** *sf* usefulness *q*; use; (*vantaggio*) benefit; **utili'tario, a** *ag* utilitarian // *sf* (*AUT*) economy car.

utiliz'zare [utilid'dzare] *vt* to use, make use of, utilize; **utilizzazi'one** *sf* utilization, use.

'uva *sf* grapes *pl*; **~ passa** raisins *pl*; **~ spina** gooseberry.

V

v. (*abbr di vedi*) v.

va'cante *ag* vacant.

va'canza [va'kantsa] *sf* (*l'essere vacante*) vacancy; (*riposo, ferie*) holiday(s *pl*); (*giorno di permesso*) day off, holiday; **~e** *sfpl* (*periodo di ferie*) holidays, vacation *sg*;

essere/andare in ~ to be/go on holiday; ~**e estive** summer holiday(s).

'vacca, che sf cow.

vacci'nare [vattʃi'nare] vt to vaccinate; **vaccinazi'one** sf vaccination.

vac'cino [vat'tʃino] sm (MED) vaccine.

vacil'lare [vatʃil'lare] vi to sway, wobble; (luce) to flicker; (fig: memoria, coraggio) to be failing, falter.

'vacuo, a ag (fig) empty, vacuous // sm vacuum.

vaga'bondo, a sm/f tramp, vagrant; (fannullone) idler, loafer.

va'gare vi to wander.

vagheggi'are [vaged'dʒare] vt to long for, dream of.

va'gina [va'dʒina] sf vagina.

va'gire [va'dʒire] vi to whimper.

'vaglia ['vaʎʎa] sm inv money order; ~ **postale** postal order.

vagli'are [vaʎ'ʎare] vt to sift; (fig) to weigh up; **'vaglio** sm sieve.

'vago, a, ghi, ghe ag vague.

va'gone sm (FERR: per passeggeri) coach; (: per merci) truck, wagon; ~ **letto** sleeper, sleeping car; ~ **ristorante** dining o restaurant car.

vai'olo sm smallpox.

va'langa, ghe sf avalanche.

va'lente ag able, talented.

va'lere vi (2) (avere forza, potenza) to have influence; (essere valido) to be valid; (avere vigore, autorità) to hold, apply; (essere capace: poeta, studente) to be good, be able // vt (prezzo, sforzo) to be worth; (corrispondere) to correspond to; (procurare): ~ **qc a qd** to earn sb sth; ~**rsi di** to make use of, take advantage of; **far** ~ (autorità etc) to assert; **vale a dire** that is to say; ~ **la pena** to be worth the effort o worth it.

va'levole ag valid.

vali'care vt to cross.

'valico, chi sm (passo) pass.

validità sf validity.

'valido, a ag valid; (in buona salute) fit; (efficace) effective; (forte) strong.

valige'ria [validʒe'ria] sf leather goods pl; leather goods factory; leather goods shop.

va'ligia, gie o ge [va'lidʒa] sf (suit)case; **fare le** ~**gie** to pack (up); ~ **diplomatica** diplomatic bag.

val'lata sf valley.

'valle sf valley; **a** ~ (di fiume) downstream; **scendere a** ~ to go downhill.

val'letto sm valet.

va'lore sm (gen) value; (merito) merit, worth; (coraggio) valour, courage; (COMM: titolo) security; ~**i** smpl (oggetti preziosi) valuables; **mettere in** ~ (bene) to exploit; (fig) to highlight, show off to advantage.

valoriz'zare [valorid'dzare] vt (terreno) to develop; (fig) to make the most of.

valo'roso, a ag valorous.

'valso, a pp di **valere**.

va'luta sf currency, money; (BANCA): ~ **15 gennaio** interest to run from January 15th.

valu'tare vt (casa, gioiello, fig) to value; (stabilire: peso, entrate, fig) to estimate; **valutazi'one** sf valuation; estimate.

'valva sf (ZOOL, BOT) valve.

'valvola sf (TECN, ANAT) valve; (ELETTR) fuse.

'valzer ['valtser] sm inv waltz.

vam'pata sf (di fiamma) blaze; (di calore) blast; (: al viso) flush.

vam'piro sm vampire.

vanda'lismo sm vandalism.

'vandalo sm vandal.

vaneggi'are [vaned'dʒare] vi to rave.

'vanga, ghe sf spade; **van'gare** vt to dig.

van'gelo [van'dʒɛlo] sm gospel.

va'niglia [va'niʎʎa] sf vanilla.

vanità sf vanity; **vani'toso, a** ag vain, conceited.

'vano, a ag vain // sm (spazio) space; (apertura) opening; (stanza) room.

van'taggio [van'taddʒo] sm advantage; **portarsi in** ~ (SPORT) to take the lead; **vantaggi'oso, a** ag advantageous; favourable.

van'tare vt to praise, speak highly of; ~**rsi** vr to boast; **vante'ria** sf boasting; **'vanto** sm boasting; (merito) virtue, merit; (gloria) pride.

'vanvera sf: **a** ~ haphazardly; **parlare a** ~ to talk nonsense.

va'pore sm vapour; (anche: ~ **acqueo**) steam; (nave) steamer; **a** ~ (turbina etc) steam cpd; **al** ~ (CUC) steamed; **vapo-'retto** sm steamer; **vapori'era** sf (FERR) steam engine; **vaporiz'zare** vt to vaporize.

va'rare vt (NAUT, fig) to launch; (DIR) to pass.

var'care vt to cross.

'varco, chi sm passage; **aprirsi un** ~ **tra la folla** to push one's way through the crowd.

vari'abile ag variable; (tempo, umore) changeable, variable // sf (MAT) variable.

vari'ante sf variant.

vari'are vt to vary // vi to vary; (subire variazioni) to vary, change; ~ **di camera/opinione** to change rooms/one's mind; **variazi'one** sf variation; change.

va'rice [va'ritʃe] sf varicose vein.

vari'cella [vari'tʃɛlla] sf chickenpox.

vari'coso, a ag varicose.

varie'gato, a ag variegated.

varietà sf inv variety // sm inv variety show.

'vario, a ag varied; (parecchi: col sostantivo al pl) various; (mutevole: umore) changeable; **vario'pinto, a** ag multicoloured.

'varo sm (NAUT, fig) launch; (di leggi) passing.

va'saio sm potter.

'vasca, sche sf basin; (anche: ~ da bagno) bathtub, bath.

va'scello [vaʃˈʃello] sm (NAUT) vessel, ship.

vase'lina sf vaseline.

vasel'lame sm china; ~ d'oro/d'argento gold/silver plate.

'vaso sm (recipiente) pot; (: barattolo) jar; (: decorativo) vase; (ANAT) vessel; ~ da fiori vase; (per piante) flowerpot.

vas'soio sm tray.

'vasto, a ag vast, immense.

Vati'cano sm: il ~ the Vatican.

ve pronome, av vedi vi.

vecchi'aia [vekˈkjaja] sf old age.

'vecchio, a [ˈvekkjo] ag old // sm/f old man/woman; i ~i the old.

'vece [ˈvetʃe] sf: in ~ di in the place of, for; fare le ~i di qd to take sb's place.

ve'dere vt, vi to see; ~rsi vr to meet, see one another; avere a che ~ con to have sth to do with; far ~ qc a qd to show sb sth; farsi ~ to show o.s.; (farsi vivo) to show one's face.

ve'detta sf (sentinella, posto) look-out; (NAUT) patrol boat.

'vedovo, a sm/f widower/widow.

ve'duta sf view.

vee'mente ag vehement; violent.

vege'tale [vedʒeˈtale] ag, sm vegetable.

vege'tare [vedʒeˈtare] vi to vegetate; vegetari'ano, a ag, sm/f vegetarian; vegetazi'one sf vegetation.

'vegeto, a [ˈvedʒeto] ag (pianta) thriving; (persona) strong, vigorous.

'veglia [ˈveʎʎa] sf wakefulness; (sorveglianza) watch; (trattenimento) evening gathering; stare a ~ to keep watch; fare la ~ a un malato to watch over a sick person.

vegli'are [veʎˈʎare] vi to be awake; to stay o sit up; (stare vigile) to watch; to keep watch // vt (malato, morto) to watch over, sit up with.

ve'icolo sm vehicle.

'vela sf (NAUT: tela) sail; (sport) sailing.

ve'lare vt to veil; ~rsi vr (occhi, luna) to mist over; (voce) to become husky; ~rsi il viso to cover one's face (with a veil); ve'lato, a ag veiled.

veleggi'are [veledˈdʒare] vi to sail; (AER) to glide.

ve'leno sm poison; vele'noso, a ag poisonous.

veli'ero sm sailing ship.

ve'lina sf (anche: carta ~: per imballare) tissue paper; (: per copie) flimsy paper; (copia) carbon copy.

ve'livolo sm aircraft.

velleità sf inv vain ambition, vain desire.

'vello sm fleece.

vel'luto sm velvet; ~ a coste cord.

'velo sm veil; (tessuto) voile.

ve'loce [veˈlotʃe] ag fast, quick // av fast, quickly; velo'cista, i, e sm/f (SPORT) sprinter; velocità sf speed; (AUT: marcia) gear; velocità di crociera cruising speed; velocità del suono speed of sound.

ve'lodromo sm velodrome.

'vena sf (gen) vein; (filone) vein, seam; (fig: ispirazione) inspiration; (: umore) mood; essere in ~ di qc to be in the mood for sth.

ve'nale ag (prezzo, valore) market cpd; (fig) venal; mercenary.

ven'demmia sf (raccolta) grape harvest; (quantità d'uva) grape crop, grapes pl; (vino ottenuto) vintage; vendemmi'are vt to harvest // vi to harvest the grapes.

'vendere vt to sell; 'vendesi' 'for sale'.

ven'detta sf revenge.

vendi'care vt to avenge; ~rsi vr: ~rsi (di) to avenge o.s. (for); (per rancore) to take one's revenge (for); vendica'tivo, a ag vindictive.

'vendita sf sale; la ~ (attività) selling; (smercio) sales pl; in ~ on sale; ~ all'asta sale by auction; vendi'tore sm seller, vendor; (gestore di negozio) trader, dealer.

ve'nefico, a, ci, che ag poisonous.

vene'rabile ag, vene'rando, a ag venerable.

vene'rare vt to venerate.

venerdì sm inv Friday; di o il ~ on Fridays; V~ Santo Good Friday.

ve'nereo, a ag venereal.

Ve'nezia [veˈnɛttsja] sf Venice; vene-zi'ano, a ag, sm/f Venetian.

veni'ale ag venial.

ve'nire vi (2) to come; (riuscire: dolce, fotografia) to turn out; (come ausiliare: essere): viene ammirato da tutti he is admired by everyone; ~ da to come from; quanto viene? how much does it cost?; far ~ (mandare a chiamare) to send for; ~ giù to come down; ~ meno (svenire) to faint; ~ meno a qc to fail in sth; ~ su to come up; ~ via to come away.

ven'taglio [venˈtaʎʎo] sm fan.

ven'tata sf gust (of wind).

ven'tenne ag: una ragazza ~ a twenty-year-old girl, a girl of twenty.

ven'tesimo, a ag, sm twentieth.

'venti num twenty.

venti'lare vt to ventilate; (fig: esaminare) to discuss; ventila'tore sm ventilator, fan; ventilazi'one sf ventilation.

ven'tina sf: una ~ (di) around twenty, twenty or so.

'vento sm wind.

ven'tosa sf (ZOOL) sucker; (di gomma) suction pad.

ven'toso, a ag windy.

'ventre sm stomach.

ven'triloquo sm ventriloquist.

ven'tura sf (good) fortune.

ven'turo, a ag next, coming.

ve'nuto, a pp di venire // sf coming, arrival.

vera'mente av really.

ve'randa sf veranda(h).

ver'bale *ag* verbal // *sm* (*di riunione*) minutes *pl*.

'verbo *sm* (*LING*) verb; (*parola*) word; (*REL*): il V~ the Word.

ver'boso, a *ag* verbose, wordy.

'verde *ag, sm* green; **essere al ~** to be broke; **~ bottiglia/oliva** *ag inv* bottle/olive green.

verde'rame *sm* verdigris.

ver'detto *sm* verdict.

ver'dura *sf* vegetables *pl*.

vere'condo, a *ag* modest.

'verga, ghe *sf* rod.

ver'gato a *ag* (*foglio*) ruled.

vergi'nale [verdʒi'nale] *ag* virginal.

'vergine ['verdʒine] *sf* virgin; (*dello zodiaco*): **V~** Virgo // *ag* virgin; (*ragazza*): **essere ~** to be a virgin; **verginità** *sf* virginity.

ver'gogna [ver'goɲɲa] *sf* shame; (*timidezza*) shyness, embarrassment; **vergo'gnarsi** *vr*: **vergognarsi (di)** to be *o* feel ashamed (of); to be shy (about), be embarrassed (about); **vergo'gnoso, a** *ag* ashamed; (*timido*) shy, embarrassed; (*causa di vergogna: azione*) shameful.

ve'ridico, a, ci, che *ag* truthful.

ve'rifica, che *sf* checking *q*, check.

verifi'care *vt* (*controllare*) to check; (*confermare*) to confirm, bear out.

verità *sf inv* truth.

veriti'ero, a *ag* (*che dice la verità*) truthful; (*conforme a verità*) true.

'verme *sm* worm.

vermi'celli [vermi'tʃelli] *smpl* vermicelli *sg*.

ver'miglio [ver'miʎʎo] *sm* vermilion, scarlet.

'vermut *sm inv* vermouth.

ver'nacolo *sm* vernacular.

ver'nice [ver'nitʃe] *sf* (*colorazione*) paint; (*trasparente*) varnish; (*pelle*) patent leather; (*fig*) veneer; **vernici'are** *vt* to paint; to varnish; **vernicia'tura** *sf* painting; varnishing.

'vero, a *ag* (*veridico: fatti, testimonianza*) true; (*autentico*) real // *sm* (*verità*) truth; (*realtà*) (real) life; **un ~ e proprio delinquente** a real criminal, an out and out criminal.

vero'simile *ag* likely, probable.

ver'ruca, che *sf* wart.

versa'mento *sm* (*pagamento*) payment; (*deposito di denaro*) deposit.

ver'sante *sm* slopes *pl*, side.

ver'sare *vt* (*fare uscire: vino, farina*) to pour (out); (*spargere: lacrime, sangue*) to shed; (*rovesciare*) to spill; (*ECON*) to pay; (: *depositare*) to deposit, pay in; **~rsi** *vr* (*rovesciarsi*) to spill; (*fiume, folla*): **~rsi (in)** to pour (into).

versa'tile *ag* versatile.

ver'sato, a *ag*: **~ in** to be (well-) versed in.

ver'setto *sm* (*REL*) verse.

versi'one *sf* version; (*traduzione*) translation.

'verso *sm* (*di poesia*) verse, line; (*di animale, uccello, venditore ambulante*) cry; (*direzione*) direction; (*modo*) way; (*di foglio di carta*) verso; (*di moneta*) reverse; **~i** *smpl* (*poesia*) verse *sg*; **non c'è ~ di persuaderlo** there's no way of persuading him, he can't be persuaded // *prep* (*in direzione di*) toward(s); (*nei pressi di*) near, around (about); (*in senso temporale*) about, around; **~ di me** towards me; **~ pagamento** (*COMM*) upon payment.

'vertebra *sf* vertebra.

verti'cale *ag, sf* vertical.

'vertice ['vertitʃe] *sm* summit, top; (*MAT*) vertex; **conferenza al ~** (*POL*) summit conference.

ver'tigine [ver'tidʒine] *sf* dizziness *q*; dizzy spell; (*MED*) vertigo; **avere le ~i** to feel dizzy; **vertigi'noso, a** *ag* (*altezza*) dizzy; (*fig*) breathtakingly high (*o* deep *etc*).

ve'scica, che [veʃ'ʃika] *sf* (*ANAT*) bladder; (*MED*) blister.

'vescovo *sm* bishop.

'vespa *sf* wasp.

'vespro *sm* (*REL*) vespers *pl*.

ves'sillo *sm* standard; (*bandiera*) flag.

ves'taglia [ves'taʎʎa] *sf* dressing gown.

'veste *sf* garment; (*rivestimento*) covering; (*qualità, facoltà*) capacity; **~i** *sfpl* clothes, clothing *sg*; **in ~ ufficiale** (*fig*) in an official capacity; **in ~ di** in the guise of, as; **vesti'ario** *sm* wardrobe, clothes *pl*.

ves'tibolo *sm* (*entrance*) hall.

ves'tigio, pl(m) gi o pl(f) gia [ves'tidʒo] *sm* trace.

ves'tire *vt* (*bambino, malato*) to dress; (*avere indosso*) to have on, wear; **~rsi** *vr* to dress, get dressed; **ves'tito, a** *ag* dressed // *sm* garment; (*da donna*) dress; (*da uomo*) suit; **vestiti** *smpl* clothes; **vestito di bianco** dressed in white.

Ve'suvio *sm*: il ~ Vesuvius.

vete'rano, a *ag, sm/f* veteran.

veteri'nario, a *ag* veterinary // *sm* veterinary surgeon, vet // *sf* veterinary medicine.

'veto *sm inv* veto.

ve'traio *sm* glassmaker; glazier.

ve'trato, a *ag* (*porta, finestra*) glazed; (*che contiene vetro*) glass *cpd* // *sf* glass door (*o* window); (*di chiesa*) stained glass window.

vetre'ria *sf* (*stabilimento*) glassworks *sg*; (*oggetti di vetro*) glassware.

ve'trina *sf* (*di negozio*) (shop) window; (*armadio*) display cabinet; **vetri'nista, i, e** *sm/f* window dresser.

vetri'olo *sm* vitriol.

'vetro *sm* glass; (*per finestra, porta*) pane (of glass); **ve'troso, a** *ag* vitreous.

'vetta *sf* peak, summit, top.

vet'tore *sm* (*MAT, FISICA*) vector; (*DIR*) carrier.

vetto'vaglie [vetto'vaʎʎe] *sfpl* supplies.

vet'tura *sf* (*carrozza, FERR*) carriage; (*autovettura*) (motor) car.

vezzeggi'are [vettsed'dʒare] *vt* to fondle,

caress; **vezzeggia'tivo** *sm* (*LING*) term of endearment.

'vezzo ['vettso] *sm* habit; **~i** *smpl* (*smancerie*) affected ways; (*leggiadria*) charms; **vez'zoso, a** *ag* (*grazioso*) charming, pretty; (*lezioso*) affected.

vi, *dav lo, la, li, le, ne diventa* **ve** *pronome* (*oggetto*) you; (*complemento di termine*) (to) you; (*riflessivo*) yourselves; (*reciproco*) each other // *av* (*lì*) there; (*qui*) here; ~ **è/sono** there is/are.

'via *sf* (*gen*) way; (*strada*) street; (*sentiero, pista*) path, track; (*AMM: procedimento*) channels *pl* // *prep* (*passando per*) via, by way of // *av* away // *escl* go away!; (*suvvia*) come on!; (*SPORT*) go! // *sm* (*SPORT*) starting signal; **per** ~ **di** (*a causa di*) because of, on account of; **per** ~ **d'esempio** by way of example; **in** *o* **per** ~ on the way; **per** ~ **aerea** by air; (*lettere*) by airmail; ~ ~ **che** (*a mano a mano*) as; **dare il** ~ (*SPORT*) to give the starting signal; **dare il** ~ **a** (*fig*) to start; **V~ lattea** (*ASTR*) Milky Way; ~ **di mezzo** middle course; **in** ~ **provvisoria** provisionally.

viabilità *sf* (*di strada*) practicability; (*rete stradale*) roads *pl*, road network.

via'dotto *sm* viaduct.

viaggi'are [viad'dʒare] *vi* to travel; **viaggia'tore, 'trice** *ag* travelling // *sm* traveller; (*passeggero*) passenger.

vi'aggio ['vjaddʒo] *sm* travel(ling); (*tragitto*) journey, trip; ~ **di nozze** honeymoon.

vi'ale *sm* avenue.

via'vai *sm* coming and going, bustle.

vi'brare *vi* to vibrate; (*agitarsi*): ~ (**di**) to quiver (with); **vibrazi'one** *sf* vibration.

vi'cario *sm* (*apostolico etc*) vicar.

'vice [vitʃe] *sm/f* deputy // *prefisso*: ~**'console** *sm* vice-consul; ~**diret'tore** *sm* assistant manager.

vi'cenda [vi'tʃɛnda] *sf* event; **a** ~ in turn; **vicen'devole** *ag* mutual, reciprocal.

vice'versa [vitʃe'vɛrsa] *av* vice versa; **da Roma a Pisa e** ~ from Rome to Pisa and back.

vici'nanza [vitʃi'nantsa] *sf* nearness, closeness; ~**e** *sfpl* neighbourhood, vicinity.

vici'nato [vitʃi'nato] *sm* neighbourhood; (*vicini*) neighbours *pl*.

vi'cino, a [vi'tʃino] *ag* (*gen*) near; (*nello spazio*) near, nearby; (*accanto*) next; (*nel tempo*) near, close at hand // *sm/f* neighbour // *av* near, close; **da** ~ (*guardare*) close up; (*esaminare, seguire*) closely; (*conoscere*) well, intimately; **a** *prep* near (to), close to; (*accanto a*) beside; ~ **di casa** neighbour.

vicissi'tudini [vitʃissi'tudini] *sfpl* trials and tribulations.

'vicolo *sm* alley; ~ **cieco** blind alley.

vie'tare *vt* to forbid; (*AMM*) to prohibit; ~ **a qd di fare** to forbid sb to do; to prohibit sb from doing; **'vietato**

fumare/l'ingresso' 'no smoking/admittance'.

vi'gente [vi'dʒɛnte] *ag* in force.

vigi'lante [vidʒi'lante] *ag* vigilant, watchful; **vigi'lanza** *sf* vigilance.

vigi'lare [vidʒi'lare] *vt* to watch over, keep an eye on // *vi*: ~ **a** to attend to, see to; ~ **che** to make sure that, see to it that.

'vigile ['vidʒile] *ag* watchful // *sm* (*anche*: ~ **urbano**) policeman (*in towns*); ~ **del fuoco** fireman.

vi'gilia [vi'dʒilja] *sf* (*giorno antecedente*) eve; **la** ~ **di Natale** Christmas Eve.

vigli'acco, a, chi, che [viʎ'ʎakko] *ag* cowardly // *sm/f* coward.

'vigna ['viɲɲa] *sf*, **vi'gneto** [viɲ'ɲeto] *sm* vineyard.

vi'gnetta [viɲ'ɲetta] *sf* cartoon.

vi'gore *sm* vigour; (*DIR*): **essere/entrare in** ~ to be in/come into force; **vigo'roso, a** *ag* vigorous.

'vile *ag* (*spregevole*) low, mean, base; (*codardo*) cowardly.

vili'pendio *sm* contempt, scorn; public insult.

'villa *sf* villa.

vil'laggio [vil'laddʒo] *sm* village.

villa'nia *sf* rudeness, lack of manners; **fare/dire una** ~ **a qd** to be rude to sb.

vil'lano, a *ag* rude, ill-mannered // *sm* boor.

villeggi'are [villed'dʒare] *vi* to holiday, spend one's holidays; **villeggia'tura** *sf* holiday(s *pl*).

vil'lino *sm* small house (with a garden), cottage.

vil'loso, a *ag* hairy.

viltà *sf* cowardice *q*; cowardly act.

'vimine *sm* wicker; **mobili di** ~**i** wicker furniture *sg*.

'vincere ['vintʃere] *vt* (*in guerra, al gioco, a una gara*) to defeat, beat; (*premio, guerra, partita*) to win; (*fig*) to overcome, conquer // *vi* to win; ~ **qd in bellezza** to be better-looking than sb; **'vincita** *sf* win; (*denaro vinto*) winnings *pl*; **vinci'tore** *sm* winner; (*MIL*) victor.

vinco'lare *vt* to bind; (*COMM: denaro*) to tie up; **'vincolo** *sm* (*fig*) bond, tie; (*DIR: servitù*) obligation.

vi'nicolo, a *ag* wine *cpd*.

'vino *sm* wine; ~ **bianco/rosso** white/red wine.

'vinto, a *pp di* **vincere**.

vi'ola *sf* (*BOT*) violet; (*MUS*) viola // *ag, sm inv* (*colore*) purple.

vio'lare *vt* (*chiesa*) to desecrate, violate; (*giuramento, legge*) to violate; **violazi'one** *sf* desecration; violation.

violen'tare *vt* to use violence on; (*donna*) to rape.

vio'lento, a *ag* violent; **vio'lenza** *sf* violence; **violenza carnale** rape.

vio'letto, a *ag, sm* (*colore*) violet // *sf* violet.

violi'nista, i, e *sm/f* violinist.

vio'lino *sm* violin.

violon'cello [violon'tʃello] sm cello.
vi'ottolo sm path, track.
'vipera sf viper, adder.
vi'raggio [vi'raddʒo] sm (NAUT, AER) turn; (FOT) toning.
vi'rare vt (NAUT) to haul (in), heave (in) // vi (NAUT, AER) to turn; (FOT) to tone; ~ **di bordo** (NAUT) to tack.
virginità [virdʒini'ta] sf = **verginità**.
'virgola sf (LING) comma; (MAT) point; **virgo'lette** sfpl inverted commas, quotation marks.
vi'rile ag (proprio dell'uomo) masculine; (non puerile, da uomo) manly, virile; **virilità** sf masculinity; manliness; (sessuale) virility.
virtù sf inv virtue; **in** o **per ~ di** by virtue of, by.
virtu'ale ag virtual.
virtu'oso, a ag virtuous // sm/f (MUS etc) virtuoso.
viru'lento, a ag virulent.
'virus sm inv virus.
'viscere ['viʃʃere] sm (ANAT) internal organ // sfpl (di animale) entrails pl; (fig) bowels pl.
'vischio ['viskjo] sm (BOT) mistletoe; (pania) birdlime; **vischi'oso, a** ag sticky.
'viscido, a ['viʃʃido] ag slimy.
vis'conte, 'essa sm/f viscount/viscountess.
vis'coso, a ag viscous.
vi'sibile ag visible.
visi'bilio sm profusion; **andare in ~ to** go into raptures.
visibilità sf visibility.
visi'era sf (di elmo) visor; (di berretto) peak.
visi'one sf vision; **prendere ~ di qc** to examine sth, look sth over; **prima/seconda ~** (CINEMA) first/second showing.
'visita sf visit; (MED) visit, call; (: esame) examination; **visi'tare** vt to visit; (MED) to visit, call on; (: esaminare) to examine; **visita'tore, 'trice** sm/f visitor.
vi'sivo, a ag visual.
'viso sm face.
vi'sone sm mink.
'vispo, a ag quick, lively.
vis'suto, a pp di **vivere**.
'vista sf (facoltà) (eye)sight; (fatto di vedere): **la ~ di** the sight of; (veduta) view; **sparare a ~** to shoot on sight; **in ~** in sight; **perdere qd di ~** to lose sight of sb; (fig) to lose touch with sb; **a ~ d'occhio** as far as the eye can see; (fig) before one's very eyes; **far ~ di fare** to pretend to do.
'visto, a pp di **vedere** // sm visa.
vis'toso, a ag gaudy, garish; (ingente) considerable.
visu'ale ag visual.
'vita sf life; (ANAT) waist; **a ~ for** life.
vi'tale ag vital; **vitalità** sf vitality; **vita'lizio, a** ag life cpd // sm life annuity.
vita'mina sf vitamin.

'vite sf (BOT) vine; (TECN) screw.
vi'tello sm (ZOOL) calf; (carne) veal; (pelle) calfskin.
vi'ticcio [vi'tittʃo] sm (BOT) tendril.
viticol'tore sm wine grower; **viticol'tura** sf wine growing.
'vitreo, a ag vitreous; (occhio, sguardo) glassy.
'vittima sf victim.
'vitto sm food; (in un albergo etc) board; ~ **e alloggio** board and lodging.
vit'toria sf victory; **vittori'oso, a** ag victorious.
vitupe'rare vt to rail at o against.
'viva escl: ~ **il re!** long live the king!
vi'vace [vi'vatʃe] ag (vivo, animato) lively; (: mente) lively, sharp; (colore) bright; **vivacità** sf vivacity; liveliness; brightness.
vi'vaio sm (di pesci) hatchery; (AGR) nursery.
vi'vanda sf food; (piatto) dish.
vi'vente ag living, alive; **i ~i** the living.
'vivere vi (2) to live // vt to live; (passare: brutto momento) to live through, go through; (sentire: gioie, pene di qd) to share // sm life; (anche: **modo di ~**) way of life; ~**i** smpl food sg, provisions; ~ **di** to live on.
'vivido, a ag (colore) vivid, bright.
vivifi'care vt to enliven, give life to; (piante etc) to revive.
vivisezi'one [vivisset'tsjone] sf vivisection.
'vivo, a ag (vivente) alive, living; (: animale) live; (fig) lively; (: colore) bright, brilliant; **i ~i** the living; ~ **e vegeto** hale and hearty; **farsi ~** to show one's face; to be heard from; **ritrarre al ~** to paint from life; **pungere qd nel ~** (fig) to cut sb to the quick.
vizi'are [vit'tsjare] vt (bambino) to spoil; (corrompere moralmente) to corrupt; **vizi'ato, a** ag spoilt; (aria, acqua) polluted.
'vizio ['vittsjo] sm vice; (cattiva abitudine) bad habit; (imperfezione) flaw, defect; (errore) fault, mistake; **vizi'oso, a** ag depraved; defective; (inesatto) incorrect, wrong.
vocabo'lario sm (dizionario) dictionary; (lessico) vocabulary.
vo'cabolo sm word.
vo'cale ag vocal // sf vowel.
vocazi'one [vokat'tsjone] sf vocation; (fig) natural bent.
'voce ['votʃe] sf voice; (diceria) rumour; (di un elenco, in bilancio) item; **aver ~ in capitolo** (fig) to have a say in the matter.
voci'are [vo'tʃare] vi to shout, yell.
'voga sf (NAUT) rowing; (usanza): **essere in ~** to be in fashion o in vogue.
vo'gare vi to row.
'voglia ['voʎʎa] sf desire, wish; (macchia) birthmark; **aver ~ di qc/di fare** to feel like sth/like doing; (più forte) to want sth/to do.
'voi pronome you; **vol'altri** pronome you (lot).

vo'lano sm (SPORT) shuttlecock; (TECN) flywheel.

vo'lante ag flying // sm (steering) wheel.

volan'tino sm leaflet.

vo'lare vi (uccello, aereo, fig) to fly; (cappello) to blow away o off, to fly away o off; ~ **via** to fly away o off.

vo'lata sf flight; (d'uccelli) flock, flight; (corsa) rush; (SPORT) final sprint.

vo'latile ag (CHIM) volatile // sm (ZOOL) bird.

volenti'eri av willingly; '~' 'with pleasure', 'I'd be glad to'.

vo'lere sm will; ~**i** smpl wishes // vt to want; (esigere, richiedere) to demand, require; **vuole un po' di formaggio?** would you like some cheese?; ~ **che qd faccia** to want sb to do; **vorrei questo I** would like this; ~**rci** (essere necessario): **quanto ci vuole per andare da Roma a Firenze?** how long does it take to go from Rome to Florence?; **ci vogliono 4 metri di stoffa** 4 metres of material are required, you will need 4 metres of material; ~ **bene a qd** to love sb; ~ **male a qd** to dislike sb; **volerne a qd** to bear sb a grudge; ~ **dire (che)** to mean (that); **senza** ~ without meaning to, unintentionally.

vol'gare ag vulgar; **l'opinione** ~ common opinion; **volgarità** sf vulgarity; **volgariz'zare** vt to popularize.

'volgere ['vɔldʒere] vt to turn // vi to turn; (tendere): ~ **a**: **il tempo volge al brutto** the weather is breaking; **un rosso che volge al viola** a red verging on purple; ~**rsi** vr to turn; ~ **al peggio** to take a turn for the worse.

'volgo sm common people.

voli'era sf aviary.

voli'tivo, a ag strong-willed.

'volo sm flight; **al** ~: **colpire qc al** ~ to hit sth as it flies past; **capire al** ~ to understand straight away.

volontà sf will; **a** ~ (mangiare, bere) as much as one likes; **buona/cattiva** ~ goodwill/lack of goodwill.

volon'tario, a ag voluntary // sm (MIL) volunteer.

volonte'roso, a ag willing.

'volpe sf fox.

'volta sf (momento, circostanza) time; (turno, giro) turn; (curva) turn, bend; (ARCHIT) vault; **a mia** (o **tua** etc) ~ in turn; **una** ~ once; **due** ~**e** twice; **una cosa per** ~ one thing at a time; **una** ~ **per tutte** once and for all; **a** ~**e** at times, sometimes; **una** ~ **che** (temporale) once; (causale) since; **3** ~**e 4** 3 times 4.

volta'faccia [volta'fattʃa] sm inv (fig) volte-face.

vol'taggio [vol'taddʒo] sm (ELETTR) voltage.

vol'tare vt to turn; (girare: moneta) to turn over; (rigirare) to turn round // vi to turn; ~**rsi** vr to turn; to turn over; to turn round.

volteggi'are [volted'dʒare] vi (volare) to

circle; (in equitazione) to do trick riding; (in ginnastica) to vault; to perform acrobatics.

'volto, a pp di **volgere** // sm face.

vo'lubile ag changeable, fickle.

vo'lume sm volume; **volumi'noso, a** ag voluminous, bulky.

voluttà sf sensual pleasure o delight; **voluttu'oso, a** ag voluptuous.

vomi'tare vt, vi to vomit; **'vomito** sm vomiting q; vomit.

'vongola sf clam.

vo'race [vo'ratʃe] ag voracious, greedy.

vo'ragine [vo'radʒine] sf abyss, chasm.

'vortice ['vortitʃe] sm whirlwind; whirlpool; (fig) whirl.

'vostro, a det: **il(la)** ~**(a)** etc your // pronome: **il(la)** ~**(a)** etc yours.

vo'tante sm/f voter.

vo'tare vi to vote // vt (sottoporre a votazione) to take a vote on; (approvare) to vote for; (REL): ~ **qc a** to dedicate sth to; **votazi'one** sf vote, voting; **votazioni** sfpl (POL) votes; (INS) marks.

vo'tivo, a ag (REL) votive.

'voto sm (POL) vote; (INS) mark; (REL) vow; (: offerta) votive offering.

vs. abbr commerciale di **vostro**.

vul'canico, a, ci, che ag volcanic.

vul'cano sm volcano.

vulne'rabile ag vulnerable.

vuo'tare vt, ~**rsi** vr to empty.

vu'oto, a ag empty; (fig: privo): ~ **di** (senso etc) devoid of // sm empty space, gap; (spazio in bianco) blank; (FISICA) vacuum; (fig: mancanza) gap, void; **a mani** ~**e** empty-handed; ~ **d'aria** air pocket; ~ **a rendere** returnable bottle.

W X Y

watt [vat] sm inv watt.

'whisky ['wiski] sm inv whisky.

'xeres ['ksɛres] sm inv sherry.

xero'copia [ksero'kɔpja] sf xerox, photocopy.

xi'lofono [ksi'lɔfono] sm xylophone.

yacht [jɔt] sm inv yacht.

'yoghurt ['jɔgurt] sm inv yoghourt.

Z

zabai'one [dzaba'jone] sm dessert made of egg yolks, sugar and marsala.

'zacchera ['tsakkera] sf splash of mud.

zaf'fata [tsaf'fata] sf (tanfo) stench.

zaffe'rano [dzaffe'rano] sm saffron.

zaf'firo [dzaf'firo] sm sapphire.

'zagara ['dzagara] sf orange blossom.

'zaino ['dzaino] sm rucksack.

'zampa ['tsampa] sf (di animale: gamba) leg; (: piede) paw; **a quattro** ~**e** on all fours.

zampil'lare [tsampil'lare] vi to gush, spurt; **zam'pillo** sm gush, spurt.

zam'pogna [tsam'poɲɲa] sf instrument similar to bagpipes.

'zanna ['tsanna] sf (di elefante) tusk; (di carnivori) fang.

zan'zara [dzan'dzara] sf mosquito; **zanzari'era** sf mosquito net.

'zappa ['tsappa] sf hoe; **zap'pare** vt to hoe.

zar, za'rina [tsar, tsa'rina] sm/f tsar/tsarina.

'zattera ['dzattera] sf raft.

za'vorra [dza'vɔrra] sf ballast.

'zazzera ['tsattsera] sf shock of hair.

'zebra ['dzɛbra] sf zebra; **~e** sfpl (AUT) zebra crossing sg.

'zecca, che ['tsekka] sf (ZOOL) tick; (officina di monete) mint.

ze'lante [dze'lante] ag zealous.

'zelo ['dzɛlo] sm zeal.

'zenit ['dzɛnit] sm zenith.

'zenzero ['dzendzero] sm ginger.

'zeppa ['tseppa] sf wedge.

'zeppo, a ['tseppo] ag: **~ di** crammed o packed with.

zer'bino [dzer'bino] sm doormat.

'zero ['dzɛro] sm zero, nought; **vincere per tre a ~** (SPORT) to win three-nil.

'zeta ['dzɛta] sm o f zed, (the letter) z.

'zia ['tsia] sf aunt.

zibel'lino [dzibel'lino] sm sable.

'zigomo ['dzigomo] sm cheekbone.

zig'zag [dzig'dzag] sm inv zigzag; **andare a ~** to zigzag.

zim'bello [dzim'bello] sm (oggetto di burle) laughing-stock.

'zinco ['dzinko] sm zinc.

'zingaro, a ['dzingaro] sm/f gipsy.

'zio ['tsio], pl **'zii** sm uncle; **zii** smpl (zio e zia) uncle and aunt.

zi'tella [dzi'tɛlla] sf spinster; (peg) old maid.

'zitto, a ['tsitto] ag quiet, silent; **sta' ~!** be quiet!

'zoccolo ['tsɔkkolo] sm (calzatura) clog; (di cavallo etc) hoof; (basamento) base; plinth.

zo'diaco [dzo'diako] sm zodiac.

'zolfo ['tsolfo] sm sulphur.

'zolla ['dzɔlla] sf clod (of earth).

zol'letta [dzol'letta] sf sugar lump.

'zona ['dzɔna] sf zone, area; **~ di depressione** (METEOR) trough of low pressure; **~ verde** (di abitato) green area.

'zonzo ['dzondzo]: **a ~** av: **andare a ~** to wander about, stroll about.

zoo ['dzɔo] sm inv zoo.

zoolo'gia [dzoolo'dʒia] sf zoology; **zoo-'logico, a, ci, che** ag zoological; **zo'ologo, a, gi, ghe** sm/f zoologist.

zoppi'care [tsoppi'kare] vi to limp; to be shaky, rickety.

'zoppo, a ['tsoppo] ag lame; (fig: mobile) shaky, rickety.

zoti'cone [dzoti'kone] sm lout.

'zucca, che ['tsukka] sf marrow; pumpkin.

zucche'rare [tsukke'rare] vt to put sugar in.

zuccheri'era [tsukkeri'rjera] sf sugar bowl.

zuccheri'ficio [tsukkeri'fitʃo] sm sugar refinery.

zucche'rino, a [tsukke'rino] ag sugary, sweet.

'zucchero ['tsukkero] sm sugar; **zucche-'roso, a** ag sugary.

zuc'chino [tsuk'kino] sm courgette, zucchini.

'zuffa ['tsuffa] sf brawl.

zufo'lare [tsufo'lare] vt, vi to whistle.

'zuppa ['tsuppa] sf soup; (fig) mixture, muddle; **~ inglese** (CUC) ≈ trifle; **zup-pi'era** sf soup tureen.

'zuppo, a ['tsuppo] ag: **~ (di)** drenched (with), soaked (with).

ENGLISH - ITALIAN
INGLESE - ITALIANO

A

a, an [eɪ, ə, æn, ən, n] *det* un (uno + *s impure, gn, pn, ps, x, z*), *f* una (un' + *vowel*); **3 a day/week** 3 al giorno/la *or* alla settimana; **10 km an hour** 10 km all'ora.

A [eɪ] *n* (*MUS*) la *m*.

A.A. *n* (*abbr of Automobile Association*) ≈ A.C.I.; *abbr of Alcoholics Anonymous.*

aback [ə'bæk] *ad*: **to be taken ~** essere sbalordito(a).

abandon [ə'bændən] *vt* abbandonare // *n* abbandono.

abashed [ə'bæʃt] *a* imbarazzato(a).

abate [ə'beɪt] *vi* calmarsi.

abattoir ['æbətwɑː*] *n* mattatoio.

abbey ['æbɪ] *n* abbazia, badia.

abbot ['æbət] *n* abate *m*.

abbreviate [ə'briːvɪeɪt] *vt* abbreviare; **abbreviation** [-'eɪʃən] *n* abbreviazione *f*.

abdicate ['æbdɪkeɪt] *vt* abdicare a // *vi* abdicare; **abdication** [-'keɪʃən] *n* abdicazione *f*.

abdomen ['æbdəmɛn] *n* addome *m*.

abduct [æb'dʌkt] *vt* rapire; **abduction** [-ʃən] *n* rapimento.

abet [ə'bɛt] *vt see* **aid**.

abeyance [ə'beɪəns] *n*: **in ~** in sospeso.

abhor [əb'hɔː*] *vt* aborrire; **~rent** *a* odioso(a.)

abide [ə'baɪd] *vt* sopportare; **to ~ by** *vt fus* conformarsi a.

ability [ə'bɪlɪtɪ] *n* abilità *f inv*.

ablaze [ə'bleɪz] *a* in fiamme; **~ with light** risplendente di luce.

able ['eɪbl] *a* capace; **to be ~ to do sth** essere capace di fare qc, poter fare qc; **~-bodied** *a* robusto(a); **ably** *ad* abilmente.

abnormal [æb'nɔːməl] *a* anormale.

aboard [ə'bɔːd] *ad a* bordo // *prep a* bordo di.

abolish [ə'bɒlɪʃ] *vt* abolire.

abolition [æbəu'lɪʃən] *n* abolizione *f*.

abominable [ə'bɒmɪnəbl] *a* abominevole.

aborigine [æbə'rɪdʒɪnɪ] *n* aborigeno/a.

abort [ə'bɔːt] *vt* abortire; **~ion** [ə'bɔːʃən] *n* aborto; **~ive** *a* abortivo(a).

abound [ə'baund] *vi* abbondare; **to ~ in** abbondare di.

about [ə'baut] *prep* intorno a, riguardo a // *ad* circa; (*here and there*) qua e là; **it takes ~ 10 hours** ci vogliono circa 10 ore; **at ~ 2 o'clock** verso le due; **it's ~ here** è qui dintorno; **to walk ~ the town** camminare per la città; **to be ~ to:** he **was ~ to cry** lui stava per piangere; **what** *or* **how ~ doing this?** che ne pensa di fare questo?; **~ turn** *n* dietro front *m inv*.

above [ə'bʌv] *ad, prep* sopra; **mentioned ~** suddetto; **costing ~ £10** che costa più di 10 sterline; **~ all** soprattutto; **~board** *a* aperto(a); onesto(a).

abrasive [ə'breɪzɪv] *a* abrasivo(a).

abreast [ə'brɛst] *ad* di fianco; **3 ~** per 3 di fronte; **to keep ~ of** tenersi aggiornato su.

abridge [ə'brɪdʒ] *vt* ridurre.

abroad [ə'brɔːd] *ad* all'estero.

abrupt [ə'brʌpt] *a* (*steep*) erto(a); (*sudden*) improvviso(a); (*gruff, blunt*) brusco(a).

abscess ['æbsɪs] *n* ascesso.

abscond [əb'skɒnd] *vi* scappare.

absence ['æbsəns] *n* assenza.

absent ['æbsənt] *a* assente; **~ee** [-'tiː] *n* assente [-'tiːɪzəm] *n* assenteismo; **~-minded** *a* distratto(a).

absolute ['æbsəluːt] *a* assoluto(a); **~ly** [-'luːtlɪ] *ad* assolutamente.

absolve [əb'zɔlv] *vt*: **to ~ sb (from)** assolvere qd (da).

absorb [əb'zɔːb] *vt* assorbire; **to be ~ed in a book** essere immerso in un libro; **~ent** *a* assorbente; **~ent cotton** *n* (*US*) cotone *m* idrofilo.

abstain [əb'steɪn] *vi*: **to ~ (from)** astenersi (da).

abstemious [əb'stiːmɪəs] *a* astemio(a).

abstention [əb'stɛnʃən] *n* astensione *f*.

abstinence ['æbstɪnəns] *n* astinenza.

abstract ['æbstrækt] *a* astratto(a) // *n* (*summary*) riassunto.

absurd [əb'sɔːd] *a* assurdo(a); **~ity** *n* assurdità *f inv*.

abundance [ə'bʌndəns] *n* abbondanza; **abundant** *a* abbondante.

abuse *n* [ə'bjuːs] abuso; (*insults*) ingiurie *fpl* // *vt* [ə'bjuːz] abusare di; **abusive** *a* ingiurioso(a).*

abysmal [ə'bɪzməl] *a* spaventoso(a).

abyss [ə'bɪs] *n* abisso.

academic [ækə'dɛmɪk] *a* accademico(a); (*pej: issue*) puramente formale // *n* universitario/a.

academy [ə'kædəmɪ] *n* (*learned body*) accademia; (*school*) scuola privata; **military/naval ~** scuola militare/navale; **~ of music** conservatorio.

accede [æk'siːd] *vi*: **to ~ to** (*request*) accedere a; (*throne*) ascendere a.

accelerate [æk'sɛləreɪt] *vt,vi* accelerare; **acceleration** [-'reɪʃən] *n* accelerazione *f*; **accelerator** *n* acceleratore *m*.

accent ['æksɛnt] *n* accento.

accept [ək'sɛpt] *vt* accettare; **~able** *a* accettabile; **~ance** *n* accettazione *f*.

access ['æksɛs] *n* accesso; **to have ~ to**

accessory [ə'sɛsərɪ] *n* accessorio; **toilet accessories** *npl* articoli *mpl* da toilette.

accident ['æksɪdənt] *n* incidente *m*; (*chance*) caso; **by ~** per caso; **~al** [-'dɛntl] *a* accidentale; **~ally** [-'dɛntlɪ] *ad* per caso; **~-prone** *a*: **he's very ~-prone** è un vero passaguai.

acclaim [ə'kleɪm] *vt* acclamare // *n* acclamazione *f*.

acclimatize [ə'klaɪmətaɪz] *vt*: **to become ~d** acclimatarsi.

accommodate [ə'kɔmədeɪt] *vt* alloggiare; (*oblige, help*) favorire.

accommodating [ə'kɔmədeɪtɪŋ] *a* compiacente.

accommodation [əkɔmə'deɪʃən] *n* alloggio.

accompaniment [ə'kʌmpənɪmənt] *n* accompagnamento.

accompany [ə'kʌmpənɪ] *vt* accompagnare.

accomplice [ə'kʌmplɪs] *n* complice *m/f*.

accomplish [ə'kʌmplɪʃ] *vt* compiere; **~ed** *a* (*person*) esperto(a); **~ment** *n* compimento; realizzazione *f*; **~ments** *npl* doti *fpl*.

accord [ə'kɔ:d] *n* accordo // *vt* accordare; **of his own ~** di propria iniziativa; **~ance** *n*: **in ~ance with** in conformità con; **~ing to** *prep* secondo; **~ingly** *ad* in conformità.

accordion [ə'kɔ:dɪən] *n* fisarmonica.

accost [ə'kɔst] *vt* avvicinare.

account [ə'kaunt] *n* (*COMM*) conto; (*report*) descrizione *f*; **by all ~s** a quanto si dice; **of little ~** di poca importanza; **on ~** in acconto; **on no ~** per nessun motivo; **on ~ of** a causa di; **to take into ~, take ~ of** tener conto di; **to ~ for** spiegare; giustificare; **~able** a responsabile.

accountancy [ə'kauntənsɪ] *n* ragioneria.

accountant [ə'kauntənt] *n* ragioniere/a.

accumulate [ə'kju:mjuleɪt] *vt* accumulare // *vi* accumularsi; **accumulation** [-'leɪʃən] *n* accumulazione *f*.

accuracy ['ækjurəsɪ] *n* precisione *f*.

accurate ['ækjurɪt] *a* preciso(a); **~ly** *ad* precisamente.

accusation [ækju'zeɪʃən] *n* accusa.

accuse [ə'kju:z] *vt* accusare; **~d** *n* accusato/a.

accustom [ə'kʌstəm] *vt* abituare; **~ed** *a* (*usual*) abituale; **~ed to** abituato(a) a.

ace [eɪs] *n* asso; **within an ~ of** a un pelo da.

ache [eɪk] *n* male *m*, dolore *m* // *vi* (*be sore*) far male, dolere; **my head ~s** mi fa male la testa; **I'm aching all over** mi duole dappertutto.

achieve [ə'tʃi:v] *vt* (*aim*) raggiungere; (*victory, success*) ottenere; (*task*) compiere; **~ment** *n* compimento; successo.

acid ['æsɪd] *a* acido(a) // *n* acido; **~ity** [ə'sɪdɪtɪ] *n* acidità.

acknowledge [ək'nɔlɪdʒ] *vt* (*letter*) confermare la ricevuta di; (*fact*) riconoscere; **~ment** *n* conferma; riconoscimento.

acne ['æknɪ] *n* acne *f*.

acorn ['eɪkɔ:n] *n* ghianda.

acoustic [ə'ku:stɪk] *a* acustico(a); **~s** *n,npl* acustica.

acquaint [ə'kweɪnt] *vt*: **to ~ sb with sth** far sapere qc a qd; **to be ~ed with** (*person*) conoscere; **~ance** *n* conoscenza; (*person*) conoscente *m/f*.

acquire [ə'kwaɪə*] *vt* acquistare.

acquisition [ækwɪ'zɪʃən] *n* acquisto.

acquisitive [ə'kwɪzɪtɪv] *a* a cui piace accumulare le cose.

acquit [ə'kwɪt] *vt* assolvere; **to ~ o.s. well** comportarsi bene; **~tal** *n* assoluzione *f*.

acre ['eɪkə*] *n* acro (= 4047 m²).

acrimonious [ækrɪ'məunɪəs] *a* astioso(a).

acrobat ['ækrəbæt] *n* acrobata *m/f*.

acrobatics [ækrəu'bætɪks] *n* acrobatica // *npl* acrobazie *fpl*.

across [ə'krɔs] *prep* (*on the other side*) dall'altra parte di; (*crosswise*) attraverso // *ad* dall'altra parte; in larghezza; **to walk ~** (**the road**) attraversare (la strada); **~ from** di fronte a.

act [ækt] *n* atto; (*in music-hall etc*) numero; (*LAW*) decreto // *vi* agire; (*THEATRE*) recitare; (*pretend*) fingere // *vt* (*part*) recitare; **to ~ Hamlet** recitare la parte di Amleto; **to ~ the fool** fare lo stupido; **to ~ as** agire da; **~ing** *a* che fa le funzioni di // *n* (*of actor*) recitazione *f*; (*activity*): **to do some ~ing** fare del teatro (*or* del cinema).

action ['ækʃən] *n* azione *f*; (*MIL*) combattimento; (*LAW*) processo; **out of ~** fuori combattimento; fuori servizio; **to take ~** agire.

activate ['æktɪveɪt] *vt* (*mechanism*) fare funzionare; (*CHEM, PHYSICS*) rendere attivo(a).

active ['æktɪv] *a* attivo(a).

activity [æk'tɪvɪtɪ] *n* attività *f inv*.

actor ['æktə*] *n* attore *m*.

actress ['æktrɪs] *n* attrice *f*.

actual ['æktjuəl] *a* reale, vero(a); **~ly** *ad* realmente; infatti.

acumen ['ækjumən] *n* acume *m*.

acupuncture ['ækjupʌŋktʃə*] *n* agopuntura.

acute [ə'kju:t] *a* acuto(a).

ad [æd] *n abbr of* **advertisement**.

A.D. *ad* (*abbr of Anno Domini*) d.C.

Adam ['ædəm] *n* Adamo; **~'s apple** *n* pomo di Adamo.

adamant ['ædəmənt] *a* adamantino(a).

adapt [ə'dæpt] *vt* adattare // *vi*: **to ~ (to)** adattarsi (a); **~able** *a* (*device*) adattabile; (*person*) che sa adattarsi; **~ation** [ædæp-'teɪʃən] *n* adattamento; **~er** *n* (*ELEC*) adattatore *m*.

add [æd] *vt* aggiungere; (*figures: also*: **to ~**

up) addizionare // vi: **to ~ to** (increase) aumentare.

adder ['ædə*] n vipera.

addict ['ædɪkt] n tossicomane m/f; (fig) fanatico/a; **~ed** [ə'dɪktɪd] a: **to be ~ed to** (drink etc) essere dedito a; (fig: football etc) essere tifoso di; **~ion** [ə'dɪkʃən] n (MED) tossicomania.

addition [ə'dɪʃən] n addizione f; **in ~** inoltre; **in ~ to** oltre; **~al** a supplementare.

additive ['ædɪtɪv] n additivo.

address [ə'drɛs] n indirizzo; (talk) discorso // vt indirizzare; (speak to) fare un discorso a.

adenoids ['ædɪnɔɪdz] npl adenoidi fpl.

adept ['ædɛpt] a: **~ at** esperto(a) in.

adequate ['ædɪkwɪt] a adeguato(a); sufficiente.

adhere [əd'hɪə*] vi: **to ~ to** aderire a; (fig: rule, decision) seguire.

adhesion [əd'hi:ʒən] n adesione f.

adhesive [əd'hi:zɪv] a adesivo(a) // n adesivo.

adjacent [ə'dʒeɪsənt] a adiacente; **~ to** accanto a.

adjective ['ædʒɛktɪv] n aggettivo.

adjoining [ə'dʒɔɪnɪŋ] a accanto inv, adiacente // prep accanto a.

adjourn [ə'dʒə:n] vt rimandare // vi aggiornare; (go) spostarsi.

adjust [ə'dʒʌst] vt aggiustare; (COMM) rettificare // vi: **to ~ (to)** adattarsi (a); **~able** a regolabile; **~ment** n adattamento; (of prices, wages) aggiustamento.

adjutant ['ædʒətənt] n aiutante m.

ad-lib [æd'lɪb] vt,vi improvvisare // n improvvisazione f.

administer [əd'mɪnɪstə*] vt amministrare; (justice) somministrare.

administration [ədmɪnɪs'treɪʃən] n amministrazione f.

administrative [əd'mɪnɪstrətɪv] a amministrativo(a).

administrator [əd'mɪnɪstreɪtə*] n amministratore/trice.

admiral ['ædmərəl] n ammiraglio; **A~ty** n Ammiragliato; Ministero della Marina.

admiration [ædmə'reɪʃən] n ammirazione f.

admire [əd'maɪə*] vt ammirare; **~r** n ammiratore/trice.

admission [əd'mɪʃən] n ammissione f; (to exhibition, night club etc) ingresso; (confession) confessione f.

admit [əd'mɪt] vt ammettere; far entrare; (agree) riconoscere; **to ~ of** lasciare adito a; **to ~ to** riconoscere; **~tance** n ingresso; **~tedly** ad bisogna pur riconoscere (che).

admonish [əd'mɒnɪʃ] vt ammonire.

ado [ə'du:] n: **without (any) more ~** senza più indugi.

adolescence [ædəu'lɛsns] n adolescenza.

adolescent [ædəu'lɛsnt] a,n adolescente (m/f).

adopt [ə'dɒpt] vt adottare; **~ed** a adottivo(a); **~ion** [ə'dɒpʃən] n adozione f.

adore [ə'dɔ:*] vt adorare.

adorn [ə'dɔ:n] vt adornare.

adrenalin [ə'drɛnəlɪn] n adrenalina.

Adriatic (Sea) [eɪdrɪ'ætɪk(si:)] n Adriatico.

adrift [ə'drɪft] ad alla deriva.

adroit [ə'drɔɪt] a abile, destro(a).

adult ['ædʌlt] n adulto/a.

adulterate [ə'dʌltəreɪt] vt adulterare.

adultery [ə'dʌltərɪ] n adulterio.

advance [əd'vɑ:ns] n avanzamento; (money) anticipo // vt avanzare; (date, money) anticipare // vi avanzare; **in ~** in anticipo; **~d** a avanzato(a); (SCOL: studies) superiore; **~ment** n avanzamento.

advantage [əd'vɑ:ntɪdʒ] n (also TENNIS) vantaggio; **to take ~ of** approfittarsi di; **~ous** [ædvən'teɪdʒəs] a vantaggioso(a).

advent ['ædvənt] n avvento; **A~** Avvento.

adventure [əd'vɛntʃə*] n avventura; **adventurous** a avventuroso(a).

adverb ['ædvə:b] n avverbio.

adversary ['ædvəsərɪ] n avversario/a.

adverse ['ædvə:s] a avverso(a); **in ~ circumstances** nelle avversità; **~ to** contrario(a) a.

adversity [əd'və:sɪtɪ] n avversità.

advert ['ædvə:t] n abbr of **advertisement**.

advertise ['ædvətaɪz] vi(vt) fare pubblicità or réclame (a); fare un'inserzione (per vendere).

advertisement [əd'və:tɪsmənt] n (COMM) réclame f inv, pubblicità f inv; (in classified ads) inserzione f.

advertising ['ædvətaɪzɪŋ] n pubblicità.

advice [əd'vaɪs] n consigli mpl; (notification) avviso; **piece of ~** consiglio.

advisable [əd'vaɪzəbl] a consigliabile.

advise [əd'vaɪz] vt consigliare; **to ~ sb of sth** informare qd di qc; **~r** n consigliere/a; **advisory** [-ərɪ] a consultivo(a).

advocate ['ædvəkeɪt] vt propugnare.

aegis ['i:dʒɪs] n: **under the ~ of** sotto gli auspici di.

aerial ['ɛərɪəl] n antenna // a aereo(a).

aeroplane ['ɛərəpleɪn] n aeroplano.

aerosol ['ɛərəsɔl] n aerosol m inv.

aesthetic [ɪs'θɛtɪk] a estetico(a).

affable ['æfəbl] a affabile.

affair [ə'fɛə*] n affare m; (also: **love ~**) relazione f amorosa.

affect [ə'fɛkt] vt toccare; (feign) fingere; **~ation** [æfɛk'teɪʃən] n affettazione f; **~ed** a affettato(a).

affection [ə'fɛkʃən] n affezione f; **~ate** a affettuoso(a).

affiliated [ə'fɪlɪeɪtɪd] a affiliato(a).

affinity [ə'fɪnɪtɪ] n affinità f inv.

affirmation [æfə'meɪʃən] n affermazione f.

affirmative [ə'fɔ:mətɪv] a affermativo(a) // n: **in the ~** affermativamente.

affix [ə'fɪks] vt apporre; attaccare.

afflict [ə'flɪkt] *vt* affliggere; ~ion [ə'flɪkʃən] *n* afflizione *f.*
affluence ['æfluəns] *n* abbondanza; opulenza.
affluent ['æfluənt] *a* abbondante; opulente; (*person*) ricco(a).
afford [ə'fɔːd] *vt* permettersi; (*provide*) fornire; **I can't ~ the time** non ho veramente il tempo.
affront [ə'frʌnt] *n* affronto; ~ed *a* insultato(a).
afield [ə'fiːld] *ad:* **far ~** lontano.
afloat [ə'fləut] *a, ad* a galla.
afoot [ə'fut] *ad:* **there is something ~** si sta preparando qualcosa.
aforesaid [ə'fɔːsɛd] *a* suddetto(a), predetto(a).
afraid [ə'freid] *a* impaurito(a); **to be ~ of** aver paura di; **to be ~ of doing** *or* **to do** aver paura di fare; **I am ~ that I'll be late** mi dispiace, ma farò tardi.
afresh [ə'frɛʃ] *ad* di nuovo.
Africa ['æfrɪkə] *n* Africa; ~n *a, n* africano(a).
aft [ɑːft] *ad* a poppa, verso poppa.
after ['ɑːftə*] *prep,ad* dopo; **what/who are you ~?** che/chi cerca?; ~ **all** dopo tutto; ~-**effects** *npl* conseguenze *fpl*; (*of illness*) postumi *mpl*; ~**life** *n* vita dell'al di là; ~**math** *n* conseguenze *fpl*; **in the ~math of** nel periodo dopo; ~**noon** *n* pomeriggio; ~-**shave** (**lotion**) *n* dopobarba *m inv*; ~**thought** *n*: **as an ~thought** come aggiunta; ~**wards** *ad* dopo.
again [ə'gɛn] *ad* di nuovo; **to begin/see ~** ricominciare/rivedere; **not ... ~** non ... più; ~ **and** ~ ripetutamente.
against [ə'gɛnst] *prep* contro; ~ **a blue background** su uno sfondo azzurro.
age [eidʒ] *n* età *f inv* // *vt,vi* invecchiare; **it's been ~s since** sono secoli che; **to come of ~** diventare maggiorenne; ~**d** *a* (*elderly:* ['eidʒɪd]) anziano(a); ~**d 10** di 10 anni; **the ~d** ['eidʒɪd] gli anziani; ~ **group** *n* generazione *f*; ~**less** *a* senza età; ~ **limit** *n* limite *m* d'età.
agency ['eidʒənsɪ] *n* agenzia; **through** *or* **by the ~ of** grazie a.
agenda [ə'dʒɛndə] *n* ordine *m* del giorno.
agent ['eidʒənt] *n* agente *m.*
aggravate ['ægrəveit] *vt* aggravare; (*annoy*) esasperare.
aggregate ['ægrɪgeit] *n* aggregato; **on ~** (*SPORT*) con punteggio complessivo.
aggression [ə'grɛʃən] *n* aggressione *f.*
aggressive [ə'grɛsɪv] *a* aggressivo(a); ~**ness** *n* aggressività.
aggrieved [ə'griːvd] *a* addolorato(a).
aghast [ə'gɑːst] *a* sbigottito(a).
agile ['ædʒaɪl] *a* agile.
agitate ['ædʒɪteɪt] *vt* turbare; agitare // *vi*: **to ~ for** agitarsi per; **agitator** *n* agitatore/trice.
ago [ə'gəu] *ad:* **2 days ~** 2 giorni fa; **not long ~** poco tempo fa.
agonizing ['ægənaɪzɪŋ] *a* straziante.

agony ['ægənɪ] *n* agonia.
agree [ə'griː] *vi*: **to ~ (with)** essere d'accordo (con); (*LING*) concordare (con); **to ~ to sth/to do sth** accettare qc/di fare qc; **to ~ that** (*admit*) ammettere che; **to ~ on sth** accordarsi su qc; **garlic doesn't ~ with me** l'aglio non mi va; ~**able** *a* gradevole; (*willing*) disposto(a); **are you ~able to this?** sei d'accordo con questo?; ~**d** *a* (*time, place*) stabilito(a); **to be ~d** essere d'accordo; ~**ment** *n* accordo; **in ~ment** d'accordo.
agricultural [ægrɪ'kʌltʃərəl] *a* agricolo(a).
agriculture ['ægrɪkʌltʃə*] *n* agricoltura.
aground [ə'graund] *ad:* **to run ~** arenarsi.
ahead [ə'hɛd] *ad* avanti; davanti; ~ **of** davanti a; (*fig: schedule etc*) in anticipo su; ~ **of time** in anticipo; **go ~!** avanti!; **go right** *or* **straight ~** tiri diritto; **they were (right) ~ of us** erano (proprio) davanti a noi.
aid [eid] *n* aiuto // *vt* aiutare; **to ~ and abet** (*LAW*) essere complice di.
aide [eid] *n* (*person*) aiutante *m.*
ailment ['eilmənt] *n* indisposizione *f.*
aim [eim] *vt*: **to ~ sth at** (*such as gun*) mirare qc a, puntare qc a; (*camera, remark*) rivolgere qc a; (*missile*) lanciare qc contro; (*blow etc*) tirare qc a // *vi* (*also:* **to take ~**) prendere la mira // *n* mira; **to ~ at** mirare; **to ~ to do** aver l'intenzione di fare; ~**less** *a*, ~**lessly** *ad* senza scopo.
air [ɛə*] *n* aria // *vt* aerare; (*grievances, ideas*) esprimere pubblicamente // *cpd* (*currents*) d'aria; (*attack*) aereo(a); ~**bed** *n* materassino gonfiabile; ~**borne** *a* in volo; aerotrasportato(a); ~ **conditioning** *n* condizionamento d'aria; ~-**cooled** *a* raffreddato(a) ad aria; ~**craft** *n, pl inv* apparecchio; ~**craft carrier** *n* portaerei *f inv*; **A~ Force** *n* aviazione *f* militare; ~**gun** *n* fucile *m* ad aria compressa; ~ **hostess** *n* hostess *f inv*; ~**ily** *ad* con disinvoltura; ~ **letter** *n* aerogramma *m*; ~**line** *n* linea aerea; ~**liner** *n* aereo di linea; ~**lock** *n* cassa d'aria; **by ~mail** per via aerea; ~**plane** *n* (*US*) aeroplano; ~**port** *n* aeroporto; ~ **raid** *n* incursione *f* aerea; ~**sick** *a* che ha il mal d'aereo; ~**strip** *n* pista d'atterraggio; ~**tight** *a* ermetico(a); ~**y** *a* arioso(a); (*manners*) non curante.
aisle [ail] *n* (*of church*) navata laterale; navata centrale.
ajar [ə'dʒɑː*] *a* socchiuso(a).
alarm [ə'lɑːm] *n* allarme *m* // *vt* allarmare; ~ **clock** *n* sveglia; ~**ist** *n* allarmista *m.*
Albania [æl'beɪnɪə] *n* Albania.
album ['ælbəm] *n* album *m inv*; (*L.P.*) 33 giri *m inv*, L.P. *m inv.*
alchemy ['ælkɪmɪ] *n* alchimia.
alcohol ['ælkəhɔl] *n* alcool *m*; ~**ic** [-'hɔlɪk] *a* alcolico(a) // *n* alcolizzato/a; ~**ism** *n* alcolismo.

alcove ['ælkəuv] *n* alcova.
alderman ['ɔːldəmən] *n* consigliere *m* comunale.
ale [eɪl] *n* birra.
alert [ə'lɔːt] *a* vivo(a); (*watchful*) vigile // *n* allarme *m*; on the ~ all'erta.
algebra ['ældʒɪbrə] *n* algebra.
Algeria [æl'dʒɪərɪə] *n* Algeria; ~n *a*, *n* algerino(a).
alias ['eɪlɪæs] *ad* alias // *n* pseudonimo, falso nome *m*.
alibi ['ælɪbaɪ] *n* alibi *m inv*.
alien ['eɪlɪən] *n* straniero/a // *a*: ~ (to) estraneo(a) a; ~ate *vt* alienare; ~ation [-'neɪʃən] *n* alienazione *f*.
alight [ə'laɪt] *a* acceso(a) // *vi* scendere; (*bird*) posarsi.
align [ə'laɪn] *vt* allineare; ~ment *n* allineamento.
alike [ə'laɪk] *a* simile // *ad* sia ... sia; to look ~ assomigliarsi.
alimony ['ælɪmənɪ] *n* (*payment*) alimenti *mpl*.
alive [ə'laɪv] *a* vivo(a); (*active*) attivo(a); ~ with pieno(a) di; ~ to conscio(a) di.
alkali ['ælkəlaɪ] *n* alcali *m inv*.
all [ɔːl] *a* tutto(a), tutti(e) *pl* // *pronoun* tutto *m*; (*pl*) tutti(e) // *ad* tutto; ~ wrong/alone tutto sbagliato/solo; ~ the time/his life tutto il tempo/tutta la sua vita; ~ five tutti e cinque; ~ of them tutti(e); ~ of it tutto; ~ of us went ci siamo andati tutti; it's not as hard *etc* as ~ that non è mica così duro *etc*; ~ in ~ in tutto sommato.
allay [ə'leɪ] *vt* (*fears*) dissipare.
allegation [ælɪ'geɪʃən] *n* asserzione *f*.
allege [ə'lɛdʒ] *vt* asserire; ~dly [ə'lɛdʒɪdlɪ] *ad* secondo che si asserisce.
allegiance [ə'liːdʒəns] *n* fedeltà.
allegory ['ælɪgərɪ] *n* allegoria.
allergic [ə'lɔːdʒɪk] *a*: ~ to allergico(a) a.
allergy ['ælədʒɪ] *n* allergia.
alleviate [ə'liːvɪeɪt] *vt* sollevare.
alley ['ælɪ] *n* vicolo; (*in garden*) vialetto.
alliance [ə'laɪəns] *n* alleanza.
allied ['ælaɪd] *a* alleato(a).
alligator ['ælɪgeɪtə*] *n* alligatore *m*.
all-important   ['ɔːlɪm'pɔːtənt] *a* importantissimo(a).
all-in ['ɔːlɪn] *a* (*also ad*: charge) tutto compreso; ~ **wrestling** *n* lotta americana.
all-night ['ɔːl'naɪt] *a* aperto(a) (*or* che dura) tutta la notte.
allocate ['æləkeɪt] *vt* (*share out*) distribuire; (*duties, sum, time*): to ~ sth to assegnare qc a; to ~ sth for stanziare qc per.
allocation [æləu'keɪʃən] *n*: ~ (of money) stanziamento.
allot [ə'lɔt] *vt* (*share out*) spartire; (*time*): to ~ sth to dare qc a; (*duties*): to ~ sth to assegnare qc a; ~ment *n* (*share*) spartizione *f*; (*garden*) lotto di terra.
all-out ['ɔːlaut] *a* (*effort etc*) totale // *ad*: to go all out for mettercela tutta per.

allow [ə'lau] *vt* (*practice, behaviour*) permettere; (*sum to spend etc*) accordare; (*sum, time estimated*) dare; (*concede*): to ~ that ammettere che; to ~ sb to do permettere a qd di fare; to ~ for *vt fus* tener conto di; ~ance *n* (*money received*) assegno; indennità *f inv*; (*TAX*) detrazione *f* di imposta; to make ~ances for tener conto di.
alloy ['ælɔɪ] *n* lega.
all right ['ɔːl'raɪt] *ad* (*feel, work*) bene; (*as answer*) va bene.
all-round ['ɔːl'raund] *a* completo(a).
all-time ['ɔːl'taɪm] *a* (*record*) assoluto(a).
allude [ə'luːd] *vi*: to ~ to alludere a.
alluring [ə'ljuərɪŋ] *a* seducente.
allusion [ə'luːʒən] *n* allusione *f*.
ally ['ælaɪ] *n* alleato.
almighty [ɔːl'maɪtɪ] *a* onnipotente.
almond ['ɑːmənd] *n* mandorla.
almost ['ɔːlməust] *ad* quasi.
alms [ɑːmz] *npl* elemosina.
alone [ə'ləun] *a* solo(a); to leave sb ~ lasciare qd in pace; to leave sth ~ lasciare stare qc.
along [ə'lɔŋ] *prep* lungo // *ad*: is he coming ~? viene con noi?; he was hopping/limping ~ lui veniva saltellando/zoppicando; ~ with insieme con; ~side *prep* accanto a; lungo // *ad* accanto.
aloof [ə'luːf] *a* distaccato(a) // *ad* a distanza, a disparte.
aloud [ə'laud] *ad* ad alta voce.
alphabet ['ælfəbɛt] *n* alfabeto.
alpine ['ælpaɪn] *a* alpino(a).
Alps [ælps] *npl*: the ~ le Alpi.
already [ɔːl'rɛdɪ] *ad* già.
alright ['ɔːl'raɪt] *ad* = **all right**.
also ['ɔːlsəu] *ad* anche.
altar ['ɔltə*] *n* altare *m*.
alter ['ɔltə*] *vt,vi* alterare; ~ation [ɔltə'reɪʃən] *n* modificazione *f*, alterazione *f*.
alternate *a* [ɔl'təːnɪt] alterno(a) // *vi* ['ɔltəːneɪt] alternare; on ~ days ogni due giorni; **alternating** *a* (*current*) alternato(a).
alternative [ɔl'təːnətɪv] *a* (*solutions*) alternativo(a); (*solution*) altro(a) // *n* (*choice*) alternativa; (*other possibility*) altra possibilità; ~ly *ad* alternativamente.
alternator ['ɔltəːneɪtə*] *n* (*AUT*) alternatore *m*.
although [ɔːl'ðəu] *cj* benché + *sub*, sebbene + *sub*.
altitude ['æltɪtjuːd] *n* altitudine *f*.
alto ['æltəu] *n* contralto.
altogether [ɔːltə'gɛðə*] *ad* del tutto, completamente; (*on the whole*) tutto considerato; (*in all*) in tutto.
altruistic [æltru'ɪstɪk] *a* altruistico(a).
aluminium [ælju'mɪnɪəm] *n* alluminio.
always ['ɔːlweɪz] *ad* sempre.
am [æm] *vb see* **be**.

a.m. ad (abbr of ante meridiem) della mattina.
amalgamate [ə'mælgəmeɪt] vt amalgamare // vi amalgamarsi; **amalgamation** [-'meɪʃən] n amalgamazione f; (COMM) fusione f.
amass [ə'mæs] vt ammassare.
amateur ['æmətə*] n dilettante m/f // a (SPORT) dilettante; ~**ish** a (pej) da dilettante.
amaze [ə'meɪz] vt stupire; ~**ment** n stupore m.
ambassador [æm'bæsədə*] n ambasciatore/trice.
amber ['æmbə*] n ambra; **at** ~ (AUT) giallo.
ambiguity [æmbɪ'gjuɪtɪ] n ambiguità f inv.
ambiguous [æm'bɪgjuəs] a ambiguo(a).
ambition [æm'bɪʃən] n ambizione f.
ambitious [æm'bɪʃəs] a ambizioso(a).
ambivalent [æm'bɪvələnt] a (attitude) ambivalente.
amble ['æmbl] vi (gen: **to** ~ **along**) camminare tranquillamente.
ambulance ['æmbjuləns] n ambulanza.
ambush ['æmbuʃ] n imboscata // vt fare un'imboscata a.
amenable [ə'mi:nəbl] a: ~ **to** (advice etc) ben disposto(a) a.
amend [ə'mend] vt (law) emendare; (text) correggere // vi emendarsi; **to make** ~**s** fare ammenda; ~**ment** n emendamento, correzione f.
amenity [ə'mi:nɪtɪ] n amenità f inv.
America [ə'merɪkə] n America; ~**n** a, n americano(a).
amethyst ['æmɪθɪst] n ametista.
amiable ['eɪmɪəbl] a amabile, gentile.
amicable ['æmɪkəbl] a amichevole.
amid(st) [ə'mɪd(st)] prep fra, tra, in mezzo a.
amiss [ə'mɪs] a,ad: **there's something** ~ c'è qualcosa che non va bene; **to take sth** ~ aversene a male.
ammunition [æmju'nɪʃən] n munizioni fpl.
amnesia [æm'ni:zɪə] n amnesia.
amnesty ['æmnɪstɪ] n amnistia.
amok [ə'mɔk] ad: **to run** ~ diventare pazzo(a) furioso(a).
among(st) [ə'mʌŋ(st)] prep fra, tra, in mezzo a.
amoral [æ'mɔrəl] a amorale.
amorous ['æmərəs] a amoroso(a).
amorphous [ə'mɔ:fəs] a amorfo(a).
amount [ə'maunt] n somma; ammontare m; quantità f inv // vi: **to** ~ **to** (total) ammontare a; (be same as) essere come.
amp(ère) ['æmp(εə*)] n ampère m inv.
amphibious [æm'fɪbɪəs] a anfibio(a).
amphitheatre ['æmfɪθɪətə*] n anfiteatro.
ample ['æmpl] a ampio(a); spazioso(a); (enough): **this is** ~ questo è più che sufficiente; **to have** ~ **time/room** avere assai tempo/posto.
amplifier ['æmplɪfaɪə*] n amplificatore m.
amplify ['æmplɪfaɪ] vt amplificare.
amply ['æmplɪ] ad ampiamente.

amputate ['æmpjuteɪt] vt amputare.
amuck [ə'mʌk] ad = **amok**.
amuse [ə'mju:z] vt divertire; ~**ment** n divertimento.
an [æn, ən, n] det see **a**.
anaemia [ə'ni:mɪə] n anemia.
anaemic [ə'ni:mɪk] a anemico(a).
anaesthetic [ænɪs'θetɪk] a anestetico(a) // n anestetico.
anaesthetist [æ'ni:sθɪtɪst] n anestesista m/f.
analogy [ə'nælədʒɪ] n analogia.
analyse ['ænəlaɪz] vt analizzare.
analysis, pl **analyses** [ə'næləsɪs, -si:z] n analisi f inv.
analyst ['ænəlɪst] n analista m/f.
analytic(al) [ænə'lɪtɪk(əl)] a analitico(a).
anarchist ['ænəkɪst] a anarchico(a) // n anarchista m/f.
anarchy ['ænəkɪ] n anarchia.
anathema [ə'næθɪmə] n anatema m.
anatomical [ænə'tɔmɪkəl] a anatomico(a).
anatomy [ə'nætəmɪ] n anatomia.
ancestor ['ænsɪstə*] n antenato/a.
ancestral [æn'sestrəl] a avito(a).
ancestry ['ænsɪstrɪ] n antenati mpl; ascendenza.
anchor ['æŋkə*] n ancora // vi (also: **to drop** ~) gettar l'ancora // vt ancorare; ~**age** n ancoraggio.
anchovy ['æntʃəvɪ] n acciuga.
ancient ['eɪnʃənt] a antico(a); (fig) anziano(a).
and [ænd] cj e (often ed before vowel); ~ **so on** e così via; **come** ~ **sit here** vieni a sedere qui; **better** ~ **better** sempre meglio.
Andes ['ændi:z] npl: **the** ~ le Ande.
anecdote ['ænɪkdəut] n aneddoto.
anemia [ə'ni:mɪə] etc = **anaemia** etc.
anesthetic [ænɪs'θetɪk] etc = **anaesthetic** etc.
anew [ə'nju:] ad di nuovo.
angel ['eɪndʒəl] n angelo.
anger ['æŋgə*] n rabbia // vt arrabbiare.
angina [æn'dʒaɪnə] n angina pectoris.
angle ['æŋgl] n angolo; from their ~ dal loro punto di vista // vi: **to** ~ **for** (fig) cercare di farsi fare; ~**r** n pescatore m con la lenza.
Anglican ['æŋglɪkən] a,n anglicano(a).
anglicize ['æŋglɪsaɪz] vt anglicizzare.
angling ['æŋglɪŋ] n pesca con la lenza.
Anglo- ['æŋgləu] prefix anglo...; ~**Saxon** a,n anglosassone (m/f).
angrily ['æŋgrɪlɪ] ad con rabbia.
angry ['æŋgrɪ] a arrabbiato(a), furioso(a); **to be** ~ **with sb/at sth** essere in collera con qd/per qc; **to get** ~ arrabbiarsi; **to make sb** ~ fare arrabbiare qd.
anguish ['æŋgwɪʃ] n angoscia.
angular ['æŋgjulə*] a angolare.
animal ['ænɪməl] a, n animale (m).
animate vt ['ænɪmeɪt] animare // a ['ænɪmɪt] animato(a); ~**d** a animato(a).
animosity [ænɪ'mɔsɪtɪ] n animosità.

aniseed ['ænisiːd] n semi mpl di anice.

ankle ['æŋkl] n caviglia.

annex n ['æneks] (also: **annexe**) edificio annesso // vt [ə'neks] annettere; ~**ation** [-'eɪʃən] n annessione f.

annihilate [ə'naɪəleɪt] vt annientare.

anniversary [æni'vɜːsəri] n anniversario.

annotate ['ænəuteɪt] vt annotare.

announce [ə'nauns] vt annunciare; ~**ment** n annuncio; (letter, card) partecipazione f; ~**r** n (RADIO, TV: between programmes) annunciatore/trice; (in a programme) presentatore/trice.

annoy [ə'nɔɪ] vt dare fastidio a; **don't get** ~**ed!** non irritarti!; ~**ance** n noia; ~**ing** a noioso(a).

annual ['ænjuəl] a annuale // n (BOT) pianta annua; (book) annuario; ~**ly** ad annualmente.

annuity [ə'njuːɪti] n annualità f inv; **life** ~ vitalizio.

annul [ə'nʌl] vt annullare; (law) rescindere; ~**ment** n annullamento; rescissione f.

annum ['ænəm] n see **per**.

anoint [ə'nɔɪnt] vt ungere.

anomaly [ə'nɒməli] n anomalia.

anonymous [ə'nɒniməs] a anonimo(a).

anorak ['ænəræk] n giacca a vento.

another [ə'nʌðə*] a: ~ **book** (one more) un altro libro, ancora un libro; (a different one) un altro libro // pronoun un altro(un'altra), ancora uno(a); see also **one**.

answer ['ɑːnsə*] n risposta; soluzione f // vi rispondere // vt (reply to) rispondere a; (problem) risolvere; (prayer) esaudire; to ~ **the phone** rispondere (al telefono); in ~ **to your letter** in risposta alla sua lettera; **to** ~ **the bell** rispondere al campanello; **to** ~ **the door** aprire la porta; **to** ~ **back** vi ribattere; **to** ~ **for** vt fus essere responsabile di; **to** ~ **to** vt fus (description) corrispondere a; ~**able** a: ~**able (to sb/for sth)** responsabile (verso qd/di qc).

ant [ænt] n formica.

antagonism [æn'tægənizəm] n antagonismo.

antagonist [æn'tægənist] n antagonista m/f; ~**ic** [æntægə'nɪstɪk] a antagonistico(a).

antagonize [æn'tægənaiz] vt provocare l'ostilità di.

Antarctic [ænt'ɑːktɪk] n Antartide f // a antartico(a).

antelope ['æntɪləup] n antilope f.

antenatal ['ænti'neɪtl] a prenatale; ~ **clinic** n assistenza medica preparto.

antenna, pl ~**e** [æn'tɛnə, -niː] n antenna.

anthem ['ænθəm] n antifona; **national** ~ inno nazionale.

ant-hill ['ænthɪl] n formicaio.

anthology [æn'θɒlədʒɪ] n antologia.

anthropology [ænθrə'pɒlədʒɪ] n antropologia.

anti- ['ænti] prefix anti... .

anti-aircraft ['ænti'ɛəkrɑːft] a antiaereo(a).

antibiotic ['æntibaɪ'ɒtɪk] a antibiotico(a) // n antibiotico.

anticipate [æn'tɪsɪpeɪt] vt prevedere; pregustare; (wishes, request) prevenire.

anticipation [æntɪsɪ'peɪʃən] n anticipazione f; (expectation) aspettative fpl; **thanking you in** ~ vi ringrazio in anticipo.

anticlimax ['ænti'klaɪmæks] n: **it was an** ~ fu una completa delusione.

anticlockwise ['ænti'klɒkwaɪz] a in senso antiorario.

antics ['æntɪks] npl buffonerie fpl.

anticyclone ['ænti'saɪkləun] n anticiclone m.

antidote ['æntidəut] n antidoto.

antifreeze ['ænti'friːz] n anticongelante m.

antipathy [æn'tɪpəθi] n antipatia.

antiquated ['æntɪkweɪtɪd] a antiquato(a).

antique [æn'tiːk] n antichità f inv // a antico(a); ~ **dealer** n antiquario/a; ~ **shop** n negozio d'antichità.

antiquity [æn'tɪkwɪti] n antichità f inv.

antiseptic [ænti'septɪk] a antisettico(a) // n antisettico.

antisocial ['ænti'səuʃəl] a antisociale.

antlers ['æntləz] npl palchi mpl.

anus ['eɪnəs] n ano.

anvil ['ænvɪl] n incudine f.

anxiety [æŋ'zaɪəti] n ansia; (keenness): ~ **to do** smania di fare.

anxious ['æŋkʃəs] a ansioso(a), inquieto(a); (keen): ~ **to do/that** impaziente di fare/che + sub.

any ['eni] det (in negative and interrogative sentences = some) del, dell', dello, dei, degli, della, delle; alcuno(a); qualche; nessuno(a); (no matter which) non importa che; (each and every) tutto(a), ogni; **I haven't** ~ **bread/books** non ho pane/libri; **come (at)** ~ **time** vieni a qualsiasi ora; **at** ~ **moment** da un momento all'altro; **in** ~ **case** in ogni caso; **at** ~ **rate** ad ogni modo // pronoun uno(a) qualsiasi; (anybody) chiunque; (in negative and interrogative sentences): **I haven't** ~ non ne ho; **have you got** ~? ne hai?; **can** ~ **of you sing?** c'è qualcuno che sa cantare? // ad (in negative sentences) per niente; (in interrogative and conditional constructions) un po'; **I can't hear him** ~ **more** non lo sento più; **are you feeling** ~ **better?** ti senti un po' meglio?; **do you want** ~ **more soup?** vuoi ancora della minestra?; ~**body** pronoun qualsiasi persona; (in interrogative sentences) qualcuno; (in negative sentences): **I don't see** ~**body** non vedo nessuno; ~**how** ad in qualsiasi modo; ~**one** = ~**body**; ~**thing** pronoun (see anybody) qualsiasi cosa; qualcosa; non ... niente, non ... nulla; ~**time** ad in qualunque momento; quando vuole; ~**way** ad in qualsiasi modo; in or ad ogni modo; ~**where** ad (see anybody) da qualsiasi parte; da qualche parte; **I don't see him ~where** non lo vedo da nessuna parte.

apart [ə'pɑːt] *ad* (*to one side*) a parte; (*separately*) separatamente; **10 miles/a long way ~** a 10 miglia di distanza/molto lontani l'uno dall'altro; **they are living ~** sono separati; **~ from** *prep* a parte, eccetto.

apartheid [ə'pɑːteɪt] *n* apartheid *f*.

apartment [ə'pɑːtmənt] *n* (*US*) appartamento; **~s** *npl* appartamento ammobiliato.

apathetic [æpə'θεtɪk] *a* apatico(a).

apathy ['æpəθɪ] *n* apatia.

ape [eɪp] *n* scimmia // *vt* scimmiottare.

aperitif [ə'pεrɪtɪv] *n* aperitivo.

aperture ['æpətʃuə*] *n* apertura.

apex ['eɪpεks] *n* apice *m*.

aphrodisiac [æfrəu'dɪzɪæk] *a* afrodisiaco(a) // *n* afrodisiaco.

apiece [ə'piːs] *ad* ciascuno(a).

aplomb [ə'plɔm] *n* disinvoltura.

apologetic [əpɔlə'dʒεtɪk] *a* (*tone, letter*) di scusa; **to be very ~ about** scusarsi moltissimo di.

apologize [ə'pɔlədʒaɪz] *vi*: **to ~ (for sth to sb)** scusarsi (di qc a qd), chiedere scusa (a qd per qc).

apology [ə'pɔlədʒɪ] *n* scuse *fpl*.

apoplexy ['æpəplεksɪ] *n* apoplessia.

apostle [ə'pɔsl] *n* apostolo.

apostrophe [ə'pɔstrəfɪ] *n* (*segno*) apostrofo.

appal [ə'pɔːl] *vt* atterrire; sgomentare; **~ling** *a* spaventoso(a).

apparatus [æpə'reɪtəs] *n* apparato.

apparent [ə'pærənt] *a* evidente; **~ly** *ad* evidentemente.

apparition [æpə'rɪʃən] *n* apparizione *f*.

appeal [ə'piːl] *vi* (*LAW*) appellarsi alla legge // *n* (*LAW*) appello; (*request*) richiesta; (*charm*) attrattiva; **to ~ for** chiedere (con insistenza); **to ~ to** (*subj: person*) appellarsi a; (*subj: thing*) piacere a; **to ~ to sb for mercy** chiedere pietà a qd; **it doesn't ~ to me** mi dice poco.

appear [ə'pɪə*] *vi* apparire; (*LAW*) comparire; (*publication*) essere pubblicato(a); (*seem*) sembrare; **it would ~ that** sembra che; **to ~ in Hamlet** recitare nell'Amleto; **to ~ on TV** presentarsi in televisione; **~ance** *n* apparizione *f*; apparenza; (*look, aspect*) aspetto; **to put in** *or* **make an ~ance** fare atto di presenza.

appease [ə'piːz] *vt* calmare, appagare.

appendage [ə'pεndɪdʒ] *n* aggiunta.

appendicitis [əpεndɪ'saɪtɪs] *n* appendicite *f*.

appendix, *pl* **appendices** [ə'pεndɪks, -siːz] *n* appendice *f*.

appetite ['æpɪtaɪt] *n* appetito.

appetizing ['æpɪtaɪzɪŋ] *a* appetitoso(a).

applaud [ə'plɔːd] *vt, vi* applaudire.

applause [ə'plɔːz] *n* applauso.

apple ['æpl] *n* mela; **~ tree** *n* melo.

appliance [ə'plaɪəns] *n* apparecchio.

applicable [ə'plɪkəbl] *a* applicabile.

applicant ['æplɪkənt] *n* candidato.

application [æplɪ'keɪʃən] *n* applicazione *f*; (*for a job, a grant etc*) domanda.

applied [ə'plaɪd] *a* applicato(a).

apply [ə'plaɪ] *vt* (*paint, ointment*): **to ~ (to)** dare (a); (*theory, technique*): **to ~ (to)** applicare (a) // *vi*: **to ~ to** (*ask*) rivolgersi a; (*be suitable for, relevant to*) riguardare, riferirsi a; **to ~ (for)** (*permit, grant, job*) fare domanda (per); **to ~ the brakes** frenare; **to ~ o.s. to** dedicarsi a.

appoint [ə'pɔɪnt] *vt* nominare; **~ment** *n* nomina; (*arrangement to meet*) appuntamento.

appraisal [ə'preɪzl] *n* valutazione *f*.

appreciable [ə'priːʃəbl] *a* apprezzabile.

appreciate [ə'priːʃɪeɪt] *vt* (*like*) apprezzare; (*be grateful for*) essere riconoscente di; (*be aware of*) rendersi conto di // *vi* (*COMM*) aumentare.

appreciation [əpriːʃɪ'eɪʃən] *n* apprezzamento; (*COMM*) aumento del valore.

appreciative [ə'priːʃɪətɪv] *a* (*person*) sensibile; (*comment*) elogiativo(a).

apprehend [æprɪ'hεnd] *vt* arrestare; (*understand*) comprendere.

apprehension [æprɪ'hεnʃən] *n* inquietudine *f*.

apprehensive [æprɪ'hεnsɪv] *a* apprensivo(a).

apprentice [ə'prεntɪs] *n* apprendista *m/f*; **~ship** *n* apprendistato.

approach [ə'prəutʃ] *vi* avvicinarsi // *vt* (*come near*) avvicinarsi a; (*ask, apply to*) rivolgersi a; (*subject, passer-by*) avvicinare // *n* approccio; accesso; (*to problem*) modo di affrontare; **~able** *a* accessibile.

appropriate *vt* [ə'prəuprɪeɪt] (*take*) appropriarsi // *a* [ə'prəuprɪɪt] appropriato(a); adatto(a); **~ly** *ad* in modo appropriato.

approval [ə'pruːvəl] *n* approvazione *f*; **on ~** (*COMM*) in prova, in esame.

approve [ə'pruːv] *vt, vi* approvare; **to ~ of** *vt fus* approvare; **~d school** *n* riformatorio; **approvingly** *ad* in approvazione.

approximate [ə'prɔksɪmɪt] *a* approssimativo(a); **~ly** *ad* circa; **approximation** [-'meɪʃən] *n* approssimazione *f*.

apricot ['eɪprɪkɔt] *n* albicocca.

April ['eɪprəl] *n* aprile *m*; **~ fool!** pesce d'aprile!

apron ['eɪprən] *n* grembiule *m*.

apt [æpt] *a* (*suitable*) adatto(a); (*able*) capace; (*likely*): **to be ~ to do** avere tendenza a fare.

aptitude ['æptɪtjuːd] *n* abilità *f inv*.

aqualung ['ækwəlʌŋ] *n* autorespiratore *m*.

aquarium [ə'kwεərɪəm] *n* acquario.

Aquarius [ə'kwεərɪəs] *n* Acquario.

aquatic [ə'kwætɪk] *a* acquatico(a).

aqueduct ['ækwɪdʌkt] *n* acquedotto.

Arab ['ærəb] n arabo/a.
Arabia [ə'reıbıə] n Arabia; ~**n** a arabo(a).
Arabic ['ærəbık] a arabico(a) // n arabo.
arable ['ærəbl] a arabile.
arbitrary ['ɑ:bıtrərı] a arbitrario(a).
arbitrate ['ɑ:bıtreıt] vi arbitrare; **arbitration** [-'treıʃən] n (LAW) arbitrato; (INDUSTRY) arbitraggio.
arbitrator ['ɑ:bıtreıtə*] n arbitro.
arc [ɑːk] n arco.
arcade [ɑː'keıd] n portico; (passage with shops) galleria.
arch [ɑːtʃ] n arco; (of foot) arco plantare // vt inarcare // a malizioso(a).
archaeologist [ɑːkı'ɔlədʒıst] n archeologo/a.
archaeology [ɑːkı'ɔlədʒı] n archeologia.
archaic [ɑː'keıık] a arcaico(a).
archbishop [ɑːtʃ'bıʃəp] n arcivescovo.
arch-enemy ['ɑːtʃ'enımı] n arcinemico/a.
archer ['ɑːtʃə*] n arciere m; ~**y** n tiro all'arco.
archetype ['ɑːkıtaıp] n archetipo.
archipelago [ɑːkı'pelıgəu] n arcipelago.
architect ['ɑːkıtekt] n architetto; ~**ural** [ɑːkı'tektʃərəl] a architettonico(a); ~**ure** ['ɑːkıtektʃə*] n architettura.
archives ['ɑːkaıvz] npl archivi mpl.
archway ['ɑːtʃweı] n arco.
Arctic ['ɑːktık] a artico(a) // n: **the** ~ l'Artico.
ardent ['ɑːdənt] a ardente.
arduous ['ɑːdjuəs] a arduo(a).
are [ɑː*] vb see **be**.
area ['ɛərıə] n (GEOM) area; (zone) zona; (: smaller) settore m; **dining** ~ n zona pranzo.
arena [ə'riːnə] n arena.
aren't [ɑːnt] = **are not**.
Argentina [ɑːdʒən'tiːnə] n Argentina; **Argentinian** [-'tınıən] a, n argentino/a.
arguable ['ɑːgjuəbl] a discutibile.
argue ['ɑːgjuː] vi (quarrel) litigare; (reason) ragionare; **to** ~ **that** sostenere che.
argument ['ɑːgjumənt] n (reasons) argomento; (quarrel) lite f; (debate) discussione f; ~**ative** [ɑːgjuːˈmentətıv] a litigioso(a).
arid ['ærıd] a arido(a).
Aries ['ɛərız] n Ariete m.
arise, pt **arose**, pp **arisen** [ə'raız, -'rəuz, -'rızn] vi alzarsi; (opportunity, problem) presentarsi; **to** ~ **from** risultare da.
aristocracy [ærıs'tɔkrəsı] n aristocrazia.
aristocrat ['ærıstəkræt] n aristocratico/a; ~**ic** [-'krætık] a aristocratico(a).
arithmetic [ə'rıθmətık] n aritmetica.
ark [ɑːk] n: **Noah's A**~ l'arca di Noè.
arm [ɑːm] n braccio; (MIL: branch) arma // vt armare; ~**s** npl (weapons) armi fpl; **in** ~ a braccetto; ~**band** n bracciale m; ~**chair** n poltrona; ~**ed** a armato(a); ~**ed robbery** n rapina a mano armata; ~**ful** n bracciata.
armistice ['ɑːmıstıs] n armistizio.
armour ['ɑːmə*] n armatura; (also:

~-**plating**) corazza, blindatura; (MIL: tanks) mezzi mpl blindati; ~**ed car** n autoblinda f inv; ~**y** n arsenale m.
armpit ['ɑːmpıt] n ascella.
army ['ɑːmı] n esercito.
aroma [ə'rəumə] n aroma; ~**tic** [ærə'mætık] a aromatico(a).
arose [ə'rəuz] pt of **arise**.
around [ə'raund] ad attorno, intorno // prep intorno a; (fig: about): ~ £5/3 **o'clock** circa 5 sterline/le 3; **is he** ~? è in giro?
arouse [ə'rauz] vt (sleeper) svegliare; (curiosity, passions) suscitare.
arrange [ə'reındʒ] vt sistemare; (programme) preparare; ~**ment** n sistemazione f; (plans etc): ~**ments** progetti mpl, piani mpl.
array [ə'reı] n: ~ **of** fila di.
arrears [ə'rıəz] npl arretrati mpl; **to be in** ~ **with one's rent** essere in arretrato con l'affitto.
arrest [ə'rest] vt arrestare; (sb's attention) attirare // n arresto; **under** ~ in arresto.
arrival [ə'raıvəl] n arrivo; (person) arrivato/a.
arrive [ə'raıv] vi arrivare; **to** ~ **at** vt fus (fig) raggiungere.
arrogance ['ærəgəns] n arroganza.
arrogant ['ærəgənt] a arrogante.
arrow ['ærəu] n freccia.
arsenal ['ɑːsınl] n arsenale m.
arsenic ['ɑːsnık] n arsenico.
arson ['ɑːsn] n incendio doloso.
art [ɑːt] n arte f; (craft) mestiere m; **A**~**s** npl (SCOL) Lettere fpl; ~ **gallery** n galleria d'arte.
artefact ['ɑːtıfækt] n manufatto.
artery ['ɑːtərı] n arteria.
artful ['ɑːtful] a furbo(a).
arthritis [ɑː'θraıtıs] n artrite f.
artichoke ['ɑːtıtʃəuk] n carciofo.
article ['ɑːtıkl] n articolo.
articulate a [ɑː'tıkjulıt] (person) che si esprime forbitamente; (speech) articolato(a) // vi [ɑː'tıkjuleıt] articolare; ~**d lorry** n autotreno.
artificial [ɑːtı'fıʃəl] a artificiale; ~ **respiration** n respirazione f artificiale.
artillery [ɑː'tılərı] n artiglieria.
artisan ['ɑːtızæn] n artigiano/a.
artist ['ɑːtıst] n artista m/f; ~**ic** [ɑː'tıstık] a artistico(a); ~**ry** n arte f.
artless ['ɑːtlıs] a semplice, ingenuo(a).
as [æz, əz] cj (cause) siccome, poiché; (time: moment) come, quando; (: duration) mentre; (manner) come; (in the capacity of) da; ~ **big** ~ tanto grande quanto; **twice** ~ **big** ~ due volte più grande che; **big** ~ **it is** grande com'è; ~ **she said** come lei ha detto; ~ **if** or **though** come se + sub; ~ **for** or **to** quanto a; ~ or **so long** ~ cj finché; purché; ~ **much** (~) **tanto**(a) (... quanto(a)); ~ **many** (~) **tanti**(e) (... quanti(e)); ~ **soon** ~ cj appena; ~ **such** ad come tale; ~ **well** ad

anche; ~ **well** ~ *cj* come pure; *see also* **so, such.**

asbestos [æz'bɛstɒs] *n* asbesto, amianto.

ascend [ə'sɛnd] *vt* salire; ~**ancy** *n* ascendente *m*.

ascent [ə'sɛnt] *n* salita.

ascertain [æsə'teɪn] *vt* accertare.

ascetic [ə'sɛtɪk] *a* ascetico(a).

ascribe [ə'skraɪb] *vt*: to ~ sth to attribuire qc a.

ash [æʃ] *n* (*dust*) cenere f; ~ (**tree**) frassino.

ashamed [ə'feɪmd] *a* vergognoso(a); to be ~ of vergognarsi di; to be ~ (of o.s.) for having done vergognarsi di aver fatto.

ashen ['æʃn] *a* (*pale*) livido(a).

ashore [ə'fɔː*] *ad* a terra; to go ~ sbarcare.

ashtray ['æʃtreɪ] *n* portacenere *m*.

Asia ['eɪʃə] *n* Asia; ~ **Minor** *n* Asia minore; ~**n** *a*, *n* asiatico(a); ~**tic** [eɪsɪ'ætɪk] *a* asiatico(a).

aside [ə'saɪd] *ad* da parte // *n* a parte *m*; to take sb ~ prendere qd a parte.

ask [ɑːsk] *vt* (*request*) chiedere; (*question*) domandare; (*invite*) invitare; to ~ sb sth/sb to do sth chiedere qc a qd/a qd di fare qc; to ~ sb about sth chiedere a qd di qc; to ~ (sb) a question fare una domanda (a qd); to ~ sb out to dinner invitare qd a mangiare fuori; to ~ after *vt fus* chiedere di; to ~ for *vt fus* chiedere.

askance [ə'skɑːns] *ad*: to look ~ at sb guardare qd di traverso.

askew [ə'skjuː] *ad* di traverso, storto.

asleep [ə'sliːp] *a* addormentato(a); to be ~ dormire; to fall ~ addormentarsi.

asparagus [əs'pærəgəs] *n* asparagi *mpl*.

aspect ['æspɛkt] *n* aspetto.

aspersions [əs'pɜːʃənz] *npl*: to cast ~ on diffamare.

asphalt ['æsfælt] *n* asfalto.

asphyxiate [æs'fɪksɪeɪt] *vt* asfissiare; **asphyxiation** [-'eɪʃən] *n* asfissia.

aspiration [æspə'reɪʃən] *n* aspirazione f.

aspire [əs'paɪə*] *vi*: to ~ to aspirare a.

aspirin ['æsprɪn] *n* aspirina.

ass [æs] *n* asino.

assail [ə'seɪl] *vt* assalire; ~**ant** *n* assalitore *m*.

assassin [ə'sæsɪn] *n* assassino; ~**ate** *vt* assassinare; ~**ation** [əsæsɪ'neɪʃən] *n* assassinio.

assault [ə'sɔːlt] *n* (MIL) assalto; (*gen*: *attack*) aggressione f, (LAW): ~ (**and battery**) minacce *fpl* e vie di fatto *fpl* // *vt* assaltare; aggredire; (*sexually*) violentare.

assemble [ə'sɛmbl] *vt* riunire; (TECH) montare // *vi* riunirsi.

assembly [ə'sɛmblɪ] *n* (*meeting*) assemblea; (*construction*) montaggio; ~ **line** *n* catena di montaggio.

assent [ə'sɛnt] *n* assenso, consenso // *vi* assentire.

assert [ə'sɜːt] *vt* asserire; (*insist on*) far valere; ~**ion** [ə'sɜːʃən] *n* asserzione f; ~**ive** *a* assertivo(a).

assess [ə'sɛs] *vt* valutare; ~**ment** *n* valutazione f.

asset ['æsɛt] *n* vantaggio; ~**s** *npl* beni *mpl*; disponibilità *fpl*; attivo.

assign [ə'saɪn] *vt* (*date*) fissare; (*task*): to ~ sth to assegnare qc a; (*resources*): to ~ sth to riservare qc a; (*cause*, *meaning*): to ~ sth to attribuire qc a; ~**ment** *n* compito.

assimilate [ə'sɪmɪleɪt] *vt* assimilare; **assimilation** [-'leɪʃən] *n* assimilazione f.

assist [ə'sɪst] *vt* assistere, aiutare; ~**ance** *n* assistenza, aiuto; ~**ant** *n* assistente *m/f*; (*also*: **shop** ~**ant**) commesso/a.

assizes [ə'saɪzɪz] *npl* assise *fpl*.

associate *a* [ə'səuʃɪt] associato(a); (*member*) aggiunto(a) // *n* collega *m/f*; (*in business*) socio/a // *vb* [ə'səuʃɪeɪt] *vt* associare // *vi*: to ~ with sb frequentare qd.

association [əsəusɪ'eɪʃən] *n* associazione f; ~ **football** *n* (gioco del) calcio.

assorted [ə'sɔːtɪd] *a* assortito(a).

assortment [ə'sɔːtmənt] *n* assortimento.

assume [ə'sjuːm] *vt* supporre; (*responsibilities etc*) assumere; (*attitude*, *name*) prendere; ~**d name** *n* nome *m* falso.

assumption [ə'sʌmpʃən] *n* supposizione f, ipotesi f *inv*.

assurance [ə'fuərəns] *n* assicurazione f; (*self-confidence*) fiducia in se stesso.

assure [ə'fuə*] *vt* assicurare.

asterisk ['æstərɪsk] *n* asterisco.

astern [ə'stɜːn] *ad* a poppa.

asthma ['æsmə] *n* asma; ~**tic** [æs'mætɪk] *a*,*n* asmatico(a).

astir [ə'stɜː*] *ad* in piedi; (*excited*) in fermento.

astonish [ə'stɒnɪʃ] *vt* stupire; ~**ment** *n* stupore *m*.

astound [ə'staund] *vt* sbalordire.

astray [ə'streɪ] *ad*: to go ~ smarrirsi; (*fig*) traviarsi.

astride [ə'straɪd] *prep* a cavalcioni di.

astrologer [əs'trɒlədʒə*] *n* astrologo/a.

astrology [əs'trɒlədʒɪ] *n* astrologia.

astronaut ['æstrənɔːt] *n* astronauta *m/f*.

astronomer [əs'trɒnəmə*] *n* astronomo/a.

astronomical [æstrə'nɒmɪkəl] *a* astronomico(a).

astronomy [əs'trɒnəmɪ] *n* astronomia.

astute [əs'tjuːt] *a* astuto(a).

asylum [ə'saɪləm] *n* asilo; (*building*) manicomio.

at [æt] *prep* a; (*because of*: *following surprised*, *annoyed etc*) di; con; ~ **Paolo's** da Paolo; ~ **the baker's** dal panettiere; ~ **times** talvolta.

ate [eɪt] *pt of* **eat.**

atheism ['eɪθɪɪzəm] *n* ateismo.

atheist ['eɪθɪɪst] *n* ateo/a.

Athens ['æθɪnz] *n* Atene f.

athlete ['æθliːt] *n* atleta *m/f*.

athletic [æθ'lɛtɪk] *a* atletico(a); ~**s** *n* atletica.

Atlantic [ət'læntɪk] *a* atlantico(a) // *n*: the

~ **(Ocean)** l'Atlantico, l'Oceano Atlantico.

atlas ['ætlæs] n atlante m.

atmosphere ['ætmɔsfiə*] n atmosfera.

atmospheric [ætmɔs'ferɪk] a atmosferico(a); ~s n (RADIO) scariche fpl.

atom ['ætɔm] n atomo; ~ic [ə'tɔmɪk] a atomico(a); ~(ic) **bomb** n bomba atomica; ~izer ['ætəmaɪzə*] n atomizzatore m.

atone [ə'təun] vi: **to** ~ **for** espiare.

atrocious [ə'trəuʃəs] a (very bad) pessimo(a).

atrocity [ə'trɔsɪtɪ] n atrocità f inv.

attach [ə'tætʃ] vt attaccare; (document, letter) allegare; (MIL: troops) assegnare; **to be** ~**ed to sb/sth** (to like) essere affezionato(a) a qd/qc; ~**é** [ə'tæʃeɪ] n addetto; ~**é case** n valigetta per documenti; ~**ment** n (tool) accessorio; (love): ~**ment** (to) affetto (per).

attack [ə'tæk] vt attaccare; (task etc) iniziare; (problem) affrontare // n attacco; (also: **heart** ~) infarto.

attain [ə'teɪn] vt (also: **to** ~ **to**) arrivare a, raggiungere; ~**ments** npl cognizioni fpl.

attempt [ə'tɛmpt] n tentativo // vt tentare; ~**ed murder** (LAW) tentato omicidio; **to make an** ~ **on sb's life** attentare alla vita di qd.

attend [ə'tɛnd] vt frequentare; (meeting, talk) andare a; (patient) assistere; **to** ~ **to** vt fus (needs, affairs etc) prendersi cura di; (customer) occuparsi di; ~**ance** n (being present) presenza; (people present) gente f presente; ~**ant** n custode m/f, persona di servizio // a concomitante.

attention [ə'tɛnʃən] n attenzione f; ~s premure fpl, attenzioni fpl; ~**!** (MIL) attenti!; **at** ~ (MIL) sull'attenti; **for the** ~ **of** (ADMIN) per l'attenzione di.

attentive [ə'tɛntɪv] a attento(a); (kind) premuroso(a); ~**ly** ad attentamente.

attest [ə'tɛst] vi: **to** ~ **to** attestare.

attic ['ætɪk] n soffitta.

attire [ə'taɪə*] n abbigliamento.

attitude ['ætɪtjuːd] n atteggiamento; posa.

attorney [ə'tɜːnɪ] n (lawyer) avvocato; (having proxy) mandatario; **A**~ **General** n (Brit) Procuratore m Generale; (US) Ministro della Giustizia; **power of** ~ n procura.

attract [ə'trækt] vt attirare; ~**ion** [ə'trækʃən] n (gen pl: pleasant things) attrattiva; (PHYSICS, fig: towards sth) attrazione f; ~**ive** a attraente.

attribute n ['ætrɪbjuːt] attributo // vt [ə'trɪbjuːt]: **to** ~ **sth** to attribuire qc a.

attrition [ə'trɪʃən] n: **war of** ~ guerra di logoramento.

aubergine ['əubəʒiːn] n melanzana.

auburn ['ɔːbən] a tizianesco(a).

auction ['ɔːkʃən] n (also: **sale by** ~) asta // vt (also: **to sell by** ~) vendere all'asta; (also: **to put up for** ~) mettere all'asta; ~**eer** [-'nɪə*] n banditore m.

audacity [ɔː'dæsɪtɪ] n audacia.

audible ['ɔːdɪbl] a udibile.

audience ['ɔːdɪəns] n (people) pubblico; spettatori mpl; ascoltatori mpl; (interview) udienza.

audio-visual [ɔːdɪəu'vɪzjuəl] a audiovisivo(a).

audit ['ɔːdɪt] n revisione f, verifica // vt rivedere, verificare.

audition [ɔː'dɪʃən] n audizione f.

auditor ['ɔːdɪtə*] n revisore m.

auditorium [ɔːdɪ'tɔːrɪəm] n sala, auditorio.

augment [ɔːg'mɛnt] vt,vi aumentare.

augur ['ɔːgə*] vt (be a sign of) predire // vi: **it** ~**s well** promette bene.

August ['ɔːgəst] n agosto.

august [ɔː'gʌst] a augusto(a).

aunt [ɑːnt] n zia; ~**ie**, ~**y** n zietta.

au pair ['əu'pɛə*] n (also: ~ **girl**) (ragazza f) alla pari inv.

aura ['ɔːrə] n aura.

auspices ['ɔːspɪsɪz] npl: **under the** ~ **of** sotto gli auspici di.

auspicious [ɔːs'pɪʃəs] a propizio(a).

austere [ɔs'tɪə*] a austero(a).

Australia [ɔs'treɪlɪə] n Australia; ~**n** a, n australiano(a).

Austria ['ɔstrɪə] n Austria; ~**n** a, n austriaco(a).

authentic [ɔː'θɛntɪk] a autentico(a).

author ['ɔːθə*] n autore/trice.

authoritarian [ɔːθɔrɪ'tɛərɪən] a autoritario(a).

authoritative [ɔː'θɔrɪtətɪv] a (account etc) autorevole; (manner) autoritario(a).

authority [ɔː'θɔrɪtɪ] n autorità f inv; (permission) autorizzazione f; **the authorities** npl le autorità.

authorize ['ɔːθəraɪz] vt autorizzare.

auto ['ɔːtəu] n (US) auto f inv.

autobiography [ɔːtəbaɪ'ɔgrəfɪ] n autobiografia.

autocratic [ɔːtə'krætɪk] a autocratico(a).

autograph ['ɔːtəgrɑːf] n autografo // vt firmare.

automatic [ɔːtə'mætɪk] a automatico(a) // n (gun) arma automatica; (car) automobile f con cambio automatico; ~**ally** ad automaticamente.

automation [ɔːtə'meɪʃən] n automazione f.

automaton, pl automata [ɔː'tɔmətɔn, -tə] n automa m.

automobile ['ɔːtəməbiːl] n (US) automobile f.

autonomy [ɔː'tɔnəmɪ] n autonomia.

autopsy ['ɔːtɔpsɪ] n autopsia.

autumn ['ɔːtəm] n autunno.

auxiliary [ɔːg'zɪlɪərɪ] a ausiliario(a) // n ausiliare m/f.

avail [ə'veɪl] vt: **to** ~ **o.s. of** servirsi di; approfittarsi di // n: **to no** ~ inutilmente.

availability [əveɪlə'bɪlɪtɪ] n disponibilità.

available [ə'veɪləbl] a disponibile; **every** ~ **means** tutti i mezzi disponibili.

avalanche ['ævəlɑːnʃ] n valanga.

avant-garde ['ævɑ̃'gɑːd] a d'avanguardia.

avarice ['ævərɪs] n avarizia.

Ave. *abbr of* **avenue**.

avenge [ə'vendʒ] *vt* vendicare.

avenue ['ævənjuː] *n* viale *m*.

average ['ævərɪdʒ] *n* media // a medio(a) // *vt* (*a certain figure*) fare di *or* in media; **on ~** in media; **above/below (the) ~** sopra/sotto la media.

averse [ə'vəːs] *a*: **to be ~ to sth/doing** essere avverso(a) a qc/a fare.

aversion [ə'vəːʃən] *n* avversione *f*.

avert [ə'vəːt] *vt* evitare, prevenire; (*one's eyes*) distogliere.

aviation [eɪvɪ'eɪʃən] *n* aviazione *f*.

avid ['ævɪd] *a* avido(a).

avocado [ævə'kɑːdəu] *n* (*also*: **~ pear**) avocado *m inv*.

avoid [ə'vɔɪd] *vt* evitare; **~able** *a* evitabile; **~ance** *n* l'evitare *m*.

await [ə'weɪt] *vt* aspettare; **~ing attention** (*COMM: letter*) in attesa di risposta; (: *order*) in attesa di essere evaso.

awake [ə'weɪk] *a* sveglio(a) // *vb* (*pt* **awoke** [ə'wəuk], *pp* **awoken** [ə'wəukən] *or* **awaked**) *vt* svegliare // *vi* svegliarsi; **~ to** consapevole di; **~ning** [ə'weɪknɪŋ] *n* risveglio.

award [ə'wɔːd] *n* premio; (*LAW*) decreto // *vt* assegnare; (*LAW: damages*) decretare.

aware [ə'wɛə*] *a*: **~ of** (*conscious*) conscio(a) di; (*informed*) informato(a) di; **to become ~ of** accorgersi di; **politically/socially ~** politicamente/socialmente preparato; **~ness** *n* consapevolezza.

awash [ə'wɔʃ] *a*: **~ (with)** inondato(a) (da).

away [ə'weɪ] *a,ad via*; lontano(a); **two kilometres ~** a due chilometri di distanza; **two hours ~ by car** a due ore di distanza in macchina; **the holiday was two weeks ~** ci mancavano due settimane alle vacanze; **~ from** lontano da; **he's ~ for a week** è andato via per una settimana; **he was working/pedalling** *etc* **~** la particella indica la continuità e l'energia dell'azione: lui lavorava/pedalava *etc* più che poteva; **to fade/wither** *etc* **~** la particella rinforza l'idea della diminuzione; **~ match** *n* (*SPORT*) partita fuori casa.

awe [ɔː] *n* timore *m*; **~-inspiring**, **~some** *a* imponente.

awful ['ɔːful] *a* terribile; **~ly** *ad* (*very*) terribilmente.

awhile [ə'waɪl] *ad* (per) un po'.

awkward ['ɔːkwəd] *a* (*clumsy*) goffo(a); (*inconvenient*) scomodo(a); (*embarrassing*) imbarazzante.

awning ['ɔːnɪŋ] *n* (*of tent*) veranda; (*of shop, hotel etc*) tenda.

awoke, awoken [ə'wəuk, -kən] *pt,pp of* **awake**.

awry [ə'raɪ] *ad* di traverso // *a* storto(a); **to go ~** andare a monte.

axe [æks] *n* scure *f* // *vt* (*project etc*) abolire; (*jobs*) sopprimere.

axiom ['æksɪəm] *n* assioma *m*.

axis, *pl* **axes** ['æksɪs, -siːz] *n* asse *m*.

axle ['æksl] *n* (*also*: **~-tree**) asse *m*.

ay(e) [aɪ] *excl* (*yes*) sì.

B

B [biː] *n* (*MUS*) si *m*.

B.A. *abbr see* **bachelor**.

babble ['bæbl] *vi* cianciare; mormorare // *n* ciance *fpl*; mormorio.

baby ['beɪbɪ] *n* bambino/a; **~ carriage** *n* (*US*) carrozzina; **~hood** *n* prima infanzia; **~ish** *a* infantile; **~-sit** *vi* fare il (*or* la) babysitter.

bachelor ['bætʃələ*] *n* scapolo; **B~ of Arts/Science (B.A./B.Sc.)** ≈ laureato/a in lettere/scienze; **~hood** *n* celibato.

back [bæk] *n* (*of person, horse*) dorso, schiena; (*of hand*) dorso; (*of house, car*) didietro; (*of train*) coda; (*of chair*) schienale *m*; (*of page*) rovescio; (*FOOTBALL*) difensore *m* // *vt* (*candidate: also*: **~ up**) appoggiare; (*horse: at races*) puntare su; (*car*) guidare a marcia indietro // *vi* indietreggiare; (*car*) fare marcia indietro // *a* (*in compounds*) posteriore, di dietro; arretrato(a); **~ seats/wheels** (*AUT*) sedili *mpl*/ruote *fpl* posteriori; **~ payments/rent** arretrati *mpl* // *ad* (*not forward*) indietro; (*returned*): **he's ~** lui è tornato; **he ran ~** tornò indietro di corsa; (*restitution*): **throw the ball ~** ritira la palla; **can I have it ~?** posso riaverlo?; (*again*): **he called ~** ha richiamato; **to ~ down** *vi* fare marcia indietro; **to ~ out** *vi* (*of promise*) tirarsi indietro; **~ache** *n* mal *m* di schiena; **~bencher** *n* membro del Parlamento senza potere amministrativo; **~biting** *n* maldicenza; **~bone** *n* spina dorsale; **~cloth** *n* scena di sfondo; **~date** *vt* (*letter*) retrodatare; **~dated pay rise** aumento retroattivo; **~er** *n* sostenitore/trice; (*COMM*) fautore *m*; **~fire** *vi* (*AUT*) far ritorno di fiamma; (*plans*) fallire; **~gammon** *n* tavola reale; **~ground** *n* sfondo; (*of events*) background *m inv*; (*basic knowledge*) base *f*; (*experience*) esperienza; **family ~ground** ambiente *m* familiare; **~ground noise** *n* rumore *m* di fondo; **~hand** *n* (*TENNIS: also*: **~hand stroke**) rovescio; **~handed** *a* (*fig*) ambiguo(a); **~hander** *n* (*bribe*) bustarella; **~ing** *n* (*fig*) appoggio; **~lash** *n* contraccolpo, ripercussione *f*; **~log** *n*: **~log of work** lavoro arretrato; **~ number** *n* (*of magazine etc*) numero arretrato; **~ pay** *n* arretrato di paga; **~side** *n* (*col*) sedere *m*; **~stroke** *n* nuoto sul dorso; **~ward** *a* (*movement*) indietro *inv*; (*person*) tardivo(a); (*country*) arretrato(a); **~ward and forward movement** movimento avanti e indietro; **~wards** *ad* indietro; (*fall, walk*) all'indietro; **~water** *n* (*fig*) posto morto; **~yard** *n* cortile *m* dietro la casa.

bacon ['beɪkən] *n* pancetta.

bacteria [bæk'tɪərɪə] *npl* batteri *mpl*.

bad [bæd] a cattivo(a); (*child*) cattivello(a); (*meat, food*) andato(a) a male; **his ~ leg** la sua gamba malata.

bade [bæd] *pt* of **bid**.

badge [bædʒ] *n* insegna; (*of policemen*) stemma *m*.

badger ['bædʒə*] *n* tasso // *vt* tormentare.

badly ['bædlɪ] *ad* (*work, dress etc*) male; **~ wounded** gravemente ferito; **he needs it ~** ne ha gran bisogno; **~ off** a povero(a).

badminton ['bædmɪntən] *n* badminton *m*.

bad-tempered ['bæd'tɛmpəd] *a* irritabile; di malumore.

baffle ['bæfl] *vt* (*puzzle*) confondere.

bag [bæg] *n* sacco; (*handbag etc*) borsa; (*of hunter*) carniere *m*; bottino // *vt* (*col: take*) mettersi in tasca; prendersi; **~s under the eyes** borse sotto gli occhi.

baggage ['bægɪdʒ] *n* bagagli *mpl*.

baggy ['bægɪ] a largo(a) largo(a).

bagpipes ['bægpaɪps] *npl* cornamusa.

Bahamas [bə'hɑːməz] *npl*: **the ~** le isole Bahama.

bail [beɪl] *n* cauzione *f* // *vt* (*prisoner: gen: to grant ~*) concedere la libertà provvisoria su cauzione a; (*boat: also: ~ out*) aggottare; *see* **bale**; **to ~ out** *vt* (*prisoner*) ottenere la libertà provvisoria su cauzione di.

bailiff ['beɪlɪf] *n* usciere *m*; fattore *m*.

bait [beɪt] *n* esca.

bake [beɪk] *vt* cuocere al forno // *vi* cuocersi al forno; **~d beans** *npl* fagioli *mpl* all'uccelletto; **~r** *n* fornaio/a; panettiere/a; **~ry** *n* panetteria; **baking powder** *n* lievito in polvere.

balaclava [bælə'klɑːvə] *n* (*also: ~ helmet*) passamontagna *m inv*.

balance ['bæləns] *n* equilibrio; (*COMM: sum*) bilancio; (*scales*) bilancia // *vt* tenere in equilibrio; (*pros and cons*) soppesare; (*budget*) far quadrare; (*account*) pareggiare; (*compensate*) contrappesare; **~ of trade/payments** bilancia commerciale/dei pagamenti; **~d** a (*personality, diet*) equilibrato(a); **~ sheet** *n* bilancio.

balcony ['bælkənɪ] *n* balcone *m*.

bald [bɔːld] a calvo(a); **~ness** *n* calvizie *f*.

bale [beɪl] *n* balla; **to ~ out** *vi* (*of a plane*) gettarsi col paracadute.

baleful ['beɪlful] a funesto(a).

balk [bɔːk] *vi*: **to ~ (at)** tirarsi indietro (davanti a); (*horse*) recalcitrare (davanti a).

ball [bɔːl] *n* palla; (*football*) pallone *m*; (*for golf*) pallina; (*dance*) ballo.

ballad ['bæləd] *n* ballata.

ballast ['bæləst] *n* zavorra.

ballerina [bælə'riːnə] *n* ballerina.

ballet ['bæleɪ] *n* balletto.

ballistics [bə'lɪstɪks] *n* balistica.

balloon [bə'luːn] *n* pallone *m*.

ballot ['bælət] *n* scrutinio; **~ box** *n* urna (per le schede); **~ paper** *n* scheda.

ball-point pen ['bɔːlpɔɪnt'pɛn] *n* penna a sfera.

ballroom ['bɔːlrum] *n* sala da ballo.

balsam ['bɔːlsəm] *n* balsamo.

Baltic [bɔːltɪk] a,n: **the ~ (Sea)** il (mare) Baltico.

bamboo [bæm'buː] *n* bambù *m*.

bamboozle [bæm'buːzl] *vt* (*col*) corbellare.

ban [bæn] *n* interdizione *f* // *vt* interdire.

banal [bə'nɑːl] a banale.

banana [bə'nɑːnə] *n* banana.

band [bænd] *n* banda; (*at a dance*) orchestra; (*MIL*) fanfara; **to ~ together** *vi* collegarsi.

bandage ['bændɪdʒ] *n* benda.

bandit ['bændɪt] *n* bandito.

bandwagon ['bændwægən] *n*: **to jump on the ~** (*fig*) seguire la corrente.

bandy ['bændɪ] *vt* (*jokes, insults*) scambiare; **to ~ about** *vt* far circolare.

bandy-legged ['bændɪ'lɛgɪd] a dalle gambe storte.

bang [bæŋ] *n* botta; (*of door*) lo sbattere; (*blow*) colpo // *vt* battere (violentemente); (*door*) sbattere // *vi* scoppiare; sbattere; **to ~ at the door** picchiare alla porta.

bangle ['bæŋgl] *n* braccialetto.

banish ['bænɪʃ] *vt* bandire.

banister(s) ['bænɪstə(z)] *n(pl)* ringhiera.

banjo, **~es** or **~s** ['bændʒəu] *n* banjo *m inv*.

bank [bæŋk] *n* (*for money*) banca, banco; (*of river, lake*) riva, sponda; (*of earth*) banco // *vi* (*AVIAT*) inclinarsi in virata; (*COMM*): **they ~ with Pitt's** sono clienti di Pitt's; **to ~ on** *vt fus* contare su; **~ account** *n* conto di banca; **~er** *n* banchiere *m*; **B~ holiday** *n* giorno di festa (*in cui le banche sono chiuse*); **~ing** *n* attività bancaria; professione *f* di banchiere; **~ing hours** *npl* orario di sportello; **~note** *n* banconota; **~ rate** *n* tasso bancario.

bankrupt ['bæŋkrʌpt] a, *n* fallito(a); **to go ~** fallire; **~cy** *n* fallimento.

banner ['bænə*] *n* bandiera.

bannister(s) ['bænɪstə(z)] *n(pl)* = **banister(s)**.

banns [bænz] *npl* pubblicazioni *fpl* di matrimonio.

banquet ['bæŋkwɪt] *n* banchetto.

banter ['bæntə*] *n* scherzi *mpl* bonari.

baptism ['bæptɪzəm] *n* battesimo.

baptize [bæp'taɪz] *vt* battezzare.

bar [bɑː*] *n* in barra; (*of window etc*) sbarra; (*of chocolate*) tavoletta; (*fig*) ostacolo; restrizione *f*; (*pub*) bar *m inv*; (*counter: in pub*) banco; (*MUS*) battuta // *vt* (*road, window*) sbarrare; (*person*) escludere; (*activity*) interdire; **~ of soap** saponetta; **the B~** (*LAW*) l'Ordine *m* degli avvocati; **~ none** senza eccezione.

barbaric [bɑː'bærɪk] a barbarico(a).

barbecue ['bɑːbɪkjuː] *n* barbecue *m inv*.

barbed wire ['bɑːbd'waɪə*] *n* filo spinato.

barber ['bɑːbə*] *n* barbiere *m*.

barbiturate [bɑː'bɪtjurɪt] *n* barbiturico.

bare [bɛə*] *a* a nudo(a) // *vt* scoprire,

denudare; (teeth) mostrare; **the ~ essentials** lo stretto necessario; **~back** ad senza sella; **~faced** a sfacciato(a); **~foot** a,ad scalzo(a); **~headed** a,ad a capo scoperto; **~ly** ad appena.

bargain ['bɑːgɪn] n (transaction) contratto; (good buy) affare m // vi trattare; **into the ~** per giunta.

barge [bɑːdʒ] n chiatta; **to ~ in** vi (walk in) piombare dentro; (interrupt talk) intromettersi a sproposito; **to ~ into** vt fus urtare contro.

baritone ['bærɪtəʊn] n baritono.

bark [bɑːk] n (of tree) corteccia; (of dog) abbaio // vi abbaiare.

barley ['bɑːlɪ] n orzo.

barmaid ['bɑːmeɪd] n cameriera al banco.

barman ['bɑːmən] n barista m.

barmy ['bɑːmɪ] a (col) tocco(a).

barn [bɑːn] n granaio.

barnacle ['bɑːnəkl] n cirripede m.

barometer [bə'rɔmɪtə*] n barometro.

baron ['bærən] n barone m; **~ess** n baronessa.

barracks ['bærəks] npl caserma.

barrage ['bærɑːʒ] n (MIL) sbarramento.

barrel ['bærəl] n barile m; (of gun) canna; **~ organ** n organetto a cilindro.

barren ['bærən] a sterile; (hills) arido(a).

barricade [bærɪ'keɪd] n barricata // vt barricare.

barrier ['bærɪə*] n barriera.

barring ['bɑːrɪŋ] prep salvo.

barrister ['bærɪstə*] n avvocato/essa (in diritto di parlare davanti a tutte le corti).

barrow ['bærəʊ] n (cart) carriola.

bartender ['bɑːtendə*] n (US) barista m.

barter ['bɑːtə*] n baratto // vt: **to ~ sth for** barattare qc con.

base [beɪs] n base f // vt: **to ~ sth on** basare qc su // a vile; **coffee-~d** a base di caffè; **a Paris-~d firm** una ditta con sede centrale a Parigi; **~ball** n baseball m; **~ment** n seminterrato; (of shop) interrato.

bases ['beɪsiːz] npl of **basis**; ['beɪsɪz] npl of **base**.

bash [bæʃ] vt (col) picchiare; **~ed in** a sfondato(a).

bashful ['bæʃful] a timido(a).

basic ['beɪsɪk] a rudimentale; essenziale; **~ally** [-lɪ] ad fondamentalmente; sostanzialmente.

basil ['bæzl] n basilico.

basin ['beɪsn] n (vessel, also GEO) bacino; (also: **wash~**) lavabo.

basis, pl **bases** ['beɪsɪs, -sɪːz] n base f.

bask [bɑːsk] vi: **to ~ in the sun** crogiolarsi al sole.

basket ['bɑːskɪt] n cesta; (smaller) cestino; (with handle) paniere m; **~ball** n pallacanestro f.

bass [beɪs] n (MUS) basso; **~ clef** n chiave f di basso.

bassoon [bə'suːn] n fagotto.

bastard ['bɑːstəd] n bastardo/a; (col!) stronzo (!).

baste [beɪst] vt (CULIN) ungere con grasso; (SEWING) imbastire.

bat [bæt] n pipistrello; (for baseball etc) mazza; (for table tennis) racchetta; **off one's own ~** di propria iniziativa; **he didn't ~ an eyelid** non battè ciglio.

batch [bætʃ] n (of bread) infornata; (of papers) cumulo.

bated ['beɪtɪd] a: **with ~ breath** col fiato sospeso.

bath [bɑːθ, pl bɑːðz] n (see also **baths**) bagno; (bathtub) vasca da bagno // vt far fare il bagno a; **to have a ~** fare un bagno; **~chair** n poltrona a rotelle.

bathe [beɪð] vi fare il bagno // vt bagnare; **~r** n bagnante m/f.

bathing ['beɪðɪŋ] n bagni mpl; **~ cap** n cuffia da bagno; **~ costume** n costume m da bagno.

bath: ~room n stanza da bagno; **~s** npl bagni mpl pubblici; **~ towel** n asciugamano da bagno.

batman ['bætmən] n (MIL) attendente m.

baton ['bætən] n bastone m; (MUS) bacchetta.

battalion [bə'tælɪən] n battaglione m.

batter ['bætə*] vt battere // n pastetta; **~ed** (hat) sformato(a); (pan) ammaccato(a); **~ed wife/baby** consorte f/bambino(a) maltrattato(a); **~ing ram** n ariete m.

battery ['bætərɪ] n batteria; (of torch) pila.

battle ['bætl] n battaglia // vi lottare; **~field** n campo di battaglia; **~ments** npl bastioni mpl; **~ship** n nave f da guerra.

baulk [bɔːlk] vi = **balk**.

bawdy ['bɔːdɪ] a piccante.

bawl [bɔːl] vi urlare.

bay [beɪ] n (of sea) baia; **to hold sb at ~** tenere qd a bada.

bayonet ['beɪənɪt] n baionetta.

bay window ['beɪ'wɪndəʊ] n bovindo.

bazaar [bə'zɑː*] n bazar m inv; vendita di beneficenza.

b. & b., B. & B. abbr see **bed**.

BBC n abbr of British Broadcasting Corporation.

B.C. ad (abbr of before Christ) a.C.

be, pt **was**, **were**, pp **been** [biː, wɔz, wɔː*, biːn] vi essere; **how are you?** come sta?; **I am warm** ho caldo; **it is cold** fa freddo; **how much is it?** quanto costa?; **he is four (years old)** ha quattro anni; **2 and 2 are 4** 2 più 2 fa 4; **where have you been?** dov'è stato?; dov'è andato?

beach [biːtʃ] n spiaggia // vt tirare in secco; **~wear** n articoli mpl da spiaggia.

beacon ['biːkən] n (lighthouse) faro; (marker) segnale m.

bead [biːd] n perlina.

beak [biːk] n becco.

beaker ['biːkə*] n coppa.

beam [biːm] n trave f; (of light) raggio // vi brillare; **~ing** a (sun, smile) raggiante.

bean [biːn] n fagiolo; (of coffee) chicco.

bear [bɛə*] n orso // vb (pt bore, pp borne)

[bɔː*, bɔːn]) vt portare; (endure) sopportare // vi: to ~ **right/left** piegare a destra/sinistra; to ~ **the responsibility of** assumersi la responsabilità di; ~**able** a sopportabile.

beard [bɪəd] n barba; ~**ed** a barbuto(a).

bearer ['bɛərə*] n portatore m.

bearing ['bɛərɪŋ] n portamento; (behaviour) condotta; (connection) rapporto; (ball) ~**s** npl cuscinetti mpl a sfere; **to take a** ~ fare un rilevamento; **to find one's** ~**s** orientarsi.

beast [biːst] n bestia; ~**ly** a meschino(a); (weather) da cani.

beat [biːt] n battimento; (MUS) tempo; battuta; (of policeman) giro // vt (pt **beat**, pp **beaten**) battere; **off the** ~**en track** fuori mano; **to** ~ **about the bush** menare il can per l'aia; **to** ~ **time** battere il tempo; **to** ~ **off** vt respingere; **to** ~ **up** vt (col: person) picchiare; (eggs) sbattere; ~**er** n (for eggs, cream) frullino; ~**ing** n bastonata.

beautician [bjuː'tɪʃən] n estetista m/f.

beautiful ['bjuːtɪful] a bello(a); ~**ly** ad splendidamente.

beauty ['bjuːtɪ] n bellezza; ~ **salon** n istituto di bellezza; ~ **spot** n neo; (TOURISM) luogo pittoresco.

beaver ['biːvə*] n castoro.

becalmed [bɪ'kɑːmd] a in bonaccia.

became [bɪ'keɪm] pt of **become**.

because [bɪ'kɔz] cj perché; ~ **of** prep a causa di.

beckon ['bɛkən] vt (also: ~ **to**) chiamare con un cenno.

become [bɪ'kʌm] vt (irg: like **come**) diventare; **to** ~ **fat/thin** ingrassarsi/dimagrire; **what has** ~ **of him?** che gli è successo?

becoming [bɪ'kʌmɪŋ] a (behaviour) che si conviene; (clothes) grazioso(a).

bed [bɛd] n letto; (of flowers) aiuola; (of coal, clay) strato; ~ **and breakfast (b. & b.)** n (terms) camera con colazione; ~**clothes** npl biancheria e coperte fpl di letto.

bedlam ['bɛdləm] n manicomio (fig).

bedraggled [bɪ'drægld] a fradicio(a).

bed: ~**ridden** a costretto(a) a letto; ~**room** n camera da letto; ~**side** n: at **sb's** ~**side** al capezzale di qd; ~**sit(ter)** n monolocale m; ~**spread** n copriletto.

bee [biː] n ape f.

beech [biːtʃ] n faggio.

beef [biːf] n manzo.

beehive ['biːhaɪv] n alveare m.

beeline ['biːlaɪn] n: **to make a** ~ **for** buttarsi a capo fitto verso.

been [biːn] pp of **be**.

beer [bɪə*] n birra.

beetle ['biːtl] n scarafaggio; coleottero.

beetroot ['biːtruːt] n barbabietola.

befall [bɪ'fɔːl] vi(vt) (irg: like **fall**) accadere (a).

before [bɪ'fɔː*] prep (in time) prima di; (in space) davanti a // cj prima che + sub; prima di' // ad prima; **the week** ~ **la**

settimana prima; **I've seen it** ~ l'ho già visto; **I've never seen it** ~ è la prima volta che lo vedo; ~**hand** ad in anticipo.

befriend [bɪ'frɛnd] vt assistere; mostrarsi amico a.

beg [bɛg] vi chiedere l'elemosina // vt chiedere in elemosina; (favour) chiedere; (entreat) pregare.

began [bɪ'gæn] pt of **begin**.

beggar ['bɛgə*] n (also: ~**man**, ~**woman**) mendicante m/f.

begin, pt **began**, pp **begun** [bɪ'gɪn, -'gæn, -'gʌn] vt, vi cominciare; ~**ner** n principiante m/f; ~**ning** n inizio, principio.

begrudge [bɪ'grʌdʒ] vt: **to** ~ **sb sth** dare qc a qd a malincuore; invidiare qd per qc.

begun [bɪ'gʌn] pp of **begin**.

behalf [bɪ'hɑːf] n: **on** ~ **of** per conto di; a nome di.

behave [bɪ'heɪv] vi comportarsi; (well: also: ~ **o.s.**) comportarsi bene.

behaviour [bɪ'heɪvjə*] n comportamento, condotta.

beheld [bɪ'hɛld] pt,pp of **behold**.

behind [bɪ'haɪnd] prep dietro; (followed by pronoun) dietro di; (time) in ritardo con // ad dietro; in ritardo // n didietro.

behold [bɪ'həuld] vt (irg: like **hold**) vedere, scorgere.

beige [beɪʒ] a beige inv.

being ['biːɪŋ] n essere m; **to come into** ~ cominciare ad esistere.

belated [bɪ'leɪtɪd] a tardo(a).

belch [bɛltʃ] vi ruttare // vt (gen: ~ **out**: smoke etc) eruttare.

belfry ['bɛlfrɪ] n campanile m.

Belgian ['bɛldʒən] a, n belga (m/f).

Belgium ['bɛldʒəm] n Belgio.

belie [bɪ'laɪ] vt smentire.

belief [bɪ'liːf] n (opinion) opinione f, convinzione f; (trust, faith) fede f; (acceptance as true) credenza.

believe [bɪ'liːv] vt,vi credere; ~**r** n credente m/f.

belittle [bɪ'lɪtl] vt sminuire.

bell [bɛl] n campana; (small, on door, electric) campanello.

belligerent [bɪ'lɪdʒərənt] a (at war) belligerante; (fig) bellicoso(a).

bellow ['bɛləu] vi muggire.

bellows ['bɛləuz] npl soffietto.

belly ['bɛlɪ] n pancia.

belong [bɪ'lɒŋ] vi: **to** ~ **to** appartenere a; (club etc) essere socio di; **this book** ~**s here** questo libro va qui; ~**ings** npl cose fpl, roba.

beloved [bɪ'lʌvɪd] a adorato(a).

below [bɪ'ləu] prep sotto, al di sotto di // ad sotto, di sotto; giù; **see** ~ vedi sotto or oltre.

belt [bɛlt] n cintura; (TECH) cinghia // vt (thrash) picchiare // vi (col) filarsela.

bench [bɛntʃ] n panca; (in workshop) banco; **the B**~ (LAW) la Corte.

bend [bɛnd] vb (pt,pp **bent** [bɛnt]) vt curvare; (leg, arm) piegare // vi curvarsi;

piegarsi // **n** (*in* road) curva; (*in* pipe, river) gomito; **to ~ down** *vi* chinarsi; **to ~ over** *vi* piegarsi.

beneath [bɪ'niːθ] *prep* sotto, al di sotto di; (*unworthy of*) indegno(a) di // *ad* sotto, di sotto.

benefactor ['bɛnɪfæktə*] *n* benefattore *m*.

beneficial [bɛnɪ'fɪʃəl] *a* che fa bene; vantaggioso(a).

benefit ['bɛnɪfɪt] *n* beneficio, vantaggio; (*allowance of money*) indennità *f inv* // *vt* far bene a // *vi*: **he'll ~ from it** ne trarrà beneficio *or* profitto.

Benelux ['bɛnɪlʌks] *n* Benelux *m*.

benevolent [bɪ'nɛvələnt] *a* benevolo(a).

bent [bɛnt] *pt,pp of* bend // *n* inclinazione *f* // *a* (col: *dishonest*) losco(a); **to be ~ on** essere deciso(a) a.

bequeath [bɪ'kwiːð] *vt* lasciare in eredità.

bequest [bɪ'kwɛst] *n* lascito.

bereavement [bɪ'riːvmənt] *n* lutto.

beret ['bɛreɪ] *n* berretto.

Bermuda [bə:'mjuːdə] *n* le Bermude.

berry ['bɛrɪ] *n* bacca.

berserk [bə'sɔːk] *a*: **to go ~** montare su tutte le furie.

berth [bə:θ] *n* (*bed*) cuccetta; (*for ship*) ormeggio // *vi* (*in harbour*) entrare in porto; (*at anchor*) gettare l'ancora.

beseech, *pt,pp* **besought** [bɪ'siːtʃ, -'sɔːt] *vt* implorare.

beset, *pt,pp* **beset** [bɪ'sɛt] *vt* assalire.

beside [bɪ'saɪd] *prep* accanto a; **to be ~ o.s. (with anger)** essere fuori di sé.

besides [bɪ'saɪdz] *ad* inoltre, per di più // *prep* oltre a; a parte.

besiege [bɪ'siːdʒ] *vt* (*town*) assediare; (*fig*) tempestare.

besought [bɪ'sɔːt] *pt,pp of* **beseech.**

best [bɛst] *a* migliore // *ad* meglio; **the ~ part of** (*quantity*) la maggior parte di; **at ~** tutt'al più; **to make the ~ of sth** cavare il meglio possibile da qc; **to the ~ of my knowledge** per quel che ne so; **to the ~ of my ability** al massimo delle mie capacità; **~ man** *n* testimone *m* dello sposo.

bestow [bɪ'stəu] *vt* accordare; (*title*) conferire.

bestseller ['bɛst'sɛlə*] *n* bestseller *m inv.*

bet [bɛt] *n* scommessa // *vt,vi* (*pt,pp* **bet** *or* **betted**) scommettere.

betray [bɪ'treɪ] *vt* tradire; **~al** *n* tradimento.

better ['bɛtə*] *a* migliore // *ad* meglio // *vt* migliorare // *n*: **to get the ~ of** avere la meglio su; **you had ~ do it** è meglio che lo faccia; **he thought ~ of it** cambiò idea; **to get ~** migliorare; **~ off** a più ricco(a); (*fig*): **you'd be ~ off this way** starebbe meglio così.

betting ['bɛtɪŋ] *n* scommesse *fpl*; **~ shop** *n* ufficio dell'allibratore.

between [bɪ'twiːn] *prep* tra // *ad* in mezzo, nel mezzo.

beverage ['bɛvərɪdʒ] *n* bevanda.

beware [bɪ'wɛə*] *vt,vi*: **to ~ (of)** stare attento(a) (a).

bewildered [bɪ'wɪldəd] *a* sconcertato(a), confuso(a).

bewitching [bɪ'wɪtʃɪŋ] *a* affascinante.

beyond [bɪ'jɔnd] *prep* (*in space*) oltre; (*exceeding*) al di sopra di // *ad* di là; **~ doubt** senza dubbio; **~ repair** irreparabile.

bias ['baɪəs] *n* (*prejudice*) pregiudizio; (*preference*) preferenza; **~(s)ed** *a* parziale.

bib [bɪb] *n* bavaglino.

Bible ['baɪbl] *n* Bibbia.

bicker ['bɪkə*] *vi* bisticciare.

bicycle ['baɪsɪkl] *n* bicicletta.

bid [bɪd] *n* offerta; (*attempt*) tentativo // *vb* (*pt* **bade** [bæd] *or* **bid**, *pp* **bidden** ['bɪdn] *or* **bid**) *vi* fare un'offerta // *vt* fare un'offerta di; **to ~ sb good day** dire buon giorno a qd; **~der** *n*: **the highest ~der** il maggior offerente; **~ding** *n* offerte *fpl.*

bide [baɪd] *vt*: **to ~ one's time** aspettare il momento giusto.

bier [bɪə*] *n* bara.

big [bɪg] *a* grande; grosso(a).

bigamy ['bɪgəmɪ] *n* bigamia.

bigheaded ['bɪg'hɛdɪd] *a* presuntuoso(a).

bigot ['bɪgət] *n* persona gretta; **~ed** *a* gretto(a); **~ry** *n* grettezza.

bigwig ['bɪgwɪg] *n* (*col*) pezzo grosso.

bike [baɪk] *n* bici *f inv.*

bikini [bɪ'kiːnɪ] *n* bikini *m inv.*

bile [baɪl] *n* bile *f.*

bilingual [baɪ'lɪŋgwəl] *a* bilingue.

bilious ['bɪlɪəs] *a* biliare; (*fig*) bilioso(a).

bill [bɪl] *n* conto; (*POL*) atto; (*US: banknote*) banconota; (*of bird*) becco; **to fit** *or* **fill the ~** (*fig*) fare al caso.

billet ['bɪlɪt] *n* alloggio.

billfold ['bɪlfəuld] *n* (*US*) portafoglio.

billiards ['bɪlɪədz] *n* biliardo.

billion ['bɪlɪən] *n* (*Brit*) bilione *m*; (*US*) miliardo.

bin [bɪn] *n* bidone *m*; **bread~** *n* cassetta *f* portapane *inv.*

bind, *pt,pp* **bound** [baɪnd, baund] *vt* legare; (*oblige*) obbligare; **~ing** *n* (*of book*) legatura // *a* (*contract*) vincolante.

bingo ['bɪŋgəu] *n* gioco simile alla tombola.

binoculars [bɪ'nɔkjuləz] *npl* binocolo.

bio... [baɪə'...] *prefix*: **~chemistry** *n* biochimica; **~graphy** [baɪ'ɔgrəfɪ] *n* biografia; **~logical** *a* biologico(a); **~logist** [baɪ'ɔlədʒɪst] *n* biologo/a; **~logy** [baɪ'ɔlədʒɪ] *n* biologia.

birch [bə:tʃ] *n* betulla.

bird [bə:d] *n* uccello; (*col: girl*) bambola; **~ watcher** *n* ornitologo/a dilettante.

birth [bə:θ] *n* nascita; **~ certificate** *n* certificato di nascita; **~ control** *n* controllo delle nascite; contraccezione *f*; **~day** *n* compleanno; **~place** *n* luogo di nascita; **~ rate** *n* indice *m* di natalità.

biscuit ['bɪskɪt] *n* biscotto.

bishop ['bɪʃəp] *n* vescovo.

bit [bɪt] *pt of* **bite** // *n* pezzo; (*of tool*) punta;

(*of horse*) morso; **a ~ of** un po' di; **a ~ mad/dangerous** un po' matto/pericoloso.

bitch [bɪtʃ] *n* (*dog*) cagna; (*col!*) vacca.

bite [baɪt] *vt,vi* (*pt* **bit** [bɪt], *pp* **bitten** ['bɪtn]) mordere // *n* morso; (*insect* ~) puntura; (*mouthful*) boccone *m*; **let's have a ~** (**to eat**) mangiamo un boccone; **to ~ one's nails** mangiarsi le unghie.

biting [ˈbaɪtɪŋ] *a* pungente.

bitten [ˈbɪtn] *pp* of **bite**.

bitter [ˈbɪtə*] *a* amaro(a); (*wind, criticism*) pungente // *n* (*beer*) birra amara; **to the ~ end** a oltranza; **~ness** *n* amarezza; gusto amaro; **~sweet** *a* agrodolce.

bivouac [ˈbɪvuæk] *n* bivacco.

bizarre [bɪˈzɑ:*] *a* bizzarro(a).

blab [blæb] *vi* parlare troppo.

black [blæk] *a* nero(a) // *n* nero // *vt* (*INDUSTRY*) boicottare; **to give sb a ~ eye** dare un occhio nero a qd; **~ and blue** *a* tutto(a) pesto(a); **~berry** *n* mora; **~bird** *n* merlo; **~board** *n* lavagna; **~currant** *n* ribes *m* nero; **~en** *vt* annerire; **~leg** *n* crumiro; **~list** *n* lista nera; **~mail** *n* ricatto // *vt* ricattare; **~mailer** *n* ricattatore/trice; **~ market** *n* mercato nero; **~out** *n* oscuramento; (*fainting*) svenimento; **the B~ Sea** il Mar Nero; **~ sheep** *n* pecora nera; **~smith** *n* fabbro ferraio.

bladder [ˈblædə*] *n* vescica.

blade [bleɪd] *n* lama; (*of oar*) pala; **~ of grass** filo d'erba.

blame [bleɪm] *n* colpa // *vt*: **to ~ sb/sth for sth** dare la colpa di qc a qd/qc; **who's to ~?** chi è colpevole?; **~less** *a* irreprensibile.

bland [blænd] *a* mite; (*taste*) blando(a).

blank [blæŋk] *a* bianco(a); (*look*) distratto(a) // *n* spazio vuoto; (*cartridge*) cartuccia a salve.

blanket [ˈblæŋkɪt] *n* coperta.

blare [blɛə*] *vi* strombettare.

blasé [ˈblɑ:zeɪ] *a* blasé *inv*.

blasphemy [ˈblæsfɪmɪ] *n* bestemmia.

blast [blɑ:st] *n* raffica di vento; esplosione *f* // *vt* far saltare; **~-off** *n* (*SPACE*) lancio.

blatant [ˈbleɪtənt] *a* flagrante.

blaze [bleɪz] *n* (*fire*) incendio; (*fig*) vampata // *vi* (*fire*) ardere, fiammeggiare; (*fig*) infiammarsi // *vt*: **to ~ a trail** (*fig*) tracciare una via nuova.

blazer [ˈbleɪzə*] *n* blazer *m inv*.

bleach [bli:tʃ] *n* (*also*: **household ~**) varechina // *vt* (*linen*) sbiancare; **~ed** *a* (*hair*) decolorato(a).

bleak [bli:k] *a* tetro(a).

bleary-eyed [ˈblɪərɪˈaɪd] *a* dagli occhi offuscati.

bleat [bli:t] *vi* belare.

bleed, *pt,pp* **bled** [bli:d, blɛd] *vt* dissanguare // *vi* sanguinare; **my nose is ~ing** mi viene fuori sangue dal naso.

blemish [ˈblemɪʃ] *n* macchia.

blend [blɛnd] *n* miscela // *vt* mescolare // *vi* (*colours etc*) armonizzare.

bless, *pt,pp* **blessed** *or* **blest** [blɛs, blɛst]

vt benedire; **~ you!** (*sneezing*) salute!; **to be ~ed with** godere di; **~ing** *n* benedizione *f*; fortuna.

blew [blu:] *pt* of **blow**.

blight [blaɪt] *n* (*of plants*) golpe *f* // *vt* (*hopes etc*) deludere.

blimey [ˈblaɪmɪ] *excl* (*col*) accidenti!

blind [blaɪnd] *a* cieco(a) // *n* (*for window*) cortina // *vt* accecare; **to turn a ~ eye** (**on** *or* **to**) chiudere gli occhi (di fronte a); **~ alley** *n* vicolo cieco, **~ corner** *n* svolta cieca; **~fold** *n* benda // *a,ad* bendato(a) // *vt* bendare gli occhi a; **~ness** *n* cecità; **~ spot** *n* (*AUT etc*) punto cieco; (*fig*) punto debole.

blink [blɪŋk] *vi* battere gli occhi; (*light*) lampeggiare; **~ers** *npl* paraocchi *mpl*.

bliss [blɪs] *n* estasi *f*.

blister [ˈblɪstə*] *n* (*on skin*) vescica; (*on paintwork*) bolla // *vi* (*paint*) coprirsi di bolle.

blithe [blaɪð] *a* gioioso(a), allegro(a).

blitz [blɪts] *n* blitz *m*.

blizzard [ˈblɪzəd] *n* bufera di neve.

bloated [ˈbləʊtɪd] *a* gonfio(a).

blob [blɔb] *n* (*drop*) goccia; (*stain, spot*) macchia.

block [blɔk] *n* blocco; (*in pipes*) ingombro; (*toy*) cubo; (*of buildings*) isolato // *vt* bloccare; **~ade** [-ˈkeɪd] *n* blocco // *vt* assediare; **~age** *n* ostacolo; **~head** *n* testa di legno; **~ of flats** *n* caseggiato; **in ~ letters** a stampatello.

bloke [bləʊk] *n* (*col*) tizio.

blonde [blɔnd] *a,n* biondo(a).

blood [blʌd] *n* sangue *m*; **~ donor** *n* donatore/trice di sangue; **~ group** *n* gruppo sanguigno; **~less** *a* (*coup*) senza sangue; **~ poisoning** *n* setticemia; **~ pressure** *n* pressione *f* sanguigna; **~shed** *n* spargimento di sangue; **~shot** *a*: **~shot eyes** occhi iniettati di sangue; **~stained** *a* macchiato(a) di sangue; **~stream** *n* flusso del sangue; **~thirsty** *a* assetato(a) di sangue; **~ transfusion** *n* trasfusione *f* di sangue; **~y** *a* sanguinoso(a); (*col!*): **this ~y ...** questo maledetto ...; **~y awful/good** (*col!*) veramente terribile/forte; **~y-minded** *a* perverso(a), ostinato(a).

bloom [blu:m] *n* fiore *m* // *vi* essere in fiore; **~ing** *a* (*col*): **this ~ing ...** questo dannato ... .

blossom [ˈblɔsəm] *n* fiore *m*; (*with pl sense*) fiori *mpl* // *vi* essere in fiore.

blot [blɔt] *n* macchia // *vt* macchiare; **to ~ out** *vt* (*memories*) cancellare; (*view*) nascondere; (*nation, city*) annientare.

blotchy [ˈblɔtʃɪ] *a* (*complexion*) coperto(a) di macchie.

blotting paper [ˈblɔtɪŋpeɪpə*] *n* carta assorbente.

blouse [blauz] *n* (*feminine garment*) camicetta.

blow [bləʊ] *n* colpo // *vb* (*pt* **blew**, *pp* **blown** [blu:, bləʊn]) *vi* soffiare // *vt* (*fuse*) far saltare; **to ~ one's nose** soffiarsi il naso; **to ~ a whistle** fischiare; **to ~**

away vt portare via; **to ~ down** vt abbattere; **to ~ off** vt far volare via; **to ~ off course** far uscire di rotta; **to ~ out** vi scoppiare; **to ~ over** vi calmarsi; **to ~ up** vi saltare in aria // vt far saltare in aria; (tyre) gonfiare; (PHOT) ingrandire; **~lamp** n lampada a benzina per saldare; **~out** n (of tyre) scoppio.

blubber ['blʌbə*] n grasso di balena // vi (pej) piangere forte.

bludgeon ['blʌdʒən] vt prendere a randellate.

blue [bluː] a azzurro(a); **~ film/joke** film/barzelletta pornografico(a); **to have the ~s** essere depresso(a); **~bell** n giacinto di bosco; **~bottle** n moscone m; **~ jeans** npl blue-jeans mpl; **~print** n (fig) progetto.

bluff [blʌf] vi bluffare // n bluff m inv // a (person) brusco(a); **to call sb's ~** mettere alla prova il bluff di qd.

blunder ['blʌndə*] n abbaglio // vi prendere un abbaglio.

blunt [blʌnt] a smussato(a); spuntato(a); (person) brusco(a) // vt smussare; spuntare; **~ly** ad chiaro; bruscamente.

blur [bləː*] n cosa offuscata // vt offuscare.

blurt [bləːt]: **to ~ out** vt lasciarsi sfuggire.

blush [blʌʃ] vi arrossire // n rossore m.

blustery ['blʌstərɪ] a (weather) burrascoso(a).

B.O. n (abbr of body odour) odori mpl del corpo.

boar [bɔː*] n cinghiale m.

board [bɔːd] n tavola; (on wall) tabellone m; (committee) consiglio, comitato; (in firm) consiglio d'amministrazione // vt (ship) salire a bordo di; (train) salire su; **~ and lodging** n vitto e alloggio; **full ~** pensione f completa; **with ~ and lodging** (job) inclusivo di vitto e alloggio; **to go by the ~** (fig): **which goes by the ~** che viene abbandonato; **to ~ up** (door) chiudere con assi; **~er** n pensionante m/f; (SCOL) convittore/trice; **~ing house** n pensione f; **~ing school** n collegio; **~ room** n sala del consiglio.

boast [bəust] vi vantare // vt vantarsi di // n vanteria; vanto; **~ful** a vanaglorioso(a).

boat [bəut] n nave f; (small) barca; **~er** n (hat) paglietta; **~ing** n canottaggio.

bob [bɔb] vi (boat, cork on water: also: **~ up and down**) andare su e giù // n (col = shilling; **to ~ up** vi saltare fuori.

bobbin ['bɔbɪn] n bobina; (of sewing machine) rocchetto.

bobby ['bɔbɪ] n (col) ≈ poliziotto.

bobsleigh ['bɔbsleɪ] n bob m inv.

bodice ['bɔdɪs] n corsetto.

bodily ['bɔdɪlɪ] a fisico(a), corporale // ad corporalmente; interamente; in persona.

body ['bɔdɪ] n corpo; (of car) carrozzeria; (of plane) fusoliera, (fig: quantity) quantità f inv; **a wine with ~** un vino corposo; **~guard** n guardia del corpo; **~work** n carrozzeria.

bog [bɔg] n palude f // vt: **to get ~ged down** (fig) impantanarsi.

boggle ['bɔgl] vi: **the mind ~s** è incredibile.

bogus ['bəugəs] a falso(a); finto(a).

boil [bɔɪl] vt, vi bollire // n (MED) foruncolo; **to ~ down** vi (fig): **to ~ down to** ridursi a; **~er** n caldaia; **~er suit** n tuta; **~ing hot** a bollente.

boisterous ['bɔɪstərəs] a chiassoso(a).

bold [bəuld] a audace; (child) impudente; (outline) chiaro(a); (colour) deciso(a); **~ness** n audacia; impudenza.

Bolivia [bə'lɪvɪə] n Bolivia.

bollard ['bɔləd] n (NAUT) bitta; (AUT) colonnina luminosa.

bolster ['bəulstə*] n capezzale m; **to ~ up** vt sostenere.

bolt [bəult] n chiavistello; (with nut) bullone m // vt serrare; (food) mangiare in fretta // vi scappare via; **a ~ from the blue** (fig) un fulmine a ciel sereno.

bomb [bɔm] n bomba // vt bombardare; **~ard** [bɔm'bɑːd] vt bombardare.

bombastic [bɔm'bæstɪk] a ampolloso(a).

bomb disposal ['bɔmdɪspəuzl] n: **~ unit** corpo degli artificieri.

bomber ['bɔmə*] n bombardiere m.

bombshell ['bɔmʃel] n (fig) notizia bomba.

bona fide ['bəunə'faɪdɪ] a sincero(a); (offer) onesto(a).

bond [bɔnd] n legame m; (binding promise, FINANCE) obbligazione f.

bone [bəun] n osso; (of fish) spina, lisca // vt disossare; togliere le spine a; **~-dry** a asciuttissimo(a).

bonfire ['bɔnfaɪə*] n falò m inv.

bonnet ['bɔnɪt] n cuffia; (Brit: of car) cofano.

bonus ['bəunəs] n premio.

bony ['bəunɪ] a (arm, face, MED: tissue) osseo(a); (meat) pieno di ossi; (fish) pieno(a) di spine.

boo [buː] excl ba! // vt fischiare // n fischio.

booby trap ['buːbɪtræp] n trappola.

book [buk] n libro; (of stamps etc) blocchetto; (COMM): **~s** conti mpl // vt (ticket, seat, room) prenotare; (driver) multare; (football player) ammonire; **~able** a: **seats are ~able** si possono prenotare i posti; **~case** n scaffale m; **~ing office** n biglietteria; **~keeping** n contabilità; **~let** n libricino; **~maker** n allibratore m; **~seller** n libraio; **~shop** n libreria; **~stall** n bancarella di libri; **~store** n = **~shop**.

boom [buːm] n (noise) rimbombo; (busy period) boom m inv // vi rimbombare; andare a gonfie vele.

boomerang ['buːməræŋ] n boomerang m inv.

boon [buːn] n vantaggio.

boorish ['buərɪʃ] a maleducato(a).

boost [buːst] n spinta // vt spingere.

boot [buːt] n stivale m; (for hiking) scarpone m da montagna; (for football etc) scarpa; (Brit: of car) portabagagli m inv; **to ~** (in addition) per giunta, in più.

booth [buːð] n (at fair) baraccone m; (of

cinema, telephone etc) cabina.
booty ['bu:tɪ] *n* bottino.
booze [bu:z] (*col*) *n* alcool *m* // *vi* trincare.
border ['bɔ:də*] *n* orlo; margine *m*; (*of a country*) frontiera; **to ~ on** *vt fus* confinare con; **~line** *n* (*fig*) linea di demarcazione; **~line case** *n* caso limite.
bore [bɔ:*] *pt of* **bear** // *vt* (*hole*) perforare; (*person*) annoiare // *n* (*person*) seccatore/trice; (*of gun*) calibro; **~dom** *n* noia.
boring ['bɔːrɪŋ] *a* noioso(a).
born [bɔ:n] *a*: **to be ~** nascere; **I was ~ in 1960** sono nato nel 1960; **~ blind** nato(a) cieco(a); **a ~ comedian** un comico nato.
borne [bɔ:n] *pp of* **bear**.
borough ['bʌrə] *n* municipio.
borrow ['bɔrəu] *vt*: **to ~ sth (from sb)** prendere in prestito qc (da qd).
borstal ['bɔ:stl] *n* riformatorio.
bosom ['buzəm] *n* petto; (*fig*) seno; **~ friend** *n* amico/a del cuore.
boss [bɔs] *n* capo // *vt* comandare; **~y** *a* prepotente.
bosun ['bəusn] *n* nostromo.
botanical [bə'tænɪkl] *a* botanico(a).
botanist ['bɔtənɪst] *n* botanico/a.
botany ['bɔtənɪ] *n* botanica.
botch [bɔtʃ] *vt* (*also*: **~ up**) fare un pasticcio di.
both [bəuθ] *a* entrambi, tutt'e due // *pronoun*: **~ (of them)** entrambi; **~ of us went, we ~ went** ci siamo andati tutt'e due // *ad*: **they sell ~ meat and poultry** vendono insieme la carne ed il pollame.
bother ['bɔðə*] *vt* (*worry*) preoccupare; (*annoy*) infastidire // *vi* (*gen*: **~ o.s.**) preoccuparsi; **can you ~ed doing it?** ti va di farlo? // *n*: **it is a ~ to have to do** è una seccatura dover fare; **it was no ~ finding** non c'era problema nel trovare.
bottle ['bɔtl] *n* bottiglia; (*baby's*) biberon *m inv* // *vt* imbottigliare; **to ~ up** *vt* contenere; **~neck** *n* ingorgo; **~-opener** *n* apribottiglie *m inv*.
bottom ['bɔtəm] *n* fondo; (*buttocks*) sedere *m* // *a* più basso(a); ultimo(a); **at the ~ of** in fondo a; **~less** *a* senza fondo.
bough [bau] *n* ramo.
bought [bɔ:t] *pt,pp of* **buy**.
boulder ['bəuldə*] *n* masso (tondeggiante).
bounce [bauns] *vi* (*ball*) rimbalzare; (*cheque*) essere restituito(a) // *vt* far rimbalzare // *n* (*rebound*) rimbalzo; **~r** *n* buttafuori *m inv*.
bound [baund] *pt,pp of* **bind** // *n* (*gen pl*) limite *m*; (*leap*) salto // *vt* (*leap*) saltare; (*limit*) delimitare // *a*: **to be ~ to do sth** (*obliged*) essere costretto a fare qc; **out of ~s** il cui accesso è vietato; **he's ~ to fail** (*likely*) è certo di fallire; **~ for** diretto(a) a.
boundary ['baundrɪ] *n* confine *m*.
boundless ['baundlɪs] *a* illimitato(a).

bout [baut] *n* periodo; (*of malaria etc*) attacco; (*BOXING etc*) incontro.
bow *n* [bəu] nodo; (*weapon*) arco; (*MUS*) archetto; [bau] inchino // *vi* [bau] inchinarsi; (*yield*): **to ~ to** *or* **before** sottomettersi a.
bowels [bauəlz] *npl* intestini *mpl*; (*fig*) viscere *fpl*.
bowl [bəul] *n* (*for eating*) scodella; (*for washing*) bacino; (*ball*) boccia; (*of pipe*) fornello // *vi* (*CRICKET*) servire (la palla); **~s** *n* gioco delle bocce; **to ~ over** *vt* (*fig*) sconcertare.
bow-legged ['bəulɛgɪd] *a* dalle gambe storte.
bowler ['bəulə*] *n* giocatore *m* di bocce; (*CRICKET*) giocatore che serve la palla; (*also*: **~ hat**) bombetta.
bowling ['bəulɪŋ] *n* (*game*) gioco delle bocce; **~ alley** *n* pista da bowling; **~ green** *n* campo di bocce.
bow tie ['bəu'taɪ] *n* cravatta a farfalla.
box [bɔks] *n* scatola; (*THEATRE*) palco // *vi* fare del pugilato; **~er** *n* (*person*) pugile *m*; (*dog*) boxer *m inv*; **~ing** *n* (*SPORT*) pugilato; **B~ing Day** *n* Santo Stefano; **~ing gloves** *npl* guantoni *mpl* da pugile; **~ office** *n* biglietteria; **~ room** *n* ripostiglio.
boy [bɔɪ] *n* ragazzo; (*servant*) servo.
boycott ['bɔɪkɔt] *n* boicottaggio // *vt* boicottare.
boyfriend ['bɔɪfrɛnd] *n* ragazzo.
boyish ['bɔɪʃ] *a* di *or* da ragazzo.
B.R. *abbr of* British Rail.
bra [brɑ:] *n* reggipetto, reggiseno.
brace [breɪs] *n* sostegno; (*on teeth*) apparecchio correttore; (*tool*) trapano // *vt* rinforzare, sostenere; **~s** *npl* bretelle *fpl*; **to ~ o.s.** (*fig*) farsi coraggio.
bracelet ['breɪslɪt] *n* braccialetto.
bracing ['breɪsɪŋ] *a* invigorante.
bracken ['brækən] *n* felce *f*.
bracket ['brækɪt] *n* (*TECH*) mensola; (*group*) gruppo; (*TYP*) parentesi *f inv* // *vt* mettere fra parentesi.
brag [bræg] *vi* vantarsi.
braid [breɪd] *n* (*trimming*) passamano; (*of hair*) treccia.
brain [breɪn] *n* cervello; **~s** *npl* cervella *fpl*; **he's got ~s** è intelligente; **~wash** *vt* fare un lavaggio di cervello a; **~wave** *n* lampo di genio; **~y** *a* intelligente.
braise [breɪz] *vt* brasare.
brake [breɪk] *n* (*on vehicle*) freno // *vt, vi* frenare.
bramble ['bræmbl] *n* rovo.
bran [bræn] *n* crusca.
branch [brɑ:ntʃ] *n* ramo; (*COMM*) succursale *f* // *vi* diramarsi.
brand [brænd] *n* marca // *vt* (*cattle*) marcare (a ferro rovente); (*fig: pej*): **to ~ sb a communist** *etc* definire qd come comunista *etc*.
brandish ['brændɪʃ] *vt* brandire.
brand-new ['brænd'nju:] *a* nuovo(a) di zecca.

brandy ['brændɪ] n brandy m inv.

brash [bræʃ] a sfacciato(a).

brass [brɑːs] n ottone m; **the ~** (MUS) gli ottoni; **~ band** n fanfara.

brassière ['bræsɪə*] n reggipetto, reggiseno.

brat [bræt] n (pej) marmocchio, monello/a.

bravado [brə'vɑːdəu] n spavalderia.

brave [breɪv] a coraggioso(a) // n guerriero m pelle rossa inv // vt affrontare; **~ry** n coraggio.

brawl [brɔːl] n rissa.

brawn [brɔːn] n muscolo; (meat) carne f di testa di maiale; **~y** a muscoloso(a).

bray [breɪ] vi ragliare.

brazen ['breɪzn] a svergognato(a) // vt: **to ~ it out** fare lo sfacciato.

brazier ['breɪzɪə*] n braciere m.

Brazil [brə'zɪl] n Brasile m; **~ian** a, n brasiliano(a); **~ nut** n noce f del Brasile.

breach [briːtʃ] vt aprire una breccia in // n (gap) breccia, varco; (breaking): **~ of contract** rottura di contratto; **~ of the peace** violazione f dell'ordine pubblico.

bread [brɛd] n pane m; **~ and butter** n pane e burro; (fig) mezzi mpl di sussistenza; **~bin** n cassetta f portapane inv; **~crumbs** npl briciole fpl; (CULIN) pangrattato; **~ line** n: **to be on the ~ line** avere appena denaro per vivere.

breadth [brɛtθ] n larghezza.

breadwinner ['brɛdwɪnə*] n chi guadagna il pane per tutta la famiglia.

break [breɪk] vb (pt **broke** [brəuk], pp **broken** ['brəukən]) vt rompere; (law) violare // vi rompersi; (weather) cambiare // n (gap) breccia; (fracture) rottura; (rest, also SCOL) intervallo; (: short) pausa; (chance) possibilità f inv; **to ~ one's leg** etc rompersi la gamba etc; **to ~ a record** battere un primato; **to ~ the news to sb** comunicare per primo la notizia a qd; **to ~ down** vt (figures, data) analizzare // vi crollare; (MED) avere un esaurimento (nervoso); (AUT) guastarsi; **to ~ even** vi coprire le spese; **to ~ free** or **loose** vi spezzare i legami; **to ~ in** vt (horse etc) domare // vi (burglar) fare irruzione; **to ~ into** vt fus (house) fare irruzione in; **to ~ off** vi (speaker) interrompersi; (branch) troncarsi; **to ~ open** vt (door etc) sfondare; **to ~ out** vi evadere; **to ~ out in spots** coprirsi di macchie; **to ~ up** vi (partnership) sciogliersi; (friends) separarsi // vt fare in pezzi, spaccare; (fight etc) interrompere, far cessare; **~able** a fragile; **~age** n rottura; **~down** n (AUT) guasto, panna; (in communications) interruzione f, (MED) esaurimento nervoso; **~down service** n servizio riparazioni; **~er** n frangente m.

breakfast ['brɛkfəst] n colazione f.

breakthrough ['breɪkθruː] n (MIL) breccia; (fig) passo avanti.

breakwater ['breɪkwɔːtə*] n frangiflutti m inv.

breast [brɛst] n (of woman) seno; (chest) petto; **~-stroke** n nuoto a rana.

breath [brɛθ] n fiato; **out of ~** senza fiato; **~alyser** n test di verifica per la sobrietà.

breathe [briːð] vt, vi respirare; **~r** n attimo di respiro.

breathless ['brɛθlɪs] a senza fiato.

breath-taking ['brɛθteɪkɪŋ] a sbalorditivo(a).

breed [briːd] vb (pt, pp **bred** [brɛd]) vt allevare // vi riprodursi // n razza, varietà f inv; **~ing** n riproduzione f; allevamento.

breeze [briːz] n brezza.

breezy ['briːzɪ] a arioso(a); allegro(a).

brevity ['brɛvɪtɪ] n brevità.

brew [bruː] vt (tea) fare un infuso di; (beer) fare; (plot) tramare // vi (tea) essere in infusione; (beer) essere in fermentazione; (fig) bollire in pentola; **~er** n birraio; **~ery** n fabbrica di birra.

bribe [braɪb] n bustarella // vt comprare; **~ry** n corruzione f.

brick [brɪk] n mattone m; **~layer** n muratore m.

bridal ['braɪdl] a nuziale.

bride [braɪd] n sposa; **~groom** n sposo; **~smaid** n damigella d'onore.

bridge [brɪdʒ] n ponte m; (NAUT) ponte di comando; (of nose) dorso; (CARDS, DENTISTRY) bridge m inv // vt (river) fare un ponte sopra; (gap) colmare.

bridle ['braɪdl] n briglia // vt tenere a freno; (horse) mettere la briglia a; **~ path** n pista per traffico animale.

brief [briːf] a breve // n (LAW) comparsa // vt dare istruzioni a; **~s** npl mutande fpl; **~case** n cartella; **~ing** n istruzioni fpl.

brigade [brɪ'geɪd] n (MIL) brigata.

brigadier [brɪgə'dɪə*] n generale m di brigata.

bright [braɪt] a luminoso(a); (person) sveglio(a); (colour) vivace; **~en** vt (room) rendere luminoso(a); ornare // vi schiarirsi; (person: gen: **~en up**) rallegrarsi.

brilliance ['brɪljəns] n splendore m.

brilliant ['brɪljənt] a splendente.

brim [brɪm] n orlo; **~ful** a pieno(a) or colmo(a) fino all'orlo; (fig) pieno(a).

brine [braɪn] n acqua salmastra; (CULIN) salamoia.

bring [brɪŋ] pt, pp **brought** [brɔːt] vt portare; **to ~ about** vt causare; **to ~ back** vt riportare; **to ~ down** vt portare giù; abbattere; **to ~ forward** vt portare avanti; (in time) anticipare; **to ~ off** vt (task, plan) portare a compimento; **to ~ out** vt (meaning) mettere in evidenza; **to ~ round** or **to** vt (unconscious person) far rinvenire; **to ~ up** vt allevare; (question) introdurre.

brink [brɪŋk] n orlo.

brisk [brɪsk] a vivace.

bristle ['brɪsl] n setola // vi rizzarsi; **bristling with** irto(a) di.

Britain ['brɪtən] n Gran Bretagna.

British ['brɪtɪʃ] a britannico(a); **the ~** npl i Britannici; **the ~ Isles** npl le Isole Britanniche.

Briton ['brɪtən] n britannico/a.
brittle ['brɪtl] a fragile.
broach [brəʊtʃ] vt (subject) affrontare.
broad [brɔːd] a largo(a); (distinction) generale; (accent) spiccato(a); **in ~ daylight** in pieno giorno; **~ hint** n allusione f esplicita; **~cast** n trasmissione f // vb (pt,pp broadcast) vt trasmettere per radio (or per televisione) // vi fare una trasmissione; **~casting** n radio f inv; televisione f; **~en** vt allargare // vi allargarsi; **~ly** ad (fig) in generale; **~-minded** a di mente aperta.
brochure ['brəʊʃjʊə*] n dépliant m inv.
broil [brɔɪl] vt cuocere a fuoco vivo.
broke [brəʊk] pt of **break** // a (col) squattrinato(a); **~n** pp of **break** // a: **~n leg** etc gamba etc rotta; **in ~n French/English** in un francese/inglese stentato; **~n-hearted** a: **to be ~n-hearted** avere il cuore spezzato.
broker ['brəʊkə*] n agente m.
bronchitis [brɔŋ'kaɪtɪs] n bronchite f.
bronze [brɔnz] n bronzo; **~d** a abbronzato(a).
brooch [brəʊtʃ] n spilla.
brood [bruːd] n covata // vi (hen) covare; (person) rimuginare.
brook [brʊk] n ruscello.
broom [brum] n scopa; **~stick** n manico di scopa.
Bros. abbr of Brothers.
broth [brɔθ] n brodo.
brothel ['brɔθl] n bordello.
brother ['brʌðə*] n fratello; **~hood** n fratellanza; confraternità f inv; **~-in-law** n cognato; **~ly** a fraterno(a).
brought [brɔːt] pt,pp of **bring**.
brow [brau] n fronte f; (rare, gen: eye~) sopracciglio; (of hill) cima; **~beat** vt intimidire.
brown [braun] a bruno(a), marrone // n (colour) color m bruno or marrone // vt (CULIN) rosolare; **~ie** n giovane esploratrice f.
browse [brauz] vi (among books) curiosare fra i libri.
bruise [bruːz] n ammaccatura // vt ammaccare // vi (fruit) ammaccarsi.
brunette [bruː'nɛt] n bruna.
brunt [brʌnt] n: **the ~ of** (attack, criticism etc) il peso maggiore di.
brush [brʌʃ] n spazzola; (quarrel) schermaglia // vt spazzolare; (gen: ~ past, ~ against) sfiorare; **to ~ aside** vt scostare; **to ~ up** vt (knowledge) rinfrescare; **~-off** n: **to give sb the ~-off** dare il ben servito a qd; **~wood** n macchia.
Brussels ['brʌslz] n Bruxelles; **~ sprout** n cavolo di Bruxelles.
brutal ['bruːtl] a brutale; **~ity** [bruː'tælɪtɪ] n brutalità.
brute [bruːt] n bestia.
B.Sc. abbr see **bachelor**.
bubble ['bʌbl] n bolla // vi ribollire; (sparkle, fig) essere effervescente.

buck [bʌk] n maschio (di camoscio, caprone, coniglio etc); (US: col) dollaro // vi sgroppare; **to pass the ~** (to sb) scaricare (su di qd) la propria responsabilità; **to ~ up** vi (cheer up) rianimarsi.
bucket ['bʌkɪt] n secchio.
buckle ['bʌkl] n fibbia // vt affibbiare; (warp) deformare.
bud [bʌd] n gemma; (of flower) boccio // vi germogliare; (flower) sbocciare.
Buddha ['bʊdə] n Budda m.
budding ['bʌdɪŋ] a (flower) in boccio; (poet etc) in erba.
buddy ['bʌdɪ] n (US) compagno.
budge [bʌdʒ] vt scostare // vi spostarsi.
budgerigar ['bʌdʒərɪgɑː*] n pappagallino.
budget ['bʌdʒɪt] n bilancio preventivo // vi: **to ~ for sth** fare il bilancio per qc.
budgie ['bʌdʒɪ] n = **budgerigar**.
buff [bʌf] a color camoscio // n (enthusiast) appassionato/a.
buffalo, pl **~** or **~es** ['bʌfələʊ] n bufalo; (US) bisonte m.
buffer ['bʌfə*] n respingente m; **~ state** n stato cuscinetto.
buffet n ['bufeɪ] (bar, food) buffet m inv // vt ['bʌfɪt] schiaffeggiare; scuotere; urtare.
buffoon [bə'fuːn] n buffone m.
bug [bʌg] n (insect) cimice f; (: gen) insetto; (fig: germ) virus m inv; (spy device) microfono spia // vt mettere sotto controllo; **~bear** n spauracchio.
bugle ['bjuːgl] n tromba.
build [bɪld] n (of person) corporatura // vt (pt,pp built [bɪlt]) costruire; **~er** n costruttore m; **~ing** n costruzione f; edificio; (also: **~ing trade**) edilizia; **~ing society** n società di credito edilizio; **to ~ up** vt accumulare; aumentare; **~-up** n (of gas etc) accumulo.
built [bɪlt] pt,pp of **build**; **well-~** a (person) robusto(a); **~-in** a (cupboard) a muro; (device) incorporato(a); **~-up area** n abitato.
bulb [bʌlb] n (BOT) bulbo; (ELEC) lampadina; **~ous** a bulboso(a).
Bulgaria [bʌl'gɛərɪə] n Bulgaria.
bulge [bʌldʒ] n rigonfiamento // vi essere protuberante or rigonfio(a); **to be bulging with** essere pieno(a) or zeppo(a) di.
bulk [bʌlk] n massa, volume m; **in ~** a pacchi (or cassette etc); (COMM) all'ingrosso; **the ~ of** il grosso di; **~head** n paratia; **~y** a grosso(a); voluminoso(a).
bull [bʊl] n toro; **~dog** n bulldog m inv.
bulldozer ['bʊldəʊzə*] n bulldozer m inv.
bullet ['bʊlɪt] n pallottola.
bulletin ['bʊlɪtɪn] n bollettino.
bullfight ['bʊlfaɪt] n corrida; **~er** n torero; **~ing** n tauromachia.
bullion ['bʊljən] n oro or argento in lingotti.
bullock ['bʊlək] n giovenco.
bull's-eye ['bʊlzaɪ] n centro del bersaglio.
bully ['bʊlɪ] n prepotente m // vt

angariare; (*frighten*) intimidire; ~**ing** *n* prepotenze *fpl*.

bum [bʌm] *n* (*col*: *backside*) culo; (*tramp*) vagabondo/a; **to** ~ **around** *vi* fare il vagabondo.

bumblebee [ˈbʌmblbiː] *n* (*ZOOL*) bombo.

bump [bʌmp] *n* (*blow*) colpo; (*jolt*) scossa; (*on road etc*) protuberanza; (*on head*) bernoccolo // *vt* battere; **to** ~ **along** *vi* procedere sobbalzando; **to** ~ **into** *vt fus* scontrarsi con; ~**er** *n* (*Brit*) paraurti *m inv* // *a*: ~**er harvest** raccolto eccezionale.

bumptious [ˈbʌmpʃəs] *a* presuntuoso(a).

bumpy [ˈbʌmpɪ] *a* dissestato(a).

bun [bʌn] *n* focaccia; (*of hair*) crocchia.

bunch [bʌntʃ] *n* (*of flowers, keys*) mazzo; (*of bananas*) ciuffo; (*of people*) gruppo; ~ **of grapes** grappolo d'uva.

bundle [ˈbʌndl] *n* fascio // *vt* (*also*: ~ **up**) legare in un fascio; (*put*): **to** ~ **sth/sb into** spingere qc/qd in; **to** ~ **off** *vt* (*person*) mandare via in gran fretta.

bung [bʌŋ] *n* tappo // *vt* (*throw*) buttare.

bungalow [ˈbʌŋgələu] *n* bungalow *m inv*.

bungle [ˈbʌŋgl] *vt* abborracciare.

bunion [ˈbʌnjən] *n* callo (al piede).

bunk [bʌŋk] *n* cuccetta; ~ **beds** *npl* letti *mpl* a castello.

bunker [ˈbʌŋkəˀ] *n* (*coal store*) ripostiglio per il carbone; (*MIL, GOLF*) bunker *m inv*.

bunny [ˈbʌnɪ] *n* (*also*: ~ **rabbit**) coniglietto; ~ **girl** *n* coniglietta.

bunting [ˈbʌntɪŋ] *n* pavesi *mpl*, bandierine *fpl*.

buoy [bɔɪ] *n* boa; **to** ~ **up** *vt* tenere a galla; (*fig*) sostenere; ~**ancy** *n* (*of ship*) galleggiabilità; ~**ant** *a* galleggiante; (*fig*) vivace.

burden [ˈbəːdn] *n* carico, fardello // *vt* caricare; (*oppress*) opprimere.

bureau, *pl* ~**x** [bjuəˈrəu, -z] *n* (*furniture*) scrivania; (*office*) ufficio, agenzia.

bureaucracy [bjuəˈrɔkrəsɪ] *n* burocrazia.

bureaucrat [ˈbjuərəkræt] *n* burocrate *m/f*; ~**ic** [-ˈkrætɪk] *a* burocratico(a).

burglar [ˈbəːgləˀ] *n* scassinatore *m*; ~ **alarm** *n* campanello antifurto; ~**ize** *vt* (*US*) svaligiare; ~**y** *n* furto con scasso.

burgle [ˈbəːgl] *vt* svaligiare.

burial [ˈberɪəl] *n* sepoltura; ~ **ground** *n* cimitero.

burly [ˈbəːlɪ] *a* robusto(a).

Burma [ˈbəːmə] *n* Birmania.

burn [bəːn] *vt, vi* (*pt, pp* **burned** *or* **burnt** [bəːnt]) bruciare // *n* bruciatura, scottatura; **to** ~ **down** *vt* distruggere col fuoco; ~**ing question** *n* questione *f* scottante.

burnish [ˈbəːnɪʃ] *vt* brunire.

burnt [bəːnt] *pt, pp of* **burn**.

burp [bəːp] (*col*) *n* rutto // *vi* ruttare.

burrow [ˈbʌrəu] *n* tana // *vt* scavare.

bursar [ˈbəːsəˀ] *n* economo/a; ~**y** *n* borsa di studio.

burst [bəːst] *vb* (*pt, pp* **burst**) *vt* far scoppiare (*or* esplodere) // *vi* esplodere;

(*tyre*) scoppiare // *n* scoppio; (*also*: ~ **pipe**) rottura nel tubo, perdita; ~ **of energy** scoppio d'energia; ~ **of laughter** scoppio di risa; ~ **blood vessel** rottura di un vaso sanguigno; **to** ~ **into flames/tears** scoppiare in fiamme/lacrime; **to be** ~**ing with** essere pronto a scoppiare di; **to** ~ **into** *vt fus* (*room etc*) irrompere in; **to** ~ **open** *vi* aprirsi improvvisamente; (*door*) spalancarsi; **to** ~ **out laughing** scoppiare a ridere; **to** ~ **out of** *vt fus* precipitarsi fuori da.

bury [ˈberɪ] *vt* seppellire; **to** ~ **one's face in one's hands** nascondere la faccia tra le mani.

bus, ~**es** [bʌs, ˈbʌsɪz] *n* autobus *m inv*.

bush [buʃ] *n* cespuglio; (*scrub land*) macchia.

bushel [ˈbuʃl] *n* staio.

bushy [ˈbuʃɪ] *a* cespuglioso(a).

business [ˈbɪznɪs] *n* (*matter*) affare *m*; (*trading*) affari *mpl*; (*firm*) azienda; (*job, duty*) lavoro; **to be away on** ~ essere andato via per affari; **it's none of my** ~ questo non mi riguarda; **it means** ~ non scherza; ~**like** *a* serio(a); efficiente; ~**man** *n* uomo d'affari.

bus-stop [ˈbʌsstɔp] *n* fermata d'autobus.

bust [bʌst] *n* busto; (*ANAT*) seno // *a* (*broken*) rotto(a); **to go** ~ fallire.

bustle [ˈbʌsl] *n* movimento, attività // *vi* darsi da fare; **bustling** *a* (*person*) indaffarato(a); (*town*) animato(a).

busy [ˈbɪzɪ] *a* occupato(a); (*shop, street*) molto frequentato(a) // *vt*: **to** ~ **o.s.** darsi da fare; ~**body** *n* ficcanaso.

but [bʌt] *cj* ma // *prep* eccetto, tranne; **nothing** ~ null'altro che; ~ **for** senza, se non fosse per; **all** ~ **finished** quasi finito; **anything** ~ **finished** tutt'altro che finito.

butane [ˈbjuːteɪn] *n* butano.

butcher [ˈbutʃəˀ] *n* macellaio // *vt* macellare.

butler [ˈbʌtləˀ] *n* maggiordomo.

butt [bʌt] *n* (*cask*) grossa botte *f*; (*thick end*) estremità *f inv* più grossa; (*of gun*) calcio; (*of cigarette*) mozzicone *m*; (*fig*: *target*) oggetto // *vt* cozzare.

butter [ˈbʌtəˀ] *n* burro // *vt* imburrare.

butterfly [ˈbʌtəflaɪ] *n* farfalla.

buttocks [ˈbʌtəks] *npl* natiche *fpl*.

button [ˈbʌtn] *n* bottone *m* // *vt* abbottonare; ~**hole** *n* asola, occhiello // *vt* attaccare un bottone a.

buttress [ˈbʌtrɪs] *n* contrafforte *f*.

buxom [ˈbʌksəm] *a* formoso(a).

buy [baɪ] *vt* (*pt, pp* **bought** [bɔːt]) comprare; **to** ~ **sb sth/sth from sb** comprare qc per qd/qc da qd; **to** ~ **sb a drink** offrire da bere a qd; **to** ~ **up** *vt* accaparrare; ~**er** *n* compratore/trice.

buzz [bʌz] *n* ronzio; (*col*: *phone call*) colpo di telefono // *vi* ronzare.

buzzard [ˈbʌzəd] *n* poiana.

buzzer [ˈbʌzəˀ] *n* cicalino.

by [baɪ] *prep* da; (*beside*) accanto a; vicino a

a, presso; (*before*): ~ **4 o'clock** entro le 4 // *ad see* **pass, go** *etc*; ~ **bus/car** in autobus/macchina; **paid** ~ **the hour** pagato(a) a ore; **to increase** *etc* ~ **the hour** aumentare di ora in ora; **(all)** ~ **oneself** tutto(a) solo(a); ~ **the way a** proposito; ~ **and large** nell'insieme; ~ **and** ~ di qui a poco o presto.

bye(-bye) ['baɪ('baɪ)] *excl* ciao!, arrivederci!

by(e)-law ['baɪlɔ:] *n* legge *f* locale.

by-election ['baɪɪlekʃən] *n* elezione *f* straordinaria.

bygone ['baɪgɔn] *a* passato(a) // *n:* **let** ~**s be** ~**s** mettiamo una pietra sopra.

bypass ['baɪpɑ:s] *n* circonvallazione *f* // *vt* fare una deviazione intorno a.

by-product ['baɪprɔdʌkt] *n* sottoprodotto; (*fig*) conseguenza secondaria.

bystander   ['baɪstændə*]   *n* spettatore/trice.

byword ['baɪwɔ:d] *n:* **to be a** ~ **for** essere sinonimo di.

C

C [si:] *n* (*MUS*) do.

C. *abbr of* centigrade.

cab [kæb] *n* taxi *m inv*; (*of train, truck*) cabina; (*horse-drawn*) carrozza.

cabaret ['kæbəreɪ] *n* cabaret *m inv*.

cabbage ['kæbɪdʒ] *n* cavolo.

cabin ['kæbɪn] *n* capanna; (*on ship*) cabina; ~ **cruiser** *n* cabinato.

cabinet ['kæbɪnɪt] *n* (*POL*) gabinetto; (*furniture*) armadietto; (*also:* **display** ~) vetrinetta; **cocktail** ~ *n* mobile *m* bar *inv*; ~-**maker** *n* stipettaio.

cable ['keɪbl] *n* cavo; fune *f*; (*TEL*) cablogramma *m* // *vt* telegrafare; ~-**car** *n* funivia; ~-**gram** *n* cablogramma *m*; ~ **railway** *n* funicolare *f*.

cache [kæʃ] *n* nascondiglio; **a** ~ **of food** *etc* un deposito segreto di viveri *etc*.

cackle ['kækl] *vi* schiamazzare.

cactus, *pl* **cacti** ['kæktəs, -taɪ] *n* cacto.

caddie ['kædɪ] *n* caddie *m inv*.

cadet [kə'dɛt] *n* (*MIL*) cadetto.

cadge [kædʒ] *vt* accattare; **to** ~ **a meal (off sb)** scroccare un pranzo (a qd).

Caesarean [si:'zɛərɪən] *a:* ~ **(section)** operazione *f* cesarea.

café ['kæfeɪ] *n* caffè *m inv*; **cafeteria** [kæfɪ'tɪərɪə] *n* self-service *m inv*.

caffein(e) ['kæfi:n] *n* caffeina.

cage [keɪdʒ] *n* gabbia.

cagey ['keɪdʒɪ] *a* (*col*) chiuso(a); guardingo(a).

cajole [kə'dʒəul] *vt* allettare.

cake [keɪk] *n* torta; ~ **of soap** saponetta; ~**d a:** ~**d with** incrostato(a) di.

calamity [kə'læmɪtɪ] *n* calamità *f inv*.

calcium ['kælsɪəm] *n* calcio.

calculate ['kælkjuleɪt] *vt* calcolare; **calculating** *a* calcolatore(trice); **calculation** [-'leɪʃən] *n* calcolo; **calculator** *n* calcolatrice *f*.

calculus ['kælkjuləs] *n* calcolo.

calendar ['kæləndə*] *n* calendario; ~ **month** *n* mese *m* (secondo il calendario); ~ **year** *n* anno civile.

calf, calves [kɑ:f, kɑ:vz] *n* (*of cow*) vitello; (*of other animals*) piccolo; (*also:* ~**skin**) (pelle *f* di) vitello; (*ANAT*) polpaccio.

calibre ['kælɪbə*] *n* calibro.

call [kɔ:l] *vt* (*gen, also TEL*) chiamare // *vi* chiamare; (*visit: also:* ~ **in**, ~ **round**): **to** ~ **(for)** passare (a prendere) // *n* (*shout*) grido, urlata; visita; (*telephone*) telefonata; **to be on** ~ essere disponibile; **to** ~ **for** *vt fus* richiedere; **to** ~ **off** *vt* disdire; **to** ~ **on** *vt fus* (*visit*) passare da; (*request*): **to** ~ **on sb to do** chiedere a qd di fare; **to** ~ **up** *vt* (*MIL*) richiamare; ~**box** *n* cabina telefonica; ~**er** *n* persona che chiama; visitatore/trice; ~ **girl** *n* ragazza *f* squillo *inv*; ~**ing** *n* vocazione *f*; ~**ing card** *n* (*US*) biglietto da visita.

callous ['kæləs] *a* indurito(a), insensibile.

calm [kɑ:m] *n* calma // *vt* calmare // *a* calmo(a); ~**ly** *ad* con calma; ~**ness** *n* calma; **to** ~ **down** *vi* calmarsi // *vt* calmare.

calorie ['kælərɪ] *n* caloria.

calve [kɑ:v] *vi* figliare.

calves [kɑ:vz] *npl of* **calf**.

camber ['kæmbə*] *n* (*of road*) bombatura.

Cambodia [kæm'bəudjə] *n* Cambogia.

came [keɪm] *pt of* **come**.

camel ['kæməl] *n* cammello.

cameo ['kæmɪəu] *n* cammeo.

camera   ['kæmərə]   *n*   macchina fotografica; (*also:* **cine**-~, **movie** ~) cinepresa; **in** ~ a porte chiuse; ~**man** *n* cameraman *m inv*.

camouflage ['kæməflɑ:ʒ] *n* camuffamento; (*MIL*) mimetizzazione *f* // *vt* camuffare; mimetizzare.

camp [kæmp] *n* campeggio; (*MIL*) campo // *vi* campeggiare; accamparsi.

campaign [kæm'peɪn] *n* (*MIL, POL etc*) campagna // *vi* (*also fig*) fare una campagna.

campbed ['kæmp'bed] *n* brandina.

camper   ['kæmpə*]   *n*   campeggiatore/trice.

camping ['kæmpɪŋ] *n* campeggio.

campsite ['kæmpsaɪt] *n* campeggio.

campus ['kæmpəs] *n* campus *m inv*.

can [kæn] *auxiliary vb* potere; (*know how to*) sapere; **I** ~ **swim** *etc* so nuotare *etc*; **I** ~ **speak French** so parlare francese // *n* (*of milk*) scatola; (*of oil*) bidone *m*; (*of water*) tanica; (*tin*) scatola // *vt* mettere in scatola.

Canada ['kænədə] *n* Canada *m*.

Canadian [kə'neɪdɪən] *a, n* canadese (*m/f*).

canal [kə'næl] *n* canale *m*.

canary [kə'nɛərɪ] *n* canarino.

cancel ['kænsəl] *vt* annullare; (*train*) sopprimere; (*cross out*) cancellare; ~**lation** [-'leɪʃən] *n* annullamento; soppressione *f*; cancellazione *f*; (*TOURISM*) prenotazione *f* annullata.

cancer ['kænsə*] n cancro; **C~** (sign) Cancro.

candid ['kændɪd] a onesto(a).

candidate ['kændɪdeɪt] n candidato.

candle ['kændl] n candela; **by ~light** a lume di candela; **~stick** n (also: **~holder**) bugia; (bigger, ornate) candeliere m.

candour ['kændə*] n sincerità.

candy ['kændɪ] n zucchero candito; (US) caramella; **~floss** n zucchero filato.

cane [keɪn] n canna; (SCOL) verga // vt punire a colpi di verga.

canine ['kænaɪn] a canino(a).

canister ['kænɪstə*] n scatola metallica.

cannabis ['kænəbɪs] n (drug) hascisc m.

canned ['kænd] a (food) in scatola.

cannibal ['kænɪbəl] n cannibale m/f; **~ism** n cannibalismo.

cannon, pl **~** or **~s** ['kænən] n (gun) cannone m; **~ball** n palla di cannone.

cannot ['kænɔt] = **can not.**

canny ['kænɪ] a furbo(a).

canoe [kə'nu:] n canoa; (SPORT) canotto; **~ing** n (SPORT) canottaggio; **~ist** n canottiere m.

canon ['kænən] n (clergyman) canonico; (standard) canone m.

canonize ['kænənaɪz] vt canonizzare.

can opener ['kænəupnə*] n apriscatole m inv.

canopy ['kænəpɪ] n baldacchino.

cant [kænt] n gergo.

can't [kænt] = **can not.**

cantankerous [kæn'tæŋkərəs] a stizzoso(a).

canteen [kæn'ti:n] n mensa; (of cutlery) portaposate m inv.

canter ['kæntə*] n piccolo galoppo.

cantilever ['kæntɪliːvə*] n trave f a sbalzo.

canvas ['kænvəs] n tela; **under ~** (camping) sotto la tenda; (NAUT) sotto la vela.

canvass ['kænvəs] vt: **~ing** sollecitazione f.

canyon ['kænjən] n canyon m inv.

cap [kæp] n (also FOOTBALL) berretto; (of pen) coperchio; (of bottle) tappo // vt tappare; (outdo) superare; **~ped with** ricoperto(a) di.

capability [keɪpə'bɪlɪtɪ] n capacità f inv, abilità f inv.

capable ['keɪpəbl] a capace; **~ of** capace di; suscettibile di.

capacity [kə'pæsɪtɪ] n capacità f inv; (of lift etc) capienza; **in his ~ as** nella sua qualità di; **to work at full ~** lavorare al massimo delle proprie capacità.

cape [keɪp] n (garment) cappa; (GEO) capo.

capital ['kæpɪtl] n (also: **~ city**) capitale f; (money) capitale m; (also: **~ letter**) (lettera) maiuscola; **~ gains** npl utili mpl di capitale; **~ism** n capitalismo; **~ist** a capitalista; **~ punishment** n pena capitale.

capitulate [kə'pɪtjuleɪt] vi capitolare.

capricious [kə'prɪʃəs] a capriccioso(a).

Capricorn ['kæprɪkɔ:n] n Capricorno.

capsize [kæp'saɪz] vt capovolgere // vi capovolgersi.

capstan ['kæpstən] n argano.

capsule ['kæpsju:l] n capsula.

captain ['kæptɪn] n capitano // vt capitanare.

caption ['kæpʃən] n leggenda.

captivate ['kæptɪveɪt] vt avvincere.

captive ['kæptɪv] a, n prigioniero(a).

captivity [kæp'tɪvɪtɪ] n prigionia; **in ~** (animal) in servitù.

capture ['kæptʃə*] vt catturare, prendere; (attention) attirare // n cattura.

car [ka:*] n macchina, automobile f.

carafe [kə'ræf] n caraffa.

caramel ['kærəml] n caramello.

carat ['kærət] n carato.

caravan ['kærəvæn] n roulotte f inv.

caraway ['kærəweɪ] n: **~ seed** seme m di cumino.

carbohydrates [ka:bəu'haɪdreɪts] npl (foods) carboidrati mpl.

carbon ['ka:bən] n carbonio; **~ copy** n copia f carbone inv; **~ paper** n carta carbone.

carburettor [ka:bju'retə*] n carburatore m.

carcass ['ka:kəs] n carcassa.

card [ka:d] n carta; (visiting **~** etc) biglietto; (Christmas **~** etc) cartolina; **~board** n cartone m; **~ game** n gioco di carte.

cardiac ['ka:dɪæk] a cardiaco(a).

cardigan ['ka:dɪgən] n cardigan m inv.

cardinal ['ka:dɪnl] a, n cardinale (m).

card index ['ka:dɪndeks] n schedario.

care [kɛə*] n cura, attenzione f; (worry) preoccupazione f // vi: **to ~ about** interessarsi di; **would you ~ to/for ...?** ti piacerebbe ...?; **I wouldn't ~ to do it** non lo vorrei fare; **in sb's ~** alle cure di qd; **to take ~** fare attenzione; **to take ~ of** vt curarsi di; **to ~ for** vt fus aver cura di; (like) volere bene a; **I don't ~** non me ne importa; **I couldn't ~** less non me ne importa un bel niente.

career [kə'rɪə*] n carriera // vi (also: **~ along**) andare di (gran) carriera.

carefree ['kɛəfri:] a sgombro(a) di preoccupazioni.

careful ['kɛəful] a attento(a); (cautious) cauto(a); **(be) ~!** attenzione!; **~ly** ad con cura; cautamente.

careless ['kɛəlɪs] a negligente; (heedless) spensierato(a); **~ly** ad trascuratamente, senza cura; **~ness** n negligenza; spensieratezza.

caress [kə'rɛs] n carezza // vt accarezzare.

caretaker ['kɛəteɪkə*] n custode m.

car-ferry ['ka:fɛrɪ] n traghetto.

cargo, **~es** ['ka:gəu] n carico.

Caribbean [kærɪ'bi:ən] a: **the ~ (Sea)** il Mar dei Caraibi.

caricature ['kærɪkətjuə*] n caricatura.

carnal ['ka:nl] a carnale.

carnation [kɑː'neɪʃən] n garofano.

carnival ['kɑːnɪvəl] n (public celebration) carnevale m.

carol ['kærəl] n: (Christmas) ~ canto di Natale.

carp [kɑːp] n (fish) carpa; **to** ~ **at** vt fus trovare a ridire su.

car park ['kɑːpɑːk] n parcheggio.

carpenter ['kɑːpɪntə*] n carpentiere m.

carpentry ['kɑːpɪntrɪ] n carpenteria.

carpet ['kɑːpɪt] n tappeto // vt coprire con tappeto.

carriage ['kærɪdʒ] n vettura; trasporto; (of typewriter) carrello; (bearing) portamento; ~**way** n (part of road) strada rotabile.

carrier ['kærɪə*] n (of disease) portatore/trice; (COMM) impresa di trasporti; (NAUT) portaerei m inv; (on car, bicycle) portabagagli m inv; ~ **bag** n sacchetto.

carrot ['kærət] n carota.

carry ['kærɪ] vt (subj: person) portare; (: vehicle) trasportare; (a motion, bill) far passare; (involve: responsibilities etc) comportare // vi (sound) farsi sentire; **to be carried away** (fig) farsi trascinare; **to** ~ **on** vi: **to** ~ **on with sth/doing** continuare qc/a fare // vt mandare avanti; **to** ~ **out** vt (orders) eseguire; (investigation) svolgere; ~**cot** n culla portabile.

cart [kɑːt] n carro // vt trasportare con carro.

cartilage ['kɑːtɪlɪdʒ] n cartilagine f.

carton ['kɑːtən] n (box) scatola di cartone; (of yogurt) cartone m; (of cigarettes) stecca.

cartoon [kɑː'tuːn] n (PRESS) disegno umoristico; (satirical) caricatura; (comic strip) fumetto; (CINEMA) disegno animato; ~**ist** n disegnatore/trice; caricaturista m/f; fumettista m/f.

cartridge ['kɑːtrɪdʒ] n (for gun, pen) cartuccia; (for camera) caricatore m; (music tape) cassetta; (of record player) testina.

carve [kɑːv] vt (meat) trinciare; (wood, stone) intagliare; **carving** n (in wood etc) scultura; **carving knife** n trinciante m.

car wash ['kɑːwɔʃ] n lavaggio auto.

cascade [kæs'keɪd] n cascata // vi scendere a cascata.

case [keɪs] n caso; (LAW) causa, processo; (box) scatola; (also: suit~) valigia; **he hasn't put forward his** ~ **very well** non ha dimostrato bene il suo caso; **in** ~ **of** in caso di; **in** ~ **he** caso mai lui; **just in** ~ in caso di bisogno.

cash [kæʃ] n denaro; (COMM) denaro liquido; (COMM: in payment) pagamento in contanti // vt incassare; **to pay (in)** ~ pagare in contanti; ~ **with order/on delivery** (COMM) pagamento all'ordinazione/contro assegno; ~**book** n giornale m di cassa; ~**desk** n cassa.

cashew [kæ'ʃuː] n (also: ~ **nut**) anacardio.

cashier [kæ'ʃɪə*] n cassiere(a).

cashmere [kæʃ'mɪə*] n cachemire m.

cash register ['kæʃrɛdʒɪstə*] n registratore m di cassa.

casing ['keɪsɪŋ] n rivestimento.

casino [kə'siːnəu] n casinò m inv.

cask [kɑːsk] n botte f.

casket ['kɑːskɪt] n cofanetto; (US: coffin) bara.

casserole ['kæsərəul] n casseruola; (food) stufato (nella casseruola).

cast [kɑːst] vt (pt, pp cast) (throw) gettare; (shed) perdere; spogliarsi di; (metal) gettare, fondere // n (THEATRE) complesso di attori; (mould) forma; (also: plaster ~) ingessatura; (THEATRE): **to** ~ **sb as Hamlet** scegliere qd per la parte di Amleto; **to** ~ **one's vote** votare, dare il voto; **to** ~ **off** vi (NAUT) salpare.

castanets [kæstə'nɛts] npl castagnette fpl.

castaway ['kɑːstəwəɪ] n naufrago/a.

caste [kɑːst] n casta.

casting ['kɑːstɪŋ] a: ~ **vote** voto decisivo.

cast iron ['kɑːst'aɪən] n ferro battuto.

castle ['kɑːsl] n castello; (fortified) rocca.

castor ['kɑːstə*] n (wheel) rotella; ~ **oil** n olio di ricino; ~ **sugar** n zucchero semolato.

castrate [kæs'treɪt] vt castrare.

casual ['kæʒjul] a (by chance) casuale, fortuito(a); (irregular: work etc) avventizio(a); (unconcerned) noncurante, indifferente; ~ **wear** n casual m; ~ **labour** n manodopera avventizia; ~**ly** ad con disinvoltura; casualmente.

casualty ['kæʒjultɪ] n ferito/a; (dead) morto/a, vittima; **heavy casualties** npl grosse perdite fpl.

cat [kæt] n gatto.

catalogue ['kætəlɔg] n catalogo.

catalyst ['kætəlɪst] n catalizzatore m.

catapult ['kætəpʌlt] n catapulta, fionda.

cataract ['kætərækt] n (also MED) cateratta.

catarrh [kə'tɑː*] n catarro.

catastrophe [kə'tæstrəfɪ] n catastrofe f; **catastrophic** [kætə'strɔfɪk] a catastrofico(a).

catch [kætʃ] vb (pt,pp caught [cɔːt]) vt (train, thief, cold) acchiappare; (ball) chiappare; (person: by surprise) sorprendere; (understand) comprendere; (get entangled) impigliare // vi (fire) prendere // n (fish etc caught) retata, presa; (trick) inganno; (TECH) gancio; **to** ~ **sb's attention** or **eye** attirare l'attenzione di qd; **to** ~ **fire** prendere fuoco; **to** ~ **sight of** scorgere; **to** ~ **up** vi mettersi in pari // vt (also: ~ **up with**) raggiungere.

catching ['kætʃɪŋ] a (MED) contagioso(a).

catchment area ['kætʃmənt'ɛərɪə] n (SCOL) circoscrizione f scolare; (GEO) bacino pluviale.

catch phrase ['kætʃfreɪz] n slogan m inv; frase f fatta.

catchy ['kætʃɪ] a orecchiabile.

catechism ['kætɪkɪzəm] *n* (*REL*) catechismo.

categoric(al) [kætɪ'gɔrɪk(əl)] *a* categorico(a).

categorize ['kætɪgəraɪz] *vt* categorizzare.

category ['kætɪgərɪ] *n* categoria.

cater ['keɪtə*] *vi* (*gen:* ~ **for**) provvedere da mangiare (per); **to** ~ **for** *vt fus* (*needs*) provvedere a; (*readers, consumers*) incontrare i gusti di; ~**er** *n* fornitore *m*; ~**ing** *n* approvvigionamento; ~**ing trade** *n* settore *m* ristoranti.

caterpillar ['kætəpɪlə*] *n* bruco; ~ **track/vehicle** *n* catena/trattore *m* a cingoli.

cathedral [kə'θiːdrəl] *n* cattedrale *f*, duomo.

catholic ['kæθəlɪk] *a* universale; aperto(a); eclettico(a); **C**~ *a,n* (*REL*) cattolico(a).

cattle ['kætl] *npl* bestiame *m*, bestie *fpl*.

caught [kɔːt] *pt,pp of* **catch**.

cauliflower ['kɒlɪflauə*] *n* cavolfiore *m*.

cause [kɔːz] *n* causa // *vt* causare; **there is no** ~ **for concern** non c'è ragione di preoccuparsi.

causeway ['kɔːzweɪ] *n* strada rialzata.

caustic ['kɔːstɪk] *a* caustico(a).

caution ['kɔːʃən] *n* prudenza; (*warning*) avvertimento // *vt* avvertire; ammonire.

cautious ['kɔːʃəs] *a* cauto(a); ~**ly** *ad* prudentemente; ~**ness** *n* cautela.

cavalry ['kævəlrɪ] *n* cavalleria.

cave [keɪv] *n* caverna, grotta; **to** ~ **in** *vi* (*roof etc*) crollare; ~**man** *n* uomo delle caverne.

cavern ['kævən] *n* caverna.

caviar(e) ['kævɪɑː*] *n* caviale *m*.

cavity ['kævɪtɪ] *n* cavità *f inv*.

cavort [kə'vɔːt] *vi* far capriole.

CBI *n* (*abbr of Confederation of British Industries*) ≈ Confindustria.

cc *abbr of cubic centimetres; carbon copy*.

cease [siːs] *vt,vi* cessare; ~**fire** *n* cessate il fuoco *m inv*; ~**less** *a* incessante, continuo(a).

cedar ['siːdə*] *n* cedro.

cede [siːd] *vt* cedere.

ceiling ['siːlɪŋ] *n* soffitto.

celebrate ['sɛlɪbreɪt] *vt,vi* celebrare; ~**d** *a* celebre; **celebration** [-'breɪʃən] *n* celebrazione *f*.

celebrity [sɪ'lɛbrɪtɪ] *n* celebrità *f inv*.

celery ['sɛlərɪ] *n* sedano.

celestial [sɪ'lɛstɪəl] *a* celeste.

celibacy ['sɛlɪbəsɪ] *n* celibato.

cell [sɛl] *n* cella; (*ELEC*) elemento (di batteria).

cellar ['sɛlə*] *n* sottosuolo, cantina.

'cello ['tʃɛləu] *n* violoncello.

cellophane ['sɛləfeɪn] *n* cellophane *m*.

cellulose ['sɛljuləus] *n* cellulosa.

Celtic ['kɛltɪk, 'sɛltɪk] *a* celtico(a).

cement [sə'mɛnt] *n* cemento // *vt* cementare.

cemetery ['sɛmɪtrɪ] *n* cimitero.

cenotaph ['sɛnətɑːf] *n* cenotafio.

censor ['sɛnsə*] *n* censore *m*; ~**ship** *n* censura.

censure ['sɛnʃə*] *vt* riprovare, censurare.

census ['sɛnsəs] *n* censimento.

cent [sɛnt] *n* (*US: coin*) centesimo, = *1:100 di un dollaro; see also* **per.**

centenary [sɛn'tiːnərɪ] *n* centenario.

centi... ['sɛntɪ] *prefix:* ~**grade** *a* centigrado(a); ~**metre** *n* centimetro.

centipede ['sɛntɪpiːd] *n* centopiedi *m inv*.

central ['sɛntrəl] *a* centrale; ~ **heating** *n* riscaldamento centrale; ~**ize** *vt* accentrare.

centre ['sɛntə*] *n* centro; ~**-forward** *n* (*SPORT*) centroavanti *m inv*; ~**-half** *n* (*SPORT*) centromediano.

centrifugal [sɛn'trɪfjugəl] *a* centrifugo(a).

century ['sɛntjurɪ] *n* secolo.

ceramic [sɪ'ræmɪk] *a* ceramico(a).

cereal ['siːrɪəl] *n* cereale *m*.

ceremony ['sɛrɪmənɪ] *n* cerimonia; **to stand on** ~ fare complimenti.

certain ['səːtən] *a* certo(a); **to make** ~ **of** assicurarsi di; **for** ~ per certo, di sicuro; ~**ly** *ad* certamente, certo; ~**ty** *n* certezza.

certificate [sə'tɪfɪkɪt] *n* certificato; diploma *m*.

certify ['səːtɪfaɪ] *vt* certificare // *vi*: **to** ~ **to** attestare a.

cervix ['səːvɪks] *n* cervice *f*.

cessation [sə'seɪʃən] *n* cessazione *f*, arresto.

cesspool ['sɛspuːl] *n* pozzo nero.

cf. (*abbr = compare*) cfr., confronta.

chafe [tʃeɪf] *vt* fregare, irritare.

chaffinch ['tʃæfɪntʃ] *n* fringuello.

chain [tʃeɪn] *n* catena // *vt* (*also:* ~ **up**) incatenare; ~ **reaction** *n* reazione *f* a catena; **to** ~ **smoke** *vi* fumare una sigaretta dopo l'altra; ~ **store** *n* negozio a catena.

chair [tʃɛə*] *n* sedia; (*armchair*) poltrona; (*of university*) cattedra // *vt* (*meeting*) presiedere; ~**lift** *n* seggiovia; ~**man** *n* presidente *m*.

chalet ['ʃæleɪ] *n* chalet *m inv*.

chalice ['tʃælɪs] *n* calice *m*.

chalk [tʃɔːk] *n* gesso.

challenge ['tʃælɪndʒ] *n* sfida // *vt* sfidare; (*statement, right*) mettere in dubbio; **to** ~ **sb to a fight/game** sfidare qd a battersi/ad una partita; **to** ~ **sb to do** sfidare qd a fare; ~**r** *n* (*SPORT*) sfidante *m/f*; **challenging** *a* sfidante; provocatorio(a).

chamber ['tʃeɪmbə*] *n* camera; ~ **of commerce** camera di commercio; ~**maid** *n* cameriera; ~ **music** *n* musica da camera.

chamois ['ʃæmwɑː] *n* camoscio; ~ **leather** *n* ['ʃæmɪleðə*] *n* pelle *f* di camoscio.

champagne [ʃæm'peɪn] *n* champagne *m inv*.

champion ['tʃæmpɪən] *n* campione/essa; ~**ship** *n* campionato.

chance [tʃɑːns] *n* caso; (*opportunity*)

occasione f; (likelihood) possibilità f inv // vt: to ~ it rischiarlo // a fortuito(a); there is little ~ of his coming è molto improbabile che venga; to take a ~ arrischiarlo; by ~ per caso.

chancel ['tʃɑ:nsəl] n coro.

chancellor ['tʃɑ:nsələ*] n cancelliere m; C~ of the Exchequer n Cancelliere dello Scacchiere.

chandelier [ʃændə'liə*] n lampadario.

change [tʃeɪndʒ] vt cambiare; (transform): to ~ sb into trasformare qd in // vi cambiarsi; (be transformed): to ~ into trasformarsi in // n cambiamento; (money) resto; to ~ one's mind cambiare idea; a ~ of clothes una cambiata; for a ~ tanto per cambiare; small ~ spiccioli mpl, moneta; ~able a (weather) variabile; ~over n cambiamento, passaggio.

changing ['tʃeɪndʒɪŋ] a che cambia; (colours) cangiante; ~ room n (in shop) camerino; (SPORT) spogliatoio.

channel ['tʃænl] n canale m; (of river, sea) alveo // vt canalizzare; through the usual ~s per le solite vie; the (English) C~ la Manica; the C~ Islands le Isole Normanne.

chant [tʃɑ:nt] n canto; salmodia // vt cantare; salmodiare.

chaos ['keɪɔs] n caos m.

chaotic [keɪ'ɔtɪk] a caotico(a).

chap [tʃæp] n (col: man) tipo // vt (skin) screpolare.

chapel ['tʃæpəl] n cappella.

chaperon ['ʃæpərəun] n accompagnatrice f // vt accompagnare.

chaplain ['tʃæplɪn] n cappellano.

chapter ['tʃæptə*] n capitolo.

char [tʃɑ:*] vt (burn) carbonizzare // vi (cleaner) lavorare come domestica (a ore) // n = charlady.

character ['kærɪktə*] n carattere m; (in novel, film) personaggio; (eccentric) originale m; ~istic [-'rɪstɪk] a caratteristico(a) // n caratteristica; ~ize vt caratterizzare.

charade [ʃə'rɑ:d] n sciarada.

charcoal ['tʃɑ:kəul] n carbone m di legna.

charge [tʃɑ:dʒ] n accusa; (cost) prezzo; (of gun, battery, MIL: attack) carica // vt (LAW): to ~ sb (with) accusare qd (di); (gun, battery, MIL: enemy) caricare; (customer) fare pagare a; (sum) fare pagare // vi (gen with: up, along etc) lanciarsi; ~s npl: bank ~s commissioni fpl bancarie; labour ~s costi mpl del lavoro; to ~ in/out precipitarsi dentro/fuori; is there a ~? c'è da pagare?; there's no ~ non c'è niente da pagare; to take ~ of incaricarsi di; to be in ~ of essere responsabile per; to have ~ of sb aver cura di qd; to ~ an expense (up) to sb addebitare una spesa a qd.

chariot ['tʃærɪət] n carro.

charitable ['tʃærɪtəbl] a caritatevole.

charity ['tʃærɪtɪ] n carità; opera pia.

charlady ['tʃɑ:leɪdɪ] n domestica a ore.

charm [tʃɑ:m] n fascino; amuleto // vt affascinare, incantare; ~ing a affascinante.

chart [tʃɑ:t] n tabella; grafico; (map) carta nautica // vt fare una carta nautica di.

charter ['tʃɑ:tə*] vt (plane) noleggiare // n (document) carta; ~ed accountant n ragioniere/a professionista; ~ flight n volo m charter inv.

chase [tʃeɪs] vt inseguire; (away) cacciare // n caccia.

chasm ['kæzəm] n abisso.

chassis ['ʃæsɪ] n telaio.

chastity ['tʃæstɪtɪ] n castità.

chat [tʃæt] vi (also: have a ~) chiacchierare // n chiacchierata.

chatter ['tʃætə*] vi (person) ciarlare // n ciarle fpl; ~box n chiacchierone/a.

chatty ['tʃætɪ] a (style) familiare; (person) chiacchierino(a).

chauffeur ['ʃəufə*] n autista m.

cheap [tʃi:p] a a buon mercato; (joke) grossolano(a); (poor quality) di cattiva qualità // ad a buon mercato; ~en vt ribassare; (fig) avvilire.

cheat [tʃi:t] vi imbrogliare; (at school) copiare // vt ingannare; (rob) defraudare // n imbroglione m; copione m; (trick) inganno.

check [tʃek] vt verificare; (passport, ticket) controllare; (halt) fermare; (restrain) contenere // n verifica; controllo; (curb) freno; (bill) conto; (pattern: gen pl) quadretti mpl; (US) = cheque; to ~ in vi (in hotel) registrare; (at airport) presentarsi all'accettazione // vt (luggage) depositare; to ~ off vt segnare; to ~ out vi (in hotel) saldare il conto // vt (luggage) ritirare; to ~ up vi: to ~ up (on sth) investigare qc; to ~ up on sb informarsi sul conto di qd; ~ers n (US) dama; ~mate n scaccomatto; ~up n (MED) controllo medico.

cheek [tʃi:k] n guancia; (impudence) faccia tosta; ~bone n zigomo; ~y a sfacciato(a).

cheer [tʃiə*] vt applaudire; (gladden) rallegrare // vi applaudire // n (gen pl) applausi mpl; evviva mpl; ~s! salute!; to ~ up vi rallegrarsi, farsi animo // vt rallegrare; ~ful a allegro(a); ~io excl ciao!

cheese [tʃi:z] n formaggio; ~board n piatto da formaggio.

chef [ʃef] n capocuoco.

chemical ['kemɪkəl] a chimico(a) // n prodotto chimico.

chemist ['kemɪst] n farmacista m/f; (scientist) chimico/a; ~ry n chimica; ~'s (shop) n farmacia.

cheque [tʃek] n assegno; ~book n libretto degli assegni.

chequered ['tʃekəd] a (fig) eclettico(a).

cherish ['tʃerɪʃ] vt aver caro; (hope etc) nutrire.

cherry ['tʃerɪ] n ciliegia.

chess [tʃes] n scacchi mpl; ~board n scacchiera; ~man n pezzo degli scacchi.

chest [tʃest] n petto; (box) cassa; ~ **of drawers** n cassettone m.

chestnut ['tʃesnʌt] n castagna; ~ **(tree)** n castagno.

chew [tʃu:] vt masticare; ~**ing gum** n chewing gum m.

chic [ʃi:k] a elegante.

chick [tʃik] n pulcino.

chicken [ˈtʃikin] n pollo; ~ **feed** n (fig) miseria; ~ **pox** n varicella.

chicory [ˈtʃikəri] n cicoria.

chief [tʃi:f] n capo // a principale; ~**ly** ad per lo più, soprattutto.

chiffon [ˈʃifɔn] n chiffon m inv.

chilblain [ˈtʃilblein] n gelone m.

child, pl ~**ren** [tʃaild, ˈtʃildrən] n bambino/a; ~**birth** n parto; ~**hood** n infanzia; ~**ish** a puerile; ~**like** a fanciullesco(a); ~ **minder** n bambinaia.

Chile [ˈtʃili] n Cile m; ~**an** a, n cileno(a).

chill [tʃil] n freddo; (MED) infreddatura // a freddo(a), gelido(a) // vt raffreddare; ~**y** a freddo(a), fresco(a); (sensitive to cold) freddoloso(a); **to feel** ~**y** sentirsi infreddolito(a).

chime [tʃaim] n carillon m inv // vi suonare, scampanare.

chimney [ˈtʃimni] n camino.

chimpanzee [tʃimpænˈzi:] n scimpanzé m inv.

chin [tʃin] n mento.

china [ˈtʃainə] n porcellana.

China [ˈtʃainə] n Cina.

Chinese [tʃaiˈni:z] a cinese // n cinese m/f; (LING) cinese m.

chink [tʃiŋk] n (opening) fessura; (noise) tintinnio.

chip [tʃip] n (gen pl: CULIN) patatina fritta; (of wood, glass, stone) scheggia // vt (cup, plate) scheggiare; ~**pings** npl: **loose** ~**pings** brecciame m.

chiropodist [kiˈrɔpədist] n pedicure m/f inv.

chirp [tʃə:p] n cinguettio // vi cinguettare.

chisel [ˈtʃizl] n cesello.

chit [tʃit] n biglietto.

chivalrous [ˈʃivəlrəs] a cavalleresco(a).

chivalry [ˈʃivlri] n cavalleria; cortesia.

chives [tʃaivz] npl erba cipollina.

chloride [ˈklɔːraid] n cloruro.

chlorine [ˈklɔːriːn] n cloro.

chock [tʃɔk] n zeppa; ~**-a-block**, ~**-full** a pieno(a) zeppo(a).

chocolate [ˈtʃɔklit] n (substance) cioccolato, cioccolata; (drink) cioccolata; (a sweet) cioccolatino.

choice [tʃɔis] n scelta // a scelto(a).

choir [ˈkwaiə*] n coro; ~**boy** n corista m fanciullo.

choke [tʃəuk] vi soffocare // vt soffocare; (block) ingombrare // n (AUT) valvola dell'aria.

cholera [ˈkɔlərə] n colera m.

choose, pt **chose**, pp **chosen** [tʃu:z, tʃəuz, ˈtʃəuzn] vt scegliere; **to ~ to do** decidere di fare; preferire fare.

chop [tʃɔp] vt (wood) spaccare; (CULIN: also:

~ **up**) tritare // n colpo netto; (CULIN) braciola; **to ~ down** vt (tree) abbattere; ~**py** a (sea) mosso(a); ~**sticks** npl bastoncini mpl cinesi.

choral [ˈkɔrəl] a corale.

chord [kɔːd] n (MUS) accordo.

chore [tʃɔː*] n faccenda; **household** ~**s** faccende fpl domestiche.

choreographer [kɔriˈɔgrəfə*] n coreografo/a.

chorister [ˈkɔristə*] n corista m/f.

chortle [ˈtʃɔːtl] vi ridacchiare.

chorus [ˈkɔːrəs] n coro; (repeated part of song, also fig) ritornello.

chose [tʃəuz] pt of **choose**.

chosen [ˈtʃəuzn] pp of **choose**.

Christ [kraist] n Cristo.

christen [ˈkrisn] vt battezzare; ~**ing** n battesimo.

Christian [ˈkristiən] a,n cristiano(a); ~**ity** [-ˈæniti] n cristianesimo; cristianità; ~ **name** n prenome m.

Christmas [ˈkrisməs] n Natale m; ~ **card** n cartolina di Natale; ~ **Eve** n la vigilia di Natale; ~ **tree** n albero di Natale.

chrome [krəum] n = **chromium plating**.

chromium [ˈkrəumiəm] n cromo; ~ **plating** n cromatura.

chromosome [ˈkrəuməsəum] n cromosoma m.

chronic [ˈkrɔnik] a cronico(a).

chronicle [ˈkrɔnikl] n cronaca.

chronological [krɔnəˈlɔdʒikəl] a cronologico(a).

chrysanthemum [kriˈsænθəməm] n crisantemo.

chubby [ˈtʃʌbi] a paffuto(a).

chuck [tʃʌk] vt buttare, gettare; **to ~ out** vt buttar fuori; **to ~ (up)** vt piantare.

chuckle [ˈtʃʌkl] vi ridere sommessamente.

chum [tʃʌm] n compagno/a.

chunk [tʃʌŋk] n pezzo; (of bread) tocco.

church [tʃə:tʃ] n chiesa; ~**yard** n sagrato.

churn [tʃə:n] n (for butter) zangola; (also: **milk** ~) bidone m.

chute [ʃu:t] n cascata; (also: **rubbish** ~) canale m di scarico; (children's slide) scivolo.

CID n (abbr of Criminal Investigation Department) ≈ polizia giudiziaria.

cider [ˈsaidə*] n sidro.

cigar [siˈgɑː*] n sigaro.

cigarette [sigəˈret] n sigaretta; ~ **case** n portasigarette m inv; ~ **end** n mozzicone m; ~ **holder** n bocchino.

cinch [sintʃ] n (col): **it's a** ~ è presto fatto.

cinder [ˈsində*] n cenere f.

cine [ˈsini]: ~**-camera** n cinepresa; ~**-film** n pellicola.

cinema [ˈsinəmə] n cinema m inv.

cine-projector [siniprəˈdʒektə*] n proiettore m.

cinnamon [ˈsinəmən] n cannella.

cipher [ˈsaifə*] n cifra; (fig: faceless

employee etc) persona di nessun conto.

circle ['sɔːkl] *n* cerchio; (*of friends etc*) circolo; (*in cinema*) galleria // *vi* girare in circolo // *vt* (*surround*) circondare; (*move round*) girare intorno a.

circuit ['sɔːkɪt] *n* circuito; ~**ous** [sɔː'kjuːtəs] *a* indiretto(a).

circular ['sɔːkjulə*] *a, n* circolare (*f*).

circulate ['sɔːkjuleɪt] *vi* circolare // *vt* far circolare; **circulation** [-'leɪʃən] *n* circolazione *f*; (*of newspaper*) tiratura.

circumcise ['sɔːkəmsaɪz] *vt* circoncidere.

circumference [sə'kʌmfərəns] *n* circonferenza.

circumstances ['sɔːkəmstənsɪz] *npl* circostanze *fpl*; (*financial condition*) condizioni *fpl* finanziarie.

circus ['sɔːkəs] *n* circo.

cistern ['sɪstən] *n* cisterna; (*in toilet*) serbatoio d'acqua.

cite [saɪt] *vt* citare.

citizen ['sɪtɪzn] *n* (*POL*) cittadino/a; (*resident*): **the ~s of this town** gli abitanti di questa città; ~**ship** *n* cittadinanza.

citrus fruit ['sɪtrəs'fruːt] *n* agrume *m*.

city ['sɪtɪ] *n* città *f inv*; **the C~** la Città di Londra (*centro commerciale*).

civic ['sɪvɪk] *a* civico(a).

civil ['sɪvɪl] *a* civile; ~ **engineer** *n* ingegnere *m* civile; ~**ian** [sɪ'vɪlɪən] *a, n* borghese (*m/f*).

civilization [sɪvɪlaɪ'zeɪʃən] *n* civiltà *f inv*.

civilized ['sɪvɪlaɪzd] *a* civilizzato(a); (*fig*) cortese.

civil: ~ **law** *n* codice *m* civile; (*study*) diritto civile; ~ **servant** *n* impiegato/a statale; **C~ Service** *n* amministrazione *f* statale; ~ **war** *n* guerra civile.

claim [kleɪm] *vt* rivendicare; sostenere, pretendere; (*damages*) richiedere // *vi* (*for insurance*) richiedere // *n* rivendicazione *f*; pretesa; (*right*) diritto; (*insurance*) ~ richiesta; ~**ant** *n* (*ADMIN, LAW*) rivendicatore/trice.

clam [klæm] *n* vongola.

clamber ['klæmbə*] *vi* arrampicarsi.

clammy ['klæmɪ] *a* (*weather*) caldo(a) umido(a); (*hands*) viscido(a).

clamp [klæmp] *n* grappa; pinza; morsa // *vt* ammorsare.

clan [klæn] *n* clan *m inv*.

clang [klæŋ] *n* fragore *m*, suono metallico.

clap [klæp] *vi* applaudire; ~**ping** *n* applausi *mpl*.

claret ['klærət] *n* vino di Bordeaux.

clarification [klærɪfɪ'keɪʃən] *n* (*fig*) chiarificazione *f*, schiarimento.

clarify ['klærɪfaɪ] *vt* chiarificare, schiarire.

clarinet [klærɪ'nɛt] *n* clarinetto.

clarity ['klærɪtɪ] *n* chiarità.

clash [klæʃ] *n* frastuono; (*fig*) scontro // *vi* scontrarsi; cozzare.

clasp [klɑːsp] *n* fermaglio, fibbia // *vt* stringere.

class [klɑːs] *n* classe *f* // *vt* classificare.

classic ['klæsɪk] *a* classico(a) // *n* classico; ~**al** *a* classico(a).

classification [klæsɪfɪ'keɪʃən] *n* classificazione *f*.

classify ['klæsɪfaɪ] *vt* classificare.

classmate ['klɑːsmeɪt] *n* compagno/a di classe.

classroom ['klɑːsrum] *n* aula.

clatter ['klætə*] *n* acciottolio; scalpitio // *vi* acciottolare; scalpitare.

clause [klɔːz] *n* clausola; (*LING*) proposizione *f*.

claustrophobia [klɔːstrə'fəubɪə] *n* claustrofobia.

claw [klɔː] *n* tenaglia; (*of bird of prey*) artiglio; (*of lobster*) pinza // *vt* graffiare; afferrare.

clay [kleɪ] *n* argilla.

clean [kliːn] *a* pulito(a); (*clear, smooth*) liscio(a) // *vt* pulire; **to** ~ **out** *vt* far piazza pulita di; **to** ~ **up** *vi* far pulizia // *vt* (*also fig*) ripulire; ~**er** *n* (*person*) donna delle pulizie; (*also*: **dry** ~**er**) tintore/a; (*product*) smacchiatore *m*; ~**ing** *n* pulizia; ~**liness** ['klɛnlɪnɪs] *n* pulizia.

cleanse [klɛnz] *vt* pulire; purificare; ~**r** *n* detergente *m*.

clean-shaven ['kliːn'ʃeɪvn] *a* sbarbato(a).

clean-up ['kliːn'ʌp] *n* pulizia.

clear [klɪə*] *a* chiaro(a); (*road, way*) libero(a) // *vt* sgombrare; liberare; (*table*) sparecchiare; (*COMM: goods*) liquidare; (*LAW: suspect*) discolpare; (*obstacle*) superare // *vi* (*weather*) rasserenarsi; (*fog*) andarsene // *ad*: ~ **of** distante da; **to** ~ **up** *vi* schiarirsi // *vt* mettere in ordine; (*mystery*) risolvere; ~**ance** *n* (*removal*) sgombro; (*free space*) spazio; (*permission*) autorizzazione *f*, permesso; ~**ance sale** *n* vendita di liquidazione; ~**-cut** *a* ben delineato(a), distinto(a); ~**ing** *n* radura; (*BANKING*) clearing *m*; ~**ly** *ad* chiaramente; ~**way** *n* (*Brit*) strada con divieto di sosta.

clef [klɛf] *n* (*MUS*) chiave *f*.

clench [klɛntʃ] *vt* stringere.

clergy ['klɔːdʒɪ] *n* clero; ~**man** *n* ecclesiastico.

clerical ['klɛrɪkəl] *a* d'impiegato; (*REL*) clericale.

clerk [klɑːk, (*US*) klɔːrk] *n* impiegato/a; (*US: salesman/ woman*) commesso/a.

clever ['klɛvə*] *a* (*mentally*) intelligente; (*deft, skilful*) abile; (*device, arrangement*) ingegnoso(a).

cliché ['kliːʃeɪ] *n* cliché *m inv*.

click [klɪk] *vi* scattare.

client ['klaɪənt] *n* cliente *m/f*; ~**ele** [kliːɑːn'tɛl] *n* clientela.

cliff [klɪf] *n* scogliera scoscesa, rupe *f*.

climate ['klaɪmɪt] *n* clima *m*.

climax ['klaɪmæks] *n* culmine *m*.

climb [klaɪm] *vi* salire; (*clamber*) arrampicarsi // *vt* salire; (*CLIMBING*) scalare // *n* salita; arrampicata; scalata; **to** ~ **down** *vi* scendere; ~**er** *n* (*also*: **rock** ~**er**) rocciatore/trice; alpinista m/f; ~ing n (also: rock ~ing) alpinismo.

clinch [klɪntʃ] vt (deal) concludere.

cling, pt, pp clung [klɪŋ, klʌŋ] vi: to ~ (to) tenersi stretto (a); (of clothes) aderire strettamente (a).

clinic ['klɪnɪk] n clinica; ~al a clinico(a).

clink [klɪŋk] vi tintinnare.

clip [klɪp] n (for hair) forcina; (also: paper ~) graffetta; (holding hose etc) anello d'attacco // vt (also: ~ together: papers) attaccare insieme; (hair, nails) tagliare; (hedge) tosare; ~pers npl macchinetta per capelli; (also: nail ~pers) forbicine fpl per le unghie.

clique [kli:k] n cricca.

cloak [kləuk] n mantello; ~room n (for coats etc) guardaroba m inv; (W.C.) gabinetti mpl.

clock [klɔk] n orologio; ~wise ad in senso orario; ~work n movimento or meccanismo a orologeria.

clog [klɔg] n zoccolo // vt intasare.

cloister ['klɔɪstə*] n chiostro.

close a, ad and derivatives [kləus] a vicino(a); (writing, texture) fitto(a); (watch) stretto(a); (examination) attento(a); (weather) afoso(a) // ad vicino, dappresso; a ~ friend un amico intimo; to have a ~ shave (fig) scamparla bella // vb and derivatives [kləuz] vt chiudere // vi (shop etc) chiudere; (lid, door etc) chiudersi; (end) finire // n (end) fine f; to ~ down vt chiudere (definitivamente) // vi cessare (definitivamente); ~d a chiuso(a); ~d shop n azienda o fabbrica che impiega solo aderenti ai sindacati; ~ly ad (examine, watch) da vicino.

closet ['klɔzɪt] n (cupboard) armadio.

close-up ['kləusʌp] n primo piano.

closure ['kləuʒə*] n chiusura.

clot [klɔt] n (also: blood ~) coagulo; (col: idiot) scemo/a // vi coagularsi; ~ted cream n panna rappresa.

cloth [klɔθ] n (material) tessuto, stoffa; (also: tea ~) strofinaccio.

clothe [kləuð] vt vestire; ~s npl abiti mpl, vestiti mpl; ~s line n corda (per stendere il bucato); ~s peg n molletta.

clothing ['kləuðɪŋ] n = clothes.

cloud [klaud] n nuvola; ~burst n acquazzone m; ~y a nuvoloso(a); (liquid) torbido(a).

clout [klaut] n (blow) colpo // vt dare un colpo a.

clove [kləuv] n chiodo di garofano; ~ of garlic spicchio d'aglio.

clover ['kləuvə*] n trifoglio.

clown [klaun] n pagliaccio // vi (also: ~ about, ~ around) fare il pagliaccio.

club [klʌb] n (society) club m inv, circolo; (weapon, GOLF) mazza // vt bastonare // vi: to ~ together associarsi; ~s npl (CARDS) fiori mpl; ~house n sede f del circolo.

cluck [klʌk] vi chiocciare.

clue [klu:] n indizio; (in crosswords)

definizione f; I haven't a ~ non ho la minima idea.

clump [klʌmp] n: ~ of trees folto d'alberi.

clumsy ['klʌmzɪ] a (person) goffo(a), maldestro(a); (object) malfatto(a), mal costruito(a).

clung [klʌŋ] pt, pp of cling.

cluster ['klʌstə*] n gruppo // vi raggrupparsi.

clutch [klʌtʃ] n (grip, grasp) presa, stretta; (AUT) frizione f // vt afferrare, stringere forte; to ~ at aggrapparsi a.

clutter ['klʌtə*] vt ingombrare.

Co. abbr of county; company.

c/o (abbr of care of) presso.

coach [kəutʃ] n (bus) pullman m inv; (horse-drawn, of train) carrozza; (SPORT) allenatore/trice // vt allenare.

coagulate [kəu'ægjuleɪt] vi coagularsi.

coal [kəul] n carbone m; ~ face n fronte f; ~field n bacino carbonifero.

coalition [kəuə'lɪʃən] n coalizione f.

coalman, coal merchant ['kəulmən, 'kəulmə:tʃənt] n negoziante m di carbone.

coalmine ['kəulmaɪn] n miniera di carbone.

coarse [kɔ:s] a (salt, sand etc) grosso(a); (cloth, person) rozzo(a).

coast [kəust] n costa // vi (with cycle etc) scendere a ruota libera; ~al a costiero(a); ~guard n guardia costiera; ~line n linea costiera.

coat [kəut] n cappotto; (of animal) pelo; (of paint) mano f // vt coprire; ~ of arms n stemma m; ~ hanger n attaccapanni m inv; ~ing n rivestimento.

coax [kəuks] vt indurre (con moine).

cobbles, cobblestones ['kɔblz, 'kɔblstəunz] npl ciottoli mpl.

cobra ['kəubrə] n cobra.

cobweb ['kɔbweb] n ragnatela.

cocaine [kə'keɪn] n cocaina.

cock [kɔk] n (rooster) gallo; (male bird) maschio // vt (gun) armare; to ~ one's ears (fig) drizzare le orecchie; ~erel n galletto; ~-eyed a (fig) storto(a); strampalato(a).

cockle ['kɔkl] n cardio.

cockney ['kɔknɪ] n cockney m/f inv (abitante dei quartieri popolari dell'East End di Londra).

cockpit ['kɔkpɪt] n (in aircraft) abitacolo.

cockroach ['kɔkrəutʃ] n blatta.

cocktail ['kɔkteɪl] n cocktail m inv; ~ shaker n shaker m inv.

cocoa ['kəukəu] n cacao.

coconut ['kəukənʌt] n noce f di cocco.

cocoon [kə'ku:n] n bozzolo.

cod [kɔd] n merluzzo.

code [kəud] n codice m.

codify ['kəudɪfaɪ] vt codificare.

coeducational ['kəuedju'keɪʃənl] a misto(a).

coerce [kəu'ə:s] vt costringere; coercion [-'ə:ʃən] n coercizione f.

coexistence ['kəuɪg'zɪstəns] n coesistenza.

coffee ['kɔfɪ] n caffè m inv; ~ **grounds** npl fondi mpl di caffè; ~**pot** n caffettiera; ~ **table** n tavolino da tè.

coffin ['kɔfɪn] n bara.

cog [kɔg] n dente m; ~**wheel** n ruota dentata.

cogent ['kəudʒənt] a convincente.

coherent [kəu'hɪərənt] a coerente.

coil [kɔɪl] n rotolo; (one loop) anello; (contraceptive) spirale f // vt avvolgere.

coin [kɔɪn] n moneta // vt (word) coniare; ~**age** n sistema m monetario.

coincide [kəuɪn'saɪd] vi coincidere; ~**nce** [kəu'ɪnsɪdəns] n combinazione f.

coke [kəuk] n coke m.

colander ['kɔləndə*] n colino.

cold [kəuld] a freddo(a) // n freddo; (MED) raffreddore m; it's ~ fa freddo; to be ~ aver freddo; to have ~ feet avere i piedi freddi; (fig) aver la fifa; to give sb the ~ shoulder ignorare qd; ~**ly** ad freddamente; ~ **sore** n erpete m.

coleslaw ['kəulslɔ:] n insalata di cavolo e di salsa maionese.

collaborate [kə'læbəreɪt] vi collaborare; **collaboration** [-'reɪʃən] n collaborazione f; **collaborator** n collaboratore/trice.

collage [kɔ'lɑ:ʒ] n collage m inv.

collapse [kə'læps] vi crollare // n crollo; (MED) collasso.

collapsible [kə'læpsəbl] a pieghevole.

collar ['kɔlə*] n (of coat, shirt) colletto; ~**bone** n clavicola.

colleague ['kɔli:g] n collega m/f.

collect [kə'lɛkt] vt adunare; raccogliere; (as a hobby) fare collezione di; (call and pick up) prendere; (mail) raccogliere; (money owed, pension) riscuotere; (donations, subscriptions) fare una colletta di // vi adunarsi, riunirsi; ammucchiarsi; ~**ed** a: ~**ed works** opere fpl raccolte; ~**ion** [kə'lɛkʃən] n collezione f; raccolta; (for money) colletta.

collector [kə'lɛktə*] n collezionista m/f; (of taxes) esattore m.

college ['kɔlɪdʒ] n collegio.

collide [kə'laɪd] vi: to ~ (with) scontrarsi (con).

colliery ['kɔlɪərɪ] n miniera di carbone.

collision [kə'lɪʒən] n collisione f, scontro.

colloquial [kə'ləukwɪəl] a familiare.

colon ['kəulən] n (sign) due punti mpl; (MED) colon m inv.

colonel ['kə:nl] n colonnello.

colonial [kə'ləunɪəl] a coloniale.

colonize ['kɔlənaɪz] vt colonizzare.

colony ['kɔlənɪ] n colonia.

colossal [kə'lɔsl] a colossale.

colour ['kʌlə*] n colore m // vt colorare; dipingere; (news) svisare; ~**s** npl (of party, club) emblemi mpl; ~ **bar** n discriminazione f razziale (in locali etc); ~**blind** a daltonico(a); ~**ed** a colorato(a); (photo) a colori // n: ~**eds** gente f di colore; ~ **film** n (for camera)

pellicola a colori; ~**ful** a pieno(a) di colore, a vivaci colori; (personality) colorato(a); ~ **television** n televisione f a colori.

colt [kəult] n puledro.

column ['kɔləm] n colonna; ~**ist** ['kɔləmnɪst] n articolista m/f.

coma ['kəumə] n coma m inv.

comb [kəum] n pettine m // vt (hair) pettinare; (area) battere a tappeto.

combat ['kɔmbæt] n combattimento // vt combattere, lottare contro.

combination [kɔmbɪ'neɪʃən] n combinazione f.

combine vb [kəm'baɪn] vt combinare; (one quality with another) unire (a) // vi unirsi; (CHEM) combinarsi // n ['kɔmbaɪn] lega; (ECON) associazione f; ~ (**harvester**) n mietitrebbia.

combustible [kəm'bʌstɪbl] a combustibile.

combustion [kəm'bʌstʃən] n combustione f.

come, pt **came**, pp **come** [kʌm, keɪm] vi venire; arrivare; to ~ **to** (decision etc) raggiungere; to ~ **about** vi succedere; to ~ **across** vt fus trovare per caso; to ~ **along** vi = to come on; to ~ **apart** vi andare in pezzi; staccarsi; to ~ **away** vi venire via; staccarsi; to ~ **back** vi ritornare; to ~ **by** vt fus (acquire) ottenere; procurarsi; to ~ **down** vi discendere; (prices) calare; (buildings) essere demolito(a); to ~ **forward** vi farsi avanti; presentarsi; to ~ **from** vt venire da; provenire da; to ~ **in** vi entrare; to ~ **in for** vt fus (criticism etc) ricevere; to ~ **into** vt fus (money) ereditare; to ~ **off** vi (button) staccarsi; (stain) andar via; (attempt) riuscire; to ~ **on** vi (pupil, undertaking) fare progressi; ~ **on!** avanti!, andiamo!, forza!; to ~ **out** vi uscire; (strike) entrare in sciopero; to ~ **to** vi rinvenire; to ~ **up** vi venire su; to ~ **up against** vt fus (resistance, difficulties) urtare contro; to ~ **up with** vt fus: **he came up with an idea** venne fuori con un'idea; to ~ **upon** vt fus trovare per caso; ~**back** n (THEATRE etc) ritorno.

comedian [kə'mi:dɪən] n comico.

comedown ['kʌmdaun] n rovescio.

comedy ['kɔmɪdɪ] n commedia.

comet ['kɔmɪt] n cometa.

comfort ['kʌmfət] n comodità f inv, benessere m; (solace) consolazione f, conforto // vt consolare, confortare; ~**s** npl comodi mpl; ~**able** a comodo(a); ~ **station** n (US) gabinetti mpl.

comic ['kɔmɪk] a (also: ~**al**) comico(a) // n comico; (magazine) giornaletto; ~ **strip** n fumetto.

coming ['kʌmɪŋ] n arrivo; ~(**s**) **and going(s)** n(pl) andirivieni m inv.

comma ['kɔmə] n virgola.

command [kə'mɑ:nd] n ordine m, comando; (MIL: authority) comando; (mastery) padronanza // vt comandare; to ~ **sb to do** ordinare a qd di fare; ~**er**

[kɔmən'dɪə*] *vt* requisire; **~er** *n* capo; (*MIL*) comandante *m*; **~ing officer** *n* comandante *m*.

commando [kə'mɑ:ndəu] *n* commando *m inv*; membro di un commando.

commemorate [kə'mɛməreit] *vt* commemorare; **commemoration** [-'reiʃən] *n* commemorazione *f*.

commence [kə'mɛns] *vt,vi* cominciare.

commend [kə'mɛnd] *vt* lodare; raccomandare; **~able** *a* lodevole; **~ation** [kɔmən'deiʃən] *n* lode *f*; raccomandazione *f*.

commensurate [kə'mɛnʃərit] *a*: **~ with** proporzionato(a) a.

comment ['kɔment] *n* commento // *vi* fare commenti; **~ary** ['kɔmentəri] *n* commentario; (*SPORT*) radiocronaca; telecronaca; **~ator** ['kɔmənteitə*] *n* commentatore/trice; radiocronista *m/f*; telecronista *m/f*.

commerce ['kɔmə:s] *n* commercio.

commercial [kə'mə:ʃəl] *a* commerciale // *n* (*TV*: *also*: **~ break**) pubblicità *f inv*; **~ize** *vt* commercializzare; **~ television** *n* televisione *f* commerciale; **~ traveller** *n* commesso viaggiatore; **~ vehicle** *n* veicolo commerciale.

commiserate [kə'mizəreit] *vi*: **to ~ with** condolersi con.

commission [kə'miʃən] *n* commissione *f* // *vt* (*MIL*) nominare (al comando); (*work of art*) commissionare; **out of ~** (*NAUT*) in disarmo; **~aire** [kəmiʃə'nɛə*] *n* (*at shop, cinema etc*) portiere *m* in livrea; **~er** *n* commissionario; (*POLICE*) questore *m*.

commit [kə'mit] *vt* (*act*) commettere; (*to sb's care*) affidare; **to ~ o.s.** (**to do**) impegnarsi (a fare); **to ~ suicide** suicidarsi; **~ment** *n* impegno; promessa.

committee [kə'miti] *n* comitato.

commodity [kə'mɔditi] *n* prodotto, articolo; (*food*) derrata.

common ['kɔmən] *a* comune; (*pej*) volgare; (*usual*) normale // *n* terreno comune; **the C~s** *npl* la Camera dei Comuni; **in ~** in comune; **it's ~ knowledge that** è di dominio pubblico che; **~er** *n* cittadino/a (non nobile); **~ ground** *n* (*fig*) terreno comune; **~ law** *n* diritto consuetudinario; **~ly** *ad* comunemente, usualmente; **C~ Market** *n* Mercato Comune; **~place** *a* banale, ordinario(a); **~room** *n* sala di riunione; (*SCOL*) sala dei professori; **~ sense** *n* buon senso; **the C~wealth** *n* il Commonwealth.

commotion [kə'məuʃən] *n* confusione *f*, tumulto.

communal ['kɔmju:nl] *a* (*life*) comunale; (*for common use*) pubblico(a).

commune *n* ['kɔmju:n] (*group*) comune *m* // *vi* [kə'mju:n]: **to ~ with** mettersi in comunione con.

communicate [kə'mju:nikeit] *vt* comunicare, trasmettere // *vi*: **to ~ (with)** comunicare (con).

communication [kəmju:ni'keiʃən] *n*

comunicazione *f*; **~ cord** *n* segnale *m* d'allarme.

communion [kə'mju:niən] *n* comunione *f*.

communiqué [kə'mju:nikei] *n* comunicato.

communism ['kɔmjunizəm] *n* comunismo; **communist** *a,n* comunista (*m/f*).

community [kə'mju:niti] *n* comunità *f inv*; **~ centre** *n* circolo ricreativo; **~ chest** *n* (*US*) fondo di beneficenza.

commutation ticket [kɔmju'teiʃəntikit] *n* (*US*) biglietto di abbonamento.

commute [kə'mju:t] *vi* fare il pendolare // *vt* (*LAW*) commutare; **~r** *n* pendolare *m/f*.

compact *a* [kəm'pækt] compatto(a) // *n* ['kɔmpækt] (*also*: **powder ~**) portacipria.

companion [kəm'pæniən] *n* compagno/a; **~ship** *n* compagnia.

company ['kʌmpəni] *n* (*also COMM, MIL, THEATRE*) compagnia; **he's good ~** è di buona compagnia; **we have ~** abbiamo ospiti; **to keep sb ~** tenere compagnia a qd; **to part ~ with** separarsi da.

comparable ['kɔmpərəbl] *a* comparabile.

comparative [kəm'pærətiv] *a* comparativo(a); (*LING*) comparato(a); **~ly** *ad* relativamente.

compare [kəm'pɛə*] *vt*: **to ~ sth/sb with/to** confrontare qc/qd con/a // *vi*: **to ~ (with)** reggere il confronto (con); **comparison** [-'pærisn] *n* confronto; **in comparison (with)** a confronto di).

compartment [kəm'pɑ:tmənt] *n* compartimento; (*RAIL*) scompartimento.

compass ['kʌmpəs] *n* bussola; **~es** *npl* compassi *mpl*.

compassion [kəm'pæʃən] *n* compassione *f*; **~ate** *a* compassionevole.

compatible [kəm'pætibl] *a* compatibile.

compel [kəm'pel] *vt* costringere, obbligare; **~ling** *a* (*fig*: *argument*) irresistibile.

compendium [kəm'pendiəm] *n* compendio.

compensate ['kɔmpənseit] *vt* risarcire // *vi*: **to ~ for** compensare; **compensation** [-'seiʃən] *n* compensazione *f*; (*money*) risarcimento.

compère ['kɔmpɛə*] *n* presentatore/trice.

compete [kəm'pi:t] *vi* (*take part*) concorrere; (*vie*): **to ~ (with)** fare concorrenza (a).

competence ['kɔmpitəns] *n* competenza.

competent ['kɔmpitənt] *a* competente.

competition [kɔmpi'tiʃən] *n* gara; concorso; (*ECON*) concorrenza.

competitive [kəm'petitiv] *a* di concorso; di concorrenza.

competitor [kəm'petitə*] *n* concorrente *m/f*.

compile [kəm'pail] *vt* compilare.

complacency [kəm'pleisnsi] *n* compiacenza di sé.

complacent [kəm'pleisənt] *a* compiaciuto(a) di sé.

complain [kəm'plein] *vi*: **to ~ (about)** lagnarsi (di); (*in shop etc*) reclamare (per); **to ~ of** vt fus (MED) accusare; **~t** n lamento; reclamo; (MED) malattia.

complement ['kɔmplɪmənt] n complemento; (especially of ship's crew etc) effettivo; **~ary** [kɔmplɪ'mɛntərɪ] a complementare.

complete [kəm'pli:t] a completo(a) // vt completare, compire; (a form) riempire; **~ly** ad completamente; **completion** n completamento.

complex ['kɔmplɛks] a complesso(a) // n (PSYCH, buildings etc) complesso.

complexion [kəm'plɛkʃən] n (of face) carnagione f; (of event etc) aspetto.

complexity [kəm'plɛksɪtɪ] n complessità f inv.

compliance [kəm'plaɪəns] n acquiescenza; **in ~ with** (orders, wishes etc) in conformità con.

compliant [kəm'plaɪənt] a acquiescente, arrendevole.

complicate ['kɔmplɪkeɪt] vt complicare; **~d** a complicato(a); **complication** [-'keɪʃən] n complicazione f.

compliment n ['kɔmplɪmənt] complimento // vt ['kɔmplɪmənt] fare un complimento a; **~s** npl complimenti mpl; rispetti mpl; **~ary** [-'mɛntəri] a complimentoso(a), elogiativo(a); (free) in omaggio; **~ary ticket** n biglietto d'omaggio.

comply [kəm'plaɪ] vi: **to ~ with** assentire a; conformarsi a.

component [kəm'pəʊnənt] n componente m.

compose [kəm'pəʊz] vt comporre; **to ~ o.s.** ricomporsi; **~d** a calmo(a); **~d of** composto(a) di; **~r** n (MUS) compositore/trice.

composition [kɔmpə'zɪʃən] n composizione f.

compost ['kɔmpɔst] n composta, concime m.

composure [kəm'pəʊʒə*] n calma.

compound ['kɔmpaʊnd] n (CHEM, LING) composto; (enclosure) recinto // a composto(a); **~ fracture** n frattura composta; **~ interest** n interesse m composto.

comprehend [kɔmprɪ'hɛnd] vt comprendere, capire; **comprehension** [-'hɛnʃən] n comprensione f.

comprehensive [kɔmprɪ'hɛnsɪv] a comprensivo(a); **~ policy** n (INSURANCE) polizza che copre tutti i rischi; **~ (school)** n scuola secondaria aperta a tutti.

compress vt [kəm'prɛs] comprimere // n ['kɔmprɛs] (MED) compressa; **~ion** [-'prɛʃən] n compressione f.

comprise [kəm'praɪz] vt (also: be **~d of**) comprendere.

compromise ['kɔmprəmaɪz] n compromesso // vt compromettere // vi venire a un compromesso.

compulsion [kəm'pʌlʃən] n costrizione f.

compulsive [kəm'pʌlsɪv] a (reason, demand) stringente; (PSYCH) inguaribile.

compulsory [kəm'pʌlsərɪ] a obbligatorio(a).

computer [kəm'pju:tə*] n computer m inv; **~ize** vt computerizzare; **~ programming** n programmazione f di computer.

comrade ['kɔmrɪd] n compagno/a; **~ship** n cameratismo.

con [kɔn] vt (col) truffare.

concave ['kɔn'keɪv] a concavo(a).

conceal [kən'si:l] vt nascondere.

concede [kən'si:d] vt concedere // vi fare una concessione.

conceit [kən'si:t] n presunzione f, vanità; **~ed** a presuntuoso(a), vanitoso(a).

conceivable [kən'si:vəbl] a concepibile.

conceive [kən'si:v] vt concepire // vi concepire un bambino.

concentrate ['kɔnsəntreɪt] vi concentrarsi // vt concentrare.

concentration [kɔnsən'treɪʃən] n concentrazione f; **~ camp** n campo di concentramento.

concept ['kɔnsɛpt] n concetto.

conception [kən'sɛpʃən] n concezione f.

concern [kən'sɔːn] n affare m; (COMM) azienda, ditta; (anxiety) preoccupazione f // vt riguardare; **to be ~ed (about)** preoccuparsi (di); **~ing** prep riguardo a, circa.

concert ['kɔnsət] n concerto; **in ~** di concerto; **~ed** [kən'sɔːtɪd] a concertato(a); **~ hall** n sala da concerti.

concertina [kɔnsə'tiːnə] n piccola fisarmonica // vi ridursi come una fisarmonica.

concerto [kən'tʃɔːtəʊ] n concerto.

concession [kən'sɛʃən] n concessione f.

conciliation [kɔnsɪlɪ'eɪʃən] n conciliazione f.

conciliatory [kən'sɪlɪətri] a conciliativo(a).

concise [kən'saɪs] a conciso(a).

conclave ['kɔnkleɪv] n riunione f segreta; (REL) conclave m.

conclude [kən'klu:d] vt concludere; **conclusion** [-'klu:ʒən] n conclusione f; **conclusive** [-'klu:sɪv] a conclusivo(a).

concoct [kən'kɔkt] vt inventare.

concourse ['kɔnkɔːs] n (hall) atrio.

concrete ['kɔnkriːt] n conglomerato (di cemento) // a concreto(a); di cemento.

concur [kən'kɔː*] vi concordare.

concurrently [kən'kʌrntlɪ] ad simultaneamente.

concussion [kən'kʌʃən] n commozione f cerebrale.

condemn [kən'dɛm] vt condannare; **~ation** [kɔndɛm'neɪʃən] n condanna.

condensation [kɔndɛn'seɪʃən] n condensazione f.

condense [kən'dɛns] vi condensarsi // vt condensare; **~d milk** n latte m condensato.

condescend [kɔndɪ'sɛnd] vi condiscendere; **~ing** a condiscendente.

condition [kən'dɪʃən] n condizione f // vt condizionare, regolare; **on ~ that** a condizione che + sub, a condizione di; ~al a condizionale.

condolences [kən'dəulənsiz] npl condoglianze fpl.

condone [kən'dəun] vt condonare.

conducive [kən'dju:siv] a: ~ to favorevole a.

conduct n ['kɔndʌkt] condotta // vt [kən'dʌkt] condurre; (manage) dirigere; amministrare; (MUS) dirigere; **to ~ o.s.** comportarsi; ~ed tour n gita accompagnata; ~or n (of orchestra) direttore m d'orchestra; (on bus) bigliettaio; (ELEC) conduttore m; ~ress n (on bus) bigliettaia.

conduit ['kɔndit] n condotto; tubo.

cone [kəun] n cono; (BOT) pigna.

confectionery [kən'fɛkʃənəri] n dolciumi mpl.

confederation [kɔnfɛdə'reiʃən] n confederazione f.

confer [kən'fə:*] vt: **to ~ sth on** conferire qc a // vi conferire.

conference ['kɔnfərns] n congresso.

confess [kən'fɛs] vt confessare, ammettere // vi confessarsi; ~ion [-'fɛʃən] n confessione f; ~ional [-'fɛʃənl] n confessionale m; ~or n confessore m.

confetti [kən'fɛti] n coriandoli mpl.

confide [kən'faid] vi: **to ~ in** confidarsi con.

confidence ['kɔnfidns] n confidenza; (trust) fiducia; (also: self-~) sicurezza di sé; ~ **trick** n truffa; **confident** a confidente, sicuro(a) di sé; **confidential** [kɔnfi'dɛnʃəl] a riservato(a).

confine [kən'fain] vt limitare; (shut up) rinchiudere; ~s ['kɔnfainz] npl confini mpl; ~d a (space) ristretto(a); ~ment n prigionia; (MIL) consegna; (MED) parto.

confirm [kən'fə:m] vt confermare; (REL) cresimare; ~ation [kɔnfə'meiʃən] n conferma; cresima; ~ed a inveterato(a).

confiscate ['kɔnfiskeit] vt confiscare; **confiscation** [-'keiʃən] n confisca.

conflict n ['kɔnflikt] conflitto // vi [kən'flikt] essere in conflitto; ~ing a contrastante.

conform [kən'fɔ:m] vi: **to ~ (to)** conformarsi (a); ~ist n conformista m/f.

confound [kən'faund] vt confondere; ~ed a maledetto(a).

confront [kən'frʌnt] vt confrontare; (enemy, danger) affrontare; ~ation [kɔnfrʌn'teiʃən] n confronto.

confuse [kən'fju:z] vt imbrogliare; (one thing with another) confondere; **confusing** a che fa confondere; **confusion** [-'fju:ʒən] n confusione f.

congeal [kən'dʒi:l] vi (blood) congelarsi.

congenial [kən'dʒi:niəl] a (person) simpatico(a); (thing) congeniale.

congenital [kən'dʒɛnitl] a congenito(a).

conger eel ['kɔngəri:l] n grongo.

congested [kən'dʒɛstid] a congestionato(a).

congestion [kən'dʒɛstʃən] n congestione f.

conglomeration [kɔnglɔmə'reiʃən] n conglomerazione f.

congratulate [kən'grætjuleit] vt: **to ~ sb (on)** congratularsi con qd (per or di); **congratulations** [-'leiʃɔnz] npl auguri mpl; (on success) complimenti mpl.

congregate [kɔngrigeit] vi congregarsi, riunirsi.

congregation [kɔngri'geiʃən] n congregazione f.

congress ['kɔngrɛs] n congresso; ~man n (US) membro del Congresso.

conical ['kɔnikl] a conico(a).

conifer ['kɔnifə*] n conifero.

conjecture [kən'dʒɛktʃə*] n congettura // vt, vi congetturare.

conjugal ['kɔndʒugl] a coniugale.

conjunction [kən'dʒʌŋkʃən] n congiunzione f.

conjunctivitis [kəndʒʌŋkti'vaitis] n congiuntivite f.

conjure ['kʌndʒə*] vt prestigiare; **to ~ up** vt (ghost, spirit) evocare; (memories) rievocare; ~r n prestidigitatore/trice; **conjuring trick** n gioco di prestigio.

conk [kɔŋk]: **to ~ out** vi (col) andare in panne.

conman ['kɔnmæn] n truffatore m.

connect [kə'nɛkt] vt connettere, collegare; (ELEC) collegare; (fig) associare // vi (train): **to ~ with** essere in coincidenza con; **to be ~ed with** aver rapporti con; essere imparentato con; ~ion [-ʃən] n relazione f, rapporto; (ELEC) connessione f; (TEL) collegamento; **in ~ion with** con riferimento a.

connexion [kə'nɛkʃən] n = connection.

conning tower ['kɔniŋtauə*] n torretta di comando.

connive [kə'naiv] vi: **to ~ at** essere connivente in.

connoisseur [kɔni'sə:*] n conoscitore/trice.

connotation [kɔnə'teiʃən] n connotazione f.

conquer ['kɔŋkə*] vt conquistare; (feelings) vincere; ~or n conquistatore m.

conquest ['kɔŋkwɛst] n conquista.

cons [kɔnz] npl see pro, convenience.

conscience ['kɔnʃəns] n coscienza.

conscientious [kɔnʃi'ɛnʃəs] a coscienzioso(a); ~ **objector** n obiettore m di coscienza.

conscious ['kɔnʃəs] a consapevole; (MED) conscio(a); ~ness n consapevolezza; coscienza; **to lose/regain** ~ness perdere/riprendere coscienza.

conscript ['kɔnskript] n coscritto; ~ion [kən'skripʃən] n coscrizione f.

consecrate ['kɔnsikreit] vt consacrare.

consecutive [kən'sɛkjutiv] a consecutivo(a).

consensus [kən'sɛnsəs] n consenso.

consent [kən'sɛnt] n consenso // vi: **to ~ (to)** acconsentire (a).

consequence ['kɔnsikwəns] n conseguenza, risultato; importanza.

consequently ['kɒnsɪkwəntlɪ] ad di conseguenza, dunque.

conservation [kɒnsɔː'veɪʃən] n conservazione f.

conservative [kən'sɔːvətɪv] a conservativo(a); (cautious) cauto(a); C~ a, n conservatore(trice).

conservatory [kən'sɔːvətrɪ] n (greenhouse) serra.

conserve [kən'sɔːv] vt conservare.

consider [kən'sɪdə*] vt considerare; (take into account) tener conto di.

considerable [kən'sɪdərəbl] a considerevole, notevole.

considerate [kən'sɪdərɪt] a premuroso(a).

consideration [kənsɪdə'reɪʃən] n considerazione f; (reward) rimunerazione f; **out of ~ for** per riguardo a; **under ~** in esame.

considering [kən'sɪdərɪŋ] prep in considerazione di.

consign [kən'saɪn] vt consegnare; (send: goods) spedire; **~ment** n consegna; spedizione f.

consist [kən'sɪst] vi: **to ~ of** constare di, essere composto(a) di.

consistency [kən'sɪstənsɪ] n consistenza; (fig) concordanza; coerenza.

consistent [kən'sɪstənt] a coerente; (constant) costante; **~ with** compatibile con.

consolation [kɒnsə'leɪʃən] n consolazione f.

console vt [kən'səul] consolare // ['kɒnsəul] mensola.

consolidate [kən'sɒlɪdeɪt] vt consolidare.

consonant ['kɒnsənənt] n consonante f.

consortium [kən'sɔːtɪəm] n consorzio.

conspicuous [kən'spɪkjuəs] a cospicuo(a).

conspiracy [kən'spɪrəsɪ] n congiura, cospirazione f.

conspire [kən'spaɪə*] vi congiurare, cospirare.

constable ['kʌnstəbl] n ≈ poliziotto, agente m di polizia; **chief ~** n capo della polizia.

constant ['kɒnstənt] a costante; continuo(a); **~ly** ad costantemente, continuamente.

constellation [kɒnstə'leɪʃən] n costellazione f.

consternation [kɒnstə'neɪʃən] n costernazione f.

constipated ['kɒnstɪpeɪtəd] a stitico(a).

constipation [kɒnstɪ'peɪʃən] n stitichezza.

constituency [kən'stɪtjuənsɪ] n collegio elettorale.

constituent [kən'stɪtjuənt] n elettore/trice; (part) elemento componente.

constitute ['kɒnstɪtjuːt] vt costituire.

constitution [kɒnstɪ'tjuːʃən] n costituzione f; **~al** a costituzionale.

constrain [kən'streɪn] vt costringere; **~ed** a costretto(a); **~t** n costrizione f.

constrict [kən'strɪkt] vt comprimere; opprimere.

construct [kən'strʌkt] vt costruire; **~ion** [-ʃən] n costruzione f; **~ive** a costruttivo(a).

construe [kən'struː] vt interpretare.

consul ['kɒnsl] n console m; **~ate** ['kɒnsjulɪt] n consolato.

consult [kən'sʌlt] vt consultare; **~ancy** n: **~ancy fee** spese fpl di consultazione; **~ant** n (MED) consulente m medico; (other specialist) consulente; **~ation** [kɒnsəl'teɪʃən] n consultazione f; (MED, LAW) consulto; **~ing room** n ambulatorio.

consume [kən'sjuːm] vt consumare; **~r** n consumatore/trice; **~r society** n società dei consumi.

consummate ['kɒnsʌmeɪt] vt consumare.

consumption [kən'sʌmpʃən] n consumo; (MED) consunzione f.

contact ['kɒntækt] n contatto; (person) conoscenza // vt mettersi in contatto con; **~ lenses** npl lenti fpl a contatto.

contagious [kən'teɪdʒəs] a contagioso(a).

contain [kən'teɪn] vt contenere; **to ~ o.s.** contenersi; **~er** n recipiente m; (for shipping etc) container m.

contaminate [kən'tæmɪneɪt] vt contaminare; **contamination** [-'neɪʃən] n contaminazione f.

cont'd abbr of continued.

contemplate ['kɒntəmpleɪt] vt contemplare; (consider) pensare a (or di); **contemplation** [-'pleɪʃən] n contemplazione f.

contemporary [kən'tempərərɪ] a contemporaneo(a); (design) moderno(a) // n contemporaneo/a.

contempt [kən'tempt] n disprezzo; **~ible** a spregevole; **~uous** a sdegnoso(a).

contend [kən'tend] vt: **to ~ that** sostenere che // vi: **to ~ with** lottare contro; **~er** n contendente m/f; concorrente m/f.

content [kən'tent] a contento(a), soddisfatto(a) // vt contentare, soddisfare // n ['kɒntent] contenuto; **~s** npl contenuto; (of barrel etc: capacity) capacità f inv; (table of) **~s** indice m; **to be ~ with** essere contento di; **~ed** a contento(a), soddisfatto(a).

contention [kən'tenʃən] n contesa; (argument) affermazione f.

contentment [kən'tentmənt] n contentezza.

contest n ['kɒntest] lotta; (competition) gara, concorso // vt [kən'test] contestare; impugnare; (compete for) contendere; **~ant** [kən'testənt] n concorrente m/f; (in fight) avversario/a.

context ['kɒntekst] n contesto.

continent ['kɒntɪnənt] n continente m; **the C~** l'Europa continentale; **~al** [-'nentl] a continentale // n abitante m/f dell'Europa continentale.

contingency [kən'tɪndʒənsɪ] n eventualità f inv; **~ plan** n misura d'emergenza.

contingent [kən'tɪndʒənt] n contingenza; **to be ~ upon** dipendere da.

continual [kən'tɪnjuəl] a continuo(a); ~**ly** ad di continuo.

continuation [kəntɪnju'eɪʃən] n continuazione f; (after interruption) ripresa; (of story) seguito.

continue [kən'tɪnju:] vi continuare // vt continuare; (start again) riprendere.

continuity [kɔntɪ'njuɪtɪ] n continuità.

continuous [kən'tɪnjuəs] a continuo(a), ininterrotto(a).

contort [kən'tɔ:t] vt contorcere; ~**ion** [-'tɔ:ʃən] n contorcimento; (of acrobat) contorsione f; ~**ionist** [-'tɔ:ʃənɪst] n contorsionista m/f.

contour ['kɔntuə*] n contorno, profilo; (also: ~ **line**) curva di livello.

contraband ['kɔntrəbænd] n contrabbando.

contraception [kɔntrə'sepʃən] n contraccezione f.

contraceptive [kɔntrə'septɪv] a contraccettivo(a) // n contraccettivo.

contract n ['kɔntrækt] contratto // vb [kən'trækt] vi (COMM): to ~ to do sth fare un contratto per fare qc; (become smaller) contrarre; ~**ion** [-ʃən] n contrazione f; ~**or** n imprenditore m.

contradict [kɔntrə'dɪkt] vt contraddire; ~**ion** [-ʃən] n contraddizione f.

contralto [kən'træltəu] n contralto.

contraption [kən'træpʃən] n (pej) aggeggio.

contrary ['kɔntrərɪ] a contrario(a); (unfavourable) avverso(a), contrario(a); [kən'trɛərɪ] (perverse) bisbetico(a) // n contrario; **on the** ~ al contrario; **unless you hear to the** ~ a meno che non si disdica.

contrast n ['kɔntrɑːst] contrasto // vt [kən'trɑːst] mettere in contrasto; ~**ing** a contrastante, di contrasto.

contravene [kɔntrə'vi:n] vt contravvenire.

contribute [kən'trɪbjuːt] vi contribuire // vt: to ~ £10/an article to dare 10 sterline/un articolo a; to ~ to contribuire a; (newspaper) scrivere per; **contribution** [kɔntrɪ'bjuːʃən] n contribuzione f; **contributor** n (to newspaper) collaboratore/trice.

contrite ['kɔntraɪt] a contrito(a).

contrivance [kən'traɪvəns] n congegno, espediente m.

contrive [kən'traɪv] vt inventare; escogitare // vi: to ~ to do fare in modo di fare.

control [kən'trəul] vt dominare; (firm, operation etc) dirigere; (check) controllare // n autorità; controllo; ~**s** npl comandi mpl; to be in ~ of aver autorità su; essere responsabile di; controllare; **circumstances beyond our** ~ circostanze fpl che non dipendono da noi; ~ **point** n punto di controllo; ~ **tower** n (AVIAT) torre f di controllo.

controversial [kɔntrə'vɜːʃl] a controverso(a), polemico(a).

controversy ['kɔntrəvɜːsɪ] n controversia, polemica.

convalesce [kɔnvə'lɛs] vi rimettersi in salute.

convalescence [kɔnvə'lɛsns] n convalescenza.

convalescent [kɔnvə'lɛsnt] a, n convalescente (m/f).

convector [kən'vɛktə*] n convettore m.

convene [kən'vi:n] vt convocare // vi convenire, adunarsi.

convenience [kən'vi:nɪəns] n convenienza; **at your** ~ a suo comodo; **all modern** ~**s**, **all mod cons** tutte le comodità moderne.

convenient [kən'vi:nɪənt] a conveniente, comodo(a).

convent ['kɔnvənt] n convento.

convention [kən'vɛnʃən] n convenzione f; (meeting) convegno; ~**al** a convenzionale.

converge [kən'vɜːdʒ] vi convergere.

conversant [kən'vɜːsnt] a: to be ~ with essere al corrente di; essere pratico(a) di.

conversation [kɔnvə'seɪʃən] n conversazione f; ~**al** a non formale; ~**al Italian** l'italiano parlato.

converse ['kɔnvɜːs] n contrario, opposto; ~**ly** [-'vɜːslɪ] ad al contrario, per contro.

conversion [kən'vɜːʃən] n conversione f; ~ **table** n tavola di equivalenza.

convert vt [kən'vɜːt] (REL, COMM) convertire; (alter) trasformare // n ['kɔnvɜːt] convertito/a; ~**ible** n macchina decappottabile.

convex ['kɔn'vɛks] a convesso(a).

convey [kən'veɪ] vt trasportare; (thanks) comunicare; (idea) dare; ~**or belt** n nastro trasportatore.

convict vt [kən'vɪkt] dichiarare colpevole // n ['kɔnvɪkt] condannato; ~**ion** [-ʃən] n condanna; (belief) convinzione f.

convince [kən'vɪns] vt convincere, persuadere; **convincing** a convincente.

convivial [kən'vɪvɪəl] a allegro(a).

convoy ['kɔnvɔɪ] n convoglio.

convulse [kən'vʌls] vt sconvolgere; **to be** ~**d with laughter** contorcersi dalle risa.

convulsion [kən'vʌlʃən] n convulsione f.

coo [ku:] vi tubare.

cook [kuk] vt cucinare, cuocere // vi cuocere; (person) cucinare // n cuoco/a; ~**book** n = ~**ery book**; ~**er** n fornello, cucina; ~**ery** n cucina; ~**ery book** n libro di cucina; ~**ie** n (US) biscotto; ~**ing** n cucina.

cool [ku:l] a fresco(a); (not afraid) calmo(a); (unfriendly) freddo(a); (impertinent) sfacciato(a) // vt raffreddare, rinfrescare // vi raffreddarsi, rinfrescarsi; ~**ing tower** n torre f di raffreddamento; ~**ness** n freschezza; sangue m freddo, calma.

coop [ku:p] n stia // vt: to ~ **up** (fig) stipare.

cooperate [kəu'ɔpəreɪt] vi cooperare, collaborare; **cooperation** [-'reɪʃən] n cooperazione f, collaborazione f.

cooperative [kəu'ɔpərətɪv] a

cooperativo(a) // n cooperativa.
coordinate [kəu'ɔːdineit] vt coordinare; **coordination** [-'neiʃən] n coordinazione f.
coot [kuːt] n folaga.
cop [kɔp] n (col) sbirro.
cope [kəup] vi farcela; **to ~ with** (problems) far fronte a.
co-pilot ['kəu'pailət] n secondo pilota m.
copious ['kəupiəs] a copioso(a), abbondante.
copper ['kɔpə*] n rame m; (col: policeman) sbirro; **~s** npl spiccioli mpl.
copse [kɔps] n bosco ceduo.
copulate ['kɔpjuleit] vi accoppiarsi.
copy ['kɔpi] n copia; (book etc) esemplare m // vt copiare; **~cat** n (pej) copione m; **~right** n diritto d'autore; **~writer** n redattore m pubblicitario.
coral ['kɔrəl] n corallo; **~ reef** n barriera corallina.
cord [kɔːd] n corda; (fabric) velluto a coste.
cordial ['kɔːdiəl] a, n cordiale (m).
cordon ['kɔːdn] n cordone m; **to ~ off** vt fare cordone a.
corduroy ['kɔːdərɔi] n fustagno.
core [kɔː*] n (of fruit) torsolo; (TECH) centro // vt estrarre il torsolo da.
cork [kɔːk] n sughero; (of bottle) tappo; **~age** n somma da pagare se il cliente porta il proprio vino; **~screw** n cavatappi m inv.
cormorant ['kɔːmərnt] n cormorano.
corn [kɔːn] n grano; (US: maize) granturco; (on foot) callo; **~ on the cob** (CULIN) pannocchia cotta.
cornea ['kɔːniə] n cornea.
corned beef ['kɔːnd'biːf] n carne f di manzo in scatola.
corner ['kɔːnə*] n angolo; (AUT) curva // vt mettere in un angolo; mettere con le spalle al muro; (COMM: market) accaparrare // vi prendere una curva; **~ flag** n (FOOTBALL) bandierina d'angolo; **~ kick** n calcio d'angolo; **~stone** n pietra angolare.
cornet ['kɔːnit] n (MUS) cornetta; (of ice-cream) cono.
cornflour ['kɔːnflauə*] n farina finissima di granturco.
cornice ['kɔːnis] n cornicione m; cornice f.
Cornwall ['kɔːnwəl] n Cornovaglia.
corny ['kɔːni] a (col) trito(a).
corollary [kə'rɔləri] n corollario.
coronary ['kɔrənəri] n trombosi f coronaria.
coronation [kɔrə'neiʃən] n incoronazione f.
coroner ['kɔrənə*] n magistrato incaricato di indagare la causa di morte in circostanze sospettose.
coronet ['kɔrənit] n diadema m.
corporal ['kɔːpərl] n caporalmaggiore m // a: **~ punishment** pena corporale.
corporate ['kɔːpərit] a costituito(a) (in corporazione); comune.
corporation [kɔːpə'reiʃən] n (of town) consiglio comunale; (COMM) ente m; **~ tax** n imposta societaria.

corps [kɔː*], pl **corps** [kɔːz] n corpo.
corpse [kɔːps] n cadavere m.
corpuscle ['kɔːpʌsl] n corpuscolo.
corral [kə'raːl] n recinto.
correct [kə'rekt] a (accurate) corretto(a), esatto(a); (proper) corretto(a) // vt correggere; **~ion** [-ʃən] n correzione f.
correlate ['kɔrileit] vt mettere in correlazione.
correspond [kɔris'pɔnd] vi corrispondere; **~ence** n corrispondenza; **~ence course** n corso per corrispondenza; **~ent** n corrispondente m/f.
corridor ['kɔridɔː*] n corridoio.
corroborate [kə'rɔbəreit] vt corroborare, confermare.
corrode [kə'rəud] vt corrodere // vi corrodersi; **corrosion** [-'rəuʒən] n corrosione f.
corrugated ['kɔrəgeitid] a increspato(a); ondulato(a); **~ iron** n lamiera di ferro ondulata.
corrupt [kə'rʌpt] a corrotto(a) // vt corrompere; **~ion** [-ʃən] n corruzione f.
corset ['kɔːsit] n busto.
Corsica ['kɔːsikə] n Corsica.
cortège [kɔː'teːʒ] n corteo.
cosh [kɔʃ] n randello (corto).
cosmetic [kɔz'metik] n cosmetico.
cosmonaut ['kɔzmənɔːt] n cosmonauta m/f.
cosmopolitan [kɔzmə'pɔlitn] a cosmopolita.
cosmos ['kɔzmɔs] n cosmo.
cosset ['kɔsit] vt vezzeggiare.
cost [kɔst] n costo // vb (pt, pp cost) vi costare // vt stabilire il prezzo di; **it ~s £5/too much** costa 5 sterline/troppo; **it ~ him his life/job** gli costò la vita/il suo lavoro; **at all ~s** a ogni costo.
co-star ['kəustɑː*] n attore/trice della stessa importanza del protagonista.
costly ['kɔstli] a costoso(a), caro(a).
cost price ['kɔst'prais] n prezzo all'ingrosso.
costume ['kɔstjuːm] n costume m; (lady's suit) tailleur m inv; (also: **swimming ~**) costume da bagno; **~ jewellery** n bigiotteria.
cosy ['kəuzi] a intimo(a).
cot [kɔt] n (child's) lettino.
cottage ['kɔtidʒ] n cottage m inv; **~ cheese** n fiocchi mpl di latte magro.
cotton ['kɔtn] n cotone m; **~ dress** etc vestito etc di cotone; **~ wool** n cotone idrofilo.
couch [kautʃ] n sofà m inv // vt esprimere.
cough [kɔf] vi tossire // n tosse f; **~ drop** n pasticca per la tosse.
could [kud] pt of **can**.
council ['kaunsl] n concilio; **city or town ~** consiglio comunale; **~ estate** n quartiere m di case popolari; **~ house** n casa popolare; **~lor** n consigliere/a.
counsel ['kaunsl] n avvocato; consultazione f; **~lor** n consigliere/a.
count [kaunt] vt, vi contare // n conto;

(*nobleman*) conte *m*; **to ~ on** *vt* fus contare su; **to ~ up** *vt* addizionare; **~down** *n* conto alla rovescia.

countenance ['kauntɪnəns] *n* volto, aspetto // *vt* approvare.

counter ['kauntə*] *n* banco // *vt* opporsi a; (*blow*) parare // *ad*: ~ **to** contro; in opposizione a; **~act** *vt* agire in opposizione a; (*poison etc*) annullare gli effetti di; **~attack** *n* contrattacco // *vi* contrattaccare; **~balance** *vt* contrappesare; **~-espionage** *n* controspionaggio.

counterfeit ['kauntəfɪt] *n* contraffazione *f*, falso // *vt* contraffare, falsificare // *a* falso(a).

counterfoil ['kauntəfɔɪl] *n* matrice *f*.

counterpart ['kauntəpɑːt] *n* (*of document etc*) copia; (*of person*) corrispondente *m/f*.

countess ['kauntɪs] *n* contessa.

countless ['kauntlɪs] *a* innumerevole.

country ['kʌntrɪ] *n* paese *m*; (*native land*) patria; (*as opposed to town*) campagna; (*region*) regione *f*; **~ dancing** *n* danza popolare; **~ house** *n* villa in campagna; **~man** *n* (*national*) compatriota *m*; (*rural*) contadino; **~ side** *n* campagna.

county ['kauntɪ] *n* contea.

coup [kuː] *n* s [kuː, -z] *n* colpo; (*also*: **~ d'état**) colpo di Stato.

coupé [kuː'peɪ] *n* coupé *m inv*.

couple ['kʌpl] *n* coppia // *vt* (*carriages*) agganciare; (*TECH*) accoppiare; (*ideas, names*) associare; **a ~ of** un paio di.

couplet ['kʌplɪt] *n* distico.

coupling ['kʌplɪŋ] *n* (*RAIL*) agganciamento.

coupon ['kuːpɔn] *n* buono; (*COMM*) coupon *m inv*.

courage ['kʌrɪdʒ] *n* coraggio; **~ous** [kə'reɪdʒəs] *a* coraggioso(a).

courier ['kurɪə*] *n* corriere *m*; (*for tourists*) guida.

course [kɔːs] *n* corso *m*; (*of ship*) rotta; (*for golf*) campo; (*part of meal*) piatto; **first ~** primo piatto; **of ~** *ad* senz'altro, naturalmente; **~ of action** modo d'agire; **~ of lectures** corso di lezioni.

court [kɔːt] *n* corte *f*; (*TENNIS*) campo // *vt* (*woman*) fare la corte a; **out of ~** (*LAW*: *settle*) in via amichevole; **to take to ~** sottoporre alla magistratura.

courteous ['kɜːtɪəs] *a* cortese.

courtesan [kɔːtɪ'zæn] *n* cortigiana.

courtesy ['kɜːtəsɪ] *n* cortesia.

court-house ['kɔːthaus] *n* (*US*) palazzo di giustizia.

courtier ['kɔːtɪə*] *n* cortigiano/a.

court-martial, *pl* **courts-martial** ['kɔːt-'mɑːʃəl] *n* corte *f* marziale.

courtroom ['kɔːtrum] *n* tribunale *m*.

courtyard ['kɔːtjɑːd] *n* cortile *m*.

cousin ['kʌzn] *n* cugino/a.

cove [kəuv] *n* piccola baia.

covenant ['kʌvənənt] *n* accordo.

cover ['kʌvə*] *vt* coprire // *n* (*of pan*) coperchio; (*over furniture*) fodera; (*of*

(*book*) copertina; (*shelter*) riparo; (*COMM*) copertura; **under ~** al riparo; **~age** *n* reportage *m*; (*INSURANCE*) copertura; **~ charge** *n* coperto; **~ing** *n* copertura; **~ing letter** *n* lettera d'accompagnamento.

covet ['kʌvɪt] *vt* bramare.

cow [kau] *n* vacca.

coward ['kauəd] *n* vigliacco/a; **~ice** [-ɪs] *n* vigliaccheria; **~ly** *a* vigliacco(a).

cowboy ['kaubɔɪ] *n* cow-boy *m inv*.

cower ['kauə*] *vi* acquattarsi.

cowshed ['kauʃɛd] *n* stalla.

coxswain ['kɔksn] *n* (*abbr*: **cox**) timoniere *m*; (*of ship*) nocchiere *m*.

coy [kɔɪ] *a* falsamente timido(a).

crab [kræb] *n* granchio; **~ apple** *n* mela selvatica.

crack [kræk] *n* fessura, crepa; incrinatura; (*noise*) schiocco; (: *of gun*) scoppio // *vt* spaccare; incrinare; (*whip*) schioccare; (*nut*) schiacciare // *a* (*troops*) fuori classe; **to ~ up** *vi* crollare; **~ed** *a* (*col*) matto(a); **~er** *n* cracker *m inv*; petardo.

crackle ['krækl] *vi* crepitare; **crackling** *n* crepitio; (*of pork*) cotenna croccante (del maiale).

cradle ['kreɪdl] *n* culla.

craft [krɑːft] *n* mestiere *m*; (*cunning*) astuzia; (*boat*) naviglio; **~sman** *n* artigiano; **~smanship** *n* abilità; **~y** *a* furbo(a), astuto(a).

crag [kræg] *n* roccia.

cram [kræm] *vt* (*fill*): **to ~ sth with** riempire qc di; (*put*): **to ~ sth into** stipare qc in; **~ming** *n* (*fig: pej*) sgobbare *m*.

cramp [kræmp] *n* crampo; **~ed** *a* ristretto(a).

crampon [kræmpɔn] *n* (*CLIMBING*) rampone *m*.

cranberry ['krænbərɪ] *n* mirtillo.

crane [kreɪn] *n* gru *f inv*.

cranium, *pl* **crania** ['kreɪnɪəm, 'kreɪnɪə] *n* cranio.

crank [kræŋk] *n* manovella; (*person*) persona stramba; **~shaft** *n* albero a manovelle.

cranny ['krænɪ] *n see* **nook**.

crash [kræʃ] *n* fragore *m*; (*of car*) incidente *m*; (*of plane*) caduta // *vt* (*car*) fracassare // *vi* (*plane*) fracassarsi; (*two cars*) scontrarsi; (*fig*) fallire, andare in rovina; **to ~ into** scontrarsi con; **~ course** *n* corso intensivo; **~ helmet** *n* casco; **~ landing** *n* atterraggio di fortuna.

crate [kreɪt] *n* gabbia.

crater ['kreɪtə*] *n* cratere *m*.

cravat(e) [krə'væt] *n* fazzoletto da collo.

crave [kreɪv] *vi*: **to ~ for** desiderare ardentemente.

crawl [krɔːl] *vi* strisciare carponi; (*vehicle*) avanzare lentamente // *n* (*SWIMMING*) crawl *m*.

crayfish ['kreɪfɪʃ] *n*, *pl inv* gambero (d'acqua dolce).

crayon ['kreɪən] *n* matita colorata.

craze [kreiz] n mania.
crazy ['kreizi] a matto(a); ~ **paving** n lastricato m a mosaico irregolare.
creak [kri:k] vi cigolare, scricchiolare.
cream [kri:m] n crema; (fresh) panna // a (colour) color crema inv; ~ **cake** n torta alla crema; ~ **cheese** n mascarpone m; ~y a cremoso(a).
crease [kri:s] n grinza; (deliberate) piega // vt sgualcire.
create [kri:'eit] vt creare; **creation** [-ʃən] n creazione f; **creative** a creativo(a); **creator** n creatore/trice.
creature ['kri:tʃə*] n creatura.
crèche, creche [krɛʃ] n asilo infantile.
credence n credenza, fede f.
credentials [kri'dɛnʃlz] npl (papers) credenziali fpl.
credibility [kredi'biliti] n credibilità.
credible ['kredibl] a credibile.
credit ['kredit] n credito; onore m // vt (COMM) accreditare; (believe: also: **give** ~ to) credere, prestar fede a; ~**s** npl (CINEMA) titoli mpl; **to** ~ **sb with** (fig) attribuire a qd; **to one's** ~ a proprio onore; **to take the** ~ **for** farsi il merito di; ~**able** a che fa onore, degno(a) di lode; ~ **card** n carta di credito; ~**or** n creditore/trice.
credulity [kri'dju:liti] n credulità.
creed [kri:d] n credo; dottrina.
creek [kri:k] n insenatura; (US) piccolo fiume m.
creep [kri:p], pt, pp **crept** [kri:p, krɛpt] vi avanzare furtivamente (or pian piano); (plant) arrampicarsi; ~**er** n pianta rampicante; ~y a (frightening) che fa accapponare la pelle.
cremate [kri'meit] vt cremare; **cremation** [-ʃən] n cremazione f.
crematorium pl **crematoria** [krɛmə'tɔːriəm, -'tɔːriə] n forno crematorio.
creosote ['kriəsəut] n creosoto.
crêpe [kreip] n crespo; ~ **bandage** n fascia elastica.
crept [krɛpt] pt, pp of **creep**.
crescendo [kri'ʃɛndəu] n crescendo.
crescent ['krɛsnt] n forma di luna crescente; strada semicircolare.
cress [krɛs] n crescione m.
crest [krɛst] n cresta; (of helmet) pennacchiera; (of coat of arms) cimiero; ~**fallen** a mortificato(a).
Crete ['kri:t] n Creta.
crevasse [kri'væs] n crepaccio.
crevice ['krɛvis] n fessura, crepa.
crew [kru:] n equipaggio; **to have a** ~**-cut** avere i capelli a spazzola; ~**-neck** n girocollo.
crib [krib] n culla; (REL) presepio // vt (col) copiare.
crick [krik] n crampo.
cricket ['krikit] n (insect) grillo; (game) cricket m; ~**er** n giocatore m di cricket.
crime [kraim] n crimine m; **criminal** ['kriminl] a, n criminale (m/f).

crimson ['krimzn] a color cremisi inv.
cringe [krindʒ] vi acquattarsi; (fig) essere servile.
crinkle ['kriŋkl] vt arricciare, increspare.
cripple ['kripl] n zoppo/a // vt azzoppare.
crisis, pl **crises** ['kraisis, -si:z] n crisi f inv.
crisp [krisp] a croccante; (fig) frizzante; vivace; deciso(a); ~**s** npl patatine fpl fritte.
criss-cross ['kriskrɔs] a incrociato(a).
criterion, pl **criteria** [krai'tiəriən, -'tiəriə] n criterio.
critic ['kritik] n critico; ~**al** a critico(a); ~**ally** ad criticamente; ~**ally ill** gravemente malato; ~**ism** ['kritisizm] n critica; ~**ize** ['kritisaiz] vt criticare.
croak [krəuk] vi gracchiare.
crochet ['krəuʃei] n lavoro all'uncinetto.
crockery ['krɔkəri] n vasellame m.
crocodile ['krɔkədail] n coccodrillo.
crocus ['krəukəs] n croco.
croft [krɔft] n piccolo podere m; ~**er** n affittuario di un piccolo podere.
crony ['krəuni] n (col) amicone/a.
crook [kruk] n truffatore m; (of shepherd) bastone m; ~**ed** ['krukid] a curvo(a), storto(a); (action) disonesto(a).
crop [krɔp] n raccolto; **to** ~ **up** vi presentarsi.
cropper ['krɔpə*] n: **to come a** ~ (col) fare fiasco.
croquet ['krəukei] n croquet m.
croquette [krə'kɛt] n crocchetta.
cross [krɔs] n croce f; (BIOL) incrocio // vt (street etc) attraversare; (arms, legs, BIOL) incrociare; (cheque) sbarrare // a di cattivo umore; **to** ~ **out** vt cancellare; **to** ~ **over** vi attraversare; ~**bar** n traversa; ~**breed** n incrocio; ~**country (race)** n cross-country m inv; ~**examination** n interrogatorio in contraddittorio; ~**examine** vt (LAW) interrogare in contraddittorio; ~**-eyed** a strabico(a); ~**ing** n incrocio; (sea-passage) traversata; (also: **pedestrian** ~**ing**) passaggio pedonale; ~**roads** n incrocio; ~ **section** n (BIOL) sezione f trasversale; (in population) settore m rappresentativo; ~**wind** n vento di traverso; ~**word** n cruciverba m inv.
crotch [krɔtʃ] n (of garment) pattina.
crotchet ['krɔtʃit] n (MUS) seminiminima.
crotchety ['krɔtʃiti] a (person) burbero(a).
crouch [krautʃ] vi acquattarsi; rannicchiarsi.
crouton ['kru:tɔn] n crostino.
crow [krəu] n (bird) cornacchia; (of cock) canto del gallo // vi (cock) cantare; (fig) vantarsi; cantar vittoria.
crowbar ['krəuba:*] n piede m di porco.
crowd [kraud] n folla // vt affollare, stipare // vi affollarsi; ~**ed** a affollato(a); ~**ed with** stipato(a) di.
crown [kraun] n corona; (of head) calotta cranica; (of hat) cocuzzolo; (of hill) cima // vt incoronare; ~ **jewels** npl gioielli mpl

della Corona; ~ **prince** *n* principe *m* ereditario.

crow's-nest ['krəuznɛst] *n* (*on sailing-ship*) coffa.

crucial ['kruːʃl] *a* cruciale, decisivo(a).

crucifix ['kruːsɪfɪks] *n* crocifisso; ~**ion** [-'fɪkʃən] *n* crocifissione *f*.

crucify ['kruːsɪfaɪ] *vt* crocifiggere, mettere in croce.

crude [kruːd] *a* (*materials*) greggio(a); non raffinato(a); (*fig: basic*) crudo(a); primitivo(a); (: *vulgar*) rozzo(a), grossolano(a); ~ (**oil**) *n* (petrolio) greggio.

cruel ['kruəl] *a* crudele; ~**ty** *n* crudeltà *f inv*.

cruet ['kruːɪt] *n* ampolla.

cruise [kruːz] *n* crociera // *vi* andare a velocità di crociera; (*taxi*) circolare; ~**r** *n* incrociatore *m*; **cruising speed** *n* velocità *f inv* di crociera.

crumb [krʌm] *n* briciola.

crumble ['krʌmbl] *vt* sbriciolare // *vi* sbriciolarsi; (*plaster etc*) sgrettolarsi; (*land, earth*) franare; (*building, fig*) crollare; **crumbly** *a* friabile.

crumpet ['krʌmpɪt] *n* crostino da tè.

crumple ['krʌmpl] *vt* raggrinzare, spiegazzare.

crunch [krʌntʃ] *vt* sgranocchiare; (*underfoot*) scricchiolare // *n* (*fig*) punto *or* momento cruciale; ~**y** *a* croccante.

crusade [kruːˈseɪd] *n* crociata; ~**r** *n* crociato.

crush [krʌʃ] *n* folla // *vt* schiacciare; (*crumple*) sgualcire; ~**ing** *a* schiacciante.

crust [krʌst] *n* crosta.

crutch [krʌtʃ] *n* gruccia.

crux [krʌks] *n* nodo.

cry [kraɪ] *vi* piangere; (*shout*) urlare // *n* urlo, grido; **to** ~ **off** *vi* ritirarsi; ~**ing** *a* (*fig*) palese; urgente.

crypt [krɪpt] *n* cripta.

cryptic ['krɪptɪk] *a* ermetico(a).

crystal ['krɪstl] *n* cristallo; ~-**clear** *a* cristallino(a); **crystallize** *vi* cristallizzarsi.

cu. *abbr*: ~ **ft.** = cubic feet; ~ **in.** = cubic inches.

cub [kʌb] *n* cucciolo.

Cuba ['kjuːbə] *n* Cuba; ~**n** *a*, *n* cubano(a).

cubbyhole ['kʌbɪhəʊl] *n* angolino.

cube [kjuːb] *n* cubo // *vt* (*MATH*) elevare al cubo; ~ **root** *n* radice *f* cubica; **cubic** *a* cubico(a).

cubicle ['kjuːbɪkl] *n* scompartimento separato; cabina.

cuckoo ['kuku:] *n* cucù *m inv*; ~ **clock** *n* orologio a cucù.

cucumber ['kjuːkʌmbə*] *n* cetriolo.

cud [kʌd] *n*: **to chew the** ~ ruminare.

cuddle ['kʌdl] *vt* abbracciare, coccolare // *vi* abbracciarsi; **cuddly** *a* da coccolare.

cudgel ['kʌdʒl] *n* randello.

cue [kjuː] *n* stecca; (*THEATRE etc*) segnale *m*.

cuff [kʌf] *n* (*of shirt, coat etc*) polsino; (*US*)

= turn-up; **off the** ~ *ad* a braccio; ~**link** *n* gemello.

cuisine [kwɪˈziːn] *n* cucina.

cul-de-sac ['kʌldəsæk] *n* vicolo cieco.

culinary ['kʌlɪnərɪ] *a* culinario(a).

culminate ['kʌlmɪneɪt] *vi* culminare; **culmination** [-'neɪʃən] *n* culmine *m*.

culpable ['kʌlpəbl] *a* colpevole.

culprit ['kʌlprɪt] *n* colpevole *m/f*.

cult [kʌlt] *n* culto.

cultivate ['kʌltɪveɪt] *vt* (*also fig*) coltivare; **cultivation** [-'veɪʃən] *n* coltivazione *f*.

cultural ['kʌltʃərəl] *a* culturale.

culture ['kʌltʃə*] *n* (*also fig*) cultura; ~**d** *a* colto(a).

cumbersome ['kʌmbəsəm] *a* ingombrante.

cumulative ['kjuːmjulətɪv] *a* cumulativo(a).

cunning ['kʌnɪŋ] *n* astuzia, furberia // *a* astuto(a), furbo(a).

cup [kʌp] *n* tazza; (*prize*) coppa.

cupboard ['kʌbəd] *n* armadio.

cupola ['kjuːpələ] *n* cupola.

cup-tie ['kʌptaɪ] *n* partita di coppa.

curable ['kjuərəbl] *a* curabile.

curate ['kjuːrɪt] *n* cappellano.

curator [kjuˈreɪtə*] *n* direttore *m* (*di museo etc*).

curb [kəːb] *vt* tenere a freno // *n* freno; (*US*) = **kerb**.

curdle ['kəːdl] *vi* cagliare.

curds [kəːds] *npl* latte *m* cagliato.

cure [kjuə*] *vt* guarire; (*CULIN*) trattare; affumicare; essiccare // *n* rimedio.

curfew ['kəːfjuː] *n* coprifuoco.

curio ['kjuərɪəu] *n* curiosità *f inv*.

curiosity [kjuərɪˈɒsɪtɪ] *n* curiosità.

curious ['kjuərɪəs] *a* curioso(a).

curl [kəːl] *n* riccio // *vt* ondulare; (*tightly*) arricciare // *vi* arricciarsi; **to** ~ **up** *vi* avvolgersi a spirale; rannicchiarsi; ~**er** *n* bigodino.

curling ['kəːlɪŋ] *n* (*SPORT*) curling *m*.

curly ['kəːlɪ] *a* ricciuto(a).

currant ['kʌrnt] *n* sultanina.

currency ['kʌrnsɪ] *n* moneta; **foreign** ~ divisa estera; **to gain** ~ (*fig*) acquistare larga diffusione.

current ['kʌrnt] *a*, *n* corrente (*f*); ~ **account** *n* conto corrente; ~ **affairs** *npl* attualità *fpl*; ~**ly** *ad* attualmente.

curriculum, *pl* ~**s** *or* **curricula** [kəˈrɪkjuləm, -lə] *n* curriculum *m inv*; ~ **vitae** *n* curriculum vitae *m inv*.

curry ['kʌrɪ] *n* curry *m inv* // *vt*: **to** ~ **favour with** cercare di attirarsi i favori di; **chicken** ~ pollo al curry.

curse [kəːs] *vt* maledire // *vi* bestemmiare // *n* maledizione *f*; bestemmia.

cursory ['kəːsərɪ] *a* superficiale.

curt [kəːt] *a* secco(a).

curtail [kəːˈteɪl] *vt* (*visit etc*) accorciare; (*expenses etc*) ridurre, decurtare.

curtain ['kəːtn] *n* tenda.

curts(e)y ['kəːtsɪ] *n* inchino, riverenza // *vi* fare un inchino *or* una riverenza.

curve [kɔːv] n curva // vi curvarsi.

cushion ['kuʃən] n cuscino // vt (shock) fare da cuscinetto a.

custard ['kʌstəd] n (for pouring) crema.

custodian [kʌs'təudiən] n custode m/f.

custody ['kʌstədi] n (of child) tutela; (for offenders) arresto.

custom ['kʌstəm] n costume m, usanza; (LAW) consuetudine f; (COMM) clientela; ~ary a consueto(a).

customer ['kʌstəmə*] n cliente m/f.

custom-made ['kʌstəm'meid] a (clothes) fatto(a) su misura; (other goods) fatto(a) su ordinazione.

customs ['kʌstəmz] npl dogana; ~ **duty** n dazio doganale; ~ **officer** n doganiere m.

cut [kʌt] vb (pt, pp **cut**) vt tagliare; (shape, make) intagliare; (reduce) ridurre // vi tagliare; (intersect) tagliarsi // n taglio; (in salary etc) riduzione f; **power** ~ mancanza di corrente elettrica; **to** ~ **a tooth** mettere un dente; **to** ~ **down (on)** vt fus ridurre; **to** ~ **off** vt tagliare; (fig) isolare; **to** ~ **out** vt tagliare fuori; eliminare; ritagliare; ~**back** n riduzione f.

cute [kjuːt] a grazioso(a); (clever) astuto(a).

cut glass [kʌt'glɑːs] n cristallo.

cuticle ['kjuːtikl] n (on nail) cuticola.

cutlery ['kʌtləri] n posate fpl.

cutlet ['kʌtlit] n costoletta.

cut: ~**out** n interruttore m; ~-**price** a a prezzo ridotto; ~**throat** n assassino.

cutting ['kʌtiŋ] a tagliente; (fig) pungente // n (PRESS) ritaglio (di giornale); (RAIL) trincea.

cuttlefish ['kʌtlfiʃ] n seppia.

cut-up ['kʌtʌp] a stravolto(a).

cwt abbr of **hundredweight(s)**.

cyanide ['saiənaid] n cianuro.

cyclamen ['sikləmən] n ciclamino.

cycle ['saikl] n ciclo; bicicletta // vi andare in bicicletta.

cycling ['saikliŋ] n ciclismo.

cyclist ['saiklist] n ciclista m/f.

cyclone ['saikləun] n ciclone m.

cygnet ['signit] n cigno giovane.

cylinder ['silində*] n cilindro; ~ **capacity** n cilindrata; ~-**head gasket** n guarnizione f della testata del cilindro.

cymbals ['simblz] npl cembali mpl.

cynic ['sinik] n cinico/a; ~**al** a cinico(a); ~**ism** ['sinisizəm] n cinismo.

cypress ['saipris] n cipresso.

Cypriot ['sipriət] a, n cipriota (m/f).

Cyprus ['saiprəs] n Cipro.

cyst [sist] n cisti f inv.

czar [zɑː*] n zar m inv.

Czech [tʃɛk] a ceco(a) // n ceco/a; (LING) ceco.

Czechoslovakia [tʃɛkəslə'vækiə] n Cecoslovacchia; ~**n** a, n cecoslovacco(a).

D

D [diː] n (MUS) re m; ~-**day** n giorno dello sbarco degli alleati in Normandia.

dab [dæb] vt (eyes, wound) tamponare; (paint, cream) applicare (con leggeri colpetti); **a** ~ **of paint** un colpetto di vernice.

dabble ['dæbl] vi: **to** ~ **in** occuparsi (da dilettante) di.

dad, daddy [dæd, 'dædi] n babbo, papà m inv; **daddy-long-legs** n tipula.

daffodil ['dæfədil] n giunchiglia.

daft [dɑːft] a sciocco(a).

dagger ['dægə*] n pugnale m.

daily ['deili] a quotidiano(a), giornaliero(a) // n quotidiano // ad tutti i giorni.

dainty ['deinti] a delicato(a), grazioso(a).

dairy ['dɛəri] n (shop) latteria; (on farm) caseificio // a caseario(a).

daisy ['deizi] n margherita.

dale [deil] n valle f.

dally ['dæli] vi trastullarsi.

dam [dæm] n diga // vt sbarrare; costruire dighe su.

damage ['dæmidʒ] n danno; danni mpl; (fig) danno // vt danneggiare; (fig) recar danno a; ~**s** npl (LAW) danni.

damn [dæm] vt condannare; (curse) maledire // n (col): **I don't give a** ~ non me ne importa un fico // a (col): **this** ~ ... questo maledetto ...; ~ **(it)!** accidenti!; ~**ing** a (evidence) schiacciante.

damp [dæmp] a umido(a) // n umidità, umido // vt (also: ~**en**) (cloth, rag) inumidire, bagnare; (enthusiasm etc) spegnere; ~**ness** n umidità, umido.

damson ['dæmzən] n susina damaschina.

dance [dɑːns] n danza, ballo; (ball) ballo // vi ballare; ~ **hall** n dancing m inv, sala da ballo; ~**r** n danzatore/trice; (professional) ballerino/a.

dancing ['dɑːnsiŋ] n danza, ballo.

dandelion ['dændilaiən] n dente m di leone.

dandruff ['dændrəf] n forfora.

Dane [dein] n danese m/f.

danger ['deindʒə*] n pericolo; **there is a** ~ **of fire** c'è pericolo di fuoco; **in** ~ in pericolo; **he was in** ~ **of falling** rischiava di cadere; ~**ous** a pericoloso(a).

dangle ['dæŋgl] vt dondolare; (fig) far balenare // vi pendolare.

Danish ['deiniʃ] a danese // n (LING) danese m.

dapper ['dæpə*] a lindo(a).

dare [dɛə*] vt: **to** ~ **sb to do** sfidare qd a fare // vi: **to** ~ **(to) do sth** osare fare qc; ~**devil** n scavezzacollo m/f; **daring** a audace, ardito(a).

dark [dɑːk] a (night, room) buio(a), scuro(a); (colour, complexion) scuro(a); (fig) cupo(a), tetro(a), nero(a) // n: **in the** ~ al buio; **in the** ~ **about** (fig)

all'oscuro di; **after** ~ a notte fatta; **~en**
vt (room) oscurare; (photo, painting) far
scuro(a) // vi oscurarsi; imbrunirsi;
~ **glasses** npl occhiali mpl scuri; **~ness** n
oscurità, buio; ~ **room** n camera oscura.

darling ['dɑːlɪŋ] a caro(a) // n tesoro.

darn [dɑːn] vt rammendare.

dart [dɑːt] n-freccetta // vi: **to ~ towards**
precipitarsi verso; **to ~ away** guizzare
via; ~**s** n tiro al bersaglio (con freccette);
~**board** n bersaglio (per freccette).

dash [dæʃ] n (sign) lineetta // vt (missile)
gettare; (hopes) infrangere // vi: **to ~
towards** precipitarsi verso; **to ~ away** vi
scappare via; ~**board** n cruscotto; ~**ing**
a ardito(a).

data ['deɪtə] npl dati mpl; ~ **processing** n
elaborazione f (elettronica) dei dati.

date [deɪt] n data; appuntamento; (fruit)
dattero // vt datare; **to ~ ad** fino a oggi;
out of ~ scaduto(a); (old-fashioned)
passato(a) di moda; **~d the 13th** datato il
13; **~d** a passato(a) di moda; ~**line** n
linea del cambiamento di data.

daub [dɔːb] vt imbrattare.

daughter ['dɔːtə*] n figlia; **~-in-law** n
nuora.

daunt [dɔːnt] vt intimidire; ~**less** a
intrepido(a).

dawdle ['dɔːdl] vi bighellonare.

dawn [dɔːn] n alba // vi (day) spuntare;
(fig) venire in mente.

day [deɪ] n giorno; (as duration) giornata;
(period of time, age) tempo, epoca; **the ~
before** il giorno avanti or prima; **by ~** di
giorno; ~**break** n spuntar m del giorno;
~**dream** n sogno a occhi aperti // vi
sognare a occhi aperti; ~**light** n luce f del
giorno; ~**time** n giorno.

daze [deɪz] vt (subject: drug) inebetire; (:
blow) stordire // n: **in a ~** inebetito(a);
stordito(a).

dazzle ['dæzl] vt abbagliare.

dead [ded] a morto(a); (numb)
intirizzito(a) // ad assolutamente,
perfettamente; **he was shot ~** fu colpito
a morte; ~ **on time** in perfetto orario; ~
tired stanco(a) morto(a); **to stop ~**
fermarsi in tronco; **the ~** i morti; ~**en** vt
(blow, sound) ammortire; (make numb)
intirizzire; ~ **end** n vicolo cieco; ~ **heat**
n (SPORT): **to finish in a ~ heat** finire
alla pari; ~**line** n scadenza; ~**lock** n
punto morto; ~**ly** a mortale; (weapon,
poison) micidiale; ~**pan** a a faccia
impassibile.

deaf [def] a sordo(a); ~**aid** n apparecchio
per la sordità; ~**en** vt assordare; ~**ening**
a fragoroso(a), assordante; ~**ness** n
sordità; ~**mute** n sordomuto/a.

deal [diːl] n accordo; affare m // vt (pt, pp
dealt [delt]) (blow, cards) dare; **a great ~
(of)** molto(a); **to ~ with** vt fus (COMM)
fare affari con, trattare con; (handle)
occuparsi di; (be about: book etc) trattarsi
di; ~**er** n commerciante m/f; ~**ings** npl
(COMM) relazioni fpl; (relations) rapporti
mpl.

dean [diːn] n (SCOL) preside m di facoltà (or
di collegio).

dear [dɪə*] a caro(a) // n: **my ~** caro
mio/cara mia; ~ **me!** Dio mio!; **D~
Sir/Madam** (in letter) Egregio(a)
Signore(a); **D~ Mr/Mrs X** Gentile
Signor/Signora X; ~**ly** ad (love)
moltissimo; (pay) a caro prezzo.

dearth [dɜːθ] n scarsità, carestia.

death [deθ] n morte f; (ADMIN) decesso;
~**bed** n letto di morte; ~ **certificate** n
atto di decesso; ~ **duties** npl (Brit)
imposta or tassa di successione; ~**ly** a di
morte; ~ **penalty** n pena di morte; ~
rate n indice m di mortalità.

debar [dɪˈbɑː*] vt: **to ~ sb from doing**
impedire a qd di fare.

debase [dɪˈbeɪs] vt (currency) adulterare;
(person) degradare.

debatable [dɪˈbeɪtəbl] a discutibile.

debate [dɪˈbeɪt] n dibattito // vt dibattere;
discutere // vi (consider): **to ~ whether**
riflettere se.

debauchery [dɪˈbɔːtʃərɪ] n dissolutezza.

debit ['debɪt] n debito // vt: **to ~ a sum
to sb** addebitare una somma a qd.

debris ['debriː] n detriti mpl.

debt [det] n debito; **to be in ~** essere
indebitato(a); ~**or** n debitore/trice.

début ['deɪbjuː] n debutto.

decade ['dekeɪd] n decennio.

decadence ['dekədəns] n decadenza.

decanter [dɪˈkæntə*] n caraffa.

decay [dɪˈkeɪ] n decadimento;
imputridimento; (fig) rovina; (also: **tooth
~**) carie f // vi (rot) imputridire; (fig)
andare in rovina.

decease [dɪˈsiːs] n decesso; ~**d** n
defunto/a.

deceit [dɪˈsiːt] n inganno; ~**ful** a
ingannevole, perfido(a).

deceive [dɪˈsiːv] vt ingannare.

decelerate [diːˈseləreɪt] vt,vi rallentare.

December [dɪˈsembə*] n dicembre m.

decency ['diːsənsɪ] n decenza.

decent ['diːsənt] a decente; **they were
very ~ about it** si sono comportati da
signori riguardo a ciò.

decentralize [diːˈsentrəlaɪz] vt
decentrare.

deception [dɪˈsepʃən] n inganno.

deceptive [dɪˈseptɪv] a ingannevole.

decibel ['desɪbel] n decibel m inv.

decide [dɪˈsaɪd] vt (person) far prendere
una decisione a; (question, argument)
risolvere, decidere // vi decidere,
decidersi; **to ~ to do/that** decidere di
fare/che; **to ~ on** decidere per; ~**d** a
(resolute) deciso(a); (clear, definite)
netto(a), chiaro(a); ~**dly** [-dɪdlɪ] ad
indubbiamente; decisamente.

deciduous [dɪˈsɪdjuːs] a deciduo(a).

decimal ['desɪməl] a, n decimale (m); ~
point n ≈ virgola.

decimate ['desɪmeɪt] vt decimare.

decipher [dɪˈsaɪfə*] vt decifrare.

decision [dɪˈsɪʒən] n decisione f.

decisive [dɪ'saɪsɪv] a decisivo(a).

deck [dɛk] n (NAUT) ponte m; (of bus): **top** ~ imperiale m; (of cards) mazzo; ~**chair** n sedia a sdraio; ~ **hand** n marinaio.

declaration [dɛklə'reɪʃən] n dichiarazione f.

declare [dɪ'klɛə*] vt dichiarare.

decline [dɪ'klaɪn] n (decay) declino; (lessening) ribasso // vt declinare; rifiutare // vi declinare; diminuire.

decode [di:'kəud] vt decifrare.

decompose [di:kəm'pəuz] vi decomporre; **decomposition** [di:kɒmpə'zɪʃən] n decomposizione f.

decontaminate [di:kən'tæmɪneɪt] vt decontaminare.

décor ['deɪkɔ:*] n decorazione f.

decorate ['dɛkəreɪt] vt (adorn, give a medal to) decorare; (paint and paper) tinteggiare e tappezzare; **decoration** [-'reɪʃən] n (medal etc, adornment) decorazione f; **decorative** ['dɛkərətɪv] a decorativo(a); **decorator** n decoratore m.

decoy ['di:kɔɪ] n zimbello.

decrease n ['di:kri:s] diminuzione f // vt, vi [di:'kri:s] diminuire.

decree [dɪ'kri:] n decreto; ~ **nisi** n sentenza provvisoria di divorzio.

decrepit [dɪ'krɛpɪt] a decrepito(a).

dedicate ['dɛdɪkeɪt] vt consacrare; (book etc) dedicare.

dedication [dɛdɪ'keɪʃən] n (devotion) dedizione f.

deduce [dɪ'dju:s] vt dedurre.

deduct [dɪ'dʌkt] vt: to ~ **sth (from)** dedurre qc (da); (from wage etc) trattenere qc (da); ~**ion** [dɪ'dʌkʃən] n (deducting) deduzione f; (from wage etc) trattenuta; (deducing) deduzione f, conclusione f.

deed [di:d] n azione f, atto; (LAW) atto.

deep [di:p] a profondo(a); **4 metres** ~ profondo(a) 4 metri // ad: ~ **in snow** affondato(a) nella neve; **spectators stood 20** ~ c'erano 20 file di spettatori; **knee-**~ **in water** in acqua fino alle ginocchia; ~**en** vt (hole) approfondire // vi approfondirsi; (darkness) farsi più buio; ~**freeze** n congelatore m // vt congelare; ~-**sea** a: ~-**sea diving** n immersione f in alto mare; ~-**sea fishing** n pesca d'alto mare; ~-**seated** a (beliefs) radicato(a); ~-**set** a (eyes) infossato(a).

deer [dɪə*] n, pl inv: **the** ~ i cervidi; **(red)** ~ cervo; **(fallow)** ~ daino; **(roe)** ~ capriolo; ~**skin** n pelle f di daino.

deface [dɪ'feɪs] vt imbrattare.

defamation [dɛfə'meɪʃən] n diffamazione f.

default [dɪ'fɔ:lt] vi (LAW) essere contumace; (gen) essere inadempiente // n: **by** ~ (LAW) in contumacia; (SPORT) per abbandono; ~**er** n (in debt) inadempiente m/f.

defeat [dɪ'fi:t] n sconfitta // vt (team, opponents) sconfiggere; (fig: plans, efforts) frustrare; ~**ist** a,n disfattista (m/f).

defect n ['di:fɛkt] difetto // vi [dɪ'fɛkt]: **to** ~ **to the enemy/the West** passare al nemico/all'Ovest; ~**ive** [dɪ'fɛktɪv] a difettoso(a).

defence [dɪ'fɛns] n difesa; **in** ~ **of** in difesa di; ~**less** a senza difesa.

defend [dɪ'fɛnd] vt difendere; ~**ant** n imputato/a; ~**er** n difensore/a.

defensive [dɪ'fɛnsɪv] a difensivo(a).

defer [dɪ'fə:*] vt (postpone) differire, rinviare.

deference ['dɛfərəns] n deferenza; riguardo.

defiance [dɪ'faɪəns] n sfida; **in** ~ **of** a dispetto di.

defiant [dɪ'faɪənt] a di sfida.

deficiency [dɪ'fɪʃənsɪ] n deficienza; carenza.

deficient [dɪ'fɪʃənt] a deficiente; insufficiente; **to be** ~ **in** mancare di.

deficit ['dɛfɪsɪt] n disavanzo.

defile vb [dɪ'faɪl] vt contaminare // vi sfilare // n ['di:faɪl] gola, stretta.

define [dɪ'faɪn] vt definire.

definite ['dɛfɪnɪt] a (fixed) definito(a), preciso(a); (clear, obvious) ben definito(a), esatto(a); (LING) determinativo(a); **he was** ~ **about it** ne era sicuro; ~**ly** ad indubbiamente.

definition [dɛfɪ'nɪʃən] n definizione f.

definitive [dɪ'fɪnɪtɪv] a definitivo(a).

deflate [di:'fleɪt] vt sgonfiare.

deflation [di:'fleɪʃən] n (ECON) deflazione f.

deflect [dɪ'flɛkt] vt deflettere, deviare.

deform [dɪ'fɔ:m] vt deformare; ~**ed** a deforme; ~**ity** n deformità f inv.

defraud [dɪ'frɔ:d] vt defraudare.

defray [dɪ'freɪ] vt: **to** ~ **sb's expenses** sostenere le spese di qd.

defrost [di:'frɒst] vt (fridge) disgelare; (milk, eggs) in polvere.

deft [dɛft] a svelto(a), destro(a).

defunct [dɪ'fʌŋkt] a defunto(a).

defuse [di:'fju:z] vt disarmare.

defy [dɪ'faɪ] vt sfidare; (efforts etc) resistere a.

degenerate vi [dɪ'dʒɛnəreɪt] degenerare // a [dɪ'dʒɛnərɪt] degenere.

degradation [dɛgrə'deɪʃən] n degradazione f.

degrading [dɪ'greɪdɪŋ] a degradante.

degree [dɪ'gri:] n grado; laurea (universitaria); **a (first)** ~ **in maths** una laurea in matematica.

dehydrated [di:haɪ'dreɪtɪd] a disidratato(a); (milk, eggs) in polvere.

de-ice [di:'aɪs] vt (windscreen) disgelare.

deign [deɪn] vi: **to** ~ **to do** degnarsi di fare.

deity ['di:ɪtɪ] n deità f inv; dio/dea.

dejected [dɪ'dʒɛktɪd] a abbattuto(a), avvilito(a).

dejection [dɪ'dʒɛkʃən] n abbattimento, avvilimento.

delay [dɪ'leɪ] vt (journey, operation) ritardare, rinviare; (travellers, trains) ritardare // n ritardo; **without** ~ senza ritardo; ~**ed-action** a a azione ritardata.

delegate n ['dɛlɪgɪt] delegato/a // vt ['dɛlɪgeɪt] delegare.
delegation [dɛlɪ'geɪʃən] n delegazione f.
delete [dɪ'liːt] vt cancellare.
deliberate a [dɪ'lɪbərɪt] (intentional) intenzionale; (slow) misurato(a) // vi [dɪ'lɪbəreɪt] deliberare, riflettere; ~ly ad (on purpose) deliberatamente.
delicacy ['dɛlɪkəsɪ] n delicatezza.
delicate ['dɛlɪkɪt] a delicato(a).
delicatessen [dɛlɪkə'tɛsn] n salumeria.
delicious [dɪ'lɪʃəs] a delizioso(a), squisito(a).
delight [dɪ'laɪt] n delizia, gran piacere m // vt dilettare; **to take ~ in** divertirsi a; ~**ful** a delizioso(a); incantevole.
delinquency [dɪ'lɪŋkwənsɪ] n delinquenza.
delinquent [dɪ'lɪŋkwənt] a,n delinquente (m/f).
delirium [dɪ'lɪrɪəm] n delirio.
deliver [dɪ'lɪvə*] vt (mail) distribuire; (goods) consegnare; (speech) pronunciare; (free) liberare; (MED) far partorire; **to ~ a message** fare un'ambasciata; **to ~ the goods** (fig) partorire; ~**y** n consegna; distribuzione f; (of speaker) modo di proporre; (MED) parto; **to take ~y of** prendere in consegna.
delta ['dɛltə] n delta m.
delude [dɪ'luːd] vt deludere, illudere.
deluge ['dɛljuːdʒ] n diluvio.
delusion [dɪ'luːʒən] n illusione f.
delve [dɛlv] vi: **to ~ into** frugare in; (subject) far ricerche in.
demagogue ['dɛməgɔg] n demagogo.
demand [dɪ'mɑːnd] vt richiedere // n domanda; (ECON, claim) richiesta; **in ~** ricercato(a), richiesto(a); **on ~** a richiesta; ~**ing** a (boss) esigente; (work) impegnativo(a).
demarcation [diːmɑː'keɪʃən] n demarcazione f.
demean [dɪ'miːn] vt: **to ~ o.s.** umiliarsi.
demeanour [dɪ'miːnə*] n comportamento; contegno.
demented [dɪ'mɛntɪd] a demente, impazzito(a).
demise [dɪ'maɪz] n decesso.
demobilize [diː'məʊbɪlaɪz] vt smobilitare.
democracy [dɪ'mɔkrəsɪ] n democrazia.
democrat ['dɛməkræt] n democratico/a; ~**ic** [dɛmə'krætɪk] a democratico(a).
demolish [dɪ'mɔlɪʃ] vt demolire.
demolition [dɛmə'lɪʃən] n demolizione f.
demonstrate ['dɛmənstreɪt] vt dimostrare, provare.
demonstration [dɛmən'streɪʃən] n dimostrazione f; (POL) manifestazione f, dimostrazione.
demonstrative [dɪ'mɔnstrətɪv] a dimostrativo(a).
demonstrator ['dɛmənstreɪtə*] n (POL) dimostrante m/f.
demoralize [dɪ'mɔrəlaɪz] vt demoralizzare.
demote [dɪ'məʊt] vt far retrocedere.
demure [dɪ'mjuə*] a contegnoso(a).

den [dɛn] n tana, covo.
denial [dɪ'naɪəl] n diniego; rifiuto.
denigrate ['dɛnɪgreɪt] vt denigrare.
denim ['dɛnɪm] n tessuto di cotone ritorto; ~**s** npl blue jeans mpl.
Denmark ['dɛnmɑːk] n Danimarca.
denomination [dɪnɔmɪ'neɪʃən] n (money) valore m; (REL) confessione f.
denominator [dɪ'nɔmɪneɪtə*] n denominatore m.
denote [dɪ'nəʊt] vt denotare.
denounce [dɪ'naʊns] vt denunciare.
dense [dɛns] a fitto(a); (stupid) ottuso(a), duro(a); ~**ly** ad: ~**ly wooded** fittamente boscoso; ~**ly populated** densamente popolato(a).
density ['dɛnsɪtɪ] n densità f inv.
dent [dɛnt] n ammaccatura // vt (also: **make a ~ in**) ammaccare.
dental ['dɛntl] a dentale; ~ **surgeon** n medico/a dentista.
dentifrice ['dɛntɪfrɪs] n dentifricio.
dentist ['dɛntɪst] n dentista m/f; ~**ry** n odontoiatria.
denture ['dɛntʃə*] n dentiera.
deny [dɪ'naɪ] vt negare; (refuse) rifiutare.
deodorant [diː'əʊdərənt] n deodorante m.
depart [dɪ'pɑːt] vi partire; **to ~ from** (leave) allontanarsi da, partire da.
department [dɪ'pɑːtmənt] n (COMM) reparto; (SCOL) sezione f, dipartimento; (POL) ministero; ~ **store** n grande magazzino.
departure [dɪ'pɑːtʃə*] n partenza; (fig): ~ **from** allontanamento da.
depend [dɪ'pɛnd] vi: **to ~ on** dipendere da; (rely on) contare su; **it ~s** dipende; ~**able** a fidato(a); (car etc) affidabile; ~**ence** n dipendenza; ~**ant**, ~**ent** n persona a carico.
depict [dɪ'pɪkt] vt (in picture) dipingere; (in words) descrivere.
depleted [dɪ'pliːtɪd] a diminuito(a).
deplorable [dɪ'plɔːrəbl] a deplorabile, lamentevole.
deplore [dɪ'plɔː*] vt deplorare.
deploy [dɪ'plɔɪ] vt dispiegare.
depopulation ['diːpɔpju'leɪʃən] n spopolamento.
deport [dɪ'pɔːt] vt deportare; espellere; ~**ation** [diːpɔː'teɪʃən] n deportazione f; ~**ment** n portamento.
depose [dɪ'pəʊz] vt deporre.
deposit [dɪ'pɔzɪt] n (COMM, GEO) deposito; (of ore, oil) giacimento; (CHEM) sedimento; (part payment) acconto; (for hired goods etc) cauzione f // vt depositare; dare in acconto; mettere o lasciare in deposito; ~ **account** n conto vincolato; ~**or** n depositante m/f.
depot ['dɛpəʊ] n deposito.
deprave [dɪ'preɪv] vt depravare, corrompere, pervertire.
depravity [dɪ'prævɪtɪ] n depravazione f.
depreciate [dɪ'priːʃɪeɪt] vt svalutare // vi svalutarsi; **depreciation** [-'eɪʃən] n svalutazione f.

depress [dɪ'prɛs] vt deprimere; (press down) premere; ~ed a (person) depresso(a), abbattuto(a); (area) depresso(a); ~ing a deprimente; ~ion [dɪ'prɛʃən] n depressione f.

deprivation [dɛprɪ'veɪʃən] n privazione f, (loss) perdita.

deprive [dɪ'praɪv] vt: to ~ sb of privare qd di; ~d a disgraziato(a).

depth [dɛpθ] n profondità f inv; in the ~s of nel profondo di; nel cuore di; in the ~s of winter in pieno inverno; ~ charge n carica di profondità.

deputation [dɛpju'teɪʃən] n deputazione f, delegazione f.

deputize ['dɛpjutaɪz] vi: to ~ for svolgere le funzioni di.

deputy ['dɛpjutɪ] a: ~ head vice-presidente m/f; (scol) vicepreside m/f // n (replacement) supplente m/f; (second in command) vice m/f.

derail [dɪ'reɪl] vt far deragliare; to be ~ed essere deragliato; ~ment n deragliamento.

deranged [dɪ'reɪndʒd] a: to be (mentally) ~ essere pazzo(a).

derelict ['dɛrɪlɪkt] a abbandonato(a).

deride [dɪ'raɪd] vt deridere.

derision [dɪ'rɪʒən] n derisione f.

derisive [dɪ'raɪsɪv] a di derisione f.

derisory [dɪ'raɪsərɪ] a (sum) irrisorio(a).

derivation [dɛrɪ'veɪʃən] n derivazione f.

derivative [dɪ'rɪvətɪv] n derivato // a derivato(a).

derive [dɪ'raɪv] vt: to ~ sth from derivare qc da; trarre qc da // vi: to ~ from derivare da.

derogatory [dɪ'rɔgətərɪ] a denigratorio(a).

derrick ['dɛrɪk] n gru f inv; (for oil) derrick m inv.

descend [dɪ'sɛnd] vt, vi discendere, scendere; to ~ from discendere da; ~ant n discendente m/f.

descent [dɪ'sɛnt] n discesa; (origin) discendenza, famiglia.

describe [dɪs'kraɪb] vt descrivere; **description** [-'krɪpʃən] n descrizione f; (sort) genere m, specie f; **descriptive** [-'krɪptɪv] a descrittivo(a).

desecrate ['dɛsɪkreɪt] vt profanare.

desert n ['dɛzət] deserto // vb [dɪ'zə:t] vt lasciare, abbandonare // vi (mil) disertare; ~er n disertore m; ~ion [dɪ'zə:ʃən] n diserzione f.

deserve [dɪ'zə:v] vt meritare; **deserving** a (person) meritevole, degno(a); (cause) meritorio(a).

design [dɪ'zaɪn] n (sketch) disegno; (layout, shape) linea; (pattern) fantasia; (comm) disegno tecnico; (intention) intenzione f // vt disegnare; progettare; to have ~s on aver mire su.

designate vt ['dɛzɪgneɪt] designare // a ['dɛzɪgnɪt] designato(a); **designation** [-'neɪʃən] n designazione f.

designer [dɪ'zaɪnə*] n (art, tech)

disegnatore/trice; (of fashion) modellista m/f.

desirability [dɪzaɪərə'bɪlɪtɪ] n desiderabilità; vantaggio.

desirable [dɪ'zaɪərəbl] a desiderabile.

desire [dɪ'zaɪə*] n desiderio, voglia // vt desiderare, volere.

desk [dɛsk] n (in office) scrivania; (for pupil) banco; (in shop, restaurant) cassa; (in hotel) ricevimento; (at airport) accettazione f.

desolate ['dɛsəlɪt] a desolato(a).

desolation [dɛsə'leɪʃən] n desolazione f.

despair [dɪs'pɛə*] n disperazione f // vi: to ~ of disperare di.

despatch [dɪs'pætʃ] n,vt = dispatch.

desperate ['dɛspərɪt] a disperato(a); (fugitive) capace di tutto; ~ly ad disperatamente; (very) terribilmente, estremamente.

desperation [dɛspə'reɪʃən] n disperazione f.

despicable [dɪs'pɪkəbl] a disprezzabile.

despise [dɪs'paɪz] vt disprezzare, sdegnare.

despite [dɪs'paɪt] prep malgrado, a dispetto di, nonostante.

despondent [dɪs'pɔndənt] a abbattuto(a), scoraggiato(a).

dessert [dɪ'zə:t] n dolce m; frutta; ~spoon n cucchiaio da dolci.

destination [dɛstɪ'neɪʃən] n destinazione f.

destine ['dɛstɪn] vt destinare.

destiny ['dɛstɪnɪ] n destino.

destitute ['dɛstɪtju:t] a indigente, bisognoso(a).

destroy [dɪs'trɔɪ] vt distruggere; ~er n (naut) cacciatorpediniere m inv.

destruction [dɪs'trʌkʃən] n distruzione f.

destructive [dɪs'trʌktɪv] a distruttivo(a).

detach [dɪ'tætʃ] vt staccare, distaccare; ~able a staccabile; ~ed a (attitude) distante; ~ed house n villa; ~ment n (mil) distaccamento; (fig) distacco.

detail ['di:teɪl] n particolare m, dettaglio // vt dettagliare, particolareggiare; in ~ nei particolari; ~ed a particolareggiato(a).

detain [dɪ'teɪn] vt trattenere; (in captivity) detenere.

detect [dɪ'tɛkt] vt scoprire, scorgere; (med, police, radar etc) individuare; ~ion [dɪ'tɛkʃən] n scoperta; individuazione f; ~ive n agente m investigativo; private ~ive investigatore m privato; ~ive story n giallo; ~or n rivelatore m.

detention [dɪ'tɛnʃən] n detenzione f; (scol) permanenza forzata per punizione.

deter [dɪ'tə:*] vt distogliere.

detergent [dɪ'tə:dʒənt] n detersivo.

deteriorate [dɪ'tɪərɪəreɪt] vi deteriorarsi; **deterioration** [-'reɪʃən] n deterioramento.

determination [dɪtə:mɪ'neɪʃən] n determinazione f.

determine [dɪ'tə:mɪn] vt determinare; ~d a (person) risoluto(a), deciso(a).

deterrent [dɪ'tɛrənt] n deterrente m.

detest [dɪ'tɛst] *vt* detestare; ~**able** *a* detestabile, abominevole.
detonate ['dɛtəneɪt] *vi* detonare; esplodere // *vt* far detonare *or* esplodere; **detonator** *n* detonatore *m*.
detour ['diːtuə*] *n* deviazione *f*.
detract [dɪ'trækt] *vt*: **to ~ from** detrarre da.
detriment ['dɛtrɪmənt] *n*: **to the ~ of** a detrimento di; ~**al** [dɛtrɪ'mɛntl] *a*: ~**al to** dannoso(a) a, nocivo(a) a.
devaluation [diːvæljuˈeɪʃən] *n* svalutazione *f*.
devalue ['diːˈvæljuː] *vt* svalutare.
devastate ['dɛvəsteɪt] *vt* devastare.
devastating ['dɛvəsteɪtɪŋ] *a* devastatore(trice).
develop [dɪ'vɛləp] *vt* sviluppare; (*habit*) prendere (gradualmente) // *vi* svilupparsi; (*facts, symptoms: appear*) manifestarsi, rivelarsi; ~**er** *n* (*PHOT*) sviluppatore *m*; (*of land*) imprenditore/trice; ~**ing country** paese *m* in via di sviluppo; ~**ment** *n* sviluppo.
deviate ['diːvɪeɪt] *vi* deviare.
deviation [diːvɪˈeɪʃən] *n* deviazione *f*.
device [dɪ'vaɪs] *n* (*apparatus*) congegno.
devil ['dɛvl] *n* diavolo; demonio; ~**ish** *a* diabolico(a).
devious ['diːvɪəs] *a* (*means*) indiretto(a), tortuoso(a); (*person*) subdolo(a).
devise [dɪ'vaɪz] *vt* escogitare, concepire.
devoid [dɪ'vɔɪd] *a*: ~ **of** privo(a) di.
devote [dɪ'vəut] *vt*: **to ~ sth to** dedicare qc a; ~**d** *a* devoto(a); **to be ~d to** essere affezionato(a) a; ~**e** [dɛvəu'tiː] *n* (*MUS, SPORT*) appassionato/a.
devotion [dɪ'vəuʃən] *n* devozione *f*, attaccamento; (*REL*) atto di devozione, preghiera.
devour [dɪ'vauə*] *vt* divorare.
devout [dɪ'vaut] *a* pio(a), devoto(a).
dew [djuː] *n* rugiada.
dexterity [dɛks'tɛrɪtɪ] *n* destrezza.
diabetes [daɪəˈbiːtiːz] *n* diabete *m*; **diabetic** [-ˈbɛtɪk] *a* diabetico(a) // *n* diabetico.
diagnose [daɪəgˈnəuz] *vt* diagnosticare.
diagnosis, pl diagnoses [daɪəgˈnəusɪs, -siːz] *n* diagnosi *f inv*.
diagonal [daɪˈægənl] *a*, *n* diagonale (*f*).
diagram ['daɪəgræm] *n* diagramma *m*.
dial ['daɪəl] *n* quadrante *m*; (*on telephone*) disco combinatore // *vt* (*number*) fare; ~**ling tone** *n* segnale *m* di linea libera.
dialect ['daɪəlɛkt] *n* dialetto.
dialogue ['daɪəlɔg] *n* dialogo.
diameter [daɪˈæmɪtə*] *n* diametro.
diamond ['daɪəmənd] *n* diamante *m*; (*shape*) rombo; ~**s** *npl* (*CARDS*) quadri *mpl*.
diaper ['daɪəpə*] *n* (*US*) pannolino.
diaphragm ['daɪəfræm] *n* diaframma *m*.
diarrhoea [daɪəˈriːə] *n* diarrea.
diary ['daɪərɪ] *n* (*daily account*) diario; (*book*) agenda.
dice [daɪs] *n*, *pl inv* dado // *vt* (*CULIN*) tagliare a dadini.

dictate *vt* [dɪk'teɪt] dettare // *n* ['dɪkteɪt] dettame *m*.
dictation [dɪk'teɪʃən] *n* dettato.
dictator [dɪk'teɪtə*] *n* dittatore *m*; ~**ship** *n* dittatura.
diction ['dɪkʃən] *n* dizione *f*.
dictionary ['dɪkʃənrɪ] *n* dizionario.
did [dɪd] *pt of* **do**.
die [daɪ] *n* (*pl*: **dies**) conio; matrice *f*; stampo // *vi* morire; **to ~ away** *vi* spegnersi a poco a poco; **to ~ down** *vi* abbassarsi; **to ~ out** *vi* estinguersi.
Diesel ['diːzəl]: ~ **engine** *n* motore *m* diesel *inv*.
diet ['daɪət] *n* alimentazione *f*; (*restricted food*) dieta // *vi* (*also*: **be on a ~**) stare a dieta.
differ ['dɪfə*] *vi*: **to ~ from sth** differire da qc; essere diverso(a) da qc; **to ~ from sb over sth** essere in disaccordo con qd su qc; ~**ence** *n* differenza; (*quarrel*) screzio; ~**ent** *a* diverso(a); ~**ential** [-'rɛnʃəl] *n* (*AUT, wages*) differenziale *m*; ~**entiate** [-'rɛnʃɪeɪt] *vi* differenziarsi; **to ~entiate between** discriminare *or* fare differenza fra; ~**ently** *ad* diversamente.
difficult ['dɪfɪkəlt] *a* difficile; ~**y** *n* difficoltà *f inv*.
diffident ['dɪfɪdənt] *a* sfiduciato(a).
diffuse *a* [dɪ'fjuːs] diffuso(a) // *vt* [dɪ'fjuːz] diffondere, emanare.
dig [dɪg] *vt* (*pt, pp* **dug** [dʌg]) (*hole*) scavare; (*garden*) vangare // *n* (*prod*) gomitata; (*fig*) frecciata; **to ~ into** (*snow, soil*) scavare; **to ~ up** *vt* scavare; (*tree etc*) sradicare.
digest *vt* [daɪ'dʒɛst] digerire; ~**ible** [dɪ'dʒɛstəbl] *a* digeribile; ~**ion** [dɪ'dʒɛstʃən] *n* digestione *f*.
digit ['dɪdʒɪt] *n* cifra; (*finger*) dito; ~**al** *a* digitale.
dignified ['dɪgnɪfaɪd] *a* dignitoso(a).
dignitary ['dɪgnɪtərɪ] *n* dignitario.
dignity ['dɪgnɪtɪ] *n* dignità.
digress [daɪ'grɛs] *vi*: **to ~ from** divagare da; ~**ion** [daɪ'grɛʃən] *n* digressione *f*.
digs [dɪgz] *npl* (*Brit*: *col*) camera ammobiliata.
dilapidated [dɪ'læpɪdeɪtɪd] *a* cadente.
dilate [daɪ'leɪt] *vt* dilatare // *vi* dilatarsi.
dilatory ['dɪlətərɪ] *a* dilatorio(a).
dilemma [daɪ'lɛmə] *n* dilemma *m*.
diligent ['dɪlɪdʒənt] *a* diligente.
dilute [daɪ'luːt] *vt* diluire; (*with water*) annacquare.
dim [dɪm] *a* (*light, eyesight*) debole; (*memory, outline*) vago(a); (*stupid*) lento(a) d'ingegno // *vt* (*light*) abbassare.
dime [daɪm] *n* (*US*) = 10 cents.
dimension [dɪ'mɛnʃən] *n* dimensione *f*.
diminish [dɪ'mɪnɪʃ] *vt*, *vi* diminuire.
diminutive [dɪ'mɪnjutɪv] *a* minuscolo(a) // *n* (*LING*) diminutivo.
dimly ['dɪmlɪ] *ad* debolmente, indistintamente.
dimple ['dɪmpl] *n* fossetta.
din [dɪn] *n* chiasso, fracasso.

dine [daɪn] vi pranzare.

dinghy ['dɪŋgɪ] n battello pneumatico; (also: **sailing ~**) dinghy m inv.

dingy ['dɪndʒɪ] a grigio(a).

dining ['daɪnɪŋ] cpd: **~ car** n vagone m ristorante; **~ room** n sala da pranzo.

dinner ['dɪnə*] n pranzo; (public) banchetto; **~ jacket** n smoking m inv; **~ party** n cena.

diocese ['daɪəsɪs] n diocesi f inv.

dip [dɪp] n discesa; (in sea) bagno // vt immergere; bagnare; (AUT: lights) abbassare // vi abbassarsi.

diphtheria [dɪf'θɪərɪə] n difterite f.

diphthong ['dɪfθɒŋ] n dittongo.

diploma [dɪ'pləumə] n diploma m.

diplomacy [dɪ'pləuməsɪ] n diplomazia.

diplomat ['dɪpləmæt] n diplomatico; **~ic** [dɪplə'mætɪk] a diplomatico(a); **~ic corps** n corpo diplomatico.

dipstick ['dɪpstɪk] n (AUT) indicatore m di livello dell'olio.

dire [daɪə*] a terribile; estremo(a).

direct [daɪ'rɛkt] a diretto(a) // vt dirigere; **can you ~ me to ...?** mi può indicare la strada per ...?; **~ current** n corrente f continua.

direction [dɪ'rɛkʃən] n direzione f; **~s** npl (advice) chiarimenti mpl; **~s for use** istruzioni fpl.

directly [dɪ'rɛktlɪ] ad (in straight line) direttamente; (at once) subito.

director [dɪ'rɛktə*] n direttore/trice; amministratore/trice; (THEATRE, CINEMA) regista m/f.

directory [dɪ'rɛktərɪ] n elenco.

dirt [dɜːt] n sporcizia; immondizia; **~-cheap** a da due soldi; **~y** a sporco(a) // vt sporcare; **~y trick** n brutto scherzo.

disability [dɪsə'bɪlɪtɪ] n invalidità f inv; (LAW) incapacità f inv.

disabled [dɪs'eɪbld] a invalido(a); (maimed) mutilato(a); (through illness, old age) inabile.

disadvantage [dɪsəd'vɑːntɪdʒ] n svantaggio; **~ous** [dɪsædvɑːn'teɪdʒəs] a svantaggioso(a).

disagree [dɪsə'griː] vi (differ) discordare; (be against, think otherwise): **to ~ (with)** essere in disaccordo (con), dissentire (da); **garlic ~s with me** l'aglio non mi va; **~able** a sgradevole; (person) antipatico(a); **~ment** n disaccordo.

disallow ['dɪsə'lau] vt respingere.

disappear [dɪsə'pɪə*] vi scomparire; **~ance** n scomparsa.

disappoint [dɪsə'pɔɪnt] vt deludere; **~ment** n delusione f.

disapproval [dɪsə'pruːvəl] n disapprovazione f.

disapprove [dɪsə'pruːv] vi: **to ~ of** disapprovare.

disarm [dɪs'ɑːm] vt disarmare; **~ament** n disarmo.

disaster [dɪ'zɑːstə*] n disastro; **disastrous** a disastroso(a).

disband [dɪs'bænd] vt sbandare; (MIL) congedare.

disbelief ['dɪsbə'liːf] n incredulità.

disc [dɪsk] n disco.

discard [dɪs'kɑːd] vt (old things) scartare; (fig) abbandonare.

disc brake [dɪs'breɪk] n freno a disco.

discern [dɪ'sɜːn] vt discernere, distinguere; **~ing** a perspicace.

discharge vt [dɪs'tʃɑːdʒ] (duties) compiere; (ELEC, waste etc) scaricare; (MED) emettere; (patient) dimettere; (employee) licenziare; (soldier) congedare; (defendant) liberare // n ['dɪstʃɑːdʒ] (ELEC) scarica; (MED) emissione f; (dismissal) licenziamento; congedo; liberazione f.

disciple [dɪ'saɪpl] n discepolo.

disciplinary ['dɪsɪplɪnərɪ] a disciplinare.

discipline ['dɪsɪplɪn] n disciplina // vt disciplinare; (punish) punire.

disc jockey ['dɪskdʒɒkɪ] n disc jockey m inv.

disclaim [dɪs'kleɪm] vt ripudiare.

disclose [dɪs'kləuz] vt rivelare, svelare; **disclosure** [-'kləuʒə*] n rivelazione f.

disco ['dɪskəu] n abbr of **discothèque.**

discoloured [dɪs'kʌləd] a scolorito(a); ingiallito(a).

discomfort [dɪs'kʌmfət] n disagio; (lack of comfort) scomodità f inv.

disconcert [dɪskən'sɜːt] vt sconcertare.

disconnect [dɪskə'nɛkt] vt sconnettere, staccare; (ELEC, RADIO) staccare; (gas, water) chiudere; **~ed** a (speech, thought) sconnesso(a).

disconsolate [dɪs'kɒnsəlɪt] a sconsolato(a).

discontent [dɪskən'tɛnt] n scontentezza; **~ed** a scontento(a).

discontinue [dɪskən'tɪnjuː] vt smettere, cessare; **'~d'** (COMM) 'sospeso'.

discord ['dɪskɔːd] n disaccordo; (MUS) dissonanza; **~ant** [dɪs'kɔːdənt] a discordante; dissonante.

discothèque ['dɪskəutɛk] n discoteca.

discount n ['dɪskaunt] sconto // vt [dɪs-'kaunt] scontare.

discourage [dɪs'kʌrɪdʒ] vt scoraggiare; **discouraging** a scoraggiante.

discourteous [dɪs'kɜːtɪəs] a scortese.

discover [dɪs'kʌvə*] vt scoprire; **~y** n scoperta.

discredit [dɪs'krɛdɪt] vt screditare; mettere in dubbio.

discreet [dɪ'skriːt] a discreto(a).

discrepancy [dɪ'skrɛpənsɪ] n discrepanza.

discretion [dɪ'skrɛʃən] n discrezione f.

discriminate [dɪ'skrɪmɪneɪt] vi: **to ~ between** distinguere tra; **to ~ against** discriminare contro; **discriminating** a fine, giudizioso(a); **discrimination** [-'neɪʃən] n discriminazione f; (judgment) discernimento.

discus ['dɪskəs] n disco.

discuss [dɪs'kʌs] vt discutere; (debate) dibattere; **~ion** [dɪ'skʌʃən] n discussione f.

disdain [dɪs'deɪn] n disdegno.

disease [dɪ'ziːz] n malattia.

disembark [dɪsɪm'bɑːk] vt, vi sbarcare.

disembodied [dɪsɪm'bɔdɪd] a disincarnato(a).

disembowel [dɪsɪm'bauəl] vt sbudellare, sventrare.

disenchanted [dɪsɪn'tʃɑːntɪd] a disincantato(a), disilluso(a).

disengage [dɪsɪn'ɡeɪdʒ] vt disimpegnare; (TECH) distaccare; (AUT) disinnestare.

disentangle [dɪsɪn'tæŋɡl] vt sbrogliare.

disfavour [dɪs'feɪvə*] n sfavore m; disgrazia.

disfigure [dɪs'fɪɡə*] vt sfigurare.

disgrace [dɪs'ɡreɪs] n vergogna; (disfavour) disgrazia // vt disonorare, far cadere in disgrazia; ~ful a scandaloso(a), vergognoso(a).

disgruntled [dɪs'ɡrʌntld] a scontento(a), di cattivo umore.

disguise [dɪs'ɡaɪz] n travestimento // vt travestire; **in ~** travestito(a).

disgust [dɪs'ɡʌst] n disgusto, nausea // vt disgustare, far schifo a; ~**ing** a disgustoso(a); ripugnante.

dish [dɪʃ] n piatto; **to do** or **wash the ~es** fare i piatti; **to ~ up** vt servire; (facts, statistics) presentare; ~**cloth** n (for drying) asciugatoio; (for washing) strofinaccio.

dishearten [dɪs'hɑːtn] vt scoraggiare.

dishevelled [dɪ'ʃevəld] a arruffato(a); scapigliato(a).

dishonest [dɪs'ɔnɪst] a disonesto(a); ~**y** n disonestà.

dishonour [dɪs'ɔnə*] n disonore m; ~**able** a disonorevole.

dishwasher ['dɪʃwɔʃə*] n lavastoviglie f inv; (person) sguattero/a.

disillusion [dɪsɪ'luːʒən] vt disilludere, disingannare // n disillusione f.

disinfect [dɪsɪn'fɛkt] vt disinfettare; ~**ant** n disinfettante m.

disintegrate [dɪs'ɪntɪɡreɪt] vi disintegrarsi.

disinterested [dɪs'ɪntrəstɪd] a disinteressato(a).

disjointed [dɪs'dʒɔɪntɪd] a sconnesso(a).

disk [dɪsk] n = **disc**.

dislike [dɪs'laɪk] n antipatia, avversione f // vt: **he ~s it** non gli piace.

dislocate ['dɪsləkeɪt] vt slogare; disorganizzare.

dislodge [dɪs'lɔdʒ] vt rimuovere, staccare; (enemy) sloggiare.

disloyal [dɪs'lɔɪəl] a sleale.

dismal ['dɪzml] a triste, cupo(a).

dismantle [dɪs'mæntl] vt smantellare, smontare; (fort, warship) disarmare.

dismay [dɪs'meɪ] n costernazione f // vt sgomentare.

dismiss [dɪs'mɪs] vt congedare; (employee) licenziare; (idea) scacciare; (LAW) respingere; ~**al** n congedo; licenziamento.

dismount [dɪs'maunt] vi scendere.

disobedience [dɪsə'biːdɪəns] n disubbidienza.

disobedient [dɪsə'biːdɪənt] a disubbidiente.

disobey [dɪsə'beɪ] vt disubbidire.

disorder [dɪs'ɔːdə*] n disordine m; (rioting) tumulto; (MED) disturbo; ~**ly** a disordinato(a); tumultuoso(a).

disorganize [dɪs'ɔːɡənaɪz] vt disorganizzare.

disown [dɪs'əun] vt ripudiare.

disparaging [dɪs'pærɪdʒɪŋ] a spregiativo(a), sprezzante.

disparity [dɪs'pærɪtɪ] n disparità f inv.

dispassionate [dɪs'pæʃənət] a calmo(a), freddo(a); imparziale.

dispatch [dɪs'pætʃ] vt spedire, inviare // n spedizione f, invio; (MIL, PRESS) dispaccio.

dispel [dɪs'pɛl] vt dissipare, scacciare.

dispensary [dɪs'pensərɪ] n farmacia; (in chemist's) dispensario.

dispense [dɪs'pɛns] vt distribuire, amministrare; **to ~ with** vt fus fare a meno di; ~**r** n (container) distributore m; **dispensing chemist** n farmacista m/f.

dispersal [dɪs'pəːsl] n dispersione f.

disperse [dɪs'pəːs] vt disperdere; (knowledge) disseminare // vi disperdersi.

dispirited [dɪs'pɪrɪtɪd] a scoraggiato(a), abbattuto(a).

displace [dɪs'pleɪs] vt spostare; ~**d person** n (POL) profugo/a.

display [dɪs'pleɪ] n mostra; esposizione f; (of feeling etc) manifestazione f; (screen) schermo; (pej) ostentazione f // vt mostrare; (goods) esporre; (results) affiggere; (departure times) indicare.

displease [dɪs'pliːz] vt dispiacere a, scontentare; **displeasure** [-'plɛʒə*] n dispiacere m.

disposable [dɪs'pəuzəbl] a (pack etc) a perdere; (income) disponibile.

disposal [dɪs'pəuzl] n (of rubbish) evacuazione f; distruzione f; **at one's ~** alla sua disposizione.

dispose [dɪs'pəuz] vt disporre; **to ~ of** vt (time, money) disporre di; (unwanted goods) sbarazzarsi di; (problem) sbrigarsi; ~**d a: ~d to do** disposto(a) a fare; **disposition** [-'zɪʃən] n disposizione f; (temperament) carattere m.

disproportionate [dɪsprə'pɔːʃənət] a sproporzionato(a).

disprove [dɪs'pruːv] vt confutare.

dispute [dɪs'pjuːt] n disputa; (also: **industrial ~**) controversia (sindacale) // vt contestare; (matter) discutere; (victory) disputare.

disqualification [dɪskwɔlɪfɪ'keɪʃən] n squalifica; ~ (**from driving**) ritiro della patente.

disqualify [dɪs'kwɔlɪfaɪ] vt (SPORT) squalificare; **to ~ sb from sth/from doing** rendere qd incapace a qc/a fare; squalificare qd da qc/da fare.

disquiet [dɪs'kwaɪət] n inquietudine f.

disregard [dɪsrɪ'ɡɑːd] vt non far caso a, non badare a.

disrepair [dɪsrɪ'pɛə*] n cattivo stato.
disreputable [dɪs'rɛpjutəbl] a (person) di cattiva fama.
disrespectful [dɪsrɪ'spɛktful] a che manca di rispetto.
disrupt [dɪs'rʌpt] vt mettere in disordine; ~ion [-'rʌpʃən] n disordine m; interruzione f.
dissatisfaction [dɪssætɪs'fækʃən] n scontentezza, insoddisfazione f.
dissatisfied [dɪs'sætɪsfaɪd] a: ~ (with) scontento(a) or insoddisfatto(a) (di).
dissect [dɪ'sɛkt] vt sezionare.
disseminate [dɪ'sɛmɪneɪt] vt disseminare.
dissent [dɪ'sɛnt] n dissenso.
disservice [dɪs'sɜːvɪs] n: to do sb a ~ fare un cattivo servizio a qd.
dissident ['dɪsɪdnt] a dissidente.
dissimilar [dɪ'sɪmɪlə*] a: ~ (to) dissimile or diverso(a) (da).
dissipate ['dɪsɪpeɪt] vt dissipare; ~d a dissipato(a).
dissociate [dɪ'səuʃɪeɪt] vt dissociare.
dissolute ['dɪsəluːt] a dissoluto(a), licenzioso(a).
dissolve [dɪ'zɒlv] vt dissolvere, sciogliere // vi dissolversi, sciogliersi; (fig) svanire.
dissuade [dɪ'sweɪd] vt: to ~ sb (from) dissuadere qd (da).
distance ['dɪstns] n distanza; in the ~ in lontananza.
distant ['dɪstnt] a lontano(a), distante; (manner) riservato(a), freddo(a).
distaste [dɪs'teɪst] n ripugnanza; ~ful a ripugnante, sgradevole.
distemper [dɪs'tɛmpə*] n (paint) tempera.
distend [dɪs'tɛnd] vt dilatare // vi dilatarsi.
distil [dɪs'tɪl] vt distillare; ~lery n distilleria.
distinct [dɪs'tɪŋkt] a distinto(a); (preference, progress) definito(a); ~ion [dɪs'tɪŋkʃən] n distinzione f; (in exam) lode f; ~ive a distintivo(a); ~ly ad chiaramente; manifestamente.
distinguish [dɪs'tɪŋgwɪʃ] vt distinguere; discernere; ~ed a (eminent) eminente; ~ing a (feature) distinto(a), caratteristico(a).
distort [dɪs'tɔːt] vt distorcere; (TECH) deformare; ~ion [dɪs'tɔːʃən] n distorsione f; deformazione f.
distract [dɪs'trækt] vt distrarre; ~ed a distratto(a); ~ion [dɪs'trækʃən] n distrazione f; to drive sb to ~ion spingere qd alla pazzia.
distraught [dɪs'trɔːt] a stravolto(a).
distress [dɪs'trɛs] n angoscia; (pain) dolore m // vt affliggere; ~ing a doloroso(a); ~ signal n segnale m di pericolo.
distribute [dɪs'trɪbjuːt] vt distribuire; **distribution** [-'bjuːʃən] n distribuzione f; **distributor** n distributore m.
district ['dɪstrɪkt] n (of country) regione f; (of town) quartiere m; (ADMIN) distretto; ~ **attorney** n (US) ≈ sostituto

procuratore m della Repubblica; ~ **nurse** n (Brit) infermiera di quartiere.
distrust [dɪs'trʌst] n diffidenza, sfiducia // vt non aver fiducia in.
disturb [dɪs'tɜːb] vt disturbare; (inconvenience) scomodare; (political etc) tumulto; (by drunks etc) disordini mpl; ~ing a sconvolgente.
disuse [dɪs'juːs] n: to fall into ~ cadere in disuso.
disused [dɪs'juːzd] a abbandonato(a).
ditch [dɪtʃ] n fossa // vt (col) piantare in asso.
dither ['dɪðə*] vi vacillare.
ditto ['dɪtəu] ad idem.
divan [dɪ'væn] n divano.
dive [daɪv] n tuffo; (of submarine) immersione f; (AVIAT) picchiata; (pej) buco // vi tuffarsi; ~r n tuffatore/trice; palombaro.
diverge [daɪ'vɜːdʒ] vi divergere.
diverse [daɪ'vɜːs] a vario(a).
diversify [daɪ'vɜːsɪfaɪ] vt diversificare.
diversion [daɪ'vɜːʃən] n (AUT) deviazione f; (distraction) divertimento; (MIL) diversione f.
diversity [daɪ'vɜːsɪtɪ] n diversità f inv, varietà f inv.
divert [daɪ'vɜːt] vt deviare; (amuse) divertire.
divide [dɪ'vaɪd] vt dividere; (separate) separare // vi dividersi.
dividend ['dɪvɪdɛnd] n dividendo.
divine [dɪ'vaɪn] a divino(a).
diving ['daɪvɪŋ] n tuffo; ~ **board** n trampolino.
divinity [dɪ'vɪnɪtɪ] n divinità f inv; teologia.
division [dɪ'vɪʒən] n divisione f; separazione f.
divorce [dɪ'vɔːs] n divorzio // vt divorziare da; ~d a divorziato(a); ~e [-'siː] n divorziato/a.
divulge [daɪ'vʌldʒ] vt divulgare, rivelare.
D.I.Y. a,n abbr of **do-it-yourself.**
dizziness ['dɪzɪnɪs] n vertigini fpl.
dizzy ['dɪzɪ] a (height) vertiginoso(a); to feel ~ avere il capogiro.
DJ n abbr of **disc jockey.**
do, pt **did,** pp **done** [duː, dɪd, dʌn] vt, vi fare; he didn't laugh non ha riso; ~ you want any? ne vuole?; he laughed, didn't he? lui ha riso, vero?; ~ they? ah sì?, vero?; who broke it? - I did chi l'ha rotto? - sono stato io; ~ you agree? - I ~ è d'accordo? - sì; to ~ one's nails farsi le unghie; to ~ one's teeth pulirsi i denti; will it ~? andrà bene?; to ~ without sth fare a meno di qc; to ~ away with vt fus abolire; to ~ up vt abbottonare; allacciare; (house etc) rimettere a nuovo.
docile ['dəusaɪl] a docile.
dock [dɔk] n bacino; (LAW) banco degli imputati // vi entrare in bacino; ~er n scaricatore m.
dockyard ['dɔkjɑːd] n cantiere m navale.
doctor ['dɔktə*] n medico/a; (Ph.D. etc) dottore/essa.

doctrine ['dɔktrɪn] n dottrina.

document ['dɔkjumənt] n documento; **~ary** [-'mentəri] a documentario(a) // n documentario; **~ation** [-'teɪʃən] n documentazione f.

doddering ['dɔdərɪŋ] a traballante.

dodge [dɔdʒ] n trucco; schivata // vt schivare, eludere.

dodgems ['dɔdʒəmz] npl autoscontro.

dog [dɔg] n cane m; **~ collar** n collare m di cane; (fig) collarino; **~-eared** a (book) con orecchie.

dogged ['dɔgɪd] a ostinato(a), tenace.

dogma ['dɔgmə] n dogma m; **~tic** [-'mætɪk] a dogmatico(a).

doings ['duɪŋz] npl attività fpl.

do-it-yourself [du:ɪtjɔ:'self] n il far da sé.

doldrums ['dɔldrəmz] npl: **to be in the ~** essere giù.

dole [dəul] n (Brit) sussidio di disoccupazione; **to be on the ~** vivere del sussidio; **to ~ out** vt distribuire.

doleful ['dəulful] a triste, doloroso(a).

doll [dɔl] n bambola; **to ~ o.s. up** farsi bello(a).

dollar ['dɔlə*] n dollaro.

dolphin ['dɔlfɪn] n delfino.

domain [də'meɪn] n dominio.

dome [dəum] n cupola.

domestic [də'mestɪk] a (duty, happiness, animal) domestico(a); (policy, affairs, flights) nazionale; **~ated** a addomesticato(a).

domicile ['dɔmɪsaɪl] n domicilio.

dominant ['dɔmɪnənt] a dominante.

dominate ['dɔmɪneɪt] vt dominare; **domination** [-'neɪʃən] n dominazione f; **domineering** [-'nɪərɪŋ] a despotico(a), autoritario(a).

dominion [də'mɪnɪən] n dominio; sovranità; dominion m inv.

domino ['dɔmɪnəu] , **~es** ['dɔmɪnəu] n domino; **~es** n (game) gioco del domino.

don [dɔn] n docente m/f universitario(a) // vt indossare.

donate [də'neɪt] vt donare; **donation** [də'neɪʃən] n donazione f.

done [dʌn] pp of do.

donkey ['dɔŋkɪ] n asino.

donor ['dəunə*] n donatore/trice.

don't [dəunt] vb = do not.

doom [du:m] n destino; rovina // vt: **to be ~ed (to failure)** essere predestinato(a) a fallire; **~sday** n il giorno del Giudizio.

door [dɔ:*] n porta; **~bell** n campanello; **~ handle** n maniglia; **~man** n (in hotel) portiere m in livrea; (in block of flats) portinaio; **~mat** n stuoia della porta; **~step** n gradino della porta.

dope [dəup] n (col: drugs) roba // vt (horse etc) drogare.

dopey ['dəupɪ] a (col) inebetito(a).

dormant ['dɔ:mənt] a inattivo(a); (fig) latente.

dormitory ['dɔ:mɪtrɪ] n dormitorio.

dormouse, pl **dormice** ['dɔ:maus, -maɪs] n ghiro.

dose [dəus] n dose f; (bout) attacco.

doss house ['dɔshaus] n asilo notturno.

dot [dɔt] n punto; macchiolina; **on the ~** in punto.

dote [dəut]: **to ~ on** vt fus essere infatuato(a) di.

dotted line [dɔtɪd'laɪn] n linea puntata.

double ['dʌbl] a doppio(a) // ad (fold) in due, doppio; (twice): **to cost ~ (sth)** costare il doppio (di qc) // n sosia m inv; (CINEMA) controfigura // vt raddoppiare; (fold) piegare doppio or in due // vi raddoppiarsi; **at the ~** a passo di corsa; **~s** n (TENNIS) doppio; **~ bass** n contrabbasso; **~ bed** n letto matrimoniale; **~ bend** n doppia curva; **~-breasted** a a doppio petto; **~cross** vt fare il doppio gioco con; **~-decker** n autobus m inv a due piani; **~ parking** n parcheggio in doppia fila; **~ room** n camera per due; **doubly** ad doppiamente.

doubt [daut] n dubbio // vt dubitare di; **to ~ that** dubitare che + sub; **~ful** a dubbioso(a), incerto(a); (person) equivoco(a); **~less** ad indubbiamente.

dough [dəu] n pasta, impasto; **~nut** n bombolone m.

dove [dʌv] n colombo/a.

dovetail ['dʌvteɪl] n: **~ joint** n incastro a coda di rondine // vi (fig) combaciare.

dowdy ['daudɪ] a trasandato(a); malvestito(a).

down [daun] n (fluff) piumino // ad giù, di sotto // prep giù per // vt (col: drink) scolarsi; **~ with XI** abbasso XI; **~-at-heel** a scalcagnato(a); (fig) trasandato(a); **~cast** a abbattuto(a); **~fall** n caduta; rovina; **~hearted** a scoraggiato(a); **~hill** ad: **to go ~hill** andare in discesa; **~ payment** n acconto; **~pour** n scroscio di pioggia; **~right** a onesto(a), franco(a); (refusal) assoluto(a); **~stairs** ad di sotto; al piano inferiore; **~stream** ad a valle; **~-to-earth** a pratico(a); **~town** ad in città // a (US): **~town Chicago** il centro di Chicago; **~ward** ['daunwəd] a,ad; **~wards** ['daunwədz] ad in giù, in discesa.

dowry ['dauri] n dote f.

doz. abbr of **dozen**.

doze [dəuz] vi sonnecchiare; **to ~ off** vi appisolarsi.

dozen ['dʌzn] n dozzina; **a ~ books** una dozzina di libri.

Dr. abbr of **doctor**.

drab [dræb] a tetro(a), grigio(a).

draft [drɑ:ft] n abbozzo; (COMM) tratta; (US: MIL) contingénte m; (: call-up) leva // vt abbozzare; see also **draught**.

drag [dræg] vt trascinare; (river) dragare // vi trascinarsi // n (col) noioso/a; noia, fatica; **to ~ on** vi tirar avanti lentamente.

dragonfly ['drægənflaɪ] n libellula.

drain [dreɪn] n canale m di scolo; (for sewage) fogna; (on resources) salasso // vt (land, marshes) prosciugare; (vegetables) scolare; (reservoir etc) vuotare // vi (water) defluire (via); **~age** n prosciugamento; fognatura; **~ing board**, **~board**

(US) n asciugapiatti m inv; ~**pipe** n tubo di scarico.

drama ['drɑːmə] n *(art)* dramma m, teatro; *(play)* commedia; *(event)* dramma; ~**tic** [drə'mætɪk] a drammatico(a); ~**tist** ['dræmətɪst] n drammaturgo/a.

drank [dræŋk] *pt of* **drink**.

drape [dreɪp] vt drappeggiare; ~**s** npl *(US)* tende fpl; ~**r** n negoziante m/f di stoffe.

drastic ['dræstɪk] a drastico(a).

draught [drɑːft] n corrente f d'aria; *(NAUT)* pescaggio; ~**s** n (gioco della) dama; **on ~** *(beer)* alla spina; ~**board** n scacchiera.

draughtsman ['drɑːftsmən] n disegnatore m.

draw [drɔː] vb *(pt* drew, *pp* drawn [druː, drɔːn])* vt tirare; *(attract)* attirare; *(picture)* disegnare; *(line, circle)* tracciare; *(money)* ritirare // vi *(SPORT)* pareggiare // n pareggio; estrazione f; attrazione f; **to ~ to a close** avvicinarsi alla conclusione; **to ~ near** vi avvicinarsi; **to ~ out** vi *(lengthen)* allungarsi // vt *(money)* ritirare; **to ~ up** vi *(stop)* arrestarsi, fermarsi // vt *(document)* compilare; ~**back** n svantaggio, inconveniente m; ~**bridge** n ponte m levatoio.

drawer [drɔː*] n cassetto.

drawing ['drɔːɪŋ] n disegno; ~ **board** n tavola da disegno; ~ **pin** n puntina da disegno; ~ **room** n salotto.

drawl [drɔːl] n pronuncia strascicata.

drawn [drɔːn] *pp of* **draw**.

dread [dred] n terrore m // vt tremare all'idea di; ~**ful** a terribile.

dream [driːm] n sogno // vt, vi *(pt, pp* dreamed *or* dreamt [dremt])* sognare; ~**er** n sognatore/trice; ~**y** a sognante.

dreary ['drɪərɪ] a tetro(a); monotono(a).

dredge [dredʒ] vt dragare; ~**r** n draga; *(also:* **sugar ~r**) spargizucchero m inv.

dregs [dregz] npl feccia.

drench [drentʃ] vt inzuppare.

dress [dres] n vestito; *(clothing)* abbigliamento // vt vestire; *(wound)* fasciare; *(food)* condire; preparare // vi vestirsi; **to ~ up** vi vestirsi a festa; *(in fancy dress)* vestirsi in costume; ~ **circle** n prima galleria; ~**er** n *(THEATRE)* assistente m/f del camerino; *(furniture)* credenza; ~**ing** n *(MED)* benda; *(CULIN)* condimento; ~**ing gown** n vestaglia; ~**ing room** n *(THEATRE)* camerino; *(SPORT)* spogliatoio; ~**ing table** n toilette f inv; ~**maker** n sarta; ~**making** n sartoria; confezioni fpl per donna; ~ **rehearsal** n prova generale; ~ **shirt** n camicia da sera.

drew [druː] *pt of* **draw**.

dribble ['drɪbl] vi gocciolare; *(baby)* sbavare.

dried [draɪd] a *(fruit, beans)* secco(a); *(eggs, milk)* in polvere.

drift [drɪft] n *(of current etc)* direzione f; forza; *(of sand etc)* turbine m; *(of snow)* cumulo; turbine; *(general meaning)* senso // vi *(boat)* essere trasportato(a) dalla corrente; *(sand, snow)* ammucchiarsi; ~**wood** n resti mpl della mareggiata.

drill [drɪl] n trapano; *(MIL)* esercitazione f // vt trapanare // vi *(for oil)* fare perforazioni.

drink [drɪŋk] n bevanda, bibita // vt, vi *(pt* drank, *pp* drunk [dræŋk, drʌŋk])* bere; **to have a ~** bere qualcosa; ~**er** n bevitore/trice; ~**ing water** n acqua potabile.

drip [drɪp] n goccia; gocciolamento; *(MED)* apparecchio per fleboclisi // vi gocciolare; *(washing)* sgocciolare; *(wall)* trasudare; ~**dry** a *(shirt)* che non si stira; ~**ping** n grasso d'arrosto; ~**ping wet** a fradicio(a).

drive [draɪv] n passeggiata *or* giro in macchina; *(also:* ~**way**) viale m d'accesso; *(energy)* energia; *(PSYCH)* impulso; bisogno; *(push)* sforzo eccezionale; campagna; *(SPORT)* drive m inv; *(TECH)* trasmissione f, propulsione f; presa // vb *(pt* drove, *pp* driven ['drɪvn])* vt guidare; *(nail)* piantare; *(push)* cacciare, spingere; *(TECH: motor)* azionare; far funzionare // vi *(AUT: at controls)* guidare; *(: travel)* andare in macchina; **left-/right-hand ~** guida a sinistra/destra.

driver ['draɪvə*] n conducente m/f; *(of taxi)* tassista m; *(of bus)* autista m.

driving ['draɪvɪŋ] a: ~ **rain** n pioggia sferzante // n guida; ~ **instructor** n istruttore/trice di scuola guida; ~ **lesson** n lezione f di guida; ~ **licence** n *(Brit)* patente f di guida; ~ **school** n scuola f guida inv; ~ **test** n esame m di guida.

drizzle ['drɪzl] n pioggerella // vi piovigginare.

droll [drəʊl] a buffo(a).

dromedary ['drɒmədərɪ] n dromedario.

drone [drəʊn] n ronzio; *(male bee)* fuco.

drool [druːl] vi sbavare.

droop [druːp] vi abbassarsi; languire.

drop [drɒp] n goccia; *(fall)* caduta; *(also:* **parachute ~**) lancio; *(of cliff)* discesa // vt lasciare cadere; *(voice, eyes, price)* abbassare; *(set down from car)* far scendere // vi cascare; **to ~ off** vi *(sleep)* addormentarsi; **to ~ out** vi *(withdraw)* ritirarsi; *(student etc)* smettere di studiare; ~**pings** npl sterco.

dross [drɒs] n scoria; scarto.

drought [draut] n siccità f inv.

drove [drəʊv] *pt of* **drive** // n: ~**s of people** una moltitudine di persone.

drown [draun] vt affogare // vi affogarsi.

drowsy ['drauzɪ] a sonnolento(a), assonnato(a).

drudge [drʌdʒ] n bestia da fatica; ~**ry** ['drʌdʒərɪ] n lavoro faticoso.

drug [drʌg] n farmaco; *(narcotic)* droga // vt drogare; ~ **addict** n tossicomane m/f; ~**gist** n *(US)* persona che gestisce un drugstore; ~**store** n *(US)* drugstore m inv.

drum [drʌm] n tamburo; *(for oil, petrol)* fusto; ~**mer** n batterista m/f.

drunk [drʌŋk] *pp of* **drink** // *a* ubriaco(a); ebbro(a) // *n* ubriacone/a; ~**ard** ['drʌŋkəd] *n* ubriacone/a; ~**en** *a* ubriaco(a); da ubriaco; ~**enness** *n* ubriachezza; ebbrezza.

dry [draɪ] *a* secco(a); (*day, clothes*) asciutto(a); // *vt* seccare; (*clothes*) asciugare // *vi* asciugarsi; **to ~ up** *vi* seccarsi; ~-**cleaner's** *n* lavasecco *m inv*; ~**er** *n* essiccatore *m*; ~ **rot** *n* fungo del legno.

dual ['djuəl] *a* doppio(a); ~ **carriageway** *n* strada a doppia carreggiata; ~ **nationality** *n* doppia nazionalità; ~-**purpose** *a* a doppio uso.

dubbed [dʌbd] *a* (*CINEMA*) doppiato(a); (*nicknamed*) soprannominato(a).

dubious ['dju:bɪəs] *a* dubbio(a).

duchess ['dʌtʃɪs] *n* duchessa.

duck [dʌk] *n* anatra // *vi* abbassare la testa; ~**ling** *n* anatroccolo.

duct [dʌkt] *n* condotto; (*ANAT*) canale *m*.

dud [dʌd] *n* (*shell*) proiettile *m* che fa cilecca; (*object, tool*): **it's a ~** è inutile, non funziona // *a* (*cheque*) a vuoto; (*note, coin*) falso(a).

due [dju:] *a* dovuto(a); (*expected*) atteso(a); (*fitting*) giusto(a) // *n* dovuto // *ad*: ~ **north** diritto verso nord; ~**s** *npl* (*for club, union*) quota; (*in harbour*) diritti *mpl* di porto; **in ~ course** a tempo debito; finalmente; ~ **to** dovuto a; a causa di.

duel ['djuəl] *n* duello.

duet [dju:'ɛt] *n* duetto.

dug [dʌg] *pt, pp of* **dig**.

duke [dju:k] *n* duca *m*.

dull [dʌl] *a* noioso(a); ottuso(a); (*sound, pain*) sordo(a); (*weather, day*) fosco(a), scuro(a); (*blade*) smussato(a) // *vt* (*pain, grief*) attutire; (*mind, senses*) intorpidire.

duly ['dju:lɪ] *ad* (*on time*) a tempo debito; (*as expected*) debitamente.

dumb [dʌm] *a* muto(a); (*stupid*) stupido(a); **dumbfounded** [dʌm'faundɪd] *a* stupito(a), stordito(a).

dummy ['dʌmɪ] *n* (*tailor's model*) manichino; (*SPORT*) finto; (*for baby*) tettarella // *a* falso(a), finto(a).

dump [dʌmp] *n* mucchio di rifiuti; (*place*) luogo di scarico; (*MIL*) deposito // *vt* (*put down*) scaricare; mettere giù; (*get rid of*) buttar via; ~**ing** *n* (*ECON*) dumping *m*; (*of rubbish*): **'no ~ing'** 'vietato lo scarico'.

dumpling ['dʌmplɪŋ] *n* specie di gnocco.

dunce [dʌns] *n* asino.

dune [dju:n] *n* duna.

dung [dʌŋ] *n* concime *m*.

dungarees [dʌŋgə'ri:z] *npl* tuta.

dungeon ['dʌndʒən] *n* prigione *f* sotterranea.

dupe [dju:p] *vt* gabbare, ingannare.

duplicate *n* ['dju:plɪkət] doppio // *vt* ['dju:plɪkeɪt] raddoppiare; (*on machine*) ciclostilare; **in ~** in duplice copia.

durable ['djuərəbl] *a* durevole; (*clothes, metal*) resistente.

duration [djuə'reɪʃən] *n* durata.

duress [djuə'rɛs] *n*: **under ~** sotto costrizione.

during ['djuərɪŋ] *prep* durante, nel corso di.

dusk [dʌsk] *n* crepuscolo; ~**y** *a* scuro(a).

dust [dʌst] *n* polvere *f* // *vt* (*furniture*) spolverare; (*cake etc*): **to ~ with** cospargere con; ~**bin** *n* (*Brit*) pattumiera; ~**er** *n* straccio per la polvere; ~ **jacket** *n* sopraccoperta; ~**man** *n* (*Brit*) netturbino; ~**y** *a* polveroso(a).

Dutch [dʌtʃ] *a* olandese // *n* (*LING*) olandese *m*; **the ~** gli Olandesi; ~**man/woman** *n* olandese *m/f.*

duty ['dju:tɪ] *n* dovere *m*; (*tax*) dazio, tassa; **duties** *npl* mansioni *fpl*; **on ~** di servizio; **off ~** libero(a), fuori servizio; ~-**free** *a* esente da dazio.

dwarf [dwɔ:f] *n* nano/a // *vt* far apparire piccolo.

dwell, *pt, pp* **dwelt** [dwɛl, dwɛlt] *vi* dimorare; **to ~ on** *vt fus* indugiare su; ~**ing** *n* dimora.

dwindle ['dwɪndl] *vi* diminuire, decrescere.

dye [daɪ] *n* tinta // *vt* tingere.

dying ['daɪɪŋ] *a* morente, moribondo(a).

dyke [daɪk] *n* diga.

dynamic [daɪ'næmɪk] *a* dinamico(a); ~**s** *n or npl* dinamica.

dynamite ['daɪnəmaɪt] *n* dinamite *f.*

dynamo ['daɪnəməu] *n* dinamo *f inv.*

dynasty ['dɪnəstɪ] *n* dinastia.

dysentery ['dɪsntrɪ] *n* dissenteria.

E

E [i:] *n* (*MUS*) mi *m*.

each [i:tʃ] *det* ogni, ciascuno(a) // *pronoun* ciascuno(a), ognuno(a); ~ **one** ognuno(a); ~ **other** si (*or ci etc*); **they hate ~ other** si odiano (l'un l'altro); **you are jealous of ~ other** siete gelosi l'uno dell'altro.

eager ['i:gə*] *a* impaziente; desideroso(a); ardente; **to be ~ to do sth** non veder l'ora di fare qc; essere desideroso di fare qc; **to be ~ for** essere desideroso di, aver gran voglia di.

eagle ['i:gl] *n* aquila.

ear [ɪə*] *n* orecchio; (*of corn*) pannocchia; ~**ache** *n* mal *m* d'orecchi; ~**drum** *n* timpano.

earl [ə:l] *n* conte *m*.

early ['ə:lɪ] *ad* presto, di buon'ora; (*ahead of time*) in anticipo // *a* precoce; anticipato(a); che si fa vedere di buon'ora; **have an ~ night/start** vada a letto/parta presto; **in the ~ or ~ in the spring/19th century** all'inizio della primavera/dell'Ottocento; ~ **retirement** *n* ritiro anticipato.

earmark ['ɪəmɑ:k] *vt*: **to ~ sth for** destinare qc a.

earn [ə:n] *vt* guadagnare; (*rest, reward*) meritare; **this ~ed him much praise, he ~ed much praise for this** si è attirato grandi lodi per questo.

earnest ['ɜːnɪst] a serio(a); **in ~ ad** sul serio.

earnings ['ɜːnɪŋz] npl guadagni mpl; (salary) stipendio.

earphones ['ɪəfəʊnz] npl cuffia.

earring ['ɪərɪŋ] n orecchino.

earshot ['ɪəʃɔt] n: **out of/within ~** fuori portata/a portata d'orecchio.

earth [ɜːθ] n (gen, also ELEC) terra; (of fox etc) tana // vt (ELEC) mettere a terra; **~enware** n terracotta; stoviglie fpl di terracotta // a di terracotta; **~quake** n terremoto; **~ tremor** n scossa sismica; **~y** a (fig) grossolano(a).

earwig ['ɪəwɪg] n forbicina.

ease [iːz] n agio, comodo // vt (soothe) calmare; (loosen) allentare; **to ~ sth out/in** tirare fuori/infilare qc con delicatezza; facilitare l'uscita/l'entrata di qc; **life of ~** vita comoda; **at ~** all'agio; (MIL) a riposo; **to ~ off** or **up** vi diminuire; (slow down) rallentarsi; (fig) rilassarsi.

easel ['iːzl] n cavalletto.

easily ['iːzɪlɪ] ad facilmente.

east [iːst] n est m // a dell'est // ad a oriente; **the E~** l'Oriente m.

Easter ['iːstə*] n Pasqua.

easterly ['iːstəlɪ] a dall'est, d'oriente.

eastern ['iːstən] a orientale, d'oriente.

East Germany [iːst'dʒɜːmənɪ] n Germania dell'Est.

eastward(s) ['iːstwəd(z)] ad verso est, verso levante.

easy ['iːzɪ] a facile; (manner) disinvolto(a) // ad: **to take it** or **things ~** prendersela con calma; **~ chair** n poltrona; **~ going** a accomodante.

eat, pt **ate**, pp **eaten** [iːt, eɪt, 'iːtn] vt mangiare; **to ~ into** vt fus rodere; **~able** a mangiabile; (safe to eat) commestibile.

eaves [iːvz] npl gronda.

eavesdrop ['iːvzdrɔp] vi: **to ~ (on a conversation)** origliare (una conversazione).

ebb [eb] n riflusso // vi rifluire; (fig: also: **~ away**) declinare.

ebony ['ebənɪ] n ebano.

ebullient [ɪ'bʌlɪənt] a esuberante.

eccentric [ɪk'sɛntrɪk] a,n eccentrico(a).

ecclesiastic [ɪkliːzɪ'æstɪk] n ecclesiastico; **~al** a ecclesiastico(a).

echo, **~es** ['ekəʊ] n eco m or f // vt ripetere; fare eco a // vi echeggiare; dare un eco.

eclipse [ɪ'klɪps] n eclissi f inv // vt eclissare.

ecology [ɪ'kɔlədʒɪ] n ecologia.

economic [iːkə'nɔmɪk] a economico(a); **~al** a economico(a); (person) economo(a); **~s** n economia.

economist [ɪ'kɔnəmɪst] n economo/a.

economize [ɪ'kɔnəmaɪz] vi risparmiare, fare economia.

economy [ɪ'kɔnəmɪ] n economia.

ecstasy ['ekstəsɪ] n estasi f inv; **to go into**

ecstasies over andare in estasi davanti a; **ecstatic** [-'tætɪk] a estatico(a), in estasi.

ecumenical [iːkjuː'mɛnɪkl] a ecumenico(a).

eczema ['eksɪmə] n eczema m.

eddy ['edɪ] n mulinello.

edge [edʒ] n margine m; (of table, plate, cup) orlo; (of knife etc) taglio // vt bordare; **on ~** (fig) = **edgy**; **to have the ~ on** essere in vantaggio su; **to ~ away from** sgattaiolare da; **~ways** ad di fianco; **he couldn't get a word in ~ways** non riuscì a dire una parola.

edgy ['edʒɪ] a nervoso(a).

edible ['edɪbl] a commestibile; (meal) mangiabile.

edict ['iːdɪkt] n editto.

edifice ['edɪfɪs] n edificio.

edit ['edɪt] vt curare; **~ion** [ɪ'dɪʃən] n edizione f; **~or** n (in newspaper) redattore/trice; redattore/trice capo; (of sb's work) curatore/trice; **~orial** [-'tɔːrɪəl] a redazionale, editoriale // n editoriale m.

educate ['edjukeɪt] vt istruire; educare.

education [edju'keɪʃən] n educazione f; (schooling) istruzione f; **~al** a pedagogico(a); scolastico(a); istruttivo(a).

EEC n (abbr of European Economic Community) C.E.E. f (Comunità Economica Europea).

eel [iːl] n anguilla.

eerie ['ɪərɪ] a che fa accapponare la pelle.

effect [ɪ'fɛkt] n effetto // vt effettuare; **~s** npl (THEATRE) effetti mpl scenici; **to take ~** (law) entrare in vigore; (drug) fare effetto; **in ~** effettivamente; **~ive** a efficace; **~iveness** n efficacia.

effeminate [ɪ'fɛmɪnɪt] a effeminato(a).

effervescent [efə'vɛsnt] a effervescente.

efficacy ['efɪkəsɪ] n efficacia.

efficiency [ɪ'fɪʃənsɪ] n efficienza; rendimento effettivo.

efficient [ɪ'fɪʃənt] a efficiente.

effigy ['efɪdʒɪ] n effigie f.

effort ['efət] n sforzo; **~less** a senza sforzo, facile.

effrontery [ɪ'frʌntərɪ] n sfrontatezza.

e.g. ad (abbr of exempli gratia) per esempio, p.es.

egalitarian [ɪgælɪ'tɛərɪən] a egualitario(a).

egg [eg] n uovo; **to ~ on** vt incitare; **~cup** n portauovo m inv; **~plant** n melanzana; **~shell** n guscio d'uovo.

ego ['iːgəʊ] n ego m inv.

egotist ['egəʊtɪst] n egotista m/f.

Egypt ['iːdʒɪpt] n Egitto; **~ian** [ɪ'dʒɪpʃən] a, n egiziano(a).

eiderdown ['aɪdədaʊn] n piumino.

eight [eɪt] num otto; **~een** num diciotto; **eighth** [eɪtθ] num ottavo(a); **~y** num ottanta.

Eire ['ɛərə] n Repubblica d'Irlanda.

either ['aɪðə*] det l'uno(a) o l'altro(a); (both, each) ciascuno(a); **on ~ side** su ciascun lato // pronoun: **~ (of them)** (o) l'uno(a) o l'altro(a); **I don't like ~** non mi piace né l'uno né l'altro // ad neanche; **no, I don't ~** no, neanch'io // cj: ~ **good or bad** o buono o cattivo.

ejaculation [ɪdʒækju'leɪʃən] n (PHYSIOL) eiaculazione f.

eject [ɪ'dʒɛkt] vt espellere; lanciare; ~**or seat** n sedile m eiettabile.

eke [iːk]: **to ~ out** vt far durare; aumentare.

elaborate a [ɪ'læbərɪt] elaborato(a), minuzioso(a) // vb [ɪ'læbəreɪt] vt elaborare // vi fornire i particolari.

elapse [ɪ'læps] vi trascorrere, passare.

elastic [ɪ'læstɪk] a elastico(a) // n elastico; ~ **band** n elastico.

elated [ɪ'leɪtɪd] a pieno(a) di gioia.

elation [ɪ'leɪʃən] n gioia.

elbow ['ɛlbəu] n gomito.

elder ['ɛldə*] a maggiore, più vecchio(a) // n (tree) sambuco; **one's ~s** i più anziani; ~**ly** a anziano(a).

eldest ['ɛldɪst] a,n: **the ~ (child)** il(la) più vecchio(a) (dei bambini).

elect [ɪ'lɛkt] vt eleggere; **to ~ to do** decidere di fare // a: **the president ~** il presidente designato; ~**ion** [ɪ'lɛkʃən] n elezione f; ~**ioneering** [ɪlɛkʃə'nɪərɪŋ] n propaganda elettorale; ~**or** n elettore/trice; ~**oral** a elettorale; ~**orate** n elettorato.

electric [ɪ'lɛktrɪk] a elettrico(a); ~**al** a elettrico(a); ~ **blanket** n coperta elettrica; ~ **chair** n sedia elettrica; ~ **cooker** n cucina elettrica; ~ **current** n corrente f elettrica; ~ **fire** n stufa elettrica.

electrician [ɪlɛk'trɪʃən] n elettricista m.

electricity [ɪlɛk'trɪsɪtɪ] n elettricità.

electrify [ɪ'lɛktrɪfaɪ] vt (RAIL) elettrificare; (audience) elettrizzare.

electro... [ɪ'lɛktrəu] prefix: **electrocute** [-kjuːt] vt fulminare; **electrode** [ɪ'lɛktrəud] n elettrodo.

electron [ɪ'lɛktrɔn] n elettrone m.

electronic [ɪlɛk'trɔnɪk] a elettronico(a); ~**s** n elettronica.

elegance ['ɛlɪgəns] n eleganza.

elegant ['ɛlɪgənt] a elegante.

element ['ɛlɪmənt] n elemento; (of heater, kettle etc) resistenza; ~**ary** [-'mɛntərɪ] a elementare.

elephant ['ɛlɪfənt] n elefante/essa.

elevate ['ɛlɪveɪt] vt elevare.

elevation [ɛlɪ'veɪʃən] n elevazione f; (height) altitudine f.

elevator ['ɛlɪveɪtə*] n elevatore m; (US: lift) ascensore m.

eleven [ɪ'lɛvn] num undici; ~**ses** npl caffè m a metà mattina; ~**th** a undicesimo(a).

elf, elves [ɛlf, ɛlvz] n elfo.

elicit [ɪ'lɪsɪt] vt: **to ~ (from)** trarre (da), cavare fuori (da).

eligible ['ɛlɪdʒəbl] a eleggibile; (for membership) che ha i requisiti.

eliminate [ɪ'lɪmɪneɪt] vt eliminare; **elimination** n eliminazione f.

élite [eɪ'liːt] n élite f inv.

ellipse [ɪ'lɪps] n ellisse f.

elm [ɛlm] n olmo.

elocution [ɛlə'kjuːʃən] n elocuzione f.

elongated ['iːlɔŋgeɪtɪd] a allungato(a).

elope [ɪ'ləup] vi (lovers) scappare; ~**ment** n fuga romantica.

eloquence ['ɛləkwəns] n eloquenza.

eloquent ['ɛləkwənt] a eloquente.

else [ɛls] ad altro; **something ~** qualcos'altro; **somewhere ~** altrove; **everywhere ~** in qualsiasi altro luogo; **where ~?** in quale altro luogo?; **little ~** poco altro; ~**where** ad altrove.

elucidate [ɪ'luːsɪdeɪt] vt delucidare.

elude [ɪ'luːd] vt eludere.

elusive [ɪ'luːsɪv] a elusivo(a); (answer) evasivo(a).

elves [ɛlvz] npl of **elf**.

emaciated [ɪ'meɪsɪeɪtɪd] a emaciato(a).

emanate ['ɛməneɪt] vi: **to ~ from** emanare da.

emancipate [ɪ'mænsɪpeɪt] vt emancipare; **emancipation** [-'peɪʃən] n emancipazione f.

embalm [ɪm'bɑːm] vt imbalsamare.

embankment [ɪm'bæŋkmənt] n (of road, railway) terrapieno; (riverside) argine m; (dyke) diga.

embargo [ɪm'bɑːgəu], ~**es** [ɪm'bɑːgəuz] n embargo.

embark [ɪm'bɑːk] vi: **to ~ (on)** imbarcarsi (su) // vt imbarcare; **to ~ on** (fig) imbarcarsi in; ~**ation** [ɛmbɑː'keɪʃən] n imbarco.

embarrass [ɪm'bærəs] vt imbarazzare; ~**ing** a imbarazzante; ~**ment** n imbarazzo.

embassy ['ɛmbəsɪ] n ambasciata.

embed [ɪm'bɛd] vt conficcare, incastrare.

embellish [ɪm'bɛlɪʃ] vt abbellire.

embers ['ɛmbəz] npl braci fpl.

embezzle [ɪm'bɛzl] vt appropriarsi indebitamente di; ~**ment** n appropriazione f indebita, malversazione f.

embitter [ɪm'bɪtə*] vt amareggiare; inasprire.

emblem ['ɛmbləm] n emblema m.

embodiment [ɪm'bɔdɪmənt] n personificazione f, incarnazione f.

embody [ɪm'bɔdɪ] vt (features) racchiudere, comprendere; (ideas) dar forma concreta a, esprimere.

embossed [ɪm'bɔst] a in rilievo; goffrato(a).

embrace [ɪm'breɪs] vt abbracciare // n abbraccio.

embroider [ɪm'brɔɪdə*] vt ricamare; (fig: story) abbellire; ~**y** n ricamo.

embryo ['ɛmbrɪəu] n (also fig) embrione m.

emerald ['ɛmərəld] n smeraldo.

emerge [ɪ'məːdʒ] vi apparire, sorgere.

emergence [ɪ'məːdʒəns] n apparizione f.

emergency [ɪ'məːdʒənsɪ] n emergenza; **in an ~** in caso di emergenza; ~ **exit** n uscita di sicurezza.

emergent [ɪ'məːdʒənt] a: ~ **nation** paese m in via di sviluppo.

emery ['ɛmərɪ] n: ~ board n limetta di carta smerigliata; ~ paper n carta smerigliata.

emetic [ɪ'mɛtɪk] n emetico.

emigrant ['ɛmɪɡrənt] n emigrante m/f.

emigrate ['ɛmɪɡreɪt] vi emigrare; emigration [-'ɡreɪʃən] n emigrazione f.

eminence ['ɛmɪnəns] n eminenza.

eminent ['ɛmɪnənt] a eminente.

emission [ɪ'mɪʃən] n emissione f.

emit [ɪ'mɪt] vt emettere.

emotion [ɪ'məʊʃən] n emozione f; ~al a (person) emotivo(a); (scene) commovente; (tone, speech) carico(a) d'emozione; ~ally ad: ~ally disturbed con turbe emotive.

emotive [ɪ'məʊtɪv] a emotivo(a).

emperor ['ɛmpərə*] n imperatore m.

emphasis, pl ases ['ɛmfəsɪs, -siːz] n enfasi f inv; importanza.

emphasize ['ɛmfəsaɪz] vt (word, point) sottolineare; (feature) mettere in evidenza.

emphatic [ɛm'fætɪk] a (strong) vigoroso(a); (unambiguous, clear) netto(a); ~ally ad vigorosamente; nettamente.

empire ['ɛmpaɪə*] n impero.

empirical [ɛm'pɪrɪkl] a empirico(a).

employ [ɪm'plɔɪ] vt impiegare; ~ee [-'iː] n impiegato/a; ~er n principale m/f, datore m di lavoro; ~ment n impiego; ~ment agency n agenzia di collocamento.

empower [ɪm'paʊə*] vt: to ~ sb to do concedere autorità a qd di fare.

empress ['ɛmprɪs] n imperatrice f.

emptiness ['ɛmptɪnɪs] n vuoto.

empty ['ɛmptɪ] a vuoto(a); (threat, promise) vano(a) // vt vuotare // vi vuotarsi; (liquid) scaricarsi; on ~ stomach a stomaco vuoto; ~-handed a a mani vuote.

emulate ['ɛmjʊleɪt] vt emulare.

emulsion [ɪ'mʌlʃən] n emulsione f; ~ (paint) n colore m a tempera.

enable [ɪ'neɪbl] vt: to ~ sb to do permettere a qd di fare.

enamel [ɪ'næməl] n smalto.

enamoured [ɪ'næməd] a: ~ of innamorato(a) di.

enchant [ɪn'tʃɑːnt] vt incantare; (subj: magic spell) catturare; ~ing a incantevole, affascinante.

encircle [ɪn'sɜːkl] vt accerchiare.

encl. (abbr of enclosed) all.

enclose [ɪn'kləʊz] vt (land) circondare, recingere; (letter etc): to ~ (with) allegare (con); please find ~d trovi qui accluso.

enclosure [ɪn'kləʊʒə*] n recinto; (COMM) allegato.

encore [ɔŋ'kɔː*] excl, n bis (m inv).

encounter [ɪn'kaʊntə*] n incontro // vt incontrare.

encourage [ɪn'kʌrɪdʒ] vt incoraggiare; ~ment n incoraggiamento.

encroach [ɪn'krəʊtʃ] vi: to ~ (up)on

(rights) usurpare; (time) abusare di; (land) oltrepassare i limiti di.

encyclop(a)edia [ɛnsaɪkləʊ'piːdɪə] n enciclopedia.

end [ɛnd] n fine f; (aim) fine m; (of table) bordo estremo // vt finire; (also: bring to an ~, put an ~ to) mettere fine a // vi finire; to come to an ~ arrivare alla fine, finire; in the ~ alla fine; at the ~ of the street in fondo alla strada; on ~ (object) ritto(a); for 5 hours on ~ per 5 ore di fila; to ~ up vi: to ~ up in finire in.

endanger [ɪn'deɪndʒə*] vt mettere in pericolo.

endearing [ɪn'dɪərɪŋ] a accattivante.

endeavour [ɪn'dɛvə*] n sforzo, tentativo // vi: to ~ to do cercare or sforzarsi di fare.

ending ['ɛndɪŋ] n fine f, conclusione f; (LING) desinenza.

endless ['ɛndlɪs] a senza fine; (patience, resources) infinito(a).

endorse [ɪn'dɔːs] vt (cheque) girare; (approve) approvare, appoggiare; ~ment n (on driving licence) contravvenzione registrata sulla patente.

endow [ɪn'daʊ] vt (provide with money) devolvere denaro a; (equip): to ~ with fornire di, dotare di.

end product ['ɛndprɒdəkt] n prodotto finito; (fig) risultato.

endurance [ɪn'djʊərəns] n resistenza; pazienza.

endure [ɪn'djʊə*] vt sopportare, resistere a // vi durare.

enemy ['ɛnəmɪ] a, n nemico(a).

energetic [ɛnə'dʒɛtɪk] a energico(a); attivo(a).

energy ['ɛnədʒɪ] n energia.

enervating ['ɛnəveɪtɪŋ] a debilitante.

enforce [ɪn'fɔːs] vt (LAW) applicare, far osservare; ~d a forzato(a).

engage [ɪn'geɪdʒ] vt assumere; (subj: activity, MIL) impegnare; (attention) occupare // vi (TECH) ingranare; to ~ in impegnarsi in; ~d a (busy, in use) occupato(a); (betrothed) fidanzato(a); to get ~d fidanzarsi; ~ment n impegno, obbligo; appuntamento; (to marry) fidanzamento; (MIL) combattimento; ~ment ring n anello di fidanzamento.

engaging [ɪn'geɪdʒɪŋ] a attraente.

engender [ɪn'dʒɛndə*] vt produrre, causare.

engine ['ɛndʒɪn] n (AUT) motore m; (RAIL) locomotiva; ~ failure n guasto al motore; ~ trouble n panne f.

engineer [ɛndʒɪ'nɪə*] n ingegnere m; (US: RAIL) macchinista m; ~ing n ingegneria; (of bridges, ships, machine) tecnica di costruzione.

England ['ɪŋɡlənd] n Inghilterra.

English ['ɪŋɡlɪʃ] a inglese // n (LING) inglese m; the ~ gli Inglesi; ~man/woman n inglese m/f.

engrave [ɪn'greɪv] vt incidere.

engraving [ɪn'greɪvɪŋ] n incisione f.

engrossed [ɪn'grəʊst] *a*: ~ **in** assorbito(a) da, preso(a) da.

engulf [ɪn'gʌlf] *vt* inghiottire.

enhance [ɪn'hɑːns] *vt* accrescere.

enigma [ɪ'nɪgmə] *n* enigma *m*; ~**tic** [ɛnɪg'mætɪk] *a* enigmatico(a).

enjoy [ɪn'dʒɔɪ] *vt* godere; (*have: success, fortune*) avere; **I** ~ **dancing** mi piace ballare; **to** ~ **oneself** godersela, divertirsi; ~**able** *a* piacevole; ~**ment** *n* piacere *m*, godimento.

enlarge [ɪn'lɑːdʒ] *vt* ingrandire // *vi*: **to** ~ **on** (*subject*) dilungarsi su; ~**ment** *n* (*PHOT*) ingrandimento.

enlighten [ɪn'laɪtn] *vt* illuminare; dare schiarimenti a; ~**ed** *a* illuminato(a); ~**ment** *n* progresso culturale; schiarimenti *mpl*; (*HISTORY*): **the E**~**ment** l'Illuminismo.

enlist [ɪn'lɪst] *vt* arruolare; (*support*) procurare // *vi* arruolarsi.

enmity ['ɛnmɪtɪ] *n* inimicizia.

enormity [ɪ'nɔːmɪtɪ] *n* enormità *f inv*.

enormous [ɪ'nɔːməs] *a* enorme.

enough [ɪ'nʌf] *a, n*: ~ **time/books** assai tempo/libri; **have you got** ~? ne ha abbastanza *or* a sufficienza? // *ad*: **big** ~ abbastanza grande; **he has not worked** ~ non ha lavorato abbastanza; ~**!** basta!; **it's hot** ~ (**as it is**)! fa caldo assai così!; ... **which, funnily** ~ ... che, strano a dirsi.

enquire [ɪn'kwaɪə*] *vt,vi* = **inquire**.

enrich [ɪn'rɪtʃ] *vt* arricchire.

enrol [ɪn'rəʊl] *vt* iscrivere // *vi* iscriversi; ~**ment** *n* iscrizione *f*.

ensign *n* (*NAUT*) ['ɛnsən] bandiera; (*MIL*) ['ɛnsaɪn] portabandiera *m inv*.

enslave [ɪn'sleɪv] *vt* fare schiavo.

ensue [ɪn'sjuː] *vi* seguire, risultare.

ensure [ɪn'ʃʊə*] *vt* assicurare; garantire; **to** ~ **that** assicurarsi che.

entail [ɪn'teɪl] *vt* comportare.

enter ['ɛntə*] *vt* (*room*) entrare in; (*club*) associarsi a; (*army*) arruolarsi in; (*competition*) partecipare a; (*sb for a competition*) iscrivere; (*write down*) registrare; **to** ~ **into** *vt fus* (*explanation*) cominciare a dare; (*debate*) partecipare a; (*agreement*) concludere; **to** ~ **(up)on** *vt fus* cominciare.

enterprise ['ɛntəpraɪz] *n* (*undertaking, company*) impresa; (*spirit*) iniziativa.

enterprising ['ɛntəpraɪzɪŋ] *a* intraprendente.

entertain [ɛntə'teɪn] *vt* divertire; (*invite*) ricevere; (*idea, plan*) nutrire; ~**er** *n* comico/a; ~**ing** *a* divertente; ~**ment** *n* (*amusement*) divertimento; (*show*) spettacolo.

enthralled [ɪn'θrɔːld] *a* affascinato(a).

enthusiasm [ɪn'θuːzɪæzəm] *n* entusiasmo.

enthusiast [ɪn'θuːzɪæst] *n* entusiasta *m/f*; ~**ic** [-'æstɪk] *a* entusiasta, entusiastico(a).

entice [ɪn'taɪs] *vt* allettare, sedurre.

entire [ɪn'taɪə*] *a* intero(a); ~**ly** *ad* completamente, interamente; ~**ty** [ɪn'taɪərətɪ] *n*: **in its** ~**ty** nel suo complesso.

entitle [ɪn'taɪtl] *vt* (*allow*): **to** ~ **sb to do** dare il diritto a qd di fare; ~**d** *a* (*book*) che si intitola; **to be** ~**d to do** avere il diritto di fare.

entrance *n* ['ɛntrns] entrata, ingresso; (*of person*) entrata // *vt* [ɪn'trɑːns] incantare, rapire; ~ **fee** *n* tassa d'iscrizione; (*to museum etc*) prezzo d'ingresso.

entrant ['ɛntrnt] *n* partecipante *m/f*; concorrente *m/f*.

entreat [ɛn'triːt] *vt* supplicare; ~**y** *n* supplica, preghiera.

entrenched [ɛn'trɛntʃd] *a* radicato(a).

entrust [ɪn'trʌst] *vt*: **to** ~ **sth to** affidare qc a.

entry ['ɛntrɪ] *n* entrata; (*way in*) entrata, ingresso; (*item: on list*) iscrizione *f*; (*in dictionary*) voce *f*; '**no** ~' 'vietato l'ingresso'; (*AUT*) 'divieto di accesso'; ~**form** *n* modulo d'iscrizione.

entwine [ɪn'twaɪn] *vt* intrecciare.

enumerate [ɪ'njuːməreɪt] *vt* enumerare.

enunciate [ɪ'nʌnsɪeɪt] *vt* enunciare; pronunciare.

envelop [ɪn'vɛləp] *vt* avvolgere, avviluppare.

envelope ['ɛnvələʊp] *n* busta.

envious ['ɛnvɪəs] *a* invidioso(a).

environment [ɪn'vaɪərnmənt] *n* ambiente *m*; ~**al** [-'mɛntl] *a* ecologico(a); ambientale.

envisage [ɪn'vɪzɪdʒ] *vt* immaginare; prevedere.

envoy ['ɛnvɔɪ] *n* inviato/a.

envy ['ɛnvɪ] *n* invidia // *vt* invidiare.

enzyme ['ɛnzaɪm] *n* enzima *m*.

ephemeral [ɪ'fɛmərl] *a* effimero(a).

epic ['ɛpɪk] *n* poema *m* epico // *a* epico(a).

epidemic [ɛpɪ'dɛmɪk] *n* epidemia.

epilepsy ['ɛpɪlɛpsɪ] *n* epilessia; **epileptic** [-'lɛptɪk] *a,n* epilettico(a).

epilogue ['ɛpɪlɔg] *n* epilogo.

Epiphany [ɪ'pɪfənɪ] *n* Epifania.

episode ['ɛpɪsəʊd] *n* episodio.

epistle [ɪ'pɪsl] *n* epistola.

epitaph ['ɛpɪtɑːf] *n* epitaffio.

epitome [ɪ'pɪtəmɪ] *n* epitome *f*; quintessenza; **epitomize** *vt* compendiare; essere l'emblema di.

epoch ['iːpɔk] *n* epoca.

equable ['ɛkwəbl] *a* uniforme; equanime.

equal ['iːkwl] *a, n* uguale (*m/f*) // *vt* uguagliare; ~ **to** (*task*) all'altezza di; ~**ity** [iː'kwɔlɪtɪ] *n* uguaglianza; ~**ize** *vt,vi* pareggiare; ~**izer** *n* pareggio; ~**ly** *ad* ugualmente; ~(**s**) **sign** *n* segno d'uguaglianza.

equanimity [ɛkwə'nɪmɪtɪ] *n* equanimità.

equate [ɪ'kweɪt] *vt*: **to** ~ **sth with** considerare qc uguale a; (*compare*) paragonare qc con; **equation** [ɪ'kweɪʃən] *n* (*MATH*) equazione *f*.

equator [ɪ'kweɪtə*] *n* equatore *m*.

equilibrium [iːkwɪ'lɪbrɪəm] *n* equilibrio.

equinox ['iːkwɪnɔks] *n* equinozio.

equip [ɪ'kwɪp] *vt* equipaggiare, attrezzare; **to** ~ **sb/sth with** fornire qd/qc di;

~**ment** *n* attrezzatura; (*electrical etc*) apparecchiatura.

equitable ['ɛkwɪtəbl] *a* equo(a), giusto(a).

equity ['ɛkwɪtɪ] *n* equità; **equities** *npl* (*comm*) azioni *fpl* ordinarie.

equivalent [ɪ'kwɪvəlnt] *a*, *n* equivalente (*m*).

equivocal [ɪ'kwɪvəkl] *a* equivoco(a); (*open to suspicion*) dubbio(a).

era ['ɪərə] *n* era, età *f inv*.

eradicate [ɪ'rædɪkeɪt] *vt* sradicare.

erase [ɪ'reɪz] *vt* cancellare; ~**r** *n* gomma.

erect [ɪ'rɛkt] *a* eretto(a) // *vt* costruire; (*monument, tent*) alzare.

erection [ɪ'rɛkʃən] *n* erezione *f*.

ermine ['ɜːmɪn] *n* ermellino.

erode [ɪ'rəud] *vt* erodere; (*metal*) corrodere; **erosion** [ɪ'rəuʒən] *n* erosione *f*.

erotic [ɪ'rɒtɪk] *a* erotico(a); ~**ism** [ɪ'rɒtɪsɪzm] *n* erotismo.

err [ɜː*] *vi* errare; (*REL*) peccare.

errand ['ɛrnd] *n* commissione *f*.

erratic [ɪ'rætɪk] *a* imprevedibile; (*person, mood*) incostante.

erroneous [ɪ'rəunɪəs] *a* erroneo(a).

error ['ɛrə*] *n* errore *m*.

erudite ['ɛrjudaɪt] *a* erudito(a).

erupt [ɪ'rʌpt] *vi* erompere; (*volcano*) mettersi (*or* essere) in eruzione; ~**ion** [ɪ'rʌpʃən] *n* eruzione *f*.

escalate ['ɛskəleɪt] *vi* intensificarsi; **escalation** [-'leɪʃən] *n* escalation *f*; (*of prices*) aumento.

escalator ['ɛskəleɪtə*] *n* scala mobile.

escapade [ɛskə'peɪd] *n* scappatella; avventura.

escape [ɪ'skeɪp] *n* evasione *f*; fuga; (*of gas etc*) fuga, fuoriuscita // *vi* fuggire; (*from jail*) evadere, scappare; (*fig*) sfuggire; (*leak*) uscire // *vt* sfuggire a; **to ~ from sb** sfuggire a qd; **escapism** *n* evasione *f* (dalla realtà).

escort *n* ['ɛskɔːt] scorta; (*male companion*) cavaliere *m* // *vt* [ɪ'skɔːt] scortare; accompagnare.

Eskimo ['ɛskɪməu] *n* esquimese *m/f*.

especially [ɪ'spɛʃlɪ] *ad* specialmente; soprattutto; espressamente.

espionage ['ɛspɪənɑːʒ] *n* spionaggio.

Esquire [ɪ'skwaɪə*] *n* (*abbr* **Esq.**): **J. Brown,** ~ Signor J. Brown.

essay ['ɛseɪ] *n* (*scol*) composizione *f*; (*literature*) saggio.

essence ['ɛsns] *n* essenza.

essential [ɪ'sɛnʃl] *a* essenziale; (*basic*) fondamentale; ~**ly** *ad* essenzialmente.

establish [ɪ'stæblɪʃ] *vt* stabilire; (*business*) mettere su; (*one's power etc*) confermare; ~**ment** *n* stabilimento; **the E**~**ment** le autorità; l'Establishment *m*.

estate [ɪ'steɪt] *n* proprietà *f inv*; beni *mpl*, patrimonio; ~ **agent** *n* agente *m* immobiliare; ~ **car** *n* (*Brit*) giardiniera.

esteem [ɪ'stiːm] *n* stima.

esthetic [ɪs'θɛtɪk] *a* (*US*) = **aesthetic**.

estimate *n* ['ɛstɪmət] stima; (*comm*) preventivo // *vt* ['ɛstɪmeɪt] stimare,

valutare; **estimation** [-'meɪʃən] *n* stima; opinione *f*.

estuary ['ɛstjuərɪ] *n* estuario.

etching ['ɛtʃɪŋ] *n* acquaforte *f*.

eternal [ɪ'tɜːnl] *a* eterno(a).

eternity [ɪ'tɜːnɪtɪ] *n* eternità.

ether ['iːθə*] *n* etere *m*.

ethical ['ɛθɪkl] *a* etico(a), morale.

ethics ['ɛθɪks] *n* etica // *npl* morale *f*.

ethnic ['ɛθnɪk] *a* etnico(a).

etiquette ['ɛtɪkɛt] *n* etichetta.

eulogy ['juːlədʒɪ] *n* elogio.

euphemism ['juːfəmɪzm] *n* eufemismo.

euphoria [juː'fɔːrɪə] *n* euforia.

Europe ['juərəp] *n* Europa; ~**an** [-'piːən] *a*, *n* europeo(a).

euthanasia [juːθə'neɪzɪə] *n* eutanasia.

evacuate [ɪ'vækjueɪt] *vt* evacuare; **evacuation** [-'eɪʃən] *n* evacuazione *f*.

evade [ɪ'veɪd] *vt* eludere; (*question, duties etc*) evadere.

evaluate [ɪ'væljueɪt] *vt* valutare.

evangelist [ɪ'vændʒəlɪst] *n* evangelista *m*.

evaporate [ɪ'væpəreɪt] *vi* evaporare // *vt* far evaporare; ~**d milk** *n* latte *m* evaporato; **evaporation** [-'reɪʃən] *n* evaporazione *f*.

evasion [ɪ'veɪʒən] *n* evasione *f*; scappatoia.

evasive [ɪ'veɪsɪv] *a* evasivo(a).

eve [iːv] *n*: **on the ~ of** alla vigilia di.

even ['iːvn] *a* regolare; (*number*) pari *inv* // *ad* anche, perfino; ~ **more** anche più; **he loves her** ~ **more** la ama anche di più; ~ **so** ciò nonostante; **to ~ out** *vi* pareggiare; **to get** ~ **with sb** dare la pari a qd.

evening ['iːvnɪŋ] *n* sera; (*as duration, event*) serata; **in the** ~ la sera; ~ **class** *n* corso serale; ~ **dress** *n* (*man's*) frac *m*, smoking *m*; (*woman's*) vestito da sera.

event [ɪ'vɛnt] *n* avvenimento; (*sport*) gara; **in the** ~ **of** in caso di; ~**ful** *a* denso(a) di eventi.

eventual [ɪ'vɛntʃuəl] *a* finale; ~**ity** ['ælɪtɪ] *n* possibilità *f inv*, eventualità *f inv*; ~**ly** *ad* finalmente.

ever ['ɛvə*] *ad* mai; (*at all times*) sempre; **the best** ~ il migliore che ci sia mai stato; **have you** ~ **seen it?** l'ha mai visto?; **hardly** ~ non ... quasi mai; ~ **since** *ad* da allora // *cj* sin da quando; ~ **so pretty** così bello(a); ~**green** *n* sempreverde *m*; ~**lasting** *a* eterno(a).

every ['ɛvrɪ] *det* ogni; ~ **day** tutti i giorni, ogni giorno; ~ **other/third day** ogni due/tre giorni; ~ **other car** una macchina su due; ~ **now and then** ogni tanto, di quando in quando; ~**body** *pronoun* ognuno, tutti *pl*; ~**day** *a* quotidiano(a); di ogni giorno; ~**one** = ~**body**; ~**thing** *pronoun* tutto, ogni cosa; ~**where** *ad* in ogni luogo, dappertutto.

evict [ɪ'vɪkt] *vt* sfrattare; ~**ion** [ɪ'vɪkʃən] *n* sfratto.

evidence ['ɛvɪdns] *n* (*proof*) prova; (*of witness*) testimonianza; (*sign*): **to show** ~ **of** dare segni di; **to give** ~ deporre; **in** ~

(obvious) in evidenza; in vista.

evident ['ɛvɪdnt] a evidente; ~ly ad evidentemente.

evil ['iːvl] a cattivo(a), maligno(a) // n male m.

evocative [ɪ'vɔkətɪv] a evocativo(a).

evoke [ɪ'vəuk] vt evocare.

evolution [iːvə'luːʃən] n evoluzione f.

evolve [ɪ'vɔlv] vt elaborare // vi svilupparsi, evolversi.

ewe [juː] n pecora.

ex- [ɛks] prefix ex.

exact [ɪg'zækt] a esatto(a) // vt: to ~ sth (from) estorcere qc (da); esigere qc (da); ~ing a esigente; (work) faticoso(a); ~itude n esattezza, precisione f; ~ly ad esattamente.

exaggerate [ɪg'zædʒəreit] vt,vi esagerare; **exaggeration** [-'reiʃən] n esagerazione f.

exalt [ɪg'zɔːlt] vt esaltare; elevare.

exam [ɪg'zæm] n (SCOL) abbr of **examination**.

examination [ɪgzæmi'neiʃən] n (SCOL) esame m; (MED) controllo.

examine [ɪg'zæmɪn] vt esaminare; (LAW: person) interrogare; ~r n esaminatore/trice.

example [ɪg'zɑːmpl] n esempio; **for** ~ ad or per esempio.

exasperate [ɪg'zɑːspəreit] vt esasperare.

excavate ['ɛkskəveit] vt scavare; **excavation** [-'veiʃən] n escavazione f; **excavator** n scavatore m, scavatrice f.

exceed [ɪk'siːd] vt superare; (one's powers, time limit) oltrepassare; ~ingly ad eccessivamente.

excel [ɪk'sɛl] vi eccellere // vt sorpassare.

excellence ['ɛksələns] n ≈ eccellenza.

Excellency ['ɛksələnsi] n: **His** ~ Sua Eccellenza.

excellent ['ɛksələnt] a eccellente.

except [ɪk'sɛpt] prep (also: ~ **for**, ~ing) salvo, all'infuori di, eccetto // vt escludere; ~ **if/when** salvo se/quando; ~ **that** salvo che; ~**ion** [ɪk'sɛpʃən] n eccezione f; **to take** ~**ion to** trovare a ridire su; ~**ional** [ɪk'sɛpʃənl] a eccezionale.

excerpt ['ɛksəːpt] n estratto.

excess [ɪk'sɛs] n eccesso; ~ **fare** n supplemento; ~ **baggage** n bagaglio in eccedenza; ~**ive** a eccessivo(a).

exchange [ɪks'tʃeindʒ] n scambio; (also: **telephone** ~) centralino // vt scambiare; ~ **market** n mercato dei cambi.

exchequer [ɪks'tʃɛkə*] n Scacchiere m, ≈ ministero delle Finanze.

excisable [ɪk'saizəbl] a soggetto a dazio.

excise n ['ɛksaiz] imposta, dazio // vt [ɛk'saiz] recidere; ~ **duties** npl dazi mpl.

excite [ɪk'sait] vt eccitare; **to get** ~**d** eccitarsi; ~**ment** n eccitazione f; agitazione f; **exciting** a avventuroso(a); (film, book) appassionante.

exclaim [ɪk'skleim] vi esclamare; **exclamation** [ɛkskla'meiʃən] n

esclamazione f; **exclamation mark** n punto esclamativo.

exclude [ɪk'skluːd] vt escludere; **exclusion** [ɪk'skluːʒən] n esclusione f.

exclusive [ɪk'skluːsiv] a esclusivo(a); (club) selettivo(a); (district) snob inv // ad (COMM) non compreso; ~ **of VAT** I.V.A. esclusa; ~**ly** ad esclusivamente; ~ **rights** npl (COMM) diritti mpl esclusivi.

excommunicate [ɛkskə'mjuːnikeit] vt scomunicare.

excrement ['ɛkskrəmənt] n escremento.

excruciating [ɪk'skruːʃieitiŋ] a straziante, atroce.

excursion [ɪk'skəːʃən] n escursione f, gita.

excuse n [ɪk'skjuːs] scusa // vt [ɪk'skjuːz] scusare; **to** ~ **sb from** (activity) dispensare qd da; ~ **me!** mi scusi!

execute ['ɛksikjuːt] vt (prisoner) giustiziare; (plan etc) eseguire.

execution [ɛksi'kjuːʃən] n esecuzione f; ~**er** n boia m inv.

executive [ɪg'zɛkjutiv] n (COMM) dirigente m; (POL) esecutivo // a esecutivo(a).

executor [ɪg'zɛkjutə*] n esecutore(trice) testamentario/a.

exemplary [ɪg'zɛmpləri] a esemplare.

exemplify [ɪg'zɛmplifai] vt esemplificare.

exempt [ɪg'zɛmpt] a esentato(a) // vt: to ~ **sb from** esentare qd da; ~**ion** [ɪg-'zɛmpʃən] n esenzione f.

exercise ['ɛksəsaiz] n esercizio // vt esercitare; (dog) portar fuori; **to take** ~ fare del movimento; ~ **book** n quaderno.

exert [ɪg'zəːt] vt esercitare; **to** ~ **o.s.** sforzarsi.

exhaust [ɪg'zɔːst] n (also: ~ **fumes**) scappamento; (also: ~ **pipe**) tubo di scappamento // vt esaurire; ~**ed** a esaurito(a); ~**ion** [ɪg'zɔːstʃən] n esaurimento; ~**ive** a esauriente.

exhibit [ɪg'zibit] n (ART) oggetto esposto; (LAW) documento or oggetto esibito // vt esporre; (courage, skill) dimostrare; ~**ion** [ɛksi'biʃən] n mostra, esposizione f; ~**ionist** [ɛksi'biʃənist] n esibizionista m/f; ~**or** n espositore/trice.

exhilarating [ɪg'ziləreitiŋ] a esilarante; stimolante.

exhort [ɪg'zɔːt] vt esortare.

exile ['ɛksail] n esilio; esiliato/a // vt esiliare; **in** ~ in esilio.

exist [ɪg'zist] vi esistere; ~**ence** n esistenza; **to be in** ~**ence** esistere.

exit ['ɛksit] n uscita.

exonerate [ɪg'zɔnəreit] vt: **to** ~ **from** discolpare da.

exorcize ['ɛksɔːsaiz] vt esorcizzare.

exotic [ɪg'zɔtik] a esotico(a).

expand [ɪk'spænd] vt espandere; estendere; allargare // vi (trade etc) svilupparsi, ampliarsi; espandersi; (gas) espandersi; (metal) dilatarsi.

expanse [ɪk'spæns] n distesa, estensione f.

expansion [ɪk'spænʃən] n sviluppo; espansione f; dilatazione f.

expatriate n [ɛks'pætriət] espatriato/a // vt [ɛks'pætrieit] espatriare.

expect [ık'spɛkt] vt (*anticipate*) prevedere, aspettarsi, prevedere *or* aspettarsi che + *sub*; (*count on*) contare su; (*hope for*) sperare; (*require*) richiedere, esigere; (*suppose*) supporre; (*await, also baby*) aspettare // vi: **to be** ∼**ing** essere in stato interessante; **to** ∼ **sb to do** aspettarsi che qd faccia; ∼**ant** a pieno(a) di aspettative; ∼**ant mother** n gestante f; ∼**ation** [ɛkspɛk'teıʃən] n aspettativa; speranza.

expedience, expediency [ɛk'spi:dıəns, ɛk'spi:dıənsı] n convenienza.

expedient [ık'spi:dıənt] a conveniente; vantaggioso(a) // n espediente m.

expedite ['ɛkspədaıt] vt sbrigare; facilitare.

expedition [ɛkspə'dıʃən] n spedizione f.

expel [ık'spɛl] vt espellere.

expend [ık'spɛnd] vt spendere; (*use up*) consumare; ∼**able** a sacrificabile; ∼**iture** [ık'spɛndıtʃə*] n spesa; spese fpl.

expense [ık'spɛns] n spesa; spese fpl; (*high cost*) costo; ∼**s** npl (*COMM*) spese fpl, indennità fpl; **at the** ∼ **of** a spese di; ∼ **account** n nota f spese inv.

expensive [ık'spɛnsıv] a caro(a), costoso(a).

experience [ık'spıərıəns] n esperienza // vt (*pleasure*) provare; (*hardship*) soffrire; ∼**d** a esperto(a).

experiment [ık'spɛrımənt] n esperimento, esperienza // vi fare esperimenti; ∼**al** [-'mɛntl] a sperimentale.

expert ['ɛkspə:t] a, n esperto(a); ∼**ise** [-'ti:z] n competenza.

expire [ık'spaıə*] vi (*period of time, licence*) scadere; **expiry** n scadenza.

explain [ık'spleın] vt spiegare; **explanation** [ɛksplə'neıʃən] n spiegazione f; **explanatory** [ık'splænətrı] a esplicativo(a).

explicit [ık'splısıt] a esplicito(a); (*definite*) netto(a).

explode [ık'spləud] vi esplodere.

exploit n ['ɛksplɔıt] impresa // vt [ık-'splɔıt] sfruttare; ∼**ation** [-'teıʃən] n sfruttamento.

exploration [ɛksplɔ'reıʃən] n esplorazione f.

exploratory [ık'splɔrətrı] a (*fig: talks*) esplorativo(a).

explore [ık'splɔ:*] vt esplorare; (*possibilities*) esaminare; ∼**r** n esploratore/trice.

explosion [ık'spləuʒən] n esplosione f.

explosive [ık'spləusıv] a esplosivo(a) // n esplosivo.

exponent [ık'spəunənt] n esponente m/f.

export vt [ɛk'spɔ:t] esportare // n ['ɛkspɔ:t] esportazione f; articolo di esportazione // cpd d'esportazione; ∼**ation** [-'teıʃən] n esportazione f; ∼**er** n esportatore m.

expose [ık'spəuz] vt esporre; (*unmask*) smascherare; **to** ∼ **o.s.** (*LAW*) oltraggiare il pudore.

exposure [ık'spəuʒə*] n esposizione f; (*PHOT*) posa; (*MED*) assideramento; ∼ **meter** n esposimetro.

expound [ık'spaund] vt esporre.

express [ık'sprɛs] a (*definite*) chiaro(a), espresso(a); (*letter etc*) espresso inv // n (*train*) espresso // ad (*send*) espresso // vt esprimere; ∼**ion** [ık'sprɛʃən] n espressione f; ∼**ive** a espressivo(a); ∼**ly** ad espressamente.

expulsion [ık'spʌlʃən] n espulsione f.

exquisite [ɛk'skwızıt] a squisito(a).

extend [ık'stɛnd] vt (*visit*) protrarre; (*street*) prolungare; (*building*) ampliare; (*offer*) offrire, porgere // vi (*land*) estendersi.

extension [ık'stɛnʃən] n prolungamento; estensione f; (*building*) annesso; (*to wire, table*) prolunga; (*telephone*) interno; (: *in private house*) apparecchio addizionale.

extensive [ık'stɛnsıv] a esteso(a), ampio(a); (*damage*) su larga scala; (*alterations*) notevole; (*inquiries*) esauriente; (*use*) grande; **he's travelled** ∼**ly** ha viaggiato molto.

extent [ık'stɛnt] n estensione f; **to some** ∼ fino a un certo punto; **to what** ∼**?** fino a che punto?

exterior [ɛk'stıərıə*] a esteriore, esterno(a) // n esteriore m, esterno; aspetto (esteriore).

exterminate [ık'stə:mıneıt] vt sterminare; **extermination** [-'neıʃən] n sterminio.

external [ɛk'stə:nl] a esterno(a), esteriore.

extinct [ık'stıŋkt] a estinto(a); ∼**ion** [ık-'stıŋkʃən] n estinzione f.

extinguish [ık'stıŋgwıʃ] vt estinguere; ∼**er** n estintore m.

extort [ık'stɔ:t] vt: **to** ∼ **sth (from)** estorcere qc (da); ∼**ion** [ık'stɔ:ʃən] n estorsione f; ∼**ionate** [ık'stɔ:ʃnət] a esorbitante.

extra ['ɛkstrə] a extra inv, supplementare // ad (*in addition*) di più // n supplemento; (*THEATRE*) comparso.

extra... ['ɛkstrə] prefix extra... .

extract vt [ık'strækt] estrarre; (*money, promise*) strappare // n ['ɛkstrækt] estratto; (*passage*) brano; ∼**ion** [ık-'strækʃən] n estrazione f; (*descent*) origine f.

extradite ['ɛkstrədaıt] vt estradare; **extradition** [-'dıʃən] n estradizione f.

extramarital [ɛkstrə'mærıtl] a extraconiugale.

extramural [ɛkstrə'mjuərl] a fuori dell'università.

extraneous [ɛk'streınıəs] a: ∼ **to** estraneo(a) a.

extraordinary [ık'strɔ:dnrı] a straordinario(a).

extra time [ɛkstrə'taım] n (*FOOTBALL*) tempo supplementare.

extravagant [ık'strævəgənt] a stravagante; (*in spending*) dispendioso(a).

extreme [ık'stri:m] a estremo(a) // n estremo; ∼**ly** ad estremamente;

extremist *a,n* estremista (*m/f*).
extremity [ɪk'strɛmətɪ] *n* estremità *f inv*.
extricate ['ɛkstrɪkeɪt] *vt*: **to ~ sth (from)** districare qc (da).
extrovert ['ɛkstrəvɜːt] *n* estroverso/a.
exuberant [ɪg'zjuːbərnt] *a* esuberante.
exude [ɪg'zjuːd] *vt* trasudare; (*fig*) emanare.
exult [ɪg'zʌlt] *vi* esultare, gioire.
eye [aɪ] *n* occhio; (*of needle*) cruna // *vt* osservare; **to keep an ~ on** tenere d'occhio; **in the public ~** esposto(a) al pubblico; **~ball** *n* globo dell'occhio; **~brow** *n* sopracciglio; **~catching** *a* che colpisce l'occhio; **~drops** *npl* gocce *fpl* oculari, collirio; **~lash** *n* ciglio; **~lid** *n* palpebra; **~opener** *n* rivelazione *f*; **~shadow** *n* ombretto; **~sight** *n* vista; **~sore** *n* pugno nell'occhio; **~ witness** *n* testimone *m/f* oculare.
eyrie ['ɪərɪ] *n* nido (d'aquila).

F

F [ɛf] *n* (*MUS*) ?a *m*.
F. *abbr of* Fahrenheit.
fable ['feɪbl] *n* favola.
fabric ['fæbrɪk] *n* stoffa, tessuto.
fabrication [fæbrɪ'keɪʃən] *n* fabbricazione *f*; falsificazione *f*.
fabulous ['fæbjuləs] *a* favoloso(a); (*col: super*) favoloso(a), fantastico(a).
façade [fə'sɑːd] *n* facciata.
face [feɪs] *n* faccia, viso, volto; (*expression*) faccia; (*grimace*) smorfia; (*of clock*) quadrante *m*; (*of building*) facciata; (*side, surface*) faccia // *vt* fronteggiare; (*fig*) affrontare; **to lose ~** perdere la faccia; **in the ~ of** (*difficulties etc*) di fronte a; **on the ~ of it** a prima vista; **to ~ up to** *vt fus* affrontare, far fronte a; **~ cloth** *n* guanto di spugna; **~ cream** *n* crema per il viso; **~ lift** *n* lifting *m inv*; (*of façade etc*) ripulita.
facet ['fæsɪt] *n* faccetta, sfaccettatura; (*fig*) sfaccettatura.
facetious [fə'siːʃəs] *a* faceto(a).
face-to-face ['feɪstə'feɪs] *ad* a faccia a faccia.
face value ['feɪs'væljuː] *n* (*of coin*) valore *m* facciale *or* nominale; **to take sth at ~** (*fig*) giudicare qc dalle apparenze.
facial ['feɪʃəl] *a* facciale.
facile ['fæsaɪl] *a* facile.
facilitate [fə'sɪlɪteɪt] *vt* facilitare.
facility [fə'sɪlɪtɪ] *n* facilità; **facilities** *npl* attrezzature *fpl*.
facsimile [fæk'sɪmɪlɪ] *n* facsimile *m inv*.
fact [fækt] *n* fatto; **in ~** infatti.
faction ['fækʃən] *n* fazione *f*.
factor ['fæktə*] *n* fattore *m*.
factory ['fæktərɪ] *n* fabbrica, stabilimento.
factual ['fæktjuəl] *a* che si attiene ai fatti.
faculty ['fækəltɪ] *n* facoltà *f inv*.
fad [fæd] *n* mania; capriccio.
fade [feɪd] *vi* sbiadire, sbiadirsi; (*light,*

sound, hope) attenuarsi, affievolirsi; (*flower*) appassire.
fag [fæg] *n* (*col: cigarette*) cicca; **~ end** *n* mozzicone *m*; **~ged out** *a* (*col*) stanco(a) morto(a).
fail [feɪl] *vt* (*exam*) non superare; (*candidate*) bocciare; (*subj: courage, memory*) mancare a // *vi* fallire; (*student*) essere respinto(a); (*supplies*) mancare; (*eyesight, health, light*) venire a mancare; **to ~ to do sth** (*neglect*) mancare di fare qc; (*be unable*) non riuscire a fare qc; **without ~** senza fallo; certamente; **~ing** *n* difetto // *prep* in mancanza di; **~ure** ['feɪljə*] *n* fallimento; (*person*) fallito/a; (*mechanical etc*) guasto.
faint [feɪnt] *a* debole; (*recollection*) vago(a); (*mark*) indistinto(a) // *vi* svenire; **to feel ~** sentirsi svenire; **~-hearted** *a* pusillanime; **~ly** *ad* debolmente; vagamente; **~ness** *n* debolezza.
fair [fɛə*] *a* (*person, decision*) giusto(a), equo(a); (*hair etc*) biondo(a); (*skin, complexion*) bianco(a); (*weather*) bello(a), clemente; (*good enough*) assai buono(a); (*sizeable*) bello(a) // *ad* (*play*) lealmente // *n* fiera; **~ copy** *n* bella copia; **~ly** *ad* equamente; (*quite*) abbastanza; **~ness** *n* equità, giustizia.
fairy ['fɛərɪ] *n* fata; **~ tale** *n* fiaba.
faith [feɪθ] *n* fede *f*; (*trust*) fiducia; (*sect*) religione *f*, fede *f*; **~ful** *a* fedele; **~fully** *ad* fedelmente.
fake [feɪk] *n* (*painting etc*) contraffazione *f*; (*photo*) trucco; (*person*) impostore/a // *a* falso(a) // *vt* simulare, falsare; (*painting*) contraffare; (*photo*) truccare; (*story*) falsificare.
falcon ['fɔːlkən] *n* falco, falcone *m*.
fall [fɔːl] *n* caduta; (*in temperature*) abbassamento; (*in price*) ribasso; (*US: autumn*) autunno // *vi* (*pt fell, pp fallen* [fɛl, 'fɔːlən]) cadere; (*temperature, price*) abbassare; **~s** *npl* (*waterfall*) cascate *fpl*; **to ~ flat** *vi* (*on one's face*) cadere bocconi; (*joke*) fare cilecca; (*plan*) fallire; **to ~ behind** *vi* rimanere indietro; **to ~ down** *vi* (*person*) cadere; (*building, hopes*) crollare; **to ~ for** *vt fus* (*trick*) cascarci dentro; (*person*) prendere una cotta per; **to ~ in** *vi* crollare; (*MIL*) mettersi in riga; **to ~ off** *vi* cadere; (*diminish*) diminuire, abbassarsi; **to ~ out** *vi* (*friends etc*) litigare; **to ~ through** *vi* (*plan, project*) fallire.
fallacy ['fæləsɪ] *n* errore *m*; falso ragionamento.
fallen ['fɔːlən] *pp of* **fall**.
fallible ['fæləbl] *a* fallibile.
fallout ['fɔːlaut] *n* fall-out *m*.
fallow ['fæləu] *a* incolto(a); a maggese.
false [fɔːls] *a* falso(a); **~ alarm** *n* falso allarme *m*; **~hood** *n* menzogna; **~ly** *ad* (*accuse*) a torto; **~ teeth** *npl* denti *mpl* finti.
falter ['fɔːltə*] *vi* esitare, vacillare.
fame [feɪm] *n* fama, celebrità.
familiar [fə'mɪlɪə*] *a* familiare; (*common*)

comune; (*close*) intimo(a); **to be ~ with** (*subject*) conoscere; **~ity** [fəmɪlɪ'ærɪtɪ] *n* familiarità; intimità; **~ize** [fə'mɪlɪəraɪz] *vt*: **to ~ize sb with sth** far conoscere qc a qd.

family ['fæmɪlɪ] *n* famiglia; **~ allowance** *n* assegni *mpl* familiari; **~ doctor** *n* medico di famiglia; **~ life** *n* vita familiare.

famine ['fæmɪn] *n* carestia.

famished ['fæmɪʃt] *a* affamato(a).

famous ['feɪməs] *a* famoso(a); **~ly** *ad* (*get on*) a meraviglia.

fan [fæn] *n* (*folding*) ventaglio; (*ELEC*) ventilatore *m*; (*person*) ammiratore/trice; tifoso/a // *vt* far vento a; (*fire, quarrel*) alimentare; **to ~ out** *vi* spargersi (a ventaglio).

fanatic [fə'nætɪk] *n* fanatico/a; **~al** *a* fanatico(a).

fan belt ['fænbɛlt] *n* cinghia del ventilatore.

fancied ['fænsɪd] *a* immaginario(a).

fanciful ['fænsɪful] *a* fantasioso(a); (*object*) di fantasia.

fancy ['fænsɪ] *n* desiderio; immaginazione *f*, fantasia; (*whim*) capriccio // *cpd* (di) fantasia *inv* // *vt* (*feel like, want*) aver voglia di; **to take a ~ to** incapricciarsi di; **~ dress** *n* costume *m* (per maschera); **~-dress ball** *n* ballo in maschera.

fang [fæŋ] *n* zanna; (*of snake*) dente *m*.

fanlight ['fænlaɪt] *n* lunetta.

fantastic [fæn'tæstɪk] *a* fantastico(a).

fantasy ['fæntəzɪ] *n* fantasia, immaginazione *f*; fantasticheria; chimera.

far [fɑ:*] *a*: **the ~ side/end** l'altra parte/l'altro capo // *ad* lontano; **~ away, ~ off** lontano, distante; **~ better** assai migliore; **~ from** lontano da; **by ~** di gran lunga; **go as ~ as the farm** vada fino alla fattoria; **as ~ as I know** per quel che so; **~ away** a lontano(a).

farce [fɑ:s] *n* farsa.

farcical ['fɑ:sɪkəl] *a* farsesco(a).

fare [fɛə*] *n* (*on trains, buses*) tariffa; (*in taxi*) prezzo della corsa; (*food*) vitto, cibo // *vi* passarsela.

Far East [fɑ:'ri:st] *n*: **the ~** l'Estremo Oriente *m*.

farewell [fɛə'wɛl] *excl, n* addio; **~ party** *n* festa di addio.

far-fetched ['fɑ:'fɛtʃt] *a* gonfiato(a).

farm [fɑ:m] *n* fattoria, podere *m* // *vt* coltivare; **~er** *n* coltivatore/trice; agricoltore/trice; **~hand** *n* bracciante *m* agricolo; **~house** *n* fattoria; **~ing** *n* agricoltura; **~land** *n* terreno da coltivare; **~yard** *n* aia.

far-reaching ['fɑ:'ri:tʃɪŋ] *a* di vasta portata.

far-sighted ['fɑ:'saɪtɪd] *a* presbite; (*fig*) lungimirante.

fart [fɑ:t] (*col!*) *n* scoreggia(!) // *vi* scoreggiare (!).

farther ['fɑ:ðə*] *ad* più lontano.

farthest ['fɑ:ðɪst] *superlative of* **far**.

fascia ['feɪʃə] *n* (*AUT*) cruscotto.

fascinate ['fæsɪneɪt] *vt* affascinare; **fascination** [-'neɪʃən] *n* fascino.

fascism ['fæʃɪzəm] *n* fascismo.

fascist ['fæʃɪst] *a,n* fascista (*m/f*).

fashion ['fæʃən] *n* moda; (*manner*) maniera, modo // *vt* foggiare, formare; **in ~** alla moda; **out of ~** passato(a) di moda; **~able** *a* alla moda, di moda; **~ show** *n* sfilata di modelli.

fast [fɑ:st] *a* rapido(a), svelto(a), veloce; (*clock*): **to be ~** andare avanti; (*dye, colour*) solido(a) // *ad* rapidamente; (*stuck, held*) saldamente // *n* digiuno // *vi* digiunare; **~ asleep** profondamente addormentato.

fasten ['fɑ:sn] *vt* chiudere, fissare; (*coat*) abbottonare, allacciare // *vi* chiudersi, fissarsi; **~er, ~ing** *n* fermaglio, chiusura.

fastidious [fæs'tɪdɪəs] *a* esigente, difficile.

fat [fæt] *a* grasso(a) // *n* grasso.

fatal ['feɪtl] *a* fatale; mortale; disastroso(a); **~ism** *n* fatalismo; **~ity** [fə'tælɪtɪ] *n* (*road death etc*) morto/a, vittima; **~ly** *ad* a morte.

fate [feɪt] *n* destino; (*of person*) sorte *f*; **~ful** *a* fatidico(a).

father ['fɑ:ðə*] *n* padre *m*; **~-in-law** *n* suocero; **~ly** *a* paterno(a).

fathom ['fæðəm] *n* braccio (= *1828 mm*) // *vt* (*mystery*) penetrare, sondare.

fatigue [fə'ti:g] *n* stanchezza; (*MIL*) corvé *f*.

fatten ['fætn] *vt,vi* ingrassare.

fatty ['fætɪ] *a* (*food*) grasso(a).

fatuous ['fætjuəs] *a* fatuo(a).

faucet ['fɔ:sɪt] *n* (*US*) rubinetto.

fault [fɔ:lt] *n* colpa; (*TENNIS*) fallo; (*defect*) difetto; (*GEO*) faglia // *vt* criticare; **it's my ~** è colpa mia; **to find ~ with** trovare da ridire su; **at ~** in fallo; **to a ~** eccessivamente; **~less** *a* perfetto(a); senza difetto; impeccabile; **~y** *a* difettoso(a).

fauna ['fɔ:nə] *n* fauna.

favour ['feɪvə*] *n* favore *m*, cortesia, piacere *m* // *vt* (*proposition*) favorire, essere favorevole a; (*pupil etc*) favorire; (*team, horse*) dare per vincente; **to do sb a ~** fare un favore *or* una cortesia a qd; **in ~ of** in favore di; **~able** *a* favorevole; (*price*) di favore; **~ably** *ad* favorevolmente; **~ite** [-rɪt] *a,n* favorito(a); **~itism** *n* favoritismo.

fawn [fɔ:n] *n* daino // *a* marrone chiaro *inv* // *vi*: **to ~ (up)on** adulare servilmente.

fear [fɪə*] *n* paura, timore *m* // *vt* aver paura di, temere; **for ~ of** per paura di; **~ful** *a* pauroso(a); (*sight, noise*) terribile, spaventoso(a); **~less** *a* intrepido(a), senza paura.

feasibility [fizə'bɪlɪtɪ] *n* praticabilità.

feasible ['fi:zəbl] *a* possibile, realizzabile.

feast [fi:st] *n* festa, banchetto; (*REL: also*: **~ day**) festa // *vi* banchettare; **to ~ on** godersi, gustare.

feat [fi:t] *n* impresa, fatto insigne.

feather ['fɛðə*] *n* penna.

feature ['fi:tʃə*] *n* caratteristica; (*article*)

articolo // vt (subj: film) avere come protagonista // vi figurare; **~s** npl (of face) fisionomia; **~ film** n film m inv principale; **~less** a anonimo(a), senza caratteri distinti.

February ['fɛbruəri] n febbraio.

fed [fɛd] pt,pp of **feed; to be ~ up** essere stufo(a).

federal ['fɛdərəl] a federale.

federation [fɛdə'reɪʃən] n federazione f.

fee [fi:] n pagamento; (of doctor, lawyer) onorario; (of school, college etc) tasse fpl scolastiche; (for examination) tassa d'esame.

feeble ['fi:bl] a debole; **~-minded** a deficiente.

feed [fi:d] n (of baby) pappa // vt (pt, pp **fed** [fɛd]) nutrire; (horse etc) dare da mangiare a; (fuel) alimentare; **to ~ material into sth** imboccare qc con materiali; **to ~ data/information into sth** nutrire qc di data/informazioni; **to ~ on** vt fus nutrirsi di; **~back** n feed-back m; **~ing bottle** n biberon m inv.

feel [fi:l] n sensazione f; (of substance) tatto // vt (pt, pp **felt** [fɛlt]) toccare; palpare; tastare; (cold, pain, anger) sentire; (grief) provare; (think, believe): **to ~ (that)** pensare che; **to ~ hungry/cold** aver fame/freddo; **to ~ lonely/better** sentirsi solo/meglio; **it ~s soft** è morbido al tatto; **to ~ like** (want) aver voglia di; **to ~ about** or **around** for cercare a tastoni; **to ~ about** or **around in one's pocket for** frugarsi in tasca per cercare; **~er** n (of insect) antenna; **to put out a ~er** fare un sondaggio; **~ing** n sensazione f; sentimento; **my ~ing is that...** ho l'impressione che... .

feet [fi:t] npl of **foot.**

feign [feɪn] vt fingere, simulare.

fell [fɛl] pt of **fall** // vt (tree) abbattere; (person) atterrare.

fellow ['fɛləu] n individuo, tipo; compagno; (of learned society) membro; **their ~ prisoners/students** i loro compagni di prigione/studio; **~ citizen** n concittadino/a; **~ countryman** n compatriota m; **~ men** npl simili mpl; **~ship** n associazione f; compagnia; specie di borsa di studio universitaria.

felony ['fɛlənɪ] n reato, crimine m.

felt [fɛlt] pt, pp of **feel** // n feltro; **~-tip pen** n pennarello.

female ['fi:meɪl] n femmina // a femminile; (BIOL, ELEC) femmina inv; **male and ~ students** studenti e studentesse; **~ impersonator** n travestito.

feminine ['fɛmɪnɪn] a, n femminile (m).

feminist ['fɛmɪnɪst] n femminista m/f.

fence [fɛns] n recinto; (col: person) ricettatore/trice // vt (also: **~ in**) recingere // vi schermire; **fencing** n (SPORT) scherma.

fend [fɛnd] vi: **to ~ for o.s.** arrangiarsi.

fender ['fɛndə*] n parafuoco; (US) parafango; paraurti m inv.

ferment vi [fə'mɛnt] fermentare // n ['fɜ:mɛnt] agitazione f, eccitazione f; **~ation** [-'teɪʃən] n fermentazione f.

fern [fɜ:n] n felce f.

ferocious [fə'rəuʃəs] a feroce.

ferocity [fə'rɒsɪtɪ] n ferocità.

ferry ['fɛrɪ] n (small) traghetto; (large: also: **~boat**) nave f traghetto inv // vt traghettare.

fertile ['fɜ:taɪl] a fertile; (BIOL) fecondo(a).

fertility [fə'tɪlɪtɪ] n fertilità; fecondità; **fertilize** ['fɜ:tɪlaɪz] vt fertilizzare; fecondare; **fertilizer** n fertilizzante m.

fervent ['fɜ:vənt] a ardente, fervente.

fester ['fɛstə*] vi suppurare.

festival ['fɛstɪvəl] n (REL) festa; (ART, MUS) festival m inv.

festive ['fɛstɪv] a di festa; **the ~ season** la stagione delle feste.

festivities [fɛs'tɪvɪtɪz] npl festeggiamenti mpl.

fetch [fɛtʃ] vt andare a prendere; (sell for) essere venduto(a) per.

fetching ['fɛtʃɪŋ] a attraente.

fête [feɪt] n festa.

fetish ['fɛtɪʃ] n feticcio.

fetters ['fɛtəz] npl catene fpl.

fetus ['fi:təs] n (US) = **foetus.**

feud [fju:d] n contesa, lotta // vi essere in lotta.

feudal ['fju:dl] a feudale; **~ism** n feudalesimo.

fever ['fi:və*] n febbre f; **~ish** a febbrile.

few [fju:] a pochi(e); **they were ~** erano pochi; **a ~** a qualche inv. // pronoun alcuni(e); **~er** a meno inv; meno numerosi(e); **~est** a il minor numero di.

fiancé [fɪ'ã:ŋseɪ] n fidanzato; **~e** n fidanzata.

fiasco [fɪ'æskəu] n fiasco.

fib [fɪb] n piccola bugia.

fibre ['faɪbə*] n fibra; **~-glass** n fibra di vetro.

fickle ['fɪkl] a incostante, capriccioso(a).

fiction ['fɪkʃən] n narrativa, romanzi mpl; finzione f; **~al** a immaginario(a).

fictitious [fɪk'tɪʃəs] a fittizio(a).

fiddle ['fɪdl] n (MUS) violino; (cheating) imbroglio; truffa // vt (accounts) falsificare, falsare; **to ~ with** vt fus gingillarsi con; **~r** n violinista m/f.

fidelity [fɪ'dɛlɪtɪ] n fedeltà; (accuracy) esattezza.

fidget ['fɪdʒɪt] vi agitarsi; **~y** a agitato(a).

field [fi:ld] n campo; **~ glasses** npl binocolo (da campagna); **~ marshal** n feldmaresciallo; **~work** n ricerche fpl esterne.

fiend [fi:nd] n demonio; **~ish** a demoniaco(a).

fierce [fɪəs] a (look, fighting) fiero(a); (wind) furioso(a); (attack) feroce; (enemy) acerrimo(a).

fiery ['faɪərɪ] a ardente; infocato(a).

fifteen [fɪf'ti:n] num quindici.

fifth [fɪfθ] num quinto(a).

fiftieth ['fɪftɪθ] num cinquantesimo(a).

fifty ['fıftı] *num* cinquanta.

fig [fıg] *n* fico.

fight [faıt] *n* zuffa, rissa; (*MIL*) battaglia, combattimento; (*against cancer etc*) lotta // *vb* (*pt, pp* **fought** [fɔ:t]) *vt* picchiare; combattere; (*cancer, alcoholism*) lottare contro, combattere // *vi* battersi, combattere; ~**er** *n* combattente *m*; (*plane*) aeroplano da caccia; ~**ing** *n* combattimento.

figment ['fıgmənt] *n*: **a** ~ **of the imagination** un parto della fantasia.

figurative ['fıgjurətıv] *a* figurato(a).

figure ['fıgə*] *n* (*DRAWING, GEOM*) figura; (*number, cipher*) cifra; (*body, outline*) forma // *vi* (*appear*) figurare; (*US: make sense*) spiegarsi; to ~ **out** *vt* riuscire a capire; calcolare; ~**head** *n* (*NAUT*) polena; (*pej*) prestanome *m/f inv*.

filament ['fıləmənt] *n* filamento.

file [faıl] *n* (*tool*) lima; (*dossier*) incartamento; (*folder*) cartellina; (*for loose leaf*) raccoglitore *m*; (*row*) fila // *vt* (*nails, wood*) limare; (*papers*) archiviare; (*LAW: claim*) presentare; passare agli atti; to ~ **in/out** *vi* entrare/uscire in fila; to ~ **past** *vt* fus marciare in fila davanti a.

filing ['faılıŋ] *n* archiviare *m*; ~**s** *npl* limatura; ~ **cabinet** *n* casellario.

fill [fıl] *vt* riempire; (*tooth*) otturare; (*job*) coprire // *n*: to eat one's ~ mangiare a sazietà; to ~ **in** *vt* (*hole*) riempire; (*form*) compilare; to ~ **up** *vt* riempire // *vi* (*AUT*) fare il pieno; ~ **it up, please** (*AUT*) mi faccia il pieno, per piacere.

fillet ['fılıt] *n* filetto.

filling ['fılıŋ] *n* (*CULIN*) impasto, ripieno; (*for tooth*) otturazione *f*; ~ **station** *n* stazione *f* di rifornimento.

fillip ['fılıp] *n* incentivo, stimolo.

film [fılm] *n* (*CINEMA*) film *m inv*; (*PHOT*) pellicola; (*thin layer*) velo // *vt* (*scene*) filmare; ~ **star** *n* divo/a dello schermo.

filter ['fıltə*] *n* filtro // *vt* filtrare; ~ **lane** *n* (*AUT*) corsia di svincolo; ~ **tip** *n* filtro.

filth [fılθ] *n* sporcizia; (*fig*) oscenità; ~**y** *a* lordo(a), sozzo(a); (*language*) osceno(a).

fin [fın] *n* (*of fish*) pinna.

final ['faınl] *a* finale, ultimo(a); definitivo(a) // *n* (*SPORT*) finale *f*; ~**s** *npl* (*SCOL*) esami *mpl* finali; ~**e** [fı'nɑ:lı] *n* finale *m*; ~**ist** *n* (*SPORT*) finalista *m/f*; ~**ize** *vt* mettere a punto; ~**ly** *ad* (*lastly*) alla fine; (*eventually*) finalmente.

finance [faı'næns] *n* finanza; ~**s** *npl* finanze *fpl* // *vt* finanziare.

financial [faı'nænʃəl] *a* finanziario(a).

financier [faı'nænsıə*] *n* finanziatore *m*.

find [faınd] *vt* (*pt, pp* **found** [faund]) trovare; (*lost object*) ritrovare // *n* trovata, scoperta; to ~ **sb guilty** (*LAW*) giudicare qd colpevole; to ~ **out** *vt* informarsi di; (*truth, secret*) scoprire; (*person*) cogliere in fallo; ~**ings** *npl* (*LAW*) sentenza, conclusioni *fpl*; (*of report*) conclusioni.

fine [faın] *a* bello(a); ottimo(a); fine // *ad* (*well*) molto bene; (*small*) finemente // *n* (*LAW*) contravvenzione *f*, ammenda; multa

// *vt* (*LAW*) fare una contravvenzione a; multare; ~ **arts** *npl* belle arti *fpl*.

finery ['faınərı] *n* abiti *mpl* eleganti.

finesse [fı'nɛs] *n* finezza.

finger ['fıŋgə*] *n* dito // *vt* toccare, tastare; ~**nail** *n* unghia; ~**print** *n* impronta digitale; ~**tip** *n* punta del dito.

finicky ['fınıkı] *a* esigente, pignolo(a); minuzioso(a).

finish ['fınıʃ] *n* fine *f*; (*polish etc*) finitura // *vt* finire; (*use up*) esaurire // *vi* finire; (*session*) terminare; to ~ **off** *vt* compiere; (*kill*) uccidere; to ~ **up** *vi, vt* finire; ~**ing line** *n* linea d'arrivo; ~**ing school** *n* scuola privata di perfezionamento (*per signorine*).

finite ['faınaıt] *a* limitato(a); (*verb*) finito(a).

Finland ['fınlənd] *n* Finlandia.

Finn [fın] *n* finlandese *m/f*; ~**ish** *a* finlandese // *n* (*LING*) finlandese *m*.

fiord [fjɔ:d] *n* fiordo.

fir [fə:*] *n* abete *m*.

fire [faıə*] *n* fuoco; incendio // *vt* (*discharge*): to ~ **a gun** scaricare un fucile; (*fig*) infiammare; (*dismiss*) licenziare // *vi* sparare, far fuoco; **on** ~ in fiamme; ~ **alarm** *n* allarme *m* d'incendio; ~**arm** *n* arma da fuoco; ~ **brigade** *n* (corpo dei) pompieri *mpl*; ~ **engine** *n* autopompa; ~ **escape** *n* scala di sicurezza; ~ **extinguisher** *n* estintore *m*; ~**man** *n* pompiere *m*; ~**place** *n* focolare *m*; ~**side** *n* angolo del focolare; ~ **station** *n* caserma dei pompieri; ~**wood** *n* legna; ~**work** *n* fuoco d'artificio.

firing ['faıərıŋ] *n* (*MIL*) spari *mpl*, tiro; ~ **squad** *n* plotone *m* d'esecuzione.

firm [fə:m] *a* fermo(a) // *n* ditta, azienda.

first [fə:st] *a* primo(a) // *ad* (*before others*) il primo, la prima; (*before other things*) per primo; (*when listing reasons etc*) per prima cosa // *n* (*person: in race*) primo/a; (*SCOL*) laurea con lode; (*AUT*) prima; at ~ dapprima, all'inizio; ~ **of all** prima di tutto; ~**-aid kit** *n* cassetta pronto soccorso; ~**-class** *a* di prima classe; ~**-hand** *a* di prima mano; ~ **lady** *n* (*US*) moglie *f* del presidente; ~**ly** *ad* in primo luogo; ~ **name** *n* prenome *m*; ~ **night** *n* (*THEATRE*) prima; ~**-rate** *a* di prima qualità, ottimo(a).

fiscal ['fıskəl] *a* fiscale.

fish [fıʃ] *n,pl inv* pesce *m* // *vi* pescare; to go ~**ing** andare a pesca; ~**erman** *n* pescatore *m*; ~**ery** *n* zona da pesca; ~ **fingers** *npl* bastoncini *mpl* di pesce (surgelati); ~**ing boat** *n* barca da pesca; ~**ing line** *n* lenza; ~**ing rod** *n* canna da pesca; ~**monger** *n* pescivendolo; ~**y** *a* (*fig*) sospetto(a).

fission ['fıʃən] *n* fissione *f*.

fissure ['fıʃə*] *n* fessura.

fist [fıst] *n* pugno.

fit [fıt] *a* (*MED, SPORT*) in forma; (*proper*) adatto(a), appropriato(a); conveniente // *vt* (*subj: clothes*) stare bene a; (*adjust*) aggiustare; (*put in*, *attach*) mettere; installare; (*equip*) fornire, equipaggiare // *vi* (*clothes*) stare bene; (*parts*) andare bene, adattarsi; (*in space*, *gap*) entrare // *n* (*MED*) accesso, attacco; ~ **to** in grado di; ~ **for** adatto(a) a; degno(a) di; **this dress is a tight/good** ~ questo vestito è stretto/sta bene; **by** ~**s and starts** a sbalzi; **to** ~ **in** *vi* accordarsi; adattarsi; **to** ~ **out** (*also:* ~ **up**) *vt* equipaggiare; ~**ful** saltuario(a); ~**ment** *n* componibile *m*; ~**ness** *n* (*MED*) forma fisica; (*of remark*) appropriatezza; ~**ter** *n* aggiustatore *m* or montatore *m* meccanico; (*DRESSMAKING*) sarto/a; ~**ting** *a* appropriato(a) // *n* (*of dress*) prova; (*of piece of equipment*) montaggio, aggiustaggio; ~**tings** *npl* impianti *mpl*.

five [faɪv] *num* cinque; ~**r** *n* (*Brit: col*) biglietto da cinque sterline.

fix [fɪks] *vt* fissare; mettere in ordine; (*mend*) riparare // *n*: **to be in a** ~ essere nei guai; ~**ed** [fɪkst] *a* (*prices etc*) fisso(a); ~**ture** ['fɪkstʃə*] *n* impianto (fisso); (*SPORT*) incontro (del calendario sportivo).

fizz [fɪz] *vi* frizzare.

fizzle ['fɪzl] *vi* frizzare; **to** ~ **out** *vi* finire in nulla.

fizzy ['fɪzɪ] *a* frizzante; gassato(a).

fjord [fjɔːd] *n* = **fiord**.

flabbergasted ['flæbəgɑːstɪd] *a* sbalordito(a).

flabby ['flæbɪ] *a* flaccido(a).

flag [flæg] *n* bandiera; (*also:* ~**stone**) pietra da lastricare // *vi* avvizzire; affievolirsi; **to** ~ **down** *vt* fare segno (di fermarsi) a.

flagon ['flægən] *n* bottiglione *m*.

flagpole ['flægpəul] *n* albero.

flagrant ['fleɪgrənt] *a* flagrante.

flair [flɛə*] *n* (*for business etc*) fiuto; (*for languages etc*) facilità.

flake [fleɪk] *n* (*of rust, paint*) scaglia; (*of snow, soap powder*) fiocco // *vi* (*also:* ~ **off**) sfaldarsi.

flamboyant [flæm'bɔɪənt] *a* sgargiante.

flame [fleɪm] *n* fiamma.

flamingo [flə'mɪŋgəu] *n* fenicottero, fiammingo.

flammable ['flæməbl] *a* infiammabile.

flan [flæn] *n* flan *m inv*.

flange [flændʒ] *n* flangia; (*on wheel*) suola.

flank [flæŋk] *n* fianco.

flannel ['flænl] *n* (*also:* **face** ~) guanto di spugna; (*fabric*) flanella; ~**s** *npl* pantaloni *mpl* di flanella.

flap [flæp] *n* (*of pocket*) patta; (*of envelope*) lembo // *vt* (*wings*) battere // *vi* (*sail, flag*) sbattere; (*col: also:* **be in a** ~) essere in agitazione.

flare [flɛə*] *n* razzo; (*in skirt etc*) svasatura; **to** ~ **up** *vi* andare in fiamma; (*fig: person*) infiammarsi di rabbia; (: *revolt*) scoppiare; ~**d** *a* (*trousers*) svasato(a).

flash [flæʃ] *n* vampata; (*also:* **news** ~) notizia / lampo *inv*; (*PHOT*) flash *m inv* // *vt* accendere e spegnere; (*send: message*) trasmettere // *vi* brillare; (*light on*

ambulance, eyes etc) lampeggiare; **in a** ~ in un lampo; **to** ~ **one's headlights** lampeggiare; **he** ~**ed by** or **past** ci passò davanti come un lampo; ~**back** *n* flashback *m inv*; ~**bulb** *n* cubo *m* flash *inv*; ~**er** *n* (*AUT*) lampeggiatore *m*.

flashy ['flæʃɪ] *a* (*pej*) vistoso(a).

flask [flɑːsk] *n* fiasco; (*CHEM*) beuta; (*also:* **vacuum** ~) thermos *m inv* ®.

flat [flæt] *a* piatto(a); (*tyre*) sgonfio(a), a terra; (*denial*) netto(a); (*MUS*) bemolle *inv*; (: *voice*) stonato(a) // *n* (*Brit: rooms*) appartamento; (*MUS*) bemolle *m*; (*AUT*) pneumatico sgonfio; ~**ly** *ad* recisamente; ~**ten** *vt* (*also:* ~ **ten out**) appiattire.

flatter ['flætə*] *vt* lusingare; ~**er** *n* adulatore/trice; ~**ing** *a* lusinghiero(a); ~**y** *n* adulazione *f*.

flaunt [flɔːnt] *vt* fare mostra di.

flavour ['fleɪvə*] *n* gusto, sapore *m* // *vt* insaporire, aggiungere sapore a; **vanilla-~ed** al gusto di vaniglia; ~**ing** *n* essenza (artificiale).

flaw [flɔː] *n* difetto; ~**less** *a* senza difetti.

flax [flæks] *n* lino; ~**en** *a* biondo(a).

flea [fliː] *n* pulce *f*.

fledg(e)ling ['fledʒlɪŋ] *n* uccellino.

flee, *pt*, *pp* **fled** [fliː, flɛd] *vt* fuggire da // *vi* fuggire, scappare.

fleece [fliːs] *n* vello // *vt* (*col*) pelare.

fleet [fliːt] *n* flotta; (*of lorries etc*) convoglio, parco.

fleeting ['fliːtɪŋ] *a* fugace, fuggitivo(a); (*visit*) volante.

Flemish ['flemɪʃ] *a* fiammingo(a) // *n* (*LING*) fiammingo.

flesh [fleʃ] *n* carne *f*.

flew [fluː] *pt of* **fly**.

flex [fleks] *n* filo (flessibile) // *vt* flettere; (*muscles*) contrarre; ~**ibility** [-'bɪlɪtɪ] *n* flessibilità; ~**ible** *a* flessibile.

flick [flɪk] *n* colpetto; scarto; **to** ~ **through** *vt fus* sfogliare.

flicker ['flɪkə*] *vi* tremolare // *n* tremolio.

flier ['flaɪə*] *n* aviatore *m*.

flight [flaɪt] *n* volo; (*escape*) fuga; (*also:* ~ **of steps**) scalinata; **to take** ~ darsi alla fuga; **to put to** ~ mettere in fuga; ~ **deck** *n* (*AVIAT*) cabina di controllo; (*NAUT*) ponte *m* di comando.

flimsy ['flɪmzɪ] *a* (*fabric*) inconsistente; (*excuse*) meschino(a).

flinch [flɪntʃ] *vi* ritirarsi; **to** ~ **from** tirarsi indietro di fronte a.

fling, *pt*, *pp* **flung** [flɪŋ, flʌŋ] *vt* lanciare, gettare.

flint [flɪnt] *n* selce *f*; (*in lighter*) pietrina.

flip [flɪp] *n* colpetto.

flippant ['flɪpənt] ~*a* senza rispetto, irriverente.

flirt [fləːt] *vi* flirtare // *n* civetta; ~**ation** [-'teɪʃən] *n* flirt *m inv*.

flit [flɪt] *vi* svolazzare.

float [fləut] *n* galleggiante *m*; (*in procession*) carro // *vi* galleggiare // *vt* far galleggiare; (*loan, business*) lanciare; ~**ing** *a* a galla.

flock [flɔk] n gregge m; (of people) folla.

flog [flɔg] vt flagellare.

flood [flʌd] n alluvione m; (of words, tears etc) diluvio // vt allagare; **in ~** in pieno; **~ing** n alluvionamento; **~light** n riflettore m // vt illuminare a giorno.

floor [flɔ:*] n pavimento; (storey) piano; (fig: at meeting): **the ~** il pubblico // vt pavimentare; (knock down) atterrare; **first ~** (Brit), **second ~** (US) primo piano; **~board** n tavellone m di legno; **~ show** n spettacolo di varietà.

flop [flɔp] n fiasco // vi (fail) far fiasco.

floppy ['flɔpɪ] a floscio(a), molle.

flora ['flɔ:rə] n flora.

floral ['flɔːrl] a floreale.

Florence ['flɔrəns] n Firenze f; **Florentine** ['flɔrəntaɪn] a fiorentino(a).

florid ['flɔrɪd] a (complexion) florido(a); (style) fiorito(a).

florist ['flɔrɪst] n fioraio/a.

flounce [flauns] n balzo; **to ~ out** vi uscire stizzito(a).

flounder ['flaundə*] vi annaspare // n (ZOOL) passera di mare.

flour ['flauə*] n farina.

flourish ['flʌrɪʃ] vi fiorire // vt brandire // n abbellimento; svolazzo; (of trumpets) fanfara; **~ing** a prosperoso(a), fiorente.

flout [flaut] vt disprezzare.

flow [fləu] n flusso; circolazione f // vi fluire; (traffic, blood in veins) circolare; (hair) scendere; **~ chart** n schema m di flusso.

flower ['flauə*] n fiore m // vi fiorire; **~ bed** n aiuola; **~pot** n vaso da fiori; **~y** a fiorito(a).

flown [fləun] pp of **fly**.

flu [flu:] n influenza.

fluctuate ['flʌktjueɪt] vi fluttuare, oscillare; **fluctuation** [-'eɪʃən] n fluttuazione f, oscillazione f.

fluency ['flu:ənsɪ] n facilità, scioltezza; (in foreign language) buona conoscenza della lingua parlata.

fluent ['flu:ənt] a (speech) facile, sciolto(a); corrente; **he speaks ~ Italian** parla l'italiano correntemente; **~ly** ad con facilità; correntemente.

fluff [flʌf] n lanugine f; **~y** a lanuginoso(a); (toy) di peluche.

fluid ['flu:ɪd] a fluido(a) // n fluido; **~ ounce** n = 0.028 l; 0.05 pints.

fluke [flu:k] n (col) colpo di fortuna.

flung [flʌŋ] pt,pp of **fling**.

fluorescent [fluə'rɛsnt] a fluorescente.

fluoride ['fluəraɪd] n fluoruro.

flurry ['flʌrɪ] n (of snow) tempesta; **a ~ of activity/excitement** una febbre di attività/improvvisa agitazione.

flush [flʌʃ] n rossore m; (fig) ebbrezza // vt ripulire con un getto d'acqua // vi arrossire // a: **~ with** a livello di, pari a; **~ against** aderente a; **to ~ the toilet** tirare la catena, tirare la scarica; **~ed** a tutto(a) rosso(a).

fluster ['flʌstə*] n agitazione f; **~ed** a sconvolto(a).

flute [flu:t] n flauto.

flutter ['flʌtə*] n agitazione f; (of wings) frullio // vi (bird) battere le ali.

flux [flʌks] n: **in a state of ~** in continuo mutamento.

fly [flaɪ] n (insect) mosca; (on trousers: also: **flies**) bracchetta // vb (pt **flew**, pp **flown** [flu:, fləun]) vt pilotare; (passengers, cargo) trasportare (in aereo); (distances) percorrere // vi volare; (passengers) andare in aereo; (escape) fuggire; (flag) sventolare; **to ~ open** vi spalancarsi all'improvviso; **~ing** n (activity) aviazione f; (action) volo // a: **~ing visit** visita volante; **with ~ing colours** con risultati brillanti; **~ing saucer** n disco volante; **~ing start** n: **to get off to a ~ing start** partire come un razzo; **~over** n (Brit: bridge) cavalcavia m inv; **~past** n parata aerea; **~sheet** n (for tent) sopratetto; **~wheel** n volano.

foal [fəul] n puledro.

foam [fəum] n schiuma // vi schiumare; **~ rubber** n gommapiuma ®.

fob [fɔb] vt: **to ~ sb off with** appioppare qd con; sbarazzarsi di qd con.

focal ['fəukəl] a focale.

focus ['fəukəs] n (pl: **~es**) fuoco; (of interest) centro // vt (field glasses etc) mettere a fuoco; **in ~** a fuoco; **out of ~** sfocato(a).

fodder ['fɔdə*] n foraggio.

foe [fəu] n nemico.

foetus ['fi:təs] n feto.

fog [fɔg] n nebbia; **~gy** a nebbioso(a); **it's ~gy** c'è nebbia.

foible ['fɔɪbl] n debolezza, punto debole.

foil [fɔɪl] vt confondere, frustrare // n lamina di metallo; (also: **kitchen ~**) foglio di alluminio; (FENCING) fioretto.

fold [fəuld] n (bend, crease) piega; (AGR) ovile m; (fig) gregge m // vt piegare; **to ~ up** vi (map etc) piegarsi; (business) crollare // vt (map etc) piegare, ripiegare; **~er** n (for papers) cartella; cartellina; (brochure) dépliant m inv; **~ing** a (chair, bed) pieghevole.

foliage ['fəulɪdʒ] n fogliame m.

folk [fəuk] npl gente f // a popolare; **~s** npl famiglia; **~lore** ['fəuklɔː*] n folclore m; **~song** n canto popolare.

follow ['fɔləu] vt seguire // vi seguire; (result) conseguire, risultare; **he ~ed suit** lui ha fatto lo stesso; **to ~ up** vt (victory) sfruttare; (letter, offer) fare seguito a; (case) seguire; **~er** n seguace m/f, discepolo/a; **~ing** a seguente, successivo(a) // n seguito, discepoli mpl.

folly ['fɔlɪ] n pazzia, follia.

fond [fɔnd] a (memory, look) tenero(a), affettuoso(a); **to be ~ of** volere bene a.

fondle ['fɔndl] vt accarezzare.

fondness ['fɔndnɪs] n affetto.

font [fɔnt] n fonte m (battesimale).

food [fu:d] n cibo; **~ poisoning** n

intossicazione *f*; ~**stuffs** *npl* generi *fpl* alimentari.

fool [fu:l] *n* sciocco/a; (HISTORY: *of king*) buffone *m*; (CULIN) frullato // *vt* ingannare // *vi* (*gen*: ~ **around**) fare lo sciocco; ~**hardy** *a* avventato(a); ~**ish** *a* scemo(a), stupido(a); imprudente; ~**proof** *a* (*plan etc*) sicurissimo/a.

foot [fut] *n* (*pl*: **feet** [fi:t]) piede *m*; (*measure*) piede (= *304 mm*; *12 inches*); (*of animal*) zampa // *vt* (*bill*) pagare; **on** ~ **a** piedi; ~ **and mouth (disease)** *n* afta epizootica; ~**ball** *n* pallone *m*; (*sport*) calcio; ~**baller** *n* calciatore *m*; ~**brake** *n* freno a pedale; ~**bridge** *n* passerella; ~**hills** *npl* contrafforti *fpl*; ~**hold** *n* punto d'appoggio; ~**ing** *n* (*fig*) posizione *f*; **to lose one's** ~**ing** mettere un piede in fallo; **on an equal** ~**ing** in condizioni di parità; ~**lights** *npl* luci *fpl* della ribalta; ~**man** *n* lacchè *m inv*; ~**note** *n* nota (a piè di pagina); ~**path** *n* sentiero, *m*; (*in street*) marciapiede *m*; ~**sore** *a* coi piedi doloranti or dolenti; ~**step** *n* passo; ~**wear** *n* calzatura.

for [fɔ:*] *prep per* // *cj* poiché; ~ **all his money, he** says ... nonostante *or* malgrado tutto il suo denaro/quel che dice ...; **I haven't seen him** ~ **a week** è una settimana che non lo vedo, non lo vedo da una settimana; **he went down** ~ **the paper** è sceso a prendere il giornale; ~ **sale** da vendere.

forage ['fɔrɪdʒ] *vi* foraggiare.

foray ['fɔreɪ] *n* incursione *f*.

forbad(e) [fə'bæd] *pt of* **forbid**.

forbearing [fɔ:'bɛərɪŋ] *a* paziente, tollerante.

forbid, *pt* **forbad(e)**, *pp* **forbidden** [fə'bɪd, -'bæd, -'bɪdn] *vt* vietare, interdire; ~**den** *a* vietato(a); ~**ding** *a* arcigno(a), d'aspetto minaccioso.

force [fɔ:s] *n* forza // *vt* forzare; **the F~s** *npl* le forze armate; **in** ~ (*in large numbers*) in gran numero; (*law*) in vigore; **to come into** ~ entrare in vigore; ~**d** [fɔ:st] *a* forzato(a); ~**ful** *a* forte, vigoroso(a).

forceps ['fɔ:seps] *npl* forcipe *m*.

forcibly ['fɔ:səblɪ] *ad* con la forza; (*vigorously*) vigorosamente.

ford [fɔ:d] *n* guado // *vt* guadare.

fore [fɔ:*] *n*: **to the** ~ in prima linea; **to come to the** ~ mettersi in evidenza.

forearm ['fɔ:rɑ:m] *n* avambraccio.

foreboding [fɔ:'bəudɪŋ] *n* presagio di male.

forecast ['fɔ:kɑ:st] *n* previsione *f* // *vt* (*irg*: *like* cast) prevedere.

forecourt ['fɔ:kɔ:t] *n* (*of garage*) corte *f* esterna.

forefathers ['fɔ:fɑ:ðəz] *npl* antenati *mpl*, avi *mpl*.

forefinger ['fɔ:fɪŋgə*] *n* (dito) indice *m*.

forego [fɔ:'gəu] *vt* = **forgo**.

foregone ['fɔ:gɔn] *a*: **it's a** ~ **conclusion** è una conclusione scontata.

foreground ['fɔ:graund] *n* primo piano.

forehead ['fɔrɪd] *n* fronte *f*.

foreign ['fɔrɪn] *a* straniero(a); (*trade*) estero(a); ~ **body** *n* corpo estraneo; ~**er** *n* straniero/a; ~ **exchange market** *n* mercato delle valute; ~ **exchange rate** *n* cambio; ~ **minister** *n* ministro degli Affari esteri.

foreman ['fɔ:mən] *n* caposquadra *m*.

foremost ['fɔ:məust] *a* principale; più in vista.

forensic [fə'rɛnsɪk] *a*: ~ **medicine** medicina legale.

forerunner ['fɔ:rʌnə*] *n* precursore *m*.

foresee, *pt* **foresaw**, *pp* **foreseen** [fɔ:'si:, -'sɔ:, -'si:n] *vt* prevedere; ~**able** *a* prevedibile.

foresight ['fɔ:saɪt] *n* previdenza.

forest ['fɔrɪst] *n* foresta.

forestall [fɔ:'stɔ:l] *vt* prevenire.

forestry ['fɔrɪstrɪ] *n* silvicoltura.

foretaste ['fɔ:teɪst] *n* pregustazione *f*.

foretell, *pt,pp* **foretold** [fɔ:'tɛl, -'təuld] *vt* predire.

forever [fə'rɛvə*] *ad* per sempre; (*fig*) sempre, di continuo.

forewent [fɔ:'wɛnt] *pt of* **forego**.

foreword ['fɔ:wə:d] *n* prefazione *f*.

forfeit ['fɔ:fɪt] *n* ammenda, pena // *vt* perdere; (*one's happiness, health*) giocarsi.

forgave [fə'geɪv] *pt of* **forgive**.

forge [fɔ:dʒ] *n* fucina // *vt* (*signature, money*) contraffare, falsificare; (*wrought iron*) fucinare, foggiare; **to** ~ **ahead** *vi* tirare avanti; ~**r** *n* contraffattore *m*; ~**ry** *n* falso; (*activity*) contraffazione *f*.

forget, *pt* **forgot**, *pp* **forgotten** [fə'gɛt, -'gɔt, -'gɔtn] *vt,vi* dimenticare; ~**ful** *a* di corta memoria; ~**ful of** dimentico(a) di.

forgive, *pt* **forgave**, *pp* **forgiven** [fə'gɪv, -'geɪv, -'gɪvn] *vt* perdonare; ~**ness** *n* perdono.

forgo, *pt* **forwent**, *pp* **forgone** [fɔ:'gəu, -'wɛnt, -'gɔn] *vt* rinunciare a.

forgot [fə'gɔt] *pt of* **forget**.

forgotten [fə'gɔtn] *pp of* **forget**.

fork [fɔ:k] *n* (*for eating*) forchetta; (*for gardening*) forca; (*of roads*) bivio; (*of railways*) inforcazione *f* // *vi* (*road*) biforcarsi; **to** ~ **out** (*col: pay*) *vt* sborsare // *vi* pagare; ~**ed** [fɔ:kt] *a* (*lightning*) a zigzag; ~**lift truck** *n* carrello elevatore.

form [fɔ:m] *n* forma; (SCOL) classe *f*; (*questionnaire*) scheda // *vt* formare; **in top** ~ in gran forma.

formal ['fɔ:məl] *a* (*offer, receipt*) vero(a) e proprio(a); (*person*) cerimonioso(a); (*occasion, dinner*) formale, ufficiale; (ART, PHILOSOPHY) formale; ~**ly** *ad* ufficialmente; formalmente; cerimoniosamente.

format ['fɔ:mæt] *n* formato.

formation [fɔ:'meɪʃən] *n* formazione *f*.

formative ['fɔ:mətɪv] *a*: ~ **years** anni *mpl* formativi.

former ['fɔ:mə*] *a* vecchio(a) (*before n*), ex *inv* (*before n*); **the** ~ ... **the latter** quello ... questo; ~**ly** *ad* in passato.

formidable ['fɔ:mɪdəbl] *a* formidabile.

formula ['fɔːmjulə] *n* formula.
formulate ['fɔːmjuleɪt] *vt* formulare.
forsake, *pt* **forsook,** *pp* **forsaken** [fəˈseɪk, -ˈsuk, -ˈseɪkən] *vt* abbandonare.
fort [fɔːt] *n* forte *m*.
forte ['fɔːtɪ] *n* forte *m*.
forth [fɔːθ] *ad* in avanti; **to go back and ~** andare avanti e indietro; **and so ~** e così via; **~coming** *a* prossimo(a); (*character*) aperto(a), comunicativo(a); **~right** *a* franco(a), schietto(a).
fortieth ['fɔːtɪɪθ] *num* quarantesimo(a).
fortification [fɔːtɪfɪˈkeɪʃən] *n* fortificazione *f*.
fortify ['fɔːtɪfaɪ] *vt* fortificare.
fortitude ['fɔːtɪtjuːd] *n* forza d'animo.
fortnight ['fɔːtnaɪt] *n* quindici giorni *mpl*, due settimane *fpl*; **~ly** *a* bimensile // *ad* ogni quindici giorni.
fortress ['fɔːtrɪs] *n* fortezza, rocca.
fortuitous [fɔːˈtjuːɪtəs] *a* fortuito(a).
fortunate ['fɔːtʃənɪt] *a* fortunato(a); **it is ~ that** è una fortuna che; **~ly** *ad* fortunatamente.
fortune ['fɔːtʃən] *n* fortuna; **~teller** *n* indovino/a.
forty ['fɔːtɪ] *num* quaranta.
forum ['fɔːrəm] *n* foro.
forward ['fɔːwəd] *a* (*ahead of schedule*) in anticipo; (*movement, position*) in avanti; (*not shy*) aperto(a); diretto(a); sfacciato(a) // *ad* avanti // *n* (*SPORT*) avanti *m inv* // *vt* (*letter*) inoltrare; (*parcel, goods*) spedire; (*fig*) promuovere, appoggiare; **to move ~** avanzare; **~(s)** *ad* avanti.
forwent [fɔːˈwent] *pt of* **forgo**.
fossil ['fɔsl] *a,n* fossile (*m*).
foster ['fɔstə*] *vt* incoraggiare, nutrire; (*child*) adottare; **~ brother** *n* fratello adottivo; fratello di latte; **~ child** *n* bambino(a) adottato(a); **~ mother** *n* madre *f* adottiva; nutrice *f*.
fought [fɔːt] *pt, pp of* **fight**.
foul [faul] *a* (*smell, food*) cattivo(a); (*weather*) sporco(a); (*language*) osceno(a); (*deed*) infame // *n* (*FOOTBALL*) fallo // *vt* sporcare; (*football player*) commettere un fallo su.
found [faund] *pt, pp of* **find** // *vt* (*establish*) fondare; **~ation** [-ˈdeɪʃən] *n* (*act*) fondazione *f*; (*base*) base *f*; (*also*: **~ation cream**) fondo tinta; **~ations** *npl* (*of building*) fondamenta *fpl*.
founder ['faundə*] *n* fondatore/ trice // *vi* affondare.
foundry ['faundrɪ] *n* fonderia.
fount [faunt] *n* fonte *f*; **~ain** ['fauntɪn] *n* fontana; **~ain pen** *n* penna stilografica.
four [fɔː*] *num* quattro; **on all ~s** a carponi; **~some** ['fɔːsəm] *n* partita a quattro; uscita in quattro; **~teen** *num* quattordici; **~th** *num* quarto(a).
fowl [faul] *n* pollame *m*; volatile *m*.
fox [fɔks] *n* volpe *f* // *vt* confondere.
foyer ['fɔɪeɪ] *n* atrio; (*THEATRE*) ridotto.
fraction ['frækʃən] *n* frazione *f*.

fracture ['fræktʃə*] *n* frattura // *vt* fratturare.
fragile ['frædʒaɪl] *a* fragile.
fragment ['frægmənt] *n* frammento; **~ary** *a* frammentario(a).
fragrance ['freɪgrəns] *n* fragranza, profumo.
fragrant ['freɪgrənt] *a* fragrante, profumato(a).
frail [freɪl] *a* debole, delicato(a).
frame [freɪm] *n* (*of building*) armatura; (*of human, animal*) ossatura, corpo; (*of picture*) cornice *f*; (*of door, window*) telaio; (*of spectacles: also*: **~s**) montatura; **~ of mind** *n* stato d'animo; **~work** *n* struttura.
France [frɑːns] *n* Francia.
franchise ['fræntʃaɪz] *n* (*POL*) diritto di voto.
frank [fræŋk] *a* franco(a), aperto(a) // *vt* (*letter*) affrancare; **~ly** *ad* francamente, sinceramente; **~ness** *n* franchezza.
frantic ['fræntɪk] *a* frenetico(a).
fraternal [frəˈtɔːnl] *a* fraterno(a).
fraternity [frəˈtɔːnɪtɪ] *n* (*club*) associazione *f*; (*spirit*) fratellanza.
fraternize ['frætənaɪz] *vi* fraternizzare.
fraud [frɔːd] *n* frode *f*, inganno, truffa; impostore/a.
fraudulent ['frɔːdjulənt] *a* fraudolento(a).
fraught [frɔːt] *a*: **~ with** pieno(a) di, intriso(a) da.
fray [freɪ] *n* baruffa // *vt* logorare // *vi* logorarsi; **her nerves were ~ed** aveva i nervi a pezzi.
freak [friːk] *n* fenomeno, mostro // *cpd* fenomenale.
freckle ['frekl] *n* lentiggine *f*.
free [friː] *a* libero(a); (*gratis*) gratuito(a); (*liberal*) generoso(a) // *vt* (*prisoner, jammed person*) liberare; (*jammed object*) districare; **~ (of charge)** *ad* gratuitamente; **~dom** ['friːdəm] *n* libertà; **~-for-all** *n* parapiglia *m* generale; **~ kick** *n* calcio libero; **~lance** *a* indipendente; **~ly** *ad* liberamente; (*liberally*) liberalmente; **~mason** *n* massone *m*; **~ trade** *n* libero scambio; **~way** *n* (*US*) superstrada; **~wheel** *vi* andare a ruota libera; **~ will** *n* libero arbitrio; **of one's own ~ will** di spontanea volontà.
freeze [friːz] *vb* (*pt* **froze,** *pp* **frozen** [frəuz, 'frəuzn]) *vi* gelare // *vt* gelare; (*food*) congelare; (*prices, salaries*) bloccare // *n* gelo; blocco; **~r** *n* congelatore *m*.
freezing ['friːzɪŋ] *a*: **~ cold** *a* gelido(a); **~ point** *n* punto di congelamento; **3 degrees below ~** 3 gradi sotto zero.
freight [freɪt] *n* (*goods*) merce *f*, merci *fpl*; (*money charged*) spese *fpl* di trasporto; **~ car** *n* (*US*) carro *m* merci *inv*; **~er** *n* (*NAUT*) nave *f* da carico.
French [frentʃ] *a* francese // *n* (*LING*) francese *m*; **the ~** i Francesi; **~ fried potatoes** *npl* patate *fpl* fritte; **~man** *n* francese *m*; **~ window** *n* portafinestra; **~woman** *n* francese *f*.
frenzy ['frenzɪ] *n* frenesia.

frequency ['fri:kwənsı] n frequenza.
frequent a ['fri:kwənt] frequente // vt [frı'kwent] frequentare; **~ly** ad frequentemente, spesso.
fresco ['freskəu] n affresco.
fresh [freʃ] a fresco(a); (new) nuovo(a); (cheeky) sfacciato(a); **~en** vi (wind, air) rinfrescare; **to ~en up** vi rinfrescarsi; **~ly** ad di recente, di fresco; **~ness** n freschezza; **~water** a (fish) d'acqua dolce.
fret [fret] vi agitarsi, affliggersi.
friar ['fraıə*] n frate m.
friction ['frıkʃən] n frizione f, attrito.
Friday ['fraıdı] n venerdì m inv.
fridge [frıdʒ] n frigo, frigorifero.
fried [fraıd] pt, pp of **fry** // a fritto(a).
friend [frend] n amico/a; **~liness** n amichevolezza; **~ly** a amichevole; **~ship** n amicizia.
frieze [fri:z] n fregio.
frigate ['frıgıt] n (NAUT: modern) fregata.
fright [fraıt] n paura, spavento; **~en** vt spaventare, far paura a; **~ening** a spaventoso(a), pauroso(a); **~ful** a orribile; **~fully** ad terribilmente.
frigid ['frıdʒıd] a (woman) frigido(a).
frill [frıl] n balza.
fringe [frındʒ] n frangia; (edge: of forest etc) margine m; (fig): **on the ~** al margine.
frisk [frısk] vt perquisire.
frisky ['frıskı] a vivace, vispo(a).
fritter ['frıtə*] n frittella; **to ~ away** vt sprecare.
frivolity [frı'volıtı] n frivolezza.
frivolous ['frıvələs] a frivolo(a).
frizzy ['frızı] a crespo(a).
fro [frəu] see **to**.
frock [frok] n vestito.
frog [frog] n rana; **~man** n uomo m rana inv.
frolic ['frolık] vi sgambettare.
from [from] prep da; **~ a pound/January** da una sterlina in su/gennaio in poi; **~ what he says** a quanto dice.
front [frʌnt] n (of house, dress) davanti m inv; (of train) testa; (of book) copertina; (promenade: also: **sea ~**) lungomare m; (MIL, POL, METEOR) fronte m; (fig: appearances) fronte f // a primo(a), anteriore, davanti inv; **~al** a frontale; **~ door** n porta d'entrata; (of car) sportello anteriore; **~ier** ['frʌntıə*] n frontiera; **~ page** n prima pagina; **~ room** n (Brit) salotto; **~-wheel drive** n trasmissione f anteriore.
frost [frost] n gelo; (also: **hoar ~**) brina; **~bite** n congelamento; **~ed** a (glass) smerigliato(a); **~y** a (window) coperto(a) di ghiaccio; (welcome) gelido(a).
froth ['froθ] n spuma; schiuma.
frown [fraun] vi accigliarsi.
froze [frəuz] pt of **freeze**; **~n** pp of **freeze** // a (food) congelato(a).
frugal ['fru:gəl] a frugale.
fruit [fru:t] n, pl inv frutto; (collectively) frutta; **~ful** a fruttuoso(a); (plant) fruttifero(a); (soil) fertile; **~ion** [fru:'ıʃən] n: **to come to ~ion** realizzarsi; **~ machine** n macchina f mangiasoldi inv; **~ salad** n macedonia.
frustrate [frʌs'treıt] vt frustrare; **~d** a frustrato(a); **frustration** [-'treıʃən] n frustrazione f.
fry, pt, pp **fried** [fraı, -d] vt friggere; **the small ~** i pesci piccoli; **~ing pan** n padella.
ft. abbr of **foot**, **feet**.
fuchsia ['fju:ʃə] n fucsia.
fudge [fʌdʒ] n (CULIN) specie di caramella a base di latte, burro e zucchero.
fuel [fjuəl] n (for heating) combustibile m; (for propelling) carburante m; **~ oil** n nafta; **~ tank** n deposito m nafta inv; (on vehicle) serbatoio (della benzina).
fugitive ['fju:dʒıtıv] n fugitivo/a, profugo/a.
fulfil [ful'fıl] vt (function) compiere; (order) eseguire; (wish, desire) soddisfare, appagare; **~ment** n (of wishes) soddisfazione f, appagamento.
full [ful] a pieno(a); (details, skirt) ampio(a) // ad: **to know ~ well** che sapere benissimo che; **~ employment** piena occupazione; **~ fare tariffa completa; a ~ two hours** due ore intere; **at ~ speed** a tutta velocità; **in ~** per intero; **~back** n (RUGBY, FOOTBALL) terzino; **~-length** a (portrait) in piedi; **~ moon** n luna piena; **~-sized** a (portrait etc) a grandezza naturale; **~ stop** n punto; **~-time** a (work) a tempo pieno // n (SPORT) fine f partita; **~y** ad interamente, pienamente, completamente.
fumble ['fʌmbl] vi brancolare, andare a tentoni // vt (ball) lasciarsi sfuggire; **to ~ with** vt fus trafficare.
fume [fju:m] vi essere furioso(a); **~s** npl esalazioni fpl, vapori mpl.
fumigate ['fju:mıgeıt] vt suffumicare.
fun [fʌn] n divertimento, spasso; **to have ~** divertirsi; **for ~** per scherzo; **it's not much ~** non è molto divertente; **to make ~ of** vt fus prendersi gioco di.
function ['fʌŋkʃən] n funzione f; cerimonia; ricevimento // vi funzionare; **~al** a funzionale.
fund [fʌnd] n fondo, cassa; (source) fondo; (store) riserva; **~s** npl fondi mpl.
fundamental [fʌndə'mentl] a fondamentale; **~s** npl basi fpl; **~ly** ad essenzialmente, fondamentalmente.
funeral ['fju:nərəl] n funerale m; **~ service** n ufficio funebre.
fun fair ['fʌnfɛə*] n luna park m inv.
fungus ['fʌŋgəs], pl **fungi** ['fʌŋgaı, -gaı] n fungo; (mould) muffa.
funnel ['fʌnl] n imbuto; (of ship) ciminiera.
funny ['fʌnı] a divertente, buffo(a); (strange) strano(a), bizzarro(a).
fur [fə:*] n pelo; pelliccia; (in kettle etc) deposito calcare; **~ coat** n pelliccia.
furious ['fjuərıəs] a furioso(a); (effort)

accanito(a); ~**ly** *ad* furiosamente; accanitamente.

furlong ['fɔːlɔŋ] *n* = 201.17 m (*termine ippico*).

furlough ['fɔːləu] *n* (*US*) congedo, permesso.

furnace ['fɔːnɪs] *n* fornace *f*.

furnish ['fɔːnɪʃ] *vt* ammobiliare; (*supply*) fornire; ~**ings** *npl* mobili *mpl*, mobilia.

furniture ['fɔːnɪtʃə*] *n* mobili *mpl*; **piece of** ~ mobile *m*.

furrow ['fʌrəu] *n* solco.

furry ['fɔːrɪ] *a* (*animal*) peloso(a).

further ['fɔːðə*] *a* supplementare, altro(a); nuovo(a); più lontano(a) // *ad* più lontano; (*more*) di più; (*moreover*) inoltre // *vt* favorire, promuovere; **until** ~ **notice** fino a nuovo avviso; **college of** ~ **education** *n* istituto statale con corsi specializzati (*di formazione professionale, aggiornamento professionale etc*); ~**more** [fɔːðə'mɔː*] *ad* inoltre, per di più.

furthest ['fɔːðɪst] *superlative of* **far**.

furtive ['fɔːtɪv] *a* furtivo(a).

fury ['fjuərɪ] *n* furore *m*.

fuse [fjuːz] *n* fusibile *m*; (*for bomb etc*) miccia, spoletta // *vt* fondere; (*ELEC*): **to** ~ **the lights** far saltare i fusibili // *vi* fondersi; ~ **box** *n* cassetta dei fusibili.

fuselage ['fjuːzəlɑːʒ] *n* fusoliera.

fusion ['fjuːʒən] *n* fusione *f*.

fuss [fʌs] *n* chiasso, trambusto, confusione *f*; (*complaining*) storie *fpl*; **to make a** ~ fare delle storie; ~**y** *a* (*person*) puntiglioso(a), esigente; che fa le storie; (*dress*) carico(a) di fronzoli; (*style*) elaborato(a).

futile ['fjuːtaɪl] *a* futile.

futility [fjuːˈtɪlɪtɪ] *n* futilità.

future ['fjuːtʃə*] *a* futuro(a) // *n* futuro, avvenire *m*; (*LING*) futuro; **in** ~ in futuro; **futuristic** [-'rɪstɪk] *a* futuristico(a).

fuzzy ['fʌzɪ] *a* (*PHOT*) indistinto(a), sfocato(a); (*hair*) crespo(a).

G

g. *abbr of* **gram(s)**.

G [dʒiː] *n* (*MUS*) sol *m*.

gabble ['gæbl] *vi* borbottare; farfugliare.

gable ['geɪbl] *n* timpano.

gadget ['gædʒɪt] *n* aggeggio.

gag [gæg] *n* bavaglio; (*joke*) facezia, scherzo // *vt* imbavagliare.

gaiety ['geɪɪtɪ] *n* gaiezza.

gaily ['geɪlɪ] *ad* allegramente.

gain [geɪn] *n* guadagno, profitto // *vt* guadagnare // *vi* (*watch*) andare avanti; **to** ~ **in/by** aumentare di/con; **to** ~ **3lbs (in weight)** crescere di 3 libbre; ~**ful** *a* profittevole, lucrativo(a).

gainsay [geɪn'seɪ] *vt irg* (*like* **say**) contraddire; negare.

gait [geɪt] *n* andatura.

gal. *abbr of* **gallon**.

gala ['gɑːlə] *n* gala.

galaxy ['gæləksɪ] *n* galassia.

gale [geɪl] *n* vento forte; burrasca.

gallant ['gælənt] *a* valoroso(a); (*towards ladies*) galante, cortese.

gall-bladder ['gɔːlblædə*] *n* cistifellea.

gallery ['gælərɪ] *n* galleria.

galley ['gælɪ] *n* (*ship's kitchen*) cambusa; (*ship*) galea.

gallon ['gæln] *n* gallone *m* (= 4.543 *l*; 8 *pints*).

gallop ['gæləp] *n* galoppo // *vi* galoppare.

gallows ['gæləuz] *n* forca.

gallstone ['gɔːlstəun] *n* calcolo biliare.

gambit ['gæmbɪt] *n* (*fig*): (**opening**) ~ prima mossa.

gamble ['gæmbl] *n* azzardo, rischio calcolato // *vt, vi* giocare; **to** ~ **on** (*fig*) giocare su; ~**r** *n* giocatore/trice d'azzardo; **gambling** *n* gioco d'azzardo.

game [geɪm] *n* gioco; (*event*) partita; (*HUNTING*) selvaggina // *a* coraggioso(a); (*ready*): **to be** ~ (**for sth/to do**) essere pronto(a) (a qc/a fare); **big** ~ *n* selvaggina grossa; ~**keeper** *n* guardiacaccia *m inv*.

gammon ['gæmən] *n* (*bacon*) prosciutto praga; (*ham*) prosciutto affumicato.

gang [gæŋ] *n* banda, squadra // *vi*: **to** ~ **up on sb** far combutta contro qd.

gangrene ['gæŋgriːn] *n* cancrena.

gangster ['gæŋstə*] *n* gangster *m inv*.

gangway ['gæŋweɪ] *n* passerella; (*of bus*) passaggio.

gaol [dʒeɪl] *n, vt* = **jail**.

gap [gæp] *n* buco; (*in time*) intervallo; (*fig*) lacuna; vuoto.

gape [geɪp] *vi* restare a bocca aperta; **gaping** *a* (*hole*) squarciato(a).

garage ['gærɑːʒ] *n* garage *m inv*.

garbage ['gɑːbɪdʒ] *n* immondizie *fpl*, rifiuti *mpl*; ~ **can** *n* (*US*) bidone *m* della spazzatura.

garbled ['gɑːbld] *a* deformato(a); ingarbugliato(a).

garden ['gɑːdn] *n* giardino // *vi* lavorare nel giardino; ~**er** *n* giardiniere/a; ~**ing** *n* giardinaggio.

gargle ['gɑːgl] *vi* fare gargarismi // *n* gargarismo.

gargoyle ['gɑːgɔɪl] *n* gargouille *f inv*.

garish ['gɛərɪʃ] *a* vistoso(a).

garland ['gɑːlənd] *n* ghirlanda; corona.

garlic ['gɑːlɪk] *n* aglio.

garment ['gɑːmənt] *n* indumento.

garnish ['gɑːnɪʃ] *vt* guarnire.

garret ['gærɪt] *n* soffitta.

garrison ['gærɪsn] *n* guarnigione *f* // *vt* guarnire.

garrulous ['gærjuləs] *a* ciarliero(a), loquace.

garter ['gɑːtə*] *n* giarrettiera.

gas [gæs] *n* gas *m inv*; (*US: gasoline*) benzina // *vt* asfissiare con il gas; (*MIL*) gasare; ~ **cooker** *n* cucina a gas; ~ **fire** *n* radiatore *m* a gas.

gash [gæʃ] *n* sfregio // *vt* sfregiare.

gasket ['gæskɪt] *n* (*AUT*) guarnizione *f*.

gasmask ['gæsmɑːsk] n maschera f antigas inv.

gas meter ['gæsmiːtə*] n contatore m del gas.

gasoline ['gæsəliːn] n (US) benzina.

gasp [gɑːsp] vi ansare, boccheggiare; (fig) tirare il fiato.

gas ring ['gæsrɪŋ] n fornello a gas.

gas stove ['gæsstəuv] n cucina a gas.

gassy ['gæsɪ] a gassoso(a).

gastric ['gæstrɪk] a gastrico(a).

gastronomy [gæs'trɒnəmɪ] n gastronomia.

gate [geɪt] n cancello; ~crash vt partecipare senza invito a; ~way n porta.

gather ['gæðə*] vt (flowers, fruit) cogliere; (pick up) raccogliere; (assemble) radunare; raccogliere; (understand) capire // vi (assemble) radunarsi; **to ~ speed** acquistare velocità; ~**ing** n adunanza.

gauche [gəuʃ] a goffo(a), maldestro(a).

gaudy ['gɔːdɪ] a vistoso(a).

gauge [geɪdʒ] n (standard measure) calibro; (RAIL) scartamento; (instrument) indicatore m // vt misurare.

gaunt [gɔːnt] a scarno(a); (grim, desolate) desolato(a).

gauntlet ['gɔːntlɪt] n (fig): **to run the ~ through an angry crowd** passare sotto il fuoco di una folla ostile.

gauze [gɔːz] n garza.

gave [geɪv] pt of **give**.

gawp [gɔːp] vi: **~ at** guardare a bocca aperta.

gay [geɪ] a (person) gaio(a), allegro(a); (colour) vivace, vivo(a); (col) omosessuale.

gaze [geɪz] n sguardo fisso; **to ~ at** vt fus guardare fisso.

gazelle [gə'zɛl] n gazzella.

gazumping [gə'zʌmpɪŋ] n il fatto di non mantenere una promessa di vendita per accettare un prezzo più alto.

G.B. abbr see **great**.

G.C.E. n (abbr of General Certificate of Education) ≈ maturità.

gear [gɪə*] n attrezzi mpl, equipaggiamento, roba; (TECH) ingranaggio; (AUT) marcia; **in top/low/bottom ~** in quarta (or quinta)/seconda/prima; **in ~** in marcia; **out of ~** in folle; ~ **box** n scatola del cambio; ~ **lever**, ~ **shift** (US) n leva del cambio.

geese [giːs] npl of **goose**.

gelatin(e) ['dʒɛlətiːn] n gelatina.

gelignite ['dʒɛlɪgnaɪt] n nitroglicerina.

gem [dʒɛm] n gemma.

Gemini ['dʒɛmɪnaɪ] n Gemelli mpl.

gender ['dʒɛndə*] n genere m.

general ['dʒɛnərl] n generale m // a generale; **in ~** in genere; ~ **election** n elezioni fpl generali; ~**ization** n generalizzazione f; ~**ize** vi generalizzare; ~**ly** ad generalmente; ~ **practitioner** (G.P.) n medico generico.

generate ['dʒɛnəreɪt] vt generare.

generation [dʒɛnə'reɪʃən] n generazione f.

generator ['dʒɛnəreɪtə*] n generatore m.

generosity [dʒɛnə'rɒsɪtɪ] n generosità.

generous ['dʒɛnərəs] a generoso(a); (copious) abbondante.

genetics [dʒɪ'nɛtɪks] n genetica.

Geneva [dʒɪ'niːvə] n Ginevra.

genial ['dʒiːnɪəl] a geniale, cordiale.

genitals ['dʒɛnɪtlz] npl genitali mpl.

genitive ['dʒɛnɪtɪv] n genitivo.

genius ['dʒiːnɪəs] n genio.

gent [dʒɛnt] n abbr of **gentleman**.

genteel [dʒɛn'tiːl] a raffinato(a), distinto(a).

gentle ['dʒɛntl] a delicato(a); (persona) dolce.

gentleman ['dʒɛntlmən] n signore m; (well-bred man) gentiluomo.

gentleness ['dʒɛntlnɪs] n delicatezza; dolcezza.

gently ['dʒɛntlɪ] ad delicatamente.

gentry ['dʒɛntrɪ] n nobiltà minore.

gents [dʒɛnts] n W.C. m (per signori).

genuine ['dʒɛnjuɪn] a autentico(a); sincero(a).

geographic(al) [dʒɪə'græfɪk(l)] a geografico(a).

geography [dʒɪ'ɒgrəfɪ] n geografia.

geological [dʒɪə'lɒdʒɪkl] a geologico(a).

geologist [dʒɪ'ɒlədʒɪst] n geologo/a.

geology [dʒɪ'ɒlədʒɪ] n geologia.

geometric(al) [dʒɪə'mɛtrɪk(l)] a geometrico(a).

geometry [dʒɪ'ɒmɪtrɪ] n geometria.

geranium [dʒɪ'reɪnjəm] n geranio.

germ [dʒɜːm] n (MED) microbo; (BIOL, fig) germe m.

German ['dʒɜːmən] a tedesco(a) // n tedesco/a; (LING) tedesco; ~ **measles** n rosolia.

Germany ['dʒɜːmənɪ] n Germania.

germination [dʒɜːmɪ'neɪʃən] n germinazione f.

gestation [dʒɛs'teɪʃən] n gestazione f.

gesticulate [dʒɛs'tɪkjuleɪt] vi gesticolare.

gesture ['dʒɛstjə*] n gesto.

get [gɛt], pt, pp got, pp gotten (US) [gɛt, gɒt, 'gɒtn] vt (obtain) avere, ottenere; (receive) ricevere; (find) trovare; (buy) comprare; (catch) chiappare; (fetch) andare a prendere; (understand) comprendere, capire; (have): **to have got** avere; (become): **to ~ rich/old** arricchirsi/invecchiarsi // vi: **to ~** (to place) andare a; arrivare a; pervenire a; **he got across the bridge/under the fence** lui ha attraversato il ponte/è passato sotto il recinto; **to ~ ready/washed/shaved etc** prepararsi/lavarsi/farsi la barba etc; **to ~ sb to do sth** far fare qc a qd; **to ~ sth through/out of** far passare qc per/uscire qc da; **to ~ about** vi muoversi; (news) diffondersi; **to ~ along** vi (agree) andare d'accordo; (depart) andarsene; (manage) = **to get by**; **to ~ at** vt fus (attack) prendersela con; (reach) raggiungere, arrivare a; **to ~ away** vi partire, andarsene; (*escape*) scappare; **to ~ away with** *vt fus* cavarsela; farla franca; **to ~ back** *vi* (*return*) ritornare, tornare // *vt* riottenere, riavere; **to ~ by** *vi* (*pass*) passare; (*manage*) farcela; **to ~ down** *vi*, *vt fus* scendere // *vt* far scendere; (*depress*) buttare giù; **to ~ down to** *vt fus* (*work*) mettersi a (fare); **to ~ in** *vi* entrare; (*train*) arrivare; (*arrive home*) ritornare, tornare; **to ~ into** *vt fus* entrare in; (*train*) arrivare; **to ~ into a rage** incavolarsi; **to ~ off** *vi* (*from train etc*) scendere; (*depart: person, car*) andare via; (*escape*) cavarsela // *vt* (*remove: clothes, stain*) levare // *vt fus* (*train, bus*) scendere da; **to ~ on** *vi* (*at exam etc*) andare; (*agree*): **to ~ on** (**with**) andare d'accordo (con) // *vt fus* montare in; (*horse*) montare su; **to ~ out** *vi* uscire; (*of vehicle*) scendere // *vt* tirar fuori, far uscire; **to ~ out of** *vt fus* uscire da; (*duty etc*) evitare; **to ~ over** *vt fus* (*illness*) riaversi da; **to ~ round** *vt fus* aggirare; (*fig: person*) rigirare; **to ~ through** *vi* riunirsi // *vt* raccogliere; **to ~ through to** *vt fus* (*TEL*) parlare a; **to ~ together** *vi* (*people*) adunarsi // *vt* raccogliere; **to ~ up** *vi* (*rise*) alzarsi // *vt* fus far alzare; **to ~ up to** *vt fus* (*reach*) raggiungere; (*prank etc*) fare; **~away** *n* fuga.

geyser ['gi:zə*] *n* scaldabagno; (*GEO*) geyser *m inv*.

Ghana ['gɑːnə] *n* Ghana *m*; **~ian** [-'neɪən] *a*, *n* ganaense (*m/f*).

ghastly ['gɑːstlɪ] *a* orribile, orrendo(a).

gherkin ['gəːkɪn] *n* cetriolino.

ghetto ['gɛtəʊ] *n* ghetto.

ghost [gəʊst] *n* fantasma *m*, spettro; **~ly** *a* spettrale.

giant ['dʒaɪənt] *n* gigante/essa // *a* gigante, enorme.

gibberish ['dʒɪbərɪʃ] *n* farfugliare *m*.

gibe [dʒaɪb] *n* frecciata.

giblets ['dʒɪblɪts] *npl* frattaglie *fpl*.

giddiness ['gɪdɪnɪs] *n* vertigine *f*.

giddy ['gɪdɪ] *a* (*dizzy*): **to be ~** aver le vertigini; (*height*) vertiginoso(a).

gift [gɪft] *n* regalo; (*donation, ability*) dono; **~ed** *a* dotato(a).

gigantic [dʒaɪ'gæntɪk] *a* gigantesco(a).

giggle ['gɪgl] *vi* ridere scioccamente.

gild [gɪld] *vt* dorare.

gill [dʒɪl] *n* (*measure*) = 0.14 l; 0.25 pints; **~s** [gɪlz] *npl* (*of fish*) branchie *fpl*.

gilt [gɪlt] *n* doratura // *a* dorato(a).

gimlet ['gɪmlɪt] *n* succhiello.

gimmick ['gɪmɪk] *n* trucco.

gin [dʒɪn] *n* (*liquor*) gin *m*.

ginger ['dʒɪndʒə*] *n* zenzero; **~ ale, ~ beer** *n* bibita gassosa allo zenzero; **~bread** *n* pan *m* di zenzero; **~-haired** *a* rossiccio(a).

gingerly ['dʒɪndʒəlɪ] *ad* cautamente.

gingham ['gɪŋəm] *n* percalle *m* a righe *or* quadretti.

gipsy ['dʒɪpsɪ] *n* zingaro/a.

giraffe [dʒɪ'rɑːf] *n* giraffa.

girder ['gəːdə*] *n* trave *f*.

girdle ['gəːdl] *n* (*corset*) guaina.

girl [gəːl] *n* ragazza; (*young unmarried woman*) signorina; (*daughter*) figlia, figliola; **~friend** *n* (*of girl*) amica; (*of boy*) ragazza; **~ish** *a* da ragazza.

girth [gəːθ] *n* circonferenza; (*of horse*) cinghia.

gist [dʒɪst] *n* succo.

give [gɪv] *n* (*of fabric*) elasticità // *vb* (*pt* **gave**, *pp* **given** [geɪv, 'gɪvn]) *vt* dare // *vi* cedere; **to ~ sb sth, ~ sth to sb** dare qc a qd; **to ~ a cry/sigh** emettere un grido/sospiro; **to ~ away** *vt* dare via; (*give free*) fare dono di; (*betray*) tradire; (*disclose*) rivelare; (*bride*) condurre all'altare; **to ~ back** *vt* rendere; **to ~ in** *vi* cedere // *vt* consegnare; **to ~ off** *vi* emettere; **to ~ out** *vt* distribuire; annunciare; **to ~ up** *vi* rinunciare // *vt* rinunciare a; **to ~ up smoking** smettere di fumare; **to ~ o.s. up** rendersi; **to ~ way** *vi* cedere; (*AUT*) dare la precedenza.

glacier ['glæsɪə*] *n* ghiacciaio.

glad [glæd] *a* lieto(a), contento(a); **~den** *vt* rallegrare, allietare.

gladly ['glædlɪ] *ad* volentieri.

glamorous ['glæmərəs] *a* attraente, seducente.

glamour ['glæmə*] *n* attrattiva.

glance [glɑːns] *n* occhiata, sguardo // *vi*: **to ~ at** dare un'occhiata a; **to ~ off** (*bullet*) rimbalzare su; **glancing** *a* (*blow*) che colpisce di striscio.

gland [glænd] *n* ghiandola.

glare [glɛə*] *n* riverbero, luce *f* abbagliante; (*look*) sguardo furioso // *vi* abbagliare; **to ~ at** guardare male; **glaring** *a* (*mistake*) madornale.

glass [glɑːs] *n* (*substance*) vetro; (*tumbler*) bicchiere *m*; (*also: looking ~*) specchio; **~es** *npl* occhiali *mpl*; **~house** *n* serra; **~ware** *n* vetrame *m*; **~y** *a* (*eyes*) vitreo(a).

glaze [gleɪz] *vt* (*door*) fornire di vetri; (*pottery*) smaltare // *n* vetrina; **~d** *a* (*eye*) vitreo(a); (*tiles, pottery*) smaltato(a).

glazier ['gleɪzɪə*] *n* vetraio.

gleam [gliːm] *n* barlume *m*; raggio // *vi* luccicare; **~ing** *a* lucente.

glee [gliː] *n* allegrezza, gioia; **~ful** *a* allegro(a), gioioso(a).

glen [glɛn] *n* valletta.

glib [glɪb] *a* dalla parola facile; facile.

glide [glaɪd] *vi* scivolare; (*AVIAT, birds*) planare // *n* scivolata; planata; **~r** *n* (*AVIAT*) aliante *m*; **gliding** *n* (*AVIAT*) volo a vela.

glimmer ['glɪmə*] *vi* luccicare // *n* barlume *m*.

glimpse [glɪmps] *n* impressione *f* fugace // *vt* vedere al volo.

glint [glɪnt] *n* luccichio // *vi* luccicare.

glisten ['glɪsn] *vi* luccicare.

glitter ['glɪtə*] *vi* scintillare // *n* scintillio.

gloat [gləʊt] *vi*: **to ~ (over)** gongolare di piacere (per).

global ['gləʊbl] *a* globale.

globe [gləʊb] *n* globo, sfera.

gloom [glu:m] *n* oscurità, buio; (*sadness*) tristezza, malinconia; **~y** *a* fosco(a), triste.

glorify ['glɔːrɪfaɪ] *vt* glorificare.

glorious ['glɔːrɪəs] *a* glorioso(a); magnifico(a).

glory ['glɔːrɪ] *n* gloria; splendore *m* // *vi*: **to ~ in** gloriarsi di *or* in.

gloss [glɔs] *n* (*shine*) lucentezza; **to ~ over** *vt fus* scivolare su.

glossary ['glɔsərɪ] *n* glossario.

glossy ['glɔsɪ] *a* lucente; **~ (magazine)** *n* rivista di lusso.

glove [glʌv] *n* guanto.

glow [gləu] *vi* ardere; (*face*) essere luminoso(a) // *n* bagliore *m*; (*of face*) rossore *m*.

glower ['glauə*] *vi*: **to ~ (at sb)** guardare (qd) in cagnesco.

glucose ['glu:kəus] *n* glucosio.

glue [glu:] *n* colla // *vt* incollare.

glum [glʌm] *a* abbattuto(a).

glut [glʌt] *n* eccesso // *vt* saziare; (*market*) saturare.

glutton ['glʌtn] *n* ghiottone/a; **a ~ for work** un(a) patito(a) del lavoro; **~ous** *a* ghiotto(a), goloso(a); **~y** *n* ghiottoneria; (*sin*) gola.

glycerin(e) ['glɪsəri:n] *n* glicerina.

gm, gms *abbr of* **gram(s)**.

gnarled [nɑːld] *a* nodoso(a).

gnat [næt] *n* moscerino.

gnaw [nɔː] *vt* rodere.

gnome [nəum] *n* gnomo.

go [gəu] *vb* (*pt* **went**, *pp* **gone** [wɛnt, gɔn]) *vi* andare; (*depart*) partire, andarsene; (*work*) funzionare; (*be sold*): **to ~ for £10** essere venduto per 10 sterline; (*fit, suit*): **to ~ with** andare bene con; (*become*): **to ~ pale** diventare pallido(a); (*break etc*) cedere // *n* (*pl*: **~es**): **to have a ~ (at)** provare; **to be on the ~** essere in moto; **whose ~ is it?** a chi tocca?; **he's going to do sta per fare; **to ~ for a walk** andare a fare una passeggiata; **to ~ dancing/shopping** andare a ballare/fare la spesa; **how did it ~?** com'è andato?; **to ~ about** *vi* (*rumour*) correre, circolare // *vt fus*: **how do I ~ about this?** qual'è la prassi per questo?; **to ~ ahead** *vi* andare avanti; **~ ahead!** faccia pure!; **to ~ along** *vi* andare, avanzare // *vt fus* percorrere; **to ~ away** *vi* partire, andarsene; **to ~ back** *vi* tornare, ritornare; (*go again*) andare di nuovo; **to ~ back on** *vt fus* (*promise*) non mantenere; **to ~ by** *vi* (*years, time*) scorrere // *vt fus* attenersi a, seguire (alla lettera); prestar fede a; **to ~ down** *vi* scendere; (*ship*) affondare; (*sun*) tramontare // *vt fus* scendere; **to ~ for** *vt fus* (*fetch*) andare a prendere; (*like*) andare matto/a per; (*attack*) attaccare; saltare addosso a; **to ~ in** *vi* entrare; **to ~ in for** *vt fus* (*competition*) iscriversi a; (*like*) interessarsi di; **to ~ into** *vt fus* entrare in; (*investigate*) indagare, esaminare; (*embark on*) lanciarsi in; **to ~ off** *vi* partire, andar

via; (*food*) guastarsi; (*explode*) esplodere, scoppiare; (*event*) passare // *vt fus*: **I've gone off chocolate** la cioccolata non mi piace più; **the gun went off** il fucile si scaricò; **to ~ on** *vi* continuare; (*happen*) succedere; **to ~ on doing** continuare a fare; **to ~ on with** *vt fus* continuare, proseguire; **to ~ out** *vi* uscire; (*fire, light*) spegnersi; **to ~ over** *vi* (*ship*) ribaltarsi // *vt fus* (*check*) esaminare; **to ~ through** *vt fus* (*town etc*) attraversare; **to ~ up** *vi*, *vt fus* salire; **to ~ without** *vt fus* fare a meno di.

goad [gəud] *vt* spronare.

go-ahead ['gəuəhɛd] *a* intraprendente // *n* via *m*.

goal [gəul] *n* (*SPORT*) gol *m*, rete *f*; (: *place*) porta; (*fig: aim*) fine *m*, scopo; **~keeper** *n* portiere *m*; **~-post** *n* palo (della porta).

goat [gəut] *n* capra.

gobble ['gɔbl] *vt* (*also*: **~ down, ~ up**) ingoiare.

go-between ['gəubɪtwi:n] *n* intermediario/a.

goblet ['gɔblɪt] *n* calice *m*, coppa.

goblin ['gɔblɪn] *n* folletto.

god [gɔd] *n* dio; **G~** *n* Dio; **~child** *n* figlioccio/a; **~dess** *n* dea; **~father** *n* padrino; **~forsaken** *a* desolato(a), sperduto(a); **~mother** *n* madrina; **~send** *n* dono del cielo; **~son** *n* figlioccio.

goggles ['gɔglz] *npl* occhiali *mpl* (di protezione).

going ['gəuɪŋ] *n* (*conditions*) andare *m*, stato del terreno // *a*: **the ~ rate** la tariffa in vigore; **a ~ concern** un'azienda avviata.

gold [gəuld] *n* oro // *a* d'oro; **~en** *a* (*made of gold*) d'oro; (*gold in colour*) dorato(a); **~en rule** regola prima; **~en age** età d'oro; **~fish** *n* pesce *m* dorato *or* rosso; **~mine** *n* miniera d'oro.

golf [gɔlf] *n* golf *m*; **~ club** *n* circolo di golf; (*stick*) bastone *m or* mazza da golf; **~ course** *n* campo di golf; **~er** *n* giocatore/trice di golf.

gondola ['gɔndələ] *n* gondola.

gone [gɔn] *pp of* **go** // *a* partito(a).

gong [gɔŋ] *n* gong *m inv*.

good [gud] *a* buono(a); (*kind*) buono(a), gentile; (*child*) bravo(a) // *n* bene *m*; **~s** *npl* beni *mpl*, merci *fpl*; **she is ~ with children/her hands** lei sa fare coi bambini/è abile nei lavori manuali; **would you be ~ enough to ...?** avrebbe la gentilezza di ...?; **a ~ deal (of)** molto(a), una buona quantità (di); **a ~ many** molti(e); **~ morning!** buon giorno!; **~ afternoon/evening!** buona sera!; **~ night!** buona notte!; **~bye!** arrivederci!; **G~ Friday** *n* Venerdì Santo; **~-looking** *a* bello(a); **~ness** *n* (*of person*) bontà; **for ~ness sake!** per amor di Dio!; **~ness!** amicizia, benevolenza; (*COMM*) avviamento.

goose, *pl* **geese** [gu:s, gi:s] *n* oca.

gooseberry ['guzbərɪ] *n* uva spina.

gooseflesh ['gu:sfleʃ] n pelle f d'oca.

gore [gɔ:*] vt incornare // n sangue m (coagulato).

gorge [gɔ:dʒ] n gola // vt: to ~ o.s. (on) ingozzarsi (di).

gorgeous ['gɔ:dʒəs] a magnifico(a).

gorilla [gə'rɪlə] n gorilla m inv.

gorse [gɔ:s] n ginestrone m.

gory ['gɔ:rɪ] a sanguinoso(a).

go-slow ['gəu'sləu] n rallentamento dei lavori (per agitazione sindacale).

gospel ['gɔspl] n vangelo.

gossamer ['gɔsəmə*] n (cobweb) fili mpl della Madonna or di ragnatela; (light fabric) stoffa sottilissima.

gossip ['gɔsɪp] n chiacchiere fpl; pettegolezzi mpl; (person) pettegolo/a // vi chiacchierare; (maliciously) pettegolare.

got [gɔt] pt,pp of get; ~ten (US) pp of get.

gout [gaut] n gotta.

govern ['gʌvən] vt governare; (LING) reggere.

governess ['gʌvənɪs] n governante f.

government ['gʌvnmənt] n governo; (ministers) ministero // cpd statale; ~al [-'mentl] a governativo(a).

governor ['gʌvənə*] n (of state, bank) governatore m; (of school, hospital) amministratore m.

Govt abbr of **government**.

gown [gaun] n vestito lungo; (of teacher, judge) toga.

G.P. n abbr see **general**.

grab [græb] vt afferrare, arraffare; (property, power) impadronirsi di.

grace [greɪs] n grazia // vt onorare; **5 days'** ~ dilazione f di 5 giorni; **to say** ~ dire il benedicite; ~ful a elegante, aggraziato(a); **gracious** ['greɪʃəs] a grazioso(a); misericordioso(a).

gradation [grə'deɪʃən] n gradazione f.

grade [greɪd] n (COMM) qualità f inv; classe f; categoria; (in hierarchy) grado; (US: SCOL) voto; classe f // vt classificare; ordinare; graduare; ~ **crossing** n (US) passaggio a livello.

gradient ['greɪdɪənt] n pendenza, inclinazione f.

gradual ['grædjuəl] a graduale; ~ly ad man mano, a poco a poco.

graduate n ['grædjuɪt] laureato/a // vi ['grædjueɪt] laurearsi; **graduation** [-'eɪʃən] n cerimonia del conferimento della laurea.

graft [grɑ:ft] n (AGR, MED) innesto // vt innestare; **hard** ~ n (col): **by sheer hard** ~ lavorando da matti.

grain [greɪn] n grano; (of sand) granello; (of wood) venatura; **it goes against the** ~ va contro la propria natura.

gram [græm] n grammo.

grammar ['græmə*] n grammatica.

grammatical [grə'mætɪkl] a grammaticale.

gramme [græm] n = **gram**.

gramophone ['græməfəun] n grammofono.

granary ['grænərɪ] n granaio.

grand [grænd] a grande, magnifico(a); grandioso(a); ~**children** npl nipoti mpl; ~**dad** n nonno; ~**daughter** n nipote f; ~**father** n nonno; ~**iose** [grændɪəuz] a grandioso(a); (pej) pomposo(a); ~**ma** n nonna; ~**mother** n nonna; ~**pa** n = ~**dad**; ~ **piano** n pianoforte m a coda; ~**son** n nipote m; ~**stand** n (SPORT) tribuna.

granite ['grænɪt] n granito.

granny ['grænɪ] n nonna.

grant [grɑ:nt] vt accordare; (a request) accogliere; (admit) ammettere, concedere // n (SCOL) borsa; (ADMIN) sussidio, sovvenzione f; **to take sth for** ~**ed** dare qc per scontato.

granulated ['grænjuleɪtɪd] a: ~ **sugar** n zucchero cristallizzato.

granule ['grænju:l] n granello.

grape [greɪp] n chicco d'uva, acino.

grapefruit ['greɪpfru:t] n pompelmo.

graph [grɑ:f] n grafico; ~**ic** a grafico(a); (vivid) vivido(a).

grapple ['græpl] vi: **to** ~ **with** essere alle prese con.

grasp [grɑ:sp] vt afferrare // n (grip) presa; (fig) potere m; comprensione f; ~**ing** a avido(a).

grass [grɑ:s] n erba; ~**hopper** n cavalletta; ~**land** n prateria; ~**y** a erboso(a).

grate [greɪt] n graticola (del focolare) // vi cigolare, stridere // vt (CULIN) grattugiare.

grateful ['greɪtful] a grato(a), riconoscente; ~**ly** ad con gratitudine.

grater ['greɪtə*] n grattugia.

gratify ['grætɪfaɪ] vt appagare; (whim) soddisfare; ~**ing** a gradito(a); soddisfacente.

grating ['greɪtɪŋ] n (iron bars) grata // a (noise) stridente, stridulo(a).

gratitude ['grætɪtju:d] n gratitudine f.

gratuity [grə'tju:ɪtɪ] n mancia.

grave [greɪv] n tomba // a grave, serio(a).

gravel ['grævl] n ghiaia.

gravestone ['greɪvstəun] n pietra tombale.

graveyard ['greɪvjɑ:d] n cimitero.

gravitate ['grævɪteɪt] vi gravitare.

gravity ['grævɪtɪ] n (PHYSICS) gravità; pesantezza; (seriousness) gravità, serietà.

gravy ['greɪvɪ] n intingolo della carne; salsa.

gray [greɪ] a = **grey**.

graze [greɪz] vi pascolare, pascere // vt (touch lightly) sfiorare; (scrape) escoriare // n (MED) escoriazione f.

grease [gri:s] n (fat) grasso; (lubricant) lubrificante m // vt ingrassare; lubrificare; ~**proof paper** n carta oleata; **greasy** a grasso(a), untuoso(a).

great [greɪt] a grande; (col) magnifico(a), meraviglioso(a); **G~ Britain** n Gran

Bretagna; **~-grandfather** n bisnonno; **~-grandmother** n bisnonna; **~ly** ad molto; **~ness** n grandezza.

Grecian ['gri:ʃən] a greco(a).

Greece [gri:s] n Grecia.

greed [gri:d] n (also: **~iness**) avarizia; (for food) golosità, ghiottoneria; **~ily** ad avidamente; golosamente; **~y** a avido(a); goloso(a), ghiotto(a).

Greek [gri:k] a greco(a) // n greco/a; (LING) greco.

green [gri:n] a verde; (inexperienced) inesperto(a), ingenuo(a) // n verde m; (stretch of grass) prato; (also: **village ~**) ≈ piazza del paese; **~s** npl verdura; **~grocer** n fruttivendolo/a, erbivendolo/a; **~house** n serra.

Greenland ['gri:nlənd] n Groenlandia.

greet [gri:t] vt salutare; **~ing** n saluto; Christmas/birthday **~ings** auguri mpl di Natale/di compleanno.

gregarious [grə'gɛərɪəs] a gregario(a); socievole.

grenade [grə'neɪd] n granata.

grew [gru:] pt of grow.

grey [greɪ] a grigio(a); **~-haired** a dai capelli grigi; **~hound** n levriere m.

grid [grɪd] n grata; (ELEC) rete f; **~iron** n graticola.

grief [gri:f] n dolore m.

grievance ['gri:vəns] n doglianza, lagnanza.

grieve [gri:v] vi addolorarsi; rattristarsi // vt addolorare.

grill [grɪl] n (on cooker) griglia // vt cuocere ai ferri; (question) interrogare senza sosta.

grille [grɪl] n grata; (AUT) griglia.

grill(room) ['grɪl(rum)] n rosticceria.

grim [grɪm] a sinistro(a), brutto(a).

grimace [grɪ'meɪs] n smorfia // vi fare smorfie; fare boccacce.

grime [graɪm] n sudiciume m.

grimy ['graɪmɪ] a sudicio(a).

grin [grɪn] n sorriso smagliante // vi sorridere.

grind [graɪnd] vt (pt, pp ground [graund]) macinare; (make sharp) arrotare // n (work) sgobbata; to **~** one's teeth digrignare i denti.

grip [grɪp] n impugnatura; presa; (holdall) borsa da viaggio // vt impugnare; afferrare; to **come to ~s with** affrontare; cercare di risolvere.

gripe(s) [graɪp(s)] n(pl) colica.

gripping ['grɪpɪŋ] a avvincente.

grisly ['grɪzlɪ] a macabro(a), orrido(a).

gristle ['grɪsl] n cartilagine f.

grit [grɪt] n ghiaia; (courage) fegato // vt (road) coprire di sabbia; to **~** one's teeth stringere i denti.

groan [grəun] n gemito // vi gemere.

grocer ['grəusə*] n negoziante m di generi alimentari; **~ies** npl provviste fpl.

groggy ['grɔgɪ] a barcollante.

groin [grɔɪn] n inguine m.

groom [gru:m] n palafreniere m; (also:

bride~) sposo // vt (horse) strigliare; (fig): to **~ sb for** avviare qd a.

groove [gru:v] n scanalatura, solco.

grope [grəup] vi andar tentoni; to **~ for** vt fus cercare a tastoni.

gross [grəus] a grossolano(a); (COMM) lordo(a) // n, pl inv (twelve dozen) grossa; **~ly** ad (greatly) molto.

grotesque [grə'tɛsk] a grottesco(a).

grotto ['grɔtəu] n grotta.

ground [graund] pt, pp of grind // n suolo, terra; (land) terreno; (SPORT) campo; (reason: gen pl) ragione f // vt (plane) tenere a terra // vi (ship) arenarsi; **~s** npl (of coffee etc) fondi mpl; (gardens etc) terreno, giardini mpl; on the **~** per/a terra; **~ floor** n pianterreno; **~ing** n (in education) basi fpl; **~sheet** n pavimento a catino per tenda; **~ staff** n personale m di terra; **~work** n preparazione f.

group [gru:p] n gruppo // vt raggruppare // vi raggrupparsi.

grouse [graus] n, pl inv (bird) tetraone m // vi (complain) brontolare.

grove [grəuv] n boschetto.

grovel ['grɔvl] vi (fig): to **~ (before)** avvilirsi (ai piedi di).

grow [grəu], pt grew, pp grown [grəu, gru:, graun] vi crescere; (increase) aumentare; (become): to **~** rich/weak arricchirsi/indebolirsi // vt coltivare, far crescere; to **~ up** vi farsi grande, crescere; **~er** n coltivatore/trice; **~ing** a (fear, amount) crescente.

growl [graul] vi ringhiare.

grown [grəun] pp of grow // a adulto(a), maturo(a); **~-up** n adulto/a, grande m/f.

growth [grəuθ] n crescita, sviluppo; (what has grown) crescita; (MED) escrescenza, tumore m.

grub [grʌb] n larva; (col: food) roba (da mangiare).

grubby ['grʌbɪ] a sporco(a).

grudge [grʌdʒ] n rancore m // vt: to **~ sb sth** dare qc a qd di malavoglia; invidiare qc a qd; to **bear sb a ~ (for)** serbar rancore a qd (per); **grudgingly** ad di malavoglia, di malincuore.

gruelling ['gruəlɪŋ] a strapazzoso(a).

gruesome ['gru:səm] a orribile.

gruff [grʌf] a rozzo(a).

grumble ['grʌmbl] vi brontolare, lagnarsi.

grumpy ['grʌmpɪ] a stizzito(a).

grunt [grʌnt] vi grugnire // n grugnito.

guarantee [gærən'ti:] n garanzia // vt garantire.

guarantor [gærən'tɔ:*] n garante m/f.

guard [gɑ:d] n guardia, custodia; (squad, FENCING) guardia; (BOXING) difesa; (one man) guardia, sentinella; (RAIL) capotreno // vt fare la guardia a; **~ed** a (fig) cauto(a), guardingo(a); **~ian** n custode m; (of minor) tutore/trice; **~'s van** n (RAIL) vagone m di servizio.

guerrilla [gə'rɪlə] n guerrigliero; **~ warfare** n guerriglia.

guess [gɛs] vi indovinare // vt indovinare; (US) credere, pensare // n congettura; to have a ~ cercare di indovinare.

guest [gɛst] n ospite m/f; (in hotel) cliente m/f; ~-**house** n pensione f; ~ **room** n camera degli ospiti.

guffaw [gʌ'fɔ:] n risata sonora // vi scoppiare in una risata sonora.

guidance ['gaɪdəns] n guida, direzione f.

guide [gaɪd] n (person, book etc) guida // vt guidare; (**girl**) ~ n giovane esploratrice f; ~**book** n guida; ~**d missile** n missile m telecomandato; ~ **dog** n cane m guida inv; ~**lines** npl (fig) indicazioni fpl, linee fpl direttive.

guild [gɪld] n arte f, corporazione f; associazione f; ~**hall** n (Brit) palazzo municipale.

guile [gaɪl] n astuzia.

guillotine ['gɪləti:n] n ghigliottina.

guilt [gɪlt] n colpevolezza; ~**y** a colpevole.

guinea ['gɪnɪ] n (Brit) ghinea (= 21 shillings: valuta ora fuori uso).

guinea pig ['gɪnɪpɪg] n cavia.

guise [gaɪz] n maschera.

guitar [gɪ'tɑ:*] n chitarra; ~**ist** n chitarrista m/f.

gulf [gʌlf] n golfo; (abyss) abisso.

gull [gʌl] n gabbiano.

gullet ['gʌlɪt] n gola.

gullible ['gʌlɪbl] a credulo(a).

gully ['gʌlɪ] n burrone m; gola; canale m.

gulp [gʌlp] vi deglutire; (from emotion) avere il nodo in gola // vt (also: ~ **down**) tracannare, inghiottire.

gum [gʌm] n (ANAT) gengiva; (glue) colla; (sweet) gelatina di frutta; (also: chewing-~) gomma americana // vt incollare; ~**boots** npl stivali mpl di gomma.

gumption ['gʌmpʃən] n buon senso, senso pratico.

gun [gʌn] n fucile m; (small) pistola, rivoltella; (rifle) carabina; (shotgun) fucile da caccia; (cannon) cannone m; ~**boat** n cannoniera; ~**fire** n spari mpl; ~**man** n bandito armato; ~**ner** n artigliere m; at ~**point** sotto minaccia di fucile; ~**powder** n polvere f da sparo; ~**shot** n sparo; **within** ~**shot** a portata di tiro.

gurgle ['gɔ:gl] n gorgoglio // vi gorgogliare.

gush [gʌʃ] n fiotto, getto // vi sgorgare; (fig) abbandonarsi ad effusioni.

gusset ['gʌsɪt] n gherone m.

gust [gʌst] n (of wind) raffica; (of smoke) buffata.

gusto ['gʌstəu] n entusiasmo.

gut [gʌt] n intestino, budello; (MUS etc) minugia; ~**s** npl (courage) fegato.

gutter ['gʌtə*] n (of roof) grondaia; (in street) cunetta.

guttural ['gʌtərl] a gutturale.

guy [gaɪ] n (also: ~**rope**) cavo or corda di fissaggio; (col: man) tipo, elemento.

guzzle ['gʌzl] vi gozzovigliare // vt trangugiare.

gym [dʒɪm] n (also: **gymnasium**) palestra; (also: **gymnastics**) ginnastica; ~ **slip** n

grembiule m da scuola (per ragazze).

gymnast ['dʒɪmnæst] n ginnasta m/f; ~**ics** [-'næstɪks] n, npl ginnastica.

gynaecology [gaɪnə'kɔlədʒɪ] n ginecologia.

gypsy ['dʒɪpsɪ] n = **gipsy**.

gyrate [dʒaɪ'reɪt] vi girare.

H

haberdashery ['hæbə'dæʃərɪ] n merceria.

habit ['hæbɪt] n abitudine f; (costume) abito; (REL) tonaca.

habitation [hæbɪ'teɪʃən] n abitazione f.

habitual [hə'bɪtjuəl] a abituale; (drinker, liar) inveterato(a); ~**ly** ad abitualmente, di solito.

hack [hæk] vt tagliare, fare a pezzi // n (cut) taglio; (blow) colpo; (pej: writer) negro.

hackney cab ['hæknɪ'kæb] n carrozza a nolo.

hackneyed ['hæknɪd] a comune, trito(a).

had [hæd] pt, pp of **have**.

haddock ['hædək] n eglefino.

haemorrhage ['hɛmərɪdʒ] n emorragia.

haemorrhoids ['hɛmərɔɪdz] npl emorroidi fpl.

haggard ['hægəd] a smunto(a).

haggle ['hægl] vi mercanteggiare.

Hague [heɪg] n: **The** ~ L'Aia.

hail [heɪl] n grandine f // vt (call) chiamare; (greet) salutare // vi grandinare; ~**stone** n chicco di grandine.

hair [hɛə*] n capelli mpl; (single hair: on head) capello; (: on body) pelo; **to do one's** ~ pettinarsi; ~**brush** n spazzola per capelli; ~**cut** n taglio di capelli; **I need a** ~**cut** ho bisogno di farmi i capelli; ~**do** ['hɛədu:] n acconciatura, pettinatura; ~**dresser** n parrucchiere/a; ~**drier** n asciugacapelli m inv; ~**net** n retina (per capelli); ~ **oil** n brillantina; ~**piece** n toupet m inv; ~**pin** n forcina; ~**pin bend** n tornante m; ~**raising** a orripilante; ~**style** n pettinatura, acconciatura; ~**y** a irsuto(a); peloso(a); (fig) spaventoso(a).

hake [heɪk] n nasello.

half [hɑ:f] n (pl: **halves** [hɑ:vz]) mezzo, metà f inv // a mezzo(a) // ad a mezzo, a metà; ~-**an-hour** mezz'ora; **two and a** ~ **due e mezzo**; **a week and a** ~ una settimana e mezza; ~ (**of it**) la metà; ~ (**of**) la metà di; ~ **the amount of** la metà di; **to cut sth in** ~ tagliare qc in due; ~**back** n (SPORT) mediano; ~**breed**, ~**caste** n meticcio/a; ~**hearted** a tiepido(a); ~**hour** n mezz'ora; ~**penny** ['heɪpnɪ] n mezzo penny m inv; (at) ~**price** a metà prezzo; ~**time** n intervallo; ~**way** ad a metà strada.

halibut ['hælɪbət] n, pl inv ippoglosso.

hall [hɔ:l] n sala, salone m; (entrance way) entrata; (corridor) corridoio; (mansion) grande villa, maniero; ~ **of residence** n casa dello studente.

hallmark ['hɔ:lmɑ:k] n marchio di garanzia; (fig) caratteristica.

hallo [hə'ləʊ] *excl* = **hello.**

hallucination [həluːsɪ'neɪʃən] *n* allucinazione *f*.

halo ['heɪləʊ] *n* (of saint etc) aureola; (of sun) alone *m*.

halt [hɔːlt] *n* fermata // *vt* fermare // *vi* fermarsi.

halve [haːv] *vt* (apple etc) dividere a metà; (expense) ridurre di metà.

halves [haːvz] *npl of* **half.**

ham [hæm] *n* prosciutto.

hamburger ['hæmbɜːgə*] *n* hamburger *m inv*.

hamlet ['hæmlɪt] *n* paesetto.

hammer ['hæmə*] *n* martello // *vt* martellare; (fig) sconfiggere duramente.

hammock ['hæmək] *n* amaca.

hamper ['hæmpə*] *vt* impedire // *n* cesta.

hand [hænd] *n* mano *f*; (of clock) lancetta; (handwriting) scrittura; (at cards) carte *fpl*; (: game) partita; (worker) operaio/a // *vt* dare, passare; **to give sb a ~** dare una mano a qd; **at ~** a portata di mano; **in ~** a disposizione; (work) in corso; **on the one ~ ..., on the other ~** da un lato ..., dall'altro; **in ~** *vt* consegnare; **to ~ out** *vt* distribuire; **to ~ over** *vt* passare; cedere; **~bag** *n* borsetta; **~ball** *n* pallamano *f*; **~basin** *n* lavandino; **~book** *n* manuale *m*; **~brake** *n* freno a mano; **~cuffs** *npl* manette *fpl*; **~ful** *n* manata, pugno.

handicap ['hændɪkæp] *n* handicap *m inv* // *vt* andicappare.

handicraft ['hændɪkraːft] *n* lavoro d'artigiano.

handkerchief ['hæŋkətʃɪf] *n* fazzoletto.

handle ['hændl] *n* (of door etc) maniglia; (of cup etc) ansa; (of knife etc) impugnatura; (of saucepan) manico; (for winding) manovella // *vt* toccare, maneggiare; (deal with) occuparsi di; (treat: people) trattare; **'~ with care'** 'fragile'; **~bar(s)** *n(pl)* manubrio.

hand-luggage ['hændlʌgɪdʒ] *n* bagagli *mpl* a mano.

handmade ['hænsmeɪd] *a* fatto(a) a mano.

handsome ['hænsəm] *a* bello(a); generoso(a); considerevole.

handwriting ['hændraɪtɪŋ] *n* scrittura.

handwritten ['hændrɪtn] *a* scritto(a) a mano, manoscritto(a).

handy ['hændɪ] *a* (person) destro(a); (close at hand) a portata di mano; (convenient) comodo(a); **~man** *n* tuttofare *m inv*; **tools for the ~man** arnesi per il fatelo-da-voi.

hang, *pt*, *pp* **hung** [hæŋ, hʌŋ] *vt* appendere; (criminal: *pt*, *pp* **hanged**) impiccare // *vi* pendere; (hair) scendere; (drapery) cadere; **to ~ about** *vi* bighellonare, ciondolare; **to ~ on** *vi* (wait) aspettare; **to ~ up** *vi* (TEL) riattaccare // *vt* appendere.

hangar ['hæŋə*] *n* hangar *m inv*.

hanger ['hæŋə*] *n* gruccia.

hanger-on [hæŋər'ɒn] *n* parassita *m*.

hang-gliding ['hæŋglaɪdɪŋ] *n* volo col deltaplano.

hangover ['hæŋəʊvə*] *n* (after drinking) postumi *mpl* di sbornia.

hang-up ['hæŋʌp] *n* complesso.

hank [hæŋk] *n* matassa.

hanker ['hæŋkə*] *vi*: **to ~ after** bramare.

hankie, hanky ['hæŋkɪ] *n* abbr of **handkerchief.**

haphazard [hæp'hæzəd] *a* a casaccio, alla carlona.

happen ['hæpən] *vi* accadere, succedere; **I ~ed to be out** mi capitò di essere fuori; **as it ~s** guarda caso; **~ing** *n* avvenimento.

happily ['hæpɪlɪ] *ad* felicemente; fortunatamente.

happiness ['hæpɪnɪs] *n* felicità, contentezza.

happy ['hæpɪ] *a* felice, contento(a); **~ with** (arrangements etc) soddisfatto(a) di; **~-go-lucky** *a* spensierato(a).

harass ['hærəs] *vt* molestare; **~ment** *n* molestia.

harbour ['haːbə*] *n* porto // *vt* dare rifugio a; **~ master** *n* capitano di porto.

hard [haːd] *a* duro(a) // *ad* (work) sodo; (think, try) bene; **to drink ~** bere forte; **~ luck!** peccato!; **no ~ feelings!** senza rancore!; **to be ~ of hearing** essere duro(a) d'orecchio; **to be ~ done by** essere trattato(a) ingiustamente; **~back** *n* libro rilegato; **~board** *n* legno precompresso; **~-boiled egg** *n* uovo sodo; **~ cash** *n* denaro in contanti; **~ en** *vt*, *vi* indurire; **~ labour** *n* lavori forzati *mpl*.

hardly ['haːdlɪ] *ad* (scarcely) appena; **it's ~ the case** non è proprio il caso; **~ anyone/ anywhere** quasi nessuno/da nessuna parte.

hardness ['haːdnɪs] *n* durezza.

hard sell ['haːd'sɛl] *n* (COMM) intensa campagna promozionale.

hardship ['haːdʃɪp] *n* avversità *f inv*; privazioni *fpl*.

hard-up [haːd'ʌp] *a* (col) al verde.

hardware ['haːdwɛə*] *n* ferramenta *fpl*; (COMPUTERS) hardware *m*; **~ shop** *n* (negozio di) ferramenta *fpl*.

hardy ['haːdɪ] *a* robusto(a); (plant) resistente al gelo.

hare [hɛə*] *n* lepre *f*; **~-brained** *a* folle; scervellato(a); **~lip** *n* (MED) labbro leporino.

harem [haː'riːm] *n* harem *m inv*.

harm [haːm] *n* male *m*; (wrong) danno // *vt* (person) fare male a; (thing) danneggiare; **to mean no ~** non avere l'intenzione d'offendere; **out of ~'s way** al sicuro; **~ful** *a* dannoso(a); **~less** *a* innocuo(a); inoffensivo(a).

harmonica [haː'mɒnɪkə] *n* armonica.

harmonics [haː'mɒnɪks] *npl* armonia.

harmonious [haː'məʊnɪəs] *a* armonioso(a).

harmonium [haː'məʊnɪəm] *n* armonium *m inv*.

harmonize ['hɑːmənaɪz] *vt, vi* armonizzare.

harmony ['hɑːmənɪ] *n* armonia.

harness ['hɑːnɪs] *n* bardatura, finimenti *mpl* // *vt* (*horse*) bardare; (*resources*) sfruttare.

harp [hɑːp] *n* arpa // *vi*: to ~ on about insistere tediosamente su; ~ist *n* arpista *m/f*.

harpoon [hɑːˈpuːn] *n* arpione *m*.

harpsichord ['hɑːpsɪkɔːd] *n* clavicembalo.

harrow ['hærəʊ] *n* (*AGR*) erpice *m*.

harrowing ['hærəʊɪŋ] *a* straziante.

harsh [hɑːʃ] *a* (*hard*) duro(a); (*severe*) severo(a); (*unpleasant: sound*) rauco(a); (: *colour*) chiassoso(a); violento(a); ~ly *ad* duramente; severamente; ~ness *n* durezza; severità.

harvest ['hɑːvɪst] *n* raccolto; (*of grapes*) vendemmia // *vt* fare il raccolto di, raccogliere; vendemmiare; ~er *n* (*machine*) mietitrice *f*.

has [hæz] *see* have.

hash [hæʃ] *n* (*CULIN*) specie di spezzatino fatto con carne già cotta; (*fig: mess*) pasticcio; *also abbr of* **hashish.**

hashish ['hæʃɪʃ] *n* hascisc *m*.

haste [heɪst] *n* fretta; precipitazione *f*; ~n ['heɪsn] *vt* affrettare // *vi* affrettarsi; **hastily** *ad* in fretta; precipitosamente; **hasty** *a* affrettato(a); precipitoso(a).

hat [hæt] *n* cappello; ~box *n* cappelliera.

hatch [hætʃ] *n* (*NAUT: also:* ~way) boccaporto; (*also:* **service** ~) portello di servizio // *vi* schiudersi // *vt* covare.

hatchback ['hætʃbæk] *n* (*AUT*) tre (*or* cinque) porte *f inv*.

hatchet ['hætʃɪt] *n* accetta.

hate [heɪt] *vt* odiare, detestare // *n* odio; to ~ to do *or* doing detestare fare; ~ful *a* odioso(a), detestabile.

hatred ['heɪtrɪd] *n* odio.

hat trick ['hættrɪk] *n* (*SPORT, also fig*) tris *m inv* (*3 reti segnate durante una partita etc*).

haughty ['hɔːtɪ] *a* altero(a), arrogante.

haul [hɔːl] *vt* trascinare, tirare // *n* (*of fish*) pescata; (*of stolen goods etc*) bottino; ~age *n* trasporto; autotrasporto; ~ier *n* trasportatore *m*.

haunch [hɔːntʃ] *n* anca.

haunt [hɔːnt] *vt* (*subj: fear*) pervadere; (: *person*) frequentare // *n* rifugio; **a ghost** ~s **this house** questa casa è abitata da un fantasma.

have *pt,pp* **had** [hæv, hæd] *vt* avere; (*meal, shower*) fare; to ~ sth done far fare qc; he had a suit made si fece fare un abito; she has to do it lo deve fare; I had better leave è meglio che io vada; to ~ it out with sb metterlo in chiaro con qd; I won't ~ it questo non mi va affatto; he's been had (*col*) c'è cascato dentro.

haven ['heɪvn] *n* porto; (*fig*) rifugio.

haversack ['hævəsæk] *n* zaino.

havoc ['hævək] *n* caos *m*.

hawk [hɔːk] *n* falco.

hawker ['hɔːkə*] *n* venditore *m* ambulante.

hay [heɪ] *n* fieno; ~ fever *n* febbre *f* da fieno; ~stack *n* mucchio di fieno.

haywire ['heɪwaɪə*] *a* (*col*): to go ~ perdere la testa; impazzire.

hazard ['hæzəd] *n* azzardo, ventura; pericolo, rischio; ~ous *a* pericoloso(a), rischioso(a).

haze [heɪz] *n* foschia.

hazelnut ['heɪzlnʌt] *n* nocciola.

hazy ['heɪzɪ] *a* fosco(a); (*idea*) vago(a); (*photograph*) indistinto(a).

he [hiː] *pronoun* lui, egli; **it is** ~ **who** ... è lui che ...; **here** ~ **is** eccolo; ~-bear *n* orso maschio.

head [hed] *n* testa, capo; (*leader*) capo // *vt* (*list*) essere in testa a; (*group*) essere a capo di; ~s (*or* **tails**) testa (o croce), pari (o gaffo); to ~ **the ball** dare di testa alla palla; to ~ **for** *vt fus* dirigersi verso; ~**ache** *n* mal *m* di testa; ~**ing** *n* titolo; intestazione *f*; ~**lamp** *n* fanale *m*; ~**land** *n* promontorio; ~**light** = ~**lamp**; ~**line** *n* titolo; ~**long** *ad* (*fall*) a capofitto; (*rush*) precipitosamente; ~**master** *n* preside *m*; ~**mistress** *n* preside *f*; ~ **office** *n* sede *f* (centrale); ~-**on** *a* (*collision*) frontale; ~**quarters** (**HQ**) *npl* ufficio centrale; (*MIL*) quartiere *m* generale; ~-**rest** *n* poggiacapo; ~**room** *n* (*in car*) altezza dell'abitacolo; (*under bridge*) altezza limite; ~**scarf** *n* foulard *m inv*; ~**strong** *a* testardo(a); ~ **waiter** *n* capocameriere *m*; ~**way** *n* progresso, cammino; ~**wind** *n* controvento; ~**y** *a* che dà alla testa; inebriante.

heal [hiːl] *vt,vi* guarire.

health [helθ] *n* salute *f*; the H~ Service ≈ il Servizio Sanitario Statale; ~y *a* (*person*) in buona salute; (*climate*) salubre; (*food*) salutare; (*attitude etc*) sano(a).

heap [hiːp] *n* mucchio // *vt* ammucchiare.

hear, *pt, pp* **heard** [hɪə*, hɜːd] *vt* sentire; (*news*) ascoltare; (*lecture*) assistere a // *vi* sentire; to ~ **about** avere notizie di; sentire parlare di; to ~ **from sb** ricevere notizie da qd; ~**ing** *n* (*sense*) udito; (*of witnesses*) audizione *f*; (*of a case*) udienza; ~**ing aid** *n* apparecchio acustico; **by** ~**say** *ad* per sentito dire.

hearse [hɜːs] *n* carro funebre.

heart [hɑːt] *n* cuore *m*; ~s *npl* (*CARDS*) cuori *mpl*; **at** ~ in fondo; **by** ~ (*learn, know*) a memoria; **to lose** ~ perdere coraggio, scoraggiarsi; ~ **attack** *n* attacco di cuore; ~**beat** *n* battito del cuore; ~**breaking** *a* straziante; **to be** ~**broken** avere il cuore spezzato; ~**burn** *n* bruciore *m* di stomaco; ~**felt** *a* sincero(a).

hearth [hɑːθ] *n* focolare *m*.

heartily ['hɑːtɪlɪ] *ad* (*laugh*) di cuore; (*eat*) di buon appetito.

heartless ['hɑːtlɪs] *a* senza cuore, insensibile; crudele.

heartwarming ['hɑːtwɔːmɪŋ] *a* confortante, che scalda il cuore.

hearty ['hɑːtɪ] a caloroso(a); robusto(a), sano(a); vigoroso(a).

heat [hiːt] n calore m; (fig) ardore m; fuoco; (SPORT: also: **qualifying ~**) prova eliminatoria // vt scaldare; **to ~ up** vi (liquids) scaldarsi; (room) riscaldarsi // vt riscaldare; **~ed** a riscaldato(a); (fig) appassionato(a); acceso(a), eccitato(a); **~er** n stufa; radiatore m.

heath [hiːθ] n (Brit) landa.

heathen ['hiːðn] a, n pagano(a).

heather ['hɛðə*] n erica.

heating ['hiːtɪŋ] n riscaldamento.

heatstroke ['hiːtstrəʊk] n colpo di sole.

heatwave ['hiːtweɪv] n ondata di caldo.

heave [hiːv] vt sollevare (con sforzo) // vi sollevarsi // n conato di vomito; (push) grande spinta.

heaven ['hɛvn] n paradiso, cielo; **~ forbid!** Dio ce ne guardi!; **~ly** a divino(a), celeste.

heavily ['hɛvɪlɪ] ad pesantemente; (drink, smoke) molto.

heavy ['hɛvɪ] a pesante; (sea) grosso(a); (rain) forte; (drinker, smoker) gran (before noun); **it's ~ going** è una gran fatica; **~ weight** n (SPORT) peso massimo.

Hebrew ['hiːbruː] a ebreo(a) // n (LING) ebraico.

heckle ['hɛkl] vt interpellare e dare noia a (un oratore).

hectic ['hɛktɪk] a movimentato(a).

he'd [hiːd] = **he would, he had.**

hedge [hɛdʒ] n siepe f // vi essere elusivo(a); **to ~ one's bets** (fig) coprirsi dai rischi.

hedgehog ['hɛdʒhɒg] n riccio.

heed [hiːd] vt (also: **take ~ of**) badare a, far conto di; **~less** a sbadato(a).

heel [hiːl] n (ANAT) calcagno; (of shoe) tacco // vt (shoe) rifare i tacchi a.

hefty ['hɛftɪ] a (person) solido(a); (parcel) pesante; (piece, price) grosso(a).

heifer ['hɛfə*] n giovenca.

height [haɪt] n altezza; (high ground) altura; (fig: of glory) apice m; (: of stupidity) colmo; **~en** vt innalzare; (fig) accrescere.

heir [ɛə*] n erede m; **~ess** n erede f; **~loom** n mobile m (or gioiello or quadro) di famiglia.

held [hɛld] pt, pp of **hold.**

helicopter ['hɛlɪkɒptə*] n elicottero.

hell [hɛl] n inferno; **a ~ of a ...** (col) un(a) maledetto(a) ... .

he'll [hiːl] = **he will, he shall.**

hellish ['hɛlɪʃ] a infernale.

hello [hə'ləʊ] excl buon giorno!; ciao! (to sb one addresses as 'tu'); (surprise) ma guarda!

helm [hɛlm] n (NAUT) timone m.

helmet ['hɛlmɪt] n casco.

helmsman ['hɛlmzmən] n timoniere m.

help [hɛlp] n aiuto; (charwoman) donna di servizio; (assistant etc) impiegato/a // vt aiutare; **~! aiuto!; ~ yourself (to bread)** si serva (del pane); **I can't ~ saying** non posso evitare di dire; **he can't ~ it** non ci

può far niente; **~er** n aiutante m/f, assistente m/f; **~ful** a di grande aiuto; (useful) utile; **~ing** n porzione f; **~less** a impotente; debole.

hem [hɛm] n orlo // vt fare l'orlo a; **to ~ in** vt cingere.

hemisphere ['hɛmɪsfɪə*] n emisfero.

hemp [hɛmp] n canapa.

hen [hɛn] n gallina.

hence [hɛns] ad (therefore) dunque; **2 years ~** di qui a 2 anni; **~forth** ad d'ora in poi.

henchman ['hɛntʃmən] n (pej) caudatario.

henpecked ['hɛnpɛkt] a dominato dalla moglie.

her [həː*] pronoun (direct) la, l' + vowel; (indirect) le; (stressed, after prep) lei; see note at **she** // a il(la) suo(a), i(le) suoi(sue); **give ~ a book** le dia un libro; **after ~** dopo (di) lei.

herald ['hɛrəld] n araldo // vt annunciare.

heraldry ['hɛrəldrɪ] n araldica.

herb [həːb] n erba; **~s** npl (CULIN) erbette fpl.

herd [həːd] n mandria.

here [hɪə*] ad qui, qua // excl ehi!; **~!** presente!; **~'s my sister** ecco mia sorella; **~ she is** eccola; **~ she comes** eccola che viene; **~ after** dopo questo // n: **the ~after** l'al di là m; **~by** ad (in letter) con la presente.

hereditary [hɪ'rɛdɪtrɪ] a ereditario(a).

heredity [hɪ'rɛdɪtɪ] n eredità.

heresy ['hɛrəsɪ] n eresia.

heretic ['hɛrətɪk] n eretico/a; **~al** [hɪ'rɛtɪkl] a eretico(a).

herewith [hɪə'wɪð] ad qui accluso.

heritage ['hɛrɪtɪdʒ] n eredità; (fig) retaggio.

hermetically [həː'mɛtɪklɪ] ad ermeticamente.

hermit ['həːmɪt] n eremita m.

hernia ['həːnɪə] n ernia.

hero, ~es ['hɪərəʊ] n eroe m; **~ic** [hɪ'rəʊɪk] a eroico(a).

heroin ['hɛrəʊɪn] n eroina.

heroine ['hɛrəʊɪn] n eroina.

heroism ['hɛrəʊɪzm] n eroismo.

heron ['hɛrən] n airone m.

herring ['hɛrɪŋ] n aringa.

hers [həːz] pronoun il(la) suo(a), i(le) suoi(sue).

herself [həː'sɛlf] pronoun (reflexive) si; (emphatic) lei stessa; (after prep) se stessa, sé.

he's [hiːz] = **he is, he has.**

hesitant ['hɛzɪtənt] a esitante, indeciso(a).

hesitate ['hɛzɪteɪt] vi: **to ~ (about/to do)** esitare (su/a fare); **hesitation** [-'teɪʃən] n esitazione f.

het up [hɛt'ʌp] a agitato(a).

hew [hjuː] vt tagliare (con l'accetta).

hexagon ['hɛksəgən] n esagono; **~al** [-'sægənl] a esagonale.

heyday ['heɪdeɪ] n: **the ~ of** i bei giorni di, l'età d'oro di.

hi [haɪ] excl ciao!

hibernate ['haibəneit] vi svernare.
hiccough, hiccup ['hikʌp] vi singhiozzare // n singhiozzo; **to have (the) ~s** avere il singhiozzo.
hid [hid] pt of **hide**.
hidden ['hidn] pp of **hide**.
hide [haid] n (skin) pelle f // vb (pt **hid**, pp **hidden** [hid, 'hidn]) vt: **to ~ sth (from sb)** nascondere qc (a qd) // vi: **to ~ (from sb)** nascondersi (da qd); **~-and-seek** n rimpiattino; **~away** n nascondiglio.
hideous ['hidiəs] a laido(a); orribile.
hiding ['haidiŋ] n (beating) bastonata; **to be in ~** (concealed) tenersi nascosto(a); **~ place** n nascondiglio.
hierarchy ['haiəra:ki] n gerarchia.
high [hai] a alto(a); (speed, respect, number) grande; (wind) forte // ad alto, in alto; **20m ~** alto(a) 20m; **~brow** a, n intellettuale (m/f); **~chair** n seggiolone m; **~-flying** a (fig) ambizioso(a); **~-handed** a prepotente; **~-heeled** a a tacchi alti; **~jack = hijack**; **~jump** n (SPORT) salto in alto; **~light** n (fig: of event) momento culminante // vt lumeggiare; **~ly** ad molto; **~ly strung** a teso(a) di nervi, eccitabile; **H~ Mass** n messa cantata or solenne; **~ness** n altezza; **Her H~ness** Sua Altezza; **~-pitched** a acuto(a); **~-rise block** n palazzone m.
high school ['haisku:l] n scuola secondaria; (US) istituto superiore d'istruzione.
high street ['haistri:t] n strada principale.
highway ['haiwei] n strada maestra.
hijack ['haidʒæk] vt dirottare; **~er** n dirottatore/trice.
hike [haik] vi fare un'escursione a piedi // n escursione f a piedi; **~r** n escursionista m/f.
hilarious [hi'lɛəriəs] a (behaviour, event) che fa schiantare dal ridere.
hilarity [hi'læriti] n ilarità.
hill [hil] n collina, colle m; (fairly high) montagna; (on road) salita; **~side** n fianco della collina; **~y** a collinoso(a); montagnoso(a).
hilt [hilt] n (of sword) elsa.
him [him] pronoun (direct) lo, l' + vowel; (indirect) gli; (stressed, after prep) lui; **I see ~** lo vedo; **give ~ a book** gli dia un libro; **after ~** dopo (di) lui; **~self** pronoun (reflexive) si; (emphatic) lui stesso; (after prep) se stesso, sé.
hind [haind] a posteriore // n cerva.
hinder ['hində*] vt ostacolare; (delay) tardare; (prevent): **to ~ sb from doing** impedire a qd di fare; **hindrance** ['hindrəns] n ostacolo, impedimento.
Hindu ['hindu:] n indù m/f inv.
hinge [hindʒ] n cardine m // vi (fig): **to ~ on** dipendere da.
hint [hint] n accenno, allusione f; (advice) consiglio // vt: **to ~ that** lasciar capire che // vi: **to ~ at** accennare a.
hip [hip] n anca, fianco.

hippopotamus [hipə'potəməs] n ippopotamo.
hire ['haiə*] vt (car, equipment) noleggiare; (worker) assumere, dare lavoro a // n nolo, noleggio; **for ~** da nolo; (taxi) libero(a); **~ purchase** (H.P.) n acquisto (or vendita) rateale.
his [hiz] a, pronoun il(la) suo(sua), i(le) suoi(sue).
hiss [his] vi fischiare; (cat, snake) sibilare // n fischio; sibilo.
historian [hi'stɔ:riən] n storico/a.
historic(al) [hi'stɔrik(l)] a storico(a).
history ['histəri] n storia.
hit [hit] vt (pt, pp **hit**) colpire, picchiare; (knock against) battere; (reach: target) raggiungere; (collide with: car) urtare contro; (fig: affect) colpire; (find) incontrare // n colpo; (success, song) successo; **to ~ it off with sb** andare molto d'accordo con qd; **~-and-run driver** n pirata m della strada.
hitch [hitʃ] vt (fasten) attaccare; (also: **~ up**) tirare su // n (difficulty) intoppo, difficoltà f inv; **to ~ a lift** fare l'autostop.
hitch-hike ['hitʃhaik] vi fare l'autostop; **~r** n autostoppista m/f.
hive [haiv] n alveare m.
H.M.S. abbr of His(Her) Majesty's Ship.
hoard [hɔ:d] n (of food) provviste fpl; (of money) gruzzolo // vt ammassare.
hoarding ['hɔ:diŋ] n tabellone m per affissioni.
hoarse [hɔ:s] a rauco(a).
hoax [həuks] n scherzo; falso allarme.
hob [hɔb] n piastra (con fornelli).
hobble ['hɔbl] vi zoppicare.
hobby ['hɔbi] n hobby m inv, passatempo.
hobo ['həubəu] n (US) vagabondo.
hock [hɔk] n vino del Reno.
hockey ['hɔki] n hockey m.
hoe [həu] n zappa.
hog [hɔg] n maiale m // vt (fig) arraffare; **to go the whole ~** farlo fino in fondo.
hoist [hɔist] n paranco // vt issare.
hold [həuld] vb (pt, pp **held** [held]) vt tenere; (contain) contenere; (keep back) trattenere; (believe) mantenere; considerare; (possess) avere, possedere; detenere // vi (withstand pressure) tenere; (be valid) essere valido(a) // n presa; (fig) potere m; (NAUT) stiva; **~ the line!** (TEL) resti in linea!; **to ~ one's own** (fig) difendersi bene; **to catch or get (a) ~ of** afferrare; **to get ~ of** (fig) trovare; **to ~ back** vt trattenere; (secret) tenere celato(a); **to ~ down** vt (person) tenere a terra; (job) tenere; **to ~ off** vt tener lontano; **to ~ on** vi tener fermo; (wait) aspettare; **to ~ on to** vt fus tenersi stretto(a) a; (keep) conservare; **to ~ out** vt offrire // vi (resist) resistere; **to ~ up** vt (raise) alzare; (support) sostenere; (delay) ritardare; **~all** n borsone m; **~er** n (of ticket, title) possessore/posseditrice; (of office etc) incaricato/a; (of record) detentore/trice; **~ing** n (share) azioni fpl, titoli mpl; (farm) podere m, tenuta; **~ing**

company n holding f inv; **~up** n (robbery) rapina a mano armata; (delay) ritardo; (in traffic) blocco.

hole [həul] n buco, buca // vt bucare.

holiday ['hɒlədɪ] n vacanza; (day off) giorno di vacanza; (public) giorno festivo; **~maker** n villeggiante m/f, **~ resort** n luogo di villeggiatura.

holiness ['həulɪnɪs] n santità.

Holland ['hɒlənd] n Olanda.

hollow ['hɒləu] a cavo(a), vuoto(a); (fig) falso(a); vano(a) // n cavità f inv; (in land) valletta, depressione f // vt: **to ~ out** scavare.

holly ['hɒlɪ] n agrifoglio.

holster ['həulstə*] n fondina (di pistola).

holy ['həulɪ] a santo(a); (bread) benedetto(a), consacrato(a); (ground) consacrato(a); **H~ Ghost** or **Spirit** n Spirito Santo; **~ orders** npl ordini mpl (sacri).

homage ['hɒmɪdʒ] n omaggio; **to pay ~ to** rendere omaggio a.

home [həum] n casa; (country) patria; (institution) casa, ricovero // a familiare; (cooking etc) casalingo(a); (ECON, POL) nazionale, interno(a) // ad a casa; in patria; (right in: nail etc) fino in fondo; **at ~ a casa; to go (or come) ~** tornare a casa (or in patria); **make yourself at ~** si metta a suo agio; **~ address** n indirizzo di casa; **~land** n patria; **~less** a senza tetto; spatriato(a); **~ly** a semplice, alla buona; accogliente; **~-made** a casalingo(a); **~ rule** n autogoverno; **H~ Secretary** n (Brit) ministro dell'Interno; **~sick** a: **to be ~sick** avere la nostalgia; **~ town** n città f inv natale; **~ward** ['həumwəd] a (journey) di ritorno; **~work** n compiti mpl (per casa).

homicide ['hɒmɪsaɪd] n (US) omicidio.

homoeopathy [həumɪ'ɒpəθɪ] n omeopatia.

homogeneous [hɒməu'dʒi:nɪəs] a omogeneo(a).

homosexual [hɒməu'sɛksjuəl] a,n omosessuale (m/f).

honest ['ɒnɪst] a onesto(a); **~ly** ad sinceramente; onestamente; sinceramente; **~y** n onestà.

honey ['hʌnɪ] n miele m; **~comb** n favo; **~moon** n luna di miele; (trip) viaggio di nozze.

honk [hɒŋk] n (AUT) colpo di clacson // vi suonare il clacson.

honorary ['ɒnərərɪ] a onorario(a); (duty, title) onorifico(a).

honour ['ɒnə*] vt onorare // n onore m; **~able** a onorevole; **~s degree** n (SCOL) laurea specializzata.

hood [hud] n cappuccio; (Brit: AUT) capote f; (US: AUT) cofano; **~wink** vt infinocchiare.

hoof, **~s** or **hooves** [hu:f, hu:vz] n zoccolo.

hook [huk] n gancio; (for fishing) amo // vt uncinare; (dress) agganciare.

hooligan ['hu:lɪgən] n giovinastro, teppista m.

hoop [hu:p] n cerchio.

hoot [hu:t] vi (AUT) suonare il clacson // n colpo di clacson; **~er** n (AUT) clacson m inv; (NAUT) sirena.

hooves [hu:vz] npl of **hoof**.

hop [hɒp] vi saltellare, saltare; (on one foot) saltare su una gamba // n salto.

hope [həup] vt,vi sperare // n speranza; **I ~ so/not** spero di sì/no; **~ful** a (person) pieno(a) di speranza; (situation) promettente; **~fully** ad con speranza; **~less** a senza speranza, disperato(a); (useless) inutile.

hops [hɒps] npl luppoli mpl.

horde [hɔ:d] n orda.

horizon [hə'raɪzn] n orizzonte m; **~tal** [hɒrɪ'zɒntl] a orizzontale.

hormone ['hɔ:məun] n ormone m.

horn [hɔ:n] n corno; (AUT) clacson m inv; **~ed** a (animal) cornuto(a).

hornet ['hɔ:nɪt] n calabrone m.

horny ['hɔ:nɪ] a corneo(a); (hands) calloso(a).

horoscope ['hɒrəskəup] n oroscopo.

horrible ['hɒrɪbl] a orribile, tremendo(a).

horrid ['hɒrɪd] a orrido(a); (person) antipatico(a).

horrify ['hɒrɪfaɪ] vt scandalizzare.

horror ['hɒrə*] n orrore m; **~ film** n film m inv dell'orrore.

hors d'œuvre [ɔ:'də:vrə] n antipasto.

horse [hɔ:s] n cavallo; **on ~back** a cavallo; **~ chestnut** n ippocastano; **~-drawn** a tirato(a) da cavalli; **~man** n cavaliere m; **~power (h.p.)** n cavallo (vapore); **~-racing** n ippica; **~radish** n barbaforte m; **~shoe** n ferro di cavallo.

horticulture ['hɔ:tɪkʌltʃə*] n orticoltura.

hose [həuz] n (also: **~pipe**) tubo; (also: **garden ~**) tubo per annaffiare.

hosiery ['həuzɪərɪ] n (in shop) (reparto di) calze fpl e calzini mpl.

hospitable [hɒs'pɪtəbl] a ospitale.

hospital ['hɒspɪtl] n ospedale m.

hospitality [hɒspɪ'tælɪtɪ] n ospitalità.

host [həust] n ospite m; (large number): **a ~ of** una schiera di; (REL) ostia.

hostage ['hɒstɪdʒ] n ostaggio/a.

hostel ['hɒstl] n ostello; (youth) **~ n** ostello della gioventù.

hostess ['həustɪs] n ospite f.

hostile ['hɒstaɪl] a ostile.

hostility [hɒ'stɪlɪtɪ] n ostilità.

hot [hɒt] a caldo(a); (as opposed to only warm) molto caldo(a); (spicy) piccante; (fig) accanito(a); ardente; violento(a), focoso(a); **~ dog** n hot dog m inv.

hotel [həu'tɛl] n albergo; **~ier** n albergatore/trice.

hot: ~headed a focoso(a), eccitabile; **~house** n serra; **~ly** ad violentemente; **~plate** n fornello; piastra riscaldante; **~-water bottle** n borsa dell'acqua calda.

hound [haund] vt perseguitare // n segugio.

hour ['auə*] n ora; **~ly** a ogni ora.

house n [haus] (pl: **~s** ['hauzɪz]) (also:

firm) casa; (POL) camera; (THEATRE) sala; pubblico; spettacolo // vt [hauz] (person) ospitare, alloggiare; **the H~ (of Commons)** la Camera dei Comuni; **on the ~** (fig) offerto(a) dalla casa; **~ arrest** n confino (a casa); **~boat** n house boat f inv; **~breaking** n furto con scasso; **~hold** n famiglia; casa; **~keeper** n governante f; **~keeping** n (work) governo della casa; **~warming party** n festa per inaugurare la casa nuova; **~wife** n massaia; **~work** n faccende fpl domestiche.

housing ['hauzɪŋ] n alloggio; **~ estate** n zona residenziale con case popolari e/o private.

hovel ['hɔvl] n casupola.

hover ['hɔvə*] vi librarsi a volo; **to ~ round sb** aggirarsi intorno a qd; **~craft** n hovercraft m inv.

how [hau] ad come; **~ are you?** come sta?; **~ long have you been here?** da quanto tempo sta qui?; **~ lovely!** che bello!; **~ many?** quanti(e)?; **~ much?** quanto(a)?; **~ many people/much milk?** quante persone/quanto latte?; **~ is it that ...?** com'è che ...? + sub; **~ever** ad in qualsiasi modo or maniera che; (+ adjective) per quanto + sub; (in questions) come // cj comunque, però.

howl [haul] n ululato // vi ululare.

howler ['haulə*] n marronata.

h.p., H.P. see hire; horse.

HQ abbr of **headquarters**.

hub [hʌb] n (of wheel) mozzo; (fig) fulcro.

hubbub ['hʌbʌb] n baccano.

huddle ['hʌdl] vi: **to ~ together** rannicchiarsi l'uno contro l'altro.

hue [hju:] n tinta; **~ and cry** n clamore m.

huff [hʌf] n: **in a ~** stizzito(a).

hug [hʌg] vt abbracciare; (shore, kerb) stringere // n abbraccio, stretta.

huge [hju:dʒ] a enorme, immenso(a).

hulk [hʌlk] n carcassa; **~ing** a: **~ing (great)** grosso(a) e goffo(a).

hull [hʌl] n (of ship) scafo.

hullo [hə'ləu] excl = hello.

hum [hʌm] vt (tune) canticchiare // vi canticchiare; (insect, plane, tool) ronzare.

human ['hju:mən] a umano(a) // n essere m umano.

humane [hju:'meɪn] a umanitario(a).

humanity [hju:'mænɪtɪ] n umanità; **the humanities** gli studi umanistici.

humble ['hʌmbl] a umile, modesto(a) // vt umiliare; **humbly** ad umilmente, modestamente.

humbug ['hʌmbʌg] n inganno; sciocchezze fpl.

humdrum ['hʌmdrʌm] a monotono(a), tedioso(a).

humid ['hju:mɪd] a umido(a); **~ity** [-'mɪdɪtɪ] n umidità.

humiliate [hju:'mɪlɪeɪt] vt umiliare; **humiliation** [-'eɪʃən] n umiliazione f.

humility [hju:'mɪlɪtɪ] n umiltà.

humorist ['hju:mərɪst] n umorista m/f.

humorous ['hju:mərəs] a umoristico(a); (person) buffo(a).

humour ['hju:mə*] n umore m // vt (person) compiacere; (sb's whims) assecondare.

hump [hʌmp] n gobba; **~back** n schiena d'asino.

hunch [hʌntʃ] n gobba; (premonition) intuizione f; **~back** n gobbo/a; **~ed** a incurvato(a).

hundred ['hʌndrəd] num cento; **~weight** n (Brit) = 50.8 kg; 112 lb; (US) = 45.3 kg; 100 lb.

hung [hʌŋ] pt, pp of hang.

Hungarian [hʌŋ'gɛərɪən] a ungherese // n ungherese m/f; (LING) ungherese m.

Hungary ['hʌŋgərɪ] n Ungheria.

hunger ['hʌŋgə*] n fame f // vi: **to ~ for** desiderare ardentemente.

hungrily ['hʌŋgrəlɪ] ad voracemente; (fig) avidamente.

hungry ['hʌŋgrɪ] a affamato(a); **to be ~** aver fame.

hunt [hʌnt] vt (seek) cercare; (SPORT) cacciare // vi andare a caccia // n caccia; **~er** n cacciatore m; **~ing** n caccia.

hurdle ['hə:dl] n (SPORT, fig) ostacolo.

hurl [hə:l] vt lanciare con violenza.

hurrah, hurray [hu'rɑ:, hu'reɪ] excl urra!, evviva!

hurricane ['hʌrɪkən] n uragano.

hurried ['hʌrɪd] a affrettato(a); (work) fatto(a) in fretta; **~ly** ad in fretta.

hurry ['hʌrɪ] n fretta // vi affrettarsi // vt (person) affrettare; (work) far in fretta; **to be in a ~** aver fretta; **to do sth in a ~** fare qc in fretta; **to ~ in/out** entrare/uscire in fretta.

hurt [hə:t] vb (pt, pp hurt) vt (cause pain to) far male a; (injure, fig) ferire // vi far male // a ferito(a); **~ful** a (remark) che ferisce.

hurtle ['hə:tl] vt scagliare // vi: **to ~ past/down** passare/scendere a razzo.

husband ['hʌzbənd] n marito.

hush [hʌʃ] n silenzio, calma // vt zittire; **~!** zitto(a)!

husk [hʌsk] n (of wheat) cartoccio; (of rice, maize) buccia.

husky ['hʌskɪ] a roco(a) // n cane m esquimese.

hustle ['hʌsl] vt spingere, incalzare // n pigia pigia m inv; **~ and bustle** n trambusto.

hut [hʌt] n rifugio; (shed) ripostiglio.

hutch [hʌtʃ] n gabbia.

hyacinth ['haɪəsɪnθ] n giacinto.

hybrid ['haɪbrɪd] a ibrido(a) // n ibrido.

hydrant ['haɪdrənt] n idrante m.

hydraulic [haɪ'drɔ:lɪk] a idraulico(a).

hydroelectric [haɪdrəu'lektrɪk] a idroelettrico(a).

hydrogen ['haɪdrədʒən] n idrogeno.

hyena [haɪ'i:nə] n iena.

hygiene ['haɪdʒi:n] n igiene f.

hygienic [haɪ'dʒi:nɪk] a igienico(a).

hymn [hɪm] n inno; cantica.

hyphen ['haɪfn] n trattino.
hypnosis [hɪp'nəʊsɪs] n ipnosi f.
hypnotism ['hɪpnətɪzm] n ipnotismo.
hypnotist ['hɪpnətɪst] n ipnotiz-zatore/trice.
hypnotize ['hɪpnətaɪz] vt ipnotizzare.
hypocrisy [hɪ'pɒkrɪsɪ] n ipocrisia.
hypocrite ['hɪpəkrɪt] n ipocrita m/f; **hypocritical** [-'krɪtɪkl] a ipocrita.
hypothesis, pl **hypotheses** [haɪ'pɒθɪsɪs, -siːz] n ipotesi f inv.
hypothetical   [haɪpəʊ'θetɪkl]   a ipotetico(a).
hysteria [hɪ'stɪərɪə] n isteria.
hysterical [hɪ'sterɪkl] a isterico(a).
hysterics [hɪ'sterɪks] npl accesso di isteria; (laughter) attacco di riso.

I

I [aɪ] pronoun io.
ice [aɪs] n ghiaccio; (on road) gelo // vt (cake) glassare; (drink) mettere in fresco // vi (also: ~ **over**) ghiacciare; (also: ~ **up**) gelare; ~ **axe** n picozza da ghiaccio; **~berg** n iceberg m inv; **~box** n (us) frigorifero; (Brit) reparto ghiaccio; (insulated box) frigo portatile; **~-cold** a gelato(a); **~ cream** n gelato; **~ hockey** n hockey m su ghiaccio.
Iceland ['aɪslənd] n Islanda; **~er** n islandese m/f; **~ic** [-'lændɪk] a islandese // n (LING) islandese m.
ice rink ['aɪsrɪŋk] n pista di pattinaggio.
icicle ['aɪsɪkl] n ghiacciolo.
icing ['aɪsɪŋ] n (AVIAT etc) patina di ghiaccio; (CULIN) glassa; ~ **sugar** n zucchero a velo.
icon ['aɪkɒn] n icona.
icy ['aɪsɪ] a ghiacciato(a); (weather, temperature) gelido(a).
I'd [aɪd] = **I would, I had.**
idea [aɪ'dɪə] n idea.
ideal [aɪ'dɪəl] a, n ideale (m); **~ist** n idealista m/f.
identical [aɪ'dentɪkl] a identico(a).
identification   [aɪdentɪfɪ'keɪʃən]   n identificazione f; **means of** ~ carta d'identità.
identify [aɪ'dentɪfaɪ] vt identificare.
identity [aɪ'dentɪtɪ] n identità f inv.
ideology [aɪdɪ'ɒlədʒɪ] n ideologia.
idiocy ['ɪdɪəsɪ] n idiozia.
idiom ['ɪdɪəm] n idioma m; (phrase) espressione f idiomatica.
idiosyncrasy   [ɪdɪəʊ'sɪŋkrəsɪ]   n idiosincrasia.
idiot ['ɪdɪət] n idiota m/f; **~ic** [-'ɒtɪk] a idiota.
idle ['aɪdl] a inattivo(a); (lazy) pigro(a), ozioso(a); (unemployed) disoccupato(a); (question, pleasures) inutile, ozioso(a); **to lie** ~ stare fermo, non funzionare; **~ness** n ozio; pigrizia; **~r** n ozioso/a; fannullone/a.
idol ['aɪdl] n idolo; **~ize** vt idoleggiare.
idyllic [ɪ'dɪlɪk] a idillico(a).

i.e. ad (abbr of id est) cioè.
if [ɪf] cj se.
igloo ['ɪgluː] n igloo m inv.
ignite [ɪg'naɪt] vt accendere // vi accendersi.
ignition [ɪg'nɪʃən] n (AUT) accensione f; **to switch on/off the** ~ accen-dere/spegnere il motore; ~ **key** n (AUT) chiave f dell'accensione.
ignorance ['ɪgnərəns] n ignoranza.
ignorant ['ɪgnərənt] a ignorante.
ignore [ɪg'nɔ:*] vt non tener conto di; (person, fact) ignorare.
I'll [aɪl] = **I will, I shall.**
ill [ɪl] a (sick) malato(a); (bad) cattivo(a) // n male m; **to take** or **be taken** ~ ammalarsi; **~-advised** a (decision) poco giudizioso(a); (person) mal consigliato(a); **~-at-ease** a a disagio.
illegal [ɪ'li:gl] a illegale.
illegible [ɪ'ledʒɪbl] a illeggibile.
illegitimate [ɪlɪ'dʒɪtɪmət] a illegittimo(a).
ill-fated [ɪl'feɪtɪd] a nefasto(a).
ill feeling [ɪl'fi:lɪŋ] n rancore m.
illicit [ɪ'lɪsɪt] a illecito(a).
illiterate [ɪ'lɪtərət] a illetterato(a); (letter) scorretto(a).
ill-mannered   [ɪl'mænəd]   a maleducato(a), sgarbato(a).
illness ['ɪlnɪs] n malattia.
illogical [ɪ'lɒdʒɪkl] a illogico(a).
ill-treat [ɪl'tri:t] vt maltrattare.
illuminate [ɪ'lu:mɪneɪt] vt illuminare; **illumination** [-'neɪʃən] n illuminazione f.
illusion [ɪ'lu:ʒən] n illusione f.
illusive, illusory [ɪ'lu:sɪv, ɪ'lu:sərɪ] a illusorio(a).
illustrate ['ɪləstreɪt] vt illustrare; **illustration** [-'streɪʃən] n illustrazione f.
illustrious [ɪ'lʌstrɪəs] a illustre.
ill will [ɪl'wɪl] n cattiva volontà.
I'm [aɪm] = **I am.**
image ['ɪmɪdʒ] n immagine f; (public face) immagine (pubblica); **~ry** n immagini fpl.
imaginary   [ɪ'mædʒɪnərɪ]   a immaginario(a).
imagination   [ɪmædʒɪ'neɪʃən]   n immaginazione f, fantasia.
imaginative   [ɪ'mædʒɪnətɪv]   a immaginoso(a).
imagine [ɪ'mædʒɪn] vt immaginare.
imbalance [ɪm'bæləns] n sbilancio.
imbecile ['ɪmbəsi:l] n imbecille m/f.
imitate ['ɪmɪteɪt] vt imitare; **imitation** [-'teɪʃən] n imitazione f; **imitator** n imitatore/trice.
immaculate   [ɪ'mækjulət]   a immacolato(a); (dress, appearance) impeccabile.
immaterial [ɪmə'tɪərɪəl] a immateriale, indifferente.
immature [ɪmə'tjuə*] a immaturo(a).
immediate [ɪ'mi:dɪət] a immediato(a); **~ly** ad (at once) subito, immediatamente; **~ly next to** proprio accanto a.
immense [ɪ'mens] a immenso(a); enorme.
immerse [ɪ'mə:s] vt immergere.

immersion heater [ı'mə:ʃnhi:tə*] n riscaldatore m a immersione.

immigrant ['ımıgrənt] n immigrante m/f; immigrato/a.

immigration [ımı'greıʃən] n immigrazione f.

imminent ['ımınənt] a imminente.

immobilize [ı'məubılaız] vt immobilizzare.

immoral [ı'mɔrl] a immorale; ~ity [-'rælıtı] n immoralità.

immortal [ı'mɔːtl] a, n immortale (m/f); ~ize vt rendere immortale.

immune [ı'mju:n] a: ~ (to) immune (da).

immunize ['ımjunaız] vt immunizzare.

impact ['ımpækt] n impatto.

impair [ım'peə*] vt danneggiare.

impale [ım'peıl] vt impalare.

impartial [ım'pɑːʃl] a imparziale; ~ity [ımpɑːʃı'ælıtı] n imparzialità.

impassable [ım'pɑːsəbl] a insuperabile; (road) impraticabile.

impatience [ım'peıʃəns] n impazienza.

impatient [ım'peıʃənt] a impaziente.

impeach [ım'piːtʃ] vt accusare, attaccare; (public official) incriminare.

impeccable [ım'pekəbl] a impeccabile.

impede [ım'piːd] vt impedire.

impediment [ım'pedımənt] n impedimento; (also: **speech** ~) difetto di pronuncia.

impending [ım'pendıŋ] a imminente.

imperative [ım'perətıv] a imperativo(a); necessario(a), urgente; (voice) imperioso(a) // n (LING) imperativo.

imperceptible [ımpə'septıbl] a impercettibile.

imperfect [ım'pəːfıkt] a imperfetto(a); (goods etc) difettoso(a) // n (LING: also: ~ **tense**) imperfetto; ~ion [-'fekʃən] n imperfezione f.

imperial [ım'pıərıəl] a imperiale; (measure) legale.

impersonal [ım'pəːsənl] a impersonale.

impersonate [ım'pəːsəneıt] vt impersonare; (THEATRE) fare la mimica di; **impersonation** [-'neıʃən] n (LAW) usurpazione f d'identità; (THEATRE) mimica.

impertinent [ım'pəːtınənt] a insolente, impertinente.

impervious [ım'pəːvıəs] a impermeabile; (fig): ~ **to** insensibile a; impassibile di fronte a.

impetuous [ım'petjuəs] a impetuoso(a), precipitoso(a).

impetus ['ımpətəs] n impeto.

impinge [ım'pındʒ]: **to** ~ **on** vt fus (person) colpire; (rights) ledere.

implausible [ım'plɔːzıbl] a non plausibile.

implement n ['ımplımənt] attrezzo; (for cooking) utensile m // vt ['ımplımənt] effettuare.

implicate ['ımplıkeıt] vt implicare; **implication** [-'keıʃən] n implicazione f.

implicit [ım'plısıt] a implicito(a); (complete) completo(a).

implore [ım'plɔː*] vt implorare.

imply [ım'plaı] vt insinuare; suggerire.

impolite [ımpə'laıt] a scortese.

imponderable [ım'pɔndərəbl] a imponderabile.

import vt [ım'pɔːt] importare // n ['ımpɔːt] (COMM) importazione f; (meaning) significato, senso.

importance [ım'pɔːtns] n importanza.

important [ım'pɔːtnt] a importante.

imported [ım'pɔːtıd] a importato(a).

importer [ım'pɔːtə*] n importatore/trice.

impose [ım'pəuz] vt imporre // vi: **to** ~ **on sb** sfruttare la bontà di qd.

imposing [ım'pəuzıŋ] a imponente.

impossibility [ımpɔsə'bılıtı] n impossibilità.

impossible [ım'pɔsıbl] a impossibile.

impostor [ım'pɔstə*] n impostore/a.

impotence ['ımpətns] n impotenza.

impotent ['ımpətnt] a impotente.

impound [ım'paund] vt confiscare.

impoverished [ım'pɔvərıʃt] a impoverito(a).

impracticable [ım'præktıkəbl] a impraticabile.

impractical [ım'præktıkl] a non pratico(a).

imprecise [ımprı'saıs] a impreciso(a).

impregnable [ım'pregnəbl] a (fortress) inespugnabile; (fig) inoppugnabile; irrefutabile.

impregnate ['ımpregneıt] vt impregnare; (fertilize) fecondare.

impresario [ımprı'sɑːrıəu] n impresario/a.

impress [ım'pres] vt impressionare; (mark) imprimere, stampare; **to** ~ **sth on sb** far capire qc a qd.

impression [ım'preʃən] n impressione f; **to be under the** ~ **that** avere l'impressione che; ~**able** a impressionabile; ~**ist** n impressionista m/f.

impressive [ım'presıv] a impressionante.

imprison [ım'prızn] vt imprigionare; ~**ment** n imprigionamento.

improbable [ım'prɔbəbl] a improbabile; (excuse) inverosimile.

impromptu [ım'prɔmptjuː] a improvvisato(a).

improper [ım'prɔpə*] a scorretto(a); (unsuitable) inadatto(a), improprio(a); sconveniente, indecente; **impropriety** [ımprə'praıətı] n sconvenienza; (of expression) improprietà.

improve [ım'pruːv] vt migliorare // vi migliorare; (pupil etc) fare progressi; ~**ment** n miglioramento; progresso.

improvisation [ımprəvaı'zeıʃən] n improvvisazione f.

improvise ['ımprəvaız] vt,vi improvvisare.

impudent ['ımpjudnt] a impudente, sfacciato(a).

impulse ['ımpʌls] n impulso.

impulsive [ım'pʌlsıv] a impulsivo(a).

impunity [ɪm'pjuːnɪtɪ] n impunità.

impure [ɪm'pjuə*] a impuro(a).

impurity [ɪm'pjuərɪtɪ] n impurità f inv.

in [ɪn] prep in; (with time: during, within): ~ **May/2 days** in maggio/2 giorni; (: after): ~ **2 weeks** entro 2 settimane; (with town) a; (with country): **it's** ~ **France** è in Francia // a entro, dentro; (fashionable) alla moda; **is he** ~? lui c'è?; ~ **town/the country** in città/campagna; ~ **the sun** al sole; ~ **the rain** sotto la pioggia; ~ **French** in francese; **a man** ~ **10** un uomo su 10; ~ **hundreds** a centinaia; **the best pupil** ~ **the class** il migliore alunno della classe; ~ **saying this** nel dire questo; **their party is** ~ il loro partito è al potere; **to run/limp** etc ~ entrare correndo/zoppicando; **the** ~**s and outs of** i dettagli di.

in., ins abbr of **inch(es)**.

inability [ɪnə'bɪlɪtɪ] n inabilità, incapacità.

inaccessible [ɪnək'sɛsɪbl] a inaccessibile.

inaccuracy [ɪn'ækjurəsɪ] n inaccuratezza; imprecisione f.

inaccurate [ɪn'ækjurət] a inesatto(a), impreciso(a).

inactivity [ɪnæk'tɪvɪtɪ] n inattività.

inadequacy [ɪn'ædɪkwəsɪ] n insufficienza.

inadequate [ɪn'ædɪkwət] a insufficiente.

inadvertently [ɪnəd'vɜːtntlɪ] ad senza volerlo.

inadvisable [ɪnəd'vaɪzəbl] a sconsigliabile.

inane [ɪ'neɪn] a vacuo(a), stupido(a).

inanimate [ɪn'ænɪmət] a inanimato(a).

inappropriate [ɪnə'prəuprɪət] a disadatto(a); (word, expression) improprio(a).

inapt [ɪn'æpt] a maldestro(a); fuori luogo; ~**itude** n improprietà.

inarticulate [ɪnɑː'tɪkjulət] a (person) che si esprime male; (speech) inarticolato(a).

inasmuch as [ɪnəz'mʌtʃæz] ad in quanto che; (seeing that) poiché.

inattention [ɪnə'tɛnʃən] n mancanza di attenzione.

inattentive [ɪnə'tɛntɪv] a disattento(a), distratto(a); negligente.

inaudible [ɪn'ɔːdɪbl] a impercettibile.

inaugural [ɪ'nɔːgjurəl] a inaugurale.

inaugurate [ɪ'nɔːgjureɪt] vt inaugurare; (president, official) insediare; **inauguration** [-'reɪʃən] n inaugurazione f; insediamento in carica.

in-between [ɪnbɪ'twiːn] a fra i (or le) due.

inborn [ɪn'bɔːn] a (feeling) innato(a); (defect) congenito(a).

inbred [ɪn'brɛd] a innato(a); (family) connaturato(a).

inbreeding [ɪn'briːdɪŋ] n incrocio ripetuto di animali consanguinei; unioni fpl fra consanguinei.

Inc. abbr see **incorporated**.

incapability [ɪnkeɪpə'bɪlɪtɪ] n incapacità.

incapable [ɪn'keɪpəbl] a incapace.

incapacitate [ɪnkə'pæsɪteɪt] vt: **to** ~ **sb from doing** rendere qd incapace di fare.

incarnate [ɪn'kɑːnɪt] a incarnato(a); **incarnation** [-'neɪʃən] n incarnazione f.

incendiary [ɪn'sɛndɪərɪ] a incendiario(a).

incense n ['ɪnsɛns] incenso // vt [ɪn'sɛns] (anger) infuriare.

incentive [ɪn'sɛntɪv] n incentivo.

incessant [ɪn'sɛsnt] a incessante; ~**ly** ad di continuo, senza sosta.

incest ['ɪnsɛst] n incesto.

inch [ɪntʃ] n pollice m (= 25 mm; 12 in a foot); **within an** ~ **of** a un pelo da.

incidence ['ɪnsɪdns] n (of crime, disease) incidenza.

incident ['ɪnsɪdnt] n incidente m; (in book) episodio.

incidental [ɪnsɪ'dɛntl] a accessorio(a), d'accompagnamento; (unplanned) incidentale; ~ **to** marginale a; ~ **expenses** npl spese fpl accessorie; ~**ly** [-'dɛntlɪ] ad (by the way) a proposito.

incinerator [ɪn'sɪnəreɪtə*] n inceneritore m.

incipient [ɪn'sɪpɪənt] a incipiente.

incision [ɪn'sɪʒən] n incisione f.

incisive [ɪn'saɪsɪv] a incisivo(a); tagliente; acuto(a).

incite [ɪn'saɪt] vt incitare.

inclination [ɪnklɪ'neɪʃən] n inclinazione f.

incline n ['ɪnklaɪn] pendenza, pendio // vb [ɪn'klaɪn] vt inclinare // vi: **to** ~ **to** tendere a; **to be** ~**d to do** tendere a fare; essere propenso(a) a fare; **to be well** ~**d towards sb** essere ben disposto(a) verso qd.

include [ɪn'kluːd] vt includere, comprendere; **including** prep compreso(a), incluso(a).

inclusion [ɪn'kluːʒən] n inclusione f.

inclusive [ɪn'kluːsɪv] a incluso(a), compreso(a).

incognito [ɪnkɒg'niːtəu] ad in incognito.

incoherent [ɪnkəu'hɪərənt] a incoerente.

income ['ɪŋkʌm] n reddito; ~ **tax** n imposta sul reddito; ~ **tax return** n dichiarazione f annuale dei redditi.

incoming ['ɪnkʌmɪŋ] a: ~ **tide** n marea montante.

incompatible [ɪnkəm'pætɪbl] a incompatibile.

incompetence [ɪn'kɒmpɪtns] n incompetenza, incapacità.

incompetent [ɪn'kɒmpɪtnt] a incompetente, incapace.

incomplete [ɪnkəm'pliːt] a incompleto(a).

incomprehensible [ɪnkɒmprɪ'hɛnsɪbl] a incomprensibile.

inconclusive [ɪnkən'kluːsɪv] a improduttivo(a); (argument) poco convincente.

incongruous [ɪn'kɒŋgruəs] a poco appropriato(a); (remark, act) incongruo(a).

inconsequential [ɪnkɒnsɪ'kwɛnʃl] a senza importanza.

inconsiderate [ɪnkən'sɪdərət] a sconsiderato(a).

inconsistent [ɪnkən'sɪstnt] a incoerente;

poco logico(a); contraddittorio(a).

inconspicuous [ɪnkən'spɪkjuəs] a incospicuo(a); (colour) poco appariscente; (dress) dimesso(a).

inconstant [ɪn'kɒnstnt] a incostante; mutevole.

incontinent [ɪn'kɒntɪnənt] a incontinente.

inconvenience [ɪnkən'viːnjəns] n inconveniente m; (trouble) disturbo // vt disturbare.

inconvenient [ɪnkən'viːnjənt] a scomodo(a).

incorporate [ɪn'kɔːpəreɪt] vt incorporare; (contain) contenere; ~d a: ~d company (US, abbr Inc.) società f inv anonima (S.A.).

incorrect [ɪnkə'rekt] a scorretto(a); (opinion, statement) impreciso(a).

incorruptible [ɪnkə'rʌptɪbl] a incorruttibile.

increase n ['ɪnkriːs] aumento // vi [ɪn-'kriːs] aumentare.

increasing [ɪn'kriːsɪŋ] a (number) crescente; ~ly ad sempre più.

incredible [ɪn'kredɪbl] a incredibile.

incredulous [ɪn'kredjuləs] a incredulo(a).

increment ['ɪnkrɪmənt] n aumento, incremento.

incriminate [ɪn'krɪmɪneɪt] vt compromettere.

incubation [ɪnkju'beɪʃən] n incubazione f.

incubator ['ɪnkjubeɪtə*] n incubatrice f.

incur [ɪn'kɔː*] vt (expenses) incorrere; (anger, risk) esporsi a; (debt) contrarre; (loss) subire.

incurable [ɪn'kjuərəbl] a incurabile.

incursion [ɪn'kɜːʃən] n incursione f.

indebted [ɪn'detɪd] a: to be ~ to sb (for) essere obbligato(a) verso qd (per).

indecent [ɪn'diːsnt] a indecente.

indecision [ɪndɪ'sɪʒən] n indecisione f.

indecisive [ɪndɪ'saɪsɪv] a indeciso(a); (discussion) non decisivo(a).

indeed [ɪn'diːd] ad infatti; veramente; yes ~! certamente!

indefinable [ɪndɪ'faɪnəbl] a indefinibile.

indefinite [ɪn'defɪnɪt] a indefinito(a); (answer) vago(a); (period, number) indeterminato(a); ~ly ad (wait) indefinitamente.

indelible [ɪn'delɪbl] a indelebile.

indemnify [ɪn'demnɪfaɪ] vt indennizzare.

indentation [ɪnden'teɪʃən] n intaccatura.

independence [ɪndɪ'pendns] n indipendenza.

independent [ɪndɪ'pendnt] a indipendente.

indescribable [ɪndɪ'skraɪbəbl] a indescrivibile.

index ['ɪndeks] n (pl: ~es: in book) indice m; (: in library etc) catalogo; (pl: indices ['ɪndɪsiːz]: ratio, sign) indice m; ~ card n scheda; ~ finger n (dito) indice m; ~-linked a legato(a) al costo della vita.

India ['ɪndɪə] n India; ~n a, n indiano(a); ~n ink n inchiostro di china; ~n Ocean n Oceano Indiano.

indicate ['ɪndɪkeɪt] vt indicare;

indication [-'keɪʃən] n indicazione f, segno.

indicative [ɪn'dɪkətɪv] a indicativo(a) // n (LING) indicativo.

indicator ['ɪndɪkeɪtə*] n indicatore m.

indices ['ɪndɪsiːz] npl of index.

indict [ɪn'daɪt] vt accusare; ~able a passibile di pena; ~ment n accusa.

indifference [ɪn'dɪfrəns] n indifferenza.

indifferent [ɪn'dɪfrənt] a indifferente; (poor) mediocre.

indigenous [ɪn'dɪdʒɪnəs] a indigeno(a).

indigestible [ɪndɪ'dʒestɪbl] a indigeribile.

indigestion [ɪndɪ'dʒestʃən] n indigestione f.

indignant [ɪn'dɪgnənt] a: ~ (at sth/with sb) indignato(a) (per qc/contro qd).

indignation [ɪndɪg'neɪʃən] n indignazione f.

indignity [ɪn'dɪgnɪtɪ] n affronto.

indirect [ɪndɪ'rekt] a indiretto(a).

indiscreet [ɪndɪ'skriːt] a indiscreto(a); (rash) imprudente.

indiscretion [ɪndɪ'skreʃən] n indiscrezione f; imprudenza.

indiscriminate [ɪndɪ'skrɪmɪnət] a (person) che non sa discernere; (admiration) cieco(a); (killings) indiscriminato(a).

indispensable [ɪndɪ'spensəbl] a indispensabile.

indisposed [ɪndɪ'spəuzd] a (unwell) indisposto(a).

indisputable [ɪndɪ'spjuːtəbl] a incontestabile, indiscutibile.

indistinct [ɪndɪ'stɪŋkt] a indistinto(a); (memory, noise) vago(a).

individual [ɪndɪ'vɪdjuəl] n individuo // a individuale; (characteristic) particolare, originale; ~ist n individualista m/f; ~ity [-'ælɪtɪ] n individualità.

indoctrinate [ɪn'dɒktrɪneɪt] vt indottrinare; **indoctrination** [-'neɪʃən] n indottrinamento.

indolent ['ɪndələnt] a indolente.

indoor ['ɪndɔː*] a da interno; (plant) d'appartamento; (swimming-pool) coperto(a); (sport, games) fatto(a) al coperto; ~s [ɪn'dɔːz] ad all'interno; (at home) in casa.

indubitable [ɪn'djuːbɪtəbl] a indubitabile.

induce [ɪn'djuːs] vt persuadere; (bring about) provocare; ~ment n incitamento; (incentive) stimolo, incentivo.

induction [ɪn'dʌkʃən] n (MED: of birth) parto indotto; ~ course n corso di avviamento.

indulge [ɪn'dʌldʒ] vt (whim) compiacere, soddisfare; (child) viziare // vi: to ~ in sth concedersi qc; abbandonarsi a qc; ~nce n lusso (che uno si permette); (leniency) indulgenza; ~nt a indulgente.

industrial [ɪn'dʌstrɪəl] a industriale; (injury) sul lavoro; (dispute) di lavoro; ~ action n azione f rivendicativa; ~ estate n zona industriale; ~ist n industriale m; ~ize vt industrializzare.

industrious [ɪn'dʌstrɪəs] a industrioso(a), assiduo(a).

industry ['ɪndəstrɪ] n industria; (diligence) operosità.

inebriated [ɪ'niːbrɪeɪtɪd] a ubriaco(a).

inedible [ɪn'edɪbl] a immangiabile.

ineffective [ɪnɪ'fektɪv] a inefficace.

ineffectual [ɪnɪ'fektʃuəl] a inefficace; incompetente.

inefficiency [ɪnɪ'fɪʃənsɪ] n inefficienza.

inefficient [ɪnɪ'fɪʃənt] a inefficiente.

ineligible [ɪn'elɪdʒɪbl] a (candidate) ineleggibile; **to be ~ for** sth non avere il diritto a qc.

inept [ɪ'nept] a inetto(a).

inequality [ɪnɪ'kwɒlɪtɪ] n ineguaglianza.

inert [ɪ'nɜːt] a inerte.

inertia [ɪ'nɜːʃə] n inerzia.

inescapable [ɪnɪ'skeɪpəbl] a inevitabile.

inestimable [ɪn'estɪməbl] a inestimabile, incalcolabile.

inevitable [ɪn'evɪtəbl] a inevitabile.

inexact [ɪnɪg'zækt] a inesatto(a).

inexhaustible [ɪnɪg'zɔːstɪbl] a inesauribile; (person) instancabile.

inexorable [ɪn'eksərəbl] a inesorabile.

inexpensive [ɪnɪk'spensɪv] a poco costoso(a).

inexperience [ɪnɪk'spɪərɪəns] n inesperienza; **~d** a inesperto(a), senza esperienza.

inexplicable [ɪnɪk'splɪkəbl] a inesplicabile.

inextricable [ɪnɪk'strɪkəbl] a inestricabile.

infallibility [ɪnfælə'bɪlɪtɪ] n infallibilità.

infallible [ɪn'fælɪbl] a infallibile.

infamous ['ɪnfəməs] a infame.

infamy ['ɪnfəmɪ] n infamia.

infancy ['ɪnfənsɪ] n infanzia.

infant ['ɪnfənt] n (baby) infante m/f; (young child) bambino/a; **~ile** a infantile; **~ school** n scuola elementare (per bambini dall'età di 5 a 7 anni).

infantry ['ɪnfəntrɪ] n fanteria; **~man** n fante m.

infatuated [ɪn'fætjueɪtɪd] a: **~ with** infatuato(a) di.

infatuation [ɪnfætju'eɪʃən] n infatuazione f.

infect [ɪn'fekt] vt infettare; **~ed with** (illness) affetto(a) da; **~ion** [ɪn'fekʃən] n infezione f; contagio; **~ious** [ɪn'fekʃəs] a infettivo(a); (also: fig) contagioso(a).

infer [ɪn'fɜː*] vt inferire, dedurre; **~ence** ['ɪnfərəns] n deduzione f, conclusione f.

inferior [ɪn'fɪərɪə*] a inferiore; (goods) di qualità scadente // n inferiore m/f; (in rank) subalterno/a; **~ity** [ɪnfɪərɪ'ɔrɪtɪ] n inferiorità; **~ity complex** n complesso di inferiorità.

infernal [ɪn'fɜːnl] a infernale.

inferno [ɪn'fɜːnəu] n inferno.

infertile [ɪn'fɜːtaɪl] a sterile; **infertility** [-'tɪlɪtɪ] n sterilità.

infested [ɪn'festɪd] a: **~ (with)** infestato(a) (di).

infidelity [ɪnfɪ'delɪtɪ] n infedeltà.

in-fighting ['ɪnfaɪtɪŋ] n lotte fpl intestine.

infiltrate ['ɪnfɪltreɪt] vt (troops etc) far penetrare; (enemy line etc) infiltrare // vi infiltrarsi.

infinite ['ɪnfɪnɪt] a infinito(a).

infinitive [ɪn'fɪnɪtɪv] n infinito.

infinity [ɪn'fɪnɪtɪ] n infinità; (also MATH) infinito.

infirmary [ɪn'fɜːmərɪ] n ospedale m; (in school, factory) infermeria.

infirmity [ɪn'fɜːmɪtɪ] n infermità f inv.

inflame [ɪn'fleɪm] vt infiammare.

inflammable [ɪn'flæməbl] a infiammabile.

inflammation [ɪnflə'meɪʃən] n infiammazione f.

inflate [ɪn'fleɪt] vt (tyre, balloon) gonfiare; (fig) esagerare; gonfiare; **to ~ the currency** far ricorso all'inflazione; **~d** a (style) gonfio(a); (value) esagerato(a); **inflation** [ɪn'fleɪʃən] n (ECON) inflazione f.

inflexible [ɪn'fleksɪbl] a inflessibile, rigido(a).

inflict [ɪn'flɪkt] vt: **to ~ on** infliggere a; **~ion** [ɪn'flɪkʃən] n infliggere m; inflizione f; afflizione f.

inflow ['ɪnfləu] n afflusso.

influence ['ɪnfluəns] n influenza // vt influenzare; **under the ~ of** sotto l'influenza di.

influential [ɪnflu'enʃl] a influente.

influenza [ɪnflu'enzə] n (MED) influenza.

influx ['ɪnflʌks] n afflusso.

inform [ɪn'fɔːm] vt: **to ~ sb (of)** informare qd (di); **to ~ sb about** mettere qd al corrente di.

informal [ɪn'fɔːml] a (person, manner) alla buona, semplice; (visit, discussion) informale; (announcement, invitation) non ufficiale; **'dress ~'** 'non è richiesto l'abito scuro'; **~ity** [-'mælɪtɪ] n semplicità, informalità; carattere m non ufficiale.

information [ɪnfə'meɪʃən] n informazioni fpl; notizie fpl; (knowledge) particolari mpl; **a piece of ~** un'informazione.

informative [ɪn'fɔːmətɪv] a istruttivo(a).

informer [ɪn'fɔːmə*] n informatore/trice.

infra-red [ɪnfrə'red] a infrarosso(a).

infrequent [ɪn'friːkwənt] a infrequente, raro(a).

infringe [ɪn'frɪndʒ] vt infrangere // vi: **to ~ on** calpestare; **~ment** n: **~ment (of)** infrazione f (di).

infuriating [ɪn'fjuərɪeɪtɪŋ] a molto irritante.

ingenious [ɪn'dʒiːnjəs] a ingegnoso(a).

ingenuity [ɪndʒɪ'njuːɪtɪ] n ingegnosità.

ingot ['ɪŋgət] n lingotto.

ingrained [ɪn'greɪnd] a radicato(a).

ingratiate [ɪn'greɪʃɪeɪt] vt: **to ~ o.s.** with ingraziarsi.

ingratitude [ɪn'grætɪtjuːd] n ingratitudine f.

ingredient [ɪn'griːdɪənt] n ingrediente m; elemento.

inhabit [ɪn'hæbɪt] vt abitare.

inhabitant [ɪnˈhæbɪtnt] n abitante m/f.
inhale [ɪnˈheɪl] vt inalare // vi (in smoking) aspirare.
inherent [ɪnˈhɪərənt] a: ~ (in or to) inerente (a).
inherit [ɪnˈhɛrɪt] vt ereditare; ~ance n eredità.
inhibit [ɪnˈhɪbɪt] vt (PSYCH) inibire; to ~ sb from doing impedire a qd di fare; ~ion [-ˈbɪʃən] n inibizione f.
inhospitable [ɪnhɔsˈpɪtəbl] a inospitale.
inhuman [ɪnˈhjuːmən] a inumano(a).
inimitable [ɪˈnɪmɪtəbl] a inimitabile.
iniquity [ɪˈnɪkwɪtɪ] n iniquità f inv.
initial [ɪˈnɪʃl] a iniziale // n iniziale f // vt siglare; ~s npl iniziali fpl; (as signature) sigla; ~ly ad inizialmente, all'inizio.
initiate [ɪˈnɪʃɪeɪt] vt (start) avviare; intraprendere; iniziare; (person) iniziare; **initiation** [-ˈeɪʃən] n (into secret etc) iniziazione f.
initiative [ɪˈnɪʃɪətɪv] n iniziativa.
inject [ɪnˈdʒɛkt] vt (liquid) iniettare; (person) fare una puntura a; ~ion [ɪnˈdʒɛkʃən] n iniezione f, puntura.
injure [ˈɪndʒə*] vt ferire; (wrong) fare male o torto a; (damage: reputation etc) nuocere a.
injury [ˈɪndʒərɪ] n ferita; (wrong) torto; ~ time n (SPORT) tempo di ricupero.
injustice [ɪnˈdʒʌstɪs] n ingiustizia.
ink [ɪŋk] n inchiostro.
inkling [ˈɪŋklɪŋ] n sentore m, vaga idea.
inlaid [ˈɪnleɪd] a incrostato(a); (table etc) intarsiato(a).
inland a [ˈɪnlənd] interno(a) // ad [ɪnˈlænd] all'interno; I~ Revenue n (Brit) fisco, entrate fpl fiscali.
in-laws [ˈɪnlɔːz] npl suoceri mpl; cognati mpl.
inlet [ˈɪnlɛt] n (GEO) insenatura, baia; ~ pipe n (TECH) tubo d'immissione.
inmate [ˈɪnmeɪt] n (in prison) carcerato/a; (in asylum) ricoverato/a.
inn [ɪn] n locanda.
innate [ɪˈneɪt] a innato(a).
inner [ˈɪnə*] a interno(a), interiore; ~ tube n camera d'aria.
innocence [ˈɪnəsns] n innocenza.
innocent [ˈɪnəsnt] a innocente.
innocuous [ɪˈnɔkjuəs] a innocuo(a).
innovation [ɪnəuˈveɪʃən] n innovazione f.
innuendo, ~es [ɪnjuˈɛndəu] n insinuazione f.
innumerable [ɪˈnjuːmrəbl] a innumerevole.
inoculation [ɪnɔkjuˈleɪʃən] n inoculazione f.
inopportune [ɪnˈɔpətjuːn] a inopportuno(a).
inordinately [ɪˈnɔːdɪnətlɪ] ad smoderatamente.
inorganic [ɪnɔːˈɡænɪk] a inorganico(a).
in-patient [ˈɪnpeɪʃənt] n ricoverato/a.
input [ˈɪnput] n (ELEC) energia, potenza; (of machine) alimentazione f; (of computer) input m.

inquest [ˈɪnkwɛst] n inchiesta.
inquire [ɪnˈkwaɪə*] vi informarsi // vt domandare, informarsi di; to ~ about vt fus informarsi di; to ~ into vt fus fare indagini su; **inquiring** a (mind) inquisitivo(a); **inquiry** n domanda; (LAW) indagine f, investigazione f.
inquisitive [ɪnˈkwɪzɪtɪv] a curioso(a).
inroad [ˈɪnrəud] n incursione f.
insane [ɪnˈseɪn] a matto(a), pazzo(a); (MED) alienato(a).
insanitary [ɪnˈsænɪtərɪ] a insalubre.
insanity [ɪnˈsænɪtɪ] n follia; (MED) alienazione f mentale.
insatiable [ɪnˈseɪʃəbl] a insaziabile.
inscribe [ɪnˈskraɪb] vt iscrivere.
inscription [ɪnˈskrɪpʃən] n iscrizione f; dedica.
inscrutable [ɪnˈskruːtəbl] a imperscrutabile.
insect [ˈɪnsɛkt] n insetto; ~icide [ɪnˈsɛktɪsaɪd] n insetticida m.
insecure [ɪnsɪˈkjuə*] a malfermo(a); malsicuro(a); (person) ansioso(a); **insecurity** n mancanza di sicurezza.
insensible [ɪnˈsɛnsɪbl] a insensibile; (unconscious) privo(a) di sensi.
insensitive [ɪnˈsɛnsɪtɪv] a insensibile.
inseparable [ɪnˈsɛprəbl] a inseparabile.
insert vt [ɪnˈsəːt] inserire, introdurre // n [ˈɪnsəːt] inserto; ~ion [ɪnˈsəːʃən] n inserzione f.
inshore [ɪnˈfɔː*] a costiero(a) // ad presso la riva; verso la riva.
inside [ˈɪnˈsaɪd] n interno, parte f interiore // a interno(a), interiore // ad dentro, all'interno // prep dentro, all'interno di; (of time): ~ 10 minutes entro 10 minuti; ~s npl (col) ventre m; ~ lane n (AUT) corsia di marcia; ~ out ad (turn) a rovescio; (know) in fondo.
insidious [ɪnˈsɪdɪəs] a insidioso(a).
insight [ˈɪnsaɪt] n acume m, perspicacia; (glimpse, idea) percezione f.
insignificant [ɪnsɪɡˈnɪfɪknt] a insignificante.
insincere [ɪnsɪnˈsɪə*] a insincero(a).
insinuate [ɪnˈsɪnjueɪt] vt insinuare; **insinuation** [-ˈeɪʃən] n insinuazione f.
insipid [ɪnˈsɪpɪd] a insipido(a), insulso(a).
insist [ɪnˈsɪst] vi insistere; to ~ on doing insistere per fare; to ~ that insistere perché + sub; (claim) sostenere che; ~ence n insistenza; ~ent a insistente.
insolence [ˈɪnsələns] n insolenza.
insolent [ˈɪnsələnt] a insolente.
insoluble [ɪnˈsɔljubl] a insolubile.
insolvent [ɪnˈsɔlvənt] a insolvente.
insomnia [ɪnˈsɔmnɪə] n insonnia.
inspect [ɪnˈspɛkt] vt ispezionare; (ticket) controllare; ~ion [ɪnˈspɛkʃən] n ispezione f; controllo; ~or n ispettore/trice; controllore m.
inspiration [ɪnspəˈreɪʃən] n ispirazione f.
inspire [ɪnˈspaɪə*] vt ispirare; **inspiring** a stimolante.
instability [ɪnstəˈbɪlɪtɪ] n instabilità.

install [ɪn'stɔːl] vt installare; ~ation [ɪnstə'leɪʃən] n installazione f.

instalment [ɪn'stɔːlmənt] n rata; (of TV serial etc) puntata.

instance ['ɪnstəns] n esempio, caso; for ~ per or ad esempio.

instant ['ɪnstənt] n istante m, attimo // a immediato(a); urgente; (coffee, food) in polvere; **the 10th** ~ il 10 corrente; ~ly ad immediatamente, subito.

instead [ɪn'sted] ad invece; ~ of invece di.

instep ['ɪnstep] n collo del piede; (of shoe) collo della scarpa.

instigation [ɪnstɪ'geɪʃən] n istigazione f.

instil [ɪn'stɪl] vt: to ~ (into) inculcare (in).

instinct ['ɪnstɪŋkt] n istinto.

instinctive [ɪn'stɪŋktɪv] a istintivo(a); ~ly ad per istinto.

institute ['ɪnstɪtjuːt] n istituto // vt istituire, stabilire; (inquiry) avviare; (proceedings) iniziare.

institution [ɪnstɪ'tjuːʃən] n istituzione f; istituto (d'istruzione); istituto (psichiatrico).

instruct [ɪn'strʌkt] vt istruire; to ~ sb in sth insegnare qc a qd; to ~ sb to do dare ordini a qd di fare; ~ion [ɪn'strʌkʃən] n istruzione f; ~ive a istruttivo(a); ~or n istruttore/trice; (for skiing) maestro/a.

instrument ['ɪnstrumənt] n strumento; ~al [-'mentl] a (MUS) strumentale; to be ~al in essere d'aiuto in; ~alist [-'mentəlɪst] n strumentista m/f; ~ panel n quadro m portastrumenti inv.

insubordinate [ɪnsə'bɔːdənɪt] a insubordinato(a); **insubordination** [-'neɪʃən] n insubordinazione f.

insufferable [ɪn'sʌfrəbl] a insopportabile.

insufficient [ɪnsə'fɪʃənt] a insufficiente.

insular ['ɪnsjulə*] a insulare; (person) di mente ristretta.

insulate ['ɪnsjuleɪt] vt isolare; **insulating tape** n nastro isolante; **insulation** [-'leɪʃən] n isolamento.

insulin ['ɪnsjulɪn] n insulina.

insult n ['ɪnsʌlt] insulto, affronto // vt [ɪn'sʌlt] insultare; ~ing a offensivo(a), ingiurioso(a).

insuperable [ɪn'sjuːprəbl] a insormontabile, insuperabile.

insurance [ɪn'fuərəns] n assicurazione f; **fire/life** ~ assicurazione contro gli incendi/sulla vita; ~ **policy** n polizza d'assicurazione.

insure [ɪn'fuə*] vt assicurare.

insurrection [ɪnsə'rekʃən] n insurrezione f.

intact [ɪn'tækt] a intatto(a).

intake ['ɪnteɪk] n (TECH) immissione f; (of food) consumo; (of pupils etc) afflusso.

intangible [ɪn'tændʒɪbl] a intangibile.

integral ['ɪntɪgrəl] a integrale; (part) integrante.

integrate ['ɪntɪgreɪt] vt integrare.

integrity [ɪn'tegrɪtɪ] n integrità.

intellect ['ɪntəlekt] n intelletto; ~ual [-'lektjuəl] a, n intellettuale (m/f).

intelligence [ɪn'telɪdʒəns] n intelligenza; (MIL etc) informazioni fpl.

intelligent [ɪn'telɪdʒənt] a intelligente.

intelligible [ɪn'telɪdʒɪbl] a intelligibile.

intemperate [ɪn'tempərət] a immoderato(a); (drinking too much) intemperante nel bere.

intend [ɪn'tend] vt (gift etc): to ~ sth for destinare qc a; to ~ to do aver l'intenzione di fare.

intense [ɪn'tens] a intenso(a); (person) di forti sentimenti; ~ly ad intensamente; profondamente.

intensify [ɪn'tensɪfaɪ] vt intensificare.

intensity [ɪn'tensɪtɪ] n intensità.

intensive [ɪn'tensɪv] a intensivo(a); ~ care unit n reparto terapia intensiva.

intent [ɪn'tent] n intenzione f // a: ~ (on) intento(a) (a), immerso(a) (in); to all ~s and purposes a tutti gli effetti; to be ~ on doing sth essere deciso a fare qc.

intention [ɪn'tenʃən] n intenzione f; ~al a intenzionale, deliberato(a); ~ally ad apposta.

intently [ɪn'tentlɪ] ad attentamente.

inter [ɪn'tɜː*] vt sotterrare.

interact [ɪntər'ækt] vi agire reciprocamente; ~ion [-'ækʃən] n azione f reciproca.

intercede [ɪntə'siːd] vi: to ~ (with) intercedere (presso).

intercept [ɪntə'sept] vt intercettare; (person) fermare; ~ion [-'sepʃən] n intercettamento.

interchange n ['ɪntətʃeɪndʒ] (exchange) scambio; (on motorway) incrocio pluridirezionale // vt [ɪntə'tʃeɪndʒ] scambiare; sostituire l'uno(a) per l'altro(a); ~able a intercambiabile.

intercom ['ɪntəkɔm] n interfono.

interconnect [ɪntəkə'nekt] vi (rooms) essere in comunicazione.

intercourse ['ɪntəkɔːs] n rapporti mpl.

interest ['ɪntrɪst] n interesse m; (COMM: stake, share) interessi mpl // vt interessare; ~ed a interessato(a); to be ~ed in interessarsi di; ~ing a interessante.

interfere [ɪntə'fɪə*] vi: to ~ in (quarrel, other people's business) immischiarsi in; to ~ with (object) toccare; (plans) ostacolare; (duty) interferire con.

interference [ɪntə'fɪərəns] n interferenza.

interim ['ɪntərɪm] a provvisorio(a) // n: in the ~ nel frattempo.

interior [ɪn'tɪərɪə*] n interno; (of country) entroterra // a interiore, interno(a).

interjection [ɪntə'dʒekʃən] n interiezione f.

interlock [ɪntə'lɔk] vi ingranarsi // vt ingranare.

interloper ['ɪntələupə*] n intruso/a.

interlude [ɪn'təluːd] n intervallo; (THEATRE) intermezzo.

intermarry [ɪntə'mærɪ] vi imparentarsi

per mezzo di matrimonio; sposarsi tra
parenti.

intermediary [ɪntə'miːdɪərɪ] n
intermediario/a.

intermediate [ɪntə'miːdɪət] a
intermedio(a); (SCOL: course, level)
medio(a).

intermission [ɪntə'mɪʃən] n pausa;
(THEATRE, CINEMA) intermissione f,
intervallo.

intermittent [ɪntə'mɪtnt] a intermittente.

intern vt [ɪn'təːn] internare // n ['ɪntəːn]
(US) medico interno.

internal [ɪn'təːnl] a interno(a); ~ly ad
all'interno; I~ Revenue n (US) fisco.

international [ɪntə'næʃənl] a
internazionale // n (SPORT) partita
internazionale.

internment [ɪn'təːnmənt] n internamento.

interplay ['ɪntəpleɪ] n azione e reazione f.

interpret [ɪn'təːprɪt] vt interpretare // vi
fare da interprete; ~ation [-'teɪʃən] n
interpretazione f; ~er n interprete m/f.

interrelated [ɪntərɪ'leɪtɪd] a correlato(a).

interrogate [ɪn'terəugeɪt] vt interrogare;
interrogation [-'geɪʃən] n interrogazione
f; (of suspect etc) interrogatorio;
interrogative [ɪntə'rɔgətɪv] a
interrogativo(a) // n (LING) interrogativo;
interrogator n interrogante m/f.

interrupt [ɪntə'rʌpt] vt interrompere;
~ion [-'rʌpʃən] n interruzione f.

intersect [ɪntə'sekt] vt intersecare // vi
(roads) intersecarsi; ~ion [-'sekʃən] n
intersezione f; (of roads) incrocio.

intersperse [ɪntə'spəːs] vt: to ~ with
costellare di.

intertwine [ɪntə'twaɪn] vt intrecciare // vi
intrecciarsi.

interval ['ɪntəvl] n intervallo; at ~s a
intervalli.

intervene [ɪntə'viːn] vi (time)
intercorrere; (event, person) intervenire;
intervention [-'venʃən] n intervento.

interview ['ɪntəvjuː] n (RADIO, TV etc)
intervista; (for job) colloquio // vt
intervistare; avere un colloquio con; ~er
n intervistatore/trice.

intestate [ɪn'testeɪt] a intestato(a).

intestine [ɪn'testɪn] n intestino.

intimacy ['ɪntɪməsɪ] n intimità.

intimate a ['ɪntɪmət] intimo(a);
(knowledge) profondo(a) // vt ['ɪntɪmeɪt]
sottintendere, suggerire; ~ly ad
intimamente.

intimation [ɪntɪ'meɪʃən] n annuncio.

intimidate [ɪn'tɪmɪdeɪt] vt intimidire,
intimorire; **intimidation** [-'deɪʃən] n inti-
midazione f.

into ['ɪntu] prep dentro, in; **come** ~ **the
house** vieni dentro la casa.

intolerable [ɪn'tɔlərəbl] a intollerabile.

intolerance [ɪn'tɔlərns] n intolleranza.

intolerant [ɪn'tɔlərnt] a intollerante.

intonation [ɪntəu'neɪʃən] n intonazione f.

intoxicate [ɪn'tɔksɪkeɪt] vt inebriare; ~d

a inebriato(a); **intoxication** [-'keɪʃən] n
ebbrezza.

intractable [ɪn'træktəbl] a intrattabile.

intransigent [ɪn'trænsɪdʒənt] a
intransigente.

intransitive [ɪn'trænsɪtɪv] a
intransitivo(a).

intravenous [ɪntrə'viːnəs] a
endovenoso(a).

intrepid [ɪn'trepɪd] a intrepido(a).

intricacy ['ɪntrɪkəsɪ] n complessità f inv.

intricate ['ɪntrɪkət] a intricato(a),
complicato(a).

intrigue [ɪn'triːg] n intrigo // vt
affascinare; **intriguing** a affascinante.

intrinsic [ɪn'trɪnsɪk] a intrinseco(a).

introduce [ɪntrə'djuːs] vt introdurre; **to** ~
sb (to sb) presentare qd (a qd); **to** ~ **sb
to** (pastime, technique) iniziare qd a;
introduction [-'dʌkʃən] n introduzione f;
(of person) presentazione f; **introductory**
a introduttivo(a).

introspective [ɪntrəu'spektɪv] a
introspettivo(a).

introvert ['ɪntrəuvəːt] a introverso(a) // n
introverso.

intrude [ɪn'truːd] vi (person) intrudersi; **to**
~ **on** or **into** intrudersi in; **am I
intruding?** disturbo?; ~r n intruso/a;
intrusion [-ʒən] n intrusione f.

intuition [ɪntjuː'ɪʃən] n intuizione f.

intuitive [ɪn'tjuːɪtɪv] a intuitivo(a);
dotato(a) di intuito.

inundate ['ɪnʌndeɪt] vt: **to** ~ **with**
inondare di.

invade [ɪn'veɪd] vt invadere; ~r n
invasore m.

invalid n ['ɪnvəlɪd] malato/a; (with
disability) invalido/a // a [ɪn'vælɪd] (not
valid) invalido(a), non valido(a); ~ate [ɪn-
'vælɪdeɪt] vt invalidare.

invaluable [ɪn'væljuəbl] a inapprezzabile,
inestimabile.

invariable [ɪn'veərɪəbl] a invariabile; (fig)
scontato(a).

invasion [ɪn'veɪʒən] n invasione f.

invective [ɪn'vektɪv] n invettiva.

invent [ɪn'vent] vt inventare; ~ion [ɪn-
'venʃən] n invenzione f; ~ive a
inventivo(a); ~or n inventore m.

inventory ['ɪnvəntrɪ] n inventario.

inverse [ɪn'vəːs] a inverso(a) // n inverso,
contrario.

invert [ɪn'vəːt] vt invertire; (cup, object)
rovesciare; ~ed commas npl virgolette
fpl.

invertebrate [ɪn'vəːtɪbrət] n invertebrato.

invest [ɪn'vest] vt investire // vi fare
investimenti.

investigate [ɪn'vestɪgeɪt] vt investigare,
indagare; (crime) fare indagini su;
investigation [-'geɪʃən] n investigazione f;
(of crime) indagine f; **investigator** n
investigatore/trice.

investiture [ɪn'vestɪtʃə*] n investitura.

investment [ɪn'vestmənt] n investimento.

investor [ɪn'vɛstə*] n investitore/trice; azionista m/f.

inveterate [ɪn'vɛtərət] a inveterato(a).

invidious [ɪn'vɪdɪəs] a odioso(a); (task) spiacevole.

invigorating [ɪn'vɪgəreɪtɪŋ] a stimolante; vivificante.

invincible [ɪn'vɪnsɪbl] a invincibile.

inviolate [ɪn'vaɪələt] a inviolato(a).

invisible [ɪn'vɪzɪbl] a invisibile.

invitation [ɪnvɪ'teɪʃən] n invito.

invite [ɪn'vaɪt] vt invitare; (opinions etc) sollecitare; (trouble) provocare; **inviting** a invitante, attraente.

invoice ['ɪnvɔɪs] n fattura // vt fatturare.

invoke [ɪn'vəuk] vt invocare.

involuntary [ɪn'vɔləntrɪ] a involontario(a).

involve [ɪn'vɔlv] vt (entail) richiedere, comportare; (associate): **to ~ sb (in)** implicare qd (in); coinvolgere qd (in); **~d** a involuto(a), complesso(a); **to feel ~d** sentirsi coinvolto(a); **~ment** n implicazione f; coinvolgimento; **~ment (in)** impegno (in); partecipazione f (in).

invulnerable [ɪn'vʌlnərəbl] a invulnerabile.

inward ['ɪnwəd] a (movement) verso l'interno; (thought, feeling) interiore, intimo(a); **~ly** ad (feel, think etc) nell'intimo, entro di sé; **~(s)** ad verso l'interno.

iodine ['aɪəudi:n] n iodio.

iota [aɪ'əutə] n (fig) ette m, briciolo.

IOU n (abbr of I owe you) pagherò m inv.

IQ n (abbr of intelligence quotient) quoziente m d'intelligenza.

Iran [ɪ'rɑ:n] n Iran m; **~ian** [ɪ'reɪnɪən] a iraniano(a) // n iraniano/a; (LING) iranico.

Iraq [ɪ'rɑ:k] n Iraq m; **~i** a iracheno(a) // n iracheno/a; (LING) iracheno.

irascible [ɪ'ræsɪbl] a irascibile.

irate [aɪ'reɪt] a irato(a).

Ireland ['aɪlənd] n Irlanda.

iris, **~es** ['aɪrɪs, -ɪz] n iride f; (BOT) giaggiolo, iride.

Irish ['aɪrɪʃ] a irlandese // npl: **the ~** gli Irlandesi; **~man** n irlandese m; **~ sea** n Mar m d'Irlanda; **~woman** n irlandese f.

irk [ə:k] vt seccare; **~some** a seccante.

iron ['aɪən] n ferro; (for clothes) ferro da stiro // a di or in ferro // vt (clothes) stirare; **~s** npl (chains) catene fpl; **to ~ out** vt (crease) appianare; (fig) spianare; far sparire; **the ~ curtain** la cortina di ferro.

ironic(al) [aɪ'rɔnɪk(l)] a ironico(a).

ironing ['aɪənɪŋ] n stiratura; **~ board** n cavalletto da stiro.

ironmonger ['aɪənmʌŋgə*] n negoziante m in ferramenta; **~'s (shop)** n (negozio di) ferramenta.

ironworks ['aɪənwə:ks] n ferriera.

irony ['aɪrənɪ] n ironia.

irrational [ɪ'ræʃənl] a irrazionale; irragionevole; illogico(a).

irreconcilable [ɪrɛkən'saɪləbl] a irreconciliabile; (opinion): **~ with** inconciliabile con.

irredeemable [ɪrɪ'di:məbl] a (COMM) irredimibile.

irrefutable [ɪrɪ'fju:təbl] a irrefutabile.

irregular [ɪ'rɛgjulə*] a irregolare; **~ity** [-'lærɪtɪ] n irregolarità f inv.

irrelevance [ɪ'rɛləvəns] n inappropriatezza.

irrelevant [ɪ'rɛləvənt] a non appropriato(a).

irreparable [ɪ'rɛprəbl] a irreparabile.

irreplaceable [ɪrɪ'pleɪsəbl] a insostituibile.

irrepressible [ɪrɪ'prɛsəbl] a irrefrenabile.

irreproachable [ɪrɪ'prəutʃəbl] a irreprensibile.

irresistible [ɪrɪ'zɪstɪbl] a irresistibile.

irresolute [ɪ'rɛzəlu:t] a irresoluto(a), indeciso(a).

irrespective [ɪrɪ'spɛktɪv]: **~ of** prep senza riguardo a.

irresponsible [ɪrɪ'spɔnsɪbl] a irresponsabile.

irreverent [ɪ'rɛvərnt] a irriverente.

irrevocable [ɪ'rɛvəkəbl] a irrevocabile.

irrigate ['ɪrɪgeɪt] vt irrigare; **irrigation** [-'geɪʃən] n irrigazione f.

irritable ['ɪrɪtəbl] a irritabile.

irritate ['ɪrɪteɪt] vt irritare; **irritation** [-'teɪʃən] n irritazione f.

is [ɪz] vb see **be**.

Islam ['ɪzlɑ:m] n Islam m.

island ['aɪlənd] n isola; (also: **traffic ~**) salvagente m inv; **~er** n isolano/a.

isle [aɪl] n isola.

isn't ['ɪznt] = **is not**.

isolate ['aɪsəleɪt] vt isolare; **~d** a isolato(a); **isolation** [-'leɪʃən] n isolamento.

isotope ['aɪsəutəup] n isotopo.

Israel ['ɪzreɪl] n Israele m; **~i** [ɪz'reɪlɪ] a, n israeliano(a).

issue ['ɪsju:] n questione f, problema m; (outcome) esito, risultato; (of banknotes etc) emissione f; (of newspaper etc) numero; (offspring) discendenza // vt (rations, equipment) distribuire; (orders) dare; (book) pubblicare; (banknotes, cheques, stamps) emettere; **at ~** in gioco, in discussione.

isthmus ['ɪsməs] n istmo.

it [ɪt] pronoun (subject) esso(a); (direct object) lo(la), l'; (indirect object) gli(le); **~'s raining** piove; **it's on ~** è lì sopra; **he's proud of ~** ne è fiero; **he agreed to ~** ha acconsentito.

Italian [ɪ'tæljən] a italiano(a) // n italiano/a; (LING) italiano; **the ~s** gli Italiani.

italic [ɪ'tælɪk] a corsivo(a); **~s** npl corsivo.

Italy ['ɪtəlɪ] n Italia.

itch [ɪtʃ] n prurito // vi (person) avere il prurito; (part of body) prudere; **I'm ~ing to do** non vedo l'ora di fare; **~y** a che prude.

it'd ['ɪtd] = **it would**; **it had**.

item ['aɪtəm] n articolo; (on agenda) punto; (in programme) numero; (also: **news** ~) notizia; ~**ize** vt specificare, dettagliare.

itinerant [ɪ'tɪnərənt] a ambulante.

itinerary [aɪ'tɪnərərɪ] n itinerario.

it'll ['ɪtl] = **it will**; **it shall**.

its [ɪts] a, pronoun il(la) suo(a), i(le) suoi(sue).

it's [ɪts] = **it is**; **it has**.

itself [ɪt'sɛlf] pronoun (emphatic) esso(a) stesso(a); (reflexive) si.

ITV n abbr of Independent Television (canale televisivo in concorrenza con la BBC).

I've [aɪv] = **I have**.

ivory ['aɪvərɪ] n avorio.

ivy ['aɪvɪ] n edera.

J

jab [dʒæb] vt: **to** ~ **sth into** affondare or piantare qc dentro // n colpo; (MED: col) puntura.

jabber ['dʒæbə*] vt,vi borbottare.

jack [dʒæk] n (AUT) cricco; (CARDS) fante m; **to** ~ **up** vt sollevare sul cricco.

jacket ['dʒækɪt] n giacca; (of book) copertura; **potatoes in their** ~**s** patate fpl con la buccia.

jack-knife ['dʒæknaɪf] vi: **the lorry** ~**d** l'autotreno si è piegato su se stesso.

jackpot ['dʒækpɔt] n bottino.

jade [dʒeɪd] n (stone) giada.

jaded ['dʒeɪdɪd] a sfinito(a), spossato(a).

jagged ['dʒægɪd] a sboccellato(a); (cliffs etc) frastagliato(a).

jail [dʒeɪl] n prigione f; ~**break** n evasione f; ~**er** n custode m del carcere.

jam [dʒæm] n marmellata; (of shoppers etc) ressa; (also: **traffic** ~) ingorgo // vt (passage etc) ingombrare, ostacolare; (mechanism, drawer etc) bloccare; (RADIO) disturbare con interferenze // vi (mechanism, sliding part) incepparsi, bloccarsi; (gun) incepparsi; **to** ~ **sth into** forzare qc dentro; infilare qc a forza dentro.

Jamaica [dʒə'meɪkə] n Giamaica.

jangle ['dʒæŋgl] vi risuonare; (bracelet) tintinnare.

janitor ['dʒænɪtə*] n (caretaker) portiere m; (: SCOL) bidello.

January ['dʒænjuərɪ] n gennaio.

Japan [dʒə'pæn] n Giappone m; ~**ese** [dʒæpə'niːz] a giapponese // n, pl inv giapponese m/f; (LING) giapponese m.

jar [dʒɑ:*] n (glass) barattolo, vasetto // vi (sound) stridere; (colours etc) stonare.

jargon ['dʒɑ:gən] n gergo.

jasmin(e) ['dʒæzmɪn] n gelsomino.

jaundice ['dʒɔ:ndɪs] n itterizia; ~**d** a (fig) invidioso(a) e critico(a).

jaunt [dʒɔ:nt] n gita; ~**y** a vivace; disinvolto(a).

javelin ['dʒævlɪn] n giavellotto.

jaw [dʒɔ:] n mascella.

jaywalker ['dʒeɪwɔ:kə*] n pedone(a) indisciplinato(a).

jazz [dʒæz] n jazz m; **to** ~ **up** vt rendere

vivace; ~**y** a vistoso(a), chiassoso(a).

jealous ['dʒɛləs] a geloso(a); ~**y** n gelosia.

jeans [dʒi:nz] npl (blue-)jeans mpl.

jeep [dʒi:p] n jeep m inv.

jeer [dʒɪə*] vi: **to** ~ **(at)** fischiare; beffeggiare.

jelly ['dʒɛlɪ] n gelatina; ~**fish** n medusa.

jeopardize ['dʒɛpədaɪz] vt mettere in pericolo.

jeopardy ['dʒɛpədɪ] n: **in** ~ in pericolo.

jerk [dʒə:k] n scossa; strappo; contrazione f, spasimo // vt dare una scossa a // vi (vehicles) sobbalzare.

jerkin ['dʒə:kɪn] n giubbotto.

jerky ['dʒə:kɪ] a a scatti; a sobbalzi.

jersey ['dʒə:zɪ] n maglia.

jest [dʒɛst] n scherzo; **in** ~ per scherzo.

jet [dʒɛt] n (of gas, liquid) getto; (AVIAT) aviogetto; ~**-black** a nero(a) come l'ebano, corvino(a); ~ **engine** n motore m a reazione.

jetsam ['dʒɛtsəm] n relitti mpl di mare.

jettison ['dʒɛtɪsn] vt gettare in mare.

jetty ['dʒɛtɪ] n molo.

Jew [dʒu:] n ebreo.

jewel ['dʒu:əl] n gioiello; ~**ler** n orefice m, gioielliere/a; ~**ler's (shop)** n oreficeria, gioielleria; ~**lery** n gioielli mpl.

Jewess ['dʒu:ɪs] n ebrea.

Jewish ['dʒu:ɪʃ] a giudeo(a); giudaico(a).

jib [dʒɪb] n (NAUT) fiocco; (of crane) braccio.

jibe [dʒaɪb] n beffa.

jiffy ['dʒɪfɪ] n (col): **in a** ~ in un batter d'occhio.

jigsaw ['dʒɪgsɔ:] n (also: ~ **puzzle**) puzzle m inv.

jilt [dʒɪlt] vt piantare in asso.

jingle ['dʒɪŋgl] n (advert) sigla pubblicitaria // vi tintinnare, scampanellare.

jinx [dʒɪŋks] n (col) iettatura; (person) iettatore/trice.

jitters ['dʒɪtəz] npl (col): **to get the** ~ aver fifa.

job [dʒɔb] n lavoro; (employment) impiego, posto; ~**less** a senza lavoro, disoccupato(a).

jockey ['dʒɔkɪ] n fantino, jockey m inv // vi: **to** ~ **for position** manovrare per una posizione di vantaggio.

jocular ['dʒɔkjulə*] a gioviale, scherzoso(a); faceto(a).

jog [dʒɔg] vt scuotere // vi (SPORT) fare il footing; **to** ~ **along** trottare; (fig) andare avanti piano piano; **to** ~ **sb's memory** stimolare la memoria di qd; ~**ging** n footing m.

join [dʒɔɪn] vt unire, congiungere; (become member of) iscriversi a; (meet) raggiungere; riunirsi a // vi (roads, rivers) confluire // n giuntura; **to** ~ **up** vi arruolarsi.

joiner ['dʒɔɪnə*] n falegname m; ~**y** n falegnameria.

joint [dʒɔɪnt] n (TECH) giuntura; giunto; (ANAT) articolazione f, giuntura; (CULIN) arrosto; (col: place) locale m // a comune; ~ly ad in comune, insieme.

joist [dʒɔɪst] n trave f.

joke [dʒəuk] n scherzo; (funny story) barzelletta; (also: **practical** ~) beffa // vi scherzare; ~r n buffone/a, burlone/a; (CARDS) matta, jolly m inv.

jolly ['dʒɔlɪ] a allegro(a), gioioso(a) // ad (col) veramente, proprio.

jolt [dʒəult] n scossa, sobbalzo // vt scossare.

Jordan [dʒɔːdən] n Giordania.

jostle ['dʒɔsl] vt spingere coi gomiti // vi farsi spazio coi gomiti.

jot [dʒɔt] n: not one ~ nemmeno un po'; to ~ down vt annotare in fretta, gettare giù; ~ter n quaderno; blocco.

journal ['dʒəːnl] n giornale m; rivista; diario; ~ese [-'liːz] n (pej) stile m giornalistico; ~ism n giornalismo; ~ist n giornalista m/f.

journey ['dʒəːnɪ] n viaggio; (distance covered) tragitto.

jowl [dʒaul] n mandibola; guancia.

joy [dʒɔɪ] n gioia; ~ful, ~ous a gioioso(a), allegro(a); ~ ride n gita in automobile (specialmente rubata).

J.P. n abbr see **justice**.

Jr, Jun., Junr abbr of **junior**.

jubilant ['dʒuːbɪlnt] a giubilante; trionfante.

jubilation [dʒuːbɪ'leɪʃən] n giubilo.

jubilee ['dʒuːbɪliː] n giubileo.

judge [dʒʌdʒ] n giudice m/f // vt giudicare; **judg(e)ment** n giudizio; (punishment) punizione f.

judicial [dʒuː'dɪʃl] a giudiziale, giudiziario(a).

judicious [dʒuː'dɪʃəs] a giudizioso(a).

judo ['dʒuːdəu] n judo m.

jug [dʒʌg] n brocca, bricco.

juggernaut ['dʒʌgənɔːt] n (huge truck) bestione m.

juggle ['dʒʌgl] vi fare giochi di destrezza; ~r n giocoliere/a.

Jugoslav ['juːgəu'slɑːv] a,n = **Yugoslav**.

juice [dʒuːs] n succo.

juicy ['dʒuːsɪ] a succoso(a).

jukebox ['dʒuːkbɔks] n juke-box m inv.

July [dʒuː'laɪ] n luglio.

jumble ['dʒʌmbl] n miscuglio // vt (also: ~ up) mischiare; ~ sale n (Brit) vendita di oggetti per beneficenza.

jumbo ['dʒʌmbəu] a: ~ jet jumbo-jet m inv.

jump [dʒʌmp] vi saltare, balzare; (start) sobbalzare; (increase) rincarare // vt saltare // n salto, balzo; sobbalzo.

jumper ['dʒʌmpə*] n maglia.

jumpy ['dʒʌmpɪ] a nervoso(a), agitato(a).

junction ['dʒʌŋkʃən] n (of roads) incrocio; (of rails) nodo ferroviario.

juncture ['dʒʌŋktʃə*] n: at this ~ in questa congiuntura.

June [dʒuːn] n giugno.

jungle ['dʒʌŋgl] n giungla.

junior ['dʒuːnɪə*] a, n: he's ~ to me (by 2 years), he's my ~ (by 2 years) è più giovane di me (di 2 anni); he's ~ to me (seniority) è al di sotto di me, ho più anzianità di lui; ~ school n scuola elementare (da 8 a 11 anni).

juniper ['dʒuːnɪpə*] n: ~ berry bacca di ginepro.

junk [dʒʌŋk] n (rubbish) chincaglia; (ship) giunca; ~shop n chincaglieria.

junta ['dʒʌntə] n giunta.

jurisdiction [dʒuərɪs'dɪkʃən] n giurisdizione f.

jurisprudence [dʒuərɪs'pruːdəns] n giurisprudenza.

juror ['dʒuərə*] n giurato.

jury ['dʒuərɪ] n giuria.

just [dʒʌst] a giusto(a) // ad: he's ~ done it/left lui lo ha appena fatto/è appena partito; ~ as I expected proprio come me lo aspettavo; ~ right proprio giusto; ~ 2 o'clock le 2 precise; it was ~ before/enough/here era poco prima/appena assai/proprio qui; it's ~ me sono solo io; it's ~ a mistake non è che uno sbaglio; ~ missed/caught appena perso/preso; ~ listen to this! senta un po' questo!

justice ['dʒʌstɪs] n giustizia; **J~ of the Peace (J.P.)** n giudice m conciliatore.

justification [dʒʌstɪfɪ'keɪʃən] n giustificazione f.

justify ['dʒʌstɪfaɪ] vt giustificare.

justly ['dʒʌstlɪ] ad giustamente.

justness ['dʒʌstnɪs] n giustezza.

jut [dʒʌt] vi (also: ~ out) sporgersi.

juvenile ['dʒuːvənaɪl] a giovane, giovanile; (court) dei minorenni; (books) per ragazzi // n giovane m/f, minorenne m/f.

juxtapose ['dʒʌkstəpəuz] vt giustapporre.

K

kaleidoscope [kə'laɪdəskəup] n caleidoscopio.

kangaroo [kæŋgə'ruː] n canguro.

keel [kiːl] n chiglia; on an even ~ (fig) in uno stato normale.

keen [kiːn] a (interest, desire) vivo(a); (eye, intelligence) acuto(a); (competition) serrato(a); (edge) affilato(a); (eager) entusiastico(a); to be ~ to do or on doing sth avere una gran voglia di fare qc; to be ~ on sth essere appassionato(a) di qc; to be ~ on sb avere un debole per qd; ~ness n (eagerness) entusiasmo.

keep [kiːp] vb (pt,pp kept [kept]) vt tenere; (hold back) trattenere; (feed: one's family etc) mantenere, sostentare; (a promise) mantenere; (chickens, bees, pigs etc) allevare // vi (food) mantenersi; (remain: in a certain state or place) restare // n (of castle) maschio; (food etc): enough for his ~ abbastanza per vitto e alloggio; to ~ doing sth continuare a fare qc; fare qc di continuo; to ~ sb from doing/sth from happening impedire a qd di fare/che qc succeda; to ~ sb happy/a

place tidy tenere qd occupato(a)/un luogo in ordine; **to ~ sth to o.s.** tenere qc per sé; **to ~ sth (back) from sb** celare qc a qd; **to ~ time** (*clock*) andar bene; **to ~ on** *vi* continuare; **to ~ on doing** continuare a fare; **to ~ out** *vt* tener fuori; '**~ out**' 'vietato l'accesso'; **to ~ up** *vi* mantenersi // *vt* continuare, mantenere; **to ~ up with** tener dietro a, andare di pari passo con; (*work etc*) farcela a seguire; **~er** *n* custode *m/f*, guardiano/a; **~ing** *n* (*care*) custodia; **in ~ing with** in armonia con; in accordo con; **~sake** *n* ricordo.

keg [kɛg] *n* barilotto.

kennel ['kɛnl] *n* canile *m*.

Kenya ['kɛnjə] *n* Kenia *m*.

kept [kɛpt] *pt,pp* of **keep**.

kerb [kɜːb] *n* orlo del marciapiede.

kernel ['kɜːnl] *n* nocciolo.

kerosene ['kɛrəsiːn] *n* cherosene *m*.

ketchup ['kɛtʃəp] *n* ketchup *m inv*.

kettle ['kɛtl] *n* bollitore *m*; **~ drum** *n* timpano.

key [kiː] *n* (*gen, MUS*) chiave *f*; (*of piano, typewriter*) tasto // *cpd* chiave *inv*; **~board** *n* tastiera; **~hole** *n* buco della serratura; **~note** *n* (*MUS*) tonica; (*fig*) nota dominante; **~ ring** *n* portachiavi *m inv*.

khaki ['kɑːkɪ] *a,n* cachi (*m*).

kick [kɪk] *vt* calciare, dare calci a // *vi* (*horse*) tirar calci // *n* calcio; (*of rifle*) contraccolpo; (*thrill*): **he does it for ~s** lo fa giusto per il piacere di farlo; **to ~ off** *vi* (*SPORT*) dare il primo calcio; **~-off** *n* (*SPORT*) calcio d'inizio.

kid [kɪd] *n* ragazzino/a; (*animal, leather*) capretto // *vi* (*col*) scherzare // *vt* (*col*) prendere in giro.

kidnap ['kɪdnæp] *vt* rapire; **~per** *n* rapitore/trice; **~ping** *n* rapimento.

kidney ['kɪdnɪ] *n* (*ANAT*) rene *m*; (*CULIN*) rognone *m*.

kill [kɪl] *vt* uccidere, ammazzare; (*fig*) sopprimere; sopraffare; ammazzare // *n* uccisione *f*; **~er** *n* uccisore *m*, killer *m inv*; assassino/a; **~ing** *n* assassinio; (*massacre*) strage *f*.

kiln [kɪln] *n* forno.

kilo ['kiːləu] *n* chilo; **~gram(me)** ['kɪləʊɡræm] *n* chilogrammo; **~metre** ['kɪləmiːtə*] *n* chilometro; **~watt** ['kɪləuwɔt] *n* chilowatt *m inv*.

kilt [kɪlt] *n* gonnellino scozzese.

kimono [kɪ'məunəu] *n* chimono.

kin [kɪn] *n* see **next, kith**.

kind [kaɪnd] *a* gentile, buono(a) // *n* sorta, specie *f*; (*species*) genere *m*; **in ~** (*COMM*) in natura; (*fig*): **to repay sb in ~** ripagare qd della stessa moneta.

kindergarten ['kɪndəɡɑːtn] *n* giardino d'infanzia.

kind-hearted [kaɪnd'hɑːtɪd] *a* di buon cuore.

kindle ['kɪndl] *vt* accendere, infiammare.

kindly ['kaɪndlɪ] *a* pieno(a) di bontà, benevolo(a) // *ad* con bontà, gentilmente;

will you ~... vuole... per favore; **he didn't take it ~** se l'è presa a male.

kindness ['kaɪndnɪs] *n* bontà, gentilezza.

kindred ['kɪndrɪd] *a* imparentato(a); **~ spirit** *n* spirito affino.

kinetic [kɪ'nɛtɪk] *a* cinetico(a).

king [kɪŋ] *n* re *m inv*; **~dom** *n* regno, reame *m*; **~fisher** *n* martin *m inv* pescatore; (*fig*) a super *inv*; gigante.

kink [kɪŋk] *n* (*of rope*) storta.

kinky ['kɪŋkɪ] *a* (*fig*) eccentrico(a); dai gusti particolari.

kiosk ['kiːɔsk] *n* edicola, chiosco; cabina (telefonica).

kipper ['kɪpə*] *n* aringa affumicata.

kiss [kɪs] *n* bacio // *vt* baciare; **to ~ (each other)** baciarsi.

kit [kɪt] *n* equipaggiamento, corredo; (*set of tools etc*) attrezzi *mpl*; (*for assembly*) scatola di montaggio; **~bag** *n* zaino; sacco militare.

kitchen ['kɪtʃɪn] *n* cucina; **~ sink** *n* acquaio.

kite [kaɪt] *n* (*toy*) aquilone *m*; (*ZOOL*) nibbio.

kith [kɪθ] *n*: **~ and kin** amici e parenti *mpl*.

kitten ['kɪtn] *n* gattino/a, micino/a.

kitty ['kɪtɪ] *n* (*money*) fondo comune.

kleptomaniac [klɛptəʊ'meɪnɪæk] *n* cleptomane *m/f*.

knack [næk] *n*: **to have a ~ (for doing)** avere una pratica (per fare); **to have the ~ of** avere l'abitudine di; **there's a ~** c'è un modo.

knapsack ['næpsæk] *n* zaino, sacco da montagna.

knave [neɪv] *n* (*CARDS*) fante *m*.

knead [niːd] *vt* impastare.

knee [niː] *n* ginocchio; **~cap** *n* rotula.

kneel [niːl] *vi* (*pt,pp* **knelt** [nɛlt]) inginocchiarsi.

knell [nɛl] *n* intocco.

knew [njuː] *pt* of **know**.

knickers ['nɪkəz] *npl* mutandine *fpl*.

knife, knives [naɪf, naɪvz] *n* coltello // *vt* accoltellare, dare una coltellata a.

knight [naɪt] *n* cavaliere *m*; (*CHESS*) cavallo; **~hood** *n* cavalleria; (*title*): **to get a ~hood** essere fatto cavaliere.

knit [nɪt] *vt* fare a maglia; (*fig*): **to ~ together** unire // *vi* lavorare a maglia; (*broken bones*) saldarsi; **~ting** *n* lavoro a maglia; **~ting needle** *n* ferro; **~wear** *n* maglieria.

knives [naɪvz] *npl* of **knife**.

knob [nɔb] *n* bottone *m*; manopola; (*fig*): **a ~ of butter** una noce di burro.

knock [nɔk] *vt* colpire; urtare; (*fig: col*) criticare // *vi* (*engine*) battere; (*at door etc*): **to ~ at/on** bussare a // *n* bussata; colpo, botta; **to ~ down** *vt* abbattere; **to ~ off** *vi* (*col: finish*) smettere (di lavorare); **to ~ out** *vt* stendere; (*BOXING*) mettere K.O.; **~er** *n* (*on door*) battente *m*; **~-kneed** *a* che ha le gambe ad x; **~out** *n* (*BOXING*) knock out *m inv*.

knot [nɔt] n nodo // vt annodare; ~ty a (fig) spinoso(a).

know [nəu] vt (pt knew, pp known [nju:, nəun]) sapere; (person, author, place) conoscere; to ~ that... sapere che...; to ~ how to do sapere fare; ~-how n tecnica; pratica; ~ing a (look etc) d'intesa; ~ingly ad consapevolmente; di complicità.

knowledge ['nɔlɪdʒ] n consapevolezza; (learning) conoscenza, sapere m; ~able a ben informato(a).

known [nəun] pp of **know**.

knuckle ['nʌkl] n nocca.

K.O. n (abbr of knockout) K.O. m // vt mettere K.O.

Koran [kɔ'ra:n] n Corano.

kw abbr of **kilowatt(s)**.

L

l. abbr of **litre**.

lab [læb] n (abbr of **laboratory**) laboratorio.

label ['leɪbl] n etichetta, cartellino; (brand: of record) casa // vt etichettare.

laboratory [lə'bɔrətərɪ] n laboratorio.

laborious [lə'bɔ:rɪəs] a laborioso(a).

labour ['leɪbə*] n (task) lavoro; (workmen) manodopera; (MED) travaglio del parto, doglie fpl // vi: to ~ (at) lavorare duro (a); in ~ (MED) in travaglio; L~, the L~ party il partito laburista, i laburisti; ~ camp n campo dei lavori forzati; ~er n manovale m; (on farm) lavoratore m agricolo; ~ force n manodopera; ~ pains npl doglie fpl.

labyrinth ['læbɪrɪnθ] n labirinto.

lace [leɪs] n merletto, pizzo; (of shoe etc) laccio // vt (shoe) allacciare.

lack [læk] n mancanza // vt mancare di; **through** or **for** ~ **of** per mancanza di; **to be** ~**ing** mancare; **to be** ~**ing in** mancare di.

lackadaisical [lækə'deɪzɪkl] a disinteressato(a), noncurante.

laconic [lə'kɔnɪk] a laconico(a).

lacquer ['lækə*] n lacca.

lad [læd] n ragazzo, giovanotto.

ladder ['lædə*] n scala; (in tights) smagliatura // vt (tights) smagliare // vi smagliarsi.

laden ['leɪdn] a: ~ (**with**) carico(a) or caricato(a) (di).

ladle ['leɪdl] n mestolo.

lady ['leɪdɪ] n signora; dama; L~ **Smith** lady Smith; **the ladies'** (toilets) gabinetti mpl per signore; ~**bird**, ~**bug** (US) n coccinella; ~-**in-waiting** n dama di compagnia; ~-**like** a da signora, distinto(a).

lag [læg] n = **time** ~ // vi (also: ~ **behind**) trascinarsi // vt (pipes) rivestire di materiale isolante.

lager ['la:gə*] n lager m inv.

lagging ['lægɪŋ] n rivestimento di materiale isolante.

lagoon [lə'gu:n] n laguna.

laid [leɪd] pt, pp of **lay**.

lain [leɪn] pp of **lie**.

lair [lɛə*] n covo, tana.

laity ['leɪətɪ] n laici mpl.

lake [leɪk] n lago.

lamb [læm] n agnello; ~ **chop** n cotoletta d'agnello; ~**swool** n lamb's wool m.

lame [leɪm] a zoppo(a).

lament [lə'mɛnt] n lamento // vt lamentare, piangere; ~**able** ['læməntəbl] a doloroso(a); deplorevole.

laminated ['læmɪneɪtɪd] a laminato(a).

lamp [læmp] n lampada.

lampoon [læm'pu:n] n pasquinata.

lamp: ~**post** n lampione m; ~**shade** n paralume m.

lance [la:ns] n lancia // vt (MED) incidere; ~ **corporal** n caporale m.

land [lænd] n (as opposed to sea) terra (ferma); (country) paese m; (soil) terreno; suolo; (estate) terreni mpl, terre fpl // vi (from ship) sbarcare; (AVIAT) atterrare; (fig: fall) cadere // vt (obtain) acchiappare; (passengers) sbarcare; (goods) scaricare; **to** ~ **up** vi andare a finire; ~**ing** n sbarco; atterraggio; (of staircase) pianerottolo; ~**ing stage** n pontile m da sbarco; ~**ing strip** n pista d'atterraggio; ~**lady** n padrona or proprietaria di casa; ~**locked** a senza sbocco sul mare; ~**lord** n padrone m or proprietario di casa; (of pub etc) oste m; ~**lubber** n marinaio d'acqua dolce; ~**mark** n punto di riferimento; ~**owner** n proprietario(a) terriero(a).

landscape ['lænskeɪp] n paesaggio.

landslide ['lændslaɪd] n (GEO) frana; (fig: POL) valanga.

lane [leɪn] n (in country) viottolo; (in town) stradetta; (AUT, in race) corsia.

language ['læŋgwɪdʒ] n lingua; (way one speaks) linguaggio; **bad** ~ linguaggio volgare.

languid ['læŋgwɪd] a languente; languido(a).

languish ['læŋgwɪʃ] vi languire.

lank [læŋk] a (hair) liscio(a) e opaco(a).

lanky ['læŋkɪ] a allampanato(a).

lantern ['læntn] n lanterna.

lap [læp] n (of track) giro; (of body): **in** or **on one's** ~ in grembo // vt (also: ~ **up**) papparsi, leccare // vi (waves) sciabordare.

lapel [lə'pɛl] n risvolto.

Lapland ['læplænd] n Lapponia.

Lapp [læp] a lappone // n lappone m/f; (LING) lappone m.

lapse [læps] n lapsus m inv; (longer) caduta // vi (law, act) passare; (ticket, passport) scadere; **to** ~ **into bad habits** pigliare cattive abitudini; ~ **of time** spazio di tempo.

larceny ['la:sənɪ] n furto.

lard [la:d] n lardo.

larder ['la:də*] n dispensa.

large [la:dʒ] a grande; (person, animal)

grosso(a); **at ~** (*free*) in libertà; (*generally*) in generale; nell'insieme; **~ly** *ad* in gran parte.

lark [lɑːk] *n* (*bird*) allodola; (*joke*) scherzo, gioco; **to ~ about** *vi* fare lo stupido.

larva, *pl* **larvae** ['lɑːvə, -iː] *n* larva.

laryngitis [lærɪn'dʒaɪtɪs] *n* laringite *f*.

larynx ['lærɪŋks] *n* laringe *f*.

lascivious [lə'sɪvɪəs] *a* lascivo(a).

laser ['leɪzə*] *n* laser *m*.

lash [læʃ] *n* frustata; (*gen:* **eyelash**) ciglio // *vt* frustare; (*tie*) assicurare con una corda; **to ~ out** *vi:* **to ~ out** (**at** *or* **against sb/sth**) attaccare violentemente (qd/qc); **to ~ out** (**on sth**) (*col: spend*) spendere un sacco di soldi (per qc).

lass [læs] *n* ragazza.

lasso [læ'suː] *n* laccio // *vt* acchiappare con il laccio.

last [lɑːst] *a* ultimo(a); (*week, month, year*) scorso(a), passato(a) // *ad* per ultimo // *vi* durare; **~ week** la settimana scorsa; **~ night** ieri sera, la notte scorsa; **at ~** finalmente, alla fine; **~ing** *a* durevole; **~-minute** *a* fatto(a) (*or* preso(a) *etc*) all'ultimo momento.

latch [lætʃ] *n* serratura a scatto; **~key** *n* chiave *f* di casa.

late [leɪt] *a* (*not on time*) in ritardo; (*far on in day etc*) tardi *inv*; tardo(a); (*recent*) recente, ultimo(a); (*former*) ex; (*dead*) defunto(a) // *ad* tardi; (*behind time, schedule*) in ritardo; **of ~** di recente; **in ~ May** verso la fine di maggio; **~comer** *n* ritardatario/a; **~ly** *ad* recentemente; **~ness** *n* (*of person*) ritardo; (*of event*) tardezza, ora tarda.

latent ['leɪtnt] *a* latente.

later ['leɪtə*] *a* (*date etc*) posteriore; (*version etc*) successivo(a) // *ad* più tardi.

lateral ['lætərl] *a* laterale.

latest ['leɪtɪst] *a* ultimo(a), più recente; **at the ~** al più tardi.

lath, **~s** [læθ, læðz] *n* assicella.

lathe [leɪð] *n* tornio.

lather ['lɑːðə*] *n* schiuma di sapone // *vt* insaponare.

Latin ['lætɪn] *n* latino // *a* latino(a); **~ America** *n* America Latina; **~-American** *a* sudamericano(a).

latitude ['lætɪtjuːd] *n* latitudine *f*.

latrine [lə'triːn] *n* latrina.

latter ['lætə*] *a* secondo(a); più recente // *n:* **the ~** quest'ultimo, il secondo; **~ly** *ad* recentemente, negli ultimi tempi.

lattice ['lætɪs] *n* traliccio; graticolato.

laudable ['lɔːdəbl] *a* lodevole.

laugh [lɑːf] *n* risata // *vi* ridere; **to ~ at** *vt fus* (*misfortune etc*) ridere di; **I ~ed at his joke** la sua barzelletta mi fece ridere; **to ~ off** *vt* prendere alla leggera; **~able** *a* ridicolo(a); **~ing** *a* (*face*) ridente; **the ~ing stock of** lo zimbello di; **~ter** *n* riso; risate *fpl*.

launch [lɔːntʃ] *n* (*of rocket etc*) lancio; (*of new ship*) varo; (*boat*) scialuppa; (*also:* **motor ~**) lancia // *vt* (*rocket*) lanciare; (*ship, plan*) varare; **~ing** *n* lancio; varo;

~(ing) pad *n* rampa di lancio.

launder ['lɔːndə*] *vt* lavare e stirare.

launderette [lɔːn'drɛt] *n* lavanderia (automatica).

laundry ['lɔːndrɪ] *n* lavanderia; (*clothes*) biancheria; **to do the ~** fare il bucato.

laureate ['lɔːrɪət] *a* see **poet**.

laurel ['lɔrl] *n* lauro.

lava ['lɑːvə] *n* lava.

lavatory ['lævətərɪ] *n* gabinetto.

lavender ['lævəndə*] *n* lavanda.

lavish ['lævɪʃ] *a* copioso(a); abbondante; (*giving freely*): **~ with** prodigo(a) di, largo(a) in // *vt:* **to ~ on sb/sth** (*care*) profondere a qd/qc.

law [lɔː] *n* legge *f*; **~-abiding** *a* ubbidiente alla legge; **~ and order** *n* l'ordine *m* pubblico; **~breaker** *n* violatore/trice della legge; **~ court** *n* tribunale *m*, corte *f* di giustizia; **~ful** *a* legale; lecito(a); **~less** *a* senza legge; illegale.

lawn [lɔːn] *n* tappeto erboso; **~mower** *n* tosaerba *m* or *f* *inv*; **~ tennis** [-'tɛnɪs] *n* tennis *m* su prato.

law: ~ school *n* facoltà di legge; **~ student** *n* studente/essa di legge.

lawsuit ['lɔːsuːt] *n* processo, causa.

lawyer ['lɔːjə*] *n* (*consultant, with company*) giurista *m/f*; (*for sales, wills etc*) ≈ notaio; (*partner, in court*) ≈ avvocato/essa.

lax [læks] *a* rilassato(a).

laxative ['læksətɪv] *n* lassativo.

laxity ['læksɪtɪ] *n* rilassamento.

lay [leɪ] *pt* of **lie** // *a* laico(a); secolare // *vt* (*pt, pp* **laid**) posare, mettere; (*eggs*) fare; (*trap*) tendere; (*plans*) fare, elaborare; **to ~ the table** apparecchiare la tavola; **to ~ aside** *or* **by** *vt* mettere da parte; **to ~ down** *vt* mettere giù; **to ~ off** *vt* (*workers*) licenziare; **to ~ on** *vt* (*water, gas*) installare, mettere; (*provide*) fornire; (*paint*) applicare; **to ~ out** *vt* (*design*) progettare; (*display*) presentare; (*spend*) sborsare; **to ~ up** *vt* (*to store*) accumulare; (*ship*) mettere in disarmo; (*subj: illness*) costringere a letto; **~about** *n* sfaccendato/a, fannullone/a; **~-by** *n* piazzola (di sosta).

layer ['leɪə*] *n* strato.

layman ['leɪmən] *n* laico; profano.

layout ['leɪaut] *n* lay-out *m* *inv*, disposizione *f*; (*PRESS*) impaginazione *f*.

laze [leɪz] *vi* oziare.

laziness ['leɪzɪnɪs] *n* pigrizia.

lazy ['leɪzɪ] *a* pigro(a).

lb. *abbr* of **pound** (*weight*).

lead [liːd] *see also next headword; n* (*front position*) posizione *f* di testa; (*distance, time ahead*) vantaggio; (*clue*) indizio; (*to battery*) filo conduttore; (*ELEC*) conduttore *m* isolato; (*for dog*) guinzaglio; (*THEATRE*) parte *f* principale // *vb* (*pt,pp* **led** [lɛd]) *vt* menare, guidare, condurre; (*induce*) indurre; (*be leader of*) essere a capo di; (*SPORT*) essere in testa a // *vi* condurre, essere in testa; **to ~ to** menare a; condurre a; portare a; **to ~ astray** *vt* sviare; **to ~ away** vt condurre via; **to ~ back** to ricondurre a; **to ~ on** vt (*tease*) tenere sulla corda; **to ~ on to** vt (*induce*) portare a; **to ~ up to** portare a; (*fig*) preparare la strada per.

lead [lɛd] *see also previous headword*; n piombo; (*in pencil*) mina; **~en** a di piombo.

leader ['liːdəˀ] n capo; direttore/trice, leader m inv; (*in newspaper*) articolo di fondo; **~ship** n direzione f; capacità di comando.

leading ['liːdɪŋ] a primo(a); principale; **~ man/lady** n (THEATRE) primo attore/prima attrice.

leaf, leaves [liːf, liːvz] n foglia; (*of table*) ribalta.

leaflet ['liːflɪt] n dépliant m inv; (POL, REL) volantino.

league [liːg] n lega; (FOOTBALL) campionato; **to be in ~ with** essere in lega con.

leak [liːk] n (*out, also fig*) fuga; (*in*) infiltrazione f // vi (*pipe, liquid etc*) perdere; (*shoes*) lasciar passare l'acqua // vt (*liquid*) spandere; (*information*) divulgare; **to ~ out** vi perdere; (*information*) trapelare.

lean [liːn] a magro(a) // n (*of meat*) carne f magra // vb (*pt,pp* leaned *or* leant [lɛnt]) vi: **to ~ sth on** appoggiare qc su // vi (*slope*) pendere; (*rest*): **to ~ against** appoggiarsi contro; essere appoggiato(a) a; **to ~ on** appoggiarsi a; **to ~ back/forward** vi sporgersi in avanti/indietro; **to ~ over** vi inclinarsi; **~ing** n: **~ing (towards)** propensione f (per).

leap [liːp] n salto, balzo // vi (*pt,pp* leaped *or* leapt [lɛpt]) saltare, balzare; **~frog** n gioco di saltamontone; **~ year** n anno bisestile.

learn, *pt,pp* learned *or* learnt [ləːn, -t] vt,vi imparare; **~ed** a ['ləːnɪd] a erudito(a), dotto(a); **~er** n principiante m/f; apprendista m/f; **~ing** n erudizione f, sapienza.

lease [liːs] n contratto d'affitto // vt affittare.

leash [liːʃ] n guinzaglio.

least [liːst] a: **the ~ +** *noun* il(la) più piccolo(a), il(la) minimo(a); (*smallest amount of*) il(la) meno; **the ~ +** *adjective*: **the ~ beautiful girl** la ragazza meno bella; **the ~ expensive** il(la) meno caro(a); **the ~ money** il meno denaro; **at ~** almeno; **not in the ~** affatto, per nulla.

leather ['lɛðəˀ] n cuoio // *cpd* di cuoio.

leave [liːv] vb (*pt,pp* left [lɛft]) vt lasciare; (*go away from*) partire da // vi partire, andarsene // n (*time off*) congedo; (MIL, *also: consent*) licenza; **to be left** rimanere; **there's some milk left over** c'è rimasto del latte; **on ~** in congedo; **to take one's ~ of** congedarsi di; **to ~ out** vt omettere, tralasciare.

leaves [liːvz] *npl of* leaf.

Lebanon ['lɛbənən] n Libano.

lecherous ['lɛtʃərəs] a lascivo(a), lubrico(a).

lectern ['lɛktəːn] n leggio.

lecture ['lɛktʃəˀ] n conferenza; (SCOL) lezione f // vi fare conferenze; fare lezioni; **to ~ on** fare una conferenza su.

lecturer ['lɛktʃərəˀ] n (*speaker*) conferenziere/a; (*at university*) professore/essa, docente m/f.

led [lɛd] *pt,pp of* lead.

ledge [lɛdʒ] n (*of window*) davanzale m; (*on wall etc*) sporgenza; (*of mountain*) cornice f, cengia.

ledger ['lɛdʒəˀ] n libro maestro, registro.

lee [liː] n lato sottovento.

leech [liːtʃ] n sanguisuga.

leek [liːk] n porro.

leer [liəˀ] vi: **to ~ at sb** gettare uno sguardo voglioso or maligno su qd.

leeway ['liːweɪ] n (*fig*): **to have some ~** avere una certa libertà di agire.

left [lɛft] *pt,pp of* leave // a sinistro(a) // *ad* a sinistra // n sinistra; **the L~** (POL) la sinistra; **~-handed** a mancino(a); **~-hand side** n lato or fianco sinistro; **~-luggage (office)** n deposito m bagagli inv; **~-overs** npl avanzi mpl, resti mpl; **~-wing** n (MIL, SPORT) ala sinistra; (POL) sinistra; **~-wing** a (POL) di sinistra.

leg [lɛg] n gamba; (*of animal*) zampa; (*of furniture*) piede m; (CULIN: *of chicken*) coscia; (*of journey*) tappa; **1st/2nd ~** (SPORT) partita di andata/ritorno.

legacy ['lɛgəsɪ] n eredità f inv.

legal ['liːgl] a legale; **~ize** vt legalizzare.

legation [lɪ'geɪʃən] n legazione f.

legend ['lɛdʒənd] n leggenda; **~ary** a leggendario(a).

leggings ['lɛgɪŋz] npl ghette fpl.

legible ['lɛdʒəbl] a leggibile.

legion ['liːdʒən] n legione f.

legislate ['lɛdʒɪsleɪt] vi legiferare; **legislation** [-'leɪʃən] n legislazione f; **legislative** ['lɛdʒɪslətɪv] a legislativo(a); **legislator** n legislatore/trice; **legislature** ['lɛdʒɪslətʃəˀ] n corpo legislativo.

legitimacy [lɪ'dʒɪtɪməsɪ] n legittimità.

legitimate [lɪ'dʒɪtɪmət] a legittimo(a).

leg-room ['lɛgruːm] n spazio per le gambe.

leisure ['lɛʒəˀ] n agio, tempo libero; ricreazioni fpl; **at ~** all'agio, a proprio comodo; **~ centre** n centro di ricreazione; **~ly** a tranquillo(a); fatto(a) con comodo or senza fretta.

lemon ['lɛmən] n limone m; **~ade** n [-'neɪd] limonata.

lend, *pt,pp* lent [lɛnd, lɛnt] vt: **to ~ sth (to sb)** prestare qc (a qd); **~er** n prestatore/trice; **~ing library** n biblioteca circolante.

length [lɛŋθ] n lunghezza; (*section: of road, pipe etc*) pezzo, tratto; **at ~** (*at last*) finalmente, alla fine; (*lengthily*) a lungo; **~en** vt allungare, prolungare // vi allungarsi; ~ways ad per il lungo; ~y a molto lungo(a).

leniency ['li:nɪənsɪ] n indulgenza, clemenza.

lenient ['li:nɪənt] a indulgente, clemente.

lens [lɛnz] n lente f; (of camera) obiettivo.

lent [lɛnt] pt,pp of **lend**.

Lent [lɛnt] n Quaresima.

lentil ['lɛntl] n lenticchia.

Leo ['li:əu] n Leone m.

leopard ['lɛpəd] n leopardo.

leotard ['li:ətɑ:d] n calzamaglia.

leper ['lɛpə*] n lebbroso/a.

leprosy ['lɛprəsɪ] n lebbra.

lesbian ['lɛzbɪən] n lesbica.

less [lɛs] det, pronoun, ad meno; ~ than you/ever meno di Lei/che mai; ~ and ~ sempre meno; the ~ he works ... meno lui lavora ... .

lessen ['lɛsn] vi diminuire, attenuarsi // vt diminuire, ridurre.

lesson ['lɛsn] n lezione f.

lest [lɛst] cj per paura di + infinitive, per paura che + sub.

let, pt,pp **let** [lɛt] vt lasciare; (lease) dare in affitto; **he ~ me go** mi ha lasciato andare; ~'s **go** andiamo; ~ **him come** lo lasci venire; '**to ~**' 'affittasi'; **to ~ down** vt (lower) abbassare; (dress) allungare; (hair) sciogliere; (disappoint) deludere; **to ~ go** vi mollare // vt lasciare andare; **to ~ in** vt lasciare entrare; (visitor etc) far entrare; **to ~ off** vt lasciare andare; (firework etc) far partire; (smell etc) emettere; **to ~ out** vt lasciare uscire; (dress) allargare; (scream) emettere; **to ~ up** vi diminuire.

lethal ['li:θl] a letale, mortale.

lethargic [lɛ'θɑ:dʒɪk] a letargico(a).

lethargy ['lɛθədʒɪ] n letargia.

letter ['lɛtə*] n lettera; ~s npl (LITERATURE) lettere; ~ **bomb** n lettera esplosiva; ~**box** n buca delle lettere; ~**ing** n iscrizione f; caratteri mpl.

lettuce ['lɛtɪs] n lattuga, insalata.

leukaemia [lu:'ki:mɪə] n leucemia.

level ['lɛvl] a piatto(a), piano(a); orizzontale // n livello // vt livellare, spianare; **to be ~ with** essere alla pari di; '**A**' ~s npl ≈ esami mpl di maturità; '**O**' ~s npl esami fatti in Inghilterra all'età di 16 anni; **on the ~** piano(a), onesto(a); **to ~ off** or **out** vi (prices etc) stabilizzarsi; ~ **crossing** n passaggio a livello; ~**-headed** a equilibrato(a).

lever ['li:və*] n leva // vt: **to ~ up/out** sollevare/estrarre con una leva; ~**age** n: ~**age** (**on** or **with**) ascendente m (su).

levity ['lɛvɪtɪ] n leggerezza, frivolità.

levy ['lɛvɪ] n tassa, imposta // vt imporre, percepire.

lewd [lu:d] a osceno(a), lascivo(a).

liability [laɪə'bɪlətɪ] n responsabilità f inv; (handicap) peso; **liabilities** npl debiti mpl; (on balance sheet) passivo.

liable ['laɪəbl] a (subject): ~ **to** soggetto(a) a; passibile di; (responsible):

~ (**for**) responsabile di; (likely): ~ **to do** propenso(a) a fare.

liaison [li:'eɪzən] n relazione f; (MIL) collegamento.

liar ['laɪə*] n bugiardo/a.

libel ['laɪbl] n libello; diffamazione f // vt diffamare.

liberal ['lɪbərl] a liberale; (generous): **to be ~ with** distribuire liberamente.

liberate ['lɪbəreɪt] vt liberare; **liberation** [-'reɪʃən] n liberazione f.

liberty ['lɪbətɪ] n libertà f inv; **at ~ to do** libero(a) di fare; **to take the ~ of** prendersi la libertà di, permettersi di.

Libra ['li:brə] n Bilancia.

librarian [laɪ'brɛərɪən] n bibliotecario/a.

library ['laɪbrərɪ] n biblioteca.

libretto [lɪ'brɛtəu] n libretto.

Libya ['lɪbɪə] n Libia; ~**n** a, n libico(a).

lice [laɪs] npl of **louse**.

licence ['laɪsns] n autorizzazione f, permesso; (COMM) licenza; (RADIO, TV) canone m, abbonamento; (also: **driving** ~) patente f di guida; (excessive freedom) licenza; ~ **plate** n targa.

license ['laɪsns] n (US) = **licence** // vt dare una licenza a; ~**d** a (for alcohol) che ha la licenza di vendere bibite alcoliche.

licentious [laɪ'sɛnʃəs] a licenzioso(a).

lichen ['laɪkən] n lichene m.

lick [lɪk] vt leccare // n leccata; **a ~ of paint** una passata di vernice.

licorice ['lɪkərɪs] n = **liquorice**.

lid [lɪd] n coperchio.

lido ['laɪdəu] n piscina all'aperto.

lie [laɪ] n bugia, menzogna // vi mentire, dire bugie; (pt **lay**, pp **lain** [leɪ, leɪn]) (rest) giacere, star disteso(a); (in grave) giacere, riposare; (of object: be situated) trovarsi, essere; **to ~ low** (fig) latitare; **to have a ~-down** sdraiarsi, riposarsi; **to have a ~-in** rimanere a letto.

lieutenant [lɛf'tɛnənt] n tenente m.

life, lives [laɪf, laɪvz] n vita // cpd di vita; della vita; ~ **assurance** n assicurazione f sulla vita; ~**belt** n cintura di salvataggio; ~**boat** n scialuppa di salvataggio; ~ **expectancy** n durata media della vita; ~**guard** n bagnino; ~ **jacket** n salvagente m, cintura di salvataggio; ~**less** a senza vita; ~**like** a verosimile; rassomigliante; ~**line** n cavo di salvataggio; ~**long** a per tutta la vita; ~ **preserver** n (US) salvagente m, cintura di salvataggio; (Brit: col) sfollagente m; ~**-raft** n zattera di salvataggio; ~**-saver** n bagnino; ~**-sized** a a grandezza naturale; ~**time** n: **in his ~time** durante la sua vita; **in a ~time** nell'arco della vita; in tutta la vita.

lift [lɪft] vt sollevare, levare; (steal) prendere, rubare // vi (fog) alzarsi // n (elevator) ascensore m; **to give sb a ~** dare un passaggio a qd; ~**-off** n decollo.

ligament ['lɪgəmənt] n legamento.

light [laɪt] n luce f, lume m; (daylight) luce f, giorno; (lamp) lampada; (AUT: rear ~) luce f di posizione; (: headlamp) fanale m;

(for cigarette etc): **have you got a ~?** ha del fuoco?; **~s** *npl* (*AUT: traffic ~s*) semaforo // *vt* (*pt, pp* **lighted** *or* **lit** [lɪt]) *(candle, cigarette, fire)* accendere; *(room)* illuminare // *a (room, colour)* chiaro(a); *(not heavy, also fig)* leggero(a); **to ~ up** *vi* illuminarsi // *vt (illuminate)* illuminare; **~bulb** *n* lampadina; **~en** *vi* schiarirsi // *vt (give light to)* illuminare; *(make lighter)* schiarire; *(make less heavy)* alleggerire; **~er** *n* (*also*: **cigarette ~**) accendino; *(boat)* chiatta; **~headed** *a* stordito(a); **~hearted** *a* gioioso(a), gaio(a); **~house** *n* faro; **~ing** *n* illuminazione f; **~ing-up time** *n* orario per l'accensione delle luci; **~ly** *ad* leggermente; **~ meter** *n* (PHOT) esposimetro; **~ness** *n* chiarezza; *(in weight)* leggerezza.

lightning ['laɪtnɪŋ] *n* lampo, fulmine *m*; **~ conductor** *n* parafulmine *m*.

lightweight ['laɪtweɪt] *a (suit)* leggero(a); *(boxer)* peso leggero *inv*.

light year ['laɪtjɪə*] *n* anno *m* luce *inv*.

like [laɪk] *vt (person)* volere bene a; *(activity, object, food)*: **I ~ swimming/that book/chocolate** mi piace nuotare/quel libro/il cioccolato // *prep* come // *a* simile, uguale // *n*: **the ~** un(a) simile; uno(a) uguale; *(pej)* una cosa simile; uno(a) uguale; **his ~s and dislikes** i suoi gusti; **I would ~**, **I'd ~** mi piacerebbe, vorrei; **to be/look ~ sb/sth** somigliare a qd/qc; **that's just ~ him** è proprio da lui; **~able** *a* simpatico(a).

likelihood ['laɪklɪhud] *n* probabilità.

likely ['laɪklɪ] *a* probabile; plausibile; **he's ~ to leave** probabilmente partirà, è probabile che parta.

like-minded [laɪk'maɪndɪd] *a* che pensa allo stesso modo.

liken ['laɪkən] *vt*: **to ~ sth to** paragonare qc a.

likewise ['laɪkwaɪz] *ad* similmente, nello stesso modo.

liking ['laɪkɪŋ] *n*: **~ (for)** simpatia (per); debole *m* (per).

lilac ['laɪlək] *n* lilla *m inv* // *a* lilla *inv*.

lilting ['lɪltɪŋ] *a* melodioso(a).

lily ['lɪlɪ] *n* giglio; **~ of the valley** *n* mughetto.

limb [lɪm] *n* membro.

limber ['lɪmbə*]: **to ~ up** *vi* riscaldarsi i muscoli.

limbo ['lɪmbəu] *n*: **to be in ~** *(fig)* essere in sospeso.

lime [laɪm] *n (tree)* tiglio; *(fruit)* limetta; *(GEO)* calce f.

limelight ['laɪmlaɪt] *n*: **in the ~** *(fig)* alla ribalta, in vista.

limerick ['lɪmərɪk] *n* poesiola umoristica di 5 versi.

limestone ['laɪmstəun] *n* pietra calcarea; *(GEO)* calce *f*.

limit ['lɪmɪt] *n* limite *m* // *vt* limitare; **~ation** [-'teɪʃən] *n* limitazione *f*, limite *m*; **~ed** *a* limitato(a), ristretto(a); **~ed (liability) company (Ltd)** *n* ≈ società *f*

inv a responsabilità limitata (S.r.l.).

limousine ['lɪməzi:n] *n* limousine *f inv*.

limp [lɪmp] *vi* zoppicare // *a* floscio(a), flaccido(a).

limpet ['lɪmpɪt] *n* patella.

line [laɪn] *n* linea; *(rope)* corda; *(wire)* filo; *(of poem)* verso; *(row, series)* fila, riga; coda // *vt (clothes)*: **to ~ (with)** foderare (di); *(box)*: **to ~ (with)** rivestire *or* foderare (di); *(subj: trees, crowd)* fiancheggiare; **in ~ with** d'accordo con; **to ~ up** *vi* allinearsi, mettersi in fila // *vt* mettere in fila.

linear ['lɪnɪə*] *a* lineare.

linen ['lɪnɪn] *n* biancheria, panni *mpl*; *(cloth)* tela di lino.

liner ['laɪnə*] *n* nave *f* di linea.

linesman ['laɪnzmən] *n* guardalinee *m inv*.

line-up ['laɪnʌp] *n* allineamento, fila; *(SPORT)* formazione *f* di gioco.

linger ['lɪŋgə*] *vi* attardarsi; indugiare; *(smell, tradition)* persistere; **~ing** *a* lungo(a); persistente; *(death)* lento(a).

lingo, ~es ['lɪŋgəu] *n (pej)* gergo.

linguist ['lɪŋgwɪst] *n* linguista *m/f*; poliglotta *m/f*; **~ic** [lɪŋ'gwɪstɪk] *a* linguistico(a); **~ics** *n* linguistica.

lining ['laɪnɪŋ] *n* fodera.

link [lɪŋk] *n (of a chain)* anello; *(connection)* legame *m*, collegamento // *vt* collegare, unire, congiungere; **~s** *npl* pista *or* terreno da golf; **to ~ up** *vt* collegare, unire // *vi* riunirsi; associarsi.

linoleum [lɪ'nəuliəm] *n* linoleum *m inv*.

lint [lɪnt] *n* garza.

lintel ['lɪntl] *n* architrave *f*.

lion ['laɪən] *n* leone *m*; **~ cub** leoncino; **~ess** *n* leonessa.

lip [lɪp] *n* labbro; *(of cup etc)* orlo; *(insolence)* sfacciataggine *f*, **~read** *vi* leggere sulle labbra; **to pay ~ service to sth** essere favorevole a qc solo a parole; **~stick** *n* rossetto.

liqueur [lɪ'kjuə*] *n* liquore *m*.

liquid ['lɪkwɪd] *n* liquido // *a* liquido(a); **~ assets** *npl* attività *fpl* liquide, crediti *mpl* liquidi.

liquidate ['lɪkwɪdeɪt] *vt* liquidare; **liquidation** [-'deɪʃən] *n* liquidazione *f*; **liquidator** *n* liquidatore *m*.

liquidize ['lɪkwɪdaɪz] *vt (CULIN)* passare al frullatore.

liquor ['lɪkə*] *n* alcool *m*.

liquorice ['lɪkərɪs] *n* liquirizia.

lisp [lɪsp] *n* difetto nel pronunciare le sibilanti.

list [lɪst] *n* lista, elenco; *(of ship)* sbandamento // *vt (write down)* mettere in lista; fare una lista di; *(enumerate)* elencare // *vi (ship)* sbandare.

listen ['lɪsn] *vi* ascoltare; **to ~ to** ascoltare; **~er** *n* ascoltatore/trice.

listless ['lɪstlɪs] *a* apatico(a).

lit [lɪt] *pt,pp of* **light**.

litany ['lɪtənɪ] *n* litania.

literacy ['lɪtərəsɪ] *n* fatto di sapere leggere e scrivere; cultura.

literal ['lɪtərl] *a* letterale; ~**ly** *ad* alla lettera, letteralmente.

literary ['lɪtərərɪ] *a* letterario(a).

literate ['lɪtərət] *a* che sa leggere e scrivere, istruito(a).

literature ['lɪtərɪtʃə*] *n* letteratura; (*brochures etc*) materiale *m*.

lithe [laɪð] *a* agile, snello(a).

litigate ['lɪtɪgeɪt] *vt* muovere causa a // *vi* litigare; **litigation** [-'geɪʃən] *n* causa.

litre ['liːtə*] *n* litro.

litter ['lɪtə*] *n* (*rubbish*) rifiuti *mpl*; (*young animals*) figliata // *vt* sparpagliare; lasciare rifiuti in; ~ **bin** *n* cestino per rifiuti; ~**ed with** coperto(a) di.

little ['lɪtl] *a* (*small*) piccolo(a); (*not much*) poco(a) // *ad* poco; **a** ~ un po' (di); **a** ~ **milk** un po' di latte; **by** ~ **by** ~ a poco a poco; **to make** ~ **of** dare poca importanza a.

liturgy ['lɪtədʒɪ] *n* liturgia.

live *vi* [lɪv] vivere, abitare // *a* [laɪv] (*animal*) vivo(a); (*wire*) sotto tensione; (*broadcast*) diretto(a); **to** ~ **down** *vt* far dimenticare (alla gente); **to** ~ **in** *vi* essere interno(a); avere vitto e alloggio; **to** ~ **on** *vt fus* (*food*) vivere di // *vi* sopravvivere, continuare a vivere; **to** ~ **up to** *vt fus* tener fede a, non venir meno a.

livelihood ['laɪvlɪhud] *n* vita, mezzi *mpl* di sussistenza.

liveliness ['laɪvlɪnəs] *n* vivacità.

lively ['laɪvlɪ] *a* vivace, vivo(a).

liver ['lɪvə*] *n* fegato.

livery ['lɪvərɪ] *n* livrea.

lives [laɪvz] *npl of* **life**.

livestock ['laɪvstɔk] *n* bestiame *m*.

livid ['lɪvɪd] *a* livido(a); (*furious*) livido(a) di rabbia, furibondo(a).

living ['lɪvɪŋ] *a* vivo(a), vivente // *n*: **to earn** *or* **make a** ~ guadagnarsi la vita; ~ **room** *n* soggiorno; ~ **standards** *npl* tenore *m* di vita; ~ **wage** *n* salario sufficiente per vivere.

lizard ['lɪzəd] *n* lucertola.

llama ['lɑːmə] *n* lama *m inv*.

load [ləud] *n* (*weight*) peso; (*ELEC, TECH, thing carried*) carico // *vt*: **to** ~ (**with**) (*lorry, ship*) caricare (di); (*gun, camera*) caricare (con); **a** ~ **of**, ~**s of** (*fig*) un sacco di; ~**ed** *a* (*dice*) falsato(a); (*question, word*) capzioso(a).

loaf, loaves [ləuf, ləuvz] *n* pane *m*, pagnotta // *vi* (*also*: ~ **about**, ~ **around**) bighellonare.

loam [ləum] *n* terra di marna.

loan [ləun] *n* prestito // *vt* dare in prestito; **on** ~ in prestito.

loath [ləuθ] *a*: **to be** ~ **to do** essere restio(a) a fare.

loathe [ləuð] *vt* detestare, aborrire; **loathing** *n* aborrimento, disgusto.

loaves [ləuvz] *npl of* **loaf**.

lobby ['lɔbɪ] *n* atrio, vestibolo; (*POL: pressure group*) gruppo di pressione // *vt* fare pressione su.

lobe [ləub] *n* lobo.

lobster ['lɔbstə*] *n* aragosta.

local ['ləukl] *a* locale // *n* (*pub*) bar *m inv or* caffè *m inv* vicino; **the** ~**s** *npl* la gente della zona; ~ **call** *n* telefonata urbana; ~ **government** *n* amministrazione *f* locale.

locality [ləu'kælɪtɪ] *n* località *f inv*; (*position*) posto, luogo.

locally ['ləukəlɪ] *ad* da queste parti; nel vicinato.

locate [ləu'keɪt] *vt* (*find*) trovare; (*situate*) collocare.

location [ləu'keɪʃən] *n* posizione *f*; **on** ~ (*CINEMA*) all'esterno.

loch [lɔx] *n* lago.

lock [lɔk] *n* (*of door, box*) serratura; (*of canal*) chiusa; (*of hair*) ciocca, riccio // *vt* (*with key*) chiudere a chiave; (*immobilize*) bloccare // *vi* (*door etc*) chiudersi a chiave; (*wheels*) bloccarsi, incepparsi.

locker ['lɔkə*] *n* armadietto.

locket ['lɔkɪt] *n* medaglione *m*.

lockjaw ['lɔkdʒɔː] *n* tetano.

locomotive [ləukə'məutɪv] *n* locomotiva.

locust ['ləukəst] *n* locusta.

lodge [lɔdʒ] *n* casetta, portineria // *vi* (*person*): **to** ~ (**with**) essere a pensione (presso *or* da) // *vt* (*appeal etc*) presentare, fare; **to** ~ **a complaint** presentare un reclamo; **to** ~ (**itself**) **in/between** piantarsi dentro/fra; ~**r** *n* affittuario/a; (*with room and meals*) pensionante *m/f*.

lodgings ['lɔdʒɪŋz] *npl* camera d'affitto; camera ammobiliata.

loft [lɔft] *n* soffitto; (*AGR*) granaio.

lofty ['lɔftɪ] *a* alto(a); (*haughty*) altezzoso(a).

log [lɔg] *n* (*of wood*) ceppo; (*book*) = **logbook**.

logbook ['lɔgbuk] *n* (*NAUT, AVIAT*) diario di bordo; (*of lorry-driver*) registro di viaggio; (*of events, movement of goods etc*) registro; (*of car*) libretto di circolazione.

loggerheads ['lɔgəhɛdz] *npl*: **at** ~ (**with**) ai ferri corti (con).

logic ['lɔdʒɪk] *n* logica; ~**al** *a* logico(a); ~**ally** *ad* logicamente.

logistics [lɔ'dʒɪstɪks] *n* logistica.

loin [lɔɪn] *n* (*CULIN*) lombata; ~**s** *npl* reni *fpl*.

loiter ['lɔɪtə*] *vi* attardarsi; **to** ~ (**about**) indugiare, bighellonare.

loll [lɔl] *vi* (*also*: ~ **about**) essere stravaccato(a).

lollipop ['lɔlɪpɔp] *n* lecca lecca *m inv*; ~ **man/lady** *n* impiegato/a che aiuta i bambini ad attraversare la strada in vicinanza di scuole.

London ['lʌndən] *n* Londra; ~**er** *n* londinese *m/f*.

lone [ləun] *a* solitario(a).

loneliness ['ləunlɪnɪs] *n* solitudine *f*, isolamento.

lonely ['ləunlɪ] *a* solo(a); solitario(a), isolato(a); **to feel** ~ sentirsi solo.

loner ['ləunə*] *n* solitario/a.

long [lɔŋ] a lungo(a) // ad a lungo, per molto tempo // vi: to ~ **for sth/to do** desiderare qc/di fare; non veder l'ora di aver qc/di fare; **he had** ~ **understood that...** aveva capito da molto tempo che...; **how** ~ **is this river/course?** quanto è lungo questo fiume/corso?; **6 metres** ~ lungo 6 metri; **6 months** ~ che dura 6 mesi, di 6 mesi; **all night** ~ tutta la notte; ~ **before** molto tempo prima; **before** ~ (+ future) presto, fra poco; (+ past) poco tempo dopo; **at** ~ **last** finalmente; ~-**distance** a (race) di fondo; (call) interurbano(a); ~-**hand** n scrittura normale; ~ing n desiderio, voglia, brama // a di desiderio; pieno(a) di nostalgia.

longitude ['lɔŋgɪtjuːd] n longitudine f.

long: ~ **jump** n salto in lunghezza; ~-**lost** a perduto(a) da tempo; ~-**playing** a: ~-**playing record (L.P.)** n (disc) 33 giri m inv; ~-**range** a a lunga portata; ~-**sighted** a presbite; (fig) lungimirante; ~-**standing** a di vecchia data; ~-**suffering** a estremamente paziente; infinitamente tollerante; ~-**term** a a lungo termine; ~ **wave** n onde fpl lunghe; ~-**winded** a prolisso(a), interminabile.

loo [luː] n (col) W.C. m inv, cesso.

look [luk] vi guardare; (seem) sembrare, parere; (building etc): to ~ **south/on to the sea** dare a sud/sul mare // n sguardo; (appearance) aspetto, aria; ~s npl aspetto; bellezza; to ~ **like** assomigliare a; to ~ **after** vt fus occuparsi di, prendere cura di; guardare, badare a; to ~ **at** vt fus guardare; to ~ **down on** vt fus (fig) guardare dall'alto, disprezzare; to ~ **for** vt fus cercare; to ~ **forward to** vt fus non veder l'ora di; to ~ **on** vi fare da spettatore; to ~ **out** vi (beware): to ~ **out (for)** stare in guardia (per); to ~ **out for** vt fus stare in aspetto per; cercare; to ~ **to** vt fus stare attento(a) a, (rely on,) contare su; to ~ **up** vi alzare gli occhi; (improve) migliorare // vt (word) cercare; (friend) andare a trovare; to ~ **up to** vt fus avere rispetto per; ~-**out** n posto d'osservazione; guardia; **to be on the** ~-**out (for)** stare in guardia (per).

loom [luːm] n telaio // vi sorgere; (fig) minacciare.

loop [luːp] n cappio; ~**hole** n via d'uscita; scappatoia.

loose [luːs] a (knot) sciolto(a); (screw) allentato(a); (stone) cadente; (clothes) ampio(a), largo(a); (animal) in libertà, scappato(a); (life, morals) dissoluto(a); (discipline) allentato(a); (thinking) poco rigoroso(a), vago(a); **to be at a** ~ **end** non saper che fare; ~**ly** ad lentamente; approssimativamente; ~**n** vt sciogliere.

loot [luːt] n bottino // vt saccheggiare; ~**ing** n saccheggio.

lop [lɔp]: **to** ~ **off** vt tagliare via, recidere.

lop-sided ['lɔp'saɪdɪd] a non equilibrato(a), assimetrico(a).

lord [lɔːd] n signore m; **L**~ **Smith** lord

Smith; **the L**~ il Signore; **the (House of) L**~**s** la Camera dei Lord; ~**ly** a nobile, maestoso(a); (arrogant) altero(a); ~**ship** n: **your L**~**ship** Sua Eccellenza.

lore [lɔː*] n tradizioni fpl.

lorry ['lɔrɪ] n camion m inv; ~ **driver** n camionista m.

lose [luːz], pt,pp **lost** [luːz, lɔst] vt perdere; (pursuers) distanziare // vi perdere; **to** ~ (**time**) (clock) ritardare; ~**r** n perdente m/f.

loss [lɔs] n perdita; **to be at a** ~ essere perplesso(a).

lost [lɔst] pt,pp of **lose** // a perduto(a); ~ **property** n oggetti mpl smarriti.

lot [lɔt] n (at auctions) lotto; (destiny) destino, sorte f; **the** ~ tutto(a) quanto(a); tutti(e) quanti(e); **a** ~ molto; **a** ~ **of** una gran quantità di, un sacco di; ~**s of** molto(a); **to draw** ~**s (for sth)** tirare a sorte (per qc).

lotion ['ləuʃən] n lozione f.

lottery ['lɔtərɪ] n lotteria.

loud [laud] a forte, alto(a); (gaudy) vistoso(a), sgargiante // ad (speak etc) forte; ~**hailer** n portavoce m inv; ~**ly** ad fortemente, ad alta voce; ~**speaker** n altoparlante m.

lounge [laundʒ] n salotto, soggiorno // vi oziare; starsene colle mani in mano; ~ **suit** n abito completo; abito da passeggio.

louse, pl **lice** [laus, laɪs] n pidocchio.

lousy ['lauzɪ] a (fig) orrendo(a), schifoso(a).

lout [laut] n zoticone m.

lovable ['lʌvəbl] a simpatico(a), carino(a); amabile.

love [lʌv] n amore m // vt amare; voler bene a; **to** ~ **to do: I** ~ **to do** mi piace fare; **to be in** ~ **with** essere innamorato(a) di; **to make** ~ fare l'amore; **'15** ~' (TENNIS) '15 a zero'; ~ **affair** n intrigo amoroso; ~ **letter** n lettera d'amore.

lovely ['lʌvlɪ] a bello(a); incantevole; gradevole, piacevole.

lover ['lʌvə*] n amante m/f; (amateur): **a** ~ **of** un(un')amante di; un(un')appassionato(a) di.

loving ['lʌvɪŋ] a affettuoso(a), amoroso(a), tenero(a).

low [ləu] a basso(a) // ad in basso // n (METEOR) depressione f // vi (cow) muggire; **to feel** ~ sentirsi giù; **he's very** ~ (ill) è molto debole; **to turn (down)** ~ vt abbassare; ~-**cut** a (dress) scollato(a); ~**ly** a umile, modesto(a); ~-**lying** a a basso livello; ~-**paid** a mal pagato(a).

loyal ['lɔɪəl] a fedele, leale; ~**ty** n fedeltà, lealtà.

lozenge ['lɔzɪndʒ] n (MED) pastiglia; (GEOM) losanga.

L.P. n abbr see **long-playing**.

Ltd abbr see **limited**.

lubricant ['luːbrɪkənt] n lubrificante m.

lubricate ['luːbrɪkeɪt] vt lubrificare.

lucid ['luːsɪd] a lucido(a); ~**ity** [-'sɪdɪtɪ] n lucidità.

luck [lʌk] n fortuna, sorte f; **bad ~** sfortuna, mala sorte; **~ily** ad fortunatamente, per fortuna; **~y** a fortunato(a); (number etc) che porta fortuna.

lucrative ['lu:krətɪv] a lucrativo(a), lucroso(a), profittevole.

ludicrous ['lu:dɪkrəs] a ridicolo(a), assurdo(a).

lug [lʌg] vt trascinare.

luggage ['lʌgɪdʒ] n bagagli mpl; **~ rack** n portabagagli m inv.

lukewarm ['lu:kwɔ:m] a tiepido(a).

lull [lʌl] n intervallo di calma // vt (child) cullare; (person, fear) acquietare, calmare.

lullaby ['lʌləbaɪ] n ninnananna.

lumbago [lʌm'beɪgəu] n lombaggine f.

lumber ['lʌmbə*] n roba vecchia; **~jack** n boscaiolo.

luminous ['lu:mɪnəs] a luminoso(a).

lump [lʌmp] n pezzo; (in sauce) grumo; (swelling) gonfiore m // vt (also: ~ together) riunire, mettere insieme; **a ~ sum** somma globale; **~y** a (sauce) grumoso(a).

lunacy ['lu:nəsɪ] n demenza, follia, pazzia.

lunar ['lu:nə*] a lunare.

lunatic ['lu:nətɪk] n, a pazzo(a), matto(a).

lunch [lʌntʃ] n pranzo.

luncheon ['lʌntʃən] n pranzo; **~ voucher** n buono m pasto inv.

lung [lʌŋ] n polmone m.

lunge [lʌndʒ] vi (also: ~ **forward**) fare un balzo in avanti.

lurch [lɜ:tʃ] vi vacillare, barcollare // n scatto improvviso.

lure [luə*] n richiamo; lusinga // vt allettare.

lurid ['luərɪd] a sgargiante; (details etc) impressionante.

lurk [lɜ:k] vi stare in agguato.

luscious ['lʌʃəs] a succulento(a); delizioso(a).

lush [lʌʃ] a lussureggiante.

lust [lʌst] n lussuria; cupidigia; desiderio; (fig): ~ **for** sete f di; **to ~ after** vt fus bramare, desiderare; **~ful** a lascivo(a), voglioso(a).

lustre ['lʌstə*] n lustro, splendore m.

lusty ['lʌstɪ] a vigoroso(a), robusto(a).

lute [lu:t] n liuto.

Luxembourg ['lʌksəmbɜ:g] n Lussemburgo.

luxuriant [lʌg'zjuərɪənt] a lussureggiante.

luxurious [lʌg'zjuərɪəs] a sontuoso(a), di lusso.

luxury ['lʌkʃərɪ] n lusso // cpd di lusso.

lying ['laɪɪŋ] n mentire m.

lynch [lɪntʃ] vt linciare.

lynx [lɪŋks] n lince f.

lyre ['laɪə*] n lira.

lyric ['lɪrɪk] a lirico(a); **~s** npl (of song) parole fpl; **~al** a lirico(a).

M

m. abbr of **metre, mile, million**.

M.A. abbr see **master**.

mac [mæk] n impermeabile m.

macaroni [mækə'rəunɪ] n maccheroni mpl.

mace [meɪs] n mazza; (spice) macis m or f.

machine [mə'ʃi:n] n macchina // vt (dress etc) cucire a macchina; **~ gun** n mitragliatrice f; **~ry** n macchinario, macchine fpl; (fig) macchina; **machinist** n macchinista m/f.

mackerel ['mækrl] n, pl inv sgombro.

mackintosh ['mækɪntɔʃ] n impermeabile m.

mad [mæd] a matto(a), pazzo(a); (foolish) sciocco(a); (angry) furioso(a).

madam ['mædəm] n signora.

madden ['mædn] vt fare infuriare.

made [meɪd] pt, pp of **make**; **~-to-measure** a fatto(a) su misura.

madly ['mædlɪ] ad follemente; (love) alla follia.

madman ['mædmən] n pazzo, alienato.

madness ['mædnɪs] n pazzia.

magazine [mægə'zi:n] n (PRESS) rivista; (MIL: store) magazzino, deposito; (of firearm) caricatore m.

maggot ['mægət] n baco, verme m.

magic ['mædʒɪk] n magia // a magico(a); **~al** a magico(a); **~ian** [mə'dʒɪʃən] n mago/a.

magistrate ['mædʒɪstreɪt] n magistrato; giudice m/f.

magnanimous [mæg'nænɪməs] a magnanimo(a).

magnate ['mægneɪt] n magnate m.

magnet ['mægnɪt] n magnete m, calamita; **~ic** [-'netɪk] a magnetico(a); **~ism** n magnetismo.

magnification [mægnɪfɪ'keɪʃən] n ingrandimento.

magnificence [mæg'nɪfɪsns] n magnificenza.

magnificent [mæg'nɪfɪsnt] a magnifico(a).

magnify ['mægnɪfaɪ] vt ingrandire; **~ing glass** n lente f d'ingrandimento.

magnitude ['mægnɪtju:d] n grandezza; importanza.

magnolia [mæg'nəulɪə] n magnolia.

magpie ['mægpaɪ] n gazza.

mahogany [mə'hɔgənɪ] n mogano // cpd di or in mogano.

maid [meɪd] n domestica; (in hotel) cameriera; **old ~** (pej) vecchia zitella.

maiden ['meɪdn] n fanciulla // a (aunt etc) nubile; (speech, voyage) inaugurale; **~ name** n nome m nubile or da ragazza.

mail [meɪl] n posta // vt spedire (per posta); **~box** n (US) cassetta per la posta; **~ing list** n elenco d'indirizzi; **~-order** n vendita (or acquisto) per corrispondenza.

maim [meɪm] vt mutilare.

main [meɪn] a principale // n (pipe)

conduttura principale; **the ~s** (ELEC) la linea principale; **~s operated** a che funziona a elettricità; **in the ~** nel complesso, nell'insieme; **~land** n continente m; **~stay** n (fig) sostegno principale.

maintain [mein'tein] vt mantenere; (affirm) sostenere; **maintenance** ['meintənəns] n manutenzione f; (alimony) alimenti mpl.

maisonette [meizə'nɛt] n appartamento a due piani.

maize [meiz] n granturco, mais m.

majestic [mə'dʒɛstik] a maestoso(a).

majesty ['mædʒisti] n maestà f inv.

major ['meidʒə*] n (MIL) maggiore m // a (greater, MUS) maggiore; (in importance) principale, importante.

majority [mə'dʒɔriti] n maggioranza.

make [meik] vt (pt, pp made [meid]) fare; (manufacture) fare, fabbricare; (cause to be): **to ~ sb sad** etc rendere qd triste etc; (force): **to ~ sb do sth** costringere qd a fare qc, far fare qc a qd; (equal): **2 and 2 ~ 4** 2 più 2 fa 4 // n fabbricazione f; (brand) marca; **to ~ do with** arrangiarsi con; **to ~ for** vt fus (place) avviarsi verso; **to ~ out** vt (write out) scrivere; (understand) capire; (see) distinguere; (: numbers) decifrare; **to ~ up** vt (invent) inventare; (parcel) fare // vi conciliarsi; (with cosmetics) truccarsi; **to ~ up for** vt fus compensare; ricuperare; **~-believe** a immaginario(a); **~r** n fabbricante m/f; creatore/trice, autore/trice; **~shift** a improvvisato(a); **~-up** n trucco; (articles) cosmetici mpl.

making ['meikiŋ] n (fig): **in the ~** in formazione.

maladjusted [mælə'dʒʌstid] a incapace di adattarsi.

malaise [mæ'leiz] n malessere m.

malaria [mə'lɛəriə] n malaria.

Malaysia [mə'leiziə] n Malaysia.

male [meil] n (BIOL, ELEC) maschio // a maschile; maschio(a); **~ and female students** studenti e studentesse; **~ sex** sesso maschile.

malevolent [mə'lɛvələnt] a malevolo(a).

malfunction [mæl'fʌŋkʃən] n funzione f difettosa.

malice ['mælis] n malevolenza; **malicious** [mə'liʃəs] a malevolo(a); (LAW) doloso(a).

malign [mə'lain] vt malignare su; calunniare.

malignant [mə'lignənt] a (MED) maligno(a).

malingerer [mə'liŋgərə*] n scansafatiche m/f inv.

malleable ['mæliəbl] a malleabile.

mallet ['mælit] n maglio.

malnutrition [mælnju:'triʃən] n denutrizione f.

malpractice [mæl'præktis] n prevaricazione f; negligenza.

malt [mɔ:lt] n malto.

Malta ['mɔ:ltə] n Malta; **Maltese** [-'ti:z] a, n (pl inv) maltese (m/f).

maltreat [mæl'tri:t] vt maltrattare.

mammal ['mæml] n mammifero.

mammoth ['mæməθ] n mammut m inv // a enorme, gigantesco(a).

man, pl **men** [mæn, mɛn] n uomo; (CHESS) pezzo; (DRAUGHTS) pedina // vt fornire d'uomini; stare a; essere di servizio a.

manage ['mænidʒ] vi farcela // vt (be in charge of) occuparsi di; gestire; **~able** a maneggevole; fattibile; **~ment** n amministrazione f, direzione f; **~r** n direttore m; (COMM) gerente m; (of artist) manager m inv; **~ress** [-ə'rɛs] n direttrice f; gerente f; **~rial** [-ə'dʒiəriəl] a dirigenziale; **managing** a: **managing director** amministratore m delegato.

mandarin ['mændərin] n mandarino.

mandate ['mændeit] n mandato.

mandatory ['mændətəri] a obbligatorio(a); (powers etc) mandatorio(a).

mandolin(e) ['mændəlin] n mandolino.

mane [mein] n criniera.

maneuver [mə'nu:və*] etc (US) = **manoeuvre** etc.

manful ['mænful] a coraggioso(a), valoroso(a).

mangle ['mæŋgl] vt straziare; mutilare // n mangano.

mango, **~es** ['mæŋgəu] n mango.

mangy ['meindʒi] a rognoso(a).

manhandle ['mænhændl] vt malmenare.

manhole ['mænhəul] n botola stradale.

manhood ['mænhud] n età virile; virilità.

manhunt ['mænhʌnt] n caccia all'uomo.

mania ['meiniə] n mania; **~c** ['meiniæk] n maniaco/a.

manicure ['mænikjuə*] n manicure f inv; **~ set** n trousse f inv della manicure.

manifest ['mænifɛst] vt manifestare // a manifesto(a), palese; **~ation** [-'teiʃən] n manifestazione f.

manifesto [mæni'fɛstəu] n manifesto.

manipulate [mə'nipjuleit] vt manipolare.

mankind [mæn'kaind] n umanità, genere m umano.

manly ['mænli] a virile; coraggioso(a).

man-made ['mæn'meid] a sintetico(a); artificiale.

manner ['mænə*] n maniera, modo; **~s** npl maniere fpl; **~ism** n vezzo, tic m inv.

manoeuvre [mə'nu:və*] vt manovrare // vi far manovre // n manovra.

manor ['mænə*] n (also: **~ house**) maniero.

manpower ['mænpauə*] n manodopera.

mansion ['mænʃən] n casa signorile.

manslaughter ['mænslɔ:tə*] n omicidio preterintenzionale.

mantelpiece ['mæntlpi:s] n mensola del caminetto.

mantle ['mæntl] n mantello.

manual ['mænjuəl] a manuale // n manuale m.

manufacture [mænju'fæktʃə*] vt fabbricare // n fabbricazione f, manifattura; **~r** n fabbricante m.

manure [mə'njuə*] n concime m.
manuscript ['mænjuskrɪpt] n manoscritto.
many ['mɛnɪ] det molti(e) // pronoun molti(e), un gran numero; **a great ~** moltissimi(e), un gran numero (di); **~ a...** molti(e)..., più di un(a)... .
map [mæp] n carta (geografica) // vt fare una carta di; **to ~ out** vt tracciare un piano di.
maple ['meɪpl] n acero.
mar [ma:*] vt sciupare.
marathon ['mærəθən] n maratona.
marauder [mə'rɔ:də*] n saccheggiatore m; predatore m.
marble ['ma:bl] n marmo; (toy) pallina, bilia; **~s** n (game) palline, bilie.
March [ma:tʃ] n marzo.
march [ma:tʃ] vi marciare; sfilare // n marcia; (demonstration) dimostrazione f; **~-past** n sfilata.
mare [mɛə*] n giumenta.
margarine [ma:dʒə'ri:n] n margarina.
margin ['ma:dʒɪn] n margine m; **~al** a marginale.
marigold ['mærɪgəʊld] n calendola.
marijuana [mærɪ'wɑ:nə] n marijuana.
marina [mə'ri:nə] n marina.
marine [mə'ri:n] a (animal, plant) marino(a); (forces, engineering) marittimo(a) // n fante m di marina; (US) marine m inv.
marital ['mærɪtl] a maritale, coniugale.
maritime ['mærɪtaɪm] a marittimo(a).
mark [ma:k] n segno; (stain) macchia; (of skid etc) traccia; (SCOL) voto; (SPORT) bersaglio; (currency) marco // vt segnare; (stain) macchiare; (SCOL) dare un voto a; correggere; **to ~ time** segnare il passo; **to ~ out** vt delimitare; **~ed** a spiccato(a), chiaro(a); **~er** n (sign) segno; (bookmark) segnalibro.
market ['ma:kɪt] n mercato // (COMM) mettere in vendita; **~ day** n giorno di mercato; **~ garden** n (Brit) orto industriale; **~ing** n marketing m; **~ place** n piazza del mercato.
marksman ['ma:ksmən] n tiratore m scelto; **~ship** n abilità nel tiro.
marmalade ['ma:məleɪd] n marmellata d'arance.
maroon [mə'ru:n] vt (fig): **to be ~ed (in** or at) essere abbandonato(a) (in) // a bordeaux inv.
marquee [ma:'ki:] n padiglione m.
marquess, marquis ['ma:kwɪs] n marchese m.
marriage ['mærɪdʒ] n matrimonio; **~ bureau** n agenzia matrimoniale.
married ['mærɪd] a sposato(a); (life, love) coniugale, matrimoniale.
marrow ['mærəʊ] n midollo; (vegetable) zucca.
marry ['mærɪ] vt sposare, sposarsi con; (subj: father, priest etc) dare in matrimonio // vi (also: **get married**) sposarsi.
Mars [ma:z] n (planet) Marte m.

marsh [ma:ʃ] n palude f.
marshal ['ma:ʃl] n maresciallo; (US: fire) capo; (: police) capitano // vt adunare.
marshy ['ma:ʃɪ] a paludoso(a).
martial ['ma:ʃl] a marziale; **~ law** n legge f marziale.
Martian ['ma:ʃən] n marziano/a.
martyr ['ma:tə*] n martire m/f // vt martirizzare; **~dom** n martirio.
marvel ['ma:vl] n meraviglia // vi: **to ~ (at)** meravigliarsi (di); **~lous** a meraviglioso(a).
Marxism ['ma:ksɪzəm] n marxismo; **Marxist** a, n marxista (m/f).
marzipan ['ma:zɪpæn] n marzapane m.
mascara [mæs'ka:rə] n mascara m.
mascot ['mæskət] n mascotte f inv.
masculine ['mæskjulɪn] a maschile // n genere m maschile; **masculinity** [-'lɪnɪtɪ] n mascolinità.
mashed [mæʃt] a: **~ potatoes** purè m di patate.
mask [ma:sk] n maschera // vt mascherare.
masochist ['mæsəʊkɪst] n masochista m/f.
mason ['meɪsn] n (also: **stone~**) scalpellino; (also: **free~**) massone m; **~ry** n muratura.
masquerade [mæskə'reɪd] n ballo in maschera; (fig) mascherata // vi: **to ~ as** farsi passare per.
mass [mæs] n moltitudine f, massa; (PHYSICS) massa; (REL) messa // vi ammassarsi; **the ~es** le masse.
massacre ['mæsəkə*] n massacro // vt massacrare.
massage ['mæsɑ:ʒ] n massaggio // vt massaggiare.
masseur [mæ'sɜ:*] n massaggiatore m; **masseuse** [-'sɜ:z] n massaggiatrice f.
massive ['mæsɪv] a enorme, massiccio(a).
mass media ['mæs'mi:dɪə] npl mass media mpl.
mass-produce ['mæsprə'dju:s] vt produrre in serie.
mast [ma:st] n albero.
master ['ma:stə*] n padrone m; (ART etc, teacher: in primary school) maestro; (: in secondary school) professore m; (title for boys): **M~ X** Signorino X // (learn) imparare a fondo; (understand) conoscere a fondo; **M~'s degree** n titolo accademico superiore al 'Bachelor'; **~ key** n chiave f maestra; **~ly** a magistrale; **~mind** n mente f superiore // vt essere il cervello di; **~piece** n capolavoro; **~ plan** n piano generale; **~ stroke** n colpo maestro; **~y** n dominio; padronanza.
masturbate ['mæstəbeɪt] vi masturbare; **masturbation** [-'beɪʃən] n masturbazione f.
mat [mæt] n stuoia; (also: **door~**) stoino, zerbino // a = **matt**.
match [mætʃ] n fiammifero; (game) partita, incontro; (fig) uguale m/f; matrimonio; partito // vt intonare; (go well with) andare benissimo con; (equal) uguagliare // vi combaciare; **to be a good**

~ andare bene; **to** ~ **up** *vt* intonare;
~**box** *n* scatola di fiammiferi; ~**ing** *a*
ben assortito(a); ~**less** *a* senza pari.

mate [meɪt] *n* compagno/a di lavoro; (*col*)
amico/a; (*animal*) compagno/a; (*in
merchant navy*) secondo // *vi* accoppiarsi
// *vt* accoppiare.

material [məˈtɪərɪəl] *n* (*substance*)
materiale *m*, materia; (*cloth*) stoffa // *a*
materiale; (*important*) essenziale; ~**s** *npl*
materiali *mpl*; ~**istic** [-əˈlɪstɪk] *a*
materialistico(a); ~**ize** *vi* realizzarsi.

maternal [məˈtəːnl] *a* materno(a).

maternity [məˈtəːnɪtɪ] *n* maternità // *cpd*
di maternità; (*clothes*) pre-maman *inv*; ~
hospital *n* ≈ clinica ostetrica.

mathematical [mæθəˈmætɪkl] *a*
matematico(a).

mathematician [mæθəməˈtɪʃən] *n*
matematico/a.

mathematics [mæθəˈmætɪks] *n*
matematica.

maths [mæθs] *n* matematica.

matinée [ˈmætɪneɪ] *n* matinée *f inv*.

mating [ˈmeɪtɪŋ] *n* accoppiamento; ~
call *n* chiamata all'accoppiamento; ~
season *n* stagione *f* degli amori.

matriarchal [meɪtrɪˈɑːkl] *a* matriarcale.

matriculation [mətrɪkjuˈleɪʃən] *n*
immatricolazione *f*.

matrimonial [mætrɪˈməunɪəl] *a*
matrimoniale, coniugale.

matrimony [ˈmætrɪmənɪ] *n* matrimonio.

matron [ˈmeɪtrən] *n* (*in hospital*)
capoinfermiera; (*in school*) infermiera;
~**ly** *a* matronale; dignitoso(a).

matt [mæt] *a* opaco(a).

matted [ˈmætɪd] *a* ingarbugliato(a).

matter [ˈmætə*] *n* questione *f*; (*PHYSICS*)
materia, sostanza; (*content*) contenuto;
(*MED: pus*) pus *m* // *vi* importare; **it
doesn't** ~ non importa; (*I don't mind*) non
fa niente; **what's the** ~? che cosa c'è?;
no ~ **what** qualsiasi cosa accada; **that's
another** ~ quello è un altro affare; **as a
** ~ **of course** come cosa naturale; **as a** ~
of fact in verità; ~-**of-fact** *a* prosaico(a).

matting [ˈmætɪŋ] *n* stuoia.

mattress [ˈmætrɪs] *n* materasso.

mature [məˈtjuə*] *a* maturo(a); (*cheese*)
stagionato(a) // *vi* maturare; stagionare;
(*COMM*) scadere; **maturity** *n* maturità.

maudlin [ˈmɔːdlɪn] *a* lacrimoso(a).

maul [mɔːl] *vt* lacerare.

mausoleum [mɔːsəˈliəm] *n* mausoleo.

mauve [məuv] *a* malva *inv*.

mawkish [ˈmɔːkɪʃ] *a* sdolcinato(a);
insipido(a).

max. *abbr of* **maximum**.

maxim [ˈmæksɪm] *n* massima.

maximum [ˈmæksɪməm] *a* massimo(a) //
n (*pl* **maxima** [ˈmæksɪmə]) massimo.

May [meɪ] *n* maggio.

may [meɪ] *vi* (*conditional:* **might**)
(*indicating possibility*): **he** ~ **come** può
darsi che venga; (*be allowed to*): ~ **I
smoke?** posso fumare?; (*wishes*): ~ **God

bless you!** Dio la benedica!; **he might be
there** può darsi che ci sia; **I might as
well go** potrei anche andarmene; **you
might like to try** forse le piacerebbe
provare.

maybe [ˈmeɪbɪ] *ad* forse, può darsi; ~
he'll... può darsi che lui... +*sub*, forse lui...

mayday [ˈmeɪdeɪ] *n* S.O.S. *m*.

May Day [ˈmeɪdeɪ] *n* il primo maggio.

mayhem [ˈmeɪhem] *n* cagnara.

mayonnaise [meɪəˈneɪz] *n* maionese *f*.

mayor [mɛə*] *n* sindaco; ~**ess** *n* sindaca;
moglie *f* del sindaco.

maze [meɪz] *n* labirinto, dedalo.

me [miː] *pronoun* mi, m' + *vowel*; (*stressed,
after prep*) me.

meadow [ˈmedəu] *n* prato.

meagre [ˈmiːgə*] *a* magro(a).

meal [miːl] *n* pasto; (*flour*) farina; ~**time**
n l'ora di mangiare; ~-**y-mouthed** *a* che
parla attraverso eufemismi.

mean [miːn] *a* (*with money*) avaro(a),
gretto(a); (*unkind*) meschino(a),
maligno(a); (*average*) medio(a) // *vt* (*pt,
pp* **meant** [ment]) (*signify*) significare,
voler dire; (*intend*): **to** ~ **to do** aver
l'intenzione di fare // *n* mezzo; (*MATH*)
media; ~**s** *npl* mezzi *mpl*; **by** ~**s of** per
mezzo di; (*person*) a mezzo di; **by all** ~**s**
ma certo, prego; **to be meant for** essere
destinato(a) a; **what do you** ~? che cosa
vuol dire?

meander [mɪˈændə*] *vi* far meandri; (*fig*)
divagare.

meaning [ˈmiːnɪŋ] *n* significato, senso;
~**ful** *a* significativo(a); ~**less** *a* senza
senso.

meanness [ˈmiːnnɪs] *n* avarizia;
meschinità.

meant [ment] *pt, pp of* **mean**.

meantime [ˈmiːntaɪm] *ad*, **meanwhile**
[ˈmiːnwaɪl] *ad* (*also:* **in the** ~) nel
frattempo.

measles [ˈmiːzlz] *n* morbillo.

measly [ˈmiːzlɪ] *a* (*col*) miserabile.

measure [ˈmɛʒə*] *vt, vi* misurare // *n*
misura; (*ruler*) metro; ~**d** *a* misurato(a);
~**ments** *npl* misure *fpl*; **chest/hip**
~**ment** giro petto/fianchi.

meat [miːt] *n* carne *f*; ~**y** *a* che sa di
carne; (*fig*) sostanzioso(a).

Mecca [ˈmekə] *n* Mecca.

mechanic [mɪˈkænɪk] *n* meccanico; ~**s** *n*
meccanica // *npl* meccanismo; ~**al** *a*
meccanico(a).

mechanism [ˈmekənɪzəm] *n* meccanismo.

mechanization [mekənaɪˈzeɪʃən] *n*
meccanizzazione *f*.

medal [ˈmedl] *n* medaglia; ~**lion**
[mɪˈdælɪən] *n* medaglione *m*; ~**list** *n*
(*SPORT*) vincitore/trice di medaglia.

meddle [ˈmedl] *vi*: **to** ~ **in** immischiarsi
in, mettere le mani in; **to** ~ **with** toccare.

media [ˈmiːdɪə] *npl* media *mpl*.

mediaeval [medɪˈiːvl] *a* = **medievale**.

mediate [ˈmiːdɪeɪt] *vi* interporsi; fare da
mediatore/trice; **mediation** [-ˈeɪʃən] *n*

mediazione   f;   **mediator**   n
mediatore/trice.
medical ['mɛdɪkl] a medico(a); ~
student n studente/essa di medicina.
medicated ['mɛdɪkeɪtɪd] a medicato(a).
medicinal [mɛ'dɪsɪnl] a medicinale.
medicine ['mɛdsɪn] n medicina; ~ **chest**
n armadietto farmaceutico.
medieval [mɛdɪ'iːvl] a medievale.
mediocre   [miːdɪ'əukə*] a mediocre;
mediocrity [-'ɔkrɪtɪ] n mediocrità.
meditate ['mɛdɪteɪt] vi: to ~ (on)
meditare (su); **meditation** [-'teɪʃən] n
meditazione f.
Mediterranean   [mɛdɪtə'reɪnɪən]   a
mediterraneo(a); **the** ~ **(Sea)** il (mare)
Mediterraneo.
medium ['miːdɪəm] a medio(a) // n (pl
media: **means**) mezzo; (pl **mediums**:
person) medium m inv; **the happy** ~ il
giusto medio.
medley ['mɛdlɪ] n selezione f.
meek [miːk] a dolce, umile.
meet, pt, pp **met** [miːt, mɛt] vt incontrare;
(for the first time) fare la conoscenza di;
(go and fetch): **I'll** ~ **you at the station**
verrò a prenderla alla stazione; (fig)
affrontare; soddisfare; raggiungere // vi
incontrarsi; (in session) riunirsi; (join:
objects) unirsi; **to** ~ **with** vt fus
incontrare; ~**ing** n incontro; (session: of
club etc) riunione f; (interview) intervista;
she's at a ~**ing** (COMM) è in riunione.
megaphone ['mɛgəfəun] n megafono.
melancholy ['mɛlənkəlɪ] n malinconia //
a malinconico(a).
mellow ['mɛləu] a (wine, sound) ricco(a);
(person, light) dolce; (colour) caldo(a);
(fruit) maturo(a) // vi (person) addolcirsi.
melodious [mɪ'ləudɪəs] a melodioso(a).
melodrama   ['mɛləudrɑːmə]   n
melodramma m.
melody ['mɛlədɪ] n melodia.
melon ['mɛlən] n melone m.
melt [mɛlt] vi (gen) sciogliersi, struggersi;
(metals) fondersi; (fig) intenerirsi // vt
sciogliere, struggere; fondere; (person)
commuovere; **to** ~ **away** vi sciogliersi
completamente; **to** ~ **down** vt fondere;
~**ing point** n punto di fusione.
member ['mɛmbə*]   n   membro; ~
country/state n paese m/stato membro;
M~ **of Parliament (M.P.)** n deputato;
~**ship** n iscrizione f; (numero d')iscritti
mpl, membri mpl.
membrane ['mɛmbreɪn] n membrana.
memento [mə'mɛntəu] n ricordo, souvenir
m inv.
memo ['mɛməu] n appunto; (COMM etc)
comunicazione f di servizio.
memoir ['mɛmwɑː*] n memoria; ~**s** npl
memorie fpl, ricordi mpl.
memorable ['mɛmərəbl] a memorabile.
memorandum,   pl   **memoranda**
[mɛmə'rændəm, -də] n appunto; (COMM etc)
comunicazione f di servizio; (DIPLOMACY)
memorandum m inv.
memorial [mɪ'mɔːrɪəl]   n   monumento

commemorativo // a commemorativo(a).
memorize ['mɛməraɪz] vt imparare a
memoria.
memory ['mɛmərɪ]   n   memoria;
(recollection) ricordo; **in** ~ **of** in memoria
di.
men [mɛn] npl of **man**.
menace ['mɛnəs] n minaccia // vt
minacciare; **menacing** a minaccioso(a).
menagerie [mɪ'nædʒərɪ] n serraglio.
mend [mɛnd] vt aggiustare, riparare;
(darn) rammendare // n rammendo; **on**
the ~ in via di guarigione.
menial ['miːnɪəl] a da servo, domestico(a);
umile.
meningitis [mɛnɪn'dʒaɪtɪs] n meningite f.
menopause ['mɛnəupɔːz] n menopausa.
menstruate ['mɛnstrueɪt] vi mestruare;
menstruation [-'eɪʃən] n mestruazione f.
mental ['mɛntl] a mentale.
mentality [mɛn'tælɪtɪ] n mentalità f inv.
mention ['mɛnʃən] n menzione f // vt
menzionare, far menzione di; **don't** ~ **it!**
non c'è di che!, prego!
menu ['mɛnjuː] n (set ~) menu m inv;
(printed) carta.
mercantile ['mɜːkəntaɪl] a mercantile;
(law) commerciale.
mercenary ['mɜːsɪnərɪ] a venale // n
mercenario.
merchandise ['mɜːtʃəndaɪz] n merci fpl.
merchant ['mɜːtʃənt] n mercante m,
commerciante m; **timber/wine** ~
negoziante m di legno/vino; ~ **bank** n
banca d'affari; ~ **navy** n marina
mercantile.
merciful ['mɜːsɪful]   a   pietoso(a),
clemente.
merciless ['mɜːsɪlɪs] a spietato(a).
mercury ['mɜːkjurɪ] n mercurio.
mercy ['mɜːsɪ] n pietà; (REL) misericordia;
to have ~ **on sb** aver pietà di qd; **at the**
~ **of** alla mercè di.
mere [mɪə*] a semplice; **by a** ~ **chance**
per mero caso; ~**ly** ad semplicemente,
non ... che.
merge [mɜːdʒ] vt unire // vi fondersi,
unirsi; (COMM) fondersi; ~**r** n (COMM)
fusione f.
meridian [mə'rɪdɪən] n meridiano.
meringue [mə'ræŋ] n meringa.
merit ['mɛrɪt] n merito, valore m // vt
meritare.
mermaid ['mɜːmeɪd] n sirena.
merriment   ['mɛrɪmənt]   n   gaiezza,
allegria.
merry ['mɛrɪ] a gaio(a), allegro(a); ~-**go-**
round n carosello.
mesh [mɛʃ] n maglia; rete f // vi (gears)
ingranarsi.
mesmerize ['mɛzməraɪz] vt ipnotizzare;
affascinare.
mess [mɛs] n confusione f, disordine m;
(fig) pasticcio; (MIL) mensa; **to** ~ **about**
vi (col) trastullarsi; **to** ~ **about with** vt
fus (col) gingillarsi con; (: plans) fare un

pasticcio di; **to ~ up** *vt* sporcare; fare un pasticcio di; rovinare.

message ['mɛsɪdʒ] *n* messaggio.

messenger ['mɛsɪndʒə*] *n* messaggero/a.

messy ['mɛsɪ] *a* sporco(a); disordinato(a).

met [mɛt] *pt, pp of* **meet**.

metabolism [mɛ'tæbəlizəm] *n* metabolismo.

metal ['mɛtl] *n* metallo // *vt* massicciare; **~lic** [-'tælɪk] *a* metallico(a); **~lurgy** [-'tælədʒɪ] *n* metallurgia.

metamorphosis, *pl* **phoses** [mɛtə'mɔːfəsɪs, -iːz] *n* metamorfosi *f inv.*

metaphor ['mɛtəfə*] *n* metafora.

metaphysics [mɛtə'fɪzɪks] *n* metafisica.

mete [miːt]: **to ~ out** *vt fus* infliggere.

meteor ['miːtɪə*] *n* meteora.

meteorology [miːtɪə'rɔlədʒɪ] *n* meteorologia.

meter ['miːtə*] *n* (*instrument*) contatore *m*; (*US*) = **metre**.

method ['mɛθəd] *n* metodo; **~ical** [mɪ'θɔdɪkl] *a* metodico(a).

methylated spirit ['mɛθɪleɪtɪd'spɪrɪt] *n* (*also:* **meths**) alcool *m* denaturato.

meticulous [mɛ'tɪkjuləs] *a* meticoloso(a).

metre ['miːtə*] *n* metro.

metric ['mɛtrɪk] *a* metrico(a); **~al** *a* metrico(a); **~ation** [-'keɪʃən] *n* conversione *f* al sistema metrico.

metronome ['mɛtrənəum] *n* metronomo.

metropolis [mɪ'trɔpəlɪs] *n* metropoli *f inv.*

mettle ['mɛtl] *n* coraggio.

mew [mjuː] *vi* (*cat*) miagolare.

Mexican ['mɛksɪkən] *a, n* messicano(a).

Mexico ['mɛksɪkəu] *n* Messico; **~ City** Città del Messico.

mezzanine ['mɛtsəniːt] *n* mezzanino.

miaow [miː'au] *vi* miagolare.

mice [maɪs] *npl of* **mouse**.

microbe ['maɪkrəub] *n* microbio.

microfilm ['maɪkrəufɪlm] *n* microfilm *m inv* // *vt* microfilmare.

microphone ['maɪkrəfəun] *n* microfono.

microscope ['maɪkrəskəup] *n* microscopio; **microscopic** [-'skɔpɪk] *a* microscopico(a).

mid [mɪd] *a*: **~ May** metà maggio; **~ afternoon** metà pomeriggio; **in ~ air** a mezz'aria; **~day** *n* mezzogiorno.

middle ['mɪdl] *n* mezzo, centro; (*waist*) vita // *a* di mezzo; **~aged** *a* di mezza età; **the M~ Ages** *npl* il Medioevo; **~-class** *a* ≈ borghese; **the ~ class(es)** ≈ la borghesia; **M~ East** *n* Medio Oriente *m*; **~man** *n* intermediario; agente *m* rivenditore.

middling ['mɪdlɪŋ] *a* medio(a).

midge [mɪdʒ] *n* moscerino.

midget ['mɪdʒɪt] *n* nano/a.

Midlands ['mɪdləndz] *npl* contee del centro dell'Inghilterra.

midnight ['mɪdnaɪt] *n* mezzanotte *f.*

midriff ['mɪdrɪf] *n* diaframma *m.*

midst [mɪdst] *n*: **in the ~ of** in mezzo a.

midsummer [mɪd'sʌmə*] *n* mezza *or* piena estate *f.*

midway [mɪd'weɪ] *a, ad*: **~ (between)** a mezza strada (fra).

midwife, midwives ['mɪdwaɪf, -vz] *n* levatrice *f*; **~ry** [-wɪfərɪ] *n* ostetricia.

midwinter [mɪd'wɪntə*] *n* pieno inverno.

might [maɪt] *vb see* **may** // *n* potere *m*, forza; **~y** *a* forte, potente // *ad* (*col*) molto.

migraine ['miːgreɪn] *n* emicrania.

migrant ['maɪgrənt] *n* (*bird, animal*) migratore *m*; (*person*) migrante *m/f*; nomade *m/f* // *a* migratore(trice); nomade; (*worker*) emigrato(a).

migrate [maɪ'greɪt] *vi* migrare; **migration** [-'greɪʃən] *n* migrazione *f.*

mike [maɪk] *n* (*abbr of* **microphone**) microfono.

mild [maɪld] *a* mite; (*person, voice*) dolce; (*flavour*) delicato(a); (*illness*) leggero(a) // *n* birra leggera.

mildew ['mɪldjuː] *n* muffa.

mildly ['maɪldlɪ] *ad* mitemente; dolcemente; delicatamente; leggeramente; **to put it ~** a dire poco.

mile [maɪl] *n* miglio; **~age** *n* distanza in miglia, ≈ chilometraggio; **~ometer** *n* = **milometer**; **~stone** *n* pietra miliare.

milieu ['miːljəː] *n* ambiente *m.*

militant ['mɪlɪtnt] *a,n* militante (*m/f*).

military ['mɪlɪtərɪ] *a* militare // *n*: **the ~** i militari, l'esercito.

militate ['mɪlɪteɪt] *vi*: **to ~ against** essere d'ostacolo a.

militia [mɪ'lɪʃə] *n* milizia.

milk [mɪlk] *n* latte *m* // *vt* (*cow*) mungere; (*fig*) sfruttare; **~ chocolate** *n* cioccolato al latte; **~ing** *n* mungitura; **~man** *n* lattaio; **~ shake** *n* frappé *m inv*; **~y** *a* lattiginoso(a); (*colour*) latteo(a); **M~y Way** *n* Via Lattea.

mill [mɪl] *n* mulino; (*small: for coffee, pepper etc*) macinino; (*factory*) fabbrica; (*spinning ~*) filatura // *vt* macinare // *vi* (*also:* **~ about**) formicolare.

millennium, *pl* **~s** *or* **millennia** [mɪ'lɛnɪəm, -'lɛnɪə] *n* millennio.

miller ['mɪlə*] *n* mugnaio.

millet ['mɪlɪt] *n* miglio.

milli... ['mɪlɪ] *prefix*: **~gram(me)** *n* milligrammo; **~litre** *n* millilitro; **~metre** *n* millimetro.

milliner ['mɪlɪnə*] *n* modista; **~y** *n* modisteria.

million ['mɪljən] *n* milione *m*; **~aire** *n* milionario, ≈ miliardario.

millstone ['mɪlstəun] *n* macina.

milometer [maɪ'lɔmɪtə*] *n* ≈ contachilometri *m inv.*

mime [maɪm] *n* mimo // *vt, vi* mimare.

mimic ['mɪmɪk] *n* imitatore/trice // *vt* fare la mimica di // *vi* fare la mimica; **~ry** *n* mimica; (*ZOOL*) mimetismo.

min. *abbr of* **minute(s)**, **minimum**.

minaret [mɪnə'rɛt] *n* minareto.

mince [mɪns] *n* tritare, macinare // *vi* (*in walking*) camminare a passettini // *n* (*CULIN*) carne *f* tritata *or* macinata; **he**

does not ~ (his) words parla chiaro e tondo; ~meat n frutta secca tritata per uso in pasticceria; ~ ple n specie di torta con frutta secca; ~r n tritacarne m inv.

mind [maɪnd] n mente f // vt (attend to, look after) badare a, occuparsi di; (be careful) fare attenzione a, stare attento(a) a; (object to): I don't ~ the noise il rumore non mi dà alcun fastidio; do you ~ if ...? le dispiace se ...?; I don't ~ non m'importa; it is on my ~ mi preoccupa; to my ~ secondo me, a mio parere; to be out of one's ~ essere uscito(a) di mente; never ~ non importa, non fa niente; to keep sth in ~ non dimenticare qc; to make up one's ~ decidersi; '~ the step' 'attenzione allo scalino'; to have in ~ to do aver l'intenzione di fare; ~ful a: ~ful of attento(a) a; memore di; ~less a idiota.

mine [maɪn] pronoun il(la) mio(a), pl i(le) miei(mie); this book is ~ questo libro è mio // n miniera; (explosive) mina // vt (coal) estrarre; (ship, beach) minare; ~ detector n rivelatore m di mine; ~field n campo minato; ~r n minatore m.

mineral ['mɪnərəl] a minerale // n minerale m; ~s npl (soft drinks) bevande fpl gasate; ~ogy [-'rælədʒɪ] n mineralogia; ~ water n acqua minerale.

minesweeper ['maɪnswiːpə*] n dragamine m inv.

mingle ['mɪŋgl] vt mescolare, mischiare // vi: to ~ with mescolarsi a, mischiarsi con.

miniature ['mɪnətʃə*] a in miniatura // n miniatura.

minibus ['mɪnɪbʌs] n minibus m inv.

minim ['mɪnɪm] n (MUS) minima.

minimal ['mɪnɪml] a minimo(a).

minimize ['mɪnɪmaɪz] vt minimizzare.

minimum ['mɪnɪməm] n (pl: minima ['mɪnɪmə]) minimo // a minimo(a).

mining ['maɪnɪŋ] n industria mineraria // a minerario(a); di minatori.

minion ['mɪnjən] n (pej) caudatario; favorito/a.

miniskirt ['mɪnɪskɜːt] n minigonna.

minister ['mɪnɪstə*] n (POL) ministro; (REL) pastore m; ~ial [-'tɪərɪəl] a (POL) ministeriale.

ministry ['mɪnɪstrɪ] n ministero; (REL): to go into the ~ diventare pastore.

mink [mɪŋk] n visone m; ~ coat n pelliccia di visone.

minnow ['mɪnəu] n pesciolino d'acqua dolce.

minor ['maɪnə*] a minore, di poca importanza; (MUS) minore // n (LAW) minorenne m/f.

minority [maɪ'nɔrɪtɪ] n minoranza.

minstrel ['mɪnstrəl] n giullare m, menestrello.

mint [mɪnt] n (plant) menta; (sweet) pasticca di menta // vt (coins) battere; the (Royal) M~ la Zecca; in ~ condition come nuovo(a) di zecca; ~ sauce n salsa di menta.

minuet [mɪnju'et] n minuetto.

minus ['maɪnəs] n (also: ~ sign) segno meno // prep meno.

minute a [maɪ'njuːt] minuscolo(a); (detail) minuzioso(a) // n ['mɪnɪt] minuto; (official record) processo verbale, resoconto sommario; ~s npl verbale m, verbali mpl.

miracle ['mɪrəkl] n miracolo; miraculous [mɪ'rækjuləs] a miracoloso(a).

mirage ['mɪrɑːʒ] n miraggio.

mirror ['mɪrə*] n specchio // vt rispecchiare, riflettere.

mirth [mɜːθ] n gaiezza.

misadventure [mɪsəd'ventʃə*] n disavventura; death by ~ morte f accidentale.

misanthropist [mɪ'zænθrəpɪst] n misantropo/a.

misapprehension ['mɪsæprɪ'henʃən] n malinteso.

misappropriate [mɪsə'prəuprɪeɪt] vt appropriarsi indebitamente di.

misbehave [mɪsbɪ'heɪv] vi comportarsi male; misbehaviour n comportamento scorretto.

miscalculate [mɪs'kælkjuleɪt] vt calcolare male; miscalculation [-'leɪʃən] n errore m di calcolo.

miscarriage ['mɪskærɪdʒ] n (MED) aborto spontaneo; ~ of justice errore m giudiziario.

miscellaneous [mɪsɪ'leɪnɪəs] a (items) vario(a); (selection) misto(a).

miscellany [mɪ'selənɪ] n raccolta.

mischief ['mɪstʃɪf] n (naughtiness) birichineria; (harm) male m, danno; (maliciousness) malizia; mischievous a (naughty) birichino(a); (harmful) dannoso(a).

misconception ['mɪskən'sepʃən] n idea sbagliata.

misconduct [mɪs'kɔndʌkt] n cattiva condotta; professional ~ reato professionale.

misconstrue [mɪskən'struː] vt interpretare male.

miscount [mɪs'kaunt] vt,vi contare male.

misdemeanour [mɪsdɪ'miːnə*] n misfatto; infrazione f.

misdirect [mɪsdɪ'rekt] vt mal indirizzare.

miser ['maɪzə*] n avaro.

miserable ['mɪzərəbl] a infelice; (wretched) miserabile.

miserly ['maɪzəlɪ] a avaro(a).

misery ['mɪzərɪ] n (unhappiness) tristezza; (pain) sofferenza; (wretchedness) miseria.

misfire [mɪs'faɪə*] vi far cilecca; (car engine) dare accensione irregolare.

misfit ['mɪsfɪt] n (person) spostato/a.

misfortune [mɪs'fɔːtʃən] n sfortuna.

misgiving(s) [mɪs'gɪvɪŋ(z)] n(pl) dubbi mpl, sospetti mpl.

misguided [mɪs'gaɪdɪd] a sbagliato(a); poco giudizioso(a).

mishandle [mɪs'hændl] vt (treat roughly) maltrattare; (mismanage) trattare male.

mishap ['mɪshæp] n disgrazia.

misinform [mɪsɪnˈfɔːm] *vt* informare male.

misinterpret [mɪsɪnˈtɜːprɪt] *vt* interpretare male.

misjudge [mɪsˈdʒʌdʒ] *vt* giudicare male.

mislay [mɪsˈleɪ] *vt irg* smarrire.

mislead [mɪsˈliːd] *vt irg* sviare; **~ing** *a* ingannevole.

mismanage [mɪsˈmænɪdʒ] *vt* gestire male; trattare male; **~ment** *n* cattiva amministrazione *f.*

misnomer [mɪsˈnəʊmə*] *n* termine *m* sbagliato *or* improprio.

misplace [mɪsˈpleɪs] *vt* smarrire; collocare fuori posto.

misprint [ˈmɪsprɪnt] *n* errore *m* di stampa.

mispronounce [mɪsprəˈnaʊns] *vt* pronunziare male.

misread [mɪsˈriːd] *vt irg* leggere male.

misrepresent [mɪsrɛprɪˈzɛnt] *vt* travisare.

miss [mɪs] *vt (fail to get)* perdere; *(regret the absence of)*: **I ~ him/it** sento la sua mancanza, lui/esso mi manca // *vi* mancare // *n (shot)* colpo mancato; *(fig)*: **that was a near ~** c'è mancato poco; **to ~ out** *vt* omettere.

Miss [mɪs] *n* Signorina.

missal [ˈmɪsl] *n* messale *m.*

misshapen [mɪsˈʃeɪpən] *a* deforme.

missile [ˈmɪsaɪl] *n (AVIAT)* missile *m*; *(object thrown)* proiettile *m.*

missing [ˈmɪsɪŋ] *a* perso(a), smarrito(a); *(after escape, disaster: person)* mancante; **to go ~** sparire.

mission [ˈmɪʃən] *n* missione *f*; **~ary** *n* missionario/a.

misspent [ˈmɪsˈspɛnt] *a*: **his ~ youth** la sua gioventù sciupata.

mist [mɪst] *n* nebbia, foschia // *vi (also: ~ over, ~ up)* annebbiarsi; *(windows)* appannarsi.

mistake [mɪsˈteɪk] *n* sbaglio, errore *m* // *vt (irg: like* **take**) sbagliarsi di; fraintendere; **to ~ for** prendere per; **~n** *a (idea etc)* sbagliato(a); **to be ~n** sbagliarsi; **~n identity** *n* errore *m* di persona.

mister [ˈmɪstə*] *n (col)* signore *m*; *see* **Mr.**

mistletoe [ˈmɪsltəʊ] *n* vischio.

mistook [mɪsˈtuk] *pt of* **mistake.**

mistranslation [mɪstrænsˈleɪʃən] *n* traduzione *f* errata.

mistreat [mɪsˈtriːt] *vt* maltrattare.

mistress [ˈmɪstrɪs] *n* padrona; *(lover)* amante *f*; *(in primary school)* maestra; *see* **Mrs.**

mistrust [mɪsˈtrʌst] *vt* diffidare di.

misty [ˈmɪstɪ] *a* nebbioso(a), brumoso(a).

misunderstand [mɪsʌndəˈstænd] *vt, vi irg* capire male, fraintendere; **~ing** *n* malinteso, equivoco.

misuse *n* [mɪsˈjuːs] cattivo uso; *(of power)* abuso // *vt* [mɪsˈjuːz] far cattivo uso di; abusare di.

mitigate [ˈmɪtɪɡeɪt] *vt* mitigare.

mitre [ˈmaɪtə*] *n* mitra; *(CARPENTRY)* ugnatura.

mitt(en) [ˈmɪt(n)] *n* mezzo guanto; manopolo.

mix [mɪks] *vt* mescolare // *vi* mescolarsi // *n* mescolanza; preparato; **to ~ up** *vt* mescolare; *(confuse)* confondere; **~ed** *a* misto(a); **~ed grill** *n* misto alla griglia; **~ed-up** *a (confused)* confuso(a); **~er** *n (for food)* sbattitore *m*; *(person)*: **he is a good ~er** è molto socievole; **~ture** *n* mescolanza; *(blend: of tobacco etc)* miscela; *(MED)* sciroppo; **~-up** *n* confusione *f.*

moan [məʊn] *n* gemito // *vi* gemere; *(col: complain)*: **to ~ (about)** lamentarsi (di); **~ing** *n* gemiti *mpl.*

moat [məʊt] *n* fossato.

mob [mɔb] *n* folla; *(disorderly)* calca; *(pej)*: **the ~** la plebaglia // *vt* accalcarsi intorno a.

mobile [ˈməʊbaɪl] *a* mobile; **~ home** *n* grande roulotte *f inv* (utilizzata come domicilio).

mobility [məʊˈbɪlɪtɪ] *n* mobilità.

moccasin [ˈmɔkəsɪn] *n* mocassino.

mock [mɔk] *vt* deridere, burlarsi di // *a* falso(a); **~ery** *n* derisione *f*; **~ing** *a* derisorio(a); **~-up** *n* modello dimostrativo; abbozzo.

mod [mɔd] *a see* **convenience.**

mode [məʊd] *n* modo.

model [ˈmɔdl] *n* modello; *(person: for fashion)* indossatore/trice; *(: for artist)* modello/a // *vt* modellare // *vi* fare l'indossatore *(or* l'indossatrice) // *a (railway: toy)* modello *inv* in scala; *(child, factory)* modello *inv*; **to ~ clothes** presentare degli abiti.

moderate *a, n* [ˈmɔdərət] moderato(a) // *vb* [ˈmɔdəreɪt] *vi* moderarsi, placarsi // *vt* moderare; **moderation** [-ˈreɪʃən] *n* moderazione *f*, misura.

modern [ˈmɔdən] *a* moderno(a); **~ize** *vt* modernizzare.

modest [ˈmɔdɪst] *a* modesto(a); **~y** *n* modestia.

modicum [ˈmɔdɪkəm] *n*: **a ~ of** un minimo di.

modification [mɔdɪfɪˈkeɪʃən] *n* modificazione *f.*

modify [ˈmɔdɪfaɪ] *vt* modificare.

module [ˈmɔdjuːl] *n* modulo.

mohair [ˈməʊhɛə*] *n* mohair *m.*

moist [mɔɪst] *a* umido(a); **~en** [ˈmɔɪsn] *vt* inumidire; **~ure** [ˈmɔɪstʃə*] *n* umidità; *(on glass)* goccioline *fpl* di vapore; **~urizer** [ˈmɔɪstʃəraɪzə*] *n* idratante *f.*

molar [ˈməʊlə*] *n* molare *m.*

molasses [məʊˈlæsɪz] *n* molassa.

mold [məʊld] *n, vt (US)* = **mould.**

mole [məʊl] *n (animal)* talpa; *(spot)* neo.

molecule [ˈmɔlɪkjuːl] *n* molecola.

molest [məʊˈlɛst] *vt* molestare.

mollusc [ˈmɔləsk] *n* mollusco.

mollycoddle [ˈmɔlɪkɔdl] *vt* coccolare, vezzeggiare.

molt [mɔult] *vi* (*US*) = **moult**.

molten ['mɔultən] *a* fuso(a).

moment ['mɔumənt] *n* momento, istante *m*; importanza; **~ary** *a* momentaneo(a), passeggero(a); **~ous** [-'mentəs] *a* di grande importanza.

momentum [mɔu'mentəm] *n* velocità acquisita, slancio; (*PHYSICS*) momento; **to gather ~** aumentare di velocità.

monarch ['mɔnək] *n* monarca/chessa; **~ist** *n* monarchista *m/f*; **~y** *n* monarchia.

monastery ['mɔnəstəri] *n* monastero.

monastic [mə'næstik] *a* monastico(a).

Monday ['mʌndi] *n* lunedì *m inv*.

monetary ['mʌnitəri] *a* monetario(a).

money ['mʌni] *n* denaro, soldi *mpl*; **~lender** *n* prestatore *m* di denaro; **~ order** *n* vaglia *m inv*.

mongol ['mɔŋgəl] *a,n* (*MED*) mongoloide (*m/f*).

mongrel ['mʌŋgrəl] *n* (*dog*) cane *m* bastardo.

monitor ['mɔnitə*] *n* (*SCOL*) capoclasse *m/f*; (*also*: **television ~**) monitor *m inv* // *vt* controllare.

monk [mʌŋk] *n* monaco.

monkey ['mʌŋki] *n* scimmia; **~ nut** *n* nocciolina americana; **~ wrench** *n* chiave *f* a rullino.

mono... ['mɔnəu] *prefix*: **~chrome** *a* monocromo(a).

monocle ['mɔnəkl] *n* monocolo.

monogram ['mɔnəgræm] *n* monogramma *m*.

monologue ['mɔnəlɔg] *n* monologo.

monopolize [mə'nɔpəlaiz] *vt* monopolizzare.

monopoly [mə'nɔpəli] *n* monopolio.

monosyllabic [mɔnəusi'læbik] *a* monosillabico(a); (*person*) che parla a monosillabi.

monotone ['mɔnətəun] *n* pronunzia (*or* voce *f*) monotona.

monotonous [mə'nɔtənəs] *a* monotono(a).

monotony [mə'nɔtəni] *n* monotonia.

monsoon [mɔn'su:n] *n* monsone *m*.

monster ['mɔnstə*] *n* mostro.

monstrosity [mɔns'trɔsiti] *n* mostruosità *f inv*.

monstrous ['mɔnstrəs] *a* mostruoso(a).

montage [mɔn'ta:ʒ] *n* montaggio.

month [mʌnθ] *n* mese *m*; **~ly** *a* mensile // *ad* al mese; ogni mese // *n* (*magazine*) rivista mensile.

monument ['mɔnjumənt] *n* monumento; **~al** [-'mentl] *a* monumentale; (*fig*) colossale.

moo [mu:] *vi* muggire, mugghiare.

mood [mu:d] *n* umore *m*; **to be in a good/bad ~** essere di buon/cattivo umore; **to be in the ~ for** essere disposto(a) a, aver voglia di; **~y** *a* (*variable*) capriccioso(a), lunatico(a); (*sullen*) imbronciato(a).

moon [mu:n] *n* luna; **~beam** *n* raggio di luna; **~light** *n* chiaro di luna; **~lit** *a* illuminato(a) dalla luna.

moor [muə*] *n* brughiera // *vt* (*ship*) ormeggiare // *vi* ormeggiarsi.

moorings ['muəriŋz] *npl* (*chains*) ormeggi *mpl*; (*place*) ormeggio.

moorland ['muələnd] *n* brughiera.

moose [mu:s] *n*, *pl inv* alce *m*.

moot [mu:t] *vt* sollevare // *a*: **~ point** punto discutibile.

mop [mɔp] *n* lavapavimenti *m inv* // *vt* lavare con lo straccio; **to ~ one's brow** asciugarsi la fronte; **to ~ up** *vt* asciugare con uno straccio; **~ of hair** *n* zazzera.

mope [mɔup] *vi* fare il broncio.

moped ['mɔupedʒ] *n* (*Brit*) ciclomotore *m*.

moral ['mɔrl] *a* morale // *n* morale *f*; **~s** *npl* moralità.

morale [mɔ'ra:l] *n* morale *m*.

morality [mə'ræliti] *n* moralità.

morass [mə'ræs] *n* palude *f*, pantano.

morbid ['mɔ:bid] *a* morboso(a).

more [mɔ:*] *det* più // *ad* più, di più; **~ people** più gente; **I want ~** ne voglio ancora *or* di più; **~ dangerous than** più pericoloso di (*or* che); **~ or less** più o meno; **~ than ever** più che mai.

moreover [mɔ:'rəuvə*] *ad* inoltre, di più.

morgue [mɔ:g] *n* obitorio.

morning ['mɔ:niŋ] *n* mattina, mattino; mattinata; **in the ~** la mattina; **7 o'clock in the ~** le 7 di *or* della mattina.

Morocco [mə'rɔkəu] *n* Marocco.

moron ['mɔ:rɔn] *n* deficiente *m/f*; **~ic** [mə'rɔnik] *a* deficiente.

morose [mə'rəus] *a* cupo(a), tetro(a).

morphine ['mɔ:fi:n] *n* morfina.

Morse [mɔ:s] *n* (*also*: **~ code**) alfabeto Morse.

morsel ['mɔ:sl] *n* boccone *m*.

mortal ['mɔ:tl] *a*, *n* mortale (*m*); **~ity** [-'tæliti] *n* mortalità.

mortar ['mɔ:tə*] *n* (*CONSTR*) malta; (*dish*) mortaio.

mortgage ['mɔ:gidʒ] *n* ipoteca; (*loan*) prestito ipotecario // *vt* ipotecare.

mortified ['mɔ:tifaid] *a* umiliato(a).

mortuary ['mɔ:tjuəri] *n* camera mortuaria; obitorio.

mosaic [mɔu'zeiik] *n* mosaico.

Moscow ['mɔskəu] *n* Mosca.

Moslem ['mɔzləm] *a, n* = **Muslim**.

mosque [mɔsk] *n* moschea.

mosquito [mɔs'ki:təu] *n* zanzara; **~ net** *n* zanzariera.

moss [mɔs] *n* muschio; **~y** *a* muscoso(a).

most [mɔust] *det* la maggior parte di; il più di // *pronoun* la maggior parte // *ad* più; (*work*, *sleep etc*) di più; (*very*) molto, estremamente; **the ~** (*also*: *+ adjective*) il(la) più; **~ fish** la maggior parte dei pesci; **~ of** la maggior parte di; **at the (very) ~** al massimo; **to make the ~ of** trarre il massimo vantaggio da; **~ly** *ad* per lo più.

MOT *n* (*abbr of Ministry of Transport*): **the**

~ (test) *revisione annuale obbligatoria degli autoveicoli.*

motel [məu'tεl] *n* motel *m inv.*

moth [mɔθ] *n* farfalla notturna; tarma; **~ball** *n* palla di canfora; **~-eaten** *a* tarmato(a).

mother ['mʌðə*] *n* madre *f* // *vt (care for)* fare da madre a; **~hood** *n* maternità; **~-in-law** *n* suocera; **~ly** *a* materno(a); **~-of-pearl** *n* madreperla; **~-to-be** *n* futura mamma; **~ tongue** *n* madrelingua.

mothproof ['mɔθpruːf] *a* antitarmico(a).

motif [məu'tiːf] *n* motivo.

motion ['məuʃən] *n* movimento, moto; *(gesture)* gesto; *(at meeting)* mozione *f* // *vt, vi*: **to ~ (to) sb to do** fare cenno a qd di fare; **~less** *a* immobile; **~ picture** *n* film *m inv.*

motivated ['məutıveıtıd] *a* motivato(a).

motivation [məutı'veıʃən] *n* motivazione *f.*

motive ['məutıv] *n* motivo // *a* motore(trice).

motley ['mɔtlı] *a* eterogeneo(a), molto vario(a).

motor ['məutə*] *n* motore *m*; *(col: vehicle)* macchina *f* a motore(trice); **~bike** *n* moto *f inv*; **~boat** *n* motoscafo; **~car** *n* automobile *f*; **~cycle** *n* motocicletta; **~cyclist** *n* motociclista *m/f*; **~ing** *n* turismo automobilistico // *a*: **~ing holiday** *n* vacanza in macchina; **~ist** *n* automobilista *m/f*, **~ racing** *n* corse *fpl* automobilistiche; **~ scooter** *n* motorscooter *m inv*; **~ vehicle** *n* autoveicolo; **~way** *n (Brit)* autostrada.

mottled ['mɔtld] *a* chiazzato(a), marezzato(a).

motto, ~es ['mɔtəu] *n* motto.

mould [məuld] *n* forma, stampo; *(mildew)* muffa // *vt* formare; *(fig)* foggiare; **~er** *vi (decay)* ammuffire; **~y** *a* ammuffito(a).

moult [məult] *vi* far la muta.

mound [maund] *n* rialzo, collinetta.

mount [maunt] *n* monte *m*, montagna; *(horse)* cavalcatura; *(for jewel etc)* montatura // *vt* montare; *(horse)* montare a // *vi* salire, montare; *(also:* **~ up)** aumentare.

mountain ['mauntın] *n* montagna // *cpd* di montagna; **~eer** [-'nıə*] *n* alpinista *m/f*; **~eering** [-'nıərıŋ] *n* alpinismo; **to go ~eering** fare dell'alpinismo; **~ous** *a* montagnoso(a); **~side** *n* fianco della montagna.

mourn [mɔːn] *vt* piangere, lamentare // *vi*: **to ~ (for)** piangere, lamentarsi (di); **~er** *n* parente *m/f* o amico/a del defunto; persona venuta a rendere omaggio al defunto; **~ful** *a* triste, lugubre; **~ing** *n* lutto // *cpd (dress)* da lutto; **in ~ing** in lutto.

mouse, *pl* **mice** [maus, maıs] *n* topo; **~trap** *n* trappola per i topi.

moustache [məs'tɑːʃ] *n* baffi *mpl.*

mousy ['mausı] *a (person)* timido(a); *(hair)* marrone indefinito(a).

mouth, **~s** [mauθ, -ðz] *n* bocca; *(of river)* bocca, foce *f*; *(opening)* orifizio; **~ful** *n*

boccata; **~ organ** *n* armonica; **~-watering** *a* che fa venire l'acquolina in bocca.

movable ['muːvəbl] *a* mobile.

move [muːv] *n (movement)* movimento; *(in game)* mossa; *(: turn to play)* turno; *(change of house)* trasloco // *vt* muovere, spostare; *(emotionally)* commuovere; *(POL: resolution etc)* proporre // *vi (gen)* muoversi, spostarsi; *(traffic)* circolare; *(also:* **~ house)** cambiar casa, traslocare; **to ~ towards** andare verso; **to ~ sb to do sth** indurre or spingere qd a fare qc; **to get a ~ on** affrettarsi, sbrigarsi; **to ~ about** *vi (fidget)* agitarsi; *(travel)* viaggiare; **to ~ along** *vi* muoversi avanti; **to ~ away** *vi* allontanarsi, andarsene; **to ~ back** *vi* indietreggiare; *(return)* ritornare; **to ~ forward** *vi* avanzare // *vt* avanzare, spostare in avanti; *(people)* far avanzare; **to ~ in** *vi (to a house)* entrare (in una nuova casa); **to ~ on** *vi* riprendere la strada // *vt (onlookers)* far circolare; **to ~ out** *vi (of house)* sgombrare; **to ~ up** *vi* avanzare.

movement ['muːvmənt] *n (gen)* movimento; *(gesture)* gesto; *(of stars, water, physical)* moto.

movie ['muːvı] *n* film *m inv*; **the ~s** il cinema; **~ camera** *n* cinepresa.

moving ['muːvıŋ] *a* mobile; commovente.

mow, *pt* **mowed**, *pp* **mowed** *or* **mown** [məu, -n] *vt* falciare; *(lawn)* mietere; **to ~ down** *vt* falciare; **~er** *n* falciatore/trice.

M.P. *n abbr see* member.

m.p.g. *abbr* = *miles per gallon (30 m.p.g. = 9.5 l. per 100 km).*

m.p.h. *abbr* = *miles per hour (60 m.p.h. = 96 km/h).*

Mr ['mıstə*] *n*: **~ X** Signor X, Sig. X.

Mrs ['mısız] *n*: **~ X** Signora X, Sig.ra X.

Ms [mız] *n (= Miss or Mrs):* **~ X** Signora X, Sig.ra X.

much [mʌtʃ] *det* molto(a) // *ad, n or pronoun* molto; **~ milk** molto latte; **how ~ is it?** quanto costa?

muck [mʌk] *n (mud)* fango; *(dirt)* sporcizia; **to ~ about** *vi (col)* fare lo stupido; *(waste time)* gingillarsi; **~y** *a (dirty)* sporco(a), lordo(a).

mucus ['mjuːkəs] *n* muco.

mud [mʌd] *n* fango.

muddle ['mʌdl] *n* confusione *f*, disordine *m*; pasticcio // *vt (also:* **~ up)** impasticciare; **to be in a ~ (person)** non riuscire a raccapezzarsi; **to get in a ~ (while explaining etc)** imbrogliarsi; **to ~ through** *vi* cavarsela alla meno peggio.

mud: ~dy *a* fangoso(a); **~guard** *n* parafango; **~-slinging** *n (fig)* infangamento.

muff [mʌf] *n* manicotto.

muffin ['mʌfın] *n* specie di pasticcino soffice da tè.

muffle ['mʌfl] *vt (sound)* smorzare, attutire; *(against cold)* imbacuccare; **~d** *a* smorzato(a), attutito(a).

mufti ['mʌftı] *n*: **in ~** in borghese.

mug [mʌg] *n* (*cup*) tazzone *m*; (: *for beer*) boccale *m*; (*col: face*) muso; (: *fool*) scemo/a // *vt* (*assault*) assalire; ~**ging** *n* assalto.

muggy ['mʌgɪ] *a* afoso(a).

mule [mju:l] *n* mulo.

mull [mʌl]: **to ~ over** *vt* rimuginare.

mulled [mʌld] *a*: ~ **wine** vino caldo.

multi... ['mʌltɪ] *prefix* multi...; ~**coloured** *a* multicolore, variopinto(a).

multiple ['mʌltɪpl] *a* multiplo(a); molteplice // *n* multiplo; ~ **sclerosis** *n* sclerosi *f* a placche.

multiplication [mʌltɪplɪ'keɪʃən] *n* moltiplicazione *f*.

multiply ['mʌltɪplaɪ] *vt* moltiplicare // *vi* moltiplicarsi.

multitude ['mʌltɪtju:d] *n* moltitudine *f*.

mum [mʌm] *n* mamma // *a*: **to keep ~** non aprire bocca; ~'s **the word!** acqua in bocca!

mumble ['mʌmbl] *vt, vi* borbottare.

mummy ['mʌmɪ] *n* (*mother*) mamma; (*embalmed*) mummia.

mumps [mʌmps] *n* orecchioni *mpl*.

munch [mʌntʃ] *vt, vi* sgranocchiare.

mundane [mʌn'deɪn] *a* terra a terra *inv*.

municipal [mju:'nɪsɪpl] *a* municipale; ~**ity** [-'pælɪtɪ] *n* municipio.

munitions [mju:'nɪʃənz] *npl* munizioni *fpl*.

mural ['mjuərl] *n* dipinto murale.

murder ['mɜ:də*] *n* assassinio, omicidio // *vt* assassinare; ~**er** *n* omicida *m*, assassino; ~**ous** *a* micidiale.

murk [mɜ:k] *n* oscurità, buio; ~**y** *a* tenebroso(a), buio(a).

murmur ['mɜ:mə*] *n* mormorio // *vt, vi* mormorare.

muscle ['mʌsl] *n* muscolo; **to ~ in** *vi* immischiarsi.

muscular ['mʌskjulə*] *a* muscolare; (*person, arm*) muscoloso(a).

muse [mju:z] *vi* meditare, sognare // *n* musa.

museum [mju:'zɪəm] *n* museo.

mushroom ['mʌʃrum] *n* fungo // *vi* (*fig*) svilupparsi rapidamente.

music ['mju:zɪk] *n* musica; ~**al** *a* musicale // *n* (*show*) commedia musicale; ~**al box** *n* scatola armonica; ~**al instrument** *n* strumento musicale; ~ **hall** *n* teatro di varietà; ~**ian** [-'zɪʃən] *n* musicista *m/f*.

musket ['mʌskɪt] *n* moschetto.

Muslim ['mʌzlɪm] *a, n* musulmano(a).

muslin ['mʌzlɪn] *n* mussolina.

mussel ['mʌsl] *n* cozza.

must [mʌst] *auxiliary vb* (*obligation*): **I ~ do it** devo farlo; (*probability*): **he ~ be there by now** dovrebbe essere arrivato ormai; **I ~ have made a mistake** devo essermi sbagliato // *n* cosa da non mancare; cosa d'obbligo.

mustard ['mʌstəd] *n* senape *f*, mostarda.

muster ['mʌstə*] *vt* radunare.

mustn't ['mʌsnt] = **must not**.

musty ['mʌstɪ] *a* che sa di muffa *or* di rinchiuso.

mute [mju:t] *a,n* muto(a).

mutilate ['mju:tɪleɪt] *vt* mutilare; **mutilation** [-'leɪʃən] *n* mutilazione *f*.

mutinous ['mju:tɪnəs] *a* (*troops*) ammutinato(a); (*attitude*) ribelle.

mutiny ['mju:tɪnɪ] *n* ammutinamento // *vi* ammutinarsi.

mutter ['mʌtə*] *vt,vi* borbottare, brontolare.

mutton ['mʌtn] *n* carne *f* di montone.

mutual ['mju:tʃuəl] *a* mutuo(a), reciproco(a).

muzzle ['mʌzl] *n* muso; (*protective device*) museruola; (*of gun*) bocca // *vt* mettere la museruola a.

my [maɪ] *a* il(la) mio(a), *pl* i(le) miei(mie).

myself [maɪ'self] *pronoun* (*reflexive*) mi; (*emphatic*) io stesso(a); (*after prep*) me.

mysterious [mɪs'tɪərɪəs] *a* misterioso(a).

mystery ['mɪstərɪ] *n* mistero; ~ **story** *n* racconto del mistero.

mystic ['mɪstɪk] *n* mistico // *a* (*mysterious*) esoterico(a); ~**al** *a* mistico(a).

mystify ['mɪstɪfaɪ] *vt* mistificare; (*puzzle*) confondere.

mystique [mɪs'ti:k] *n* fascino.

myth [mɪθ] *n* mito; ~**ology** [mɪ'θɔlədʒɪ] *n* mitologia.

N

nab [næb] *vt* (*col*) beccare, acchiappare.

nag [næg] *n* (*pej: horse*) ronzino; (: *person*) brontolone/a // *vt* tormentare // *vi* brontolare in continuazione; ~**ging** *a* (*doubt, pain*) persistente.

nail [neɪl] *n* (*human*) unghia; (*metal*) chiodo // *vt* inchiodare; **to ~ sb down to a date/price** costringere qd a un appuntamento/ad accettare un prezzo; ~**brush** *n* spazzolino da *or* per unghie; ~**file** *n* lima da *or* per unghie; ~ **polish** *n* smalto da *or* per unghie; ~ **scissors** *npl* forbici *fpl* da *or* per unghie; ~ **varnish** *n* = ~ **polish**.

naïve [naɪ'i:v] *a* ingenuo(a).

naked ['neɪkɪd] *a* nudo(a).

name [neɪm] *n* nome *m*; (*reputation*) nome, reputazione *f* // *vt* (*baby etc*) chiamare; (*plant, illness*) nominare; (*person, object*) identificare; (*price, date*) fissare; **in the ~ of** in nome di; ~ **dropping** *n* menzionare qd *o* qc per fare bella figura; ~**less** *a* senza nome; ~**ly** *ad* cioè; ~**sake** *n* omonimo.

nanny ['nænɪ] *n* bambinaia.

nap [næp] *n* (*sleep*) pisolino; (*of cloth*) peluria; **to have a ~** schiacciare un pisolino; **to be caught ~ping** essere preso alla sprovvista.

napalm ['neɪpɑ:m] *n* napalm *m*.

nape [neɪp] *n*: ~ **of the neck** nuca.

napkin ['næpkɪn] *n* tovagliolo; (*Brit: for baby*) pannolino.

nappy ['næpɪ] *n* pannolino.

narcotic [nɑ:'kɔtɪk] *n* narcotico.

nark [nɑːk] *vt* (*col*) scocciare.

narrate [nə'reɪt] *vt* raccontare, narrare.

narrative ['nærətɪv] *n* narrativa // *a* narrativo(a).

narrow ['nærəu] *a* stretto(a); (*fig*): **to take a ~ view** di avere una visione limitata di // *vi* restringersi; **to have a ~ escape** farcela per un pelo; **to ~ sth down to** ridurre qc a; **~ly** *ad* per un pelo; (*time*) per poco; **~-minded** *a* meschino(a).

nasal ['neɪzl] *a* nasale.

nasty ['nɑːstɪ] *a* (*person*, *remark*) cattivo(a); (*smell*, *wound*, *situation*) brutto(a).

nation ['neɪʃən] *n* nazione *f*.

national ['næʃənl] *a* nazionale // *n* cittadino/a; **~ dress** *n* costume *m* nazionale; **~ism** *n* nazionalismo; **~ist** *a,n* nazionalista (*m/f*); **~ity** [-'nælɪtɪ] *n* nazionalità *f inv*; **~ization** [-aɪ'zeɪʃən] *n* nazionalizzazione *f*; **~ize** *vt* nazionalizzare; **~ly** *ad* a livello nazionale.

nation-wide ['neɪʃənwaɪd] *a* diffuso(a) in tutto il paese // *ad* in tutto il paese.

native ['neɪtɪv] *n* abitante *m/f* del paese; (*in colonies*) indigeno/a // *a* indigeno(a); (*country*) natio(a); (*ability*) innato(a); **a ~ of Russia** un nativo della Russia; **a ~ speaker of French** una persona di madrelingua francese; **~ language** madrelingua.

natter ['nætə*] *vi* chiacchierare.

natural ['nætʃrəl] *a* naturale; (*ability*) innato(a); (*manner*) semplice; **~ gas** *n* gas *m* metano; **~ist** *n* naturalista *m/f*; **~ize** *vt* naturalizzare; **~ly** *ad* naturalmente; (*by nature*): **gifted** di natura.

nature ['neɪtʃə*] *n* natura; (*character*) carattere *m*; **by ~** di natura.

naught [nɔːt] *n* zero.

naughty ['nɔːtɪ] *a* (*child*) birichino(a), cattivello(a); (*story*, *film*) spinto(a).

nausea ['nɔːsɪə] *n* (*MED*) nausea; (*fig*: *disgust*) schifo; **~te** ['nɔːsɪeɪt] *vt* nauseare; far schifo a.

nautical ['nɔːtɪkl] *a* nautico(a).

naval ['neɪvl] *a* navale; **~ officer** *n* ufficiale *m* di marina.

nave [neɪv] *n* navata centrale.

navel ['neɪvl] *n* ombelico.

navigable ['nævɪgəbl] *a* navigabile.

navigate ['nævɪgeɪt] *vt* percorrere navigando // *vi* navigare; **navigation** [-'geɪʃən] *n* navigazione *f*, **navigator** *n* (*NAUT*, *AVIAT*) ufficiale *m* di rotta; (*explorer*) navigatore *m*; (*AUT*) copilota *m/f*.

navvy ['nævɪ] *n* manovale *m*.

navy ['neɪvɪ] *n* marina; **~(-blue)** *a* blu scuro *inv*.

near [nɪə*] *a* vicino(a); (*relation*) prossimo(a) // *ad* vicino // *prep* (*also*: **~ to**) vicino a, presso; (*time*) verso // *vt* avvicinarsi a; **to come ~** *vi* avvicinarsi; **~by** [nɪə'baɪ] *a* vicino(a); **N~ East** *n* Medio Oriente *m*; **~ly** *ad* quasi; **~ miss** *n*: **that was a ~ miss** c'è mancato poco; **~ness** *n* vicinanza; **~side** *n* (*AUT*: *right-hand drive*) lato

sinistro; **~-sighted** *a* miope.

neat [niːt] *a* (*person*, *room*) ordinato(a); (*work*) pulito(a); (*solution*, *plan*) ben indovinato(a), azzeccato(a); (*spirits*) liscio(a); **~ly** *ad* con ordine; (*skilfully*) abilmente.

nebulous ['nɛbjuləs] *a* nebuloso(a); (*fig*) vago(a).

necessarily ['nɛsɪsrɪlɪ] *ad* necessariamente.

necessary ['nɛsɪsrɪ] *a* necessario(a).

necessitate [nɪ'sɛsɪteɪt] *vt* rendere necessario(a).

necessity [nɪ'sɛsɪtɪ] *n* necessità *f inv*.

neck [nɛk] *n* collo; (*of garment*) colletto; **~ and ~** testa a testa.

necklace ['nɛklɪs] *n* collana.

neckline ['nɛklaɪn] *n* scollatura.

née [neɪ] *a*: **~ Scott** nata Scott.

need [niːd] *n* bisogno // *vt* aver bisogno di.

needle ['niːdl] *n* ago // *vt* punzecchiare.

needless ['niːdlɪs] *a* inutile.

needlework ['niːdlwəːk] *n* cucito.

needy ['niːdɪ] *a* bisognoso(a).

negation [nɪ'geɪʃən] *n* negazione *f*.

negative ['nɛgətɪv] *n* negativo // *a* negativo(a).

neglect [nɪ'glɛkt] *vt* trascurare // *n* (*of person*, *duty*) negligenza; (*state of*) **~** stato di abbandono.

negligee ['nɛglɪʒeɪ] *n* négligé *m inv*.

negligence ['nɛglɪdʒəns] *n* negligenza.

negligent ['nɛglɪdʒənt] *a* negligente; **~ly** *ad* con negligenza.

negligible ['nɛglɪdʒɪbl] *a* insignificante, trascurabile.

negotiable [nɪ'gəuʃɪəbl] *a* negoziabile; (*cheque*) trasferibile; (*road*) transitabile.

negotiate [nɪ'gəuʃɪeɪt] *vi* negoziare // *vt* (*COMM*) negoziare; (*obstacle*) superare; **negotiation** [-'eɪʃən] *n* negoziato, trattativa; **negotiator** *n* negoziatore/trice.

Negress ['niːgrɪs] *n* negra.

Negro ['niːgrəu] *a*, *n* (*pl*: **~es**) negro(a).

neighbour ['neɪbə*] *n* vicino/a; **~hood** *n* vicinato; **~ing** *a* vicino(a); **~ly** *a*: **he is a ~ly person** fa da buon vicino.

neither ['naɪðə*] *a*, *pronoun* né l'uno(a) né l'altro(a), nessuno(a) dei(delle) due // *cj* neanche, nemmeno, neppure // *ad*: **~ good nor bad** né buono né cattivo; **I didn't move and ~ did Claude** io non mi mossi e nemmeno Claude.

neon ['niːɔn] *n* neon *m*; **~ light** *n* luce *f* al neon; **~ sign** *n* insegna al neon.

nephew ['nɛvjuː] *n* nipote *m*.

nerve [nəːv] *n* nervo; (*fig*) coraggio; (*impudence*) faccia tosta; **a fit of ~s** una crisi di nervi; **~-racking** *a* che spezza i nervi.

nervous ['nəːvəs] *a* nervoso(a); **~ breakdown** *n* esaurimento nervoso; **~ness** *n* nervosismo.

nest [nɛst] *n* nido.

nestle ['nɛsl] *vi* accoccolarsi.

net [nɛt] n rete f // a netto(a); ~**ball** n specie di pallacanestro.

Netherlands ['nɛðələndz] npl: the ~ i Paesi Bassi.

nett [nɛt] a = **net**.

netting ['nɛtɪŋ] n (for fence etc) reticolato.

nettle ['nɛtl] n ortica.

network ['nɛtwə:k] n rete f.

neurosis ['njuə'rəusɪs, -si:z] pl **neuroses** [njuə'rəusɪs, -si:z] n nevrosi f inv.

neurotic [njuə'rɔtɪk] a, n nevrotico(a).

neuter ['nju:tə*] a neutro(a) // n neutro // vt (cat etc) castrare.

neutral ['nju:trəl] a neutro(a); (person, nation) neutrale // n (AUT): **in** ~ in folle; ~**ity** [-'trælɪtɪ] n neutralità.

never ['nɛvə*] ad (non...) mai; ~ **again** mai più; I'll ~ **go there again** non ci vado più; ~**ending** a interminabile; ~**theless** [nɛvəðə'lɛs] ad tuttavia, ciò nonostante, ciò nondimeno.

new [nju:] a nuovo(a); (brand new) nuovo(a) di zecca; ~**born** a neonato(a); ~**comer** ['nju:kʌmə*] n nuovo(a) venuto(a); ~**ly** ad di recente; ~ **moon** n luna nuova.

news [nju:z] n notizie fpl; (RADIO) giornale m radio; (TV) telegiornale m; **a piece of** ~ una notizia; ~ **agency** n agenzia di stampa; ~**agent** n giornalaio; ~ **flash** n notizia f lampo inv; ~**paper** n giornale m; ~ **stand** n edicola.

New Year ['nju:'jɪə*] n Anno Nuovo; ~'s **Day** n il Capodanno; ~'s **Eve** n la vigilia di Capodanno.

New Zealand [nju:'zi:lənd] n Nuova Zelanda.

next [nɛkst] a prossimo(a) // ad accanto; (in time) dopo; **when do we meet** ~? quando ci rincontriamo?; ~ **door** ad accanto; ~-**of-kin** n parente m/f prossimo(a); ~ **time** ad la prossima volta; ~ **to** prep accanto a; ~ **to nothing** quasi niente.

N.H.S. n abbr of National Health Service.

nib [nɪb] n (of pen) pennino.

nibble ['nɪbl] vt mordicchiare.

nice [naɪs] a (holiday, trip) piacevole; (flat, picture) simpatico(a); (person) simpatico(a), gentile; (distinction, point) sottile; ~-**looking** a bello(a); ~**ly** ad bene.

niceties ['naɪsɪtɪz] npl finezze fpl.

nick [nɪk] n tacca f // vt (col) rubare; **in the** ~ **of time** appena in tempo.

nickel ['nɪkl] n nichel m; (US) moneta da cinque centesimi di dollaro.

nickname ['nɪkneɪm] n soprannome m // vt soprannominare.

nicotine ['nɪkəti:n] n nicotina.

niece [ni:s] n nipote f.

Nigeria [naɪ'dʒɪərɪə] n Nigeria.

niggling ['nɪglɪŋ] a pignolo(a).

night [naɪt] n notte f; (evening) sera; **at** ~ la sera; **by** ~ di notte; ~**cap** n bicchierino prima di andare a letto; ~ **club** n locale m; ~**dress** n camicia da notte; ~**fall** n crepuscolo; ~**ie** ['naɪtɪ] n camicia da notte.

nightingale ['naɪtɪŋgeɪl] n usignolo.

night life ['naɪtlaɪf] n vita notturna.

nightly ['naɪtlɪ] a di ogni notte or sera; (by night) notturno(a) // ad ogni notte or sera.

nightmare ['naɪtmɛə*] n incubo.

night school ['naɪtsku:l] n scuola serale.

night-time ['naɪttaɪm] n notte f.

night watchman ['naɪt'wɔtʃmən] n guardiano notturno.

nil [nɪl] n nulla m; (SPORT) zero.

nimble ['nɪmbl] a agile.

nine [naɪn] num nove; ~**teen** num diciannove; ~**ty** num novanta.

ninth [naɪnθ] a nono(a).

nip [nɪp] vt pizzicare.

nipple ['nɪpl] n (ANAT) capezzolo.

nippy ['nɪpɪ] a (weather) pungente; (car, person) svelto(a).

nitrogen ['naɪtrədʒən] n azoto.

no [nəu] det nessuno(a), non; **I have** ~ **money** non ho soldi; **there is** ~ **reason to believe...** non c'è nessuna ragione per credere...; **I have** ~ **books** non ho libri // ad non; **I have** ~ **more wine** non ho più vino // excl, n no (m inv); ~ **entry** vietata l'entrata.

nobility [nəu'bɪlɪtɪ] n nobiltà.

noble ['nəubl] a, n nobile (m).

nobody ['nəubədɪ] pronoun nessuno.

nod [nɔd] vi accennare col capo, fare un cenno; (sleep) sonnecchiare // n cenno; **to** ~ **off** vi assopirsi.

noise [nɔɪz] n rumore m; (din, racket) chiasso; **noisy** a (street, car) rumoroso(a); (person) chiassoso(a).

nomad ['nəumæd] n nomade m/f.

no man's land ['nəumænzlænd] n terra di nessuno.

nominal ['nɔmɪnl] a nominale.

nominate ['nɔmɪneɪt] vt (propose) proporre come candidato; (elect) nominare.

nomination [nɔmɪ'neɪʃən] n nomina; candidatura.

nominee [nɔmɪ'ni:] n persona nominata; candidato.

non... [nɔn] prefix non...; ~-**alcoholic** a analcolico(a).

nonchalant ['nɔnʃələnt] a incurante, indifferente.

non-committal ['nɔnkə'mɪtl] a evasivo(a).

nondescript ['nɔndɪskrɪpt] a qualunque inv.

none [nʌn] pronoun (not one thing) niente; (not one person) nessuno(a).

nonentity [nɔ'nentɪtɪ] n persona insignificante.

non: ~-**fiction** n saggistica; ~-**flammable** a ininfiammabile.

nonplussed [nɔn'plʌst] a sconcertato(a).

nonsense ['nɔnsəns] n sciocchezze fpl.

non: ~-**smoker** n non fumatore/trice; ~-**stick** a antiaderente, antiadesivo(a); ~-**stop** a continuo(a); (train, bus) direttissimo(a) // ad senza sosta.

noodles ['nu:dlz] npl taglierini mpl.

nook [nuk] *n*: ~s and crannies angoli *mpl.*

noon [nu:n] *n* mezzogiorno.

no one ['nəuwʌn] *pronoun* = **nobody**.

nor [nɔː*] *cj* = **neither** // *ad see* **neither.**

norm [nɔːm] *n* norma.

normal ['nɔːml] *a* normale; ~ly *ad* normalmente.

north [nɔːθ] *n* nord *m*, settentrione *m* // *a* nord *inv*, del nord, settentrionale // *ad* verso nord; N~ **America** *n* America del Nord; ~**east** *n* nord-est *m*; ~**ern** ['nɔːðən] *a* del nord, settentrionale; N~**ern Ireland** *n* Irlanda del Nord; N~ **Pole** *n* Polo Nord; N~ **Sea** *n* Mare *m* del Nord; ~**ward(s)** ['nɔːθwəd(z)] *ad* verso nord; ~**west** *n* nord-ovest *m.*

Norway ['nɔːweɪ] *n* Norvegia.

Norwegian [nɔː'wiːdʒən] *a* norvegese // *n* norvegese *m/f*; (LING) norvegese *m.*

nose [nəuz] *n* naso; (*of animal*) muso; ~**dive** *n* picchiata; ~**y** *a* curioso(a).

nostalgia [nɔs'tældʒɪə] *n* nostalgia; **nostalgic** *a* nostalgico(a).

nostril ['nɔstrɪl] *n* narice *f*; (*of horse*) frogia.

nosy ['nəuzɪ] *a* = **nosey**.

not [nɔt] *ad* non; ~ **at all** niente affatto; **you must** ~ **or mustn't do this** non deve fare questo; **he isn't...** egli non è... .

notable ['nəutəbl] *a* notevole.

notably ['nəutəblɪ] *ad* notevolmente.

notch [nɔtʃ] *n* tacca.

note [nəut] *n* nota; (*letter, banknote*) biglietto // *vt* prendere nota di; **to take** ~**s** prendere appunti; ~**book** *n* taccuino; ~**d** ['nəutɪd] *a* celebre; ~**paper** *n* carta da lettere.

nothing ['nʌθɪŋ] *n* nulla *m*, niente *m*; ~ **new** niente di nuovo; **for** ~ (*free*) per niente.

notice ['nəutɪs] *n* avviso; (*of leaving*) preavviso // *vt* notare, accorgersi di; **to take** ~ **of** fare attenzione a; **to bring sth to sb's** ~ far notare qc a qd; ~**able** *a* evidente; ~ **board** *n* (*Brit*) tabellone *m* per affissi.

notify ['nəutɪfaɪ] *vt*: **to** ~ **sth to sb** far sapere qc a qd; **to** ~ **sb of sth** avvisare qd di qc.

notion ['nəuʃən] *n* idea; (*concept*) nozione *f.*

notorious [nəu'tɔːrɪəs] *a* famigerato(a).

notwithstanding [nɔtwɪθ'stændɪŋ] *ad* nondimeno // *prep* nonostante, malgrado.

nougat ['nuːgɑː] *n* torrone *m.*

nought [nɔːt] *n* zero.

noun [naun] *n* nome *m*, sostantivo.

nourish ['nʌrɪʃ] *vt* nutrire; ~**ing** *a* nutriente; ~**ment** *n* nutrimento.

novel ['nɔvl] *n* romanzo // *a* nuovo(a); ~**ist** *n* romanziere/a; ~**ty** *n* novità *f inv.*

November [nəu'vembə*] *n* novembre *m.*

novice ['nɔvɪs] *n* principiante *m/f*; (REL) novizio/a.

now [nau] *ad* ora, adesso; ~ **and then,** ~ **and again** ogni tanto; **from** ~ **on** da ora in poi; ~**adays** ['nauədeɪz] *ad* oggidì.

nowhere ['nəuwɛə*] *ad* in nessun luogo, da nessuna parte.

nozzle ['nɔzl] *n* (*of hose*) boccaglio.

nuance ['njuːɑːns] *n* sfumatura.

nuclear ['njuːklɪə*] *a* nucleare.

nucleus, *pl* **nuclei** ['njuːklɪəs, 'njuːklɪaɪ] *n* nucleo.

nude [njuːd] *a* nudo(a) // *n* (ART) nudo; **in the** ~ tutto(a) nudo(a).

nudge [nʌdʒ] *vt* dare una gomitata a.

nudist ['njuːdɪst] *n* nudista *m/f.*

nudity ['njuːdɪtɪ] *n* nudità.

nuisance ['njuːsns] *n*: **it's a** ~ è una seccatura; **he's a** ~ lui dà fastidio.

null [nʌl] *a*: ~ **and void** nullo(a); ~**ify** ['nʌlɪfaɪ] *vt* annullare.

numb [nʌm] *a* intormentito(a).

number ['nʌmbə*] *n* numero // *vt* numerare; (*include*) contare; **a** ~ **of** un certo numero di; **the staff** ~**s 20** gli impiegati sono in 20; ~ **plate** *n* targa.

numeral ['njuːmərəl] *n* numero, cifra.

numerical [njuː'merɪkl] *a* numerico(a).

numerous ['njuːmərəs] *a* numeroso(a).

nun [nʌn] *n* suora, monaca.

nurse [nɜːs] *n* infermiere/a // *vt* (*patient, cold*) curare; (*hope*) nutrire; ~(**maid**) *n* bambinaia.

nursery ['nɜːsərɪ] *n* (*room*) camera dei bambini; (*institution*) asilo; (*for plants*) vivaio; ~ **rhyme** *n* filastrocca; ~ **school** *n* scuola materna; ~ **slope** *n* (SKI) pista per principianti.

nursing ['nɜːsɪŋ] *n* (*profession*) professione *f* di infermiere (*or* di infermiera); ~ **home** *n* casa di cura.

nut [nʌt] *n* (*of metal*) dado; (*fruit*) noce *f*; **he's** ~**s** (*col*) è matto; ~**case** *n* (*col*) mattarello/a; ~**crackers** *npl* schiaccianoci *m inv*; ~**meg** *n* ['nʌtmeg] *n* noce *f* moscata.

nutrition [njuː'trɪʃən] *n* nutrizione *f.*

nutritious [njuː'trɪʃəs] *a* nutriente.

nutshell ['nʌtʃel] *n* guscio di noce; **in a** ~ in poche parole.

nylon ['naɪlɔn] *n* nailon *m*; ~**s** *npl* calze *fpl* di nailon.

O

oaf [əuf] *n* zoticone *m.*

oak [əuk] *n* quercia.

O.A.P. *abbr see* **old.**

oar [ɔː*] *n* remo.

oasis, *pl* **oases** [əu'eɪsɪs, əu'eɪsiːz] *n* oasi *f inv.*

oath [əuθ] *n* giuramento; (*swear word*) bestemmia; **on** ~ sotto giuramento; giurato(a).

oatmeal ['əutmiːl] *n* farina d'avena.

oats [əuts] *n* avena.

obedience [ə'biːdɪəns] *n* ubbidienza; **in** ~ **to** conformemente a.

obedient [ə'biːdɪənt] *a* ubbidiente.

obelisk ['ɔbɪlɪsk] *n* obelisco.

obesity [əu'biːsɪtɪ] *n* obesità.

obey [ə'beɪ] *vt* ubbidire a; (*instructions,*

regulations) osservare // *vi* ubbidire.
obituary [ə'bɪtjʊərɪ] *n* necrologia.
object *n* ['ɔbdʒɪkt] oggetto; (*purpose*) scopo, intento; (*LING*) complemento oggetto // *vi* [əb'dʒɛkt]: **to ~ to** (*attitude*) disapprovare; (*proposal*) protestare contro, sollevare delle obiezioni contro; **I ~!** mi oppongo!; **he ~ed that ...** obiettò che ...; **~ion** [əb'dʒɛkʃən] *n* obiezione *f*; (*drawback*) inconveniente *m*; **~ionable** [əb'dʒɛkʃənəbl] *a* antipatico(a); (*smell*) sgradevole; (*language*) scostumato(a); **~ive** *n* obiettivo // *a* obiettivo(a); **~ivity** [ɔbdʒɪk'tɪvɪtɪ] *n* obiettività; **~or** *n* oppositore/trice.
obligation [ɔblɪ'geɪʃən] *n* obbligo, dovere *m*; (*debt*) obbligo (di riconoscenza).
obligatory [ə'blɪgətərɪ] *a* obbligatorio(a).
oblige [ə'blaɪdʒ] *vt* (*force*): **to ~ sb to do** costringere qd a fare; (*do a favour*) fare una cortesia a; **to be ~d to sb for sth** essere grato a qd per qc; **obliging** *a* servizievole, compiacente.
oblique [ə'bliːk] *a* obliquo(a); (*allusion*) indiretto(a).
obliterate [ə'blɪtəreɪt] *vt* cancellare.
oblivion [ə'blɪvɪən] *n* oblio.
oblivious [ə'blɪvɪəs] *a*: **~ of** incurante di; inconscio(a) di.
oblong ['ɔblɔŋ] *a* oblungo(a) // *n* rettangolo.
obnoxious [əb'nɔkʃəs] *a* odioso(a); (*smell*) disgustoso(a), ripugnante.
oboe ['əubəu] *n* oboe *m*.
obscene [əb'siːn] *a* osceno(a).
obscenity [əb'sɛnɪtɪ] *n* oscenità *f inv*.
obscure [əb'skjuə*] *a* oscuro(a) // *vt* oscurare; (*hide: sun*) nascondere; **obscurity** *n* oscurità.
obsequious [əb'siːkwɪəs] *a* ossequioso(a).
observable [əb'zɔːvəbl] *a* osservabile; (*appreciable*) notevole.
observance [əb'zɔːvns] *n* osservanza.
observant [əb'zɔːvnt] *a* attento(a).
observation [ɔbzə'veɪʃən] *n* osservazione *f*; (*by police etc*) sorveglianza.
observatory [əb'zɔːvətrɪ] *n* osservatorio.
observe [əb'zɔːv] *vt* osservare; (*remark*) fare osservare; **~r** *n* osservatore/trice.
obsess [əb'sɛs] *vt* ossessionare; **~ion** [əb'sɛʃən] *n* ossessione *f*; **~ive** *a* ossessivo(a).
obsolescence [ɔbsə'lɛsns] *n* obsolescenza.
obsolete ['ɔbsəliːt] *a* obsoleto(a); (*word*) desueto(a).
obstacle ['ɔbstəkl] *n* ostacolo; **~ race** *n* corsa agli ostacoli.
obstetrics [ɔb'stɛtrɪks] *n* ostetrica.
obstinacy ['ɔbstɪnəsɪ] *n* ostinatezza.
obstinate ['ɔbstɪnɪt] *a* ostinato(a).
obstreperous [əb'strɛpərəs] *a* turbolento(a).
obstruct [əb'strʌkt] *vt* (*block*) ostruire, ostacolare; (*halt*) fermare; (*hinder*) impedire; **~ion** [əb'strʌkʃən] *n* ostruzione *f*; ostacolo; **~ive** *a* ostruttivo(a).
obtain [əb'teɪn] *vt* ottenere // *vi* essere in uso; **~able** *a* ottenibile.

obtrusive [əb'truːsɪv] *a* (*person*) importuno(a); (*smell*) invadente; (*building etc*) imponente e invadente.
obtuse [əb'tjuːs] *a* ottuso(a).
obviate ['ɔbvɪeɪt] *vt* ovviare a, evitare.
obvious ['ɔbvɪəs] *a* ovvio(a), evidente; **~ly** *ad* ovviamente; certo.
occasion [ə'keɪʒən] *n* occasione *f*; (*event*) avvenimento // *vt* cagionare; **~al** *a* occasionale; **I smoke an ~al cigarette** ogni tanto fumo una sigaretta.
occupation [ɔkju'peɪʃən] *n* occupazione *f*; (*job*) mestiere *m*, professione *f*; **~al hazard** *n* rischio del mestiere.
occupier ['ɔkjupaɪə*] *n* occupante *m/f*.
occupy ['ɔkjupaɪ] *vt* occupare; **to ~ o.s. by doing** occuparsi a fare.
occur [ə'kəː*] *vi* accadere; (*difficulty, opportunity*) capitare; (*phenomenon, error*) trovarsi; **to ~ to sb** venire in mente a qd; **~rence** *n* caso, fatto; presenza.
ocean ['əuʃən] *n* oceano; **~-going** *a* d'alto mare.
ochre ['əukə*] *a* ocra *inv*.
o'clock [ə'klɔk] *ad*: **it is 5 ~** sono le 5.
octagonal [ɔk'tægənl] *a* ottagonale.
octane ['ɔkteɪn] *n* ottano.
octave ['ɔktɪv] *n* ottavo.
October [ɔk'təubə*] *n* ottobre *m*.
octopus ['ɔktəpəs] *n* polpo, piovra.
odd [ɔd] *a* (*strange*) strano(a), bizzarro(a); (*number*) dispari *inv*; (*left over*) in più; (*not of a set*) spaiato(a); **60-~** 60 e oltre; **at ~ times** di tanto in tanto; **the ~ one out** l'eccezione *f*; **~ity** *n* bizzarria; (*person*) originale *m*; **~-job man** *n* tuttofare *m inv*; **~ jobs** *npl* lavori *mpl* occasionali; **~ly** *ad* stranamente; **~ments** *npl* (*COMM*) rimanenze *fpl*; **~s** *npl* (*in betting*) quota; **the ~s are against his coming** c'è poca probabilità che venga; **it makes no ~s** non importa; **at ~s** in contesa.
ode [əud] *n* ode *f*.
odious ['əudɪəs] *a* odioso(a), ripugnante.
odour ['əudə*] *n* odore *m*; **~less** *a* inodoro(a).
of [ɔv, əv] *prep* di; **a friend ~ ours** un nostro amico; **3 ~ them** went 3 di loro sono andati; **the 5th ~ July** il 5 luglio; **a boy ~ 10** un ragazzo di 10 anni.
off [ɔf] *a,ad* (*engine*) spento(a); (*tap*) chiuso(a); (*food:* bad) andato a male; (*absent*) assente; (*cancelled*) sospeso(a) // *prep* da; a poca distanza di; **to be ~** (*to leave*) partire, andarsene; **to be ~ sick** essere assente per malattia; **a day ~** un giorno di vacanza; **to have an ~ day** non essere in forma; **he had his coat ~** si era tolto il cappotto; **10% ~** (*COMM*) con uno sconto di 10%; **5 km ~ (the road)** a 5 km (dalla strada); **~ the coast** al largo della costa; **a house ~ the main road** una casa fuori della strada maestra; **I'm ~ meat** la carne non mi va più; non mangio più la carne; **on the ~ chance** a caso.
offal ['ɔfl] *n* (*CULIN*) frattaglie *fpl*.
offbeat ['ɔfbiːt] *a* eccentrico(a).

off-colour ['ɔf'kʌlə*] a (ill) malato(a), indisposto(a).

offence, offense (US) [ə'fɛns] n (LAW) contravvenzione f; (: more serious) reato; **to take ~ at** offendersi per.

offend [ə'fɛnd] vt (person) offendere; ~**er** n delinquente m/f; (against regulations) contravventore/trice.

offensive [ə'fɛnsɪv] a offensivo(a); (smell etc) sgradevole, ripugnante // n (MIL) offensiva.

offer ['ɔfə*] n offerta, proposta // vt offrire; **'on ~'** (COMM) 'in offerta speciale'; ~**ing** n offerta.

offhand [ɔf'hænd] a disinvolto(a), noncurante // ad all'improvviso.

office ['ɔfɪs] n (place) ufficio; (position) carica; **to take ~** entrare in carica; ~ **block** n complesso di uffici; ~ **boy** n garzone m; ~**r** n (MIL etc) ufficiale m; (of organization) funzionario; (also: **police** ~**r**) agente m di polizia; ~ **worker** n impiegato/a d'ufficio.

official [ə'fɪʃl] a (authorized) ufficiale // n ufficiale m; (civil servant) impiegato/a statale; funzionario; ~**ly** ad ufficialmente.

officious [ə'fɪʃəs] a invadente.

offing ['ɔfɪŋ] n: **in the ~** (fig) in vista.

off: ~-**licence** n (Brit: shop) spaccio di bevande alcoliche; ~-**peak** a (ticket etc) a tariffa ridotta; (time) non di punta; ~-**season** a, ad fuori stagione.

offset ['ɔfsɛt] vt irg . (counteract) controbilanciare, compensare.

offshore [ɔf'ʃɔː*] a (breeze) di terra; . (island) vicino alla costa; (fishing) costiero(a).

offside ['ɔf'saɪd] a (SPORT) fuori gioco // n (AUT: with right-hand drive) lato destro.

offspring ['ɔfsprɪŋ] n prole f, discendenza.

off: ~**stage** ad nelle quinte; ~-**white** a bianco sporco inv.

often ['ɔfn] ad spesso; **as ~ as not** quasi sempre.

ogle ['əugl] vt occhieggiare.

oil [ɔɪl] n olio; (petroleum) petrolio; (for central heating) nafta f // vt (machine) lubrificare; ~**can** n oliatore m a mano; (for storing) latta da olio; ~**field** n giacimento petrolifero; ~-**fired** a a nafta; ~ **level** n livello dell'olio; ~ **painting** n quadro a olio; ~ **refinery** n raffineria di petrolio; ~ **rig** n derrick mar inv; (at sea) piattaforma per trivellazioni subacquee; ~**skins** npl indumenti mpl di tela cerata; ~ **slick** n chiazza d'olio; ~ **tanker** n petroliera; ~ **well** n pozzo petrolifero; ~**y** a unto(a), oleoso(a); (food) untuoso(a).

ointment ['ɔɪntmənt] n unguento.

O.K., okay ['əu'keɪ] excl d'accordo! // vt approvare; **is it ~?, are you ~?** tutto bene?

old [əuld] a vecchio(a); (ancient) antico(a), vecchio(a); (person) vecchio(a), anziano(a); **how ~ are you?** quanti anni ha?; **he's 10 years ~** ha 10 anni; ~ **age** n vecchiaia; ~-**age pensioner (O.A.P.)** n

pensionato/a; ~**er brother/sister** fratello/sorella maggiore; ~-**fashioned** a antiquato(a), fuori moda; (person) all'antica.

olive ['ɔlɪv] n (fruit) oliva; (tree) olivo // a (also: ~-**green**) verde oliva inv; ~ **oil** n olio d'oliva.

Olympic [əu'lɪmpɪk] a olimpico(a); **the ~ Games, the ~s** i giochi olimpici, le Olimpiadi.

omelet(te) ['ɔmlɪt] n omelette f inv.

omen ['əumən] n presagio, augurio.

ominous ['ɔmɪnəs] a minaccioso(a); (event) di malaugurio.

omission [əu'mɪʃən] n omissione f.

omit [əu'mɪt] vt omettere.

on [ɔn] prep su; (on top of) sopra // ad (machine) in moto; (light, radio) acceso(a); (tap) aperto(a); **is the meeting still ~?** terrà sempre luogo la riunione?; la riunione è ancora in corso?; **when is this film ~?** quando c'è questo film?; ~ **the train** in treno; ~ **the wall** sul or al muro; ~ **television** alla televisione; ~ **learning this** imparando questo; ~ **arrival** all'arrivo; ~ **the left** sulla or a sinistra; ~ **Friday** venerdì; ~ **Fridays** di or il venerdì; **a week** ~ **Friday** venerdì fra otto giorni; **put your coat** ~ mettiti il cappotto; **to walk** etc ~ continuare a camminare etc; **it's not** ~! non è possibile!; ~ **and off** ogni tanto.

once [wʌns] ad una volta // cj non appena, quando; **at** ~ subito; (simultaneously) a un tempo; **all at** ~ ad (all to) ad un tratto; ~ **a week** una volta alla settimana; ~ **more** ancora una volta; ~ **and for all** una volta per sempre.

oncoming ['ɔnkʌmɪŋ] a (traffic) che viene in senso opposto.

one [wʌn] det, num un(uno) m, una(un') f // pronoun uno(a); (impersonal) si; **this** ~ questo(a) qui; **that** ~ quello(a) là; **the ~ book which...** l'unico libro che...; ~ **by** ~ a uno(a) a uno(a); ~ **never knows** non si sa mai; **to express** ~**'s opinion** esprimere la propria opinione; ~ **another** l'un(a) l'altro(a); ~-**man** a (business) diretto(a) etc da un solo uomo; ~-**self** pronoun si; (after prep, also emphatic) sé, se stesso(a); ~-**way** a (street, traffic) a senso unico.

ongoing ['ɔngəuɪŋ] a in corso; in attuazione.

onion ['ʌnjən] n cipolla.

onlooker ['ɔnlukə*] n spettatore/trice.

only ['əunlɪ] ad solo, soltanto // a solo(a), unico(a) // cj solo che, ma; **an** ~ **child** un figlio unico; **not** ~ non solo; **I** ~ **took one** ne ho preso soltanto uno, non ne ho preso che uno.

onset ['ɔnsɛt] n inizio; (of winter, old age) approssimarsi m.

onshore ['ɔnʃɔː*] a (wind) di mare.

onslaught ['ɔnslɔːt] n attacco, assalto.

onto ['ɔntu] prep = on to.

onus ['əunəs] n onere m, peso.

onward(s) ['ɔnwəd(z)] ad (move) in

avanti; **from this time** ~ d'ora in poi.

onyx ['ɔnɪks] n onice f.

ooze [uːz] vi stillare.

opal ['əʊpl] n opale m or f.

opaque [əʊ'peɪk] a opaco(a).

open ['əʊpn] a aperto(a); (road) libero(a); (meeting) pubblico(a); (admiration) evidente, franco(a); (question) insoluto(a); (enemy) dichiarato(a) // vt aprire // vi (eyes, door, debate) aprirsi; (flower) sbocciare; (shop, bank, museum) aprire; (book etc: commence) cominciare; **to ~ on to** vt fus (subj: room, door) dare su; **to ~ out** vt aprire // vi aprirsi; **to ~ up** vt aprire; (blocked road) sgombrare // vi aprirsi; **in the ~ (air)** all'aperto; ~-**air** a all'aperto; ~**ing** n apertura; (opportunity) occasione f, opportunità f inv; sbocco; (job) posto vacante; ~**ly** ad apertamente; ~-**minded** a che ha la mente aperta; ~ **sandwich** n canapè m inv; **the ~ sea** il mare aperto, l'alto mare.

opera ['ɔpərə] n opera; ~ **glasses** npl binocolo da teatro; ~ **house** n opera.

operate ['ɔpəreɪt] vt (machine) azionare, far funzionare; (system) usare // vi funzionare; (drug) essere efficace; **to ~ on sb (for)** (MED) operare qd (di).

operatic [ɔpə'rætɪk] a dell'opera, lirico(a).

operating ['ɔpəreɪtɪŋ] a: ~ **table** tavolo operatorio; ~ **theatre** sala operatoria.

operation [ɔpə'reɪʃən] n operazione f; **to be in ~** (machine) essere in azione or funzionamento; (system) essere in vigore; ~**al** a in funzione; d'esercizio.

operative ['ɔpərətɪv] a (measure) operativo(a) // n (in factory) operaio/a.

operator ['ɔpəreɪtə*] n (of machine) operatore/trice; (TEL) centralinista m/f.

operetta [ɔpə'rɛtə] n operetta.

opinion [ə'pɪnɪən] n opinione f, parere m; **in my ~** secondo me, a mio avviso; ~**ated** a dogmatico(a).

opium ['əʊpɪəm] n oppio.

opponent [ə'pəʊnənt] n avversario/a.

opportune ['ɔpətjuːn] a opportuno(a); **opportunist** [-'tjuːnɪst] n opportunista m/f.

opportunity [ɔpə'tjuːnɪtɪ] n opportunità f inv, occasione f.

oppose [ə'pəʊz] vt opporsi a; ~**d to** a contrario(a) a; **as ~d to** in contrasto con; **opposing** a opposto(a); (team) avversario(a).

opposite ['ɔpəzɪt] a opposto(a); (house etc) di fronte // ad di fronte, dirimpetto // prep di fronte a // n opposto, contrario; (of word) contrario; **his ~ number** il suo corrispondente.

opposition [ɔpə'zɪʃən] n opposizione f.

oppress [ə'prɛs] vt opprimere; ~**ion** [ə'prɛʃən] n oppressione f; ~**ive** a oppressivo(a).

opt [ɔpt] vi: **to ~ for** optare per; **to ~ to do** scegliere di fare; **to ~ out of** ritirarsi da.

optical ['ɔptɪkl] a ottico(a).

optician [ɔp'tɪʃən] n ottico.

optimism ['ɔptɪmɪzəm] n ottimismo.

optimist ['ɔptɪmɪst] n ottimista m/f; ~**ic** [-'mɪstɪk] a ottimistico(a).

optimum ['ɔptɪməm] a ottimale.

option ['ɔpʃən] n scelta; (SCOL) materia facoltativa; (COMM) opzione f; **to keep one's ~s open** (fig) non impegnarsi; ~**al** a facoltativo(a); (COMM) a scelta.

opulence ['ɔpjʊləns] n opulenza; abbondanza.

or [ɔː*] cj o, oppure; (with negative): **he hasn't seen ~ heard anything** non ha visto nè sentito niente; ~ **else** se no, altrimenti; oppure.

oracle ['ɔrəkl] n oracolo.

oral ['ɔːrəl] a orale // n esame m orale.

orange ['ɔrɪndʒ] n (fruit) arancia // a arancione.

oration [ɔː'reɪʃən] n orazione f.

orator ['ɔrətə*] n oratore/trice.

oratorio [ɔrə'tɔːrɪəʊ] n oratorio.

orb [ɔːb] n orbe m.

orbit ['ɔːbɪt] n orbita // vt orbitare intorno a.

orchard ['ɔːtʃəd] n frutteto.

orchestra ['ɔːkɪstrə] n orchestra; ~**l** [-'kɛstrəl] a orchestrale; (concert) sinfonico(a).

orchid ['ɔːkɪd] n orchidea.

ordain [ɔː'deɪn] vt (REL) ordinare; (decide) decretare.

ordeal [ɔː'diːl] n prova, travaglio.

order ['ɔːdə*] n ordine m; (COMM) ordinazione f // vt ordinare; **in ~** in ordine; (of document) in regola; **in ~ of size** in ordine di grandezza; **in ~ to do** per fare; **in ~ that** affinché +sub; **to ~ sb to do** ordinare a qd di fare; **the lower ~s** (pej) i ceti inferiori; ~ **form** n modulo d'ordinazione; ~**ly** n (MIL) attendente m // a (room) in ordine; (mind) metodico(a); (person) ordinato(a), metodico(a).

ordinal ['ɔːdɪnl] a (number) ordinale.

ordinary ['ɔːdnrɪ] a normale, comune, (pej) mediocre.

ordination [ɔːdɪ'neɪʃən] n ordinazione f.

ore [ɔː*] n minerale m grezzo.

organ ['ɔːgən] n organo; ~**ic** [ɔː'gænɪk] a organico(a).

organism ['ɔːgənɪzəm] n organismo.

organist ['ɔːgənɪst] n organista m/f.

organization [ɔːgənaɪ'zeɪʃən] n organizzazione f.

organize ['ɔːgənaɪz] vt organizzare; ~**r** n organizzatore/trice.

orgasm ['ɔːgæzəm] n orgasmo.

orgy ['ɔːdʒɪ] n orgia.

Orient ['ɔːrɪənt] n: **the ~** l'Oriente m; **oriental** [-'ɛntl] a, n orientale (m/f).

orientate ['ɔːrɪənteɪt] vt orientare.

orifice ['ɔrɪfɪs] n orifizio.

origin ['ɔrɪdʒɪn] n origine f.

original [ə'rɪdʒɪnl] a originale; (earliest) originario(a) // n originale m; ~**ity** [-'nælɪtɪ] n originalità f; ~**ly** ad (at first) all'inizio.

originate [ə'rɪdʒɪneɪt] vi: **to ~ from**

venire da, essere originario(a) di; (*suggestion*) provenire da.

ornament ['ɔːnəmənt] *n* ornamento; (*trinket*) ninnolo; **~al** [-'mentl] *a* ornamentale.

ornate [ɔː'neɪt] *a* molto ornato(a).

ornithologist [ɔːnɪ'θɒlədʒɪst] *n* ornitologo/a.

ornithology [ɔːnɪ'θɒlədʒɪ] *n* ornitologia.

orphan ['ɔːfn] *n* orfano/a // *vt*: **to be ~ed** diventare orfano; **~age** *n* orfanotrofio.

orthodox ['ɔːθədɒks] *a* ortodosso(a).

orthopaedic [ɔːθə'piːdɪk] *a* ortopedico(a).

oscillate ['ɒsɪleɪt] *vi* oscillare.

ostensible [ɒs'tensɪbl] *a* preteso(a); apparente; **ostensibly** *ad* all'apparenza.

ostentation [ɒsten'teɪʃən] *n* ostentazione *f*.

ostentatious [ɒsten'teɪʃəs] *a* pretenzioso(a); ostentato(a).

osteopath ['ɒstɪəpæθ] *n* specialista *m/f* di osteopatia.

ostracize ['ɒstrəsaɪz] *vt* dare l'ostracismo a.

ostrich ['ɒstrɪtʃ] *n* struzzo.

other ['ʌðə*] *a* altro(a); **~ than** altro che; a parte; **~wise** *ad,cj* altrimenti.

otter ['ɒtə*] *n* lontra.

ought [ɔːt], *pt* **ought** [ɔːt] *auxiliary vb*: **I ~ to do it** dovrei farlo; **this ~ to have been corrected** questo avrebbe dovuto essere corretto; **he ~ to win** dovrebbe vincere.

ounce [auns] *n* oncia (= 28.35 g; 16 in a pound).

our ['auə*] *a* il(la) nostro(a), *pl* i(le) nostri(e); **~s** *pronoun* il(la) nostro(a), *pl* i(le) nostri(e); **~selves** *pronoun pl* (*reflexive*) ci; (*after preposition*) noi; (*emphatic*) noi stessi(e).

oust [aust] *vt* cacciare, espellere.

out [aut] *ad* fuori; (*published, not at home etc*) uscito(a); (*light, fire*) spento(a); **~ here** qui fuori; **~ there** là fuori; **he's ~** è uscito; (*unconscious*) ha perso conoscenza; **to be ~ in one's calculations** essersi sbagliato nei calcoli; **to run/back etc ~** uscire di corsa/a marcia indietro *etc*; **~ loud** *ad* ad alta voce; **~ of** (*outside*) fuori di; (*because of: anger etc*) per; (*from among*): **~ of 10** su 10; (*without*): **~ of petrol** senza benzina, a corto di benzina; **made ~ of wood** di *or* in legno; **~ of order** (*machine etc*) guasto(a).

outboard ['autbɔːd] *n*: **~ (motor)** (motore *m*) fuoribordo.

outbreak ['autbreɪk] *n* scoppio; epidemia.

outbuilding ['autbɪldɪŋ] *n* dipendenza.

outburst ['autbɔːst] *n* scoppio.

outcast ['autkɑːst] *n* esule *m/f*, (*socially*) paria *m inv*.

outclass [aut'klɑːs] *vt* surclassare.

outcome ['autkʌm] *n* esito, risultato.

outcry ['autkraɪ] *n* protesta, clamore *m*.

outdated [aut'deɪtɪd] *a* (*custom, clothes*) fuori moda; (*idea*) sorpassato(a).

outdo [aut'duː] *vt irg* sorpassare.

outdoor [aut'dɔː*] *a* all'aperto; **~s** *ad* fuori; all'aria aperta.

outer ['autə*] *a* esteriore; **~ space** *n* spazio cosmico.

outfit ['autfɪt] *n* equipaggiamento; (*clothes*) abito; **'~ter's'** 'confezioni da uomo'.

outgoings ['autgəuɪŋz] *npl* (*expenses*) spese *fpl*.

outgrow [aut'grəu] *vt irg* (*clothes*) diventare troppo grande per.

outing ['autɪŋ] *n* gita; escursione *f*.

outlandish [aut'lændɪʃ] *a* strano(a).

outlaw ['autlɔː] *n* fuorilegge *m/f* // *vt* (*person*) mettere fuori della legge; (*practice*) proscrivere.

outlay ['autleɪ] *n* spese *fpl*; (*investment*) sborsa, spesa.

outlet ['autlet] *n* (*for liquid etc*) sbocco, scarico; (*for emotion*) sfogo; (*for goods*) sbocco; (*also*: **retail ~**) punto di vendita.

outline ['autlaɪn] *n* contorno, profilo; (*summary*) abbozzo, grandi linee *fpl*.

outlive [aut'lɪv] *vt* sopravvivere a.

outlook ['autluk] *n* prospettiva, vista.

outlying ['autlaɪɪŋ] *a* periferico(a).

outmoded [aut'məudɪd] *a* passato(a) di moda; antiquato(a).

outnumber [aut'nʌmbə*] *vt* superare in numero.

outpatient ['autpeɪʃənt] *n* paziente *m/f* ambulatoriale.

outpost ['autpəust] *n* avamposto.

output ['autput] *n* produzione *f*.

outrage ['autreɪdʒ] *n* oltraggio; scandalo // *vt* oltraggiare; **~ous** [-'reɪdʒəs] *a* oltraggioso(a); scandaloso(a).

outrider ['autraɪdə*] *n* (*on motorcycle*) battistrada *m inv*.

outright *ad* [aut'raɪt] completamente; schiettamente; apertamente; sul colpo // *a* ['autraɪt] completo(a); schietto(a) e netto(a).

outset ['autset] *n* inizio.

outside [aut'saɪd] *n* esterno, esteriore *m* // *a* esterno(a), esteriore // *ad* fuori, all'esterno // *prep* fuori di, all'esterno di; **at the ~** (*fig*) al massimo; **~ lane** *n* (AUT) corsia di sorpasso; **~r** *n* (*in race etc*) outsider *m inv*; (*stranger*) straniero/a.

outsize ['autsaɪz] *a* enorme; (*clothes*) per taglie forti.

outskirts ['autskɜːts] *npl* sobborghi *mpl*.

outspoken [aut'spəukən] *a* molto franco(a).

outstanding [aut'stændɪŋ] *a* eccezionale, di rilievo; (*unfinished*) non completo(a); non evaso(a); non regolato(a).

outstay [aut'steɪ] *vt*: **to ~ one's welcome** diventare un ospite sgradito.

outstretched [aut'stretʃt] *a* (*hand*) teso(a); (*body*) disteso(a).

outward [aut'wəd] *a* (*sign, appearances*) esteriore; (*journey*) d'andata; **~ly** *ad* esteriormente; in apparenza.

outweigh [aut'weɪ] *vt* avere maggior peso di.

outwit [aut'wɪt] *vt* superare in astuzia.

oval ['əuvl] *a,n* ovale (*m*).

ovary ['əuvərɪ] *n* ovaia.

ovation [əu'veɪʃən] *n* ovazione *f*.

oven ['ʌvn] *n* forno; ~**proof** *a* da forno.

over ['əuvə*] *ad* al di sopra // *a* (*or ad*) (*finished*) finito(a), terminato(a); (*too*) troppo; (*remaining*) che avanza // *prep* su; sopra; (*above*) al di sopra di; (*on the other side of*) di là di; (*more than*) più di; (*during*) durante; ~ **here** qui; ~ **there** là; **all** ~ (*everywhere*) dappertutto; (*finished*) tutto(a) finito(a); ~ **and** ~ (**again**) più e più volte; ~ **and** above oltre (a); **to ask sb** ~ invitare qd (a passare).

over... ['əuvə*] *prefix:* ~**abundant** sovrabbondante.

overact [əuvər'ækt] *vi* (THEATRE) esagerare o strafare la propria parte.

overall *a,n* ['əuvərɔːl] *a* totale // *n* (Brit) grembiule *m* // *ad* [əuvər'ɔːl] nell'insieme, complessivamente; ~**s** *npl* tuta (da lavoro).

overawe [əuvər'ɔː] *vt* intimidire.

overbalance [əuvə'bæləns] *vi* perdere l'equilibrio.

overbearing [əuvə'beərɪŋ] *a* imperioso(a), prepotente.

overboard ['əuvəbɔːd] *ad* (NAUT) fuori bordo, in mare.

overcast ['əuvəkɑːst] *a* coperto(a).

overcharge [əuvə'tʃɑːdʒ] *vt*: **to** ~ **sb for sth** far pagare troppo caro a qd per qc.

overcoat ['əuvəkəut] *n* soprabito, cappotto.

overcome [əuvə'kʌm] *vt irg* superare; sopraffare.

overcrowded [əuvə'kraudɪd] *a* sovraffollato(a).

overcrowding [əuvə'kraudɪŋ] *n* sovraffollamento; (*in bus*) calca.

overdo [əuvə'duː] *vt irg* esagerare; (*overcook*) cuocere troppo.

overdose ['əuvədəus] *n* dose *f* eccessiva.

overdraft ['əuvədrɑːft] *n* scoperto (di conto).

overdrawn [əuvə'drɔːn] *a* (*account*) scoperto(a).

overdue [əuvə'djuː] *a* in ritardo; (*recognition*) tardivo(a).

overestimate [əuvər'estɪmeɪt] *vt* sopravvalutare.

overexertion [əuvərɪg'zəːʃən] *n* logorio (fisico).

overexpose [əuvərɪk'spəuz] *vt* (PHOT) sovraesporre.

overflow [əuvə'fləu] *vi* traboccare.

overgrown [əuvə'grəun] *a* (*garden*) ricoperto(a) di vegetazione.

overhaul *vt* [əuvə'hɔːl] revisionare // *n* ['əuvəhɔːl] revisione *f*.

overhead *ad* [əuvə'hed] di sopra // *a* ['əuvəhed] aereo(a); (*lighting*) verticale; ~**s** *npl* spese *fpl* generali.

overhear [əuvə'hɪə*] *vt irg* sentire (per caso).

overjoyed [əuvə'dʒɔɪd] *a* pazzo(a) di gioia.

overland ['əuvəlænd] *a, ad* per via di terra.

overlap [əuvə'læp] *vi* sovrapporsi.

overload [əuvə'ləud] *vt* sovraccaricare.

overlook [əuvə'luk] *vt* (*have view of*) dare su; (*miss*) trascurare; (*forgive*) passare sopra a.

overnight [əuvə'naɪt] *ad* (*happen*) durante la notte; (*fig*) tutto ad un tratto // *a* di notte; fulmineo(a); **he stayed there** ~ ci ha passato la notte; **if you travel** ~... se viaggia di notte... .

overpass ['əuvəpɑːs] *n* cavalcavia *m inv*.

overpower [əuvə'pauə*] *vt* sopraffare; ~**ing** *a* irresistibile; (*heat, stench*) soffocante.

overrate [əuvə'reɪt] *vt* sopravvalutare.

overreact [əuvəriː'ækt] *vi* reagire in modo esagerato.

override [əuvə'raɪd] *vt* (*irg: like* ride) (*order, objection*) passar sopra a; (*decision*) annullare; **overriding** *a* preponderante.

overrule [əuvə'ruːl] *vt* (*decision*) annullare; (*claim*) respingere.

overseas [əuvə'siːz] *ad* oltremare; (*abroad*) all'estero // *a* (*trade*) estero(a); (*visitor*) straniero(a).

overseer ['əuvəsɪə*] *n* (*in factory*) caposquadra *m*.

overshadow [əuvə'ʃædəu] *vt* (*fig*) eclissare.

overshoot [əuvə'ʃuːt] *vt irg* superare.

oversight ['əuvəsaɪt] *n* omissione *f*, svista.

oversimplify [əuvə'sɪmplɪfaɪ] *vt* rendere troppo semplice.

oversleep [əuvə'sliːp] *vi irg* dormire troppo a lungo.

overspill ['əuvəspɪl] *n* eccedenza di popolazione.

overstate [əuvə'steɪt] *vt* esagerare; ~**ment** *n* esagerazione *f*.

overt [əu'vəːt] *a* palese.

overtake [əuvə'teɪk] *vt irg* sorpassare; **overtaking** *n* (AUT) sorpasso.

overthrow [əuvə'θrəu] *vt irg* (*government*) rovesciare.

overtime ['əuvətaɪm] *n* (lavoro) straordinario.

overtone ['əuvətəun] *n* (*also:* ~**s**) sottinteso.

overture ['əuvətʃuə*] *n* (MUS) ouverture *f inv*; (*fig*) approccio.

overturn [əuvə'təːn] *vt* rovesciare // *vi* rovesciarsi.

overweight [əuvə'weɪt] *a* (*person*) troppo grasso(a); (*luggage*) troppo pesante.

overwhelm [əuvə'welm] *vt* sopraffare; sommergere; schiacciare; ~**ing** *a* (*victory, defeat*) schiacciante; (*desire*) irresistibile.

overwork [əuvə'wəːk] *vt* far lavorare troppo // *vi* lavorare troppo, strapazzarsi.

overwrought [əuvə'rɔːt] *a* molto agitato(a).

owe [əu] *vt* dovere; **to** ~ **sb sth, to** ~ **sth to sb** dovere qc a qd.

owing to ['əuɪŋtuː] *prep* a causa di, a motivo di.

owl [aul] *n* gufo.

own [əun] *vt* possedere // *a* proprio(a); **a**

room of my ~ la mia propria camera; **to get one's** ~ **back** vendicarsi; **on one's** ~ tutto(a) solo(a); **to** ~ **up** *vi* confessare; ~**er** *n* proprietario/a; ~**ership** *n* possesso.

ox, *pl* **oxen** [ɔks, 'ɔksn] *n* bue *m*.

oxide ['ɔksaɪd] *n* ossido.

oxtail ['ɔksteɪl] *n*: ~ **soup** minestra di coda di bue.

oxygen ['ɔksɪdʒən] *n* ossigeno; ~ **mask/tent** *n* maschera/tenda ad ossigeno.

oyster ['ɔɪstə*] *n* ostrica.

oz. *abbr of* **ounce(s)**.

ozone ['əuzəun] *n* ozono.

P

p [piː] *abbr of* **penny, pence**.

p.a. *abbr of* **per annum**.

pa [pɑː] *n* (*col*) papà *m inv*, babbo.

pace [peɪs] *n* passo; (*speed*) passo; velocità // *vi*: **to** ~ **up and down** camminare su e giù; **to keep** ~ **with** camminare di pari passo a; (*events*) tenersi al corrente di; ~**maker** *n* (*MED*) segnapasso.

pacific [pə'sɪfɪk] *n*: **the P**~ (**Ocean**) il Pacifico, l'Oceano Pacifico.

pacifist ['pæsɪfɪst] *n* pacifista *m/f*.

pacify ['pæsɪfaɪ] *vt* pacificare; (*soothe*) calmare.

pack [pæk] *n* pacco; balla; (*of hounds*) muta; (*of thieves etc*) banda; (*of cards*) mazzo // *vt* (*goods*) impaccare, imballare; (*in suitcase etc*) mettere; (*box*) riempire; (*cram*) stipare, pigiare; (*press down*) tamponare; turare; **to** ~ (**one's bags**) fare la valigia.

package ['pækɪdʒ] *n* pacco; balla; (*also:* ~ **deal**) pacchetto; forfait *m inv*; ~ **tour** *n* viaggio organizzato.

packet ['pækɪt] *n* pacchetto.

pack ice ['pækaɪs] *n* banchisa.

packing ['pækɪŋ] *n* imballaggio; ~ **case** *n* cassa da imballaggio.

pact [pækt] *n* patto, accordo; trattato.

pad [pæd] *n* blocco; (*for inking*) tampone *m*; (*col: flat*) appartamentino // *vt* imbottire; ~**ding** *n* imbottitura; (*fig*) riempitivo.

paddle ['pædl] *n* (*oar*) pagaia // *vi* sguazzare; ~ **steamer** *n* vapore *m* con ruote a pala; **paddling pool** *n* piscina per bambini.

paddock ['pædək] *n* recinto; paddock *m inv*.

paddy ['pædɪ] *n*: ~ **field** *n* risaia.

padlock ['pædlɔk] *n* lucchetto.

padre ['pɑːdrɪ] *n* cappellano.

paediatrics [piːdɪ'ætrɪks] *n* pediatria.

pagan ['peɪgən] *a,n* pagano(a).

page [peɪdʒ] *n* pagina; (*also:* ~ **boy**) fattorino; (*at wedding*) paggio // *vt* (*in hotel etc*) (far) chiamare.

pageant ['pædʒənt] *n* spettacolo storico; grande cerimonia; ~**ry** *n* pompa.

paid [peɪd] *pt*, *pp of* **pay** // *a* (*work, official*)

rimunerato(a); **to put** ~ **to** mettere fine a.

pail [peɪl] *n* secchio.

pain [peɪn] *n* dolore *m*; **to be in** ~ soffrire, aver male; **to have a** ~ **in** aver male *or* un dolore a; **to take** ~**s to do** mettercela tutta per fare; ~**ed** *a* addolorato(a), afflitto(a); ~**ful** *a* doloroso(a), che fa male; difficile, penoso(a); ~**killer** *n* antalgico, antidolorifico; ~**less** *a* indolore; ~**staking** ['peɪnzteɪkɪŋ] *a* sollecito(a).

paint [peɪnt] *n* vernice *f*, colore *m* // *vt* dipingere; (*walls, door etc*) verniciare; **to** ~ **the door blue** verniciare la porta di azzurro; ~**brush** *n* pennello; ~**er** *n* pittore *m*; imbianchino; ~**ing** *n* pittura; verniciatura; (*picture*) dipinto, quadro; ~-**stripper** *n* prodotto sverniciante.

pair [pɛə*] *n* (*of shoes, gloves etc*) paio; (*of people*) coppia; duo *m inv*; **a** ~ **of scissors** delle forbici.

pajamas [pɪ'dʒɑːməz] *npl* (*US*) pigiama *m*.

Pakistan [pɑːkɪ'stɑːn] *n* Pakistan *m*; ~**i** *a, n* pakistano(a).

pal [pæl] *n* (*col*) amico/a, compagno/a.

palace ['pæləs] *n* palazzo.

palatable ['pælɪtəbl] *a* gustoso(a).

palate ['pælɪt] *n* palato.

palaver [pə'lɑːvə*] *n* chiacchiere *fpl*; storie *fpl*.

pale [peɪl] *a* pallido(a); ~ **blue** *a* azzurro *or* blu pallido *inv*; ~**ness** *n* pallidezza.

Palestine ['pælɪstaɪn] *n* Palestina; **Palestinian** [-'tɪnɪən] *a, n* palestinese (*m/f*).

palette ['pælɪt] *n* tavolozza.

palisade [pælɪ'seɪd] *n* palizzata.

pall [pɔːl] *n* (*of smoke*) cappa // *vi*: **to** ~ (**on**) diventare noioso(a) (a).

pallid ['pælɪd] *a* pallido(a), smorto(a).

pally ['pælɪ] *a* (*col*) amichevole.

palm [pɑːm] *n* (*ANAT*) palma, palmo; (*also:* ~ **tree**) palma // *vt*: **to** ~ **sth off on sb** (*col*) rifilare qc a qd; ~**ist** *n* chiromante *m/f*; **P**~ **Sunday** *n* la Domenica delle Palme.

palpable ['pælpəbl] *a* palpabile.

palpitation [pælpɪ'teɪʃən] *n* palpitazione *f*.

paltry ['pɔːltrɪ] *a* derisorio(a); insignificante.

pamper ['pæmpə*] *vt* viziare, accarezzare.

pamphlet ['pæmflət] *n* dépliant *m inv*.

pan [pæn] *n* (*also:* **sauce**~) casseruola; (*also:* **frying** ~) padella // *vi* (*CINEMA*) fare una panoramica.

panacea [pænə'sɪə] *n* panacea.

Panama ['pænəmɑː] *n* Panama; ~ **canal** *n* canale *m* di Panama.

pancake ['pænkeɪk] *n* frittella.

panda ['pændə] *n* panda *m inv*.

pandemonium [pændɪ'məunɪəm] *n* pandemonio.

pander ['pændə*] *vi*: **to** ~ **to** lusingare; concedere tutto a.

pane [peɪn] *n* vetro.

panel ['pænl] *n* (*of wood, cloth etc*)

pannello; (RADIO, TV) giuria; ~ling n rivestimento a pannelli.

pang [pæŋ] n: ~s of hunger spasimi mpl della fame; ~s of conscience morsi mpl di coscienza.

panic ['pænɪk] n panico // vi perdere il sangue freddo; ~ky a (person) pauroso(a).

pannier ['pænɪə*] n (on animal) bisaccia; (on bicycle) borsa.

panorama [pænə'rɑːmə] n panorama m.

pansy ['pænzɪ] n (BOT) viola del pensiero, pensée f inv; (col) femminuccia.

pant [pænt] vi ansare.

panther ['pænθə*] n pantera.

panties ['pæntɪz] npl slip m, mutandine fpl.

pantomime ['pæntəmaɪm] n pantomima.

pantry ['pæntrɪ] n dispensa.

pants [pænts] npl mutande fpl, slip m; (US: trousers) pantaloni mpl.

papacy ['peɪpəsɪ] n papato.

papal ['peɪpəl] a papale, pontificio(a).

paper ['peɪpə*] n carta; (also: wall~) carta da parati, tappezzeria; (also: news~) giornale m; (study, article) saggio; (exam) prova scritta // a di carta // vt tappezzare; (identity) ~s npl carte fpl, documenti mpl; ~back n tascabile m; edizione f economica; ~ bag n sacchetto di carta; ~ clip n graffetta, clip f inv; ~ mill n cartiera; ~weight n fermacarte m inv; ~work n lavoro amministrativo.

papier-mâché ['pæpɪeɪ'mæʃeɪ] n cartapesta.

paprika ['pæprɪkə] n paprica.

par [pɑː*] n parità, pari f; (GOLF) norma; on a ~ with alla pari con.

parable ['pærəbl] n parabola.

parachute ['pærəʃuːt] n paracadute m inv // vi scendere col paracadute; parachutist n paracadutista m/f.

parade [pə'reɪd] n parata; (inspection) rivista, rassegna // vt (fig) fare sfoggio di // vi sfilare in parata.

paradise ['pærədaɪs] n paradiso.

paradox ['pærədɔks] n paradosso; ~ical [-'dɔksɪkl] a paradossale.

paraffin ['pærəfɪn] n: ~ (oil) paraffina.

paragraph ['pærəgrɑːf] n paragrafo.

parallel ['pærəlɛl] a parallelo(a); (fig) analogo(a) // n (line) parallela; (fig, GEO) parallelo.

paralysis [pə'rælɪsɪs] n paralisi f inv.

paralyze ['pærəlaɪz] vt paralizzare.

paramount ['pærəmaunt] a: of ~ importance di capitale importanza.

paranoia [pærə'nɔɪə] n paranoia.

paraphernalia [pærəfə'neɪlɪə] n attrezzi mpl, roba.

paraphrase ['pærəfreɪz] vt parafrasare.

paraplegic [pærə'pliːdʒɪk] n paraplegico(a).

parasite ['pærəsaɪt] n parassita m.

paratrooper ['pærətruːpə*] n paracadutista m (soldato).

parcel ['pɑːsl] n pacco, pacchetto // vt (also: ~ up) impaccare.

parch [pɑːtʃ] vt riardere; ~ed a (person) assetato(a).

parchment ['pɑːtʃmənt] n pergamena.

pardon ['pɑːdn] n perdono; grazia // vt perdonare; (LAW) graziare; ~! scusi; ~ me! mi scusi!; I beg your ~! scusi!; I beg your ~? prego?

parent ['pɛərənt] n genitore m; ~s npl genitori mpl; ~al [pə'rɛntl] a dei genitori.

parenthesis, pl parentheses [pə'rɛnθɪsɪs, -siːz] n parentesi f inv.

Paris ['pærɪs] n Parigi.

parish ['pærɪʃ] n parrocchia; (civil) ≈ municipio // a parrocchiale; ~ioner [pə'rɪʃənə*] n parrocchiano/a.

parity ['pærɪtɪ] n parità.

park [pɑːk] n parco // vt, vi parcheggiare; ~ing n parcheggio; ~ing lot n (US) posteggio, parcheggio; ~ing meter n parchimetro; ~ing place n posto di parcheggio.

parliament ['pɑːləmənt] n parlamento; ~ary [-'mɛntərɪ] a parlamentare.

parlour ['pɑːlə*] n salotto.

parochial [pə'rəukɪəl] a parrocchiale; (pej) provinciale.

parody ['pærədɪ] n parodia.

parole [pə'rəul] n: on ~ lasciato(a) libero(a) sulla parola.

parquet ['pɑːkeɪ] n: ~ floor(ing) parquet m.

parrot ['pærət] n pappagallo; ~ fashion ad in modo pappagallesco.

parry ['pærɪ] vt parare.

parsimonious [pɑːsɪ'məunɪəs] a parsimonioso(a).

parsley ['pɑːslɪ] n prezzemolo.

parsnip ['pɑːsnɪp] n pastinaca.

parson ['pɑːsn] n prete m; (Church of England) parroco.

part [pɑːt] n parte f; (of machine) pezzo; (MUS) voce f; parte // a in parte // ad partly // vt separare // vi (people) separarsi; (roads) dividersi; to take ~ in prendere parte a; on his ~ da parte sua; for my ~ per parte mia; for the most ~ in generale; nella maggior parte dei casi; to ~ with vt fus separarsi da; rinunciare a; (take leave) lasciare; in ~ exchange in pagamento parziale.

partial ['pɑːʃl] a parziale; to be ~ to avere un debole per.

participate [pɑː'tɪsɪpeɪt] vi: to ~ (in) prendere parte (a), partecipare (a); participation [-'peɪʃən] n partecipazione f.

participle ['pɑːtɪsɪpl] n participio.

particle ['pɑːtɪkl] n particella.

particular [pə'tɪkjulə*] a particolare, speciale; (fussy) difficile; meticoloso(a); ~s npl particolari mpl, dettagli mpl; (information) informazioni fpl; ~ly ad particolarmente; in particolare.

parting ['pɑːtɪŋ] n separazione f; (in hair) scriminatura // a d'addio.

partisan [pɑːtɪ'zæn] n partigiano/a // a partigiano(a); di parte.

partition [pɑːˈtɪʃən] n (POL) partizione f; (wall) tramezzo.

partly [ˈpɑːtlɪ] ad parzialmente; in parte.

partner [ˈpɑːtnə*] n (COMM) socio/a; (SPORT) compagno/a; (at dance) cavaliere/dama; ~ship n associazione f; (COMM) società f inv.

partridge [ˈpɑːtrɪdʒ] n pernice f.

part-time [ˈpɑːtˈtaɪm] a,ad a orario ridotto.

party [ˈpɑːtɪ] n (POL) partito; (team) squadra; gruppo; (LAW) parte f; (celebration) ricevimento; serata; festa.

pass [pɑːs] vt (gen) passare; (place) passare davanti a; (exam) superare, promuovere; (candidate) promuovere; (overtake, surpass) sorpassare, superare; (approve) approvare // vi passare // n (permit) lasciapassare m inv; permesso; (in mountains) passo, gola; (SPORT) passaggio; (SCOL: also: ~ mark): to get a ~ prendere la sufficienza; could you ~ the vegetables round? potrebbe far passare i contorni?; to ~ away vi morire; to ~ by vi passare // vt trascurare; to ~ for passare per; to ~ out vi svenire; ~able a (road) praticabile; (work) accettabile.

passage [ˈpæsɪdʒ] n (gen) passaggio; (also: ~way) corridoio; (in book) brano, passo; (by boat) traversata.

passenger [ˈpæsɪndʒə*] n passeggero/a.

passer-by [pɑːsəˈbaɪ] n passante m/f.

passing [ˈpɑːsɪŋ] a (fig) fuggevole; **a ~ reference** un accenno; **in ~** incidentalmente.

passion [ˈpæʃən] n passione f; amore m; ~ate a appassionato(a).

passive [ˈpæsɪv] a (also LING) passivo(a).

passport [ˈpɑːspɔːt] n passaporto.

password [ˈpɑːswɜːd] n parola d'ordine.

past [pɑːst] prep (further than) oltre, di là di; dopo; (later than) dopo // a passato(a); (president etc) ex inv // n passato; **he's ~ forty** ha più di quarant'anni; **for the ~ few days** da qualche giorno; **in questi ultimi giorni; to run ~** passare di corsa.

pasta [ˈpæstə] n pasta.

paste [peɪst] n (glue) colla; (CULIN) pâté m inv; pasta // vt collare.

pastel [ˈpæstl] a pastello(a).

pasteurized [ˈpæstəraɪzd] a pastorizzato(a).

pastille [ˈpæstl] n pastiglia.

pastime [ˈpɑːstaɪm] n passatempo.

pastoral [ˈpɑːstərl] a pastorale.

pastry [ˈpeɪstrɪ] n pasta.

pasture [ˈpɑːstʃə*] n pascolo.

pasty n [ˈpæstɪ] pasticcio di carne // a [ˈpeɪstɪ] (complexion) pallido(a).

pat [pæt] vt accarezzare, dare un colpetto (affettuoso) a // n: **a ~ of butter** un panetto di burro.

patch [pætʃ] n (of material) toppa; (spot) macchia; (of land) pezzo // vt (clothes) rattoppare; **a bad ~** un brutto periodo; **to ~ up** vt rappezzare; ~**work** n patchwork m; ~**y** a irregolare.

pâté [ˈpæteɪ] n pâté m inv.

patent [ˈpeɪtnt] n brevetto // vt brevettare // a patente, manifesto(a); ~ **leather** n cuoio verniciato.

paternal [pəˈtɜːnl] a paterno(a).

paternity [pəˈtɜːnɪtɪ] n paternità.

path [pɑːθ] n sentiero, viottolo; viale m; (fig) via, strada; (of planet, missile) traiettoria.

pathetic [pəˈθetɪk] a (pitiful) patetico(a); (very bad) penoso(a).

pathologist [pəˈθɒlədʒɪst] n patologo/a.

pathology [pəˈθɒlədʒɪ] n patologia.

pathos [ˈpeɪθɒs] n pathos m.

pathway [ˈpɑːθweɪ] n sentiero, viottolo.

patience [ˈpeɪʃns] n pazienza; (CARDS) solitario.

patient [ˈpeɪʃnt] n paziente m/f; malato/a // a paziente.

patio [ˈpætɪəu] n terrazza.

patriot [ˈpeɪtrɪət] n patriota m/f; ~**ic** [pætrɪˈɒtɪk] a patriottico(a).

patrol [pəˈtrəul] n pattuglia // vt pattugliare; ~ **car** n autoradio f inv (della polizia); ~**man** n (US) poliziotto.

patron [ˈpeɪtrən] n (in shop) cliente m/f; (of charity) benefattore/trice; ~**age** [ˈpætrənɪdʒ] n patronato; ~**ize** [ˈpætrənaɪz] vt essere cliente abituale di; (fig) trattare con condiscendenza; ~ **saint** n patrono.

patter [ˈpætə*] n picchiettio; (sales talk) propaganda di vendita // vi picchiettare.

pattern [ˈpætən] n modello; (design) disegno, motivo; (sample) campione m.

paunch [pɔːntʃ] n pancione m.

pauper [ˈpɔːpə*] n indigente m/f.

pause [pɔːz] n pausa // vi fare una pausa, arrestarsi.

pave [peɪv] vt pavimentare; **to ~ the way for** aprire la via a.

pavement [ˈpeɪvmənt] n (Brit) marciapiede m.

pavilion [pəˈvɪlɪən] n padiglione m; tendone m.

paving [ˈpeɪvɪŋ] n pavimentazione f; ~**stone** n lastra di pietra.

paw [pɔː] n zampa // vt dare una zampata a; (subj: person: pej) palpare.

pawn [pɔːn] n pegno; (CHESS) pedone m; (fig) pedina // vt dare in pegno; ~**broker** n prestatore m su pegno; ~**shop** n monte m di pietà.

pay [peɪ] n stipendio; paga // vb (pt,pp **paid** [peɪd]) vt pagare // vi pagare; (be profitable) rendere; **to ~ attention (to)** fare attenzione (a); **to ~ back** vt rimborsare; **to ~ for** vt fus pagare; **to ~ in** vt versare; **to ~ up** vt saldare; ~**able** a pagabile; ~ **day** n giorno di paga; ~**ee** n beneficiario/a; ~**ment** n pagamento; versamento; saldamento; ~ **packet** n busta f paga inv; ~**roll** n ruolo (organico).

p.c. abbr of **per cent**.

pea [piː] n pisello.

peace [pi:s] n pace f; (calm) calma, tranquillità; ~**able** a pacifico(a); ~**ful** a pacifico(a), calmo(a); ~**keeping** n mantenimento della pace.

peach [pi:tʃ] n pesca.

peacock ['pi:kɔk] n pavone m.

peak [pi:k] n (of mountain) cima, vetta; (mountain itself) picco; (fig) massimo; (: of career) acme f; ~ **period** n periodo di punta.

peal [pi:l] n (of bells) scampanio, carillon m inv; ~**s of laughter** scoppi mpl di risa.

peanut ['pi:nʌt] n arachide f, nocciolina americana; ~ **butter** n burro di arachidi.

pear [pɛə*] n pera.

pearl [pɜːl] n perla.

peasant ['pɛznt] n contadino/a.

peat [pi:t] n torba.

pebble ['pɛbl] n ciottolo.

peck [pɛk] vt (also: ~ **at**) beccare; (food) mangiucchiare // n colpo di becco; (kiss) bacetto; ~**ish** a (col): **I feel** ~**ish** ho un languorino.

peculiar [pɪ'kju:lɪə*] a strano(a), bizzarro(a); peculiare; ~ **to** peculiare di; ~**ity** [pɪkju:lɪ'ærɪtɪ] n peculiarità f inv; (oddity) bizzarria.

pecuniary [pɪ'kju:nɪərɪ] a pecuniario(a).

pedal ['pɛdl] n pedale m // vi pedalare.

pedantic [pɪ'dæntɪk] a pedantesco(a).

pedestal ['pɛdəstl] n piedestallo.

pedestrian [pɪ'dɛstrɪən] n pedone/a // a pedonale; (fig) prosaico(a), pedestre.

pediatrics [pi:dɪ'ætrɪks] n (US) = **paediatrics**.

pedigree ['pɛdɪgri:] n stirpe f; (of animal) pedigree m inv // cpd (animal) di razza.

pedlar ['pɛdlə*] n venditore m ambulante.

peek [pi:k] vi guardare furtivamente.

peel [pi:l] n buccia; (of orange, lemon) scorza // vt sbucciare // vi (paint etc) staccarsi.

peep [pi:p] n (look) sguardo furtivo, sbirciata; (sound) pigolio // vi guardare furtivamente; **to** ~ **out** vi mostrarsi furtivamente; ~**hole** n spioncino.

peer [pɪə*] vi: **to** ~ **at** scrutare // n (noble) pari m inv; (equal) pari m/f inv, uguale m/f; ~**age** n dignità di pari; pari mpl.

peeved [pi:vd] a stizzito(a).

peevish ['pi:vɪʃ] a stizzoso(a).

peg [pɛg] n caviglia; (for coat etc) attaccapanni m inv; (also: **clothes** ~) molletta; **off the** ~ ad confezionato(a).

pejorative [pɪ'dʒɔrətɪv] a peggiorativo(a).

pekingese [pi:kɪ'ni:z] n pechinese m.

pelican ['pɛlɪkən] n pellicano.

pellet ['pɛlɪt] n pallottola, pallina.

pelmet ['pɛlmɪt] n mantovana; cassonetto.

pelt [pɛlt] vt: **to** ~ **sb (with)** bombardare qd (con) // vi (rain) piovere a dirotto // n pelle f.

pelvis ['pɛlvɪs] n pelvi f inv, bacino.

pen [pɛn] n penna; (for sheep) recinto.

penal ['pi:nl] a penale; ~**ize** vt punire; (SPORT) penalizzare; (fig) svantaggiare.

penalty ['pɛnltɪ] n penalità f inv; sanzione f penale; (fine) ammenda; (SPORT) penalizzazione f; ~ (**kick**) n (FOOTBALL) calcio di rigore.

penance ['pɛnəns] n penitenza.

pence [pɛns] npl of **penny**.

pencil ['pɛnsl] n matita; ~ **sharpener** n temperamatite m inv.

pendant ['pɛndnt] n pendaglio.

pending ['pɛndɪŋ] prep in attesa di // a in sospeso.

pendulum ['pɛndjuləm] n pendolo.

penetrate ['pɛnɪtreɪt] vt penetrare; **penetrating** a penetrante; **penetration** [-'treɪʃən] n penetrazione f.

penfriend ['pɛnfrɛnd] n corrispondente m/f.

penguin ['pɛŋgwɪn] n pinguino.

penicillin [pɛnɪ'sɪlɪn] n penicillina.

peninsula [pə'nɪnsjulə] n penisola.

penis ['pi:nɪs] n pene m.

penitence ['pɛnɪtns] n penitenza.

penitent ['pɛnɪtnt] a penitente.

penitentiary [pɛnɪ'tɛnʃərɪ] n (US) carcere m.

penknife ['pɛnnaɪf] n temperino.

pennant ['pɛnənt] n banderuola.

penniless ['pɛnɪlɪs] a senza un soldo.

penny, pl **pennies** or **pence** ['pɛnɪ, 'pɛnɪz, pɛns] n penny m (pl pence).

pension ['pɛnʃən] n pensione f; ~**able** a che ha diritto a una pensione; ~**er** n pensionato/a.

pensive ['pɛnsɪv] a pensoso(a).

pentagon ['pɛntəgən] n pentagono.

Pentecost ['pɛntɪkɔst] n Pentecoste f.

penthouse ['pɛnthaus] n appartamento (di lusso) nell'attico.

pent-up ['pɛntʌp] a (feelings) represso(a).

penultimate [pɛ'nʌltɪmət] a penultimo(a).

people ['pi:pl] npl gente f; persone fpl; (citizens) popolo // n (nation, race) popolo // vt popolare; **4/several** ~ **came** 4/parecchie persone sono venute; **the room was full of** ~ la stanza era piena di gente; ~ **say that...** si dice or la gente dice che... .

pep [pɛp] n (col) dinamismo; **to** ~ **up** vt vivacizzare; (food) rendere più gustoso(a).

pepper ['pɛpə*] n pepe m; (vegetable) peperone m // vt pepare; ~**mint** n (plant) menta peperita; (sweet) pasticca di menta.

peptalk ['pɛptɔk] n (col) discorso di incoraggiamento.

per [pə:*] prep per; a; ~ **hour** all'ora; ~ **kilo** etc il chilo etc; ~ **day** al giorno; ~ **cent** per cento; ~ **annum** all'anno.

perceive [pə'si:v] vt percepire; (notice) accorgersi di.

percentage [pə'sɛntɪdʒ] n percentuale f.

perceptible [pə'sɛptɪbl] a percettibile.

perception [pə'sɛpʃən] n percezione f; sensibilità; perspicacia.

perceptive [pə'sɛptɪv] a percettivo(a); perspicace.

perch [pə:tʃ] n (fish) pesce m persico; (for

bird) sostegno, ramo // *vi* appollaiarsi.

percolator ['pɜːkəleɪtə*] *n* caffettiera a pressione; caffettiera elettrica.

percussion [pə'kʌʃən] *n* percussione *f.*

peremptory [pə'remptərɪ] *a* perentorio(a).

perennial [pə'renɪəl] *a* perenne // *n* pianta perenne.

perfect *a,n* ['pɜːfɪkt] *a* perfetto(a) // *n* (*also:* ~ **tense**) perfetto, passato prossimo // *vt* [pə'fekt] perfezionare; mettere a punto; ~**ion** [-'fekʃən] *n* perfezione *f;* ~**ionist** *n* perfezionista *m/f.*

perforate ['pɜːfəreɪt] *vt* perforare; **perforation** [-'reɪʃən] *n* perforazione *f;* (*line of holes*) dentellatura.

perform [pə'fɔːm] *vt* (*carry out*) eseguire, fare; (*symphony etc*) suonare; (*play, ballet*) dare; (*opera*) fare // *vi* suonare; recitare; ~**ance** *n* esecuzione *f;* (*at theatre etc*) rappresentazione *f,* spettacolo; (*of an artist*) interpretazione *f;* (*of player etc*) performance *f;* (*of car, engine*) prestazione *f;* ~**er** *n* artista *m/f;* ~**ing** *a* (*animal*) ammaestrato(a).

perfume ['pɜːfjuːm] *n* profumo.

perfunctory [pə'fʌŋktərɪ] *a* superficiale, per la forma.

perhaps [pə'hæps] *ad* forse.

peril ['perɪl] *n* pericolo; ~**ous** *a* pericoloso(a).

perimeter [pə'rɪmɪtə*] *n* perimetro; ~ **wall** *n* muro di cinta.

period ['pɪərɪəd] *n* periodo; (*HISTORY*) epoca; (*SCOL*) lezione *f;* (*full stop*) punto; (*MED*) mestruazioni *fpl* // *a* (*costume, furniture*) d'epoca; ~**ic** [-'ɔdɪk] *a* periodico(a); ~**ical** [-'ɔdɪkl] *a* periodico(a) // *n* periodico.

peripheral [pə'rɪfərəl] *a* periferico(a).

periphery [pə'rɪfərɪ] *n* periferia.

periscope ['perɪskəup] *n* periscopio.

perish ['perɪʃ] *vi* perire, morire; (*decay*) deteriorarsi; ~**able** *a* deperibile; ~**ing** *a* (*col: cold*) da morire.

perjure ['pɜːdʒə*] *vt:* **to ~ o.s.** spergiurare; **perjury** *n* spergiuro.

perk [pɜːk] *n* vantaggio; **to ~ up** *vi* (*cheer up*) rianimarsi; ~**y** *a* (*cheerful*) vivace, allegro(a).

perm [pɜːm] *n* (*for hair*) permanente *f.*

permanence ['pɜːmənəns] *n* permanenza.

permanent ['pɜːmənənt] *a* permanente.

permeate ['pɜːmɪeɪt] *vi* penetrare // *vt* permeare.

permissible [pə'mɪsɪbl] *a* permissibile, ammissibile.

permission [pə'mɪʃən] *n* permesso.

permissive [pə'mɪsɪv] *a* tollerante; **the ~ society** la società permissiva.

permit *n* ['pɜːmɪt] permesso // *vt* [pə'mɪt] permettere; **to ~ sb to do** permettere a qd di fare, dare il permesso a qd di fare.

permutation [pɜːmjuː'teɪʃən] *n* permutazione *f.*

pernicious [pə'nɪʃəs] *a* pernicioso(a), nocivo(a).

perpendicular [pɜːpən'dɪkjulə*] *a,n* perpendicolare (*f*).

perpetrate ['pɜːpɪtreɪt] *vt* perpetrare, commettere.

perpetual [pə'petjuəl] *a* perpetuo(a).

perpetuity [pɜːpɪ'tjuːɪtɪ] *n:* **in ~ in** perpetuo.

perplex [pə'pleks] *vt* rendere perplesso(a); (*complicate*) imbrogliare.

persecute ['pɜːsɪkjuːt] *vt* perseguitare; **persecution** [-'kjuːʃən] *n* persecuzione *f.*

persevere [pɜːsɪ'vɪə*] *vi* perseverare.

Persian ['pɜːʃən] *a* persiano(a) // *n* (*LING*) persiano; **the (~) Gulf** *n* il Golfo Persico.

persist [pə'sɪst] *vi:* **to ~ (in doing)** persistere (nel fare); ostinarsi (a fare); ~**ence** *n* persistenza; ostinazione *f;* ~**ent** *a* persistente; ostinato(a).

person ['pɜːsn] *n* persona; ~**able** *a* di bell'aspetto; ~**al** *a* personale; individuale; ~**ality** [-'nælɪtɪ] *n* personalità *f inv;* ~**ally** *ad* personalmente; ~**ify** [-'sɔnɪfaɪ] *vt* personificare.

personnel [pɜːsə'nel] *n* personale *m;* ~ **manager** *n* direttore/trice del personale.

perspective [pə'spektɪv] *n* prospettiva.

perspicacity [pɜːspɪ'kæsɪtɪ] *n* perspicacia.

perspiration [pɜːspɪ'reɪʃən] *n* traspirazione *f,* sudore *m.*

perspire [pə'spaɪə*] *vi* traspirare.

persuade [pə'sweɪd] *vt* persuadere.

persuasion [pə'sweɪʒən] *n* persuasione *f.*

persuasive [pə'sweɪsɪv] *a* persuasivo(a).

pert [pɜːt] *a* (*bold*) sfacciato(a), impertinente.

pertaining [pə'teɪnɪŋ]: ~ **to** *prep* che riguarda.

pertinent ['pɜːtɪnənt] *a* pertinente.

perturb [pə'tɜːb] *vt* turbare.

Peru [pə'ruː] *n* Perù *m.*

perusal [pə'ruːzl] *n* attenta lettura.

Peruvian [pə'ruːvjən] *a, n* peruviano(a).

pervade [pə'veɪd] *vt* pervadere.

perverse [pə'vɜːs] *a* perverso(a).

perversion [pə'vɜːʃn] *n* pervertimento, perversione *f.*

perversity [pə'vɜːsɪtɪ] *n* perversità.

pervert *n* ['pɜːvɜːt] pervertito/a // *vt* [pə'vɜːt] pervertire.

pessimism ['pesɪmɪzəm] *n* pessimismo.

pessimist ['pesɪmɪst] *n* pessimista *m/f;* ~**ic** [-'mɪstɪk] *a* pessimistico(a).

pest [pest] *n* animale *m* (*or* insetto) pestifero; (*fig*) peste *f.*

pester ['pestə*] *vt* tormentare, molestare.

pesticide ['pestɪsaɪd] *n* pesticida *m.*

pestle ['pesl] *n* pestello.

pet [pet] *n* animale *m* domestico; (*favourite*) favorito/a // *vt* accarezzare // *vi* (*col*) fare il petting; ~ **lion** *n* leone *m* ammaestrato.

petal ['petl] *n* petalo.

peter ['piːtə*]: **to ~ out** *vi* esaurirsi; estinguersi.

petite [pə'tiːt] *a* piccolo(a) e aggraziato(a).

petition [pə'tɪʃən] *n* petizione *f.*

petrified ['petrɪfaɪd] *a* (*fig*) morto(a) di paura.

petrol ['petrəl] *n* (*Brit*) benzina.

petroleum [pə'trəuliəm] *n* petrolio.

petrol: ~ **pump** *n* (*in car, at garage*) pompa di benzina; ~ **station** *n* stazione *f* di rifornimento; ~ **tank** *n* serbatoio della benzina.

petticoat ['petɪkəut] *n* sottana.

pettiness ['petɪnɪs] *n* meschinità.

petty ['petɪ] *a* (*mean*) meschino(a); (*unimportant*) insignificante; ~ **cash** *n* piccola cassa; ~ **officer** *n* sottufficiale *m* di marina.

petulant ['petjulənt] *a* irritabile.

pew [pju:] *n* panca (di chiesa).

pewter ['pju:tə*] *n* peltro.

phallic ['fælɪk] *a* fallico(a).

phantom ['fæntəm] *n* fantasma *m*.

Pharaoh ['fɛərəu] *n* faraone *m*.

pharmacist ['fɑ:məsɪst] *n* farmacista *m/f*.

pharmacy ['fɑ:məsɪ] *n* farmacia.

phase [feɪz] *n* fase *f*, periodo // *vt*: **to** ~ **sth in/out** introdurre/eliminare qc progressivamente.

Ph.D. (*abbr* = *Doctor of Philosophy*) *n* (*degree*) dottorato di ricerca.

pheasant ['feznt] *n* fagiano.

phenomenon, *pl* **phenomena** [fə'nɔmɪnən, -nə] *n* fenomeno.

phew [fju:] *excl* uff!

phial ['faɪəl] *n* fiala.

philanthropic [fɪlən'θrɔpɪk] *a* filantropico(a).

philanthropist [fɪ'lænθrəpɪst] *n* filantropo.

philately [fɪ'lætəlɪ] *n* filatelia.

Philippines ['fɪlɪpi:nz] *npl* (*also:* **Philippine Islands**) Filippine *fpl*.

philosopher [fɪ'lɔsəfə*] *n* filosofo/a.

philosophical [fɪlə'sɔfɪkl] *a* filosofico(a).

philosophy [fɪ'lɔsəfɪ] *n* filosofia.

phlegm [flɛm] *n* flemma; ~**atic** [flɛg-'mætɪk] *a* flemmatico(a).

phobia ['fəubjə] *n* fobia.

phone [fəun] *n* telefono // *vt* telefonare; **to** ~ **back** *vt, vi* richiamare.

phonetics [fə'netɪks] *n* fonetica.

phon(e)y ['fəunɪ] *a* falso(a), fasullo(a) // *n* (*person*) ciarlatano.

phonograph ['fəunəgrɑ:f] *n* (*US*) giradischi *m*.

phosphate ['fɔsfeɪt] *n* fosfato.

phosphorus ['fɔsfərəs] *n* fosforo.

photo ['fəutəu] *n* foto *f inv*.

photo... ['fəutəu] *prefix*: ~**copier** *n* fotocopiatrice *f*; ~**copy** *n* fotocopia // *vt* fotocopiare; ~**genic** [-'dʒenɪk] *a* fotogenico(a); ~**graph** *n* fotografia // *vt* fotografare; ~**grapher** [fə'tɔgrɑfə*] *n* fotografo; ~**graphic** [-'græfɪk] *a* fotografico(a); ~**graphy** [fə'tɔgrəfɪ] *n* fotografia.

phrase [freɪz] *n* espressione *f*; (*LING*) locuzione *f*; (*MUS*) frase *f* // *vt* esprimere; ~ **book** *n* vocabolarietto.

physical ['fɪzɪkl] *a* fisico(a); ~**ly** *ad* fisicamente.

physician [fɪ'zɪʃən] *n* medico.

physicist ['fɪzɪsɪst] *n* fisico.

physics ['fɪzɪks] *n* fisica.

physiology [fɪzɪ'ɔlədʒɪ] *n* fisiologia.

physiotherapist [fɪzɪəu'θerəpɪst] *n* fisioterapista *m/f*.

physiotherapy [fɪzɪəu'θerəpɪ] *n* fisioterapia.

physique [fɪ'zi:k] *n* fisico; costituzione *f*.

pianist ['pi:ənɪst] *n* pianista *m/f*.

piano [pɪ'ænəu] *n* pianoforte *m*.

piccolo ['pɪkələu] *n* ottavino.

pick [pɪk] *n* (*tool: also:* ~**-axe**) piccone *m* // *vt* scegliere; (*gather*) cogliere; **take your** ~ scelga; **the** ~ **of** il fior fiore di; **to** ~ **one's teeth** stuzzicarsi i denti; **to** ~ **pockets** borseggiare; **to** ~ **on** *vt fus* (*person*) avercela con; **to** ~ **out** *vt* scegliere; (*distinguish*) distinguere; **to** ~ **up** *vi* (*improve*) migliorarsi // *vt* raccogliere; (*collect*) passare a prendere; (*AUT: give lift to*) far salire; (*learn*) imparare; **to** ~ **up speed** acquistare velocità; **to** ~ **o.s. up** rialzarsi.

picket ['pɪkɪt] *n* (*in strike*) scioperante *m/f* che fa parte di un picchetto; picchetto // *vt* picchettare; ~ **line** *n* controllo del picchetto.

pickle ['pɪkl] *n* (*also:* ~**s:** *as condiment*) sottaceti *mpl* // *vt* mettere sottaceto; mettere in salamoia.

pick-me-up ['pɪkmiːʌp] *n* tiramisù *m inv*.

pickpocket ['pɪkpɔkɪt] *n* borsaiolo.

pickup ['pɪkʌp] *n* (*on record player*) pick-up *m inv*; (*small truck*) camioncino.

picnic ['pɪknɪk] *n* picnic *m inv* // *vi* fare un picnic.

pictorial [pɪk'tɔ:rɪəl] *a* illustrato(a).

picture ['pɪktʃə*] *n* quadro; (*painting*) pittura; (*photograph*) foto(grafia) *f*; (*drawing*) disegno; (*film*) film *m inv* // *vt* raffigurarsi; **the** ~**s** il cinema; ~ **book** *n* libro illustrato.

picturesque [pɪktʃə'resk] *a* pittoresco(a).

piddling ['pɪdlɪŋ] *a* (*col*) insignificante.

pidgin ['pɪdʒɪn] *a*: ~ **English** *n* inglese semplificato misto ad elementi indigeni.

pie [paɪ] *n* torta; (*of meat*) pasticcio.

piebald ['paɪbɔ:ld] *a* pezzato(a).

piece [pi:s] *n* pezzo; (*of land*) appezzamento; (*item*): **a** ~ **of furniture/advice** un mobile/ consiglio // *vt*: **to** ~ **together** mettere insieme; **in** ~**s** (*broken*) in pezzi; (*not yet assembled*) smontato(a); **to take to** ~**s** smontare; ~**meal** *ad* pezzo a pezzo, a spizzico; ~**work** *n* (lavoro a) cottimo.

pier [pɪə*] *n* molo; (*of bridge etc*) pila.

pierce [pɪəs] *vt* forare; (*with arrow etc*) trafiggere.

piercing ['pɪəsɪŋ] *a* (*cry*) acuto(a).

piety ['paɪətɪ] *n* pietà, devozione *f*.

pig [pɪg] *n* maiale *m*, porco.

pigeon ['pɪdʒən] *n* piccione *m*; ~**hole** *n*

casella; ~-toed a che cammina con i piedi in dentro.

piggy bank ['pɪgɪbæŋk] n salvadanaro.

pigheaded ['pɪg'hedɪd] a caparbio(a), cocciuto(a).

piglet ['pɪglɪt] n porcellino.

pigment ['pɪgmənt] n pigmento.

pigmy ['pɪgmɪ] n = pygmy.

pigsty ['pɪgstaɪ] n porcile m.

pigtail ['pɪgteɪl] n treccina.

pike [paɪk] n (spear) picca; (fish) luccio.

pilchard ['pɪltʃəd] n specie di sardina.

pile [paɪl] n (pillar, of books) pila; (heap) mucchio; (of carpet) pelo // vb (also: ~ up) vt ammucchiare // vi ammucchiarsi.

piles [paɪlz] npl emorroidi fpl.

pileup ['paɪlʌp] n (AUT) tamponamento a catena.

pilfering ['pɪlfərɪŋ] n rubacchiare m.

pilgrim ['pɪlgrɪm] n pellegrino/a; ~age n pellegrinaggio.

pill [pɪl] n pillola; **the ~** la pillola.

pillage ['pɪlɪdʒ] vt saccheggiare.

pillar ['pɪlə*] n colonna; ~ **box** n (Brit) cassetta postale.

pillion ['pɪljən] n (of motor cycle) sellino posteriore.

pillory ['pɪlərɪ] n berlina // vt mettere alla berlina.

pillow ['pɪləʊ] n guanciale m; ~**case** n federa.

pilot ['paɪlət] n pilota m/f // cpd (scheme etc) pilota inv // vt pilotare; ~ **boat** n battello pilota; ~ **light** n fiamma pilota.

pimp [pɪmp] n mezzano.

pimple ['pɪmpl] n foruncolo.

pin [pɪn] n spillo; (TECH) perno // vt attaccare con uno spillo; ~**s and needles** formicolio; to ~ **sb down** (fig) obbligare qd a pronunziarsi.

pinafore ['pɪnəfɔ:*] n grembiule m (senza maniche); ~ **dress** n scamiciato.

pincers ['pɪnsəz] npl pinzette fpl.

pinch [pɪntʃ] n pizzicotto, pizzico // vt pizzicare; (col: steal) grattare // vi (shoe) stringere; **at a ~** in caso di bisogno.

pincushion ['pɪnkuʃən] n puntaspilli m inv.

pine [paɪn] n (also: ~ **tree**) pino // vi: to ~ **for** struggersi dal desiderio di; **to ~ away** vi languire.

pineapple ['paɪnæpl] n ananas m inv.

ping [pɪŋ] n (noise) tintinnio; ~-**pong** n ® ping-pong m ®.

pink [pɪŋk] a rosa inv // n (colour) rosa m inv; (BOT) garofano.

pinnacle ['pɪnəkl] n pinnacolo.

pinpoint ['pɪnpɔɪnt] vt indicare con precisione.

pinstripe ['pɪnstraɪp] n stoffa gessata.

pint [paɪnt] n pinta (=0.56 l).

pinup ['pɪnʌp] n pin-up girl f inv.

pioneer [paɪə'nɪə*] n pioniere/a.

pious ['paɪəs] a pio(a).

pip [pɪp] n (seed) seme m; (time signal on radio) segnale m orario.

pipe [paɪp] n tubo; (for smoking) pipa; (MUS) piffero // vt portare per mezzo di tubazione; ~**s** npl (also: **bag~s**) cornamusa (scozzese); to ~ **down** vi (col) calmarsi; ~ **dream** n vana speranza; ~**line** n conduttura; (for oil) oleodotto; ~**r** n piffero; suonatore/trice di cornamusa.

piping ['paɪpɪŋ] ad: ~ **hot** caldo bollente.

pique [pi:k] n picca.

piracy ['paɪərəsɪ] n pirateria.

pirate ['paɪərət] n pirata m; ~ **radio** n radio pirata f inv.

pirouette [pɪru'et] n piroetta // vi piroettare.

Pisces ['paɪsi:z] n Pesci mpl.

pistol ['pɪstl] n pistola.

piston ['pɪstən] n pistone m.

pit [pɪt] n buca, fossa; (also: **coal ~**) miniera; (also: **orchestra ~**) orchestra // vt: to ~ **sb against sb** opporre qd a qd; ~**s** npl (AUT) box m; to ~ **o.s. against** opporsi a.

pitch [pɪtʃ] n (throw) lancia; (MUS) tono; (of voice) altezza; (SPORT) campo; (NAUT) beccheggio; (tar) pece f // vt (throw) lanciare // vi (fall) cascare; (NAUT) beccheggiare; **to ~ a tent** piantare una tenda; ~-**black** a nero(a) come la pece; ~**ed battle** n battaglia campale.

pitcher ['pɪtʃə*] n brocca.

pitchfork ['pɪtʃfɔ:k] n forcone m.

piteous ['pɪtɪəs] a pietoso(a).

pitfall ['pɪtfɔ:l] n trappola.

pith [pɪθ] n (of plant) midollo; (of orange) parte f interna della scorza; (fig) essenza, succo; vigore m.

pithy ['pɪθɪ] a conciso(a); vigoroso(a).

pitiable ['pɪtɪəbl] a pietoso(a).

pitiful ['pɪtɪful] a (touching) pietoso(a); (contemptible) miserabile.

pitiless ['pɪtɪlɪs] a spietato(a).

pittance ['pɪtns] n miseria, magro salario.

pity ['pɪtɪ] n pietà // vt aver pietà di; **what a ~!** che peccato!; ~**ing** a compassionevole.

pivot ['pɪvət] n perno // vi imperniarsi.

pixie ['pɪksɪ] n folletto.

placard ['plækɑ:d] n affisso.

placate [plə'keɪt] vt placare, calmare.

place [pleɪs] n posto, luogo; (proper position, rank, seat) posto; (house) casa, alloggio; (home): **at/to his ~** a casa sua // vt (object) posare, mettere; (identify) riconoscere; individuare; **to take ~** aver luogo; succedere; **to ~ an order** dare un'ordinazione; **out of ~** (not suitable) inopportuno(a); **in the first ~** in primo luogo; ~ **mat** n sottopiatto.

placid ['plæsɪd] a placido(a), calmo(a).

plagiarism ['pleɪdʒjərɪzm] n plagio.

plagiarize ['pleɪdʒjəraɪz] vt plagiare.

plague [pleɪg] n piaga; (MED) peste f.

plaice [pleɪs] n, pl inv pianuzza.

plaid [plæd] n plaid m inv.

plain [pleɪn] a (clear) chiaro(a), palese; (simple) semplice; (frank) franco(a), aperto(a); (not handsome) bruttino(a); (without seasoning etc) scondito(a);

naturale; (in one colour) tinta unita inv // ad francamente, chiaramente // in pianura; in ~ clothes (police) in borghese; ~ly ad chiaramente; (frankly) francamente; ~ness n semplicità.

plaintiff ['pleintif] n attore/trice.

plait [plæt] n treccia.

plan [plæn] n pianta; (scheme) progetto, piano // vt (think in advance) progettare; (prepare) organizzare // vi far piani or progetti; to ~ to do progettare di fare.

plane [plein] n (AVIAT) aereo; (tree) platano; (tool) pialla; (ART, MATH etc) piano // a piano(a), piatto(a) // vt (with tool) piallare.

planet ['plænit] n pianeta m.

planetarium [plænɪˈtɛərɪəm] n planetario.

plank [plæŋk] n tavola, asse f.

plankton ['plæŋktən] n plancton m.

planner ['plænə*] n pianificatore/trice.

planning ['plæniŋ] n progettazione f; family ~ pianificazione f delle nascite.

plant [plɑːnt] n pianta; (machinery) impianto; (factory) fabbrica // vt piantare; (bomb) mettere.

plantation [plæn'teiʃən] n piantagione f.

plaque [plæk] n placca.

plasma ['plæzmə] n plasma m.

plaster ['plɑːstə*] n intonaco; (also: ~ of Paris) gesso; (also: sticking ~) cerotto // vt intonacare; ingessare; (cover): to ~ with coprire di; in ~ (leg etc) ingessato(a); ~ed a (col) ubriaco(a) fradicio(a); ~er n intonacatore m.

plastic ['plæstik] n plastica // a (made of plastic) di or in plastica; (flexible) plastico(a), malleabile; (art) plastico(a).

plasticine ['plæstɪsiːn] n (®) plastilina (®).

plastic surgery ['plæstɪk'sɜːdʒəri] n chirurgia plastica.

plate [pleit] n (dish) piatto; (sheet of metal) lamiera; (PHOT) lastra; (in book) tavola; gold ~ (dishes) vasellame m d'oro; silver ~ (dishes) argenteria.

plateau, ~s or ~x ['plætəu, -z] n altipiano.

plateful ['pleitful] n piatto.

plate glass [pleit'glɑːs] n vetro piano.

platform ['plætfɔːm] n (at meeting) piattaforma; (stage) palco; (RAIL) marciapiede m; ~ ticket n biglietto d'ingresso ai binari.

platinum ['plætinəm] n platino.

platitude ['plætɪtjuːd] n luogo comune.

platoon [plə'tuːn] n plotone m.

platter ['plætə*] n piatto.

plausible ['plɔːzɪbl] a plausibile, credibile; (person) convincente.

play [plei] n gioco; (THEATRE) commedia // vt (game) giocare a; (team, opponent) giocare contro; (instrument, piece of music) suonare; (play, part) interpretare // vi giocare; suonare; recitare; to ~ down vt minimizzare; to ~ up vi (cause trouble) fare i capricci; to ~act vi fare la commedia; ~ed-out a spossato(a); ~er n giocatore/trice; (THEATRE) attore/trice; (MUS) musicista m/f; ~ful a gioioso(a);

~ground n campo di ricreazioni; ~group n giardino d'infanzia; ~ing card n carta da gioco; ~ing field n campo sportivo; ~mate n compagno/a di gioco; ~off n (SPORT) bella; ~ on words n gioco di parole; ~pen n box m inv; ~thing n giocattolo; ~wright n drammaturgo/a.

plea [pliː] n (request) preghiera, domanda; (excuse) scusa; (LAW) (argomento di) difesa.

plead [pliːd] vt patrocinare; (give as excuse) addurre a pretesto // vi (LAW) perorare la causa; (beg): to ~ with sb implorare qd.

pleasant ['pleznt] a piacevole, gradevole; ~ly ad piacevolmente; ~ness n (of person) amabilità; (of place) amenità; ~ry n (joke) scherzo.

please [pliːz] vt piacere a // vi (think fit): do as you ~ faccia come le pare; ~! per piacere!; my bill, ~ il conto, per piacere; ~ yourself! come ti (or le) pare!; ~d a: ~d (with) contento(a) di; pleasing a piacevole, che fa piacere.

pleasurable ['plɛʒərəbl] a molto piacevole, molto gradevole.

pleasure ['plɛʒə*] n piacere m; 'it's a ~' 'prego'; ~ steamer n vapore m da diporto.

pleat [pliːt] n piega.

plebiscite ['plebɪsɪt] n plebiscito.

plectrum ['plektrəm] n plettro.

pledge [pledʒ] n pegno; (promise) promessa // vt impegnare; promettere.

plentiful ['plentiful] a abbondante, copioso(a).

plenty ['plenti] n abbondanza; ~ of tanto(a), molto(a); un'abbondanza di.

pleurisy ['pluərisi] n pleurite f.

pliable ['plaiəbl] a flessibile; (person) malleabile.

pliers ['plaiəz] npl pinza.

plight [plait] n situazione f critica.

plimsolls ['plimsəlz] npl scarpe fpl da tennis.

plinth [plinθ] n plinto; piedistallo.

plod [plɔd] vi camminare a stento; (fig) sgobbare; ~der n sgobbone m.

plonk [plɔŋk] (col) n (wine) vino da poco // vt: to ~ sth down buttare giù qc bruscamente.

plot [plɔt] n congiura, cospirazione f; (of story, play) trama; (of land) lotto // vt (mark out) fare la pianta di; rilevare; (: diagram etc) tracciare; (conspire) congiurare, cospirare // vi congiurare; ~ter n cospiratore/trice.

plough, plow (US) [plau] n aratro // vt (earth) arare; to ~ back vt (COMM) reinvestire; to ~ through vt fus (snow etc) procedere a fatica in.

ploy [plɔi] n stratagemma m.

pluck [plʌk] vt (fruit) cogliere; (musical instrument) pizzicare; (bird) spennare // n coraggio, fegato; to ~ up courage farsi coraggio; ~y a coraggioso(a).

plug [plʌg] n tappo; (ELEC) spina; (AUT)

candela // vt (hole) tappare; (col: advertise) spingere.

plum [plʌm] n (fruit) susina // a: ~ **job** n (col) impiego ottimo or favoloso.

plumb [plʌm] a verticale // n piombo // ad (exactly) esattamente // vt sondare.

plumber ['plʌmə*] n idraulico.

plumbing ['plʌmɪŋ] n (trade) lavoro di idraulico; (piping) tubature fpl.

plumbline ['plʌmlaɪn] n filo a piombo.

plume [plu:m] n piuma, penna; (decorative) pennacchio.

plummet ['plʌmɪt] vi cadere a piombo.

plump [plʌmp] a grassoccio(a); **to ~ for** vt fus (col: choose) decidersi per.

plunder ['plʌndə*] n saccheggio // vt saccheggiare.

plunge [plʌndʒ] n tuffo // vt immergere // vi (fall) cadere, precipitare; **to take the ~** saltare il fosso; **plunging** a (neckline) profondo(a).

pluperfect [plu:'pə:fɪkt] n piucchepperfetto.

plural ['pluərl] a, n plurale (m).

plus [plʌs] n (also: ~ **sign**) segno più // prep più; **ten/twenty** ~ più di dieci/venti; ~ **fours** npl calzoni mpl alla zuava.

plush [plʌʃ] a lussuoso(a).

ply [plaɪ] n (of wool) capo; (of wood) strato // vt (tool) maneggiare; (a trade) esercitare // vi (ship) fare il servizio; **to ~ sb with drink** dare di bere continuamente a qd; ~**wood** n legno compensato.

P.M. abbr see **prime**.

p.m. ad (abbr of post meridiem) del pomeriggio.

pneumatic [nju:'mætɪk] a pneumatico(a).

pneumonia [nju:'məunɪə] n polmonite f.

P.O. abbr see **post office**.

poach [pəutʃ] vt (cook) affogare; (steal) cacciare (or pescare) di frodo // vi fare il bracconiere; ~**ed** a (egg) affogato(a); ~**er** n bracconiere m; ~**ing** n caccia (or pesca) di frodo.

pocket ['pɔkɪt] n tasca // vt intascare; **to be out of** ~ rimetterci; ~**book** n (wallet) portafoglio; (notebook) taccuino; ~ **knife** n temperino; ~ **money** n paghetta, settimana.

pockmarked ['pɔkmɑ:kt] a (face) butterato(a).

pod [pɔd] n guscio // vt sgusciare.

podgy ['pɔdʒɪ] a grassoccio(a).

poem ['pəuɪm] n poesia.

poet ['pəuɪt] n poeta/essa; ~**ic** [-'ɛtɪk] a poetico(a); ~ **laureate** n poeta m laureato (nominato dalla Corte Reale); ~**ry** n poesia.

poignant ['pɔɪnjənt] a struggente; (sharp) pungente.

point [pɔɪnt] n (gen) punto; (tip: of needle etc) punta; (in time) punto, momento; (SCOL) voto; (main idea, important part) nocciolo; (also: **decimal** ~): **2 ~ 3 (2.3)** 2 virgola 3 (2,3) // vt (show) indicare; (gun etc): **to ~ sth at** puntare qc contro // vi

mostrare a dito; ~**s** npl (AUT) puntine fpl; (RAIL) scambio; **to make a ~** fare un'osservazione; **to get the ~** capire; **to come to the ~** venire al fatto; **there's no ~ (in doing)** è inutile (fare); **good** ~**s** vantaggi mpl; (of person) qualità fpl; **to ~ out** vt far notare; **to ~** indicare; (fig) dimostrare; ~**-blank** ad (also: **at** ~**-blank range**) a bruciapelo; (fig) categoricamente; ~**ed** a (shape) aguzzo(a), appuntito(a); (remark) specifico(a), inequivocabile; ~**er** n (stick) bacchetta; (needle) lancetta; (dog) pointer m, cane m da punta; ~**less** a inutile, vano(a); ~ **of view** n punto di vista.

poise [pɔɪz] n (balance) equilibrio; (of head, body) portamento; (calmness) calma // vt tenere in equilibrio; **to be ~d for** (fig) essere pronto(a) a.

poison ['pɔɪzn] n veleno // vt avvelenare; ~**ing** n avvelenamento; ~**ous** a velenoso(a).

poke [pəuk] vt (fire) attizzare; (jab with finger, stick etc) punzecchiare; (put): **to ~ sth in(to)** spingere qc dentro; **to ~ about** vi frugare.

poker ['pəukə*] n attizzatoio; (CARDS) poker m; ~**-faced** a dal viso impassibile.

poky ['pəukɪ] a piccolo(a) e stretto(a).

Poland ['pəulənd] n Polonia.

polar ['pəulə*] a polare; ~ **bear** n orso bianco.

polarize ['pəuləraɪz] vt polarizzare.

pole [pəul] n (of wood) palo; (ELEC, GEO) polo.

Pole [pəul] n polacco/a.

polecat ['pəulkæt] n (US) puzzola.

polemic [pɔ'lɛmɪk] n polemica.

pole star ['pəulstɑ:*] n stella polare.

pole vault ['pəulvɔ:lt] n salto con l'asta.

police [pə'li:s] n polizia // vt mantenere l'ordine in; ~ **car** n macchina della polizia; ~**man** n poliziotto, agente m di polizia; ~ **station** n posto di polizia; ~**woman** n donna f poliziotto inv.

policy ['pɔlɪsɪ] n politica; (also: **insurance** ~) polizza (d'assicurazione).

polio ['pəulɪəu] n polio f.

Polish ['pəulɪʃ] a polacco(a) // n (LING) polacco.

polish ['pɔlɪʃ] n (for shoes) lucido; (for floor) cera; (for nails) smalto; (shine) lucentezza, lustro; (fig: refinement) raffinatezza // vt lucidare; (fig: improve) raffinare; **to ~ off** vt (work) sbrigare; (food) mangiarsi; ~**ed** a (fig) raffinato(a).

polite [pə'laɪt] a cortese; ~**ly** ad cortesemente; ~**ness** n cortesia.

politic ['pɔlɪtɪk] a diplomatico(a); ~**al** [pə'lɪtɪkl] a politico(a); ~**ian** [-'tɪʃən] n politico; ~**s** npl politica.

polka ['pɔlkə] n polca; ~ **dot** n pois m inv.

poll [pəul] n scrutinio; (votes cast) voti mpl; (also: **opinion** ~) sondaggio (d'opinioni) // vt ottenere.

pollen ['pɔlən] n polline m.

pollination [pɒlɪ'neɪʃən] n impollinazione f.

polling ['pəʊlɪŋ]: ~ **booth** n cabina elettorale; ~ **day** n giorno delle elezioni; ~ **station** n sezione f elettorale.

pollute [pə'luːt] vt inquinare.

pollution [pə'luːʃən] n inquinamento.

polo ['pəʊləʊ] n polo; ~-**neck** a a collo alto risvoltato.

polyester [pɒlɪ'ɛstə*] n poliestere m.

polygamy [pə'lɪgəmɪ] n poligamia.

Polynesia [pɒlɪ'niːzɪə] n Polinesia.

polytechnic [pɒlɪ'tɛknɪk] n (college) istituto superiore di tendenza tecnologica.

polythene ['pɒlɪθiːn] n politene m; ~ **bag** n sacco di plastica.

pomegranate ['pɒmɪgrænɪt] n melagrana.

pommel ['pɒml] n pomo.

pomp [pɒmp] n pompa, fasto.

pompous ['pɒmpəs] a pomposo(a).

pond [pɒnd] n pozza; stagno.

ponder ['pɒndə*] vt ponderare, riflettere su; ~**ous** a ponderoso(a), pesante.

pontiff ['pɒntɪf] n pontefice m.

pontificate [pɒn'tɪfɪkeɪt] vi (fig): to ~ (about) pontificare (su).

pontoon [pɒn'tuːn] n pontone m.

pony ['pəʊnɪ] n pony m inv; ~**tail** n coda di cavallo.

poodle ['puːdl] n barboncino, barbone m.

pooh-pooh ['puː'puː] vt deridere.

pool [puːl] n (of rain) pozza; (pond) stagno; (artificial) vasca; (also: **swimming** ~) piscina; (sth shared) fondo comune; (billiards) specie di biliardo a buca // vt mettere in comune.

poor [pʊə*] a povero(a); (mediocre) mediocre, cattivo(a) // npl: **the** ~ i poveri; ~**ly** ad poveramente; male // a indisposto(a), malato(a).

pop [pɒp] n (noise) schiocco; (MUS) musica pop; (US: col: father) babbo // vt (put) mettere (in fretta) // vi scoppiare; (cork) schioccare; to ~ **in** vi passare; to ~ **out** vi fare un salto fuori; to ~ **up** vi apparire, sorgere; ~ **concert** n concerto m pop inv; ~**corn** n pop-corn m.

pope [pəʊp] n papa m.

poplar ['pɒplə*] n pioppo.

poplin ['pɒplɪn] n popeline f.

poppy ['pɒpɪ] n papavero.

populace ['pɒpjʊləs] n popolo.

popular ['pɒpjʊlə*] a popolare; (fashionable) in voga; ~**ity** ['lærɪtɪ] n popolarità; ~**ize** vt divulgare; (science) volgarizzare.

population [pɒpjʊ'leɪʃən] n popolazione f.

populous ['pɒpjʊləs] a popolato(a).

porcelain ['pɔːslɪn] n porcellana.

porch [pɔːtʃ] n veranda.

porcupine ['pɔːkjʊpaɪn] n porcospino.

pore [pɔː*] n poro // vi: to ~ **over** essere immerso(a) in.

pork [pɔːk] n carne f di maiale.

pornographic [pɔːnə'græfɪk] a pornografico(a).

pornography [pɔː'nɒgrəfɪ] n pornografia.

porous ['pɔːrəs] a poroso(a).

porpoise ['pɔːpəs] n focena.

porridge ['pɒrɪdʒ] n porridge m.

port [pɔːt] n porto; (opening in ship) portello; (NAUT: left side) babordo; (wine) porto.

portable ['pɔːtəbl] a portatile.

portal ['pɔːtl] n portale m.

portcullis [pɔːt'kʌlɪs] n saracinesca.

portent ['pɔːtɛnt] n presagio.

porter ['pɔːtə*] n (for luggage) facchino, portabagagli m inv; (doorkeeper) portiere m, portinaio.

porthole ['pɔːthəʊl] n oblò m inv.

portico ['pɔːtɪkəʊ] n portico.

portion ['pɔːʃən] n porzione f.

portly ['pɔːtlɪ] a corpulento(a).

portrait ['pɔːtreɪt] n ritratto.

portray [pɔː'treɪ] vt fare il ritratto di; (character on stage) rappresentare; (in writing) ritrarre; ~**al** n ritratto; rappresentazione f.

Portugal ['pɔːtjʊgl] n Portogallo.

Portuguese [pɔːtjʊ'giːz] a portoghese // n, pl inv portoghese m/f; (LING) portoghese m.

pose [pəʊz] n posa // vi posare; (pretend): to ~ **as** atteggiarsi a, posare a // vt porre.

posh [pɒʃ] a (col) elegante; (family) per bene.

position [pə'zɪʃən] n posizione f; (job) posto // vt mettere in posizione, collocare.

positive ['pɒzɪtɪv] a positivo(a); (certain) sicuro(a), certo(a); (definite) preciso(a); definitivo(a).

posse ['pɒsɪ] n (US) drappello.

possess [pə'zɛs] vt possedere; ~**ion** [pə'zɛʃən] n possesso; (object) bene m; ~**ive** a possessivo(a); ~**or** n possessore/posseditrice.

possibility [pɒsɪ'bɪlɪtɪ] n possibilità f inv.

possible ['pɒsɪbl] a possibile; **if** ~ se possibile; **as big as** ~ il più grande possibile.

possibly ['pɒsɪblɪ] ad (perhaps) forse; **if you** ~ **can** se le è possibile; **I cannot** ~ **come** proprio non posso venire.

post [pəʊst] n posta; (collection) levata; (job, situation) posto; (pole) palo // vt (send by post) impostare; (MIL) appostare; (appoint): to ~ **to** assegnare a; (notice) affiggere; ~**age** n affrancatura; ~**al** a postale; ~**al order** n vaglia m inv postale; ~**box** n cassetta postale; ~**card** n cartolina.

postdate ['pəʊst'deɪt] vt (cheque) postdatare.

poster ['pəʊstə*] n manifesto, affisso.

poste restante [pəʊst'rɛstɑːnt] n fermo posta m.

posterity [pɒs'tɛrɪtɪ] n posterità.

postgraduate ['pəʊst'grædjʊət] n ≈ laureato/a che continua gli studi.

posthumous ['pɒstjʊməs] a postumo(a); ~**ly** ad dopo la mia (or sua etc) morte.

postman ['pəʊstmən] n postino.

postmark ['pəʊstmɑːk] n bollo or timbro postale.

postmaster ['pəʊstmɑːstə*] n direttore m d'un ufficio postale.

post-mortem [pəʊst'mɔːtəm] n autopsia.

post office ['pəʊstɔfis] n (building) ufficio postale; (organization) poste fpl; ~ **box** (P.O. box) n casella postale (C.P.).

postpone [pəs'pəʊn] vt rinviare; ~**ment** n rinvio.

postscript ['pəʊstskrıpt] n poscritto.

postulate ['pɔstjuleit] vt postulare.

posture ['pɔstʃə*] n portamento; (pose) posa, atteggiamento // vi posare.

postwar ['pəʊst'wɔː*] a del dopoguerra.

posy ['pəʊzı] n mazzetto di fiori.

pot [pɔt] n (for cooking) pentola; casseruola; (for plants, jam) vaso; (col: marijuana) erba // vt (plant) piantare in vaso; **to go to** ~ andare in malora.

potash ['pɔtæʃ] n potassa.

potato, ~**es** [pə'teitəu] n patata.

potency ['pəʊtnsı] n potenza; (of drink) forza.

potent ['pəʊtnt] a potente, forte.

potentate ['pəʊtnteit] n potentato.

potential [pə'tɛnʃl] a potenziale // n possibilità fpl; ~**ly** ad potenzialmente.

pothole ['pɔthəʊl] n (in road) buca; (underground) marmitta; ~**r** n speleologo/a; **potholing** n: **to go potholing** fare la speleologia.

potion ['pəʊʃən] n pozione f.

potluck [pɔt'lʌk] n: **to take** ~ tentare la sorte.

potshot ['pɔtʃɔt] n: **to take** ~**s** at tirare a vanvera contro.

potted ['pɔtid] a (food) in conserva; (plant) in vaso.

potter ['pɔtə*] n vasaio // vi: **to** ~ **around,** ~ **about** lavoracchiare; ~**y** n ceramiche fpl.

potty ['pɔtı] a (col: mad) tocco(a) // n (child's) vasino.

pouch [pautʃ] n borsa; (ZOOL) marsupio.

pouf(fe) [puːf] n (stool) pouf m inv.

poultice ['pəʊltıs] n impiastro, cataplasma.

poultry ['pəʊltrı] n pollame m.

pounce [pauns] vi: **to** ~ **(on)** balzare addosso a, piombare su // n balzo.

pound [paund] n (weight) libbra; (money) (lira) sterlina; (for dogs) canile m municipale // vt (beat) battere; (crush) pestare, polverizzare // vi (beat) battere, martellare.

pour [pɔː*] vt versare // vi riversarsi; (rain) piovere a dirotto; **to** ~ **away** vt vuotare; **to** ~ **in** vi (people) entrare a flotti; **to** ~ **out** vt vuotare; versare; (serve: a drink) mescere; ~**ing** a: ~**ing rain** pioggia torrenziale.

pout [paut] vi sporgere le labbra; fare il broncio.

poverty ['pɔvətı] n povertà, miseria;

~**-stricken** a molto povero(a), misero(a).

powder ['paudə*] n polvere f // vt spolverizzare; (face) incipriare; ~ **room** n toilette f inv (per signore); ~**y** a polveroso(a).

power ['pauə*] n (strength) potenza, forza; (ability, POL: of party, leader) potere m; (MATH) potenza; (ELEC) corrente f // vt fornire di energia; **mental** ~**s** capacità fpl mentali; ~ **cut** n interruzione f or mancanza di corrente; ~**ed a:** ~**ed by** azionato(a) da; ~**ful** a potente, forte; ~**less** a impotente, senza potere; ~ **point** n presa di corrente; ~ **station** n centrale f elettrica.

powwow ['pauwau] n riunione f.

pox [pɔks] n see **chicken**.

p.p. abbr: ~ **J. Smith** per il Signor J. Smith.

P.R. abbr of **public relations.**

practicability [præktıkə'bılıtı] n praticabilità.

practicable ['præktıkəbl] a (scheme) praticabile.

practical ['præktıkl] a pratico(a); ~ **joke** n beffa; ~**ly** ad (almost) quasi.

practice ['præktıs] n pratica; (of profession) esercizio; (at football etc) allenamento; (business) gabinetto; clientela // vt,vi (US) = **practise;** in ~ (in reality) in pratica; **out of** ~ fuori esercizio; **2 hours' piano** ~ 2 ore di esercizio al pianoforte.

practise, (US) **practice** ['præktıs] vt (work at: piano, one's backhand etc) esercitarsi a; (train for: skiing, running etc) allenarsi a; (a sport, religion) praticare; (method) usare; (profession) esercitare // vi esercitarsi; (train) allenarsi; **practising** a (Christian etc) praticante; (lawyer) che esercita la professione.

practitioner [præk'tıʃənə*] n professionista m/f.

pragmatic [præg'mætık] a prammatico(a).

prairie ['prɛərı] n prateria.

praise [preiz] n elogio, lode f // vt elogiare, lodare; ~**worthy** a lodevole.

pram [præm] n carrozzina.

prance [prɑːns] vi (horse) impennarsi.

prank [præŋk] n burla.

prattle ['prætl] vi cinguettare.

prawn [prɔːn] n gamberetto.

pray [prei] vi pregare.

prayer [prɛə*] n preghiera; ~ **book** n libro di preghiere.

preach [priːtʃ] vt,vi predicare; ~**er** n predicatore/trice.

preamble [prı'æmbl] n preambolo.

precarious [prı'kɛərıəs] a precario(a).

precaution [prı'kɔːʃən] n precauzione f; ~**ary** a (measure) precauzionale.

precede [prı'siːd] vt, vi precedere.

precedence ['prɛsıdəns] n precedenza; **to take** ~ **over** avere la precedenza su.

precedent ['prɛsıdənt] n precedente m.

preceding [prı'siːdıŋ] a precedente.

precept ['pri:sεpt] *n* precetto.
precinct ['pri:sɪŋkt] *n* (*round cathedral*) recinto; ~s *npl* (*neighbourhood*) dintorni *mpl*, vicinanze *fpl*; **pedestrian** ~ *n* zona pedonale.
precious ['prεʃəs] *a* prezioso(a).
precipice ['prεsɪpɪs] *n* precipizio.
precipitate [prɪ'sɪpɪtɪt] *a* (*hasty*) precipitoso(a); **precipitation** [-'teɪʃən] *n* precipitazione *f*.
precipitous [prɪ'sɪpɪtəs] *a* (*steep*) erto(a), ripido(a).
précis, *pl* **précis** ['preɪsɪ:, -z] *n* riassunto.
precise [prɪ'saɪs] *a* preciso(a); ~ly *ad* precisamente; ~ly! appunto!
preclude [prɪ'klu:d] *vt* precludere, impedire; to ~ **sb from doing** impedire a qd di fare.
precocious [prɪ'kəuʃəs] *a* precoce.
preconceived [pri:kən'si:vd] *a* (*idea*) preconcetto(a).
precondition [pri:kən'dɪʃən] *n* condizione *f* necessaria.
precursor [pri:'kə:sə*] *n* precursore *m*.
predator ['prεdətə*] *n* predatore *m*; ~y *a* predatore(trice).
predecessor ['pri:dɪsεsə*] *n* predecessore/a.
predestination [pri:dεstɪ'neɪʃən] *n* predestinazione *f*.
predetermine [pri:dɪ'tə:mɪn] *vt* predeterminare.
predicament [prɪ'dɪkəmənt] *n* situazione *f* difficile.
predicate ['prεdɪkɪt] *n* (LING) predicativo.
predict [prɪ'dɪkt] *vt* predire; ~ion [-'dɪkʃən] *n* predizione *f*.
predominant [prɪ'dɔmɪnənt] *a* predominante; ~ly *ad* in maggior parte; soprattutto.
predominate [prɪ'dɔmɪneɪt] *vi* predominare.
pre-eminent [pri:'εmɪnənt] *a* preminente.
pre-empt [pri:'εmt] *vt* acquistare per diritto di prelazione.
preen [pri:n] *vt*: to ~ **itself** (*bird*) lisciarsi le penne.
prefab ['pri:fæb] *n* casa prefabbricata.
prefabricated [pri:'fæbrɪkeɪtɪd] *a* prefabbricato(a).
preface ['prεfəs] *n* prefazione *f*.
prefect ['pri:fεkt] *n* (*Brit: in school*) studente/essa con funzioni disciplinari; (*in Italy*) prefetto.
prefer [prɪ'fə:*] *vt* preferire; ~able ['prεfrəbl] *a* preferibile; ~ably ['prεfrəbl] *ad* preferibilmente; ~ence ['prεfrəns] *n* preferenza; ~ential [prεfə'rεnʃəl] *a* preferenziale.
prefix ['pri:fɪks] *n* prefisso.
pregnancy ['prεgnənsɪ] *n* gravidanza.
pregnant ['prεgnənt] *a* incinta *a*.
prehistoric ['pri:hɪs'tɔrɪk] *a* preistorico(a).
prejudge [pri:'dʒʌdʒ] *vt* pregiudicare.
prejudice ['prεdʒudɪs] *n* pregiudizio; (*harm*) torto, danno // *vt* pregiudicare,

ledere; ~**d** *a* (*person*) pieno(a) di pregiudizi; (*view*) prevenuto(a).
prelate ['prεlət] *n* prelato.
preliminary [prɪ'lɪmɪnərɪ] *a* preliminare; **preliminaries** *npl* preliminari *mpl*.
prelude ['prεlju:d] *n* preludio.
premarital ['pri:'mærɪtl] *a* prematrimoniale.
premature ['prεmətʃuə*] *a* prematuro(a).
premeditated [pri:'mεdɪteɪtɪd] *a* premeditato(a).
premier ['prεmɪə*] *a* primo(a) // *n* (POL) primo ministro.
première ['prεmɪεə*] *n* première *f inv*.
premise ['prεmɪs] *n* premessa; ~s *npl* locale *m*; **on the** ~s sul posto.
premium ['pri:mɪəm] *n* premio.
premonition [prεmə'nɪʃən] *n* premonizione *f*.
preoccupation [pri:ɔkju'peɪʃən] *n* preoccupazione *f*.
preoccupied [pri:'ɔkjupaɪd] *a* preoccupato(a).
prep [prεp] *n* (SCOL: *study*) studio; ~ **school** *n* = **preparatory school.**
prepaid [pri:'peɪd] *a* pagato(a) in anticipo.
preparation [prεpə'reɪʃən] *n* preparazione *f*; ~s *npl* (*for trip, war*) preparativi *mpl*.
preparatory [prɪ'pærətərɪ] *a* preparatorio(a); ~ **school** *n* scuola elementare privata.
prepare [prɪ'pεə*] *vt* preparare // *vi*: to ~ **for** prepararsi a; ~**d for** preparato(a) a; ~**d to** pronto(a) a.
preponderance [prɪ'pɔndərns] *n* preponderanza.
preposition [prεpə'zɪʃən] *n* preposizione *f*.
preposterous [prɪ'pɔstərəs] *a* assurdo(a).
prerequisite [pri:'rεkwɪzɪt] *n* requisito indispensabile.
prerogative [prɪ'rɔgətɪv] *n* prerogativa.
presbytery ['prεzbɪtərɪ] *n* presbiterio.
prescribe [prɪ'skraɪb] *vt* prescrivere; (MED) ordinare.
prescription [prɪ'skrɪpʃən] *n* prescrizione *f*; (MED) ricetta.
presence ['prεzns] *n* presenza; ~ **of mind** *n* presenza di spirito.
present ['prεznt] *a* presente; (*wife, residence, job*) attuale // *n* regalo; (*also*: ~ **tense**) tempo presente // *vt* [prɪ'zεnt] presentare; (*give*): to ~ **sb with sth** offrire qc a qd; **at** ~ al momento; ~**able** [prɪ'zεntəbl] *a* presentabile; ~**ation** [-'teɪʃən] *n* presentazione *f*; (*gift*) regalo, dono; (*ceremony*) cerimonia per il conferimento di un regalo; ~**-day** *a* attuale, d'oggigiorno; ~**ly** *ad* (*soon*) fra poco, presto; (*at present*) al momento.
preservation [prεzə'veɪʃən] *n* preservazione *f*, conservazione *f*.
preservative [prɪ'zə:vətɪv] *n* conservante *m*.
preserve [prɪ'zə:v] *vt* (*keep safe*) preservare, proteggere; (*maintain*) conservare; (*food*) mettere in conserva //

n (for game, fish) riserva; (*often pl: jam*) marmellata; (: *fruit*) frutta sciroppata.

preside [prɪ'zaɪd] *vi* presiedere.

presidency ['prɛzɪdənsɪ] *n* presidenza.

president ['prɛzɪdənt] *n* presidente *m*; ~**ial** [-'dɛnʃl] *a* presidenziale.

press [prɛs] *n* (*tool, machine*) pressa; (*for wine*) torchio; (*newspapers*) stampa; (*crowd*) folla // *vt* (*push*) premere, pigiare; (*squeeze*) spremere; (: *hand*) stringere; (*clothes: iron*) stirare; (*pursue*) incalzare; (*insist*): to ~ **sth on sb** far accettare qc da qd // *vi* premere; accalcare; **we are** ~**ed for time** ci manca il tempo; **to** ~ **for sth** insistere per avere qc; **to** ~ **on** *vi* continuare; ~ **agency** *n* agenzia di stampa; ~ **conference** *n* conferenza stampa; ~ **cutting** *n* ritaglio di giornale; ~**ing** *a* urgente // *n* stiratura; ~ **stud** *n* bottone *m* a pressione.

pressure ['prɛʃə*] *n* pressione *f*; ~ **cooker** *n* pentola a pressione; ~ **gauge** *n* manometro; ~ **group** *n* gruppo di pressione; **pressurized** *a* pressurizzato(a).

prestige [prɛs'ti:ʒ] *n* prestigio.

prestigious [prɛs'tɪdʒəs] *a* prestigioso(a).

presumably [prɪ'zju:məblɪ] *ad* presumibilmente.

presume [prɪ'zju:m] *vt* supporre; **to** ~ **to do** (*dare*) permettersi di fare.

presumption [prɪ'zʌmpʃən] *n* presunzione *f*; (*boldness*) audacia.

presumptuous [prɪ'zʌmpʃəs] *a* presuntuoso(a).

presuppose [pri:sə'pəuz] *vt* presupporre.

pretence, pretense (*US*) [prɪ'tɛns] *n* (*claim*) pretesa; **to make a** ~ **of doing** far finta di fare.

pretend [prɪ'tɛnd] *vt* (*feign*) fingere // *vi* (*feign*) far finta; (*claim*): **to** ~ **to sth** pretendere a qc; **to** ~ **to do** far finta di fare.

pretentious [prɪ'tɛnʃəs] *a* pretenzioso(a).

preterite ['prɛtərɪt] *n* preterito.

pretext ['pri:tɛkst] *n* pretesto.

pretty ['prɪtɪ] *a* grazioso(a), carino(a) // *ad* abbastanza, assai.

prevail [prɪ'veɪl] *vi* (*win, be usual*) prevalere; (*persuade*): **to** ~ **(up)on sb to do** persuadere qd a fare; ~**ing** *a* dominante.

prevalent ['prɛvələnt] *a* (*belief*) predominante; (*customs*) diffuso(a); (*fashion*) corrente; (*disease*) comune.

prevarication [prɪværɪ'keɪʃən] *n* tergiversazione *f*.

prevent [prɪ'vɛnt] *vt* prevenire; **to** ~ **sb from doing** impedire a qd di fare; ~**able** *a* evitabile; ~**ative** *a* preventivo(a); ~**ion** [-'vɛnʃən] *n* prevenzione *f*; ~**ive** *a* preventivo(a).

preview ['pri:vju:] *n* (*of film*) anteprima.

previous ['pri:vɪəs] *a* precedente; anteriore; ~**ly** *ad* prima.

prewar ['pri:'wɔ:*] *a* anteguerra *inv*.

prey [preɪ] *n* preda // *vi*: **to** ~ **on** far

preda di; **it was** ~**ing on his mind** gli rodeva la mente.

price [praɪs] *n* prezzo // *vt* (*goods*) fissare il prezzo di; valutare; ~**less** *a* inapprezzabile.

prick [prɪk] *n* puntura // *vt* pungere; **to** ~ **up one's ears** drizzare gli orecchi.

prickle ['prɪkl] *n* (*of plant*) spina; (*sensation*) pizzicore *m*.

prickly ['prɪklɪ] *a* spinoso(a); (*fig: person*) permaloso(a); ~ **heat** *n* sudamina.

pride [praɪd] *n* orgoglio; superbia // *vt*: **to** ~ **o.s. on** essere orgoglioso(a) di; vantarsi di.

priest [pri:st] *n* prete *m*, sacerdote *m*; ~**ess** *n* sacerdotessa; ~**hood** *n* sacerdozio.

prig [prɪg] *n*: **he's a** ~ è compiaciuto di se stesso.

prim [prɪm] *a* pudico(a); contegnoso(a).

primarily ['praɪmərɪlɪ] *ad* principalmente, essenzialmente.

primary ['praɪmərɪ] *a* primario(a); (*first in importance*) primo(a); ~ **school** *n* scuola elementare.

primate *n* (*REL*: ['praɪmɪt], *ZOOL*: ['praɪmeɪt]) primate *m*.

prime [praɪm] *a* primario(a), fondamentale; (*excellent*) di prima qualità // *vt* (*gun*) innescare; (*pump*) adescare; (*fig*) mettere al corrente; **in the** ~ **of life** nel fiore della vita; ~ **minister (P.M.)** *n* primo ministro; ~**r** *n* (*book*) testo elementare.

primeval [praɪ'mi:vl] *a* primitivo(a).

primitive ['prɪmɪtɪv] *a* primitivo(a).

primrose ['prɪmrəuz] *n* primavera.

primus (stove) ['praɪməs(stəuv)] *n* ⒶⓇ fornello a petrolio.

prince [prɪns] *n* principe *m*.

princess [prɪn'sɛs] *n* principessa.

principal ['prɪnsɪpl] *a* principale // *n* (*headmaster*) preside *m*.

principality [prɪnsɪ'pælɪtɪ] *n* principato.

principle ['prɪnsɪpl] *n* principio.

print [prɪnt] *n* (*mark*) impronta; (*letters*) caratteri *mpl*; (*fabric*) tessuto stampato; (*ART, PHOT*) stampa // *vt* imprimere; (*publish*) stampare, pubblicare; (*write in capitals*) scrivere in stampatello; **out of** ~ esaurito(a); ~**ed matter** *n* stampe *fpl*; ~**er** *n* tipografo; ~**ing** *n* stampa; ~**ing press** *n* macchina tipografica; ~**-out** *n* tabulato.

prior ['praɪə*] *a* precedente // *n* priore *m*; ~ **to doing** prima di fare.

priority [praɪ'ɔrɪtɪ] *n* priorità *f inv*; precedenza.

priory ['praɪərɪ] *n* monastero.

prise [praɪz] *vt*: **to** ~ **open** forzare.

prism ['prɪzəm] *n* prisma *m*.

prison ['prɪzn] *n* prigione *f*; ~**er** *n* prigioniero/a.

pristine ['prɪsti:n] *a* originario(a); intatto(a); puro(a).

privacy ['prɪvəsɪ] *n* solitudine *f*, intimità.

private ['praɪvɪt] *a* privato(a); personale

// n soldato semplice; '~' (on envelope) 'riservata'; **in ~ in** privato; ~ **eye** n investigatore m privato; ~**ly** ad in privato; (within oneself) dentro di sé.

privet ['prɪvɪt] n ligustro.

privilege ['prɪvɪlɪdʒ] n privilegio; ~**d** a privilegiato(a).

privy ['prɪvɪ] a: **to be ~ to** essere al corrente di; **P~ Council** n Consiglio della Corona.

prize [praɪz] n premio // a (example, idiot) perfetto(a); (bull, novel) premiato(a) // vt apprezzare, pregiare; ~ **fight** n incontro di pugilato tra professionisti; ~ **giving** n premiazione f; ~**winner** n premiato/a.

pro [prəu] n (SPORT) professionista m/f; **the ~s and cons** il pro e il contro.

probability [prɒbə'bɪlɪtɪ] n probabilità f inv.

probable ['prɒbəbl] a probabile; **probably** ad probabilmente.

probation [prə'beɪʃən] n (in employment) periodo di prova; (LAW) libertà vigilata; **on ~** (employee) in prova; (LAW) in libertà vigilata.

probe [prəub] n (MED, SPACE) sonda; (enquiry) indagine f, investigazione f // vt sondare, esplorare; indagare.

probity ['prəubɪtɪ] n probità.

problem ['prɒbləm] n problema m; ~**atic** ['-'mætɪk] a problematico(a).

procedure [prə'si:dʒə*] n (ADMIN, LAW) procedura; (method) metodo, procedimento.

proceed [prə'si:d] vi (go forward) avanzare, andare avanti; (go about it) procedere; (continue): **to ~ (with)** continuare; **to ~ to** andare a; passare a; **to ~ to do** mettersi a fare; ~**ing** n procedimento, modo d'agire; ~**ings** npl misure fpl; (LAW) procedimento; (meeting) riunione f; (records) rendiconti mpl; atti mpl; ~**s** ['prəusi:dz] npl profitto, incasso.

process ['prəuses] n processo; (method) metodo, sistema m // vt trattare; (information) elaborare; ~**ing** n trattamento; elaborazione f.

procession [prə'sɛʃən] n processione f, corteo.

proclaim [prə'kleɪm] vt proclamare, dichiarare.

proclamation [prɒklə'meɪʃən] n proclamazione f.

procrastination [prəukræstɪ'neɪʃən] n procrastinazione f.

procreation [prəukrɪ'eɪʃən] n procreazione f.

procure [prə'kjuə*] vt (for o.s.) procurarsi; (for sb) procurare.

prod [prɒd] vt pungolare // n (push, jab) pungolo.

prodigal ['prɒdɪgl] a prodigo(a).

prodigious [prə'dɪdʒəs] a prodigioso(a).

prodigy ['prɒdɪdʒɪ] n prodigio.

produce n ['prɒdju:s] (AGR) prodotto, prodotti mpl // vt ['prə'dju:s] produrre; (to show) esibire, mostrare; (cause) cagionare, causare; (THEATRE) mettere in

scena; ~**r** n (THEATRE) direttore/trice; (AGR, CINEMA) produttore m.

product ['prɒdʌkt] n prodotto.

production [prə'dʌkʃən] n produzione f; (THEATRE) messa in scena; ~ **line** n catena di lavorazione.

productive [prə'dʌktɪv] a produttivo(a).

productivity [prɒdʌk'tɪvɪtɪ] n produttività.

profane [prə'feɪn] a profano(a); (language) empio(a).

profess [prə'fɛs] vt professare.

profession [prə'fɛʃən] n professione f; ~**al** n (SPORT) professionista m/f // a professionale; (work) da professionista; ~**alism** n professionismo.

professor [prə'fɛsə*] n professore m (titolare di una cattedra).

proficiency [prə'fɪʃənsɪ] n competenza, abilità.

proficient [prə'fɪʃənt] a competente, abile.

profile ['prəufaɪl] n profilo.

profit ['prɒfɪt] n profitto; beneficio // vi: **to ~ (by or from)** approfittare (di); ~**ability** ['-bɪlɪtɪ] n redditività; ~**able** a redditizio(a).

profiteering [prɒfɪ'tɪərɪŋ] n (pej) affarismo.

profound [prə'faund] a profondo(a).

profuse [prə'fju:s] a profuso(a), abbondante; ~**ly** ad con grande effusione; **profusion** ['-'fju:ʒən] n profusione f, abbondanza.

progeny ['prɒdʒɪnɪ] n progenie f; discendenti mpl.

programme, program (US) ['prəugræm] n programma m // vt programmare; **programming, programing** (US) n programmazione f.

progress n ['prəugres] progresso // vi [prə'gres] avanzare, procedere; **in ~** in corso; **to make ~** far progressi; ~**ion** ['-'greʃən] n progressione f; ~**ive** ['-'gresɪv] a progressivo(a); (person) progressista m/f; ~**ively** ['-'gresɪvlɪ] ad progressivamente.

prohibit [prə'hɪbɪt] vt proibire, vietare; ~**ion** [prəuɪ'bɪʃən] n (US) proibizionismo; ~**ive** a (price etc) proibitivo(a).

project n ['prɒdʒekt] (plan) piano; (venture) progetto; (SCOL) studio // vb [prə'dʒekt] vt proiettare // vi (stick out) sporgere.

projectile [prə'dʒektaɪl] n proiettile m.

projection [prə'dʒekʃən] n proiezione f; sporgenza.

projector [prə'dʒektə*] n proiettore m.

proletarian [prəulɪ'tɛərɪən] a, n proletario(a).

proletariat [prəulɪ'tɛərɪət] n proletariato.

proliferate [prə'lɪfəreɪt] vi proliferare; **proliferation** ['-'reɪʃən] n proliferazione f.

prolific [prə'lɪfɪk] a prolifico(a).

prologue ['prəulɒg] n prologo.

prolong [prə'lɒŋ] vt prolungare.

prom [prɒm] n abbr of **promenade**; (US: ball) ballo studentesco.

promenade [prɒmə'nɑ:d] n (by sea)

lungomare m; ~ **concert** n concerto di musica classica.

prominence ['prɒmɪnəns] n prominenza; importanza.

prominent ['prɒmɪnənt] a (standing out) prominente; (important) importante.

promiscuity [prɒmɪsˈkjuːɪtɪ] n (sexual) rapporti mpl multipli.

promiscuous [prəˈmɪskjuəs] a (sexually) di facili costumi.

promise ['prɒmɪs] n promessa // vt,vi promettere; **promising** a promettente.

promontory ['prɒməntrɪ] n promontorio.

promote [prəˈməʊt] vt promuovere; (venture, event) organizzare; ~r n (of sporting event) organizzatore/trice; **promotion** [-ˈməʊʃən] n promozione f; (of new product) promotion m.

prompt [prɒmpt] a rapido(a), svelto(a); puntuale; (reply) sollecito(a) // ad (punctually) in punto // vt incitare; provocare; (THEATRE) suggerire a; **to ~ sb to do** spingere qd a fare; ~er n (THEATRE) suggeritore m; ~ly ad prontamente; puntualmente; ~ness n prontezza; puntualità.

prone [prəʊn] a (lying) prono(a); ~ **to** propenso(a) a, incline a.

prong [prɒŋ] n rebbio, punta.

pronoun ['prəʊnaʊn] n pronome m.

pronounce [prəˈnaʊns] vt pronunziare // vi: **to ~ (up)on** pronunziare su; ~**d** a (marked) spiccato(a); ~**ment** n dichiarazione f.

pronunciation [prənʌnsɪˈeɪʃən] n pronunzia.

proof [pruːf] n prova; (of book) bozza; (PHOT) provino; (of alcohol) grado // a: ~ **against** a prova di.

prop [prɒp] n sostegno, appoggio // vt (also: ~ **up**) sostenere, appoggiare; (lean): **to ~ sth against** appoggiare qc contro or a.

propaganda [prɒpəˈgændə] n propaganda.

propagation [prɒpəˈgeɪʃən] n propagazione f.

propel [prəˈpɛl] vt spingere (in avanti), muovere; ~**ler** n elica; ~**ling pencil** n matita a mina.

propensity [prəˈpɛnsɪtɪ] n tendenza.

proper ['prɒpə*] a (suited, right) adatto(a), appropriato(a); (seemly) decente; (authentic) vero(a); (col: real) noun + vero(a) e proprio(a); ~**ly** ad decentemente; proprio, del tutto; ~ **noun** n nome m proprio.

property ['prɒpətɪ] n (things owned) beni mpl; proprietà fpl; bene m immobile; tenuta, terra; (CHEM etc: quality) proprietà f inv; ~ **owner** n proprietario/a.

prophecy ['prɒfɪsɪ] n profezia.

prophesy ['prɒfɪsaɪ] vt predire.

prophet ['prɒfɪt] n profeta m; ~**ic** [prəˈfɛtɪk] a profetico(a).

proportion [prəˈpɔːʃən] n proporzione f; (share) parte f // vt proporzionare, commisurare; ~**al** a proporzionale; ~**ate** a proporzionato(a).

proposal [prəˈpəʊzəl] n proposta; (plan) progetto; (of marriage) proposta di matrimonio.

propose [prəˈpəʊz] vt proporre, suggerire // vi fare una proposta di matrimonio; **to ~ to do** proporsi di fare, aver l'intenzione di fare.

proposition [prɒpəˈzɪʃən] n proposizione f.

propound [prəˈpaʊnd] vt proporre, presentare.

proprietor [prəˈpraɪətə*] n proprietario/a.

propulsion [prəˈpʌlʃən] n propulsione f.

prosaic [prəʊˈzeɪɪk] a prosaico(a).

prose [prəʊz] n prosa; (SCOL: translation) traduzione f dalla madrelingua.

prosecute ['prɒsɪkjuːt] vt processare; **prosecution** [-ˈkjuːʃən] n processo; (accusing side) accusa; **prosecutor** n accusatore/trice; (also: **public ~**) pubblico ministero.

prospect n ['prɒspɛkt] prospettiva; (hope) speranza // vb [prəˈspɛkt] vt fare assaggi in // vi fare assaggi; ~**s** npl (for work etc) prospettive fpl; **prospecting** n prospezione f; **prospective** a possibile; futuro(a); **prospector** n prospettore m.

prospectus [prəˈspɛktəs] n prospetto, programma m.

prosper ['prɒspə*] vi prosperare; ~**ity** [-ˈspɛrɪtɪ] n prosperità; ~**ous** a prospero(a).

prostitute ['prɒstɪtjuːt] n prostituta.

prostrate ['prɒstreɪt] a prostrato(a).

protagonist [prəˈtægənɪst] n protagonista m/f.

protect [prəˈtɛkt] vt proteggere, salvaguardare; ~**ion** n protezione f; ~**ive** a protettivo(a); ~**or** n protettore/trice.

protégé ['prəʊtɛʒeɪ] n protetto; ~**e** n protetta.

protein ['prəʊtiːn] n proteina.

protest n ['prəʊtɛst] protesta // vi [prəˈtɛst] protestare.

Protestant ['prɒtɪstənt] a,n protestante (m/f).

protocol ['prəʊtəkɔl] n protocollo.

prototype ['prəʊtətaɪp] n prototipo.

protracted [prəˈtræktɪd] a tirato(a) per le lunghe.

protrude [prəˈtruːd] vi sporgere.

protuberance [prəˈtjuːbərəns] n sporgenza.

proud [praʊd] a fiero(a), orgoglioso(a); (pej) superbo(a).

prove [pruːv] vt provare, dimostrare // vi: **to ~ correct** etc risultare vero(a) etc; **to ~ o.s.** mostrare le proprie capacità; **to ~ o.s./itself (to be) useful** etc mostrarsi or rivelarsi utile etc.

proverb ['prɒvɜːb] n proverbio; ~**ial** [prəˈvɜːbɪəl] a proverbiale.

provide [prəˈvaɪd] vt fornire, provvedere; **to ~ sb with sth** fornire or provvedere qd di qc; **to ~ for** vt provvedere a; ~**d (that)** cj purché + sub, a condizione che + sub.

Providence ['prɔvɪdəns] n Provvidenza.
providing [prə'vaɪdɪŋ] cj purché + sub, a condizione che + sub.
province ['prɔvɪns] n provincia; **provincial** [prə'vɪnʃəl] a provinciale.
provision [prə'vɪʒən] n (supply) riserva; (supplying) provvista; rifornimento; (stipulation) condizione f; ~s npl (food) provviste fpl; ~al a provvisorio(a).
proviso [prə'vaɪzəu] n condizione f.
provocation [prɔvə'keɪʃən] n provocazione f.
provocative [prə'vɔkətɪv] a (aggressive) provocatorio(a); (thought-provoking) stimolante; (seductive) provocante.
provoke [prə'vəuk] vt provocare; incitare.
prow [prau] n prua.
prowess ['prauɪs] n prodezza.
prowl [praul] vi (also: ~ about, ~ around) aggirarsi furtivamente; ~er n tipo sospetto (che s'aggira con l'intenzione di rubare, aggredire etc).
proximity [prɔk'sɪmɪtɪ] n prossimità.
proxy ['prɔksɪ] n procura; **by** ~ per procura.
prudence ['pru:dns] n prudenza.
prudent ['pru:dnt] a prudente.
prudish ['pru:dɪʃ] a puritano(a).
prune [pru:n] n prugna secca // vt potare.
pry [praɪ] vi: **to** ~ **into** ficcare il naso in.
psalm [sɑ:m] n salmo.
pseudo- ['sju:dəu] prefix pseudo...; ~**nym** n pseudonimo.
psyche ['saɪkɪ] n psiche f.
psychiatric [saɪkɪ'ætrɪk] a psichiatrico(a).
psychiatrist [saɪ'kaɪətrɪst] n psichiatra m/f.
psychiatry [saɪ'kaɪətrɪ] n psichiatria.
psychic ['saɪkɪk] a (also: ~**al**) psichico(a); (person) dotato(a) di qualità telepatiche.
psychoanalyse [saɪkəu'ænəlaɪz] vt psicanalizzare.
psychoanalysis, pl lyses [saɪkəu-'næləsɪs, -sɪz] n psicanalisi f inv.
psychoanalyst [saɪkəu'ænəlɪst] n psicanalista m/f.
psychological [saɪkə'lɔdʒɪkl] a psicologico(a).
psychologist [saɪ'kɔlədʒɪst] n psicologo/a.
psychology [saɪ'kɔlədʒɪ] n psicologia.
psychopath ['saɪkəupæθ] n psicopatico/a.
psychotic [saɪ'kɔtɪk] a,n psicotico(a).
P.T.O. abbr (= please turn over) v.r. (vedi retro).
pub [pʌb] n (abbr of **public house**) pub m inv.
puberty ['pju:bətɪ] n pubertà.
public ['pʌblɪk] a pubblico(a) // n pubblico; **the general** ~ il pubblico.
publican ['pʌblɪkən] n proprietario di un pub.
publication [pʌblɪ'keɪʃən] n pubblicazione f.
public: ~ **company** n società f inv per azioni (costituita tramite pubblica

sottoscrizione); ~ **convenience** n gabinetti mpl; ~ **house** n pub m inv.
publicity [pʌb'lɪsɪtɪ] n pubblicità.
publicly ['pʌblɪklɪ] ad pubblicamente.
public: ~ **opinion** n opinione f pubblica; ~ **relations** n pubbliche relazioni fpl; ~ **school** n (Brit) scuola privata; ~**spirited** a che ha senso civico.
publish ['pʌblɪʃ] vt pubblicare; ~**er** n editore m; ~**ing** n (industry) editoria; (of a book) pubblicazione f.
puce [pju:s] a color pulce inv.
puck [pʌk] n (ICE HOCKEY) disco.
pucker ['pʌkə*] vt corrugare.
pudding ['pudɪŋ] n budino; (dessert) dolce m.
puddle ['pʌdl] n pozza, pozzanghera.
puerile ['pjuəraɪl] a puerile.
puff [pʌf] n sbuffo; (also: **powder** ~) piumino // vt: **to** ~ **one's pipe** tirare sboccate di fumo // vi uscire a sbuffi; (pant) ansare; **to** ~ **out smoke** mandar fuori sbuffi di fumo; ~**ed** a (col: out of breath) senza fiato.
puffin ['pʌfɪn] n puffino.
puff pastry ['pʌf'peɪstrɪ] n pasta sfoglia.
puffy ['pʌfɪ] a gonfio(a).
pugnacious [pʌg'neɪʃəs] a combattivo(a).
pull [pul] n (tug): **to give sth a** ~ tirare su qc; (fig) influenza // vt tirare; (muscle) strappare // vi tirare; **to** ~ **to pieces** fare a pezzi; **to** ~ **one's punches** (BOXING) risparmiare l'avversario; **not to** ~ **one's punches** (fig) non avere peli sulla lingua; **to** ~ **one's weight** dare il proprio contributo; **to** ~ **o.s. together** ricomporsi, riprendersi; **to** ~ **sb's leg** prendere in giro qd; **to** ~ **apart** vt (break) fare a pezzi; **to** ~ **down** vt (house) demolire; (tree) abbattere; **to** ~ **in** vi (AUT: at the kerb) accostarsi; (RAIL) entrare in stazione; **to** ~ **off** vt (deal etc) portare a compimento; **to** ~ **out** vi partire; (AUT: come out of line) spostarsi sulla mezzeria // vt staccare; far uscire; (withdraw) ritirare; **to** ~ **through** vi farcela; **to** ~ **up** vi (stop) fermarsi // vt (uproot) sradicare; (stop) fermare.
pulley ['pulɪ] n puleggia, carrucola.
pullover ['puləuvə*] n pullover m inv.
pulp [pʌlp] n (of fruit) polpa; (for paper) pasta per carta.
pulpit ['pulpɪt] n pulpito.
pulsate [pʌl'seɪt] vi battere, palpitare.
pulse [pʌls] n polso.
pulverize ['pʌlvəraɪz] vt polverizzare.
puma ['pju:mə] n puma m inv.
pummel ['pʌml] vt dare pugni a.
pump [pʌmp] n pompa; (shoe) scarpetta // vt pompare; (fig: col) far parlare; **to** ~ **up** vt gonfiare.
pumpkin ['pʌmpkɪn] n zucca.
pun [pʌn] n gioco di parole.
punch [pʌntʃ] n (blow) pugno; (fig: force) forza; (tool) punzone m; (drink) ponce m // vt (hit): **to** ~ **sb/sth** dare un pugno a qd/qc; **to** ~ **a hole (in)** fare un buco (in); ~**up** n (col) rissa.

punctual ['pʌŋktjuəl] a puntuale; ~ity [-'æliti] n puntualità.

punctuate ['pʌŋktjueit] vt punteggiare; **punctuation** [-'eiʃən] n interpunzione f, punteggiatura.

puncture ['pʌŋktʃə*] n foratura // vt forare.

pundit ['pʌndit] n sapientone/a.

pungent ['pʌndʒənt] a piccante; (fig) mordace, caustico(a).

punish ['pʌniʃ] vt punire; ~able a punibile; ~ment n punizione f.

punt [pʌnt] n (boat) barchino; (FOOTBALL) colpo a volo.

puny ['pju:ni] a gracile.

pup [pʌp] n cucciolo/a.

pupil ['pju:pl] n allievo/a; alunno/a.

puppet ['pʌpit] n burattino.

puppy ['pʌpi] n cucciolo/a, cagnolino/a.

purchase ['pɜ:tʃis] n acquisto, compera // vt comprare; ~r n compratore/trice.

pure [pjuə*] a puro(a).

purge [pɜ:dʒ] n (MED) purga; (POL) epurazione f // vt purgare; (fig) epurare.

purification [pjuərifi'keiʃən] n purificazione f.

purify ['pjuərifai] vt purificare.

purist ['pjuərist] n purista m/f.

puritan ['pjuəritən] n puritano/a; ~ical [-'tænikl] a puritano(a).

purity ['pjuəriti] n purità.

purl [pɜ:l] n punto rovescio.

purple ['pɜ:pl] a di porpora; viola inv.

purport [pɜː'pɔːt] vi: **to ~ to be/do** pretendere di essere/fare.

purpose ['pɜ:pəs] n intenzione f, scopo; **on ~** apposta; ~**ful** a deciso(a), risoluto(a); ~**ly** ad apposta.

purr [pɜ:*] vi fare le fusa.

purse [pɜ:s] n borsellino // vt contrarre.

purser ['pɜ:sə*] n (NAUT) commissario di bordo.

pursue [pə'sju:] vt inseguire; ~**r** n inseguitore/trice.

pursuit [pə'sju:t] n inseguimento; (occupation) occupazione f, attività f inv; **scientific ~s** ricerche fpl scientifiche.

purveyor [pə'veiə*] n fornitore/trice.

pus [pʌs] n pus m.

push [puʃ] n spinta; (effort) grande sforzo; (drive) energia f // vt spingere; (button) premere; (thrust): **to ~ sth (into)** ficcare qc (in); (fig) fare pubblicità a // vi spingere; premere; **to ~ aside** vt scostare; **to ~ off** vi (col) filare; **to ~ on** vi (continue) continuare; **to ~ through** vt (measure) far approvare; **to ~ up** vt (total, prices) far salire; ~**chair** n passeggino; ~**over** n (col): **it's a ~over** è un lavoro da bambini; ~**y** a (pej) opportunista.

puss, pussy(-cat) [pus, 'pusi(kæt)] n micio.

put, pt, pp **put** [put] vt mettere, porre; (say) dire, esprimere; (a question) fare; (estimate) stimare; **to ~ about** vi (NAUT) virare di bordo // vt (rumour) diffondere;

to ~ across vt (ideas etc) comunicare; far capire; **to ~ away** vt (return) mettere a posto; **to ~ back** vt (replace) rimettere (a posto); (postpone) rinviare; (delay) ritardare; **to ~ by** vt (money) mettere da parte; **to ~ down** vt (parcel etc) posare, mettere giù; (pay) versare; (in writing) mettere per iscritto; (suppress: revolt etc) reprimere, sopprimere; (attribute) attribuire; **to ~ forward** vt (ideas) avanzare, proporre; (date) anticipare; **to ~ in** vt (application, complaint) presentare; **to ~ off** vt (postpone) rimandare, rinviare; (discourage) dissuadere; **to ~ on** vt (clothes, lipstick etc) mettere; (light etc) accendere; (play etc) mettere in scena; (food, meal) servire; (brake) mettere; **to ~ on weight** ingrassare; **to ~ on airs** darsi delle arie; **to ~ out** vt mettere fuori; (one's hand) porgere; (light etc) spegnere; (person: inconvenience) scomodare; **to ~ up** vt (raise) sollevare, alzare; (pin up) affiggere; (hang) appendere; (build) costruire, erigere; (increase) aumentare; (accommodate) alloggiare; **to ~ up with** vt fus sopportare.

putrid ['pju:trid] a putrido(a).

putt [pʌt] vt (ball) colpire leggermente // n colpo leggero; ~**er** n (GOLF) putter m inv; ~**ing green** n green m inv; campo da putting.

putty ['pʌti] n stucco.

put-up ['putʌp] a: ~ **job** n montatura.

puzzle ['pʌzl] n enigma m, mistero; (jigsaw) puzzle m // vt confondere, rendere perplesso(a) // vi scervellarsi; **puzzling** a sconcertante, inspiegabile.

pygmy ['pigmi] n pigmeo/a.

pyjamas [pi'dʒɑːməz] npl pigiama m.

pylon ['pailən] n pilone m.

pyramid ['pirəmid] n piramide f.

python ['paiθən] n pitone m.

Q

quack [kwæk] n (of duck) qua qua m inv; (pej: doctor) dottoruccio/a.

quad [kwɔd] abbr of **quadrangle, quadruplet**.

quadrangle ['kwɔdræŋgl] n (MATH) quadrilatero; (courtyard) cortile m.

quadruped ['kwɔdrupəd] n quadrupede m.

quadruple [kwɔ'drupl] a quadruplo(a) // n quadruplo // vt quadruplicare // vi quadruplicarsi; ~**t** [-'dru:plit] n uno/a di quattro gemelli.

quagmire ['kwægmaiə*] n pantano.

quail [kweil] n (ZOOL) quaglia.

quaint [kweint] a bizzarro(a); (old-fashioned) antiquato(a); grazioso(a), pittoresco(a).

quake [kweik] vi tremare // n abbr of **earthquake**.

Quaker ['kweikə*] n quacchero/a.

qualification [kwɔlifi'keiʃən] n (degree etc) qualifica, titolo; (ability) competenza, qualificazione f; (limitation) riserva, restrizione f.

qualified ['kwɔlɪfaɪd] a qualificato(a); (able) competente, qualificato(a); (limited) condizionato(a).

qualify ['kwɔlɪfaɪ] vt abilitare; (limit: statement) modificare, precisare // vi: to ~ (as) qualificarsi (come); to ~ (for) acquistare i requisiti necessari (per); (SPORT) qualificarsi (per or a).

qualitative ['kwɔlɪtətɪv] a qualitativo(a).

quality ['kwɔlɪtɪ] n qualità f inv.

qualm [kwɑːm] n dubbio; scrupolo.

quandary ['kwɔndrɪ] n: in a ~ in un dilemma.

quantitative ['kwɔntɪtətɪv] a quantitativo(a).

quantity ['kwɔntɪtɪ] n quantità f inv; ~ surveyor n geometra m (specializzato nel calcolare la quantità e il costo del materiale da costruzione).

quarantine ['kwɔrntiːn] n quarantena.

quarrel ['kwɔrl] n lite f, disputa (f) // vi litigare; ~some a litigioso(a).

quarry ['kwɔrɪ] n (for stone) cava; (animal) preda // vt (marble etc) estrarre.

quart [kwɔːt] n ≈ litro (= 2 pints).

quarter ['kwɔːtə*] n quarto; (of year) trimestre m; (district) quartiere m // vt dividere in quattro; (MIL) alloggiare; ~s npl alloggio; (MIL) alloggi mpl, quadrato; a ~ of an hour un quarto d'ora; ~ final n quarto di finale; ~ly a trimestrale // ad trimestralmente; ~master n (MIL) furiere m.

quartet(te) [kwɔː'tɛt] n quartetto.

quartz [kwɔːts] n quarzo; ~ watch n orologio al quarzo.

quash [kwɔʃ] vt (verdict) annullare.

quasi- ['kweɪzaɪ] prefix quasi + noun; quasi, pressoché + adjective.

quaver ['kweɪvə*] n (MUS) croma // vi tremolare.

quay [kiː] n (also: ~side) banchina.

queasy ['kwiːzɪ] a (stomach) delicato(a); to feel ~ aver la nausea.

queen [kwiːn] n (gen) regina; (CARDS etc) regina, donna; ~ mother n regina madre.

queer [kwɪə*] a strano(a), curioso(a); (suspicious) dubbio(a), sospetto(a); (sick): I feel ~ mi sento poco bene // n (col) finocchio.

quell [kwɛl] vt domare.

quench [kwɛntʃ] vt (flames) spegnere; to ~ one's thirst dissetarsi.

query ['kwɪərɪ] n domanda, questione f; (doubt) dubbio // vt mettere in questione.

quest [kwɛst] n cerca, ricerca.

question ['kwɛstʃən] n domanda, questione f // vt (person) interrogare; (plan, idea) mettere in questione or in dubbio; it's a ~ of doing si tratta di fare; beyond ~ fuori di dubbio; out of the ~ fuori discussione, impossibile; ~able a discutibile; ~ing a interrogativo(a) // n interrogatorio; ~ mark n punto interrogativo.

questionnaire [kwɛstʃə'nɛə*] n questionario.

queue [kjuː] n coda, fila // vi fare la coda.

quibble ['kwɪbl] vi cavillare.

quick [kwɪk] a rapido(a), veloce; (reply) pronto(a); (mind) pronto(a), acuto(a) // ad rapidamente, presto // n: cut to the ~ (fig) toccato(a) sul vivo; be ~! fa presto!; ~en vt accelerare, affrettare; (rouse) animare, stimolare // vi accelerare, affrettarsi; ~ly ad rapidamente, velocemente; ~ness n rapidità; prontezza; acutezza; ~sand n sabbie fpl mobili; ~step n (dance) fox-trot m inv; ~witted a pronto(a) d'ingegno.

quid [kwɪd] n, pl inv (Brit: col) sterlina.

quiet ['kwaɪət] a tranquillo(a), quieto(a); (ceremony) semplice; (colour) discreto(a) // n tranquillità, calma; keep ~! sta zitto!; on the ~ di nascosto; ~en (also: ~en down) vi calmarsi, chetarsi // vt calmare, chetare; ~ly ad tranquillamente, calmamente; sommessamente; discretamente; ~ness n tranquillità, calma; silenzio.

quill [kwɪl] n penna d'oca.

quilt [kwɪlt] n piumino; (continental) ~ n sofficcione m imbottito.

quin [kwɪn] abbr of **quintuplet**.

quinine [kwɪ'niːn] n chinino.

quintet(te) [kwɪn'tɛt] n quintetto.

quintuplet [kwɪn'tjuːplɪt] n uno/a di cinque gemelli.

quip [kwɪp] n frizzo.

quirk [kwəːk] n ghiribizzo.

quit, pt, pp **quit** or **quitted** [kwɪt] vt lasciare, partire da // vi (give up) mollare; (resign) dimettersi; **notice to** ~ preavviso (dato all'inquilino).

quite [kwaɪt] ad (rather) assai; (entirely) completamente, del tutto; **I** ~ **understand** capisco perfettamente; ~ **a few of them** non pochi di loro; ~ **(so)!** esatto!

quits [kwɪts] a: ~ (with) pari (con).

quiver ['kwɪvə*] vi tremare, fremere // n (for arrows) faretra.

quiz [kwɪz] n (game) quiz m inv; indovinello // vt interrogare; ~zical a enigmatico(a).

quoits [kwɔɪts] npl gioco degli anelli.

quorum ['kwɔːrəm] n quorum m.

quota ['kwɔːtə] n quota.

quotation [kwəu'teɪʃən] n citazione f; (of shares etc) quotazione f; (estimate) preventivo; ~ **marks** npl virgolette fpl.

quote [kwəut] n citazione f // vt (sentence) citare; (price) dare, fissare; (shares) quotare // vi: to ~ **from** citare; to ~ **for a job** dare un preventivo per un lavoro.

R

rabbi ['ræbaɪ] n rabbino.

rabbit ['ræbɪt] n coniglio; ~ **hutch** n conigliera.

rabble ['ræbl] n (pej) canaglia, plebaglia.

rabid ['ræbɪd] a rabbioso(a);   (fig) fanatico(a).

rabies ['reɪbiːz] n rabbia.

RAC n abbr of Royal Automobile Club.

raccoon [rə'kuːn] n procione m.

race [reɪs] n corsa; (competition) gara, corsa // vi (person) gareggiare (in corsa) con; (horse) far correre; (engine) imballare // vi correre; ~**course** n campo di corse, ippodromo; ~**horse** n cavallo da corsa;   ~ **relations** npl rapporto fra le razze.

racial ['reɪʃl] a razziale; ~ **discrimination** n discriminazione f razziale; ~**ism** n razzismo; ~**ist** a, n razzista (m/f).

racing ['reɪsɪŋ] n corsa; ~ **car** n macchina da corsa; ~ **driver** n corridore m automobilista.

racist ['reɪsɪst] a,n (pej) razzista (m/f).

rack [ræk] n rastrelliera; (also: **luggage** ~) rete f, portabagagli m inv; (also: **roof** ~) portabagagli // vt torturare, tormentare; **toast** ~ n portatoast m inv.

racket ['rækɪt] n (for tennis) racchetta; (noise) fracasso; baccano; (swindle) imbroglio, truffa; (organized crime) racket m inv.

racoon [rə'kuːn] n = **raccoon**.

racquet ['rækɪt] n racchetta.

racy ['reɪsɪ] a brioso(a); piccante.

radar ['reɪdɑː*] n radar m // cpd radar inv.

radiance ['reɪdɪəns] n splendore m, radiosità.

radiant ['reɪdɪənt] a raggiante; (PHYSICS) radiante.

radiate ['reɪdɪeɪt] vt (heat) irraggiare, irradiare // vi (lines) irradiarsi.

radiation [reɪdɪ'eɪʃən] n irradiamento; (radioactive) radiazione f.

radiator ['reɪdɪeɪtə*] n radiatore m; ~ **cap** n tappo del radiatore.

radical ['rædɪkl] a radicale.

radii ['reɪdɪaɪ] npl of **radius**.

radio ['reɪdɪəu] n radio f inv; **on the** ~ alla radio; ~ **station** n stazione f radio inv.

radio... ['reɪdɪəu] prefix: ~**active** a radioattivo(a); ~**activity** n radioattività; ~**grapher** [-'ɔgrəfə*] n radiologo/a; ~**graphy** [-'ɔgrəfɪ] n radiografia; ~**logy** [-'ɔlədʒɪ] n radiologia.

radish ['rædɪʃ] n ravanello.

radium ['reɪdɪəm] n radio.

radius ['reɪdɪəs], pl **radii** ['reɪdɪaɪ, -ɪaɪ] n raggio; (ANAT) radio.

raffia ['ræfɪə] n rafia.

raffle ['ræfl] n lotteria.

raft [rɑːft] n zattera.

rafter ['rɑːftə*] n trave f.

rag [ræg] n straccio, cencio; (pej: newspaper) giornalaccio, bandiera; (for charity) iniziativa studentesca a scopo caritativo // vt prendere in giro; ~**s** npl stracci mpl, brandelli mpl;   ~**-and-bone man** n straccivendolo;   ~**bag**   n   (fig) guazzabuglio.

rage [reɪdʒ] n (fury) collera, furia // vi (person) andare su tutte le furie; (storm) infuriare; **it's all the** ~ fa furore.

ragged ['rægɪd] a (edge) irregolare; (cuff) logoro(a); (appearance) pezzente.

raid [reɪd] n (MIL) incursione f; (criminal) rapina; (by police) irruzione f // vt fare un'incursione in; rapinare; fare irruzione in; ~**er** n rapinatore/trice; (plane) aeroplano da incursione.

rail [reɪl] n (on stair) ringhiera; (on bridge, balcony) parapetto; (of ship) battagliola; (for train) rotaia; ~**s** npl binario, rotaie fpl; **by** ~ per ferrovia; ~**ing(s)** n(pl) ringhiere fpl; ~**road** n (US), ~**way** n ferrovia; ~**wayman** n ferroviere m; ~**way station** n stazione f ferroviaria.

rain [reɪn] n pioggia // vi piovere; **in the** ~ sotto la pioggia; ~**bow** n arcobaleno; ~**coat** n impermeabile m; ~**drop** n goccia di pioggia; ~**fall** n pioggia; (measurement)   piovosità;   ~**proof**   a impermeabile; ~**y** a piovoso(a).

raise [reɪz] n aumento // vt (lift) alzare; sollevare; (build) erigere; (increase) aumentare; (a protest, doubt, question) sollevare; (cattle, family) allevare; (crop) coltivare; (army, funds) raccogliere; (loan) ottenere; **to** ~ **one's voice** alzare la voce.

raisin ['reɪzn] n uva secca.

rajah ['rɑːdʒə] n ragià m inv.

rake [reɪk] n (tool) rastrello; (person) libertino // vt (garden) rastrellare; (with machine gun) spazzare.

rakish ['reɪkɪʃ] a dissoluto(a); disinvolto(a).

rally ['rælɪ] n (POL etc) riunione f; (AUT) rally m inv; (TENNIS) scambio // vt riunire, radunare // vi raccogliersi, radunarsi; (sick person, Stock Exchange) riprendersi; **to** ~ **round** vt fus raggrupparsi intorno a; venire in aiuto di.

ram [ræm] n montone m; (also: device) ariete m // vt conficcare; (crash into) cozzare, sbattere contro; percuotere; speronare.

ramble ['ræmbl] n escursione f // vi (pej: also: ~ **on**) divagare; ~**r** n escursionista m/f; (BOT) rosa rampicante; **rambling** a (speech) sconnesso(a); (BOT) rampicante.

ramification   [ræmɪfɪ'keɪʃən]   n ramificazione f.

ramp [ræmp] n rampa.

rampage [ræm'peɪdʒ] n: **to be on the** ~ scatenarsi in modo violento // vi: **they went rampaging through the town** si sono scatenati in modo violento per la città.

rampant ['ræmpənt] a (disease etc) che infierisce.

rampart ['ræmpɑːt] n bastione m.

ramshackle ['ræmʃækl] a (house) cadente; (car etc) sgangherato(a).

ran [ræn] pt of **run**.

ranch [rɑːntʃ] n ranch m inv; ~**er** n proprietario di un ranch; cowboy m inv.

rancid ['rænsɪd] a rancido(a).

rancour ['ræŋkə*] *n* rancore *m*.

random ['rændəm] *a* fatto(a) *or* detto(a) per caso // *n*: **at ~ a** casaccio.

randy ['rændɪ] *a* (*col*) arrapato(a); lascivo(a).

rang [ræŋ] *pt of* **ring**.

range [reɪndʒ] *n* (*of mountains*) catena; (*of missile, voice*) portata; (*of products*) gamma; (*MIL: also:* **shooting ~**) campo di tiro; (*also:* **kitchen ~**) fornello, cucina economica // *vi*: **to ~ over** coprire; **to ~ from ... to** andare da ... a; **~r** *n* guardia forestale.

rank [ræŋk] *n* fila; (*MIL*) grado; (*also:* **taxi ~**) posteggio di taxi // *vi*: **to ~ among** essere nel numero di // *a* a puzzolente; vero(a) e proprio(a); **the ~s** (*MIL*) la truppa; **the ~ and file** (*fig*) la gran massa.

rankle ['ræŋkl] *vi* bruciare.

ransack ['rænsæk] *vt* rovistare; (*plunder*) saccheggiare.

ransom ['rænsəm] *n* riscatto; **to hold sb to ~** (*fig*) esercitare pressione su qd.

rant [rænt] *vi* vociare; **~ing** *n* vociare *m*.

rap [ræp] *n* colpo secco e lieve; picchio // *vt* bussare a; picchiare su.

rape [reɪp] *n* violenza carnale, stupro // *vt* violentare.

rapid ['ræpɪd] *a* rapido(a); **~s** *npl* (*GEO*) rapida.

rapist ['reɪpɪst] *n* violentatore *m*.

rapport [ræ'pɔ:*] *n* rapporto.

rapture ['ræptʃə*] *n* estasi *f inv*; **to go into ~s over** andare in solluchero per; **rapturous** *a* estatico(a).

rare [rɛə*] *a* raro(a); (*CULIN: steak*) - al sangue.

rarefied ['rɛərɪfaɪd] *a* (*air, atmosphere*) rarefatto(a).

rarely ['rɛəlɪ] *ad* raramente.

rarity ['rɛərɪtɪ] *n* rarità *f inv*.

rascal ['rɑ:skl] *n* mascalzone *m*.

rash [ræʃ] *a* imprudente, sconsiderato(a) // *n* (*MED*) eruzione *f*.

rasher ['ræʃə*] *n* fetta sottile (di lardo *or* prosciutto).

rasp [rɑ:sp] *n* (*tool*) lima.

raspberry ['rɑːzbərɪ] *n* lampone *m*.

rasping ['rɑːspɪŋ] *a* stridulo(a).

rat [ræt] *n* ratto.

ratchet ['rætʃɪt] *n* (*TECH*) dente *m* d'arresto.

rate [reɪt] *n* (*proportion*) tasso, percentuale *f*; (*speed*) velocità *f inv*; (*price*) tariffa // *vt* giudicare; stimare; **to ~ sb/sth as** valutare qd/qc come; **to ~ sb/sth among** annoverare qd/qc tra; **~s** *npl* (*Brit*) imposte *fpl* comunali; (*fees*) tariffe *fpl*; **~able value** *n* valore *m* imponibile *or* locativo (di una proprietà); **~ of exchange** *n* corso dei cambi; **~payer** *n* contribuente *m/f* (che paga le imposte comunali).

rather ['rɑːðə*] *ad* piuttosto; **it's ~ expensive** è piuttosto caro; (*too much*) è un po' caro; **I would** *or* **I'd ~ go** preferirei andare.

ratification [rætɪfɪ'keɪʃən] *n* ratificazione *f*.

ratify ['rætɪfaɪ] *vt* ratificare.

rating ['reɪtɪŋ] *n* classificazione *f*; punteggio di merito; (*NAUT: sailor*) marinaio semplice.

ratio ['reɪʃɪəu] *n* proporzione *f*.

ration ['ræʃən] *n* (*gen pl*) razioni *fpl* // *vt* razionare.

rational ['ræʃənl] *a* razionale, ragionevole; (*solution, reasoning*) logico(a); **~e** [-'nɑːl] *n* fondamento logico; giustificazione *f*; **~ize** *vt* razionalizzare; **~ly** *ad* razionalmente; logicamente.

rat race ['rætreɪs] *n* mondo cane.

rattle ['rætl] *n* tintinnio; (*louder*) strepito; (*object: of baby*) sonaglino; (: *of sports fan*) raganella // *vi* risuonare, tintinnare; fare un rumore di ferraglia // *vt* scuotere (con strepito); **~snake** *n* serpente *m* a sonagli.

raucous ['rɔːkəs] *a* rauco(a).

ravage ['rævɪdʒ] *vt* devastare; **~s** *npl* danni *mpl*.

rave [reɪv] *vi* (*in anger*) infuriarsi; (*with enthusiasm*) andare in estasi; (*MED*) delirare.

raven ['reɪvən] *n* corvo.

ravenous ['rævənəs] *a* affamato(a).

ravine [rə'viːn] *n* burrone *m*.

raving ['reɪvɪŋ] *a*: **~ lunatic** *n* pazzo(a) furioso(a).

ravioli [rævɪ'əulɪ] *n* ravioli *mpl*.

ravish ['rævɪʃ] *vt* (*delight*) estasiare; **~ing** *a* incantevole.

raw [rɔː] *a* (*uncooked*) crudo(a); (*not processed*) greggio(a); (*sore*) vivo(a); (*inexperienced*) inesperto(a); **~ material** *n* materia prima.

ray [reɪ] *n* raggio.

rayon ['reɪon] *n* raion *m*.

raze [reɪz] *vt* radere, distruggere.

razor ['reɪzə*] *n* rasoio; **~ blade** *n* lama di rasoio.

Rd *abbr of* **road**.

re [riː] *prep* con riferimento a.

reach [riːtʃ] *n* portata; (*of river etc*) tratto // *vt* raggiungere; arrivare a // *vi* stendersi; **out of/within ~** (*object*) fuori/a portata di mano; **within easy ~ (of)** (*place*) a breve distanza (di), vicino (a); **to ~ out** *vi*: **to ~ out for** stendere la mano per prendere.

react [riː'ækt] *vi* reagire; **~ion** [-'ækʃən] *n* reazione *f*; **~ionary** [-'ækʃənrɪ] *a,n* reazionario(a).

reactor [riː'æktə*] *n* reattore *m*.

read, *pt,pp* **read** [riːd, rɛd] *vi* leggere // *vt* leggere; (*understand*) intendere, interpretare; (*study*) studiare; **to ~ out** *vt* leggere ad alta voce; **~er** *n* lettore/trice; (*book*) libro di lettura; (*at university*) professore con funzioni preminenti di ricerca; **~ership** *n* (*of paper etc*) numero di lettori.

readily ['rɛdɪlɪ] *ad* volentieri; (*easily*) facilmente.

readiness ['rɛdɪnɪs] *n* prontezza; **in ~** (*prepared*) pronto(a).

reading ['ri:dɪŋ] n lettura; (understanding) interpretazione f; (on instrument) indicazione f; ~ **lamp** n lampada da studio; ~ **room** n sala di lettura.

readjust [ri:ə'dʒʌst] vt raggiustare // vi (person): **to ~ (to)** riadattarsi (a).

ready ['rɛdɪ] a pronto(a); (willing) pronto(a), disposto(a); (quick) rapido(a); (available) disponibile // ad: ~-**cooked** già cotto(a) // n: **at the ~** (MIL) pronto a sparare; (fig) tutto(a) pronto(a); ~ **cash** n denaro in contanti; ~-**made** a prefabbricato(a); (clothes) confezionato(a).

real [rɪəl] a reale; vero(a); **in ~ terms** in realtà; ~ **estate** n beni mpl immobili; ~**ism** n (also ART) realismo; ~**ist** n realista m/f; ~**istic** [-'lɪstɪk] a realistico(a).

reality [ri:'ælɪtɪ] n realtà f inv; **in ~** in realtà, in effetti.

realization [rɪəlaɪ'zeɪʃən] n presa di coscienza; realizzazione f.

realize ['rɪəlaɪz] vt (understand) rendersi conto di; (a project, COMM: asset) realizzare.

really ['rɪəlɪ] ad veramente, davvero.

realm [rɛlm] n reame m, regno.

ream [ri:m] n risma.

reap [ri:p] vt mietere; (fig) raccogliere.

reappear [ri:ə'pɪə*] vi ricomparire, riapparire; ~**ance** n riapparizione f.

rear [rɪə*] a di dietro; (AUT: wheel etc) posteriore // n didietro, parte f posteriore // vt (cattle, family) allevare // vi (also: ~ **up**) (animal) impennarsi; ~**guard** n retroguardia.

rearm [ri:'ɑ:m] vt, vi riarmare; ~**ament** n riarmo.

rearrange [ri:ə'reɪndʒ] vt riordinare.

rear-view ['rɪəvju:] a: ~ **mirror** n (AUT) specchio retrovisivo.

reason ['ri:zn] n ragione f; (cause, motive) ragione, motivo // vi: **to ~ with sb** far ragionare qd; **to have ~ to think** aveıe motivi per pensare; **it stands to ~ that** è ovvio che; ~**able** a ragionevole; (not bad) accettabile; ~**ably** ad ragionevolmente; ~**ed** a (argument) ponderato(a); ~**ing** n ragionamento.

reassert [ri:ə'sə:t] vt riaffermare.

reassure [ri:ə'ʃuə*] vt rassicurare; **to ~ sb of** rassicurare qd di or su; **reassuring** a rassicurante.

rebate ['ri:beɪt] n (on product) ribasso; (on tax etc) sgravio; (repayment) rimborso.

rebel n ['rɛbl] ribelle m/f // vi [rɪ'bɛl] ribellarsi; ~**lion** n ribellione f; ~**lious** a ribelle.

rebirth [ri:'bə:θ] n rinascita.

rebound vi [rɪ'baund] (ball) rimbalzare // n ['ri:baund] rimbalzo.

rebuff [rɪ'bʌf] n secco rifiuto // vt respingere.

rebuild [ri:'bɪld] vt irg ricostruire.

rebuke [rɪ'bju:k] n rimprovero // vt rimproverare.

rebut [rɪ'bʌt] vt rifiutare; ~**tal** n rifiuto.

recall [rɪ'kɔ:l] vt richiamare; (remember) ricordare, richiamare alla mente // n richiamo; **beyond ~** a irrevocabile.

recant [rɪ'kænt] vi ritrattarsi; (REL) fare abiura.

recap ['ri:kæp] n ricapitolazione f // vt ricapitolare // vi riassumere.

recapture [ri:'kæptʃə*] vt riprendere; (atmosphere) ricreare.

recede [rɪ'si:d] vi allontanarsi; ritirarsi; calare; **receding** a (forehead, chin) sfuggente; **he's got a receding hairline** sta stempiando.

receipt [rɪ'si:t] n (document) ricevuta; (act of receiving) ricevimento; ~**s** npl (COMM) introiti mpl.

receive [rɪ'si:v] vt ricevere; (guest) ricevere, accogliere.

receiver [rɪ'si:və*] n (TEL) ricevitore m; (of stolen goods) ricettatore/trice; (LAW) curatore m fallimentare.

recent ['ri:snt] a recente; ~**ly** ad recentemente.

receptacle [rɪ'sɛptɪkl] n recipiente m.

reception [rɪ'sɛpʃən] n ricevimento; (welcome) accoglienza; (TV etc) ricezione f; ~ **desk** n ricevimento; ~**ist** n receptionist m/f inv.

receptive [rɪ'sɛptɪv] a ricettivo(a).

recess [rɪ'sɛs] n (in room) alcova; (POL etc: holiday) vacanze fpl.

recharge [ri:'tʃɑ:dʒ] vt (battery) ricaricare.

recipe ['rɛsɪpɪ] n ricetta.

recipient [rɪ'sɪpɪənt] n beneficiario/a; (of letter) destinatario.

reciprocal [rɪ'sɪprəkl] a reciproco(a).

reciprocate [rɪ'sɪprəkeɪt] vt ricambiare, contraccambiare.

recital [rɪ'saɪtl] n recital m inv.

recite [rɪ'saɪt] vt (poem) recitare.

reckless ['rɛkləs] a (driver etc) spericolato(a).

reckon ['rɛkən] vt (count) calcolare; (consider) considerare, stimare; (think): **I ~ that ...** penso che ...; **to ~ on** vt fus contare su; ~**ing** n conto; stima; **the day of ~ing** il giorno del giudizio.

reclaim [rɪ'kleɪm] vt (land) bonificare; (demand back) richiedere, reclamare; **reclamation** [rɛklə'meɪʃən] n bonifica.

recline [rɪ'klaɪn] vi stare sdraiato(a); **reclining** a (seat) ribaltabile.

recluse [rɪ'klu:s] n eremita m, appartato/a.

recognition [rɛkəg'nɪʃən] n riconoscimento; **to gain ~** essere riconosciuto(a); **transformed beyond ~** irriconoscibile.

recognizable ['rɛkəgnaɪzəbl] a riconoscibile.

recognize ['rɛkəgnaɪz] vt: **to ~ (by/as)** riconoscere (a or da/come).

recoil [rɪ'kɔɪl] vi (gun) rinculare; (spring) balzare indietro; (person): **to ~ (from)** indietreggiare (davanti a) // n rinculo; contraccolpo.

recollect [rɛkə'lɛkt] vt ricordare; ~**ion** [-'lɛkʃən] n ricordo.

recommend [rekə'mɛnd] *vt* raccomandare; (*advise*) consigliare; ~**ation** [-'deiʃən] *n* raccomandazione *f*; consiglio.

recompense ['rɛkɔmpɛns] *vt* ricompensare; (*compensate*) risarcire.

reconcile ['rɛkɔnsail] *vt* (*two people*) riconciliare; (*two facts*) conciliare, quadrare; **to** ~ **o.s. to** rassegnarsi a; **reconciliation** [-sili'eiʃən] *n* riconciliazione *f*; conciliazione *f*.

recondition [riːkən'diʃən] *vt* rimettere a nuovo; rifare.

reconnaissance [ri'kɔnisns] *n* (MIL) ricognizione *f*.

reconnoitre [rɛkə'nɔitə*] (MIL) *vt* fare una ricognizione di // *vi* fare una ricognizione.

reconsider [riːkən'sidə*] *vt* riconsiderare.

reconstruct [riːkən'strʌkt] *vt* ricostruire; ~**ion** [-kʃən] *n* ricostruzione *f*.

record *n* ['rɛkɔːd] ricordo, documento; (*of meeting etc*) nota, verbale *m*; (*register*) registro; (*file*) pratica, dossier *m inv*; (*also*: **police** ~) fedina penale sporca; (MUS: *disc*) disco; (SPORT) record *m inv*, primato // *vt* [ri'kɔːd] (*set down*) prendere nota di, registrare; (*relate*) raccontare; (MUS: *song etc*) registrare; **in** ~ **time** a tempo di record; **to keep a** ~ **of** tener nota di; **off the** ~ *a* ufficioso(a); ~ **card** *n* (*in file*) scheda; ~**er** *n* avvocato che funge da giudice; (MUS) flauto diritto; ~ **holder** *n* (SPORT) primatista *m/f*, ~**ing** *n* (MUS) registrazione *f*; ~ **library** *n* discoteca; ~ **player** *n* giradischi *m inv*.

recount [ri'kaunt] *vt* raccontare, narrare.

re-count ['riːkaunt] *n* (POL: *of votes*) nuovo computo.

recoup [ri'kuːp] *vt* ricuperare.

recourse [ri'kɔːs] *n* ricorso; rimedio; **to have** ~ **to** ricorrere a.

recover [ri'kʌvə*] *vt* ricuperare // *vi* (*from illness*) rimettersi (in salute), ristabilirsi; (*country, person: from shock*) riprendersi.

re-cover [riː'kʌvə*] *vt* (*chair etc*) ricoprire.

recovery [ri'kʌvəri] *n* ricupero; ristabilimento; ripresa.

recreate [riːkri'eit] *vt* ricreare.

recreation [rɛkri'eiʃən] *n* ricreazione *f*; svago; ~**al** *a* ricreativo(a).

recrimination [rikrimi'neiʃən] *n* recriminazione *f*.

recruit [ri'kruːt] *n* recluta // *vt* reclutare; ~**ment** *n* reclutamento.

rectangle ['rɛktæŋgl] *n* rettangolo; **rectangular** [-'tæŋgjulə*] *a* rettangolare.

rectify ['rɛktifai] *vt* (*error*) rettificare; (*omission*) riparare.

rector ['rɛktə*] *n* (REL) parroco (anglicano); **rectory** *n* presbiterio.

recuperate [ri'kjuːpəreit] *vi* ristabilirsi.

recur [ri'kəː*] *vi* riaccadere; (*idea, opportunity*) riapparire; (*symptoms*) ripresentarsi; ~**rence** *n* recrudescenza; riapparizione *f*; rinnovo; ~**rent** *a*

ricorrente, periodico(a); ~**ring** *a* (MATH) periodico(a).

red [rɛd] *n* rosso; (POL: *pej*) rosso/a // *a* rosso(a); **in the** ~ (*account*) scoperto; (*business*) in deficit; ~ **carpet treatment** *n* cerimonia col gran pavese; **R** ~ **Cross** *n* Croce *f* Rossa; ~**currant** *n* ribes *m inv*; ~**den** *vt* arrossare // *vi* arrossire; ~**dish** *a* rossiccio(a).

redeem [ri'diːm] *vt* (*debt*) riscattare; (*sth in pawn*) ritirare; (*fig, also* REL) redimere; ~**ing** *a* (*feature*) che salva.

redeploy [riːdi'plɔi] *vt* (*resources*) riorganizzare.

red-haired [rɛd'hɛəd] *a* dai capelli rossi.

red-handed [rɛd'hændid] *a*: **to be caught** ~ essere preso(a) in flagrante *or* con le mani nel sacco.

redhead ['rɛdhɛd] *n* rosso/a.

red herring ['rɛd'hɛriŋ] *n* (*fig*) falsa pista.

red-hot [rɛd'hɔt] *a* arrovente.

redirect [riːdai'rɛkt] *vt* (*mail*) far seguire.

redistribute [riːdi'stribjuːt] *vt* ridistribuire.

red light ['rɛd'lait] *n*: **to go through a** ~ (AUT) passare col rosso; **red-light district** *n* quartiere *m* luce rossa *inv*.

redness ['rɛdnis] *n* rossore *m*; (*of hair*) rosso.

redo [riː'duː] *vt irg* rifare.

redolent ['rɛdəulnt] *a*: ~ **of** che sa di; (*fig*) che ricorda.

redouble [riː'dʌbl] *vt*: **to** ~ **one's efforts** raddoppiare gli sforzi.

redress [ri'drɛs] *n* riparazione *f*.

red tape ['rɛd'teip] *n* (*fig*) burocrazia.

reduce [ri'djuːs] *vt* ridurre; (*lower*) ridurre, abbassare; **reduction** [ri'dʌkʃən] *n* riduzione *f*; (*of price*) ribasso; (*discount*) sconto.

redundancy [ri'dʌndənsi] *n* licenziamento.

redundant [ri'dʌndnt] *a* (*worker*) licenziato(a); (*detail, object*) superfluo(a); **to make** ~ licenziare.

reed [riːd] *n* (BOT) canna; (MUS: *of clarinet etc*) ancia.

reef [riːf] *n* (*at sea*) scogliera.

reek [riːk] *vi*: **to** ~ (**of**) puzzare (di).

reel [riːl] *n* bobina, rocchetto; (TECH) aspo; (FISHING) mulinello; (CINEMA) rotolo // *vt* (TECH) annaspare; (*also*: ~ **up**) avvolgere // *vi* (*sway*) barcollare.

re-election [riːi'lɛkʃən] *n* rielezione *f*.

ref [rɛf] *n* (*col: abbr of* **referee**) arbitro.

refectory [ri'fɛktəri] *n* refettorio.

refer [ri'fəː*] *vt*: **to** ~ **sb** (*or* **sth**) **to** (*dispute, decision*) deferire qc a; (*inquirer: for information*) indirizzare qd a; (*reader: to text*) rimandare qd a; **to** ~ **to** *vt fus* (*allude to*) accennare a; (*apply to*) riferire a; (*consult*) rivolgersi a; ~**ring to your letter** (COMM) in riferimento alla Vostra lettera.

referee [rɛfə'riː] *n* arbitro; (*for job application*) referenza // *vt* arbitrare.

reference ['rɛfrəns] *n* riferimento;

(*mention*) menzione f, allusione f; (*for job application: letter*) referenza; lettera di raccomandazione; (: *person*) referenza; **with ~ to** a riguardo; (*COMM: in letter*) in or con riferimento a; ~ **book** n libro di consultazione.

referendum,   pl   **referenda** [rɛfə'rɛndəm, -də] n referendum m inv.

refill vt [ri:'fɪl] riempire di nuovo; (*pen, lighter etc*) ricaricare // n ['ri:fɪl] (*for pen etc*) ricambio.

refine [rɪ'faɪn] vt raffinare; ~**d** a (*person, taste*) raffinato(a); ~**ment** n (*of person*) raffinatezza; ~**ry** n raffineria.

reflect [rɪ'flɛkt] vt (*light, image*) riflettere; (*fig*) rispecchiare // vi (*think*) riflettere, considerare; **to ~ on** vt fus (*discredit*) rispecchiarsi su; ~**ion** [-'flɛkʃən] n riflessione f; (*image*) riflesso; (*criticism*): ~**ion on** giudizio su; attacco a; **on ~ion** pensandoci sopra; ~**or** n (*also* AUT) catarifrangente m.

reflex [ri:flɛks] a riflesso(a) // n riflesso; ~**ive** [rɪ'flɛksɪv] a (LING) riflessivo(a).

reform [rɪ'fɔ:m] n riforma // vt riformare; **the R~ation** [rɛfə'meɪʃən] n la Riforma; ~**ed** a cambiato(a) (per il meglio); ~**er** n riformatore/trice.

refrain [rɪ'freɪn] vi: **to ~ from doing** trattenersi dal fare // n ritornello.

refresh [rɪ'frɛʃ] vt rinfrescare; ~**er course** n corso di aggiornamento; ~**ment room** n posto di ristoro; ~**ments** npl rinfreschi mpl.

refrigeration [rɪfrɪdʒə'reɪʃən]   n refrigerazione f.

refrigerator [rɪ'frɪdʒəreɪtə*]   n frigorifero.

refuel [ri:'fjuəl] vt rifornire (di carburante) // vi far rifornimento (di carburante).

refuge ['rɛfju:dʒ] n rifugio; **to take ~ in** rifugiarsi in.

refugee [rɛfju'dʒi:]   n   rifugiato/a, profugo/a.

refund n ['ri:fʌnd] rimborso // vt [rɪ'fʌnd] rimborsare.

refurbish [ri:'fə:bɪʃ] vt rimettere a nuovo.

refusal [rɪ'fju:zəl] n rifiuto.

refuse n ['rɛfju:s] rifiuti mpl // vt, vi [rɪ'fju:z] rifiutare; ~ **collector** n netturbino.

refute [rɪ'fju:t] vt confutare.

regain [rɪ'geɪn] vt riguadagnare; riacquistare, ricuperare.

regal ['ri:gl] a regio(a); ~**ia** [rɪ'geɪlɪə] n insegne fpl regie.

regard [rɪ'gɑ:d] n riguardo, stima // vt considerare, stimare; **to give one's ~s to** porgere i suoi saluti a; ~**ing, as ~s, with ~ to** riguardo a; ~**less** ad lo stesso; ~**less of** a dispetto di, nonostante.

regatta [rɪ'gætə] n regata.

regency ['ri:dʒənsɪ] n reggenza.

regent ['ri:dʒənt] n reggente m.

régime [reɪ'ʒi:m] n regime m.

regiment ['rɛdʒɪmənt] n reggimento; ~**al** [-'mɛntl] a reggimentale; ~**ation** [-'teɪʃən] n irreggimentazione f.

region ['ri:dʒən] n regione f; **in the ~ of** (*fig*) all'incirca di; ~**al** a regionale.

register ['rɛdʒɪstə*] n registro; (*also: electoral ~*) lista elettorale // vt registrare; (*vehicle*) immatricolare; (*luggage*) spedire assicurato(a); (*letter*) raccomandare; (*subj: instrument*) segnare // vi iscriversi; (*at hotel*) firmare il registro; (*make impression*) entrare in testa; ~**ed** a (*design*) depositato(a); (*letter*) raccomandato(a).

registrar ['rɛdʒɪstrɑ:*] n ufficiale m di stato civile; segretario.

registration [rɛdʒɪs'treɪʃən] n (*act*) registrazione f; iscrizione f; (AUT: *also: ~ number*) numero di targa.

registry ['rɛdʒɪstrɪ] n ufficio del registro; ~ **office** n anagrafe f.

regret [rɪ'grɛt]   n   rimpianto, rincrescimento // vt rimpiangere; **I ~ that I/he cannot help** mi rincresce di non poter aiutare/che lui non possa aiutare; ~**fully** ad con rincrescimento; ~**table** a deplorevole.

regroup [ri:'gru:p] vt raggruppare // vi raggrupparsi.

regular ['rɛgjulə*] a regolare; (*usual*) abituale, normale; (*soldier*) dell'esercito regolare; (COMM: *size*) normale // n (*client etc*) cliente m/f abituale; ~**ity** [-'lærɪtɪ] n regolarità f inv; ~**ly** ad regolarmente.

regulate ['rɛgjuleɪt]   vt   regolare; **regulation** [-'leɪʃən] n (*rule*) regola, regolamento; (*adjustment*) regolazione f.

rehabilitation ['ri:həbɪlɪ'teɪʃən] n (*of offender*) riabilitazione f; (*of disabled*) riadattamento.

rehash [ri:'hæʃ] vt (*col*) rimaneggiare.

rehearsal [rɪ'hə:səl] n prova.

rehearse [rɪ'hə:s] vt provare.

reign [reɪn] n regno // vi regnare; ~**ing** a (*monarch*) regnante; (*champion*) attuale.

reimburse [ri:ɪm'bə:s] vt rimborsare.

rein [reɪn] n (*for horse*) briglia.

reincarnation [ri:ɪnkɑ:'neɪʃən] n reincarnazione f.

reindeer ['reɪndɪə*] n, pl inv renna.

reinforce [ri:ɪn'fɔ:s] vt rinforzare; ~**d concrete** n cemento armato; ~**ment** n (*action*) rinforzamento; ~**ments** npl (MIL) rinforzi mpl.

reinstate [ri:ɪn'steɪt] vt reintegrare.

reissue [ri:'ɪʃju:] vt (*book*) ristampare, ripubblicare; (*film*) distribuire di nuovo.

reiterate [ri:'ɪtəreɪt] vt reiterare, ripetere.

reject n ['ri:dʒɛkt] (COMM) scarto // vt [rɪ'dʒɛkt] rifiutare, respingere; (COMM: *goods*) scartare; ~**ion** [rɪ'dʒɛkʃən] n rifiuto.

rejoice [rɪ'dʒɔɪs] vi: **to ~ (at or over)** provare diletto in.

rejuvenate [rɪ'dʒu:vəneɪt] vt ringiovanire.

rekindle [ri:'kɪndl] vt riaccendere.

relapse [rɪ'læps] n (MED) ricaduta.

relate [rɪ'leɪt] vt (*tell*) raccontare; (*connect*) collegare; ~**d** a imparentato(a);

collegato(a), connesso(a); ~**d** to imparentato(a) con; collegato(a) *or* connesso(a) con; **relating: relating to** *prep* che riguarda, rispetto a.

relation [rɪ'leɪʃən] *n* (*person*) parente *m/f*; (*link*) rapporto, relazione *f*; ~**ship** *n* rapporto; (*personal ties*) rapporti *mpl*, relazioni *fpl*.

relative ['rɛlətɪv] *n* parente *m/f* // *a* relativo(a); (*respective*) rispettivo(a); ~**ly** *ad* relativamente.

relax [rɪ'læks] *vi* rilasciarsi; (*person: unwind*) rilassarsi // *vt* rilasciare; (*mind, person*) rilassare; ~**ation** [riːlæk'seɪʃən] *n* rilasciamento; rilassamento; (*entertainment*) ricreazione *f*, svago; ~**ed** *a* rilasciato(a); rilassato(a); ~**ing** *a* rilassante.

relay ['riːleɪ] *n* (*SPORT*) corsa a staffetta // *vt* (*message*) trasmettere.

release [rɪ'liːs] *n* (*from prison*) rilascio; (*from obligation*) liberazione *f*; (*of gas etc*) emissione *f*; (*of film etc*) distribuzione *f*; (*record*) disco; (*device*) disinnesto // *vt* (*prisoner*) rilasciare; (*from obligation, wreckage etc*) liberare; (*book, film*) fare uscire; (*news*) rendere pubblico(a); (*gas etc*) emettere; (*TECH: catch, spring etc*) disinnestare; (*let go*) rilasciare; lasciar andare; sciogliere; **to ~ one's grip** mollare la presa; **to ~ the clutch** (*AUT*) staccare la frizione.

relegate ['rɛləɡeɪt] *vt* relegare.

relent [rɪ'lɛnt] *vi* cedere; ~**less** *a* implacabile.

relevance ['rɛləvəns] *n* pertinenza; ~ **of sth to sth** rapporto tra qc e qc.

relevant ['rɛləvənt] *a* pertinente; (*chapter*) in questione; ~ **to** pertinente a.

reliability [rɪlaɪə'bɪlɪtɪ] *n* fidabilità; affidabilità.

reliable [rɪ'laɪəbl] *a* (*person, firm*) fidato(a), che dà affidamento; (*method*) sicuro(a); (*machine*) affidabile; **reliably** *ad*: **to be reliably informed** sapere da fonti sicure.

reliance [rɪ'laɪəns] *n*: ~ **(on)** fiducia (in); bisogno (di).

relic ['rɛlɪk] *n* (*REL*) reliquia; (*of the past*) resto.

relief [rɪ'liːf] *n* (*from pain, anxiety*) sollievo; (*help, supplies*) soccorsi *mpl*; (*of guard*) cambio; (*ART, GEO*) rilievo.

relieve [rɪ'liːv] *vt* (*pain, patient*) sollevare; (*bring help*) soccorrere; (*take over from: gen*) sostituire; (: *guard*) rilevare; **to ~ sb of sth** alleggerire qd di qc.

religion [rɪ'lɪdʒən] *n* religione *f*; **religious** *a* religioso(a).

relinquish [rɪ'lɪŋkwɪʃ] *vt* abbandonare; (*plan, habit*) rinunziare a.

relish ['rɛlɪʃ] *n* (*CULIN*) condimento; (*enjoyment*) gran piacere *m* // *vt* (*food etc*) godere; **to ~ doing** adorare fare.

relive [riː'lɪv] *vt* rivivere.

reload [riː'ləud] *vt* ricaricare.

reluctance [rɪ'lʌktəns] *n* riluttanza.

reluctant [rɪ'lʌktənt] *a* riluttante, mal

disposto(a); ~**ly** *ad* di mala voglia, a malincuore.

rely [rɪ'laɪ]: **to ~ on** *vt fus* contare su; (*be dependent*) dipendere da.

remain [rɪ'meɪn] *vi* restare, rimanere; ~**der** *n* resto; (*COMM*) rimanenza; ~**ing** *a* che rimane; ~**s** *npl* resti *mpl*.

remand [rɪ'mɑːnd] *n*: **on ~** in detenzione preventiva // *vt*: **to ~ in custody** rinviare in carcere; trattenere a disposizione della legge.

remark [rɪ'mɑːk] *n* osservazione *f* // *vt* osservare, dire; (*notice*) notare; ~**able** *a* notevole; eccezionale.

remedial [rɪ'miːdɪəl] *a* (*tuition, classes*) di riparazione.

remedy ['rɛmədɪ] *n*: ~ **(for)** rimedio (per) // *vt* rimediare a.

remember [rɪ'mɛmbə*] *vt* ricordare, ricordarsi di; ~ **me to** (*in letter*) ricordami a; **remembrance** *n* memoria; ricordo.

remind [rɪ'maɪnd] *vt*: **to ~ sb of sth** ricordare qc a qd; **to ~ sb to do** ricordare a qd di fare; ~**er** *n* richiamo; (*note etc*) promemoria *m inv*.

reminisce [rɛmɪ'nɪs] *vi*: **to ~ (about)** abbandonarsi ai ricordi (di).

reminiscences [rɛmɪ'nɪsnsɪz] *npl* reminiscenze *fpl*, memorie *fpl*.

reminiscent [rɛmɪ'nɪsnt] *a*: ~ **of** che fa pensare a, che richiama.

remission [rɪ'mɪʃən] *n* remissione *f*; (*of fee*) esonero.

remit [rɪ'mɪt] *vt* (*send: money*) rimettere; ~**tance** *n* rimessa.

remnant ['rɛmnənt] *n* resto, avanzo; ~**s** *npl* (*COMM*) scampoli *mpl*; fine *f* serie.

remorse [rɪ'mɔːs] *n* rimorso; ~**ful** *a* pieno(a) di rimorsi; ~**less** *a* (*fig*) spietato(a).

remote [rɪ'məut] *a* remoto(a), lontano(a); (*person*) distaccato(a); ~ **control** *n* telecomando; ~**ly** *ad* remotamente; (*slightly*) vagamente; ~**ness** *n* lontananza.

remould ['riːməuld] *n* (*tyre*) gomma rivestita.

removable [rɪ'muːvəbl] *a* (*detachable*) staccabile.

removal [rɪ'muːvəl] *n* (*taking away*) rimozione *f*; soppressione *f*; (*from house*) trasloco; (*from office: sacking*) destituzione *f*; (*MED*) ablazione *f*; ~ **van** *n* furgone *m* per traslochi.

remove [rɪ'muːv] *vt* togliere, rimuovere; (*employee*) destituire; (*stain*) far sparire; (*doubt, abuse*) sopprimere, eliminare.

remuneration [rɪmjuːnə'reɪʃən] *n* rimunerazione *f*.

rend, *pt, pp* **rent** [rɛnd, rɛnt] *vt* lacerare.

render ['rɛndə*] *vt* rendere; (*CULIN: fat*) struggere; ~**ing** *n* (*MUS etc*) interpretazione *f*.

rendez-vous ['rɒndɪvuː] *n* appuntamento; (*place*) luogo d'incontro; (*meeting*) incontro.

renegade ['rɛnɪɡeɪd] *n* rinnegato/a.

renew [rɪ'njuː] vt rinnovare; (negotiations) riprendere; ~al n rinnovamento; ripresa.

renounce [rɪ'naʊns] vt rinunziare a; (disown) ripudiare.

renovate ['rɛnəveɪt] vt rinnovare; (art work) restaurare; **renovation** [-'veɪʃən] n rinnovamento; restauro.

renown [rɪ'naʊn] n rinomanza; ~ed a rinomato(a).

rent [rɛnt] pt, pp of rend // n affitto // vt (take for rent) prendere in affitto; (also: ~ out) dare in affitto; ~al n (for television, car) fitto.

renunciation [rɪnʌnsɪ'eɪʃən] n rinnegamento; (self-denial) rinunzia.

reopen [riː'əʊpən] vt riaprire; ~ing n riapertura.

reorder [riː'ɔːdə*] vt ordinare di nuovo; (rearrange) riorganizzare.

reorganize [riː'ɔːɡənaɪz] vt riorganizzare.

rep [rɛp] n (COMM: abbr of **representative**) rappresentante m/f; (THEATRE: abbr of **repertory**) teatro di repertorio.

repair [rɪ'pɛə*] n riparazione f // vt riparare; **in good/bad** ~ in buona/cattiva condizione; ~ **kit** n corredo per riparazioni; ~ **shop** n (AUT etc) officina.

repartee [rɛpɑː'tiː] n risposta pronta.

repay [riː'peɪ] vt irg (money, creditor) rimborsare, ripagare; (sb's efforts) ricompensare; ~ment n rimborsamento; ricompensa.

repeal [rɪ'piːl] n (of law) abrogazione f; (of sentence) annullamento // vt abrogare; annullare.

repeat [rɪ'piːt] n (RADIO, TV) replica // vt ripetere; (pattern) riprodurre; (promise, attack, also COMM: order) rinnovare; ~edly ad ripetutamente, spesso.

repel [rɪ'pɛl] vt respingere; ~lent a repellente // n: **insect** ~lent prodotto m anti-insetti inv.

repent [rɪ'pɛnt] vi: to ~ (of) pentirsi (di); ~ance n pentimento.

repercussion [riːpə'kʌʃən] n (consequence) ripercussione f.

repertoire ['rɛpətwɑː*] n repertorio.

repertory ['rɛpətərɪ] n (also: ~ theatre) teatro di repertorio.

repetition [rɛpɪ'tɪʃən] n ripetizione f; (COMM: order etc) rinnovo.

repetitive [rɪ'pɛtɪtɪv] a (movement) che si ripete; (work) monotono(a); (speech) pieno(a) di ripetizioni.

replace [rɪ'pleɪs] vt (put back) rimettere a posto; (take the place of) sostituire; (TEL): '~ the receiver' 'riattaccare'; ~ment n rimessa; sostituzione f; (person) sostituto/a; ~ment part n pezzo di ricambio.

replenish [rɪ'plɛnɪʃ] vt (glass) riempire; (stock etc) rifornire.

replete [rɪ'pliːt] a ripieno(a); (well-fed) sazio(a).

replica ['rɛplɪkə] n replica, copia.

reply [rɪ'plaɪ] n risposta // vi rispondere.

report [rɪ'pɔːt] n rapporto; (PRESS etc)

cronaca; (also: **school** ~) pagella // vt riportare; (PRESS etc) fare una cronaca su; (bring to notice: occurrence) segnalare; (: person) denunciare // vi (make a report) fare un rapporto (or una cronaca); (present o.s.): to ~ (to sb) presentarsi (a qd); **it is** ~ed that si dice che; ~ed **speech** n (LING) discorso indiretto; ~er n reporter m inv.

reprehensible [rɛprɪ'hɛnsɪbl] a riprensibile.

represent [rɛprɪ'zɛnt] vt rappresentare; ~ation [-'teɪʃən] n rappresentazione f; ~ations npl (protest) protesta; ~ative n rappresentativo/a; (US: POL) deputato/a // a rappresentativo(a), caratteristico(a).

repress [rɪ'prɛs] vt reprimere; ~ion [-'prɛʃən] repressione f; ~ive a repressivo(a).

reprieve [rɪ'priːv] n (LAW) sospensione f dell'esecuzione della condanna; (fig) dilazione f // vt sospendere l'esecuzione della condanna a; accordare una dilazione a.

reprimand ['rɛprɪmɑːnd] n rampogna // vt rampognare.

reprisal [rɪ'praɪzl] n rappresaglia.

reproach [rɪ'prəʊtʃ] n rimprovero // vt: to ~ **sb with sth** rimproverare qd di qc; **beyond** ~ irreprensibile; ~ful a di rimprovero.

reproduce [riːprə'djuːs] vt riprodurre // vi riprodursi; **reproduction** [-'dʌkʃən] n riproduzione f; **reproductive** [-'dʌktɪv] a riproduttore(trice); riproduttivo(a).

reprove [rɪ'pruːv] vt (action) disapprovare; (person): to ~ (for) biasimare (per); **reproving** a di disapprovazione.

reptile ['rɛptaɪl] n rettile m.

republic [rɪ'pʌblɪk] n repubblica; ~an a,n repubblicano(a).

repudiate [rɪ'pjuːdɪeɪt] vt ripudiare.

repugnant [rɪ'pʌɡnənt] a ripugnante.

repulse [rɪ'pʌls] vt respingere.

repulsion [rɪ'pʌlʃən] n ripulsione f.

repulsive [rɪ'pʌlsɪv] a ripugnante, ripulsivo(a).

reputable ['rɛpjutəbl] a di buona reputazione; (occupation) rispettabile.

reputation [rɛpju'teɪʃən] n reputazione f.

repute [rɪ'pjuːt] n reputazione f; ~d a reputato(a); ~dly ad secondo che si dice.

request [rɪ'kwɛst] n domanda; (formal) richiesta // vt: to ~ (of or from sb) chiedere (a qd).

requiem ['rɛkwɪəm] n requiem m or f inv.

require [rɪ'kwaɪə*] vt (need: subj: person) aver bisogno di; (: thing, situation) richiedere; (want) volere; esigere; (order) obbligare; ~d a richiesto(a); **if** ~d in caso di bisogno; ~ment n esigenza; bisogno; requisito.

requisite ['rɛkwɪzɪt] n cosa necessaria // a necessario(a); **toilet** ~s articoli mpl da toletta.

requisition [rɛkwɪ'zɪʃən] n: ~ (for) richiesta (di) // vt (MIL) requisire.

rescind [rɪ'sɪnd] *vt* annullare; *(law)* abrogare; *(judgment)* rescindere.

rescue ['rɛskjuː] *n* salvataggio; *(help)* soccorso // *vt* salvare; ~ **party** *n* squadra di salvataggio; ~**r** *n* salvatore/trice.

research [rɪ'sɜːtʃ] *n* ricerca, ricerche *fpl* // *vt* fare ricerche su; ~**er** *n* ricercatore/trice; ~ **work** *n* ricerche *fpl*.

resemblance [rɪ'zɛmbləns] *n* somiglianza.

resemble [rɪ'zɛmbl] *vt* assomigliare a.

resent [rɪ'zɛnt] *vt* risentirsi di; ~**ful** *a* pieno(a) di risentimento; ~**ment** *n* risentimento.

reservation [rɛzə'veɪʃən] *n* *(booking)* prenotazione *f*; *(doubt)* dubbio; *(protected area)* riserva; *(on road: also:* **central** ~) spartitraffico *m inv*; **to make a** ~ *(in an hotel/a restaurant/on a plane)* prenotare una camera/una tavola/un posto.

reserve [rɪ'zɜːv] *n* riserva // *vt* *(seats etc)* prenotare; ~**s** *npl* (MIL) riserve *fpl*; **in** ~ in serbo; ~**d** *a* *(shy)* riservato(a); *(seat)* prenotato(a).

reservoir ['rɛzəvwaː*] *n* serbatoio.

reshape [riː'ʃeɪp] *vt* *(policy)* ristrutturare.

reshuffle [riː'ʃʌfl] *n*: **Cabinet** ~ (POL) rimpasto governativo.

reside [rɪ'zaɪd] *vi* risiedere.

residence ['rɛzɪdəns] *n* residenza; ~ **permit** *n* permesso di soggiorno.

resident ['rɛzɪdənt] *n* residente *m/f*; *(in hotel)* cliente *m/f* fisso(a) // *a* residente.

residential [rɛzɪ'dɛnʃl] *a* di residenza; *(area)* residenziale.

residue ['rɛzɪdjuː] *n* resto; (CHEM, PHYSICS) residuo.

resign [rɪ'zaɪn] *vt* *(one's post)* dimettersi da // *vi* dimettersi; **to** ~ **o.s. to** rassegnarsi a; ~**ation** [rɛzɪg'neɪʃən] *n* dimissioni *fpl*; rassegnazione *f*; ~**ed** *a* rassegnato(a).

resilience [rɪ'zɪlɪəns] *n* *(of material)* elasticità, resilienza; *(of person)* capacità di recupero.

resilient [rɪ'zɪlɪənt] *a* *(person)* che si riprende facilmente.

resin ['rɛzɪn] *n* resina.

resist [rɪ'zɪst] *vt* resistere a; ~**ance** *n* resistenza.

resolute ['rɛzəluːt] *a* risoluto(a).

resolution [rɛzə'luːʃən] *n* risoluzione *f*.

resolve [rɪ'zɔlv] *n* risoluzione *f* // *vt* *(decide)*: **to** ~ **to do** decidere di fare; ~**d** *a* risoluto(a).

resonant ['rɛzənənt] *a* risonante.

resort [rɪ'zɔːt] *n* *(town)* stazione *f*; *(recourse)* ricorso // *vi*: **to** ~ **to** aver ricorso a; **as a last** ~ come ultimo ricorso.

resound [rɪ'zaund] *vi*: **to** ~ **(with)** risonare (di); ~**ing** *a* risonante.

resource [rɪ'sɔːs] *n* risorsa; ~**s** *npl* risorse *fpl*; ~**ful** *a* pieno(a) di risorse, intraprendente.

respect [rɪs'pɛkt] *n* rispetto // *vt* rispettare; **with** ~ **to** rispetto a, riguardo a; **in this** ~ per questo riguardo;

~**ability** [-ə'bɪlɪtɪ] *n* rispettabilità; ~**able** *a* rispettabile; ~**ful** *a* rispettoso(a).

respective [rɪs'pɛktɪv] *a* rispettivo(a); ~**ly** *ad* rispettivamente.

respiration [rɛspɪ'reɪʃən] *n* respirazione *f*.

respite ['rɛspaɪt] *n* respiro, tregua.

resplendent [rɪs'plɛndənt] *a* risplendente.

respond [rɪs'pɔnd] *vi* rispondere.

response [rɪs'pɔns] *n* risposta.

responsibility [rɪspɔnsɪ'bɪlɪtɪ] *n* responsabilità *f inv*.

responsible [rɪs'pɔnsɪbl] *a* *(liable)*: ~ **(for)** responsabile (di); *(trustworthy)* fidato(a); *(job)* di (grande) responsabilità; **responsibly** *ad* responsabilmente.

responsive [rɪs'pɔnsɪv] *a* che reagisce.

rest [rɛst] *n* riposo; *(stop)* sosta, pausa; (MUS) pausa; *(support)* appoggio, sostegno; *(remainder)* resto, avanzi *mpl* // *vi* riposarsi; *(be supported)*: **to** ~ **on** appoggiarsi su; *(remain)* rimanere, restare // *vt* *(lean)*: **to** ~ **sth on/against** appoggiare qc su/contro; **the** ~ **of them** gli altri; **it** ~**s with him to decide** sta a lui decidere.

restart [riː'staːt] *vt* *(engine)* rimettere in marcia; *(work)* ricominciare.

restaurant ['rɛstərɔŋ] *n* ristorante *m*; ~ **car** *n* vagone *m* ristorante.

restful ['rɛstful] *a* riposante.

rest home ['rɛsthəum] *n* casa di riposo.

restitution [rɛstɪ'tjuːʃən] *n* *(act)* restituzione *f*; *(reparation)* riparazione *f*.

restive ['rɛstɪv] *a* agitato(a), impaziente; *(horse)* restio(a).

restless ['rɛstlɪs] *a* agitato(a), irrequieto(a).

restock [riː'stɔk] *vt* rifornire.

restoration [rɛstə'reɪʃən] *n* restauro; restituzione *f*.

restore [rɪ'stɔː*] *vt* *(building)* restaurare; *(sth stolen)* restituire; *(peace, health)* ristorare.

restrain [rɪs'treɪn] *vt* *(feeling)* contenere, frenare; *(person)*: **to** ~ **(from doing)** trattenere (dal fare); ~**ed** *a* *(style)* contenuto(a), sobrio(a); *(manner)* riservato(a); ~**t** *n* *(restriction)* limitazione *f*; *(moderation)* ritegno.

restrict [rɪs'trɪkt] *vt* restringere, limitare; ~**ed area** *n* (AUT) zona a velocità limitata; ~**ion** [-kʃən] *n* restrizione *f*, limitazione *f*; ~**ive** *a* restrittivo(a).

rest room ['rɛstrum] *n* (US) toletta.

result [rɪ'zʌlt] *n* risultato // *vi*: **to** ~ **in** avere per risultato.

resume [rɪ'zjuːm] *vt*, *vi* *(work, journey)* riprendere.

resumption [rɪ'zʌmpʃən] *n* ripresa.

resurgence [rɪ'sɜːdʒəns] *n* rinascita.

resurrection [rɛzə'rɛkʃən] *n* risurrezione *f*.

resuscitate [rɪ'sʌsɪteɪt] *vt* (MED) risuscitare; **resuscitation** [-'teɪʃən] *n* rianimazione *f*.

retail ['riːteɪl] *n* (vendita al) minuto // *cpd* al minuto // *vt* vendere al minuto; ~**er** *n* commerciante *m/f* al minuto, dettagliante *m*; ~ **price** *n* prezzo al minuto.

retain [rɪ'teɪn] *vt* (*keep*) tenere, serbare; ~**er** *n* (*servant*) servitore *m*; (*fee*) onorario.

retaliate [rɪ'tælɪeɪt] *vi*: to ~ (**against**) vendicarsi (di); **retaliation** [-'eɪʃən] *n* vendetta, rappresaglie *fpl*.

retarded [rɪ'tɑːdɪd] *a* ritardato(a); (*also*: **mentally** ~) tardo(a) (di mente).

retch [rɛtʃ] *vi* aver conati di vomito.

rethink ['riː'θɪŋk] *vt* ripensare.

reticence ['rɛtɪsns] *n* reticenza.

reticent ['rɛtɪsnt] *a* reticente.

retina ['rɛtɪnə] *n* retina.

retinue ['rɛtɪnjuː] *n* seguito, scorta.

retire [rɪ'taɪə*] *vi* (*give up work*) andare in pensione; (*withdraw*) ritirarsi, andarsene; (*go to bed*) andare a letto, ritirarsi; ~**d** *a* (*person*) pensionato(a); ~**ment** *n* pensione *f*; **retiring** *a* (*person*) riservato(a).

retort [rɪ'tɔːt] *n* (*reply*) rimbecco; (*container*) storta // *vi* rimbeccare.

retrace [riː'treɪs] *vt* ricostruire; to ~ **one's steps** tornare sui passi.

retract [rɪ'trækt] *vt* (*statement*) ritrattare; (*claws, undercarriage, aerial*) ritrarre, ritirare // *vi* ritrarsi; ~**able** *a* retrattile.

retrain [rɪ'treɪn] *vt* (*worker*) riaddestrare; ~**ing** *n* riaddestramento.

retreat [rɪ'triːt] *n* ritirata; (*place*) rifugio // *vi* battere in ritirata; (*flood*) ritirarsi.

retrial [riː'traɪəl] *n* nuovo processo.

retribution [rɛtrɪ'bjuːʃən] *n* castigo.

retrieval [rɪ'triːvəl] *n* ricupero; riparazione *f*.

retrieve [rɪ'triːv] *vt* (*sth lost*) ricuperare, ritrovare; (*situation, honour*) salvare; (*error, loss*) riparare; (*COMPUTERS*) ricuperare; ~**r** *n* cane *m* da riporto.

retrospect ['rɛtrəspɛkt] *n*: **in** ~ guardando indietro; ~**ive** [-'spɛktɪv] *a* retrospettivo(a); (*law*) retroattivo(a).

return [rɪ'tɜːn] *n* (*going or coming back*) ritorno; (*of sth stolen etc*) restituzione *f*; (*recompense*) ricompensa; (*FINANCE: from land, shares*) profitto, reddito; (*report*) rapporto // *cpd* (*journey, match*) di ritorno; (*ticket*) di andata e ritorno // *vi* tornare, ritornare // *vt* rendere, restituire; (*bring back*) riportare; (*send back*) mandare indietro; (*put back*) rimettere; (*POL: candidate*) eleggere; ~**s** *npl* (*COMM*) incassi *mpl*; profitti *mpl*; **many happy** ~**s** (**of the day**)! auguri!, buon compleanno!

reunion [riː'juːnɪən] *n* riunione *f*.

reunite [riːjuː'naɪt] *vt* riunire.

rev [rɛv] *n* (*abbr of* **revolution**: *AUT*) giro // *vb* (*also*: ~ **up**) *vt* imballare // *vi* imballarsi.

revamp ['riː'væmp] *vt* rinnovare; riorganizzare.

reveal [rɪ'viːl] *vt* (*make known*) rivelare, svelare; (*display*) rivelare, mostrare; ~**ing** *a* rivelatore(trice); (*dress*) scollato(a).

reveille [rɪ'vælɪ] *n* (*MIL*) sveglia.

revel ['rɛvl] *vi*: to ~ **in sth/in doing** dilettarsi di qc/a fare.

revelation [rɛvə'leɪʃən] *n* rivelazione *f*.

reveller ['rɛvlə*] *n* crapulone/a, festaiolo/a.

revelry ['rɛvlrɪ] *n* crapula, baldoria.

revenge [rɪ'vɛndʒ] *n* vendetta; (*in game etc*) rivincita // *vt* vendicare; to **take** ~ vendicarsi; ~**ful** *a* vendicatore(trice); vendicativo(a).

revenue ['rɛvənjuː] *n* reddito.

reverberate [rɪ'vɜːbəreɪt] *vi* (*sound*) rimbombare; (*light*) riverberarsi; **reverberation** [-'reɪʃən] *n* (*of light, sound*) riverberazione *f*.

reverence ['rɛvərəns] *n* venerazione *f*, riverenza.

reverent ['rɛvərənt] *a* riverente.

reverie ['rɛvərɪ] *n* fantasticheria.

reversal [rɪ'vɜːsl] *n* capovolgimento.

reverse [rɪ'vɜːs] *n* contrario, opposto; (*back*) rovescio; (*AUT*: *also*: ~ **gear**) marcia indietro // *a* (*order, direction*) contrario(a), opposto(a) // *vt* (*turn*) invertire, rivoltare; (*change*) capovolgere, rovesciare; (*LAW*: *judgment*) cassare // *vi* (*AUT*) fare marcia indietro; ~**d charge call** *n* (*TEL*) telefonata con addebito al ricevente.

reversion [rɪ'vɜːʃən] *n* ritorno.

revert [rɪ'vɜːt] *vi*: to ~ **to** tornare a.

review [rɪ'vjuː] *n* rivista; (*of book, film*) recensione *f* // *vt* passare in rivista; fare la recensione di; ~**er** *n* recensore/a.

revise [rɪ'vaɪz] *vt* (*manuscript*) rivedere, correggere; (*opinion*) emendare, modificare; (*study*: *subject, notes*) ripassare; **revision** [rɪ'vɪʒən] *n* revisione *f*; ripasso.

revitalize [riː'vaɪtəlaɪz] *vt* ravvivare.

revival [rɪ'vaɪvəl] *n* ripresa; ristabilimento; (*of faith*) risveglio.

revive [rɪ'vaɪv] *vt* (*person*) rianimare; (*custom*) far rivivere; (*hope, courage*) ravvivare; (*play, fashion*) riesumare // *vi* (*person*) rianimarsi; (*hope*) ravvivarsi; (*activity*) riprendersi.

revoke [rɪ'vəuk] *vt* revocare; (*promise, decision*) rinvenire su.

revolt [rɪ'vəult] *n* rivolta, ribellione *f* // *vi* rivoltarsi, ribellarsi; ~**ing** *a* ripugnante.

revolution [rɛvə'luːʃən] *n* rivoluzione *f*; (*of wheel etc*) rivoluzione, giro; ~**ary** *a, n* rivoluzionario(a); ~**ize** *vt* rivoluzionare.

revolve [rɪ'vɔlv] *vi* girare.

revolver [rɪ'vɔlvə*] *n* rivoltella.

revolving [rɪ'vɔlvɪŋ] *a* girevole.

revue [rɪ'vjuː] *n* (*THEATRE*) rivista.

revulsion [rɪ'vʌlʃən] *n* ripugnanza.

reward [rɪ'wɔːd] *n* ricompensa, premio // *vt*: to ~ (**for**) ricompensare (per); ~**ing** *a* (*fig*) soddisfacente.

rewind [riː'waɪnd] *vt* *irg* (*watch*) ricaricare; (*ribbon etc*) riavvolgere.

rewire [riː'waɪə*] *vt* (*house*) rifare l'impianto elettrico di.

reword [ri:'wɔːd] *vt* formulare *or* esprimere con altre parole.

rewrite [ri:'raɪt] *vt irg* riscrivere.

rhapsody ['ræpsədɪ] *n* (*MUS*) rapsodia; (*fig*) elogio stravagante.

rhetoric ['rɛtərɪk] *n* retorica; ~**al** [rɪ'tɔrɪkl] *a* retorico(a).

rheumatic [ruː'mætɪk] *a* reumatico(a).

rheumatism ['ruːmətɪzəm] *n* reumatismo.

Rhine [raɪn] *n*: **the** ~ il Reno.

rhinoceros [raɪ'nɔsərəs] *n* rinoceronte *m*.

rhododendron [rəʊdə'dɛndrn] *n* rododendro.

Rhone [rəʊn] *n*: **the** ~ il Rodano.

rhubarb ['ruːbɑːb] *n* rabarbaro.

rhyme [raɪm] *n* rima; (*verse*) poesia.

rhythm ['rɪðm] *n* ritmo; ~**ic(al)** *a* ritmico(a); ~**ically** *ad* con ritmo.

rib [rɪb] *n* (*ANAT*) costola // *vt* (*tease*) punzecchiare.

ribald ['rɪbəld] *a* licenzioso(a), volgare.

ribbed [rɪbd] *a* (*knitting*) a coste.

ribbon ['rɪbən] *n* nastro; **in** ~**s** (*torn*) a brandelli.

rice [raɪs] *n* riso; ~**field** *n* risaia; ~ **pudding** *n* budino di riso.

rich [rɪtʃ] *a* ricco(a); (*clothes*) sontuoso(a); **the** ~ i ricchi; ~**es** *npl* ricchezze *fpl*; ~**ness** *n* ricchezza.

rickets ['rɪkɪts] *n* rachitismo.

rickety ['rɪkɪtɪ] *a* zoppicante.

rickshaw ['rɪkʃɔː] *n* risció *m inv*.

ricochet ['rɪkəʃeɪ] *n* rimbalzo // *vi* rimbalzare.

rid, *pt*, *pp* **rid** [rɪd] *vt*: **to** ~ **sb of** sbarazzare *or* liberare qd di; **to get** ~ **of** sbarazzarsi di; **good riddance!** che liberazione!

ridden ['rɪdn] *pp of* **ride**.

riddle ['rɪdl] *n* (*puzzle*) indovinello // *vt*: **to be** ~**d with** essere crivellato(a) di.

ride [raɪd] *n* (*on horse*) cavalcata; (*outing*) passeggiata; (*distance covered*) cavalcata; corsa // *vb* (*pt* **rode**, *pp* **ridden** [rəʊd, 'rɪdn]) *vi* (*as sport*) cavalcare; (**to go somewhere**: *on horse, bicycle*) andare (a cavallo *or* in bicicletta *etc*); (*journey*: *on bicycle, motor cycle, bus*) andare, viaggiare // *vt* (*a horse*) montare, cavalcare; **we rode all day** abbiamo cavalcato tutto il giorno; **to** ~ **a horse/bicycle/camel** montare a cavallo/in bicicletta/in groppa a un cammello; **to** ~ **at anchor** (*NAUT*) essere alla fonda; **horse** ~ cavalcata; **car** ~ passeggiata in macchina; **to take sb for a** ~ (*fig*) prendere in giro qd; fregare qd; ~**r** *n* cavalcatore/trice; (*in race*) fantino; (*on bicycle*) ciclista *m/f*; (*on motorcycle*) motociclista *m/f*; (*in document*) clausola addizionale, aggiunta.

ridge [rɪdʒ] *n* (*of hill*) cresta; (*of roof*) colmo; (*of mountain*) giogo; (*on object*) riga (in rilievo).

ridicule ['rɪdɪkjuːl] *n* ridicolo; scherno // *vt* mettere in ridicolo.

ridiculous [rɪ'dɪkjuləs] *a* ridicolo(a).

riding ['raɪdɪŋ] *n* equitazione *f*; ~ **school** *n* scuola d'equitazione.

rife [raɪf] *a* diffuso(a); **to be** ~ **with** abbondare di.

riffraff ['rɪfræf] *n* canaglia.

rifle ['raɪfl] *n* carabina // *vt* vuotare; ~ **range** *n* campo di tiro; (*indoor*) tiro al bersaglio.

rift [rɪft] *n* fessura, crepatura; (*fig: disagreement*) incrinatura, disaccordo.

rig [rɪg] *n* (*also*: **oil** ~: *on land*) derrick *m inv*; (: *at sea*) piattaforma per trivellazioni subacquee // *vt* (*election etc*) truccare; **to** ~ **out** *vt* attrezzare; (*pej*) abbigliare, agghindare; **to** ~ **up** *vt* allestire; ~**ging** *n* (*NAUT*) attrezzatura.

right [raɪt] *a* giusto(a); (*suitable*) appropriato(a); (*not left*) destro(a) // *n* (*title, claim*) diritto; (*not left*) destra // *ad* (*answer*) correttamente; (*not on the left*) a destra // *vt* raddrizzare; (*fig*) riparare // *excl* bene!; **to be** ~ (*person*) aver ragione; (*answer*) essere giusto(a) *or* corretto(a); ~ **now** proprio adesso; subito; ~ **against the wall** proprio contro il muro; ~ **ahead** sempre diritto; proprio davanti; ~ **in the middle** proprio nel mezzo; ~ **away** subito; **by** ~**s** di diritto; **on the** ~ a destra; ~ **angle** *n* angolo retto; ~**eous** ['raɪtʃəs] *a* retto(a), virtuoso(a); (*anger*) giusto(a), giustificato(a); ~**eousness** ['raɪtʃəsnɪs] *n* rettitudine *f*, virtù *f*; ~**ful** *a* (*heir*) legittimo(a); ~**handed** *a* (*person*) che adopera la mano destra; ~**hand man** *n* braccio destro; **the** ~**hand side** il lato destro; ~**ly** *ad* bene, correttamente; (*with reason*) a ragione; ~**minded** *a* sensato(a); ~ **of way** *n* diritto di passaggio; (*AUT*) precedenza; ~ **wing** *n* (*MIL, SPORT*) ala destra; (*POL*) destra; ~**wing** *a* (*POL*) di destra.

rigid ['rɪdʒɪd] *a* rigido(a); (*principle*) rigoroso(a); ~**ity** [rɪ'dʒɪdɪtɪ] *n* rigidità; ~**ly** *ad* rigidamente.

rigmarole ['rɪgmərəʊl] *n* tiritera; commedia.

rigorous ['rɪgərəs] *a* rigoroso(a).

rigour ['rɪgə*] *n* rigore *m*.

rim [rɪm] *n* orlo; (*of spectacles*) montatura; (*of wheel*) cerchione *m*; ~**less** *a* (*spectacles*) senza montatura; ~**med** *a* bordato(a); cerchiato(a).

rind [raɪnd] *n* (*of bacon*) cotenna; (*of lemon etc*) scorza.

ring [rɪŋ] *n* anello; (*also*: **wedding** ~) fede *f*; (*of people, objects*) cerchio; (*of spies*) giro; (*of smoke etc*) spirale *m*; (*arena*) pista, arena; (*for boxing*) ring *m inv*; (*sound of bell*) scampanio; (*telephone call*) colpo di telefono // *vb* (*pt* **rang**, *pp* **rung** [ræŋ, rʌŋ]) *vi* (*person, bell, telephone*) suonare; (*also*: ~ **out**: *voice, words*) risuonare; (*TEL*) telefonare // *vt* (*TEL*: *also*: ~ **up**) telefonare a; **to** ~ **the bell** suonare; **to** ~ **back** *vt, vi* (*TEL*) richiamare; **to** ~ **off** *vi* (*TEL*) mettere giù, riattaccare; ~**leader** *n* (*of gang*) capobanda *m*.

ringlets ['rɪŋlɪts] *npl* boccoli *mpl*.

ring road ['rɪŋrəud] n raccordo anulare.

rink [rɪŋk] n (also: **ice** ~) pista di pattinaggio.

rinse [rɪns] n risciacquatura; (hair tint) colorito // vt sciacquare; darsi il colorito a.

riot ['raɪət] n sommossa, tumulto // vi tumultuare; **a ~ of colours** un'orgia di colori; **to run** ~ creare disordine; ~**ous** a tumultuoso(a); che fa crepare dal ridere; ~**ously funny** che fa crepare dal ridere.

rip [rɪp] n strappo // vt strappare // vi strapparsi; ~**cord** n cavo di sfilamento.

ripe [raɪp] a (fruit) maturo(a); (cheese) stagionato(a); ~**n** vt maturare // vi maturarsi; stagionarsi; ~**ness** n maturità.

ripple ['rɪpl] n increspamento, ondulazione f; mormorio // vi incresparsi.

rise [raɪz] n (slope) salita, pendio; (hill) altura; (increase: in wages) aumento; (: in prices, temperature) rialzo, aumento; (fig: to power etc) ascesa // vi (pt **rose**, pp **risen** [rauz, 'rɪzn]) alzarsi, levarsi; (prices) aumentarsi; (waters, river) crescere; (sun, wind, person: from chair, bed) levarsi; (also: ~ **up**: rebel) insorgere; ribellarsi; **to give** ~ **to** provocare, dare origine a; **to** ~ **to the occasion** essere all'altezza.

risk [rɪsk] n rischio, pericolo // vt rischiare; **to take** or **run the** ~ **of doing** correre il rischio di fare; **at** ~ in pericolo; ~**y** a rischioso(a).

risqué ['ri:skeɪ] a (joke) spinto(a).

rissole ['rɪsəul] n crocchetta.

rite [raɪt] n rito.

ritual ['rɪtjuəl] a, n rituale (m).

rival ['raɪvl] a rivale m/f; (in business) concorrente m/f // a rivale; che fa concorrenza // vt essere in concorrenza con; **to** ~ **sb/sth** in competere con qd/qc in; ~**ry** n rivalità; concorrenza.

river ['rɪvə*] n fiume m // cpd (port, traffic) fluviale; ~**bank** n argine m; ~**bed** n alveo (fluviale); ~**side** n sponda del fiume.

rivet ['rɪvɪt] n ribattino, rivetto // vt ribadire; (fig) concentrare, fissare.

Riviera [rɪvɪ'ɛərə] n: **the (French)** ~ la Costa Azzurra.

RN abbr of **Royal Navy**.

road [rəud] n strada; (small) cammino; (in town) via; ~**block** n blocco stradale; ~**hog** n guidatore m egoista e spericolato; ~ **map** n carta stradale; ~**side** n margine m della strada; ~**sign** n cartello stradale; ~**way** n carreggiata; ~**worthy** a in buono stato di marcia.

roam [rəum] vi errare, vagabondare // vt vagare per.

roar [rɔ:*] n ruggito; (of crowd) tumulto; (of thunder, storm) muggito // vi ruggire; tumultuare; muggire; **to** ~ **with laughter** scoppiare dalle risa; **a** ~**ing fire** un bel fuoco; **to do a** ~**ing trade** fare affari d'oro.

roast [rəust] n arrosto // vt (meat) arrostire.

rob [rɔb] vt (person) rubare; (bank) svaligiare; **to** ~ **sb of sth** derubare qd di qc; (fig: deprive) privare qd di qc; ~**ber** n ladro; (armed) rapinatore m; ~**bery** n furto; rapina.

robe [rəub] n (for ceremony etc) abito; (also: **bath** ~) accappatoio // vt vestire.

robin ['rɔbɪn] n pettirosso.

robot ['rəubɔt] n robot m inv.

robust [rəu'bʌst] a robusto(a); (material) solido(a).

rock [rɔk] n (substance) roccia; (boulder) masso; roccia; (in sea) scoglio; (sweet) zucchero candito // vt (swing gently: cradle) dondolare; (: child) cullare; (shake) scrollare, far tremare // vi dondolarsi; scrollarsi, tremare; **on the** ~**s** (drink) col ghiaccio; (ship) sugli scogli; (marriage etc) in crisi; ~-**bottom** n (fig) stremo; ~**ery** n giardino roccioso.

rocket ['rɔkɪt] n razzo; (MIL) razzo, missile m.

rock face ['rɔkfeɪs] n parete f della roccia.

rock fall ['rɔkfɔ:l] n caduta di massa.

rocking chair ['rɔkɪŋtʃɛə*] n sedia a dondolo.

rocking horse ['rɔkɪŋhɔ:s] n cavallo a dondolo.

rocky ['rɔkɪ] a (hill) roccioso(a); (path) sassoso(a); (unsteady: table) traballante.

rod [rɔd] n (metallic, TECH) asta; (wooden) bacchetta; (also: **fishing** ~) canna da pesca.

rode [rəud] pt of **ride**.

rodent ['rəudnt] n roditore m.

rodeo ['rəudɪəu] n rodeo.

roe [rəu] n (species: also: ~ **deer**) capriolo; (of fish) uova fpl di pesce; **soft** ~ latte m di pesce.

rogue [rəug] n mascalzone m; **roguish** a birbantesco(a).

role [rəul] n ruolo.

roll [rəul] n rotolo; (of banknotes) mazzo; (also: **bread** ~) panino; (register) lista; (sound: of drums etc) rullo; (movement: of ship) rullio // vt rotolare; (also: ~ **up**: string) aggomitolare; (also: ~ **out**: pastry) stendere // vi rotolare; (wheel) girare; **to** ~ **in** vi (mail, cash) arrivare a bizzeffe; **to** ~ **over** vi rivoltarsi; **to** ~ **up** vi (col: arrive) arrivare // vt (carpet) arrotolare; ~ **call** n appello; ~**ed gold** a d'oro laminato; ~**er** n rullo; (wheel) rotella; ~**er skates** npl pattini mpl a rotelle.

rolling ['rəulɪŋ] a (landscape) ondulato(a); ~ **pin** n matterello; ~ **stock** n (RAIL) materiale m rotabile.

Roman ['rəumən] a, n romano(a); ~ **Catholic** a, n cattolico(a).

romance [rə'mæns] n storia (or avventura or film m inv) romantico(a); (charm) poesia; (love affair) idillio.

Romanesque [rəumə'nɛsk] a romanico(a).

Romania [rəu'meɪnɪə] n Romania; ~**n** a, n romeno(a).

romantic [rə'mæntɪk] a romantico(a); sentimentale.

romanticism [rə'mæntısızəm] n romanticismo.

Rome [rəum] n Roma.

romp [rɔmp] n gioco rumoroso // vi (also: ~ **about**) far chiasso, giocare in un modo rumoroso.

rompers ['rɔmpəz] npl pagliaccetto.

roof [ru:f] n tetto; (of tunnel, cave) volta // vt coprire (con un tetto); ~ **garden** n giardino pensile; ~**ing** n materiale m per copertura; ~ **rack** n (AUT) portabagagli m inv.

rook [ruk] n (bird) corvo nero; (CHESS) torre f // vt (cheat) truffare, spennare.

room [ru:m] n (in house) stanza, camera; (in school etc) sala; (space) posto, spazio; ~**s** npl (lodging) alloggio; ~**ing house** n (US) casa in cui si affittano camere o appartamentini ammobiliati; ~**mate** n compagno/a di stanza; ~ **service** n servizio da camera; ~**y** a spazioso(a); (garment) ampio(a).

roost [ru:st] n appollaiato // vi appollaiarsi.

rooster ['ru:stə*] n gallo.

root [ru:t] n radice f // vt (plant, belief) far radicare; to ~ **about** vi (fig) frugare; to ~ **for** vt fus fare il tifo per; to ~ **out** vt estirpare.

rope [rəup] n corda, fune f; (NAUT) cavo // vt (box) legare; (climbers) legare in cordata; to ~ **sb in** (fig) coinvolgere qd; to know the ~**s** (fig) conoscere i trucchi del mestiere; ~ **ladder** n scala di corda.

rosary ['rəuzərı] n rosario; roseto.

rose [rəuz] pt of **rise** // n rosa; (on watering can) rosetta // a rosa inv.

rosé ['rəuzeı] n vino rosato.

rose: ~**bed** n roseto; ~**bud** n bocciolo di rosa; ~**bush** n rosaio.

rosemary ['rəuzmərı] n rosmarino.

rosette [rəu'zet] n rosetta; (larger) coccarda.

roster ['rɔstə*] n: **duty** ~ ruolino di servizio.

rostrum ['rɔstrəm] n tribuna.

rosy ['rəuzı] a roseo(a).

rot [rɔt] n (decay) putrefazione f; (fig: pej) stupidaggini fpl // vt, vi imputridire, marcire.

rota ['rəutə] n ruolino di servizio.

rotary ['rəutərı] a rotante.

rotate [rəu'teıt] vt (revolve) far girare; (change round: crops) avvicendare; (: jobs) fare a turno // vi (revolve) girare; **rotating** a (movement) rotante; **rotation** [-'teıʃən] n rotazione f.

rotor ['rəutə*] n rotore m.

rotten ['rɔtn] a (decayed) putrido(a), marcio(a); (dishonest) corrotto(a); (col: bad) brutto(a); (: action) vigliacco(a); to feel ~ (ill) sentirsi proprio male.

rotund [rəu'tʌnd] a grassoccio(a); tondo(a).

rouble ['ru:bl] n rublo.

rouge [ru:ʒ] n rossetto.

rough [rʌf] a aspro(a); (person, manner: coarse) rozzo(a), aspro(a); (: violent) brutale; (district) malfamato(a); (weather) cattivo(a); (plan) abbozzato(a); (guess) approssimativo(a) // n (GOLF) macchia; (person) duro; to ~ **it** far vita dura; to **play** ~ far il gioco pesante; to **sleep** ~ dormire all'addiaccio; to **feel** ~ sentirsi male; to ~ **out** vt (draft) abbozzare; ~**en** vt (a-surface) rendere ruvido(a); ~**ly** ad (handle) rudemente, brutalmente; (make) grossolanamente; (approximately) approssimativamente; ~**ness** n asprezza; rozzezza; brutalità; ~ **work** n (at school etc) brutta copia.

roulette [ru:'let] n roulette f.

Roumania [ru:'meınıə] n = **Romania**.

round [raund] a rotondo(a) // n tondo, cerchio; (of toast) fetta; (duty: of policeman, milkman etc) giro; (: of doctor) visite fpl; (game: of cards, in competition) partita; (BOXING) round m inv; (of talks) serie f inv // vt (corner) girare; (bend) prendere; (cape) doppiare // prep intorno a // ad: ~ **right**, ~ **all** ~ tutt'attorno; all the year ~ tutto l'anno; it's just ~ the corner (also fig) è dietro l'angolo; to go ~ fare il giro; to go ~ **an obstacle** aggirare un ostacolo; to go ~ **a house** visitare una casa; to ~ **off** vt (speech etc) finire; to ~ **up** vt radunare; (criminals) fare una retata di; (prices) arrotondare; ~**about** n (AUT) rotatoria; (at fair) giostra // a (route, means) indiretto(a); ~ **of ammunition** n cartuccia; ~ **of applause** n applausi mpl; ~ **of drinks** n giro di bibite; ~ **of sandwiches** n sandwich m inv; ~**ed** a arrotondato(a); (style) armonioso(a); ~**ly** ad (fig) chiaro e tondo; ~**-shouldered** a dalle spalle tonde; ~ **trip** n (viaggio di) andata e ritorno; ~**up** n raduno; (of criminals) retata.

rouse [rauz] vt (wake up) svegliare; (stir up) destare; provocare; risvegliare; **rousing** a (speech, applause) entusiastico(a).

rout [raut] n (MIL) rotta // vt mettere in rotta.

route [ru:t] n itinerario; (of bus) percorso; (of trade, shipping) rotta.

routine [ru:'ti:n] a (work) corrente, abituale; (procedure) solito(a) // n (pej) routine f, tran tran m; (THEATRE) numero; **daily** ~ orario quotidiano.

roving ['rəuvıŋ] a (life) itinerante.

row [rəu] n (line) riga, fila; (KNITTING) ferro; (behind one another: of cars, people) fila // n (in boat) remare; (as sport) vogare // vi (boat) manovrare a remi; **in a** ~ (fig) di fila.

row [rau] n (noise) baccano, chiasso; (dispute) lite f // vi litigare.

rowdiness ['raudınıs] n baccano; (fighting) zuffa.

rowdy ['raudı] a chiassoso(a); turbolento(a) // n teppista m/f.

rowing ['rəuıŋ] n canottaggio; ~ **boat** n barca a remi.

rowlock ['rɔlək] n scalmo.

royal ['rɔɪəl] *a* reale; ~**ist** *a, n* realista (*m/f*).

royalty ['rɔɪəltɪ] *n* (*royal persons*) (membri *mpl* della) famiglia reale; (*payment: to author*) diritti *mpl* d'autore; (: *to inventor*) diritti di brevetto.

r.p.m. *abbr* (= *revs per minute*) giri/min. (giri/minuto).

R.S.V.P. *abbr* (= *répondez s'il vous plaît*) R.S.V.P.

Rt Hon. *abbr* (= *Right Honourable*) ≈ Onorevole.

rub [rʌb] *n* (*with cloth*) fregata, strofinata; (*on person*) frizione *f*, massaggio // *vt* fregare, strofinare, frizionare; **to ~ sb up the wrong way** lisciare qd contro pelo; **to ~ off** *vi* andare via; **to ~ off on** lasciare una traccia su.

rubber ['rʌbə*] *n* gomma; ~ **band** *n* elastico; ~ **plant** *n* ficus elastica *m inv*; ~ **stamp** *n* timbro di gomma; ~**y** *a* gommoso(a).

rubbish ['rʌbɪʃ] *n* (*from household*) immondizie *fpl*, rifiuti *mpl*; (*fig: pej*) cose *fpl* senza valore; robaccia; sciocchezze *fpl*; ~ **bin** *n* pattumiera; ~ **dump** *n* (*in town*) immondezzaio.

rubble ['rʌbl] *n* macerie *fpl*; (*smaller*) pietrisco.

ruble ['ru:bl] *n* (*US*) = **rouble**.

ruby ['ru:bɪ] *n* rubino.

rucksack ['rʌksæk] *n* zaino.

rudder ['rʌdə*] *n* timone *m*.

ruddy ['rʌdɪ] *a* (*face*) fresco(a); (*col: damned*) maledetto(a).

rude [ru:d] *a* (*impolite: person*) scortese, rozzo(a); (: *word, manners*) grossolano(a), rozzo(a); (*shocking*) indecente; ~**ly** *ad* scortesemente; grossolanamente; ~**ness** *n* scortesia; grossolanità.

rudiment ['ru:dɪmənt] *n* rudimento; ~**ary** [-'mentərɪ] *a* rudimentale.

rueful ['ru:ful] *a* mesto(a), triste.

ruff [rʌf] *n* gorgiera.

ruffian ['rʌfɪən] *n* briccone *m*, furfante *m*.

ruffle ['rʌfl] *vt* (*hair*) scompigliare; (*clothes, water*) increspare; (*fig: person*) turbare.

rug [rʌg] *n* tappeto; (*for knees*) coperta.

rugby ['rʌgbɪ] *n* (*also*: ~ **football**) rugby *m*.

rugged ['rʌgɪd] *a* (*landscape*) aspro(a); (*features, determination*) duro(a); (*character*) brusco(a).

rugger ['rʌgə*] *n* (*col*) rugby *m*.

ruin ['ru:ɪn] *n* rovina // *vt* rovinare; (*spoil: clothes*) sciupare; ~**s** *npl* rovine *fpl*, ruderi *mpl*; ~**ation** [-'neɪʃən] *n* rovina; ~**ous** *a* rovinoso(a); (*expenditure*) inverosimile.

rule [ru:l] *n* regola; (*regulation*) regolamento, regola; (*government*) governo // *vt* (*country*) governare; (*person*) dominare; (*decide*) decidere // *vi* regnare; decidere; (*LAW*) dare una sentenza; **as a ~** normalmente; ~**d** *a* (*paper*) vergato(a); ~**r** *n* (*sovereign*) sovrano/a; (*leader*) capo (dello Stato); (*for measuring*) regolo, riga; **ruling** *a* (*party*) al potere;

(*class*) dirigente // *n* (*LAW*) decisione *f*.

rum [rʌm] *n* rum *m* // *a* (*col*) strano(a).

Rumania [ru:'meɪnɪə] *n* = **Romania**.

rumble ['rʌmbl] *n* rimbombo; brontolio // *vi* rimbombare; (*stomach, pipe*) brontolare.

rummage ['rʌmɪdʒ] *vi* frugare.

rumour ['ru:mə*] *n* voce *f* // *vt*: **it is** ~**ed that** corre voce che.

rump [rʌmp] *n* (*of animal*) groppa; ~ **steak** *n* bistecca di girello.

rumpus ['rʌmpəs] *n* (*col*) baccano; (: *quarrel*) rissa.

run [rʌn] *n* corsa; (*outing*) gita in macchina; (*distance travelled*) percorso, tragitto; (*series*) serie *f*; (*THEATRE*) periodo di rappresentazione; (*SKI*) pista // *vb* (*pt* **ran**, *pp* **run** [ræn, rʌn]) *vt* (*operate: business*) gestire, dirigere; (: *competition, course*) organizzare; (: *hotel*) gestire; (: *house*) governare; (*force through: rope, pipe*): **to ~ sth through** far passare qc attraverso; (*to pass: hand, finger*): **to ~ sth over** passare qc su; (*water, bath*) far scorrere // *vi* correre; (*pass: road etc*) passare; (*work: machine, factory*) funzionare, andare; (*bus, train: operate*) far servizio; (: *travel*) circolare; (*continue: play, contract*) durare; (*slide: drawer; flow: river, bath*) scorrere; (*colours, washing*) stemperarsi; (*in election*) presentarsi candidato; **there was a ~ on …** c'era una corsa a …; **in the long ~** alla lunga; in fin dei conti; **on the ~** in fuga; **I'll ~ you to the station** la porto alla stazione; **to ~ a risk** correre un rischio; **to ~ about** *vi* (*children*) correre qua e là; **to ~ across** *vt fus* (*find*) trovare per caso; **to ~ away** *vi* fuggire; **to ~ down** *vi* (*clock*) scaricarsi // *vt* (*AUT*) investire; (*criticize*) criticare; **to be ~ down** essere esausto(a) or a zero; **to ~ off** *vi* fuggire; **to ~ out** *vi* (*person*) uscire di corsa; (*liquid*) colare; (*lease*) scadere; (*money*) esaurirsi; **to ~ out of** *vt fus* rimanere a corto di; **to ~ over** *vt sep* (*AUT*) investire, arrotare // *vt fus* (*revise*) rivedere; **to ~ through** *vt fus* (*instructions*) dare una scorsa a; **to ~ up** *vt* (*debt*) lasciar accumulare; **to ~ up against** (*difficulties*) incontrare; ~**away** *a* (*person*) fuggiasco(a); (*horse*) in libertà; (*truck*) fuori controllo; (*inflation*) galoppante.

rung [rʌŋ] *pp of* **ring** // *n* (*of ladder*) piolo.

runner ['rʌnə*] *n* (*in race*) corridore *m*; (*on sledge*) pattino; (*for drawer etc, carpet: in hall etc*) guida; ~ **bean** *n* (*BOT*) fagiolo rampicante; ~**-up** *n* secondo(a) arrivato(a).

running ['rʌnɪŋ] *n* corsa; direzione *f*; organizzazione *f*; funzionamento // *a* (*water*) corrente; (*commentary*) simultaneo(a); **6 days ~** 6 giorni di seguito.

runny ['rʌnɪ] *a* che cola.

run-of-the-mill ['rʌnəvðə'mɪl] *a* solito(a), banale.

runt [rʌnt] *n* (*also: pej*) omuncolo; (*ZOOL*)

animale *m* più piccolo del normale.
run-through ['rʌnθruː] *n* prova.
runway ['rʌnweɪ] *n* (*AVIAT*) pista (di decollo).
rupture ['rʌptʃə*] *n* (*MED*) ernia // *vt*: **to ~ o.s.** darsi un'ernia.
rural ['ruərl] *a* rurale.
ruse [ruːz] *n* trucco.
rush [rʌʃ] *n* corsa precipitosa; (*of crowd*) afflusso; (*hurry*) furia, fretta; (*current*) flusso // *vt* mandare or spedire velocemente; (*attack: town etc*) prendere d'assalto // *vi* precipitarsi; **don't ~ me!** non mi affrettate!; **~es** *npl* (*BOT*) giunchi *mpl*; **~ hour** *n* ora di punta.
rusk [rʌsk] *n* biscotto.
Russia ['rʌʃə] *n* Russia; **~n** *a* russo(a) // *n* russo/a; (*LING*) russo.
rust [rʌst] *n* ruggine *f* // *vi* arrugginirsi.
rustic ['rʌstɪk] *a* rustico(a) // *n* (*pej*) cafone/a.
rustle ['rʌsl] *vi* frusciare // *vt* (*paper*) far frusciare; (*US: cattle*) rubare.
rustproof ['rʌstpruːf] *a* inossidabile.
rusty ['rʌstɪ] *a* arrugginito(a).
rut [rʌt] *n* solco; (*ZOOL*) fregola.
ruthless ['ruːθlɪs] *a* spietato(a).
rye ['raɪ] *n* segale *f.*

S

Sabbath ['sæbəθ] *n* (*Jewish*) sabato; (*Christian*) domenica.
sabbatical [sə'bætɪkl] *a*: **~ year** *n* anno sabbatico.
sabotage ['sæbətɑːʒ] *n* sabotaggio // *vt* sabotare.
saccharin(e) ['sækərɪn] *n* saccarina.
sack [sæk] *n* (*bag*) sacco // *vt* (*dismiss*) licenziare, mandare a spasso; (*plunder*) saccheggiare; **to get the ~** essere mandato a spasso; **a ~ful of** un sacco di; **~ing** *n* tela di sacco; (*dismissal*) licenziamento.
sacrament ['sækrəmənt] *n* sacramento.
sacred ['seɪkrɪd] *a* sacro(a).
sacrifice ['sækrɪfaɪs] *n* sacrificio // *vt* sacrificare.
sacrilege ['sækrɪlɪdʒ] *n* sacrilegio.
sacrosanct ['sækrəʊsæŋkt] *a* sacrosanto(a).
sad [sæd] *a* triste; **~den** *vt* rattristare.
saddle ['sædl] *n* sella // *vt* (*horse*) sellare; **to be ~d with sth** (*col*) avere qc sulle spalle; **~bag** *n* bisaccia; (*on bicycle*) borsa.
sadism ['seɪdɪzm] *n* sadismo; **sadist** *n* sadico/a; **sadistic** [sə'dɪstɪk] *a* sadico(a).
sadness ['sædnɪs] *n* tristezza.
safari [sə'fɑːrɪ] *n* safari *m inv.*
safe [seɪf] *a* sicuro(a); (*out of danger*) salvo(a), al sicuro; (*cautious*) prudente // *n* cassaforte *f*; **~ from** al sicuro da; **~ and sound** sano(a) e salvo(a); **(just) to be on the ~ side** per non correre rischi; **~guard** *n* salvaguardia // *vt* salvaguardare; **~keeping** *n* custodia;

~ly *ad* sicuramente; sano(a) e salvo(a); prudentemente.
safety ['seɪftɪ] *n* sicurezza; **~ belt** *n* cintura di sicurezza; **~ pin** *n* spilla di sicurezza.
saffron ['sæfrən] *n* zafferano.
sag [sæg] *vi* incurvarsi; afflosciarsi.
sage [seɪdʒ] *n* (*herb*) salvia; (*man*) saggio.
Sagittarius [sædʒɪ'teərɪəs] *n* Sagittario.
sago ['seɪɡəʊ] *n* sagù *m.*
said [sɛd] *pt, pp of* **say.**
sail [seɪl] *n* (*on boat*) vela; (*trip*): **to go for a ~** fare un giro in barca a vela // *vt* (*boat*) condurre, governare // *vi* (*travel: ship*) navigare; (: *passenger*) viaggiare per mare; (*set off*) salpare; (*SPORT*) fare della vela; **they ~ed into Genoa** entrarono nel porto di Genova; **to ~ through** (*fig*) *vt fus* superare senza difficoltà // *vi* farcela senza difficoltà; **~boat** *n* (*US*) barca a vela; **~ing** *n* (*SPORT*) vela; **to go ~ing** fare della vela; **~ing boat** *n* barca a vela; **~ing ship** *n* veliero; **~or** *n* marinaio.
saint [seɪnt] *n* santo/a.
sake [seɪk] *n*: **for the ~ of** per, per amore di, per il bene di; **for pity's ~** per pietà.
salad ['sæləd] *n* insalata; **~ bowl** *n* insalatiera; **~ cream** *n* (tipo di) maionese *f*; **~ dressing** *n* condimento per insalata; **~ oil** *n* olio da tavola.
salary ['sælərɪ] *n* stipendio.
sale [seɪl] *n* vendita; (*at reduced prices*) svendita, liquidazione *f*; **'for ~'** 'in vendita'; **on ~ or return** da vendere o rimandare; **~room** *n* sala delle aste; **~sman** *n* commesso; (*representative*) rappresentante *m*; **~swoman** *n* commessa.
salient ['seɪlɪənt] *a* saliente.
saliva [sə'laɪvə] *n* saliva.
sallow ['sæləʊ] *a* giallastro(a).
salmon ['sæmən] *n, pl inv* salmone *m.*
saloon [sə'luːn] *n* (*US*) saloon *m inv*, bar *m inv*; (*AUT*) berlina; (*ship's lounge*) salone *m.*
salt [sɔlt] *n* sale *m* // *vt* salare // *cpd* di sale; (*CULIN*) salato(a); **~ cellar** *n* saliera; **~y** *a* salato(a).
salutary ['sæljutərɪ] *a* salutare.
salute [sə'luːt] *n* saluto // *vt* salutare.
salvage ['sælvɪdʒ] *n* (*saving*) salvataggio; (*things saved*) beni *mpl* salvati or recuperati // *vt* salvare, mettere in salvo.
salvation [sæl'veɪʃən] *n* salvezza; **S~ Army** *n* Esercito della Salvezza.
salvo ['sælvəʊ] *n* salva.
same [seɪm] *a* stesso(a), medesimo(a) // *pronoun*: **the ~** lo(la) stesso(a), gli(le) stessi(e); **the ~ book** as lo stesso libro di (or che); **all or just the ~** tuttavia; **to do the ~** fare la stessa cosa; **to do the ~ as sb** fare come qd.
sample ['sɑːmpl] *n* campione *m* // *vt* (*food*) assaggiare; (*wine*) degustare.
sanatorium, *pl* **sanatoria** [sænə'tɔːrɪəm, -rɪə] *n* sanatorio.
sanctimonious [sæŋktɪ'məʊnɪəs] *a* bigotto(a), bacchettone(a).

sanction ['sæŋkʃən] n sanzione f // vt sancire, sanzionare.

sanctity ['sæŋktıtı] n santità.

sanctuary ['sæŋktjuərı] n (holy place) santuario; (refuge) rifugio; (for wildlife) riserva.

sand [sænd] n sabbia // vt cospargere di sabbia; ~s npl spiaggia.

sandal ['sændl] n sandalo.

sandcastle ['sændkɑ:sl] n castello di sabbia.

sand dune ['sænddju:n] n duna di sabbia.

sandpaper ['sændpeıpə*] n carta vetrata.

sandpit ['sændpıt] n (for children) buca di sabbia per i giochi dei bambini.

sandstone ['sændstəun] n arenaria.

sandwich ['sændwıtʃ] n tramezzino, panino, sandwich m inv // vt (also: ~ in) intramezzare, interporre; **cheese/ham ~ sandwich** al formaggio/prosciutto; **~ course** n corso di formazione professionale.

sandy ['sændı] a sabbioso(a); (colour) color sabbia inv, biondo(a) rossiccio(a).

sane [seın] a (person) sano(a) di mente; (outlook) sensato(a).

sang [sæŋ] pt of **sing.**

sanguine ['sæŋgwın] a ottimista.

sanitary ['sænıtərı] a (system, arrangements) sanitario(a); (clean) igienico(a); **~ towel, ~ napkin** (US) n assorbente m (igienico).

sanitation [sænı'teıʃən] n (in house) impianti mpl sanitari; (in town) fognature fpl.

sanity ['sænıtı] n sanità mentale; (common sense) buon senso.

sank [sæŋk] pt of **sink.**

Santa Claus [sæntə'klɔ:z] n Babbo Natale.

sap [sæp] n (of plants) linfa // vt (strength) fiaccare.

sapling ['sæplıŋ] n alberello.

sapphire ['sæfaıə*] n zaffiro.

sarcasm ['sɑ:kæzm] n sarcasmo.

sarcastic [sɑ:'kæstık] a sarcastico(a).

sardine [sɑ:'di:n] n sardina.

Sardinia [sɑ:'dınıə] n Sardegna f.

sash [sæʃ] n fascia; **~ window** n finestra a ghigliottina.

sat [sæt] pt,pp of **sit.**

Satan ['seıtən] n Satana m.

satchel ['sætʃl] n cartella.

satellite ['sætəlaıt] a, n satellite (m).

satin ['sætın] n raso, satin m // a di o in satin.

satire ['sætaıə*] n satira; **satirical** [sə'tırıkl] a satirico(a).

satisfaction [sætıs'fækʃən] n soddisfazione f.

satisfactory [sætıs'fæktərı] a soddisfacente.

satisfy ['sætısfaı] vt soddisfare; (convince) convincere; **~ing** a soddisfacente.

saturate ['sætʃəreıt] vt: **to ~ (with)** saturare (di).

Saturday ['sætədı] n sabato.

sauce [sɔ:s] n salsa; (containing meat, fish) sugo; **~pan** n casseruola.

saucer ['sɔ:sə*] n sottocoppa m, piattino.

saucy ['sɔ:sı] a impertinente.

saunter ['sɔ:ntə*] vi andare a zonzo, bighellonare.

sausage ['sɔsıdʒ] n salsiccia; **~ roll** n rotolo di pasta sfoglia ripiena di salsiccia.

savage ['sævıdʒ] a (cruel, fierce) selvaggio(a), feroce; (primitive) primitivo(a) // n selvaggio/a // vt attaccare selvaggiamente; **~ry** n crudeltà, ferocia.

save [seıv] vt (person, belongings) salvare; (money) risparmiare, mettere da parte; (time) risparmiare; (food) conservare; (avoid: trouble) evitare // vi (also: ~ up) economizzare // n (SPORT) parata // prep salvo, a eccezione di.

saving ['seıvıŋ] n risparmio // a: **the ~ grace of** l'unica cosa buona di; **~s** npl risparmi mpl; **~s bank** n cassa di risparmio.

saviour ['seıvjə*] n salvatore m.

savour ['seıvə*] n sapore m, gusto // vt gustare; **~y** a saporito(a); (dish: not sweet) salato(a).

saw [sɔ:] pt of **see** // n (tool) sega // vt (pt **sawed**, pp **sawed** or **sawn** [sɔ:n]) segare; **~dust** n segatura; **~mill** n segheria.

saxophone ['sæksəfəun] n sassofono.

say [seı] n: **to have one's ~** fare sentire il proprio parere; **to have a ~** avere voce in capitolo // vt (pt, pp **said** [sɛd]) dire; **could you ~ that again?** potrebbe ripeterlo?; **that is to ~** cioè, vale a dire; **to ~ nothing of** per non parlare di; **~ that ...** mettiamo or diciamo che ...; **that goes without ~ing** va da sé; **~ing** n proverbio, detto.

scab [skæb] n crosta; (pej) crumiro/a; **~by** a crostoso(a).

scaffold ['skæfəuld] n impalcatura; (gallows) patibolo; **~ing** n impalcatura.

scald [skɔ:ld] n scottatura // vt scottare.

scale [skeıl] n scala; (of fish) squama // vt (mountain) scalare; **~s** npl bilancia; **on a large ~** su vasta scala; **~ model** n modello in scala; **small-~ model** n modello in scala ridotta.

scallop ['skɔləp] n pettine m.

scalp [skælp] n cuoio capelluto // vt scotennare.

scalpel ['skælpl] n bisturi m inv.

scamper ['skæmpə*] vi: **to ~ away, ~ off** darsela a gambe.

scan [skæn] vt scrutare; (glance at quickly) scorrere, dare un'occhiata a; (poetry) scandire; (TV) analizzare; (RADAR) esplorare.

scandal ['skændl] n scandalo; (gossip) pettegolezzi mpl; **~ize** vt scandalizzare; **~ous** a scandaloso(a).

Scandinavia [skændı'neıvıə] n Scandinavia; **~n** a, n scandinavo(a).

scant [skænt] a scarso(a); **~y** a insufficiente; (swimsuit) ridotto(a).

scapegoat ['skeıpgəut] n capro espiatorio.

scar [skɑ:] n cicatrice f // vt sfregiare.
scarce [skɛəs] a scarso(a); (copy, edition)
raro(a); ~**ly** ad appena; **scarcity** n
scarsità, mancanza.
scare [skɛə*] n spavento; panico // vt
spaventare, atterrire; **to ~ sb stiff**
spaventare a morte qd; ~**crow** n
spaventapasseri m inv; ~**d** a: **to be ~d**
aver paura; ~**monger** n allarmista m/f.
scarf, scarves [skɑ:f, skɑ:vz] n (long)
sciarpa; (square) fazzoletto da testa,
foulard m inv.
scarlet [skɑ:lɪt] a scarlatto(a); ~ **fever** n
scarlattina.
scarves [skɑ:vz] npl of **scarf**.
scathing [skeɪðɪŋ] a aspro(a).
scatter [skætə*] vt spargere; (crowd)
disperdere // vi disperdere; ~**brained** a
scervellato(a), sbadato(a); ~**ed** a
sparso(a), sparpagliato(a).
scatty [skætɪ] a (col) scervellato(a),
sbadato(a).
scavenger [skævəndʒə*] n spazzino.
scene [si:n] n (THEATRE, fig etc) scena; (of
crime, accident) scena, luogo; (sight, view)
vista, veduta; ~**ry** n (THEATRE) scenario;
(landscape) panorama m; **scenic** a
scenico(a); panoramico(a).
scent [sɛnt] n odore m, profumo; (fig:
track) pista; (sense of smell) olfatto,
odorato.
sceptic [skɛptɪk] n scettico/a; ~**al** a
scettico(a); ~**ism** [skɛptɪsɪzm] n
scetticismo.
sceptre [sɛptə*] n scettro.
schedule [ʃɛdju:l] n programma m, piano;
(of trains) orario; (of prices etc) lista,
tabella // vt stabilire; **as ~d** come
stabilito; **on ~** in orario; in regola con la
tabella di marcia; **to be ahead of/behind
~** essere in anticipo/ritardo sul previsto.
scheme [ski:m] n piano, progetto; (method) sistema m; (dishonest plan, plot)
intrigo, trama; (arrangement) disposizione
f, sistemazione f // vt progettare; (plot)
ordire // vi fare progetti; (intrigue)
complottare; **scheming** a intrigante // n
intrighi mpl, macchinazioni fpl.
schism [skɪzəm] n scisma m.
schizophrenic [skɪtsə'frɛnɪk] a
schizofrenico(a).
scholar [skɔlə*] n erudito/a; ~**ly** a
dotto(a), erudito(a); ~**ship** n erudizione f;
(grant) borsa di studio.
school [sku:l] n scuola; (in university)
scuola, facoltà f inv // cpd scolare,
scolastico(a) // vt (animal) addestrare;
~**book** n libro scolastico; ~**boy** n
scolaro; ~**days** npl giorni mpl di scuola;
~**girl** n scolara; ~**ing** n istruzione f;
~**leaving age** n età dell'adempimento
dell'obbligo scolastico; ~**master** n
(primary) maestro; (secondary) insegnante
m; ~**mistress** n maestra; insegnante f;
~**teacher** n insegnante m/f, docente m/f;
(primary) maestro/a.
schooner [sku:nə*] n (ship) goletta,

schooner m inv; (glass) bicchiere m alto da
sherry.
sciatica [saɪætɪkə] n sciatica.
science [saɪəns] n scienza; ~ **fiction** n
fantascienza; **scientific** [-tɪfɪk] a
scientifico(a); **scientist** n scienziato/a.
scintillating [sɪntɪleɪtɪŋ] a scintillante.
scissors [sɪzəz] npl forbici fpl; **a pair of
~** un paio di forbici.
scoff [skɔf] vt (col: eat) trangugiare,
ingozzare // vi: **to ~ (at)** (mock) farsi
beffe (di).
scold [skəuld] vt rimproverare.
scone [skɔn] n focaccina da tè.
scoop [sku:p] n mestolo; (for ice cream)
cucchiaio dosatore; (PRESS) colpo
giornalistico, notizia (in) esclusiva; **to ~
out** vt scavare; **to ~ up** vt tirare su,
sollevare.
scooter [sku:tə*] n (motor cycle)
motoretta, scooter m inv; (toy)
monopattino.
scope [skəup] n (capacity: of plan, undertaking) portata; (: of person) competenza;
(opportunity) opportunità; **within the ~
of** entro la competenza di.
scorch [skɔ:tʃ] vt (clothes) strinare,
bruciacchiare; (earth, grass) seccare,
bruciare; ~**er** n (col: hot day) giornata
torrida; ~**ing** a cocente, scottante.
score [skɔ:*] n punti mpl, punteggio; (MUS)
partitura, spartito; (twenty) venti // vt
(goal, point) segnare, fare; (success)
ottenere // vi segnare; (FOOTBALL) fare un
gol; (keep score) segnare i punti; **on that
~** a questo riguardo; ~**board** n tabellone
m segnapunti; ~**card** n (SPORT)
cartoncino segnapunti; ~**r** n marca-
tore/trice; (keeping score) segnapunti m
inv.
scorn [skɔ:n] n disprezzo // vt disprezzare.
Scorpio [skɔ:pɪəu] n Scorpione m.
scorpion [skɔ:pɪən] n scorpione m.
Scot [skɔt] n scozzese m/f.
scotch [skɔtʃ] vt (rumour etc) soffocare;
S~ n whisky m scozzese, scotch m.
scot-free [skɔt'fri:] a impunito(a).
Scotland [skɔtlənd] n Scozia.
Scots [skɔts] a scozzese; ~**man/woman** n
scozzese m/f.
Scottish [skɔtɪʃ] a scozzese.
scoundrel [skaundrl] n farabutto/a;
(child) furfantello/a.
scour [skauə*] vt (clean) pulire
strofinando; raschiare via; ripulire;
(search) battere, perlustrare.
scourge [skə:dʒ] n flagello.
scout [skaut] n (MIL) esploratore m; (also:
boy ~) giovane esploratore, scout m inv;
to ~ around vi cercare in giro.
scowl [skaul] vi acciglarsi, aggrottare le
sopracciglia; **to ~ at** guardare torvo.
scraggy [skrægɪ] a scarno(a), molto
magro(a).
scram [skræm] vi (col) filare via.
scramble [skræmbl] n arrampicata // vi
inerpicarsi; **to ~ for** azzuffarsi per; ~**d
eggs** npl uova fpl strapazzate.

scrap [skræp] n pezzo, pezzetto; (fight) zuffa; (also: ~ iron) rottami mpl di ferro, ferraglia // vt demolire; (fig) scartare; ~s npl (waste) scarti mpl; ~book n album m inv di ritagli.

scrape [skreip] vt,vi raschiare, grattare // n: to get into a ~ cacciarsi in un guaio; ~r n raschietto.

scrap: ~ heap n mucchio di rottami; ~ merchant n commerciante m di ferraglia; ~ paper n cartaccia; ~py a frammentario(a), sconnesso(a).

scratch [skrætʃ] n graffio // a: ~ team n squadra raccogliticcia // vt graffiare, rigare // vi grattare, graffiare; to start from ~ cominciare or partire da zero; to be up to ~ essere all'altezza.

scrawl [skrɔːl] n scarabocchio // vi scarabocchiare.

scrawny ['skrɔːnɪ] a scarno(a), pelle e ossa inv.

scream [skriːm] n grido, urlo // vi urlare, gridare.

scree [skriː] n ghiaione m.

screech [skriːtʃ] n strido; (of tyres, brakes) stridore m // vi stridere.

screen [skriːn] n schermo; (fig) muro, cortina, velo // vt schermare, fare schermo a; (from the wind etc) riparare; (film) proiettare; (book) adattare per lo schermo; (candidates etc) selezionare; ~ing n (MED) dépistage m inv.

screw [skruː] n vite f; (propeller) elica // vt avvitare; ~driver n cacciavite m; ~y a (col) svitato(a).

scribble ['skrɪbl] n scarabocchio // vt scribacchiare in fretta // vi scarabocchiare.

script [skrɪpt] n (CINEMA etc) copione m; (in exam) elaborato or compito d'esame.

Scripture ['skrɪptʃə*] n sacre Scritture fpl.

scriptwriter ['skrɪptraɪtə*] n soggettista m/f.

scroll [skrəul] n rotolo di carta.

scrounge [skraundʒ] vt (col): to ~ sth (off or from sb) scroccare (qc a qd) // vi: to ~ on sb vivere alle spalle di qd; ~r n scroccone/a.

scrub [skrʌb] n (clean) strofinata; (land) boscaglia // vt pulire strofinando; (reject) annullare.

scruff [skrʌf] n: by the ~ of the neck per la collottola.

scruffy ['skrʌfɪ] a sciatto(a).

scrum(mage) ['skrʌm(ɪdʒ)] n mischia.

scruple ['skruːpl] n scrupolo.

scrupulous ['skruːpjuləs] a scrupoloso(a).

scrutinize ['skruːtɪnaɪz] vt scrutare, esaminare attentamente.

scrutiny ['skruːtɪnɪ] n esame m accurato.

scuff [skʌf] vt (shoes) consumare strascicando.

scuffle ['skʌfl] n baruffa, tafferuglio.

scullery ['skʌlərɪ] n retrocucina m or f.

sculptor ['skʌlptə*] n scultore m.

sculpture ['skʌlptʃə*] n scultura.

scum [skʌm] n schiuma; (pej: people) feccia.

scurrilous ['skʌrɪləs] a scurrile, volgare.

scurry ['skʌrɪ] vi sgambare, affrettarsi.

scurvy ['skəːvɪ] n scorbuto.

scuttle ['skʌtl] n (also: coal ~) secchio del carbone // vt (ship) autoaffondare // vi (scamper): to ~ away, ~ off darsela a gambe, scappare.

scythe [saɪð] n falce f.

sea [siː] n mare m // cpd marino(a), del mare; (ship, sailor, port) marittimo(a), di mare; on the ~ (boat) in mare; (town) di mare; to be all at ~ (fig) non sapere che pesci pigliare; ~bird n uccello di mare; ~board n costa; ~ breeze n brezza di mare; ~farer n navigante m; ~food n frutti mpl di mare; ~ front n lungomare m; ~going a (ship) d'alto mare; ~gull n gabbiano.

seal [siːl] n (animal) foca; (stamp) sigillo; (impression) impronta del sigillo // vt sigillare.

sea level n livello del mare.

sea lion ['siːlaɪən] n leone m marino.

seam [siːm] n cucitura; (of coal) filone m.

seaman ['siːmən] n marinaio.

seamy ['siːmɪ] a orribile.

seance ['seɪɔns] n seduta spiritica.

seaplane ['siːpleɪn] n idrovolante m.

seaport ['siːpɔːt] n porto di mare.

search [səːtʃ] n (for person, thing) ricerca; (of drawer, pockets) esame m accurato; (LAW: at sb's home) perquisizione f // vt perlustrare, frugare; (examine) esaminare minuziosamente // vi: to ~ for ricercare; to ~ through vt fus frugare; in ~ of alla ricerca di; ~ing a minuzioso(a); penetrante; ~light n proiettore m; ~ party n squadra di soccorso; ~ warrant n mandato di perquisizione.

seashore ['siːʃɔː*] n spiaggia.

seasick ['siːsɪk] a che soffre il mal di mare.

seaside ['siːsaɪd] n spiaggia; ~ resort n stazione f balneare.

season ['siːzn] n stagione f // vt condire, insaporire; ~al a stagionale; ~ing n condimento; ~ ticket n abbonamento.

seat [siːt] n sedile m; (in bus, train: place) posto; (PARLIAMENT) seggio; (buttocks) didietro; (of trousers) fondo // vt far sedere; (have room for) avere or essere fornito(a) di posti a sedere per; ~ belt n cintura di sicurezza.

sea water ['siːwɔːtə*] n acqua di mare.

seaweed ['siːwiːd] n alga.

seaworthy ['siːwəːðɪ] a atto(a) alla navigazione.

sec. abbr of second(s).

secluded [sɪ'kluːdɪd] a isolato(a), appartato(a).

seclusion [sɪ'kluːʒən] n isolamento.

second ['sekənd] num secondo(a) // ad (in race etc) al secondo posto; (RAIL) in seconda // n (unit of time) secondo; (in series, position) secondo/a; (AUT: also: ~ gear) seconda; (COMM: imperfect) scarto

// vt (motion) appoggiare; ~ary a secondario(a); ~ary school n scuola secondaria; ~-class a di seconda classe; ~er n sostenitore/trice; ~hand a di seconda mano, usato(a); ~ hand n (on clock) lancetta dei secondi; ~ly ad in secondo luogo; ~-rate a scadente; ~ thoughts npl ripensamenti mpl; on ~ thoughts ripensandoci bene.

secrecy ['si:krəsɪ] n segretezza.

secret ['si:krɪt] a segreto(a) // n segreto.

secretariat [sɛkrɪ'tɛərɪət] n segretariato.

secretary ['sɛkrətərɪ] n segretario/a; S~ of State (for) (Brit: POL) ministro (di).

secretive ['si:krətɪv] a riservato(a).

sect [sɛkt] n setta; ~arian [-'tɛərɪən] a settario(a).

section ['sɛkʃən] n sezione f // vt sezionare, dividere in sezioni.

sector ['sɛktə*] n settore m.

secular ['sɛkjulə*] a secolare.

secure [sɪ'kjuə*] a (free from anxiety) sicuro(a); (firmly fixed) assicurato(a), ben fermato(a); (in safe place) al sicuro // vt (fix) fissare, assicurare; (get) ottenere, assicurarsi.

security [sɪ'kjuərɪtɪ] n sicurezza; (for loan) garanzia.

sedate [sɪ'deɪt] a posato(a); calmo(a) // vt calmare.

sedation [sɪ'deɪʃən] n (MED) l'effetto dei sedativi.

sedative ['sɛdɪtɪv] n sedativo, calmante m.

sediment ['sɛdɪmənt] n sedimento.

seduce [sɪ'dju:s] vt sedurre; seduction [-'dʌkʃən] n seduzione f; seductive [-'dʌktɪv] a seducente.

see [si:] vb (pt saw, pp seen [sɔ:, si:n]) vt vedere; (accompany): to ~ sb to the door accompagnare qd alla porta // vi vedere; (understand) capire // n sede f vescovile; to ~ that (ensure) badare che + sub, fare in modo che + sub; to ~ off vt salutare alla partenza; to ~ through vt portare a termine // vt fus non lasciarsi ingannare da; to ~ to vt fus occuparsi di.

seed [si:d] n seme m; (fig) germe m; (TENNIS) testa di serie; to go to ~ fare seme; (fig) scadere; ~ling n piantina di semenzaio; ~y a (shabby: person) sciatto(a); (: place) cadente.

seeing ['si:ɪŋ] cj: ~ (that) visto che.

seek, pt,pp sought [si:k, sɔ:t] vt cercare.

seem [si:m] vi sembrare, parere; there seems to be ... sembra che ci sia ...; ~ingly ad apparentemente.

seen [si:n] pp of see.

seep [si:p] vi filtrare, trapelare.

seer [sɪə*] n profeta/essa, veggente m/f.

seesaw ['si:sɔ:] n altalena a bilico.

seethe [si:ð] vi ribollire; to ~ with anger fremere di rabbia.

see-through ['si:θru:] a trasparente.

segment ['sɛgmənt] n segmento.

segregate ['sɛgrɪgeɪt] vt segregare, isolare.

seismic ['saɪzmɪk] a sismico(a).

seize [si:z] vt (grasp) afferrare; (take possession of) impadronirsi di; (LAW) sequestrare; to ~ (up)on vt fus ricorrere a; to ~ up vi (TECH) grippare.

seizure ['si:ʒə*] n (MED) attacco; (LAW) confisca, sequestro.

seldom ['sɛldəm] ad raramente.

select [sɪ'lɛkt] a scelto(a) // vt scegliere, selezionare; ~ion [-'lɛkʃən] n selezione f, scelta; ~ive a selettivo(a).

self [sɛlf] n (pl selves [sɛlvz]): the ~ l'io m // prefix auto...; ~-assured a sicuro(a) di sé; ~-catering a in cui ci si cucina da sé; ~-centred a egocentrico(a); ~-coloured a monocolore; ~-confidence n sicurezza di sé; ~-conscious a timido(a); ~-contained a (flat) indipendente; ~-control n autocontrollo; ~-defence n autodifesa; (LAW) legittima difesa; ~-discipline n autodisciplina; ~-employed a che lavora in proprio; ~-evident a evidente; ~-explanatory a ovvio(a); ~-indulgent a indulgente verso se stesso(a); ~-interest n interesse m personale; ~-ish a egoista; ~-ishness n egoismo; ~-lessly ad altruisticamente; ~-pity n autocommiserazione f; ~-portrait n autoritratto; ~-possessed a controllato(a); ~-preservation n istinto di conservazione; ~-respect n rispetto di sé, amor proprio; ~-respecting a che ha rispetto di sé; ~-righteous a soddisfatto(a) di sé; ~-sacrifice n abnegazione f; ~-satisfied a compiaciuto(a) di sé; ~-seal a autosigillante; ~-service n autoservizio, self-service m; ~-sufficient a autosufficiente; ~-supporting a economicamente indipendente.

sell, pt,pp sold [sɛl, səuld] vt vendere // vi vendersi; to ~ at or for 1000 lire essere in vendita a 1000 lire; to ~ off vt svendere, liquidare; ~er n venditore/trice; ~ing price n prezzo di vendita.

sellotape ['sɛləuteɪp] n ® nastro adesivo, scotch m ®.

sellout ['sɛlaut] n tradimento; (of tickets): it was a ~ registrò un tutto esaurito.

selves [sɛlvz] npl of self.

semantic [sɪ'mæntɪk] a semantico(a); ~s n semantica.

semaphore ['sɛməfɔ:*] n segnali mpl con bandiere; (RAIL) semaforo.

semen ['si:mən] n sperma m.

semi ['sɛmɪ] prefix semi...; ~-breve n semibreve f; ~-circle n semicerchio; ~-colon n punto e virgola; ~-conscious a parzialmente cosciente; ~-detached (house) n casa gemella; ~-final n semifinale f.

seminar ['sɛmɪnɑ:*] n seminario.

semiquaver ['sɛmɪkweɪvə*] n semicroma.

semiskilled ['sɛmɪ'skɪld] a: ~ worker n operaio(a) non specializzato(a).

semitone ['sɛmɪtəun] n (MUS) semitono.

semolina [semə'li:nə] n semolino.
senate ['senɪt] n senato; **senator** n senatore/trice.
send, pt,pp **sent** [send, sent] vt mandare; **to ~ sb to Coventry** dare l'ostracismo a qd; **to ~ away** vt (letter, goods) spedire; (person) mandare via; **to ~ away for** vt fus richiedere per posta, farsi spedire; **to ~ back** vt rimandare; **to ~ for** vt fus mandare a chiamare, far venire; **to ~ off** vt (goods) spedire; (SPORT: player) espellere; **to ~ out** vt (invitation) diramare; **to ~ up** vt (person, price) far salire; (parody) mettere in ridicolo; **~er** n mittente m/f.
senile ['si:naɪl] a senile.
senior ['si:nɪə*] a (older) più vecchio(a); (of higher rank) di grado più elevato // n persona più anziana; (in service) persona con maggiore anzianità; **~ity** [-'ɔrɪtɪ] n anzianità.
sensation [sen'seɪʃən] n sensazione f; **to create a ~** fare scalpore; **~al** a sensazionale; (marvellous) eccezionale.
sense [sens] n senso; (feeling) sensazione f, senso; (meaning) senso, significato; (wisdom) buonsenso // vt sentire, percepire; **it makes ~** ha senso; **~s** npl ragione f; **~less** a sciocco(a); (unconscious) privo(a) di sensi.
sensibility [sensɪ'bɪlɪtɪ] n sensibilità; **sensibilities** npl sensibilità sg.
sensible ['sensɪbl] a sensato(a), ragionevole.
sensitive ['sensɪtɪv] a: **~ (to)** sensibile (a); **sensitivity** [-'tɪvɪtɪ] n sensibilità.
sensual ['sensjʊəl] a sensuale.
sensuous ['sensjʊəs] a sensuale.
sent [sent] pt,pp of **send**.
sentence ['sentns] n (LING) frase f; (LAW: judgment) sentenza; (: punishment) condanna // vt: **to ~ sb to death/to 5 years** condannare qd a morte/a 5 anni.
sentiment ['sentɪmənt] n sentimento; (opinion) opinione f; **~al** [-'mentl] a sentimentale.
sentry ['sentrɪ] n sentinella.
separate a ['seprɪt] separato(a) // vb ['sepəreɪt] vt separare // vi separarsi; **~ly** ad separatamente; **~s** npl (clothes) coordinati mpl; **separation** [-'reɪʃən] n separazione f.
September [sep'tembə*] n settembre m.
septic ['septɪk] a settico(a); (wound) infettato(a).
sequel ['si:kwl] n conseguenza; (of story) seguito.
sequence ['si:kwəns] n (series) serie f; (order) ordine m.
sequin ['si:kwɪn] n lustrino, paillette f inv.
serenade [serə'neɪd] n serenata.
serene [sɪ'ri:n] a sereno(a), calmo(a); **serenity** [sə'renɪtɪ] n serenità, tranquillità.
sergeant ['sɑːdʒənt] n sergente m; (POLICE) brigadiere m.
serial ['sɪərɪəl] n (PRESS) romanzo a puntate; (RADIO, TV) trasmissione f a

puntate // a (number) di serie; **~ize** vt pubblicare a puntate; trasmettere a puntate.
series ['sɪəri:s] n serie f inv; (PUBLISHING) collana.
serious ['sɪərɪəs] a serio(a), grave; **~ly** ad seriamente; **~ness** n serietà, gravità.
sermon ['sə:mən] n sermone m.
serrated [sɪ'reɪtɪd] a seghettato(a).
serum ['sɪərəm] n siero.
servant ['sə:vənt] n domestico/a.
serve [sə:v] vt (employer etc) servire, essere a servizio di; (purpose) servire a; (customer, food, meal) servire; (apprenticeship) fare; (prison term) scontare // vi (also TENNIS) servire; (be useful): **to ~ as/for/to do** servire da/per/per fare // n (TENNIS) servizio; **it ~s him right** ben gli sta, se l'èmeritata; **to ~ out, ~ up** vt (food) servire.
service ['sə:vɪs] n servizio; (AUT: maintenance) assistenza, revisione f // vt (car, washing machine) revisionare; **the S~s** le forze armate; **to be of ~ to sb, to do sb a ~** essere d'aiuto a qd; **to put one's car in for (a) ~** portare la macchina in officina per una revisione; **dinner ~** n servizio da tavola; **~able** a pratico(a), utile; **~ area** n (on motorway) area di servizio; **~man** n militare m; **~ station** n stazione f di servizio.
serviette [sə:vi'et] n tovagliolo.
servile ['sə:vaɪl] a servile.
session ['seʃən] n (sitting) seduta, sessione f; (SCOL) anno scolastico (or accademico); **to be in ~** essere in seduta.
set [set] n serie f inv; (RADIO, TV) apparecchio; (TENNIS) set m inv; (group of people) mondo, ambiente m; (CINEMA) scenario; (THEATRE: stage) scene fpl; (: scenery) scenario; (MATH) insieme m; (HAIRDRESSING) messa in piega // a (fixed) stabilito(a), determinato(a); (ready) pronto(a) // vb (pt, pp set) (place) posare, mettere; (fix) fissare; (adjust) regolare; (decide: rules etc) stabilire, fissare; (TYP) comporre // vi (sun) tramontare; (jam, jelly) rapprendersi; (concrete) fare presa; **to be ~ on doing** essere deciso a fare; **to be ~ against** essere completamente contrario a; **to ~ (to music)** mettere in musica; **to ~ on fire** dare fuoco a; **to ~ free** liberare; **to ~ sail** prendere il mare; **to ~ about** vt fus (task) intraprendere, mettersi a; **to ~ aside** vt mettere da parte; **to ~ back** vt (in time): **to ~ back (by)** mettere indietro (di); **to ~ off** vi partire // vt (bomb) far scoppiare; (cause to start) mettere in moto; (show up well) dare risalto a; **to ~ out** vi: **to ~ out to do** proporsi di fare // vt (arrange) disporre; (state) esporre, presentare; **to ~ up** vt (organization) fondare, costituire; (record) stabilire; (monument) innalzare; **~back** n (hitch) contrattempo, inconveniente m.
settee [se'ti:] n divano, sofà m inv.

setting ['sɛtɪŋ] *n* ambiente *m*; (*of jewel*) montatura.

settle ['sɛtl] *vt* (*argument, matter*) appianare; (*problem*) risolvere; (*MED: calm*) calmare // *vi* (*bird, dust etc*) posarsi; (*sediment*) depositarsi; (*also:* ~ **down**) sistemarsi, stabilirsi; calmarsi; **to** ~ **to** **sth** applicarsi a qc; **to** ~ **for sth** accontentarsi di qc; **to** ~ **in** *vi* sistemarsi; **to** ~ **on sth** decidersi per qc; **to** ~ **up** **with sb** regolare i conti con qd; ~**ment** *n* (*payment*) pagamento, saldo; (*agreement*) accordo; (*colony*) colonia; (*village etc*) villaggio, comunità *f inv*; ~**r** *n* colonizzatore/trice.

setup ['sɛtʌp] *n* (*arrangement*) situazione *f*; sistemazione *f*; (*situation*) situazione.

seven ['sɛvn] *num* sette; ~**teen** *num* diciassette; ~**th** *num* settimo(a); ~**ty** *num* settanta.

sever ['sɛvə*] *vt* recidere, tagliare; (*relations*) troncare.

several ['sɛvərl] *a, pronoun* alcuni(e), diversi(e); ~ **of us** alcuni di noi.

severe [sɪ'vɪə*] *a* severo(a); (*serious*) serio(a), grave; (*hard*) duro(a); (*plain*) semplice, sobrio(a); **severity** [sɪ'vɛrɪtɪ] *n* severità; gravità; (*of weather*) rigore *m*.

sew, *pt* **sewed**, *pp* **sewn** [səu, səud, səun] *vt, vi* cucire; **to** ~ **up** *vt* ricucire.

sewage ['su:ɪdʒ] *n* acque *fpl* di scolo.

sewer ['su:ə*] *n* fogna.

sewing ['səuɪŋ] *n* cucitura; cucito; ~ **machine** *n* macchina da cucire.

sewn [səun] *pp* of **sew**.

sex [sɛks] *n* sesso; **to have** ~ **with** avere rapporti sessuali con; ~ **act** *n* atto sessuale.

sexual ['sɛksjuəl] *a* sessuale.

sexy ['sɛksɪ] *a* provocante, sexy *inv*.

shabby ['ʃæbɪ] *a* malandato(a); (*behaviour*) vergognoso(a).

shack [ʃæk] *n* baracca, capanna.

shackles ['ʃæklz] *npl* ferri *mpl*, catene *fpl*.

shade [ʃeɪd] *n* ombra; (*for lamp*) paralume *m*; (*of colour*) tonalità *f inv*; (*small quantity*): **a** ~ **of** un po' or un'ombra di // *vt* ombreggiare, fare ombra a; **in the** ~ all'ombra; **a** ~ **smaller** un tantino più piccolo.

shadow ['ʃædəu] *n* ombra // *vt* (*follow*) pedinare; ~ **cabinet** *n* (*POL*) governo *m* ombra *inv*; ~**y** *a* ombreggiato(a), ombroso(a); (*dim*) vago(a), indistinto(a).

shady ['ʃeɪdɪ] *a* ombroso(a); (*fig: dishonest*) losco(a), equivoco(a).

shaft [ʃɑːft] *n* (*of arrow, spear*) asta; (*AUT, TECH*) albero; (*of mine*) pozzo; (*of lift*) tromba; (*of light*) raggio.

shaggy ['ʃægɪ] *a* ispido(a).

shake [ʃeɪk] *vb* (*pt* **shook**, *pp* **shaken** [ʃuk, 'ʃeɪkn]) *vt* scuotere; (*bottle, cocktail*) agitare // *vi* tremare // *n* scossa; **to** ~ **hands with sb** stringere or dare la mano a qd; **to** ~ **off** *vt* scrollare (via); (*fig*) sbarazzarsi di; **to** ~ **up** *vt* scuotere; ~-**up** *n* riorganizzazione *f* drastica; **shaky** *a*

(*hand, voice*) tremante; (*building*) traballante.

shale [ʃeɪl] *n* roccia scistosa.

shall [ʃæl] *auxiliary vb*: **I** ~ **go** andrò.

shallow ['ʃæləu] *a* poco profondo(a); (*fig*) superficiale.

sham [ʃæm] *n* finzione *f*, messinscena; (*jewellery, furniture*) imitazione *f* // *a* finto(a) // *vt* fingere, simulare.

shambles ['ʃæmblz] *n* confusione *f*, baraonda, scompiglio.

shame [ʃeɪm] *n* vergogna // *vt* far vergognare; **it is a** ~ (**that/to do**) è un peccato (che + *sub*/fare); **what a** ~! che peccato!; ~**faced** *a* vergognoso(a); ~**ful** *a* vergognoso(a); ~**less** *a* sfrontato(a); (*immodest*) spudorato(a).

shampoo [ʃæm'puː] *n* shampoo *m inv* // *vt* fare lo shampoo a.

shamrock ['ʃæmrɔk] *n* trifoglio (*simbolo nazionale dell'Irlanda*).

shandy ['ʃændɪ] *n* birra con gassosa.

shanty ['ʃæntɪ] *n* baracca, capanna; ~**town** *n* bidonville *f inv*.

shape [ʃeɪp] *n* forma // *vt* formare; (*statement*) formulare; (*sb's ideas*) condizionare // *vi* (*also:* ~ **up**) (*events*) andare, mettersi; (*person*) cavarsela; **to** **take** ~ prendere forma; -**shaped** *suffix*: **heart-shaped** *a* a forma di cuore; ~**less** *a* senza forma, informe; ~**ly** *a* ben proporzionato(a).

share [ʃɛə*] *n* (*thing received, contribution*) parte *f*; (*COMM*) azione *f* // *vt* dividere; (*have in common*) condividere, avere in comune; **to** ~ **out** (**among** or **between**) dividere (tra); ~**holder** *n* azionista *m/f*.

shark [ʃɑːk] *n* squalo, pescecane *m*.

sharp [ʃɑːp] *a* (*razor, knife*) affilato(a); (*point*) acuto(a), acuminato(a); (*nose, chin*) aguzzo(a); (*outline*) netto(a); (*cold, pain*) pungente; (*MUS*) diesis; (*voice*) stridulo(a); (*person*: *quick-witted*) sveglio(a); (: *unscrupulous*) disonesto(a) // *n* (*MUS*) diesis *m inv* // *ad*: **at 2 o'clock** ~ alle due in punto; ~**en** *vt* affilare; (*pencil*) fare la punta a; (*fig*) aguzzare; ~**ener** *n* (*also:* **pencil** ~**ener**) temperamatite *m* *inv*; (*also:* **knife** ~**ener**) affilacoltelli *m* *inv*; ~**eyed** *a* dalla vista acuta.

shatter ['ʃætə*] *vt* mandare in frantumi, frantumare; (*fig: upset*) distruggere; (: *ruin*) rovinare // *vi* frantumarsi, andare in pezzi.

shave [ʃeɪv] *vt* radere, rasare // *vi* radersi, farsi la barba // *n*: **to have a** ~ farsi la barba; ~ **n** *a* (*head*) rasato(a), tonsurato(a); ~**r** *n* (*also:* **electric** ~) rasoio elettrico.

shaving ['ʃeɪvɪŋ] *n* (*action*) rasatura; ~**s** *npl* (*of wood etc*) trucioli *mpl*; ~ **brush** *n* pennello da barba; ~ **cream** *n* crema da barba; ~ **soap** *n* sapone *m* da barba.

shawl [ʃɔːl] *n* scialle *m*.

she [ʃiː] *pronoun* ella, lei, essa; ~-**cat** *n* gatta; ~-**elephant** *n* elefantessa; *NB: for ships, countries follow the gender of your translation.*

sheaf, sheaves [ʃiːf, ʃiːvz] n covone m.
shear [ʃiə*] vt (pt ~ed, pp ~ed or shorn [ʃɔːn]) (sheep) tosare; to ~ off vt tosare; (branch) tagliare; ~s npl (for hedge) cesoie fpl.
sheath [ʃiːθ] n fodero, guaina; (contraceptive) preservativo.
sheaves [ʃiːvz] npl of sheaf.
shed [ʃɛd] n capannone m // vt (pt,pp shed) (leaves, fur etc) perdere; (tears) versare.
sheep [ʃiːp] n, pl inv pecora; ~dog n cane m da pastore; ~ish a vergognoso(a), timido(a); ~skin n pelle f di pecora.
sheer [ʃiə*] a (utter) vero(a) (e proprio(a)); (steep) a picco, perpendicolare; (almost transparent) sottile // ad a picco.
sheet [ʃiːt] n (on bed) lenzuolo; (of paper) foglio; (of glass) lastra; (of metal) foglio, lamina; ~ lightning n lampo diffuso.
sheik(h) [ʃeɪk] n sceicco.
shelf, shelves [ʃɛlf, ʃɛlvz] n scaffale m, mensola.
shell [ʃɛl] n (on beach) conchiglia; (of egg, nut etc) guscio; (explosive) granata; (of building) scheletro // vt (peas) sgranare; (MIL) bombardare, cannoneggiare.
shellfish [ˈʃɛlfɪʃ] n, pl inv (crab etc) crostaceo; (scallop etc) mollusco; (pl: as food) crostacei; molluschi.
shelter [ˈʃɛltə*] n riparo, rifugio // vt riparare, proteggere; (give lodging to) dare rifugio or asilo a // vi ripararsi, mettersi al riparo; ~ed a (life) ritirato(a); (spot) riparato(a), protetto(a).
shelve [ʃɛlv] vt (fig) accantonare, rimandare; ~s npl of shelf.
shepherd [ˈʃɛpəd] n pastore m // vt (guide) guidare.
sheriff [ˈʃɛrɪf] n sceriffo.
sherry [ˈʃɛrɪ] n sherry m.
shield [ʃiːld] n scudo // vt: to ~ (from) riparare (da), proteggere (da or contro).
shift [ʃɪft] n (change) cambiamento; (of workers) turno // vt spostare, muovere; (remove) rimuovere // vi spostarsi, muoversi; ~ work n lavoro a squadre; ~y a ambiguo(a); (eyes) sfuggente.
shilling [ˈʃɪlɪŋ] n scellino (= 12 old pence; 20 in a pound).
shilly-shally [ˈʃɪlɪʃælɪ] vi tentennare, esitare.
shimmer [ˈʃɪmə*] vi brillare, luccicare.
shin [ʃɪn] n tibia.
shine [ʃaɪn] n splendore m, lucentezza // vb (pt, pp shone [ʃɔn]) vi (ri)splendere, brillare // vt far brillare, far risplendere; (torch): to ~ sth on puntare qc verso.
shingle [ˈʃɪŋgl] n (on beach) ciottoli mpl; (on roof) assicella di copertura; ~s n (MED) erpete m.
shiny [ˈʃaɪnɪ] a lucente, lucido(a).
ship [ʃɪp] n nave f // vt trasportare (via mare); (send) spedire (via mare); (load) imbarcare, caricare; ~building n costruzione f navale; ~ment n carico; ~ping n (ships) naviglio; (traffic)

navigazione f; ~shape a in perfetto ordine; ~wreck n relitto; (event) naufragio; ~yard n cantiere m navale.
shire [ˈʃaɪə*] n contea.
shirk [ʃəːk] vt sottrarsi a, evitare.
shirt [ʃəːt] n (man's) camicia; in ~ sleeves in maniche di camicia; ~y a (col) incavolato(a).
shiver [ˈʃɪvə*] n brivido // vi rabbrividire, tremare.
shoal [ʃəʊl] n (of fish) banco.
shock [ʃɔk] n (impact) urto, colpo; (ELEC) scossa; (emotional) colpo, shock m inv; (MED) shock // vt colpire, scioccare; scandalizzare; ~ absorber n ammortizzatore m; ~ing a scioccante, traumatizzante; scandaloso(a), oltraggioso(a); ~proof a antiurto inv.
shod [ʃɔd] pt, pp of shoe.
shoddy [ˈʃɔdɪ] a scadente.
shoe [ʃuː] n scarpa; (also: horse~) ferro di cavallo // vt (pt,pp shod [ʃɔd]) (horse) ferrare; ~brush n spazzola per le scarpe; ~horn n calzante m; ~lace n stringa; ~ polish n lucido per scarpe; ~shop n calzoleria; ~tree n forma per scarpe.
shone [ʃɔn] pt,pp of shine.
shook [ʃʊk] pt of shake.
shoot [ʃuːt] n (on branch, seedling) germoglio // vb (pt,pp shot [ʃɔt]) vt (game) cacciare, andare a caccia di; (person) sparare a; (execute) fucilare; (film) girare // vi (with gun): to ~ (at) sparare (a), fare fuoco (su); (with bow): to ~ (at) tirare (su); (FOOTBALL) sparare, tirare (forte); to ~ down vt (plane) abbattere; to ~ in/out vi entrare/uscire come una freccia; to ~ up vi (fig) salire alle stelle; ~ing n (shots) sparatoria; (HUNTING) caccia; ~ing range n poligono (di tiro), tirassegno; ~ing star n stella cadente.
shop [ʃɔp] n negozio; (workshop) officina // vi (also: go ~ping) fare spese; ~ assistant n commesso/a; ~ floor n officina; (fig) operai mpl, maestranze fpl; ~keeper n negoziante m/f, bottegaio/a; ~lifting n taccheggio; ~per n compratore/trice; ~ping n (goods) spesa, acquisti mpl; ~ping bag n borsa per la spesa; ~ping centre n centro commerciale; ~soiled a sciupato(a) a forza di stare in vetrina; ~ steward n (INDUSTRY) rappresentante m sindacale; ~ window n vetrina.
shore [ʃɔː*] n (of sea) riva, spiaggia; (of lake) riva // vt: to ~ (up) puntellare.
shorn [ʃɔːn] pp of shear.
short [ʃɔːt] a (not long) corto(a); (soon finished) breve; (person) basso(a); (curt) brusco(a), secco(a); (insufficient) insufficiente // n (also: ~ film) cortometraggio; (a pair of) ~s (i) calzoncini; to be ~ of sth essere a corto di or mancare di qc; I'm 3 ~ me ne mancano 3; in ~ in breve; ~ of doing a meno che non si faccia; everything ~ of tutto fuorché; it is ~ for è

l'abbreviazione *or* il diminutivo di; **to cut ~** (*speech, visit*) accorciare, abbreviare; (*person*) interrompere; **to fall ~ of** non essere all'altezza di; **to stop ~** fermarsi di colpo; **to stop ~ of** non arrivare fino a; **~age** *n* scarsezza, carenza; **~bread** *n* biscotto di pasta frolla; **~circuit** *n* cortocircuito // *vt* cortocircuitare // *vi* fare cortocircuito; **~coming** *n* difetto; **~(crust) pastry** *n* pasta frolla; **~cut** *n* scorciatoia; **~en** *vt* accorciare, ridurre; **~hand** *n* stenografia; **~hand typist** *n* stenodattilografo/a; **~ list** *n* (*for job*) rosa dei candidati; **~-lived** *a* effimero(a), di breve durata; **~ly** *ad* fra poco; **~-sighted** *a* miope; **~ story** *n* racconto, novella; **~-tempered** *a* irascibile; **~-term** *a* (*effect*) di *or* a breve durata; **~wave** *n* (*RADIO*) onde *fpl* corte.

shot [ʃɔt] *pt,pp of* **shoot** // *n* sparo, colpo; (*person*) tiratore *m*; (*try*) prova; (*injection*) iniezione *f*; (*PHOT*) foto *f inv*; **like a ~** come un razzo; (*very readily*) immediatamente; **~gun** *n* fucile *m* da caccia.

should [ʃud] *auxiliary vb*: **I ~ go now** dovrei andare ora; **he ~ be there now** dovrebbe essere arrivato ora; **I ~ go if I were you** se fossi in te andrei; **I ~ like** to mi piacerebbe.

shoulder [ˈʃəuldə*] *n* spalla; (*of road*): **hard ~** banchina // *vt* (*fig*) addossarsi, prendere sulle proprie spalle; **~ bag** *n* borsa a tracolla; **~ blade** *n* scapola; **~ strap** *n* bretella, spallina.

shout [ʃaut] *n* urlo, grido // *vt* gridare // *vi* urlare, gridare; **to give sb a ~** chiamare qd gridando; **to ~ down** *vt* zittire gridando; **~ing** *n* urli *mpl*.

shove [ʃʌv] *vt* spingere; (*col: put*): **to ~ sth in** ficcare qc in; **to ~ off** *vi* (*NAUT*) scostarsi.

shovel [ˈʃʌvl] *n* pala // *vt* spalare.

show [ʃəu] *n* (*of emotion*) dimostrazione *f*, manifestazione *f*; (*semblance*) apparenza *f*; (*exhibition*) mostra, esposizione *f*; (*THEATRE, CINEMA*) spettacolo // *vb* (*pt* **~ed**, *pp* **shown** [ʃəun]) *vt* far vedere, mostrare; (*courage etc*) dimostrare, dar prova di; (*exhibit*) esporre // *vi* vedersi, essere visibile; **to ~ sb in** far entrare qd; **to ~ off** *vi* (*pej*) esibirsi, mettersi in mostra // *vt* (*display*) mettere in risalto; (*pej*) mettere in mostra; **to ~ sb out** accompagnare qd alla porta; **to ~ up** *vi* (*stand out*) essere ben visibile; (*col: turn up*) farsi vedere // *vt* mettere in risalto; (*unmask*) smascherare; **~ business** *n* industria dello spettacolo; **~down** *n* prova di forza.

shower [ˈʃauə*] *n* (*rain*) acquazzone *m*; (*of stones etc*) pioggia; (*also*: **~bath**) doccia // *vi* fare la doccia // *vt*: **to ~ sb with** (*gifts, abuse etc*) coprire qd di; (*missiles*) lanciare contro qd una pioggia di.

showground [ˈʃəugraund] *n* terreno d'esposizione.

showing [ˈʃəuiŋ] *n* (*of film*) proiezione *f*.

show jumping [ˈʃəudʒʌmpiŋ] *n* concorso ippico (di salto ad ostacoli).

showmanship [ˈʃəumənʃip] *n* abilità d'impresario.

shown [ʃəun] *pp of* **show**.

show-off [ˈʃəuɔf] *n* (*col: person*) esibizionista *m/f*.

showroom [ˈʃəurum] *n* sala d'esposizione.

shrank [ʃræŋk] *pt of* **shrink**.

shrapnel [ˈʃræpnl] *n* shrapnel *m*.

shred [ʃred] *n* (*gen pl*) brandello // *vt* fare a brandelli; (*CULIN*) sminuzzare, tagliuzzare.

shrewd [ʃruːd] *a* astuto(a), scaltro(a).

shriek [ʃriːk] *n* strillo // *vt, vi* strillare.

shrift [ʃrift] *n*: **to give sb short ~** sbrigare qd.

shrill [ʃril] *a* acuto(a), stridulo(a), stridente.

shrimp [ʃrimp] *n* gamberetto.

shrine [ʃrain] *n* reliquario; (*place*) santuario.

shrink [ʃriŋk] *vb* (*pt* **shrank**, *pp* **shrunk** [ʃræŋk, ʃrʌŋk]) *vi* restringersi; (*fig*) ridursi // *vt* (*wool*) far restringere // *n* (*col: pej*) psicanalista *m/f*; **~age** *n* restringimento.

shrivel [ˈʃrivl] (*also*: **~ up**) *vt* raggrinzare, avvizzire // *vi* raggrinzirsi, avvizzire.

shroud [ʃraud] *n* sudario // *vt*: **~ed in mystery** avvolto(a) nel mistero.

Shrove Tuesday [ˈʃrəuvˈtjuːzdi] *n* martedì *m* grasso.

shrub [ʃrʌb] *n* arbusto; **~bery** *n* arbusti *mpl*.

shrug [ʃrʌg] *n* scrollata di spalle // *vt,vi*: **to ~ (one's shoulders)** alzare le spalle, fare spallucce; **to ~ off** *vt* passare sopra a.

shrunk [ʃrʌŋk] *pp of* **shrink**; **~en** *a* rattrappito(a).

shudder [ˈʃʌdə*] *n* brivido // *vi* rabbrividire.

shuffle [ˈʃʌfl] *vt* (*cards*) mescolare; **to ~ (one's feet)** strascicare i piedi.

shun [ʃʌn] *vt* sfuggire, evitare.

shunt [ʃʌnt] *vt* (*RAIL: direct*) smistare; (: *divert*) deviare // *vi*: **to ~ (to and fro)** fare la spola.

shut, *pt, pp* **shut** [ʃʌt] *vt* chiudere // *vi* chiudersi, chiudere; **to ~ down** *vt, vi* chiudere definitivamente; **to ~ off** *vt* fermare, bloccare; **to ~ up** *vi* (*col: keep quiet*) stare zitto(a), fare silenzio // *vt* (*close*) chiudere; (*silence*) far tacere; **~ter** *n* imposta; (*PHOT*) otturatore *m*.

shuttle [ˈʃʌtl] *n* spola, navetta; (*also*: **~ service**) servizio *m* navetta *inv*.

shuttlecock [ˈʃʌtlkɔk] *n* volano.

shy [ʃai] *a* timido(a).

Siamese [saiəˈmiːz] *a*: **~ cat** gatto siamese.

Sicily [ˈsisili] *n* Sicilia.

sick [sik] *a* (*ill*) malato(a); (*vomiting*): **to be ~** vomitare; (*humour*) macabro(a); **to feel ~** avere la nausea; **to be ~ of** (*fig*) averne abbastanza di; **~ bay** *n* infermeria; ~**en** vt nauseare; ~**ening** a (fig) disgustoso(a), rivoltante.

sickle ['sɪkl] n falcetto.

sick: ~ **leave** n congedo per malattia; ~**ly** a malaticcio(a); (causing nausea) nauseante; ~**ness** n malattia; (vomiting) vomito; ~ **pay** n sussidio per malattia.

side [saɪd] n lato; (of lake) riva // cpd (door, entrance) laterale // vi: to ~ **with sb** parteggiare per qd, prendere le parti di qd; **by the** ~ **of** a fianco di; (road) sul ciglio di; ~ **by** ~ fianco a fianco; **to take** ~**s (with)** schierarsi (con); ~**board** n credenza; ~**boards**, ~**burns** npl (whiskers) basette fpl; ~ **effect** n (MED) effetto collaterale; ~**light** n (AUT) luce f di posizione; ~**line** n (SPORT) linea laterale; (fig) attività secondaria; ~**long** a obliquo(a); ~ **road** n strada secondaria; ~**saddle** ad all'amazzone; ~ **show** n attrazione f; ~**track** vt (fig) distrarre; ~**walk** n (US) marciapiede m; ~**ways** ad di traverso.

siding ['saɪdɪŋ] n (RAIL) binario di raccordo.

sidle ['saɪdl] vi: to ~ **up (to)** avvicinarsi furtivamente (a).

siege [si:dʒ] n assedio.

sieve [sɪv] n setaccio // vt setacciare.

sift [sɪft] vt passare al crivello; (fig) vagliare.

sigh [saɪ] n sospiro // vi sospirare.

sight [saɪt] n (faculty) vista; (spectacle) spettacolo; (on gun) mira // vt avvistare; **in** ~ in vista; **out of** ~ non visibile; ~**seeing** n giro turistico; **to go** ~**seeing** visitare una località; ~**seer** n turista m/f.

sign [saɪn] n segno; (with hand etc) segno, gesto; (notice) insegna, cartello // vt firmare; **to** ~ **in/out** vi firmare il registro (all'arrivo/alla partenza); **to** ~ **up** (MIL) vt arruolarsi // vi arruolarsi.

signal ['sɪɡnl] n segnale m // vt (person) fare segno a; (message) segnalare.

signature ['sɪɡnətʃə*] n firma; ~ **tune** n sigla musicale.

signet ring ['sɪɡnətrɪŋ] n anello con sigillo.

significance [sɪɡ'nɪfɪkəns] n significato; importanza.

significant [sɪɡ'nɪfɪkənt] a significante.

signify ['sɪɡnɪfaɪ] vt significare.

signpost ['saɪnpəust] n cartello indicatore.

silence ['saɪləns] n silenzio // vt far tacere, ridurre al silenzio; ~**r** n (on gun, AUT) silenziatore m.

silent ['saɪlnt] a silenzioso(a); (film) muto(a).

silhouette [sɪlu:'ɛt] n silhouette f inv.

silicon chip ['sɪlɪkən'tʃɪp] n piastrina di silicio.

silk [sɪlk] n seta // cpd di seta; ~**y** a di seta.

silly ['sɪlɪ] a stupido(a), sciocco(a).

silt [sɪlt] n limo.

silver ['sɪlvə*] n argento; (money) monete da 5, 10 o 50 pence; (also: ~**ware**) argenteria // cpd d'argento; ~ **paper** n carta argentata, (carta) stagnola; ~**-plated** a argentato(a); ~**smith** n argentiere m; ~**y** a (colour) argenteo(a); (sound) argentino(a).

similar ['sɪmɪlə*] a: ~ **(to)** simile (a); ~**ity** [-'lærɪtɪ] n somiglianza, rassomiglianza.

simile ['sɪmɪlɪ] n similitudine f.

simmer ['sɪmə*] vi cuocere a fuoco lento.

simple ['sɪmpl] a semplice; **simplicity** [-'plɪsɪtɪ] n semplicità; **simplify** ['sɪmplɪfaɪ] vt semplificare; **simply** ad semplicemente.

simulate ['sɪmjuleɪt] vt fingere, simulare.

simultaneous [sɪməl'teɪnɪəs] a simultaneo(a).

sin [sɪn] n peccato // vi peccare.

since [sɪns] ad da allora // prep da // cj (time) da quando; (because) poiché, dato che; ~ **then** da allora.

sincere [sɪn'sɪə*] a sincero(a); **sincerity** [-'sɛrɪtɪ] n sincerità.

sine [saɪn] n (MATH) seno.

sinew ['sɪnju:] n tendine m; ~**s** npl muscoli mpl.

sinful ['sɪnful] a peccaminoso(a).

sing, pt **sang**, pp **sung** [sɪŋ, sæŋ, sʌŋ] vt,vi cantare.

singe [sɪndʒ] vt bruciacchiare.

singer ['sɪŋə*] n cantante m/f.

single ['sɪŋgl] a solo(a), unico(a); (unmarried: man) celibe; (: woman) nubile; (not double) semplice // n (also: ~ **ticket**) biglietto di (sola) andata; (record) 45 giri m; ~**s** npl (TENNIS) singolo; **to** ~ **out** vt scegliere; (distinguish) distinguere; ~**-breasted** a a un petto; **in** ~ **file** in fila indiana; ~**-handed** ad senza aiuto, da solo(a); ~**-minded** a tenace, risoluto(a); ~ **room** n camera singola.

singlet ['sɪŋglɪt] n canottiera.

singly ['sɪŋglɪ] ad separatamente.

singular ['sɪŋgjulə*] a (exceptional, LING) singolare; (unusual) strano(a) // n (LING) singolare m.

sinister ['sɪnɪstə*] a sinistro(a).

sink [sɪŋk] n lavandino, acquaio // vb (pt **sank**, pp **sunk** [sæŋk, sʌŋk]) vt (ship) (fare) affondare, colare a picco; (foundations) scavare; (piles etc): to ~ **sth into** conficcare qc in // vi affondare, andare a fondo; (ground etc) cedere, avvallarsi; **to** ~ **in** vi conficcarsi, penetrare.

sinner ['sɪnə*] n peccatore/trice.

sinuous ['sɪnjuəs] a sinuoso(a).

sinus ['saɪnəs] n (ANAT) seno.

sip [sɪp] n sorso // vt sorseggiare.

siphon ['saɪfən] n sifone m; **to** ~ **off** vt travasare (con un sifone).

sir [sə*] n signore m; S~ **John Smith** Sir John Smith; **yes** ~ sì, signore.

siren ['saɪərn] n sirena.

sirloin ['sə:lɔɪn] n lombata di manzo.

sirocco [sɪ'rɔkəu] n scirocco.

sissy ['sɪsɪ] n (col) femminuccia.

sister ['sɪstə*] n sorella; (nun) suora;

(*nurse*) infermiera *f* caposala *inv*; ~-in-law *n* cognata.

sit, *pt,pp* **sat** [sɪt, sæt] *vi* sedere, sedersi; (*assembly*) essere in seduta // *vt* (*exam*) sostenere, dare; **to ~ down** *vi* sedersi; **to ~ up** *vi* tirarsi su a sedere; (*not go to bed*) stare alzato(a) fino a tardi.

site [saɪt] *n* posto; (*also*: **building ~**) cantiere *m* // *vt* situare.

sit-in ['sɪtɪn] *n* (*demonstration*) sit-in *m inv*, manifestazione *f* di protesta con occupazione.

sitting ['sɪtɪŋ] *n* (*of assembly etc*) seduta; (*in canteen*) turno; **~ room** *n* soggiorno.

situated ['sɪtjueɪtɪd] *a* situato(a).

situation [sɪtju'eɪʃən] *n* situazione *f*.

six [sɪks] *num* sei; **~teen** *num* sedici; **~th** *a* sesto(a); **~ty** *num* sessanta.

size [saɪz] *n* dimensioni *fpl*; (*of clothing*) taglia, misura; (*of shoes*) numero; (*glue*) colla; **to ~ up** *vt* giudicare, farsi un'idea di; **~able** *a* considerevole.

sizzle ['sɪzl] *vi* sfrigolare.

skate [skeɪt] *n* pattino; (*fish*: *pl inv*) razza // *vi* pattinare; **~board** *n* skateboard *m inv*; **~r** *n* pattinatore/trice; **skating** *n* pattinaggio; **skating rink** *n* pista di pattinaggio.

skeleton ['skelɪtn] *n* scheletro; **~ staff** *n* personale *m* ridotto.

sketch [sketʃ] *n* (*drawing*) schizzo, abbozzo; (*THEATRE*) scenetta comica, sketch *m inv* // *vt* abbozzare, schizzare; **~ book** *n* album *m inv* per schizzi; **~ pad** *n* blocco per schizzi; **~y** *a* incompleto(a), lacunoso(a).

skewer ['skjuːə*] *n* spiedo.

ski [skiː] *n* sci *m inv* // *vi* sciare; **~ boot** *n* scarpone *m* da sci.

skid [skɪd] *n* slittamento // *vi* slittare.

skier ['skiːə*] *n* sciatore/trice.

skiing ['skiːɪŋ] *n* sci *m*.

skilful ['skɪlful] *a* abile.

ski lift ['skiːlɪft] *n* sciovia.

skill [skɪl] *n* abilità *f inv*, capacità *f inv*; **~ed** *a* esperto(a); (*worker*) qualificato(a), specializzato(a).

skim [skɪm] *vt* (*milk*) scremare; (*soup*) schiumare; (*glide over*) sfiorare // *vi*: **to ~ through** (*fig*) scorrere, dare una scorsa a.

skimp [skɪmp] *vt* (*work*) fare alla carlona; (*cloth etc*) lesinare; **~y** *a* misero(a); striminzito(a); frugale.

skin [skɪn] *n* pelle *f* // *vt* (*fruit etc*) sbucciare; (*animal*) scuoiare, spellare; **~-deep** *a* superficiale; **~ diving** *n* nuoto subacqueo; **~ graft** *n* innesto epidermico; **~ny** *a* molto magro(a), pelle e ossa *inv*; **~ test** *n* prova di reazione cutanea.

skip [skɪp] *n* saltello, balzo; (*container*) benna // *vi* saltare; (*with rope*) saltare la corda // *vt* (*pass over*) saltare.

skipper ['skɪpə*] *n* (*NAUT, SPORT*) capitano.

skipping rope ['skɪpɪŋrəup] *n* corda per saltare.

skirmish ['skəːmɪʃ] *n* scaramuccia.

skirt [skəːt] *n* gonna, sottana // *vt*

fiancheggiare, costeggiare; **~ing board** *n* zoccolo.

skit [skɪt] *n* parodia; scenetta satirica.

ski tow ['skiːtəu] *n* = **ski lift**.

skittle ['skɪtl] *n* birillo; **~s** *n* (*game*) (gioco dei) birilli *mpl*.

skive [skaɪv] *vi* (*Brit*: *col*) fare il lavativo.

skulk [skʌlk] *vi* muoversi furtivamente.

skull [skʌl] *n* cranio, teschio.

skunk [skʌŋk] *n* moffetta.

sky [skaɪ] *n* cielo; **~light** *n* lucernario; **~scraper** *n* grattacielo.

slab [slæb] *n* lastra.

slack [slæk] *a* (*loose*) allentato(a); (*slow*) lento(a); (*careless*) negligente // *n* (*in rope etc*) parte *f* non tesa; **~s** *npl* pantaloni *mpl*; **~en** (*also*: **~en off**) *vi* rallentare, diminuire // *vt* allentare.

slag [slæg] *n* scorie *fpl*; **~ heap** *n* ammasso di scorie.

slam [slæm] *vt* (*door*) sbattere; (*throw*) scaraventare; (*criticize*) stroncare // *vi* sbattere.

slander ['slɑːndə*] *n* calunnia; diffamazione *f* // *vt* calunniare; diffamare.

slang [slæŋ] *n* gergo; slang *m*.

slant [slɑːnt] *n* pendenza, inclinazione *f*; (*fig*) angolazione *f*, punto di vista; **~ed** *a* tendenzioso(a); **~ing** *a* in pendenza, inclinato(a).

slap [slæp] *n* manata, pacca; (*on face*) schiaffo // *vt* dare una manata a; schiaffeggiare // *ad* (*directly*) in pieno; **~dash** *a* abborracciato(a); **~stick** *n* (*comedy*) farsa grossolana; **a ~up meal** un pranzo (*or* una cena) coi fiocchi.

slash [slæʃ] *vt* squarciare; (*face*) sfregiare; (*fig*: *prices*) ridurre drasticamente, tagliare.

slate [sleɪt] *n* ardesia // *vt* (*fig*: *criticize*) stroncare, distruggere.

slaughter ['slɔːtə*] *n* strage *f*, massacro // *vt* (*animal*) macellare; (*people*) trucidare, massacrare; **~house** *n* macello, mattatoio.

Slav [slɑːv] *a* slavo(a).

slave [sleɪv] *n* schiavo/a // *vi* (*also*: **~ away**) lavorare come uno schiavo; **~ry** *n* schiavitù *f*.

sleazy ['sliːzɪ] *a* trasandato(a).

sledge [sledʒ] *n* slitta; **~hammer** *n* mazza, martello da fabbro.

sleek [sliːk] *a* (*hair, fur*) lucido(a), lucente; (*car, boat*) slanciato(a), affusolato(a).

sleep [sliːp] *n* sonno // *vi* (*pt, pp* **slept** [slept]) dormire; **to go to ~** addormentarsi; **to ~ in** (*lie late*) alzarsi tardi; (*oversleep*) dormire fino a tardi; **~er** *n* (*person*) dormiente *m/f*; (*RAIL*: *on track*) traversina; (: *train*) treno di vagoni letto; **~ing** *a* addormentato(a); **~ing bag** *n* sacco a pelo; **~ing car** *n* vagone *m* letto *inv*, carrozza *f* letto *inv*; **~ing pill** *n* sonnifero; **~lessness** *n* insonnia; **a ~less night** una notte in bianco; **~walker** *n* sonnambulo/a; **~y** *a* assonnato(a), sonnolento(a); (*fig*) addormentato(a).

sleet [sli:t] *n* nevischio.

sleeve [sli:v] *n* manica; **~less** *a* (*garment*) senza maniche.

sleigh [sleɪ] *n* slitta.

sleight [slaɪt] *n*: ~ **of hand** gioco di destrezza.

slender ['slɛndə*] *a* snello(a), sottile; (*not enough*) scarso(a), esiguo(a).

slept [slɛpt] *pt,pp* of **sleep**.

slice [slaɪs] *n* fetta // *vt* affettare, tagliare a fette.

slick [slɪk] *a* (*clever*) brillante; (*insincere*) untuoso(a), falso(a) // *n* (*also:* **oil ~**) chiazza di petrolio.

slid [slɪd] *pt,pp* of **slide**.

slide [slaɪd] *n* (*in playground*) scivolo; (PHOT) diapositiva; (*also:* **hair ~**) fermaglio (per capelli); (*in prices*) caduta // *vb* (*pt,pp* **slid** [slɪd]) *vt* far scivolare // *vi* scivolare; ~ **rule** *n* regolo calcolatore; **sliding** *a* (*door*) scorrevole; **sliding scale** *n* scala mobile.

slight [slaɪt] *a* (*slim*) snello(a), sottile; (*frail*) delicato(a), fragile; (*trivial*) insignificante; (*small*) piccolo(a) // *n* offesa, affronto // *vt* (*offend*) offendere, fare un affronto a; **the ~est** il minimo (*or* la minima); **not in the ~est** affatto, neppure per sogno; **~ly** *ad* lievemente, un po'.

slim [slɪm] *a* magro(a), snello(a) // *vi* dimagrire; fare (*or* seguire) una dieta dimagrante.

slime [slaɪm] *n* limo, melma; viscidume *m*.

sling [slɪŋ] *n* (MED) benda al collo // *vt* (*pt,pp* **slung** [slʌŋ]) lanciare, tirare.

slip [slɪp] *n* scivolata, scivolone *m*; (*mistake*) errore *m*, sbaglio; (*underskirt*) sottoveste *f*; (*of paper*) striscia di carta; tagliando, scontrino // *vt* (*slide*) far scivolare // *vi* (*slide*) scivolare; (*move smoothly*) **to ~ into/out of** scivolare in/via da; (*decline*) declinare; **to give sb the ~** sfuggire qd; **a ~ of the tongue** un lapsus linguae; **to ~ away** *vi* svignarsela; **to ~ in** *vt* introdurre casualmente; **to ~ out** *vi* uscire furtivamente; **~ped disc** *n* spostamento delle vertebre.

slipper ['slɪpə*] *n* pantofola.

slippery ['slɪpərɪ] *a* scivoloso(a).

slip road ['slɪprəud] *n* (*to motorway*) rampa di accesso.

slipshod ['slɪpʃɔd] *a* sciatto(a), trasandato(a).

slip-up ['slɪpʌp] *n* granchio.

slipway ['slɪpweɪ] *n* scalo di costruzione.

slit [slɪt] *n* fessura, fenditura; (*cut*) taglio; (*tear*) squarcio; strappo // *vt* (*pt,pp* **slit**) tagliare; (*make a slit*) squarciare; strappare.

slither ['slɪðə*] *vi* scivolare, sdrucciolare.

slog [slɔg] *n* faticata // *vi* lavorare con accanimento, sgobbare.

slogan ['sləugən] *n* motto, slogan *m inv*.

slop [slɔp] *vi* (*also:* ~ **over**) traboccare; versarsi // *vt* spandere; versare; **~s** *npl* acqua sporca; sbobba.

slope [sləup] *n* pendio; (*side of mountain*) versante *m*; (*of roof*) pendenza; (*of floor*) inclinazione *f* // *vi*: **to ~ down** declinare; **to ~ up** essere in salita.

sloppy ['slɔpɪ] *a* (*work*) tirato(a) via; (*appearance*) sciatto(a); (*film etc*) sdolcinato(a).

slot [slɔt] *n* fessura // *vt*: **to ~ into** introdurre in una fessura; ~ **machine** *n* distributore *m* automatico.

slouch [slautʃ] *vi* ciondolare.

slovenly ['slʌvənlɪ] *a* sciatto(a), trasandato(a).

slow [sləu] *a* lento(a); (*watch*): **to be ~** essere indietro // *ad* lentamente // *vt,vi* (*also:* ~ **down**, ~ **up**) rallentare; ' ~ ' (*road sign*) 'rallentare'; **~ly** *ad* lentamente; **in ~ motion** al rallentatore.

sludge [slʌdʒ] *n* fanghiglia.

slug [slʌg] *n* lumaca; (*bullet*) pallottola; **~gish** *a* lento(a).

sluice [slu:s] *n* chiusa.

slum [slʌm] *n* catapecchia.

slumber ['slʌmbə*] *n* sonno.

slump [slʌmp] *n* crollo, caduta; depressione *f*, crisi *f inv* // *vi* crollare.

slung [slʌŋ] *pt,pp* of **sling**.

slur [slɔ:*] *n* pronuncia indistinta; (*stigma*) diffamazione *f*, calunnia; (*smear*): ~ (**on**) macchia (su); (MUS) legatura // *vt* pronunciare in modo indistinto.

slush [slʌʃ] *n* neve mista a fango.

slut [slʌt] *n* donna trasandata, sciattona.

sly [slaɪ] *a* furbo(a), scaltro(a); **on the ~** di soppiatto.

smack [smæk] *n* (*slap*) pacca; (*on face*) schiaffo // *vt* schiaffeggiare; (*child*) picchiare // *vi*: **to ~ of** puzzare di; **to ~ one's lips** fare uno schiocco con le labbra.

small [smɔ:l] *a* piccolo(a); ~ **ads** *npl* piccola pubblicità; **in the ~ hours** alle ore piccole; **~pox** *n* vaiolo; ~ **talk** *n* chiacchiere *fpl*.

smarmy ['sma:mɪ] *a* (*col*) untuoso(a), strisciante.

smart [sma:t] *a* elegante; (*clever*) intelligente; (*quick*) sveglio(a) // *vi* bruciare; **to ~en up** *vi* farsi bello(a) // *vt* (*people*) fare bello(a); (*things*) abbellire.

smash [smæʃ] *n* (*also:* **~-up**) scontro, collisione *f* // *vt* frantumare, fracassare; (*opponent*) annientare, schiacciare; (*hopes*) distruggere; (SPORT: *record*) battere // *vi* frantumarsi, andare in pezzi; **~ing** *a* (*col*) favoloso(a), formidabile.

smattering ['smætərɪŋ] *n*: **a ~ of** un'infarinatura di.

smear [smɪə*] *n* macchia; (MED) striscio // *vt* ungere; (*fig*) denigrare, diffamare.

smell [smɛl] *n* odore *m*; (*sense*) olfatto, odorato // *vb* (*pt,pp* **smelt** *or* **smelled** [smɛlt, smɛld]) *vt* sentire (l')odore di // *vi* (*food etc*): **to ~ (of)** avere odore (di); (*pej*) puzzare, avere un cattivo odore; **~y** *a* puzzolente.

smile [smaɪl] *n* sorriso // *vi* sorridere.

smirk [smə:k] *n* sorriso furbo; sorriso compiaciuto.

smith [smɪθ] n fabbro; ~**y** n fucina.

smitten ['smɪtn] a: ~ **with** colpito(a) da.

smock [smɔk] n grembiule m, camice m.

smog [smɔg] n smog m.

smoke [sməuk] n fumo // vt, vi fumare; **to have a** ~ fumarsi una sigaretta; ~**d** a (bacon, glass) affumicato(a); ~**r** n (person) fumatore/trice; (RAIL) carrozza per fumatori; **smoking** n: '**no smoking**' (sign) 'vietato fumare'; **smoky** a fumoso(a); (surface) affumicato(a).

smooth [smuːð] a liscio(a); (sauce) omogeneo(a); (flavour, whisky) amabile; (movement) regolare; (person) mellifluo(a) // vt lisciare, spianare; (also: ~ **out**: difficulties) appianare.

smother ['smʌðə*] vt soffocare.

smoulder ['sməuldə*] vi covare sotto la cenere.

smudge [smʌdʒ] n macchia; sbavatura // vt imbrattare, sporcare.

smug [smʌg] a soddisfatto(a), compiaciuto(a).

smuggle ['smʌgl] vt contrabbandare ~**r** n contrabbandiere/a; **smuggling** n contrabbando.

smutty ['smʌtɪ] a (fig) osceno(a), indecente.

snack [snæk] n spuntino; ~ **bar** n tavola calda, snack bar m inv.

snag [snæg] n intoppo, ostacolo imprevisto.

snail [sneɪl] n chiocciola.

snake [sneɪk] n serpente m.

snap [snæp] n (sound) schianto, colpo secco; (photograph) istantanea; (game) rubamazzo // a improvviso(a) // vt schioccare; (break) spezzare di netto; (photograph) scattare un'istantanea di // vi spezzarsi con un rumore secco; **to** ~ **open/shut** aprirsi/chiudersi di scatto; **to** ~ **at** vt fus (subj: dog) cercare di mordere; **to** ~ **off** vt (break) schiantare; **to** ~ **up** vt afferrare; ~**py** a rapido(a); ~**shot** n istantanea.

snare [snɛə*] n trappola.

snarl [snɑːl] vi ringhiare.

snatch [snætʃ] n (fig) furto con strappo, scippo; (small amount): ~**es of** frammenti mpl di // vt strappare (con violenza); (steal) rubare.

sneak [sniːk] vi: **to** ~ **in/out** entrare/uscire di nascosto; ~**y** a falso(a), disonesto(a).

sneer [snɪə*] n ghigno, sogghigno // vi ghignare, sogghignare.

sneeze [sniːz] n starnuto // vi starnutire.

snide [snaɪd] a maligno(a).

sniff [snɪf] n fiutata, annusata // vi fiutare, annusare; tirare su col naso; (in contempt) arricciare il naso // vt fiutare, annusare.

snigger ['snɪgə*] n riso represso // vi ridacchiare, ridere sotto i baffi.

snip [snɪp] n pezzetto; (bargain) (buon) affare m, occasione f // vt tagliare.

sniper ['snaɪpə*] n (marksman) franco tiratore m, cecchino.

snippet ['snɪpɪt] n frammento.

snivelling ['snɪvlɪŋ] a (whimpering) piagnucoloso(a).

snob [snɔb] n snob m/f inv; ~**bery** n snobismo; ~**bish** a snob inv.

snooker ['snuːkə*] n tipo di gioco del biliardo.

snoop ['snuːp] vi: **to** ~ **on sb** spiare qd.

snooty ['snuːtɪ] a borioso(a), snob inv.

snooze [snuːz] n sonnellino, pisolino // vi fare un sonnellino.

snore [snɔː*] vi russare.

snorkel ['snɔːkl] n (of swimmer) respiratore m a tubo.

snort [snɔːt] n sbuffo // vi sbuffare.

snout [snaut] n muso.

snow [snəu] n neve f // vi nevicare; ~**ball** n palla di neve; ~**bound** a bloccato(a) dalla neve; ~**drift** n cumulo di neve (ammucchiato dal vento); ~**drop** n bucaneve m inv; ~**fall** n nevicata; ~**flake** n fiocco di neve; ~**man** n pupazzo di neve; ~**plough** n spazzaneve m inv; ~**storm** n tormenta.

snub [snʌb] vt snobbare // n offesa, affronto; ~-**nosed** a dal naso camuso.

snuff [snʌf] n tabacco da fiuto.

snug [snʌg] a comodo(a); (room, house) accogliente, comodo(a).

so [səu] ad (degree) così, tanto; (manner: thus) così, in questo modo // cj perciò; ~ **as to** do in modo da or così da fare; ~ **that** (purpose) affinché + sub; (result) così che; ~ **do I,** ~ **am I** etc anch'io etc; **if** ~ se è così; **I hope** ~ spero di sì; **10 or** ~ circa 10; ~ **far** fin qui, finora; (in past) fino ad allora; ~ **long!** arrivederci!; ~ **many** tanti(e); ~ **much** ad tanto // det tanto(a); ~ **and** ~ n tale m/f dei tali.

soak [səuk] vt inzuppare; (clothes) mettere a mollo // vi inzupparsi; (clothes) essere a mollo; **to be** ~**ed through** essere fradicio; **to** ~ **in** vi penetrare; **to** ~ **up** vt assorbire.

soap [səup] n sapone m; ~ **powder** n detersivo; ~**y** a insaponato(a).

soar [sɔː*] vi volare in alto.

sob [sɔb] n singhiozzo // vi singhiozzare.

sober ['səubə*] a non ubriaco(a); (sedate) serio(a); (moderate) moderato(a); (colour, style) sobrio(a); **to** ~ **up** vt far passare la sbornia a // vi farsi passare la sbornia.

Soc. abbr of **society.**

so-called ['səu'kɔːld] a cosiddetto(a).

soccer ['sɔkə*] n calcio.

sociable ['səuʃəbl] a socievole.

social ['səuʃl] a sociale // n festa, serata; ~ **club** n club m inv sociale; ~**ism** n socialismo; ~**ist** a,n socialista (m/f); ~ **science** n scienze fpl sociali; ~ **security** n previdenza sociale; ~ **welfare** n assistenza sociale; ~ **work** n servizio sociale; ~ **worker** n assistente m/f sociale.

society [sə'saɪətɪ] n società f inv; (club) società, associazione f; (also: **high** ~) alta società.

sociology [səusɪ'ɔlədʒɪ] n sociologia.

sock [sɔk] n calzino // vt (hit) dare un pugno a.

socket ['sɔkɪt] n cavità f inv; (of eye) orbita; (ELEC: also: **wall** ~) presa di corrente; (: for light bulb) portalampada m inv.

sod [sɔd] n (of earth) zolla erbosa; (col!) bastardo/a (!).

soda ['səudə] n (CHEM) soda; (also: ~ **water**) acqua di seltz.

sodden ['sɔdn] a fradicio(a).

sodium ['səudiəm] n sodio.

sofa ['səufə] n sofà m inv.

soft [sɔft] a (not rough) morbido(a); (not hard) soffice; (not loud) sommesso(a); (kind) gentile; (weak) debole; (stupid) stupido(a); ~ **drink** n analcolico; ~**en** ['sɔfn] vt ammorbidire; addolcire; attenuare // vi ammorbidirsi; addolcirsi; attenuarsi; ~**hearted** a sensibile; ~**ly** ad dolcemente; morbidamente; ~**ness** n dolcezza; morbidezza; ~**ware** n software m.

soggy ['sɔgɪ] a inzuppato(a).

soil [sɔɪl] n (earth) terreno, suolo // vt sporcare; (fig) macchiare.

solar ['səulə*] a solare.

sold [səuld] pt,pp of sell; ~ **out** a (COMM) esaurito(a).

solder ['səuldə*] vt saldare // n saldatura.

soldier ['səuldʒə*] n soldato, militare m.

sole [səul] n (of foot) pianta (del piede); (of shoe) suola; (fish: pl inv) sogliola // a solo(a), unico(a).

solemn ['sɔləm] a solenne; grave; serio(a).

solicitor [sə'lɪsɪtə*] n (for wills etc) ≈ notaio; (in court) ≈ avvocato.

solid ['sɔlɪd] a (not hollow) pieno(a); (strong, sound, reliable, not liquid) solido(a); (meal) sostanzioso(a) // n solido.

solidarity [sɔlɪ'dærɪtɪ] n solidarietà.

solidify [sə'lɪdɪfaɪ] vi solidificarsi // vt solidificare.

solitaire [sɔlɪ'tɛə*] n (game, gem) solitario.

solitary ['sɔlɪtərɪ] a solitario(a).

solitude ['sɔlɪtjuːd] n solitudine f.

solo ['səuləu] n assolo; ~**ist** n solista m/f.

solstice ['sɔlstɪs] n solstizio.

soluble ['sɔljubl] a solubile.

solution [sə'luːʃən] n soluzione f.

solve [sɔlv] vt risolvere.

solvent ['sɔlvənt] a (COMM) solvibile // n (CHEM) solvente m.

sombre, (US) **somber** ['sɔmbə*] a (dark) a scuro(a); (mood, person) triste.

some [sʌm] det (a few) alcuni(e), qualche; (certain) certi(e); (a certain number or amount) ... qualunque // pronoun alcuni(e); un po' // ad: ~ **10 people** circa 10 persone; **I have** ~ **books** ho qualche libro o alcuni libri; **have** ~ **tea/ice-cream/water** prendi un po' di tè/gelato/acqua; **there's** ~ **milk in the fridge** c'è un po' di latte nel frigo; ~ **(of it) was left** ne è rimasto un po'; **I've got** ~ (i.e. books etc) ne ho

alcuni; (i.e. milk, money etc) ne ho un po'; ~**body** pronoun qualcuno; ~ **day** ad uno di questi giorni, un giorno o l'altro; ~**how** ad in un modo o nell'altro, in qualche modo; (for some reason) per qualche ragione; ~**one** pronoun = **somebody**; ~**place** ad (US) = **somewhere**.

somersault ['sʌməsɔːlt] n capriola; salto mortale // vi fare una capriola (or un salto mortale); (car) cappottare.

something ['sʌmθɪŋ] pronoun qualcosa; ~ **interesting** qualcosa di interessante.

sometime ['sʌmtaɪm] ad (in future) una volta o l'altra; (in past): ~ **last month** durante il mese scorso.

sometimes ['sʌmtaɪmz] ad qualche volta.

somewhat ['sʌmwɔt] ad piuttosto.

somewhere ['sʌmwɛə*] ad in or da qualche parte.

son [sʌn] n figlio.

song [sɔŋ] n canzone f; ~**book** n canzoniere m.

sonic ['sɔnɪk] a (boom) sonico(a).

son-in-law ['sʌnɪnlɔː] n genero.

sonnet ['sɔnɪt] n sonetto.

sonny ['sʌnɪ] n (col) ragazzo mio.

soon [suːn] ad presto, fra poco; (early) presto; ~ **afterwards** subito dopo; see also **as**; ~**er** ad (time) prima; (preference): **I would** ~**er do** preferirei fare; ~**er or later** prima o poi.

soot [sut] n fuliggine f.

soothe [suːð] vt calmare.

sop [sɔp] n: **that's only a** ~ è soltanto un'offa.

sophisticated [sə'fɪstɪkeɪtɪd] a sofisticato(a); raffinato(a); altamente perfezionato(a); complesso(a).

sopping ['sɔpɪŋ] a (also: ~ **wet**) bagnato(a) fradicio(a).

soppy ['sɔpɪ] a (pej) sentimentale.

soprano [sə'prɑːnəu] n (voice) soprano m; (singer) soprano m/f.

sorcerer ['sɔːsərə*] n stregone m, mago.

sordid ['sɔːdɪd] a sordido(a).

sore [sɔː*] a (painful) dolorante; (col: offended) offeso(a) // n piaga; ~**ly** ad (tempted) fortemente.

sorrow ['sɔrəu] n dolore m; ~**ful** a triste.

sorry ['sɔrɪ] a spiacente; (condition, excuse) misero(a); ~**!** scusa! (or scusi! or scusate!); **to feel** ~ **for sb** rincrescersi per qd.

sort [sɔːt] n specie f, genere m // vt (also: ~ **out**: papers) classificare; ordinare; (: letters etc) smistare; (: problems) risolvere; ~**ing office** n ufficio m smistamento inv.

SOS n (abbr of save our souls) S.O.S. m inv.

so-so ['səusəu] ad così così.

soufflé ['suːfleɪ] n soufflé m inv.

sought [sɔːt] pt,pp of seek.

soul [səul] n anima; ~**-destroying** a demoralizzante; ~**ful** a pieno(a) di sentimento.

sound [saund] a (healthy) sano(a); (safe, not damaged) solido(a), in buono stato; (reliable, not superficial) solido(a); (sensible) giudizioso(a), di buon senso //

ad: ~ **asleep** profondamente addormentato // n (noise) suono; rumore m; (GEO) stretto // vt (alarm) suonare; (also: ~ **out**: opinions) sondare // vi suonare; (fig: seem) sembrare; **to ~ like** rassomigliare a; **~ barrier** n muro del suono; **~ing** n (NAUT etc) scandagliamento; **~ly** ad (sleep) profondamente; (beat) duramente; **~proof** vt insonorizzare, isolare acusticamente // a insonorizzato(a), isolato(a) acusticamente; **~track** n (of film) colonna sonora.

soup [su:p] n minestra; brodo; zuppa; **in the ~** (fig) nei guai; **~spoon** n cucchiaio da minestra.

sour ['sauə*] a aspro(a); (fruit) acerbo(a); (milk) acido(a), fermentato(a); (fig) arcigno(a); acido(a); **it's ~ grapes** è soltanto invidia.

source [sɔ:s] n fonte f, sorgente f; (fig) fonte.

south [sauθ] n sud m, meridione m, mezzogiorno // a del sud, sud inv, meridionale // ad verso sud; **S~ Africa** n Sudafrica m; **S~ African** a, n sudafricano(a); **S~ America** n Sudamerica, America del sud; **S~ American** a, n sudamericano(a); **~-east** n sud-est m; **~erly** ['sʌðəlɪ] a dal sud, meridionale; **~ern** ['sʌðən] a del sud, meridionale; esposto(a) a sud; **S~ Pole** n Polo Sud; **~ward(s)** ad verso sud; **~-west** n sud-ovest m.

souvenir [su:və'nɪə*] n ricordo, souvenir m inv.

sovereign ['sɔvrɪn] a,n sovrano(a); **~ty** n sovranità.

soviet ['səuvɪət] a sovietico(a); **the S~ Union** l'Unione f Sovietica.

sow n [sau] scrofa // vt [səu] (pt ~**ed**, pp **sown** [səun]) seminare.

soya bean ['sɔɪəbi:n] n seme m di soia.

spa [spɑ:] n (resort) stazione f termale.

space [speɪs] n spazio; (room) posto; spazio; (length of time) intervallo // cpd spaziale // vt (also: ~ **out**) distanziare; **~craft** n veicolo spaziale; **~man/woman** n astronauta m/f, cosmonauta m/f; **spacing** n spaziatura.

spacious ['speɪʃəs] a spazioso(a), ampio(a).

spade [speɪd] n (tool) vanga; pala; (child's) paletta; **~s** npl (CARDS) picche fpl; **~work** n (fig) duro lavoro preparatorio.

Spain [speɪn] n Spagna.

span [spæn] pt of **spin** // n (of bird, plane) apertura alare; (of arch) campata; (in time) periodo; durata // vt attraversare; (fig) abbracciare.

Spaniard ['spænjəd] n spagnolo/a.

spaniel ['spænjəl] n spaniel m inv.

Spanish ['spænɪʃ] a spagnolo // n (LING) spagnolo.

spank [spæŋk] vt sculacciare.

spanner ['spænə*] n chiave f inglese.

spare [spɛə*] a di riserva, di scorta; (surplus) in più, d'avanzo // n (part) pezzo di ricambio // vt (do without) fare a meno di; (afford to give) concedere; (refrain from hurting, using) risparmiare; **to ~** (surplus) d'avanzo; **~ part** n pezzo di ricambio; **~ time** n tempo libero.

sparing ['spɛərɪŋ] a (amount) scarso(a); (use) parsimonioso(a); **~ of words** che risparmia le proprie parole; **~ly** ad moderatamente.

spark [spɑ:k] n scintilla; **~(ing) plug** n candela.

sparkle ['spɑ:kl] n scintillio, sfavillio // vi scintillare, sfavillare; (bubble) spumeggiare, frizzare; **sparkling** a scintillante, sfavillante; (wine) spumante.

sparrow ['spærəu] n passero.

sparse [spɑ:s] a sparso(a), rado(a).

spasm ['spæzəm] n (MED) spasmo; (fig) accesso, attacco; **~odic** [spæz'mɔdɪk] a spasmodico(a); (fig) intermittente.

spastic ['spæstɪk] n spastico/a.

spat [spæt] pt,pp of **spit**.

spate [speɪt] n (fig): ~ **of** diluvio or fiume m di; **in ~** (river) in piena.

spatter ['spætə*] vt, vi schizzare.

spatula ['spætjulə] n spatola.

spawn [spɔ:n] vt deporre // vi deporre le uova // n uova fpl.

speak, pt **spoke**, pp **spoken** [spi:k, spəuk, 'spəukn] vt (language) parlare; (truth) dire // vi parlare; **to ~ to sb/of or about sth** parlare a qd/di qc; **~ up!** parla più forte!; **~er** n (in public) oratore/trice; (also: **loud~er**) altoparlante m; (POL): **the S~er** il presidente della Camera dei Comuni; **to be on ~ing terms** parlarsi.

spear [spɪə*] n lancia.

spec [spɛk] n (col): **on ~** sperando bene.

special ['spɛʃl] a speciale; **take ~ care** siate particolarmente prudenti; **~ist** n specialista m/f; **~ity** [spɛʃɪ'ælɪtɪ] n specialità f inv; **~ize** vi: **to ~ize (in)** specializzarsi (in); **~ly** ad specialmente, particolarmente.

species ['spi:ʃi:z] n, pl inv specie f inv.

specific [spə'sɪfɪk] a specifico(a); preciso(a); **~ation** [spɛsɪfɪ'keɪʃən] n specificazione f.

specify ['spɛsɪfaɪ] vt specificare, precisare.

specimen ['spɛsɪmən] n esemplare m, modello; (MED) campione m.

speck [spɛk] n puntino, macchiolina; (particle) granello.

speckled ['spɛkld] a macchiettato(a).

specs [spɛks] npl (col) occhiali mpl.

spectacle ['spɛktəkl] n spettacolo; **~s** npl occhiali mpl; **spectacular** [-'tækjulə*] a spettacolare // n (CINEMA etc) film m inv etc spettacolare.

spectator [spɛk'teɪtə*] n spettatore m.

spectre ['spɛktə*] n spettro.

spectrum, pl **spectra** ['spɛktrəm, -rə] n spettro; (fig) gamma.

speculate ['spɛkjuleɪt] vi speculare; (try to guess): **to ~ about** fare ipotesi su; **speculation** [-'leɪʃən] n speculazione f;

congettura; **speculative** [-lətɪv] *a* speculativo(a).

speech [spiːtʃ] *n* (*faculty*) parola; (*talk*) discorso; (*manner of speaking*) parlata; (*enunciation*) elocuzione *f*; ~**less** *a* ammutolito(a), muto(a); ~ **therapy** *n* cura dei disturbi del linguaggio.

speed [spiːd] *n* velocità *f inv*; (*promptness*) prontezza; **at full** *or* **top** ~ a tutta velocità; **to** ~ **up** *vi*, *vt* accelerare; ~**boat** *n* motoscafo; fuoribordo *m inv*; ~**ily** *ad* velocemente; prontamente; ~**ing** *n* (AUT) eccesso di velocità; ~ **limit** *n* limite *m* di velocità; ~**ometer** [spɪ'dɔmɪtə*] *n* tachimetro; ~**way** *n* (SPORT) pista per motociclismo; ~**y** *a* veloce, rapido(a); pronto(a).

spell [spɛl] *n* (*also:* **magic** ~) incantesimo; (*period of time*) (breve) periodo // *vt* (*pt,pp* **spelt** *or* ~**ed** [spɛlt, spɛld]) (*in writing*) scrivere (lettera per lettera); (*aloud*) dire il nome delle lettere di; (*fig*) significare; **to cast a** ~ **on sb** fare un incantesimo a qd; **he can't** ~ lui fa errori di ortografia; ~**bound** *a* incantato(a); affascinato(a); ~**ing** *n* ortografia.

spelt [spɛlt] *pt,pp of* **spell.**

spend, *pt,pp* **spent** [spɛnd, spɛnt] *vt* (*money*) spendere; (*time, life*) passare; ~**ing money** *n* denaro per le piccole spese; ~**thrift** *n* spendaccione/a.

spent [spɛnt] *pt,pp of* **spend** // *a* (*patience*) esaurito(a).

sperm [spəːm] *n* spermatozoo; (*semen*) sperma *m*; ~ **whale** *n* capodoglio.

spew [spjuː] *vt* vomitare.

sphere [sfɪə*] *n* sfera.

spice [spaɪs] *n* spezia // *vt* aromatizzare.

spick-and-span   ['spɪkən'spæn]   *a* impeccabile.

spicy ['spaɪsɪ] *a* piccante.

spider ['spaɪdə*] *n* ragno.

spike [spaɪk] *n* punta.

spill, *pt,pp* **spilt** *or* ~**ed** [spɪl, -t, -d] *vt* versare, rovesciare // *vi* versarsi, rovesciarsi.

spin [spɪn] *n* (*revolution of wheel*) rotazione *f*; (AVIAT) avvitamento; (*trip in car*) giretto // *vb* (*pt* **spun, span,** *pp* **spun** [spʌn, spæn]) *vt* (*wool etc*) filare; (*wheel*) far girare // *vi* girare; **to** ~ **a yarn** raccontare una storia; **to** ~ **out** far durare.

spinach ['spɪnɪtʃ] *n* spinacio; (*as food*) spinaci *mpl.*

spinal ['spaɪnl] *a* spinale; ~ **cord** *n* midollo spinale.

spindly ['spɪndlɪ] *a* lungo(a) e sottile, filiforme.

spin-drier [spɪn'draɪə*] *n* centrifuga.

spine [spaɪn] *n* spina dorsale; (*thorn*) spina; ~**less** *a* invertebrato(a), senza spina dorsale; (*fig*) smidollato(a).

spinning ['spɪnɪŋ] *n* filatura; ~ **top** *n* trottola; ~ **wheel** *n* filatoio.

spinster ['spɪnstə*] *n* nubile *f*; zitella.

spiral ['spaɪərl] *n* spirale *f* // *a* a spirale //

vi (*fig*) salire a spirale; ~ **staircase** *n* scala a chiocciola.

spire ['spaɪə*] *n* guglia.

spirit ['spɪrɪt] *n* (*soul*) spirito, anima; (*ghost*) spirito, fantasma *m*; (*mood*) stato d'animo, umore *m*; (*courage*) coraggio; ~**s** *npl* (*drink*) alcolici *mpl*; **in good** ~**s** di buon umore; **in low** ~**s** triste, abbattuto(a); ~**ed** *a* vivace, vigoroso(a); (*horse*) focoso(a); ~ **level** *n* livella a bolla (d'aria).

spiritual ['spɪrɪtjuəl] *a* spirituale // *n* (*also:* **Negro** ~) spiritual *m inv*; ~**ism** *n* spiritismo.

spit [spɪt] *n* (*for roasting*) spiedo // *vi* (*pt, pp* .**spat** [spæt]) sputare; (*fire, fat*) scoppiettare.

spite [spaɪt] *n* dispetto // *vt* contrariare, far dispetto a; **in** ~ **of** nonostante, malgrado; ~**ful** *a* dispettoso(a).

spittle ['spɪtl] *n* saliva; sputo.

splash [splæʃ] *n* spruzzo; (*sound*) ciac *m inv*; (*of colour*) schizzo // *vt* spruzzare // *vi* (*also:* ~ **about**) sguazzare.

spleen [spliːn] *n* (ANAT) milza.

splendid   ['splɛndɪd]   *a* splendido(a), magnifico(a).

splendour ['splɛndə*] *n* splendore *m.*

splice [splaɪs] *vt* (*rope*) impiombare; (*wood*) calettare.

splint [splɪnt] *n* (MED) stecca.

splinter ['splɪntə*] *n* scheggia // *vi* scheggiarsi.

split [splɪt] *n* spaccatura; (*fig:* POL) scissione *f* // *vb* (*pt, pp* **split**) *vt* spaccare; (*party*) dividere; (*work, profits*) spartire, ripartire // *vi* (*divide*) dividersi; **to** ~ **up** *vi* (*couple*) separarsi, rompere; (*meeting*) sciogliersi; ~**ting headache** *n* mal *m* di testa da impazzire.

splutter   ['splʌtə*]   *vi*   farfugliare; sputacchiare.

spoil, *pt,pp* **spoilt** *or* ~**ed** [spɔɪl, -t, -d] *vt* (*damage*) rovinare, guastare; (*mar*) sciupare; (*child*) viziare; ~**s** *npl* bottino; ~**sport** *n* guastafeste *m/f inv.*

spoke [spəʊk] *pt of* **speak** // *n* raggio.

spoken ['spəʊkn] *pp of* **speak.**

spokesman ['spəʊksmən] *n* portavoce *m inv.*

sponge [spʌndʒ] *n* spugna // *vt* spugnare, pulire con una spugna // *vi*: **to** ~ **on** scroccare a; ~ **cake** *n* pan *m* di Spagna; ~**r** *n* (*pej*) parassita *m/f*, scroccone/a; **spongy** *a* spugnoso(a).

sponsor   ['spɔnsə*]   *n*   (RADIO,   TV) finanziatore/trice (a scopo pubblicitario) // *vt* sostenere; patrocinare; ~**ship** *n* finanziamento (a scopo pubblicitario); patrocinio.

spontaneous   [spɔn'teɪnɪəs]   *a* spontaneo(a).

spooky ['spuːkɪ] *a* che fa accapponare la pelle.

spool [spuːl] *n* bobina.

spoon [spuːn] *n* cucchiaio; ~**-feed** *vt* nutrire con il cucchiaio; (*fig*) imboccare; ~**ful** *n* cucchiaiata.

sporadic [spə'rædɪk] *a* sporadico(a).
sport [spɔːt] *n* sport *m inv*; (*person*) sportivo/a // *vt* sfoggiare; ~**ing** *a* sportivo(a); **to give sb a ~ing chance** dare a qd una possibilità (di vincere); ~**s car** *n* automobile *f* sportiva; ~**s jacket** *n* giacca sportiva; ~**sman** *n* sportivo; ~**smanship** *n* spirito sportivo; ~**s page** *n* pagina sportiva; ~**swear** *n* abiti *mpl* sportivi; ~**swoman** *n* sportiva; ~**y** *a* sportivo(a).
spot [spɔt] *n* punto; (*mark*) macchia; (*dot: on pattern*) pallino; (*pimple*) foruncolo; (*place*) posto; (*small amount*): **a ~ of** un po' di // *vt* (*notice*) individuare, distinguere; **on the ~** sul posto; su due piedi; ~ **check** *n* controllo senza preavviso; ~**less** *a* immacolato(a); ~**light** *n* proiettore *m*; (*AUT*) faro ausiliario; ~**ted** *a* macchiato(a); a puntini, a pallini; ~**ted with** punteggiato(a) di; ~**ty** *a* (*face*) foruncoloso(a).
spouse [spauz] *n* sposo/a.
spout [spaut] *n* (*of jug*) beccuccio; (*of liquid*) zampillo, getto // *vi* zampillare.
sprain [spreɪn] *n* storta, distorsione *f* // *vt*: **to ~ one's ankle** storcersi una caviglia.
sprang [spræŋ] *pt of* **spring**.
sprawl [sprɔːl] *vi* sdraiarsi (in modo scomposto).
spray [spreɪ] *n* spruzzo; (*container*) nebulizzatore *m*, spray *m inv*; (*of flowers*) mazzetto // *vt* spruzzare; (*crops*) irrorare.
spread [sprɛd] *n* diffusione *f*; (*distribution*) distribuzione *f*; (*CULIN*) pasta (da spalmare) // *vb* (*pt,pp* **spread**) *vt* (*cloth*) stendere, distendere; (*butter etc*) spalmare; (*disease, knowledge*) propagare, diffondere // *vi* stendersi, distendersi; spalmarsi; propagarsi, diffondersi.
spree [spriː] *n*: **to go on a ~** fare baldoria.
sprig [sprɪg] *n* ramoscello.
sprightly ['spraɪtlɪ] *a* vivace.
spring [sprɪŋ] *n* (*leap*) salto, balzo; (*coiled metal*) molla; (*season*) primavera; (*of water*) sorgente *f* // *vi* (*pt* **sprang**, *pp* **sprung** [spræŋ, sprʌŋ]) saltare, balzare; **to ~ from** provenire da; **to ~ up** *vi* (*problem*) presentarsi; ~**board** *n* trampolino; ~-**clean** *n* (*also*: ~-**cleaning**) grandi pulizie *fpl* di primavera; ~**time** *n* primavera; ~**y** *a* elastico(a).
sprinkle ['sprɪŋkl] *vt* spruzzare; spargere; **to ~ water etc on**, ~ **with water etc** spruzzare dell'acqua *etc* su; **to ~ sugar etc on**, ~ **with sugar etc** spolverizzare di zucchero *etc*; ~**d with** (*fig*) cosparso(a) di.
sprint [sprɪnt] *n* volata, scatto // *vi* correre di volata, scattare; ~**er** *n* velocista *m/f*.
sprite [spraɪt] *n* elfo, folletto.
sprout [spraut] *vi* germogliare; (**Brussels**) ~**s** *npl* cavolini *mpl* di Bruxelles.

spruce [spruːs] *n* abete *m* rosso // *a* lindo(a); azzimato(a).
sprung [sprʌŋ] *pp of* **spring**.
spry [spraɪ] *a* arzillo(a), sveglio(a).
spun [spʌn] *pt, pp of* **spin**.
spur [spəː*] *n* sperone *m*; (*fig*) sprone *m*, incentivo // *vt* (*also*: ~ **on**) spronare; **on the ~ of the moment** lì per lì.
spurious ['spjuərɪəs] *a* falso(a).
spurn [spəːn] *vt* rifiutare con disprezzo, sdegnare.
spurt [spəːt] *n* getto; (*of energy*) esplosione *f* // *vi* sgorgare; zampillare.
spy [spaɪ] *n* spia // *vi*: **to ~ on** spiare // *vt* (*see*) scorgere; ~**ing** *n* spionaggio.
sq. (*MATH*), **Sq.** (*in address*) *abbr of* **square**.
squabble ['skwɔbl] *vi* bisticciarsi.
squad [skwɔd] *n* (*MIL*) plotone *m*; (*POLICE*) squadra.
squadron ['skwɔdrn] *n* (*MIL*) squadrone *m*; (*AVIAT, NAUT*) squadriglia.
squalid ['skwɔlɪd] *a* sordido(a).
squall [skwɔːl] *n* raffica; burrasca.
squalor ['skwɔlə*] *n* squallore *m*.
squander ['skwɔndə*] *vt* dissipare.
square [skwɛə*] *n* quadrato; (*in town*) piazza; (*instrument*) squadra // *a* quadrato(a); (*honest*) onesto(a); (*col: ideas, tastes*) di vecchio stampo // *vt* (*arrange*) regolare; (*MATH*) elevare al quadrato // *vi* (*agree*) accordarsi; **all ~** pari; **a ~ meal** un pasto abbondante; **2 metres ~** di 2 metri per 2; **1 ~ metre** 1 metro quadrato; ~**ly** *ad* diritto; fermamente.
squash [skwɔʃ] *n* (*drink*): **lemon/orange ~** sciroppo di limone/arancia; (*SPORT*) squash *m* // *vt* schiacciare.
squat [skwɔt] *a* tarchiato(a), tozzo(a) // *vi* accovacciarsi; ~**ter** *n* occupante *m/f* abusivo(a).
squawk [skwɔːk] *vi* emettere strida rauche.
squeak [skwiːk] *vi* squittire.
squeal [skwiːl] *vi* strillare.
squeamish ['skwiːmɪʃ] *a* schizzinoso(a); disgustato(a).
squeeze [skwiːz] *n* pressione *f*; (*also ECON*) stretta // *vt* premere; (*hand, arm*) stringere; **to ~ out** *vt* spremere.
squelch [skwɛltʃ] *vi* fare ciac; sguazzare.
squib [skwɪb] *n* petardo.
squid [skwɪd] *n* calamaro.
squint [skwɪnt] *vi* essere strabico(a) // *n*: **he has a ~** è strabico.
squire ['skwaɪə*] *n* proprietario terriero.
squirm [skwəːm] *vi* contorcersi.
squirrel ['skwɪrəl] *n* scoiattolo.
squirt [skwəːt] *n* schizzo // *vi* schizzare; zampillare.
Sr *abbr of* **senior**.
St *abbr of* **saint**, **street**.
stab [stæb] *n* (*with knife etc*) pugnalata; (*col: try*): **to have a ~ at (doing) sth** provare a fare qc // *vt* pugnalare.
stability [stə'bɪlɪtɪ] *n* stabilità.
stabilize ['steɪbəlaɪz] *vt* stabilizzare.

stable ['steɪbl] n (for horses) scuderia; (for cattle) stalla // a stabile.

stack [stæk] n catasta, pila // vt accatastare, ammucchiare.

stadium ['steɪdɪəm] n stadio.

staff [stɑːf] n (work force) personale m; (: SCOL) personale insegnante; (: servants) personale di servizio; (MIL) stato maggiore; (stick) bastone m // vt fornire di personale.

stag [stæg] n cervo.

stage [steɪdʒ] n palcoscenico; (profession): **the ~**. il teatro, la scena; (point) punto; (platform) palco // vt (play) allestire, mettere in scena; (demonstration) organizzare; (fig: perform: recovery etc) effettuare; **in ~s** per gradi; a tappe; **~coach** n diligenza; **~ door** n ingresso degli artisti; **~ fright** n paura del pubblico; **~ manager** n direttore m di scena.

stagger ['stægə*] vi barcollare // vt (person) sbalordire; (hours, holidays) scaglionare; **~ing** a (amazing) incredibile, sbalorditivo(a).

stagnant ['stægnənt] a stagnante.

stagnate [stæg'neɪt] vi stagnare.

stag party ['stægpɑːtɪ] n festa di addio al celibato.

staid [steɪd] a posato(a), serio(a).

stain [steɪn] n macchia; (colouring) colorante m // vt macchiare; (wood) tingere; **~ed glass window** n vetrata; **~less** a (steel) inossidabile; **~ remover** n smacchiatore m.

stair [stɛə*] n (step) gradino; **~s** npl scale fpl, scala; **on the ~s** sulle scale; **~case, ~way** n scale fpl, scala.

stake [steɪk] n palo, piolo; (BETTING) puntata, scommessa // vt (bet) scommettere; (risk) rischiare; **to be at ~** essere in gioco.

stalactite ['stæləktaɪt] n stalattite f.

stalagmite ['stæləgmaɪt] n stalagmite f.

stale [steɪl] a (bread) raffermo(a), stantio(a); (beer) svaporato(a); (smell) di chiuso.

stalemate ['steɪlmeɪt] n stallo; (fig) punto morto.

stalk [stɔːk] n gambo, stelo // vt inseguire // vi camminare con sussiego.

stall [stɔːl] n bancarella; (in stable) box m inv di stalla // vt (AUT) far spegnere // vi (AUT) spegnersi, fermarsi; (fig) temporeggiare; **~s** npl (in cinema, theatre) platea.

stalwart ['stɔːlwət] n membro fidato.

stamina ['stæmɪnə] n vigore m, resistenza.

stammer ['stæmə*] n balbuzie f // vi balbettare.

stamp [stæmp] n (postage ~) francobollo; (implement) timbro; (mark, also fig) marchio, impronta; (on document) bollo; timbro // vt battere il piede // vt battere; (letter) affrancare; (mark with a ~) timbrare; **~ album** n album m inv per francobolli; **~ collecting** n filatelia.

stampede [stæm'piːd] n fuggi fuggi m inv.

stance [stæns] n posizione f.

stand [stænd] n (position) posizione f; (MIL) resistenza; (structure) supporto, sostegno; (at exhibition) stand m inv; (in shop) banco; (at market) bancarella; (booth) chiosco; (SPORT) tribuna // vb (pt,pp stood [stud]) vi stare in piedi; (rise) alzarsi in piedi; (be placed) trovarsi // vt (place) mettere, porre; (tolerate, withstand) resistere, sopportare; **to make a ~** prendere posizione; **to ~ for parliament** presentarsi come candidato (per il parlamento); **it ~s to reason** è logico; **to ~ by** vi (be ready) tenersi pronto // vt fus (opinion) sostenere; **to ~ for** vt fus (signify) rappresentare, significare; (tolerate) sopportare, tollerare; **to ~ in for** vt fus sostituire; **to ~ out** vi (be prominent) spiccare; **to ~ up** vi (rise) alzarsi in piedi; **to ~ up for** vt fus difendere; **to ~ up to** vt fus tener testa a, resistere a.

standard ['stændəd] n modello, standard m inv; (level) livello; (flag) stendardo // a (size etc) normale, standard inv; **~s** npl (morals) principi mpl, valori mpl; **~ize** vt normalizzare, standardizzare; **~ lamp** n lampada a stelo; **~ of living** n livello di vita.

stand-by ['stændbaɪ] n riserva, sostituto; **~ ticket** n (AVIAT) biglietto senza garanzia.

stand-in ['stændɪn] n sostituto/a; (CINEMA) controfigura.

standing ['stændɪŋ] a diritto(a), in piedi // n rango, condizione f, posizione f; **of many years' ~** che esiste da molti anni; **~ committee** n commissione f permanente; **~ order** n (at bank) ordine m permanente (di pagamento periodico); **~ orders** npl (MIL) regolamento; **~ room** n posto all'impiedi.

stand-offish [stænd'ɔfɪʃ] a scostante, freddo(a).

standpoint ['stændpɔɪnt] n punto di vista.

standstill ['stændstɪl] n: **at a ~** alla fermata; (fig) a un punto morto; **to come to a ~** fermarsi; giungere a un punto morto.

stank [stæŋk] pt of **stink**.

staple ['steɪpl] n (for papers) graffetta // a (food etc) di base // vt cucire; **~r** n cucitrice f.

star [stɑː*] n stella; (celebrity) divo/a; (principal actor) vedette f inv // vi: **to ~ (in)** essere il (or la) protagonista di // vt (CINEMA) essere interpretato(a) da.

starboard ['stɑːbəd] n dritta; **to ~ a** dritta.

starch [stɑːtʃ] n amido; **~ed** a (collar) inamidato(a).

stardom ['stɑːdəm] n celebrità.

stare [stɛə*] n sguardo fisso // vi: **to ~ at** fissare.

starfish ['stɑːfɪʃ] n stella di mare.

stark [stɑːk] a (bleak) desolato(a) // ad: **~ naked** completamente nudo(a).

starling ['stɑːlɪŋ] n storno.

start [stɑːt] n inizio; (of race) partenza; (sudden movement) sobbalzo // vt cominciare, iniziare // vi partire, mettersi in viaggio; (jump) sobbalzare; **to ~ doing sth** (in)cominciare a fare qc; **to ~ off** vi cominciare; (leave) partire; **to ~ up** vi cominciare; (car) avviarsi // vt iniziare; (car) avviare; **~er** n (AUT) motorino d'avviamento; (SPORT: official) starter m inv; (: runner, horse) partente m/f; (CULIN) primo piatto; **~ing point** n punto di partenza.

startle ['stɑːtl] vt far trasalire; **startling** a sorprendente, sbalorditivo(a).

starvation [stɑːˈveɪʃən] n fame f, inedia.

starve [stɑːv] vi morire di fame; soffrire la fame // vt far morire di fame, affamare; **I'm starving** muoio di fame.

state [steɪt] n stato // vt dichiarare, affermare; annunciare; **the S~s** gli Stati Uniti; **to be in a ~** essere agitato(a); **~d** a fissato(a), stabilito(a); **~ly** a maestoso(a), imponente; **~ment** n dichiarazione f; (LAW) deposizione f; **~sman** n statista m.

static ['stætɪk] n (RADIO) scariche fpl // a statico(a); **~ electricity** n elettricità statica.

station ['steɪʃən] n stazione f; (rank) rango, condizione f // vt collocare, disporre.

stationary ['steɪʃənərɪ] a fermo(a), immobile.

stationer ['steɪʃənə*] n cartolaio/a; **~'s (shop)** n cartoleria; **~y** n articoli mpl di cancelleria.

station master ['steɪʃənmɑːstə*] n (RAIL) capostazione m.

station wagon ['steɪʃənwægən] n (US) giardinetta.

statistic [stəˈtɪstɪk] n statistica; **~s** npl (science) statistica; **~al** a statistico(a).

statue ['stætjuː] n statua.

stature ['stætʃə*] n statura.

status ['steɪtəs] n posizione f, condizione f sociale; prestigio; stato; **the ~ quo** lo statu quo; **~ symbol** n simbolo di prestigio.

statute ['stætjuːt] n legge f; **~s** npl (of club etc) statuto; **statutory** a stabilito(a) dalla legge, statutario(a).

staunch [stɔːntʃ] a fidato(a), leale.

stave [steɪv] n (MUS) rigo // vt: **to ~ off** (attack) respingere; (threat) evitare.

stay [steɪ] n (period of time) soggiorno, permanenza // vi rimanere; (reside) alloggiare, stare; (spend some time) trattenersi, soggiornare; **to ~ put** non muoversi; **to ~ with friends** stare presso amici; **to ~ the night** passare la notte; **to ~ behind** vi restare indietro; **to ~ in** vi (at home) stare in casa; **to ~ on** vi restare, rimanere; **to ~ out** vi (of house) rimanere fuori (di casa); **to ~ up** vi (at night) rimanere alzato(a).

STD n (abbr of Subscriber Trunk Dialling) teleselezione f.

steadfast ['stedfɑːst] a fermo(a), risoluto(a).

steadily ['stedɪlɪ] ad continuamente; (walk) con passo sicuro.

steady ['stedɪ] a stabile, solido(a), fermo(a); (regular) costante; (person) calmo(a), tranquillo(a) // vt stabilizzare; calmare; **to ~ oneself** ritrovare l'equilibrio.

steak [steɪk] n (meat) bistecca; (fish) trancia.

steal, pt **stole**, pp **stolen** [stiːl, stəul, 'stəuln] rubare.

stealth [stelθ] n: **by ~** furtivamente; **~y** a furtivo(a).

steam [stiːm] n vapore m // vt trattare con vapore; (CULIN) cuocere a vapore // vi fumare; (ship): **to ~ along** filare; **~ engine** n macchina a vapore; (RAIL) locomotiva a vapore; **~er** n piroscafo, vapore m; **~roller** n rullo compressore.

steel [stiːl] n acciaio // cpd di acciaio; **~works** n acciaieria.

steep [stiːp] a ripido(a), scosceso(a); (price) eccessivo(a) // vt inzuppare; (washing) mettere a molo.

steeple ['stiːpl] n campanile m; **~chase** n corsa a ostacoli, steeplechase m inv.

steer [stɪə*] n manzo // vt (ship) governare; (car) guidare // vi (NAUT: person) governare; (: ship) rispondere al timone; (car) guidarsi; **~ing** n (AUT) sterzo; **~ing column** n piantone m dello sterzo; **~ing wheel** n volante m.

stem [stem] n (of flower, plant) stelo; (of tree) fusto; (of glass) gambo; (of fruit, leaf) picciolo; (NAUT) prua, prora // vt contenere, arginare; **to ~ from** vt fus provenire da, derivare da.

stench [stentʃ] n puzzo, fetore m.

stencil ['stensl] n (of metal, cardboard) stampino, mascherina; (in typing) matrice f.

step [step] n passo; (stair) gradino, scalino; (action) mossa, azione f // vi: **to ~ forward** fare un passo avanti; **~s** npl = **stepladder; to ~ down** vi (fig) ritirarsi; **to ~ off** vt fus scendere da; **to ~ up** vt aumentare; intensificare; **~brother** n fratellastro; **~child** n figliastro/a; **~father** n patrigno; **~ladder** n scala a libretto; **~mother** n matrigna; **stepping stone** n pietra di un guado; (fig) trampolino; **~sister** n sorellastra.

stereo ['stɛrɪəu] n (system) sistema m stereofonico; (record player) stereo m inv // a (also: **~phonic**) stereofonico(a).

stereotype ['stɪərɪətaɪp] n stereotipo.

sterile ['sterail] a sterile; **sterilize** ['sterilaiz] vt sterilizzare.

sterling ['stɜːlɪŋ] a (gold, silver) di buona lega; (fig) autentico(a), genuino(a) // n (ECON) (lira) sterlina; **a pound ~** una lira sterlina.

stern [stɜːn] a severo(a) // n (NAUT) poppa.

stethoscope ['steθəskəup] n stetoscopio.

stew [stjuː] n stufato // vt, vi cuocere in umido.

steward ['stjuːəd] n (AVIAT, NAUT, RAIL)

steward *m inv*; (*in club etc*) dispensiere *m*; ~ess *n* assistente *f* di volo, hostess *f inv*.

stick [stɪk] *n* stecco; bastone *m* // *vb* (*pt, pp* **stuck** [stʌk]) *vt* (*glue*) attaccare; (*thrust*): **to ~ sth into** conficcare *or* piantare *or* infiggere qc in; (*col: put*) ficcare; (*col: tolerate*) sopportare // *vi* conficcarsi; tenere; (*remain*) restare, rimanere; **to ~ out, to ~ up** *vi* sporgere, spuntare; **to ~ up for** *vt fus* difendere; ~**er** *n* cartellino adesivo.

stickler ['stɪklə*] *n*: **to be a ~ for** essere pignolo(a) su, tenere molto a.

sticky ['stɪkɪ] *a* attaccaticcio(a), vischioso(a); (*label*) adesivo(a).

stiff [stɪf] *a* rigido(a), duro(a); (*muscle*) legato(a), indolenzito(a); (*difficult*) difficile, arduo(a); (*cold*) freddo(a), formale; (*strong*) forte; (*high: price*) molto alto(a); ~**en** *vt* irrigidire; rinforzare // *vi* irrigidirsi; indurirsi; ~ **neck** *n* torcicollo.

stifle ['staɪfl] *vt* soffocare; **stifling** *a* (*heat*) soffocante.

stigma ['stɪɡmə] *n* (*BOT, fig*) stigma *m*; ~**ta** [stɪɡ'mɑːtə] *npl* (*REL*) stigmate *fpl*.

stile [staɪl] *n* cavalcasiepe *m*; cavalcasteccato.

stiletto [stɪ'letəu] *n* (*also:* ~ **heel**) tacco a spillo.

still [stɪl] *a* fermo(a); silenzioso(a) // *ad* (*up to this time, even*) ancora; (*nonetheless*) tuttavia, ciò nonostante; ~**born** *a* nato(a) morto(a); ~ **life** *n* natura morta.

stilt [stɪlt] *n* trampolo; (*pile*) palo.

stilted ['stɪltɪd] *a* freddo(a), formale; artificiale.

stimulate ['stɪmjuleɪt] *vt* stimolare; **stimulating** *a* stimolante.

stimulus, *pl* **stimuli** ['stɪmjuləs, 'stɪmjulaɪ] *n* stimolo.

sting [stɪŋ] *n* puntura; (*organ*) pungiglione *m* // *vt* (*pt, pp* **stung** [stʌŋ]) pungere.

stingy ['stɪndʒɪ] *a* spilorcio(a), tirchio(a).

stink [stɪŋk] *n* fetore *m*, puzzo // *vi* (*pt* **stank**, *pp* **stunk** [stæŋk, stʌŋk]) puzzare; ~**er** *n* (*col*) porcheria; fetente *m/f*; ~**ing** *a* (*col*): **a ~ing...** uno schifo di..., un(a) maledetto(a)...

stint [stɪnt] *n* lavoro, compito // *vi*: **to ~ on** lesinare su.

stipulate ['stɪpjuleɪt] *vt* stipulare.

stir [stə:*] *n* agitazione *f*, clamore *m* // *vt* rimescolare; (*move*) smuovere, agitare // *vi* muoversi; **to ~ up** *vt* provocare, suscitare; ~**ring** *a* eccitante; commovente.

stirrup ['stɪrəp] *n* staffa.

stitch [stɪtʃ] *n* (*SEWING*) punto; (*KNITTING*) maglia; (*MED*) punto (di sutura); (*pain*) fitta // *vt* cucire, attaccare; suturare.

stoat [stəut] *n* ermellino.

stock [stɔk] *n* riserva, provvista; (*COMM*) giacenza, stock *m inv*; (*AGR*) bestiame *m*; (*CULIN*) brodo; (*FINANCE*) titoli *mpl*, azioni *fpl* // *a* (*fig: reply etc*) consueto(a), classico(a) // *vt* (*have in stock*) avere, vendere; **well-~ed** ben fornito(a); **to**

take ~ (*fig*) fare il punto; **to ~ up with** *vt fus* fare provvista di.

stockade [stɔ'keɪd] *n* palizzata.

stockbroker ['stɔkbrəukə*] *n* agente *m* di cambio.

stock exchange ['stɔkɪkstʃeɪndʒ] *n* Borsa (Valori).

stocking ['stɔkɪŋ] *n* calza.

stockist ['stɔkɪst] *n* fornitore *m*.

stock market ['stɔkmɑːkɪt] *n* Borsa, mercato finanziario.

stock phrase ['stɔk'freɪz] *n* cliché *m inv*.

stockpile ['stɔkpaɪl] *n* riserva // *vt* accumulare riserve.

stocktaking ['stɔkteɪkɪŋ] *n* (*COMM*) inventario.

stocky ['stɔkɪ] *a* tarchiato(a), tozzo(a).

stodgy ['stɔdʒɪ] *a* pesante, indigesto(a).

stoical ['stəuɪkəl] *a* stoico(a).

stoke [stəuk] *vt* alimentare; ~**r** *n* fochista *m*.

stole [stəul] *pt of* **steal** // *n* stola.

stolen ['stəuln] *pp of* **steal**.

stolid ['stɔlɪd] *a* impassibile.

stomach ['stʌmək] *n* stomaco; (*abdomen*) ventre *m* // *vt* sopportare, digerire; ~**ache** *n* mal *m* di stomaco.

stone [stəun] *n* pietra; (*pebble*) sasso, ciottolo; (*in fruit*) nocciolo; (*MED*) calcolo; (*weight*) misura di peso = 6.348 kg.; 14 libbre // *cpd* di pietra // *vt* lapidare; ~**-cold** *a* gelido(a), ~**-deaf** *a* sordo(a) come una campana; ~**work** *n* muratura; **stony** *a* pietroso(a), sassoso(a).

stood [stud] *pt,pp of* **stand**.

stool [stuːl] *n* sgabello.

stoop [stuːp] *vi* (*also:* **have a ~**) avere una curvatura; (*bend*) chinarsi, curvarsi.

stop [stɔp] *n* arresto; (*stopping place*) fermata; (*in punctuation*) punto // *vt* arrestare, fermare; (*break off*) interrompere; (*also:* **put a ~ to**) porre fine a // *vi* fermarsi; (*rain, noise etc*) cessare, finire; **to ~ doing sth** cessare *or* finire di fare qc; **to ~ dead** fermarsi di colpo; **to ~ off** *vi* sostare brevemente; **to ~ up** *vt* (*hole*) chiudere, turare; ~**lights** *npl* (*AUT*) stop *mpl*; ~**over** *n* breve sosta; (*AVIAT*) scalo.

stoppage ['stɔpɪdʒ] *n* arresto, fermata; (*of pay*) trattenuta; (*strike*) interruzione *f* del lavoro.

stopper ['stɔpə*] *n* tappo.

stop-press ['stɔp'pres] *n* ultimissime *fpl*.

stopwatch ['stɔpwɔtʃ] *n* cronometro.

storage ['stɔːrɪdʒ] *n* immagazzinamento; (*COMPUTERS*) memoria.

store [stɔː*] *n* provvista, riserva; (*depot*) deposito; (*large shop*) grande magazzino // *vt* immagazzinare; **to ~ up** *vt* mettere in serbo, conservare; ~**room** *n* dispensa.

storey ['stɔːrɪ] *n* piano.

stork [stɔːk] *n* cicogna.

storm [stɔːm] *n* tempesta, temporale *m*, burrasca; uragano // *vi* (*fig*) infuriarsi // *vt* prendere d'assalto; ~**y** *a* tempestoso(a), burrascoso(a).

story ['stɔːrɪ] *n* storia; favola; racconto; (*US*) = **storey**; ~**book** *n* libro di racconti.

stout [staut] *a* solido(a), robusto(a); (*brave*) coraggioso(a); (*fat*) corpulento(a), grasso(a) // *n* birra scura.

stove [stəuv] *n* (*for cooking*) fornello; (: *small*) fornelletto; (*for heating*) stufa.

stow [stəu] *vt* mettere via; ~**away** *n* passeggero(a) clandestino(a).

straddle ['strædl] *vt* stare a cavalcioni di.

strafe [strɑːf] *vt* mitragliare.

straggle ['strægl] *vi* crescere (*or* estendersi) disordinatamente; trascinarsi; rimanere indietro; ~**d along the coast** disseminati(e) lungo la costa; ~**r** *n* sbandato/a; **straggling, straggly** *a* (*hair*) in disordine.

straight [streit] *a* dritto(a); (*frank*) onesto(a), franco(a) // *ad* diritto; (*drink*) liscio // *n*: **the** ~ **linea retta**; (*RAIL*) il rettilineo; (*SPORT*) la dirittura d'arrivo; **to put** *or* **get** ~ mettere in ordine, mettere ordine in; ~ **away**, ~**off** (*at once*) immediatamente; ~ **off**, ~ **out** senza esitare; ~**en** *vt* (*also*: ~**en out**) raddrizzare; ~**forward** *a* semplice; onesto(a), franco(a).

strain [strein] *n* (*TECH*) sollecitazione *f*; (*physical*) sforzo; (*mental*) tensione *f*; (*MED*) strappo; distorsione *f*; (*streak, trace*) tendenza; elemento // *vt* tendere; (*muscle*) sforzare; (*ankle*) storcere; (*friendship, marriage*) mettere a dura prova; (*filter*) colare, filtrare // *vi* sforzarsi; ~**s** *npl* (*MUS*) motivo; ~**ed** *a* (*laugh etc*) forzato(a); (*relations*) teso(a); ~**er** *n* passino, colino.

strait [streit] *n* (*GEO*) stretto; ~**jacket** *n* camicia di forza; ~**-laced** *a* bacchettone(a).

strand [strænd] *n* (*of thread*) filo; ~**ed** *a* nei guai; senza mezzi di trasporto.

strange [streindʒ] *a* (*not known*) sconosciuto(a); (*odd*) strano(a), bizzarro(a); ~**r** *n* sconosciuto/a; estraneo/a.

strangle ['stræŋgl] *vt* strangolare; ~**hold** *n* (*fig*) stretta (mortale).

strap [stræp] *n* cinghia; (*of slip, dress*) spallina, bretella // *vt* legare con una cinghia; (*child etc*) punire (con una cinghia).

strapping ['stræpɪŋ] *a* ben piantato(a).

strata ['strɑːtə] *npl of* **stratum**.

strategic [strəˈtiːdʒɪk] *a* strategico(a).

strategy ['strætɪdʒɪ] *n* strategia.

stratum, pl strata ['strɑːtəm, 'strɑːtə] *n* strato.

straw [strɔː] *n* paglia.

strawberry ['strɔːbərɪ] *n* fragola.

stray [strei] *a* (*animal*) randagio(a) // *vi* perdersi; ~ **bullet** *n* proiettile *m* vagante.

streak [striːk] *n* striscia; (*fig: of madness etc*): **a** ~ **of** una vena di // *vt* striare, screziare // *vi*: **to** ~ **past** passare vicino(a) come un fulmine; ~**y** *a*

screziato(a), striato(a); ~**y bacon** *n* ≈ pancetta.

stream [striːm] *n* ruscello; corrente *f*; (*of people*) fiume *m* // *vt* (*SCOL*) dividere in livelli di rendimento // *vi* scorrere; **to** ~ **in/out** entrare/uscire a fiotti.

streamer ['striːmə*] *n* (*flag*) fiamma; (*of paper*) stella filante.

streamlined ['striːmlaɪnd] *a* aerodinamico(a); affusolato(a); (*fig*) razionalizzato(a).

street [striːt] *n* strada, via; ~**car** *n* (*US*) tram *m inv*; ~ **lamp** *n* lampione *m*.

strength [streŋθ] *n* forza; (*of girder, knot etc*) resistenza, solidità; ~**en** *vt* rinforzare; fortificare; consolidare.

strenuous ['strenjuəs] *a* vigoroso(a), energico(a); (*tiring*) duro(a), pesante.

stress [stres] *n* (*force, pressure*) pressione *f*; (*mental strain*) tensione *f*; (*accent*) accento // *vt* insistere su, sottolineare.

stretch [stretʃ] *n* (*of sand etc*) distesa // *vi* stirarsi; (*extend*): **to** ~ **to/as far as** estendersi fino a // *vt* tendere, allungare; (*spread*) distendere; (*fig*) spingere (al massimo); **at a** ~ ininterrottamente; **to** ~ **out** *vi* allungarsi, estendersi // *vt* (*arm etc*) allungare, tendere; (*to spread*) distendere; **to** ~ **out for sth** allungare la mano per prendere qc.

stretcher ['stretʃə*] *n* barella, lettiga.

strewn [struːn] *a*: ~ **with** cosparso(a) di.

stricken ['strɪkən] *a* provato(a); affranto(a); ~ **with** colpito(a) da.

strict [strɪkt] *a* (*severe*) rigido(a), severo(a); (*precise*) preciso(a), stretto(a); ~**ly** *ad* severamente; strettamente, assolutamente.

stride [straɪd] *n* passo lungo // *vi* (*pt* **strode**, *pp* **stridden** [strəud, 'strɪdn]) camminare a grandi passi.

strident ['straɪdnt] *a* stridente.

strife [straɪf] *n* conflitto; litigi *mpl*.

strike [straɪk] *n* sciopero; (*of oil etc*) scoperta; (*attack*) attacco // *vb* (*pt,pp* **struck** [strʌk]) *vt* colpire; (*oil etc*) scoprire, trovare // *vi* far sciopero, scioperare; (*attack*) attaccare; (*clock*) suonare; **to** ~ **a match** accendere un fiammifero; **to** ~ **down** *vt* (*fig*) atterrare; **to** ~ **out** *vt* depennare; **to** ~ **up** *vt* (*MUS*) attaccare; **to** ~ **up a friendship with** fare amicizia con; ~**breaker** *n* crumiro/a; ~**r** *n* scioperante *m/f*; (*SPORT*) attaccante *m*; **striking** *a* impressionante.

string [strɪŋ] *n* spago; (*row*) fila; sequenza; catena; (*MUS*) corda // *vt* (*pt,pp* **strung** [strʌŋ]): **to** ~ **out** disporre di fianco; **the** ~**s** *npl* (*MUS*) gli archi; ~ **bean** *n* fagiolino; ~**(ed) instrument** *n* (*MUS*) strumento a corda; ~ **of pearls** filo di perle.

stringent ['strɪndʒənt] *a* rigoroso(a); (*need*) stringente, impellente.

strip [strɪp] *n* striscia // *vt* spogliare; (*also*: ~ **down**: *machine*) smontare // *vi* spogliarsi; ~ **cartoon** *n* fumetto.

stripe [straɪp] *n* striscia, riga; **~d** *a* a strisce *or* righe.

strip light ['strɪplaɪt] *n* tubo al neon.

stripper ['strɪpə⁰] *n* spogliarellista.

striptease ['strɪptiːz] *n* spogliarello.

strive, *pt* **strove**, *pp* **striven** [straɪv, strəʊv, 'strɪvn] *vi*: **to ~ to do** sforzarsi di fare.

strode [strəʊd] *pt of* **stride.**

stroke [strəʊk] *n* colpo; (MED) colpo apoplettico; (*caress*) carezza // *vt* accarezzare; **at a ~** in un attimo; **on the ~ of 5** alle 5 in punto, allo scoccare delle 5.

stroll [strəʊl] *n* giretto, passeggiatina // *vi* andare a spasso.

strong [strɔŋ] *a* forte; vigoroso(a); solido(a); vivo(a); **they are 50 ~** sono in 50; **~hold** *n* fortezza, roccaforte *f*; **~ly** *ad* fortemente, con forza; energicamente; vivamente; **~room** *n* camera di sicurezza.

strove [strəʊv] *pt of* **strive.**

struck [strʌk] *pt,pp of* **strike.**

structural ['strʌktʃərəl] *a* strutturale; (CONSTR) di costruzione; di struttura.

structure ['strʌktʃə⁰] *n* struttura; (*building*) costruzione *f*, fabbricato.

struggle ['strʌgl] *n* lotta // *vi* lottare.

strum [strʌm] *vt* (*guitar*) strimpellare.

strung [strʌŋ] *pt,pp of* **string.**

strut [strʌt] *n* sostegno, supporto // *vi* pavoneggiarsi.

stub [stʌb] *n* mozzicone *m*; (*of ticket etc*) matrice *f*, talloncino; **to ~ out** *vt* schiacciare.

stubble ['stʌbl] *n* stoppia; (*on chin*) barba ispida.

stubborn ['stʌbən] *a* testardo(a), ostinato(a).

stuck [stʌk] *pt,pp of* **stick** // *a* (*jammed*) bloccato(a); **~-up** *a* presuntuoso(a).

stud [stʌd] *n* bottoncino; borchia; (*of horses*) scuderia, allevamento di cavalli; (*also:* **~ horse**) stallone *m* // *vt* (*fig*): **~ded with** tempestato(a) di.

student ['stjuːdənt] *n* studente/essa // *cpd* studentesco(a); universitario(a); degli studenti.

studied ['stʌdɪd] *a* studiato(a), calcolato(a).

studio ['stjuːdɪəu] *n* studio.

studious ['stjuːdɪəs] *a* studioso(a); (*studied*) studiato(a), voluto(a); **~ly** *ad* (*carefully*) deliberatamente, di proposito.

study ['stʌdɪ] *n* studio // *vt* studiare; esaminare // *vi* studiare.

stuff [stʌf] *n* cosa, roba; (*belongings*) cose *fpl*, roba; (*substance*) sostanza, materiale *m* // *vt* imbottire; (CULIN) farcire; **~ing** *n* imbottitura, (CULIN) ripieno; **~y** *a* (*room*) mal ventilato(a), senz'aria; (*ideas*) antiquato(a).

stumble ['stʌmbl] *vi* inciampare; **to ~ across** (*fig*) imbattersi in; **stumbling block** *n* ostacolo, scoglio.

stump [stʌmp] *n* ceppo; (*of limb*) moncone *m*.

stun [stʌn] *vt* stordire; sbalordire.

stung [stʌŋ] *pt, pp of* **sting.**

stunk [stʌŋk] *pp of* **stink.**

stunning ['stʌnɪŋ] *a* (*piece of news etc*) sbalorditivo(a); (*girl, dress*) favoloso(a), stupendo(a).

stunt [stʌnt] *n* bravata; trucco pubblicitario; (AVIAT) acrobazia // *vt* arrestare; **~ed** a stentato(a), rachitico(a); **~man** *n* cascatore *m*.

stupefy ['stjuːpɪfaɪ] *vt* stordire; intontire; (*fig*) stupire.

stupendous [stjuː'pɛndəs] *a* stupendo(a), meraviglioso(a).

stupid ['stjuːpɪd] *a* stupido(a); **~ity** [-'pɪdɪtɪ] *n* stupidità *f* inv, stupidaggine *f*.

stupor ['stjuːpə⁰] *n* torpore *m*.

sturdy ['stɜːdɪ] *a* robusto(a), vigoroso(a); solido(a).

sturgeon ['stɜːdʒən] *n* storione *m*.

stutter ['stʌtə⁰] *n* balbuzie *f* // *vi* balbettare.

sty [staɪ] *n* (*of pigs*) porcile *m*.

stye [staɪ] *n* (MED) orzaiolo.

style [staɪl] *n* stile *m*; (*distinction*) eleganza, classe *f*; **stylish** *a* elegante.

stylized ['staɪlaɪzd] *a* stilizzato(a).

stylus ['staɪləs] *n* (*of record player*) puntina.

suave [swɑːv] *a* untuoso(a).

sub... [sʌb] *prefix* **sub...**, **sotto...**; **subconscious** *a, n* subcosciente (*m*); **subdivide** *vt* suddividere.

subdue [səb'djuː] *vt* sottomettere, soggiogare; **~d** *a* pacato(a); (*light*) attenuato(a); (*person*) poco esuberante.

subject *n* ['sʌbdʒɪkt] soggetto; (*citizen etc*) cittadino/a; (SCOL) materia // *vt* [səb'dʒɛkt]: **to ~ to** sottomettere a; esporre a; **to be ~ to** (*law*) essere sottomesso(a) a; (*disease*) essere soggetto(a) a; **~ive** *a* soggettivo(a); **~ matter** *n* argomento; contenuto.

subjunctive [səb'dʒʌŋktɪv] *a* congiuntivo(a) // *n* congiuntivo.

sublime [sə'blaɪm] *a* sublime.

submachine gun ['sʌbmə'ʃiːngʌn] *n* mitra *m* inv.

submarine [sʌbmə'riːn] *n* sommergibile *m*.

submerge [səb'mɜːdʒ] *vt* sommergere; immergere // *vi* immergersi.

submission [səb'mɪʃən] *n* sottomissione *f*.

submissive [səb'mɪsɪv] *a* remissivo(a).

submit [səb'mɪt] *vt* sottomettere // *vi* sottomettersi.

subordinate [sə'bɔːdɪnət] *a,n* subordinato(a).

subscribe [səb'skraɪb] *vi* contribuire; **to ~ to** (*opinion*) approvare, condividere; (*fund*) sottoscrivere; (*newspaper*) abbonarsi a; essere abbonato(a) a; **~r** *n* (*to periodical, telephone*) abbonato/a.

subscription [səb'skrɪpʃən] *n* sottoscrizione *f*; abbonamento.

subsequent ['sʌbsɪkwənt] *a* successivo(a),

seguente; conseguente; ~ly ad in seguito, successivamente.

subside [səb'saɪd] vi cedere, abbassarsi; (flood) decrescere; (wind) calmarsi; ~nce [-'saɪdns] n cedimento, abbassamento.

subsidiary [səb'sɪdɪərɪ] a sussidiario(a); accessorio(a) // n filiale f.

subsidize ['sʌbsɪdaɪz] vt sovvenzionare.

subsidy ['sʌbsɪdɪ] n sovvenzione f.

subsistence [səb'sɪstəns] n esistenza; mezzi mpl di sostentamento.

substance ['sʌbstəns] n sostanza; (fig) essenza.

substantial [səb'stænʃl] a solido(a); (amount, progress etc) notevole; (meal) sostanzioso(a).

substantiate [səb'stænʃɪeɪt] vt comprovare.

substitute ['sʌbstɪtjuːt] n (person) sostituto/a; (thing) succedaneo, surrogato // vt: to ~ sth/sb for sostituire qc/qd con; **substitution** [-'tjuːʃən] n sostituzione f.

subtitle ['sʌbtaɪtl] n (CINEMA) sottotitolo.

subtle ['sʌtl] a sottile; ~ty n sottigliezza.

subtract [səb'trækt] vt sottrarre; ~ion [-'trækʃən] n sottrazione f.

suburb ['sʌbəːb] n sobborgo; the ~s la periferia; ~an [sə'bəːbən] a suburbano(a).

subversive [səb'vəːsɪv] a sovversivo(a).

subway ['sʌbweɪ] n (US) metropolitana; (Brit) sottopassaggio.

succeed [sək'siːd] vi riuscire; avere successo // vt succedere a; to ~ in doing riuscire a fare; ~ing a (following) successivo(a).

success [sək'sɛs] n successo; ~ful a (venture) coronato(a) da successo, riuscito(a); **to be ~ful (in doing)** riuscire (a fare).

succession [sək'sɛʃən] n successione f.

successive [sək'sɛsɪv] a successivo(a); consecutivo(a).

successor [sək'sɛsə*] n successore m.

succinct [sək'sɪŋkt] a succinto(a), breve.

succulent ['sʌkjulənt] a succulento(a).

succumb [sə'kʌm] vi soccombere.

such [sʌtʃ] a, det tale; (of that kind): ~ a book un tale libro, un libro del genere; ~ books tali libri, libri del genere; (so much): ~ courage tanto coraggio; ~ a long trip un viaggio così lungo; ~ good books libri così buoni; ~ a lot of talmente or così tanto(a); **making ~ a noise** che facendo un rumore tale che; ~ as (like) come; a noise ~ as to un rumore tale da; as ~ ad come or in quanto tale; ~-and-~ det tale (after noun).

suck [sʌk] vt succhiare; (breast, bottle) poppare; ~er n (ZOOL, TECH) ventosa; (BOT) pollone m; (col) gonzo/a, babbeo/a.

suckle ['sʌkl] vt allattare.

suction ['sʌkʃən] n succhiamento; (TECH) aspirazione f.

sudden ['sʌdn] a improvviso(a); **all of a ~** improvvisamente, all'improvviso; ~ly

ad bruscamente, improvvisamente, di colpo.

suds [sʌdz] npl schiuma (di sapone).

sue [suː] vt citare in giudizio.

suede [sweɪd] n pelle f scamosciata // cpd scamosciato(a).

suet ['suɪt] n grasso di rognone.

suffer ['sʌfə*] vt soffrire, patire; (bear) sopportare, tollerare // vi soffrire; ~ing n sofferenza.

suffice [sə'faɪs] vi essere sufficiente, bastare.

sufficient [sə'fɪʃənt] a sufficiente; ~ money abbastanza soldi; ~ly ad sufficientemente, abbastanza.

suffix ['sʌfɪks] n suffisso.

suffocate ['sʌfəkeɪt] vi (have difficulty breathing) soffocare; (die through lack of air) asfissiare; **suffocation** [-'keɪʃən] n soffocamento; (MED) asfissia.

sugar ['ʃugə*] n zucchero // vt zuccherare; ~ beet n barbabietola da zucchero; ~ cane n canna da zucchero; ~y a zuccherino(a), dolce; (fig) sdolcinato(a).

suggest [sə'dʒɛst] vt proporre, suggerire; indicare; ~ion [-'dʒɛstʃən] n suggerimento, proposta; ~ive a suggestivo(a).

suicide ['suɪsaɪd] n (person) suicida m/f; (act) suicidio.

suit [suːt] n (man's) vestito; (woman's) completo, tailleur m inv; (CARDS) seme m, colore m // vt andar bene a or per; essere adatto(a) a or per; (adapt): **to ~ sth to** adattare qc a; ~able a adatto(a); appropriato(a).

suitcase ['suːtkeɪs] n valigia.

suite [swiːt] n (of rooms) appartamento; (MUS) suite f inv; (furniture): **bedroom/dining room ~** arredo or mobilia per la camera da letto/sala da pranzo.

sulk [sʌlk] vi fare il broncio; ~y a imbronciato(a).

sullen ['sʌlən] a scontroso(a); cupo(a).

sulphur ['sʌlfə*] n zolfo; ~ic [-'fjuərɪk] a: ~ic acid acido solforico.

sultana [sʌl'tɑːnə] n (fruit) uva (secca) sultanina.

sultry ['sʌltrɪ] a afoso(a).

sum [sʌm] n somma; (SCOL etc) addizione f; **to ~ up** vt,vi ricapitolare.

summarize ['sʌməraɪz] vt riassumere, riepilogare.

summary ['sʌmərɪ] n riassunto // a (justice) sommario(a).

summer ['sʌmə*] n estate f // cpd d'estate, estivo(a); ~house n (in garden) padiglione m; ~time n (season) estate f; ~ time n (by clock) ora legale (estiva).

summit ['sʌmɪt] n cima, sommità; vertice m; ~ (conference) n (conferenza al) vertice.

summon ['sʌmən] vt chiamare, convocare; **to ~ up** vt raccogliere, fare appello a; ~s n ordine m di comparizione // vt citare.

sump [sʌmp] n (AUT) coppa dell'olio.

sumptuous ['sʌmptjuəs] a sontuoso(a).

sun [sʌn] n sole m; in the ~ al sole;
~bathe vi prendere un bagno di sole;
~burnt a abbronzato(a); (painfully) scottato(a) dal sole; ~ cream n crema solare.

Sunday ['sʌndɪ] n domenica.

sundial ['sʌndaɪəl] n meridiana.

sundry ['sʌndrɪ] a vari(e), diversi(e); all
and ~ tutti quanti; sundries npl articoli
diversi, cose diverse.

sunflower ['sʌnflauə*] n girasole m.

sung [sʌŋ] pp of sing.

sunglasses ['sʌnglɑːsɪz] npl occhiali mpl
da sole.

sunk [sʌŋk] pp of sink; ~en a
sommerso(a); infossato(a).

sun: ~light n (luce f del) sole m; ~lit a
assolato(a), soleggiato(a); ~ny a
assolato(a), soleggiato(a); (fig) allegro(a),
felice; ~rise n levata del sole, alba; ~set
n tramonto; ~shade n parasole m;
~shine n (luce f del) sole m; ~stroke n
insolazione f, colpo di sole; ~tan n
abbronzatura; ~tan oil n olio solare;
~trap n luogo molto assolato, angolo
pieno di sole.

super ['suːpə*] a (col) fantastico(a).

superannuation [suːpərænjuˈeɪʃən] n
contributi mpl pensionistici; pensione f.

superb [suːˈpɔːb] a magnifico(a).

supercilious [suːpəˈsɪlɪəs] a sprezzante,
sdegnoso(a).

superficial [suːpəˈfɪʃəl] a superficiale.

superfluous [suˈpɔːfluəs] a superfluo(a).

superhuman [suːpəˈhjuːmən] a
sovrumano(a).

superimpose ['suːpərɪmˈpəuz] vt
sovrapporre.

superintendent [suːpərɪnˈtɛndənt] n
direttore/trice; (POLICE) ≈ commissario
(capo).

superior [suˈpɪərɪə*] a,n superiore (m/f);
~ity [-ˈɔrɪtɪ] n superiorità.

superlative [suˈpɔːlətɪv] a superlativo(a),
supremo(a) // n (LING) superlativo.

superman ['suːpəmæn] n superuomo.

supermarket ['suːpəmɑːkɪt] n
supermercato.

supernatural [suːpəˈnætʃərəl] a
soprannaturale.

superpower ['suːpəpauə*] n (POL)
superpotenza.

supersede [suːpəˈsiːd] vt sostituire,
soppiantare.

supersonic ['suːpəˈsɒnɪk] a
supersonico(a).

superstition [suːpəˈstɪʃən] n superstizione
f.

superstitious [suːpəˈstɪʃəs] a
superstizioso(a).

supervise ['suːpəvaɪz] vt (person etc)
sorvegliare; (organization) soprintendere
a; supervision [-ˈvɪʒən] n sorveglianza;
supervisione f; supervisor n sorvegliante
m/f; soprintendente m/f; (in shop)
capocommesso/a.

supper ['sʌpə*] n cena.

supple ['sʌpl] a flessibile; agile.

supplement n ['sʌplɪmənt] supplemento
// vt [sʌplɪˈmɛnt] completare, integrare;
~ary [-ˈmɛntərɪ] a supplementare.

supplier [səˈplaɪə*] n fornitore m.

supply [səˈplaɪ] vt (provide) fornire;
(equip): to ~ (with) approvvigionare
(di); attrezzare (con) // n riserva,
provvista; (supplying) approvvigionamento; (TECH) alimentazione f // cpd
(teacher etc) supplente; supplies npl
(food) viveri mpl; (MIL) sussistenza; ~
and demand la domanda e l'offerta.

support [səˈpɔːt] n (moral, financial etc)
sostegno, appoggio; (TECH) supporto // vt
sostenere; (financially) mantenere;
(uphold) sostenere, difendere; ~er n (POL
etc) sostenitore/trice, fautore/ trice;
(SPORT) tifoso/a.

suppose [səˈpəuz] vt, vi supporre;
immaginare; to be ~d to do essere
tenuto(a) a fare; ~dly [səˈpəuzɪdlɪ] ad
presumibilmente; (seemingly) apparentemente; supposing cj se, ammesso che +
sub; supposition [sʌpəˈzɪʃən] n
supposizione f, ipotesi f inv.

suppress [səˈprɛs] vt reprimere;
sopprimere; tenere segreto(a); ~ion
[səˈprɛʃən] n repressione f; soppressione f;
~or n (ELEC etc) soppressore m.

supremacy [suˈprɛməsɪ] n supremazia.

supreme [suˈpriːm] a supremo(a).

surcharge [ˈsɔːtʃɑːdʒ] n supplemento;
(extra tax) soprattassa.

sure [ʃuə*] a sicuro(a); (definite, convinced)
sicuro(a), certo(a); ~! (of course)
senz'altro!, certo!; ~ enough infatti; to
make ~ of assicurarsi di; ~-footed a
dal passo sicuro; ~ly ad sicuramente;
certamente.

surety ['ʃuərətɪ] n garanzia.

surf [sɔːf] n risacca; cresta dell'onda;
frangenti mpl.

surface ['sɔːfɪs] n superficie f // vt (road)
asfaltare // vi risalire alla superficie; (fig:
person) venire a galla, farsi vivo(a); ~
mail n posta ordinaria.

surfboard ['sɔːfbɔːd] n tavola per surfing.

surfeit ['sɔːfɪt] n: a ~ of un eccesso di;
un'indigestione di.

surfing ['sɔːfɪŋ] n surfing m.

surge [sɔːdʒ] n (strong movement) ondata;
(of feeling) impeto // vi (waves) gonfiarsi;
(ELEC: power) aumentare improvvisamente; (fig) sollevarsi.

surgeon ['sɔːdʒən] n chirurgo.

surgery ['sɔːdʒərɪ] n chirurgia; (room)
studio or gabinetto medico, ambulatorio;
~ hours npl orario delle visite or di
consultazione.

surgical ['sɔːdʒɪkl] a chirurgico(a); ~
spirit n alcool denaturato.

surly ['sɔːlɪ] a scontroso(a), burbero(a).

surmise [sɔːˈmaɪz] vt supporre,
congetturare.

surmount [sɔːˈmaunt] vt sormontare.

surname ['sɔːneɪm] n cognome m.

surpass [sɔːˈpɑːs] vt superare.

surplus ['sɔːpləs] n eccedenza; (ECON) surplus m inv // a eccedente, d'avanzo.

surprise [sə'praɪz] n sorpresa; (astonishment) stupore m // vt sorprendere; stupire; **surprising** a sorprendente, stupefacente.

surrender [sə'rendə*] n resa, capitolazione f // vi arrendersi.

surreptitious [sʌrəp'tɪʃəs] a furtivo(a).

surround [sə'raund] vt circondare; (MIL etc) accerchiare; **~ing** a circostante; **~ings** npl dintorni mpl; (fig) ambiente m.

surveillance [sɔː'veɪləns] n sorveglianza, controllo.

survey n ['sɔːveɪ] vista; (study) esame m; (in housebuying etc) perizia; (of land) rilevamento, rilievo topografico // vt [sɔː'veɪ] osservare; esaminare; valutare; rilevare; **~ing** n (of land) agrimensura; **~or** n perito; geometra m; (of land) agrimensore m.

survival [sə'vaɪvl] n sopravvivenza; (relic) reliquia, vestigio.

survive [sə'vaɪv] vi sopravvivere // vt sopravvivere a; **survivor** n superstite m/f, sopravvissuto/a.

susceptible [sə'septəbl] a: ~ (to) sensibile a; (disease) predisposto(a) (a).

suspect a, n ['sʌspekt] a sospetto(a) // n persona sospetta // vt [səs'pekt] sospettare; (think likely) supporre; (doubt) dubitare.

suspend [səs'pend] vt sospendere; **~ed sentence** n condanna con la condizionale; **~er belt** n reggicalze m inv; **~ers** npl giarrettiere fpl; (US) bretelle fpl.

suspense [səs'pens] n apprensione f; (in film etc) suspense m.

suspension [səs'penʃən] n (gen AUT) sospensione f; (of driving licence) ritiro temporaneo; ~ **bridge** n ponte m sospeso.

suspicion [səs'pɪʃən] n sospetto.

suspicious [səs'pɪʃəs] a (suspecting) sospettoso(a); (causing suspicion) sospetto(a).

sustain [səs'teɪn] vt sostenere; sopportare; (LAW: charge) confermare; (suffer) subire; **~ed** a (effort) prolungato(a).

sustenance ['sʌstɪnəns] n nutrimento; mezzi mpl di sostentamento.

swab [swɔb] n (MED) tampone m.

swagger ['swægə*] vi pavoneggiarsi.

swallow ['swɔləu] n (bird) rondine f // vt inghiottire; (fig: story) bere; **to ~ up** vt inghiottire.

swam [swæm] pt of **swim**.

swamp [swɔmp] n palude f // vt sommergere.

swan [swɔn] n cigno.

swap [swɔp] n scambio // vt: **to ~ (for)** scambiare (con).

swarm [swɔːm] n sciame m // vi formicolare; (bees) sciamare.

swarthy ['swɔːðɪ] a di carnagione scura.

swastika ['swɔstɪkə] n croce f uncinata, svastica.

swat [swɔt] vt schiacciare.

sway [sweɪ] vi (building) oscillare; (tree) ondeggiare; (person) barcollare // vt (influence) influenzare, dominare.

swear, pt **swore,** pp **sworn** [swɛə*, swɔː*, swɔːn] vi (witness etc) giurare; (curse) bestemmiare, imprecare; **to ~ to sth** giurare qc; **~word** n parolaccia.

sweat [swet] n sudore m, traspirazione f // vi sudare; **in a** ~ in un bagno di sudore.

sweater ['swetə*] n maglione m.

sweaty ['swetɪ] a sudato(a); bagnato(a) di sudore.

swede [swiːd] n rapa svedese.

Swede [swiːd] n svedese m/f.

Sweden ['swiːdn] n Svezia.

Swedish ['swiːdɪʃ] a svedese // n (LING) svedese m.

sweep [swiːp] n spazzata; (curve) curva; (expanse) distesa; (range) portata; (also: **chimney** ~) spazzacamino // vb (pt, pp swept [swept]) vt spazzare, scopare // vi camminare maestosamente; precipitarsi, lanciarsi; (e)stendersi; **to ~ away** vt spazzare via; trascinare via; **to ~ past** vi sfrecciare accanto; passare accanto maestosamente; **to ~ up** vt, vi spazzare; **~ing** a (gesture) largo(a); circolare; **a ~ing statement** una affermazione generica.

sweet [swiːt] n dolce m; (candy) caramella // a dolce; (fresh) fresco(a); (fig) piacevole; delicato(a), grazioso(a); gentile; **~bread** n animella; **~corn** n granturco dolce; **~en** vt addolcire; zuccherare; **~heart** n innamorato/a; **~ness** n sapore m dolce; dolcezza; **~pea** n pisello odoroso; **to have a ~ tooth** avere un debole per i dolci.

swell [swel] n (of sea) mare m lungo // a (col: excellent) favoloso(a) // vb (pt **~ed,** pp swollen, **~ed** ['swəulən]) vt gonfiare, ingrossare; aumentare // vi gonfiarsi, ingrossarsi; (sound) crescere; (MED) gonfiarsi; **~ing** n (MED) tumefazione f, gonfiore m.

sweltering ['sweltərɪŋ] a soffocante.

swept [swept] pt,pp of **sweep.**

swerve [swɔːv] vi deviare; (driver) sterzare; (boxer) scartare.

swift [swift] n (bird) rondone m // a rapido(a), veloce.

swig [swig] n (col: drink) sorsata.

swill [swil] n broda // vt (also: ~ **out,** ~ **down**) risciacquare.

swim [swim] n: **to go for a** ~ andare a fare una nuotata // vb (pt swam, pp swum [swæm, swʌm]) vi nuotare; (SPORT) fare del nuoto; (head, room) girare // vt (river, channel) attraversare o percorrere a nuoto; (length) nuotare; **~mer** n nuotatore/trice; **~ming** n nuoto; **~ming baths** npl piscina; **~ming cap** n cuffia; **~ming costume** n costume m da bagno; **~ming pool** n piscina; **~suit** n costume m da bagno.

swindle ['swindl] n truffa // vt truffare; **~r** n truffatore/trice.

swine [swaɪn] *n*, *pl inv* maiale *m*, porco; (*col!*) porco.

swing [swɪŋ] *n* altalena; (*movement*) oscillazione *f*; (*MUS*) ritmo; swing *m* // *vb* (*pt*, *pp* **swung** [swʌŋ]) *vt* dondolare, far oscillare; (*also*: ~ **round**) far girare // *vi* oscillare, dondolare; (*also*: ~ **round**) (*object*) roteare; (*person*) girarsi, voltarsi; **to be in full** ~ (*activity*) essere in piena attività; (*party etc*) essere nel pieno; ~ **bridge** *n* ponte *m* girevole; ~ **door** *n* porta battente.

swingeing [ˈswɪndʒɪŋ] *a* (*defeat*) violento(a); (*price increase*) enorme.

swinging [ˈswɪŋɪŋ] *a* (*step*) cadenzato(a), ritmico(a); (*rhythm, music*) trascinante.

swipe [swaɪp] *n* forte colpo; schiaffo // *vt* (*hit*) colpire con forza; dare uno schiaffo a; (*col: steal*) sgraffignare.

swirl [swə:l] *n* turbine *m*, mulinello // *vi* turbinare, far mulinello.

swish [swɪʃ] *a* (*col: smart*) all'ultimo grido, alla moda // *vi* sibilare.

Swiss [swɪs] *a*, *n*, *pl inv* svizzero(a); ~ **German** *a* svizzero(a) tedesco(a).

switch [swɪtʃ] *n* (*for light, radio etc*) interruttore *m*; (*change*) cambiamento // *vt* (*change*) cambiare; scambiare; **to** ~ **off** *vt* spegnere; **to** ~ **on** *vt* accendere; (*engine, machine*) mettere in moto, avviare; ~**back** *n* montagne *fpl* russe; ~**board** *n* (*TEL*) centralino; ~**board operator** centralinista *m/f*.

Switzerland [ˈswɪtsələnd] *n* Svizzera.

swivel [ˈswɪvl] *vi* (*also*: ~ **round**) girare.

swollen [ˈswəʊlən] *pp* of **swell** // *a* (*ankle etc*) gonfio(a).

swoon [swu:n] *vi* svenire.

swoop [swu:p] *n* (*by police etc*) incursione *f* // *vi* (*also*: ~ **down**) scendere in picchiata, piombare.

swop [swɒp] *n*, *vt* = **swap**.

sword [sɔ:d] *n* spada; ~**fish** *n* pesce *m* spada *inv*.

swore [swɔ:*] *pt* of **swear**.

sworn [swɔ:n] *pp* of **swear**.

swot [swɒt] *vt* sgobbare su // *vi* sgobbare.

swum [swʌm] *pp* of **swim**.

swung [swʌŋ] *pt*, *pp* of **swing**.

sycamore [ˈsɪkəmɔ:*] *n* sicomoro.

syllable [ˈsɪləbl] *n* sillaba.

syllabus [ˈsɪləbəs] *n* programma *m*.

symbol [ˈsɪmbl] *n* simbolo; ~**ic(al)** [-ˈbɔlɪk(l)] *a* simbolico(a); ~**ism** *n* simbolismo; ~**ize** *vt* simbolizzare.

symmetrical [sɪˈmetrɪkl] *a* simmetrico(a).

symmetry [ˈsɪmɪtrɪ] *n* simmetria.

sympathetic [sɪmpəˈθetɪk] *a* (*showing pity*) compassionevole; (*kind*) comprensivo(a); ~ **towards** ben disposto(a) verso.

sympathize [ˈsɪmpəθaɪz] *vi*: **to** ~ **with sb** compatire qd; partecipare al dolore di qd; ~**r** *n* (*POL*) simpatizzante *m/f*.

sympathy [ˈsɪmpəθɪ] *n* compassione *f*; **in** ~ **with** d'accordo con; (*strike*) per solidarietà con; **with our deepest** ~ con

le nostre più sincere condoglianze.

symphony [ˈsɪmfənɪ] *n* sinfonia.

symposium [sɪmˈpəʊzɪəm] *n* simposio.

symptom [ˈsɪmptəm] *n* sintomo; indizio.

synagogue [ˈsɪnəgɔg] *n* sinagoga.

synchronize [ˈsɪŋkrənaɪz] *vt* sincronizzare // *vi*: **to** ~ **with** essere contemporaneo(a) a.

syncopated [ˈsɪŋkəpeɪtɪd] *a* sincopato(a).

syndicate [ˈsɪndɪkɪt] *n* sindacato.

syndrome [ˈsɪndrəʊm] *n* sindrome *f*.

synonym [ˈsɪnənɪm] *n* sinonimo; ~**ous** [sɪˈnɒnɪməs] *a*: ~**ous** (**with**) sinonimo(a) (di).

synopsis, *pl* **synopses** [sɪˈnɒpsɪs, -si:z] *n* sommario, sinossi *f inv*.

syntax [ˈsɪntæks] *n* sintassi *f inv*.

synthesis, *pl* **syntheses** [ˈsɪnθəsɪs, -si:z] *n* sintesi *f inv*.

synthetic [sɪnˈθetɪk] *a* sintetico(a).

syphilis [ˈsɪfɪlɪs] *n* sifilide *f*.

syphon [ˈsaɪfən] *n*, *vb* = **siphon**.

Syria [ˈsɪrɪə] *n* Siria; ~**n** *a*, *n* siriano(a).

syringe [sɪˈrɪndʒ] *n* siringa.

syrup [ˈsɪrəp] *n* sciroppo; (*also*: **golden** ~) melassa raffinata.

system [ˈsɪstəm] *n* sistema *m*; (*order*) metodo; (*ANAT*) organismo; ~**atic** [-ˈmætɪk] *a* sistematico(a); metodico(a); ~**s analyst** *n* analista programmatore *m*.

T

ta [ta:] *excl* (*Brit: col*) grazie!

tab [tæb] *n* (*loop on coat etc*) laccetto; (*label*) etichetta; **to keep** ~**s on** (*fig*) tenere d'occhio.

tabby [ˈtæbɪ] *n* (*also*: ~ **cat**) (gatto) soriano, gatto tigrato.

table [ˈteɪbl] *n* tavolo, tavola // *vt* (*motion etc*) presentare; **to lay** *or* **set the** ~ apparecchiare *or* preparare la tavola; ~ **of contents** *n* indice *m*; ~**cloth** *n* tovaglia; ~ **d'hôte** [ta:blˈdəʊt] *a* (*meal*) a prezzo fisso; ~ **lamp** *n* lampada da tavolo; ~**mat** *n* sottopiatto; ~ **salt** *n* sale *m* fino *or* da tavola; ~**spoon** *n* cucchiaio da tavola; (*also*: ~**spoonful**: *as measurement*) cucchiaiata.

tablet [ˈtæblɪt] *n* (*MED*) compressa; (: *for sucking*) pastiglia; (*for writing*) blocco; (*of stone*) targa.

table: ~ **tennis** *n* tennis *m* da tavolo, ping-pong *m* ®; ~ **wine** *n* vino da tavola.

taboo [təˈbu:] *a*, *n* tabù (*m inv*).

tabulate [ˈtæbjuleɪt] *vt* (*data, figures*) tabulare, disporre in tabelle.

tacit [ˈtæsɪt] *a* tacito(a).

taciturn [ˈtæsɪtə:n] *a* taciturno(a).

tack [tæk] *n* (*nail*) bulletta; (*stitch*) punto d'imbastitura; (*NAUT*) bordo, bordata // *vt* imbullettare; imbastire // *vi* bordeggiare; **to change** ~ virare di bordo; **on the wrong** ~ (*fig*) sulla strada sbagliata.

tackle [ˈtækl] *n* attrezzatura, equipaggiamento; (*for lifting*) paranco; (*RUGBY*) placcaggio // *vt* (*difficulty*)

affrontare; (*RUGBY*) placcare.
tacky ['tækɪ] *a* colloso(a),
appiccicaticcio(a); ancora bagnato(a).
tact [tækt] *n* tatto; ~**ful** *a* delicato(a),
discreto(a).
tactical ['tæktɪkl] *a* tattico(a).
tactics ['tæktɪks] *n,npl* tattica.
tactless ['tæktlɪs] *a* che manca di tatto.
tadpole ['tædpəul] *n* girino.
tag [tæg] *n* etichetta; **to** ~ **along** *vi*
seguire.
tail [teɪl] *n* coda; (*of shirt*) falda //
(*follow*) seguire, pedinare; **to** ~ **away**, ~
off *vi* (*in size, quality etc*) diminuire grada-
tamente; ~**back** *n* ingorgo; ~ **coat** *n*
marsina; ~ **end** *n* (*of train, procession etc*)
coda; (*of meeting etc*) fine *f*.
tailor ['teɪlə*] *n* sarto; ~**ing** *n* (*cut*) stile
m; ~-**made** *a* (*also fig*) fatto(a) su misura.
tailwind ['teɪlwɪnd] *n* vento di coda.
tainted ['teɪntɪd] *a* (*food*) guasto(a);
(*water, air*) infetto(a); (*fig*) corrotto(a).
take [teɪk], *pt* **took**, *pp* **taken** [teɪk, tuk, 'teɪkn]
vt prendere; (*gain: prize*) ottenere,
vincere; (*require: effort, courage*)
occorrere, volerci; (*tolerate*) accettare,
sopportare; (*hold: passengers etc*)
contenere; (*accompany*) accompagnare;
(*bring, carry*) portare; (*exam*) sostenere,
presentarsi a; **it** ~**s a lot of
time/courage** occorre *or* ci vuole molto
tempo/coraggio; **I** ~ **it** that suppongo
che; **to** ~ **for a walk** (*child, dog*) portare
a fare una passeggiata; **to** ~ **after** *vt fus*
assomigliare a; **to** ~ **apart** *vt* smontare;
to ~ **away** *vt* portare via; togliere; **to** ~
back *vt* (*return*) restituire; riportare;
(*one's words*) ritirare; **to** ~ **down** *vt*
(*building*) demolire; (*letter etc*) scrivere;
to ~ **in** *vt* (*deceive*) imbrogliare,
abbindolare; (*understand*) capire; (*include*)
comprendere, includere; (*lodger*)
prendere, ospitare; **to** ~ **off** *vi* (*AVIAT*)
decollare // *vt* (*remove*) togliere; (*imitate*)
imitare; **to** ~ **on** *vt* (*work*) accettare, intraprendere; (*employee*) assumere;
prendere; (*opponent*) sfidare, affrontare;
to ~ **out** *vt* portare fuori; (*remove*)
togliere; (*licence*) prendere, ottenere; **to**
~ **sth out of** tirare qc fuori da; estrarre
qc da; **to** ~ **over** *vt* (*business*) rilevare //
vi: **to** ~ **over from sb** prendere le
consegne *or* il controllo da qd; **to** ~ **to** *vt
fus* (*person*) prendere in simpatia;
(*activity*) prendere gusto a; **to** ~ **up** *vt*
(*one's story*) riprendere; · (*dress*)
accorciare; (*occupy: time, space*) occupare;
(*engage in: hobby etc*) mettersi a; ~**away**
a (*food*) da portar via; ~-**home pay** *n*
stipendio netto; ~**off** *n* (*AVIAT*) decollo;
~**over** *n* (*COMM*) rilevamento.
takings ['teɪkɪŋz] *npl* (*COMM*) incasso.
talc [tælk] *n* (*also:* ~ **um powder**) talco.
tale [teɪl] *n* racconto, storia; (*pej*) fandonia.
talent ['tælnt] *n* talento.
talk [tɔːk] *n* discorso; (*gossip*) chiacchiere
fpl; (*conversation*) conversazione *f*;
(*interview*) discussione *f* // *vi* (*chatter*)

chiacchierare; **to** ~ **about** parlare di;
(*converse*) discorrere *or* conversare su; **to**
~ **sb out of/into doing** dissuadere qd
da/convincere qd a fare; **to** ~ **shop**
parlare del lavoro *or* degli affari; **to** ~
over *vt* discutere; ~**ative** *a* loquace,
ciarliero(a).
tall [tɔːl] *a* alto(a); **to be 6 feet** ~ ≈
essere alto 1 metro e 80; ~**boy** *n*
cassettone *m* alto; ~ **story** *n* panzana,
frottola.
tally ['tælɪ] *n* conto, conteggio // *vi*: **to** ~
(**with**) corrispondere (con).
tambourine [tæmbə'riːn] *n* tamburello.
tame [teɪm] *a* addomesticato(a); (*fig: story,
style*) insipido(a), scialbo(a).
tamper ['tæmpə*] *vi*: **to** ~ **with**
manomettere.
tampon ['tæmpɔn] *n* assorbente *m* interno.
tan [tæn] *n* (*also:* **sun**~) abbronzatura //
vt abbronzare // *vi* abbronzarsi // *a*
(*colour*) marrone rossiccio *inv*.
tandem ['tændəm] *n* tandem *m inv*.
tang [tæŋ] *n* odore *m* penetrante; sapore *m*
piccante.
tangent ['tændʒənt] *n* (*MATH*) tangente *f*.
tangerine [tændʒə'riːn] *n* mandarino.
tangible ['tændʒəbl] *a* tangibile.
tangle ['tæŋgl] *n* groviglio // *vt*
aggrovigliare; **to get in(to) a** ~ finire in
un groviglio.
tango ['tæŋgəu] *n* tango.
tank [tæŋk] *n* serbatoio; (*for processing*)
vasca; (*for fish*) acquario; (*MIL*) carro
armato.
tankard ['tæŋkəd] *n* boccale *m*.
tanker ['tæŋkə*] *n* (*ship*) nave *f* cisterna
inv; (*truck*) autobotte *f*, autocisterna.
tantalizing ['tæntəlaɪzɪŋ] *a* allettante.
tantamount ['tæntəmaunt] *a*: ~ **to**
equivalente a.
tantrum ['tæntrəm] *n* accesso di collera.
tap [tæp] *n* (*on sink etc*) rubinetto; (*gentle
blow*) colpetto // *vt* dare un colpetto a;
(*resources*) sfruttare, utilizzare;
~-**dancing** *n* tip tap *m*.
tape [teɪp] *n* nastro; (*also:* **magnetic** ~)
nastro (magnetico) // *vt* (*record*)
registrare (su nastro); ~ **measure** *n*
metro a nastro.
taper ['teɪpə*] *n* candelina // *vi*
assottigliarsi.
tape recorder ['teɪprɪkɔːdə*] *n*
registratore *m* (a nastro).
tapestry ['tæpɪstrɪ] *n* arazzo; tappezzeria.
tapioca [tæpɪ'əukə] *n* tapioca.
tar [tɑː] *n* catrame *m*.
tarantula [tə'ræntjulə] *n* tarantola.
tardy ['tɑːdɪ] *a* tardo(a); tardivo(a).
target ['tɑːgɪt] *n* bersaglio; (*fig: objective*)
obiettivo; ~ **practice** *n* tiro al bersaglio.
tariff ['tærɪf] *n* (*COMM*) tariffa; (*taxes*)
tariffe *fpl* doganali.
tarmac ['tɑːmæk] *n* macadam *m* al
catrame; (*AVIAT*) pista di decollo.
tarnish ['tɑːnɪʃ] *vt* offuscare, annerire;
(*fig*) macchiare.

tarpaulin [tɑːˈpɔːlin] n tela incatramata.

tart [tɑːt] n (CULIN) crostata; (col: pej: woman) sgualdrina // a (flavour) aspro(a), agro(a).

tartan ['tɑːtn] n tartan m inv.

tartar ['tɑːtə*] n (on teeth) tartaro; ~ **sauce** n salsa tartara.

task [tɑːsk] n compito; **to take to** ~ rimproverare; ~ **force** n (MIL, POLICE) unità operativa.

Tasmania [tæzˈmeɪnɪə] n Tasmania.

tassel ['tæsl] n fiocco.

taste [teist] n gusto; (flavour) sapore m, gusto; (fig: glimpse, idea) idea // vt gustare; (sample) assaggiare // vi: **to** ~ **of** (fish etc) sapere or avere sapore di; **it** ~s **like fish** sa di pesce; **can I have a** ~ **of this wine?** posso assaggiare un po' di questo vino?; **to have a** ~ **of sth** assaggiare qc; **to have a** ~ **for sth** avere un'inclinazione per qc; ~**ful** a di buon gusto; ~**less** a (food) insipido(a); (remark) di cattivo gusto; **tasty** a saporito(a), gustoso(a).

tatters ['tætəz] npl: **in** ~ (also: **tattered**) a brandelli, sbrindellato(a).

tattoo [təˈtuː] n tatuaggio; (spectacle) parata militare // vt tatuare.

tatty ['tæti] a (col) malandato(a).

taught [tɔːt] pt,pp of **teach**.

taunt [tɔːnt] n scherno // vt schernire.

Taurus ['tɔːrəs] n Toro.

taut [tɔːt] a teso(a).

tavern ['tævən] n taverna.

tawdry ['tɔːdri] a pacchiano(a).

tawny ['tɔːni] a fulvo(a).

tax [tæks] n (on goods) imposta; (on services) tassa; (on income) imposte fpl, tasse fpl // vt tassare; (fig: strain: patience etc) mettere alla prova; ~**ation** [-ˈseiʃən] n tassazione f; tasse fpl, imposte fpl; ~ **avoidance** n l'evitare legalmente il pagamento di imposte; ~ **collector** n esattore m delle imposte; ~ **evasion** n evasione f fiscale; ~ **exile** n chi ripara all'estero per evadere le imposte; ~**free** a esente da imposte.

taxi ['tæksi] n taxi m inv // vi (AVIAT) rullare; ~ **driver** n tassista m/f; ~ **rank**, ~ **stand** n posteggio dei taxi.

tax: ~ **payer** n contribuente m/f; ~ **return** n dichiarazione f dei redditi.

TB abbr of **tuberculosis**.

tea [tiː] n tè m inv; (snack: for children) merenda; **high** ~ cena leggera (presa nel tardo pomeriggio); ~ **bag** n bustina di tè; ~ **break** n intervallo per il tè.

teach, pt, pp **taught** [tiːtʃ, tɔːt] vt: **to** ~ **sb sth**, ~ **sth to sb** insegnare qc a qd // vi insegnare; ~**er** n insegnante m/f; (in secondary school) professore/essa; (in primary school) maestro/a; ~**ing** n insegnamento; ~**ing staff** n insegnanti mpl, personale m insegnante.

tea cosy ['tiːkəuzi] n copriteiera m inv.

teacup ['tiːkʌp] n tazza da tè.

teak [tiːk] n teak m.

tea leaves ['tiːliːvz] npl foglie fpl di tè.

team [tiːm] n squadra; (of animals) tiro; ~ **games/work** giochi mpl/lavoro di squadra.

tea party ['tiːpɑːti] n tè m inv (ricevimento).

teapot ['tiːpɔt] n teiera.

tear n [tɛə*] strappo; [tiə*] lacrima // vb [tɛə*] (pt **tore**, pp **torn** [tɔː*, tɔːn]) vt strappare // vi strapparsi; **in** ~**s** in lacrime; **to burst into** ~**s** scoppiare in lacrime; **to** ~ **along** vi (rush) correre all'impazzata; ~**ful** a piangente, lacrimoso(a); ~ **gas** n gas m lacrimogeno.

tearoom ['tiːruːm] n sala da tè.

tease [tiːz] vt canzonare; (unkindly) tormentare.

tea set ['tiːset] n servizio da tè.

teaspoon ['tiːspuːn] n cucchiaino da tè; (also: ~**ful**: as measurement) cucchiaino.

tea strainer ['tiːstreinə*] n colino da tè.

teat [tiːt] n capezzolo.

teatime ['tiːtaim] n l'ora del tè.

tea towel ['tiːtauəl] n strofinaccio (per i piatti).

technical ['tɛknikl] a tecnico(a); ~**ity** [-ˈkælɪti] n tecnicità; (detail) dettaglio tecnico.

technician [tɛkˈniʃən] n tecnico/a.

technique [tɛkˈniːk] n tecnica.

technological [tɛknəˈlɔdʒikl] a tecnologico(a).

technology [tɛkˈnɔlədʒi] n tecnologia.

teddy (bear) ['tɛdi(bɛə*)] n orsacchiotto.

tedious ['tiːdiəs] a noioso(a), tedioso(a).

tedium ['tiːdiəm] n noia, tedio.

tee [tiː] n (GOLF) tee m inv.

teem [tiːm] vi abbondare, brulicare; **to** ~ **with** brulicare di; **it is** ~**ing (with rain)** piove a dirotto.

teenage ['tiːneidʒ] a (fashions etc) per giovani, per adolescenti; ~**r** n adolescente m/f.

teens [tiːnz] npl: **to be in one's** ~ essere adolescente.

tee-shirt ['tiːʃəːt] n = **T-shirt**.

teeter ['tiːtə*] vi barcollare, vacillare.

teeth [tiːθ] npl of **tooth**.

teethe [tiːð] vi mettere i denti.

teething ['tiːðiŋ] a: ~ **ring** n dentaruolo; ~ **troubles** npl (fig) difficoltà fpl iniziali.

teetotal ['tiːˈtəutl] a astemio(a).

telecommunications ['tɛlikəmjuːniˈkeiʃənz] n telecomunicazioni fpl.

telegram ['tɛligræm] n telegramma m.

telegraph ['tɛligrɑːf] n telegrafo; ~**ic** [-ˈgræfik] a telegrafico(a); ~ **pole** n palo del telegrafo.

telepathy [təˈlɛpəθi] n telepatia.

telephone ['tɛlifəun] n telefono // vt (person) telefonare a; (message) telefonare; ~ **booth**, ~ **box** n cabina telefonica; ~ **call** n telefonata; ~ **directory** n elenco telefonico; ~ **exchange** n centralino telefonico; ~ **number** n numero di telefono;

telephonist [tə'lɛfənɪst] n telefonista m/f.
telephoto ['tɛlɪ'fəʊtəʊ] a: ~ **lens** n teleobiettivo.
teleprinter ['tɛlɪprɪntə*] n telescrivente f.
telescope ['tɛlɪskəʊp] n telescopio // vt incastrare a cannocchiale.
televise ['tɛlɪvaɪz] vt teletrasmettere.
television ['tɛlɪvɪʒən] n televisione f; ~ **programme** n programma m televisivo; ~ **set** n televisore m.
tell, pt, pp **told** [tɛl, təʊld] vt dire; (relate: story) raccontare; (distinguish): **to ~ sth from** distinguere qc da // vi (have effect) farsi sentire, avere effetto; **to ~ sb to do** dire a qd di fare; **to ~ on** vt fus (inform against) denunciare; **to ~ off** vt rimproverare, sgridare; ~**er** n (in bank) cassiere/a; ~**ing** a (remark, detail) rivelatore(trice); ~**tale** a (sign) significativo(a) // n malalingua, pettegolo/a.
telly ['tɛlɪ] n (col: abbr of **television**) tivù f inv.
temerity [tə'mɛrɪtɪ] n temerarietà.
temp [tɛmp] n (abbr of **temporary**) segretaria temporanea.
temper ['tɛmpə*] n (nature) carattere m; (mood) umore m; (fit of anger) collera // vt (moderate) temperare, moderare; **to be in a ~** essere in collera; **to lose one's ~** andare in collera.
temperament ['tɛmprəmənt] n (nature) temperamento; ~**al** [-'mɛntl] a capriccioso(a).
temperance ['tɛmpərns] n moderazione f; (in drinking) temperanza nel bere.
temperate ['tɛmprət] a moderato(a); (climate) temperato(a).
temperature ['tɛmprətʃə*] n temperatura; **to have** or **run a ~** avere la febbre.
tempered ['tɛmpəd] a (steel) temprato(a).
tempest ['tɛmpɪst] n tempesta.
tempi ['tɛmpiː] npl of **tempo.**
template ['tɛmplɪt] n sagoma.
temple ['tɛmpl] n (building) tempio; (ANAT) tempia.
tempo, ~**s** or **tempi** ['tɛmpəʊ, 'tɛmpiː] n tempo; (fig: of life etc) ritmo.
temporal ['tɛmpərl] a temporale.
temporary ['tɛmpərərɪ] a temporaneo(a); (job, worker) avventizio(a), temporaneo(a); ~ **secretary** n segretaria temporanea.
tempt [tɛmpt] vt tentare; **to ~ sb into doing** indurre qd a fare; ~**ation** [-'teɪʃən] n tentazione f; ~**ing** a allettante, seducente.
ten [tɛn] num dieci.
tenacious [tə'neɪʃəs] a tenace.
tenacity [tə'næsɪtɪ] n tenacia.
tenancy ['tɛnənsɪ] n affitto; condizione f di inquilino.
tenant ['tɛnənt] n inquilino/a.
tend [tɛnd] vt badare a, occuparsi di // vi: **to ~ to do** tendere a fare; (colour): **to ~ to** tendere a.
tendency ['tɛndənsɪ] n tendenza.

tender ['tɛndə*] a tenero(a); (delicate) fragile; (sore) dolorante; (affectionate) affettuoso(a) // n (COMM: offer) offerta; (money): **legal ~** valuta (a corso legale) // vt offrire; ~**ize** vt (CULIN) far intenerire.
tendon ['tɛndən] n tendine m.
tenement ['tɛnəmənt] n casamento.
tenet ['tɛnət] n principio.
tennis ['tɛnɪs] n tennis m; ~ **ball** n palla da tennis; ~ **court** n campo da tennis; ~ **racket** n racchetta da tennis.
tenor ['tɛnə*] n (MUS, of speech etc) tenore m.
tense [tɛns] a teso(a) // n (LING) tempo.
tension ['tɛnʃən] n tensione f.
tent [tɛnt] n tenda.
tentacle ['tɛntəkl] n tentacolo.
tentative ['tɛntətɪv] a esitante, incerto(a); (conclusion) provvisorio(a).
tenterhooks ['tɛntəhʊks] npl: **on ~** sulle spine.
tenth [tɛnθ] num decimo(a).
tent: ~ **peg** n picchetto da tenda; ~ **pole** n palo da tenda, montante m.
tenuous ['tɛnjʊəs] a tenue.
tenure ['tɛnjʊə*] n (of property) possesso; (of job) permanenza; titolarità.
tepid ['tɛpɪd] a tiepido(a).
term [təːm] n (limit) termine m; (word) vocabolo, termine; (SCOL) trimestre m; (LAW) sessione f // vt chiamare, definire; ~**s** npl (conditions) condizioni fpl; (COMM) prezzi mpl, tariffe fpl; ~ **of imprisonment** periodo di prigionia; **in the short/long ~** a breve/lunga scadenza; **to be on good ~s with** essere in buoni rapporti con; **to come to ~s with** (person) arrivare a un accordo con; (problem) affrontare.
terminal ['təːmɪnl] a finale, terminale; (disease) nella fase terminale // n (ELEC) morsetto; (for oil, ore etc) terminal m inv; (also: **air ~**) aerostazione f; (also: **coach ~**) capolinea m.
terminate ['təːmɪneɪt] vt mettere fine a // vi: **to ~ in** finire in or con.
terminology [təːmɪ'nɔlədʒɪ] n terminologia.
terminus, pl **termini** ['təːmɪnəs, 'təːmɪnaɪ] n (for buses) capolinea m; (for trains) stazione f terminale.
termite ['təːmaɪt] n termite f.
terrace ['tɛrəs] n terrazza; (row of houses) fila di case (unite); **the ~s** (SPORT) le gradinate; ~**d** a (garden) a terrazze.
terrain [tɛ'reɪn] n terreno.
terrible ['tɛrɪbl] a terribile; (weather) bruttissimo(a); (work) orribile; **terribly** ad terribilmente; (very badly) spaventosamente male.
terrier ['tɛrɪə*] n terrier m inv.
terrific [tə'rɪfɪk] a incredibile, fantastico(a); (wonderful) formidabile, eccezionale.
terrify ['tɛrɪfaɪ] vt terrorizzare.
territory ['tɛrɪtərɪ] n territorio.

terror ['tɛrə*] n terrore m; ~**ism** n terrorismo; ~**ist** n terrorista m/f; ~**ize** vt terrorizzare.

terse [tə:s] a (style) conciso(a); (reply) laconico(a).

test [tɛst] n (trial, check, of courage etc) prova, (: of goods in factory) controllo, collaudo; (MED) esame m; (CHEM) analisi f inv; (exam: of intelligence etc) test m inv; (: in school) saggio; (also: **driving** ~) esame m di guida // vt provare; controllare, collaudare; esaminare; analizzare; saggiare; sottoporre ad esame.

testament ['tɛstəmənt] n testamento; **the Old/New T~** il Vecchio/Nuovo testamento.

test: ~ **case** n (LAW, fig) caso da annali or che farà testo; ~ **flight** n volo di prova.

testicle ['tɛstɪkl] n testicolo.

testify ['tɛstɪfaɪ] vi (LAW) testimoniare, deporre.

testimonial [tɛstɪ'məunɪəl] n (reference) benservito; (gift) testimonianza di stima.

testimony ['tɛstɪmənɪ] n (LAW) testimonianza, deposizione f.

test: ~ **match** n (CRICKET, RUGBY) partita internazionale; ~ **paper** n (SCOL) interrogazione f scritta; ~ **pilot** n pilota m collaudatore; ~ **tube** n provetta.

testy ['tɛstɪ] a irritabile.

tetanus ['tɛtənəs] n tetano.

tether ['tɛðə*] vt legare, impastoiare // n: **at the end of one's** ~ al limite (della pazienza).

text [tɛkst] n testo; ~**book** n libro di testo.

textile ['tɛkstaɪl] n tessile m.

texture ['tɛkstʃə*] n tessitura; (of skin, paper etc) struttura.

Thai [taɪ] a tailandese // n tailandese m/f; (LING) tailandese m; ~**land** n Tailandia.

Thames [tɛmz] n: **the** ~ il Tamigi.

than [ðæn, ðən] cj che; (with numerals, pronouns, proper names): **more** ~ **10/me/Maria** più di 10/me/Maria; **you know her better** ~ **I do** la conosce meglio di me or di quanto non la conosca io; **she has more apples** ~ **pears** ha più mele che pere.

thank [θæŋk] vt ringraziare; ~ **you (very much)** grazie (tante); ~**s** npl ringraziamenti mpl, grazie fpl // excl grazie!; ~**s to** prep grazie a; ~**ful** a: ~**ful (for)** riconoscente (per); ~**less** a ingrato(a); **T~sgiving (Day)** n giorno del ringraziamento.

that [ðæt, ðət] cj che // det quel (quell', quello) m; quella(quell') f // pronoun ciò; (the one, not 'this one') quello(a); (relative) che; prep + il(la) quale; (with time): **on the day** ~ **he came** il giorno in cui or quando venne // ad: ~ **high** così alto; alto così; ~ **one** quello(a) (là); **what's** ~? cos'è?; **who's** ~? chi è?; **is** ~ **you?** sei tu?; ~**'s what he said** questo è or ecco quello che ha detto; ~ **is...** cio è..., vale a dire...; **I can't work** ~ **much** non posso lavorare così tanto.

thatched [θætʃt] a (roof) di paglia; ~

cottage n cottage m inv col tetto di paglia.

thaw [θɔ:] n disgelo // vi (ice) sciogliersi; (food) scongelarsi // vt (food) (fare) scongelare; **it's** ~**ing** (weather) sta sgelando.

the [ði:, ðə] det il(lo, l') m; la(l') f; i(gli) mpl; le fpl.

theatre ['θɪətə*] n teatro; ~-**goer** n frequentatore/trice di teatri.

theatrical [θɪ'ætrɪkl] a teatrale.

theft [θɛft] n furto.

their [ðɛə*] a il(la) loro, pl i(le) loro; ~**s** pronoun il(la) loro, pl i(le) loro; **it is** ~**s** è loro; **a friend of** ~**s** un loro amico.

them [ðɛm, ðəm] pronoun (direct) li(le); (indirect) gli, loro (after vb); (stressed, after prep: people) loro; (: people, things) essi(e); **I see** ~ li vedo; **give** ~ **the book** dà loro or dagli il libro.

theme [θi:m] n tema m; ~ **song/tune** n tema musicale.

themselves [ðəm'sɛlvz] pl pronoun (reflexive) si; (emphatic) loro stessi(e); (after prep) se stessi(e); **between** ~ tra (di) loro.

then [ðɛn] ad (at that time) allora; (next) poi, dopo; (and also) e poi // cj (therefore) perciò, dunque, quindi // a: **the** ~ **president** il presidente di allora; **from** ~ **on** da allora in poi.

theologian [θɪə'ləudʒən] n teologo/a.

theology [θɪ'ɔlədʒɪ] n teologia.

theorem ['θɪərəm] n teorema m.

theoretical [θɪə'rɛtɪkl] a teorico(a).

theorize ['θɪəraɪz] vi teorizzare.

theory ['θɪərɪ] n teoria.

therapeutic(al) [θɛrə'pju:tɪk(l)] a terapeutico(a).

therapy ['θɛrəpɪ] n terapia.

there [ðɛə*] ad là, lì; ~, ~! su, su!; **it's** ~ è lì; **he went** ~ ci è andato; ~ **is** c'è; ~ **are** ci sono; ~ **he is** eccolo; ~ **has been** c'è stato; **on/in** ~ lassù/lì dentro; **to go** ~ **and back** andarci e ritornare; ~**abouts** ad (place) nei pressi, da quelle parti; (amount) giù di lì, all'incirca; ~**after** ad da allora in poi; ~**fore** ad perciò, quindi.

thermal ['θə:ml] a termico(a).

thermometer [θə'mɔmɪtə*] n termometro.

thermonuclear ['θə:məu'nju:klɪə*] a termonucleare.

Thermos ['θə:məs] n ® (also: ~ **flask**) thermos m inv ®.

thermostat ['θə:məstæt] n termostato.

thesaurus [θɪ'sɔ:rəs] n dizionario dei sinonimi.

these [ði:z] pl pronoun, det questi(e).

thesis, pl **theses** ['θi:sɪs, 'θi:si:z] n tesi f inv.

they [ðeɪ] pl pronoun essi(esse); (people only) loro; ~ **say that...** (it is said that) si dice che... .

thick [θɪk] a spesso(a); (crowd) compatto(a); (stupid) ottuso(a), lento(a) // n: **in the** ~ **of** nel folto di; **it's 20 cm** ~ ha uno spessore di 20 cm; ~**en** vi ispessire // vt (sauce etc) ispessire, rendere più denso(a); ~ness n spessore m; ~set a tarchiato(a), tozzo(a); ~skinned a (fig) insensibile.

thief, thieves [θiːf, θiːvz] n ladro/a.

thigh [θaɪ] n coscia; ~bone n femore m.

thimble ['θɪmbl] n ditale m.

thin [θɪn] a sottile; (person) magro(a); (soup) brodoso(a); (hair, crowd) rado(a); (fog) leggero(a) // vt (hair) sfoltire; to ~ (down) (sauce, paint) diluire.

thing [θɪŋ] n cosa; (object) oggetto; (contraption) aggeggio; ~s npl (belongings) cose fpl; for one ~ tanto per cominciare; the best ~ would be to la cosa migliore sarebbe di; how are ~s? come va?

think, pt, pp thought [θɪŋk, θɔːt] vi pensare, riflettere // vt pensare, credere; (imagine) immaginare; to ~ of pensare a; what did you ~ of them? cosa ne ha pensato?; to ~ about sth/sb pensare a qc/qd; I'll ~ about it ci penserò; to ~ of doing pensare di fare; I ~ so penso di sì; to ~ well of avere una buona opinione di; to ~ over vt riflettere su; to ~ up vt ideare.

third [θɔːd] num terzo(a) // n terzo/a; (fraction) terzo, terza parte f; (SCOL: degree) ≈ laurea col minimo dei voti; ~ly ad in terzo luogo; ~ party insurance n assicurazione f contro terzi; ~-rate a di qualità scadente; the T-World n il Terzo Mondo.

thirst [θɔːst] n sete f; ~y a (person) assetato(a), che ha sete.

thirteen ['θɔː'tiːn] num tredici.

thirty ['θɔːtɪ] num trenta.

this [ðɪs] det, pronoun questo(a); ~ one questo(a) (qui); ~ is what he said questo è quello or ciò che ha detto.

thistle ['θɪsl] n cardo.

thong [θɒŋ] n cinghia.

thorn [θɔːn] n spina; ~y a spinoso(a).

thorough ['θʌrə] a (search) minuzioso(a); (knowledge, research) approfondito(a), profondo(a); coscienzioso(a); (cleaning) a fondo; ~bred n ' (horse) purosangue m/f inv; ~fare n strada transitabile; 'no ~fare' 'divieto di transito'; ~ly ad minuziosamente; in profondità; a fondo; he ~ly agreed fu completamente d'accordo.

those [ðəʊz] pl pronoun quelli(e) // pl det quei(quegli) mpl; quelle fpl.

though [ðəʊ] cj benché, sebbene // ad comunque.

thought [θɔːt] pt, pp of think // n pensiero; (opinion) opinione f; (intention) intenzione f; ~ful a pensieroso(a), pensoso(a); ponderato(a); (considerate) premuroso(a); ~less a irriguardoso(a).

thousand ['θaʊzənd] num mille; ~th num millesimo(a); one ~ mille; ~s of migliaia di.

thrash [θræʃ] vt picchiare; bastonare; (defeat) battere; to ~ about vi dibattersi; to ~ out vi dibattere, sviscerare.

thread [θrɛd] n filo; (of screw) filetto // vt

(needle) infilare; to ~ one's way between infilarsi tra; ~bare a consumato(a). logoro(a).

threat [θrɛt] n minaccia; ~en vi (storm) minacciare // vt: to ~en sb with sth/to do minacciare qd con qc/di fare.

three [θriː] num tre; ~-dimensional a tridimensionale; (film) stereoscopico(a); ~-piece suit n completo (con gilè); ~-piece suite n salotto comprendente un divano e due poltrone; ~-ply (wool) a tre strati; (wool) a tre fili; ~-wheeler n (car) veicolo a tre ruote.

thresh [θreʃ] vt (AGR) trebbiare; ~ing machine n trebbiatrice f.

threshold ['θreʃhəʊld] n soglia.

threw [θruː] pt of throw.

thrifty ['θrɪftɪ] a economico(a).

thrill [θrɪl] n brivido // vi eccitarsi, tremare // vt (audience) elettrizzare; to be ~ed (with gift etc) essere commosso(a); ~er n film m inv (or dramma m or libro) del brivido.

thrive, pt thrived, throve pp thrived, thriven [θraɪv, θrəʊv, 'θrɪvn] vi crescere or svilupparsi bene; (business) prosperare; he ~s on it gli fa bene, ne gode.

throat [θrəʊt] n gola; to have a sore ~ avere (un or il) mal di gola.

throb [θrɒb] n (of heart) battito; (of engine) vibrazione f; (of pain) fitta // vi (heart) palpitare; (engine) vibrare; (with pain) pulsare.

throes [θrəʊz] npl: in the ~ of alle prese con; in preda a; in the ~ of death in agonia.

thrombosis [θrɒm'bəʊsɪs] n trombosi f.

throne [θrəʊn] n trono.

throttle ['θrɒtl] n (AUT) valvola a farfalla // vt strangolare.

through [θruː] prep attraverso; (time) per, durante; (by means of) per mezzo di; (owing to) a causa di // a (ticket, train, passage) diretto(a) // ad attraverso; to put sb ~ to sb (TEL) passare qd a qd; to be ~ (TEL) ottenere la comunicazione; (have finished) avere finito; 'no ~ way' 'strada senza sbocco'; ~out prep (place) dappertutto in; (time) per or durante tutto(a) // ad dappertutto; sempre.

throve [θrəʊv] pt of thrive.

throw [θrəʊ] n tiro, getto; (SPORT) lancio // vt (pt threw, pp thrown [θruː, θrəʊn]) tirare, gettare; (rider) disarcionare; (fig) confondere; (pottery) formare al tornio; to ~ a party dare una festa; to ~ away vt gettare or buttare via; to ~ off vt sbarazzarsi di; to ~ out vt buttare fuori; (reject) respingere; to ~ up vi vomitare; ~away a da buttare; ~-in n (SPORT) rimessa in gioco.

thru [θruː] prep, a, ad (US) = through.

thrush [θrʌʃ] n tordo.

thrust [θrʌst] n (TECH) spinta // vt (pt, pp thrust) spingere con forza; (push in) conficcare.

thud [θʌd] n tonfo.

thug [θʌg] n delinquente m.

thumb [θʌm] n (ANAT) pollice m // vt (book) sfogliare; **to ~ a lift** fare l'autostop; **~ index** n indice m a rubrica; **~tack** n (US) puntina da disegno.

thump [θʌmp] n colpo forte; (sound) tonfo // vt battere su // vi picchiare, battere.

thunder ['θʌndə*] n tuono // vi tuonare; (train etc): **to ~ past** passare con un rombo; **~clap** n rombo di tuono; **~ous** a fragoroso(a); **~storm** n temporale m; **~y** a temporalesco(a).

Thursday ['θɔːzdɪ] n giovedì m inv.

thus [ðʌs] ad così.

thwart [θwɔːt] vt contrastare.

thyme [taɪm] n timo.

thyroid ['θaɪrɔɪd] n tiroide f.

tiara [tɪ'ɑːrə] n (woman's) diadema m.

Tiber ['taɪbə*] n: **the ~** il Tevere.

tic [tɪk] n tic m inv.

tick [tɪk] n (sound: of clock) tic tac m inv; (mark) segno; spunta; (ZOOL) zecca; (col): **in a ~** in un attimo // vi fare tic tac // vt spuntare; **to ~ off** vt spuntare; (person) sgridare.

ticket ['tɪkɪt] n biglietto; (in shop: on goods) etichetta; (: from cash register) scontrino; (for library) scheda; **~ collector** n bigliettaio; **~ holder** n persona munita di biglietto; **~ office** n biglietteria.

tickle ['tɪkl] n solletico // vt fare il solletico a, solleticare; (fig) stuzzicare; piacere a; far ridere; **ticklish** a che soffre il solletico.

tidal ['taɪdl] a di marea.

tiddlywinks ['tɪdlɪwɪŋks] n gioco della pulce.

tide [taɪd] n marea; (fig: of events) corso.

tidy ['taɪdɪ] a (room) ordinato(a), lindo(a); (dress, work) curato(a), in ordine; (person) ordinato(a) // vt (also: **~ up**) riordinare, mettere in ordine; **to ~ o.s. up** rassettarsi.

tie [taɪ] n (string etc) legaccio; (also: **neck~**) cravatta; (fig: link) legame m; (SPORT: draw) pareggio // vt (parcel) legare; (ribbon) annodare // vi (SPORT) pareggiare; **'black/white ~'** 'smoking/abito di rigore'; **to ~ sth in a bow** annodare qc; **to ~ a knot in sth** fare un nodo a qc; **to ~ down** vt fissare con una corda; (fig): **to ~ sb down to** costringere qd a accettare; **to ~ up** vt (parcel, dog) legare; (boat) ormeggiare; (arrangements) concludere; **to be ~d up** (busy) essere occupato or preso.

tier [tɪə*] n fila; (of cake) piano, strato.

tiff [tɪf] n battibecco.

tiger ['taɪgə*] n tigre f.

tight [taɪt] a (rope) teso(a), tirato(a); (clothes) stretto(a); (budget, programme, bend) stretto(a); (control) severo(a), fermo(a); (col: drunk) sbronzo(a) // ad (squeeze) fortemente; (shut) ermeticamente; **~s** npl collant m inv; **~en** vt (rope) tendere; (screw) stringere; (control) rinforzare // vi tendersi; stringersi; **~-fisted** a avaro(a); **~ly** ad

(grasp) bene, saldamente; **~-rope** n corda (da acrobata).

tile [taɪl] n (on roof) tegola; (on wall or floor) piastrella, mattonella.

till [tɪl] n registratore m di cassa // vt (land) coltivare // prep, cj = **until**.

tiller ['tɪlə*] n (NAUT) barra del timone.

tilt [tɪlt] vt inclinare, far pendere // vi inclinarsi, pendere.

timber ['tɪmbə*] n (material) legname m; (trees) alberi mpl da legname.

time [taɪm] n tempo; (epoch: often pl) epoca, tempo; (by clock) ora; (moment) momento; (occasion, also MATH) volta; (MUS) tempo // vt (race) cronometrare; (programme) calcolare la durata di; (remark etc) dire (or fare) al momento giusto; **a long ~** molto tempo; **for the ~ being** per il momento; **from ~ to ~** ogni tanto; **in ~** (soon enough) in tempo; (after some time) col tempo; (MUS) a tempo; **in a week's ~** fra una settimana; **on ~** puntualmente; **5 ~s 5** 5 volte or per 5; **what ~ is it?** che ora è?, che ore sono?; **to have a good ~** divertirsi; **~'s up!** è (l')ora!; **~ bomb** n bomba a orologeria; **~ keeper** n (SPORT) cronometrista m/f; **~ lag** n intervallo, ritardo; (in travel) differenza di fuso orario; **~less** a eterno(a); **~ limit** n limite m di tempo; **~ly** a opportuno(a); **~ off** n tempo libero; **~r** n (in kitchen) contaminuti m inv; **~-saving** a che fa risparmiare tempo; **~ switch** n interruttore m a tempo; **~table** n orario; **~ zone** n fuso orario.

timid ['tɪmɪd] a timido(a); (easily scared) pauroso(a).

timing ['taɪmɪŋ] n sincronizzazione f; (fig) scelta del momento opportuno, tempismo; (SPORT) cronometraggio.

timpani ['tɪmpənɪ] npl timpani mpl.

tin [tɪn] n stagno; (also: **~ plate**) latta; (can) barattolo (di latta), lattina, scatola; (for baking) teglia; **~ foil** n stagnola.

tinge [tɪndʒ] n sfumatura // vt: **~d with** tinto(a) di.

tingle ['tɪŋgl] vi pizzicare.

tinker ['tɪŋkə*] n calderaio ambulante; (gipsy) zingaro/a; **to ~ with** vt fus armeggiare intorno a; cercare di riparare.

tinkle ['tɪŋkl] vi tintinnare.

tinned [tɪnd] a (food) in scatola.

tinny ['tɪnɪ] a metallico(a).

tin opener ['tɪnəupnə*] n apriscatole m inv.

tinsel ['tɪnsl] n decorazioni fpl natalizie (argentate).

tint [tɪnt] n tinta.

tiny ['taɪnɪ] a minuscolo(a).

tip [tɪp] n (end) punta; (protective: on umbrella etc) puntale m; (gratuity) mancia; (for coal) discarica; (for rubbish) immondezzaio; (advice) suggerimento // vt (waiter) dare la mancia a; (tilt) inclinare; (overturn: also: **~ over**) capovolgere; (empty: also: **~ out**) scaricare; **~-off** n (hint) soffiata; **~ped** a (cigarette) col

filtro; **steel-~ped** con la punta d'acciaio.
tipple ['tɪpl] *vi* sbevazzare // *n*: **to have a ~** prendere un bicchierino.
tipsy ['tɪpsɪ] *a* brillo(a).
tiptoe ['tɪptəʊ] *n*: **on ~** in punta di piedi.
tiptop ['tɪp'tɒp] *a*: **in ~ condition** in ottime condizioni.
tire ['taɪə*] *vt* stancare // *vi* stancarsi; **~d a** stanco(a); **to be ~d of** essere stanco or stufo di; **~less** *a* instancabile; **~some** *a* noioso(a); **tiring** *a* faticoso(a).
tissue ['tɪʃuː] *n* tessuto; (*paper handkerchief*) fazzoletto di carta; **~ paper** *n* carta velina.
tit [tɪt] *n* (*bird*) cinciallegra; **to give ~ for tat** rendere pan per focaccia.
titbit ['tɪtbɪt] *n* (*food*) leccornia; (*news*) notizia ghiotta.
titillate ['tɪtɪleɪt] *vt* titillare.
titivate ['tɪtɪveɪt] *vt* agghindare.
title ['taɪtl] *n* titolo; **~ deed** *n* (*LAW*) titolo di proprietà; **~ role** *n* ruolo or parte *f* principale.
titter ['tɪtə*] *vi* ridere scioccamente.
tittle-tattle ['tɪtltætl] *n* chiacchiere *fpl*, pettegolezzi *mpl*.
tizzy ['tɪzɪ] *n*: **to be in a ~** essere in agitazione.
to [tuː, tə] *prep* a; (*towards*) verso; **give it ~ me** dammelo; **the key ~ the front door** la chiave della porta d'ingresso; **the main thing is ~ ...** l'importante è di...; **to go ~ France/Portugal** andare in Francia/Portogallo; **I went ~ Claudia's** sono andato da Claudia; **to go ~ town/school** andare in città/a scuola; **to pull/push the door ~** tirare/spingere la porta; **to go ~ and fro** andare e tornare.
toad [təʊd] *n* rospo; **~stool** *n* fungo (velenoso); **~y** *vi* adulare.
toast [təʊst] *n* (*CULIN*) toast *m*, pane *m* abbrustolito; (*drink, speech*) brindisi *m inv* // *vt* (*CULIN*) abbrustolire; (*drink to*) brindare a; **a piece** or **slice of ~** una fetta di pane abbrustolito; **~er** *n* tostapane *m inv*; **~master** *n* direttore *m* dei brindisi.
tobacco [tə'bækəʊ] *n* tabacco; **~nist** *n* tabaccaio/a; **~nist's (shop)** *n* tabaccheria.
toboggan [tə'bɒgən] *n* toboga *m inv*; (*child's*) slitta.
today [tə'deɪ] *ad,n* (*also fig*) oggi (*m*).
toddler ['tɒdlə*] *n* bambino/a che impara a camminare.
toddy ['tɒdɪ] *n* grog *m inv*.
to-do [tə'duː] *n* (*fuss*) storie *fpl*.
toe [təʊ] *n* dito del piede; (*of shoe*) punta; **to ~ the line** (*fig*) stare in riga, conformarsi; **~nail** *n* unghia del piede.
toffee ['tɒfɪ] *n* caramella.
toga ['təʊgə] *n* toga.
together [tə'geðə*] *ad* insieme; (*at same time*) allo stesso tempo; **~ with** *prep* insieme a; **~ness** *n* solidarietà; intimità.
toil [tɔɪl] *n* travaglio, fatica // *vi* affannarsi; sgobbare.
toilet ['tɔɪlət] *n* (*lavatory*) gabinetto // *cpd*

(*bag, soap etc*) da toletta; **~ bowl** *n* vaso or tazza del gabinetto; **~ paper** *n* carta igienica; **~ries** *npl* articoli *mpl* da toletta; **~ roll** *n* rotolo di carta igienica; **~ water** *n* colonia.
token ['təʊkən] *n* (*sign*) segno; (*voucher*) buono; **book/record ~** *n* buono-libro/disco.
told [təʊld] *pt, pp of* **tell**.
tolerable ['tɒlərəbl] *a* (*bearable*) tollerabile; (*fairly good*) passabile.
tolerance ['tɒlərns] *n* (*also: TECH*) tolleranza.
tolerant ['tɒlərnt] *a*: **~ (of)** tollerante (nei confronti di).
tolerate ['tɒləreɪt] *vt* sopportare; (*MED, TECH*) tollerare; **toleration** [-'reɪʃən] *n* tolleranza.
toll [təʊl] *n* (*tax, charge*) pedaggio // *vi* (*bell*) suonare; **the accident ~ on the roads** il numero delle vittime della strada; **~bridge** *n* ponte *m* a pedaggio.
tomato, **~es** [tə'mɑːtəʊ] *n* pomodoro.
tomb [tuːm] *n* tomba.
tombola [tɒm'bəʊlə] *n* tombola.
tomboy ['tɒmbɔɪ] *n* maschiaccio.
tombstone ['tuːmstəʊn] *n* pietra tombale.
tomcat ['tɒmkæt] *n* gatto.
tomorrow [tə'mɒrəʊ] *ad,n* (*also fig*) domani (*m inv*); **the day after ~** dopodomani; **~ morning** domani mattina.
ton [tʌn] *n* tonnellata (*=1016 kg; 20 cwt*); (*NAUT: also: register ~*) tonnellata di stazza (*=2.83 cu.m; 100 cu. ft*); **~s of** (*col*) un mucchio or sacco di.
tone [təʊn] *n* tono // *vi* intonarsi; **to ~ down** *vt* (*colour, criticism, sound*) attenuare; **to ~ up** *vt* (*muscles*) tonificare; **~-deaf** *a* che non ha orecchio (musicale).
tongs [tɒŋz] *npl* tenaglie *fpl*; (*for coal*) molle *fpl*; (*for hair*) arricciacapelli *m inv*.
tongue [tʌŋ] *n* lingua; **~ in cheek** *ad* ironicamente; **~-tied** *a* (*fig*) muto(a); **~-twister** *n* scioglilingua *m inv*.
tonic ['tɒnɪk] *n* (*MED*) tonico; (*MUS*) nota tonica; (*also: ~ water*) acqua tonica.
tonight [tə'naɪt] *ad* stanotte; (*this evening*) stasera // *n* questa notte; questa sera.
tonnage ['tʌnɪdʒ] *n* (*NAUT*) tonnellaggio, stazza.
tonne [tʌn] *n* (*metric ton*) tonnellata.
tonsil ['tɒnsl] *n* tonsilla; **~litis** [-'laɪtɪs] *n* tonsillite *f*.
too [tuː] *ad* (*excessively*) troppo; (*also*) anche; **~ much** *ad* troppo // *det* troppo(a); **~ many** *det* troppi(e); **~ bad!** tanto peggio!, peggio così!
took [tʊk] *pt of* **take**.
tool [tuːl] *n* utensile *m*, attrezzo // *vt* lavorare con un attrezzo; **~ box/kit** *n* cassetta *f* portautensili/attrezzi *inv*.
toot [tuːt] *vi* suonare; (*with car-horn*) suonare il clacson.
tooth, *pl* **teeth** [tuːθ, tiːθ] *n* (*ANAT, TECH*) dente *m*; **~ache** *n* mal *m* di denti; **~brush** *n* spazzolino da denti; **~paste** *n*

dentifricio (in pasta); ~pick n stuzzicadenti m inv.

top [tɔp] n (of mountain, page, ladder) cima; (of box, cupboard, table) sopra m inv, parte f superiore; (lid: of box, jar) coperchio; (: of bottle) tappo; (toy) trottola // a più alto(a); (in rank) primo(a); (best) migliore // vt (exceed) superare; (be first in) essere in testa a; on ~ of sopra, in cima a; (in addition to) oltre a; from ~ to toe dalla testa ai piedi; to ~ up vt riempire; ~ floor n ultimo piano; ~ hat n cilindro; ~-heavy a (object) con la parte superiore troppo pesante.

topic ['tɔpɪk] n argomento; ~al a d'attualità.

top: ~less a (bather etc) col seno scoperto; ~less swimsuit n topless m inv; ~-level a (talks) ad alto livello; ~most a il(la) più alto(a).

topple ['tɔpl] vt rovesciare, far cadere // vi cadere; traballare.

topsy-turvy ['tɔpsɪ'tə:vɪ] a,ad sottosopra.

torch [tɔ:tʃ] n torcia; (electric) lampadina tascabile.

tore [tɔ:*] pt of tear.

torment n ['tɔ:mɛnt] tormento // vt [tɔ:'mɛnt] tormentare; (fig: annoy) infastidire.

torn [tɔ:n] pp of tear // a: ~ between (fig) combattuto(a) tra.

tornado, ~es [tɔ:'neɪdəu] n tornado.

torpedo, ~es [tɔ:'pi:dəu] n siluro.

torpor ['tɔ:pə*] n torpore m.

torque [tɔ:k] n coppia di torsione.

torrent ['tɔrnt] n torrente m; ~ial [-'rɛnʃl] a torrenziale.

torso ['tɔ:səu] n torso.

tortoise ['tɔ:təs] n tartaruga; ~shell ['tɔ:təʃɛl] a di tartaruga.

tortuous ['tɔ:tjuəs] a tortuoso(a).

torture ['tɔ:tʃə*] n tortura // vt torturare.

Tory ['tɔ:rɪ] a dei tories, conservatore(trice) // n tory m inv, conservatore/trice.

toss [tɔs] vt gettare, lanciare; (pancake) far saltare; (head) scuotere; to ~ a coin fare a testa o croce; to ~ up for sth fare a testa o croce per qc; to ~ and turn (in bed) girarsi e rigirarsi.

tot [tɔt] n (drink) bicchierino; (child) bimbo/a.

total ['təutl] a totale // n totale m // vt (add up) sommare; (amount to) ammontare a.

totalitarian [təutæli'tɛərɪən] a totalitario(a).

totem pole ['təutəmpəul] n totem m inv.

totter ['tɔtə*] vi barcollare.

touch [tʌtʃ] n tocco, (sense) tatto; (contact) contatto; (FOOTBALL) fuori gioco m // vt toccare; a ~ of (fig) un tocco di; un pizzico di; in ~ with in contatto con; to get in ~ with mettersi in contatto con; to lose ~ (friends) perdersi di vista; to ~ on vt fus (topic) sfiorare, accennare a; to ~ up vt (paint) ritoccare; ~-and-go a incerto(a); it was ~-and-go whether

we did it c'è mancato poco che non lo facessimo; ~down n atterraggio; (on sea) ammaraggio; ~ed a commosso(a); (col) tocco(a), toccato(a); ~ing a commovente; ~line n (SPORT) linea laterale; ~y a (person) suscettibile.

tough [tʌf] a duro(a); (resistant) resistente; (meat) duro(a), tiglioso(a); ~ luck! che disdetta!, peggio per me (or te etc)!; ~en vt indurire, rendere più resistente.

toupee ['tu:peɪ] n parrucchino.

tour ['tuə*] n viaggio; (also: package ~) viaggio organizzato or tutto compreso; (of town, museum) visita; (by artist) tournée f inv // vt visitare; ~ing n turismo.

tourism ['tuərɪzəm] n turismo.

tourist ['tuərɪst] n turista m/f // ad (travel) in classe turistica // cpd turistico(a); ~ office n pro loco f inv.

tournament ['tuənəmənt] n torneo.

tousled ['tauzld] a (hair) arruffato(a).

tout [taut] vi: to ~ for procacciare, raccogliere; cercare clienti per; to ~ sth (around) cercare di (ri)vendere qc.

tow [təu] vt rimorchiare; 'on ~' (AUT) 'veicolo rimorchiato'.

toward(s) [tə'wɔ:d(z)] prep verso; (of attitude) nei confronti di; (of purpose) per.

towel ['tauəl] n asciugamano; (also: tea ~) strofinaccio; ~ling n (fabric) spugna; ~ rail n portasciugamano.

tower ['tauə*] n torre f; ~ block n palazzone m; ~ing a altissimo(a), imponente.

town [taun] n città f inv; to go to ~ andare in città; (fig) mettercela tutta; ~ clerk n segretario comunale; ~ council n consiglio comunale; ~ hall n ≈ municipio; ~ planner n urbanista m/f; ~ planning n urbanistica.

towpath ['təupɑ:θ] n alzaia.

towrope ['təurəup] n (cavo da) rimorchio.

toxic ['tɔksɪk] a tossico(a).

toy [tɔɪ] n giocattolo; to ~ with vt fus giocare con; (idea) accarezzare, trastullarsi con; ~shop n negozio di giocattoli.

trace [treɪs] n traccia // vt (draw) tracciare; (follow) seguire; (locate) rintracciare.

track [træk] n (mark) traccia; (on tape, SPORT, path: gen) pista; (: of bullet etc) traiettoria; (: of suspect, animal) pista, tracce fpl; (RAIL) binario, rotaie fpl // vt seguire le tracce di; to keep ~ of seguire; to ~ down vt (prey) scovare; snidare; (sth lost) rintracciare; ~er dog n cane m poliziotto inv; ~ suit n tuta sportiva.

tract [trækt] n (GEO) tratto, estensione f; (pamphlet) opuscolo, libretto; respiratory ~ (ANAT) apparato respiratorio.

tractor ['træktə*] n trattore m.

trade [treɪd] n commercio; (skill, job) mestiere m // vi commerciare; to ~ with/in commerciare con/in; to ~ in vt (old car etc) dare come pagamento parziale; ~mark n marchio di fabbrica;

~**name** n marca, nome m depositato; ~**r** n commerciante m/f; ~**sman** n (shopkeeper) negoziante m; ~ **union** n sindacato; ~ **unionist** sindacalista m/f; **trading** n commercio; **trading estate** n zona industriale.

tradition [trə'dıʃən] n tradizione f; ~**s** npl tradizioni, usanze fpl; ~**al** a tradizionale.

traffic ['træfık] n traffico // vi: **to ~ in** (pej: liquor, drugs) trafficare in; ~ **circle** n (US) isola rotatoria; ~ **jam** n ingorgo (del traffico); ~ **lights** npl semaforo; ~ **warden** n addetto/a al controllo del traffico e del parcheggio.

tragedy ['trædʒıdı] n tragedia.

tragic ['trædʒık] a tragico(a).

trail [treıl] n (tracks) tracce fpl, pista; (path) sentiero; (of smoke etc) scia // vt trascinare, strascicare; (follow) seguire // vi essere al traino; (dress etc) strusciare; (plant) arrampicarsi; strisciare; **to ~ behind** vi essere al traino; ~**er** n (AUT) rimorchio; (US) roulotte f inv; (CINEMA) prossimamente m inv.

train [treın] n treno; (of dress) coda, strascico // vt (apprentice, doctor etc) formare; (sportsman) allenare; (dog) addestrare; (memory) esercitare; (point: gun etc): **to ~ sth on** puntare qc contro // vi formarsi; allenarsi; **one's ~ of thought** il filo dei propri pensieri; ~**ed** a qualificato(a); allenato(a); addestrato(a); ~**ee** [treı'ni:] n allievo/a; (in trade) apprendista m/f; ~**er** n (SPORT) allenatore/trice; (of dogs etc) addestratore/trice; ~**ing** n formazione f; allenamento; addestramento; **in ~ing** (SPORT) in allenamento; (fit) in forma; ~**ing college** n istituto professionale; (for teachers) ≈ istituto magistrale.

traipse [treıps] vi girovagare, andare a zonzo.

trait [treıt] n tratto.

traitor ['treıtə*] n traditore m.

tram [træm] n (also: ~**car**) tram m inv; ~**line** n linea tranviaria.

tramp [træmp] n (person) vagabondo/a // vi camminare con passo pesante // vt (walk through: town, streets) percorrere a piedi.

trample ['træmpl] vt: **to ~ (underfoot)** calpestare.

trampoline ['træmpəlı:n] n trampolino.

trance [trɑːns] n trance f inv; (MED) catalessi f inv.

tranquil ['træŋkwıl] a tranquillo(a); ~**lity** n tranquillità; ~**lizer** n (MED) tranquillante m.

transact [træn'zækt] vt (business) trattare; ~**ion** [-'zækʃən] n transazione f; ~**ions** npl (minutes) atti mpl.

transatlantic ['trænzət'læntık] a transatlantico(a).

transcend [træn'send] vt trascendere; (excel over) superare.

transcript ['trænskrıpt] n trascrizione f; ~**ion** [-'skrıpʃən] n trascrizione f.

transept ['trænsept] n transetto.

transfer n ['trænsfə*] (gen, also SPORT) trasferimento; (POL: of power) passaggio; (picture, design) decalcomania; (: stick-on) autoadesivo // vt [træns'fə:*] trasferire; passare; decalcare; **to ~ the charges** (TEL) telefonare con addebito al ricevente; ~**able** [-'fɔːrəbl] a trasferibile.

transform [træns'fɔːm] vt trasformare; ~**ation** [-'meıʃən] n trasformazione f; ~**er** n (ELEC) trasformatore m.

transfusion [træns'fjuːʒən] n trasfusione f.

transient ['trænzıənt] a transitorio(a), fugace.

transistor [træn'zıstə*] n (ELEC) transistor m inv; (also: ~ **radio**) radio f inv a transistor.

transit ['trænzıt] n: **in ~** in transito; ~ **lounge** n sala di transito.

transition [træn'zıʃən] n passaggio, transizione f; ~**al** a di transizione.

transitive ['trænzıtıv] a (LING) transitivo(a).

transitory ['trænzıtərı] a transitorio(a).

translate [trænz'leıt] vt tradurre; **translation** [-'leıʃən] n traduzione f; (SCOL: as opposed to prose) versione f; **translator** n traduttore/trice.

transmission [trænz'mıʃən] n trasmissione f.

transmit [trænz'mıt] vt trasmettere; ~**ter** n trasmettitore m.

transparency [træns'pɛərnsı] n (PHOT) diapositiva.

transparent [træns'pærnt] a trasparente.

transplant vt [træns'plɑːnt] trapiantare // n ['trænsplɑːnt] (MED) trapianto.

transport n ['trænspɔːt] trasporto // vt [træns'pɔːt] trasportare; ~**ation** [-'teıʃən] n (mezzo di) trasporto; (of prisoners) deportazione f; ~ **café** n trattoria per camionisti.

transvestite [trænz'vestaıt] n travestito/a.

trap [træp] n (snare, trick) trappola; (carriage) calesse m // vt prendere in trappola, intrappolare; (immobilize) bloccare; (jam) chiudere, schiacciare; ~ **door** n botola.

trapeze [trə'piːz] n trapezio.

trapper ['træpə*] n cacciatore m di animali da pelliccia.

trappings ['træpıŋz] npl ornamenti mpl; indoratura, sfarzo.

trash [træʃ] n (pej: goods) ciarpame m; (: nonsense) sciocchezze fpl; ~ **can** n (US) secchio della spazzatura.

trauma ['trɔːmə] n trauma m; ~**tic** [-'mætık] a traumatico(a).

travel ['trævl] n viaggio; viaggi mpl; // vi viaggiare; (move) andare, spostarsi // vt (distance) percorrere; ~**ler** n viaggiatore/trice; ~**ler's cheque** n assegno turistico; ~**ling** n viaggi mpl // cpd (bag, clock) da viaggio; (expenses) di viaggio; ~ **sickness** n mal m d'auto (or di mare or d'aria).

travesty ['trævəstı] n parodia.

trawler ['trɔːlə*] n peschereccio (a strascico etc).

tray [treɪ] n (for carrying) vassoio; (on desk) vaschetta.

treacherous ['tretʃərəs] a traditore(trice).

treachery ['tretʃərɪ] n tradimento.

treacle ['triːkl] n melassa.

tread [tred] n passo; (sound) rumore m di passi; (of tyre) battistrada m inv // vi (pt **trod**, pp **trodden** [trɔd, 'trɔdn]) camminare; **to ~ on** vt fus calpestare.

treason ['triːzn] n tradimento.

treasure ['treʒə*] n tesoro // vt (value) tenere in gran conto, apprezzare molto; (store) custodire gelosamente.

treasurer ['treʒərə*] n tesoriere/a.

treasury ['treʒərɪ] n tesoreria; **the T~** (POL) il ministero del tesoro.

treat [triːt] n regalo // vt trattare; (MED) curare; **it was a ~** mi (or ci etc) ha fatto veramente piacere; **to ~ sb to sth** offrire qc a qd.

treatise ['triːtɪz] n trattato.

treatment ['triːtmənt] n trattamento.

treaty ['triːtɪ] n patto, trattato.

treble ['trebl] a triplo(a), triplice // n (MUS) soprano m/f // vt triplicare // vi triplicarsi; ~ **clef** n chiave f di violino.

tree [triː] n albero; ~ **trunk** n tronco d'albero.

trek [trek] n viaggio; camminata; (tiring walk) tirata a piedi // vi (as holiday) fare dell'escursionismo.

trellis ['trelɪs] n graticcio, pergola.

tremble ['trembl] vi tremare; (machine) vibrare.

tremendous [trɪ'mendəs] a (enormous) enorme; (excellent) meraviglioso(a), formidabile.

tremor ['tremə*] n tremore m, tremito; (also: **earth ~**) scossa sismica.

trench [trentʃ] n trincea.

trend [trend] n (tendency) tendenza; (of events) corso; (fashion) moda; ~**y** a (idea) di moda; (clothes) all'ultima moda.

trepidation [trepɪ'deɪʃən] n trepidazione f, agitazione f.

trespass ['trespəs] vi: **to ~ on** entrare abusivamente in; (fig) abusare di; **'no ~ing'** 'proprietà privata', 'vietato l'accesso'.

trestle ['tresl] n cavalletto; ~ **table** n tavolo su cavalletti.

trial ['traɪəl] n (LAW) processo; (test: of machine etc) collaudo; (hardship) prova, difficoltà f inv; (worry) cruccio; **to be on ~** essere sotto processo; **by ~ and error** a tentoni.

triangle ['traɪæŋgl] n (MATH, MUS) triangolo.

tribe [traɪb] n tribù f inv; ~**sman** n membro della tribù.

tribulation [trɪbju'leɪʃən] n tribolazione f.

tribunal [traɪ'bjuːnl] n tribunale m.

tributary ['trɪbjutərɪ] n (river) tributario, affluente m.

tribute ['trɪbjuːt] n tributo, omaggio; **to**

pay ~ to rendere omaggio a.

trice [traɪs] n: **in a ~** in un attimo.

trick [trɪk] n trucco; (clever act) stratagemma m; (joke) tiro; (CARDS) presa // vt imbrogliare, ingannare; **to play a ~ on sb** giocare un tiro a qd; ~**ery** n inganno.

trickle ['trɪkl] n (of water etc) rivolo; gocciolio // vi gocciolare; **to ~ in/out** (people) entrare/uscire alla spicciolata.

tricky ['trɪkɪ] a difficile, delicato(a).

tricycle ['traɪsɪkl] n triciclo.

trifle ['traɪfl] n sciocchezza; (CULIN) ≈ zuppa inglese // ad: **a ~ long** un po' lungo; **trifling** a insignificante.

trigger ['trɪgə*] n (of gun) grilletto; **to ~ off** vt dare l'avvio a.

trigonometry [trɪgə'nɔmətrɪ] n trigonometria.

trim [trɪm] a ordinato(a); (house, garden) ben tenuto(a); (figure) snello(a) // n (haircut etc) spuntata, regolata; (embellishment) finiture fpl; (on car) guarnizioni fpl // vt spuntare; (decorate): **to ~ (with)** decorare (con); (NAUT: a sail) orientare; ~**mings** npl decorazioni fpl; (extras: gen CULIN) guarnizione f.

Trinity ['trɪnɪtɪ] n: **the ~** la Trinità.

trinket ['trɪŋkɪt] n gingillo; (piece of jewellery) ciondolo.

trio ['triːəu] n trio.

trip [trɪp] n viaggio; (excursion) gita, escursione f; (stumble) passo falso // vi inciampare; (go lightly) camminare con passo leggero; **on a ~** in viaggio; **to ~ up** vi inciampare // vt fare lo sgambetto a.

tripe [traɪp] n (CULIN) trippa; (pej: rubbish) sciocchezze fpl, fesserie fpl.

triple ['trɪpl] a triplo(a).

triplets ['trɪplɪts] npl bambini(e) trigemini(e).

triplicate ['trɪplɪkət] n: **in ~** in triplice copia.

tripod ['traɪpɔd] n treppiede m.

trite [traɪt] a banale, trito(a).

triumph ['traɪʌmf] n trionfo // vi: **to ~ (over)** trionfare (su); ~**al** [-'ʌmfl] a trionfale; ~**ant** [-'ʌmfənt] a trionfante.

trivia ['trɪvɪə] npl banalità fpl.

trivial ['trɪvɪəl] a insignificante; (commonplace) banale.

trod [trɔd] pt of **tread**; ~**den** pp of **tread**.

trolley ['trɔlɪ] n carrello; ~ **bus** n filobus m inv.

trollop ['trɔləp] n prostituta.

trombone [trɔm'bəun] n trombone m.

troop [truːp] n gruppo, truppa; ~**s** npl (MIL) truppe fpl; **to ~ in/out** vi entrare/uscire a frotte; ~**er** n (MIL) soldato di cavalleria; ~**ing the colour** (ceremony) sfilata della bandiera.

trophy ['trəufɪ] n trofeo.

tropic ['trɔpɪk] n tropico; **in the ~s** ai tropici; **T~ of Cancer/Capricorn** n tropico del Cancro/Capricorno; ~**al** a tropicale.

trot [trɔt] n trotto // vi trottare; **on the ~**

(fig: col) di fila, uno(a) dopo l'altro(a).

trouble ['trʌbl] *n* difficoltà *f inv*, problema *m*; difficoltà *fpl*, problemi *m*; *(worry)* preoccupazione *f*; *(bother, effort)* sforzo; *(POL)* conflitti *mpl*, disordine *m*; *(MED):* stomach *etc* ~ disturbi *mpl* gastrici *etc* // *vt* disturbare; *(worry)* preoccupare // *vi:* to ~ to do disturbarsi a fare; ~s *npl* *(POL etc)* disordini *mpl*; to be in ~ avere dei problemi; to go to the ~ of doing darsi la pena di fare; it's no ~! di niente!; what's the ~? cosa c'è che non va?; ~d *a (person)* preoccupato(a), inquieto(a); *(epoch, life)* agitato(a), difficile; ~**-free** *a* senza problemi; ~**maker** *n* elemento disturbatore, agitatore/trice; ~**shooter** *n* *(in conflict)* conciliatore *m*; ~**some** *a* fastidioso(a), seccante.

trough [trɔf] *n (also:* drinking ~) abbeveratoio; *(also:* feeding ~) trogolo, mangiatoia; *(channel)* canale *m*; ~ of low pressure *n (GEO)* depressione *f*.

trounce [trauns] *vt (defeat)* sgominare.

troupe [tru:p] *n* troupe *f inv*.

trousers ['trauzəz] *npl* pantaloni *mpl*, calzoni *mpl*; short ~ *npl* calzoncini *mpl*.

trousseau, *pl* ~x *or* ~s ['tru:səu, -z] *n* corredo da sposa.

trout [traut] *n, pl inv* trota.

trowel ['trauəl] *n* cazzuola.

truant ['truənt] *n*: to play ~ marinare la scuola.

truce [tru:s] *n* tregua.

truck [trʌk] *n* autocarro, camion *m inv*; *(RAIL)* carro merci aperto; *(for luggage)* carrello *m* portabagagli *inv*; ~ **driver** *n* camionista *m/f*.

trudge [trʌdʒ] *vi* arrancare.

true [tru:] *a* vero(a); *(accurate)* accurato(a), esatto(a); *(genuine)* reale; *(faithful)* fedele.

truffle ['trʌfl] *n* tartufo.

truly ['tru:lɪ] *ad* veramente; *(truthfully)* sinceramente; *(faithfully)* fedelmente.

trump [trʌmp] *n* briscola; ~**ed-up** *a* inventato(a).

trumpet ['trʌmpɪt] *n* tromba.

truncated [trʌŋ'keɪtɪd] *a* tronco(a).

truncheon ['trʌntʃən] *n* sfollagente *m inv*.

trundle ['trʌndl] *vt, vi*: to ~ along rotolare rumorosamente.

trunk [trʌŋk] *n (of tree, person)* tronco; *(of elephant)* proboscide *f*; *(case)* baule *m*; ~s *npl (also:* swimming ~s) calzoncini *mpl* da bagno; ~ call *n (TEL)* (telefonata) interurbana.

truss [trʌs] *n (MED)* cinto erniario; to ~ (up) *vt (CULIN)* legare.

trust [trʌst] *n* fiducia; *(LAW)* amministrazione *f* fiduciaria; *(COMM)* trust *m inv* // *vt (rely on)* contare su; *(entrust):* to ~ sth to sb affidare qc a qd; ~**ed** *a* fidato(a); ~**ee** [trʌs'ti:] *n (LAW)* amministratore(trice) fiduciario; *(of school etc)* amministratore *m*; ~**ful,** ~**ing** *a* fiducioso(a); ~**worthy** *a* fidato(a), degno(a) di fiducia; ~**y** *a* fidato(a).

truth, ~s [tru:θ, tru:ðz] *n* verità *f inv*; ~**ful** *a (person)* sincero(a); *(description)* veritiero(a), esatto(a).

try [traɪ] *n* prova, tentativo; *(RUGBY)* meta // *vt (LAW)* giudicare; *(test: sth new)* provare; *(strain)* mettere alla prova // *vi* provare; to ~ to do provare a fare; *(seek)* cercare di fare; to ~ on *vt (clothes)* provare; to ~ it on (with sb) *(fig)* cercare di farla a qd; to ~ out *vt* provare, mettere alla prova; ~**ing** *a (day, experience)* logorante, pesante; *(child)* difficile, insopportabile.

tsar [za:*] *n* zar *m inv*.

T-shirt ['ti:ʃət] *n* maglietta.

T-square ['ti:skwɛə*] *n* riga a T.

tub [tʌb] *n* tinozza; mastello; *(bath)* bagno.

tuba ['tju:bə] *n* tuba.

tubby ['tʌbɪ] *a* grassoccio(a).

tube [tju:b] *n* tubo; *(underground)* metropolitana; *(for tyre)* camera d'aria.

tuberculosis [tjubə:kju'ləusɪs] *n* tubercolosi *f*.

tubing ['tju:bɪŋ] *n* tubazione *f*; a piece of ~ un tubo.

tubular ['tju:bjulə*] *a* tubolare.

TUC *n (abbr of Trades Union Congress)* confederazione *f* dei sindacati britannici.

tuck [tʌk] *n (SEWING)* piega // *vt (put)* mettere; to ~ away *vt* riporre; to ~ in *vt* mettere dentro; *(child)* rimboccare // *vi (eat)* mangiare di buon appetito; abbuffarsi; to ~ up *vt (child)* rimboccare; ~ shop *n* negozio di pasticceria *(in una scuola)*.

Tuesday ['tju:zdɪ] *n* martedì *m inv*.

tuft [tʌft] *n* ciuffo.

tug [tʌg] *n (ship)* rimorchiatore *m* // *vt* tirare con forza; ~**-of-war** *n* tiro alla fune.

tuition [tju:'ɪʃən] *n* lezioni *fpl*.

tulip ['tju:lɪp] *n* tulipano.

tumble ['tʌmbl] *n (fall)* capitombolo // *vi* capitombolare, ruzzolare; *(somersault)* fare capriole // *vt* far cadere; ~**down** *a* cadente, diroccato(a); ~ dryer *n* asciugatrice *f*.

tumbler ['tʌmblə*] *n* bicchiere *m* (senza piede); acrobata *m/f*.

tummy ['tʌmɪ] *n (col)* pancia.

tumour ['tju:mə*] *n* tumore *m*.

tumult ['tju:mʌlt] *n* tumulto; ~**uous** [-'mʌltjuəs] *a* tumultuoso(a).

tuna ['tju:nə] *n, pl inv (also:* ~ fish) tonno.

tune [tju:n] *n (melody)* melodia, aria // *vt (MUS)* accordare; *(RADIO, TV, AUT)* regolare, mettere a punto; to be in/out of ~ *(instrument)* essere accordato(a)/scordato(a); *(singer)* essere intonato(a)/stonato(a); to ~ in (to) *(RADIO, TV)* sintonizzarsi (su); to ~ up *vi (musician)* accordare lo strumento; ~**ful** *a* melodioso(a); ~**r** *n (radio set)* sintonizzatore *m*; piano ~**r** accordatore/trice di pianoforte.

tungsten ['tʌŋstn] *n* tungsteno.

tunic ['tju:nɪk] *n* tunica.

tuning ['tju:nɪŋ] n messa a punto; ~ **fork** n diapason m inv.

Tunisia [tju:'nɪzɪə] n Tunisia.

tunnel ['tʌnl] n galleria // vi scavare una galleria.

tunny ['tʌnɪ] n tonno.

turban ['tɜːbən] n turbante m.

turbine ['tɜːbaɪn] n turbina.

turbojet ['tɜːbəʊ'dʒɛt] n turboreattore m.

turbot ['tɜːbət] n, pl inv rombo gigante.

turbulence ['tɜːbjʊləns] n (AVIAT) turbolenza.

turbulent ['tɜːbjʊlənt] a turbolento(a); (sea) agitato(a).

tureen [tə'riːn] n zuppiera.

turf [tɜːf] n terreno erboso; (clod) zolla // vt coprire di zolle erbose; **the T~** n l'ippodromo; **to ~ out** vt (col) buttar fuori.

turgid ['tɜːdʒɪd] a (speech) ampolloso(a), pomposo(a).

Turk [tɜːk] n turco/a.

turkey ['tɜːkɪ] n tacchino.

Turkey ['tɜːkɪ] n Turchia.

Turkish ['tɜːkɪʃ] a turco(a) // n (LING) turco; ~ **bath** n bagno turco.

turmoil ['tɜːmɔɪl] n confusione f, tumulto.

turn [tɜːn] n giro; (in road) curva; (tendency: of mind, events) tendenza; (performance) numero; (MED) crisi f inv, attacco // vt girare, voltare; (milk) far andare a male; (change): **to ~ sth into** trasformare qc in // vi girare; (person: look back) girarsi, voltarsi; (reverse direction) girarsi indietro; (change) cambiare; (become) diventare; **to ~ into** trasformarsi in; **a good ~** un buon servizio; **a bad ~** un brutto tiro; **it gave me quite a ~** mi ha fatto prendere un bello spavento; **'no left ~'** (AUT) 'divieto di svolta a sinistra'; **it's your ~** tocca a lei; **in ~** a sua volta; **a turno; to take ~s (at sth)** fare (qc) a turno; **to ~ about** vi girarsi indietro; **to ~ away** vi girarsi (dall'altra parte); **to ~ back** vi ritornare, tornare indietro; **to ~ down** vt (refuse) rifiutare; (reduce) abbassare; (fold) ripiegare; **to ~ in** vi (col: go to bed) andare a letto // vt (fold) voltare in dentro; **to ~ off** vi (from road) girare, voltare // vt (light, radio, engine etc) spegnere; **to ~ on** vt (light, radio etc) accendere; (engine) avviare; **to ~ out** vt (light, gas) chiudere, spegnere // vi: **to ~ out to be...** rivelarsi ..., risultare ...; **to ~ up** vi (person) arrivare, presentarsi; (lost object) saltar fuori // vt (collar, sound) alzare; ~**ed-up** a (nose) all'insù; ~**ing** n (in road) curva; ~**ing point** n (fig) svolta decisiva.

turnip ['tɜːnɪp] n rapa.

turnout ['tɜːnaʊt] n presenza, affluenza.

turnover ['tɜːnəʊvə*] n (COMM) giro di affari.

turnpike ['tɜːnpaɪk] n (US) autostrada a pedaggio.

turnstile ['tɜːnstaɪl] n tornella.

turntable ['tɜːnteɪbl] n (on record player) piatto.

turn-up ['tɜːnʌp] n (on trousers) risvolto.

turpentine ['tɜːpəntaɪn] n (also: **turps**) acqua ragia.

turquoise ['tɜːkwɔɪz] n (stone) turchese m // a color turchese; di turchese.

turret ['tʌrɪt] n torretta.

turtle ['tɜːtl] n testuggine f; ~**neck (sweater)** n maglione m con il collo alto.

tusk [tʌsk] n zanna.

tussle ['tʌsl] n baruffa, mischia.

tutor ['tjuːtə*] n (in college) docente m/f (responsabile di un gruppo di studenti); (private teacher) precettore m; ~**ial** [-'tɔːrɪəl] n (SCOL) lezione f con discussione (a un gruppo limitato).

tuxedo [tʌk'siːdəʊ] n (US) smoking m inv.

T.V. [tiː'viː] n (abbr of **television**) tivù f inv.

twang [twæŋ] n (of instrument) suono vibrante; (of voice) accento nasale.

tweed [twiːd] n tweed m inv.

tweezers ['twiːzəz] npl pinzette fpl.

twelfth [twelfθ] num dodicesimo(a).

twelve [twelv] num dodici; **at ~** alle dodici, a mezzogiorno; (midnight) a mezzanotte.

twentieth ['twɛntɪɪθ] num ventesimo(a).

twenty ['twɛntɪ] num venti.

twice [twaɪs] ad due volte; ~ **as much** due volte tanto.

twig [twɪg] n ramoscello // vt, vi (col) capire.

twilight ['twaɪlaɪt] n crepuscolo.

twill [twɪl] n spigato.

twin [twɪn] a,n gemello(a).

twine [twaɪn] n spago, cordicella // vi (plant) attorcigliarsi; (road) serpeggiare.

twinge [twɪndʒ] n (of pain) fitta; **a ~ of conscience/regret** un rimorso/rimpianto.

twinkle ['twɪŋkl] n scintillio; guizzo // vi scintillare; (eyes) brillare.

twirl [twɜːl] n mulinello; piroetta // vt mulinare // vi roteare.

twist [twɪst] n torsione f; (in wire, flex) storta; (in story) colpo di scena // vt attorcigliare; (weave) intrecciare; (roll around) arrotolare; (fig) deformare // vi attorcigliarsi; arrotolarsi; (road) serpeggiare.

twit [twɪt] n (col) minchione/a.

twitch [twɪtʃ] n strattone m; (nervous) tic m inv // vi contrarsi; avere un tic.

two [tuː] num due; **to put ~ and ~ together** (fig) trarre le conclusioni; ~**-door** a (AUT) a due porte; ~**-faced** a (pej: person) falso(a); ~**-piece (suit)** n due pezzi m inv; ~**-piece (swimsuit)** n (costume m da bagno a) due pezzi m inv; ~**-seater** n (plane) biposto; (car) macchina a due posti; ~**some** n (people) coppia; ~**-way** a (traffic) a due sensi.

tycoon [taɪ'kuːn] n: **(business) ~** magnate m.

type [taɪp] n (category) genere m; (model) modello; (example) tipo; (TYP) tipo,

carattere m // vt (letter etc) battere (a
macchina), dattilografare; ~-cast a
(actor) a ruolo fisso; ~script n
dattiloscritto; ~writer n macchina da
scrivere.
typhoid ['taɪfɔɪd] n tifoidea.
typhoon [taɪ'fuːn] n tifone m.
typhus ['taɪfəs] n tifo.
typical ['tɪpɪkl] a tipico(a).
typify ['tɪpɪfaɪ] vt essere tipico(a) di.
typing ['taɪpɪŋ] n dattilografia.
typist ['taɪpɪst] n dattilografo/a.
tyranny ['tɪrənɪ] n tirannia.
tyrant ['taɪərnt] n tiranno.
tyre ['taɪə*] n pneumatico, gomma; ~
pressure n pressione f (delle gomme).
tzar [zɑː*] n = tsar.

U

ubiquitous [juː'bɪkwɪtəs] a onnipresente.
udder ['ʌdə*] n mammella.
UFO ['juːfəu] n (abbr of unidentified flying
object) UFO m inv.
ugh [əːh] excl puah!
ugliness ['ʌɡlɪnɪs] n bruttezza.
ugly ['ʌɡlɪ] a brutto(a).
UHF abbr of ultra-high frequency.
U.K. n abbr see united.
ulcer ['ʌlsə*] n ulcera.
Ulster ['ʌlstə*] n Ulster m.
ulterior [ʌl'tɪərɪə*] a ulteriore; ~ motive
n secondo fine m.
ultimate ['ʌltɪmət] a ultimo(a), finale;
(authority) massimo(a), supremo(a); ~ly
ad alla fine; in definitiva, in fin dei conti.
ultimatum [ʌltɪ'meɪtəm] n ultimatum m
inv.
ultraviolet ['ʌltrə'vaɪəlɪt] a
ultravioletto(a).
umbilical [ʌm'bɪlɪkl] a: ~ cord cordone
m ombelicale.
umbrage ['ʌmbrɪdʒ] n: to take ~
offendersi, impermalirsi.
umbrella [ʌm'brɛlə] n ombrello.
umpire ['ʌmpaɪə*] n arbitro.
umpteen [ʌmp'tiːn] a non so quanti(e); for
the ~th time per l'ennesima volta.
UN, UNO abbr see united.
unabashed [ʌnə'bæʃt] a imperturbato(a).
unabated [ʌnə'beɪtɪd] a non diminuito(a).
unable [ʌn'eɪbl] a: to be ~ to non potere,
essere nell'impossibilità di; essere
incapace di.
unaccompanied [ʌnə'kʌmpənɪd] a (child,
lady) non accompagnato(a).
unaccountably [ʌnə'kauntəblɪ] ad
inesplicabilmente.
unaccustomed [ʌnə'kʌstəmd] a
insolito(a); to be ~ to sth non essere
abituato a qc.
unanimity [juːnə'nɪmɪtɪ] n unanimità.
unanimous [juː'nænɪməs] a unanime;
~ly ad all'unanimità.
unashamed [ʌnə'ʃeɪmd] a sfacciato(a);
senza vergogna.

unassuming [ʌnə'sjuːmɪŋ] a modesto(a),
senza pretese.
unattached [ʌnə'tætʃt] a senza legami,
libero(a).
unattended [ʌnə'tɛndɪd] a (car, child, luggage) incustodito(a).
unattractive [ʌnə'træktɪv] a privo(a) di
attrattiva, poco attraente.
unauthorized [ʌn'ɔːθəraɪzd] a non
autorizzato(a).
unavoidable [ʌnə'vɔɪdəbl] a inevitabile.
unaware [ʌnə'wɛə*] a: to be ~ of non
sapere, ignorare; ~s ad di sorpresa, alla
sprovvista.
unbalanced [ʌn'bælənst] a squilibrato(a).
unbearable [ʌn'bɛərəbl] a insopportabile.
unbeatable [ʌn'biːtəbl] a imbattibile.
unbeknown(st) [ʌnbɪ'nəun(st)] ad: ~ to
all'insaputa di.
unbelievable [ʌnbɪ'liːvəbl] a incredibile.
unbend [ʌn'bɛnd] vb (irg) vi distendersi //
vt (wire) raddrizzare.
unbreakable [ʌn'breɪkəbl] a infrangibile.
unbridled [ʌn'braɪdld] a sbrigliato(a).
unbroken [ʌn'brəukən] a intero(a);
continuo(a).
unburden [ʌn'bəːdn] vt: to ~ o.s.
sfogarsi.
unbutton [ʌn'bʌtn] vt sbottonare.
uncalled-for [ʌn'kɔːldfɔː*] a (remark)
fuori luogo inv; (action) ingiustificato(a).
uncanny [ʌn'kænɪ] a misterioso(a),
strano(a).
unceasing [ʌn'siːsɪŋ] a incessante.
uncertain [ʌn'səːtn] a incerto(a);
dubbio(a); ~ty n incertezza.
unchanged [ʌn'tʃeɪndʒd] a immutato(a).
uncharitable [ʌn'tʃærɪtəbl] a duro(a),
severo(a).
uncharted [ʌn'tʃɑːtɪd] a inesplorato(a).
unchecked [ʌn'tʃɛkt] a incontrollato(a).
uncle ['ʌŋkl] n zio.
uncomfortable [ʌn'kʌmfətəbl] a
scomodo(a); (uneasy) a disagio, agitato(a);
fastidioso(a).
uncommon [ʌn'kɔmən] a raro(a),
insolito(a), non comune.
uncompromising [ʌn'kɔmprəmaɪzɪŋ] a
intransigente, inflessibile.
unconditional [ʌnkən'dɪʃənl] a
incondizionato(a), senza condizioni.
unconscious [ʌn'kɔnʃəs] a privo(a) di
sensi, svenuto(a); (unaware) inconsa-
pevole, inconscio(a) // n: the ~
l'inconscio; ~ly ad inconsciamente.
uncontrollable [ʌnkən'trəuləbl] a
incontrollabile; indisciplinato(a).
uncouth [ʌn'kuːθ] a maleducato(a),
grossolano(a).
uncover [ʌn'kʌvə*] vt scoprire.
unctuous ['ʌŋktjuəs] a untuoso(a).
undaunted [ʌn'dɔːntɪd] a intrepido(a).
undecided [ʌndɪ'saɪdɪd] a indeciso(a).
undeniable [ʌndɪ'naɪəbl] a innegabile,
indiscutibile.
under ['ʌndə*] prep sotto; (less than) meno
di; al disotto di; (according to) secondo, in

conformità a // ad (al) disotto; **from ~ sth** da sotto a o dal disotto di qc; **~ there** là sotto; **~ repair** in riparazione.

under... ['ʌndə*] prefix sotto..., sub...; **~age** a minorenne; **~carriage** n carrello (d'atterraggio); **~clothes** npl biancheria (intima); **~coat** n (paint) mano f di fondo; **~cover** a segreto(a), clandestino(a); **~current** n corrente f sottomarina; **~cut** vt irg vendere a prezzo minore di; **~developed** a sottosviluppato(a); **~dog** n oppresso/a; **~done** a (CULIN) al sangue; (pej) poco cotto(a); **~estimate** vt sottovalutare; **~exposed** a (PHOT) sottoesposto(a); **~fed** a denutrito(a); **~foot** ad sotto i piedi; **~go** vt irg subire; (treatment) sottoporsi a; **~graduate** n studente(essa) universitario(a); **~ground** n metropolitana; (POL) movimento clandestino // ad sottoterra; clandestinamente; **~growth** n sottobosco; **~hand(ed)** a (fig) furtivo(a), subdolo(a); **~lie** vt irg essere alla base di; **~line** vt sottolineare; **~ling** ['ʌndəlɪŋ] n (pej) subalterno/a, tirapiedi m/f inv; **~mine** vt minare; **~neath** [ʌndə'niːθ] ad sotto, disotto // prep sotto, al di sotto di; **~paid** a mal pagato(a); **~pants** npl (Brit) mutande fpl, slip m inv; **~pass** n sottopassaggio; **~play** vt minimizzare; **~privileged** a non abbiente; meno favorito(a); **~rate** vt sottovalutare; **~shirt** n (US) maglietta; **~shorts** npl (US) mutande fpl, slip m inv; **~side** n disotto; **~skirt** n sottoveste f.

understand [ʌndə'stænd] vb (irg: like **stand**) vt, vi capire, comprendere; **I ~ that...** sento che...; credo di capire che...; **~able** a comprensibile; **~ing** a comprensivo(a) // n comprensione f; (agreement) accordo.

understatement [ʌndə'steɪtmənt] n: **that's an ~!** a dire poco!

understood [ʌndə'stud] pt, pp of **understand** // a inteso(a); (implied) sottinteso(a); **to make o.s. ~** farsi capire.

understudy ['ʌndəstʌdɪ] n sostituto/a, attore/trice supplente.

undertake [ʌndə'teɪk] vt irg intraprendere; impegnarsi a.

undertaker ['ʌndəteɪkə*] n impresario di pompe funebri.

undertaking [ʌndə'teɪkɪŋ] n impresa; (promise) promessa.

underwater [ʌndə'wɔːtə*] ad sott'acqua // a subacqueo(a).

underwear ['ʌndəwɛə*] n biancheria (intima).

underworld ['ʌndəwəːld] n (of crime) malavita.

underwriter ['ʌndəraɪtə*] n (INSURANCE) sottoscrittore/trice.

undesirable [ʌndɪ'zaɪərəbl] a indesiderabile; sgradito(a).

undies ['ʌndɪz] npl (col) robina, biancheria intima da donna.

undisputed [ʌndɪs'pjuːtɪd] a indiscusso(a).

undistinguished [ʌndɪs'tɪŋgwɪʃt] a mediocre, qualunque.

undo [ʌn'duː] vt irg disfare; **~ing** n rovina, perdita.

undoubted [ʌn'dautɪd] a sicuro(a), certo(a); **~ly** ad senza alcun dubbio.

undress [ʌn'drɛs] vi spogliarsi.

undue [ʌn'djuː] a eccessivo(a).

undulating ['ʌndjuleɪtɪŋ] a ondeggiante; ondulato(a).

unduly [ʌn'djuːlɪ] ad eccessivamente.

unearth [ʌn'əːθ] vt dissotterrare; (fig) scoprire.

unearthly [ʌn'əːθlɪ] a soprannaturale; (hour) impossibile.

uneasy [ʌn'iːzɪ] a a disagio; (worried) preoccupato(a).

uneconomic(al) ['ʌniːkə'nɔmɪk(l)] a non economico(a); antieconomico(a).

unemployed [ʌnɪm'plɔɪd] a disoccupato(a) // n: **the ~** i disoccupati.

unemployment [ʌnɪm'plɔɪmənt] n disoccupazione f.

unending [ʌn'ɛndɪŋ] a senza fine.

unerring [ʌn'əːrɪŋ] a infallibile.

uneven [ʌn'iːvn] a ineguale; irregolare.

unexpected [ʌnɪk'spɛktɪd] a inatteso(a), imprevisto(a).

unfailing [ʌn'feɪlɪŋ] a inesauribile; infallibile.

unfair [ʌn'fɛə*] a: **~ (to)** ingiusto(a) (nei confronti di).

unfaithful [ʌn'feɪθful] a infedele.

unfamiliar [ʌnfə'mɪlɪə*] a sconosciuto(a), strano(a).

unfasten [ʌn'fɑːsn] vt slacciare; sciogliere.

unfavourable [ʌn'feɪvərəbl] a sfavorevole.

unfeeling [ʌn'fiːlɪŋ] a insensibile, duro(a).

unfinished [ʌn'fɪnɪʃt] a incompiuto(a).

unfit [ʌn'fɪt] a inadatto(a); (ill) malato(a), in cattiva salute; (incompetent): **~ (for)** incompetente (in); (: work, service) inabile (a); **~ for habitation** inabitabile.

unflagging [ʌn'flægɪŋ] a instancabile.

unflappable [ʌn'flæpəbl] a calmo(a), composto(a).

unflinching [ʌn'flɪntʃɪŋ] a che non indietreggia, risoluto(a).

unfold [ʌn'fəuld] vt spiegare; (fig) rivelare // vi (view, countryside) distendersi; (story, plot) svelarsi.

unforeseen ['ʌnfɔː'siːn] a imprevisto(a).

unforgivable [ʌnfə'gɪvəbl] a imperdonabile.

unfortunate [ʌn'fɔːtʃnət] a sfortunato(a); (event, remark) infelice; **~ly** ad sfortunatamente, purtroppo.

unfounded [ʌn'faundɪd] a infondato(a).

unfriendly [ʌn'frɛndlɪ] a poco amichevole, freddo(a).

ungainly [ʌn'geɪnlɪ] a goffo(a), impacciato(a).

ungodly [ʌn'gɔdlɪ] a empio(a); **at an ~ hour** a un'ora impossibile.

unguarded [ʌn'gɑːdɪd] a: **~ moment** n

momento di distrazione *or* di disattenzione.

unhappiness [ʌn'hæpɪnɪs] *n* infelicità.
unhappy [ʌn'hæpɪ] *a* infelice; ~ **with** (*arrangements etc*) insoddisfatto(a) di.
unharmed [ʌn'hɑːmd] *a* incolume, sano(a) e salvo(a).
unhealthy [ʌn'hɛlθɪ] *a* (*gen*) malsano(a); (*person*) malaticcio(a).
unheard-of [ʌn'hɜːdɔv] *a* inaudito(a), senza precedenti.
unhook [ʌn'huk] *vt* sganciare; sfibbiare.
unhurt [ʌn'hɜːt] *a* incolume, sano(a) e salvo(a).
unicorn ['juːnɪkɔːn] *n* unicorno.
unidentified [ʌnaɪ'dɛntɪfaɪd] *a* non identificato(a).
uniform ['juːnɪfɔːm] *n* uniforme *f*, divisa // *a* uniforme; ~**ity** [-'fɔːmɪtɪ] *n* uniformità.
unify ['juːnɪfaɪ] *vt* unificare.
unilateral [juːnɪ'lætərəl] *a* unilaterale.
unimaginable [ʌnɪ'mædʒɪnəbl] *a* inimmaginabile, inconcepibile.
uninhibited [ʌnɪn'hɪbɪtɪd] *a* senza inibizioni; senza ritegno.
unintentional [ʌnɪn'tɛnʃənəl] *a* involontario(a).
union ['juːnjən] *n* unione *f*; (*also*: **trade ~**) sindacato // *cpd* sindacale, dei sindacati; **U~ Jack** *n* bandiera nazionale britannica.
unique [juː'niːk] *a* unico(a).
unison ['juːnɪsn] *n*: **in ~** all'unisono.
unit ['juːnɪt] *n* unità *f inv*; (*section: of furniture etc*) elemento; (*team, squad*) reparto, squadra.
unite [juː'naɪt] *vt* unire // *vi* unirsi; ~**d** *a* unito(a); unificato(a); (*efforts*) congiunto(a); **U~d Kingdom (U.K.)** *n* Regno Unito; **U~d Nations (Organization) (UN, UNO)** *n* (Organizzazione *f* delle) Nazioni Unite (O.N.U.); **U~d States (of America) (US, USA)** *n* Stati *mpl* Uniti (d'America) (USA).
unit trust ['juːnɪttrʌst] *n* (*Brit*) fondo d'investimento.
unity ['juːnɪtɪ] *n* unità.
universal [juːnɪ'vɜːsl] *a* universale.
universe ['juːnɪvɜːs] *n* universo.
university [juːnɪ'vɜːsɪtɪ] *n* università *f inv*.
unjust [ʌn'dʒʌst] *a* ingiusto(a).
unkempt [ʌn'kɛmpt] *a* trasandato(a); spettinato(a).
unkind [ʌn'kaɪnd] *a* scortese; crudele.
unknown [ʌn'nəun] *a* sconosciuto(a).
unladen [ʌn'leɪdn] *a* (*ship, weight*) a vuoto.
unlawful [ʌn'lɔːful] *a* illecito(a), illegale.
unleash [ʌn'liːʃ] *vt* sguinzagliare; (*fig*) scatenare.
unleavened [ʌn'lɛvnd] *a* non lievitato(a), azzimo(a).
unless [ʌn'lɛs] *cj* a meno che (non) + *sub*; ~ **otherwise stated** salvo indicazione contraria.
unlicensed [ʌn'laɪsənst] *a* senza licenza per la vendita di alcolici.
unlike [ʌn'laɪk] *a* diverso(a) // *prep* a differenza di, contrariamente a.

unlikely [ʌn'laɪklɪ] *a* improbabile; inverosimile.
unlimited [ʌn'lɪmɪtɪd] *a* illimitato(a).
unload [ʌn'ləud] *vt* scaricare.
unlock [ʌn'lɔk] *vt* aprire.
unlucky [ʌn'lʌkɪ] *a* sfortunato(a); (*object, number*) che porta sfortuna, di malaugurio.
unmarried [ʌn'mærɪd] *a* non sposato(a); (*man only*) scapolo, celibe; (*woman only*) nubile; ~ **mother** *n* ragazza *f* madre *inv*.
unmask [ʌn'mɑːsk] *vt* smascherare.
unmistakable [ʌnmɪs'teɪkəbl] *a* indubbio(a); facilmente riconoscibile.
unmitigated [ʌn'mɪtɪgeɪtɪd] *a* non mitigato(a), assoluto(a), vero(a) e proprio(a).
unnatural [ʌn'nætʃrəl] *a* innaturale; contro natura.
unnecessary [ʌn'nɛsəsərɪ] *a* inutile, superfluo(a).
unobtainable [ʌnəb'teɪnəbl] *a* (*TEL*) non ottenibile.
unofficial [ʌnə'fɪʃl] *a* non ufficiale; (*strike*) non dichiarato(a) dal sindacato.
unorthodox [ʌn'ɔːθədɔks] *a* non ortodosso(a).
unpack [ʌn'pæk] *vi* disfare la valigia (*or* le valigie).
unpalatable [ʌn'pælətəbl] *a* (*truth*) sgradevole.
unparalleled [ʌn'pærəleld] *a* incomparabile, impareggiabile.
unpleasant [ʌn'plɛznt] *a* spiacevole.
unplug [ʌn'plʌg] *vt* staccare.
unpopular [ʌn'pɔpjulə*] *a* impopolare.
unprecedented [ʌn'prɛsɪdəntɪd] *a* senza precedenti.
unpredictable [ʌnprɪ'dɪktəbl] *a* imprevedibile.
unpretentious [ʌnprɪ'tɛnʃəs] *a* senza pretese.
unqualified [ʌn'kwɔlɪfaɪd] *a* (*teacher*) non abilitato(a); (*success*) assoluto(a), senza riserve.
unravel [ʌn'rævl] *vt* dipanare, districare.
unreal [ʌn'rɪəl] *a* irreale.
unreasonable [ʌn'riːznəbl] *a* irragionevole.
unrelated [ʌnrɪ'leɪtɪd] *a*: ~ **(to)** senza rapporto (con); non imparentato(a) (con).
unrelenting [ʌnrɪ'lɛntɪŋ] *a* implacabile; accanito(a).
unreliable [ʌnrɪ'laɪəbl] *a* (*person, machine*) che non dà affidamento; (*news, source of information*) inattendibile.
unrelieved [ʌnrɪ'liːvd] *a* (*monotony*) uniforme.
unremitting [ʌnrɪ'mɪtɪŋ] *a* incessante, infaticabile.
unrepentant [ʌnrɪ'pɛntənt] *a* impenitente.
unrest [ʌn'rɛst] *n* agitazione *f*.
unroll [ʌn'rəul] *vt* srotolare.
unruly [ʌn'ruːlɪ] *a* indisciplinato(a).
unsafe [ʌn'seɪf] *a* pericoloso(a), rischioso(a).

unsaid [ʌn'sɛd] a: **to leave sth ~** passare qc sotto silenzio.

unsatisfactory ['ʌnsætis'fæktəri] a che lascia a desiderare, insufficiente.

unsavoury [ʌn'seivəri] a (fig: person) losco(a); (: reputation, subject) disgustoso(a), ripugnante.

unscathed [ʌn'skeiðd] a incolume.

unscrew [ʌn'skru:] vt svitare.

unscrupulous [ʌn'skru:pjuləs] a senza scrupoli.

unseemly [ʌn'si:mli] a sconveniente.

unsettled [ʌn'sɛtld] a turbato(a); instabile; indeciso(a).

unsightly [ʌn'saitli] a brutto(a), sgradevole a vedersi.

unskilled [ʌn'skild] a: ~ **worker** n manovale m.

unsophisticated [ʌnsə'fistikeitid] a semplice, naturale.

unspeakable [ʌn'spi:kəbl] a (bad) abominevole.

unsteady [ʌn'stɛdi] a instabile, malsicuro(a).

unstuck [ʌn'stʌk] a: **to come ~** scollarsi; (fig) fare fiasco.

unsuccessful [ʌnsək'sɛsful] a (writer, proposal) che non ha successo; (marriage, attempt) mal riuscito(a), fallito(a); **to be ~** (in attempting sth) non riuscire; non avere successo; (application) non essere considerato(a); **~ly** ad senza successo.

unsuitable [ʌn'su:təbl] a inadatto(a); inopportuno(a); sconveniente.

unsuspecting [ʌnsə'spɛktiŋ] a che non sospetta niente.

unswerving [ʌn'swə:viŋ] a fermo(a).

untangle [ʌn'tæŋgl] vt sbrogliare.

untapped [ʌn'tæpt] a (resources) non sfruttato(a).

unthinkable [ʌn'θiŋkəbl] a impensabile, inconcepibile.

untidy [ʌn'taidi] a (room) in disordine; (appearance, work) trascurato(a); (person, writing) disordinato(a).

untie [ʌn'tai] vt (knot, parcel) disfare; (prisoner, dog) slegare.

until [ən'til] prep fino a; (after negative) prima di // cj finché, fino a quando; (in past, after negative) prima che + sub, prima di + infinitive.

untimely [ʌn'taimli] a intempestivo(a), inopportuno(a); (death) prematuro(a).

untold [ʌn'təuld] a incalcolabile; indescrivibile.

untoward [ʌntə'wɔ:d] a sfortunato(a), sconveniente.

unused [ʌn'ju:zd] a nuovo(a).

unusual [ʌn'ju:ʒuəl] a insolito(a), eccezionale, raro(a).

unveil [ʌn'veil] vt scoprire; svelare.

unwavering [ʌn'weivəriŋ] a fermo(a), incrollabile.

unwell [ʌn'wel] a indisposto(a).

unwieldy [ʌn'wi:ldi] a poco maneggevole.

unwilling [ʌn'wiliŋ] a: **to be ~ to do** non voler fare; **~ly** ad malvolentieri.

unwind [ʌn'waind] vb (irg) vt svolgere, srotolare // vi (relax) rilassarsi.

unwitting [ʌn'witiŋ] a involontario(a).

unworthy [ʌn'wə:ði] a indegno(a).

unwrap [ʌn'ræp] vt disfare; aprire.

unwritten [ʌn'ritn] a (agreement) tacito(a).

up [ʌp] prep: **to go/be ~ sth** salire/essere su qc // ad su, (di) sopra; in alto; **~ there** lassù; **~ above** al di sopra; **~ to** fino a; **to be ~** (out of bed) essere alzato(a) or in piedi; **it is ~ to you** tocca a lei decidere; **what is he ~ to?** cosa sta tramando?; **he is not ~ to it** non ne è capace; **~-and-coming** a pieno(a) di promesse, promettente; **~s and downs** npl (fig) alti e bassi mpl.

upbringing ['ʌpbriŋiŋ] n educazione f.

update [ʌp'deit] vt aggiornare.

upgrade [ʌp'greid] vt promuovere; (job) rivalutare.

upheaval [ʌp'hi:vl] n sconvolgimento; tumulto.

uphill [ʌp'hil] a in salita; (fig: task) difficile // ad: **to go ~** andare in salita, salire.

uphold [ʌp'həuld] vt irg approvare; sostenere.

upholstery [ʌp'həulstəri] n tappezzeria.

upkeep ['ʌpki:p] n manutenzione f.

upon [ə'pɔn] prep su.

upper ['ʌpə*] a superiore // n (of shoe) tomaia; **the ~ class** ≈ l'alta borghesia; **~-class** a dell'alta borghesia; **~most** a il(la) più alto(a); predominante.

upright ['ʌprait] a diritto(a); verticale; (fig) diritto(a), onesto(a) // n montante m.

uprising ['ʌpraiziŋ] n insurrezione f, rivolta.

uproar ['ʌprɔ:*] n tumulto, clamore m.

uproot [ʌp'ru:t] vt sradicare.

upset n ['ʌpsɛt] turbamento // vt [ʌp'sɛt] (irg: like set) (glass etc) rovesciare; (plan, stomach) scombussolare; (person: offend) contrariare; (: grieve) addolorare; sconvolgere // a [ʌp'sɛt] contrariato(a); addolorato(a); (stomach) scombussolato(a), disturbato(a).

upshot ['ʌpʃɔt] n risultato.

upside ['ʌpsaid]: **~-down** ad sottosopra; **to turn ~-down** capovolgere; (fig) mettere sottosopra.

upstairs [ʌp'stɛəz] ad, a di sopra, al piano superiore.

upstart ['ʌpstɑ:t] n nuovo(a) ricco(a).

upstream [ʌp'stri:m] ad a monte.

uptake ['ʌpteik] n: **he is quick/slow on the ~** è pronto/lento di comprendonio.

up-to-date ['ʌptə'deit] a moderno(a); aggiornato(a).

upturn ['ʌptə:n] n (in luck) svolta favorevole.

upward ['ʌpwəd] a ascendente; verso l'alto; **~(s)** ad in su, verso l'alto.

uranium [juə'reiniəm] n uranio.

urban ['ə:bən] a urbano(a).

urbane [ə:'bein] a civile, urbano(a), educato(a).

urchin ['ɔ:tʃin] n monello; **sea** ~ n riccio di mare.

urge [ɜ:dʒ] n impulso; stimolo; forte desiderio // vt: **to** ~ **sb to do** esortare qd a fare, spingere qd a fare; raccomandare a qd di fare; **to** ~ **on** vt spronare.

urgency ['ɜːdʒənsɪ] n urgenza; (of tone) insistenza.

urgent ['ɜːdʒənt] a urgente.

urinate ['juərɪneɪt] vi orinare.

urn [ɜːn] n urna; (also: **tea** ~) bollitore m per il tè.

us [ʌs] pronoun ci; (stressed, after prep) noi.

US, USA n abbr see **united**.

usage ['juːzɪdʒ] n uso.

use n [juːs] uso; impiego, utilizzazione f // vt [juːz] usare, utilizzare, servirsi di; **she** ~d **to do it** lo faceva (una volta), era solita farlo; **in** ~ in uso; **out of** ~ fuori uso; **it's no** ~ non serve, è inutile; **to be** ~d **to** avere l'abitudine di; **to** ~ **up** vt consumare; esaurire; ~d a (car) d'occasione; ~**ful** a utile; ~**fulness** n utilità; ~**less** a inutile; ~ r n utente m/f.

usher ['ʌʃə*] n usciere m; (in cinema) maschera; ~**ette** [-'ret] n (in cinema) maschera.

USSR n: **the** ~ l'URSS f.

usual ['juːʒuəl] a solito(a); ~**ly** ad di solito.

usurer ['juːʒərə*] n usuraio/a.

usurp [juːˈzɜːp] vt usurpare.

utensil [juːˈtensl] n utensile m.

uterus ['juːtərəs] n utero.

utilitarian [juːtɪlɪˈtɛərɪən] a utilitario(a).

utility [juːˈtɪlɪtɪ] n utilità; (also: **public** ~) servizio pubblico.

utilization [juːtɪlaɪˈzeɪʃən] n utilizzazione f.

utilize ['juːtɪlaɪz] vt utilizzare; sfruttare.

utmost ['ʌtməust] a estremo(a) // n: **to do one's** ~ fare il possibile or di tutto.

utter ['ʌtə*] a assoluto(a), totale // vt pronunciare, proferire; emettere; ~**ance** n espressione f; parole fpl.

U-turn ['juːˈtɜːn] n inversione f a U.

V

v. abbr of **verse, versus, volt**; (abbr of vide) vedi, vedere.

vacancy ['veɪkənsɪ] n (job) posto libero; (room) stanza libera; **'no vacancies'** 'completo'.

vacant ['veɪkənt] a (job, seat etc) libero(a); (expression) assente.

vacate [vəˈkeɪt] vt lasciare libero(a).

vacation [vəˈkeɪʃən] n vacanze fpl; ~ **course** n corso estivo.

vaccinate ['væksɪneɪt] vt vaccinare; **vaccination** [-ˈneɪʃən] n vaccinazione f.

vaccine ['væksiːn] n vaccino.

vacuum ['vækjum] n vuoto; ~ **cleaner** n aspirapolvere m inv; ~ **flask** n thermos m inv ®.

vagina [vəˈdʒaɪnə] n vagina.

vagrant ['veɪgrnt] n vagabondo/a.

vague [veɪg] a vago(a); (blurred: photo, memory) sfocato(a); ~**ly** ad vagamente.

vain [veɪn] a (useless) inutile, vano(a); (conceited) vanitoso(a); **in** ~ inutilmente, invano.

valentine ['væləntain] n (also: ~ **card**) cartolina or biglietto di San Valentino.

valiant ['væliənt] a valoroso(a), coraggioso(a).

valid ['vælɪd] a valido(a), valevole; (excuse) valido(a); ~**ity** [-ˈlɪdɪtɪ] n validità.

valley ['vælɪ] n valle f.

valuable ['væljuəbl] a (jewel) di (grande) valore; (time) prezioso(a); ~**s** npl oggetti mpl di valore.

valuation [væljuˈeɪʃən] n valutazione f, stima.

value ['væljuː] n valore m // vt (fix price) valutare, dare un prezzo a; (cherish) apprezzare, tenere a; ~ **added tax (VAT)** n imposta sul valore aggiunto (I.V.A.); ~**d** a (appreciated) stimato(a), apprezzato(a).

valve [vælv] n valvola.

van [væn] n (AUT) furgone m; (RAIL) vagone m.

vandal ['vændl] n vandalo/a; ~**ism** n vandalismo.

vanguard ['vængɑːd] n avanguardia.

vanilla [vəˈnɪlə] n vaniglia // cpd (ice cream) alla vaniglia.

vanish ['vænɪʃ] vi svanire, scomparire.

vanity ['vænɪtɪ] n vanità; ~ **case** n valigetta per cosmetici.

vantage ['vɑːntɪdʒ] n: ~ **point** n posizione f or punto di osservazione; (fig) posizione vantaggiosa.

vapour ['veɪpə*] n vapore m.

variable ['vɛərɪəbl] a variabile; (mood) mutevole.

variance ['vɛərɪəns] n: **to be at** ~ (**with**) essere in disaccordo (con); (facts) essere in contraddizione (con).

variant ['vɛərɪənt] n variante f.

variation [vɛərɪˈeɪʃən] n variazione f; (in opinion) cambiamento.

varicose ['værɪkəus] a: ~ **veins** npl varici fpl.

varied ['vɛərɪd] a vario(a), diverso(a).

variety [vəˈraɪətɪ] n varietà f inv; (quantity) quantità, numero; ~ **show** n varietà m inv.

various ['vɛərɪəs] a vario(a), diverso(a); (several) parecchi(e), molti(e).

varnish ['vɑːnɪʃ] n vernice f // vt verniciare.

vary ['vɛərɪ] vt, vi variare, mutare; ~**ing** a variabile.

vase [vɑːz] n vaso.

vast [vɑːst] a vasto(a); (amount, success) enorme; ~**ly** ad enormemente.

vat [væt] n tino.

VAT [væt] n abbr see **value**.

Vatican ['vætɪkən] n: **the** ~ il Vaticano.

vault [vɔːlt] n (of roof) volta; (tomb) tomba; (in bank) camera blindata; (jump) salto // vt (also: ~ **over**) saltare (d'un balzo).

vaunted ['vɔːntɪd] a: **much-~** tanto celebrato(a).

VD n abbr see **venereal**.

veal [viːl] n vitello.

veer [vɪə*] vi girare; virare.

vegetable ['vedʒtəbl] n verdura, ortaggio // a vegetale.

vegetarian [vedʒɪ'tɛərɪən] a, n vegetariano(a).

vegetate ['vedʒɪteɪt] vi vegetare.

vegetation [vedʒɪ'teɪʃən] n vegetazione f.

vehemence ['viːɪməns] n veemenza, violenza.

vehicle ['viːɪkl] n veicolo.

veil [veɪl] n velo // vt velare.

vein [veɪn] n vena; (on leaf) nervatura; (fig: mood) vena, umore m.

velocity [vɪ'lɔsɪti] n velocità.

velvet ['velvɪt] n velluto.

vending machine ['vendɪŋməʃiːn] n distributore m automatico.

vendor ['vendɔ*] n venditore/trice.

veneer [və'nɪə*] n impiallacciatura; (fig) vernice f.

venerable ['venərəbl] a venerabile.

venereal [vɪ'nɪərɪəl] a: **~ disease (VD)** n malattia venerea.

Venetian [vɪ'niːʃən] a veneziano(a); **~ blind** n (tenda alla) veneziana.

Venezuela [vene'zweɪlə] n Venezuela m; **~n** a, n venezuelano(a).

vengeance ['vendʒəns] n vendetta; **with a ~** (fig) davvero; furiosamente.

Venice ['venɪs] n Venezia.

venison ['venɪsn] n carne f di cervo.

venom ['venəm] n veleno; **~ous** a velenoso(a).

vent [vent] n foro, apertura; (in dress, jacket) spacco // vt (fig: one's feelings) sfogare, dare sfogo a.

ventilate ['ventɪleɪt] vt (room) dare aria a, arieggiare; **ventilation** [-'leɪʃən] n ventilazione f; **ventilator** n ventilatore m.

ventriloquist [ven'trɪləkwɪst] n ventriloquo/a.

venture ['ventʃə*] n impresa (rischiosa) // vt rischiare, azzardare // vi arrischiarsi, azzardarsi.

venue ['venjuː] n luogo di incontro; (SPORT) luogo (designato) per l'incontro.

veranda(h) [və'rændə] n veranda.

verb [vəːb] n verbo; **~al** a verbale; (translation) letterale.

verbose [vəː'bəus] a verboso(a).

verdict ['vəːdɪkt] n verdetto.

verge [vəːdʒ] n bordo, orlo; **on the ~ of doing** sul punto di fare; **to ~ on** vt fus rasentare.

verger ['vəːdʒə*] n (REL) sagrestano.

verification [verɪfɪ'keɪʃən] n verifica.

verify ['verɪfaɪ] vt verificare.

vermin ['vəːmɪn] npl animali mpl nocivi; (insects) insetti mpl parassiti.

vermouth ['vəːməθ] n vermut m inv.

vernacular [və'nækjulə*] n vernacolo.

versatile ['vəːsətaɪl] a (person) versatile;

(machine, tool etc) (che si presta) a molti usi.

verse [vəːs] n versi mpl; (stanza) stanza, strofa; (in bible) versetto.

versed [vəːst] a: **(well-)~ in** versato(a) in.

version ['vəːʃən] n versione f.

versus ['vəːsəs] prep contro.

vertebra, pl **~e** ['vəːtɪbrə, -briː] n vertebra.

vertebrate ['vəːtɪbrɪt] n vertebrato.

vertical ['vəːtɪkl] a, n verticale (m); **~ly** ad verticalmente.

vertigo ['vəːtɪgəu] n vertigine f.

verve [vəːv] n brio; entusiasmo.

very ['verɪ] ad molto // a: **the ~ book which** proprio il libro che; **at the ~ end** proprio alla fine; **the ~ last** proprio l'ultimo; **at the ~ least** almeno; **~ much** moltissimo.

vespers ['vespəz] npl vespro.

vessel ['vesl] n (ANAT) vaso; (NAUT) nave f; (container) recipiente m.

vest [vest] n maglia; (sleeveless) canottiera; (US: waistcoat) gilè m inv // vt: **to ~ sb with sth, to ~ sth in sb** conferire qc a qd; **~ed interests** npl (COMM) diritti mpl acquisiti.

vestibule ['vestɪbjuːl] n vestibolo.

vestige ['vestɪdʒ] n vestigio.

vestment ['vestmənt] n (REL) paramento liturgico.

vestry ['vestrɪ] n sagrestia.

vet [vet] n (abbr of **veterinary surgeon**) veterinario // vt esaminare minuziosamente; (text) rivedere.

veteran ['vetərn] n veterano; (also: **war ~**) reduce m; **~ car** n auto f inv d'epoca.

veterinary ['vetrɪnərɪ] a veterinario(a); **~ surgeon** n veterinario.

veto ['viːtəu] n, pl **~es** veto // vt opporre il veto a.

vex [veks] vt irritare, contrariare; **~ed** a (question) controverso(a), dibattuto(a).

VHF abbr of very high frequency.

via ['vaɪə] prep (by way of) via; (by means of) tramite.

viable ['vaɪəbl] a attuabile; vitale.

viaduct ['vaɪədʌkt] n viadotto.

vibrate [vaɪ'breɪt] vi: **to ~ (with)** vibrare (di); (resound) risonare (di); **vibration** [-'breɪʃən] n vibrazione f.

vicar ['vɪkə*] n pastore m; **~age** n presbiterio.

vice [vaɪs] n (evil) vizio; (TECH) morsa.

vice- [vaɪs] prefix vice...; **~chairman** n vicepresidente m.

vice squad ['vaɪsskwɔd] n (squadra del) buon costume f.

vice versa ['vaɪsɪ'vəːsə] ad viceversa.

vicinity [vɪ'sɪnɪti] n vicinanze fpl.

vicious ['vɪʃəs] a (remark) maligno(a), cattivo(a); (blow) violento(a); **~ness** n malignità, cattiveria; ferocia.

vicissitudes [vɪ'sɪsɪtjuːdz] npl vicissitudini fpl.

victim ['vɪktɪm] n vittima; **~ization**

[-aɪzeɪʃən] n persecuzione f; rappresaglie fpl; ~ize vt perseguitare; compiere delle rappresaglie contro.

victor ['vɪktə*] n vincitore m.

Victorian [vɪk'tɔːrɪən] a vittoriano(a).

victorious [vɪk'tɔːrɪəs] a vittorioso(a).

victory ['vɪktərɪ] n vittoria.

video ['vɪdɪəʊ] cpd video...; ~-(-tape) recorder n videoregistratore m.

vie [vaɪ] vi: to ~ with competere con, rivaleggiare con.

Vienna [vɪ'enə] n Vienna.

view [vjuː] n vista, veduta; (opinion) opinione f // vt (situation) considerare; (house) visitare; **on** ~ (in museum etc) esposto(a); **in my** ~ a mio avviso, secondo me; **in** ~ **of the fact that** considerato che; ~**er** n (viewfinder) mirino; (small projector) visore m; (TV) telespettatore/trice; ~**finder** n mirino; ~**point** n punto di vista.

vigil ['vɪdʒɪl] n veglia; ~**ance** n vigilanza; ~**ant** a vigile.

vigorous ['vɪgərəs] a vigoroso(a).

vigour ['vɪgə*] n vigore m.

vile [vaɪl] a (action) vile; (smell) disgustoso(a), nauseante; (temper) pessimo(a).

villa ['vɪlə] n villa.

village ['vɪlɪdʒ] n villaggio; ~**r** n abitante m/f di villaggio.

villain ['vɪlən] n (scoundrel) canaglia; (criminal) criminale m; (in novel etc) cattivo.

vindicate ['vɪndɪkeɪt] vt comprovare; giustificare.

vindictive [vɪn'dɪktɪv] a vendicativo(a).

vine [vaɪn] n vite f; (climbing plant) rampicante m.

vinegar ['vɪnɪgə*] n aceto.

vineyard ['vɪnjɑːd] n vigna, vigneto.

vintage ['vɪntɪdʒ] n (year) annata, produzione f; ~ **wine** n vino d'annata.

vinyl ['vaɪnl] n vinile m.

viola [vɪ'əʊlə] n viola.

violate ['vaɪəleɪt] vt violare; **violation** [-'leɪʃən] n violazione f.

violence ['vaɪələns] n violenza; (POL etc) incidenti mpl violenti.

violent ['vaɪələnt] a violento(a); ~**ly** ad violentemente; estremamente.

violet ['vaɪələt] a (colour) viola inv, violetto(a) // n (plant) violetta.

violin [vaɪə'lɪn] n violino; ~**ist** n violinista m/f.

VIP n (abbr of very important person) V.I.P. m/f inv.

viper ['vaɪpə*] n vipera.

virgin ['vɜːdʒɪn] n vergine f // a vergine; **the Blessed V~** la Beatissima Vergine; ~**ity** [-'dʒɪnɪtɪ] n verginità.

Virgo ['vɜːgəʊ] n (sign) Vergine f.

virile ['vɪraɪl] a virile.

virility [vɪ'rɪlɪtɪ] n virilità.

virtually ['vɜːtjʊəlɪ] ad (almost) praticamente.

virtue ['vɜːtjuː] n virtù f inv; (advantage)

pregio, vantaggio; **by** ~ **of** grazie a.

virtuoso [vəːtjʊ'əʊzəʊ] n virtuoso.

virtuous ['vɜːtjʊəs] a virtuoso(a).

virus ['vaɪərəs] n virus m inv.

visa ['viːzə] n visto.

vis-à-vis [viːzə'viː] prep rispetto a, nei riguardi di.

viscount ['vaɪkaʊnt] n visconte m.

visibility [vɪzɪ'bɪlɪtɪ] n visibilità.

visible ['vɪzəbl] a visibile.

vision ['vɪʒən] n (sight) vista; (foresight, in dream) visione f; ~**ary** n visionario/a.

visit ['vɪzɪt] n visita; (stay) soggiorno // vt (person) andare a trovare; (place) visitare; ~**ing card** n biglietto da visita; ~**or** n visitatore/trice; (guest) ospite m/f; (in hotel) cliente m/f; ~**ors' book** n libro d'oro; (in hotel) registro.

visor ['vaɪzə*] n visiera.

vista ['vɪstə] n vista, prospettiva.

visual ['vɪzjʊəl] a visivo(a); visuale; ottico(a); ~ **aid** n sussidio visivo.

visualize ['vɪzjʊəlaɪz] vt immaginare, figurarsi; (foresee) prevedere.

vital ['vaɪtl] a vitale; ~**ity** [-'tælɪtɪ] n vitalità; ~**ly** ad estremamente; ~ **statistics** npl (fig) misure fpl.

vitamin ['vɪtəmɪn] n vitamina.

vivacious [vɪ'veɪʃəs] a vivace.

vivacity [vɪ'væsɪtɪ] n vivacità.

vivid ['vɪvɪd] a vivido(a); ~**ly** ad (describe) vividamente; (remember) con precisione.

vivisection [vɪvɪ'sekʃən] n vivisezione f.

vocabulary [vəʊ'kæbjʊlərɪ] n vocabolario.

vocal ['vəʊkl] a (MUS) vocale; (communication) verbale; (noisy) rumoroso(a); ~**ist** n cantante m/f di musica vocale, vocalist m/f inv.

vocation [vəʊ'keɪʃən] n vocazione f; ~**al** a professionale.

vociferous [vəˈsɪfərəs] a rumoroso(a).

vodka ['vɒdkə] n vodka f inv.

vogue [vəʊg] n moda; (popularity) popolarità, voga.

voice [vɔɪs] n voce f // vt (opinion) esprimere.

void [vɔɪd] n vuoto // a: ~ **of** privo(a) di.

volatile ['vɒlətaɪl] a volatile; (fig) volubile.

volcanic [vɒl'kænɪk] a vulcanico(a).

volcano, ~**es** [vɒl'keɪnəʊ] n vulcano.

volition [və'lɪʃən] n: **of one's own** ~ di sua volontà.

volley ['vɒlɪ] n (of gunfire) salva; (of stones etc) raffica, gragnola; (TENNIS etc) volata; ~**ball** n pallavolo f.

volt [vəʊlt] n volt m inv; ~**age** n tensione f, voltaggio.

voluble ['vɒljʊbl] a loquace, ciarliero(a).

volume ['vɒljuːm] n volume m; ~ **control** n (RADIO, TV) regolatore m or manopola del volume.

voluntarily ['vɒləntrɪlɪ] ad volontariamente; gratuitamente.

voluntary ['vɒləntərɪ] a volontario(a); (unpaid) gratuito(a), non retribuito(a).

volunteer [vɒlən'tɪə*] n volontario/a // vi

(MIL) arruolarsi volontario; **to ~ to do** offrire (volontariamente) di fare.

voluptuous [vəˈlʌptjuəs] a voluttuoso(a).

vomit [ˈvɔmit] n vomito // vt, vi vomitare.

vote [vəut] n voto, suffragio; (cast) voto; (franchise) diritto di voto // vi votare; **~ of thanks** n discorso di ringraziamento; **~r** n elettore/trice; **voting** n scrutinio.

vouch [vautʃ]: **to ~ for** vt farsi garante di.

voucher [ˈvautʃə*] n (for meal, petrol) buono; (receipt) ricevuta.

vow [vau] n voto, promessa solenne // vi giurare.

vowel [ˈvauəl] n vocale f.

voyage [ˈvɔidʒ] n viaggio per mare, traversata.

vulgar [ˈvʌlgə*] a volgare; **~ity** [-ˈgæriti] n volgarità.

vulnerable [ˈvʌlnərəbl] a vulnerabile.

vulture [ˈvʌltʃə*] n avvoltoio.

W

wad [wɔd] n (of cotton wool, paper) tampone m; (of banknotes etc) fascio.

wade [weid] vi: **to ~ through** camminare a stento in // vt guadare.

wafer [ˈweifə*] n (CULIN) cialda; (REL) ostia.

waffle [ˈwɔfl] n (CULIN) cialda; (col) ciance fpl; riempitivo // vi cianciare; parlare a vuoto.

waft [wɔft] vt portare // vi diffondersi.

wag [wæg] vt agitare, muovere // vi agitarsi.

wage [weidʒ] n salario, paga // vt: **to ~ war** fare la guerra; **~s** npl salario, paga.

wager [ˈweidʒə*] n scommessa.

waggle [ˈwægl] vt dimenare, agitare // vi dimenarsi, agitarsi.

wag(g)on [ˈwægən] n (horse-drawn) carro; (truck) furgone m; (RAIL) vagone m (merci).

wail [weil] n gemito; (of siren) urlo // vi gemere; urlare.

waist [weist] n vita, cintola; **~coat** n panciotto, gilè m inv; **~line** n (giro di) vita.

wait [weit] n attesa // vi aspettare, attendere; **to lie in ~ for** stare in agguato a; **I can't ~ to** (fig) non vedo l'ora di; **to ~ behind** vi rimanere (ad aspettare); **to ~ for** aspettare; **to ~ on** vt fus servire; **~er** n cameriere m; **'no ~ing'** (AUT) 'divieto di sosta'; **~ing list** n lista di attesa; **~ing room** n sala d'aspetto or d'attesa; **~ress** n cameriera.

waive [weiv] vt rinunciare a, abbandonare.

wake [weik] vb (pt woke, ~d, pp woken, ~d) [wəuk, ˈwəukn] vt (also: ~ up) svegliare // vi (also: ~ up) svegliarsi // n (for dead person) veglia funebre; (NAUT) scia; **~n** vt, vi = **wake**.

Wales [weilz] n Galles m.

walk [wɔ:k] n passeggiata; (short) giretto; (gait) passo, andatura; (path) sentiero; (in park etc) sentiero, vialetto // vi camminare; (for pleasure, exercise) passeggiare // vt (distance) fare or percorrere a piedi; (dog) accompagnare, portare a passeggiare; **10 minutes' ~ from** 10 minuti di cammino or a piedi da; **from all ~s of life** di tutte le condizioni sociali; **~er** n (person) camminatore/trice; **~ie-talkie** [ˈwɔ:kiˈtɔ:ki] n radiotelefono portatile; **~ing** n camminare m; **~ing stick** n bastone m da passeggio; **~out** n (of workers) sciopero senza preavviso or a sorpresa; **~over** n (col) vittoria facile, gioco da ragazzi.

wall [wɔ:l] n muro; (internal, of tunnel, cave) parete f; **~ed** a (city) fortificato(a).

wallet [ˈwɔlit] n portafoglio.

wallflower [ˈwɔ:lflauə*] n violacciocca; **to be a ~** (fig) fare da tappezzeria.

wallop [ˈwɔləp] vt (col) pestare.

wallow [ˈwɔləu] vi sguazzare, voltolarsi.

wallpaper [ˈwɔ:lpeipə*] n carta da parati.

walnut [ˈwɔ:lnʌt] n noce f; (tree) noce m.

walrus [ˈwɔ:lrəs], pl ~ or ~es n tricheco.

waltz [wɔ:lts] n valzer m inv // vi ballare il valzer.

wan [wɔn] a pallido(a), smorto(a); triste.

wand [wɔnd] n (also: **magic ~**) bacchetta (magica).

wander [ˈwɔndə*] vi (person) girare senza meta, girovagare; (thoughts) vagare; (river) serpeggiare; **~er** n vagabondo/a.

wane [wein] vi (moon) calare; (reputation) declinare.

want [wɔnt] vt volere; (need) aver bisogno di; (lack) mancare di // n: **for ~ of** per mancanza di; **~s** npl (needs) bisogni mpl; **to ~ to do** volere fare; **to ~ sb to do** volere che qd faccia; **to be found ~ing** non risultare all'altezza.

wanton [ˈwɔntn] a sfrenato(a); senza motivo.

war [wɔ:*] n guerra; **to go to ~** entrare in guerra.

ward [wɔ:d] n (in hospital: room) corsia; (: section) reparto; (POL) circoscrizione f; (LAW: child) pupillo/a; **to ~ off** vt parare, schivare.

warden [ˈwɔ:dn] n (of institution) direttore/trice; (of park, game reserve) guardiano/a; (also: **traffic ~**) addetto/a al controllo del traffico e del parcheggio.

warder [ˈwɔ:də*] n guardia carceraria.

wardrobe [ˈwɔ:drəub] n (cupboard) guardaroba m inv, armadio; (clothes) guardaroba; (THEATRE) costumi mpl.

warehouse [ˈwɛəhaus] n magazzino.

wares [wɛəz] npl merci fpl.

warfare [ˈwɔ:fɛə*] n guerra.

warhead [ˈwɔ:hed] n (MIL) testata, ogiva.

warily [ˈwɛərili] ad cautamente, con prudenza.

warlike [ˈwɔ:laik] a guerriero(a).

warm [wɔ:m] a caldo(a); (thanks, welcome, applause) caloroso(a); **it's ~** fa caldo; **I'm ~** ho caldo; **to ~ up** vi scaldarsi, riscaldarsi; (athlete, discussion) riscaldarsi

// vt scaldare, riscaldare; (engine) far scaldare; ~-hearted a affettuoso(a); ~ly ad caldamente; calorosamente; vivamente; ~ th n calore m.

warn [wɔ:n] vt avvertire, avvisare; ~ing n avvertimento; (notice) avviso; ~ing light n spia luminosa.

warp [wɔ:p] vi deformarsi // vt deformare; (fig) corrompere.

warrant ['wɔrnt] n (LAW: to arrest) mandato di cattura; (: to search) mandato di perquisizione.

warranty ['wɔrənti] n garanzia.

warrior ['wɔriə*] n guerriero/a.

warship ['wɔ:ʃip] n nave f da guerra.

wart [wɔ:t] n verruca.

wartime ['wɔ:taim] n: in ~ in tempo di guerra.

wary ['wɛəri] a prudente.

was [wɔz] pt of be.

wash [wɔʃ] vt lavare // vi lavarsi // n: to give sth a ~ lavare qc, dare una lavata a qc; to **have a** ~ lavarsi; to ~ **away** vt (stain) togliere lavando; (subj: river etc) trascinare via; to ~ **down** vt lavare; to ~ **off** vi andare via con il lavaggio; to ~ **up** vi lavare i piatti; ~**basin** n lavabo; ~**er** n (TECH) rondella; ~**ing** n (linen etc) bucato; ~**ing machine** n lavatrice f; ~**ing powder** n detersivo (in polvere); ~**ing-up** n rigovernatura, lavatura dei piatti; ~**-out** n (col) disastro; ~**room** n gabinetto.

wasn't ['wɔznt] = was not.

wasp [wɔsp] n vespa.

wastage ['weistidʒ] n spreco; (in manufacturing) scarti mpl.

waste [weist] n spreco; (of time) perdita; (rubbish) rifiuti mpl // a (material) di scarto; (food) avanzato(a) // vt sprecare; (time, opportunity) perdere; ~s npl distesa desolata; to ~ **away** vi deperire; ~**bin** n bidone m or secchio della spazzatura; ~ **disposal unit** n eliminatore m di rifiuti; ~**ful** a sprecone(a); (process) dispendioso(a); ~ **ground** n terreno incolto or abbandonato; ~**paper basket** n cestino per la carta straccia.

watch [wɔtʃ] n orologio; (act of watching) sorveglianza; (guard: MIL, NAUT) guardia; (NAUT: spell of duty) quarto // vt (look at) osservare; (: match, programme) guardare; (spy on, guard) sorvegliare, tenere d'occhio; (be careful of) fare attenzione a // vi osservare, guardare; (keep guard) fare or montare la guardia; to ~ **out** vi fare attenzione; ~**dog** n cane m da guardia; ~**ful** a attento(a), vigile; ~**maker** n orologiaio/a; ~**man** n guardiano; (also: **night** ~**man**) guardiano notturno; ~ **strap** n cinturino da orologio.

water ['wɔ:tə*] n acqua // vt (plant) annaffiare; **in British** ~**s** nelle acque territoriali britanniche; to ~ **down** vt (milk) diluire; (fig: story) edulcorare; ~ **closet** n W.C. m inv, gabinetto; ~**colours** npl colori mpl per acquarello; ~**cress** n crescione m; ~**fall** n cascata; ~**ing can**

n annaffiatoio; ~ **level** n livello dell'acqua; (of flood) livello delle acque; ~ **lily** n ninfea; ~**line** n (NAUT) linea di galleggiamento; ~**logged** a saturo(a) d'acqua; imbevuto(a) d'acqua; (football pitch etc) allagato(a); ~ **main** n conduttura dell'acqua; ~**mark** n (on paper) filigrana; ~**melon** n anguria, cocomero; ~ **polo** n pallanuoto f; ~**proof** a impermeabile; ~**shed** n (GEO, fig) spartiacque m; ~**-skiing** n sci m acquatico; ~**tight** a stagno(a); ~**works** npl impianto idrico; ~**y** a (colour) slavato(a); (coffee) acquoso(a).

watt [wɔt] n watt m inv.

wave [weiv] n onda; (of hand) gesto, segno; (in hair) ondulazione f // vi fare un cenno con la mano; (flag) sventolare // vt (handkerchief) sventolare; (stick) brandire; (hair) ondulare; ~**length** n lunghezza d'onda.

waver ['weivə*] vi vacillare; (voice) tremolare.

wavy ['weivi] a ondulato(a); ondeggiante.

wax [wæks] n cera // vt dare la cera a; (car) lucidare // vi (moon) crescere; ~**works** npl cere fpl; museo delle cere.

way [wei] n via, strada; (path, access) passaggio; (distance) distanza; (direction) parte f, direzione f; (manner) modo, stile m; (habit) abitudine f; (condition) condizione f; **which** ~? – **this** ~ da che parte or in quale direzione? – da questa parte, per di qua; to **be on one's** ~ essere in cammino or sulla strada; to **be in the** ~ bloccare il passaggio; (fig) essere tra i piedi or d'impiccio; to **go out of one's** ~ **to do** (fig) mettercela tutta or fare di tutto per fare; **in a** ~ in un certo senso; **in some** ~**s** sotto certi aspetti; '~ **in**' 'entrata', 'ingresso'; '~ **out**' 'uscita'; **the** ~ **back** la via del ritorno.

waylay [wei'lei] vt irg tendere un agguato a; attendere al passaggio.

wayward ['weiwəd] a capriccioso(a); testardo(a).

W.C. ['dʌblju:'si:] n W.C. m inv, gabinetto.

we [wi:] pl pronoun noi.

weak [wi:k] a debole; (health) precario(a); (beam etc) fragile; ~**en** vi indebolirsi // vt indebolire; ~**ling** ['wi:kliŋ] n smidollato/a; debole m/f; ~**ness** n debolezza; (fault) punto debole, difetto.

wealth [wɛlθ] n (money, resources) ricchezza, ricchezze fpl; (of details) abbondanza, profusione f; ~**y** a ricco(a).

wean [wi:n] vt svezzare.

weapon ['wɛpən] n arma.

wear [wɛə*] n (use) uso; (deterioration through use) logorio, usura; (clothing): **sports/baby~** abbigliamento sportivo/per neonati // vb (pt **wore**, pp **worn** [wɔ:*, wɔ:n]) vt (clothes) portare; mettersi; (damage: through use) consumare // vi (last) durare; (rub etc through) consumarsi; **town/evening** ~ n abiti mpl or tenuta da città/sera; ~ **and tear** n usura, consumo; to ~ **away** vt consumare; erodere // vi consumarsi; essere eroso(a); **to** ~ **down** vt consumare; (strength) esaurire; **to** ~ **off** vi sparire lentamente; **to** ~ **on** vi passare; **to** ~ **out** vt consumare; (person, strength) esaurire.

weariness ['wɪərɪnɪs] n stanchezza.

weary ['wɪərɪ] a stanco(a); (tiring) faticoso(a) // vi: **to** ~ **of** stancarsi di.

weasel ['wi:zl] n (ZOOL) donnola.

weather ['wɛðə*] n tempo // vt (wood) stagionare; (storm, crisis) superare; ~**-beaten** a (person) segnato(a) dalle intemperie; (building) logorato(a) dalle intemperie; ~ **cock** n banderuola; ~ **forecast** n previsioni fpl del tempo, bollettino meteorologico.

weave, pt **wove**, pp **woven** [wi:v, wəuv, 'wəuvn] vt (cloth) tessere; (basket) intrecciare; ~**r** n tessitore/trice; **weaving** n tessitura.

web [wɛb] n (of spider) ragnatela; (on foot) palma; (fabric, also fig) tessuto; ~**bed** a (foot) palmato(a).

wed [wɛd] vt (pt, pp **wedded**) sposare // n: **the newly-**~**s** gli sposi novelli.

we'd [wi:d] = **we had, we would**.

wedding ['wɛdɪŋ] n matrimonio; **silver/golden** ~ n nozze fpl d'argento/d'oro; ~ **day** n giorno delle nozze or del matrimonio; ~ **dress** n abito nuziale; ~ **present** n regalo di nozze; ~ **ring** n fede f.

wedge [wɛdʒ] n (of wood etc) cuneo; (under door etc) zeppa; (of cake) spicchio, fetta // vt (fix) fissare con zeppe; (push) incuneare.

wedlock ['wɛdlɔk] n vincolo matrimoniale.

Wednesday ['wɛdnzdi] n mercole-dì m inv.

wee [wi:] a (Scottish) piccolo(a); piccolissimo(a).

weed [wi:d] n erbaccia // vt diserbare; ~**-killer** n diserbante m.

week [wi:k] n settimana; ~**day** n giorno feriale; (COMM) giornata lavorativa; ~**end** n fine settimana m or f inv, weekend m inv; ~**ly** ad ogni settimana, settimanalmente // a,n settimanale (m).

weep, pt, pp **wept** [wi:p, wɛpt] vi (person) piangere; ~**ing** willow n salice m piangente.

weigh [wei] vt,vi pesare; **to** ~ **anchor** salpare or levare l'ancora; **to** ~ **down** vt (branch) piegare; (fig: with worry) opprimere, caricare; **to** ~ **up** vt valutare.

weight [weit] n peso; **sold by** ~ venduto(a) a peso; ~**lessness** n mancanza di peso; ~ **lifter** n pesista m; ~**y** a pesante; (fig) importante, grave.

weir [wɪə*] n diga.

weird [wɪəd] a strano(a), bizzarro(a); (eerie) soprannaturale.

welcome ['wɛlkəm] a benvenuto(a) // n accoglienza, benvenuto // vt accogliere cordialmente; (also: **bid** ~) dare il benvenuto a; (be glad of) rallegrarsi di; **to**

be ~ essere il(la) benvenuto(a); **welcoming** a accogliente.

weld [wɛld] n saldatura // vt saldare; ~**er** n (person) saldatore m; ~**ing** n saldatura (autogena).

welfare ['wɛlfɛə*] n benessere m; ~ **state** n stato assistenziale; ~ **work** n assistenza sociale.

well [wɛl] n pozzo // ad bene // a: **to be** ~ andare bene; (person) stare bene // excl allora!; ma!; ebbene!; ~ **done!** bravo(a)!; **get** ~ **soon!** guarisci presto!; **to do** ~ **in** sth riuscire in qc.

we'll [wi:l] = **we will, we shall**.

well: ~**-behaved** a ubbidiente; ~**-being** n benessere m; ~**-built** a (person) ben fatto(a); ~**-developed** a (girl) sviluppata; ~**-earned** a (rest) meritato(a); ~**-groomed** a curato(a), azzimato(a); ~**-heeled** a (col: wealthy) agiato(a), facoltoso(a).

wellingtons ['wɛlɪŋtənz] npl (also: **wellington boots**) stivali mpl di gomma.

well: ~**-known** a (person) ben noto(a); (: famous) famoso(a); ~**-meaning** a ben intenzionato(a); ~**-off** a benestante, danaroso(a); ~**-read** a colto(a); ~**-to-do** a abbiente, benestante.

Welsh [wɛlʃ] a gallese // n (LING) gallese m; ~**man/woman** n gallese m/f; ~ **rarebit** n crostino al formaggio.

went [wɛnt] pt of **go**.

wept [wɛpt] pt, pp of **weep**.

were [wə:*] pt of **be**.

we're [wɪə*] = **we are**.

weren't [wə:nt] = **were not**.

west [wɛst] n ovest m, occidente m, ponente m // a (a) ovest inv, occidentale // ad verso ovest; **the W**~ n l'Occidente m; **the W**~ **Country** n il sud-ovest dell'Inghilterra; ~**erly** a (wind) occidentale, da ovest; ~**ern** a occidentale, dell'ovest // n (CINEMA) western m inv; **W**~ **Germany** n Germania occidentale or ovest; **W**~ **Indies** npl Indie fpl occidentali; ~**ward(s)** ad verso ovest.

wet [wɛt] a umido(a), bagnato(a); (soaked) fradicio(a); (rainy) piovoso(a); **to get** ~ bagnarsi; ~ **blanket** n (fig) guastafeste m/f; '~ **paint**' 'vernice fresca'; ~ **suit** n tuta da sub.

we've [wi:v] = **we have**.

whack [wæk] vt picchiare, battere; ~**ed** a (col: tired) sfinito(a), a pezzi.

whale [weil] n (ZOOL) balena.

wharf, wharves [wɔ:f, wɔ:vz] n banchina.

what [wɔt] excl cosa!, come! // det quale o che; (interrogative) che cosa, cosa, che; (relative) quello che, ciò che; ~ **a mess!** che disordine!; ~ **is it called?** come si chiama?; ~ **about doing ...?** cosa ne diresti di fare ...?; ~ **about me?** e io?; ~**ever** det: ~**ever book** qualunque or qualsiasi libro + sub // pronoun: **do** ~**ever is necessary/you want** faccia qualunque or qualsiasi cosa sia necessaria/lei voglia; ~**ever happens**

qualunque cosa accada; **no reason**
~**ever** *or* ~**soever** nessuna ragione
affatto *or* al mondo.
wheat [wi:t] *n* grano, frumento.
wheel [wi:l] *n* ruota; (AUT: *also:* **steering**
~) volante *m*; (NAUT) (ruota del) timone
m // *vt* spingere // *vi* (*also:* ~ **round**)
girare; ~**barrow** *n* carriola, ~**chair** *n*
sedia a rotelle.
wheeze [wi:z] *n* respiro affannoso // *vi*
ansimare.
when [wɛn] *ad* quando // *cj* quando, nel
momento in cui; (*whereas*) mentre;
~**ever** *ad* quando mai // *cj* quando;
(*every time that*) ogni volta che.
where [wɛə*] *ad,cj* dove; **this is** ~ è qui
che; ~**abouts** *ad* dove // *n:* sb's
~**abouts** luogo dove qd si trova; ~**as** *cj*
mentre; ~**ver** [-'ɛvə*] *ad* dove mai // *cj*
dovunque + *sub*.
whet [wɛt] *vt* (*tool*) affilare; (*appetite etc*)
stimolare.
whether [ˈwɛðə*] *cj* se; **I don't know** ~
to accept or not non so se accettare o no;
it's doubtful ~ è dubbio che; ~
you go or not che lei vada o no.
which [wɪtʃ] *det* (*interrogative*) che, quale;
~ **one of you?** chi di voi?; **tell me** ~
one you want mi dica quale vuole //
pronoun (*interrogative, indirect*) quale;
(*relative: subject*) che; (: *object*) che, *prep* +
cui, il(la) quale; **I don't mind** ~ non mi
importa quale; **the apple** ~ **you ate/**~
is on the table la mela che ha
mangiato/che è sul tavolo; **the chair on**
~ la sedia sulla quale *or* su cui; **the book**
of ~ il libro del quale *or* di cui; **he said**
he knew, ~ **is true/I feared** disse che
lo sapeva, il che è vero/ciò che temevo;
after ~ dopo di che; **in** ~ **case** nel qual
caso; ~**ever** *det:* take ~**ever book you**
prefer prenda qualsiasi libro che
preferisce; ~**ever book you take**
qualsiasi libro prenda.
whiff [wɪf] *n* soffio; sbuffo; odore *m*.
while [waɪl] *n* momento // *cj* mentre; (*as*
long as) finché; (*although*) sebbene + *sub*;
per quanto + *sub*; **for a** ~ per un po'.
whim [wɪm] *n* capriccio.
whimper [ˈwɪmpə*] *n* piagnucolio // *vi*
piagnucolare.
whimsical [ˈwɪmzɪkl] *a* (*person*)
capriccioso(a); (*look*) strano(a).
whine [waɪn] *n* gemito // *vi* gemere;
uggiolare; piagnucolare.
whip [wɪp] *n* frusta; (*for riding*) frustino;
(*Brit: POL: person*) capogruppo (*che*
sovrintende alla disciplina dei colleghi di
partito) // *vt* frustare; (*snatch*) sollevare
(*or* estrarre) bruscamente; ~**ped cream**
n panna montata; ~**round** *n* colletta.
whirl [wə:l] *n* turbine *m* // *vt* (far) girare
rapidamente; (far) turbinare // *vi*
turbinare; ~**pool** *n* mulinello; ~**wind** *n*
turbine *m*.
whirr [wə:*] *vi* ronzare; rombare; frullare.
whisk [wɪsk] *n* (CULIN) frusta; frullino // *vt*
sbattere, frullare; **to** ~ **sb away** *or* **off**

portar via qd a tutta velocità.
whisker [ˈwɪskə*] *n:* ~s *npl* (*of animal*)
baffi *mpl*; (*of man*) favoriti *mpl*.
whisk(e)y [ˈwɪskɪ] *n* whisky *m inv*.
whisper [ˈwɪspə*] *n* sussurro; (*rumour*)
voce *f* // *vt,vi* sussurrare.
whist [wɪst] *n* whist *m*.
whistle [ˈwɪsl] *n* (*sound*) fischio; (*object*)
fischietto // *vi* fischiare.
white [waɪt] *a* bianco(a); (*with fear*)
pallido(a) // *n* bianco; (*person*) bianco/a;
~**-collar worker** *n* impiegato; ~ **lie** *n*
bugia pietosa; ~**ness** *n* bianchezza;
~**wash** *n* (*paint*) bianco di calce // *vt*
imbiancare; (*fig*) coprire.
Whitsun [ˈwɪtsn] *n* la Pentecoste.
whittle [ˈwɪtl] *vt:* **to** ~ **away,** ~ **down**
ridurre, tagliare.
whizz [wɪz] *vi* sfrecciare; ~ **kid** *n* (*col*)
ragazzo/a prodigio.
WHO *n* (*abbr of World Health Organization*)
O.M.S. *f* (Organizzazione mondiale della
sanità).
who [hu:] *pronoun* (*interrogative*) chi;
(*relative*) che; ~**dunit** [hu:ˈdʌnɪt] *n* (*col*)
giallo; ~**ever** *pronoun:* ~**ever finds it**
chiunque lo trovi; **ask** ~**ever you like** io
chieda a chiunque vuole; ~**ever told you**
that? chi mai gliel'ha detto?
whole [həʊl] *a* (*complete*) tutto(a),
completo(a); (*not broken*) intero(a),
intatto(a) // *n* (*total*) totale *m*; (*sth not*
broken) tutto; **the** ~ **of the time** tutto il
tempo; **on the** ~, **as a** ~ nel complesso,
nell'insieme; ~**hearted** *a* sincero(a);
~**sale** *n* commercio *or* vendita
all'ingrosso // *a* all'ingrosso; (*destruction*)
totale; ~**saler** *n* grossista *m/f*; ~**some** *a*
sano(a); salutare; **wholly** *ad*
completamente, del tutto.
whom [hu:m] *pronoun* che, *prep* + il(la)
quale; (*interrogative*) chi.
whooping cough [ˈhu:pɪŋkɔf] *n* pertosse *f*.
whopping [ˈwɔpɪŋ] *a* (*col: big*) enorme.
whore [hɔ:*] *n* (*pej*) puttana.
whose [hu:z] *det:* ~ **book is this?** di chi è
questo libro?; ~ **pencil have you taken?**
di chi è la matita che ha preso?; **the man**
~ **son you rescued** l'uomo di cui *or* del
quale ha salvato il figlio; **the girl** ~
sister you were speaking to la ragazza
alla sorella di cui *or* della quale stava
parlando // *pronoun:* ~ **is this?** di chi è
questo?; **I know** ~ **it is** so di chi è.
why [waɪ] *ad* perché // *excl* oh!; ma come!;
the reason ~ la ragione perché *or* per la
quale; ~**ever** *ad* perché mai.
wick [wɪk] *n* lucignolo, stoppino.
wicked [ˈwɪkɪd] *a* cattivo(a), malvagio(a);
maligno(a); perfido(a); (*mischievous*) mali-
zioso(a).
wicker [ˈwɪkə*] *n* vimine *m*; (*also:*
~**work**) articoli *mpl* di vimini.
wicket [ˈwɪkɪt] *n* (CRICKET) porta; area tra
le due porte.
wide [waɪd] *a* largo(a); (*region, knowledge*)
vasto(a); (*choice*) ampio(a) // *ad:* **to open**
~ spalancare; **to shoot** ~ tirare a vuoto

or fuori bersaglio; ~-**angle lens** n grandangolare m; ~-**awake** a completamente sveglio(a); ~**ly** ad (different) molto, completamente; (believed) generalmente; ~**ly spaced** molto distanziati(e); ~**n** vt allargare, ampliare; ~ **open** a spalancato(a); ~**spread** a (belief etc) molto or assai diffuso(a).

widow ['wɪdəu] n vedova; ~**ed** a (che è rimasto(a)) vedovo(a); ~**er** n vedovo.

width [wɪdθ] n larghezza.

wield [wi:ld] vt (sword) maneggiare; (power) esercitare.

wife, wives [waɪf, waɪvz] n moglie f.

wig [wɪg] n parrucca.

wiggle ['wɪgl] vt dimenare, agitare // vi (loose screw etc) traballare; (worm) torcersi.

wild [waɪld] a selvatico(a); selvaggio(a); (sea) tempestoso(a); (idea, life) folle; stravagante; ~**s** npl regione f selvaggia; ~**erness** ['wɪldənɪs] n deserto; ~-**goose chase** n (fig) pista falsa; ~**life** n natura; ~**ly** ad (applaud) freneticamente; (hit, guess) a casaccio; (happy) follemente.

wilful ['wɪlful] a (person) testardo(a), ostinato(a); (action) intenzionale; (crime) premeditato(a).

will [wɪl] auxiliary vb: **he** ~ **come** verrà // vt (pt, pp ~**ed**): **to** ~ **sb to do** volere che qd faccia; **he** ~**ed himself to go on** continuò grazie a un grande sforzo di volontà // n volontà; testamento; ~**ing** a volonteroso(a); ~**ing to do** disposto(a) a fare; ~**ingly** ad volentieri; ~**ingness** n buona volontà.

willow ['wɪləu] n salice m.

will power ['wɪlpauə*] n forza di volontà.

wilt [wɪlt] vi appassire.

wily ['waɪlɪ] a furbo(a).

win [wɪn] n (in sports etc) vittoria // vb (pt, pp **won** [wʌn]) vt (battle, prize) vincere; (money) guadagnare; (popularity) conquistare // vi vincere; **to** ~ **over**, ~ **round** vt convincere.

wince [wɪns] n trasalimento, sussulto // vi trasalire.

winch [wɪntʃ] n verricello, argano.

wind n [wɪnd] vento; (MED) flatulenza, ventosità // vb [waɪnd] (pt, pp **wound** [waund]) vt attorcigliare; (wrap) avvolgere; (clock, toy) caricare; (take breath away: subj: [wɪnd]) far restare senza fiato // vi (road, river) serpeggiare; **to** ~ **up** vt (clock) caricare; (debate) concludere; ~**break** n frangivento; ~**fall** n colpo di fortuna; ~**ing** ['waɪndɪŋ] a (road) serpeggiante; (staircase) a chiocciola; ~ **instrument** n (MUS) strumento a fiato; ~**mill** n mulino a vento.

window ['wɪndəu] n finestra; (in car, train) finestrino; (in shop etc) vetrina; (also: ~**pane**) vetro; ~ **box** n cassetta da fiori; ~**cleaner** n (person) pulitore m di finestre; ~ **ledge** n davanzale m; ~ **pane** n vetro; ~ **sill** n davanzale m.

windpipe ['wɪndpaɪp] n trachea.

windscreen, windshield (US) ['wɪndskri:n, 'wɪndʃi:ld] n parabrezza m inv; ~ **washer** n lavacristallo; ~ **wiper** n tergicristallo.

windswept ['wɪndswɛpt] a spazzato(a) dal vento.

windy ['wɪndɪ] a ventoso(a); **it's** ~ c'è vento.

wine [waɪn] n vino; ~ **cellar** n cantina; ~ **glass** n bicchiere m da vino; ~ **list** n lista dei vini; ~ **tasting** n degustazione f dei vini; ~ **waiter** n sommelier m inv.

wing [wɪŋ] n ala; ~**s** npl (THEATRE) quinte fpl; ~**er** n (SPORT) ala.

wink [wɪŋk] n ammiccamento // vi ammiccare, fare l'occhiolino.

winner ['wɪnə*] n vincitore/trice.

winning ['wɪnɪŋ] a (team) vincente; (goal) decisivo(a); ~**s** npl vincite fpl; ~ **post** n traguardo.

winter ['wɪntə*] n inverno; ~ **sports** npl sport mpl invernali.

wintry ['wɪntrɪ] a invernale.

wipe [waɪp] n pulita, passata // vt pulire (strofinando); (dishes) asciugare; **to** ~ **off** vt cancellare; (stains) togliere strofinando; **to** ~ **out** vt (debt) pagare, liquidare; (memory) cancellare; (destroy) annientare; **to** ~ **up** vt asciugare.

wire ['waɪə*] n filo; (ELEC) filo elettrico; (TEL) telegramma m.

wireless ['waɪəlɪs] n telegrafia senza fili; (set) (apparecchio m) radio f inv.

wiry ['waɪərɪ] a magro e nerboruto(a).

wisdom ['wɪzdəm] n saggezza; (of action) prudenza; ~ **tooth** n dente m del giudizio.

wise [waɪz] a saggio(a); prudente; giudizioso(a).

...wise [waɪz] suffix: **time**~ per quanto riguarda il tempo, in termini di tempo.

wisecrack ['waɪzkræk] n battuta spiritosa.

wish [wɪʃ] n (desire) desiderio; (specific desire) richiesta // vt desiderare, volere; **best** ~**es** (on birthday etc) i migliori auguri; **with best** ~**es** (in letter) cordiali saluti, con i migliori saluti; **to** ~ **sb goodbye** dire arrivederci a qd; **he** ~**ed me well** mi augurò di riuscire; **to** ~ **to do/sb to do** desiderare o volere fare/che qd faccia; **to** ~ **for** desiderare; **it's** ~**ful thinking** è prendere i desideri per realtà.

wisp [wɪsp] n ciuffo, ciocca; (of smoke, straw) filo.

wistful ['wɪstful] a malinconico(a).

wit [wɪt] n (gen pl) intelligenza; presenza di spirito; (wittiness) spirito, arguzia; (person) bello spirito; **to be at one's** ~**s' end** (fig) non sapere più cosa fare; **to** ~ ad cioè.

witch [wɪtʃ] n strega; ~**craft** n stregoneria.

with [wɪð, wɪθ] prep con; **red** ~ **anger** rosso dalla or per la rabbia; **covered** ~ **snow** coperto di neve; **the man** ~ **the grey hat** l'uomo dal cappello grigio; **to be** ~ **it** (fig) essere al corrente; essere sveglio(a); **I am ~ you** (*I understand*) la seguo.

withdraw [wɪθˈdrɔ:] *vb* (*irg*) *vt* ritirare; (*money from bank*) ritirare; prelevare // *vi* ritirarsi; (*go back on promise*) ritrattarsi; **~al** *n* ritiro; prelievo; (*of army*) ritirata; (*MED*) stato di privazione.

wither [ˈwɪðə*] *vi* appassire; **~ed** *a* appassito(a); (*limb*) atrofizzato(a).

withhold [wɪθˈhəuld] *vt* *irg* (*money*) trattenere; (*decision*) rimettere, rimandare; (*permission*): **to ~ (from)** rifiutare (a); (*information*): **to ~ (from)** nascondere (a).

within [wɪðˈɪn] *prep* all'interno, (*in time, distances*) entro // *ad* all'interno, dentro; **~ sight of** in vista di; **~ a mile of** entro un miglio da; **~ the week** prima della fine della settimana.

without [wɪðˈaut] *prep* senza.

withstand [wɪθˈstænd] *vt* *irg* resistere a.

witness [ˈwɪtnɪs] *n* (*person*) testimone *m/f* // *vt* (*event*) essere testimone di; (*document*) attestare l'autenticità di; **to bear ~ to sth** testimoniare qc; **~ box, ~ stand** (*US*) *n* banco dei testimoni.

witticism [ˈwɪtɪsɪzm] *n* spiritosaggine *f*.

witty [ˈwɪtɪ] *a* spiritoso(a).

wives [waɪvz] *npl* of **wife**.

wizard [ˈwɪzəd] *n* mago.

wk *abbr* of **week**.

wobble [ˈwɔbl] *vi* tremare; (*chair*) traballare.

woe [wəu] *n* dolore *m*; disgrazia.

woke [wəuk] *pt* of **wake**; **~n** *pp* of **wake**.

wolf, wolves [wulf, wulvz] *n* lupo.

woman, *pl* **women** [ˈwumən, ˈwɪmɪn] *n* donna; **~ doctor** *n* dottoressa; **~ly** *a* femminile.

womb [wu:m] *n* (*ANAT*) utero.

women [ˈwɪmɪn] *npl* of **woman**.

won [wʌn] *pt,pp* of **win**.

wonder [ˈwʌndə*] *n* meraviglia // *vi*: **to ~ whether** domandarsi se; **to ~ at** essere sorpreso/a di; meravigliarsi di; **to ~ about** domandarsi di; pensare a; **it's no ~ that** c'è poco *or* non c'è da meravigliarsi che **+ sub**; **~ful** *a* meraviglioso(a); **~fully** *ad* (**+ adjective**) meravigliosamente; (**+ vb**) a meraviglia.

wonky [ˈwɔŋkɪ] *a* (*col*) traballante.

won't [wəunt] = **will not**.

woo [wu:] *vt* (*woman*) fare la corte a.

wood [wud] *n* legno; (*timber*) legname *m*; (*forest*) bosco; **~ carving** *n* scultura in legno, intaglio; **~ed** *a* boschivo(a); boscoso(a); **~en** *a* di legno; (*fig*) rigido(a); inespressivo(a); **~pecker** *n* picchio; **~wind** *n* (*MUS*) strumento a fiato in legno; **the ~wind** (*MUS*) i legni; **~work** *n* parti *fpl* in legno; (*craft, subject*) falegnameria; **~worm** *n* tarlo del legno.

wool [wul] *n* lana; **to pull the ~ over sb's eyes** (*fig*) imbrogliare qd; **~len** *a* di lana; **~lens** *npl* indumenti *mpl* di lana; **~ly** *a* lanoso(a); (*fig*: *ideas*) confuso(a).

word [wɔ:d] *n* parola; (*news*) notizie *fpl* // *vt* esprimere, formulare; **in other ~s** in

altre parole; **to break/keep one's ~** non mantenere/mantenere la propria parola; **I'll take your ~ for it** la crederò sulla parola; **~ing** *n* formulazione *f*; **~y** *a* verboso(a).

wore [wɔ:*] *pt* of **wear**.

work [wɔ:k] *n* lavoro; (*ART, LITERATURE*) opera // *vi* lavorare; (*mechanism, plan etc*) funzionare; (*medicine*) essere efficace // *vt* (*clay, wood etc*) lavorare; (*mine etc*) sfruttare; (*machine*) far funzionare; **to be out of ~** essere disoccupato(a); **~s** *n* (*factory*) fabbrica // *npl* (*of clock, machine*) meccanismo; **to ~ loose** *vi* allentarsi; **to ~ on** *vt fus* lavorare a; (*principle*) basarsi su; **to ~ out** *vi* (*plans etc*) riuscire, andare bene // *vt* (*problem*) risolvere; (*plan*) elaborare; **it ~s out at £100** fa 100 sterline; **to get ~ed up** andare su tutte le furie; eccitarsi; **~able** *a* (*solution*) realizzabile; **~er** *n* lavoratore/trice, operaio/a; **~ing class** *n* classe *f* operaia *or* lavoratrice; **~ing-class** *a* operaio(a); **~ing man** *n* lavoratore *m*; **in ~ing order** funzionante; **~man** *n* operaio; **~manship** *n* abilità; lavoro; fattura; **~shop** *n* officina; **~-to-rule** *n* sciopero bianco.

world [wɔ:ld] *n* mondo // *cpd* (*champion*) del mondo; (*power, war*) mondiale; **to think the ~ of sb** (*fig*) pensare un gran bene di qd; **out of this ~ a** formidabile; **~ly** *a* di questo mondo; **~-wide** *a* universale.

worm [wɔ:m] *n* verme *m*.

worn [wɔ:n] *pp* of **wear** // *a* usato(a); **~-out** *a* (*object*) consumato(a), logoro(a); (*person*) sfinito(a).

worried [ˈwʌrɪd] *a* preoccupato(a).

worrier [ˈwʌrɪə*] *n* ansioso/a.

worry [ˈwʌrɪ] *n* preoccupazione *f* // *vt* preoccupare // *vi* preoccuparsi; **~ing** *a* preoccupante.

worse [wɔ:s] *a* peggiore // *ad, n* peggio; **a change for the ~** un peggioramento; **~n** *vt, vi* peggiorare; **~ off** *a* in condizioni (economiche) peggiori.

worship [ˈwɔ:ʃɪp] *n* culto // *vt* (*God*) adorare, venerare; (*person*) adorare; **Your W~** (*to mayor*) signor sindaco; (*to judge*) signor giudice; **~per** *n* adoratore/trice; (*in church*) fedele *m/f*, devoto/a.

worst [wɔ:st] *a* il(la) peggiore // *ad, n* peggio; **at ~** al peggio, per male che vada.

worsted [ˈwustɪd] *n*: **(wool) ~** lana pettinata.

worth [wɔ:θ] *n* valore *m* // *a*: **to be ~** valere; **it's ~ it** ne vale la pena; **50 pence ~ of apples** 50 pence di mele; **~less** *a* di nessun valore; **~while** *a* (*activity*) utile; (*cause*) lodevole; **a ~while book** un libro che vale la pena leggere.

worthy [ˈwɔ:ðɪ] *a* (*person*) degno(a); (*motive*) lodevole; **~ of** degno di.

would [wud] *auxiliary vb*: **she ~ come** verrebbe; **he ~ have come** sarebbe venuto; **~ you like a biscuit?** vuole *or* vorrebbe un biscotto?; **he ~ go there on Mondays** ci andava il lunedì; **~-be** *a* (*pej*) sedicente.

wound *vb* [waund] *pt, pp of* **wind** // *n,vt* [wu:nd] *n* ferita // *vt* ferire; **~ed in the leg** ferito(a) alla gamba.

wove [wɔuv] *pt of* **weave**; **~n** *pp of* **weave**.

wrangle ['ræŋgl] *n* litigio // *vi* litigare.

wrap [ræp] *n* (*stole*) scialle *m*; (*cape*) mantellina // *vt* (*also*: **~ up**) avvolgere; (*parcel*) incartare; **~per** *n* (*of book*) copertina; **~ping paper** *n* carta da pacchi; (*for gift*) carta da regali.

wrath [rɔθ] *n* collera, ira.

wreath, **~s** [ri:θ, ri:ðz] *n* corona.

wreck [rɛk] *n* (*sea disaster*) naufragio; (*ship*) relitto; (*pej: person*) rottame *m* // *vt* demolire; (*ship*) far naufragare; (*fig*) rovinare; **~age** *n* rottami *mpl*; (*of building*) macerie *fpl*; (*of ship*) relitti *mpl*.

wren [rɛn] *n* (ZOOL) scricciolo.

wrench [rɛntʃ] *n* (TECH) chiave *f*; (*tug*) torsione *f* brusca; (*fig*) strazio // *vt* strappare; storcere; **to ~ sth from** strappare qc a *or* da.

wrestle ['rɛsl] *vi*: **to ~ (with sb)** lottare (con qd); **to ~ with** (*fig*) combattere *or* lottare contro; **~r** *n* lottatore/trice; **wrestling** *n* lotta; (*also*: **all-in wrestling**) catch *m*, lotta libera.

wretched ['rɛtʃid] *a* disgraziato(a); (*col: weather, holiday*) orrendo(a), orribile; (: *child, dog*) pestifero(a).

wriggle ['rigl] *n* contorsione *f* // *vi* dimenarsi; (*snake, worm*) serpeggiare, muoversi serpeggiando.

wring, *pt, pp* **wrung** [riŋ, rʌŋ] *vt* torcere; (*wet clothes*) strizzare; (*fig*): **to ~ sth out of** strappare qc a.

wrinkle ['riŋkl] *n* (*on skin*) ruga; (*on paper etc*) grinza // *vt* corrugare; raggrinzire // *vi* corrugarsi; raggrinzirsi.

wrist [rist] *n* polso // **~ watch** *n* orologio da polso.

writ [rit] *n* ordine *m*; mandato.

write, *pt* **wrote,** *pp* **written** [rait, rəut, 'ritn] *vt, vi* scrivere; **to ~ down** *vt* annotare; (*put in writing*) mettere per iscritto; **to ~ off** *vt* (*debt*) cancellare; (*depreciate*) deprezzare; **to ~ out** *vt* scrivere; (*copy*) ricopiare; **to ~ up** *vt* redigere; **~-off** *n* perdita completa; **the car is a ~-off** la macchina a bene per il demolitore; **~r** *n* autore/trice, scrittore/trice.

writhe [raið] *vi* contorcersi.

writing ['raitiŋ] *n* scrittura; (*of author*) scritto, opera; **in ~** per iscritto; **~ paper** *n* carta da scrivere.

written ['ritn] *pp of* **write**.

wrong [rɔŋ] *a* sbagliato(a); (*not suitable*) inadatto(a); (*wicked*) cattivo(a); (*unfair*) ingiusto(a) // *ad* in modo sbagliato, erroneamente // *n* (*evil*) male *m*;

(*injustice*) torto // *vt* fare torto a; **you are ~ to do it** ha torto a farlo; **you are ~ about that** si sbaglia; **to be in the ~** avere torto; **what's ~?** cosa c'è che non va?; **to go ~** (*person*) sbagliarsi; (*plan*) fallire, non riuscire; (*machine*) guastarsi; **~ful** *a* illegittimo(a); ingiusto(a); **~ly** *ad* a torto.

wrote [rəut] *pt of* **write**.

wrought [rɔːt] *a*: **~ iron** ferro battuto.

wrung [rʌŋ] *pt, pp of* **wring**.

wry [rai] *a* storto(a).

wt. *abbr of* **weight**.

X Y Z

Xmas ['ɛksməs] *n abbr of* **Christmas**.

X-ray ['ɛks'rei] *n* raggio X; (*photograph*) radiografia // *vt* radiografare.

xylophone ['zailəfəun] *n* xilofono.

yacht [jɔt] *n* panfilo, yacht *m inv*; **~ing** *n* yachting *m*, sport *m* della vela; **~sman** *n* yachtsman *m inv*.

Yank [jæŋk] *n* (*pej*) yankee *m/f inv*.

yap [jæp] *vi* (*dog*) guaire, abbaiare.

yard [jɑːd] *n* (*of house etc*) cortile *m*; (*measure*) iarda (= 914 *mm*; 3 *feet*); **~stick** *n* (*fig*) misura, criterio.

yarn [jɑːn] *n* filato; (*tale*) lunga storia.

yawn [jɔːn] *n* sbadiglio // *vi* sbadigliare; **~ing** *a* (*gap*) spalancato(a).

yd. *abbr of* **yard(s)**.

year [jiə*] *n* anno; (*referring to harvest, wine etc*) annata; **~ly** *a* annuale // *ad* annualmente.

yearn [jə:n] *vi*: **to ~ for sth/to do** desiderare ardentemente qc/di fare; **~ing** *n* desiderio intenso.

yeast [ji:st] *n* lievito.

yell [jɛl] *n* urlo // *vi* urlare.

yellow ['jɛləu] *a* giallo(a).

yelp [jɛlp] *n* guaito, uggiolio // *vi* guaire, uggiolare.

yes [jɛs] *ad*, *n* sì (*m inv*).

yesterday ['jɛstədi] *ad*,*n* ieri (*m inv*).

yet [jɛt] *ad* ancora; già // *cj* ma, tuttavia; **it is not finished ~** non è ancora finito; **the best ~** finora il migliore; **as ~** finora.

yew [ju:] *n* tasso.

Yiddish ['jidiʃ] *n* yiddish *m*.

yield [ji:ld] *n* produzione *f*, resa; reddito // *vt* produrre, rendere; (*surrender*) cedere // *vi* cedere.

yodel ['jəudl] *vi* cantare lo jodel *or* alla tirolese.

yoga ['jəugə] *n* yoga *m*.

yog(h)ourt, yog(h)urt ['jəugət] *n* iogurt *m inv*.

yoke [jəuk] *n* giogo.

yolk [jəuk] *n* tuorlo, rosso d'uovo.

yonder ['jɔndə*] *ad* là.

you [ju:] *pronoun* tu; (*polite form*) lei; (*pl*) voi; (: *very formal*) loro; (*complement: direct*) ti; la; vi; li; (: *indirect*) ti; le; vi; gli; (*stressed*) te; lei; voi; loro; (*one*): **fresh air**

does ~ **good** l'aria fresca fa bene; ~ **never know** non si sa mai.

you'd [juːd] = **you had; you would.**

you'll [juːl] = **you will; you shall.**

young [jʌŋ] a giovane // npl (of animal) piccoli mpl; (people): **the** ~ i giovani, la gioventù; ~**ster** n giovanotto, ragazzo; (child) bambino/a.

your [jɔː*] a il(la) tuo(a), pl i(le) tuoi(tue); il(la) suo(a), pl i(le) suoi(sue); il(la) vostro(a), pl i(le) vostri(e); il(la) loro, pl i(le) loro.

you're [juə*] = **you are.**

yours [jɔːz] pronoun il(la) tuo(a), pl i(le) tuoi(tue); (polite form) il(la) suo(a), pl i(le) suoi(sue); (pl) il(la) vostro(a), pl i(le) vostri(e); (: very formal) il(la) loro, pl i(le) loro; ~ **sincerely/faithfully** cordiali/distinti saluti.

yourself [jɔː'sɛlf] pronoun (reflexive) ti; si; (after prep) te; sé; (emphatic) tu stesso(a); lei stesso(a); **yourselves** pl pronoun (reflexive) vi; si; (after prep) voi; loro; (emphatic) voi stessi(e); loro stessi(e).

youth [juːθ] n gioventù f; (young man: pl ~**s** [juːðz]) giovane m, ragazzo; ~**ful** a giovane; da giovane; giovanile; ~ **hostel** n ostello della gioventù.

you've [juːv] = **you have.**

Yugoslav ['juːgəu'slɑːv] a, n jugoslavo(a).

Yugoslavia ['juːgəu'slɑːvɪə] n Jugoslavia.

zany ['zeɪnɪ] a un po' pazzo(a).

zeal [ziːl] n zelo; entusiasmo; ~**ous** ['zɛləs] a zelante; premuroso(a).

zebra ['ziːbrə] n zebra; ~ **crossing** n (passaggio pedonale a) strisce fpl, zebre fpl.

zero ['zɪərəu] n zero; ~ **hour** n l'ora zero.

zest [zɛst] n gusto; (CULIN) buccia.

zigzag ['zɪgzæg] n zigzag m inv // vi zigzagare.

zinc [zɪŋk] n zinco.

zip [zɪp] n (also: ~ **fastener,** ~**per**) chiusura f or cerniera f lampo inv // vt (also: ~ **up**) chiudere con una cerniera lampo.

zither ['zɪðə*] n cetra.

zodiac ['zəudɪæk] n zodiaco.

zombie ['zɒmbɪ] n (fig): **like a** ~ come un morto che cammina.

zone [zəun] n zona; (subdivision of town) quartiere m.

zoo [zuː] n zoo m inv.

zoologist [zuː'ɒlədʒɪst] n zoologo/a.

zoology [zuː'ɒlədʒɪ] n zoologia.

zoom [zuːm] vi: **to** ~ **past** sfrecciare; ~ **lens** n zoom m inv, obiettivo a focale variabile.

ITALIAN VERBS

NB: **Verbi inglesi:** le forme irregolari di verbi inglesi si trovano in ordine alfabetico nella nomenclatura con rimando alla forma di base.

1 Gerundio *2* Participio passato *3* Presente *4* Imperfetto *5* Passato remoto *6* Futuro *7* Condizionale *8* Congiuntivo presente *9* Congiuntivo passato *10* Imperativo

andare *3* vado, vai, va, andiamo, andate, vanno *6* andrò *etc* *8* vada *10* va'!, vada!, andate!, vadano!

apparire *2* apparso *3* appaio, appari *o* apparisci, appare *o* apparisce, appaiono *o* appariscono *5* apparvi *o* apparsi, apparisti, apparve *o* apparì *o* apparse, apparvero *o* apparirono *o* apparsero *8* appaia *o* apparisca

aprire *2* aperto *3* apro *5* aprii *o* apersi, apristi *8* apra

AVERE *3* ho, hai, ha, abbiamo, avete, hanno *5* ebbi, avesti, ebbe, avemmo, aveste, ebbero *6* avrò *etc* *8* abbia *etc* *10* abbi!, abbia!, abbiate!, abbiano!

bere *1* bevendo *2* bevuto *3* bevo *etc* *4* bevevo *etc* *5* bevvi *o* bevetti, bevesti *6* berrò *etc* *8* beva *etc* *9* bevessi *etc*

cadere *5* caddi, cadesti *6* cadrò *etc*

cogliere *2* colto *3* colgo, colgono *5* colsi, cogliesti *8* colga

correre *2* corso *5* corsi, corresti

cuocere *2* cotto *3* cuocio, cociamo, cuociono *5* cossi, cocesti

dare *3* do, dai, da, diamo, date, danno *5* diedi *o* detti, desti *6* darò *etc* *8* dia *etc* *9* dessi *etc* *10* da'!, dia!, date!, diano!

dire *1* dicendo *2* detto *3* dìco, dici, dice, diciamo, dite, dicono *4* dicevo *etc* *5* dissi, dicesti *6* dirò *etc* *8* dica, diciamo, dìciate, dicano *9* dicessi *etc* *10* di'!, dica!, dite!, dicano!

dolere *3* dolgo, duoli, duole, dolgono *5* dolsi, dolesti *6* dorrò *etc* *8* dolga

dovere *3* devo *o* debbo, devi, deve, dobbiamo, dovete, devono *o* debbono *6* dovrò *etc* *8* debba, dobbiamo, dobbiate, devano *o* debbano

ESSERE *2* stato *3* sono, sei, è, siamo, siete, sono *4* ero, eri, era, eravamo, eravate, erano *5* fui, fosti, fu, fummo, foste, furono *6* sarò *etc* *8* sia *etc* *9* fossi, fossi, fosse, fossimo, foste, fossero *10* sii!, sia!, siate!, siano!

fare *1* facendo *2* fatto *3* faccio, fai, fa, facciamo, fate, fanno *4* facevo *etc* *5* feci, facesti *6* farò *etc* *8* faccia *etc* *9* facessi *etc* *10* fa'!, faccia!, fate!, facciano!

FINIRE *1* finendo *2* finito *3* finisco, finisci, finisce, finiamo, finite, finiscono *4* finivo, finivi, finiva, finivamo, finivate, finivano *5* finii, finisti, finì, finimmo, finiste, finirono *6* finirò, finirai, finirà, finiremo, finirete, finiranno *7* finirei, finiresti, finirebbe, finiremmo, finireste, finirebbero *8* finisca, finisca, finisca, finiamo, finiate, finiscano *9* finissi, finissi, finisse, finissimo, finiste, finissero *10* finisci!, finisca!, finite!, finiscano!

giungere *2* giunto *5* giunsi, giungesti

leggere *2* letto *5* lessi, leggesti

mettere *2* messo *5* misi, mettesti

morire *2* morto *3* muoio, muori, muore, moriamo, morite, muoiono *6* morirò *o* morrò *etc* *8* muoia

muovere *2* mosso *5* mossi, movesti

nascere *2* nato *5* nacqui, nascesti

nuocere *2* nuociuto *3* nuoccio, nuoci, nuoce, nociamo *o* nuociamo, nuocete, nuocciono *4* nuocevo *etc* *5* nocqui, nuocesti *6* nuocerò *etc* *7* nuoccia

offrire *2* offerto *3* offro *5* offersi *o* offrii, offristi *8* offra

parere *2* parso *3* paio, paiamo, paiono *5* parvi *o* parsi, paresti *6* parrò *etc* *8* paia, paiamo, pariate, paiano

PARLARE *1* parlando *2* parlato *3* parlo, parli, parla, parliamo, parlate, parlano *4* parlavo, parlavi, parlava, parlavamo, parlavate, parlavano *5* parlai, parlasti, parlò, parlammo, parlaste, parlarono *6* parlerò, parlerai, parlerà, parleremo, parlerete, parleranno *7* parlerei, parleresti, parlerebbe, parleremmo, parlereste, parlerebbero *8* parli, parli, parli, parliamo, parliate, parlino *9* parlassi, parlassi, parlasse, parlassimo, parlaste, parlassero *10* parla!, parli!, parlate!, parlino!

piacere *2* piaciuto *3* piaccio, piacciamo, piacciono *5* piacqui, piacesti *8* piaccia *etc*

porre *1* ponendo *2* posto *3* pongo, poni, pone, poniamo, ponete, pongono *4* ponevo *etc* *5* posi, ponesti *6* porrò *etc* *8* ponga, poniamo, poniate, pongano *9* ponessi *etc*

potere *3* posso, puoi, può, possiamo, potete, possono *6* potrò *etc* *8* possa, possiamo, possiate, possano

prendere *2* preso *5* presi, prendesti

ridurre *1* riducendo *2* ridotto *3* riduco *etc* *4* riducevo *etc* *5* ridussi, riducesti *6* ridurrò *etc* *8* riduca *etc* *9* riducessi *etc*

riempire *2* riempiendo *3* riempio, riempi, riempie, riempiono

rimanere *2* rimasto *3* rimango, rimangono *5* rimasi, rimanesti *6* rimarrò *etc* *8* rimanga

rispondere *2* risposto *5* risposi, rispondesti

salire *3* salgo, sali, salgono *8* salga

sapere *3* so, sai, sa, sappiamo, sapete, sanno *5* seppi, sapesti *6* saprò *etc* *8* sappia *etc* *10* sappi!, sappia!, sappiate!, sappiano!

scrivere *2* scritto *5* scrissi, scrivesti

sedere *3* siedo, siedi, siede, siedono *8* sieda

spegnere *2* spento *3* spengo, spengono *5* spensi, spegnesti *8* spenga

stare *2* stato *3* sto, stai, sta, stiamo, state, stanno *5* stetti, stesti *6* starò *etc* *8* stia *etc* *9* stessi *etc* *10* sta'!, stia!, state!, stiano!

tacere *2* taciuto *3* taccio, tacciono *5* tacqui, tacesti *8* .accia

tenere *3* tengo, tieni, tiene, tengono *5* tenni, tenesti *6* terrò *etc* *8* tenga

trarre *1* traendo *2* tratto *3* traggo, trai, trae, traiamo, traete, traggono *4* traevo *etc* *5* trassi, traesti *6* trarrò *etc* *8* tragga *9* traessi *etc*

udire *3* odo, odi, ode, odono *8* oda

uscire *3* esco, esci, esce, escono *8* esca

valere *2* valso *3* valgo, valgono *5* valsi, valesti *6* varrò *etc* *8* valga

vedere *2* visto *o* veduto *5* vidi, vedesti *6* vedrò *etc*

VENDERE *1* vendendo *2* venduto *3* vendo, vendi, vende, vendiamo, vendete, vendono *4* vendevo, vendevi, vendeva, vendevamo, vendevate, vendevano *5* vendei *o* vendetti, vendesti, vendé *o* vendette, vendemmo, vendeste, venderono *o* vendettero *6* venderò, venderai, venderà, venderemo, venderete, venderanno *7* venderei, venderesti, venderebbe, venderemmo, vendereste, venderebbero *8* venda, venda, venda, vendiamo, vendiate, vendano *9* vendessi, vendessi, vendesse, vendessimo, vendeste, vendessero *10* vendi!, venda!, vendete!, vendano!

venire *2* venuto *3* vengo, vieni, viene, vengono *5* venni, venisti *6* verrò *etc* *8* venga

vivere *2* vissuto *5* vissi, vivesti

volere *3* voglio, vuoi, vuole, vogliamo, volete, vogliono *5* volli, volesti *6* vorrò *etc* *8* voglia *etc* *10* vogli!, voglia!, vogliate!, vogliano!

VERBI INGLESI

present	pt	pp	present	pt	pp
arise	arose	arisen	eat	ate	eaten
awake	awoke	awaked	fall	fell	fallen
be (am,	was,	been	feed	fed	fed
is, are;	were		feel	felt	felt
being)			fight	fought	fought
bear	bore	born(e)	find	found	found
beat	beat	beaten	flee	fled	fled
become	became	become	fling	flung	flung
befall	befell	befallen	fly	flew	flown
begin	began	begun	forbid	forbade	forbidden
behold	beheld	beheld	forecast	forecast	forecast
bend	bent	bent	forget	forgot	forgotten
beset	beset	beset	forgive	forgave	forgiven
bet	bet,	bet,	forsake	forsook	forsaken
	betted	betted	freeze	froze	frozen
bid	bid	bid	get	got	got, (US)
bind	bound	bound			gotten
bite	bit	bitten	give	gave	given
bleed	bled	bled	go	went	gone
blow	blew	blown	(goes)		
break	broke	broken	grind	ground	ground
breed	bred	bred	grow	grew	grown
bring	brought	brought	hang	hung,	hung,
build	built	built		hanged	hanged
burn	burnt,	burnt,	have	had	had
	burned	burned	hear	heard	heard
burst	burst	burst	hide	hid	hidden
buy	bought	bought	hit	hit	hit
can	could	(been able)	hold	held	held
cast	cast	cast	hurt	hurt	hurt
catch	caught	caught	keep	kept	kept
choose	chose	chosen	kneel	knelt,	knelt,
cling	clung	clung		kneeled	kneeled
come	came	come	know	knew	known
cost	cost	cost	lay	laid	laid
creep	crept	crept	lead	led	led
cut	cut	cut	lean	leant,	leant,
deal	dealt	dealt		leaned	leaned
dig	dug	dug	leap	leapt,	leapt,
do (3rd	did	done		leaped	leaped
person;			learn	learnt,	learnt,
he/she/				learned	learned
it/does)			leave	left	left
draw	drew	drawn	lend	lent	lent
dream	dreamed,	dreamed,	let	let	let
	dreamt	dreamt	lie	lay	lain
drink	drank	drunk	(lying)		
drive	drove	driven	light	lit,	lit,
dwell	dwelt	dwelt		lighted	lighted

present	pt	pp	present	pt	pp
lose	lost	lost	speed	sped,	sped,
make	made	made		speeded	speeded
may	might	—	spell	spelt,	spelt,
mean	meant	meant		spelled	spelled
meet	met	met	spend	spent	spent
mistake	mistook	mistaken	spill	spilt,	spilt,
mow	mowed	mown,		spilled	spilled
		mowed	spin	spun	spun
must	(had to)	(had to)	spit	spat	spat
pay	paid	paid	split	split	split
put	put	put	spoil	spoiled,	spoiled,
quit	quit,	quit,		spoilt	spoilt
	quitted	quitted	spread	spread	spread
read	read	read	spring	sprang	sprung
rend	rent	rent	stand	stood	stood
rid	rid	rid	steal	stole	stolen
ride	rode	ridden	stick	stuck	stuck
ring	rang	rung	sting	stung	stung
rise	rose	risen	stink	stank	stunk
run	ran	run	stride	strode	strode
saw	sawed	sawn	strike	struck	struck,
say	said	said			stricken
see	saw	seen	strive	strove	striven
seek	sought	sought	swear	swore	sworn
sell	sold	sold	sweep	swept	swept
send	sent	sent	swell	swelled	swollen,
set	set	set			swelled
shake	shook	shaken	swim	swam	swum
shall	should	—	swing	swung	swung
shear	sheared	shorn,	take	took	taken
		sheared	teach	taught	taught
shed	shed	shed			
shine	shone	shone	tear	tore	torn
shoot	shot	shot	tell	told	told
show	showed	shown	think	thought	thought
shrink	shrank	shrunk	throw	threw	thrown
shut	shut	shut	thrust	thrust	thrust
sing	sang	sung	tread	trod	trodden
sink	sank	sunk	wake	woke,	woken,
sit	sat	sat		waked	waked
slay	slew	slain	wear	wore	worn
sleep	slept	slept	weave	wove,	woven,
slide	slid	slid		weaved	weaved
sling	slung	slung	wed	wedded,	wedded,
slit	slit	slit		wed	wed
smell	smelt,	smelt,	weep	wept	wept
	smelled	smelled	win	won	won
sow	sowed	sown,	wind	wound	wound
		sowed	wring	wrung	wrung
speak	spoke	spoken	write	wrote	written

405

NUMBERS

I NUMERI

one/first	uno(a)/primo(a)
two/second	due/secondo(a)
three/third	tre/terzo(a)
four/fourth	quattro/quarto(a)
five/fifth	cinque/quinto(a)
six/sixth	sei/sesto(a)
seven/seventh	sette/settimo(a)
eight/eighth	otto/ottavo(a)
nine/ninth	nove/nono(a)
ten/tenth	dieci/decimo(a)
eleven/eleventh	undici/undicesimo(a)
twelve/twelfth	dodici/dodicesimo(a)
thirteen/thirteenth	tredici/tredicesimo(a)
fourteen/fourteenth	quattordici/ quattordicesimo(a)
fifteen/fifteenth	quindici/quindicesimo(a)
sixteen/sixteenth	sedici/sedicesimo(a)
seventeen/seventeenth	diciassette/diciassettesimo(a)
eighteen/eighteenth	diciotto/diciottesimo(a)
nineteen/nineteenth	diciannove/diciannovesimo(a)
twenty/twentieth	venti/ventesimo(a)
twenty-one/twenty-first	ventuno/ventunesimo(a)
twenty-two/twenty-second	ventidue/ventiduesimo(a)
twenty-three/twenty-third	ventitré/ventitreesimo(a)
twenty-eight/twenty-eighth	ventotto/ventottesimo(a)
thirty/thirtieth	trenta/trentesimo(a)
forty	quaranta
fifty	cinquanta
sixty	sessanta
seventy	settanta
eighty	ottanta
ninety	novanta
a hundred, one hundred/hundredth	cento/centesimo(a)
a hundred and one/hundred-and-first	cento uno/centunesimo(a)
two hundred	duecento
a thousand, one thousand/thousandth	mille/millesimo(a)
one thousand two hundred and two	milleduecentodue
five thousand	cinquemila
a million, one million/millionth	un milione/milionesimo(a)

THE TIME	L'ORA
what time is it? it's 0 it is ...	*che ora è?, che ore sono? è/sono ...*
midnight	mezzanotte, le dodici di sera
one (o'clock) (a.m. *o* in the morning), 1 a.m.	l'una
ten past one	l'una e dieci
a quarter past one, one fifteen	l'una e un quarto, l'una e quindici
half past one, one thirty	l'una e mezzo *o* mezza, l'una e trenta
a quarter to two, one forty-five	le due meno un quarto, l'una e quarantacinque
ten to two, one fifty	le due meno dieci, l'una e cinquanta
twelve (o'clock), midday, noon	mezzogiorno, le dodici
one (o'clock) (p.m. *o* in the afternoon), 1 p.m.	l'una, il tocco, le tredici
seven (o'clock) (p.m. *o* at night)	le sette (di sera), le diciannove
(at) what time?	*a che ora?*
at midnight	a mezzanotte
at one (o'clock)	all'una
at seven (o'clock)	alle sette

There's an epidemic with 27 million victims. And no visible symptoms.

It's an epidemic of people who can't read.

Believe it or not, 27 million Americans are functionally illiterate, about one adult in five.

The solution to this problem is you... when you join the fight against illiteracy. So call the Coalition for Literacy at toll-free **1-800-228-8813** and volunteer.

Volunteer Against Illiteracy. The only degree you need is a degree of caring.